Collins

# Collins
# French
# Dictionary

D0964425

**HarperCollins Publishers**
Westerhill Road
Bishopbriggs
Glasgow
G64 2QT
Great Britain

Second Edition 2006

© HarperCollins Publishers 2005, 2006

ISBN 978-0-00-787413-2

Collins® and Bank of English® are
registered trademarks of
HarperCollins Publishers Limited

www.collinslanguage.com

A catalogue record for this book is available
from the British Library

Typeset by Thomas Callan
Verb supplement typeset by
Davidson Publishing Solutions, Glasgow

Printed in Great Britain by
Clays Ltd, St Ives, plc

#### Acknowledgements
We would like to thank those authors and
publishers who kindly gave permission
for copyright material to be used in the
Collins Word Web. We would also like to
thank Times Newspapers Ltd for providing
valuable data.

**MANAGING EDITOR**
Michela Clari

**CONTRIBUTORS**
Maree Airlie
Jean-François Allain
Gaëlle Amiot-Cadey
Cécile Aubinière-Robb
Sabine Citron
Wendy Lee
Catherine Love
Rose Rociola

**SERIES EDITOR**
Lorna Knight

# TABLE DES MATIÈRES    CONTENTS

William Collins' dream of knowledge for all began with the publication of his first book in 1819. A self-educated mill worker, he not only enriched millions of lives, but also founded a flourishing publishing house. Today, staying true to this spirit, Collins books are packed with inspiration, innovation, and practical expertise. They place you at the centre of a world of possibility and give you exactly what you need to explore it.

Language is the key to this exploration, and at the heart of Collins Dictionaries is language as it is really used. New words, phrases, and meanings spring up every day, and all of them are captured and analysed by the Collins Word Web. Constantly updated, and with over 2.5 billion entries, this living language resource is unique to our dictionaries.

Words are tools for life. And a Collins Dictionary makes them work for you.

**Collins. Do more**

# INTRODUCTION

Nous sommes très heureux que vous ayez choisi ce dictionnaire et espérons que vous aimerez l'utiliser et que vous en tirerez profit au lycée, à la maison, en vacances ou au travail.

Cette introduction a pour but de vous donner quelques conseils sur la façon d'utiliser au mieux votre dictionnaire, en vous référant non seulement à son importante nomenclature mais aussi aux informations contenues dans chaque entrée. Ceci vous aidera à lire et à comprendre, mais aussi à communiquer et à vous exprimer en anglais contemporain.

Au début du dictionnaire, vous trouverez la liste des abréviations utilisées dans le texte et celle de la transcription des sons par des symboles phonétiques. Vous y trouverez également la liste des verbes irréguliers en anglais, suivis d'une section finale sur les nombres et sur les expressions de temps.

## COMMENT UTILISER VOTRE DICTIONNAIRE

Ce dictionnaire offre une richesse d'informations et utilise diverses formes et tailles de caractères, symboles, abréviations, parenthèses et crochets. Les conventions et symboles utilisés sont expliqués dans les sections qui suivent.

## ENTRÉES

Les mots que vous cherchez dans le dictionnaire - les entrées - sont classés par ordre alphabétique. Ils sont imprimés en charactères gras à la ligne pour pouvoir être repérés rapidement. Les entrées figurant en haut de page indiquent le premier (sur la page de gauche) et le dernier mot (sur la page de droite) des deux pages en question.

Des informations sur l'usage ou sur la forme de certaines entrées sont données entre parenthèses, après la transcription phonétique. Ces indications apparaissent sous forme abrégée et en italiques (par ex. (*fam*), (*Comm*)).

Pour plus de facilité, les mots de la même famille sont regroupés sous la même entrée (**ronger, rongeur; accept, acceptance**) et apparaissent également en charactères gras.

Les expressions courantes dans lesquelles apparaît l'entrée sont indiquées par des caractères romains gras différents (par exemple **retard** : [...] **avoir du ~**).

### TRANSCRIPTION PHONÉTIQUE
La transcription phonétique de chaque entrée (indiquant sa prononciation) est indiquée entre crochets immédiatement après l'entrée (par ex. **fumer** [fyme]; **knee** [ni:]). La liste des symboles phonétiques figure page xiii.

### TRADUCTIONS
Les traductions des entrées apparaissent en caractères ordinaires ; lorsque plusieurs sens ou usages coexistent, ces traductions sont séparées par un point-virgule. Vous trouverez des synonymes de l'entrée en italiques entre parenthèses avant les traductions  (par ex. **poser** (*installer : moquette, carrelage*)) ou des mots qui fournissent le contexte dans lequel l'entrée est susceptible d'être utilisée (par ex. **poser** (*question*)).

Une importance particulière est accordée à certains mots français et anglais qui sont considérés comme des « mots-clés » dans chacune des langues. Cela peut être dû à leur utilisation très fréquente ou au fait qu'ils ont divers types d'usage (par ex. **vouloir, plus**; **get, that**). L'utilisation de triangles et de chiffres aide à distinguer différentes catégories grammaticales et différents sens. D'autres renseignements utiles apparaissent en italiques et entre parenthèses dans la langue de l'utilisateur.

**DONNÉES GRAMMATICALES**
Les catégories grammaticales sont données sous forme abrégée et en italiques après la transcription phonétique (par ex. *vt*, *adv*, *conj*). Les genres des noms français sont indiqués de la manière suivante : *nm* pour un nom masculin et *nf* pour un nom féminin. Le féminin et le pluriel irréguliers de certains noms sont également indiqués (par ex. **directeur, -trice** ; **cheval, -aux**).

Le masculin et le féminin des adjectifs sont indiqués lorsque ces deux formes sont différentes (par ex. **noir, e**). Lorsque l'adjectif a un féminin ou un pluriel irrégulier, ces formes sont clairement indiquées (par ex. **net, nette**). Les pluriels irréguliers des noms, et les formes irrégulières des verbes anglais sont indiqués entre parenthèses, avant la catégorie grammaticale (par ex. **man** [...] (*pl* **men**) *n* ; **give** (*pt* **gave**; *pp* **~n**) *vt*).

## INTRODUCTION

We are delighted that you have decided to buy this dictionary and hope you will enjoy and benefit from using it at school, at home, on holiday or at work.

This introduction gives you a few tips on how to get the most out of your dictionary – not simply from its comprehensive wordlist but also from the information provided in each entry. This will help you to read and understand modern French, as well as communicate and express yourself in the language. This dictionary begins by listing the abbreviations used in the text and illustrating the sounds shown by the phonetic symbols. You will also find French verb tables, followed by a final section on numbers and time expressions.

### USING YOUR DICTIONARY

A wealth of information is presented in the dictionary, using various typefaces, sizes of type, symbols, abbreviations and brackets. The various conventions and symbols used are explained in the following sections.

### HEADWORDS

The words you look up in a dictionary – 'headwords' – are listed alphabetically. They are printed in **bold** and on a new line for rapid identification. The headwords appearing at the top of each page indicate the first (if it appears on a left-hand page) and last word (if it appears on a right-hand page) dealt with on the page in question.

Information about the usage or form of certain headwords is given in brackets after the phonetic spelling. This usually appears in abbreviated form and in italics (e.g. (*fam*), (*Comm*)).

Where appropriate, words related to headwords are grouped in the same entry (**ronger, rongeur; accept, acceptance**) and are also in bold. Common expressions in which the headword appears are shown in a bold roman type (e.g. **retard:** [...] **avoir du ~**).

## PHONETIC SPELLINGS

The phonetic spelling of each headword (indicating its pronunciation) is given in square brackets immediately after the headword (e.g. **fumer** [fyme]; **knee** [ni:]). A list of these symbols is given on page xiii.

## TRANSLATIONS

Headword translations are given in ordinary type and, where more than one meaning or usage exists, these are separated by a semi-colon. You will often find other words in italics in brackets before the translations. These offer suggested contexts in which the headword might appear (e.g. **rough** *(voice)*, [...] *(weather)*) or provide synonyms (e.g. **rough** *(violent)*). The gender of the translation also appears in italics immediately following the key element of the translation.

## KEY WORDS

Special status is given to certain French and English words which are considered as 'key' words in each language. They may, for example, occur very frequently or have several types of usage (e.g. **vouloir, plus; get, that**). A combination of triangles and numbers helps you to distinguish different parts of speech and different meanings. Further helpful information is provided in brackets and italics.

## GRAMMATICAL INFORMATION

Parts of speech are given in abbreviated form in italics after the phonetic spellings of headwords (e.g. *vt, adv, conj*). Genders of French nouns are indicated as follows: *nm* for a masculine and *nf* for a feminine noun. Feminine and irregular plural forms of nouns are also shown (**directeur, -trice; cheval, -aux**).

Adjectives are given in both masculine and feminine forms where these forms are different (e.g. **noir, e**). Clear information is provided where adjectives have an irregular feminine or plural form (e.g. **net, nette**).

## ABRÉVIATIONS

## ABBREVIATIONS

| | | |
|---|---|---|
| abréviation | *ab(b)r* | abbreviation |
| adjectif, locution adjectivale | *adj* | adjective, adjectival phrase |
| administration | *Admin* | administration |
| adverbe, locution adverbiale | *adv* | adverb, adverbial phrase |
| agriculture | *Agr* | agriculture |
| anatomie | *Anat* | anatomy |
| architecture | *Archit* | architecture |
| article défini | *art déf* | definite article |
| article indéfini | *art indéf* | indefinite article |
| automobile | *Aut(o)* | the motor car and motoring |
| aviation, voyages aériens | *Aviat* | flying, air travel |
| biologie | *Bio(l)* | biology |
| botanique | *Bot* | botany |
| anglais britannique | *BRIT* | British English |
| chimie | *Chem* | chemistry |
| commerce, finance, banque | *Comm* | commerce, finance, banking |
| informatique | *Comput* | computing |
| conjonction | *conj* | conjunction |
| construction | *Constr* | building |
| nom utilisé comme adjectif | *cpd* | compound element |
| cuisine | *Culin* | cookery |
| article défini | *def art* | definite article |
| déterminant: article; adjectif démonstratif ou indéfini *etc* | *dét* | determiner: article, demonstrative *etc* |
| économie | *Écon, Econ* | economics |
| électricité, électronique | *Élec, Elec* | electricity, electronics |
| en particulier | *esp* | especially |
| exclamation, interjection | *excl* | exclamation, interjection |
| féminin | *f* | feminine |
| langue familière (! emploi vulgaire) | *fam(!)* | colloquial usage (! particularly offensive) |
| emploi figuré | *fig* | figurative use |
| (verbe anglais) dont la particule est inséparable | *fus* | (phrasal verb) where the particle is inseparable |
| généralement | *gén, gen* | generally |
| géographie, géologie | *Géo, Geo* | geography, geology |
| géométrie | *Géom, Geom* | geometry |
| langue familière (! emploi vulgaire) | *inf(!)* | colloquial usage (! particularly offensive) |
| infinitif | *infin* | infinitive |
| informatique | *Inform* | computing |
| invariable | *inv* | invariable |
| irrégulier | *irreg* | irregular |
| domaine juridique | *Jur* | law |

## ABRÉVIATIONS

| | | |
|---|---|---|
| grammaire, linguistique | Ling | grammar, linguistics |
| masculin | m | masculine |
| mathématiques, algèbre | Math | mathematics, calculus |
| médecine | Méd, Med | medical term, medicine |
| masculin ou féminin | m/f | masculine or feminine |
| domaine militaire, armée | Mil | military matters |
| musique | Mus | music |
| nom | n | noun |
| navigation, nautisme | Navig, Naut | sailing, navigation |
| nom ou adjectif numéral | num | numeral noun or adjective |
| | o.s. | oneself |
| péjoratif | péj, pej | derogatory, pejorative |
| photographie | Phot(o) | photography |
| physiologie | Physiol | physiology |
| pluriel | pl | plural |
| politique | Pol | politics |
| participe passé | pp | past participle |
| préposition | prép, prep | preposition |
| pronom | pron | pronoun |
| psychologie, psychiatrie | Psych | psychology, psychiatry |
| temps du passé | pt | past tense |
| quelque chose | qch | |
| quelqu'un | qn | |
| religion, domaine ecclésiastique | Rel | religion |
| | sb | somebody |
| enseignement, système scolaire et universitaire | Scol | schooling, schools and universities |
| singulier | sg | singular |
| | sth | something |
| subjonctif | sub | subjunctive |
| sujet (grammatical) | su(b)j | (grammatical) subject |
| superlatif | superl | superlative |
| techniques, technologie | Tech | technical term, technology |
| télécommunications | Tél, Tel | telecommunications |
| télévision | TV | television |
| typographie | Typ(o) | typography, printing |
| anglais des USA | US | American English |
| verbe (auxiliare) | vb (aux) | (auxiliary) verb |
| verbe intransitif | vi | intransitive verb |
| verbe transitif | vt | transitive verb |
| zoologie | Zool | zoology |
| marque déposée | ® | registered trademark |
| indique une équivalence culturelle | ≈ | introduces a cultural equivalent |

## ABBREVIATIONS

# TRANCRIPTION PHONÉTIQUE

## CONSONNES

NB. **p, b, t, d, k, g** sont suivis d'une aspiration en anglais.

## CONSONANTS

NB. **p, b, t, d, k, g** are not aspirated in French.

| | | |
|---|---|---|
| poupée | p | puppy |
| bombe | b | baby |
| tente thermal | t | tent |
| dinde | d | daddy |
| coq qui képi | k | cork kiss chord |
| gage bague | g | gag guess |
| sale ce nation | s | so rice kiss |
| zéro rose | z | cousin buzz |
| tache chat | ʃ | sheep sugar |
| gilet juge | ʒ | pleasure beige |
| | tʃ | church |
| | dʒ | judge general |
| fer phare | f | farm raffle |
| verveine | v | very revel |
| | θ | thin maths |
| | ð | that other |
| lent salle | l | little ball |
| rare rentrer | ʀ | |
| | r | rat rare |
| maman femme | m | mummy comb |
| non bonne | n | no ran |
| agneau vigne | ɲ | |
| | ŋ | singing bank |
| | h | hat rehearse |
| yeux paille pied | j | yet |
| nouer oui | w | wall wail |
| huile lui | ɥ | |
| | x | loch |

### DIVERS

pour l'anglais: le r final se prononce en liaison devant une voyelle

pour l'anglais: précède la syllabe accentuée

### MISCELLANEOUS

in English transcription: final r can be pronounced before a vowel

in French wordlist: no liaison before aspirate h

| | |
|---|---|
| r | |
| ' | |

En règle générale, la prononciation est donnée entre crochets après chaque entrée. Toutefois, du côté anglais-français et dans le cas des expressions composées de deux ou plusieurs mots non réunis par un trait d'union et faisant l'objet d'une entrée séparée, la prononciation doit être cherchée sous chacun des mots constitutifs de l'expression en question.

# PHONETIC TRANSCRIPTION

| VOYELLES | | VOWELS |
|---|---|---|
| NB. La mise en équivalence de certains sons n'indique qu'une ressemblance approximative. | | NB. The pairing of some vowel sounds only indicates approximate equivalence. |
| ici vie lyrique | i iː | heel bead |
| | ɪ | hit pity |
| jouer été | e | |
| lait jouet merci | ɛ | set tent |
| plat amour | a æ | bat apple |
| bas pâte | ɑ ɑː | after car calm |
| | ʌ | fun cousin |
| le premier | ə | over above |
| beurre peur | œ | |
| peu deux | ø əː | urgent fern work |
| or homme | ɔ | wash pot |
| mot eau gauche | o ɔː | born cork |
| genou roue | u | full hook |
| | uː | boom shoe |
| rue urne | y | |

| DIPHTONGUES | | DIPHTHONGS |
|---|---|---|
| | ɪə | beer tier |
| | ɛə | tear fair there |
| | eɪ | date plaice day |
| | aɪ | life buy cry |
| | au | owl foul now |
| | əu | low no |
| | ɔɪ | boil boy oily |
| | uə | poor tour |

| NASALES | | NASAL VOWELS |
|---|---|---|
| matin plein | ɛ̃ | |
| brun | œ̃ | |
| sang an dans | ɑ̃ | |
| non pont | ɔ̃ | |

In general, we give the pronunciation of each entry in square brackets after the word in question. However, on the English-French side, where the entry is composed of two or more unhyphenated words, each of which is given elsewhere in this dictionary, you will find the pronunciation of each word in its alphabetical position.

# FRENCH VERB TABLES

1 Present participle 2 Past participle 3 Present 4 Imperfect 5 Future
6 Conditional 7 Present subjunctive

**acquérir** 1 acquérant 2 acquis
3 acquiers, acquérons,
acquièrent 4 acquérais
5 acquerrai 7 acquière

**ALLER** 1 allant 2 allé 3 vais, vas, va,
allons, allez, vont 4 allais 5 irai
6 irais 7 aille

**asseoir** 1 asseyant 2 assis 3 assieds,
asseyons, asseyez, asseyent
4 asseyais 5 assiérai 7 asseye

**atteindre** 1 atteignant 2 atteint
3 atteins, atteignons
4 atteignais 7 atteigne

**AVOIR** 1 ayant 2 eu 3 ai, as, a,
avons, avez, ont 4 avais 5 aurai
6 aurais 7 aie, aies, ait, ayons,
ayez, aient

**battre** 1 battant 2 battu 3 bats, bat,
battons 4 battais 7 batte

**boire** 1 buvant 2 bu 3 bois, buvons,
boivent 4 buvais 7 boive

**bouillir** 1 bouillant 2 bouilli 3 bous,
bouillons 4 bouillais 7 bouille

**conclure** 1 concluant 2 conclu
3 conclus, concluons
4 concluais 7 conclue

**conduire** 1 conduisant 2 conduit
3 conduis, conduisons
4 conduisais 7 conduise

**connaître** 1 connaissant 2 connu
3 connais, connaît, connaissons
4 connaissais 7 connaisse

**coudre** 1 cousant 2 cousu 3 couds,
cousons, cousez, cousent
4 cousais 7 couse

**courir** 1 courant 2 couru 3 cours,
courons 4 courais 5 courrai
7 coure

**couvrir** 1 couvrant 2 couvert
3 couvre, couvrons 4 couvrais
7 couvre

**craindre** 1 craignant 2 craint
3 crains, craignons 4 craignais
7 craigne

**croire** 1 croyant 2 cru 3 crois,
croyons, croient 4 croyais
7 croie

**croître** 1 croissant 2 crû, crue, crus,
crues 3 croîs, croissons
4 croissais 7 croisse

**cueillir** 1 cueillant 2 cueilli
3 cueille, cueillons 4 cueillais
5 cueillerai 7 cueille

**devoir** 1 devant 2 dû, due, dus,
dues 3 dois, devons, doivent
4 devais 5 devrai 7 doive

**dire** 1 disant 2 dit 3 dis, disons,
dites, disent 4 disais 7 dise

**dormir** 1 dormant 2 dormi 3 dors,
dormons 4 dormais 7 dorme

**écrire** 1 écrivant 2 écrit 3 écris,
écrivons 4 écrivais 7 écrive

**ÊTRE** 1 étant 2 été 3 suis, es, est,
sommes, êtes, sont 4 étais
5 serai 6 serais 7 sois, sois, soit,
soyons, soyez, soient

**FAIRE** 1 faisant 2 fait 3 fais, fais,
fait, faisons, faites, font
4 faisais 5 ferai 6 ferais 7 fasse

**falloir** 2 fallu 3 faut 4 fallait
5 faudra 7 faille

**FINIR** 1 finissant 2 fini 3 finis,
finis, finit, finissons, finissez,
finissent 4 finissais 5 finirai
6 finirais 7 finisse

**fuir** 1 fuyant 2 fui 3 fuis, fuyons,
fuient 4 fuyais 7 fuie

**joindre** 1 joignant 2 joint 3 joins,
joignons 4 joignais 7 joigne

**lire** 1 lisant 2 lu 3 lis, lisons 4 lisais
7 lise

**luire** 1 luisant 2 lui 3 luis, luisons

**4** luisais **7** luise

**maudire 1** maudissant **2** maudit
**3** maudis, maudissons
**4** maudissait **7** maudisse

**mentir 1** mentant **2** menti **3** mens,
mentons **4** mentais **7** mente

**mettre 1** mettant **2** mis **3** mets,
mettons **4** mettais **7** mette

**mourir 1** mourant **2** mort **3** meurs,
mourons, meurent **4** mourais
**5** mourrai **7** meure

**naître 1** naissant **2** né **3** nais, naît,
naissons **4** naissais **7** naisse

**offrir 1** offrant **2** offert **3** offre,
offrons **4** offrais **7** offre

**PARLER 1** parlant **2** parlé **3** parle,
parles, parle, parlons, parlez,
parlent **4** parlais, parlais,
parlait, parlions, parliez,
parlaient **5** parlerai, parleras,
parlera, parlerons, parlerez,
parleront **6** parlerais, parlerais,
parlerait, parlerions, parleriez,
parleraient **7** parle, parles,
parle, parlions, parliez, parlent
*impératif* parle! parlons! parlez!

**partir 1** partant **2** parti **3** pars,
partons **4** partais **7** parte

**plaire 1** plaisant **2** plu **3** plais, plaît,
plaisons **4** plaisais **7** plaise

**pleuvoir 1** pleuvant **2** plu **3** pleut,
pleuvent **4** pleuvait **5** pleuvra
**7** pleuve

**pourvoir 1** pourvoyant **2** pourvu
**3** pourvois, pourvoyons,
pourvoient **4** pourvoyais
**7** pourvoie

**pouvoir 1** pouvant **2** pu **3** peux,
peut, pouvons, peuvent **4**
pouvais **5** pourrai **7** puisse

**prendre 1** prenant **2** pris **3** prends,
prenons, prennent **4** prenais
**7** prenne

**prévoir** like voir **5** prévoirai

**RECEVOIR 1** recevant **2** reçu
**3** reçois, reçois, reçoit, recevons,
recevez, rerçoivent **4** recevais

**5** recevrai **6** recevrais **7** reçoive

**RENDRE 1** rendant **2** rendu
**3** rends, rends, rend, rendons,
rendez, rendent **4** rendais
**5** rendrai **6** rendrais **7** rende

**résoudre 1** résolvant **2** résolu
**3** résous, résout, résolvons
**4** résolvais **7** résolve

**rire 1** riant **2** ri **3** ris, rions **4** riais
**7** rie

**savoir 1** sachant **2** su **3** sais,
savons, savent **4** savais **5** saurai
**7** sache *impératif* sache! sachons!
sachez!

**servir 1** servant **2** servi **3** sers,
servons **4** servais **7** serve

**sortir 1** sortant **2** sorti **3** sors,
sortons **4** sortais **7** sorte

**souffrir 1** souffrant **2** souffert
**3** souffre, souffrons **4** souffrais
**7** souffre

**suffire 1** suffisant **2** suffi **3** suffis,
suffisons **4** suffisais **7** suffise

**suivre 1** suivant **2** suivi **3** suis,
suivons **4** suivais **7** suive

**taire 1** taisant **2** tu **3** tais, taisons
**4** taisais **7** taise

**tenir 1** tenant **2** tenu **3** tiens,
tenons, tiennent **4** tenais
**5** tiendrai **7** tienne

**vaincre 1** vainquant **2** vaincu
**3** vaincs, vainc, vainquons
**4** vainquais **7** vainque

**valoir 1** valant **2** valu **3** vaux, vaut,
valons **4** valais **5** vaudrai **7** vaille

**venir 1** venant **2** venu **3** viens,
venons, viennent **4** venais
**5** viendrai **7** vienne

**vivre 1** vivant **2** vécu **3** vis, vivons
**4** vivais **7** vive

**voir 1** voyant **2** vu **3** vois, voyons,
voient **4** voyais **5** verrai **7** voie

**vouloir 1** voulant **2** voulu **3** veux,
veut, voulons, veulent **4** voulais
**5** voudrai **7** veuille; *impératif*
veuillez!

# VERBES IRRÉGULIERS ANGLAIS

| PRÉSENT | PASSÉ | PARTICIPE | PRÉSENT | PASSÉ | PARTICIPE |
|---|---|---|---|---|---|
| arise | arose | arisen | fight | fought | fought |
| awake | awoke | awoken | find | found | found |
| be | was, were | been | flee | fled | fled |
| (am, is, | | | fling | flung | flung |
| are; being) | | | fly | flew | flown |
| bear | bore | born(e) | forbid | forbad(e) | forbidden |
| beat | beat | beaten | forecast | forecast | forecast |
| become | became | become | forget | forgot | forgotten |
| begin | began | begun | forgive | forgave | forgiven |
| bend | bent | bent | forsake | forsook | forsaken |
| bet | bet, | bet, | freeze | froze | frozen |
| | betted | betted | get | got | got, |
| bid (at auction, | bid | bid | | | (US) gotten |
| cards) | | | give | gave | given |
| bid (say) | bade | bidden | go (goes) | went | gone |
| bind | bound | bound | grind | ground | ground |
| bite | bit | bitten | grow | grew | grown |
| bleed | bled | bled | hang | hung | hung |
| blow | blew | blown | hang (execute) | hanged | hanged |
| break | broke | broken | have | had | had |
| breed | bred | bred | hear | heard | heard |
| bring | brought | brought | hide | hid | hidden |
| build | built | built | hit | hit | hit |
| burn | burnt, | burnt, | hold | held | held |
| | burned | burned | hurt | hurt | hurt |
| burst | burst | burst | keep | kept | kept |
| buy | bought | bought | kneel | knelt, | knelt, |
| can | could | (been able) | | kneeled | kneeled |
| cast | cast | cast | know | knew | known |
| catch | caught | caught | lay | laid | laid |
| choose | chose | chosen | lead | led | led |
| cling | clung | clung | lean | leant, | leant, |
| come | came | come | | leaned | leaned |
| cost | cost | cost | leap | leapt, | leapt, |
| cost (work | costed | costed | | leaped | leaped |
| out price of) | | | learn | learnt, | learnt, |
| creep | crept | crept | | learned | learned |
| cut | cut | cut | leave | left | left |
| deal | dealt | dealt | lend | lent | lent |
| dig | dug | dug | let | let | let |
| do (does) | did | done | lie (lying) | lay | lain |
| draw | drew | drawn | light | lit, | lit, |
| dream | dreamed, | dreamed, | | lighted | lighted |
| | dreamt | dreamt | lose | lost | lost |
| drink | drank | drunk | make | made | made |
| drive | drove | driven | may | might | – |
| dwell | dwelt | dwelt | mean | meant | meant |
| eat | ate | eaten | meet | met | met |
| fall | fell | fallen | mistake | mistook | mistaken |
| feed | fed | fed | mow | mowed | mown, |
| feel | felt | felt | | | mowed |

| PRÉSENT | PASSÉ | PARTICIPE | PRÉSENT | PASSÉ | PARTICIPE |
|---------|-------|-----------|---------|-------|-----------|
| **must** | (had to) | (had to) | **spend** | spent | spent |
| **pay** | paid | paid | **spill** | spilt, | spilt, |
| **put** | put | put | | spilled | spilled |
| **quit** | quit, | quit, | **spin** | spun | spun |
| | quitted | quitted | **spit** | spat | spat |
| **read** | read | read | **spoil** | spoiled, | spoiled, |
| **rid** | rid | rid | | spoilt | spoilt |
| **ride** | rode | ridden | **spread** | spread | spread |
| **ring** | rang | rung | **spring** | sprang | sprung |
| **rise** | rose | risen | **stand** | stood | stood |
| **run** | ran | run | **steal** | stole | stolen |
| **saw** | sawed | sawed, | **stick** | stuck | stuck |
| | | sawn | **sting** | stung | stung |
| **say** | said | said | **stink** | stank | stunk |
| **see** | saw | seen | **stride** | strode | stridden |
| **seek** | sought | sought | **strike** | struck | struck |
| **sell** | sold | sold | **strive** | strove | striven |
| **send** | sent | sent | **swear** | swore | sworn |
| **set** | set | set | **sweep** | swept | swept |
| **sew** | sewed | sewn | **swell** | swelled | swollen, |
| **shake** | shook | shaken | | | swelled |
| **shear** | sheared | shorn, | **swim** | swam | swum |
| | | sheared | **swing** | swung | swung |
| **shed** | shed | shed | **take** | took | taken |
| **shine** | shone | shone | **teach** | taught | taught |
| **shoot** | shot | shot | **tear** | tore | torn |
| **show** | showed | shown | **tell** | told | told |
| **shrink** | shrank | shrunk | **think** | thought | thought |
| **shut** | shut | shut | **throw** | threw | thrown |
| **sing** | sang | sung | **thrust** | thrust | thrust |
| **sink** | sank | sunk | **tread** | trod | trodden |
| **sit** | sat | sat | **wake** | woke, | woken, |
| **slay** | slew | slain | | waked | waked |
| **sleep** | slept | slept | **wear** | wore | worn |
| **slide** | slid | slid | **weave** | wove | woven |
| **sling** | slung | slung | **weave** (*wind*) | weaved | weaved |
| **slit** | slit | slit | **wed** | wedded, | wedded, |
| **smell** | smelt, | smelt, | | wed | wed |
| | smelled | smelled | **weep** | wept | wept |
| **sow** | sowed | sown, | **win** | won | won |
| | | sowed | **wind** | wound | wound |
| **speak** | spoke | spoken | **wring** | wrung | wrung |
| **speed** | sped, | sped, | **write** | wrote | written |
| | speeded | speeded | | | |
| **spell** | spelt, | spelt, | | | |
| | spelled | spelled | | | |

## LES NOMBRES

| | | NUMBERS |
|---|---|---|
| un (une) | 1 | one |
| deux | 2 | two |
| trois | 3 | three |
| quatre | 4 | four |
| cinq | 5 | five |
| six | 6 | six |
| sept | 7 | seven |
| huit | 8 | eight |
| neuf | 9 | nine |
| dix | 10 | ten |
| onze | 11 | eleven |
| douze | 12 | twelve |
| treize | 13 | thirteen |
| quatorze | 14 | fourteen |
| quinze | 15 | fifteen |
| seize | 16 | sixteen |
| dix-sept | 17 | seventeen |
| dix-huit | 18 | eighteen |
| dix-neuf | 19 | nineteen |
| vingt | 20 | twenty |
| vingt et un (une) | 21 | twenty-one |
| vingt-deux | 22 | twenty-two |
| trente | 30 | thirty |
| quarante | 40 | forty |
| cinquante | 50 | fifty |
| soixante | 60 | sixty |
| soixante-dix | 70 | seventy |
| soixante-et-onze | 71 | seventy-one |
| soixante-douze | 72 | seventy |
| quatre-vingts | 80 | eighty |
| quatre-vingt-un (-une) | 81 | eighty-one |
| quatre-vingt-dix | 90 | ninety |
| cent | 100 | a hundred, one hundred |
| cent un (une) | 101 | a hundred and one |
| deux cents | 200 | two hundred |
| deux cent un (une) | 201 | two hundred and one |
| quatre cents | 400 | four hundred |
| mille | 1000 | a thousand |
| cinq mille | 5000 | five thousand |
| un million | 1000000 | a million |

## LES NOMBRES

premier (première), 1$^{er}$ (1$^{ère}$)
deuxième, 2$^e$ or 2$^{ème}$
troisième, 3$^e$ or 3$^{ème}$
quatrième, 4$^e$ or 4$^{ème}$
cinquième, 5$^e$ or 5$^{ème}$
sixième, 6$^e$ or 6$^{ème}$
septième
huitième
neuvième
dixième
onzième
douzième
treizième
quartorzième
quinzième
seizième
dix-septième
dix-huitième
dix-neuvième
vingtième
vingt-et-unième
vingt-deuxième
trentième
centième
cent-unième
millième

## LES FRACTIONS ETC

un demi
un tiers
un quart
un cinquième
zéro virgule cinq, 0,5
trois virgule quatre, 3,4
dix pour cent
cent pour cent

## EXEMPLES

elle habite au septième (étage)
il habite au sept
au chapitre/à la page sept
il est arrivé (le) septième

## NUMBERS

first, 1st
second, 2nd
third, 3rd
fourth, 4th
fifth, 5th
sixth, 6th
seventh
eighth
ninth
tenth
eleventh
twelfth
thirteenth
fourteenth
fifteenth
sixteenth
seventeenth
eighteenth
nineteenth
twentieth
twenty-first
twenty-second
thirtieth
hundredth
hundred-and-first
thousandth

## FRACTIONS ETC

a half
a third
a quarter
a fifth
(nought) point five, 0.5
three point four, 3.4
ten per cent
a hundred per cent

## EXAMPLES

she lives on the 7th floor
he lives at number 7
chapter/page 7
he came in 7th

## L'HEURE

*quelle heure est-il?*

il est ...

minuit
une heure (du matin)

une heure cinq
une heure dix
une heure et quart

une heure vingt-cinq

une heure et demie, une heure trente
deux heures moins vingt-cinq, une
    heure trente-cinq
deux heures moins vingt, une heure
    quarante
deux heures moins le quart, une heure
    quarante-cinq
deux heures moins dix, une heure
    cinquante
midi

deux heures (de l'après-midi),
    quatorze heures
sept heures (du soir), dix-sept heures

*à quelle heure?*

à minuit
à sept heures

dans vingt minutes
il y a un quart d'heure

## THE TIME

*what time is it?*

it's ou it is ...

midnight, twelve p.m.
one o'clock (in the
    morning), one (a.m.)

five past one
ten past one
a quarter past one,
    one fifteen

twenty-five past one,
    one twenty-five

half-past one, one thirty
twenty-five to two,
    one thirty-five
twenty to two, one forty

a quarter to two,
    one forty-five
ten to two, one fifty

twelve o'clock, midday,
    noon
two o'clock (in the
    afternoon), two (p.m.)
seven o'clock (in the
    evening), seven (p.m.)

*(at) what time?*

at midnight
at seven o'clock

in twenty minutes
fifteen minutes ago

friend of mine; **donner qch à qn** to give sth to sb

**5** (*moyen*) with; **se chauffer au gaz** to have gas heating; **à bicyclette** on a *ou* by bicycle; **à pied** on foot; **à la main/machine** by hand/machine

**6** (*provenance*) from; **boire à la bouteille** to drink from the bottle

**7** (*caractérisation, manière*): **l'homme aux yeux bleus** the man with the blue eyes; **à leur grande surprise** much to their surprise; **à ce qu'il prétend** according to him, from what he says; **à la russe** the Russian way; **à nous deux nous n'avons pas su le faire** we couldn't do it, even between the two of us

**8** (*but, destination*): **tasse à café** coffee cup; **maison à vendre** house for sale; **je n'ai rien à lire** I don't have anything to read; **à bien réfléchir …** thinking about it …, on reflection …

**9** (*rapport, évaluation, distribution*): **100 km/unités à l'heure** 100 km/units per *ou* an hour; **payé au mois/à l'heure** paid monthly/by the hour; **cinq à six** five to six; **ils sont arrivés à quatre** four of them arrived

**a** [a] *vb voir* **avoir**

 **MOT-CLÉ**

**à** [a] (*à + le = **au**, à + les = **aux***) *prép*
**1** (*endroit, situation*) at, in; **être à Paris/au Portugal** to be in Paris/Portugal; **être à la maison/à l'école** to be at home/at school; **à la campagne** in the country; **c'est à 10 km/à 20 minutes (d'ici)** it's 10 km/20 minutes away

**2** (*direction*) to; **aller à Paris/au Portugal** to go to Paris/Portugal; **aller à la maison/à l'école** to go home/to school; **à la campagne** to the country

**3** (*temps*) at; **à 3 heures/minuit** at 3 o'clock/midnight; **au printemps/mois de juin** in the spring/the month of June; **à Noël/Pâques** at Christmas/Easter; **à demain/lundi!** see you tomorrow/on Monday!

**4** (*attribution, appartenance*) to; **le livre est à Paul/à lui/à nous** this book is Paul's/his/ours; **un ami à moi** a

**abaisser** [abese] *vt* to lower, bring down; (*manette*) to pull down; **s'abaisser** *vi* to go down; (*fig*) to demean o.s.

**abandon** [abɑ̃dɔ̃] *nm* abandoning; giving up; withdrawal; **être à l'~** to be in a state of neglect; **laisser à l'~** to abandon

**abandonner** [abɑ̃dɔne] *vt* (*personne*) to abandon; (*projet, activité*) to abandon, give up; (*Sport*) to retire *ou* withdraw from; (*céder*) to surrender; **s'~ à** (*paresse, plaisirs*) to give o.s. up to

**abat-jour** [abaʒuʀ] *nm inv* lampshade

**abats** [aba] *nmpl* (*de bœuf, porc*) offal *sg*; (*de volaille*) giblets

**abattement** [abatmɑ̃] *nm*: **abattement fiscal** ≈ tax allowance

**abattoir** [abatwaʀ] *nm*

slaughterhouse

**abattre** [abatʀ] vt (arbre) to cut down, fell; (mur, maison) to pull down; (avion, personne) to shoot down; (animal) to shoot, kill; (fig) to wear out, tire out; to demoralize; **s'abattre** vi to crash down; **ne pas se laisser ~** to keep one's spirits up, not to let things get one down; **s'~ sur** to beat down on; (fig) to rain down on; **~ du travail** ou **de la besogne** to get through a lot of work

**abbaye** [abei] nf abbey

**abbé** [abe] nm priest; (d'une abbaye) abbot

**abcès** [apsɛ] nm abscess

**abdiquer** [abdike] vi to abdicate

**abdominaux** [abdɔmino] nmpl: **faire des ~** to do sit-ups

**abeille** [abɛj] nf bee

**aberrant, e** [abeʀɑ̃, ɑ̃t] adj absurd

**aberration** [abeʀasjɔ̃] nf aberration

**abîme** [abim] nm abyss, gulf

**abîmer** [abime] vt to spoil, damage; **s'abîmer** vi to get spoilt ou damaged

**aboiement** [abwamɑ̃] nm bark, barking

**abolir** [abɔliʀ] vt to abolish

**abominable** [abɔminabl] adj abominable

**abondance** [abɔ̃dɑ̃s] nf abundance

**abondant, e** [abɔ̃dɑ̃, ɑ̃t] adj plentiful, abundant, copious; **abonder** vi to abound, be plentiful; **abonder dans le sens de qn** to concur with sb

**abonné, e** [abɔne] nm/f subscriber; season ticket holder

**abonnement** [abɔnmɑ̃] nm subscription; (transports, concerts) season ticket

**abonner** [abɔne] vt: **s'~ à** to subscribe to, take out a subscription to

**abord** [abɔʀ] nm: **au premier ~** at first sight, initially; **abords** nmpl (environs) surroundings; **d'~** first

**abordable** [abɔʀdabl] adj (prix) reasonable; (personne) approachable

**aborder** [abɔʀde] vi to land ▷ vt (sujet, difficulté) to tackle; (personne) to approach; (rivage etc) to reach

**aboutir** [abutiʀ] vi (négociations etc) to succeed; **~ à** to end up at; **n'~ à rien** to come to nothing

**aboyer** [abwaje] vi to bark

**abréger** [abʀeʒe] vt to shorten

**abreuver** [abʀœve]: **s'abreuver** vi to drink; **abreuvoir** nm watering place

**abréviation** [abʀevjasjɔ̃] nf abbreviation

**abri** [abʀi] nm shelter; **être à l'~** to be under cover; **se mettre à l'~** to shelter; **à l'~ de** (vent, soleil) sheltered from; (danger) safe from

**abricot** [abʀiko] nm apricot

**abriter** [abʀite] vt to shelter; **s'abriter** vt to shelter, take cover

**abrupt, e** [abʀypt] adj sheer, steep; (ton) abrupt

**abruti, e** [abʀyti] adj stunned, dazed ▷ nm/f (fam) idiot, moron; **~ de travail** overworked

**absence** [apsɑ̃s] nf absence; (Méd) blackout; **avoir des ~s** to have mental blanks

**absent, e** [apsɑ̃, ɑ̃t] adj absent ▷ nm/f absentee; **absenter: s'absenter** vi to take time off work; (sortir) to leave, go out

**absolu, e** [apsɔly] adj absolute; **absolument** adv absolutely

**absorbant, e** [apsɔʀbɑ̃, ɑ̃t] adj absorbent

**absorber** [apsɔʀbe] vt to absorb; (gén Méd: manger, boire) to take

**abstenir** [apstəniʀ] vb: **s'~ de qch/de faire** to refrain from sth/from doing

**abstrait, e** [apstʀɛ, ɛt] adj abstract

**absurde** [apsyʀd] adj absurd

**abus** [aby] nm abuse; **~ de confiance** breach of trust; **il y a de l'~!** (fam) that's a bit much!; **abuser** vi to go too far, overstep the mark; (duper) to take advantage of; **s'abuser** vi (se méprendre) to be mistaken; **abusif, -ive** adj exorbitant; (punition) excessive

**académie** [akademi] nf academy; (Scol: circonscription) ≈ regional education authority

● **ACADÉMIE FRANÇAISE**
●
● The **Académie française** was
● founded by Cardinal Richelieu in
● 1635, during the reign of Louis XIII. It
● is made up of forty elected scholars
● and writers who are known as 'les
● Quarante' or 'les Immortels'. One
● of the **Académie**'s functions is to
● keep an eye on the development
● of the French language, and its
● recommendations are frequently
● the subject of lively public debate. It
● has produced several editions of its
● famous dictionary and also awards
● various literary prizes.

**acajou** [akaʒu] *nm* mahogany
**acariâtre** [akarjɑtr] *adj* cantankerous
**accablant, e** [akablɑ̃, ɑ̃t] *adj* (*chaleur*)
oppressive; (*témoignage, preuve*)
overwhelming
**accabler** [akable] *vt* to overwhelm,
overcome; **~ qn d'injures** to heap *ou*
shower abuse on sb; **~ qn de travail** to
overwork sb
**accalmie** [akalmi] *nf* lull
**accaparer** [akapare] *vt* to
monopolize; (*suj: travail etc*) to take up
(all) the time *ou* attention of
**accéder** [aksede]: **~ à** *vt* (*lieu*) to reach;
(*accorder: requête*) to grant, accede to
**accélérateur** [akseleratœr] *nm*
accelerator
**accélérer** [akselere] *vt* to speed up ▷ *vi*
to accelerate
**accent** [aksɑ̃] *nm* accent; (*Phonétique,
fig*) stress; **mettre l'~ sur** (*fig*) to stress;
**~ aigu/grave/circonflexe** acute/
grave/circumflex accent; **accentuer**
*vt* (*Ling*) to accent; (*fig*) to accentuate,
emphasize; **s'accentuer** *vi* to become
more marked *ou* pronounced
**acceptation** [akseptasjɔ̃] *nf*
acceptance
**accepter** [aksepte] *vt* to accept; **~ de**

**faire** to agree to do; **acceptez-vous
les cartes de crédit?** do you take
credit cards?
**accès** [aksɛ] *nm* (*à un lieu*) access; (*Méd:
de toux*) fit; (: *de fièvre*) bout; **d'~ facile**
easily accessible; **facile d'~** easy to
get to; **accès de colère** fit of anger;
**accessible** *adj* accessible; (*livre, sujet*):
**accessible à qn** within the reach of sb
**accessoire** [akseswar] *adj* secondary;
incidental ▷ *nm* accessory; (*Théâtre*)
prop
**accident** [aksidɑ̃] *nm* accident; **par
~** by chance; **j'ai eu un ~** I've had an
accident; **accident de la route** road
accident; **accidenté, e** *adj* damaged;
injured; (*relief, terrain*) uneven; hilly;
**accidentel, le** *adj* accidental
**acclamer** [aklame] *vt* to cheer,
acclaim
**acclimater** [aklimate]: **s'acclimater**
*vi* (*personne*) to adapt (o.s.)
**accolade** [akɔlad] *nf* (*amicale*)
embrace; (*signe*) brace
**accommoder** [akɔmɔde] *vt* (*Culin*)
to prepare; **s'accommoder de** *vt* to
put up with; (*se contenter de*) to make
do with
**accompagnateur, -trice**
[akɔ̃paɲatœr, tris] *nm/f* (*Mus*)
accompanist; (*de voyage: guide*) guide;
(*de voyage organisé*) courier
**accompagner** [akɔ̃paɲe] *vt* to
accompany, be *ou* go *ou* come with;
(*Mus*) to accompany
**accompli, e** [akɔ̃pli] *adj*
accomplished; *voir aussi* **fait**
**accomplir** [akɔ̃plir] *vt* (*tâche, projet*) to
carry out; (*souhait*) to fulfil; **s'accomplir**
*vi* to be fulfilled
**accord** [akɔr] *nm* agreement; (*entre des
styles, tons etc*) harmony; (*Mus*) chord;
**d'~!** OK!; **se mettre d'~** to come to an
agreement; **être d'~ (pour faire qch)**
to agree (to do sth)
**accordéon** [akɔrdeɔ̃] *nm* (*Mus*)
accordion
**accorder** [akɔrde] *vt* (*faveur, délai*) to

grant; (*harmoniser*) to match; (*Mus*) to tune; (*valeur, importance*) attach

**accoster** [akɔste] vt (*Navig*) to draw alongside ▷ vi to berth

**accouchement** [akuʃmã] nm delivery, (child)birth; labour

**accoucher** [akuʃe] vi to give birth, have a baby; **~ d'un garçon** to give birth to a boy

**accouder** [akude]: **s'accouder** vi: **s'~ à/contre/sur** to rest one's elbows on/ against/on; **accoudoir** nm armrest

**accoupler** [akuple] vt to couple; (*pour la reproduction*) to mate; **s'accoupler** vt to mate

**accourir** [akuʀiʀ] vi to rush *ou* run up

**accoutumance** [akutymãs] nf (*gén*) adaptation; (*Méd*) addiction

**accoutumé, e** [akutyme] adj (*habituel*) customary, usual

**accoutumer** [akutyme] vt: **s'~ à** to get accustomed *ou* used to

**accroc** [akʀo] nm (*déchirure*) tear; (*fig*) hitch, snag

**accrochage** [akʀɔʃaʒ] nm (*Auto*) collision; (*dispute*) clash, brush

**accrocher** [akʀɔʃe] vt (*fig*) to catch, attract; **s'accrocher** (*se disputer*) to have a clash *ou* brush; **~ qch à** (*suspendre*) to hang sth (up) on; (*attacher: remorque*) to hitch sth (up) to; **~ qch (à)** (*déchirer*) to catch sth (on); **il a accroché ma voiture** he bumped into my car; **s'~ à** (*rester pris à*) to catch on; (*agripper, fig*) to hang on *ou* cling to

**accroissement** [akʀwasmã] nm increase

**accroître** [akʀwatʀ]: **s'accroître** vi to increase

**accroupir** [akʀupiʀ]: **s'accroupir** vi to squat, crouch (down)

**accru, e** [akʀy] pp de **accroître**

**accueil** [akœj] nm welcome; **comité d'~** reception committee; **accueillir** vt to welcome; (*aller chercher*) to meet, collect

**accumuler** [akymyle] vt to accumulate, amass; **s'accumuler** vi to accumulate; to pile up

**accusation** [akyzasjõ] nf (*gén*) accusation; (*Jur*) charge; (*partie*): **l'~** the prosecution

**accusé, e** [akyze] nm/f accused; defendant; **accusé de réception** acknowledgement of receipt

**accuser** [akyze] vt to accuse; (*fig*) to emphasize, bring out; **~ qn de** to accuse sb of; (*Jur*) to charge sb with; **~ réception de** to acknowledge receipt of

**acéré, e** [asere] adj sharp

**acharné, e** [aʃarne] adj (*efforts*) relentless; (*lutte, adversaire*) fierce, bitter

**acharner** [aʃarne] vb: **s'~ contre** to set o.s. against; (*suj: malchance*) to dog; **s'~ à faire** to try doggedly to do; (*persister*) to persist in doing; **s'~ sur qn** to hound sb

**achat** [aʃa] nm purchase; **faire des ~s** to do some shopping; **faire l'~ de qch** to purchase sth

**acheter** [aʃ(ə)te] vt to buy, purchase; (*soudoyer*) to buy; **~ qch à** (*marchand*) to buy *ou* purchase sth from; (*ami etc: offrir*) to buy sth for; **où est-ce que je peux ~ des cartes postales?** where can I buy (some) postcards?; **acheteur, -euse** nm/f buyer; shopper; (*Comm*) buyer

**achever** [aʃ(ə)ve] vt to complete, finish; (*blessé*) to finish off; **s'achever** vi to end

**acide** [asid] adj sour, sharp; (*Chimie*) acid(ic) ▷ nm (*Chimie*) acid; **acidulé, e** adj slightly acid; **bonbons acidulés** acid drops

**acier** [asje] nm steel; **aciérie** nf steelworks sg

**acné** [akne] nf acne

**acompte** [akɔ̃t] nm deposit

**à-côté** [akote] nm side-issue; (*argent*) extra

**à-coup** [aku] nm: **par ~s** by fits and starts

**acoustique** [akustik] nf (*d'une salle*) acoustics pl

**acquéreur** [akerœr] nm buyer, purchaser

**acquérir** [akerir] vt to acquire

**acquis, e** [aki, iz] pp de **acquérir** ▷ nm (accumulated) experience; **son aide nous est ~e** we can count on her help

**acquitter** [akite] vt (Jur) to acquit; (facture) to pay, settle; **s'acquitter de** vt (devoir) to discharge; (promesse) to fulfil

**âcre** [akr] adj acrid, pungent

**acrobate** [akrobat] nm/f acrobat; **acrobatie** nf acrobatics sg

**acte** [akt] nm act, action; (Théâtre) act; **prendre ~ de** to note, take note of; **faire ~ de candidature** to apply; **faire ~ de présence** to put in an appearance; **acte de naissance** birth certificate

**acteur** [aktœr] nm actor

**actif, -ive** [aktif, iv] adj active ▷ nm (Comm) assets pl; (fig): **avoir à son ~** to have to one's credit; **population active** working population

**action** [aksjɔ̃] nf (gén) action; (Comm) share; **une bonne ~** a good deed; **actionnaire** nm/f shareholder; **actionner** vt (mécanisme) to activate; (machine) to operate

**activer** [aktive] vt to speed up; **s'activer** vi to bustle about; to hurry up

**activité** [aktivite] nf activity; **en ~** (volcan) active; (fonctionnaire) in active life

**actrice** [aktris] nf actress

**actualité** [aktɥalite] nf (d'un problème) topicality; (événements): **l'~** current events; **actualités** nfpl (Cinéma, TV) the news; **d'~** topical

**actuel, le** [aktɥɛl] adj (présent) present; (d'actualité) topical; **à l'heure ~le** at the present time; **actuellement** adv at present, at the present time

▌ Attention à ne pas traduire *actuellement* par *actually*.

**acuponcture** [akypɔ̃ktyr] nf acupuncture

**adaptateur** [adaptatœr] nm (Élec) adapter

**adapter** [adapte] vt to adapt; **s'adapter (à)** (suj: personne) to adapt (to); **~ qch à** (approprier) to adapt sth to (fit); **~ qch sur/dans/à** (fixer) to fit sth on/into/to

**addition** [adisjɔ̃] nf addition; (au café) bill; **l'~, s'il vous plaît** could I have the bill, please?; **additionner** vt to add (up)

**adepte** [adɛpt] nm/f follower

**adéquat, e** [adekwa(t), at] adj appropriate, suitable

**adhérent, e** [aderã, ãt] nm/f member

**adhérer** [adere]: **~ à** vt (coller) to adhere ou stick to; (se rallier à) to join; **adhésif, -ive** adj adhesive, sticky; **ruban adhésif** sticky ou adhesive tape

**adieu, x** [adjø] excl goodbye ▷ nm farewell

**adjectif** [adʒɛktif] nm adjective

**adjoint, e** [adʒwɛ̃, wɛ̃t] nm/f assistant; **adjoint au maire** deputy mayor; **directeur adjoint** assistant manager

**admettre** [admɛtr] vt (laisser entrer) to admit; (candidat: Scol) to pass; (tolérer) to allow, accept; (reconnaître) to admit, acknowledge

**administrateur, -trice** [administratœr, tris] nm/f (Comm) director; (Admin) administrator

**administration** [administrasjɔ̃] nf administration; **l'A~** ≈ the Civil Service

**administrer** [administre] vt (firme) to manage, run; (biens, remède, sacrement etc) to administer

**admirable** [admirabl] adj admirable, wonderful

**admirateur, -trice** [admiratœr, tris] nm/f admirer

**admiration** [admirasjɔ̃] nf admiration

**admirer** [admire] vt to admire

**admis, e** [admi, iz] pp de **admettre**

**admissible** [admisibl] adj (candidat) eligible; (comportement) admissible, acceptable

**ADN** sigle m (= acide désoxyribonucléique) DNA

**adolescence** [adɔlesɑ̃s] *nf* adolescence

**adolescent, e** [adɔlesɑ̃, ɑ̃t] *nm/f* adolescent, teenager

**adopter** [adɔpte] *vt* to adopt; **adoptif, -ive** *adj* (*parents*) adoptive; (*fils, patrie*) adopted

**adorable** [adɔrabl] *adj* delightful, adorable

**adorer** [adɔre] *vt* to adore; (*Rel*) to worship

**adosser** [adose] *vt*: **~ qch à** ou **contre** to stand sth against; **s'adosser à/contre** to lean with one's back against

**adoucir** [adusiʀ] *vt* (*goût, température*) to make milder; (*avec du sucre*) to sweeten; (*peau, voix*) to soften; (*caractère*) to mellow

**adresse** [adʀɛs] *nf* (*domicile*) address; (*dextérité*) skill, dexterity; **~ électronique** email address

**adresser** [adʀese] *vt* (*lettre: expédier*) to send; (: *écrire l'adresse sur*) to address; (*injure, compliments*) to address; **s'adresser à** (*parler à*) to speak to, address; (*s'informer auprès de*) to go and see; (: *bureau*) to inquire at; (*suj: livre, conseil*) to be aimed at; **~ la parole à** to speak to, address

**adroit, e** [adʀwa, wat] *adj* skilful, skilled.

**ADSL** *sigle m* (= *asymmetrical digital subscriber line*) ADSL, broadband

**adulte** [adylt] *nm/f* adult, grown-up ▷ *adj* (*chien, arbre*) fully-grown, mature; (*attitude*) adult, grown-up

**adverbe** [advɛrb] *nm* adverb

**adversaire** [advɛʀsɛʀ] *nm/f* (*Sport, gén*) opponent, adversary

**aération** [aeʀasjɔ̃] *nf* airing; (*circulation de l'air*) ventilation

**aérer** [aeʀe] *vt* to air; (*fig*) to lighten

**aérien, ne** [aeʀjɛ̃, jɛn] *adj* (*Aviat*) air *cpd*, aerial; (*câble, métro*) overhead; (*fig*) light; **compagnie ~ne** airline

**aéro...** [aeʀɔ] *préfixe*: **aérobic** *nm* aerobics *sg*; **aérogare** *nf* airport (buildings); (*en ville*) air terminal;

**aéroglisseur** *nm* hovercraft; **aérophagie** *nf* (*Méd*) wind, aerophagia (*Méd*); **aéroport** *nm* airport; **aérosol** *nm* aerosol

**affaiblir** [afeblir]: **s'affaiblir** *vi* to weaken

**affaire** [afɛʀ] *nf* (*problème, question*) matter; (*criminelle, judiciaire*) case; (*scandaleuse etc*) affair; (*entreprise*) business; (*marché, transaction*) deal; business *no pl*; (*occasion intéressante*) bargain; **affaires** *nfpl* (*intérêts publics et privés*) affairs; (*activité commerciale*) business *sg*; (*effets personnels*) things, belongings; **ce sont mes ~s** (*cela me concerne*) that's my business; **occupe-toi de tes ~s!** mind your own business!; **ça fera l'~** that will do (nicely); **se tirer d'~** to sort it ou things out for o.s.; **avoir ~ à** (*être en contact*) to be dealing with; **les A~s étrangères** Foreign Affairs; **affairer: s'affairer** *vi* to busy o.s., bustle about

**affamé, e** [afame] *adj* starving

**affecter** [afɛkte] *vt* to affect; **~ qch à** to allocate ou allot sth to; **~ qn à** to appoint sb to; (*diplomate*) to post sb to

**affectif, -ive** [afɛktif, iv] *adj* emotional

**affection** [afɛksjɔ̃] *nf* affection; (*mal*) ailment; **affectionner** *vt* to be fond of; **affectueux, -euse** *adj* affectionate

**affichage** [afiʃaʒ] *nm* billposting; (*électronique*) display; **"~ interdit"** "stick no bills"; **affichage à cristaux liquides** liquid crystal display, LCD

**affiche** [afiʃ] *nf* poster; (*officielle*) notice; (*Théâtre*) bill; **être à l'~** to be on

**afficher** [afiʃe] *vt* (*affiche*) to put up; (*réunion*) to put up a notice about; (*électroniquement*) to display; (*fig*) to exhibit, display; **"défense d'~"** "no bill posters"; **s'afficher** *vr* (*péj*) to flaunt o.s.; (*électroniquement*) to be displayed

**affilée** [afile]: **d'~** *adv* at a stretch

**affirmatif, -ive** [afiʀmatif, iv] *adj* affirmative

**affirmer** [afiʀme] *vt* to assert

**affligé, e** [aflize] adj distressed, grieved; **~ de** (maladie, tare) afflicted with

**affliger** [aflize] vt (peiner) to distress, grieve

**affluence** [aflyãs] nf crowds pl; **heures d'~** rush hours; **jours d'~** busiest days

**affluent** [aflyã] nm tributary

**affolement** [afɔlmã] nm panic

**affoler** [afɔle] vt to throw into a panic; **s'affoler** vi to panic

**affranchir** [afrãʃir] vt to put a stamp ou stamps on; (à la machine) to frank (BRIT), meter (US); (fig) to free, liberate; **affranchissement** nm postage

**affreux, -euse** [afrø, øz] adj dreadful, awful

**affront** [afrɔ̃] nm affront; **affrontement** nm clash, confrontation

**affronter** [afrɔ̃te] vt to confront, face

**affût** [afy] nm: **à l'~ (de)** (gibier) lying in wait (for); (fig) on the look-out (for)

**Afghanistan** [afganistã] nm: **l'~** Afghanistan

**afin** [afɛ̃]: **~ que** conj so that, in order that; **~ de faire** in order to do, so as to do

**africain, e** [afrikɛ̃, ɛn] adj African ▷ nm/f: **A~, e** African

**Afrique** [afrik] nf: **l'~** Africa; **l'Afrique du Nord/Sud** North/South Africa

**agacer** [agase] vt to irritate

**âge** [aʒ] nm age; **quel ~ as-tu?** how old are you?; **prendre de l'~** to be getting on (in years); **le troisième ~** (période) retirement; (personnes âgées) senior citizens; **âgé, e** adj old, elderly; **âgé de 10 ans** 10 years old

**agence** [aʒãs] nf agency, office; (succursale) branch; **agence de voyages** travel agency; **agence immobilière** estate agent (BRIT) ou real estate (US) agent's (office)

**agenda** [aʒɛ̃da] nm diary; **~ électronique** PDA

▌ Attention à ne pas traduire **agenda** par le mot anglais **agenda**.

**agenouiller** [aʒ(ə)nuje]: **s'agenouiller** vi to kneel (down)

**agent, e** [aʒã, ãt] nm/f (aussi: **~(e) de police**) policeman(policewoman); (Admin) official, officer; **agent immobilier** estate agent (BRIT), realtor (US)

**agglomération** [aglɔmerasjɔ̃] nf town; built-up area; **l'~ parisienne** the urban area of Paris

**aggraver** [agrave]: **s'aggraver** vi to worsen

**agile** [aʒil] adj agile, nimble

**agir** [aʒir] vi to act; **il s'agit de** (ça traite de) it is about; (il est important de) it's a matter ou question of; **il s'agit de faire** we (ou you etc) must do; **de quoi s'agit-il?** what is it about?

**agitation** [aʒitasjɔ̃] nf (hustle and) bustle; (trouble) agitation, excitement; (politique) unrest, agitation

**agité, e** [aʒite] adj fidgety, restless; (troublé) agitated, perturbed; (mer) rough

**agiter** [aʒite] vt (bouteille, chiffon) to shake; (bras, mains) to wave; (préoccuper, exciter) to perturb

**agneau, x** [aɲo] nm lamb

**agonie** [agɔni] nf mortal agony, death pangs pl; (fig) death throes pl

**agrafe** [agraf] nf (de vêtement) hook, fastener; (de bureau) staple; **agrafer** vt to fasten; to staple; **agrafeuse** nf stapler

**agrandir** [agrãdir] vt to enlarge; **s'agrandir** vi (ville, famille) to grow, expand; (trou, écart) to get bigger; **agrandissement** nm (Photo) enlargement

**agréable** [agreabl] adj pleasant, nice

**agréé, e** [agree] adj: **concessionnaire ~** registered dealer

**agréer** [agree] vt (requête) to accept; **~ à** to please, suit; **veuillez ~, Monsieur/Madame, mes salutations distinguées** (personne nommée) yours sincerely; (personne non nommée) yours faithfully

**agrégation** [agʁegasjɔ̃] nf highest teaching diploma in France; **agrégé, e** nm/f holder of the agrégation

**agrément** [agʁemɑ̃] nm (accord) consent, approval; (attraits) charm, attractiveness; (plaisir) pleasure

**agresser** [agʁese] vt to attack; **agresseur** nm aggressor, attacker; (Pol, Mil) aggressor; **agressif, -ive** adj aggressive

**agricole** [agʁikɔl] adj agricultural; **agriculteur** nm farmer; **agriculture** nf agriculture, farming

**agripper** [agʁipe] vt to grab, clutch; **s'agripper à** to cling (on) to, clutch, grip

**agro-alimentaire** [agʁoalimɑ̃tɛʁ] nm farm-produce industry

**agrumes** [agʁym] nmpl citrus fruit(s)

**aguets** [agɛ] nmpl: **être aux ~** to be on the look out

**ai** [ɛ] vb voir **avoir**

**aide** [ɛd] nm/f assistant; carer ▷ nf assistance, help; (secours financier) aid; **à l'~ de** (avec) with the help ou aid of; **appeler (qn) à l'~** to call for help (from sb); **à l'~!** help!; **aide judiciaire** legal aid; **aide ménagère** ≈ home help (BRIT) ou helper (US); **aide-mémoire** nm inv memoranda pages pl; (key facts) handbook; **aide-soignant, e** nm/f auxiliary nurse

**aider** [ede] vt to help; **~ à qch** to help (towards) sth; **~ qn à faire qch** to help sb to do sth; **pouvez-vous m'~?** can you help me?; **s'aider de** (se servir de) to use, make use of

**aïe** [aj] excl ouch!

**aie** etc [ɛ] vb voir **avoir**

**aigle** [ɛgl] nm eagle

**aigre** [ɛgʁ] adj sour, sharp; (fig) sharp, cutting; **aigre-doux, -ce** adj (sauce) sweet and sour; **aigreur** nf sourness; sharpness; **aigreurs d'estomac** heartburn sg

**aigu, ë** [egy] adj (objet, douleur) sharp; (son, voix) high-pitched, shrill; (note) high(-pitched)

**aiguille** [eguij] nf needle; (de montre) hand; **aiguille à tricoter** knitting needle

**aiguiser** [egize] vt to sharpen; (fig) to stimulate; (: sens) to excite

**ail** [aj] nm garlic

**aile** [ɛl] nf wing; **aileron** nm (de requin) fin; **ailier** nm winger

**aille** etc [aj] vb voir **aller**

**ailleurs** [ajœʁ] adv elsewhere, somewhere else; **partout/nulle part ~** everywhere/nowhere else; **d'~** (du reste) moreover, besides; **par ~** (d'autre part) moreover, furthermore

**aimable** [ɛmabl] adj kind, nice

**aimant** [ɛmɑ̃] nm magnet

**aimer** [eme] vt to love; (d'amitié, affection, par goût) to like; (souhait): **j'aimerais ...** I would like ...; **j'aime faire du ski** I like skiing; **je t'aime** I love you; **bien ~ qn/qch** to like sb/sth; **j'aime mieux Paul (que Pierre)** I prefer Paul (to Pierre); **j'aimerais mieux faire** I'd much rather do

**aine** [ɛn] nf groin

**aîné, e** [ene] adj elder, older; (le plus âgé) eldest, oldest ▷ nm/f oldest child ou one, oldest boy ou son/girl ou daughter

**ainsi** [ɛ̃si] adv (de cette façon) like this, in this way, thus; (ce faisant) thus ▷ conj thus, so; **~ que** (comme) (just) as; (et aussi) as well as; **pour ~ dire** so to speak; **et ~ de suite** and so on

**air** [ɛʁ] nm air; (mélodie) tune; (expression) look, air; **prendre l'~** to get some (fresh) air; **avoir l'~** (sembler) to look, appear; **il a l'~ triste/malade** he looks sad/ill; **avoir l'~ de** to look like; **il a l'~ de dormir** he looks as if he's sleeping; **en l'~** (promesses) empty

**airbag** [ɛʁbag] nm airbag

**aisance** [ɛzɑ̃s] nf ease; (richesse) affluence

**aise** [ɛz] nf comfort; **être à l'~** ou **à son ~** to be comfortable; (pas embarrassé) to be at ease; (financièrement) to be comfortably off; **se mettre à l'~** to make o.s. comfortable; **être mal à l'~**

to be uncomfortable; (*gêné*) to be ill at ease; **en faire à son ~** to do as one likes; **aisé, e** *adj* easy; (*assez riche*) well-to-do, well-off

**aisselle** [ɛsɛl] *nf* armpit

**ait** [ɛ] *vb voir* **avoir**

**ajonc** [aʒɔ̃] *nm* gorse *no pl*

**ajourner** [aʒuʀne] *vt* (*réunion*) to adjourn; (*décision*) to defer, postpone

**ajouter** [aʒute] *vt* to add

**alarme** [alaʀm] *nf* alarm; **donner l'~** to give *ou* raise the alarm; **alarmer** *vt* to alarm; **s'alarmer** *vi* to become alarmed

**Albanie** [albani] *nf*: **l'~** Albania

**album** [albɔm] *nm* album

**alcool** [alkɔl] *nm*: **l'~** alcohol; **un ~** a spirit, a brandy; **bière sans ~** non-alcoholic *ou* alcohol-free beer; **alcool à brûler** methylated spirits (*BRIT*), wood alcohol (*US*); **alcool à 90°** surgical spirit; **alcoolique** *adj*, *nm/f* alcoholic; **alcoolisé, e** *adj* alcoholic; **une boisson non alcoolisée** a soft drink; **alcoolisme** *nm* alcoholism; **alco(o)test®** *nm* Breathalyser®; (*test*) breath-test

**aléatoire** [aleatwaʀ] *adj* uncertain; (*Inform*) random

**alentour** [alɑ̃tuʀ] *adv* around, round about; **alentours** *nmpl* (*environs*) surroundings; **aux ~s de** in the vicinity *ou* neighbourhood of, round about; (*temps*) round about

**alerte** [alɛʀt] *adj* agile, nimble; brisk, lively ▷ *nf* alert; warning; **alerte à la bombe** bomb scare; **alerter** *vt* to alert

**algèbre** [alʒɛbʀ] *nf* algebra

**Alger** [alʒe] *n* Algiers

**Algérie** [alʒeʀi] *nf*: **l'~** Algeria; **algérien, ne** *adj* Algerian ▷ *nm/f*: **Algérien, ne** Algerian

**algue** [alg] *nf* (*gén*) seaweed *no pl*; (*Bot*) alga

**alibi** [alibi] *nm* alibi

**aligner** [aliɲe] *vt* to align, line up; (*idées, chiffres*) to string together; (*adapter*): **~ qch sur** to bring sth into

alignment with; **s'aligner** (*soldats etc*) to line up; **s'~ sur** (*Pol*) to align o.s. on

**aliment** [alimɑ̃] *nm* food; **alimentation** *nf* (*commerce*) food trade; (*magasin*) grocery store; (*régime*) diet; (*en eau etc, de moteur*) supplying; (*Inform*) feed; **alimenter** *vt* to feed; (*Tech*): **alimenter (en)** to supply (with); to feed (with); (*fig*) to sustain, keep going

**allaiter** [alete] *vt* to (breast-)feed, nurse; (*suj: animal*) to suckle

**allécher** [aleʃe] *vt*: **~ qn** to make sb's mouth water; to tempt *ou* entice sb

**allée** [ale] *nf* (*de jardin*) path; (*en ville*) avenue, drive; **~s et venues** comings and goings

**allégé, e** [aleʒe] *adj* (*yaourt etc*) low-fat

**alléger** [aleʒe] *vt* (*voiture*) to make lighter; (*chargement*) to lighten; (*souffrance*) to alleviate, soothe

**Allemagne** [alman] *nf*: **l'~** Germany; **allemand, e** *adj* German ▷ *nm/f*: **Allemand, e** German ▷ *nm* (*Ling*) German

**aller** [ale] *nm* (*trajet*) outward journey; (*billet: aussi*: **~ simple**) single (*BRIT*) *ou* one-way (*US*) ticket; **~ (et) retour** return (ticket) (*BRIT*), round-trip ticket (*US*) ▷ *vi* (*gén*) to go; **~ à** (*convenir*) to suit; (*suj: forme, pointure etc*) to fit; **~ (bien) avec** (*couleurs, style etc*) to go (well) with; **je vais y ~/me fâcher** I'm going to go/to get angry; **~ chercher qn** to go and get *ou* fetch (*BRIT*) sb; **~ voir** to go and see, go to see; **allez!** come on!; **allons!** come now!; **comment allez-vous?** how are you?; **comment ça va?** how are you?; (*affaires etc*) how are things?; **il va bien/mal** he's well/not well, he's fine/ill; **ça va bien/mal** (*affaires etc*) it's going well/not going well; **~ mieux** to be better; **s'en ~** (*partir*) to be off, go, leave; (*disparaître*) to go away

**allergie** [alɛʀʒi] *nf* allergy

**allergique** [alɛʀʒik] *adj*: **~ à** allergic to; **je suis ~ à la pénicilline** I'm allergic to penicillin

**alliance** [aljɑ̃s] *nf* (*Mil, Pol*) alliance;
(*bague*) wedding ring

**allier** [alje] *vt* (*Pol, gén*) to ally; (*fig*) to
combine; **s'allier** to become allies; to
combine

**allô** [alo] *excl* hullo, hallo

**allocation** [alɔkasjɔ̃] *nf* allowance;
**allocation (de) chômage**
unemployment benefit; **allocations
familiales** ≈ child benefit

**allonger** [alɔ̃ʒe] *vt* to lengthen, make
longer; (*étendre: bras, jambe*) to stretch
(out); **s'allonger** *vi* to get longer; (*se
coucher*) to lie down, stretch out; **~ le
pas** to hasten one's step(s)

**allumage** [alymaʒ] *nm* (*Auto*) ignition

**allume-cigare** [alymsigaʀ] *nm inv*
cigar lighter

**allumer** [alyme] *vt* (*lampe, phare, radio*)
to put *ou* switch on; (*pièce*) to put *ou*
switch the light(s) on in; (*feu*) to light;
**s'allumer** *vi* (*lumière, lampe*) to come *ou*
go on; **je n'arrive pas à ~ le chauffage**
I can't turn the heating on

**allumette** [alymɛt] *nf* match

**allure** [alyʀ] *nf* (*vitesse*) speed, pace;
(*démarche*) walk; (*aspect, air*) look;
**avoir de l'~** to have style; **à toute ~** at
top speed

**allusion** [a(l)lyzjɔ̃] *nf* allusion; (*sous-
entendu*) hint; **faire ~ à** to allude *ou* refer
to; to hint at

⭘ **MOT-CLÉ**

**alors** [alɔʀ] *adv* **1** (*à ce moment-là*) then,
at that time; **il habitait alors à Paris**
he lived in Paris at that time
**2** (*par conséquent*) then; **tu as fini?**
**je m'en vais** have you finished? I'm
going then; **et alors?** so what?
▷ *conj:* **alors que 1** (*au moment où*)
when, as; **il est arrivé alors que je
partais** he arrived as I was leaving
**2** (*tandis que*) whereas, while; **alors
que son frère travaillait dur, lui
se reposait** while his brother was

working hard, HE would rest
**3** (*bien que*) even though; **il a été
puni alors qu'il n'a rien fait** he was
punished, even though he had done
nothing

**alourdir** [aluʀdiʀ] *vt* to weigh down,
make heavy

**Alpes** [alp] *nfpl*: **les ~** the Alps

**alphabet** [alfabɛ] *nm* alphabet; (*livre*)
ABC (book)

**alpinisme** [alpinism] *nm*
mountaineering, climbing

**Alsace** [alzas] *nf* Alsace; **alsacien, ne**
*adj* Alsatian ▷ *nm/f:* **Alsacien, ne**
Alsatian

**altermondialisme** [altɛʀmɔ̃djalism]
*nm* anti-globalism; **altermondialiste**
*adj, nm/f* anti-globalist

**alternatif, -ive** [altɛʀnatif, iv] *adj*
alternating; **alternative** *nf* (*choix*)
alternative; **alterner** *vi* to alternate

**altitude** [altityd] *nf* altitude, height

**alto** [alto] *nm* (*instrument*) viola

**aluminium** [alyminjɔm] *nm*
aluminium (BRIT), aluminum (US)

**amabilité** [amabilite] *nf* kindness

**amaigrissant, e** [amegʀisɑ̃, ɑ̃t] *adj*
(*régime*) slimming

**amande** [amɑ̃d] *nf* (*de l'amandier*)
almond; **amandier** *nm* almond (tree)

**amant** [amɑ̃] *nm* lover

**amas** [ama] *nm* heap, pile; **amasser**
*vt* to amass

**amateur** [amatœʀ] *nm* amateur;
**en ~** (*péj*) amateurishly; **amateur de
musique/sport** music/sport lover

**ambassade** [ɑ̃basad] *nf* embassy;
**l'~ de France** the French Embassy;
**ambassadeur, -drice** *nm/f*
ambassador(-dress)

**ambiance** [ɑ̃bjɑ̃s] *nf* atmosphere; **il y a
de l'~** there's a great atmosphere

**ambigu, ë** [ɑ̃bigy] *adj* ambiguous

**ambitieux, -euse** [ɑ̃bisjø, jøz] *adj*
ambitious

**ambition** [ɑ̃bisjɔ̃] *nf* ambition

**ambulance** [ɑ̃bylɑ̃s] *nf* ambulance;

**appelez une ~!** call an ambulance!;
**ambulancier, -ière** nm/f ambulance
man(-woman) (BRIT), paramedic (US)
**âme** [ɑm] nf soul; **âme sœur** kindred
spirit
**amélioration** [ameljɔrasjɔ̃] nf
improvement
**améliorer** [ameljɔre] vt to improve;
**s'améliorer** vi to improve, get better
**aménager** [amenaʒe] vt (agencer,
transformer) to fit out; to lay out;
(: quartier, territoire) to develop;
(installer) to fix up, put in; **ferme
aménagée** converted farmhouse
**amende** [amɑ̃d] nf fine; **faire ~
honorable** to make amends
**amener** [am(ə)ne] vt to bring; (causer)
to bring about; **s'amener** vi to show
up (fam), turn up; **~ qn à faire qch** to
lead sb to do sth
**amer, amère** [amɛr] adj bitter
**américain, e** [amerikɛ̃, ɛn] adj
American ▷ nm/f: **A~, e** American
**Amérique** [amerik] nf: **l'~** America;
**Amérique centrale/latine** Central/
Latin America; **l'Amérique du Nord/
Sud** North/South America
**amertume** [amɛrtym] nf bitterness
**ameublement** [amœbləmɑ̃] nm
furnishing; (meubles) furniture
**ami, e** [ami] nm/f friend; (amant/
maîtresse) boyfriend/girlfriend ▷ adj:
**pays/groupe ~** friendly country/
group; **petit ~/petite ~e** boyfriend/
girlfriend
**amiable** [amjabl]: **à l'~** adv (Jur) out of
court; (gén) amicably
**amiante** [amjɑ̃t] nm asbestos
**amical, e, -aux** [amikal, o] adj
friendly; **amicalement** adv in a
friendly way; (dans une lettre) (with)
best wishes
**amincir** [amɛ̃sir] vt: **~ qn** to make sb
thinner ou slimmer; (suj: vêtement) to
make sb look slimmer
**amincissant, e** [amɛ̃sisɑ̃, ɑ̃t] adj:
**régime ~** (slimming) diet; **crème ~e**
slimming cream

**amiral, -aux** [amiral, o] nm admiral
**amitié** [amitje] nf friendship; **prendre
en ~** to befriend; **faire ou présenter
ses ~s à qn** to send sb one's best
wishes; **"~s"** (dans une lettre) "(with)
best wishes"
**amonceler** [amɔ̃s(ə)le] vt to pile ou
heap up; **s'amonceler** vi to pile ou
heap up; (fig) to accumulate
**amont** [amɔ̃]: **en ~** adv upstream
**amorce** [amɔrs] nf (sur un hameçon)
bait; (explosif) cap; primer; priming; (fig:
début) beginning(s), start
**amortir** [amɔrtir] vt (atténuer: choc)
to absorb, cushion; (bruit, douleur) to
deaden; (Comm: dette) to pay off; **~ un
achat** to make a purchase pay for itself;
**amortisseur** nm shock absorber
**amour** [amur] nm love; **faire l'~** to
make love; **amoureux, -euse** adj
(regard, tempérament) amorous; (vie,
problèmes) love cpd; (personne): **être
amoureux (de qn)** to be in love (with
sb); **tomber amoureux (de qn)** to
fall in love (with sb) ▷ nmpl courting
couple(s); **amour-propre** nm self-
esteem, pride
**ampère** [ɑ̃pɛr] nm amp(ere)
**amphithéâtre** [ɑ̃fiteɑtr] nm
amphitheatre; (d'université) lecture hall
ou theatre
**ample** [ɑ̃pl] adj (vêtement) roomy,
ample; (gestes, mouvement) broad;
(ressources) ample; **amplement** adv:
**c'est amplement suffisant** that's
more than enough; **ampleur** nf (de
dégâts, problème) extent
**amplificateur** [ɑ̃plifikatœr] nm
amplifier
**amplifier** [ɑ̃plifje] vt (fig) to expand,
increase
**ampoule** [ɑ̃pul] nf (électrique) bulb;
(de médicament) phial; (aux mains, pieds)
blister
**amusant, e** [amyzɑ̃, ɑ̃t] adj
(divertissant, spirituel) entertaining,
amusing; (comique) funny, amusing
**amuse-gueule** [amyzgœl] nm inv

appetizer, snack

**amusement** [amyzmã] *nm*
(*divertissement*) amusement; (*jeu etc*)
pastime, diversion

**amuser** [amyze] *vt* (*divertir*) to
entertain, amuse; (*égayer, faire rire*) to
amuse; **s'amuser** *vi* (*jouer*) to play; (*se
divertir*) to enjoy o.s., have fun; (*fig*) to
mess around

**amygdale** [amidal] *nf* tonsil

**an** [ã] *nm* year; **avoir quinze ans** to be
fifteen (years old); **le jour de l'an, le
premier de l'an, le nouvel an** New
Year's Day

**analphabète** [analfabɛt] *nm/f*
illiterate

**analyse** [analiz] *nf* analysis; (*Méd*) test;
**analyser** *vt* to analyse; to test

**ananas** [anana(s)] *nm* pineapple

**anatomie** [anatɔmi] *nf* anatomy

**ancêtre** [ãsɛtʀ] *nm/f* ancestor

**anchois** [ãʃwa] *nm* anchovy

**ancien, ne** [ãsjɛ̃, jɛn] *adj* old; (*de
jadis, de l'antiquité*) ancient; (*précédent,
ex-*) former, old; (*par l'expérience*)
senior ▷ *nm/f* (*dans une tribu*) elder;
**ancienneté** *nf* (*Admin*) (length of)
service; (*privilèges obtenus*) seniority

**ancre** [ãkʀ] *nf* anchor; **jeter/lever l'~** to
cast/weigh anchor; **ancrer** *vt* (*Constr:
câble etc*) to anchor; (*fig*) to fix firmly

**Andorre** [ãdɔʀ] *nf* Andorra

**andouille** [ãduj] *nf* (*Culin*) *sausage made
of chitterlings*; (*fam*) clot, nit

**âne** [ɑn] *nm* donkey, ass; (*péj*) dunce

**anéantir** [aneãtiʀ] *vt* to annihilate,
wipe out; (*fig*) to obliterate, destroy

**anémie** [anemi] *nf* anaemia;
**anémique** *adj* anaemic

**anesthésie** [anɛstezi] *nf* anaesthesia;
**faire une ~ locale/générale à qn** to
give sb a local/general anaesthetic

**ange** [ãʒ] *nm* angel; **être aux ~s** to be
over the moon

**angine** [ãʒin] *nf* throat infection;
**angine de poitrine** angina

**anglais, e** [ãglɛ, ɛz] *adj* English ▷ *nm/f*:
**A~, e** Englishman(-woman) ▷ *nm*

(*Ling*) English; **les A~** the English; **filer à
l'~e** to take French leave

**angle** [ãgl] *nm* angle; (*coin*) corner;
**angle droit** right angle

**Angleterre** [ãglətɛʀ] *nf*: **l'~** England

**anglo...** [ãglɔ] *préfixe* Anglo-, anglo(-);
**anglophone** *adj* English-speaking

**angoisse** [ãgwas] *nf* anguish, distress;
**angoissé, e** *adj* (*personne*) distressed

**anguille** [ãgij] *nf* eel

**animal, e, -aux** [animal, o] *adj, nm*
animal

**animateur, -trice** [animatœʀ, tʀis]
*nm/f* (*de télévision*) host; (*de groupe*)
leader, organizer

**animation** [animasjõ] *nf* (*voir animé*)
busyness; liveliness; (*Cinéma: technique*)
animation

**animé, e** [anime] *adj* (*lieu*) busy, lively;
(*conversation, réunion*) lively, animated

**animer** [anime] *vt* (*ville, soirée*) to liven
up; (*mener*) to lead

**anis** [ani(s)] *nm* (*Culin*) aniseed; (*Bot*)
anise

**ankyloser** [ãkiloze]: **s'ankyloser** *vi*
to get stiff

**anneau, x** [ano] *nm* (*de rideau, bague*)
ring; (*de chaîne*) link

**année** [ane] *nf* year

**annexe** [anɛks] *adj* (*problème*) related;
(*document*) appended; (*salle*) adjoining
▷ *nf* (*bâtiment*) annex(e); (*jointe à une
lettre*) enclosure

**anniversaire** [anivɛʀsɛʀ] *nm*
birthday; (*d'un événement, bâtiment*)
anniversary

**annonce** [anõs] *nf* announcement;
(*signe, indice*) sign; (*aussi:* **~ publicitaire**)
advertisement; **les petites ~s** the
classified advertisements, the small
ads

**annoncer** [anõse] *vt* to announce; (*être
le signe de*) to herald; **s'~ bien/difficile**
to look promising/difficult

**annuaire** [anɥɛʀ] *nm* yearbook,
annual; **annuaire téléphonique**
(telephone) directory, phone book

**annuel, le** [anɥɛl] *adj* annual, yearly

**annulation** [anylasjɔ̃] nf cancellation

**annuler** [anyle] vt (rendez-vous, voyage) to cancel, call off; (jugement) to quash (BRIT), repeal (US); (Math, Physique) to cancel out; **je voudrais ~ ma réservation** I'd like to cancel my reservation

**anonymat** [anɔnima] nm anonymity; **garder l'~** to remain anonymous

**anonyme** [anɔnim] adj anonymous; (fig) impersonal

**anorak** [anɔrak] nm anorak

**anorexie** [anɔrɛksi] nf anorexia

**anormal, e, -aux** [anɔrmal, o] adj abnormal

**ANPE** sigle f (= Agence nationale pour l'emploi) national employment agency

**antarctique** [ãtarktik] adj Antarctic ▷ nm: **l'A~** the Antarctic

**antenne** [ãtɛn] nf (de radio) aerial; (d'insecte) antenna, feeler; (poste avancé) outpost; (petite succursale) sub-branch; **passer à l'~** to go on the air; **antenne parabolique** satellite dish

**antérieur, e** [ãterjœr] adj (d'avant) previous, earlier; (de devant) front

**anti...** [ãti] préfixe anti...; **antialcoolique** adj anti-alcohol; **antibiotique** nm antibiotic; **antibrouillard** adj: **phare antibrouillard** fog lamp (BRIT) ou light (US)

**anticipation** [ãtisipasjɔ̃] nf: **livre/ film d'~** science fiction book/film

**anticipé, e** [ãtisipe] adj: **avec mes remerciements ~s** thanking you in advance ou anticipation

**anticiper** [ãtisipe] vt (événement, coup) to anticipate, foresee

**anti...: anticorps** nm antibody; **antidote** nm antidote; **antigel** nm antifreeze; **antihistaminique** nm antihistamine

**antillais, e** [ãtijɛ, ɛz] adj West Indian, Caribbean ▷ nm/f: **A~, e** West Indian, Caribbean

**Antilles** [ãtij] nfpl: **les ~** the West Indies; **les Grandes/Petites ~** the Greater/Lesser Antilles

**antilope** [ãtilɔp] nf antelope

**anti...: antimite(s)** adj, nm: **(produit) antimite(s)** mothproofer; moth repellent; **antimondialisation** nf anti-globalization; **antipathique** adj unpleasant, disagreeable; **antipelliculaire** adj anti-dandruff

**antiquaire** [ãtikɛr] nm/f antique dealer

**antique** [ãtik] adj antique; (très vieux) ancient, antiquated; **antiquité** nf (objet) antique; **l'Antiquité** Antiquity; **magasin d'antiquités** antique shop

**anti...: antirabique** adj rabies cpd; **antirouille** adj inv anti-rust cpd; **antisémite** adj anti-Semitic; **antiseptique** adj, nm antiseptic

**antivirus** [ãti'virus] nm (Inform) antivirus; **antivol** adj, nm: **(dispositif) antivol** anti-theft device

**anxieux, -euse** [ãksjø, jøz] adj anxious, worried

**AOC** sigle f (= appellation d'origine contrôlée) label guaranteeing the quality of wine

**août** [u(t)] nm August

**apaiser** [apeze] vt (colère, douleur) to soothe; (personne) to calm (down), pacify; **s'apaiser** vi (tempête, bruit) to die down, subside; (personne) to calm down

**apercevoir** [apɛrsəvwar] vt to see; **s'apercevoir de** vt to notice; **s'~ que** to notice that

**aperçu** [apɛrsy] nm (vue d'ensemble) general survey

**apéritif** [aperitif] nm (boisson) aperitif; (réunion) drinks pl

**à-peu-près** [apøprɛ] (péj) nm inv vague approximation

**apeuré, e** [apœre] adj frightened, scared

**aphte** [aft] nm mouth ulcer

**apitoyer** [apitwaje] vt to move to pity; **s'apitoyer (sur)** to feel pity (for)

**aplatir** [aplatir] vt to flatten; **s'aplatir** vi to become flatter; (écrasé) to be flattened

**aplomb** [aplɔ̃] nm (équilibre) balance, equilibrium; (fig) self-assurance; nerve; **d'~** steady

**apostrophe** [apɔstʀɔf] nf (signe) apostrophe

**apparaître** [apaʀɛtʀ] vi to appear

**appareil** [apaʀɛj] nm (outil, machine) piece of apparatus, device; (électrique, ménager) appliance; (avion) (aero)plane, aircraft inv; (téléphonique) phone; (dentier) brace (BRIT), braces (US); **"qui est à l'~?"** "who's speaking?"; **dans le plus simple ~** in one's birthday suit; **appareil(-photo)** camera; **appareiller** vi (Navig) to cast off, get under way ▷ vt (assortir) to match up

**apparemment** [apaʀamɑ̃] adv apparently

**apparence** [apaʀɑ̃s] nf appearance; **en ~** apparently

**apparent, e** [apaʀɑ̃, ɑ̃t] adj visible; (évident) obvious; (superficiel) apparent

**apparenté, e** [apaʀɑ̃te] adj: **~ à** related to; (fig) similar to

**apparition** [apaʀisjɔ̃] nf appearance; (surnaturelle) apparition

**appartement** [apaʀtəmɑ̃] nm flat (BRIT), apartment (US)

**appartenir** [apaʀtəniʀ]: **~ à** vt to belong to; **il lui appartient de** it is his duty to

**apparu, e** [apaʀy] pp de **apparaître**

**appât** [apa] nm (Pêche) bait; (fig) lure, bait

**appel** [apɛl] nm call; (nominal) roll call; (: Scol) register; (Mil: recrutement) call-up; **faire ~ à** (invoquer) to appeal to; (avoir recours à) to call on; (nécessiter) to call for, require; **faire ou interjeter ~** (Jur) to appeal; **faire l'~** to call the roll; (Scol) to call the register; **sans ~** (fig) final, irrevocable; **faire un ~ de phares** to flash one's headlights; **appel d'offres** (Comm) invitation to tender; **appel (téléphonique)** (tele)phone call

**appelé** [ap(ə)le] nm (Mil) conscript

**appeler** [ap(ə)le] vt to call; (faire venir: médecin etc) to call, send for; **s'appeler** vi: **elle s'appelle Gabrielle** her name is Gabrielle, she's called Gabrielle; **comment vous appelez-vous?** what's your name?; **comment ça s'appelle?** what is it called?; **être appelé à** (fig) to be destined to

**appendicite** [apɛ̃disit] nf appendicitis

**appesantir** [apəzɑ̃tiʀ]: **s'appesantir** vi to grow heavier; **s'~ sur** (fig) to dwell on

**appétissant, e** [apetisɑ̃, ɑ̃t] adj appetizing, mouth-watering

**appétit** [apeti] nm appetite; **bon ~!** enjoy your meal!

**applaudir** [aplodiʀ] vt to applaud ▷ vi to applaud, clap; **applaudissements** nmpl applause sg, clapping sg

**application** [aplikasjɔ̃] nf application

**appliquer** [aplike] vt to apply; (loi) to enforce; **s'appliquer** vi (élève etc) to apply o.s.; **s'~ à** to apply to

**appoint** [apwɛ̃] nm (extra) contribution ou help; **avoir/faire l'~** to have/give the right change ou money; **chauffage d'~** extra heating

**apporter** [apɔʀte] vt to bring

**appréciable** [apʀesjabl] adj appreciable

**apprécier** [apʀesje] vt to appreciate; (évaluer) to estimate, assess

**appréhender** [apʀeɑ̃de] vt (craindre) to dread; (arrêter) to apprehend

**apprendre** [apʀɑ̃dʀ] vt to learn; (événement, résultats) to learn of, hear of; **~ qch à qn** (informer) to tell sb (of) sth; (enseigner) to teach sb sth; **~ à faire qch** to learn to do sth; **~ à qn à faire qch** to teach sb to do sth; **apprenti, e** nm/f apprentice; **apprentissage** nm learning; (Comm, Scol: période) apprenticeship

**apprêter** [apʀete] vt: **s'~ à faire qch** to get ready to do sth

**appris, e** [apʀi, iz] pp de **apprendre**

**apprivoiser** [apʀivwaze] vt to tame

**approbation** [apʀɔbasjɔ̃] nf approval

**approcher** [apʀɔʃe] vi to approach, come near ▷ vt to approach; (rapprocher): **~ qch (de qch)** to bring ou put sth near (to sth); **s'approcher de** to approach, go ou come near to; **~ de** (lieu, but) to draw near to; (quantité, moment) to approach

**approfondir** [apʀɔfɔ̃diʀ] vt to deepen; (question) to go further into

**approprié, e** [apʀɔpʀije] adj: **~ (à)** appropriate (to), suited to

**approprier** [apʀɔpʀije]: **s'approprier** vt to appropriate, take over; **s'~ en** to stock up with

**approuver** [apʀuve] vt to agree with; (trouver louable) to approve of

**approvisionner** [apʀɔvizjɔne] vt to supply; (compte bancaire) to pay funds into; **s'approvisionner en** to stock up with

**approximatif, -ive** [apʀɔksimatif, iv] adj approximate, rough; (termes) vague

**appt** abr = **appartement**

**appui** [apɥi] nm support; **prendre ~ sur** to lean on; (objet) to rest on; **l'~ de la fenêtre** the windowsill, the window ledge

**appuyer** [apɥije] vt (poser): **~ qch sur/contre** to lean ou rest sth on/against; (soutenir: personne, demande) to support, back (up) ▷ vi: **~ sur** (bouton) to press, push; (mot, détail) to stress, emphasize; **~ sur le frein** to brake, to apply the brakes; **s'appuyer sur** to lean on; (fig: compter sur) to rely on

**après** [apʀɛ] prép after ▷ adv afterwards; **2 heures ~** 2 hours later; **~ qu'il est** ou **soit parti** after he left; **~ avoir fait** after having done; **d'~** (selon) according to; **~ coup** after the event, afterwards; **~ tout** (au fond) after all; **et (puis) ~?** so what?; **après-demain** adv the day after tomorrow; **après-midi** nm ou nf inv afternoon; **après-rasage** nm inv aftershave; **après-shampooing** nm inv conditioner; **après-ski** nm inv snow boot

**après-soleil** [apʀɛsɔlɛj] adj inv after-sun cpd ▷ nm after-sun cream ou lotion

**apte** [apt] adj capable; **~ à qch/faire qch** capable of sth/doing sth; **~ (au service)** (Mil) fit (for service)

**aquarelle** [akwaʀɛl] nf watercolour

**aquarium** [akwaʀjɔm] nm aquarium

**arabe** [aʀab] adj Arabic; (désert, cheval) Arabian; (nation, peuple) Arab ▷ nm/f: **A~** Arab ▷ nm (Ling) Arabic

**Arabie** [aʀabi] nf: **l'~ (Saoudite)** Saudi Arabia

**arachide** [aʀaʃid] nf (plante) groundnut (plant); (graine) peanut, groundnut

**araignée** [aʀeɲe] nf spider

**arbitraire** [aʀbitʀɛʀ] adj arbitrary

**arbitre** [aʀbitʀ] nm (Sport) referee; (: Tennis, Cricket) umpire; (fig) arbiter, judge; (Jur) arbitrator; **arbitrer** vt to referee; to umpire; to arbitrate

**arbre** [aʀbʀ] nm tree; (Tech) shaft

**arbuste** [aʀbyst] nm small shrub

**arc** [aʀk] nm (arme) bow; (Géom) arc; (Archit) arch; **en ~ de cercle** semi-circular

**arcade** [aʀkad] nf arch(way); **arcades** nfpl (série) arcade sg, arches

**arc-en-ciel** [aʀkɑ̃sjɛl] nm rainbow

**arche** [aʀʃ] nf arch; **arche de Noé** Noah's Ark

**archéologie** [aʀkeɔlɔʒi] nf arch(a)eology; **archéologue** nm/f arch(a)eologist

**archet** [aʀʃɛ] nm bow

**archipel** [aʀʃipɛl] nm archipelago

**architecte** [aʀʃitɛkt] nm architect

**architecture** [aʀʃitɛktyʀ] nf architecture

**archives** [aʀʃiv] nfpl (collection) archives

**arctique** [aʀktik] adj Arctic ▷ nm: **l'A~** the Arctic

**ardent, e** [aʀdɑ̃, ɑ̃t] adj (soleil) blazing; (amour) ardent, passionate; (prière) fervent

**ardoise** [aʀdwaz] nf slate

**ardu, e** [aʀdy] adj (travail) arduous; (problème) difficult

**arène** [aʀɛn] nf arena; **arènes** nfpl
(*amphithéâtre*) bull-ring *sg*

**arête** [aʀɛt] nf (*de poisson*) bone; (*d'une
montagne*) ridge

**argent** [aʀʒɑ̃] nm (*métal*) silver;
(*monnaie*) money; **argent de poche**
pocket money; **argent liquide** ready
money, (ready) cash; **argenterie** nf
silverware

**argentin, e** [aʀʒɑ̃tɛ̃, in] adj
Argentinian ▷ nm/f: **A~, e** Argentinian

**Argentine** [aʀʒɑ̃tin] nf: **l'~** Argentina

**argentique** [aʀʒɑ̃tik] adj (*appareil-
photo*) film *cpd*

**argile** [aʀʒil] nf clay

**argot** [aʀgo] nm slang; **argotique** adj
slang *cpd*; (*très familier*) slangy

**argument** [aʀgymɑ̃] nm argument

**argumenter** [aʀgymɑ̃te] vi to argue

**aride** [aʀid] adj arid

**aristocratie** [aʀistɔkʀasi] nf
aristocracy; **aristocratique** adj
aristocratic

**arithmétique** [aʀitmetik] adj
arithmetic(al) ▷ nf arithmetic

**arme** [aʀm] nf weapon; **armes** nfpl
(*armement*) weapons, arms; (*blason*)
(coat of) arms; **~s de destruction
massive** weapons of mass destruction;
**arme à feu** firearm

**armée** [aʀme] nf army; **armée de l'air**
Air Force; **armée de terre** Army

**armer** [aʀme] vt to arm; (*arme à feu*) to
cock; (*appareil-photo*) to wind on; **~ qch
de** to reinforce sth with; **s'armer de** to
arm o.s. with

**armistice** [aʀmistis] nm armistice;
**l'A~** ≈ Remembrance (BRIT) ou Veterans
(US) Day

**armoire** [aʀmwaʀ] nf (tall) cupboard;
(*penderie*) wardrobe (BRIT), closet (US)

**armure** [aʀmyʀ] nf armour *no pl*, suit
of armour; **armurier** nm gunsmith

**arnaque** [aʀnak] nf swindling;
**c'est de l'~** it's a rip-off; **arnaquer** (*fam*)
vt to swindle

**arobase** [aʀɔbaz] nf (*symbole*) at
symbol; **"paul ~ société point fr"** "paul

at société dot fr"

**aromates** [aʀɔmat] nmpl seasoning
*sg*, herbs (and spices)

**aromathérapie** [aʀɔmateʀapi] nf
aromatherapy

**aromatisé, e** [aʀɔmatize] adj
flavoured

**arôme** [aʀom] nm aroma

**arracher** [aʀaʃe] vt to pull out; (*page
etc*) to tear off, tear out; (*légumes,
herbe*) to pull up; (*bras etc*) to tear off;
**s'arracher** vt (*article recherché*) to fight
over; **~ qch à qn** to snatch sth from sb;
(fig) to wring sth out of sb

**arrangement** [aʀɑ̃ʒmɑ̃] nm
agreement, arrangement

**arranger** [aʀɑ̃ʒe] vt (*gén*) to arrange;
(*réparer*) to fix, put right; (*régler:
différend*) to settle, sort out; (*convenir
à*) to suit, be convenient for; **cela
m'arrange** that suits me (fine);
**s'arranger** vi (*se mettre d'accord*) to
come to an agreement; **je vais m'~** I'll
manage; **ça va s'~** it'll sort itself out

**arrestation** [aʀɛstasjɔ̃] nf arrest

**arrêt** [aʀɛ] nm stopping; (*de bus etc*)
stop; (*Jur*) judgment, decision; **à l'~**
stationary; **tomber en ~ devant**
to stop short in front of; **sans ~**
(*sans interruption*) non-stop; (*très
fréquemment*) continually; **arrêt de
travail** stoppage (of work)

**arrêter** [aʀete] vt to stop; (*chauffage
etc*) to turn off, switch off; (*fixer: date
etc*) to appoint, decide on; (*criminel,
suspect*) to arrest; **s'arrêter** vi to stop;
**~ de faire** to stop doing; **arrêtez-vous
ici/au coin, s'il vous plaît** could you
stop here/at the corner, please?

**arrhes** [aʀ] nfpl deposit *sg*

**arrière** [aʀjɛʀ] nm back; (*Sport*) fullback
▷ adj inv: **siège/roue ~** back ou rear
seat/wheel; **à l'~** behind, at the back;
**en ~** behind; (*regarder*) back, behind;
(*tomber, aller*) backwards; **arrière-goût**
nm aftertaste; **arrière-grand-mère**
nf great-grandmother; **arrière-
grand-père** nm great-grandfather;

**arrière-pays** *nm inv* hinterland;
**arrière-pensée** *nf* ulterior motive;
mental reservation; **arrière-plan** *nm*
background; **à l'arrière-plan** in the
background; **arrière-saison** *nf* late
autumn
**arrimer** [aʀime] *vt* to secure;
*(cargaison)* to stow
**arrivage** [aʀivaʒ] *nm* consignment
**arrivée** [aʀive] *nf* arrival; *(ligne d'arrivée)*
finish
**arriver** [aʀive] *vi* to arrive; *(survenir)*
to happen, occur; **il arrive à Paris à
8h** he gets to *ou* arrives in Paris at 8; **à
quelle heure arrive le train de Lyon?**
what time does the train from Lyons
get in?; **~ à** *(atteindre)* to reach; **~ à faire
qch** to succeed in doing sth; **en ~ à**
*(finir par)* to come to; **il arrive que** it
happens that; **il lui arrive de faire** he
sometimes does
**arrobase** [aʀɔbaz] *nf* (*Inform*) @,
'at' sign
**arrogance** [aʀɔgɑ̃s] *nf* arrogance
**arrogant, e** [aʀɔgɑ̃, ɑ̃t] *adj* arrogant
**arrondissement** [aʀɔ̃dismɑ̃] *nm*
(*Admin*) ≈ district
**arroser** [aʀoze] *vt* to water; *(victoire)* to
celebrate (over a drink); *(Culin)* to baste;
**arrosoir** *nm* watering can
**arsenal, -aux** [aʀsənal, o] *nm* (*Navig*)
naval dockyard; *(Mil)* arsenal; *(fig)* gear,
paraphernalia
**art** [aʀ] *nm* art
**artère** [aʀtɛʀ] *nf* (*Anat*) artery; *(rue)*
main road
**arthrite** [aʀtʀit] *nf* arthritis
**artichaut** [aʀtiʃo] *nm* artichoke
**article** [aʀtikl] *nm* article; *(Comm)*
item, article; **à l'~ de la mort** at the
point of death
**articulation** [aʀtikylasjɔ̃] *nf*
articulation; *(Anat)* joint
**articuler** [aʀtikyle] *vt* to articulate
**artificiel, le** [aʀtifisjɛl] *adj* artificial
**artisan** [aʀtizɑ̃] *nm* artisan, (self-
employed) craftsman; **artisanal, e,
-aux** *adj* of *ou* made by craftsmen; *(péj)*

cottage industry *cpd*; **de fabrication
artisanale** home-made; **artisanat** *nm*
arts and crafts *pl*
**artiste** [aʀtist] *nm/f* artist; *(de variétés)*
entertainer; *(musicien etc)* performer;
**artistique** *adj* artistic
**as¹** [a] *vb voir* **avoir**
**as²** [ɑs] *nm* ace
**ascenseur** [asɑ̃sœʀ] *nm* lift (BRIT),
elevator (US)
**ascension** [asɑ̃sjɔ̃] *nf* ascent;
*(de montagne)* climb; **l'A~** *(Rel)* the
Ascension

● **ASCENSION**
●
● The **fête de l'Ascension** is a public
● holiday in France. It always falls on
● a Thursday, usually in May. Many
● French people take the following
● Friday off work too and enjoy a long
● weekend.

**asiatique** [azjatik] *adj* Asiatic, Asian
▷ *nm/f*: **A~** Asian
**Asie** [azi] *nf*: **l'~** Asia
**asile** [azil] *nm* (*refuge*) refuge,
sanctuary; *(Pol)*: **droit d'~** (political)
asylum
**aspect** [aspɛ] *nm* appearance, look;
*(fig)* aspect, side; **à l'~ de** at the sight of
**asperge** [aspɛʀʒ] *nf* asparagus *no pl*
**asperger** [aspɛʀʒe] *vt* to spray, sprinkle
**asphalte** [asfalt] *nm* asphalt
**asphyxier** [asfiksje] *vt* to suffocate,
asphyxiate; *(fig)* to stifle
**aspirateur** [aspiʀatœʀ] *nm* vacuum
cleaner; **passer l'~** to vacuum
**aspirer** [aspiʀe] *vt* (*air*) to inhale;
*(liquide)* to suck (up); *(suj: appareil)* to
suck up; **~ à** to aspire to
**aspirine** [aspiʀin] *nf* aspirin
**assagir** [asaʒiʀ]: **s'assagir** *vi* to
quieten down, settle down
**assaisonnement** [asɛzɔnmɑ̃] *nm*
seasoning
**assaisonner** [asɛzɔne] *vt* to season
**assassin** [asasɛ̃] *nm* murderer;

assassin; **assassiner** vt to murder; (esp Pol) to assassinate

**assaut** [aso] nm assault, attack; **prendre d'~** to storm, assault; **donner l'~ à** to attack

**assécher** [aseʃe] vt to drain

**assemblage** [asɑ̃blaʒ] nm (action) assembling; (de couleurs, choses) collection

**assemblée** [asɑ̃ble] nf (réunion) meeting; (assistance) gathering; (Pol) assembly; **l'A~ nationale** the National Assembly (the lower house of the French Parliament)

**assembler** [asɑ̃ble] vt (joindre, monter) to assemble, put together; (amasser) to gather (together), collect (together); **s'assembler** vi to gather

**asseoir** [aswaR] vt (malade, bébé) to sit up; (personne debout) to sit down; (autorité, réputation) to establish; **s'asseoir** vi to sit (o.s.) down

**assez** [ase] adv (suffisamment) enough, sufficiently; (passablement) rather, quite, fairly; **~ de pain/livres** enough ou sufficient bread/books; **vous en avez ~?** have you got enough?; **j'en ai ~!** I've had enough!

**assidu, e** [asidy] adj (appliqué) assiduous, painstaking; (ponctuel) regular

**assied** etc [asje] vb voir **asseoir**

**assiérai** etc [asjeRe] vb voir **asseoir**

**assiette** [asjɛt] nf plate; (contenu) plate(ful); **il n'est pas dans son ~** he's not feeling quite himself; **assiette à dessert** dessert plate; **assiette anglaise** assorted cold meats; **assiette creuse** (soup) dish, soup plate; **assiette plate** (dinner) plate

**assimiler** [asimile] vt to assimilate, absorb; (comparer): **~ qch/qn à** to liken ou compare sth/sb to; **s'assimiler** vr (s'intégrer) to be assimilated, assimilate

**assis, e** [asi, iz] pp de **asseoir** ▷ adj sitting (down), seated

**assistance** [asistɑ̃s] nf (public) audience; (aide) assistance; **enfant de l'A~ publique** child in care

**assistant, e** [asistɑ̃, ɑ̃t] nm/f assistant; (d'université) probationary lecturer; **assistant(e) social(e)** social worker

**assisté, e** [asiste] adj (Auto) power assisted; **~ par ordinateur** computer-assisted; **direction ~e** power steering

**assister** [asiste] vt (aider) to assist; **~ à** (scène, événement) to witness; (conférence, séminaire) to attend, be at; (spectacle, match) to be at, see

**association** [asɔsjasjɔ̃] nf association

**associé, e** [asɔsje] nm/f associate; (Comm) partner

**associer** [asɔsje] vt to associate; **s'associer** vi to join together; **s'~ à qn pour faire** to join (forces) with sb to do; **s'~ à** (couleurs, qualités) to be combined with; (opinions, joie de qn) to share in; **~ qn à** (profits) to give sb a share of; (affaire) to make sb a partner in; (joie, triomphe) to include sb in; **~ qch à** (allier à) to combine sth with

**assoiffé, e** [aswafe] adj thirsty

**assommer** [asɔme] vt (étourdir, abrutir) to knock out, stun

**Assomption** [asɔ̃psjɔ̃] nf: **l'~** the Assumption

● **ASSOMPTION**
●
● The **fête de l'Assomption**, more
● commonly known as 'le 15 août',
● is a national holiday in France.
● Traditionally, large numbers of
● holidaymakers leave home on 15
● August, frequently causing chaos
● on the roads.

**assorti, e** [asɔʀti] adj matched, matching; (varié) assorted; **~ à** matching; **assortiment** nm assortment, selection

**assortir** [asɔʀtiʀ] vt to match; **~ qch à** to match sth with; **~ qch de** to accompany sth with

**assouplir** [asupliʀ] vt to make supple;

(*fig*) to relax; **assouplissant** *nm* (fabric) softener

**assumer** [asyme] *vt* (*fonction, emploi*) to assume, take on

**assurance** [asyʀɑ̃s] *nf* (*certitude*) assurance; (*confiance en soi*) (self-)confidence; (*contrat*) insurance (policy); (*secteur commercial*) insurance; **assurance au tiers** third-party insurance; **assurance maladie** health insurance; **assurance tous risques** (*Auto*) comprehensive insurance; **assurances sociales** ≈ National Insurance (BRIT), ≈ Social Security (US); **assurance-vie** *nf* life assurance *ou* insurance

**assuré, e** [asyʀe] *adj* (*certain: réussite, échec*) certain, sure; (*air*) assured; (*pas*) steady ▷ *nm/f* insured (person); **assurément** *adv* assuredly, most certainly

**assurer** [asyʀe] *vt* (*Finance*) to insure; (*victoire etc*) to ensure; (*frontières, pouvoir*) to make secure; (*service*) to provide, operate; **s'assurer (contre)** (*Comm*) to insure o.s. (against); **s'~ de/ que** (*vérifier*) to make sure of/that; **s'~ (de)** (*aide de qn*) to secure; **~ à qn que** to assure sb that; **~ qn de** to assure sb of

**asthmatique** [asmatik] *adj, nm/f* asthmatic

**asthme** [asm] *nm* asthma

**asticot** [astiko] *nm* maggot

**astre** [astʀ] *nm* star

**astrologie** [astʀɔlɔʒi] *nf* astrology

**astronaute** [astʀonot] *nm/f* astronaut

**astronomie** [astʀɔnɔmi] *nf* astronomy

**astuce** [astys] *nf* shrewdness, astuteness; (*truc*) trick, clever way; **astucieux, -euse** *adj* clever

**atelier** [atəlje] *nm* workshop; (*de peintre*) studio

**athée** [ate] *adj* atheistic ▷ *nm/f* atheist

**Athènes** [atɛn] *n* Athens

**athlète** [atlɛt] *nm/f* (*Sport*) athlete; **athlétisme** *nm* athletics *sg*

**atlantique** [atlɑ̃tik] *adj* Atlantic ▷ *nm*: **l'(océan) A~** the Atlantic (Ocean)

**atlas** [atlɑs] *nm* atlas

**atmosphère** [atmɔsfɛʀ] *nf* atmosphere

**atome** [atom] *nm* atom; **atomique** *adj* atomic, nuclear

**atomiseur** [atɔmizœʀ] *nm* atomizer

**atout** [atu] *nm* trump; (*fig*) asset

**atroce** [atʀɔs] *adj* atrocious

**attachant, e** [ataʃɑ̃, ɑ̃t] *adj* engaging, lovable, likeable

**attache** [ataʃ] *nf* clip, fastener; (*fig*) tie

**attacher** [ataʃe] *vt* to tie up; (*étiquette*) to attach, tie on; (*ceinture*) to fasten ▷ *vi* (*poêle, riz*) to stick; **s'attacher à** (*par affection*) to become attached to; **~ qch à** to tie *ou* attach sth to

**attaque** [atak] *nf* attack; (*cérébrale*) stroke; (*d'épilepsie*) fit

**attaquer** [atake] *vt* to attack ▷ *vi* to attack; **s'attaquer à** *vt* (*personne*) to attack; (*problème*) to tackle; **~ qn en justice** to bring an action against sb, sue sb

**attarder** [ataʀde]: **s'attarder** *vi* to linger

**atteindre** [atɛ̃dʀ] *vt* to reach; (*blesser*) to hit; (*émouvoir*) to affect; **atteint, e** *adj* (*Méd*): **être atteint de** to be suffering from; **atteinte** *nf*: **hors d'atteinte** out of reach; **porter atteinte à** to strike a blow at

**attendant** [atɑ̃dɑ̃] *adv*: **en ~** meanwhile, in the meantime

**attendre** [atɑ̃dʀ] *vt* (*gén*) to wait for; (*être destiné ou réservé à*) to await, be in store for ▷ *vi* to wait; **s'attendre à (ce que)** to expect (that); **attendez-moi, s'il vous plaît** wait for me, please; **~ un enfant** to be expecting a baby; **~ de faire/d'être** to wait until one does/is; **attendez qu'il vienne** wait until he comes; **~ qch de** to expect sth of

Attention à ne pas traduire *attendre* par **to attend**.

**attendrir** [atɑ̃dʀiʀ] *vt* to move (to pity); (*viande*) to tenderize

**attendu, e** [atɑ̃dy] *adj* (*visiteur*) expected; (*événement*) long-awaited; **~ que** considering that, since

**attentat** [atɑ̃ta] *nm* assassination attempt; **attentat à la pudeur** indecent assault *no pl*; **attentat suicide** suicide bombing

**attente** [atɑ̃t] *nf* wait; (*espérance*) expectation

**attenter** [atɑ̃te]: **~ à** *vt* (*liberté*) to violate; **~ à la vie de qn** to make an attempt on sb's life

**attentif, -ive** [atɑ̃tif, iv] *adj* (*auditeur*) attentive; (*examen*) careful; **~ à** careful to

**attention** [atɑ̃sjɔ̃] *nf* attention; (*prévenance*) attention, thoughtfulness *no pl*; **à l'~ de** for the attention of; **faire ~ (à)** to be careful (of); **faire ~ (à ce) que** to be sure that; **~!** careful!, watch out!; **~ à la voiture!** watch out for that car!; **attentionné, e** *adj* thoughtful, considerate

**atténuer** [atenɥe] *vt* (*douleur*) to alleviate, ease; (*couleurs*) to soften; **s'atténuer** *vi* to ease; (*violence etc*) to abate

**atterrir** [ateʀiʀ] *vi* to land; **atterrissage** *nm* landing

**attestation** [atɛstasjɔ̃] *nf* certificate

**attirant, e** [atiʀɑ̃, ɑ̃t] *adj* attractive, appealing

**attirer** [atiʀe] *vt* to attract; (*appâter*) to lure, entice; **~ qn dans un coin/vers soi** to draw sb into a corner/towards one; **~ l'attention de qn** to attract sb's attention; **~ l'attention de qn sur** to draw sb's attention to; **s'~ des ennuis** to bring trouble upon o.s., get into trouble

**attitude** [atityd] *nf* attitude; (*position du corps*) bearing

**attraction** [atʀaksjɔ̃] *nf* (*gén*) attraction; (*de cabaret, cirque*) number

**attrait** [atʀɛ] *nm* appeal, attraction

**attraper** [atʀape] *vt* (*gén*) to catch; (*habitude, amende*) to get, pick up; (*fam: duper*) to con; **se faire ~** (*fam*) to be told off

**attrayant, e** [atʀɛjɑ̃, ɑ̃t] *adj* attractive

**attribuer** [atʀibɥe] *vt* (*prix*) to award; (*rôle, tâche*) to allocate, assign; (*imputer*): **~ qch à** to attribute sth to; **s'attribuer** *vt* (*s'approprier*) to claim for o.s.

**attrister** [atʀiste] *vt* to sadden

**attroupement** [atʀupmɑ̃] *nm* crowd

**attrouper** [atʀupe]: **s'attrouper** *vi* to gather

**au** [o] *prép +dét* = **à +le**

**aubaine** [obɛn] *nf* godsend

**aube** [ob] *nf* dawn, daybreak; **à l'~** at dawn ou daybreak

**aubépine** [obepin] *nf* hawthorn

**auberge** [obɛʀʒ] *nf* inn; **auberge de jeunesse** youth hostel

**aubergine** [obɛʀʒin] *nf* aubergine

**aucun, e** [okœ̃ yn] *dét* no, *tournure négative* +any; (*positif*) any ▷ *pron* none, *tournure négative* +any; any(one); **sans ~ doute** without any doubt; **plus qu'~ autre** more than any other; **il le fera mieux qu'~ de nous** he'll do it better than any of us; **~ des deux** neither of the two; **~ d'entre eux** none of them

**audace** [odas] *nf* daring, boldness; (*péj*) audacity; **audacieux, -euse** *adj* daring, bold

**au-delà** [od(ə)la] *adv* beyond ▷ *nm*: **l'~** the hereafter; **~ de** beyond

**au-dessous** [odsu] *adv* underneath; below; **~ de** under(neath), below; (*limite, somme etc*) below, under; (*dignité, condition*) below

**au-dessus** [odsy] *adv* above; **~ de** above

**au-devant** [od(ə)vɑ̃]: **~ de** *prép*: **aller ~ de** (*personne, danger*) to go (out) and meet; (*souhaits de qn*) to anticipate

**audience** [odjɑ̃s] *nf* audience; (*Jur: séance*) hearing

**audiovisuel, le** [odjovizɥɛl] *adj* audiovisual

**audition** [odisjɔ̃] *nf* (*ouïe, écoute*)

hearing; (*Jur: de témoins*) examination; (*Mus, Théâtre: épreuve*) audition

**auditoire** [oditwar] *nm* audience

**augmentation** [ɔgmɑ̃tasjɔ̃] *nf* increase; **augmentation (de salaire)** rise (in salary) (*BRIT*), (pay) raise (*US*)

**augmenter** [ɔgmɑ̃te] *vt* (*gén*) to increase; (*salaire, prix*) to increase, raise, put up; (*employé*) to increase the salary of ▷ *vi* to increase

**augure** [ogyʀ] *nm*: **de bon/mauvais ~** of good/ill omen

**aujourd'hui** [oʒuʀdɥi] *adv* today

**aumône** [omon] *nf inv* alms *sg*; **aumônier** *nm* chaplain

**auparavant** [oparavɑ̃] *adv* before(hand)

**auprès** [opʀɛ]: **~ de** *prép* next to, close to; (*recourir, s'adresser*) to; (*en comparaison de*) compared with

**auquel** [okɛl] *prép +pron* = **à +lequel**

**aurai** *etc* [ɔʀe] *vb voir* **avoir**

**aurons** *etc* [oʀɔ̃] *vb voir* **avoir**

**aurore** [`ʀ] *nf* dawn, daybreak

**ausculter** [ɔskylte] *vt* to sound (the chest of)

**aussi** [osi] *adv* (*également*) also, too; (*de comparaison*) as ▷ *conj* therefore, consequently; **~ fort que** as strong as; **moi ~** me too

**aussitôt** [osito] *adv* straight away, immediately; **~ que** as soon as

**austère** [ostɛʀ] *adj* austere

**austral, e** [ɔstʀal] *adj* southern

**Australie** [ɔstʀali] *nf*: **l'~** Australia; **australien, ne** *adj* Australian ▷ *nm/f*: **Australien, ne** Australian

**autant** [otɑ̃] *adv* (*intensité*) so much; **je ne savais pas que tu la détestais ~** I didn't know you hated her so much; (*comparatif*): **~ (que)** as much (as); (*nombre*) as many (as); **~ (de)** so much (*ou* many); as much (*ou* many); **~ partir** we (*ou* you *etc*) may as well leave; **~ dire que ...** one might as well say that ...; **pour ~** for all that; **d'~ plus/mieux (que)** all the more/the

better (since)

**autel** [otɛl] *nm* altar

**auteur** [otœʀ] *nm* author

**authentique** [otɑ̃tik] *adj* authentic, genuine

**auto** [oto] *nf* car

**auto...**: **autobiographie** *nf* autobiography; **autobronzant** *nm* self-tanning cream (*or* lotion *etc*); **autobus** *nm* bus; **autocar** *nm* coach

**autochtone** [ɔtɔktɔn] *nm/f* native

**auto...**: **autocollant, e** *adj* self-adhesive; (*enveloppe*) self-seal ▷ *nm* sticker; **autocuiseur** *nm* pressure cooker; **autodéfense** *nf* self-defence; **autodidacte** *nm/f* self-taught person; **auto-école** *nf* driving school; **autographe** *nm* autograph

**automate** [ɔtɔmat] *nm* (*machine*) (automatic) machine

**automatique** [ɔtɔmatik] *adj* automatic ▷ *nm*: **l'~** direct dialling

**automne** [otɔn] *nm* autumn (*BRIT*), fall (*US*)

**automobile** [ɔtɔmɔbil] *adj* motor *cpd*, car *cpd* ▷ *nf* (motor) car; **automobiliste** *nm/f* motorist

**autonome** [ɔtɔnɔm] *adj* autonomous; **autonomie** *nf* autonomy; (*Pol*) self-government, autonomy

**autopsie** [ɔtɔpsi] *nf* post-mortem (examination), autopsy

**autoradio** [otoʀadjo] *nm* car radio

**autorisation** [ɔtɔʀizasjɔ̃] *nf* permission, authorization; (*papiers*) permit

**autorisé, e** [ɔtɔʀize] *adj* (*opinion, sources*) authoritative

**autoriser** [ɔtɔʀize] *vt* to give permission for, authorize; (*fig*) to allow (of)

**autoritaire** [ɔtɔʀitɛʀ] *adj* authoritarian

**autorité** [ɔtɔʀite] *nf* authority; **faire ~** to be authoritative; **les ~s** the authorities

**autoroute** [otoʀut] *nf* motorway (*BRIT*), highway (*US*); **~ de**

**l'information** (*Inform*) information superhighway

- **AUTOROUTE**
-
- Motorways in France, indicated
- by blue road signs with the letter A
- followed by a number, are toll roads.
- The speed limit is 130 km/h (110 km/
- h when it is raining). At the tollgate,
- the lanes marked 'réservé' and with
- an orange 't' are reserved for people
- who subscribe to 'télépéage', an
- electronic payment system.

**auto-stop** [otostɔp] *nm*: **faire de l'~** to hitch-hike; **prendre qn en ~** to give sb a lift; **auto-stoppeur, -euse** *nm/f* hitch-hiker

**autour** [otuʀ] *adv* around; **~ de** around; **tout ~** all around

 **MOT-CLÉ**

**autre** [otʀ] *adj* **1** (*différent*) other, different; **je préférerais un autre verre** I'd prefer another *ou* a different glass

**2** (*supplémentaire*) other; **je voudrais un autre verre d'eau** I'd like another glass of water

**3**: **autre chose** something else; **autre part** somewhere else; **d'autre part** on the other hand

▷ *pron*: **un autre** another (one); **nous/vous autres** us/you; **d'autres** others; **l'autre** the other (one); **les autres** the others; (*autrui*) others; **l'un et l'autre** both of them; **se détester l'un l'autre/les uns les autres** to hate each other *ou* one another; **d'une semaine à l'autre** from one week to the next; (*incessamment*) any week now; **entre autres** (*personnes*) among others; (*choses*) among other things

**autrefois** [otʀəfwa] *adv* in the past
**autrement** [otʀəmɑ̃] *adv* differently;

(*d'une manière différente*) in another way; (*sinon*) otherwise; **~ dit** in other words

**Autriche** [otʀiʃ] *nf*: **l'~** Austria; **autrichien, ne** *adj* Austrian ▷ *nm/f*: **Autrichien, ne** Austrian

**autruche** [otʀyʃ] *nf* ostrich

**aux** [o] *prép* +*dét* = **à +les**

**auxiliaire** [oksiljɛʀ] *adj, nm/f* auxiliary

**auxquelles** [okɛl] *prép* +*pron* = **à +lesquelles**

**auxquels** [okɛl] *prép* +*pron* = **à +lesquels**

**avalanche** [avalɑ̃ʃ] *nf* avalanche

**avaler** [avale] *vt* to swallow

**avance** [avɑ̃s] *nf* (*de troupes etc*) advance; progress; (*d'argent*) advance; (*sur un concurrent*) lead; **avances** *nfpl* (*amoureuses*) advances; **(être) en ~** (to be) early; (*sur un programme*) (to be) ahead of schedule; **à l'~, d'~** in advance

**avancé, e** [avɑ̃se] *adj* advanced; (*travail*) well on, well under way

**avancement** [avɑ̃smɑ̃] *nm* (*professionnel*) promotion

**avancer** [avɑ̃se] *vi* to move forward, advance; (*projet, travail*) to make progress; (*montre, réveil*) to be fast; to gain ▷ *vt* to move forward, advance; (*argent*) to advance; (*montre, pendule*) to put forward; **s'avancer** *vi* to move forward, advance; (*fig*) to commit o.s.

**avant** [avɑ̃] *prép, adv* before ▷ *adj inv*: **siège/roue ~** front seat/wheel ▷ *nm* (*d'un véhicule, bâtiment*) front; (*Sport*: *joueur*) forward; **~ qu'il (ne) parte** before he goes *ou* leaves; **~ de partir** before leaving; **~ tout** (*surtout*) above all; **à l'~** (*dans un véhicule*) in (the) front; **en ~** (*se pencher, tomber*) forward(s); **partir en ~** to go on ahead; **en ~ de** in front of

**avantage** [avɑ̃taʒ] *nm* advantage; **avantages sociaux** fringe benefits; **avantager** *vt* (*favoriser*) to favour; (*embellir*) to flatter; **avantageux, -euse** *adj* (*prix*) attractive

**avant...**: **avant-bras** *nm inv* forearm; **avant-coureur** *adj inv*: **signe avant-**

**coureur** advance indication *ou* sign;
**avant-dernier, -ière** *adj, nm/f* next
to last, last but one; **avant-goût** *nm*
foretaste; **avant-hier** *adv* the day
before yesterday; **avant-première**
*nf* (*de film*) preview; **avant-veille** *nf*:
**l'avant-veille** two days before
**avare** [avaʀ] *adj* miserly, avaricious
▷ *nm/f* miser; **~ de** (*compliments etc*)
sparing of
**avec** [avɛk] *prép* with; (*à l'égard de*)
to(wards), with; **et ~ ça?** (*dans magasin*)
anything else?
**avenir** [avniʀ] *nm* future; **à l'~**
in future; **politicien/métier d'~**
politician/job with prospects *ou* a
future
**aventure** [avɑ̃tyʀ] *nf* adventure;
(*amoureuse*) affair; **aventureux, -euse**
*adj* adventurous, venturesome; (*projet*)
risky, chancy
**avenue** [avny] *nf* avenue
**avérer** [aveʀe]: **s'avérer** *vb +attrib* to
prove (to be)
**averse** [avɛʀs] *nf* shower
**averti, e** [avɛʀti] *adj* (well-)informed
**avertir** [avɛʀtiʀ] *vt*: **~ qn (de qch/que)**
to warn sb (of sth/that); (*renseigner*) to
inform sb (of sth/that); **avertissement**
*nm* warning; **avertisseur** *nm* horn,
siren
**aveu, x** [avø] *nm* confession
**aveugle** [avœgl] *adj* blind ▷ *nm/f* blind
man/woman
**aviation** [avjasjɔ̃] *nf* aviation; (*sport*)
flying; (*Mil*) air force
**avide** [avid] *adj* eager; (*péj*) greedy,
grasping
**avion** [avjɔ̃] *nm* (aero)plane (BRIT),
(air)plane (US); **aller (quelque part)**
**en ~** to go (somewhere) by plane, fly
(somewhere); **par ~** by airmail; **avion à**
**réaction** jet (plane)
**aviron** [aviʀɔ̃] *nm* oar; (*sport*): **l'~**
rowing
**avis** [avi] *nm* opinion; (*notification*)
notice; **à mon ~** in my opinion;
**changer d'~** to change one's mind;

**jusqu'à nouvel ~** until further notice
**aviser** [avize] *vt* (*informer*): **~ qn de/que**
to advise *ou* inform sb of/that ▷ *vi*
to think about things, assess the
situation; **nous ~ons sur place** we'll
work something out once we're there;
**s'~ de qch/que** to become suddenly
aware of sth/that; **s'~ de faire** to take
it into one's head to do
**avocat, e** [avɔka, at] *nm/f* (*Jur*)
barrister (BRIT), lawyer ▷ *nm* (*Culin*)
avocado (pear); **~ de la défense**
counsel for the defence; **avocat**
**général** assistant public prosecutor
**avoine** [avwan] *nf* oats *pl*

O **MOT-CLÉ**

**avoir** [avwaʀ] *nm* assets *pl*, resources
*pl*; (*Comm*) credit
▷ *vt* **1** (*posséder*) to have; **elle a 2**
**enfants/une belle maison** she has
(got) 2 children/a lovely house; **il a les**
**yeux bleus** he has (got) blue eyes; **vous**
**avez du sel?** do you have any salt?;
**avoir du courage/de la patience** to
be brave/patient
**2** (*âge, dimensions*) to be; **il a 3 ans** he
is 3 (years old); **le mur a 3 mètres de**
**haut** the wall is 3 metres high; *voir aussi*
**faim**; **peur** *etc*
**3** (*fam: duper*) to do, have; **on vous a**
**eu!** (*dupé*) you've been done *ou* had!;
(*fait une plaisanterie*) we *ou* they had
you there
**4**: **en avoir après** *ou* **contre qn** to have
a grudge against sb; **en avoir assez** to
be fed up; **j'en ai pour une demi-heure**
it'll take me half an hour
**5** (*obtenir, attraper*) to get; **j'ai réussi**
**à avoir mon train** I managed to
get *ou* catch my train; **j'ai réussi à**
**avoir le renseignement qu'il me**
**fallait** I managed to get (hold of) the
information I needed
**6** (*éprouver*): **avoir de la peine** to be
*ou* feel sad
▷ *vb aux* **1** to have; **avoir mangé/dormi**

to have eaten/slept
**2** (*avoir +à +infinitif*): **avoir à faire qch**
to have to do sth; **vous n'avez qu'à lui
demander** you only have to ask him
▷ *vb impers* **1: il y a** (+ *singulier*) there is; (+
*pluriel*) there are; **il y avait du café/des
gâteaux** there was coffee/there were
cakes; **qu'y-a-t-il?, qu'est-ce qu'il y a?**
what's the matter?, what is it?; **il doit
y avoir une explication** there must be
an explanation; **il n'y a qu'à ...** we (*ou*
you *etc*) will just have to ...; **il ne peut y
en avoir qu'un** there can only be one
**2** (*temporel*): **il y a 10 ans** 10 years ago;
**il y a 10 ans/longtemps que je le sais**
I've known it for 10 years/a long time; **il
y a 10 ans qu'il est arrivé** it's 10 years
since he arrived

**avortement** [avɔRtəmɑ̃] *nm* abortion
**avouer** [avwe] *vt* (*crime, défaut*) to
confess (to); **~ avoir fait/que** to admit
*ou* confess to having done/that
**avril** [avRil] *nm* April
**axe** [aks] *nm* axis; (*de roue etc*) axle;
(*fig*) main line; **axe routier** main road,
trunk road (BRIT), highway (US)
**ayons** *etc* [ɛjɔ̃] *vb voir* **avoir**

# b

**bâbord** [babɔR] *nm*: **à ~** to port, on the
port side
**baby-foot** [babifut] *nm* table football
**bac** [bak] *abr m* = **baccalauréat** ▷ *nm*
(*récipient*) tub
**baccalauréat** [bakalɔRea] *nm* high
school diploma
**bâcler** [bakle] *vt* to botch (up)
**baffe** [baf] (*fam*) *nf* slap, clout
**bafouiller** [bafuje] *vi, vt* to stammer
**bagage** [bagaʒ] *nm* piece of luggage;
(*connaissances*) background,
knowledge; **nos ~s ne sont pas arrivés**
our luggage hasn't arrived; **bagage à
main** piece of hand-luggage
**bagarre** [bagaR] *nf* fight, brawl;
**bagarrer**: **se bagarrer** *vi* to have a
fight *ou* scuffle, fight
**bagnole** [baɲɔl] (*fam*) *nf* car
**bague** [bag] *nf* ring; **bague de
fiançailles** engagement ring
**baguette** [bagɛt] *nf* stick; (*cuisine
chinoise*) chopstick; (*de chef d'orchestre*)
baton; (*pain*) stick of (French) bread;

**baguette magique** magic wand
**baie** [bɛ] nf (Géo) bay; (fruit) berry; **baie (vitrée)** picture window
**baignade** [bɛɲad] nf bathing; **"~ interdite"** "no bathing"
**baigner** [beɲe] vt (bébé) to bath; **se baigner** vi to have a swim, go swimming ou bathing; **baignoire** nf bath(tub)
**bail** [baj, bo] (pl **baux**) nm lease
**bâiller** [baje] vi to yawn; (être ouvert) to gape
**bain** [bɛ̃] nm bath; **prendre un ~** to have a bath; **se mettre dans le ~** (fig) to get into it ou things; **bain de bouche** mouthwash; **bain moussant** bubble bath; **bain de soleil: prendre un bain de soleil** to sunbathe; **bain-marie** nm: **faire chauffer au bain-marie** (boîte etc) to immerse in boiling water
**baiser** [beze] nm kiss ▷ vt (main, front) to kiss; (fam!) to screw (!)
**baisse** [bɛs] nf fall, drop; **être en ~** to be falling, be declining
**baisser** [bese] vt to lower; (radio, chauffage) to turn down ▷ vi to fall, drop, go down; (vue, santé) to fail, dwindle; **se baisser** vi to bend down
**bal** [bal] nm dance; (grande soirée) ball; **bal costumé** fancy-dress ball
**balade** [balad] (fam) nf (à pied) walk, stroll; (en voiture) drive; **balader** (fam): **se balader** vi to go for a walk ou stroll; to go for a drive; **baladeur** nm personal stereo, Walkman®
**balai** [balɛ] nm broom, brush
**balance** [balɑ̃s] nf scales pl; (signe): **la B~** Libra; **balance commerciale** balance of trade
**balancer** [balɑ̃se] vt to swing; (fam: lancer) to fling, chuck; (: jeter) to chuck out; **se balancer** vi to swing, rock; **se ~ de** (fam) not to care about; **balançoire** nf swing; (sur pivot) seesaw
**balayer** [baleje] vt (feuilles etc) to sweep up, brush up; (pièce) to sweep; (objections) to sweep aside; (suj: radar) to scan; **balayeur, -euse** nm/f

roadsweeper
**balbutier** [balbysje] vi, vt to stammer
**balcon** [balkɔ̃] nm balcony; (Théâtre) dress circle; **avez-vous une chambre avec ~?** do you have a room with a balcony?
**Bâle** [bɑl] n Basle, Basel
**Baléares** [baleaʀ] nfpl: **les ~** the Balearic Islands, the Balearics
**baleine** [balɛn] nf whale
**balise** [baliz] nf (Navig) beacon; (marker) buoy; (Aviat) runway light, beacon; (Auto, Ski) sign, marker; **baliser** vt to mark out (with lights etc)
**balle** [bal] nf (de fusil) bullet; (de sport) ball; (fam: franc) franc
**ballerine** [bal(ə)ʀin] nf (danseuse) ballet dancer; (chaussure) ballet shoe
**ballet** [balɛ] nm ballet
**ballon** [balɔ̃] nm (de sport) ball; (jouet, Aviat) balloon; **ballon de football** football
**balnéaire** [balneɛʀ] adj seaside cpd; **station ~** seaside resort
**balustrade** [balystʀad] nf railings pl, handrail
**bambin** [bɑ̃bɛ̃] nm little child
**bambou** [bɑ̃bu] nm bamboo
**banal, e** [banal] adj banal, commonplace; (péj) trite; **banalité** nf banality
**banane** [banan] nf banana; (sac) waist-bag, bum-bag
**banc** [bɑ̃] nm seat, bench; (de poissons) shoal; **banc d'essai** (fig) testing ground
**bancaire** [bɑ̃kɛʀ] adj banking; (chèque, carte) bank cpd
**bancal, e** [bɑ̃kal] adj wobbly
**bandage** [bɑ̃daʒ] nm bandage
**bande** [bɑ̃d] nf (de tissu etc) strip; (Méd) bandage; (motif) stripe; (magnétique etc) tape; (groupe) band; (: péj) bunch; **faire ~ à part** to keep to o.s.; **bande dessinée** comic strip; **bande sonore** sound track
**bande-annonce** [bɑ̃danɔ̃s] nf trailer
**bandeau, x** [bɑ̃do] nm headband; (sur les yeux) blindfold
**bander** [bɑ̃de] vt (blessure) to bandage;

**~ les yeux à qn** to blindfold sb
**bandit** [bɑ̃di] nm bandit
**bandoulière** [bɑ̃duljɛʀ] nf: **en ~** (slung ou worn) across the shoulder
**Bangladesh** [bɑ̃ɡladɛʃ] nm: **le ~** Bangladesh
**banlieue** [bɑ̃ljø] nf suburbs pl; **lignes/ quartiers de ~** suburban lines/areas; **trains de ~** commuter trains
**bannir** [baniʀ] vt to banish
**banque** [bɑ̃k] nf bank; (activités) banking; **banque de données** data bank
**banquet** [bɑ̃kɛ] nm dinner; (d'apparat) banquet
**banquette** [bɑ̃kɛt] nf seat
**banquier** [bɑ̃kje] nm banker
**banquise** [bɑ̃kiz] nf ice field
**baptême** [batɛm] nm christening; baptism; **baptême de l'air** first flight
**baptiser** [batize] vt to baptize, christen
**bar** [baʀ] nm bar
**baraque** [baʀak] nf shed; (fam) house; (dans une fête foraine) stall, booth; **baraqué, e** (fam) adj well-built, hefty
**barbare** [baʀbaʀ] adj barbaric
**barbe** [baʀb] nf beard; **la ~!** (fam) damn it!; **quelle ~!** (fam) what a drag ou bore!; **à la ~ de qn** under sb's nose; **barbe à papa** candy-floss (BRIT), cotton candy (US)
**barbelé** [baʀbəle] adj, nm: **(fil de fer) ~** barbed wire no pl
**barbiturique** [baʀbityʀik] nm barbiturate
**barbouiller** [baʀbuje] vt to daub; **avoir l'estomac barbouillé** to feel queasy
**barbu, e** [baʀby] adj bearded
**barder** [baʀde] (fam) vi: **ça va ~** sparks will fly, things are going to get hot
**barème** [baʀɛm] nm (Scol) scale; (table de référence) table
**baril** [baʀi(l)] nm barrel; (poudre) keg
**bariolé, e** [baʀjɔle] adj gaudily-coloured
**baromètre** [baʀɔmɛtʀ] nm barometer

**baron, ne** [baʀɔ̃] nm/f baron(ess)
**baroque** [baʀɔk] adj (Art) baroque; (fig) weird
**barque** [baʀk] nf small boat
**barquette** [baʀkɛt] nf (pour repas) tray; (pour fruits) punnet
**barrage** [baʀaʒ] nm dam; (sur route) roadblock, barricade
**barre** [baʀ] nf bar; (Navig) helm; (écrite) line, stroke
**barreau, x** [baʀo] nm bar; (Jur): **le ~** the Bar
**barrer** [baʀe] vt (route etc) to block; (mot) to cross out; (chèque) to cross (BRIT); (Navig) to steer; **se barrer** (fam) ▷ vi to clear off
**barrette** [baʀɛt] nf (pour cheveux) (hair) slide (BRIT) ou clip (US)
**barricader** [baʀikade]: **se barricader** vi to barricade o.s.
**barrière** [baʀjɛʀ] nf fence; (obstacle) barrier; (porte) gate
**barrique** [baʀik] nf barrel, cask
**bar-tabac** [baʀtaba] nm bar (which sells tobacco and stamps)
**bas, basse** [bɑ, bɑs] adj low ▷ nm bottom, lower part; (vêtement) stocking ▷ adv low; (parler) softly; **au ~ mot** at the lowest estimate; **en ~** down below; (d'une liste, d'un mur etc) at/to the bottom; (dans une maison) downstairs; **en ~ de** at the bottom of; **un enfant en ~ âge** a young child; **à ~ ...!** down with ...!
**bas-côté** [bakote] nm (de route) verge (BRIT), shoulder (US)
**basculer** [baskyle] vi to fall over, topple (over); (benne) to tip up ▷ vt (contenu) to tip out; (benne) to tip up
**base** [bɑz] nf base; (Pol) rank and file; (fondement, principe) basis; **de ~** basic; **à ~ de café** etc coffee etc -based; **base de données** database; **baser** vt to base; **se baser sur** vt (preuves) to base one's argument on
**bas-fond** [bafɔ̃] nm (Navig) shallow; **bas-fonds** nmpl (fig) dregs
**basilic** [bazilik] nm (Culin) basil

**basket** [baskɛt] nm trainer (BRIT), sneaker (US); (aussi: **~-ball**) basketball

**basque** [bask] adj Basque ▷ nm/f: **B~** Basque; **le Pays Basque** the Basque Country

**basse** [bɑs] adj voir **bas** ▷ nf (Mus) bass; **basse-cour** nf farmyard

**bassin** [basɛ̃] nm (pièce d'eau) pond, pool; (de fontaine;: Géo) basin; (Anat) pelvis; (portuaire) dock

**bassine** [basin] nf (ustensile) basin; (contenu) bowl(ful)

**basson** [basɔ̃] nm bassoon

**bat** [ba] vb voir **battre**

**bataille** [bataj] nf (Mil) battle; (rixe) fight; **elle avait les cheveux en ~** her hair was a mess

**bateau, x** [bato] nm boat, ship; **bateau-mouche** nm passenger pleasure boat (on the Seine)

**bâti, e** [bɑti] adj: **bien ~** well-built; **terrain ~** piece of land that has been built on

**bâtiment** [bɑtimɑ̃] nm building; (Navig) ship, vessel; (industrie) building trade

**bâtir** [bɑtiʀ] vt to build

**bâtisse** [bɑtis] nf building

**bâton** [bɑtɔ̃] nm stick; **parler à ~s rompus** to chat about this and that

**bats** [ba] vb voir **battre**

**battement** [batmɑ̃] nm (de cœur) beat; (intervalle) interval; **10 minutes de ~** 10 minutes to spare

**batterie** [batʀi] nf (Mil, Élec) battery; (Mus) drums pl, drum kit; **batterie de cuisine** pots and pans pl, kitchen utensils pl

**batteur** [batœʀ] nm (Mus) drummer; (appareil) whisk

**battre** [batʀ] vt to beat; (blé) to thresh; (passer au peigne fin) to scour; (cartes) to shuffle ▷ vi (cœur) to beat; (volets etc) to bang, rattle; **se battre** vi to fight; **~ la mesure** to beat time; **~ son plein** to be at its height, be going full swing; **~ des mains** to clap one's hands

**baume** [bom] nm balm

**bavard, e** [bavaʀ, aʀd] adj (very) talkative; gossipy; **bavarder** vi to chatter; (commérer) to gossip; (divulguer un secret) to blab

**baver** [bave] vi to dribble; (chien) to slobber; **en ~** (fam) to have a hard time (of it)

**bavoir** [bavwaʀ] nm bib

**bavure** [bavyʀ] nf smudge; (fig) hitch; (policière etc) blunder

**bazar** [bazaʀ] nm general store; (fam) jumble; **bazarder** (fam) vt to chuck out

**BCBG** sigle adj (= bon chic bon genre) preppy, smart and trendy

**BD** sigle f = **bande dessinée**

**bd** abr = **boulevard**

**béant, e** [beɑ̃, ɑ̃t] adj gaping

**beau, bel, belle** [bo, bɛl] (mpl **~x**) adj beautiful, lovely; (homme) handsome; (femme) beautiful ▷ adv: **il fait ~** the weather's fine ▷ nm: **faire le ~** (chien) to sit up and beg; **un ~ jour** one (fine) day; **de plus belle** more than ever, even more; **on a ~ essayer** however hard we try; **bel et bien** well and truly; **le plus ~ c'est que ...** the best of it is that ...

 **MOT-CLÉ**

**beaucoup** [boku] adv **1** a lot; **il boit beaucoup** he drinks a lot; **il ne boit pas beaucoup** he doesn't drink much ou a lot

**2** (suivi de plus, trop etc) much, a lot; **il est beaucoup plus grand** he is much ou a lot taller; **c'est beaucoup plus cher** it's a lot ou much more expensive; **il a beaucoup plus de temps que moi** he has much ou a lot more time than me; **il y a beaucoup plus de touristes ici** there are a lot ou many more tourists here; **beaucoup trop vite** much too fast; **il fume beaucoup trop** he smokes far too much

**3**: **beaucoup de** (nombre) many, a lot of; (quantité) a lot of; **beaucoup d'étudiants/de touristes** a lot of ou many students/tourists; **beaucoup**

**de courage** a lot of courage; **il n'a pas beaucoup d'argent** he hasn't got much *ou* a lot of money
**4**: **de beaucoup** by far

**beau…**: **beau-fils** nm son-in-law; (remariage) stepson; **beau-frère** nm brother-in-law; **beau-père** nm father-in-law; (remariage) stepfather
**beauté** [bote] nf beauty; **de toute ~** beautiful; **finir qch en ~** to complete sth brilliantly
**beaux-arts** [bozar] nmpl fine arts
**beaux-parents** [boparā] nmpl wife's/husband's family, in-laws
**bébé** [bebe] nm baby
**bec** [bɛk] nm beak, bill; (de théière) spout; (de casserole) lip; (fam) mouth; **bec de gaz** (street) gaslamp
**bêche** [bɛʃ] nf spade; **bêcher** vt to dig
**bedaine** [bədɛn] nf paunch
**bedonnant, e** [bədɔnā, āt] adj potbellied
**bée** [be] adj: **bouche ~** gaping
**bégayer** [begeje] vt, vi to stammer
**beige** [bɛʒ] adj beige
**beignet** [bɛɲɛ] nm fritter
**bel** [bɛl] adj voir **beau**
**bêler** [bele] vi to bleat
**belette** [bəlɛt] nf weasel
**belge** [bɛlʒ] adj Belgian ▷ nm/f: **B~** Belgian
**Belgique** [bɛlʒik] nf: **la ~** Belgium
**bélier** [belje] nm ram; (signe): **le B~** Aries
**belle** [bɛl] adj voir **beau** ▷ nf (Sport): **la ~** the decider; **belle-fille** nf daughter-in-law; (remariage) stepdaughter; **belle-mère** nf mother-in-law; stepmother; **belle-sœur** nf sister-in-law
**belvédère** [bɛlvedɛr] nm panoramic viewpoint (or small building there)
**bémol** [bemɔl] nm (Mus) flat
**bénédiction** [benediksjɔ̃] nf blessing
**bénéfice** [benefis] nm (Comm) profit; (avantage) benefit; **bénéficier**: **bénéficier de** vt to enjoy; (situation) to benefit by *ou* from; **bénéfique** adj beneficial

**Benelux** [benelyks] nm: **le ~** Benelux, the Benelux countries
**bénévole** [benevɔl] adj voluntary, unpaid
**bénin, -igne** [benɛ̃, iɲ] adj minor, mild; (tumeur) benign
**bénir** [benir] vt to bless; **bénit, e** adj consecrated; **eau bénite** holy water
**benne** [bɛn] nf skip; (de téléphérique) (cable) car; **benne à ordures** (amovible) skip
**béquille** [bekij] nf crutch; (de bicyclette) stand
**berceau, x** [bɛrso] nm cradle, crib
**bercer** [bɛrse] vt to rock, cradle; (suj: musique etc) to lull; **~ qn de** (promesses etc) to delude sb with; **berceuse** nf lullaby
**béret** [berɛ] nm (aussi: **~ basque**) beret
**berge** [bɛrʒ] nf bank
**berger, -ère** [bɛrʒe, ɛr] nm/f shepherd(-ess); **berger allemand** alsatian (BRIT), German shepherd
**Berlin** [bɛrlɛ̃] n Berlin
**Bermudes** [bɛrmyd] nfpl: **les (îles) ~** Bermuda
**Berne** [bɛrn(ə)] n Bern
**berner** [bɛrne] vt to fool
**besogne** [bəzɔɲ] nf work no pl, job
**besoin** [bəzwɛ̃] nm need; **avoir ~ de qch/faire qch** to need sth/to do sth; **au ~** if need be; **le ~** (pauvreté) need, want; **être dans le ~** to be in need *ou* want; **faire ses ~s** to relieve o.s.
**bestiole** [bɛstjɔl] nf (tiny) creature
**bétail** [betaj] nm livestock, cattle pl
**bête** [bɛt] nf animal; (bestiole) insect, creature ▷ adj stupid, silly; **il cherche la petite ~** he's being pernickety *ou* over fussy; **bête noire** pet hate; **bête sauvage** wild beast *ou* animal
**bêtise** [betiz] nf stupidity; (action) stupid thing (to say *ou* do)
**béton** [betɔ̃] nm concrete; **(en) ~** (alibi, argument) cast iron; **béton armé** reinforced concrete
**betterave** [bɛtrav] nf beetroot (BRIT), beet (US); **betterave sucrière**

sugar beet

**Beur** [bœʀ] nm/f person of North African origin living in France

**beurre** [bœʀ] nm butter; **beurrer** vt to butter; **beurrier** nm butter dish

**biais** [bjɛ] nm (moyen) device, expedient; (aspect) angle; **en ~, de ~** (obliquement) at an angle; **par le ~ de** by means of

**bibelot** [biblo] nm trinket, curio

**biberon** [bibʀɔ̃] nm (feeding) bottle; **nourrir au ~** to bottle-feed

**bible** [bibl] nf bible

**biblio...** [biblio] préfixe: **bibliobus** nm mobile library van; **bibliothécaire** nm/f librarian; **bibliothèque** nf library; (meuble) bookcase

**bic®** [bik] nm Biro®

**bicarbonate** [bikaʀbɔnat] nm: **~ (de soude)** bicarbonate of soda

**biceps** [bisɛps] nm biceps

**biche** [biʃ] nf doe

**bicolore** [bikɔlɔʀ] adj two-coloured

**bicoque** [bikɔk] (péj) nf shack

**bicyclette** [bisiklɛt] nf bicycle

**bidet** [bidɛ] nm bidet

**bidon** [bidɔ̃] nm can ▷ adj inv (fam) phoney

**bidonville** [bidɔ̃vil] nm shanty town

**bidule** [bidyl] (fam) nm thingumajig

⚫ **MOT-CLÉ**

**bien** [bjɛ̃] nm **1** (avantage, profit): **faire du bien à qn** to do sb good; **dire du bien de** to speak well of; **c'est pour son bien** it's for his own good

**2** (possession, patrimoine) possession, property; **son bien le plus précieux** his most treasured possession; **avoir du bien** to have property; **biens (de consommation etc)** (consumer etc) goods

**3** (moral): **le bien** good; **distinguer le bien du mal** to tell good from evil

▷ adv **1** (de façon satisfaisante) well; **elle travaille/mange bien** she works/eats well; **croyant bien faire, je/il ...** thinking I/he was doing the

right thing, I/he ...; **tiens-toi bien!** (assieds-toi correctement) sit up straight!; (debout) stand up straight!; (sois sage) behave yourself!; (prépare-toi) wait for it!; **c'est bien fait!** it serves him (ou her etc) right!

**2** (valeur intensive) quite; **bien jeune** quite young; **bien assez** quite enough; **bien mieux** (very) much better; **j'espère bien y aller** I do hope to go; **je veux bien le faire** (concession) I'm quite willing to do it; **il faut bien le faire** it has to be done; **Paul est bien venu, n'est-ce pas?** Paul did come, didn't he?; **où peut-il bien être passé?** where can he have got to?

**3** (beaucoup): **bien du temps/des gens** quite a time/a number of people

**4** (au moins) at least; **cela fait bien deux ans que je ne l'ai pas vu** I haven't seen him for at least ou a good two years

▷ adj inv **1** (en bonne forme, à l'aise): **je me sens bien** I feel fine; **je ne me sens pas bien** I don't feel well; **on est bien dans ce fauteuil** this chair is very comfortable

**2** (joli, beau) good-looking; **tu es bien dans cette robe** you look good in that dress

**3** (satisfaisant) good; **elle est bien, cette maison/secrétaire** it's a good house/she's a good secretary; **c'est bien?** is that ou it O.K.?; **c'est très bien (comme ça)** it's fine (like that)

**4** (moralement) right; (: personne) good, nice; (: respectable) respectable; **ce n'est pas bien de ...** it's not right to ...; **elle est bien, cette femme** she's a nice woman, she's a good sort; **des gens bien** respectable people

**5** (en bons termes): **être bien avec qn** to be on good terms with sb

▷ préfixe: **bien-aimé, e** adj, nm/f beloved; **bien-être** nm well-being; **bienfaisance** nf charity; **bienfait** nm act of generosity, benefaction; (de la science etc) benefit; **bienfaiteur, -trice** *nm/f* benefactor/benefactress; **bien-fondé** *nm* soundness; **bien que** *conj* (al)though; **bien sûr** *adv* certainly

**bientôt** [bjɛ̃to] *adv* soon; **à ~** see you soon

**bienveillant, e** [bjɛ̃vejã, ãt] *adj* kindly

**bienvenu, e** [bjɛ̃vny] *adj* welcome; **bienvenue** *nf*: **souhaiter la bienvenue à** to welcome; **bienvenue à** welcome to

**bière** [bjɛʀ] *nf* (*boisson*) beer; (*cercueil*) bier; **bière blonde** lager; **bière brune** brown ale (BRIT), dark beer (US); **bière (à la) pression** draught beer

**bifteck** [biftɛk] *nm* steak

**bigorneau, x** [bigɔʀno] *nm* winkle

**bigoudi** [bigudi] *nm* curler

**bijou, x** [biʒu] *nm* jewel; **bijouterie** *nf* jeweller's (shop); **bijoutier, -ière** *nm/f* jeweller

**bikini** [bikini] *nm* bikini

**bilan** [bilã] *nm* (*fig*) (net) outcome; (: *de victimes*) toll; (*Comm*) balance sheet(s); **un ~ de santé** a (medical) checkup; **faire le ~ de** to assess, review; **déposer son ~** to file a bankruptcy statement

**bile** [bil] *nf* bile; **se faire de la ~** (*fam*) to worry o.s. sick

**bilieux, -euse** [biljø, øz] *adj* bilious; (*fig: colérique*) testy

**bilingue** [bilɛ̃g] *adj* bilingual

**billard** [bijaʀ] *nm* (*jeu*) billiards *sg*; (*table*) billiard table

**bille** [bij] *nf* (*gén*) ball; (*du jeu de billes*) marble

**billet** [bijɛ] *nm* (*aussi*: **~ de banque**) (bank)note; (*de cinéma, de bus etc*) ticket; (*courte lettre*) note; **billet électronique** e-ticket; **billetterie** *nf* ticket office; (*distributeur*) ticket machine; (*Banque*) cash dispenser

**billion** [biljɔ̃] *nm* billion (BRIT), trillion (US)

**bimensuel, le** [bimãsɥɛl] *adj* bimonthly

**bio** [bjo] *adj inv* organic

**bio...** [bjo] *préfixe* bio...; **biochimie**

*nf* biochemistry; **biographie** *nf* biography; **biologie** *nf* biology; **biologique** *adj* biological; (*produits, aliments*) organic; **biométrie** *nf* biometrics; **biotechnologie** *nf* biotechnology; **bioterrorisme** *nm* bioterrorism

**Birmanie** [biʀmani] *nf* Burma

**bis** [bis] *adv*: **12 ~** 12a ou A ▷ *excl, nm* encore

**biscotte** [biskɔt] *nf* toasted bread (*sold in packets*)

**biscuit** [biskɥi] *nm* biscuit (BRIT), cookie (US)

**bise** [biz] *nf* (*fam: baiser*) kiss; (*vent*) North wind; **grosses ~s (de)** (*sur lettre*) love and kisses (from)

**bisexuel, le** [bisɛksɥɛl] *adj* bisexual

**bisou** [bizu] (*fam*) *nm* kiss

**bissextile** [bisɛkstil] *adj*: **année ~** leap year

**bistro(t)** [bistʀo] *nm* bistro, café

**bitume** [bitym] *nm* asphalt

**bizarre** [bizaʀ] *adj* strange, odd

**blague** [blag] *nf* (*propos*) joke; (*farce*) trick; **sans ~!** no kidding!; **blaguer** *vi* to joke

**blaireau, x** [blɛʀo] *nm* (*Zool*) badger; (*brosse*) shaving brush

**blâme** [blɑm] *nm* blame; (*sanction*) reprimand; **blâmer** *vt* to blame

**blanc, blanche** [blɑ̃, blɑ̃ʃ] *adj* white; (*non imprimé*) blank ▷ *nm/f* white, white man(-woman) ▷ *nm* (*couleur*) white; (*espace non écrit*) blank; (*aussi*: **~ d'œuf**) (egg-)white; (*aussi*: **~ de poulet**) breast, white meat; (*aussi*: **vin ~**) white wine; **~ cassé** off-white; **chèque en ~** blank cheque; **à ~** (*chauffer*) white-hot; (*tirer, charger*) with blanks; **blanche** *nf* (*Mus*) minim (BRIT), half-note (US); **blancheur** *nf* whiteness

**blanchir** [blɑ̃ʃiʀ] *vt* (*gén*) to whiten; (*linge*) to launder; (*Culin*) to blanch; (*fig: disculper*) to clear ▷ *vi* (*cheveux*) to go white; **blanchisserie** *nf* laundry

**blason** [blazɔ̃] *nm* coat of arms

**blasphème** [blasfɛm] *nm* blasphemy

**blazer** [blazɛʀ] nm blazer

**blé** [ble] nm wheat; **blé noir** buckwheat

**bled** [blɛd] (péj) nm hole

**blême** [blɛm] adj pale

**blessé, e** [blese] adj injured ▷ nm/f injured person, casualty

**blesser** [blese] vt to injure; (délibérément) to wound; (offenser) to hurt; **se blesser** to injure o.s.; **se ~ au pied** to injure one's foot; **blessure** nf (accidentelle) injury; (intentionnelle) wound

**bleu, e** [blø] adj blue; (bifteck) very rare ▷ nm (couleur) blue; (contusion) bruise; (vêtement: aussi **~s**) overalls pl; (fromage) blue cheese; **bleu marine** navy blue; **bleuet** nm cornflower

**bloc** [blɔk] nm (de pierre etc) block; (de papier à lettres) pad; (ensemble) group, block; **serré à ~** tightened right down; **en ~** as a whole; **bloc opératoire** operating ou theatre block; **blocage** nm (des prix) freezing; (Psych) hang-up; **bloc-notes** nm note pad

**blog, blogue** [blɔg] nm blog; **bloguer** vi to blog

**blond, e** [blɔ̃, blɔ̃d] adj fair, blond; (sable, blés) golden

**bloquer** [blɔke] vt (passage) to block; (pièce mobile) to jam; (crédits, compte) to freeze

**blottir** [blɔtiʀ]: **se blottir** vi to huddle up

**blouse** [bluz] nf overall

**blouson** [bluzɔ̃] nm blouson jacket; **blouson noir** (fig) ≈ rocker

**bluff** [blœf] nm bluff

**bobine** [bɔbin] nf reel; (Élec) coil

**bobo** [bobo] abr m/f = bourgeois bohème (fam) boho

**bocal, -aux** [bɔkal, o] nm jar

**bock** [bɔk] nm glass of beer

**bœuf** [bœf] nm ox; (Culin) beef

**bof** [bɔf] (fam) excl don't care!; (pas terrible) nothing special

**bohémien, ne** [bɔemjɛ̃, -ɛn] nm/f gipsy

**boire** [bwaʀ] vt to drink; (s'imprégner de) to soak up; **~ un coup** (fam) to have a drink

**bois** [bwa] nm wood; **de ~, en ~** wooden; **boisé, e** adj woody, wooded

**boisson** [bwasɔ̃] nf drink

**boîte** [bwat] nf box; (fam: entreprise) firm; **aliments en ~** canned ou tinned (BRIT) foods; **boîte à gants** glove compartment; **boîte à ordures** dustbin (BRIT), trashcan (US); **boîte aux lettres** letter box; **boîte d'allumettes** box of matches; (vide) matchbox; **boîte de conserves** can ou tin (BRIT) of food; **boîte (de nuit)** night club; **boîte de vitesses** gear box; **boîte postale** PO Box; **boîte vocale** (Tél) voice mail

**boiter** [bwate] vi to limp; (fig: raisonnement) to be shaky

**boîtier** [bwatje] nm case

**boive** etc [bwav] vb voir **boire**

**bol** [bɔl] nm bowl; **un ~ d'air** a breath of fresh air; **j'en ai ras le ~** (fam) I'm fed up with this; **avoir du ~** (fam) to be lucky

**bombarder** [bɔ̃baʀde] vt to bomb; **~ qn de** (cailloux, lettres) to bombard sb with

**bombe** [bɔ̃b] nf bomb; (atomiseur) (aerosol) spray

 **MOT-CLÉ**

**bon, bonne** [bɔ̃, bɔn] adj **1** (agréable, satisfaisant) good; **un bon repas/ restaurant** a good meal/restaurant; **être bon en maths** to be good at maths (BRIT) ou math (US)

**2** (charitable): **être bon (envers)** to be good (to)

**3** (correct) right; **le bon numéro/ moment** the right number/moment

**4** (souhaits): **bon anniversaire!** happy birthday!; **bon voyage!** have a good trip!; **bonne chance!** good luck!; **bonne année!** happy New Year!; **bonne nuit!** good night!

**5** (approprié, apte): **bon à/pour** fit to/for; **à quoi bon?** what's the use?

**6**: **bon enfant** adj inv accommodating,

easy-going; **bonne femme** (*péj*) woman; **de bonne heure** early; **bon marché** *adj inv, adv* cheap; **bon mot** witticism; **bon sens** common sense; **bon vivant** jovial chap; **bonnes œuvres** charitable works, charities ▷ *nm* **1** (*billet*) voucher; (*aussi:* **bon cadeau**) gift voucher; **bon d'essence** petrol coupon; **bon du Trésor** Treasury bond **2**: **avoir du bon** to have its good points; **pour le bon** for good ▷ *adv*: **il fait bon** it's *ou* the weather is fine; **sentir bon** to smell good; **tenir bon** to stand firm ▷ *excl* good!; **ah bon?** really?; **bon, je reste** right then, I'll stay; *voir aussi* **bonne**

**bonbon** [bɔ̃bɔ̃] *nm* (boiled) sweet
**bond** [bɔ̃] *nm* leap; **faire un ~** to leap in the air
**bondé, e** [bɔ̃de] *adj* packed (full)
**bondir** [bɔ̃diʀ] *vi* to leap
**bonheur** [bɔnœʀ] *nm* happiness; **porter ~ (à qn)** to bring sb luck; **au petit ~** haphazardly; **par ~** fortunately
**bonhomme** [bɔnɔm] (*pl* **bonshommes**) *nm* fellow; **bonhomme de neige** snowman
**bonjour** [bɔ̃ʒuʀ] *excl, nm* hello; (*selon l'heure*) good morning/afternoon; **c'est simple comme ~!** it's easy as pie!
**bonne** [bɔn] *adj voir* **bon** ▷ *nf* (*domestique*) maid
**bonnet** [bɔnɛ] *nm* hat; (*de soutien-gorge*) cup; **bonnet de bain** bathing cap
**bonsoir** [bɔ̃swaʀ] *excl* good evening
**bonté** [bɔ̃te] *nf* kindness *no pl*
**bonus** [bɔnys] *nm* no-claims bonus; (*de DVD*) extras *pl*
**bord** [bɔʀ] *nm* (*de table, verre, falaise*) edge; (*de rivière, lac*) bank; (*de route*) side; (**monter**) **à ~** (to go) on board; **jeter par-dessus ~** to throw overboard; **le commandant de/les hommes du ~** the ship's master/crew; **au ~ de la mer** at the seaside; **au ~ de la route** at the

roadside; **être au ~ des larmes** to be on the verge of tears
**bordeaux** [bɔʀdo] *nm* Bordeaux (wine) ▷ *adj inv* maroon
**bordel** [bɔʀdɛl] *nm* brothel; (*fam!*) bloody mess (!)
**border** [bɔʀde] *vt* (*être le long de*) to line; (*qn dans son lit*) to tuck up; (*garnir*): **~ qch de** to edge sth with
**bordure** [bɔʀdyʀ] *nf* border; **en ~ de** on the edge of
**borne** [bɔʀn] *nf* boundary stone; (*aussi:* **~ kilométrique**) kilometre-marker, ≈ milestone; **bornes** *nfpl* (*fig*) limits; **dépasser les ~s** to go too far
**borné, e** [bɔʀne] *adj* (*personne*) narrow-minded
**borner** [bɔʀne] *vt*: **se ~ à faire** (*se contenter de*) to content o.s. with doing; (*se limiter à*) to limit o.s. to doing
**bosniaque** [bɔsnjak] *adj* Bosnian ▷ *nm/f*: **B~** Bosnian
**Bosnie-Herzégovine** [bɔsniɛʀzegɔvin] *nf* Bosnia-Herzegovina
**bosquet** [bɔskɛ] *nm* grove
**bosse** [bɔs] *nf* (*de terrain etc*) bump; (*enflure*) lump; (*du bossu, du chameau*) hump; **avoir la ~ des maths** *etc* (*fam*) to have a gift for maths *etc*; **il a roulé sa ~** (*fam*) he's been around
**bosser** [bɔse] *vi* (*travailler*) to work; (*travailler dur*) to slave (away)
**bossu, e** [bɔsy] *nm/f* hunchback
**botanique** [bɔtanik] *nf* botany ▷ *adj* botanic(al)
**botte** [bɔt] *nf* (*soulier*) (high) boot; (*gerbe*): **~ de paille** bundle of straw; **botte de radis/d'asperges** bunch of radishes/asparagus; **bottes de caoutchouc** wellington boots
**bottin** [bɔtɛ̃] *nm* directory
**bottine** [bɔtin] *nf* ankle boot
**bouc** [buk] *nm* goat; (*barbe*) goatee; **bouc émissaire** scapegoat
**boucan** [bukã] (*fam*) *nm* din, racket
**bouche** [buʃ] *nf* mouth; **faire du ~ à ~ à qn** to give sb the kiss of life *ou* mouth-

to-mouth resuscitation (BRIT); **rester ~ bée** to stand open-mouthed; **bouche d'égout** manhole; **bouche d'incendie** fire hydrant; **bouche de métro** métro entrance

**bouché, e** [buʃe] adj (flacon etc) stoppered; (temps, ciel) overcast; (péj fam: personne) thick (fam); **c'est un secteur ~** there's no future in that area; **avoir le nez ~** to have a blocked(-up) nose; **l'évier est ~** the sink's blocked

**bouchée** [buʃe] nf mouthful; **bouchées à la reine** chicken vol-au-vents

**boucher, -ère** [buʃe] nm/f butcher ▷ vt (trou) to fill up; (obstruer) to block (up); **se boucher** vi (tuyau etc) to block up, get blocked up; **j'ai le nez bouché** my nose is blocked; **se ~ le nez** to hold one's nose; **boucherie** nf butcher's (shop); (fig) slaughter

**bouchon** [buʃɔ̃] nm stopper; (de tube) top; (en liège) cork; (fig: embouteillage) holdup; (Pêche) float

**boucle** [bukl] nf (forme, figure) loop; (objet) buckle; **boucle (de cheveux)** curl; **boucle d'oreille** earring

**bouclé, e** [bukle] adj (cheveux) curly

**boucler** [bukle] vt (fermer: ceinture etc) to fasten; (terminer) to finish off; (fam: enfermer) to shut away; (quartier) to seal off ▷ vi to curl

**bouder** [bude] vi to sulk ▷ vt to stay away from

**boudin** [budɛ̃] nm: **~ (noir)** black pudding; **boudin blanc** white pudding

**boue** [bu] nf mud

**bouée** [bwe] nf buoy; **bouée (de sauvetage)** lifebuoy

**boueux, -euse** [bwø, øz] adj muddy

**bouffe** [buf] (fam) nf grub (fam), food

**bouffée** [bufe] nf (de cigarette) puff; **une ~ d'air pur** a breath of fresh air; **bouffée de chaleur** hot flush (BRIT) ou flash (US)

**bouffer** [bufe] (fam) vi to eat

**bouffi, e** [bufi] adj swollen

**bouger** [buʒe] vi to move; (dent etc) to be loose; (s'activer) to get moving ▷ vt

to move; **les prix/les couleurs n'ont pas bougé** prices/colours haven't changed

**bougie** [buʒi] nf candle; (Auto) spark(ing) plug

**bouillabaisse** [bujabɛs] nf type of fish soup

**bouillant, e** [bujɑ̃, ɑ̃t] adj (qui bout) boiling; (très chaud) boiling (hot)

**bouillie** [buji] nf (de bébé) cereal; **en ~** (fig) crushed

**bouillir** [bujiʀ] vi, vt to boil; **~ d'impatience** to seethe with impatience

**bouilloire** [bujwaʀ] nf kettle

**bouillon** [bujɔ̃] nm (Culin) stock no pl; **bouillonner** vi to bubble; (fig: idées) to bubble up

**bouillotte** [bujɔt] nf hot-water bottle

**boulanger, -ère** [bulɑ̃ʒe, ɛʀ] nm/f baker; **boulangerie** nf bakery

**boule** [bul] nf (gén) ball; (de pétanque) bowl; **boule de neige** snowball

**boulette** [bulɛt] nf (de viande) meatball

**boulevard** [bulvaʀ] nm boulevard

**bouleversement** [bulvɛʀsəmɑ̃] nm upheaval

**bouleverser** [bulvɛʀse] vt (émouvoir) to overwhelm; (causer du chagrin) to distress; (pays, vie) to disrupt; (papiers, objets) to turn upside down

**boulimie** [bulimi] nf bulimia

**boulimique** [bulimik] adj bulimic

**boulon** [bulɔ̃] nm bolt

**boulot, te** [bulo, ɔt] adj plump, tubby ▷ nm (fam: travail) work

**boum** [bum] nm bang ▷ nf (fam) party

**bouquet** [bukɛ] nm (de fleurs) bunch (of flowers), bouquet; (de persil etc) bunch; **c'est le ~!** (fam) that takes the biscuit!

**bouquin** [bukɛ̃] (fam) nm book; **bouquiner** (fam) vi to read

**bourdon** [buʀdɔ̃] nm bumblebee

**bourg** [buʀ] nm small market town

**bourgeois, e** [buʀʒwa, waz] (péj) adj ≈ (upper) middle class; **bourgeoisie** nf ≈ upper middle classes pl

**bourgeon** [buʀʒɔ̃] nm bud

**Bourgogne** [buʀgɔɲ] *nf*: **la ~** Burgundy
▷ *nm*: **bourgogne** burgundy (wine)
**bourguignon, ne** [buʀgiɲɔ̃, ɔn] *adj* of
ou from Burgundy, Burgundian
**bourrasque** [buʀask] *nf* squall
**bourratif, -ive** [buʀatif, iv] *(fam) adj*
filling, stodgy *(pej)*
**bourré, e** [buʀe] *adj (fam: ivre)*
plastered, tanked up *(BRIT)*; *(rempli)*: **~
de** crammed full of
**bourrer** [buʀe] *vt (pipe)* to fill; *(poêle)* to
pack; *(valise)* to cram (full)
**bourru, e** [buʀy] *adj* surly, gruff
**bourse** [buʀs] *nf (subvention)* grant;
*(porte-monnaie)* purse; **la B~** the Stock
Exchange
**bous** [bu] *vb voir* **bouillir**
**bousculade** [buskylad] *nf (hâte)* rush;
*(cohue)* crush; **bousculer** *vt (heurter)* to
knock into; *(fig)* to push, rush
**boussole** [busɔl] *nf* compass
**bout** [bu] *vb voir* **bouillir** ▷ *nm* bit; *(d'un
bâton etc)* tip; *(d'une ficelle, table, rue,
période)* end; **au ~ de** at the end of, after;
**pousser qn à ~** to push sb to the limit;
**venir à ~ de** to manage to finish; **à ~
portant** (at) point-blank *(range)*
**bouteille** [butɛj] *nf* bottle; *(de gaz
butane)* cylinder
**boutique** [butik] *nf* shop
**bouton** [butɔ̃] *nm* button; *(sur la
peau)* spot; *(Bot)* bud; **boutonner**
*vt* to button up; **boutonnière** *nf*
buttonhole; **bouton-pression** *nm*
press stud
**bovin, e** [bɔvɛ̃, in] *adj* bovine; **bovins**
*nmpl* cattle *pl*
**bowling** [buliŋ] *nm* (tenpin) bowling;
*(salle)* bowling alley
**boxe** [bɔks] *nf* boxing
**BP** *abr* = **boîte postale**
**bracelet** [bʀaslɛ] *nm* bracelet
**braconnier** [bʀakɔnje] *nm* poacher
**brader** [bʀade] *vt* to sell off; **braderie**
*nf* cut-price shop/stall
**braguette** [bʀagɛt] *nf* fly ou flies *pl*
*(BRIT)*, zipper *(US)*
**braise** [bʀɛz] *nf* embers *pl*

**brancard** [bʀɑ̃kaʀ] *nm (civière)*
stretcher; **brancardier** *nm* stretcher-
bearer
**branche** [bʀɑ̃ʃ] *nf* branch
**branché, e** [bʀɑ̃ʃe] *(fam) adj* trendy
**brancher** [bʀɑ̃ʃe] *vt* to connect (up); *(en
mettant la prise)* to plug in
**brandir** [bʀɑ̃diʀ] *vt* to brandish
**braquer** [bʀake] *vi (Auto)* to turn (the
wheel) ▷ *vt (revolver etc)*: **~ qch sur**
to aim sth at, point sth at; *(mettre en
colère)*: **~ qn** to put sb's back up
**bras** [bʀɑ] *nm* arm; **~ dessus, ~ dessous**
arm in arm; **se retrouver avec qch sur
les ~** *(fam)* to be landed with sth; **bras
droit** *(fig)* right hand man
**brassard** [bʀasaʀ] *nm* armband
**brasse** [bʀas] *nf (nage)* breast-stroke;
**brasse papillon** butterfly (stroke)
**brassée** [bʀase] *nf* armful
**brasser** [bʀase] *vt* to mix; **~ l'argent/
les affaires** to handle a lot of money/
business
**brasserie** [bʀasʀi] *nf (restaurant)* café-
restaurant; *(usine)* brewery
**brave** [bʀav] *adj (courageux)* brave; *(bon,
gentil)* good, kind
**braver** [bʀave] *vt* to defy
**bravo** [bʀavo] *excl* bravo ▷ *nm* cheer
**bravoure** [bʀavuʀ] *nf* bravery
**break** [bʀɛk] *nm (Auto)* estate car
**brebis** [bʀəbi] *nf* ewe; **brebis galeuse**
black sheep
**bredouiller** [bʀəduje] *vi, vt* to
mumble, stammer
**bref, brève** [bʀɛf, ɛv] *adj* short, brief
▷ *adv* in short; **d'un ton ~** sharply,
curtly; **en ~** in short, in brief
**Brésil** [bʀezil] *nm* Brazil
**Bretagne** [bʀətaɲ] *nf* Brittany
**bretelle** [bʀətɛl] *nf (de vêtement, de
sac)* strap; *(d'autoroute)* slip road *(BRIT)*,
entrance/exit ramp *(US)*; **bretelles**
*nfpl (pour pantalon)* braces *(BRIT)*,
suspenders *(US)*
**breton, ne** [bʀətɔ̃, ɔn] *adj* Breton
▷ *nm/f*: **B~, ne** Breton
**brève** [bʀɛv] *adj voir* **bref**

**brevet** [bʀəvɛ] nm diploma, certificate; **brevet des collèges** exam taken at the age of 15; **brevet (d'invention)** patent; **breveté, e** adj patented

**bricolage** [bʀikɔlaʒ] nm: **le ~** do-it-yourself

**bricoler** [bʀikɔle] vi (petits travaux) to do DIY jobs; (passe-temps) to potter about ▷ vt (réparer) to fix up; **bricoleur, -euse** nm/f handyman(-woman), DIY enthusiast

**bridge** [bʀidʒ] nm (Cartes) bridge

**brièvement** [bʀijɛvmɑ̃] adv briefly

**brigade** [bʀigad] nf (Police) squad; (Mil) brigade; **brigadier** nm sergeant

**brillamment** [bʀijamɑ̃] adv brilliantly

**brillant, e** [bʀijɑ̃, ɑ̃t] adj (remarquable) bright; (luisant) shiny, shining

**briller** [bʀije] vi to shine

**brin** [bʀɛ̃] nm (de laine, ficelle etc) strand; (fig): **un ~ de** a bit of

**brindille** [bʀɛ̃dij] nf twig

**brioche** [bʀijɔʃ] nf brioche (bun); (fam: ventre) paunch

**brique** [bʀik] nf brick; (de lait) carton

**briquet** [bʀikɛ] nm (cigarette) lighter

**brise** [bʀiz] nf breeze

**briser** [bʀize] vt to break; **se briser** vi to break

**britannique** [bʀitanik] adj British ▷ nm/f: **B~** British person, Briton; **les B~s** the British

**brocante** [bʀɔkɑ̃t] nf junk, second-hand goods pl; **brocanteur, -euse** nm/f junkshop owner; junk dealer

**broche** [bʀɔʃ] nf brooch; (Culin) spit; (Méd) pin; **à la ~** spit-roasted

**broché, e** [bʀɔʃe] adj (livre) paper-backed

**brochet** [bʀɔʃɛ] nm pike inv

**brochette** [bʀɔʃɛt] nf (ustensile) skewer; (plat) kebab

**brochure** [bʀɔʃyʀ] nf pamphlet, brochure, booklet

**broder** [bʀɔde] vt to embroider ▷ vi: **~ (sur les faits ou une histoire)** to embroider the facts; **broderie** nf embroidery

**bronches** [bʀɔ̃ʃ] nfpl bronchial tubes; **bronchite** nf bronchitis

**bronze** [bʀɔ̃z] nm bronze

**bronzer** [bʀɔ̃ze] vi to get a tan; **se bronzer** to sunbathe

**brosse** [bʀɔs] nf brush; **coiffé en ~** with a crewcut; **brosse à cheveux** hairbrush; **brosse à dents** toothbrush; **brosse à habits** clothesbrush; **brosser** vt (nettoyer) to brush; (fig: tableau etc) to paint; **se brosser les dents** to brush one's teeth

**brouette** [bʀuɛt] nf wheelbarrow

**brouillard** [bʀujaʀ] nm fog

**brouiller** [bʀuje] vt (œufs, message) to scramble; (idées) to mix up; (rendre trouble) to cloud; (désunir: amis) to set at odds; **se brouiller** vi (vue) to cloud over; (gens): **se ~ (avec)** to fall out (with)

**brouillon, ne** [bʀujɔ̃, ɔn] adj (sans soin) untidy; (qui manque d'organisation) disorganized ▷ nm draft; **(papier) ~** rough paper

**broussailles** [bʀusaj] nfpl undergrowth sg; **broussailleux, -euse** adj bushy

**brousse** [bʀus] nf: **la ~** the bush

**brouter** [bʀute] vi to graze

**brugnon** [bʀynɔ̃] nm (Bot) nectarine

**bruiner** [bʀɥine] vb impers: **il bruine** it's drizzling, there's a drizzle

**bruit** [bʀɥi] nm: **un ~** a noise, a sound; (fig: rumeur) a rumour; **le ~** noise; **sans ~** without a sound, noiselessly; **bruit de fond** background noise

**brûlant, e** [bʀylɑ̃, ɑ̃t] adj burning; (liquide) boiling (hot)

**brûlé, e** [bʀyle] adj (fig: démasqué) blown ▷ nm: **odeur de ~** smell of burning

**brûler** [bʀyle] vt to burn; (suj: eau bouillante) to scald; (consommer: électricité, essence) to use; (feu rouge, signal) to go through ▷ vi to burn; **tu brûles!** you're getting hot!; **se brûler** to burn o.s.; (s'ébouillanter) to scald o.s.

**brûlure** [bʀylyʀ] nf (lésion) burn; **brûlures d'estomac** heartburn sg

**brume** [bʀym] nf mist

**brun, e** [bʀœ̃ bʀyn] adj (gén, bière) brown; (cheveux, tabac) dark; **elle est ~e** she's got dark hair

**brunch** [bʀœntʃ] nm brunch

**brushing** [bʀœʃiŋ] nm blow-dry

**brusque** [bʀysk] adj abrupt

**brut, e** [bʀyt] adj (minerai, soie) raw; (diamant) rough; (Comm) gross; **(pétrole) ~** crude (oil)

**brutal, e, -aux** [bʀytal, o] adj brutal

**Bruxelles** [bʀysɛl] n Brussels

**bruyamment** [bʀɥjamɑ̃] adv noisily

**bruyant, e** [bʀɥjɑ̃, ɑ̃t] adj noisy

**bruyère** [bʀyjɛʀ] nf heather

**BTS** sigle m (= brevet de technicien supérieur) vocational training certificate taken at the end of a higher education course

**bu, e** [by] pp de **boire**

**buccal, e, -aux** [bykal, o] adj: **par voie ~e** orally

**bûche** [byʃ] nf log; **prendre une ~** (fig) to come a cropper; **bûche de Noël** Yule log

**bûcher** [byʃe] nm (funéraire) pyre; (supplice) stake ▷ vi (fam) to swot (BRIT), slave (away) ▷ vt (fam) to swot up (BRIT), slave away at

**budget** [bydʒɛ] nm budget

**buée** [bɥe] nf (sur une vitre) mist

**buffet** [byfɛ] nm (meuble) sideboard; (de réception) buffet; **buffet (de gare)** (station) buffet, snack bar

**buis** [bɥi] nm box tree; (bois) box(wood)

**buisson** [bɥisɔ̃] nm bush

**bulbe** [bylb] nm (Bot, Anat) bulb

**Bulgarie** [bylgaʀi] nf Bulgaria

**bulle** [byl] nf bubble

**bulletin** [byltɛ̃] nm (communiqué, journal) bulletin; (Scol) report; **bulletin d'informations** news bulletin; **bulletin (de vote)** ballot paper; **bulletin météorologique** weather report

**bureau, x** [byʀo] nm (meuble) desk; (pièce, service) office; **bureau de change** (foreign) exchange office

ou bureau; **bureau de poste** post office; **bureau de tabac** tobacconist's (shop); **bureaucratie** [byʀokʀasi] nf bureaucracy

**bus¹** [by] vb voir **boire**

**bus²** [bys] nm bus; **à quelle heure part le ~?** what time does the bus leave?

**buste** [byst] nm (torse) chest; (seins) bust

**but¹** [by] vb voir **boire**

**but²** [by(t)] nm (cible) target; (fig) goal, aim; (Football etc) goal; **de ~ en blanc** point-blank; **avoir pour ~ de faire** to aim to do; **dans le ~ de** with the intention of

**butane** [bytan] nm (camping) butane; (usage domestique) Calor gas®

**butiner** [bytine] vi (abeilles) to gather nectar

**buvais** etc [byvɛ] vb voir **boire**

**buvard** [byvaʀ] nm blotter

**buvette** [byvɛt] nf bar

# C

**c'** [s] dét voir **ce**

**ça** [sa] pron (pour désigner) this; (: plus loin) that; (comme sujet indéfini) it; **ça m'étonne que ...** it surprises me that ...; **comment ça va?** how are you?; **ça va?** (d'accord?) O.K.?, all right?; **où ça?** where's that?; **pourquoi ça?** why's that?; **qui ça?** who's that?; **ça alors!** well really!; **ça fait 10 ans (que)** it's 10 years (since); **c'est ça** that's right; **ça y est** that's it

**cabane** [kaban] nf hut, cabin

**cabaret** [kabaʀɛ] nm night club

**cabillaud** [kabijo] nm cod inv

**cabine** [kabin] nf (de bateau) cabin; (de piscine etc) cubicle; (de camion, train) cab; (d'avion) cockpit; **cabine d'essayage** fitting room; **cabine (téléphonique)** call ou (tele)phone box

**cabinet** [kabinɛ] nm (petite pièce) closet; (de médecin) surgery (BRIT), office (US); (de notaire etc) office; (: clientèle) practice; (Pol) Cabinet; **cabinets** nmpl (w.-c.) toilet sg; **cabinet de toilette** toilet

**câble** [kɑbl] nm cable; **le ~** (TV) cable television, cablevision (US)

**cacahuète** [kakaɥɛt] nf peanut

**cacao** [kakao] nm cocoa

**cache** [kaʃ] nm mask, card (for masking)

**cache-cache** [kaʃkaʃ] nm: **jouer à ~** to play hide-and-seek

**cachemire** [kaʃmiʀ] nm cashmere

**cacher** [kaʃe] vt to hide, conceal; **se cacher** vi (volontairement) to hide; (être caché) to be hidden ou concealed; **~ qch à qn** to hide ou conceal sth from sb

**cachet** [kaʃɛ] nm (comprimé) tablet; (de la poste) postmark; (rétribution) fee; (fig) style, character

**cachette** [kaʃɛt] nf hiding place; **en ~** on the sly, secretly

**cactus** [kaktys] nm cactus

**cadavre** [kadɑvʀ] nm corpse, (dead) body

**caddie®** [kadi] nm (supermarket) trolley (BRIT), (grocery) cart (US)

**cadeau, x** [kado] nm present, gift; **faire un ~ à qn** to give sb a present ou gift; **faire ~ de qch à qn** to make a present of sth to sb, give sb sth as a present

**cadenas** [kadnɑ] nm padlock

**cadet, te** [kadɛ, ɛt] adj younger; (le plus jeune) youngest ▷ nm/f youngest child ou one

**cadran** [kadʀɑ̃] nm dial; **cadran solaire** sundial

**cadre** [kadʀ] nm frame; (environnement) surroundings pl ▷ nm/f (Admin) managerial employee, executive; **dans le ~ de** (fig) within the framework ou context of

**cafard** [kafaʀ] nm cockroach; **avoir le ~** (fam) to be down in the dumps

**café** [kafe] nm coffee; (bistro) café ▷ adj inv coffee(-coloured); **café au lait** white coffee; **café noir** black coffee; **café tabac** tobacconist's or newsagent's serving coffee and spirits; **cafetière** nf (pot) coffee-pot

**cage** [kaʒ] nf cage; **cage (d'escalier)** stairwell; **cage thoracique** rib cage

**cageot** [kaʒo] nm crate

**cagoule** [kagul] nf (passe-montagne) balaclava

**cahier** [kaje] nm notebook; **cahier de brouillon** jotter (BRIT), rough notebook; **cahier d'exercices** exercise book

**caille** [kaj] nf quail

**caillou, x** [kaju] nm (little) stone; **cailllouteux, -euse** adj (route) stony

**Caire** [kɛR] nm: **le ~** Cairo

**caisse** [kɛs] nf box; (tiroir où l'on met la recette) till; (où l'on paye) cash desk (BRIT), check-out; (de banque) cashier's desk; **caisse d'épargne** savings bank; **caisse de retraite** pension fund; **caisse enregistreuse** cash register; **caissier, -ière** nm/f cashier

**cake** [kɛk] nm fruit cake

**calandre** [kalɑ̃dR] nf radiator grill

**calcaire** [kalkɛR] nm limestone ▷ adj (eau) hard; (Géo) limestone cpd

**calcul** [kalkyl] nm calculation; **le ~** (Scol) arithmetic; **calcul (biliaire)** (gall)stone; **calculatrice** nf calculator; **calculer** vt to calculate, work out; **calculette** nf pocket calculator

**cale** [kal] nf (de bateau) hold; (en bois) wedge

**calé, e** [kale] (fam) adj clever, bright

**caleçon** [kalsɔ̃] nm (d'homme) boxer shorts; (de femme) leggings

**calendrier** [kalɑ̃dRije] nm calendar; (fig) timetable

**calepin** [kalpɛ̃] nm notebook

**caler** [kale] vt to wedge ▷ vi (moteur, véhicule) to stall

**calibre** [kalibR] nm calibre

**câlin, e** [kɑlɛ̃, in] adj cuddly, cuddlesome; (regard, voix) tender

**calmant** [kalmɑ̃] nm tranquillizer, sedative; (pour la douleur) painkiller

**calme** [kalm] adj calm, quiet ▷ nm calm(ness), quietness; **sans perdre son ~** without losing one's cool (inf) ou composure; **calmer** vt to calm (down); (douleur, inquiétude) to ease, soothe; **se calmer** vi to calm down

**calorie** [kaloRi] nf calorie

**camarade** [kamaRad] nm/f friend, pal; (Pol) comrade

**Cambodge** [kɑ̃bɔdʒ] nm: **le ~** Cambodia

**cambriolage** [kɑ̃bRijɔlaʒ] nm burglary; **cambrioler** vt to burgle (BRIT), burglarize (US); **cambrioleur, -euse** nm/f burglar

**camelote** [kamlɔt] (fam) nf rubbish, trash, junk

**caméra** [kameRa] nf (Cinéma, TV) camera; (d'amateur) cine-camera

**Cameroun** [kamRun] nm: **le ~** Cameroon

**caméscope®** [kameskɔp] nm camcorder®

**camion** [kamjɔ̃] nm lorry (BRIT), truck; **camion de dépannage** breakdown (BRIT) ou tow (US) truck; **camionnette** nf (small) van; **camionneur** nm (chauffeur) lorry (BRIT) ou truck driver; (entrepreneur) haulage contractor (BRIT), trucker (US)

**camomille** [kamɔmij] nf camomile; (boisson) camomile tea

**camp** [kɑ̃] nm camp; (fig) side

**campagnard, e** [kɑ̃paɲaR, aRd] adj country cpd

**campagne** [kɑ̃paɲ] nf country, countryside; (Mil, Pol, Comm) campaign; **à la ~** in the country

**camper** [kɑ̃pe] vi to camp ▷ vt to sketch; **se ~ devant** to plant o.s. in front of; **campeur, -euse** nm/f camper

**camping** [kɑ̃piŋ] nm camping; **faire du ~** to go camping; **(terrain de) camping** campsite, camping site; **camping-car** nm camper, motorhome (US); **camping-gaz®** nm inv camp(ing) stove

**Canada** [kanada] nm: **le ~** Canada; **canadien, ne** adj Canadian ▷ nm/f: **Canadien, ne** Canadian; **canadienne** nf (veste) fur-lined jacket

**canal, -aux** [kanal, o] nm canal;

(*naturel*, TV) channel; **canalisation** *nf* (*tuyau*) pipe

**canapé** [kanape] *nm* settee, sofa

**canard** [kanaʀ] *nm* duck; (*fam: journal*) rag

**cancer** [kɑ̃sɛʀ] *nm* cancer; (*signe*): **le C~** Cancer

**cancre** [kɑ̃kʀ] *nm* dunce

**candidat, e** [kɑ̃dida, at] *nm/f* candidate; (*à un poste*) applicant, candidate; **candidature** *nf* (*Pol*) candidature; (*à poste*) application; **poser sa candidature à un poste** to apply for a job

**cane** [kan] *nf* (female) duck

**canette** [kanɛt] *nf* (*de bière*) (flip-top) bottle

**canevas** [kanvɑ] *nm* (*Couture*) canvas

**caniche** [kaniʃ] *nm* poodle

**canicule** [kanikyl] *nf* scorching heat

**canif** [kanif] *nm* penknife, pocket knife

**canne** [kan] *nf* (walking) stick; **canne à pêche** fishing rod; **canne à sucre** sugar cane

**cannelle** [kanɛl] *nf* cinnamon

**canoë** [kanɔe] *nm* canoe; (*sport*) canoeing; **canoë (kayak)** kayak

**canot** [kano] *nm* ding(h)y; **canot de sauvetage** lifeboat; **canot pneumatique** inflatable ding(h)y

**cantatrice** [kɑ̃tatʀis] *nf* (opera) singer

**cantine** [kɑ̃tin] *nf* canteen

**canton** [kɑ̃tɔ̃] *nm* *district consisting of several communes*; (*en Suisse*) canton

**caoutchouc** [kautʃu] *nm* rubber; **caoutchouc mousse** foam rubber

**cap** [kap] *nm* (*Géo*) cape; (*promontoire*) headland; (*fig: tournant*) watershed; (*Navig*): **changer de ~** to change course; **mettre le ~ sur** to head *ou* steer for

**CAP** *sigle m* (= *Certificat d'aptitude professionnelle*) *vocational training certificate taken at secondary school*

**capable** [kapabl] *adj* able, capable; **~ de qch/faire** capable of sth/doing

**capacité** [kapasite] *nf* (*compétence*) ability; (*Jur, contenance*) capacity

**cape** [kap] *nf* cape, cloak; **rire sous ~** to laugh up one's sleeve

**CAPES** [kapɛs] *sigle m* (= *Certificat d'aptitude pédagogique à l'enseignement secondaire*) *teaching diploma*

**capitaine** [kapitɛn] *nm* captain

**capital, e, -aux** [kapital, o] *adj* (*œuvre*) major; (*question, rôle*) fundamental ▷ *nm* capital; (*fig*) stock; **d'une importance ~e** of capital importance; **capitaux** *nmpl* (*fonds*) capital *sg*; **capital (social)** authorized capital; **capitale** *nf* (*ville*) capital; (*lettre*) capital (letter); **capitalisme** *nm* capitalism; **capitaliste** *adj, nm/f* capitalist

**caporal, -aux** [kapɔʀal, o] *nm* lance corporal

**capot** [kapo] *nm* (*Auto*) bonnet (BRIT), hood (US)

**câpre** [kɑpʀ] *nf* caper

**caprice** [kapʀis] *nm* whim, caprice; **faire des ~s** to make a fuss; **capricieux, -euse** *adj* (*fantasque*) capricious, whimsical; (*enfant*) awkward

**Capricorne** [kapʀikɔʀn] *nm*: **le ~** Capricorn

**capsule** [kapsyl] *nf* (*de bouteille*) cap; (*Bot etc, spatiale*) capsule

**capter** [kapte] *vt* (*ondes radio*) to pick up; (*fig*) to win, capture

**captivant, e** [kaptivɑ̃, ɑ̃t] *adj* captivating

**capturer** [kaptyʀe] *vt* to capture

**capuche** [kapyʃ] *nf* hood

**capuchon** [kapyʃɔ̃] *nm* hood; (*de stylo*) cap, top

**car** [kaʀ] *nm* coach ▷ *conj* because, for

**carabine** [kaʀabin] *nf* rifle

**caractère** [kaʀaktɛʀ] *nm* (*gén*) character; **avoir bon/mauvais ~** to be good-/ill-natured; **en ~s gras** in bold type; **en petits ~s** in small print; **~s d'imprimerie** (block) capitals

**caractériser** [kaʀakteʀize] *vt* to be characteristic of; **se ~ par** to be characterized *ou* distinguished by

**caractéristique** [kaʀakteʀistik] *adj,*

*nf* characteristic

**carafe** [kaʀaf] *nf* (*pour eau, vin ordinaire*)
carafe

**caraïbe** [kaʀaib] *adj* Caribbean ▷ *n*: **les
C~s** the Caribbean (Islands)

**carambolage** [kaʀɑ̃bɔlaʒ] *nm*
multiple crash, pileup

**caramel** [kaʀamɛl] *nm* (*bonbon*)
caramel, toffee; (*substance*) caramel

**caravane** [kaʀavan] *nf* caravan;
**caravaning** *nm* caravanning

**carbone** [kaʀbɔn] *nm* carbon; (*double*)
carbon (copy)

**carbonique** [kaʀbɔnik] *adj*: **gaz ~**
carbon dioxide; **neige ~** dry ice

**carbonisé, e** [kaʀbɔnize] *adj* charred

**carburant** [kaʀbyʀɑ̃] *nm* (motor) fuel

**carburateur** [kaʀbyʀatœʀ] *nm*
carburettor

**cardiaque** [kaʀdjak] *adj* cardiac, heart
*cpd* ▷ *nm/f* heart patient; **être ~** to have
heart trouble

**cardigan** [kaʀdigɑ̃] *nm* cardigan

**cardiologue** [kaʀdjɔlɔg] *nm/f*
cardiologist, heart specialist

**carême** [kaʀɛm] *nm*: **le C~** Lent

**carence** [kaʀɑ̃s] *nf* (*manque*) deficiency

**caresse** [kaʀɛs] *nf* caress

**caresser** [kaʀese] *vt* to caress; (*animal*)
to stroke

**cargaison** [kaʀgɛzɔ̃] *nf* cargo, freight

**cargo** [kaʀgo] *nm* cargo boat, freighter

**caricature** [kaʀikatyʀ] *nf* caricature

**carie** [kaʀi] *nf*: **la ~ (dentaire)** tooth
decay; **une ~** a bad tooth

**carnaval** [kaʀnaval] *nm* carnival

**carnet** [kaʀnɛ] *nm* (*calepin*) notebook;
(*de tickets, timbres etc*) book; **carnet de
chèques** cheque book

**carotte** [kaʀɔt] *nf* carrot

**carré, e** [kaʀe] *adj* square; (*fig: franc*)
straightforward ▷ *nm* (Math) square;
**mètre/kilomètre ~** square metre/
kilometre

**carreau, x** [kaʀo] *nm* (*par terre*) (floor)
tile; (*au mur*) (wall) tile; (*de fenêtre*)
(window) pane; (*motif*) check, square;
(*Cartes: couleur*) diamonds *pl*; **tissu à ~x**

checked fabric

**carrefour** [kaʀfuʀ] *nm* crossroads *sg*

**carrelage** [kaʀlaʒ] *nm* (*sol*) (tiled) floor

**carrelet** [kaʀlɛ] *nm* (*poisson*) plaice

**carrément** [kaʀemɑ̃] *adv* (*franchement*)
straight out, bluntly; (*sans hésiter*)
straight; (*intensif*) completely; **c'est ~
impossible** it's completely impossible

**carrière** [kaʀjɛʀ] *nf* (*métier*) career;
(*de roches*) quarry; **militaire de ~**
professional soldier

**carrosserie** [kaʀɔsʀi] *nf* body,
coachwork *no pl*

**carrure** [kaʀyʀ] *nf* build; (*fig*) stature,
calibre

**cartable** [kaʀtabl] *nm* satchel,
(school) bag

**carte** [kaʀt] *nf* (*de géographie*) map;
(*marine, du ciel*) chart; (*d'abonnement,
à jouer*) card; (*au restaurant*) menu;
(*aussi*: **~ de visite**) (visiting) card;
**pouvez-vous me l'indiquer sur la
~?** can you show me (it) on the map?;
**à la ~** (*au restaurant*) à la carte; **est-ce
qu'on peut voir la ~?** can we see the
menu?; **donner ~ blanche à qn** to give
sb a free rein; **carte bancaire** cash
card; **Carte Bleue®** debit card; **carte à
puce** smart card; **carte de crédit** credit
card; **carte de fidélité** loyalty card;
**carte d'identité** identity card; **carte
de séjour** residence permit; **carte
grise** (*Auto*) ≈ (car) registration book,
logbook; **carte memoire** (*d'appareil-
photo numérique*) memory card; **carte
postale** postcard; **carte routière**
road map

**carter** [kaʀtɛʀ] *nm* sump

**carton** [kaʀtɔ̃] *nm* (*matériau*)
cardboard; (*boîte*) (cardboard) box;
**faire un ~** (*fam*) to score a hit; **carton (à
dessin)** portfolio

**cartouche** [kaʀtuʃ] *nf* cartridge; (*de
cigarettes*) carton

**cas** [kɑ] *nm* case; **ne faire aucun ~ de**
to take no notice of; **en aucun ~** on no
account; **au ~ où** in case; **en ~ de** in
case of, in the event of; **en ~ de besoin**

if need be; **en tout ~** in any case, at
any rate
**cascade** [kaskad] nf waterfall, cascade
**case** [kɑz] nf (hutte) hut; (compartiment)
compartment; (sur un formulaire, de
mots croisés etc) box
**caser** [kɑze] (fam) vt (placer) to put
(away); (loger) to put up; **se caser** vi
(se marier) to settle down; (trouver un
emploi) to find a (steady) job
**caserne** [kazɛʀn] nf barracks pl
**casier** [kazje] nm (pour courrier)
pigeonhole; (compartiment)
compartment; (à clef) locker; **casier
judiciaire** police record
**casino** [kazino] nm casino
**casque** [kask] nm helmet; (chez le
coiffeur) (hair-)drier; (pour audition)
(head-)phones pl, headset
**casquette** [kaskɛt] nf cap
**casse...**: **casse-croûte** nm inv snack;
**casse-noix** nm inv nutcrackers pl;
**casse-pieds** (fam) adj inv: **il est casse-
pieds** he's a pain in the neck
**casser** [kɑse] vt to break; (Jur) to quash;
**se casser** vi to break; **~ les pieds à qn**
(fam: irriter) to get on sb's nerves; **se ~ la
tête** (fam) to go to a lot of trouble
**casserole** [kasʀɔl] nf saucepan
**casse-tête** [kɑstɛt] nm inv (difficultés)
headache (fig)
**cassette** [kasɛt] nf (bande magnétique)
cassette; (coffret) casket
**cassis** [kasis] nm blackcurrant
**cassoulet** [kasulɛ] nm bean and sausage
hot-pot
**catalogue** [katalɔg] nm catalogue
**catalytique** [katalitik] adj: **pot ~**
catalytic convertor
**catastrophe** [katastʀɔf] nf
catastrophe, disaster
**catéchisme** [kateʃism] nm catechism
**catégorie** [kategɔʀi] nf category;
**catégorique** adj categorical
**cathédrale** [katedʀal] nf cathedral
**catholique** [katɔlik] adj, nm/f
(Roman) Catholic; **pas très ~** a bit
shady ou fishy

**cauchemar** [koʃmaʀ] nm nightmare
**cause** [koz] nf cause; (Jur) lawsuit,
case; **à ~ de** because of, owing to;
**pour ~ de** on account of; **(et) pour ~**
and for (a very) good reason; **être en ~**
(intérêts) to be at stake; **remettre en ~**
to challenge; **causer** vt to cause ▷ vi
to chat, talk
**caution** [kosjɔ̃] nf guarantee, security;
(Jur) bail (bond); (fig) backing, support;
**libéré sous ~** released on bail
**cavalier, -ière** [kavalje, jɛʀ] adj
(désinvolte) offhand ▷ nm/f rider; (au
bal) partner ▷ nm (Échecs) knight
**cave** [kav] nf cellar
**CD** sigle m (=compact disc) CD
**CD-ROM** [sedeʀɔm] sigle m CD-ROM

 **MOT-CLÉ**

**ce, cette** [sə, sɛt] (devant nm **cet** +
voyelle ou h aspiré; pl **ces**) dét (proximité)
this; these pl; (non-proximité) that; those
pl; **cette maison(-ci/là)** this/that
house; **cette nuit** (qui vient) tonight;
(passée) last night
▷ pron 1: **c'est** it's ou it is; **c'est un
peintre** he's ou he is a painter; **ce
sont des peintres** they're ou they are
painters; **c'est le facteur** etc (à la porte)
it's the postman; **c'est toi qui lui a
parlé** it was you who spoke to him; **qui
est-ce?** who is it?; (en désignant) who is
he/she?; **qu'est-ce?** what is it?
2: **ce qui, ce que**: **ce qui me plaît,
c'est sa franchise** what I like about
him ou her is his ou her frankness; **il est
bête, ce qui me chagrine** he's stupid,
which saddens me; **tout ce qui bouge**
everything ou that which moves; **tout
ce que je sais** all I know; **ce dont j'ai
parlé** what I talked about; **ce que c'est
grand!** it's so big!; voir aussi **-ci**; **est-ce
que**; **n'est-ce pas**; **c'est-à-dire**

**ceci** [səsi] pron this
**céder** [sede] vt (donner) to give up ▷ vi
(chaise, barrage) to give way; (personne)

to give in; **~ à** to yield to, give in to
**CEDEX** [sedɛks] *sigle m* (= *courrier d'entreprise à distribution exceptionnelle*) postal service for bulk users
**cédille** [sedij] *nf* cedilla
**ceinture** [sɛ̃tyʀ] *nf* belt; (*taille*) waist; **ceinture de sécurité** safety *ou* seat belt
**cela** [s(ə)la] *pron* that; (*comme sujet indéfini*) it; **~ m'étonne que ...** it surprises me that ...; **quand/où ~?** when/where (was that)?
**célèbre** [selɛbʀ] *adj* famous; **célébrer** *vt* to celebrate
**céleri** [sɛlʀi] *nm*: **~(-rave)** celeriac; **céleri en branche** celery
**célibataire** [selibatɛʀ] *adj* single, unmarried ▷ *nm* bachelor ▷ *nf* unmarried woman
**celle, celles** [sɛl] *pron voir* **celui**
**cellule** [selyl] *nf* (*gén*) cell; **~ souche** stem cell
**cellulite** [selylit] *nf* cellulite

**⬤ MOT-CLÉ**

**celui, celle** [səlɥi, sɛl] (*mpl* **ceux**, *fpl* **celles**) *pron* **1**: **celui-ci/là, celle-ci/là** this one/that one; **ceux-ci, celles-ci** these (ones); **ceux-là, celles-là** those (ones)
**2**: **celui qui bouge** the one which *ou* that moves; (*personne*) the one who moves; **celui que je vois** the one (which *ou* that) I see; (*personne*) the one (whom) I see; **celui dont je parle** the one I'm talking about; **celui de mon frère** my brother's; **celui du salon/du dessous** the one in (*ou* from) the lounge/below
**3** (*valeur indéfinie*): **celui qui veut** whoever wants

**cendre** [sɑ̃dʀ] *nf* ash; **cendres** *nfpl* (*d'un défunt*) ashes; **sous la ~** (*Culin*) in (the) embers; **cendrier** *nm* ashtray
**censé, e** [sɑ̃se] *adj*: **être ~ faire** to be supposed to do
**censeur** [sɑ̃sœʀ] *nm* (*Scol*) deputy-head

(*BRIT*), vice-principal (*US*)
**censure** [sɑ̃syʀ] *nf* censorship; **censurer** *vt* (*Cinéma, Presse*) to censor; (*Pol*) to censure
**cent** [sɑ̃] *num* a hundred, one hundred ▷ *nm* (*US, Canada etc*) cent; (*partie de l'euro*) cent; **centaine** *nf*: **une centaine (de)** about a hundred, a hundred or so; **des centaines (de)** hundreds (of); **centenaire** *adj* hundred-year-old ▷ *nm* (*anniversaire*) centenary; (*monnaie*) cent; **centième** *num* hundredth; **centigrade** *nm* centigrade; **centilitre** *nm* centilitre; **centime** *nm* centime; **centime d'euro** *nm* euro cent; **centimètre** *nm* centimetre; (*ruban*) tape measure, measuring tape
**central, e, -aux** [sɑ̃tʀal, o] *adj* central ▷ *nm*: **~ (téléphonique)** (telephone) exchange; **centrale** *nf* power station; **centrale électrique/nucléaire** power/nuclear power station
**centre** [sɑ̃tʀ] *nm* centre; **centre commercial/sportif/culturel** shopping/sports/arts centre; **centre d'appels** call centre; **centre-ville** *nm* town centre, downtown (area) (*US*)
**cèpe** [sɛp] *nm* (edible) boletus
**cependant** [s(ə)pɑ̃dɑ̃] *adv* however
**céramique** [seʀamik] *nf* ceramics *sg*
**cercle** [sɛʀkl] *nm* circle; **cercle vicieux** vicious circle
**cercueil** [sɛʀkœj] *nm* coffin
**céréale** [seʀeal] *nf* cereal
**cérémonie** [seʀemɔni] *nf* ceremony; **sans ~** (*inviter, manger*) informally
**cerf** [sɛʀ] *nm* stag
**cerf-volant** [sɛʀvɔlɑ̃] *nm* kite
**cerise** [s(ə)ʀiz] *nf* cherry; **cerisier** *nm* cherry (tree)
**cerner** [sɛʀne] *vt* (*Mil etc*) to surround; (*fig: problème*) to delimit, define
**certain, e** [sɛʀtɛ̃, ɛn] *adj* certain ▷ *dét* certain; **d'un ~ âge** past one's prime, not so young; **un ~ temps** (quite) some time; **un ~ Georges** someone called Georges; **~s** *pron* some; **certainement** *adv* (*probablement*) most probably *ou*

likely; (*bien sûr*) certainly, of course
**certes** [sɛʀt] *adv* (*sans doute*)
admittedly; (*bien sûr*) of course
**certificat** [sɛʀtifika] *nm* certificate
**certifier** [sɛʀtifje] *vt*: ~ **qch à qn**
to assure sb of sth; **copie certifiée
conforme** certified copy of the original
**certitude** [sɛʀtityd] *nf* certainty
**cerveau, x** [sɛʀvo] *nm* brain
**cervelas** [sɛʀvəla] *nm* saveloy
**cervelle** [sɛʀvɛl] *nf* (*Anat*) brain; (*Culin*)
brains
**ces** [se] *dét voir* **ce**
**CES** *sigle m* (= *collège d'enseignement
secondaire*) ≈ (junior) secondary school
(BRIT)
**cesse** [sɛs]: **sans ~** *adv* (*tout le temps*)
continually, constantly; (*sans
interruption*) continuously; **il n'a eu de
~ que** he did not rest until; **cesser** *vt*
to stop ▷ *vi* to stop, cease; **cesser de
faire** to stop doing; **cessez-le-feu** *nm
inv* ceasefire
**c'est-à-dire** [sɛtadiʀ] *adv* that is (to say)
**cet, cette** [sɛt] *dét voir* **ce**
**ceux** [sø] *pron voir* **celui**
**chacun, e** [ʃakœ̃, yn] *pron* each; (*indéfini*)
everyone, everybody
**chagrin** [ʃagʀɛ̃] *nm* grief, sorrow; **avoir
du ~** to be grieved
**chahut** [ʃay] *nm* uproar; **chahuter** *vt*
to rag, bait ▷ *vi* to make an uproar
**chaîne** [ʃɛn] *nf* chain; (*Radio, TV:
stations*) channel; **travail à la ~**
production line work; **réactions
en ~** chain reaction *sg*; **chaîne de
montagnes** mountain range; **chaîne
(hi-fi)** hi-fi system
**chair** [ʃɛʀ] *nf* flesh; **avoir la ~ de poule**
to have goosepimples *ou* gooseflesh;
**bien en ~** plump, well-padded; **en
~ et en os** in the flesh; **~ à saucisse**
sausage meat
**chaise** [ʃɛz] *nf* chair; **chaise longue**
deckchair
**châle** [ʃɑl] *nm* shawl
**chaleur** [ʃalœʀ] *nf* heat; (*fig: accueil*)
warmth; **chaleureux, -euse** *adj* warm

**chamailler** [ʃamaje]: **se chamailler** *vi*
to squabble, bicker
**chambre** [ʃɑ̃bʀ] *nf* bedroom; (*Pol,
Comm*) chamber; **faire ~ à part** to sleep
in separate rooms; **je voudrais une ~
pour deux personnes** I'd like a double
room; **chambre à air** (*de pneu*) (inner)
tube; **chambre à coucher** bedroom;
**chambre à un lit/à deux lits** (à
*l'hôtel*) single-/twin-bedded room;
**chambre d'amis** spare *ou* guest room;
**chambre d'hôte** ≈ bed and breakfast;
**chambre meublée** bedsit(ter) (BRIT),
furnished room; **chambre noire** (*Photo*)
darkroom
**chameau, x** [ʃamo] *nm* camel
**chamois** [ʃamwa] *nm* chamois
**champ** [ʃɑ̃] *nm* field; **champ de bataille**
battlefield; **champ de courses**
racecourse
**champagne** [ʃɑ̃paɲ] *nm* champagne
**champignon** [ʃɑ̃piɲɔ̃] *nm* mushroom;
(*terme générique*) fungus; **champignon
de Paris** *ou* **de couche** button
mushroom
**champion, ne** [ʃɑ̃pjɔ̃, jɔn] *adj,
nm/f* champion; **championnat** *nm*
championship
**chance** [ʃɑ̃s] *nf*: **la ~** luck; **chances** *nfpl*
(*probabilités*) chances; **avoir de la ~** to
be lucky; **il a des ~s de réussir** he's got
a good chance of passing; **bonne ~!**
good luck!
**change** [ʃɑ̃ʒ] *nm* (*devises*) exchange
**changement** [ʃɑ̃ʒmɑ̃] *nm* change;
**changement de vitesses** gears *pl*
**changer** [ʃɑ̃ʒe] *vt* (*modifier*) to change,
alter; (*remplacer, Comm*) to change ▷ *vi*
to change, alter; **se changer** *vi* to
change (o.s.); **~ de** (*remplacer: adresse,
nom, voiture etc*) to change one's;
(*échanger: place, train etc*) to change;
**~ d'avis** to change one's mind; **~ de
vitesse** to change gear; **il faut ~ à Lyon**
you *ou* we *etc* have to change in Lyons;
**où est-ce que je peux ~ de l'argent?**
where can I change some money?
**chanson** [ʃɑ̃sɔ̃] *nf* song

**chant** [ʃɑ̃] nm song; (art vocal) singing; (d'église) hymn

**chantage** [ʃɑ̃taʒ] nm blackmail; **faire du ~** to use blackmail

**chanter** [ʃɑ̃te] vt, vi to sing; **si cela lui chante** (fam) if he feels like it; **chanteur, -euse** nm/f singer

**chantier** [ʃɑ̃tje] nm (building) site; (sur une route) roadworks pl; **mettre en ~** to put in hand; **chantier naval** shipyard

**chantilly** [ʃɑ̃tiji] nf voir **crème**

**chantonner** [ʃɑ̃tɔne] vi, vt to sing to oneself, hum

**chapeau, x** [ʃapo] nm hat; **~!** well done!

**chapelle** [ʃapɛl] nf chapel

**chapitre** [ʃapitʀ] nm chapter

**chaque** [ʃak] dét each, every; (indéfini) every

**char** [ʃaʀ] nm (Mil): **~ (d'assaut)** tank; **~ à voile** sand yacht

**charbon** [ʃaʀbɔ̃] nm coal; **charbon de bois** charcoal

**charcuterie** [ʃaʀkytʀi] nf (magasin) pork butcher's shop and delicatessen; (produits) cooked pork meats pl; **charcutier, -ière** nm/f pork butcher

**chardon** [ʃaʀdɔ̃] nm thistle

**charge** [ʃaʀʒ] nf (fardeau) load, burden; (Élec, Mil, Jur) charge; (rôle, mission) responsibility; **charges** nfpl (du loyer) service charges; **à la ~ de** (dépendant de) dependent upon; (aux frais de) chargeable to; **prendre en ~** to take charge of; (suj: véhicule) to take on; (dépenses) to take care of; **charges sociales** social security contributions

**chargement** [ʃaʀʒəmɑ̃] nm (objets) load

**charger** [ʃaʀʒe] vt (voiture, fusil, caméra) to load; (batterie) to charge ▷ vi (Mil etc) to charge; **se ~ de** to see to, take care of

**chariot** [ʃaʀjo] nm trolley; (charrette) waggon

**charité** [ʃaʀite] nf charity; **faire la ~ à** to give (something) to

**charmant, e** [ʃaʀmɑ̃, ɑ̃t] adj charming

**charme** [ʃaʀm] nm charm; **charmer** vt to charm

**charpente** [ʃaʀpɑ̃t] nf frame(work); **charpentier** nm carpenter

**charrette** [ʃaʀɛt] nf cart

**charter** [ʃaʀtɛʀ] nm (vol) charter flight

**chasse** [ʃas] nf hunting; (au fusil) shooting; (poursuite) chase; (aussi: **~ d'eau**) flush; **prendre en ~** to give chase to; **tirer la ~ (d'eau)** to flush the toilet, pull the chain; **~ à courre** hunting; **chasse-neige** nm inv snowplough (BRIT), snowplow (US); **chasser** vt to hunt; (expulser) to chase away ou out, drive away ou out; **chasseur, -euse** nm/f hunter ▷ nm (avion) fighter

**chat¹** [ʃa] nm cat

**chat²** [tʃat] nm (Internet) chat room

**châtaigne** [ʃatɛɲ] nf chestnut

**châtain** [ʃatɛ̃] adj inv (cheveux) chestnut (brown); (personne) chestnut-haired

**château, x** [ʃato] nm (forteresse) castle; (résidence royale) palace; (manoir) mansion; **château d'eau** water tower; **château fort** stronghold, fortified castle

**châtiment** [ʃatimɑ̃] nm punishment

**chaton** [ʃatɔ̃] nm (Zool) kitten

**chatouiller** [ʃatuje] vt to tickle; **chatouilleux, -euse** adj ticklish

**chatte** [ʃat] nf (she-)cat

**chatter** [tʃate] vi (Internet) to chat

**chaud, e** [ʃo, ʃod] adj (gén) warm; (très chaud) hot; **il fait ~** it's warm; it's hot; **avoir ~** to be warm; to be hot; **ça me tient ~** it keeps me warm; **rester au ~** to stay in the warm

**chaudière** [ʃodjɛʀ] nf boiler

**chauffage** [ʃofaʒ] nm heating; **chauffage central** central heating

**chauffe-eau** [ʃofo] nm inv water-heater

**chauffer** [ʃofe] vt to heat ▷ vi to heat up, warm up; (trop chauffer: moteur) to overheat; **se chauffer** vi (au soleil) to warm o.s.

**chauffeur** [ʃofœʀ] nm driver; (privé) chauffeur

**chaumière** [ʃomjɛʀ] nf (thatched) cottage

**chaussée** [ʃose] nf road(way)

**chausser** [ʃose] vt (bottes, skis) to put on; (enfant) to put shoes on; **~ du 38/42** to take size 38/42

**chaussette** [ʃosɛt] nf sock

**chausson** [ʃosɔ̃] nm slipper; (de bébé) bootee; **chausson (aux pommes)** (apple) turnover

**chaussure** [ʃosyʀ] nf shoe; **chaussures basses** flat shoes; **chaussures montantes** ankle boots; **chaussures de ski** ski boots

**chauve** [ʃov] adj bald; **chauve-souris** nf bat

**chauvin, e** [ʃovɛ̃, in] adj chauvinistic

**chaux** [ʃo] nf lime; **blanchi à la ~** whitewashed

**chef** [ʃɛf] nm head, leader; (de cuisine) chef; **commandant en ~** commander-in-chief; **chef d'accusation** charge; **chef d'entreprise** company head; **chef d'État** head of state; **chef de famille** head of the family; **chef de file** (de parti etc) leader; **chef de gare** station master; **chef d'orchestre** conductor; **chef-d'œuvre** nm masterpiece; **chef-lieu** nm county town

**chemin** [ʃ(ə)mɛ̃] nm path; (itinéraire, direction, trajet) way; **en ~** on the way; **chemin de fer** railway (BRIT), railroad (US)

**cheminée** [ʃ(ə)mine] nf chimney; (à l'intérieur) chimney piece, fireplace; (de bateau) funnel

**chemise** [ʃ(ə)miz] nf shirt; (dossier) folder; **chemise de nuit** nightdress

**chemisier** [ʃ(ə)mizje] nm blouse

**chêne** [ʃɛn] nm oak (tree); (bois) oak

**chenil** [ʃ(ə)nil] nm kennels pl

**chenille** [ʃ(ə)nij] nf (Zool) caterpillar

**chèque** [ʃɛk] nm cheque (BRIT), check (US); **est-ce que je peux payer par ~?** can I pay by cheque?; **chèque sans provision** bad cheque; **chèque de voyage** traveller's cheque; **chéquier** [ʃekje] nm cheque book

**cher, -ère** [ʃɛʀ] adj (aimé) dear; (coûteux) expensive, dear ▷ adv: **ça coûte ~** it's expensive

**chercher** [ʃɛʀʃe] vt to look for; (gloire etc) to seek; **aller ~** to go for, go and fetch; **à faire** to try to do; **chercheur, -euse** nm/f researcher, research worker

**chéri, e** [ʃeʀi] adj beloved, dear; **(mon) ~** darling

**cheval, -aux** [ʃ(ə)val, o] nm horse; (Auto): **~ (vapeur)** horsepower no pl; **faire du ~** to ride; **à ~** on horseback; **à ~ sur** astride; (fig) overlapping; **cheval de course** racehorse

**chevalier** [ʃ(ə)valje] nm knight

**chevalière** [ʃ(ə)valjɛʀ] nf signet ring

**chevaux** [ʃəvo] nmpl de **cheval**

**chevet** [ʃ(ə)vɛ] nm: **au ~ de qn** at sb's bedside; **lampe de chevet** bedside lamp

**cheveu, x** [ʃ(ə)vø] nm hair; **cheveux** nmpl (chevelure) hair sg; **avoir les ~x courts** to have short hair

**cheville** [ʃ(ə)vij] nf (Anat) ankle; (de bois) peg; (pour une vis) plug

**chèvre** [ʃɛvʀ] nf (she-)goat

**chèvrefeuille** [ʃɛvʀəfœj] nm honeysuckle

**chevreuil** [ʃəvʀœj] nm roe deer inv; (Culin) venison

 **MOT-CLÉ**

**chez** [ʃe] prép **1** (à la demeure de) at; (: direction) to; **chez qn** at/to sb's house ou place; **je suis chez moi** I'm at home; **je rentre chez moi** I'm going home; **allons chez Nathalie** let's go to Nathalie's

**2** (+profession) at; (: direction) to; **chez le boulanger/dentiste** at ou to the baker's/dentist's

**3** (dans le caractère, l'œuvre de) in; **chez ce poète** in this poet's work; **c'est ce que je préfère chez lui** that's what I like best about him

**chic** [ʃik] adj inv chic, smart; (fam:

généreux) nice, decent ▷ nm stylishness;
**~ (alors)!** (fam) great!; **avoir le ~ de** to
have the knack of

**chicorée** [ʃikɔʀe] nf (café) chicory;
(salade) endive

**chien** [ʃjɛ̃] nm dog; **chien d'aveugle**
guide dog; **chien de garde** guard dog

**chienne** [ʃjɛn] nf dog, bitch

**chiffon** [ʃifɔ̃] nm (piece of) rag;
**chiffonner** vt to crumple; (fam:
tracasser) to concern

**chiffre** [ʃifʀ] nm (représentant un nombre)
figure, numeral; (montant, total) total,
sum; **en ~s ronds** in round figures;
**chiffre d'affaires** turnover; **chiffrer**
vt (dépense) to put a figure to, assess;
(message) to (en)code, cipher; **se
chiffrer à** to add up to, amount to

**chignon** [ʃiɲɔ̃] nm chignon, bun

**Chili** [ʃili] nm: **le ~** Chile; **chilien, ne** adj
Chilean ▷ nm/f: **Chilien, ne** Chilean

**chimie** [ʃimi] nf chemistry;
**chimiothérapie** [ʃimjɔteʀapi]
nf chemotherapy; **chimique** adj
chemical; **produits chimiques**
chemicals

**chimpanzé** [ʃɛ̃pɑ̃ze] nm chimpanzee

**Chine** [ʃin] nf: **la ~** China; **chinois, e** adj
Chinese ▷ nm/f: **Chinois, e** Chinese
▷ nm (Ling) Chinese

**chiot** [ʃjo] nm pup(py)

**chips** [ʃips] nfpl crisps (BRIT), (potato)
chips (US)

**chirurgie** [ʃiʀyʀʒi] nf surgery;
**chirurgie esthétique** plastic surgery;
**chirurgien, ne** nm/f surgeon

**chlore** [klɔʀ] nm chlorine

**choc** [ʃɔk] nm (heurt) impact, shock;
(collision) crash; (moral) shock;
(affrontement) clash

**chocolat** [ʃɔkɔla] nm chocolate;
**chocolat au lait** milk chocolate

**chœur** [kœʀ] nm (chorale) choir; (Opéra,
Théâtre) chorus; **en ~** in chorus

**choisir** [ʃwaziʀ] vt to choose, select

**choix** [ʃwa] nm choice, selection; **avoir
le ~** to have the choice; **premier ~**
(Comm) class one; **de ~** choice, selected;

**au ~** as you wish

**chômage** [ʃomaʒ] nm unemployment;
**mettre au ~** to make redundant,
put out of work; **être au ~** to be
unemployed ou out of work; **chômeur,
-euse** nm/f unemployed person

**choquer** [ʃɔke] vt (offenser) to shock;
(deuil) to shake

**chorale** [kɔʀal] nf choir

**chose** [ʃoz] nf thing; **c'est peu de ~** it's
nothing (really)

**chou, x** [ʃu] nm cabbage; **mon petit
~** (my) sweetheart; **chou à la crème**
choux bun; **chou de Bruxelles** Brussels
sprout; **choucroute** nf sauerkraut

**chouette** [ʃwɛt] nf owl ▷ adj (fam)
great, smashing

**chou-fleur** [ʃuflœʀ] nm cauliflower

**chrétien, ne** [kʀetjɛ̃, jɛn] adj, nm/f
Christian

**Christ** [kʀist] nm: **le ~** Christ;
**christianisme** nm Christianity

**chronique** [kʀɔnik] adj chronic ▷ nf
(de journal) column, page; (historique)
chronicle; (Radio, TV): **la ~ sportive** the
sports review

**chronologique** [kʀɔnɔlɔʒik] adj
chronological

**chronomètre** [kʀɔnɔmɛtʀ] nm
stopwatch; **chronométrer** vt to time

**chrysanthème** [kʀizɑ̃tɛm] nm
chrysanthemum

● **CHRYSANTHÈME**
●
● Chrysanthemums are strongly
● associated with funerals in France,
● and therefore should not be given
● as gifts.

**chuchotement** [ʃyʃɔtmɑ̃] nm whisper

**chuchoter** [ʃyʃɔte] vt, vi to whisper

**chut** [ʃyt] excl sh!

**chute** [ʃyt] nf fall; (déchet) scrap; **faire
une ~ (de 10 m)** to fall (10 m); **chute
(d'eau)** waterfall; **chute libre** free
fall; **chutes de pluie/neige** rainfall/
snowfall

**Chypre** [ʃipʀ] nm/f Cyprus

**-ci** [si] adv voir **par** ▷ dét: **ce garçon~** this boy; **ces femmes~** these women

**cible** [sibl] nf target

**ciboulette** [sibulɛt] nf (small) chive

**cicatrice** [sikatʀis] nf scar; **cicatriser** vt to heal

**ci-contre** [sikɔ̃tʀ] adv opposite

**ci-dessous** [sidəsu] adv below

**ci-dessus** [sidəsy] adv above

**cidre** [sidʀ] nm cider

**Cie** abr (= compagnie) Co.

**ciel** [sjɛl] nm sky; (Rel) heaven

**cieux** [sjø] nmpl de **ciel**

**cigale** [sigal] nf cicada

**cigare** [sigaʀ] nm cigar

**cigarette** [sigaʀɛt] nf cigarette

**ci-inclus, e** [siɛ̃kly, yz] adj, adv enclosed

**ci-joint, e** [siʒwɛ̃, ɛ̃t] adj, adv enclosed

**cil** [sil] nm (eye)lash

**cime** [sim] nf top; (montagne) peak

**ciment** [simã] nm cement

**cimetière** [simtjɛʀ] nm cemetery; (d'église) churchyard

**cinéaste** [sineast] nm/f film-maker

**cinéma** [sinema] nm cinema

**cinq** [sɛ̃k] num five; **cinquantaine** nf: **une cinquantaine (de)** about fifty; **avoir la cinquantaine** (âge) to be around fifty; **cinquante** num fifty; **cinquantenaire** adj, nm/f fifty-year-old; **cinquième** num fifth ▷ nf (Scol) year 8 (BRIT), seventh grade (US)

**cintre** [sɛ̃tʀ] nm coat-hanger

**cintré, e** [sɛ̃tʀe] adj (chemise) fitted

**cirage** [siʀaʒ] nm (shoe) polish

**circonflexe** [siʀkɔ̃flɛks] adj: **accent ~** circumflex accent

**circonstance** [siʀkɔ̃stãs] nf circumstance; (occasion) occasion; **circonstances atténuantes** mitigating circumstances

**circuit** [siʀkɥi] nm (Élec, Tech) circuit; (trajet) tour, (round) trip

**circulaire** [siʀkylɛʀ] adj, nf circular

**circulation** [siʀkylasjɔ̃] nf circulation; (Auto): **la ~** (the) traffic

**circuler** [siʀkyle] vi (sang, devises) to circulate; (véhicules) to drive (along); (passants) to walk along; (train, bus) to run; **faire ~** (nouvelle) to spread (about), circulate; (badauds) to move on

**cire** [siʀ] nf wax; **ciré** nm oilskin; **cirer** vt to wax, polish

**cirque** [siʀk] nm circus; (fig) chaos, bedlam; **quel ~!** what a carry-on!

**ciseau, x** [sizo] nm: **~ (à bois)** chisel; **ciseaux** nmpl (paire de ciseaux) (pair of) scissors

**citadin, e** [sitadɛ̃, in] nm/f city dweller

**citation** [sitasjɔ̃] nf (d'auteur) quotation; (Jur) summons sg

**cité** [site] nf town; (plus grande) city; **cité universitaire** students' residences pl

**citer** [site] vt (un auteur) to quote (from); (nommer) to name; (Jur) to summon

**citoyen, ne** [sitwajɛ̃, jɛn] nm/f citizen

**citron** [sitʀɔ̃] nm lemon; **citron pressé** (fresh) lemon juice; **citron vert** lime; **citronnade** nf still lemonade

**citrouille** [sitʀuj] nf pumpkin

**civet** [sivɛ] nm: **~ de lapin** rabbit stew

**civière** [sivjɛʀ] nf stretcher

**civil, e** [sivil] adj (mariage, poli) civil; (non militaire) civilian; **en ~** in civilian clothes; **dans le ~** in civilian life

**civilisation** [sivilizasjɔ̃] nf civilization

**clair, e** [klɛʀ] adj light; (pièce) light, bright; (eau, son, fig) clear ▷ adv: **voir ~** to see clearly; **tirer qch au ~** to clear sth up, clarify sth; **mettre au ~** (notes etc) to tidy up ▷ nm: **~ de lune** moonlight; **clairement** adv clearly

**clairière** [klɛʀjɛʀ] nf clearing

**clandestin, e** [klãdɛstɛ̃, in] adj clandestine, secret; (mouvement) underground; (travailleur, immigration) illegal; **passager ~** stowaway

**claque** [klak] nf (gifle) slap; **claquer** vi (porte) to bang, slam; (fam: mourir) to snuff it ▷ vt (porte) to slam, bang; (doigts) to snap; (fam: dépenser) to blow; **il claquait des dents** his teeth were chattering; **être claqué** (fam) to be dead tired; **se claquer un muscle** to pull ou strain a muscle; **claquettes** nfpl tap-dancing sg; (chaussures) flip-flops

**clarinette** [klaʀinɛt] nf clarinet

**classe** [klɑs] nf class; (Scol: local) class(room); (: leçon, élèves) class; **aller en ~** to go to school; **classement** nm (rang: Scol) place; (: Sport) placing; (liste: Scol) class list (in order of merit); (: Sport) placings pl

**classer** [klɑse] vt (idées, livres) to classify; (papiers) to file; (candidat, concurrent) to grade; (Jur: affaire) to close; **se ~ premier/dernier** to come first/last; (Sport) to finish first/last; **classeur** nm (cahier) file

**classique** [klasik] adj classical; (sobre: coupe etc) classic(al); (habituel) standard, classic

**clavecin** [klav(ə)sɛ̃] nm harpsichord

**clavicule** [klavikyl] nf collarbone

**clavier** [klavje] nm keyboard

**clé** [kle] nf key; (Mus) clef; (de mécanicien) spanner (BRIT), wrench (US); **prix ~s en main** (d'une voiture) on-the-road price; **clé de contact** ignition key; **clé USB** USB key

**clef** [kle] nf = **clé**

**clergé** [klɛʀʒe] nm clergy

**cliché** [kliʃe] nm (fig) cliché; (négatif) negative; (photo) print

**client, e** [klijɑ̃, klijɑ̃t] nm/f (acheteur) customer, client; (d'hôtel) guest, patron; (du docteur) patient; (de l'avocat) client; **clientèle** nf (du magasin) customers pl, clientèle; (du docteur, de l'avocat) practice

**cligner** [kliɲe] vi: **~ des yeux** to blink (one's eyes); **~ de l'œil** to wink; **clignotant** nm (Auto) indicator; **clignoter** vi (étoiles etc) to twinkle; (lumière) to flicker

**climat** [klima] nm climate

**climatisation** [klimatizasjɔ̃] nf air conditioning; **climatisé, e** adj air-conditioned

**clin d'œil** [klɛ̃dœj] nm wink; **en un clin d'œil** in a flash

**clinique** [klinik] nf private hospital

**clip** [klip] nm (boucle d'oreille) clip-on; **(vidéo) ~** (pop) video

**cliquer** [klike] vt to click; **~ sur** to click on

**clochard, e** [klɔʃaʀ, aʀd] nm/f tramp

**cloche** [klɔʃ] nf (d'église) bell; (fam) clot; **clocher** nm church tower; (en pointe) steeple ▷ vi (fam) to be ou go wrong; **de clocher** (péj) parochial

**cloison** [klwazɔ̃] nf partition (wall)

**clonage** [klɔnaʒ] nm cloning

**cloner** [klɔne] vt to clone

**cloque** [klɔk] nf blister

**clore** [klɔʀ] vt to close

**clôture** [klotyʀ] nf closure; (barrière) enclosure

**clou** [klu] nm nail; **clous** nmpl (passage clouté) pedestrian crossing; **pneus à ~s** studded tyres; **le ~ du spectacle** the highlight of the show; **clou de girofle** clove

**clown** [klun] nm clown

**club** [klœb] nm club

**CNRS** sigle m (= Centre nationale de la recherche scientifique) ≈ SERC (BRIT), ≈ NSF (US)

**coaguler** [kɔagyle] vt, vi (aussi: **se ~**: sang) to coagulate

**cobaye** [kɔbaj] nm guinea-pig

**coca** [kɔka] nm Coke®

**cocaïne** [kɔkain] nf cocaine

**coccinelle** [kɔksinɛl] nf ladybird (BRIT), ladybug (US)

**cocher** [kɔʃe] vt to tick off

**cochon, ne** [kɔʃɔ̃, ɔn] nm pig ▷ adj (fam) dirty, smutty; **cochon d'Inde** guinea-pig; **cochonnerie** (fam) nf (saleté) filth; (marchandise) rubbish, trash

**cocktail** [kɔktɛl] nm cocktail; (réception) cocktail party

**cocorico** [kɔkɔriko] excl, nm cock-a-doodle-do

**cocotte** [kɔkɔt] nf (en fonte) casserole; **ma ~** (fam) sweetie (pie); **cocotte (minute)®** pressure cooker

**code** [kɔd] nm code ▷ adj: **phares ~s** dipped lights; **se mettre en ~(s)** to dip one's (head)lights; **code à barres** bar code; **code civil** Common Law; **code de la route** highway code; **code pénal** penal code; **code postal** (*numéro*) post (BRIT) *ou* zip (US) code

**cœur** [kœʀ] *nm* heart; (*Cartes: couleur*) hearts *pl*; (: *carte*) heart; **avoir bon ~** to be kind-hearted; **avoir mal au ~** to feel sick; **par ~** by heart; **de bon ~** willingly; **cela lui tient à ~** that's (very) close to his heart

**coffre** [kɔfʀ] *nm* (*meuble*) chest; (*d'auto*) boot (BRIT), trunk (US); **coffre-fort** *nm* safe; **coffret** *nm* casket

**cognac** [kɔɲak] *nm* brandy, cognac

**cogner** [kɔɲe] *vi* to knock; **se ~ contre** to knock *ou* bump into; **se ~ la tête** to bang one's head

**cohérent, e** [kɔeʀɑ̃, ɑ̃t] *adj* coherent, consistent

**coiffé, e** [kwafe] *adj*: **bien/mal ~** with tidy/untidy hair; **~ d'un chapeau** wearing a hat

**coiffer** [kwafe] *vt* (*fig: surmonter*) to cover, top; **se coiffer** *vi* to do one's hair; **~ qn** to do sb's hair; **coiffeur, -euse** *nm/f* hairdresser; **coiffeuse** *nf* (*table*) dressing table; **coiffure** *nf* (*cheveux*) hairstyle, hairdo; (*art*): **la coiffure** hairdressing

**coin** [kwɛ̃] *nm* corner; (*pour coincer*) wedge; **l'épicerie du ~** the local grocer; **dans le ~** (*aux alentours*) in the area, around about; (*habiter*) locally; **je ne suis pas du ~** I'm not from here; **au ~ du feu** by the fireside; **regard en ~** sideways glance

**coincé, e** [kwɛ̃se] *adj* stuck, jammed; (*fig: inhibé*) inhibited, hung up (*fam*)

**coïncidence** [kɔɛ̃sidɑ̃s] *nf* coincidence

**coing** [kwɛ̃] *nm* quince

**col** [kɔl] *nm* (*de chemise*) collar; (*encolure, cou*) neck; (*de montagne*) pass; **col de l'utérus** cervix; **col roulé** polo-neck

**colère** [kɔlɛʀ] *nf* anger; **une ~** a fit of anger; **(se mettre) en ~ (contre qn)** (to get) angry (with sb); **coléreux, -euse, colérique** *adj* quick-tempered, irascible

**colin** [kɔlɛ̃] *nm* hake

**colique** [kɔlik] *nf* diarrhoea

**colis** [kɔli] *nm* parcel

**collaborer** [kɔ(l)labɔʀe] *vi* to collaborate; **~ à** to collaborate on; (*revue*) to contribute to

**collant, e** [kɔlɑ̃, ɑ̃t] *adj* sticky; (*robe etc*) clinging, skintight; (*péj*) clinging ▷ *nm* (*bas*) tights *pl*; (*de danseur*) leotard

**colle** [kɔl] *nf* glue; (*à papiers peints*) (wallpaper) paste; (*fam: devinette*) teaser, riddle; (*Scol: fam*) detention

**collecte** [kɔlɛkt] *nf* collection; **collectif, -ive** *adj* collective; (*visite, billet*) group *cpd*

**collection** [kɔlɛksjɔ̃] *nf* collection; (*Édition*) series; **collectionner** *vt* to collect; **collectionneur, -euse** *nm/f* collector

**collectivité** [kɔlɛktivite] *nf* group; **collectivités locales** (*Admin*) local authorities

**collège** [kɔlɛʒ] *nm* (*école*) (secondary) school; (*assemblée*) body; **collégien** *nm* schoolboy

**collègue** [kɔ(l)lɛg] *nm/f* colleague

**coller** [kɔle] *vt* (*papier, timbre*) to stick (on); (*affiche*) to stick up; (*enveloppe*) to stick down; (*morceaux*) to stick *ou* glue together; (*Comput*) to paste; (*fam: mettre, fourrer*) to stick, shove; (*Scol: fam*) to keep in ▷ *vi* (*être collant*) to be sticky; (*adhérer*) to stick; **~ à** to stick to; **être collé à un examen** (*fam*) to fail an exam

**collier** [kɔlje] *nm* (*bijou*) necklace; (*de chien, Tech*) collar

**colline** [kɔlin] *nf* hill

**collision** [kɔlizjɔ̃] *nf* collision, crash; **entrer en ~ (avec)** to collide (with)

**collyre** [kɔliʀ] *nm* eye drops

**colombe** [kɔlɔ̃b] *nf* dove

**Colombie** [kɔlɔ̃bi] *nf*: **la ~** Colombia

**colonie** [kɔlɔni] *nf* colony; **colonie (de vacances)** holiday camp (*for children*)

**colonne** [kɔlɔn] *nf* column; **se mettre en ~ par deux** to get into twos;

**colonne (vertébrale)** spine, spinal column

**colorant** [kɔlɔrɑ̃] *nm* colouring

**colorer** [kɔlɔre] *vt* to colour

**colorier** [kɔlɔrje] *vt* to colour (in)

**coloris** [kɔlɔri] *nm* colour, shade

**colza** [kɔlza] *nm* rape(seed)

**coma** [kɔma] *nm* coma; **être dans le ~** to be in a coma

**combat** [kɔ̃ba] *nm* fight, fighting *no pl*; **combat de boxe** boxing match; **combattant** *nm*: **ancien combattant** war veteran; **combattre** *vt* to fight; (*épidémie, ignorance*) to combat, fight against

**combien** [kɔ̃bjɛ̃] *adv* (*quantité*) how much; (*nombre*) how many; **~ de** (*quantité*) how much; (*nombre*) how many; **~ de temps** how long; **~ ça coûte/pèse?** how much does it cost/weigh?; **on est le ~ aujourd'hui?** (*fam*) what's the date today?

**combinaison** [kɔ̃binezɔ̃] *nf* combination; (*astuce*) scheme; (*de femme*) slip; (*de plongée*) wetsuit; (*bleu de travail*) boiler suit (BRIT), coveralls *pl* (US)

**combiné** [kɔ̃bine] *nm* (*aussi:* **~ téléphonique**) receiver

**comble** [kɔ̃bl] *adj* (*salle*) packed (full) ▷ *nm* (*du bonheur, plaisir*) height; **combles** *nmpl* (*Constr*) attic *sg*, loft *sg*; **c'est le ~!** that beats everything!

**combler** [kɔ̃ble] *vt* (*trou*) to fill in; (*besoin, lacune*) to fill; (*déficit*) to make good; (*satisfaire*) to fulfil

**comédie** [kɔmedi] *nf* comedy; (*fig*) playacting *no pl*; **faire la ~** (*fam*) to make a fuss; **comédie musicale** musical; **comédien, ne** *nm/f* actor(-tress)

**comestible** [kɔmɛstibl] *adj* edible

**comique** [kɔmik] *adj* (*drôle*) comical; (*Théâtre*) comic ▷ *nm* (*artiste*) comic, comedian

**commandant** [kɔmɑ̃dɑ̃] *nm* (*gén*) commander, commandant; (*Navig, Aviat*) captain

**commande** [kɔmɑ̃d] *nf* (*Comm*) order; **commandes** *nfpl* (*Aviat etc*) controls; **sur ~** to order; **commander** *vt* (*Comm*) to order; (*diriger, ordonner*) to command; **commander à qn de faire** to command *ou* order sb to do; **je peux commander, s'il vous plaît?** can I order, please?

🔵 **MOT-CLÉ**

**comme** [kɔm] *prép* **1** (*comparaison*) like; **tout comme son père** just like his father; **fort comme un bœuf** as strong as an ox; **joli comme tout** ever so pretty

**2** (*manière*) like; **faites-le comme ça** do it like this, do it this way; **comme ci, comme ça** so-so, middling; **comme il faut** (*correctement*) properly

**3** (*en tant que*) as a; **donner comme prix** to give as a prize; **travailler comme secrétaire** to work as a secretary

▷ *conj* **1** (*ainsi que*) as; **elle écrit comme elle parle** she writes as she talks; **comme si** as if

**2** (*au moment où, alors que*) as; **il est parti comme j'arrivais** he left as I arrived

**3** (*parce que, puisque*) as; **comme il était en retard, il ...** as he was late, he ...

▷ *adv*: **comme il est fort/c'est bon!** he's so strong/it's so good!

**commencement** [kɔmɑ̃smɑ̃] *nm* beginning, start

**commencer** [kɔmɑ̃se] *vt, vi* to begin, start; **~ à** *ou* **de faire** to begin *ou* start doing

**comment** [kɔmɑ̃] *adv* how; **~?** (*que dites-vous*) pardon?; **et ~!** and how!

**commentaire** [kɔmɑ̃tɛr] *nm* (*remarque*) comment, remark; (*exposé*) commentary

**commerçant, e** [kɔmɛrsɑ̃, ɑ̃t] *nm/f* shopkeeper, trader

**commerce** [kɔmɛrs] *nm* (*activité*) trade, commerce; (*boutique*) business; **~ électronique** e-commerce; **~**

**équitable** fair trade; **commercial, e,
-aux** adj commercial, trading; (péj)
commercial; **les commerciaux** the
sales people; **commercialiser** vt to
market

**commissaire** [kɔmisɛʀ] nm (de
police) ≈ (police) superintendent;
**commissaire aux comptes** (Admin)
auditor; **commissariat** nm police
station

**commission** [kɔmisjɔ̃] nf (comité,
pourcentage) commission; (message)
message; (course) errand; **commissions**
nfpl (achats) shopping sg

**commode** [kɔmɔd] adj (pratique)
convenient, handy; (facile) easy;
(personne): **pas ~** awkward (to deal
with) ▷ nf chest of drawers

**commun, e** [kɔmœ̃, yn] adj common;
(pièce) communal, shared; (effort) joint;
**ça sort du ~** it's out of the ordinary;
**le ~ des mortels** the common run
of people; **en ~** (faire) jointly; **mettre
en ~** to pool, share; **communs** nmpl
(bâtiments) outbuildings; **d'un ~ accord**
by mutual agreement

**communauté** [kɔmynote] nf
community

**commune** [kɔmyn] nf (Admin)
commune, ≈ district; (: urbaine)
≈ borough

**communication** [kɔmynikasjɔ̃] nf
communication

**communier** [kɔmynje] vi (Rel) to
receive communion

**communion** [kɔmynjɔ̃] nf
communion

**communiquer** [kɔmynike] vt
(nouvelle, dossier) to pass on, convey;
(peur etc) to communicate ▷ vi to
communicate; **se communiquer à** (se
propager) to spread to

**communisme** [kɔmynism] nm
communism; **communiste** adj, nm/f
communist

**commutateur** [kɔmytatœʀ] nm (Élec)
(change-over) switch, commutator

**compact, e** [kɔ̃pakt] adj (dense) dense;
(appareil) compact

**compagne** [kɔ̃paɲ] nf companion

**compagnie** [kɔ̃paɲi] nf (firme, Mil)
company; **tenir ~ à qn** to keep sb
company; **fausser ~ à qn** to give
sb the slip, slip ou sneak away from
sb; **compagnie aérienne** airline
(company)

**compagnon** [kɔ̃paɲɔ̃] nm companion

**comparable** [kɔ̃paʀabl] adj: **~ (à)**
comparable (to)

**comparaison** [kɔ̃paʀɛzɔ̃] nf
comparison

**comparer** [kɔ̃paʀe] vt to compare; **~
qch/qn à** ou **et** (pour choisir) to compare
sth/sb with ou and; (pour établir une
similitude) to compare sth/sb to

**compartiment** [kɔ̃paʀtimɑ̃] nm
compartment; **un ~ non-fumeurs** a
non-smoking compartment (BRIT)
ou car (US)

**compas** [kɔ̃pa] nm (Géom) (pair of)
compasses pl; (Navig) compass

**compatible** [kɔ̃patibl] adj compatible

**compatriote** [kɔ̃patʀijɔt] nm/f
compatriot

**compensation** [kɔ̃pɑ̃sasjɔ̃] nf
compensation

**compenser** [kɔ̃pɑ̃se] vt to compensate
for, make up for

**compétence** [kɔ̃petɑ̃s] nf competence

**compétent, e** [kɔ̃petɑ̃, ɑ̃t] adj (apte)
competent, capable

**compétition** [kɔ̃petisjɔ̃] nf (gén)
competition; (Sport: épreuve) event; **la ~
automobile** motor racing

**complément** [kɔ̃plemɑ̃] nm
complement; (reste) remainder;
**complément d'information** (Admin)
supplementary ou further information;
**complémentaire** adj complementary;
(additionnel) supplementary

**complet, -ète** [kɔ̃plɛ, ɛt] adj
complete; (plein: hôtel etc) full ▷ nm
(aussi: **~-veston**) suit; **pain complet**
wholemeal bread; **complètement**
adv completely; **compléter** vt (porter
à la quantité voulue) to complete;

(*augmenter*: *connaissances*, *études*) to complement, supplement; (: *garde-robe*) to add to

**complexe** [kɔ̃plɛks] *adj*, *nm* complex; **complexe hospitalier/industriel** hospital/industrial complex; **complexé, e** *adj* mixed-up, hung-up

**complication** [kɔ̃plikasjɔ̃] *nf* complexity, intricacy; (*difficulté*, *ennui*) complication; **complications** *nfpl* (*Méd*) complications

**complice** [kɔ̃plis] *nm* accomplice

**compliment** [kɔ̃plimɑ̃] *nm* (*louange*) compliment; **compliments** *nmpl* (*félicitations*) congratulations

**compliqué, e** [kɔ̃plike] *adj* complicated, complex; (*personne*) complicated

**comportement** [kɔ̃pɔrtəmɑ̃] *nm* behaviour

**comporter** [kɔ̃pɔrte] *vt* (*consister en*) to consist of, comprise; (*inclure*) to have; **se comporter** *vi* to behave

**composer** [kɔ̃poze] *vt* (*musique*, *texte*) to compose; (*mélange*, *équipe*) to make up; (*numéro*) to dial; (*constituer*) to make up, form ▷ *vi* (*transiger*) to come to terms; **se composer de** to be composed of, be made up of; **compositeur, -trice** *nm/f* (*Mus*) composer; **composition** *nf* composition; (*Scol*) test

**composter** [kɔ̃pɔste] *vt* (*billet*) to punch

⬤ **COMPOSTER**
⬤
⬤ In France you have to punch your
⬤ ticket on the platform to validate it
⬤ before getting onto the train.

**compote** [kɔ̃pɔt] *nf* stewed fruit *no pl*; **compote de pommes** stewed apples

**compréhensible** [kɔ̃preɑ̃sibl] *adj* comprehensible; (*attitude*) understandable

**compréhensif, -ive** [kɔ̃preɑ̃sif, iv] *adj* understanding

▌ Attention à ne pas traduire *compréhensif* par *comprehensive*.

**comprendre** [kɔ̃prɑ̃dr] *vt* to understand; (*se composer de*) to comprise, consist of

**compresse** [kɔ̃prɛs] *nf* compress

**comprimé** [kɔ̃prime] *nm* tablet

**compris, e** [kɔ̃pri, iz] *pp de* **comprendre** ▷ *adj* (*inclus*) included; **~ entre** (*situé*) contained between; **l'électricité ~e/non ~e, y/non ~ l'électricité** including/excluding electricity; **100 euros tout ~** 100 euros all inclusive *ou* all-in

**comptabilité** [kɔ̃tabilite] *nf* (*activité*) accounting, accountancy; (*comptes*) accounts *pl*, books *pl*; (*service*) accounts office

**comptable** [kɔ̃tabl] *nm/f* accountant

**comptant** [kɔ̃tɑ̃] *adv*: **payer ~** to pay cash; **acheter ~** to buy for cash

**compte** [kɔ̃t] *nm* count; (*total*, *montant*) count, (right) number; (*bancaire*, *facture*) account; **comptes** *nmpl* (*Finance*) accounts, books; (*fig*) explanation *sg*; **en fin de ~** all things considered; **s'en tirer à bon ~** to get off lightly; **pour le ~ de** on behalf of; **pour son propre ~** for one's own benefit; **régler un ~** (*s'acquitter de qch*) to settle an account; (*se venger*) to get one's own back; **rendre des ~s à qn** (*fig*) to be answerable to sb; **tenir ~ de** to take account of; **travailler à son ~** to work for oneself; **rendre ~ (à qn) de qch** to give (sb) an account of sth; *voir aussi* **rendre**; **compte à rebours** countdown; **compte courant** current account; **compte rendu** account, report; (*de film*, *livre*) review; **compte-gouttes** *nm inv* dropper

**compter** [kɔ̃te] *vt* to count; (*facturer*) to charge for; (*avoir à son actif*, *comporter*) to have; (*prévoir*) to allow, reckon; (*penser*, *espérer*): **~ réussir** to expect to succeed ▷ *vi* to count; (*être économe*) to economize; (*figurer*): **~ parmi** to be *ou* rank among; **~ sur** to count (up)on;

**~ avec qch/qn** to reckon with *ou* take account of sth/sb; **sans ~ que** besides which

**compteur** [kɔ̃tœʀ] *nm* meter; **compteur de vitesse** speedometer

**comptine** [kɔ̃tin] *nf* nursery rhyme

**comptoir** [kɔ̃twaʀ] *nm* (*de magasin*) counter; (*bar*) bar

**con, ne** [kɔ̃, kɔn] (*fam!*) *adj* damned *ou* bloody (BRIT) stupid (*!*)

**concentrer** [kɔ̃sɑ̃tʀe] *vt* to concentrate; **se concentrer** *vi* to concentrate

**concerner** [kɔ̃sɛʀne] *vt* to concern; **en ce qui me concerne** as far as I am concerned

**concert** [kɔ̃sɛʀ] *nm* concert; **de ~** (*décider*) unanimously

**concessionnaire** [kɔ̃sesjɔnɛʀ] *nm/f* agent, dealer

**concevoir** [kɔ̃s(ə)vwaʀ] *vt* (*idée, projet*) to conceive (of); (*comprendre*) to understand; (*enfant*) to conceive; **bien/mal conçu** well-/badly-designed

**concierge** [kɔ̃sjɛʀʒ] *nm/f* caretaker

**concis, e** [kɔ̃si, iz] *adj* concise

**conclure** [kɔ̃klyʀ] *vt* to conclude; **conclusion** *nf* conclusion

**conçois** *etc* [kɔ̃swa] *vb voir* **concevoir**

**concombre** [kɔ̃kɔ̃bʀ] *nm* cucumber

**concours** [kɔ̃kuʀ] *nm* competition; (*Scol*) competitive examination; (*assistance*) aid, help; **concours de circonstances** combination of circumstances; **concours hippique** horse show

**concret, -ète** [kɔ̃kʀɛ, ɛt] *adj* concrete

**conçu, e** [kɔ̃sy] *pp de* **concevoir**

**concubinage** [kɔ̃kybinaʒ] *nm* (*Jur*) cohabitation

**concurrence** [kɔ̃kyʀɑ̃s] *nf* competition; **faire ~ à** to be in competition with; **jusqu'à ~ de** up to

**concurrent, e** [kɔ̃kyʀɑ̃, ɑ̃t] *nm/f* (*Sport, Écon etc*) competitor; (*Scol*) candidate

**condamner** [kɔ̃dane] *vt* (*blâmer*) to condemn; (*Jur*) to sentence; (*porte,*

*ouverture*) to fill in, block up; **~ qn à 2 ans de prison** to sentence sb to 2 years' imprisonment

**condensation** [kɔ̃dɑ̃sasjɔ̃] *nf* condensation

**condition** [kɔ̃disjɔ̃] *nf* condition; **conditions** *nfpl* (*tarif, prix*) terms; (*circonstances*) conditions; **sans ~s** unconditionally; **à ~ de ou que** provided that; **conditionnel, le** *nm* conditional (tense)

**conditionnement** [kɔ̃disjɔnmɑ̃] *nm* (*emballage*) packaging

**condoléances** [kɔ̃dɔleɑ̃s] *nfpl* condolences

**conducteur, -trice** [kɔ̃dyktœʀ, tʀis] *nm/f* driver ▷ *nm* (*Élec etc*) conductor

**conduire** [kɔ̃dɥiʀ] *vt* to drive; (*délégation, troupeau*) to lead; **se conduire** *vi* to behave; **~ à** to lead to; **~ qn quelque part** to take sb somewhere; to drive sb somewhere

**conduite** [kɔ̃dɥit] *nf* (*comportement*) behaviour; (*d'eau, de gaz*) pipe; **sous la ~ de** led by

**confection** [kɔ̃fɛksjɔ̃] *nf* (*fabrication*) making; (*Couture*): **la ~** the clothing industry

**conférence** [kɔ̃feʀɑ̃s] *nf* conference; (*exposé*) lecture; **conférence de presse** press conference

**confesser** [kɔ̃fese] *vt* to confess; **confession** *nf* confession; (*culte: catholique etc*) denomination

**confetti** [kɔ̃feti] *nm* confetti *no pl*

**confiance** [kɔ̃fjɑ̃s] *nf* (*en l'honnêteté de qn*) confidence, trust; (*en la valeur de qch*) faith; **avoir ~ en** to have confidence *ou* faith in, trust; **faire ~ à qn** to trust sb; **mettre qn en ~** to win sb's trust; **confiance en soi** self-confidence

**confiant, e** [kɔ̃fjɑ̃, jɑ̃t] *adj* confident; trusting

**confidence** [kɔ̃fidɑ̃s] *nf* confidence; **confidentiel, le** *adj* confidential

**confier** [kɔ̃fje] *vt*: **~ à qn** (*objet, travail*) to entrust sb; (*secret, pensée*) to confide to sb; **se ~ à qn** to confide in sb

**confirmation** [kɔ̃fiʀmasjɔ̃] nf
confirmation

**confirmer** [kɔ̃fiʀme] vt to confirm

**confiserie** [kɔ̃fizʀi] nf (magasin)
confectioner's ou sweet shop;
**confiseries** nfpl (bonbons)
confectionery sg

**confisquer** [kɔ̃fiske] vt to confiscate

**confit, e** [kɔ̃fi, it] adj: **fruits ~s**
crystallized fruits; **confit d'oie** nm
conserve of goose

**confiture** [kɔ̃fityʀ] nf jam

**conflit** [kɔ̃fli] nm conflict

**confondre** [kɔ̃fɔ̃dʀ] vt (jumeaux, faits)
to confuse, mix up; (témoin, menteur) to
confound; **se confondre** vi to merge;
**se ~ en excuses** to apologize profusely

**conforme** [kɔ̃fɔʀm] adj: **~ à** (loi, règle)
in accordance with; **conformément**
adv: **conformément à** in accordance
with; **conformer** vt: **se conformer à**
to conform to

**confort** [kɔ̃fɔʀ] nm comfort; **tout ~**
(Comm) with all modern conveniences;
**confortable** adj comfortable

**confronter** [kɔ̃fʀɔ̃te] vt to confront

**confus, e** [kɔ̃fy, yz] adj (vague)
confused; (embarrassé) embarrassed;
**confusion** nf (voir confus) confusion;
embarrassment; (voir confondre)
confusion, mixing up

**congé** [kɔ̃ʒe] nm (vacances) holiday; **en**
**~** on holiday; **semaine/jour de ~** week/
day off; **prendre ~ de qn** to take one's
leave of sb; **donner son ~ à** to give in
one's notice to; **congé de maladie** sick
leave; **congé de maternité** maternity
leave; **congés payés** paid holiday

**congédier** [kɔ̃ʒedje] vt to dismiss

**congélateur** [kɔ̃ʒelatœʀ] nm freezer

**congeler** [kɔ̃ʒ(ə)le] vt to freeze; **les**
**produits congelés** frozen foods

**congestion** [kɔ̃ʒɛstjɔ̃] nf congestion

**Congo** [kɔ̃o] nm: **le ~** Congo, the
Democratic Republic of the Congo

**congrès** [kɔ̃gʀɛ] nm congress

**conifère** [kɔnifɛʀ] nm conifer

**conjoint, e** [kɔ̃ʒwɛ̃, wɛ̃t] adj joint
▷ nm/f spouse

**conjonctivite** [kɔ̃ʒɔ̃ktivit] nf
conjunctivitis

**conjoncture** [kɔ̃ʒɔ̃ktyʀ] nf
circumstances pl; **la ~ actuelle** the
present (economic) situation

**conjugaison** [kɔ̃ʒygɛzɔ̃] nf (Ling)
conjugation

**connaissance** [kɔnɛsɑ̃s] nf (savoir)
knowledge no pl; (personne connue)
acquaintance; **être sans ~** to be
unconscious; **perdre/reprendre ~** to
lose/regain consciousness; **à ma/sa**
**~** to (the best of) my/his knowledge;
**faire la ~ de qn** to meet sb

**connaisseur, -euse** [kɔnɛsœʀ, øz]
nm/f connoisseur

**connaître** [kɔnɛtʀ] vt to know;
(éprouver) to experience; (avoir: succès)
to have, enjoy; **~ de nom/vue** to know
by name/sight; **ils se sont connus à**
**Genève** they (first) met in Geneva; **s'y**
**~ en qch** to know a lot about sth

**connecter** [kɔnɛkte] vt to connect; **se**
**~ à Internet** to log onto the Internet

**connerie** [kɔnʀi] (fam!) nf stupid thing
(to do/say)

**connexion** [kɔnɛksjɔ̃] nf connection

**connu, e** [kɔny] adj (célèbre) well-
known

**conquérir** [kɔ̃keʀiʀ] vt to conquer;
**conquête** nf conquest

**consacrer** [kɔ̃sakʀe] vt (employer) to
devote, dedicate; (Rel) to consecrate; **se**
**~ à qch** to dedicate ou devote o.s. to sth

**conscience** [kɔ̃sjɑ̃s] nf conscience;
**avoir/prendre ~ de** to be/become
aware of; **perdre ~** to lose
consciousness; **avoir bonne/**
**mauvaise ~** to have a clear/guilty
conscience; **consciencieux, -euse**
adj conscientious; **conscient, e** adj
conscious

**consécutif, -ive** [kɔ̃sekytif, iv] adj
consecutive; **~ à** following upon

**conseil** [kɔ̃sɛj] nm (avis) piece of
advice; (assemblée) council; **des ~s**

advice; **prendre ~ (auprès de qn)**
to take advice (from sb); **conseil
d'administration** board (of directors);
**conseil des ministres** ≈ the Cabinet;
**conseil municipal** town council

**conseiller, -ère** [kɔ̃seje, ɛʀ]
*nm/f* adviser ▷ *vt* (*personne*) to advise;
(*méthode, action*) to recommend, advise;
**~ à qn de** to advise sb to; **pouvez-vous
me ~ un bon restaurant?** can you
suggest a good restaurant?

**consentement** [kɔ̃sɑ̃tmɑ̃] *nm*
consent

**consentir** [kɔ̃sɑ̃tiʀ] *vt* to agree,
consent

**conséquence** [kɔ̃sekɑ̃s] *nf*
consequence; **en ~** (*donc*) consequently;
(*de façon appropriée*) accordingly;
**conséquent, e** *adj* logical, rational;
(*fam: important*) substantial; **par
conséquent** consequently

**conservateur, -trice** [kɔ̃sɛʀvatœʀ,
tʀis] *nm/f* (*Pol*) conservative; (*de
musée*) curator ▷ *nm* (*pour aliments*)
preservative

**conservatoire** [kɔ̃sɛʀvatwaʀ] *nm*
academy

**conserve** [kɔ̃sɛʀv] *nf* (*gén pl*) canned
*ou* tinned (*BRIT*) food; **en ~** canned,
tinned (*BRIT*)

**conserver** [kɔ̃sɛʀve] *vt* (*faculté*) to
retain, keep; (*amis, livres*) to keep;
(*préserver, Culin*) to preserve

**considérable** [kɔ̃sideʀabl] *adj*
considerable, significant, extensive

**considération** [kɔ̃sideʀasjɔ̃] *nf*
consideration; (*estime*) esteem

**considérer** [kɔ̃sideʀe] *vt* to consider; **~
qch comme** to regard sth as

**consigne** [kɔ̃siɲ] *nf* (*de gare*) left
luggage (office) (*BRIT*), checkroom
(*US*); (*ordre, instruction*) instructions *pl*;
**consigne automatique** left-luggage
locker

**consister** [kɔ̃siste] *vi*: **~ en/à faire** to
consist of/in doing

**consoler** [kɔ̃sɔle] *vt* to console

**consommateur, -trice** [kɔ̃sɔmatœʀ,

tʀis] *nm/f* (*Écon*) consumer; (*dans un
café*) customer

**consommation** [kɔ̃sɔmasjɔ̃] *nf*
(*boisson*) drink; (*Écon*) consumption; **de
~** (*biens, sociétés*) consumer *cpd*

**consommer** [kɔ̃sɔme] *vt* (*suj: personne*)
to eat *ou* drink, consume; (*: voiture,
machine*) to use, consume; (*mariage*)
to consummate ▷ *vi* (*dans un café*) to
(have a) drink

**consonne** [kɔ̃sɔn] *nf* consonant

**constamment** [kɔ̃stamɑ̃] *adv*
constantly

**constant, e** [kɔ̃stɑ̃, ɑ̃t] *adj* constant;
(*personne*) steadfast

**constat** [kɔ̃sta] *nm* (*de police, d'accident*)
report; **~ (à l')amiable** *jointly-agreed
statement for insurance purposes*; **~
d'échec** acknowledgement of failure

**constatation** [kɔ̃statasjɔ̃] *nf*
(*observation*) (observed) fact,
observation

**constater** [kɔ̃state] *vt* (*remarquer*) to
note; (*Admin, Jur: attester*) to certify

**consterner** [kɔ̃stɛʀne] *vt* to dismay

**constipé, e** [kɔ̃stipe] *adj* constipated

**constitué, e** [kɔ̃stitɥe] *adj*: **~ de** made
up *ou* composed of

**constituer** [kɔ̃stitɥe] *vt* (*équipe*)
to set up; (*dossier, collection*) to put
together; (*suj: éléments: composer*)
to make up, constitute; (*représenter,
être*) to constitute; **se ~ prisonnier** to
give o.s. up

**constructeur, -trice** [kɔ̃stʀyktœʀ,
tʀis] *nm/f* manufacturer, builder

**constructif, -ive** [kɔ̃stʀyktif, iv] *adj*
constructive

**construction** [kɔ̃stʀyksjɔ̃] *nf*
construction, building

**construire** [kɔ̃stʀɥiʀ] *vt* to build,
construct

**consul** [kɔ̃syl] *nm* consul; **consulat**
*nm* consulate

**consultant** [kɔ̃syltɑ̃] *adj, nm*
consultant

**consultation** [kɔ̃syltasjɔ̃] *nf*
consultation; **heures de ~** (*Méd*)

surgery (BRIT) ou office (US) hours

**consulter** [kɔ̃sylte] vt to consult ▷ vi (médecin) to hold surgery (BRIT), be in (the office) (US)

**contact** [kɔ̃takt] nm contact; **au ~ de** (air, peau) on contact with; (gens) through contact with; **mettre/couper le ~** (Auto) to switch on/off the ignition; **entrer en** ou **prendre ~ avec** to get in touch ou contact with; **contacter** vt to contact, get in touch with

**contagieux, -euse** [kɔ̃taʒjø, jøz] adj infectious; (par le contact) contagious

**contaminer** [kɔ̃tamine] vt to contaminate

**conte** [kɔ̃t] nm tale; **conte de fées** fairy tale

**contempler** [kɔ̃tɑ̃ple] vt to contemplate, gaze at

**contemporain, e** [kɔ̃tɑ̃pɔrɛ̃, ɛn] adj, nm/f contemporary

**contenir** [kɔ̃t(ə)nir] vt to contain; (avoir une capacité de) to hold

**content, e** [kɔ̃tɑ̃, ɑ̃t] adj pleased, glad; **~ de** pleased with; **contenter** vt to satisfy, please; **se contenter de** to content o.s. with

**contenu** [kɔ̃t(ə)ny] nm (d'un récipient) contents pl; (d'un texte) content

**conter** [kɔ̃te] vt to recount, relate

**conteste** [kɔ̃tɛst]: **sans ~** adv unquestionably, indisputably; **contester** vt to question ▷ vi (Pol, gén) rebel (against established authority)

**contexte** [kɔ̃tɛkst] nm context

**continent** [kɔ̃tinɑ̃] nm continent

**continu, e** [kɔ̃tiny] adj continuous; **faire la journée ~e** to work without taking a full lunch break; **(courant) continu** direct current, DC

**continuel, le** [kɔ̃tinɥɛl] adj (qui se répète) constant, continual; (continu) continuous

**continuer** [kɔ̃tinɥe] vt (travail, voyage etc) to continue (with), carry on (with), go on (with); (prolonger: alignement, rue) to continue ▷ vi (vie, bruit) to continue,

go on; **~ à** ou **de faire** to go on ou continue doing

**contourner** [kɔ̃turne] vt to go round; (difficulté) to get round

**contraceptif, -ive** [kɔ̃traseptif, iv] adj, nm contraceptive; **contraception** nf contraception

**contracté, e** [kɔ̃trakte] adj tense

**contracter** [kɔ̃trakte] vt (muscle etc) to tense, contract; (maladie, dette) to contract; (assurance) to take out; **se contracter** vi (muscles) to contract

**contractuel, le** [kɔ̃traktɥɛl] nm/f (agent) traffic warden

**contradiction** [kɔ̃tradiksjɔ̃] nf contradiction; **contradictoire** adj contradictory, conflicting

**contraignant, e** [kɔ̃trɛɲɑ̃, ɑ̃t] adj restricting

**contraindre** [kɔ̃trɛdr] vt: **~ qn à faire** to compel sb to do; **contrainte** nf constraint

**contraire** [kɔ̃trɛr] adj, nm opposite; **~ à** contrary to; **au ~** on the contrary

**contrarier** [kɔ̃trarje] vt (personne: irriter) to annoy; (fig: projets) to thwart, frustrate; **contrariété** nf annoyance

**contraste** [kɔ̃trast] nm contrast

**contrat** [kɔ̃tra] nm contract

**contravention** [kɔ̃travɑ̃sjɔ̃] nf parking ticket

**contre** [kɔ̃tr] prép against; (en échange) (in exchange) for; **par ~** on the other hand

**contrebande** [kɔ̃trəbɑ̃d] nf (trafic) contraband, smuggling; (marchandise) contraband, smuggled goods pl; **faire la ~ de** to smuggle

**contrebas** [kɔ̃trəba]: **en ~** adv (down) below

**contrebasse** [kɔ̃trəbas] nf (double) bass

**contre...**: **contrecoup** nm repercussions pl; **contredire** vt (personne) to contradict; (faits) to refute

**contrefaçon** [kɔ̃trəfasɔ̃] nf forgery

**contre...**: **contre-indication** (pl **contre-indications**) nf (Méd) contraindication; **"contre-indication en cas d'eczéma"** "should not be used by people with eczema"; **contre-indiqué, e** adj (Méd) contraindicated; (déconseillé) unadvisable, ill-advised

**contremaître** [kɔ̃trəmɛtr] nm foreman

**contre-plaqué** [kɔ̃trəplake] nm plywood

**contresens** [kɔ̃trəsɑ̃s] nm (erreur) misinterpretation; (de traduction) mistranslation; **à ~** the wrong way

**contretemps** [kɔ̃trətɑ̃] nm hitch; **à ~** (fig) at an inopportune moment

**contribuer** [kɔ̃tribɥe] : **~ à** vt to contribute towards; **contribution** nf contribution; **mettre à contribution** to call upon; **contributions directes/ indirectes** direct/indirect taxation

**contrôle** [kɔ̃trol] nm checking no pl, check; (des prix) monitoring, control; (test) test, examination; **perdre le ~ de** (véhicule) to lose control of; **contrôle continu** (Scol) continuous assessment; **contrôle d'identité** identity check

**contrôler** [kɔ̃trole] vt (vérifier) to check; (surveiller: opérations) to supervise; (: prix) to monitor, control; (maîtriser, Comm: firme) to control; **contrôleur, -euse** nm/f (de train) (ticket) inspector; (de bus) (bus) conductor(-tress)

**controversé, e** [kɔ̃trɔvɛrse] adj (personnage, question) controversial

**contusion** [kɔ̃tyzjɔ̃] nf bruise, contusion

**convaincre** [kɔ̃vɛ̃kr] vt: **~ qn (de qch)** to convince sb (of sth); **~ qn (de faire)** to persuade sb (to do)

**convalescence** [kɔ̃valesɑ̃s] nf convalescence

**convenable** [kɔ̃vnabl] adj suitable; (assez bon, respectable) decent

**convenir** [kɔ̃vnir] vi to be suitable; **~ à** to suit; **~ de** (bien-fondé de qch) to admit (to), acknowledge; (date, somme etc) to agree upon; **~ que** (admettre) to admit that; **~ de faire** to agree to do

**convention** [kɔ̃vɑ̃sjɔ̃] nf convention; **conventions** nfpl (convenances) convention sg; **convention collective** (Écon) collective agreement; **conventionné, e** adj (Admin) applying charges laid down by the state

**convenu, e** [kɔ̃vny] pp de **convenir** ▷ adj agreed

**conversation** [kɔ̃vɛrsasjɔ̃] nf conversation

**convertir** [kɔ̃vɛrtir] vt: **~ qn (à)** to convert sb (to); **se convertir (à)** to be converted (to); **~ qch en** to convert sth into

**conviction** [kɔ̃viksjɔ̃] nf conviction

**convienne** etc [kɔ̃vjɛn] vb voir **convenir**

**convivial, e, -aux** [kɔ̃vivjal, jo] adj (Inform) user-friendly

**convocation** [kɔ̃vɔkasjɔ̃] nf (document) notification to attend; (: Jur) summons sg

**convoquer** [kɔ̃vɔke] vt (assemblée) to convene; (subordonné) to summon; (candidat) to ask to attend

**coopération** [kɔɔperasjɔ̃] nf co-operation; (Admin): **la C~** ≈ Voluntary Service Overseas (BRIT), ≈ Peace Corps (US)

**coopérer** [kɔɔpere] vi: **~ (à)** to co-operate (in)

**coordonné, e** [kɔɔrdɔne] adj coordinated; **coordonnées** nfpl (adresse etc) address and telephone number

**coordonner** [kɔɔrdɔne] vt to coordinate

**copain** [kɔpɛ̃] (fam) nm mate, pal; (petit ami) boyfriend

**copie** [kɔpi] nf copy; (Scol) script, paper; **copier** vt, vi to copy; **copier coller** (Comput) copy and paste; **copier sur** to copy from; **copieur** nm (photo)copier

**copieux, -euse** [kɔpjø, jøz] adj copious

**copine** [kɔpin] (fam) nf mate, pal; (petite amie) girlfriend

**coq** [kɔk] nm cock, rooster

**coque** [kɔk] nf (de noix, mollusque) shell; (de bateau) hull; **à la ~** (Culin) (soft-)boiled

**coquelicot** [kɔkliko] nm poppy

**coqueluche** [kɔklyʃ] nf whooping-cough

**coquet, te** [kɔkɛ, ɛt] adj appearance-conscious; (logement) smart, charming

**coquetier** [kɔk(ə)tje] nm egg-cup

**coquillage** [kɔkijaʒ] nm (mollusque) shellfish inv; (coquille) shell

**coquille** [kɔkij] nf shell; (Typo) misprint; **coquille St Jacques** scallop

**coquin, e** [kɔkɛ̃, in] adj mischievous, roguish; (polisson) naughty

**cor** [kɔr] nm (Mus) horn; (Méd): **~ (au pied)** corn

**corail, -aux** [kɔraj, o] nm coral no pl

**Coran** [kɔrɑ̃] nm: **le ~** the Koran

**corbeau, x** [kɔrbo] nm crow

**corbeille** [kɔrbɛj] nf basket; **corbeille à papier** waste paper basket ou bin

**corde** [kɔrd] nf rope; (de violon, raquette) string; **usé jusqu'à la ~** threadbare; **corde à linge** washing ou clothes line; **corde à sauter** skipping rope; **cordes vocales** vocal cords; **cordée** nf (d'alpinistes) rope, roped party

**cordialement** [kɔrdjalmɑ̃] adv (formule épistolaire) (kind) regards

**cordon** [kɔrdɔ̃] nm cord, string; **cordon de police** police cordon; **cordon ombilical** umbilical cord

**cordonnerie** [kɔrdɔnri] nf shoe repairer's (shop); **cordonnier** nm shoe repairer

**Corée** [kɔre] nf: **la ~ du Sud/du Nord** South/North Korea

**coriace** [kɔrjas] adj tough

**corne** [kɔrn] nf horn; (de cerf) antler

**cornée** [kɔrne] nf cornea

**corneille** [kɔrnɛj] nf crow

**cornemuse** [kɔrnəmyz] nf bagpipes pl

**cornet** [kɔrnɛ] nm (paper) cone; (de glace) cornet, cone

**corniche** [kɔrniʃ] nf (route) coast road

**cornichon** [kɔrniʃɔ̃] nm gherkin

**Cornouailles** [kɔrnwaj] nf Cornwall

**corporel, le** [kɔrpɔrɛl] adj bodily; (punition) corporal

**corps** [kɔr] nm body; **à ~ perdu** headlong; **prendre ~** to take shape; **corps électoral** the electorate; **corps enseignant** the teaching profession

**correct, e** [kɔrɛkt] adj correct; (fam: acceptable: salaire, hôtel) reasonable, decent; **correcteur, -trice** nm/f (Scol) examiner; **correction** nf (voir corriger) correction; (voir correct) correctness; (coups) thrashing

**correspondance** [kɔrɛspɔ̃dɑ̃s] nf correspondence; (de train, d'avion) connection; **cours par ~** correspondence course; **vente par ~** mail-order business

**correspondant, e** [kɔrɛspɔ̃dɑ̃, ɑ̃t] nm/f correspondent; (Tél) person phoning (ou being phoned)

**correspondre** [kɔrɛspɔ̃dr] vi to correspond, tally; **~ à** to correspond to; **~ avec qn** to correspond with sb

**corrida** [kɔrida] nf bullfight

**corridor** [kɔridɔr] nm corridor

**corrigé** [kɔriʒe] nm (Scol: d'exercice) correct version

**corriger** [kɔriʒe] vt (devoir) to correct; (punir) to thrash; **~ qn de** (défaut) to cure sb of

**corrompre** [kɔrɔ̃pr] vt to corrupt; (acheter: témoin etc) to bribe

**corruption** [kɔrypsjɔ̃] nf corruption; (de témoins) bribery

**corse** [kɔrs] adj, nm/f Corsican ▷ nf: **la C~** Corsica

**corsé, e** [kɔrse] adj (café) full-flavoured; (sauce) spicy; (problème) tough

**cortège** [kɔrtɛʒ] nm procession

**cortisone** [kɔrtizɔn] nf cortisone

**corvée** [kɔrve] nf chore, drudgery no pl

**cosmétique** [kɔsmetik] nm beauty care product

**cosmopolite** [kɔsmɔpɔlit] adj cosmopolitan

**costaud, e** [kɔsto, od] (fam) adj strong, sturdy

**costume** [kɔstym] *nm* (*d'homme*) suit; (*de théâtre*) costume; **costumé, e** *adj* dressed up; **bal costumé** fancy dress ball

**cote** [kɔt] *nf* (*en Bourse*) quotation; **cote d'alerte** danger *ou* flood level; **cote de popularité** (popularity) rating

**côte** [kot] *nf* (*rivage*) coast(line); (*pente*) hill; (*Anat*) rib; (*d'un tricot, tissu*) rib, ribbing *no pl*; **~ à ~** side by side; **la Côte (d'Azur)** the (French) Riviera

**côté** [kote] *nm* (*gén*) side; (*direction*) way, direction; **de chaque ~ (de)** on each side (of); **de tous les ~s** from all directions; **de quel ~ est-il parti?** which way did he go?; **de ce/de l'autre ~** this/the other way; **du ~ de** (*provenance*) from; (*direction*) towards; (*proximité*) near; **de ~** (*regarder*) sideways; **mettre qch de ~** to put sth aside; **mettre de l'argent de ~** to save some money; **à ~** (right) nearby; (*voisins*) next door; **à ~ de** beside, next to; (*en comparaison*) compared to; **être aux ~s de** to be by the side of

**Côte d'Ivoire** [kotdivwaʀ] *nf*: **la Côte d'Ivoire** Côte d'Ivoire, the Ivory Coast

**côtelette** [kotlɛt] *nf* chop

**côtier, -ière** [kotje, jɛʀ] *adj* coastal

**cotisation** [kɔtizasjɔ̃] *nf* subscription, dues *pl*; (*pour une pension*) contributions *pl*

**cotiser** [kɔtize] *vi*: **~ (à)** to pay contributions (to); **se cotiser** *vi* to club together

**coton** [kɔtɔ̃] *nm* cotton; **coton hydrophile** cotton wool (BRIT), absorbent cotton (US); **Coton-tige®** *nm* cotton bud

**cou** [ku] *nm* neck

**couchant** [kuʃɑ̃] *adj*: **soleil ~** setting sun

**couche** [kuʃ] *nf* layer; (*de peinture, vernis*) coat; (*de bébé*) nappy (BRIT), diaper (US); **couches sociales** social levels *ou* strata

**couché, e** [kuʃe] *adj* lying down; (*au lit*) in bed

**coucher** [kuʃe] *vt* (*personne*) to put to bed; (: *loger*) to put up; (*objet*) to lay on its side ▷ *vi* to sleep; **~ avec qn** to sleep with sb; **se coucher** *vi* (*pour dormir*) to go to bed; (*pour se reposer*) to lie down; (*soleil*) to set; **coucher de soleil** sunset

**couchette** [kuʃɛt] *nf* couchette; (*pour voyageur, sur bateau*) berth

**coucou** [kuku] *nm* cuckoo

**coude** [kud] *nm* (*Anat*) elbow; (*de tuyau, de la route*) bend; **~ à ~** shoulder to shoulder, side by side

**coudre** [kudʀ] *vt* (*bouton*) to sew on ▷ *vi* to sew

**couette** [kwɛt] *nf* duvet, quilt; **couettes** *nfpl* (*cheveux*) bunches

**couffin** [kufɛ̃] *nm* Moses basket

**couler** [kule] *vi* to flow, run; (*fuir: stylo, récipient*) to leak; (*nez*) to run; (*sombrer: bateau*) to sink ▷ *vt* (*cloche, sculpture*) to cast; (*bateau*) to sink; (*faire échouer: personne*) to bring down

**couleur** [kulœʀ] *nf* colour (BRIT), color (US); (*Cartes*) suit; **film/télévision en ~s** colo(u)r film/television; **de ~** (*homme, femme: vieilli*) colo(u)red

**couleuvre** [kulœvʀ] *nf* grass snake

**coulisses** [kulis] *nfpl* (*Théâtre*) wings; (*fig*): **dans les ~** behind the scenes

**couloir** [kulwaʀ] *nm* corridor, passage; (*d'avion*) aisle; (*de bus*) gangway; **~ aérien/de navigation** air/shipping lane

**coup** [ku] *nm* (*heurt, choc*) knock; (*affectif*) blow, shock; (*agressif*) blow; (*avec arme à feu*) shot; (*de l'horloge*) stroke; (*tennis, golf*) stroke; (*boxe*) blow; (*fam: fois*) time; **donner un ~ de balai** to give the floor a sweep; **boire un ~** (*fam*) to have a drink; **être dans le ~** (*impliqué*) to be in on it; (*à la page*) to be hip *ou* trendy; **du ~ ...** as a result; **d'un seul ~** (*subitement*) suddenly; (*à la fois*) at one go; **du premier ~** first time; **du même ~** at the same time; **à tous les ~s** (*fam*) every time; **tenir le ~** to hold out; **après ~** afterwards; **à ~ sûr** definitely, without fail; **~ sur** in

quick succession; **sur le ~** outright;
**sous le ~ de** (*surprise etc*) under the
influence of; **coup de chance** stroke
of luck; **coup de coude** nudge (with
the elbow); **coup de couteau** stab (of
a knife); **coup d'envoi** kick-off; **coup
d'essai** first attempt; **coup d'État**
coup; **coup de feu** shot; **coup de filet**
(*Police*) haul; **coup de foudre** (*fig*) love
at first sight; **coup de frein** (sharp)
braking *no pl*; **coup de grâce** coup
de grâce, death blow; **coup de main:
donner un coup de main à qn** to give
sb a (helping) hand; **coup d'œil** glance;
**coup de pied** kick; **coup de poing**
punch; **coup de soleil** sunburn *no pl*;
**coup de sonnette** ring of the bell;
**coup de téléphone** phone call; **coup
de tête** (*fig*) (sudden) impulse; **coup de
théâtre** (*fig*) dramatic turn of events;
**coup de tonnerre** clap of thunder;
**coup de vent** gust of wind; **en coup
de vent** (*rapidement*) in a tearing hurry;
**coup franc** free kick

**coupable** [kupabl] *adj* guilty ▷ *nm/f*
(*gén*) culprit; (*Jur*) guilty party

**coupe** [kup] *nf* (*verre*) goblet; (*à
fruits*) dish; (*Sport*) cup; (*de cheveux, de
vêtement*) cut; (*graphique, plan*) (cross)
section

**couper** [kupe] *vt* to cut; (*retrancher*)
to cut (out); (*route, courant*) to cut off;
(*appétit*) to take away; (*vin à table*) to
dilute ▷ *vi* to cut; (*prendre un raccourci*)
to take a short-cut; **se couper** *vi* (*se
blesser*) to cut o.s.; **~ la parole à qn** to
cut sb short; **nous avons été coupés**
we've been cut off

**couple** [kupl] *nm* couple

**couplet** [kuplɛ] *nm* verse

**coupole** [kupɔl] *nf* dome

**coupon** [kupɔ̃] *nm* (*ticket*) coupon;
(*reste de tissu*) remnant

**coupure** [kupyʀ] *nf* cut; (*billet de
banque*) note; (*de journal*) cutting;
**coupure de courant** power cut

**cour** [kuʀ] *nf* (*de ferme, jardin*)
(court)yard; (*d'immeuble*) back yard; (*Jur,

*royale*) court; **faire la ~ à qn** to court sb;
**cour d'assises** court of assizes; **cour
de récréation** playground

**courage** [kuʀaʒ] *nm* courage,
bravery; **courageux, -euse** *adj* brave,
courageous

**couramment** [kuʀamɑ̃] *adv*
commonly; (*parler*) fluently

**courant, e** [kuʀɑ̃, ɑ̃t] *adj* (*fréquent*)
common; (*Comm, gén: normal*) standard;
(*en cours*) current ▷ *nm* current; (*fig*)
movement; **être
au ~ (de)** (*fait, nouvelle*) to know
(about); **mettre qn au ~ (de)** to tell sb
(about); (*nouveau travail etc*) to teach
sb the basics (of); **se tenir au ~ (de)**
(*techniques etc*) to keep o.s. up-to-date
(on); **dans le ~ de** (*pendant*) in the
course of; **le 10 ~** (*Comm*) the 10th
inst.; **courant d'air** draught; **courant
électrique** (electric) current, power

**courbature** [kuʀbatyʀ] *nf* ache

**courbe** [kuʀb] *adj* curved ▷ *nf* curve

**coureur, -euse** [kuʀœʀ, øz]
*nm/f* (*Sport*) runner (*ou* driver); (*péj*)
womanizer; manhunter

**courge** [kuʀʒ] *nf* (*Culin*) marrow;
**courgette** *nf* courgette (BRIT),
zucchini (US)

**courir** [kuʀiʀ] *vi* to run ▷ *vt* (*Sport:
épreuve*) to compete in; (*risque*) to run;
(*danger*) to face; **~ les magasins** to go
round the shops; **le bruit court que** the
rumour is going round that

**couronne** [kuʀɔn] *nf* crown; (*de fleurs*)
wreath, circlet

**courons** *etc* [kuʀɔ̃] *vb voir* **courir**

**courriel** [kuʀjɛl] *nm* e-mail

**courrier** [kuʀje] *nm* mail, post; (*lettres
à écrire*) letters *pl*; **est-ce que j'ai du ~?**
are there any letters for me?; **courrier
électronique** e-mail

▌ Attention à ne pas traduire *courrier*
par le mot anglais *courier*.

**courroie** [kuʀwa] *nf* strap; (*Tech*) belt

**courrons** *etc* [kuʀɔ̃] *vb voir* **courir**

**cours** [kuʀ] *nm* (*leçon*) class;
(*: particulier*) lesson; (*série de leçons,

*cheminement*) course; (*écoulement*) flow; (*Comm: de devises*) rate; (: *de denrées*) price; **donner libre ~ à** to give free expression to; **avoir ~** (*Scol*) to have a class *ou* lecture; **en ~** (*année*) current; (*travaux*) in progress; **en ~ de route** on the way; **au ~ de** in the course of, during; **le ~ de change** the exchange rate; **cours d'eau** waterway; **cours du soir** night school

**course** [kuRs] *nf* running; (*Sport: épreuve*) race; (*d'un taxi*) journey, trip; (*commission*) errand; **courses** *nfpl* (*achats*) shopping *sg*; **faire des ~s** to do some shopping

**court, e** [kuR, kuRt(ə)] *adj* short ▷ *adv* short ▷ *nm*: **~ (de tennis)** (tennis) court; **à ~ de** short of; **prendre qn de ~** to catch sb unawares; **court-circuit** *nm* short-circuit

**courtoisie** [kuRtwazi] *nf* courtesy

**couru, e** [kuRy] *pp de* **courir**

**cousais** *etc* [kuzɛ] *vb voir* **coudre**

**couscous** [kuskus] *nm* couscous

**cousin, e** [kuzɛ̃, in] *nm/f* cousin

**coussin** [kusɛ̃] *nm* cushion

**cousu, e** [kuzy] *pp de* **coudre**

**coût** [ku] *nm* cost; **le ~ de la vie** the cost of living

**couteau, x** [kuto] *nm* knife

**coûter** [kute] *vt, vi* to cost; **combien ça coûte?** how much is it?, what does it cost?; **ça coûte trop cher** it's too expensive; **coûte que coûte** at all costs; **coûteux, -euse** *adj* costly, expensive

**coutume** [kutym] *nf* custom

**couture** [kutyR] *nf* sewing; (*profession*) dressmaking; (*points*) seam; **couturier** *nm* fashion designer; **couturière** *nf* dressmaker

**couvent** [kuvã] *nm* (*de sœurs*) convent; (*de frères*) monastery

**couver** [kuve] *vt* to hatch; (*maladie*) to be coming down with ▷ *vi* (*feu*) to smoulder; (*révolte*) to be brewing

**couvercle** [kuvɛRkl] *nm* lid; (*de bombe aérosol etc, qui se visse*) cap, top

**couvert, e** [kuvɛR, ɛRt] *pp de* **couvrir** ▷ *adj* (*ciel*) overcast ▷ *nm* place setting; (*place à table*) place; **couverts** *nmpl* (*ustensiles*) cutlery *sg*; **~ de** covered with *ou* in; **mettre le ~** to lay the table

**couverture** [kuvɛRtyR] *nf* blanket; (*de livre, assurance, fig*) cover; (*presse*) coverage

**couvre-lit** [kuvRəli] *nm* bedspread

**couvrir** [kuvRiR] *vt* to cover; **se couvrir** *vi* (*s'habiller*) to cover up; (*se coiffer*) to put on one's hat; (*ciel*) to cloud over

**cow-boy** [koboj] *nm* cowboy

**crabe** [kRab] *nm* crab

**cracher** [kRaʃe] *vi, vt* to spit

**crachin** [kRaʃɛ̃] *nm* drizzle

**craie** [kRɛ] *nf* chalk

**craindre** [kRɛ̃dR] *vt* to fear, be afraid of; (*être sensible à: chaleur, froid*) to be easily damaged by

**crainte** [kRɛ̃t] *nf* fear; **de ~ de/que** for fear of/that; **craintif, -ive** *adj* timid

**crampe** [kRãp] *nf* cramp; **j'ai une ~ à la jambe** I've got cramp in my leg

**cramponner** [kRãpɔne] *vb*: **se ~ (à)** to hang *ou* cling on (to)

**cran** [kRã] *nm* (*entaille*) notch; (*de courroie*) hole; (*fam: courage*) guts *pl*

**crâne** [kRɑn] *nm* skull

**crapaud** [kRapo] *nm* toad

**craquement** [kRakmã] *nm* crack, snap; (*du plancher*) creak, creaking *no pl*

**craquer** [kRake] *vi* (*bois, plancher*) to creak; (*fil, branche*) to snap; (*couture*) to come apart; (*fig: accusé*) to break down; (: *fam*) to crack up ▷ *vt* (*allumette*) to strike; **j'ai craqué** (*fam*) I couldn't resist it

**crasse** [kRas] *nf* grime, filth; **crasseux, -euse** *adj* grimy, filthy

**cravache** [kRavaʃ] *nf* (riding) crop

**cravate** [kRavat] *nf* tie

**crawl** [kRol] *nm* crawl; **dos ~é** backstroke

**crayon** [kRɛjõ] *nm* pencil; **crayon à bille** ball-point pen; **crayon de couleur** crayon, colouring pencil; **crayon-feutre** (*pl* **crayons-feutres**) *nm* felt(-tip) pen

**création** [kʀeasjɔ̃] *nf* creation

**crèche** [kʀɛʃ] *nf* (*de Noël*) crib; (*garderie*) crèche, day nursery

**crédit** [kʀedi] *nm* (*gén*) credit; **crédits** *nmpl* (*fonds*) funds; **payer/acheter à ~** to pay/buy on credit *ou* on easy terms; **faire ~ à qn** to give sb credit; **créditer** *vt*: **créditer un compte (de)** to credit an account (with)

**créer** [kʀee] *vt* to create

**crémaillère** [kʀemajɛʀ] *nf*: **pendre la ~** to have a house-warming party

**crème** [kʀɛm] *nf* cream; (*entremets*) cream dessert ▷ *adj inv* cream(-coloured); **un (café) ~** ≈ a white coffee; **crème anglaise** (egg) custard; **crème Chantilly** whipped cream; **crème à raser** shaving cream; **crème solaire** suntan lotion

**créneau, x** [kʀeno] *nm* (*de fortification*) crenel(le); (*dans marché*) gap, niche; (*Auto*): **faire un ~** to reverse into a parking space (*between two cars alongside the kerb*)

**crêpe** [kʀɛp] *nf* (*galette*) pancake ▷ *nm* (*tissu*) crêpe; **crêperie** *nf* pancake shop *ou* restaurant

**crépuscule** [kʀepyskyl] *nm* twilight, dusk

**cresson** [kʀesɔ̃] *nm* watercress

**creuser** [kʀøze] *vt* (*trou, tunnel*) to dig; (*sol*) to dig a hole in; (*fig*) to go (deeply) into; **ça creuse** that gives you a real appetite; **se ~ la cervelle** (*fam*) to rack one's brains

**creux, -euse** [kʀø, kʀøz] *adj* hollow ▷ *nm* hollow; **heures creuses** slack periods; (*électricité, téléphone*) off-peak periods; **avoir un ~** (*fam*) to be hungry

**crevaison** [kʀəvɛzɔ̃] *nf* puncture

**crevé, e** [kʀəve] (*fam*) *adj* (*fatigué*) shattered (BRIT), exhausted

**crever** [kʀəve] *vt* (*ballon*) to burst ▷ *vi* (*pneu*) to burst; (*automobiliste*) to have a puncture (BRIT) *ou* a flat (tire) (US); (*fam*) to die

**crevette** [kʀəvɛt] *nf*: **~ (rose)** prawn;

**~ grise** shrimp

**cri** [kʀi] *nm* cry, shout; (*d'animal: spécifique*) cry, call; **c'est le dernier ~** (*fig*) it's the latest fashion

**criard, e** [kʀijaʀ, kʀijaʀd] *adj* (*couleur*) garish, loud; (*voix*) yelling

**cric** [kʀik] *nm* (*Auto*) jack

**crier** [kʀije] *vi* (*pour appeler*) to shout, cry (out); (*de douleur etc*) to scream, yell ▷ *vt* (*injure*) to shout (out), yell (out)

**crime** [kʀim] *nm* crime; (*meurtre*) murder; **criminel, le** *nm/f* criminal; (*assassin*) murderer

**crin** [kʀɛ̃] *nm* (*de cheval*) hair *no pl*

**crinière** [kʀinjɛʀ] *nf* mane

**crique** [kʀik] *nf* creek, inlet

**criquet** [kʀikɛ] *nm* grasshopper

**crise** [kʀiz] *nf* crisis; (*Méd*) attack; (: *d'épilepsie*) fit; **piquer une ~ de nerfs** to go hysterical; **crise cardiaque** heart attack; **crise de foie**: **avoir une crise de foie** to have really bad indigestion

**cristal, -aux** [kʀistal, o] *nm* crystal

**critère** [kʀitɛʀ] *nm* criterion

**critiquable** [kʀitikabl] *adj* open to criticism

**critique** [kʀitik] *adj* critical ▷ *nm/f* (*de théâtre, musique*) critic ▷ *nf* criticism; (*Théâtre etc*: *article*) review

**critiquer** [kʀitike] *vt* (*dénigrer*) to criticize; (*évaluer*) to assess, examine (critically)

**croate** [kʀɔat] *adj* Croatian ▷ *nm/f*: **C~** Croat, Croatian

**Croatie** [kʀɔasi] *nf*: **la ~** Croatia

**crochet** [kʀɔʃɛ] *nm* hook; (*détour*) detour; (*Tricot: aiguille*) crochet hook; (: *technique*) crochet; **vivre aux ~s de qn** to live *ou* sponge off sb

**crocodile** [kʀɔkɔdil] *nm* crocodile

**croire** [kʀwaʀ] *vt* to believe; **se ~ fort** to think one is strong; **~ que** to believe *ou* think that; **~ à, ~ en** to believe in

**croisade** [kʀwazad] *nf* crusade

**croisement** [kʀwazmɑ̃] *nm* (*carrefour*) crossroads *sg*; (*Bio*) crossing; (: *résultat*) crossbreed

**croiser** [kʀwaze] *vt* (*personne, voiture*)

to pass; (*route*) to cross, cut across; (*Bio*) to cross; **se croiser** vi (*personnes, véhicules*) to pass each other; (*routes, lettres*) to cross; (*regards*) to meet; **~ les jambes/bras** to cross one's legs/fold one's arms

**croisière** [kʀwazjɛʀ] nf cruise

**croissance** [kʀwasɑ̃s] nf growth

**croissant** [kʀwasɑ̃] nm (*à manger*) croissant; (*motif*) crescent

**croître** [kʀwatʀ] vi to grow

**croix** [kʀwa] nf cross; **la Croix Rouge** the Red Cross

**croque-monsieur** [kʀɔkməsjø] nm inv toasted ham and cheese sandwich

**croquer** [kʀɔke] vt (*manger*) to crunch; (: *fruit*) to munch; (*dessiner*) to sketch; **chocolat à croquer** plain dessert chocolate

**croquis** [kʀɔki] nm sketch

**crotte** [kʀɔt] nf droppings pl; **crottin** nm dung, manure; (*fromage*) (small round) cheese (*made of goat's milk*)

**croustillant, e** [kʀustijɑ̃, ɑ̃t] adj crisp

**croûte** [kʀut] nf crust; (*du fromage*) rind; (*Méd*) scab; **en ~** (*Culin*) in pastry

**croûton** [kʀutɔ̃] nm (*Culin*) crouton; (*bout du pain*) crust, heel

**croyant, e** [kʀwajɑ̃, ɑ̃t] nm/f believer

**CRS** sigle fpl (= *Compagnies républicaines de sécurité*) state security police force ▷ sigle m member of the CRS

**cru, e** [kʀy] pp de **croire** ▷ adj (*non cuit*) raw; (*lumière, couleur*) harsh; (*paroles*) crude ▷ nm (*vignoble*) vineyard; (*vin*) wine; **un grand ~** a great vintage; **jambon ~** Parma ham

**crû** [kʀy] pp de **croître**

**cruauté** [kʀyote] nf cruelty

**cruche** [kʀyʃ] nf pitcher, jug

**crucifix** [kʀysifi] nm crucifix

**crudités** [kʀydite] nfpl (*Culin*) selection of raw vegetables

**crue** [kʀy] nf (*inondation*) flood

**cruel, le** [kʀyɛl] adj cruel

**crus** etc [kʀy] vb voir **croire**; **croître**

**crûs** etc [kʀy] vb voir **croître**

**crustacés** [kʀystase] nmpl shellfish

**Cuba** [kyba] nf Cuba; **cubain, e** adj Cuban ▷ nm/f: **Cubain, e** Cuban

**cube** [kyb] nm cube; (*jouet*) brick; **mètre ~** cubic metre; **2 au ~** 2 cubed

**cueillette** [kœjɛt] nf picking; (*quantité*) crop, harvest

**cueillir** [kœjiʀ] vt (*fruits, fleurs*) to pick, gather; (*fig*) to catch

**cuiller** [kɥijɛʀ], **cuillère** [kɥijɛʀ] nf spoon; **cuiller à café** coffee spoon; (*Culin*) ≈ teaspoonful; **cuiller à soupe** soup-spoon; (*Culin*) ≈ tablespoonful; **cuillerée** nf spoonful

**cuir** [kɥiʀ] nm leather; **cuir chevelu** scalp

**cuire** [kɥiʀ] vt (*aliments*) to cook; (*au four*) to bake ▷ vi to cook; **bien cuit** (*viande*) well done; **trop cuit** overdone

**cuisine** [kɥizin] nf (*pièce*) kitchen; (*art culinaire*) cookery, cooking; (*nourriture*) cooking, food; **faire la ~** to cook; **cuisiné, e** adj: **plat cuisiné** ready-made meal ou dish; **cuisiner** vt to cook; (*fam*) to grill ▷ vi to cook; **cuisinier, -ière** nm/f cook; **cuisinière** nf (*poêle*) cooker

**cuisse** [kɥis] nf thigh; (*Culin*) leg

**cuisson** [kɥisɔ̃] nf cooking

**cuit, e** [kɥi, kɥit] pp de **cuire**

**cuivre** [kɥivʀ] nm copper; **les cuivres** (*Mus*) the brass

**cul** [ky] (*fam!*) nm arse (!)

**culminant, e** [kylminɑ̃, ɑ̃t] adj: **point ~** highest point

**culot** [kylo] (*fam*) nm (*effronterie*) cheek

**culotte** [kylɔt] nf (*de femme*) knickers pl (*BRIT*), panties pl

**culte** [kylt] nm (*religion*) religion; (*hommage, vénération*) worship; (*protestant*) service

**cultivateur, -trice** [kyltivatœʀ, tʀis] nm/f farmer

**cultivé, e** [kyltive] adj (*personne*) cultured, cultivated

**cultiver** [kyltive] vt to cultivate; (*légumes*) to grow, cultivate

**culture** [kyltyʀ] nf cultivation; (*connaissances etc*) culture; **les ~s**

**intensives** intensive farming; **culture physique** physical training; **culturel, le** *adj* cultural

**cumin** [kymɛ̃] *nm* cumin

**cure** [kyʀ] *nf* (*Méd*) course of treatment; **cure d'amaigrissement** slimming (*BRIT*) *ou* weight-loss (*US*) course; **cure de repos** rest cure

**curé** [kyʀe] *nm* parish priest

**cure-dent** [kyʀdɑ̃] *nm* toothpick

**curieux, -euse** [kyʀjø, jøz] *adj* (*indiscret*) curious, inquisitive; (*étrange*) strange, curious ▷ *nmpl* (*badauds*) onlookers; **curiosité** *nf* curiosity; (*site*) unusual feature

**curriculum vitae** [kyʀikylɔmvite] *nm inv* curriculum vitae

**cutané, e** [kytane] *adj* skin

**cuve** [kyv] *nf* vat; (*à mazout etc*) tank

**cuvée** [kyve] *nf* vintage

**cuvette** [kyvɛt] *nf* (*récipient*) bowl, basin; (*Géo*) basin

**CV** *sigle m* (*Auto*) = **cheval vapeur**; (*Comm*) = **curriculum vitae**

**cybercafé** [sibɛʀkafe] *nm* Internet café

**cyberespace** [sibɛʀɛspas] *nm* cyberspace

**cybernaute** [sibɛʀnot] *nm/f* Internet user

**cyclable** [siklabl] *adj*: **piste ~** cycle track

**cycle** [sikl] *nm* cycle; **cyclisme** *nm* cycling; **cycliste** *nm/f* cyclist ▷ *adj* cycle *cpd*; **coureur cycliste** racing cyclist

**cyclomoteur** [siklomɔtœʀ] *nm* moped

**cyclone** [siklon] *nm* hurricane

**cygne** [siɲ] *nm* swan

**cylindre** [silɛ̃dʀ] *nm* cylinder; **cylindrée** *nf* (*Auto*) (cubic) capacity; **une (voiture de) grosse cylindrée** a big-engined car

**cymbale** [sɛ̃bal] *nf* cymbal

**cynique** [sinik] *adj* cynical

**cystite** [sistit] *nf* cystitis

# d

**d'** [d] *prép voir* **de**

**dactylo** [daktilo] *nf* (*aussi*: **~graphe**) typist; (*aussi*: **~graphie**) typing

**dada** [dada] *nm* hobby-horse

**daim** [dɛ̃] *nm* (fallow) deer *inv*; (*cuir suédé*) suede

**daltonien, ne** [daltɔnjɛ̃, jɛn] *adj* colour-blind

**dame** [dam] *nf* lady; (*Cartes, Échecs*) queen; **dames** *nfpl* (*jeu*) draughts *sg* (*BRIT*), checkers *sg* (*US*)

**Danemark** [danmaʀk] *nm* Denmark

**danger** [dɑ̃ʒe] *nm* danger; **être en ~** (*personne*) to be in danger; **mettre en ~** (*personne*) to put in danger; (*projet, carrière*) to jeopardize; **dangereux, -euse** *adj* dangerous

**danois, e** [danwa, waz] *adj* Danish ▷ *nm/f*: **D~, e** Dane ▷ *nm* (*Ling*) Danish

 **MOT-CLÉ**

**dans** [dɑ̃] *prép* **1** (*position*) in; (*à l'intérieur de*) inside; **c'est dans le tiroir/le salon**

it's in the drawer/lounge; **dans la boîte** in *ou* inside the box; **je l'ai lu dans le journal** I read it in the newspaper; **marcher dans la ville** to walk about the town

**2** (*direction*) into; **elle a couru dans le salon** she ran into the lounge; **monter dans une voiture/le bus** to get into a car/on to the bus

**3** (*provenance*) out of, from; **je l'ai pris dans le tiroir/salon** I took it out of *ou* from the drawer/lounge; **boire dans un verre** to drink out of *ou* from a glass

**4** (*temps*) in; **dans 2 mois** in 2 months, in 2 months' time

**5** (*approximation*) about; **dans les 20 euros** about 20 euros

**danse** [dãs] *nf*: **la ~** dancing; **une ~** a dance; **la ~ classique** ballet; **danser** *vi, vt* to dance; **danseur, -euse** *nm/f* ballet dancer; (*au bal etc*) dancer; (*: cavalier*) partner

**date** [dat] *nf* date; **de longue ~** longstanding; **date de naissance** date of birth; **date limite** deadline; **dater** *vt, vi* to date; **dater de** to date from; **à dater de** (*as*) from

**datte** [dat] *nf* date

**dauphin** [dofɛ̃] *nm* (*Zool*) dolphin

**davantage** [davãtaʒ] *adv* more; (*plus longtemps*) longer; **~ de** more

🔘 **MOT-CLÉ**

**de, d'** [də] (*de +le* = **du**, *de +les* = **des**) *prép*
**1** (*appartenance*) of; **le toit de la maison** the roof of the house; **la voiture d'Ann/de mes parents** Ann's/my parents' car

**2** (*provenance*) from; **il vient de Londres** he comes from London; **elle est sortie du cinéma** she came out of the cinema

**3** (*caractérisation, mesure*) : **un mur de brique/bureau d'acajou** a brick wall/mahogany desk; **un billet de 50 euros** a 50 euro note; **une pièce de 2 m de large** *ou* **large de 2 m** a room 2m wide,

a 2m-wide room; **un bébé de 10 mois** a 10-month-old baby; **12 mois de crédit/travail** 12 months' credit/work; **être payé 20 euros de l'heure** to be paid 20 euros an *ou* per hour; **augmenter de 10 euros** to increase by 10 euros; **de 14 à 18** from 14 to 18

**4** (*moyen*) with; **je l'ai fait de mes propres mains** I did it with my own two hands

**5** (*cause*): **mourir de faim** to die of hunger; **rouge de colère** red with fury

**6** (*devant infinitif*) to; **il m'a dit de rester** he told me to stay

▷ *dét* **1** (*phrases affirmatives*) some (*souvent omis*); **du vin, de l'eau, des pommes** (some) wine, (some) water, (some) apples; **des enfants sont venus** some children came; **pendant des mois** for months

**2** (*phrases interrogatives et négatives*) any; **a-t-il du vin?** has he got any wine?; **il n'a pas de pommes/d'enfants** he hasn't (got) any apples/children, he has no apples/children

**dé** [de] *nm* (*à jouer*) die *ou* dice; (*aussi*: **dé à coudre**) thimble

**déballer** [debale] *vt* to unpack

**débarcadère** [debaʀkadɛʀ] *nm* wharf

**débardeur** [debaʀdœʀ] *nm* (*maillot*) tank top

**débarquer** [debaʀke] *vt* to unload, land ▷ *vi* to disembark; (*fig: fam*) to turn up

**débarras** [debaʀɑ] *nm* (*pièce*) lumber room; (*placard*) junk cupboard; **bon ~!** good riddance!; **débarrasser** *vt* to clear; **se débarrasser de** *vt* to get rid of; **débarrasser qn de** (*vêtements, paquets*) to relieve sb of; **débarrasser (la table)** to clear the table

**débat** [deba] *nm* discussion, debate; **débattre** *vt* to discuss, debate; **se débattre** *vi* to struggle

**débit** [debi] *nm* (*d'un liquide, fleuve*) flow; (*d'un magasin*) turnover (of goods); (*élocution*) delivery; (*bancaire*) debit; **débit de boissons** drinking establishment; **débit de tabac** tobacconist's

**déblayer** [debleje] vt to clear

**débloquer** [deblɔke] vt (prix, crédits) to free

**déboîter** [debwate] vt (Auto) to pull out; **se ~ le genou** etc to dislocate one's knee etc

**débordé, e** [debɔrde] adj: **être ~ (de)** (travail, demandes) to be snowed under (with)

**déborder** [debɔrde] vi to overflow; (lait etc) to boil over; **~ (de) qch** (dépasser) to extend beyond sth; **~ de** (joie, zèle) to be brimming over with ou bursting with

**débouché** [debuʃe] nm (pour vendre) outlet; (perspective d'emploi) opening

**déboucher** [debuʃe] vt (évier, tuyau etc) to unblock; (bouteille) to uncork ▷ vi: **~ de** to emerge from; **~ sur** (études) to lead on to

**debout** [d(ə)bu] adv: **être ~** (personne) to be standing, stand; (: levé, éveillé) to be up; **se mettre ~** to stand up; **se tenir ~** to stand; **~!** stand up!; (du lit) get up!; **cette histoire ne tient pas ~** this story doesn't hold water

**déboutonner** [debutɔne] vt to undo, unbutton

**débraillé, e** [debraje] adj slovenly, untidy

**débrancher** [debrãʃe] vt to disconnect; (appareil électrique) to unplug

**débrayage** [debrɛjaʒ] nm (Auto) clutch; **débrayer** vi (Auto) to declutch; (cesser le travail) to stop work

**débris** [debri] nmpl fragments; **des ~ de verre** bits of glass

**débrouillard, e** [debrujar, ard] (fam) adj smart, resourceful

**débrouiller** [debruje] vt to disentangle, untangle; **se débrouiller** vi to manage; **débrouillez-vous** you'll have to sort things out yourself

**début** [deby] nm beginning, start; **débuts** nmpl (de carrière) début sg; **~**

**juin** in early June; **débutant, e** nm/f beginner, novice; **débuter** vi to begin, start; (faire ses débuts) to start out

**décaféiné, e** [dekafeine] adj decaffeinated

**décalage** [dekalaʒ] nm gap; **décalage horaire** time difference

**décaler** [dekale] vt to shift

**décapotable** [dekapɔtabl] adj convertible

**décapsuleur** [dekapsylœr] nm bottle-opener

**décédé, e** [desede] adj deceased

**décéder** [desede] vi to die

**décembre** [desãbr] nm December

**décennie** [deseni] nf decade

**décent, e** [desã, ãt] adj decent

**déception** [desɛpsjɔ̃] nf disappointment

**décès** [desɛ] nm death

**décevoir** [des(ə)vwar] vt to disappoint

**décharge** [deʃarʒ] nf (dépôt d'ordures) rubbish tip ou dump; (électrique) electrical discharge; **décharger** vt (marchandise, véhicule) to unload; (tirer) to discharge; **décharger qn de** (responsabilité) to relieve sb of, release sb from

**déchausser** [deʃose] vt (skis) to take off; **se déchausser** vi to take off one's shoes; (dent) to come ou work loose

**déchet** [deʃɛ] nm (reste) scrap; **déchets** nmpl (ordures) refuse sg, rubbish sg; **~s nucléaires** nuclear waste

**déchiffrer** [deʃifre] vt to decipher

**déchirant, e** [deʃirã, ãt] adj heart-rending

**déchirement** [deʃirmã] nm (chagrin) wrench, heartbreak; (gén pl: conflit) rift, split

**déchirer** [deʃire] vt to tear; (en morceaux) to tear up; (arracher) to tear out; (fig: conflit) to tear (apart); **se déchirer** vi to tear, rip; **se ~ un muscle** to tear a muscle

**déchirure** [deʃiryr] nf (accroc) tear, rip; **déchirure musculaire** torn muscle

**décidé, e** [deside] adj (personne, air) determined; **c'est ~** it's decided; **décidément** adv really

**décider** [deside] vt: **~ qch** to decide on sth; **~ de faire/que** to decide to do/that; **~ qn (à faire qch)** to persuade sb (to do sth); **se décider (à faire)** to decide (to do), make up one's mind (to do); **se ~ pour** to decide on ou in favour of

**décimal, e, -aux** [desimal, o] adj decimal

**décimètre** [desimetR] nm decimetre

**décisif, -ive** [desizif, iv] adj decisive

**décision** [desizjɔ̃] nf decision

**déclaration** [deklaRasjɔ̃] nf declaration; (discours: Pol etc) statement; **déclaration d'impôts** ou **de revenus** ≈ tax return; **déclaration de vol: faire une déclaration de vol** to report a theft

**déclarer** [deklaRe] vt to declare; (décès, naissance) to register; **se déclarer** vi (feu) to break out

**déclencher** [deklɑ̃ʃe] vt (mécanisme etc) to release; (sonnerie) to set off; (attaque, grève) to launch; (provoquer) to trigger off; **se déclencher** vi (sonnerie) to go off

**décliner** [dekline] vi to decline ▷ vt (invitation) to decline; (nom, adresse) to state

**décoiffer** [dekwafe] vt: **~ qn** to mess up sb's hair; **je suis toute décoiffée** my hair is in a real mess

**déçois** etc [deswa] vb voir **décevoir**

**décollage** [dekɔlaʒ] nm (Aviat) takeoff

**décoller** [dekɔle] vt to unstick ▷ vi (avion) to take off; **se décoller** vi to come unstuck

**décolleté, e** [dekɔlte] adj low-cut ▷ nm low neck(line); (plongeant) cleavage

**décolorer** [dekɔlɔRe]: **se décolorer** vi to fade; **se faire ~ les cheveux** to have one's hair bleached

**décommander** [dekɔmɑ̃de] vt to cancel; **se décommander** vi to cry off

**déconcerter** [dekɔ̃seRte] vt to disconcert, confound

**décongeler** [dekɔ̃ʒ(ə)le] vt to thaw

**déconner** [dekɔne] (fam) vi to talk rubbish

**déconseiller** [dekɔ̃seje] vt: **~ qch (à qn)** to advise (sb) against sth; **c'est déconseillé** it's not recommended

**décontracté, e** [dekɔ̃tRakte] adj relaxed, laid-back (fam)

**décontracter** [dekɔ̃tRakte]: **se décontracter** vi to relax

**décor** [dekɔR] nm décor; (paysage) scenery; **décorateur** nm (interior) decorator; **décoration** nf decoration; **décorer** vt to decorate

**décortiquer** [dekɔRtike] vt to shell; (fig: texte) to dissect

**découdre** [dekudR]: **se découdre** vi to come unstitched

**découper** [dekupe] vt (papier, tissu etc) to cut up; (viande) to carve; (article) to cut out

**décourager** [dekuRaʒe] vt to discourage; **se décourager** vi to lose heart, become discouraged

**décousu, e** [dekuzy] adj unstitched; (fig) disjointed, disconnected

**découvert, e** [dekuvɛR, ɛRt] adj (tête) bare, uncovered; (lieu) open, exposed ▷ nm (bancaire) overdraft; **découverte** nf discovery; **faire la découverte de** to discover

**découvrir** [dekuvRiR] vt to discover; (enlever ce qui couvre) to uncover; (dévoiler) to reveal; **se découvrir** vi (chapeau) to take off one's hat; (vêtement) to take something off; (ciel) to clear

**décrire** [dekRiR] vt to describe

**décrocher** [dekRɔʃe] vt (détacher) to take down; (téléphone) to take off the hook; (: pour répondre) to lift the receiver; (fam: contrat etc) to get, land ▷ vi (fam: abandonner) to drop out; (: cesser d'écouter) to switch off

**déçu, e** [desy] pp de **décevoir**

**dédaigner** [dedeɲe] vt to despise, scorn; (négliger) to disregard, spurn;

**dédaigneux, -euse** *adj* scornful, disdainful; **dédain** *nm* scorn, disdain

**dedans** [dədɑ̃] *adv* inside; (*pas en plein air*) indoors, inside ▷ *nm* inside; **au ~** inside

**dédicacer** [dedikase] *vt*: **~ (à qn)** to sign (for sb), autograph (for sb)

**dédier** [dedje] *vt*: **~ à** to dedicate to

**dédommagement** [dedɔmaʒmɑ̃] *nm* compensation

**dédommager** [dedɔmaʒe] *vt*: **~ qn (de)** to compensate sb (for)

**dédouaner** [dedwane] *vt* to clear through customs

**déduire** [deduiʀ] *vt*: **~ qch (de)** (*ôter*) to deduct sth (from); (*conclure*) to deduce ou infer sth (from)

**défaillance** [defajɑ̃s] *nf* (*syncope*) blackout; (*fatigue*) (sudden) weakness *no pl*; (*technique*) fault, failure; **défaillance cardiaque** heart failure

**défaire** [defɛʀ] *vt* to undo; (*installation*) to take down, dismantle; **se défaire** *vi* to come undone; **se ~ de** to get rid of

**défait, e** [defɛ, ɛt] *adj* (*visage*) haggard, ravaged; **défaite** *nf* defeat

**défaut** [defo] *nm* (*moral*) fault, failing, defect; (*tissus*) fault, flaw; (*manque, carence*): **~ de** shortage of; **prendre qn en ~** to catch sb out; **faire ~** (*manquer*) to be lacking; **à ~ de** for lack ou want of

**défavorable** [defavɔʀabl] *adj* unfavourable (BRIT), unfavorable (US)

**défavoriser** [defavɔʀize] *vt* to put at a disadvantage

**défectueux, -euse** [defɛktɥø, øz] *adj* faulty, defective

**défendre** [defɑ̃dʀ] *vt* to defend; (*interdire*) to forbid; **se défendre** *vi* to defend o.s.; **à qn qch/de faire** to forbid sb sth/to do; **il se défend** (*fam: se débrouille*) he can hold his own; **se ~ de/contre** (*se protéger*) to protect o.s. from/against; **se ~ de** (*se garder de*) to refrain from

**défense** [defɑ̃s] *nf* defence; (*d'éléphant etc*) tusk; **ministre de la ~** Minister of Defence (BRIT), Defence Secretary (US);

**"~ de fumer"** "no smoking"

**défi** [defi] *nm* challenge; **lancer un ~ à qn** to challenge sb; **sur un ton de ~** defiantly

**déficit** [defisit] *nm* (*Comm*) deficit

**défier** [defje] *vt* (*provoquer*) to challenge; (*mort, autorité*) to defy; **~ qn de faire qch** to challenge ou defy sb to do sth

**défigurer** [defigyʀe] *vt* to disfigure

**défilé** [defile] *nm* (*Géo*) (narrow) gorge ou pass; (*soldats*) parade; (*manifestants*) procession, march

**défiler** [defile] *vi* (*troupes*) to march past; (*sportifs*) to parade; (*manifestants*) to march; (*visiteurs*) to pour, stream; **faire ~ un document** (*Comput*) to scroll a document; **se défiler** *vi*: **il s'est défilé** (*fam*) he wriggled out of it

**définir** [definiʀ] *vt* to define

**définitif, -ive** [definitif, iv] *adj* (*final*) final, definitive; (*pour longtemps*) permanent, definitive; (*refus*) definite; **définitive** *nf*: **en définitive** eventually; (*somme toute*) in fact; **définitivement** *adv* (*partir, s'installer*) for good

**déformer** [defɔʀme] *vt* to put out of shape; (*pensée, fait*) to distort; **se déformer** *vi* to lose its shape

**défouler** [defule]: **se défouler** *vi* to unwind, let off steam

**défunt, e** [defœ̃, œ̃t] *adj* (*mort*) late *before n* ▷ *nm/f* deceased

**dégagé, e** [degaʒe] *adj* (*route, ciel*) clear; **sur un ton ~** casually

**dégager** [degaʒe] *vt* (*exhaler*) to give off; (*délivrer*) to free, extricate; (*désencombrer*) to clear; (*isoler: idée, aspect*) to bring out; **~ qn de** (*engagement, parole etc*) to release ou free sb from; **se dégager** *vi* (*passage, ciel*) to clear

**dégâts** [dega] *nmpl* damage *sg*; **faire des ~** to cause damage

**dégel** [deʒɛl] *nm* thaw; **dégeler** *vt* to thaw (out)

**dégivrer** [deʒivʀe] *vt* (*frigo*) to defrost; (*vitres*) to de-ice

**dégonflé, e** [degɔ̃fle] *adj* (*pneu*) flat

**dégonfler** [degɔ̃fle] *vt* (*pneu, ballon*) to let down, deflate; **se dégonfler** *vi* (*fam*) to chicken out

**dégouliner** [deguline] *vi* to trickle, drip

**dégourdi, e** [degurdi] *adj* smart, resourceful

**dégourdir** [degurdir] *vt*: **se ~ les jambes** to stretch one's legs (*fig*)

**dégoût** [degu] *nm* disgust, distaste; **dégoûtant, e** *adj* disgusting; **dégoûté, e** *adj* disgusted; **dégoûté de** sick of; **dégoûter** *vt* to disgust; **dégoûter qn de qch** to put sb off sth

**dégrader** [degrade] *vt* (*Mil: officier*) to degrade; (*abîmer*) to damage, deface; **se dégrader** *vi* (*relations, situation*) to deteriorate

**degré** [dəgre] *nm* degree

**dégressif, -ive** [degresif, iv] *adj* on a decreasing scale

**dégringoler** [degrɛ̃gɔle] *vi* to tumble (down)

**déguisement** [degizmɑ̃] *nm* (*pour s'amuser*) fancy dress

**déguiser** [degize]: **se déguiser (en)** *vi* (*se costumer*) to dress up (as); (*pour tromper*) to disguise o.s. (as)

**dégustation** [degystasjɔ̃] *nf* (*de fromages etc*) sampling; **~ de vins** wine-tasting session

**déguster** [degyste] *vt* (*vins*) to taste; (*fromages etc*) to sample; (*savourer*) to enjoy, savour

**dehors** [dəɔr] *adv* outside; (*en plein air*) outdoors ▷ *nm* outside ▷ *nmpl* (*apparences*) appearances; **mettre ou jeter ~** (*expulser*) to throw out; **au ~** outside; **au ~ de** outside; **en ~ de** (*hormis*) apart from

**déjà** [deʒa] *adv* already; (*auparavant*) before, already

**déjeuner** [deʒœne] *vi* to (have) lunch; (*le matin*) to have breakfast ▷ *nm* lunch

**delà** [dəla] *adv*: **en ~ (de), au ~ (de)** beyond

**délacer** [delase] *vt* (*chaussures*) to undo

**délai** [delɛ] *nm* (*attente*) waiting period; (*sursis*) extension (of time); (*temps accordé*) time limit; **sans ~** without delay; **dans les ~s** within the time limit

**délaisser** [delese] *vt* to abandon, desert

**délasser** [delase] *vt* to relax; **se délasser** *vi* to relax

**délavé, e** [delave] *adj* faded

**délayer** [deleje] *vt* (*Culin*) to mix (with water *etc*); (*peinture*) to thin down

**delco(r)** [dɛlko] *nm* (*Auto*) distributor

**délégué, e** [delege] *nm/f* representative

**déléguer** [delege] *vt* to delegate

**délibéré, e** [delibere] *adj* (*conscient*) deliberate

**délicat, e** [delika, at] *adj* delicate; (*plein de tact*) tactful; (*attention*) thoughtful; **délicatement** *adv* delicately; (*avec douceur*) gently

**délice** [delis] *nm* delight

**délicieux, -euse** [delisjø, jøz] *adj* (*au goût*) delicious; (*sensation*) delightful

**délimiter** [delimite] *vt* (*terrain*) to delimit, demarcate

**délinquant, e** [delɛ̃kɑ̃, -ɑ̃t] *adj, nm/f* delinquent

**délirer** [delire] *vi* to be delirious; **tu délires!** (*fam*) you're crazy!

**délit** [deli] *nm* (*criminal*) offence

**délivrer** [delivre] *vt* (*prisonnier*) to (set) free, release; (*passeport*) to issue

**deltaplane(r)** [dɛltaplan] *nm* hang-glider

**déluge** [delyʒ] *nm* (*pluie*) downpour; (*biblique*) Flood

**demain** [d(ə)mɛ̃] *adv* tomorrow; **~ matin/soir** tomorrow morning/ evening

**demande** [d(ə)mɑ̃d] *nf* (*requête*) request; (*revendication*) demand; (*d'emploi*) application; (*Écon*): **la ~** demand; **"~s d'emploi"** (*annonces*) "situations wanted"

**demandé, e** [d(ə)mɑ̃de] *adj* (*article etc*): **très ~** (very) much in demand

**demander** [d(ə)mɑ̃de] *vt* to ask for;

(*chemin, heure etc*) to ask; (*nécessiter*) to require, demand; **~ qch à qn** to ask sb for sth; **~ un service à qn** to ask sb a favour; **~ à qn de faire qch** to ask sb to do sth; **je ne demande pas mieux que de ...** I'll be only too pleased to ...; **se ~ si/pourquoi** *etc* to wonder whether/why *etc*; **demandeur, -euse** *nm/f*: **demandeur d'emploi** job-seeker; **demandeur d'asile** asylum-seeker

**démangeaison** [demãʒɛzõ] *nf* itching; **avoir des ~s** to be itching

**démanger** [demãʒe] *vi* to itch

**démaquillant** [demakijã] *nm* make-up remover

**démaquiller** [demakije] *vt*: **se démaquiller** to remove one's make-up

**démarche** [demarʃ] *nf* (*allure*) gait, walk; (*intervention*) step; (*fig: intellectuelle*) thought processes *pl*; **faire les ~s nécessaires (pour obtenir qch)** to take the necessary steps (to obtain sth)

**démarrage** [demaraʒ] *nm* start

**démarrer** [demare] *vi* (*conducteur*) to start (up); (*véhicule*) to move off; (*travaux*) to get moving; **démarreur** *nm* (*Auto*) starter

**démêlant** [demɛlã] *nm* conditioner

**démêler** [demele] *vt* to untangle; **démêlés** *nmpl* problems

**déménagement** [demenaʒmã] *nm* move; **camion de déménagement** removal van

**déménager** [demenaʒe] *vt* (*meubles*) to (re)move ▷ *vi* to move (house); **déménageur** *nm* removal man

**démerder** [demɛrde] (*fam*): **se démerder** *vi* to sort things out for o.s.

**démettre** [demɛtr] *vt*: **~ qn de** (*fonction, poste*) to dismiss sb from; **se ~ l'épaule** *etc* to dislocate one's shoulder *etc*

**demeurer** [d(ə)mœre] *vi* (*habiter*) to live; (*rester*) to remain

**demi, e** [dəmi] *adj* half ▷ *nm* (*bière*) ≈ half-pint (0,25 litres) ▷ *préfixe*: **~...** half-, semi..., demi-; **trois heures/bouteilles**

**et ~es** three and a half hours/bottles, three hours/bottles and a half; **il est 2 heures et ~e/midi et ~** it's half past 2/half past 12; **à ~** half-; **à la ~e** (*heure*) on the half-hour; **demi-douzaine** *nf* half-dozen, half a dozen; **demi-finale** *nf* semifinal; **demi-frère** *nm* half-brother; **demi-heure** *nf* half-hour, half an hour; **demi-journée** *nf* half-day, half a day; **demi-litre** *nm* half-litre, half a litre; **demi-livre** *nf* half-pound, half a pound; **demi-pension** *nf* (*à l'hôtel*) half-board; **demi-pensionnaire** *nm/f*: **être demi-pensionnaire** to take school lunches

**démis, e** [demi, iz] *adj* (*épaule etc*) dislocated

**demi-sœur** [dəmisœr] *nf* half-sister

**démission** [demisjõ] *nf* resignation; **donner sa ~** to give *ou* hand in one's notice; **démissionner** *vi* to resign

**demi-tarif** [dəmitarif] *nm* half-price; **voyager à ~** to travel half-fare

**demi-tour** [dəmitur] *nm* about-turn; **faire ~** to turn (and go) back

**démocratie** [demɔkrasi] *nf* democracy; **démocratique** *adj* democratic

**démodé, e** [demɔde] *adj* old-fashioned

**demoiselle** [d(ə)mwazɛl] *nf* (*jeune fille*) young lady; (*célibataire*) single lady, maiden lady; **demoiselle d'honneur** bridesmaid

**démolir** [demɔlir] *vt* to demolish

**démon** [demõ] *nm* (*enfant turbulent*) devil, demon; **le D~** the Devil

**démonstration** [demõstrasjõ] *nf* demonstration

**démonter** [demõte] *vt* (*machine etc*) to take down, dismantle; **se démonter** (*meuble*) to be dismantled, be taken to pieces; (*personne*) to lose countenance

**démontrer** [demõtre] *vt* to demonstrate

**démouler** [demule] *vt* to turn out

**démuni, e** [demyni] *adj* (*sans argent*) impoverished; **~ de** without

**dénicher** [deniʃe] (*fam*) *vt* (*objet*) to

unearth; (*restaurant etc*) to discover
**dénier** [denje] *vt* to deny
**dénivellation** [denivelasjɔ̃] *nf* (*pente*) slope
**dénombrer** [denɔ̃bʀe] *vt* to count
**dénomination** [denɔminasjɔ̃] *nf* designation, appellation
**dénoncer** [denɔ̃se] *vt* to denounce; **se dénoncer** to give o.s. up, come forward
**dénouement** [denumɑ̃] *nm* outcome
**dénouer** [denwe] *vt* to unknot, undo
**denrée** [dɑ̃ʀe] *nf*: **denrées alimentaires** foodstuffs
**dense** [dɑ̃s] *adj* dense; **densité** *nf* density
**dent** [dɑ̃] *nf* tooth; **dent de lait/de sagesse** milk/wisdom tooth; **dentaire** *adj* dental; **cabinet dentaire** dental surgery (BRIT), dentist's office (US)
**dentelle** [dɑ̃tɛl] *nf* lace *no pl*
**dentier** [dɑ̃tje] *nm* denture
**dentifrice** [dɑ̃tifʀis] *nm* toothpaste
**dentiste** [dɑ̃tist] *nm/f* dentist
**dentition** [dɑ̃tisjɔ̃] *nf* teeth
**dénué, e** [denɥe] *adj*: **~ de** devoid of
**déodorant** [deɔdɔʀɑ̃] *nm* deodorant
**déontologie** [deɔ̃tɔlɔʒi] *nf* code of practice
**dépannage** [depanaʒ] *nm*: **service de ~** (*Auto*) breakdown service
**dépanner** [depane] *vt* (*voiture, télévision*) to fix, repair; (*fig*) to bail out, help out; **dépanneuse** *nf* breakdown lorry (BRIT), tow truck (US)
**dépareillé, e** [depaʀeje] *adj* (*collection, service*) incomplete; (*objet*) odd
**départ** [depaʀ] *nm* departure; (*Sport*) start; **au ~** at the start; **la veille de son ~** the day before he leaves/left
**département** [depaʀtəmɑ̃] *nm* department

• **DÉPARTEMENT**
•
• France is divided into 96
• administrative units called
• **départements**. These local
• government divisions are headed

• by a state-appointed 'préfet',
• and administered by an elected
• 'Conseil général'. **Départements**
• are usually named after prominent
• geographical features such as rivers
• or mountain ranges.

**dépassé, e** [depase] *adj* superseded, outmoded; **il est complètement ~** he's completely out of his depth, he can't cope
**dépasser** [depase] *vt* (*véhicule, concurrent*) to overtake; (*endroit*) to pass, go past; (*somme, limite*) to exceed; (*fig: en beauté etc*) to surpass, outshine ▷ *vi* (*jupon etc*) to show; **se dépasser** to excel o.s.
**dépaysé, e** [depeize] *adj* disoriented
**dépaysement** [depeizmɑ̃] *nm* (*changement*) change of scenery
**dépêcher** [depeʃe]: **se dépêcher** *vi* to hurry
**dépendance** [depɑ̃dɑ̃s] *nf* dependence; (*bâtiment*) outbuilding
**dépendre** [depɑ̃dʀ]: **~ de** *vt* to depend on; (*financièrement etc*) to be dependent on; **ça dépend** it depends
**dépens** [depɑ̃] *nmpl*: **aux ~ de** at the expense of
**dépense** [depɑ̃s] *nf* spending *no pl*, expense, expenditure *no pl*; **dépenser** *vt* to spend; (*énergie*) to expend, use up; **se dépenser** *vi* to exert o.s.
**dépeupler** [depœple]: **se dépeupler** *vi* to become depopulated
**dépilatoire** [depilatwaʀ] *adj*: **crème ~** hair-removing *ou* depilatory cream
**dépister** [depiste] *vt* to detect; (*voleur*) to track down
**dépit** [depi] *nm* vexation, frustration; **en ~ de** in spite of; **en ~ du bon sens** contrary to all good sense; **dépité, e** *adj* vexed, frustrated
**déplacé, e** [deplase] *adj* (*propos*) out of place, uncalled-for
**déplacement** [deplasmɑ̃] *nm* (*voyage*) trip, travelling *no pl*; **en ~** away
**déplacer** [deplase] *vt* (*table, voiture*) to

move, shift; **se déplacer** vi to move;
(voyager) to travel; **se ~ une vertèbre**
to slip a disc

**déplaire** [deplɛʀ] vt: **ça me déplaît** I
don't like this, I dislike this; **se déplaire**
vi to be unhappy; **déplaisant, e** adj
disagreeable

**dépliant** [deplijɑ̃] nm leaflet

**déplier** [deplije] vt to unfold

**déposer** [depoze] vt (gén: mettre,
poser) to lay ou put down; (à la banque,
à la consigne) to deposit; (passager) to
drop (off), set down; (roi) to depose;
(plainte) to lodge; (marque) to register;
**se déposer** vi to settle; **dépositaire**
nm/f (Comm) agent; **déposition** nf
statement

**dépôt** [depo] nm (à la banque, sédiment)
deposit; (entrepôt) warehouse, store

**dépourvu, e** [depuʀvy] adj: **~ de**
lacking in, without; **prendre qn au ~** to
catch sb unprepared

**dépression** [depʀesjɔ̃] nf depression;
**dépression (nerveuse)** (nervous)
breakdown

**déprimant, e** [depʀimɑ̃, ɑ̃t] adj
depressing

**déprimer** [depʀime] vi to be/get
depressed

 **MOT-CLÉ**

**depuis** [dəpɥi] prép **1** (point de départ
dans le temps) since; **il habite Paris
depuis 1983/l'an dernier** he has been
living in Paris since 1983/last year;
**depuis quand?** since when?; **depuis
quand le connaissez-vous?** how long
have you known him?

**2** (temps écoulé) for; **il habite Paris
depuis 5 ans** he has been living in Paris
for 5 years; **je le connais depuis 3 ans**
I've known him for 3 years

**3** (lieu): **il a plu depuis Metz** it's been
raining since Metz; **elle a téléphoné
depuis Valence** she rang from Valence

**4** (quantité, rang) from; **depuis les plus
petits jusqu'aux plus grands** from the

youngest to the oldest
▷ adv (temps) since (then); **je ne lui
ai pas parlé depuis** I haven't spoken
to him since (then); **depuis que** conj
(ever) since; **depuis qu'il m'a dit ça**
(ever) since he said that to me

**député, e** [depyte] nm/f (Pol)
≈ Member of Parliament (BRIT),
≈ Member of Congress (US)

**dérangement** [deʀɑ̃ʒmɑ̃] nm (gêne)
trouble; (gastrique etc) disorder; **en ~**
(téléphone, machine) out of order

**déranger** [deʀɑ̃ʒe] vt (personne) to
trouble, bother; (projets) to disrupt,
upset; (objets, vêtements) to disarrange;
**se déranger** vi: **surtout ne vous
dérangez pas pour moi** please don't
put yourself out on my account; **est-ce
que cela vous dérange si …?** do you
mind if …?

**déraper** [deʀape] vi (voiture) to skid;
(personne, semelles) to slip

**dérégler** [deʀegle] vt (mécanisme) to
put out of order; (estomac) to upset

**dérisoire** [deʀizwaʀ] adj derisory

**dérive** [deʀiv] nf: **aller à la ~** (Navig,
fig) to drift

**dérivé, e** [deʀive] nm (Tech) by-product

**dermatologue** [dɛʀmatɔlɔɡ] nm/f
dermatologist

**dernier, -ière** [dɛʀnje, jɛʀ] adj last; (le
plus récent) latest, last; **lundi/le mois ~**
last Monday/month; **c'est le ~ cri** it's
the very latest thing; **en ~** last; **ce ~** the
latter; **dernièrement** adv recently

**dérogation** [deʀɔɡasjɔ̃] nf (special)
dispensation

**dérouiller** [deʀuje] vt: **se ~ les jambes**
to stretch one's legs (fig)

**déroulement** [deʀulmɑ̃] nm (d'une
opération etc) progress

**dérouler** [deʀule] vt (ficelle) to unwind;
**se dérouler** vi (avoir lieu) to take
place; (se passer) to go (off); **tout s'est
déroulé comme prévu** everything
went as planned

**dérouter** [deʀute] vt (avion, train) to

reroute, divert; (*étonner*) to disconcert,
throw (out)

**derrière** [dɛʀjɛʀ] *adv, prép* behind ▷ *nm*
(*d'une maison*) back; (*postérieur*) behind,
bottom; **les pattes de ~** the back *ou*
hind legs; **par ~** from behind; (*fig*)
behind one's back

**des** [de] *dét voir de* ▷ *prép* +*dét* = **de** +**les**

**dès** [dɛ] *prép* from; **~ que** as soon as;
**~ son retour** as soon as he was (*ou*
is) back

**désaccord** [dezakɔʀ] *nm*
disagreement

**désagréable** [dezagʀeabl] *adj*
unpleasant

**désagrément** [dezagʀemã] *nm*
annoyance, trouble *no pl*

**désaltérer** [dezalteʀe] *vt*: **se
désaltérer** to quench one's thirst

**désapprobateur, -trice**
[dezapʀɔbatœʀ, tʀis] *adj* disapproving

**désapprouver** [dezapʀuve] *vt* to
disapprove of

**désarmant, e** [dezaʀmã, ãt] *adj*
disarming

**désastre** [dezastʀ] *nm* disaster;
**désastreux, -euse** *adj* disastrous

**désavantage** [dezavãtaʒ] *nm*
disadvantage; **désavantager** *vt* to put
at a disadvantage

**descendre** [desãdʀ] *vt* (*escalier,
montagne*) to go (*ou* come) down; (*valise,
paquet*) to take *ou* get down; (*étagère etc*)
to lower; (*fam: abattre*) to shoot down
▷ *vi* to go (*ou* come) down; (*passager:
s'arrêter*) to get out, alight; **~ à pied/en
voiture** to walk/drive down; **~ de**
(*famille*) to be descended from; **~ du
train** to get out of *ou* get off the train; **~
de cheval** to dismount; **~ d'un arbre** to
climb down from a tree; **~ à l'hôtel** to
stay at a hotel

**descente** [desãt] *nf* descent, going
down; (*chemin*) way down; (*Ski*)
downhill (race); **au milieu de la ~**
halfway down; **descente de lit** bedside
rug; **descente (de police)** (police) raid

**description** [dɛskʀipsjõ] *nf*

description

**déséquilibre** [dezekilibʀ] *nm*
(*position*): **en ~** unsteady; (*fig: des forces,
du budget*) imbalance

**désert, e** [dezɛʀ, ɛʀt] *adj* deserted
▷ *nm* desert; **désertique** *adj* desert *cpd*

**désespéré, e** [dezɛspeʀe] *adj*
desperate

**désespérer** [dezɛspeʀe] *vi*: **~ (de)** to
despair (of); **désespoir** *nm* despair; **en
désespoir de cause** in desperation

**déshabiller** [dezabije] *vt* to undress;
**se déshabiller** *vi* to undress (o.s.)

**déshydraté, e** [dezidʀate] *adj*
dehydrated

**désigner** [deziɲe] *vt* (*montrer*) to point
out, indicate; (*dénommer*) to denote;
(*candidat etc*) to name

**désinfectant, e** [dezɛ̃fɛktã, ãt] *adj,
nm* disinfectant

**désinfecter** [dezɛ̃fɛkte] *vt* to disinfect

**désintéressé, e** [dezɛ̃teʀese] *adj*
disinterested, unselfish

**désintéresser** [dezɛ̃teʀese] *vt*: **se ~
(de)** to lose interest (in)

**désintoxication** [dezɛ̃tɔksikasjõ]
*nf*: **faire une cure de ~** to undergo
treatment for alcoholism (*ou* drug
addiction)

**désinvolte** [dezɛ̃vɔlt] *adj* casual,
off-hand

**désir** [deziʀ] *nm* wish; (*sensuel*)
desire; **désirer** *vt* to want, wish for;
(*sexuellement*) to desire; **je désire ...**
(*formule de politesse*) I would like ...

**désister** [deziste]: **se désister** *vi* to
stand down, withdraw

**désobéir** [dezɔbeiʀ] *vi*: **~ (à qn/qch)** to
disobey (sb/sth); **désobéissant, e** *adj*
disobedient

**désodorisant** [dezɔdɔʀizã] *nm* air
freshener, deodorizer

**désolé, e** [dezɔle] *adj* (*paysage*)
desolate; **je suis ~** I'm sorry

**désordonné, e** [dezɔʀdɔne] *adj*
untidy

**désordre** [dezɔʀdʀ] *nm*
disorder(liness), untidiness; (*anarchie*)

disorder; **en ~** in a mess, untidy

**désormais** [dezɔRmɛ] *adv* from now on

**desquelles** [dekɛl] *prép +pron* = **de +lesquelles**

**desquels** [dekɛl] *prép +pron* = **de +lesquels**

**dessécher** [deseʃe]: **se dessécher** *vi* to dry out

**desserrer** [deseRe] *vt* to loosen; (*frein*) to release

**dessert** [deseR] *nm* dessert, pudding

**desservir** [deseRviR] *vt* (*ville, quartier*) to serve; (*débarrasser*): **~ (la table)** to clear the table

**dessin** [desɛ̃] *nm* (*œuvre, art*) drawing; (*motif*) pattern, design; **dessin animé** cartoon (film); **dessin humoristique** cartoon; **dessinateur, -trice** *nm/f* drawer; (*de bandes dessinées*) cartoonist; (*industriel*) draughtsman(-woman) (BRIT), draftsman(-woman) (US); **dessiner** *vt* to draw; (*concevoir*) to design; **se dessiner** *vi* (*forme*) to be outlined; (*fig: solution*) to emerge

**dessous** [d(ə)su] *adv* underneath, beneath ▷ *nm* underside ▷ *nmpl* (*sous-vêtements*) underwear *sg*; **en ~, par ~** underneath; **au-~ (de)** below; (*peu digne de*) beneath; **avoir le ~** to get the worst of it; **les voisins du ~** the downstairs neighbours; **dessous-de-plat** *nm inv* tablemat

**dessus** [d(ə)sy] *adv* on top; (*collé, écrit*) on it ▷ *nm* top; **en ~** above; **par ~** *adv* over it ▷ *prép* over; **au-~ (de)** above; **les voisins de ~** the upstairs neighbours; **avoir le ~** to get the upper hand; **sens ~** upside down; **dessus-de-lit** *nm inv* bedspread

**destin** [destɛ̃] *nm* fate; (*avenir*) destiny

**destinataire** [destinatɛR] *nm/f* (*Postes*) addressee; (*d'un colis*) consignee

**destination** [destinasjɔ̃] *nf* (*lieu*) destination; (*usage*) purpose; **à ~ de** bound for, travelling to

**destiner** [destine] *vt*: **~ qch à qn** (*envisager de donner*) to intend sb to have sth; (*adresser*) to intend sth for sb; **être destiné à** (*usage*) to be meant for; **se ~ à l'enseignement** to intend to become a teacher

**détachant** [detaʃɑ̃] *nm* stain remover

**détacher** [detaʃe] *vt* (*enlever*) to detach, remove; (*délier*) to untie; (*Admin*): **~ qn (auprès de** *ou* **à)** to post sb (to); **se détacher** *vi* (*se séparer*) to come off; (: *page*) to come out; (*se défaire*) to come undone; **se ~ sur** to stand out against; **se ~ de** (*se désintéresser*) to grow away from

**détail** [detaj] *nm* detail; (*Comm*): **le ~** retail; **en ~** in detail; **au ~** (*Comm*) retail; **détaillant** *nm* retailer; **détaillé, e** *adj* (*plan, explications*) detailed; (*facture*) itemized; **détailler** *vt* (*expliquer*) to explain in detail

**détecter** [detɛkte] *vt* to detect

**détective** [detɛktiv] *nm*: **détective (privé)** private detective

**déteindre** [detɛ̃dR] *vi* (*au lavage*) to run, lose its colour; **~ sur** (*vêtement*) to run into; (*fig*) to rub off on

**détendre** [detɑ̃dR] *vt* (*corps, esprit*) to relax; **se détendre** *vi* (*ressort*) to lose its tension; (*personne*) to relax

**détenir** [det(ə)niR] *vt* (*record, pouvoir, secret*) to hold; (*prisonnier*) to detain, hold

**détente** [detɑ̃t] *nf* relaxation

**détention** [detɑ̃sjɔ̃] *nf* (*d'armes*) possession; (*captivité*) detention; **détention préventive** custody

**détenu, e** [det(ə)ny] *nm/f* prisoner

**détergent** [deteRʒɑ̃] *nm* detergent

**détériorer** [deteRjɔRe] *vt* to damage; **se détériorer** *vi* to deteriorate

**déterminé, e** [detɛRmine] *adj* (*résolu*) determined; (*précis*) specific, definite

**déterminer** [detɛRmine] *vt* (*fixer*) to determine; **~ qn à faire qch** to decide sb to do sth; **se ~ à faire qch** to make up one's mind to do sth

**détester** [detɛste] *vt* to hate, detest

**détour** [detuR] *nm* detour; (*tournant*)

bend, curve; **ça vaut le ~** it's worth the trip; **sans ~** (fig) plainly

**détourné, e** [deturne] adj (moyen) roundabout

**détourner** [deturne] vt to divert; (par la force) to hijack; (yeux, tête) to turn away; (de l'argent) to embezzle; **se détourner** vi to turn away

**détraquer** [detrake] vt to put out of order; (estomac) to upset; **se détraquer** vi (machine) to go wrong

**détriment** [detrimã] nm: **au ~ de** to the detriment of

**détroit** [detrwa] nm strait

**détruire** [detrɥir] vt to destroy

**dette** [dɛt] nf debt

**DEUG** sigle m (= diplôme d'études universitaires générales) diploma taken after 2 years at university

**deuil** [dœj] nm (perte) bereavement; (période) mourning; **être en ~** to be in mourning

**deux** [dø] num two; **tous les ~** both; **ses ~ mains** both his hands, his two hands; **~ fois** twice; **deuxième** num second; **deuxièmement** adv secondly; **deux-pièces** nm inv (tailleur) two-piece suit; (de bain) two-piece (swimsuit); (appartement) two-roomed flat (BRIT) ou apartment (US); **deux-points** nm inv colon sg; **deux-roues** nm inv two-wheeled vehicle

**devais** [dəvɛ] vb voir **devoir**

**dévaluation** [devalɥasjɔ̃] nf devaluation

**devancer** [d(ə)vɑ̃se] vt (coureur, rival) to get ahead of; (arriver) to arrive before; (prévenir: questions, désirs) to anticipate

**devant** [d(ə)vɑ̃] adv in front; (à distance: en avant) ahead ▷ prép in front of; (en avant) ahead of; (avec mouvement: passer) past; (en présence de) before, in front of; (étant donné) in view of ▷ nm front; **prendre les ~s** to make the first move; **les pattes de ~** the front legs, the forelegs; **par ~** (boutonner) at the front; (entrer) the front way; **aller au-~ de**

qn to go out to meet sb; **aller au-~ de** (désirs de qn) to anticipate

**devanture** [d(ə)vɑ̃tyr] nf (étalage) display; (vitrine) (shop) window

**développement** [dev(ə)lɔpmɑ̃] nm development; **pays en voie de ~** developing countries

**développer** [dev(ə)lɔpe] vt to develop; **se développer** vi to develop

**devenir** [dəv(ə)nir] vb +attrib to become; **que sont-ils devenus?** what has become of them?

**devez** [dəve] vb voir **devoir**

**déviation** [devjasjɔ̃] nf (Auto) diversion (BRIT), detour (US)

**devienne** etc [dəvjɛn] vb voir **devenir**

**deviner** [d(ə)vine] vt to guess; (apercevoir) to distinguish; **devinette** nf riddle

**devis** [d(ə)vi] nm estimate, quotation

**devise** [dəviz] nf (formule) motto, watchword; **devises** nfpl (argent) currency sg

**dévisser** [devise] vt to unscrew, undo; **se dévisser** vi to come unscrewed

**devoir** [d(ə)vwar] nm duty; (Scol) homework no pl; (: en classe) exercise ▷ vt (argent, respect): to owe (sb) sth; (+infin: obligation): **il doit le faire** he has to do it, he must do it; (: intention): **le nouveau centre commercial doit ouvrir en mai** the new shopping centre is due to open in May; (: probabilité): **il doit être tard** it must be late; (: fatalité): **cela devait arriver** it was bound to happen; **combien est-ce que je vous dois?** how much do I owe you?

**dévorer** [devɔre] vt to devour

**dévoué, e** [devwe] adj devoted

**dévouer** [devwe]: **se dévouer** vi (se sacrifier): **se ~ (pour)** to sacrifice o.s. (for); (se consacrer): **se ~ à** to devote ou dedicate o.s. to

**devrai** [dəvre] vb voir **devoir**

**dézipper** [dezipe] vt to unzip

**diabète** [djabɛt] nm diabetes sg; **diabétique** nm/f diabetic

**diable** [djɑbl] nm devil
**diabolo** [djabolo] nm (boisson) lemonade with fruit cordial
**diagnostic** [djagnɔstik] nm diagnosis sg; **diagnostiquer** vt to diagnose
**diagonal, e, -aux** [djagɔnal, o] adj diagonal; **diagonale** nf diagonal; **en diagonale** diagonally
**diagramme** [djagram] nm chart, graph
**dialecte** [djalɛkt] nm dialect
**dialogue** [djalɔg] nm dialogue
**diamant** [djamɑ̃] nm diamond
**diamètre** [djamɛtr] nm diameter
**diapositive** [djapozitiv] nf transparency, slide
**diarrhée** [djare] nf diarrhoea
**dictateur** [diktatœr] nm dictator; **dictature** nf dictatorship
**dictée** [dikte] nf dictation
**dicter** [dikte] vt to dictate
**dictionnaire** [diksjɔnɛr] nm dictionary
**dièse** [djɛz] nm sharp
**diesel** [djezɛl] nm diesel ▷ adj inv diesel
**diète** [djɛt] nf (jeûne) starvation diet; (régime) diet; **diététique** adj: **magasin diététique** health food shop (BRIT) ou store (US)
**dieu, x** [djø] nm god; **D~** God; **mon D~!** good heavens!
**différemment** [diferamɑ̃] adv differently
**différence** [diferɑ̃s] nf difference; **à la ~ de** unlike; **différencier** vt to differentiate
**différent, e** [diferɑ̃, ɑ̃t] adj (dissemblable) different; **~ de** different from; (divers) different, various
**différer** [difere] vt to postpone, put off ▷ vi: **~ (de)** to differ (from)
**difficile** [difisil] adj difficult; (exigeant) hard to please; **difficilement** adv with difficulty
**difficulté** [difikylte] nf difficulty; **en ~** (bateau, alpiniste) in difficulties
**diffuser** [difyze] vt (chaleur) to diffuse;

(émission, musique) to broadcast; (nouvelle) to circulate; (Comm) to distribute
**digérer** [diʒere] vt to digest; (fam: accepter) to stomach, put up with; **digestif** nm (after-dinner) liqueur; **digestion** nf digestion
**digne** [diɲ] adj dignified; **~ de** worthy of; **~ de foi** trustworthy; **dignité** nf dignity
**digue** [dig] nf dike, dyke
**dilemme** [dilɛm] nm dilemma
**diligence** [diliʒɑ̃s] nf stagecoach
**diluer** [dilɥe] vt to dilute
**dimanche** [dimɑ̃ʃ] nm Sunday
**dimension** [dimɑ̃sjɔ̃] nf (grandeur) size; (dimensions) dimensions
**diminuer** [diminɥe] vt to reduce, decrease; (ardeur etc) to lessen; (dénigrer) to belittle ▷ vi to decrease, diminish; **diminutif** nm (surnom) pet name
**dinde** [dɛ̃d] nf turkey
**dindon** [dɛ̃dɔ̃] nm turkey
**dîner** [dine] nm dinner ▷ vi to have dinner
**dingue** [dɛ̃g] (fam) adj crazy
**dinosaure** [dinɔzɔr] nm dinosaur
**diplomate** [diplɔmat] adj diplomatic ▷ nm diplomat; (fig) diplomatist; **diplomatie** nf diplomacy
**diplôme** [diplom] nm diploma; **avoir des ~s** to have qualifications; **diplômé, e** adj qualified
**dire** [dir] nm: **au ~ de** according to ▷ vt to say; (secret, mensonge, heure) to tell; **~ qch à qn** to tell sb sth; **~ à qn qu'il fasse** ou **de faire** to tell sb to do; **on dit que** they say that; **ceci** ou **cela dit** that being said; **si cela lui dit** (plaire) if he fancies it; **que dites-vous de** (penser) what do you think of; **on dirait que** it looks (ou sounds etc) as if; **dis/dites (donc)!** I say!; **se ~ malade** (se prétendre) to claim one is ill; **ça ne se dit pas** (impoli) you shouldn't say that; (pas en usage) you don't say that
**direct, e** [dirɛkt] adj direct ▷ nm (TV):

en ~ live; **directement** adv directly
**directeur, -trice** [dirɛktœr, tris] nm/f (d'entreprise) director; (de service) manager(-eress); (d'école) head(teacher) (BRIT), principal (US)
**direction** [dirɛksjɔ̃] nf (sens) direction; (d'entreprise) management; (Auto) steering; **"toutes ~s"** "all routes"
**dirent** [dir] vb voir **dire**
**dirigeant, e** [diriʒɑ̃, ɑ̃t] adj (classe) ruling ▷ nm/f (d'un parti etc) leader
**diriger** [diriʒe] vt (entreprise) to manage, run; (véhicule) to steer; (orchestre) to conduct; (recherches, travaux) to supervise; **~ sur** (arme) to point ou level ou aim at; **~ son regard sur** to look in the direction of; **se diriger** vi (s'orienter) to find one's way; **se ~ vers** ou **sur** to make ou head for
**dis** [di] vb voir **dire**
**discerner** [disɛrne] vt to discern, make out
**discipline** [disiplin] nf discipline; **discipliner** vt to discipline
**discontinu, e** [diskɔ̃tiny] adj intermittent
**discontinuer** [diskɔ̃tinɥe] vi: **sans ~** without stopping, without a break
**discothèque** [diskɔtɛk] nf (boîte de nuit) disco(thèque)
**discours** [diskur] nm speech
**discret, -ète** [diskrɛ, ɛt] adj discreet; (parfum, maquillage) unobtrusive; **discrétion** nf discretion; **à discrétion** as much as one wants
**discrimination** [diskriminasjɔ̃] nf discrimination; **sans ~** indiscriminately
**discussion** [diskysjɔ̃] nf discussion
**discutable** [diskytabl] adj debatable
**discuter** [diskyte] vt (débattre) to discuss; (contester) to question, dispute ▷ vi to talk; (protester) to argue; **~ de** to discuss
**dise** [diz] vb voir **dire**
**disjoncteur** [disʒɔ̃ktœr] nm (Élec) circuit breaker
**disloquer** [dislɔke]: **se disloquer** vi

(parti, empire) to break up; (meuble) to come apart; (épaule) to be dislocated
**disons** [dizɔ̃] vb voir **dire**
**disparaître** [disparɛtr] vi to disappear; (se perdre: traditions etc) to die out; **faire ~** (tache) to remove; (douleur) to get rid of
**disparition** [disparisjɔ̃] nf disappearance; **espèce en voie de ~** endangered species
**disparu, e** [dispary] nm/f missing person ▷ adj: **être porté ~** to be reported missing
**dispensaire** [dispɑ̃sɛr] nm community clinic
**dispenser** [dispɑ̃se] vt: **~ qn de** to exempt sb from
**disperser** [dispɛrse] vt to scatter; **se disperser** vi to break up
**disponible** [dispɔnibl(ə)] adj available
**disposé, e** [dispoze] adj: **bien/mal ~** (humeur) in a good/bad mood; **~ à** (prêt à) willing ou prepared to
**disposer** [dispoze] vt to arrange ▷ vi: **vous pouvez ~** you may leave; **~ de** to have (at one's disposal); **se ~ à faire** to prepare to do, be about to do
**dispositif** [dispozitif] nm device; (fig) system, plan of action
**disposition** [dispozisjɔ̃] nf (arrangement) arrangement, layout; (humeur) mood; **prendre ses ~s** to make arrangements; **avoir des ~s pour la musique** etc to have a special aptitude for music etc; **à la ~ de qn** at sb's disposal; **je suis à votre ~** I am at your service
**disproportionné, e** [disprɔpɔrsjɔne] adj disproportionate, out of all proportion
**dispute** [dispyt] nf quarrel, argument; **disputer** vt (match) to play; (combat) to fight; **se disputer** vi to quarrel
**disqualifier** [diskalifje] vt to disqualify
**disque** [disk] nm (Mus) record; (forme, pièce) disc; (Sport) discus; **disque compact** compact disc; **disque dur**

hard disk; **disquette** nf floppy disk, diskette

**dissertation** [disɛʀtasjɔ̃] nf (Scol) essay

**dissimuler** [disimyle] vt to conceal

**dissipé, e** [disipe] adj (élève) undisciplined, unruly

**dissolvant** [disɔlvɑ̃] nm nail polish remover

**dissuader** [disɥade] vt: ~ qn de faire to dissuade sb from doing

**distance** [distɑ̃s] nf distance; (fig: écart) gap; **à ~** at ou from a distance; **distancer** vt to outdistance

**distant, e** [distɑ̃, ɑ̃t] adj (réservé) distant; **~ de** (lieu) far away from

**distillerie** [distilʀi] nf distillery

**distinct, e** [distɛ̃(kt), ɛ̃kt] adj distinct; **distinctement** adv distinctly, clearly; **distinctif, -ive** adj distinctive

**distingué, e** [distɛ̃ge] adj distinguished

**distinguer** [distɛ̃ge] vt to distinguish; **se ~ de** to be distinguished by

**distraction** [distraksjɔ̃] nf (inattention) absent-mindedness; (passe-temps) distraction, entertainment

**distraire** [distʀɛʀ] vt (divertir) to entertain, divert; (déranger) to distract; **se distraire** vi to amuse ou enjoy o.s.; **distrait, e** adj absent-minded

**distrayant, e** [distʀɛjɑ̃, ɑ̃t] adj entertaining

**distribuer** [distribɥe] vt to distribute, hand out; (Cartes) to deal (out); (courrier) to deliver; **distributeur** nm (Comm) distributor; **distributeur (automatique)** (vending) machine; **distributeur de billets** (cash) dispenser

**dit, e** [di, dit] pp de **dire** ▷ adj (fixé): **le jour ~** the arranged day; (surnommé): **X, ~ Pierrot** X, known as Pierrot

**dites** [dit] vb voir **dire**

**divan** [divɑ̃] nm divan

**divers, e** [divɛʀ, ɛʀs] adj (varié) diverse, varied; (différent) different, various; **~es personnes** various ou several people

**diversité** [divɛʀsite] nf (variété) diversity

**divertir** [divɛʀtiʀ]: **se divertir** vi to amuse ou enjoy o.s.; **divertissement** nm distraction, entertainment

**diviser** [divize] vt to divide; **division** nf division

**divorce** [divɔʀs] nm divorce; **divorcé, e** nm/f divorcee; **divorcer** vi to get a divorce, get divorced; **divorcer de** ou **d'avec qn** to divorce sb

**divulguer** [divylge] vt to disclose

**dix** [dis] num ten; **dix-huit** num eighteen; **dix-huitième** num eighteenth; **dixième** num tenth; **dix-neuf** num nineteen; **dix-neuvième** num nineteenth; **dix-sept** num seventeen; **dix-septième** num seventeenth

**dizaine** [dizɛn] nf: **une ~ (de)** about ten, ten or so

**do** [do] nm (note) C; (en chantant la gamme) do(h)

**docile** [dɔsil] adj docile

**dock** [dɔk] nm dock; **docker** nm docker

**docteur** [dɔktœʀ] nm doctor; **doctorat** nm doctorate

**doctrine** [dɔktʀin] nf doctrine

**document** [dɔkymɑ̃] nm document; **documentaire** adj, nm documentary; **documentation** nf documentation, literature; **documenter** vt: **se documenter (sur)** to gather information (on)

**dodo** [dodo] nm (langage enfantin): **aller faire ~** to go to beddy-byes

**dogue** [dɔg] nm mastiff

**doigt** [dwa] nm finger; **à deux ~s de** within an inch of; **un ~ de lait/ whiskey** a drop of milk/whisky; **doigt de pied** toe

**doit** etc [dwa] vb voir **devoir**

**dollar** [dɔlaʀ] nm dollar

**domaine** [dɔmɛn] nm estate, property; (fig) domain, field

**domestique** [dɔmɛstik] adj domestic ▷ nm/f servant, domestic

**domicile** [dɔmisil] *nm* home, place of residence; **à ~** at home; **livrer à ~** to deliver; **domicilié, e** *adj*: **"domicilié à ..."** "address ..."

**dominant, e** [dɔminɑ̃, ɑ̃t] *adj* (*opinion*) predominant

**dominer** [dɔmine] *vt* to dominate; (*sujet*) to master; (*surpasser*) to outclass, surpass; (*surplomber*) to tower above, dominate ▷ *vi* to be in the dominant position; **se dominer** *vi* to control o.s.

**domino** [dɔmino] *nm* domino; **dominos** *nmpl* (*jeu*) dominoes *sg*

**dommage** [dɔmaʒ] *nm*: **~s** (*dégâts*) damage *no pl*; **c'est ~!** what a shame!; **c'est ~ que** it's a shame ou pity that

**dompter** [dɔ̃(p)te] *vt* to tame; **dompteur, -euse** *nm/f* trainer

**DOM-ROM** [dɔmʀɔm] *sigle m* (= *départements et régions d'outre-mer*) French overseas departments and regions

**don** [dɔ̃] *nm* gift; (*charité*) donation; **avoir des ~s pour** to have a gift ou talent for; **elle a le ~ de m'énerver** she's got a knack of getting on my nerves

**donc** [dɔ̃k] *conj* therefore, so; (*après une digression*) so, then

**donné, e** [dɔne] *adj* (*convenu: lieu, heure*) given; (*pas cher: fam*): **c'est ~** it's a gift; **étant ~ que ...** given that ...; **données** *nfpl* data

**donner** [dɔne] *vt* to give; (*vieux habits etc*) to give away; (*spectacle*) to put on; **~ qch à qn** to give sb sth, give sth to sb; **~ sur** (*suj: fenêtre, chambre*) to look (out) onto; **ça donne soif/faim** it makes you (feel) thirsty/hungry; **se ~ à fond** to give one's all; **se ~ du mal** to take (great) trouble; **s'en ~ à cœur joie** (*fam*) to have a great time

 **MOT-CLÉ**

**dont** [dɔ̃] *pron relatif* **1** (*appartenance: objets*) whose, of which; (*appartenance: êtres animés*) whose; **la maison dont le toit est rouge** the house the roof of which is red, the house whose roof is red; **l'homme dont je connais la sœur** the man whose sister I know

**2** (*parmi lesquel(le)s*): **2 livres, dont l'un est ...** 2 books, one of which is ...; **il y avait plusieurs personnes, dont Gabrielle** there were several people, among them Gabrielle; **10 blessés, dont 2 grièvement** 10 injured, 2 of them seriously

**3** (*complément d'adjectif, de verbe*): **le fils dont il est si fier** the son he's so proud of; **le pays dont il est originaire** the country he's from; **la façon dont il l'a fait** the way he did it; **ce dont je parle** what I'm talking about

**dopage** [dɔpaʒ] *nm* (*Sport*) drug use; (*de cheval*) doping

**doré, e** [dɔʀe] *adj* golden; (*avec dorure*) gilt, gilded

**dorénavant** [dɔʀenavɑ̃] *adv* henceforth

**dorer** [dɔʀe] *vt* to gild; **(faire) ~** (*Culin*) to brown

**dorloter** [dɔʀlɔte] *vt* to pamper

**dormir** [dɔʀmiʀ] *vi* to sleep; (*être endormi*) to be asleep

**dortoir** [dɔʀtwaʀ] *nm* dormitory

**dos** [do] *nm* back; (*de livre*) spine; **"voir au ~"** "see over"; **de ~** from the back

**dosage** [dozaʒ] *nm* mixture

**dose** [doz] *nf* dose; **doser** *vt* to measure out; **il faut savoir doser ses efforts** you have to be able to pace yourself

**dossier** [dosje] *nm* (*documents*) file; (*de chaise*) back; (*Presse*) feature; (*Comput*) folder; **un ~ scolaire** a school report

**douane** [dwan] *nf* customs *pl*; **douanier, -ière** *adj* customs *cpd* ▷ *nm* customs officer

**double** [dubl] *adj, adv* double ▷ *nm* (2 *fois plus*): **le ~ (de)** twice as much (ou many) (as); (*autre exemplaire*) duplicate, copy; (*sosie*) double; (*Tennis*) doubles *sg*; **en ~ (exemplaire)** in duplicate; **faire ~ emploi** to be redundant; **double-cliquer** *vi* (*Inform*) to double-click

**doubler** [duble] vt (*multiplier par 2*) to double; (*vêtement*) to line; (*dépasser*) to overtake, pass; (*film*) to dub; (*acteur*) to stand in for ▷ vi to double

**doublure** [dublyʀ] nf lining; (*Cinéma*) stand-in

**douce** [dus] adj voir **doux**; **douceâtre** adj sickly sweet; **doucement** adv gently; (*lentement*) slowly; **douceur** nf softness; (*de quelqu'un*) gentleness; (*de climat*) mildness

**douche** [duʃ] nf shower; **prendre une ~** to have ou take a shower; **doucher: se doucher** vi to have ou take a shower

**doué, e** [dwe] adj gifted, talented; **être ~ pour** to have a gift for

**douille** [duj] nf (*Élec*) socket

**douillet, te** [dujɛ, ɛt] adj cosy; (*péj: à la douleur*) soft

**douleur** [dulœʀ] nf pain; (*chagrin*) grief, distress; **douloureux, -euse** adj painful

**doute** [dut] nm doubt; **sans ~** no doubt; (*probablement*) probably; **sans aucun ~** without a doubt; **douter** vt to doubt; **douter de** (*sincérité de qn*) to have (one's) doubts about; (*réussite*) to be doubtful of; **douter que** to doubt if ou whether; **se douter de qch/que** to suspect sth/that; **je m'en doutais** I suspected as much; **douteux, -euse** adj (*incertain*) doubtful; (*péj*) dubious-looking

**Douvres** [duvʀ] n Dover

**doux, douce** [du, dus] adj soft; (*sucré*) sweet; (*peu fort*: moutarde, clément: climat*) mild; (*pas brusque*) gentle

**douzaine** [duzɛn] nf (12) dozen; (*environ 12*): **une ~ (de)** a dozen or so

**douze** [duz] num twelve; **douzième** num twelfth

**dragée** [dʀaʒe] nf sugared almond

**draguer** [dʀage] vt (*rivière*) to dredge; (*fam*) to try to pick up

**dramatique** [dʀamatik] adj dramatic; (*tragique*) tragic ▷ nf (TV) (television) drama

**drame** [dʀam] nm drama

**drap** [dʀa] nm (*de lit*) sheet; (*tissu*) woollen fabric

**drapeau, x** [dʀapo] nm flag

**drap-housse** [dʀaus] nm fitted sheet

**dresser** [dʀese] vt (*mettre vertical, monter*) to put up, erect; (*liste*) to draw up; (*animal*) to train; **se dresser** vi (*obstacle*) to stand; (*personne*) to draw o.s. up; **~ qn contre qn** to set sb against sb; **~ l'oreille** to prick up one's ears

**drogue** [dʀɔg] nf drug; **la ~** drugs pl; **drogué, e** nm/f drug addict; **droguer** vt (*victime*) to drug; **se droguer** vi (*aux stupéfiants*) to take drugs; (*péj: de médicaments*) to dose o.s. up; **droguerie** nf hardware shop; **droguiste** nm keeper/owner of a hardware shop

**droit, e** [dʀwa, dʀwat] adj (*non courbe*) straight; (*vertical*) upright, straight; (*fig: loyal*) upright, straight(forward); (*opposé à gauche*) right, right-hand ▷ adv straight ▷ nm (*prérogative*) right; (*taxe*) duty, tax; (: d'inscription) fee; (*Jur*): **le ~** law; **avoir le ~ de** to be allowed to; **avoir ~ à** to be entitled to; **être dans son ~** to be within one's rights; **à ~e** on the right; (*direction*) (to the) right; **droits d'auteur** royalties; **droits d'inscription** enrolment fee; **droite** nf (*Pol*): **la droite** the right (wing); **droitier, -ière** adj right-handed

**drôle** [dʀol] adj funny; **une ~ d'idée** a funny idea

**dromadaire** [dʀɔmadɛʀ] nm dromedary

**du** [dy] dét voir **de** ▷ prép +dét = **de + le**

**dû, due** [dy] vb voir **devoir** ▷ adj (*somme*) owing, owed; (*causé par*) **dû à** due to ▷ nm due

**dune** [dyn] nf dune

**duplex** [dyplɛks] nm (*appartement*) split-level apartment, duplex

**duquel** [dykɛl] prép +pron = **de +lequel**

**dur, e** [dyʀ] adj (*pierre, siège, travail, problème*) hard; (*voix, climat*) harsh; (*sévère*) hard, harsh; (*cruel*) hard(-hearted); (*porte, col*) stiff; (*viande*) tough ▷ adv hard ▷ nm (*fam*:

*meneur*) tough nut; **~ d'oreille** hard of hearing

**durant** [dyʀɑ̃] *prép* (*au cours de*) during; (*pendant*) for; **des mois ~** for months

**durcir** [dyʀsiʀ] *vt, vi* to harden; **se durcir** *vi* to harden

**durée** [dyʀe] *nf* length; (*d'une pile etc*) life; **de courte ~** (*séjour*) short

**durement** [dyʀmɑ̃] *adv* harshly

**durer** [dyʀe] *vi* to last

**dureté** [dyʀte] *nf* hardness; harshness; stiffness; toughness

**durit(r)** [dyʀit] *nf* (car radiator) hose

**duvet** [dyvɛ] *nm* down; (*sac de couchage*) down-filled sleeping bag

**DVD** *sigle m* (= *digital versatile disc*) DVD

**dynamique** [dinamik] *adj* dynamic; **dynamisme** *nm* dynamism

**dynamo** [dinamo] *nf* dynamo

**dyslexie** [dislɛksi] *nf* dyslexia, word-blindness

# e

**eau, x** [o] *nf* water; **eaux** *nfpl* (*Méd*) waters; **prendre l'~** to leak, let in water; **tomber à l'~** (*fig*) to fall through; **eau de Cologne** eau de Cologne; **eau courante** running water; **eau de javel** bleach; **eau de toilette** toilet water; **eau douce** fresh water; **eau gazeuse** sparkling (mineral) water; **eau minérale** mineral water; **eau plate** still water; **eau salée** salt water; **eau-de-vie** *nf* brandy

**ébène** [ebɛn] *nf* ebony; **ébéniste** *nm* cabinetmaker

**éblouir** [ebluiʀ] *vt* to dazzle

**éboueur** [ebwœʀ] *nm* dustman (*BRIT*), garbageman (*US*)

**ébouillanter** [ebujɑ̃te] *vt* to scald; (*Culin*) to blanch

**éboulement** [ebulmɑ̃] *nm* rock fall

**ébranler** [ebʀɑ̃le] *vt* to shake; (*affaiblir*) to weaken; **s'ébranler** *vi* (*partir*) to move off

**ébullition** [ebylisjɔ̃] *nf* boiling point; **en ~** boiling

**écaille** [ekɑj] nf (de poisson) scale; (matière) tortoiseshell; **écailler** vt (poisson) to scale; **s'écailler** vi to flake ou peel (off)

**écart** [ekaʀ] nm gap; **à l'~** out of the way; **à l'~ de** away from; **faire un ~** (voiture) to swerve

**écarté, e** [ekaʀte] adj (lieu) out-of-the-way, remote; (ouvert): **les jambes ~es** legs apart; **les bras ~s** arms outstretched

**écarter** [ekaʀte] vt (séparer) to move apart, separate; (éloigner) to push back, move away; (ouvrir: bras, jambes) to spread, open; (: rideau) to draw (back); (éliminer: candidat, possibilité) to dismiss; **s'écarter** vi to part; (s'éloigner) to move away; **s'~ de** to wander from

**échafaudage** [eʃafodaʒ] nm scaffolding

**échalote** [eʃalɔt] nf shallot

**échange** [eʃɑ̃ʒ] nm exchange; **en ~ de** in exchange ou return for; **échanger** vt: **échanger qch (contre)** to exchange sth (for)

**échantillon** [eʃɑ̃tijɔ̃] nm sample

**échapper** [eʃape]: **~ à** vt (gardien) to escape (from); (punition, péril) to escape; **s'échapper** vi to escape; **~ à qn** (détail, sens) to escape sb; (objet qu'on tient) to slip out of sb's hands; **laisser ~** (cri etc) to let out; **l'~ belle** to have a narrow escape

**écharde** [eʃaʀd] nf splinter (of wood)

**écharpe** [eʃaʀp] nf scarf; **avoir le bras en ~** to have one's arm in a sling

**échauffer** [eʃofe] vt (moteur) to overheat; **s'échauffer** vi (Sport) to warm up; (dans la discussion) to become heated

**échéance** [eʃeɑ̃s] nf (d'un paiement: date) settlement date; (fig) deadline; **à brève ~** in the short term; **à longue ~** in the long run

**échéant** [eʃeɑ̃]: **le cas ~** adv if the case arises

**échec** [eʃɛk] nm failure; (Échecs): **~ et mat/au roi** checkmate/check; **échecs** nmpl (jeu) chess sg; **tenir en ~** to hold in check

**échelle** [eʃɛl] nf ladder; (fig, d'une carte) scale

**échelon** [eʃ(ə)lɔ̃] nm (d'échelle) rung; (Admin) grade; **échelonner** vt to space out

**échiquier** [eʃikje] nm chessboard

**écho** [eko] nm echo; **échographie** nf: **passer une échographie** to have a scan

**échouer** [eʃwe] vi to fail; **s'échouer** vi to run aground

**éclabousser** [eklabuse] vt to splash

**éclair** [eklɛʀ] nm (d'orage) flash of lightning, lightning no pl; (gâteau) éclair

**éclairage** [eklɛʀaʒ] nm lighting

**éclaircie** [eklɛʀsi] nf bright interval

**éclaircir** [eklɛʀsiʀ] vt to lighten; (fig: mystère) to clear up; (: point) to clarify; **s'éclaircir** vi (ciel) to clear; **s'~ la voix** to clear one's throat; **éclaircissement** nm (sur un point) clarification

**éclairer** [eklɛʀe] vt (lieu) to light (up); (personne: avec une lampe etc) to light the way for; (fig: problème) to shed light on ▷ vi: **~ mal/bien** to give a poor/good light; **s'~ à la bougie** to use candlelight

**éclat** [ekla] nm (de bombe, de verre) fragment; (du soleil, d'une couleur etc) brightness, brilliance; (d'une cérémonie) splendour; (scandale): **faire un ~** to cause a commotion; **éclats de voix** shouts; **éclat de rire** roar of laughter

**éclatant, e** [eklatɑ̃, ɑ̃t] adj brilliant

**éclater** [eklate] vi (pneu) to burst; (bombe) to explode; (guerre) to break out; (groupe, parti) to break up; **~ en sanglots/de rire** to burst out sobbing/laughing

**écluse** [eklyz] nf lock

**écœurant, e** [ekœʀɑ̃, ɑ̃t] adj (gâteau etc) sickly; (fig) sickening

**écœurer** [ekœʀe] vt: **~ qn** (nourriture) to make sb feel sick; (conduite, personne) to disgust sb

**école** [ekɔl] nf school; **aller à l'~** to go

to school; **école maternelle** nursery school; **école primaire** primary (BRIT) ou grade (US) school; **école secondaire** secondary (BRIT) ou high (US) school; **écolier, -ière** nm/f schoolboy(-girl)

**écologie** [ekɔlɔʒi] nf ecology; **écologique** adj environment-friendly; **écologiste** nm/f ecologist

**économe** [ekɔnɔm] adj thrifty ▷ nm/f (de lycée etc) bursar (BRIT), treasurer (US)

**économie** [ekɔnɔmi] nf economy; (gain: d'argent, de temps etc) saving; (science) economics sg; **économies** nfpl (pécule) savings; **économique** adj (avantageux) economical; (Écon) economic; **économiser** vt, vi to save

**écorce** [ekɔʀs] nf bark; (de fruit) peel

**écorcher** [ekɔʀʃe] vt: **s'~ le genou/la main** to graze one's knee/one's hand; **écorchure** nf graze

**écossais, e** [ekɔsɛ, ɛz] adj Scottish ▷ nm/f: É-, e Scot

**Écosse** [ekɔs] nf: **l'~** Scotland

**écouter** [ekute] vt to listen to; **s'écouter** (malade) to be a bit of a hypochondriac; **si je m'écoutais** if I followed my instincts; **écouteur** nm (Tél) receiver; **écouteurs** nmpl (casque) headphones pl, headset

**écran** [ekʀɑ̃] nm screen; **petit ~** television; **~ total** sunblock

**écrasant, e** [ekʀazɑ̃, ɑ̃t] adj overwhelming

**écraser** [ekʀaze] vt to crush; (piéton) to run over; **s'écraser** vi to crash; **s'~ contre** to crash into

**écrémé, e** [ekʀeme] adj (lait) skimmed

**écrevisse** [ekʀəvis] nf crayfish inv

**écrire** [ekʀiʀ] vt to write; **s'écrire** to write to each other; **ça s'écrit comment?** how is it spelt?; **écrit** nm (examen) written paper; **par écrit** in writing

**écriteau, x** [ekʀito] nm notice, sign

**écriture** [ekʀityʀ] nf writing; **écritures** nfpl (Comm) accounts, books; **l'É-~ (sainte), les É-s** the Scriptures

**écrivain** [ekʀivɛ̃] nm writer

**écrou** [ekʀu] nm nut

**écrouler** [ekʀule]: **s'écrouler** vi to collapse

**écru, e** [ekʀy] adj (couleur) off-white, écru

**écume** [ekym] nf foam

**écureuil** [ekyʀœj] nm squirrel

**écurie** [ekyʀi] nf stable

**eczéma** [ɛgzema] nm eczema

**EDF** sigle f (= Électricité de France) national electricity company

**Édimbourg** [edɛ̃buʀ] n Edinburgh

**éditer** [edite] vt (publier) to publish; (annoter) to edit; **éditeur, -trice** nm/f publisher; **édition** nf edition; (industrie du livre) publishing

**édredon** [edʀədɔ̃] nm eiderdown

**éducateur, -trice** [edykatœʀ, tʀis] nm/f teacher; (en école spécialisée) instructor

**éducatif, -ive** [edykatif, iv] adj educational

**éducation** [edykasjɔ̃] nf education; (familiale) upbringing; (manières) (good) manners pl; **éducation physique** physical education

**éduquer** [edyke] vt to educate; (élever) to bring up

**effacer** [efase] vt to erase, rub out; **s'effacer** vi (inscription etc) to wear off; (pour laisser passer) to step aside

**effarant, e** [efaʀɑ̃, ɑ̃t] adj alarming

**effectif, -ive** [efɛktif, iv] adj real ▷ nm (Scol) (pupil) numbers pl; (entreprise) staff, workforce; **effectivement** adv (réellement) actually, really; (en effet) indeed

**effectuer** [efɛktɥe] vt (opération) to carry out; (trajet) to make

**effervescent, e** [efɛʀvesɑ̃, ɑ̃t] adj effervescent

**effet** [efɛ] nm effect; (impression) impression; **effets** nmpl (vêtements etc) things; **faire ~** (médicament) to take effect; **faire de l'~** (impressionner) to make an impression; **faire bon/mauvais ~ sur qn** to make a good/bad impression on sb; **en ~** indeed; **effet de**

**serre** greenhouse effect

**efficace** [efikas] *adj (personne)* efficient; *(action, médicament)* effective; **efficacité** *nf* efficiency; effectiveness

**effondrer** [efɔ̃dʀe]: **s'effondrer** *vi* to collapse

**efforcer** [efɔʀse]: **s'efforcer de** *vt*: **s'~ de faire** to try hard to do

**effort** [efɔʀ] *nm* effort

**effrayant, e** [efʀɛjɑ̃, ɑ̃t] *adj* frightening

**effrayer** [efʀeje] *vt* to frighten, scare; **s'~ (de)** to be frightened *ou* scared (by)

**effréné, e** [efʀene] *adj* wild

**effronté, e** [efʀɔ̃te] *adj* cheeky

**effroyable** [efʀwajabl] *adj* horrifying, appalling

**égal, e, -aux** [egal, o] *adj* equal; *(constant: vitesse)* steady ▷ *nm/f* equal; **être ~ à** *(prix, nombre)* to be equal to; **ça lui est ~** it's all the same to him, he doesn't mind; **sans ~** matchless, unequalled; **d'~ à ~** as equals; **également** *adv* equally; *(aussi)* too, as well; **égaler** *vt* to equal; **égaliser** *vt (sol, salaires)* to level (out); *(chances)* to equalize ▷ *vi (Sport)* to equalize; **égalité** *nf* equality; **être à égalité** to be level

**égard** [egaʀ] *nm*: **~s** *mpl* consideration *sg*; **à cet ~** in this respect; **par ~ pour** out of consideration for; **à l'~ de** towards

**égarer** [egaʀe] *vt* to mislay; **s'égarer** *vi* to get lost, lose one's way; *(objet)* to go astray

**églefin** [egləfɛ̃] *nm* haddock

**église** [egliz] *nf* church; **aller à l'~** to go to church

**égoïsme** [egɔism] *nm* selfishness; **égoïste** *adj* selfish

**égout** [egu] *nm* sewer

**égoutter** [egute] *vt* to drip; **s'égoutter** *vi* to drip; **égouttoir** *nm* draining board; *(mobile)* draining rack

**égratignure** [egʀatiɲyʀ] *nf* scratch

**Égypte** [eʒipt] *nf*: **l'~** Egypt; **égyptien, ne** *adj* Egyptian ▷ *nm/f*:

**Égyptien, ne** Egyptian

**eh** [e] *excl* hey!; **eh bien!** well!

**élaborer** [elabɔʀe] *vt* to elaborate; *(projet, stratégie)* to work out; *(rapport)* to draft

**élan** [elɑ̃] *nm (Zool)* elk, moose; *(Sport)* run up; *(fig: de tendresse etc)* surge; **prendre de l'~** to gather speed

**élancer** [elɑ̃se]: **s'élancer** *vi* to dash, hurl o.s.

**élargir** [elaʀʒiʀ] *vt* to widen; **s'élargir** *vi* to widen; *(vêtement)* to stretch

**élastique** [elastik] *adj* elastic ▷ *nm (de bureau)* rubber band; *(pour la couture)* elastic *no pl*

**élection** [elɛksjɔ̃] *nf* election

**électricien, ne** [elɛktʀisjɛ̃, jɛn] *nm/f* electrician

**électricité** [elɛktʀisite] *nf* electricity; **allumer/éteindre l'~** to put on/off the light

**électrique** [elɛktʀik] *adj* electric(al)

**électrocuter** [elɛktʀɔkyte] *vt* to electrocute

**électroménager** [elɛktʀomenaʒe] *adj, nm*: **appareils ~s, l'~** domestic (electrical) appliances

**électronique** [elɛktʀɔnik] *adj* electronic ▷ *nf* electronics *sg*

**élégance** [elegɑ̃s] *nf* elegance

**élégant, e** [elegɑ̃, ɑ̃t] *adj* elegant

**élément** [elemɑ̃] *nm* element; *(pièce)* component, part; **élémentaire** *adj* elementary

**éléphant** [elefɑ̃] *nm* elephant

**élevage** [el(ə)vaʒ] *nm* breeding; *(de bovins)* cattle rearing; **truite d'~** farmed trout

**élevé, e** [el(ə)ve] *adj* high; **bien/mal ~** well-/ill-mannered

**élève** [elɛv] *nm/f* pupil

**élever** [el(ə)ve] *vt (enfant)* to bring up, raise; *(animaux)* to breed; *(hausser: taux, niveau)* to raise; *(édifier: monument)* to put up, erect; **s'élever** *vi (avion)* to go up; *(niveau, température)* to rise; **s'~ à** *(suj: frais, dégâts)* to amount to, add up to; **s'~ contre qch** to rise up against

sth; **~ la voix** to raise one's voice;
**éleveur, -euse** nm/f breeder
**éliminatoire** [eliminatwaʀ] nf
(Sport) heat
**éliminer** [elimine] vt to eliminate
**élire** [eliʀ] vt to elect
**elle** [ɛl] pron (sujet) she; (: chose) it;
(complément) her; it; **~s** (sujet) they;
(complément) them; **~-même** herself;
itself; **~s-mêmes** themselves; voir
aussi **il**
**éloigné, e** [elwaɲe] adj distant, far-off;
(parent) distant
**éloigner** [elwaɲe] vt (échéance) to put
off, postpone; (soupçons, danger) to
ward off; (objet): **~ qch (de)** to move
ou take sth away (from); (personne):
**~ qn (de)** to take sb away ou remove
sb (from); **s'éloigner (de)** (personne)
to go away (from); (véhicule) to move
away (from); (affectivement) to grow
away (from)
**élu, e** [ely] pp de **élire** ▷ nm/f (Pol)
elected representative
**Élysée** [elize] nm: **(le palais de) l'~**
the Élysée Palace (the French president's
residence)
**émail, -aux** [emaj, o] nm enamel
**e-mail** [imɛl] nm e-mail; **envoyer qch
par ~** to e-mail sth
**émanciper** [emãsipe] **s'émanciper**
vi (fig) to become emancipated ou
liberated
**emballage** [ãbalaʒ] nm (papier)
wrapping; (boîte) packaging
**emballer** [ãbale] vt to wrap (up); (dans
un carton) to pack (up); (fig: fam) to thrill
(to bits); **s'emballer** vi (moteur) to race;
(cheval) to bolt; (fig: personne) to get
carried away
**embarcadère** [ãbaʀkadɛʀ] nm
wharf, pier
**embarquement** [ãbaʀkəmã] nm (de
passagers) boarding; (de marchandises)
loading
**embarquer** [ãbaʀke] vt (personne) to
embark; (marchandise) to load; (fam)
to cart off ▷ vi (passager) to board;

**s'embarquer** vi to board; **s'~ dans**
(affaire, aventure) to embark upon
**embarras** [ãbaʀa] nm (gêne)
embarrassment; **mettre qn dans
l'~** to put sb in an awkward position;
**vous n'avez que l'~ du choix** the only
problem is choosing
**embarrassant, e** [ãbaʀasã, ãt] adj
embarrassing
**embarrasser** [ãbaʀase] vt (encombrer)
to clutter (up); (gêner) to hinder,
hamper; **~ qn** to put sb in an awkward
position; **s'~ de** to burden o.s. with
**embaucher** [ãboʃe] vt to take on, hire
**embêter** [ãbete] vt to bother;
**s'embêter** vi (s'ennuyer) to be bored
**emblée** [ãble]: **d'~** adv straightaway
**embouchure** [ãbuʃyʀ] nf (Géo) mouth
**embourber** [ãbuʀbe]: **s'embourber** vi
to get stuck in the mud
**embouteillage** [ãbutɛjaʒ] nm
traffic jam
**embranchement** [ãbʀãʃmã] nm
(routier) junction
**embrasser** [ãbʀase] vt to kiss; (sujet,
période) to embrace, encompass
**embrayage** [ãbʀɛjaʒ] nm clutch
**embrouiller** [ãbʀuje] vt to muddle up;
(fils) to tangle (up); **s'embrouiller** vi
(personne) to get in a muddle
**embruns** [ãbʀœ̃] nmpl sea spray sg
**embué, e** [ãbɥe] adj misted up
**émeraude** [em(ə)ʀod] nf emerald
**émerger** [emɛʀʒe] vi to emerge; (faire
saillie, aussi fig) to stand out
**émeri** [em(ə)ʀi] nm: **toile** ou **papier ~**
emery paper
**émerveiller** [emɛʀveje] vt to fill with
wonder; **s'émerveiller de** to marvel at
**émettre** [emɛtʀ] vt (son, lumière) to
give out, emit; (message etc: Radio) to
transmit; (billet, timbre, emprunt) to
issue; (hypothèse, avis) to voice, put
forward ▷ vi to broadcast
**émeus** etc [emø] vb voir **émouvoir**
**émeute** [emøt] nf riot
**émigrer** [emigʀe] vi to emigrate
**émincer** [emɛ̃se] vt to cut into thin

slices

**émission** [emisjɔ̃] nf (Radio, TV) programme, broadcast; (d'un message) transmission; (de timbre) issue

**emmêler** [ɑ̃mele] vt to tangle (up); (fig) to muddle up; **s'emmêler** vi to get in a tangle

**emménager** [ɑ̃menaʒe] vi to move in; **~ dans** to move into

**emmener** [ɑ̃m(ə)ne] vt to take (with one); (comme otage, capture) to take away; **~ qn au cinéma** to take sb to the cinema

**emmerder** [ɑ̃mɛʀde] (fam!) vt to bug, bother; **s'emmerder** vi to be bored stiff

**émoticone** [emotikon] nm smiley

**émotif, -ive** [emotif, iv] adj emotional

**émotion** [emosjɔ̃] nf emotion

**émouvoir** [emuvwaʀ] vt to move; **s'émouvoir** vi to be moved; (s'indigner) to be roused

**empaqueter** [ɑ̃pakte] vt to parcel up

**emparer** [ɑ̃paʀe]: **s'emparer de** vt (objet) to seize, grab; (comme otage, MIL) to seize; (suj: peur etc) to take hold of

**empêchement** [ɑ̃pɛʃmɑ̃] nm (unexpected) obstacle, hitch

**empêcher** [ɑ̃peʃe] vt to prevent; **~ qn de faire** to prevent ou stop sb (from) doing; **il n'empêche que** nevertheless; **il n'a pas pu s'~ de rire** he couldn't help laughing

**empereur** [ɑ̃pʀœʀ] nm emperor

**empiffrer** [ɑ̃pifʀe]: **s'~** (fam) vi to stuff o.s.

**empiler** [ɑ̃pile] vt to pile (up)

**empire** [ɑ̃piʀ] nm empire; (fig) influence

**empirer** [ɑ̃piʀe] vi to worsen, deteriorate

**emplacement** [ɑ̃plasmɑ̃] nm site

**emploi** [ɑ̃plwa] nm (utilisation) use; (Comm, Écon) employment; (poste) job, situation; **mode d'~** directions for use; **emploi du temps** timetable, schedule

**employé, e** [ɑ̃plwaje] nm/f employee; **employé de bureau** office employee ou clerk

**employer** [ɑ̃plwaje] vt to use; (ouvrier, main-d'œuvre) to employ; **s'~ à faire** to apply ou devote o.s. to doing; **employeur, -euse** nm/f employer

**empoigner** [ɑ̃pwaɲe] vt to grab

**empoisonner** [ɑ̃pwazɔne] vt to poison; (empester: air, pièce) to stink out; (fam): **~ qn** to drive sb mad

**emporter** [ɑ̃pɔʀte] vt to take (with one); (en dérobant ou enlevant, emmener: blessés, voyageurs) to take away; (entraîner) to carry away; **s'emporter** vi (de colère) to lose one's temper; **l'~ (sur)** to get the upper hand (of); **plats à ~** take-away meals

**empreinte** [ɑ̃pʀɛ̃t] nf: **~ (de pas)** footprint; **empreintes (digitales)** fingerprints

**empressé, e** [ɑ̃pʀese] adj attentive

**empresser** [ɑ̃pʀese]: **s'empresser** vi: **s'~ auprès de qn** to surround sb with attentions; **s'~ de faire** (se hâter) to hasten to do

**emprisonner** [ɑ̃pʀizɔne] vt to imprison

**emprunt** [ɑ̃pʀœ̃] nm loan

**emprunter** [ɑ̃pʀœ̃te] vt to borrow; (itinéraire) to take, follow

**ému, e** [emy] pp de **émouvoir** ▷ adj (gratitude) touched; (compassion) moved

 **MOT-CLÉ**

**en** [ɑ̃] prép **1** (endroit, pays) in; (direction) to; **habiter en France/ville** to live in France/town; **aller en France/ville** to go to France/town

**2** (moment, temps) in; **en été/juin** in summer/June; **en 3 jours** in 3 days

**3** (moyen) by; **en avion/taxi** by plane/taxi

**4** (composition) made of; **c'est en verre** it's (made of) glass; **un collier en argent** a silver necklace

**5** (description, état): **une femme (habillée) en rouge** a woman (dressed) in red; **peindre qch en rouge** to paint sth red; **en T/étoile** T/star-shaped; **en**

**chemise/chaussettes** in one's shirt-sleeves/socks; **en soldat** as a soldier; **cassé en plusieurs morceaux** broken into several pieces; **en réparation** being repaired, under repair; **en vacances** on holiday; **en deuil** in mourning; **le même en plus grand** the same but *ou* only bigger

6 *(avec gérondif)* while, on, by; **en dormant** while sleeping, as one sleeps; **en sortant** on going out, as he *etc* went out; **sortir en courant** to run out

7 *(comme)* as; **je te parle en ami** I'm talking to you as a friend

▷ *pron* 1 *(indéfini)*: **j'en ai/veux** I have/want some; **en as-tu?** have you got any?; **je n'en veux pas** I don't want any; **j'en ai 2** I've got 2; **combien y en a-t-il?** how many (of them) are there?; **j'en ai assez** I've got enough (of it *ou* them); *(j'en ai marre)* I've had enough

2 *(provenance)* from there; **j'en viens** I've come from there

3 *(cause)*: **il en est malade/perd le sommeil** he is ill/can't sleep because of it

4 *(complément de nom, d'adjectif, de verbe)*: **j'en connais les dangers** I know its *ou* the dangers; **j'en suis fier** I am proud of it *ou* him *ou* her *ou* them; **j'en ai besoin** I need it *ou* them

**encadrer** [ãkadʀe] *vt (tableau, image)* to frame; *(fig: entourer)* to surround; *(personnel, soldats etc)* to train

**encaisser** [ãkese] *vt (chèque)* to cash; *(argent)* to collect; *(fam: coup, défaite)* to take

**en-cas** [ãkɑ] *nm* snack

**enceinte** [ãsɛ̃t] *adj f*: **~ (de 6 mois)** (6 months) pregnant ▷ *nf (mur)* wall; *(espace)* enclosure; **enceinte (acoustique)** (loud)speaker

**encens** [ãsã] *nm* incense

**enchaîner** [ãʃene] *vt* to chain up; *(mouvements, séquences)* to link (together) ▷ *vi* to carry on

**enchanté, e** [ãʃãte] *adj (ravi)* delighted; *(magique)* enchanted; **~ (de faire votre connaissance)** pleased to meet you

**enchère** [ãʃɛʀ] *nf* bid; **mettre/vendre aux ~s** to put up for (sale by)/sell by auction

**enclencher** [ãklãʃe] *vt (mécanisme)* to engage; **s'enclencher** *vi* to engage

**encombrant, e** [ãkɔ̃bʀã, ãt] *adj* cumbersome, bulky

**encombrement** [ãkɔ̃bʀəmã] *nm*: **être pris dans un ~** to be stuck in a traffic jam

**encombrer** [ãkɔ̃bʀe] *vt* to clutter (up); *(gêner)* to hamper; **s'~ de** *(bagages etc)* to load *ou* burden o.s. with

 **MOT-CLÉ**

**encore** [ãkɔʀ] *adv* 1 *(continuation)* still; **il y travaille encore** he's still working on it; **pas encore** not yet

2 *(de nouveau)* again; **j'irai encore demain** I'll go again tomorrow; **encore une fois** (once) again; **(et puis) quoi encore?** what next?

3 *(en plus)* more; **encore un peu de viande?** a little more meat?; **encore deux jours** two more days

4 *(intensif)* even, still; **encore plus fort/mieux** even louder/better, louder/better still

5 *(restriction)* even so *ou* then, only; **encore pourrais-je le faire si ...** even so, I might be able to do it if ...; **si encore** if only

**encourager** [ãkuʀaʒe] *vt* to encourage; **~ qn à faire qch** to encourage sb to do sth

**encourir** [ãkuʀiʀ] *vt* to incur

**encre** [ãkʀ] *nf* ink; **encre de Chine** Indian ink

**encyclopédie** [ãsiklɔpedi] *nf* encyclopaedia

**endetter** [ãdete]: **s'endetter** *vi* to get into debt

**endive** [ãdiv] *nf* chicory *no pl*

**endormi, e** [ɑ̃dɔʀmi] adj asleep
**endormir** [ɑ̃dɔʀmiʀ] vt to put to sleep; (suj: chaleur etc) to send to sleep; (Méd: dent, nerf) to anaesthetize; (fig: soupçons) to allay; **s'endormir** vi to fall asleep, go to sleep
**endroit** [ɑ̃dʀwa] nm place; (opposé à l'envers) right side; **à l'~** (vêtement) the right way out; (objet posé) the right way round
**endurance** [ɑ̃dyʀɑ̃s] nf endurance
**endurant, e** [ɑ̃dyʀɑ̃, ɑ̃t] adj tough, hardy
**endurcir** [ɑ̃dyʀsiʀ] **s'endurcir** vi (physiquement) to become tougher; (moralement) to become hardened
**endurer** [ɑ̃dyʀe] vt to endure, bear
**énergétique** [enɛʀʒetik] adj (aliment) energy-giving
**énergie** [enɛʀʒi] nf (Physique) energy; (Tech) power; (morale) vigour, spirit; **énergique** adj energetic, vigorous; (mesures) drastic, stringent
**énervant, e** [enɛʀvɑ̃, ɑ̃t] adj irritating, annoying
**énerver** [enɛʀve] vt to irritate, annoy; **s'énerver** vi to get excited, get worked up
**enfance** [ɑ̃fɑ̃s] nf childhood
**enfant** [ɑ̃fɑ̃] nm/f child; **enfantin, e** adj (puéril) childlike; (langage, jeu etc) children's cpd
**enfer** [ɑ̃fɛʀ] nm hell
**enfermer** [ɑ̃fɛʀme] vt to shut up; (à clef, interner) to lock up; **s'enfermer** to shut o.s. away
**enfiler** [ɑ̃file] vt (vêtement) to slip on, slip into; (perles) to string; (aiguille) to thread
**enfin** [ɑ̃fɛ̃] adv at last; (en énumérant) lastly; (toutefois) still; (pour conclure) in a word; (somme toute) after all
**enflammer** [ɑ̃flame] **s'enflammer** vi to catch fire; (Méd) to become inflamed
**enflé, e** [ɑ̃fle] adj swollen
**enfler** [ɑ̃fle] vi to swell (up)
**enfoncer** [ɑ̃fɔ̃se] vt (clou) to drive in; (faire pénétrer): **~ qch dans** to push (ou

drive) sth into; (forcer: porte) to break open; **s'enfoncer** vi to sink; **s'~ dans** to sink into; (forêt, ville) to disappear into
**enfouir** [ɑ̃fwiʀ] vt (dans le sol) to bury; (dans un tiroir etc) to tuck away
**enfuir** [ɑ̃fɥiʀ] **s'enfuir** vi to run away ou off
**engagement** [ɑ̃gaʒmɑ̃] nm commitment; **sans ~** without obligation
**engager** [ɑ̃gaʒe] vt (embaucher) to take on; (: artiste) to engage; (commencer) to start; (lier) to bind, commit; (impliquer) to involve; (investir) to invest, lay out; (inciter) to urge; (introduire: clé) to insert; **s'engager** vi (promettre) to commit o.s.; (Mil) to enlist; (débuter: conversation etc) to start (up); **s'~ à faire** to undertake to do; **s'~ dans** (rue, passage) to turn into; (fig: affaire, discussion) to enter into, embark on
**engelures** [ɑ̃ʒlyʀ] nfpl chilblains
**engin** [ɑ̃ʒɛ̃] nm machine; (outil) instrument; (Auto) vehicle; (Aviat) aircraft inv

> ⬛ Attention à ne pas traduire **engin** par le mot anglais **engine**.

**engloutir** [ɑ̃glutiʀ] vt to swallow up
**engouement** [ɑ̃gumɑ̃] nm (sudden) passion
**engouffrer** [ɑ̃gufʀe] vt to swallow up, devour; **s'engouffrer dans** to rush into
**engourdir** [ɑ̃guʀdiʀ] vt to numb; (fig) to dull, blunt; **s'engourdir** vi to go numb
**engrais** [ɑ̃gʀɛ] nm manure; **engrais chimique** chemical fertilizer
**engraisser** [ɑ̃gʀese] vt to fatten (up)
**engrenage** [ɑ̃gʀənaʒ] nm gears pl, gearing; (fig) chain
**engueuler** [ɑ̃gœle] (fam) vt to bawl at
**enhardir** [ɑ̃aʀdiʀ] **s'enhardir** vi to grow bolder
**énigme** [enigm] nf riddle
**enivrer** [ɑ̃nivʀe] vt: **s'~** to get drunk
**enjamber** [ɑ̃ʒɑ̃be] vt to stride over
**enjeu, x** [ɑ̃ʒø] nm stakes pl
**enjoué, e** [ɑ̃ʒwe] adj playful

**enlaidir** [ɑ̃lediʀ] vt to make ugly ▷ vi to become ugly

**enlèvement** [ɑ̃lɛvmɑ̃] nm (rapt) abduction, kidnapping

**enlever** [ɑ̃l(ə)ve] vt (ôter: gén) to remove; (: vêtement, lunettes) to take off; (emporter: ordures etc) to take away; (kidnapper) to abduct, kidnap; (obtenir: prix, contrat) to win; (prendre): **~ qch à qn** to take sth (away) from sb

**enliser** [ɑ̃lize]: **s'enliser** vi to sink, get stuck

**enneigé, e** [ɑ̃neʒe] adj (route, maison) snowed-up; (paysage) snowy

**ennemi, e** [ɛnmi] adj hostile; (Mil) enemy cpd ▷ nm/f enemy

**ennui** [ɑ̃nɥi] nm (lassitude) boredom; (difficulté) trouble no pl; **avoir des ~s** to have problems; **ennuyer** vt to bother; (lasser) to bore; **s'ennuyer** vi to be bored; **si cela ne vous ennuie pas** if it's no trouble (to you); **ennuyeux, -euse** adj boring, tedious; (embêtant) annoying

**énorme** [enɔʀm] adj enormous, huge; **énormément** adv enormously; **énormément de neige/gens** an enormous amount of snow/number of people

**enquête** [ɑ̃kɛt] nf (de journaliste, de police) investigation; (judiciaire, administrative) inquiry; (sondage d'opinion) survey; **enquêter** vi: **enquêter (sur)** to investigate

**enragé, e** [ɑ̃ʀaʒe] adj (Méd) rabid, with rabies; (fig) fanatical

**enrageant, e** [ɑ̃ʀaʒɑ̃, ɑ̃t] adj infuriating

**enrager** [ɑ̃ʀaʒe] vi to be in a rage

**enregistrement** [ɑ̃ʀ(ə)ʒistʀəmɑ̃] nm recording; **enregistrement des bagages** baggage check-in

**enregistrer** [ɑ̃ʀ(ə)ʒistʀe] vt (Mus etc) to record; (fig: mémoriser) to make a mental note of; (bagages: à l'aéroport) to check in

**enrhumer** [ɑ̃ʀyme] vt: **s'~, être enrhumé** to catch a cold

**enrichir** [ɑ̃ʀiʃiʀ] vt to make rich(er); (fig) to enrich; **s'enrichir** vi to get rich(er)

**enrouer** [ɑ̃ʀwe]: **s'enrouer** vi to go hoarse

**enrouler** [ɑ̃ʀule] vt (fil, corde) to wind (up); **s'~ (autour de qch)** to wind (around sth)

**enseignant, e** [ɑ̃sɛɲɑ̃, ɑ̃t] nm/f teacher

**enseignement** [ɑ̃sɛɲ(ə)mɑ̃] nm teaching; (Admin) education

**enseigner** [ɑ̃sɛɲe] vt, vi to teach; **~ qch à qn** to teach sb sth

**ensemble** [ɑ̃sɑ̃bl] adv together ▷ nm (groupement) set; (vêtements) outfit; (totalité): **l'~ du/de la** the whole ou entire; (unité, harmonie) unity; **impression/idée d'~** overall ou general impression/idea; **dans l'~** (en gros) on the whole

**ensoleillé, e** [ɑ̃sɔleje] adj sunny

**ensuite** [ɑ̃sɥit] adv then, next; (plus tard) afterwards, later

**entamer** [ɑ̃tame] vt (pain, bouteille) to start; (hostilités, pourparlers) to open

**entasser** [ɑ̃tase] vt (empiler) to pile up, heap up; **s'entasser** vi (s'amonceler) to pile up; **s'~ dans** (personnes) to cram into

**entendre** [ɑ̃tɑ̃dʀ] vt to hear; (comprendre) to understand; (vouloir dire) to mean; **s'entendre** vi (sympathiser) to get on; (se mettre d'accord) to agree; **j'ai entendu dire que** I've heard (it said) that; **~ parler de** to hear of

**entendu, e** [ɑ̃tɑ̃dy] adj (réglé) agreed; (au courant: air) knowing; **(c'est) ~** all right, agreed; **bien ~** of course

**entente** [ɑ̃tɑ̃t] nf understanding; (accord, traité) agreement; **à double ~** (sens) with a double meaning

**enterrement** [ɑ̃tɛʀmɑ̃] nm (cérémonie) funeral, burial

**enterrer** [ɑ̃teʀe] vt to bury

**entêtant, e** [ɑ̃tɛtɑ̃, ɑ̃t] adj heady

**en-tête** [ɑ̃tɛt] nm heading; **papier à ~** headed notepaper

**entêté, e** [ãtete] *adj* stubborn
**entêter** [ãtete]: **s'entêter** *vi*: **s'~ (à faire)** to persist (in doing)
**enthousiasme** [ãtuzjasm] *nm* enthusiasm; **enthousiasmer** *vt* to fill with enthusiasm; **s'enthousiasmer (pour qch)** to get enthusiastic (about sth); **enthousiaste** *adj* enthusiastic
**entier, -ère** [ãtje, jɛʀ] *adj* whole; *(total: satisfaction etc)* complete; *(fig: caractère)* unbending ▷ *nm (Math)* whole; **en ~** totally; **lait ~** full-cream milk; **entièrement** *adv* entirely, wholly
**entonnoir** [ãtɔnwaʀ] *nm* funnel
**entorse** [ãtɔʀs] *nf (Méd)* sprain; *(fig)*: **~ au règlement** infringement of the rule
**entourage** [ãtuʀaʒ] *nm* circle; *(famille)* circle of family/friends; *(ce qui enclôt)* surround
**entourer** [ãtuʀe] *vt* to surround; *(apporter son soutien à)* to rally round; **~ de** to surround with; **s'~ de** to surround o.s. with
**entracte** [ãtʀakt] *nm* interval
**entraide** [ãtʀɛd] *nf* mutual aid
**entrain** [ãtʀɛ̃] *nm* spirit; **avec/sans ~** spiritedly/half-heartedly
**entraînement** [ãtʀɛnmã] *nm* training
**entraîner** [ãtʀene] *vt (charrier)* to carry *ou* drag along; *(Tech)* to drive; *(emmener: personne)* to take (off); *(influencer)* to lead; *(Sport)* to train; *(impliquer)* to entail; **s'entraîner** *vi (Sport)* to train; **s'~ à qch/à faire** to train o.s. for sth/to do; **~ qn à faire** *(inciter)* to lead sb to do; **entraîneur, -euse** *nm/f (Sport)* coach, trainer ▷ *nm (Hippisme)* trainer
**entre** [ãtʀ] *prép* between; *(parmi)* among(st); **l'un d'~ eux/nous** one of them/us; **ils se battent ~ eux** they are fighting among(st) themselves; **~ autres (choses)** among other things; **entrecôte** *nf* entrecôte *ou* rib steak
**entrée** [ãtʀe] *nf* entrance; *(accès: au cinéma etc)* admission; *(billet)* (admission) ticket; *(Culin)* first course
**entre...**: **entrefilet** *nm* paragraph *(short*

*article)*; **entremets** *nm* (cream) dessert
**entrepôt** [ãtʀəpo] *nm* warehouse
**entreprendre** [ãtʀəpʀãdʀ] *vt (se lancer dans)* to undertake; *(commencer)* to begin *ou* start (upon)
**entrepreneur, -euse** [ãtʀəpʀənœʀ, øz] *nm/f*: **entrepreneur (en bâtiment)** (building) contractor
**entreprise** [ãtʀəpʀiz] *nf (société)* firm, concern; *(action)* undertaking, venture
**entrer** [ãtʀe] *vi* to go *(ou* come) in, enter ▷ *vt (Inform)* to enter, input; **~ qch dans** to get sth into; **~ dans** *(gén)* to enter; *(pièce)* to go *(ou* come) into, enter; *(club)* to join; *(heurter)* to run into; **~ à l'hôpital** to go into hospital; **faire ~** *(visiteur)* to show in
**entre-temps** [ãtʀətã] *adv* meanwhile
**entretenir** [ãtʀət(ə)niʀ] *vt* to maintain; *(famille, maîtresse)* to support, keep; **~ qn (de)** to speak to sb (about)
**entretien** [ãtʀətjɛ̃] *nm* maintenance; *(discussion)* discussion, talk; *(pour un emploi)* interview
**entrevoir** [ãtʀəvwaʀ] *vt (à peine)* to make out; *(brièvement)* to catch a glimpse of
**entrevue** [ãtʀəvy] *nf (audience)* interview
**entrouvert, e** [ãtʀuvɛʀ, ɛʀt] *adj* half-open
**énumérer** [enymeʀe] *vt* to list
**envahir** [ãvaiʀ] *vt* to invade; *(suj: inquiétude, peur)* to come over; **envahissant, e** *(péj) adj (personne)* intrusive
**enveloppe** [ãv(ə)lɔp] *nf (de lettre)* envelope; *(crédits)* budget; **envelopper** *vt* to wrap; *(fig)* to envelop, shroud
**enverrai** *etc* [ãveʀe] *vb voir* **envoyer**
**envers** [ãvɛʀ] *prép* towards, to ▷ *nm* other side; *(d'une étoffe)* wrong side; **à l'~** *(verticalement)* upside down; *(pull)* back to front; *(chaussettes)* inside out
**envie** [ãvi] *nf (sentiment)* envy; *(souhait)* desire, wish; **avoir ~ de (faire)** to feel like (doing); *(plus fort)* to want (to

do); **avoir ~ que** to wish that; **cette glace me fait ~** I fancy some of that ice cream; **envier** vt to envy; **envieux, -euse** adj envious

**environ** [ãvirɔ̃] adv: **~ 3 h/2 km** (around) about 3 o'clock/2 km; voir aussi **environs**

**environnant, e** [ãvirɔnã, ãt] adj surrounding

**environnement** [ãvirɔnmã] nm environment

**environs** [ãvirɔ̃] nmpl surroundings; **aux ~ de** (round) about

**envisager** [ãvizaʒe] vt to contemplate, envisage; **~ de faire** to consider doing

**envoler** [ãvɔle]: **s'envoler** vi (oiseau) to fly away ou off; (avion) to take off; (papier, feuille) to blow away; (fig) to vanish (into thin air)

**envoyé, e** [ãvwaje] nm/f (Pol) envoy; (Presse) correspondent; **envoyé spécial** special correspondent

**envoyer** [ãvwaje] vt to send; (lancer) to hurl, throw; **~ chercher** to send for; **~ promener qn** (fam) to send sb packing

**épagneul, e** [epaɲœl] nm/f spaniel

**épais, se** [epɛ, ɛs] adj thick; **épaisseur** nf thickness

**épanouir** [epanwir]: **s'épanouir** vi (fleur) to bloom, open out; (visage) to light up; (personne) to blossom

**épargne** [eparɲ] nf saving

**épargner** [eparɲe] vt to save; (ne pas tuer ou endommager) to spare ▷ vi to save; **~ qch à qn** to spare sb sth

**éparpiller** [eparpije] vt to scatter; **s'éparpiller** vi to scatter; (fig) to dissipate one's efforts

**épatant, e** [epatã, ãt] (fam) adj super

**épater** [epate] (fam) vt (étonner) to amaze; (impressionner) to impress

**épaule** [epol] nf shoulder

**épave** [epav] nf wreck

**épée** [epe] nf sword

**épeler** [ep(ə)le] vt to spell

**éperon** [eprɔ̃] nm spur

**épervier** [epɛrvje] nm sparrowhawk

**épi** [epi] nm (de blé, d'orge) ear; (de maïs) cob

**épice** [epis] nf spice

**épicé, e** [epise] adj spicy

**épicer** [epise] vt to spice

**épicerie** [episri] nf grocer's shop; (denrées) groceries pl; **épicerie fine** delicatessen; **épicier, -ière** nm/f grocer

**épidémie** [epidemi] nf epidemic

**épiderme** [epidɛrm] nm skin

**épier** [epje] vt to spy on, watch closely

**épilepsie** [epilɛpsi] nf epilepsy

**épiler** [epile] vt (jambes) to remove the hair from; (sourcils) to pluck

**épinards** [epinar] nmpl spinach sg

**épine** [epin] nf thorn, prickle; (d'oursin etc) spine

**épingle** [epɛ̃gl] nf pin; **épingle de nourrice** ou **de sûreté** safety pin

**épisode** [epizɔd] nm episode; **film/roman à ~s** serial; **épisodique** adj occasional

**épluche-légumes** [eplyʃlegym] nm inv (potato) peeler

**éplucher** [eplyʃe] vt (fruit, légumes) to peel; (fig) to go over with a fine-tooth comb; **épluchures** nfpl peelings

**éponge** [epɔ̃ʒ] nf sponge; **éponger** vt (liquide) to mop up; (surface) to sponge; (fig: déficit) to soak up

**époque** [epɔk] nf (de l'histoire) age, era; (de l'année, la vie) time; **d'~** (meuble) period cpd

**épouse** [epuz] nf wife; **épouser** vt to marry

**épousseter** [epuste] vt to dust

**épouvantable** [epuvãtabl] adj appalling, dreadful

**épouvantail** [epuvãtaj] nm scarecrow

**épouvante** [epuvãt] nf terror; **film d'~** horror film; **épouvanter** vt to terrify

**époux** [epu] nm husband ▷ nmpl (married) couple

**épreuve** [eprœv] nf (d'examen) test; (malheur, difficulté) trial, ordeal; (Photo) print; (Typo) proof; (Sport) event; **à toute ~** unfailing; **mettre à l'~** to put to the test

**éprouver** [epruve] vt (tester) to

test; (*marquer, faire souffrir*) to afflict, distress; (*ressentir*) to experience

**épuisé, e** [epɥize] *adj* exhausted; (*livre*) out of print; **épuisement** *nm* exhaustion

**épuiser** [epɥize] *vt* (*fatiguer*) to exhaust, wear *ou* tire out; (*stock, sujet*) to exhaust; **s'épuiser** *vi* to wear *ou* tire o.s. out, exhaust o.s.

**épuisette** [epɥizɛt] *nf* shrimping net

**équateur** [ekwatœʀ] *nm* equator; (**la république de) l'É~** Ecuador

**équation** [ekwasjɔ̃] *nf* equation

**équerre** [ekɛʀ] *nf* (*à dessin*) (set) square

**équilibre** [ekilibʀ] *nm* balance; **garder/perdre l'~** to keep/lose one's balance; **être en ~** to be balanced; **équilibré, e** *adj* well-balanced; **équilibrer** *vt* to balance

**équipage** [ekipaʒ] *nm* crew

**équipe** [ekip] *nf* team; **travailler en ~** to work as a team

**équipé, e** [ekipe] *adj*: **bien/mal ~** well-/poorly-equipped

**équipement** [ekipmã] *nm* equipment

**équiper** [ekipe] *vt* to equip; **~ qn/qch de** to equip sb/sth with

**équipier, -ière** [ekipje, jɛʀ] *nm/f* team member

**équitation** [ekitasjɔ̃] *nf* (horse-)riding; **faire de l'~** to go riding

**équivalent, e** [ekivalɑ̃, ɑ̃t] *adj, nm* equivalent

**équivaloir** [ekivalwaʀ]: **~ à** *vt* to be equivalent to

**érable** [eʀabl] *nm* maple

**érafler** [eʀafle] *vt* to scratch; **éraflure** *nf* scratch

**ère** [eʀ] *nf* era; **en l'an 1050 de notre ~** in the year 1050 A.D.

**érection** [eʀɛksjɔ̃] *nf* erection

**éroder** [eʀɔde] *vt* to erode

**érotique** [eʀɔtik] *adj* erotic

**errer** [eʀe] *vi* to wander

**erreur** [eʀœʀ] *nf* mistake, error; **faire ~** to be mistaken; **par ~** by mistake

**éruption** [eʀypsjɔ̃] *nf* eruption; (*Méd*) rash

**es** [ɛ] *vb voir* **être**

**ès** [ɛs] *prép*: **licencié ès lettres/sciences** ≈ Bachelor of Arts/Science

**ESB** *sigle f* (= *encéphalopathie spongiforme bovine*) BSE

**escabeau, x** [ɛskabo] *nm* (*tabouret*) stool; (*échelle*) stepladder

**escalade** [ɛskalad] *nf* climbing *no pl*; (*Pol etc*) escalation; **escalader** *vt* to climb

**escale** [ɛskal] *nf* (*Navig: durée*) call; (*endroit*) port of call; (*Aviat*) stop(over); **faire ~ à** (*Navig*) to put in at; (*Aviat*) to stop over at; **vol sans ~** nonstop flight

**escalier** [ɛskalje] *nm* stairs *pl*; **dans l'~** *ou* **les ~s** on the stairs; **escalier mécanique** *ou* **roulant** escalator

**escapade** [ɛskapad] *nf*: **faire une ~** to go on a jaunt; (*s'enfuir*) to run away *ou* off

**escargot** [ɛskaʀgo] *nm* snail

**escarpé, e** [ɛskaʀpe] *adj* steep

**esclavage** [ɛsklavaʒ] *nm* slavery

**esclave** [ɛsklav] *nm/f* slave

**escompte** [ɛskɔ̃t] *nm* discount

**escrime** [ɛskʀim] *nf* fencing

**escroc** [ɛskʀo] *nm* swindler, conman; **escroquer** *vt*: **escroquer qch (à qn)** to swindle sth (out of sb); **escroquerie** *nf* swindle

**espace** [ɛspas] *nm* space; **espacer** *vt* to space out; **s'espacer** *vi* (*visites etc*) to become less frequent

**espadon** [ɛspadɔ̃] *nm* swordfish *inv*

**espadrille** [ɛspadʀij] *nf* rope-soled sandal

**Espagne** [ɛspaɲ] *nf*: **l'~** Spain; **espagnol, e** *adj* Spanish ▷ *nm/f*: **Espagnol, e** Spaniard ▷ *nm* (*Ling*) Spanish

**espèce** [ɛspɛs] *nf* (*Bio, Bot, Zool*) species *inv*; (*gén: sorte*) sort, kind, type; (*péj*): **~ de maladroit/de brute!** you clumsy oaf/you brute!; **espèces** *nfpl* (*Comm*) cash *sg*; **payer en ~** to pay (in) cash

**espérance** [ɛspeʀɑ̃s] *nf* hope; **espérance de vie** life expectancy

**espérer** [ɛspeʀe] *vt* to hope for;

**j'espère (bien)** I hope so; **~ que/faire** to hope that/to do

**espiègle** [ɛspjɛgl] *adj* mischievous

**espion, ne** [ɛspjɔ̃, jɔn] *nm/f* spy; **espionnage** *nm* espionage, spying; **espionner** *vt* to spy (up)on

**espoir** [ɛspwaʀ] *nm* hope; **dans l'~ de/que** in the hope of/that; **reprendre ~** not to lose hope

**esprit** [ɛspʀi] *nm* (*intellect*) mind; (*humour*) wit; (*mentalité, d'une loi etc, fantôme etc*) spirit; **faire de l'~** to try to be witty; **reprendre ses ~s** to come to; **perdre l'~** to lose one's mind

**esquimau, de, -x** [ɛskimo, od] *adj* Eskimo ▷ *nm/f*: **E~, de** Eskimo ▷ *nm*: **E~®** ice lolly (BRIT), popsicle (US)

**essai** [ese] *nm* (*tentative*) attempt, try; (*de produit*) testing; (*Rugby*) try; (*Littérature*) essay; **à l'~** on a trial basis; **mettre à l'~** to put to the test

**essaim** [esɛ̃] *nm* swarm

**essayer** [eseje] *vt* to try; (*vêtement, chaussures*) to try (on); (*méthode, voiture*) to try (out) ▷ *vi* to try; **~ de faire** to try *ou* attempt to do

**essence** [esɑ̃s] *nf* (*de voiture*) petrol (BRIT), gas(oline) (US); (*extrait de plante*) essence; (*espèce: d'arbre*) species *inv*

**essentiel, le** [esɑ̃sjɛl] *adj* essential; **c'est l'~** (*ce qui importe*) that's the main thing; **l'~ de** the main part of

**essieu, x** [esjø] *nm* axle

**essor** [esɔʀ] *nm* (*de l'économie etc*) rapid expansion

**essorer** [esɔʀe] *vt* (*en tordant*) to wring (out); (*par la force centrifuge*) to spin-dry; **essoreuse** *nf* spin-dryer

**essouffler** [esufle]: **s'essouffler** *vi* to get out of breath

**essuie-glace** [esɥiglas] *nm inv* windscreen (BRIT) *ou* windshield (US) wiper

**essuyer** [esɥije] *vt* to wipe; (*fig: échec*) to suffer; **s'essuyer** *vi* (*après le bain*) to dry o.s.; **~ la vaisselle** to dry up

**est¹** [ɛ] *vb voir* **être**

**est²** [ɛst] *nm* east ▷ *adj inv* east; (*région*) east(ern); **à l'~** in the east; (*direction*) to the east, east(wards); **à l'~ de** (to the) east of

**est-ce que** [ɛskə] *adv*: **~ c'est cher/ c'était bon?** is it expensive/was it good?; **quand est-ce qu'il part?** when does he leave?, when is he leaving?; *voir aussi* **que**

**esthéticienne** [ɛstetisjɛn] *nf* beautician

**esthétique** [ɛstetik] *adj* attractive

**estimation** [ɛstimasjɔ̃] *nf* valuation; (*chiffre*) estimate

**estime** [ɛstim] *nf* esteem, regard; **estimer** *vt* (*respecter*) to esteem; (*expertiser: bijou etc*) to value; (*évaluer: coût etc*) to assess, estimate; (*penser*): **estimer que/être** to consider that/o.s. to be

**estival, e, -aux** [ɛstival, o] *adj* summer *cpd*

**estivant, e** [ɛstivɑ̃, ɑ̃t] *nm/f* (summer) holiday-maker

**estomac** [ɛstɔma] *nm* stomach

**estragon** [ɛstʀagɔ̃] *nm* tarragon

**estuaire** [ɛstɥɛʀ] *nm* estuary

**et** [e] *conj* and; **et lui?** what about him?; **et alors!** so what!

**étable** [etabl] *nf* cowshed

**établi** [etabli] *nm* (work)bench

**établir** [etabliʀ] *vt* (*papiers d'identité, facture*) to make out; (*liste, programme*) to draw up; (*entreprise*) to set up; (*réputation, usage, fait, culpabilité*) to establish; **s'établir** *vi* to be established; **s'~ (à son compte)** to set up in business; **s'~ à/près de** to settle in/near

**établissement** [etablismɑ̃] *nm* (*entreprise, institution*) establishment; **établissement scolaire** school, educational establishment

**étage** [etaʒ] *nm* (*d'immeuble*) storey, floor; **à l'~** upstairs; **au 2ème ~** on the 2nd (BRIT) *ou* 3rd (US) floor; **c'est à quel ~?** what floor is it on?

**étagère** [etaʒɛʀ] *nf* (*rayon*) shelf; (*meuble*) shelves *pl*

**étai** [etɛ] nm stay, prop

**étain** [etɛ̃] nm pewter no pl

**étais** etc [etɛ] vb voir **être**

**étaler** [etale] vt (carte, nappe) to spread (out); (peinture) to spread; (échelonner: paiements, vacances) to spread, stagger; (marchandises) to display; (connaissances) to parade; **s'étaler** vi (liquide) to spread out; (fam) to fall flat on one's face; **s'~ sur** (suj: paiements etc) to be spread out over

**étalon** [etalɔ̃] nm (cheval) stallion

**étanche** [etɑ̃ʃ] adj (récipient) watertight; (montre, vêtement) waterproof

**étang** [etɑ̃] nm pond

**étant** [etɑ̃] vb voir **être**; **donné**

**étape** [etap] nf stage; (lieu d'arrivée) stopping place; (: Cyclisme) staging point

**état** [eta] nm (Pol, condition) state; **en mauvais ~** in poor condition; **en ~ (de marche)** in (working) order; **remettre en ~** to repair; **hors d'~** out of order; **être en ~/hors d'~ de faire** to be in a/in no fit state to do; **être dans tous ses ~s** to be in a state; **faire ~ de** (alléguer) to put forward; **l'É~** the State; **état civil** civil status; **état des lieux** inventory of fixtures; **États-Unis** nmpl: **les États-Unis** the United States

**etc.** [ɛtsetera] adv etc

**et c(a)etera** [ɛtsetera] adv et cetera, and so on

**été** [ete] pp de **être** ▷ nm summer

**éteindre** [etɛ̃dr] vt (lampe, lumière, radio) to turn ou switch off; (cigarette, feu) to put out, extinguish; **s'éteindre** vi (feu, lumière) to go out; (mourir) to pass away; **éteint, e** adj (fig) lacklustre, dull; (volcan) extinct

**étendre** [etɑ̃dr] vt (pâte, liquide) to spread; (carte etc) to spread out; (linge) to hang up; (bras, jambes) to stretch out; (fig: agrandir) to extend; **s'étendre** vi (augmenter, se propager) to spread; (terrain, forêt etc) to stretch; (s'allonger) to stretch out; (se coucher) to lie down;

(fig: expliquer) to elaborate

**étendu, e** [etɑ̃dy] adj extensive

**éternel, le** [etɛrnɛl] adj eternal

**éternité** [etɛrnite] nf eternity; **ça a duré une ~** it lasted for ages

**éternuement** [etɛrnymɑ̃] nm sneeze

**éternuer** [etɛrnɥe] vi to sneeze

**êtes** [ɛt(z)] vb voir **être**

**Éthiopie** [etjɔpi] nf: **l'~** Ethiopia

**étiez** [etje] vb voir **être**

**étinceler** [etɛ̃s(ə)le] vi to sparkle

**étincelle** [etɛ̃sɛl] nf spark

**étiquette** [etikɛt] nf label; (protocole): **l'~** etiquette

**étirer** [etire] s'étirer vi (personne) to stretch; (convoi, route): **s'~ sur** to stretch out over

**étoile** [etwal] nf star; **à la belle ~** in the open; **étoile de mer** starfish; **étoile filante** shooting star; **étoilé, e** adj starry

**étonnant, e** [etɔnɑ̃, ɑ̃t] adj amazing

**étonnement** [etɔnmɑ̃] nm surprise, amazement

**étonner** [etɔne] vt to surprise, amaze; **s'étonner que/de** to be amazed that/at; **cela m'~ait (que)** (j'en doute) I'd be very surprised (if)

**étouffer** [etufe] vt to suffocate; (bruit) to muffle; (scandale) to hush up ▷ vi to suffocate; **s'étouffer** vi (en mangeant etc) to choke; **on étouffe** it's stifling

**étourderie** [eturdəri] nf (caractère) absent-mindedness no pl; (faute) thoughtless blunder

**étourdi, e** [eturdi] adj (distrait) scatterbrained, heedless

**étourdir** [eturdir] vt (assommer) to stun, daze; (griser) to make dizzy ou giddy; **étourdissement** nm dizzy spell

**étrange** [etrɑ̃ʒ] adj strange

**étranger, -ère** [etrɑ̃ʒe, ɛr] adj foreign; (pas de la famille, non familier) strange ▷ nm/f foreigner; stranger ▷ nm: **à l'~** abroad

**étrangler** [etrɑ̃gle] vt to strangle; **s'étrangler** vi (en mangeant etc) to choke

○ **MOT-CLÉ**

**être** [ɛtʀ] nm being; **être humain** human being
▷ vb +attrib **1** (état, description) to be; **il est instituteur** he is ou he's a teacher; **vous êtes grand/intelligent/fatigué** you are ou you're tall/clever/tired
**2** (+à: appartenir) to be; **le livre est à Paul** the book is Paul's ou belongs to Paul; **c'est à moi/eux** it is ou it's mine/theirs
**3** (+de: provenance): **il est de Paris** he is from Paris; (: appartenance): **il est des nôtres** he is one of us
**4** (date): **nous sommes le 10 janvier** it's the 10th of January (today)
▷ vi to be; **je ne serai pas ici demain** I won't be here tomorrow
▷ vb aux **1** to have; to be; **être arrivé/allé** to have arrived/gone; **il est parti** he has left, he has gone
**2** (forme passive) to be; **être fait par** to be made by; **il a été promu** he has been promoted
**3** (+à: obligation): **c'est à réparer** it needs repairing; **c'est à essayer** it should be tried; **il est à espérer que ...** it is ou it's to be hoped that ...
▷ vb impers **1**: **il est** +adjectif it is +adjective; **il est impossible de le faire** it's impossible to do it
**2** (heure, date): **il est 10 heures** it is ou it's 10 o'clock
**3** (emphatique): **c'est moi** it's me; **c'est à lui de le faire** it's up to him to do it

**étrennes** [etʀɛn] nfpl Christmas box sg
**étrier** [etʀije] nm stirrup
**étroit, e** [etʀwa, wat] adj narrow; (vêtement) tight; (fig: liens, collaboration) close; **à l'~** cramped; **~ d'esprit** narrow-minded
**étude** [etyd] nf studying; (ouvrage, rapport) study; (Scol: salle de travail) study room; **études** nfpl (Scol) studies; **être à l'~** (projet etc) to be under consideration; **faire des ~s (de droit/**médecine) to study (law/medicine)
**étudiant, e** [etydjɑ̃, jɑ̃t] nm/f student
**étudier** [etydje] vt, vi to study
**étui** [etɥi] nm case
**eu, eue** [y] pp de **avoir**
**euh** [ø] excl er
**euro** [øʀo] nm euro
**Europe** [øʀɔp] nf: **l'~** Europe; **européen, ne** adj European ▷ nm/f: **Européen, ne** European
**eus** etc [y] vb voir **avoir**
**eux** [ø] pron (sujet) they; (objet) them
**évacuer** [evakɥe] vt to evacuate
**évader** [evade]: **s'évader** vi to escape
**évaluer** [evalɥe] vt (expertiser) to appraise, evaluate; (juger approximativement) to estimate
**évangile** [evɑ̃ʒil] nm gospel; **É~** Gospel
**évanouir** [evanwiʀ]: **s'évanouir** vi to faint; (disparaître) to vanish, disappear; **évanouissement** nm (syncope) fainting fit
**évaporer** [evapɔʀe]: **s'évaporer** vi to evaporate
**évasion** [evazjɔ̃] nf escape
**éveillé, e** [eveje] adj awake; (vif) alert, sharp; **éveiller** vt to (a)waken; (soupçons etc) to arouse; **s'éveiller** vi to (a)waken; (fig) to be aroused
**événement** [evɛnmɑ̃] nm event
**éventail** [evɑ̃taj] nm fan; (choix) range
**éventualité** [evɑ̃tɥalite] nf eventuality; possibility; **dans l'~ de** in the event of
**éventuel, le** [evɑ̃tɥɛl] adj possible
▌ Attention à ne pas traduire
*éventuel* par *eventual*.
**éventuellement** adv possibly
▌ Attention à ne pas traduire
*éventuellement* par *eventually*.
**évêque** [evɛk] nm bishop
**évidemment** [evidamɑ̃] adv (bien sûr) of course; (certainement) obviously
**évidence** [evidɑ̃s] nf obviousness; (fait) obvious fact; **de toute ~** quite obviously ou evidently; **être en ~** to be clearly visible; **mettre en ~** (fait) to highlight; **évident, e** adj obvious,

evident; **ce n'est pas évident!** (*fam*) it's not that easy!

**évier** [evje] *nm* (kitchen) sink

**éviter** [evite] *vt* to avoid; **~ de faire** to avoid doing; **~ qch à qn** to spare sb sth

**évoluer** [evɔlɥe] *vi* (*enfant, maladie*) to develop; (*situation, moralement*) to evolve, develop; (*aller et venir*) to move about; **évolution** *nf* development, evolution

**évoquer** [evɔke] *vt* to call to mind, evoke; (*mentionner*) to mention

**ex-** [ɛks] *préfixe* ex-; **son ~mari** her ex-husband; **son ~femme** his ex-wife

**exact, e** [ɛgza(kt), ɛgzakt] *adj* exact; (*correct*) correct; (*ponctuel*) punctual; **l'heure ~** the right *ou* exact time; **exactement** *adv* exactly

**ex aequo** [ɛgzeko] *adj* equally placed; **arriver ~** to finish neck and neck

**exagéré, e** [ɛgzaʒeʀe] *adj* (*prix etc*) excessive

**exagérer** [ɛgzaʒeʀe] *vt* to exaggerate ▷ *vi* to exaggerate; (*abuser*) to go too far

**examen** [ɛgzamɛ̃] *nm* examination; (*Scol*) exam, examination; **à l'~** under consideration; **examen médical** (medical) examination; (*analyse*) test

**examinateur, -trice** [ɛgzaminatœʀ, tʀis] *nm/f* examiner

**examiner** [ɛgzamine] *vt* to examine

**exaspérant, e** [ɛgzaspeʀɑ̃, ɑ̃t] *adj* exasperating

**exaspérer** [ɛgzaspeʀe] *vt* to exasperate

**exaucer** [ɛgzose] *vt* (*vœu*) to grant

**excéder** [ɛksede] *vt* (*dépasser*) to exceed; (*agacer*) to exasperate

**excellent, e** [ɛkselɑ̃, ɑ̃t] *adj* excellent

**excentrique** [ɛksɑ̃tʀik] *adj* eccentric

**excepté, e** [ɛksɛpte] *adj, prép*: **les élèves ~s, ~ les élèves** except for the pupils

**exception** [ɛksɛpsjɔ̃] *nf* exception; **à l'~ de** except for, with the exception of; **d'~** (*mesure, loi*) special, exceptional; **exceptionnel, le** *adj* exceptional; **exceptionnellement** *adv* exceptionally

**excès** [ɛksɛ] *nm* surplus ▷ *nmpl* excesses; **faire des ~** to overindulge; **excès de vitesse** speeding *no pl*; **excessif, -ive** *adj* excessive

**excitant, e** [ɛksitɑ̃, ɑ̃t] *adj* exciting ▷ *nm* stimulant; **excitation** *nf* (*état*) excitement

**exciter** [ɛksite] *vt* to excite; (*suj: café etc*) to stimulate; **s'exciter** *vi* to get excited

**exclamer** [ɛksklame]: **s'exclamer** *vi* to exclaim

**exclure** [ɛksklyʀ] *vt* (*faire sortir*) to expel; (*ne pas compter*) to exclude, leave out; (*rendre impossible*) to exclude, rule out; **il est exclu que** it's out of the question that ...; **il n'est pas exclu que ...** it's not impossible that ...; **exclusif, -ive** *adj* exclusive; **exclusion** *nf* exclusion; **à l'exclusion de** with the exclusion *ou* exception of; **exclusivité** *nf* (*Comm*) exclusive rights *pl*; **film passant en exclusivité à** film showing only at

**excursion** [ɛkskyʀsjɔ̃] *nf* (*en autocar*) excursion, trip; (*à pied*) walk, hike

**excuse** [ɛkskyz] *nf* excuse; **excuses** *nfpl* (*regret*) apology *sg*, apologies; **excuser** *vt* to excuse; **s'excuser (de)** to apologize (for); **excusez-moi** I'm sorry; (*pour attirer l'attention*) excuse me

**exécuter** [ɛgzekyte] *vt* (*tuer*) to execute; (*tâche etc*) to execute, carry out; (*Mus: jouer*) to perform, execute; **s'exécuter** *vi* to comply

**exemplaire** [ɛgzɑ̃plɛʀ] *nm* copy

**exemple** [ɛgzɑ̃pl] *nm* example; **par ~** for instance, for example; **donner l'~** to set an example

**exercer** [ɛgzɛʀse] *vt* (*pratiquer*) to exercise, practise; (*influence, contrôle*) to exert; (*former*) to exercise, train; **s'exercer** *vi* (*sportif, musicien*) to practise

**exercice** [ɛgzɛʀsis] *nm* exercise

**exhiber** [ɛgzibe] *vt* (*montrer: papiers, certificat*) to present, produce; (*péj*) to display, flaunt; **s'exhiber** vi to parade; (suj: exhibitionniste) to expose o.s; **exhibitionniste** nm/f flasher

**exigeant, e** [εgziʒɑ̃, ɑ̃t] adj demanding; (péj) hard to please

**exiger** [εgziʒe] vt to demand, require

**exil** [εgzil] nm exile; **exiler** vt to exile; **s'exiler** vi to go into exile

**existence** [εgzistɑ̃s] nf existence

**exister** [εgziste] vi to exist; **il existe un/des** there is a/are (some)

**exorbitant, e** [εgzɔrbitɑ̃, ɑ̃t] adj exorbitant

**exotique** [εgzɔtik] adj exotic; **yaourt aux fruits ~s** tropical fruit yoghurt

**expédier** [εkspedje] vt (lettre, paquet) to send; (troupes) to dispatch; (fam: travail etc) to dispose of, dispatch; **expéditeur, -trice** nm/f sender; **expédition** nf sending; (scientifique, sportive, Mil) expedition

**expérience** [εksperjɑ̃s] nf (de la vie) experience; (scientifique) experiment

**expérimenté, e** [εksperimɑ̃te] adj experienced

**expérimenter** [εksperimɑ̃te] vt to test out, experiment with

**expert, e** [εkspεr, εrt] adj, nm expert; **~ en objets d'art** art appraiser; **expert-comptable** nm ≈ chartered accountant (BRIT), ≈ certified public accountant (US)

**expirer** [εkspire] vi (prendre fin, mourir) to expire; (respirer) to breathe out

**explication** [εksplikasjɔ̃] nf explanation; (discussion) discussion; (dispute) argument

**explicite** [εksplisit] adj explicit

**expliquer** [εksplike] vt to explain; **s'expliquer** to explain o.s.); **s'~ avec qn** (discuter) to explain o.s. to sb; **son erreur s'explique** one can understand his mistake

**exploit** [εksplwa] nm exploit, feat; **exploitant, e** nm/f: **exploitant (agricole)** farmer; **exploitation** nf exploitation; (d'une entreprise) running; **exploitation agricole** farming

concern; **exploiter** vt (personne, don) to exploit; (entreprise, ferme) to run, operate; (mine) to exploit, work

**explorer** [εksplɔre] vt to explore

**exploser** [εksploze] vi to explode, blow up; (engin explosif) to go off; (personne: de colère) to flare up; **explosif, -ive** adj, nm explosive; **explosion** nf explosion; (de joie, colère) outburst

**exportateur, -trice** [εkspɔrtatœr, tris] adj export cpd, exporting ▷ nm exporter

**exportation** [εkspɔrtasjɔ̃] nf (action) exportation; (produit) export

**exporter** [εkspɔrte] vt to export

**exposant** [εkspozɑ̃] nm exhibitor

**exposé, e** [εkspoze] nm talk ▷ adj: **~ au sud** facing south

**exposer** [εkspoze] vt (marchandise) to display; (peinture) to exhibit, show; (parler de) to explain, set out; (mettre en danger, orienter, Photo) to expose; **s'~ à** (soleil, danger) to expose o.s. to; **exposition** nf (manifestation) exhibition; (Photo) exposure

**exprès¹** [εksprε] adv (délibérément) on purpose; (spécialement) specially; **faire ~ de faire qch** to do sth on purpose

**exprès², -esse** [εksprεs] adj inv (lettre, colis) express

**express** [εksprεs] adj, nm: **(café) ~** espresso (coffee); **(train)** ~ fast train

**expressif, -ive** [εkspresif, iv] adj expressive

**expression** [εkspresjɔ̃] nf expression

**exprimer** [εksprime] vt (sentiment, idée) to express; (jus, liquide) to press out; **s'exprimer** vi (personne) to express o.s

**expulser** [εkspylse] vt to expel; (locataire) to evict; (Sport) to send off

**exquis, e** [εkski, iz] adj exquisite

**extasier** [εkstazje]: **s'extasier sur** vt to go into raptures over

**exténuer** [εkstenɥe] vt to exhaust

**extérieur, e** [εksterjœr] adj (porte, mur etc) outer, outside; (au dehors: escalier, w.-c.) outside; (commerce) foreign; (*influences*) external; (*apparent: calme, gaieté etc*) surface *cpd* ▷ *nm* (*d'une maison, d'un récipient etc*) outside, exterior; (*apparence*) exterior; **à l'~** outside; (*à l'étranger*) abroad

**externat** [ɛkstɛʁna] *nm* day school

**externe** [ɛkstɛʁn] *adj* external, outer ▷ *nm/f* (*Méd*) non-resident medical student (*BRIT*), extern (*US*); (*Scol*) day pupil

**extincteur** [ɛkstɛ̃ktœʁ] *nm* (fire) extinguisher

**extinction** [ɛkstɛ̃ksjɔ̃] *nf*: **extinction de voix** loss of voice

**extra** [ɛkstʁa] *adj inv* first-rate; (*fam*) fantastic ▷ *nm inv* extra help

**extraire** [ɛkstʁɛʁ] *vt* to extract; **~ qch de** to extract sth from; **extrait** *nm* extract; **extrait de naissance** birth certificate

**extraordinaire** [ɛkstʁaɔʁdinɛʁ] *adj* extraordinary; (*Pol: mesures etc*) special

**extravagant, e** [ɛkstʁavagɑ̃, ɑ̃t] *adj* extravagant

**extraverti, e** [ɛkstʁavɛʁti] *adj* extrovert

**extrême** [ɛkstʁɛm] *adj, nm* extreme; **d'un ~ à l'autre** from one extreme to another; **extrêmement** *adv* extremely; **Extrême-Orient** *nm* Far East

**extrémité** [ɛkstʁemite] *nf* end; (*situation*) straits *pl*, plight; (*geste désespéré*) extreme action; **extrémités** *nfpl* (*pieds et mains*) extremities

**exubérant, e** [ɛgzybeʁɑ̃, ɑ̃t] *adj* exuberant

# f

**F** *abr* = **franc**; (*appartement*): **un F2/F3** a one-/two-bedroom flat (*BRIT*) *ou* apartment (*US*)

**fa** [fa] *nm inv* (*Mus*) F; (*en chantant la gamme*) fa

**fabricant, e** [fabʁikɑ̃, ɑ̃t] *nm/f* manufacturer

**fabrication** [fabʁikasjɔ̃] *nf* manufacture

**fabrique** [fabʁik] *nf* factory; **fabriquer** *vt* to make; (*industriellement*) to manufacture; (*fig*): **qu'est-ce qu'il fabrique?** (*fam*) what is he doing?

**fac** [fak] (*fam*) *abr f* (*Scol*) = **faculté**

**façade** [fasad] *nf* front, façade

**face** [fas] *nf* face; (*fig: aspect*) side ▷ *adj*: **le côté ~** heads; **en ~ de** opposite; (*fig*) in front of; **de ~** (*voir*) face on; **~ à** facing; (*fig*) faced with, in the face of; **faire ~ à** to face; **~ à ~** *adv* facing each other ▷ *nm inv* encounter

**fâché, e** [fɑʃe] *adj* angry; (*désolé*) sorry

**fâcher** [fɑʃe] *vt* to anger; **se fâcher (contre qn)** *vi* to get angry (with sb);

se ~ avec (*se brouiller*) to fall out with

**facile** [fasil] *adj* easy; (*caractère*) easy-going; **facilement** *adv* easily; **facilité** *nf* easiness; (*disposition, don*) aptitude; **facilités** (*possibilités*) facilities; (*Comm*) terms; **faciliter** *vt* to make easier

**façon** [fasɔ̃] *nf* (*manière*) way; (*d'une robe etc*) making-up, cut; **façons** *nfpl* (*péj*) fuss *sg*; **de ~ à/à ce que** so as to/that; **de toute ~** anyway, in any case; **sans ~** (*accepter*) without fuss; **non merci, sans ~** no thanks, honestly

**facteur, -trice** [faktœʁ]
*nm/f* postman(-woman) (BRIT),
mailman(-woman) (US) ▷ *nm* (*Math, fig: élément*) factor

**facture** [faktyʁ] *nf* (*à payer: gén*) bill; (*Comm*) invoice

**facultatif, -ive** [fakyltatif, iv] *adj* optional

**faculté** [fakylte] *nf* (*intellectuelle, d'université*) faculty; (*pouvoir, possibilité*) power

**fade** [fad] *adj* insipid

**faible** [fɛbl] *adj* weak; (*voix, lumière, vent*) faint; (*rendement, revenu*) low ▷ *nm* (*pour quelqu'un*) weakness, soft spot; **faiblesse** *nf* weakness; **faiblir** *vi* to weaken; (*lumière*) to dim; (*vent*) to drop

**faïence** [fajɑ̃s] *nf* earthenware *no pl*

**faillir** [fajiʁ] *vi*: **j'ai failli tomber** I almost *ou* very nearly fell

**faillite** [fajit] *nf* bankruptcy; **faire ~** to go bankrupt

**faim** [fɛ̃] *nf* hunger; **avoir ~** to be hungry; **rester sur sa ~** (*aussi fig*) to be left wanting more

**fainéant, e** [fɛneɑ̃, ɑ̃t] *nm/f* idler, loafer

 **MOT-CLÉ**

**faire** [fɛʁ] *vt* **1** (*fabriquer, être l'auteur de*) to make; **faire du vin/une offre/un film** to make wine/an offer/a film; **faire du bruit** to make a noise
**2** (*effectuer: travail, opération*) to do; **que faites-vous?** (*quel métier etc*) what do

you do?; (*quelle activité: au moment de la question*) what are you doing?; **faire la lessive** to do the washing
**3** (*études*) to do; (*sport, musique*) to play; **faire du droit/du français** to do law/French; **faire du rugby/piano** to play rugby/the piano
**4** (*simuler*): **faire le malade/l'innocent** to act the invalid/the innocent
**5** (*transformer, avoir un effet sur*): **faire de qn un frustré/avocat** to make sb frustrated/a lawyer; **ça ne me fait rien** (*m'est égal*) I don't care *ou* mind; (*me laisse froid*) it has no effect on me; **ça ne fait rien** it doesn't matter; **faire que** (*impliquer*) to mean that
**6** (*calculs, prix, mesures*): **2 et 2 font 4** 2 and 2 are *ou* make 4; **ça fait 10 m/15 euros** it's 10 m/15 euros; **je vous le fais 10 euros** I'll let you have it for 10 euros; **je fais du 40** I take a size 40
**7** (*distance*): **faire du 50 (à l'heure)** to do 50 (km an hour); **nous avons fait 1000 km en 2 jours** we did *ou* covered 1000 km in 2 days; **faire l'Europe** to tour *ou* do Europe; **faire les magasins** to go shopping
**8**: **qu'a-t-il fait de sa valise?** what has he done with his case?
**9**: **ne faire que**: **il ne fait que critiquer** (*sans cesse*) all he (ever) does is criticize; (*seulement*) he's only criticizing
**10** (*dire*) to say; **"vraiment?" fit-il** "really?" he said
**11** (*maladie*) to have; **faire du diabète** to have diabetes *sg*
▷ *vi* **1** (*agir, s'y prendre*) to act, do; **il faut faire vite** we (*ou* you *etc*) must act quickly; **comment a-t-il fait pour?** how did he manage to?; **faites comme chez vous** make yourself at home
**2** (*paraître*) to look; **faire vieux/démodé** to look old/old-fashioned; **ça fait bien** it looks good
▷ *vb substitut* to do; **ne le casse pas comme je l'ai fait** don't break it as I did; **je peux le voir? — faites!** can I see

it? — please do!
▷ vb impers 1: **il fait beau** etc the weather is fine etc; voir aussi **jour**; **froid** etc
2 (temps écoulé, durée): **ça fait 2 ans qu'il est parti** it's 2 years since he left; **ça fait 2 ans qu'il y est** he's been there for 2 years
▷ vb semi-aux 1: **faire** (+infinitif: action directe) to make; **faire tomber/bouger qch** to make sth fall/move; **faire démarrer un moteur/chauffer de l'eau** to start up an engine/heat some water; **cela fait dormir** it makes you sleep; **faire travailler les enfants** to make the children work ou get the children to work; **il m'a fait traverser la rue** he helped me to cross the street
2 (indirectement, par un intermédiaire): **faire réparer qch** to get ou have sth repaired; **faire punir les enfants** to have the children punished
**se faire** vi 1 (être convenable): **cela se fait beaucoup/ne se fait pas** it's done a lot/not done
2: **se faire** +nom ou pron: **se faire une jupe** to make o.s. a skirt; **se faire des amis** to make friends; **se faire du souci** to worry; **il ne s'en fait pas** he doesn't worry
3: **se faire** +adj (devenir): **se faire vieux** to be getting old; **se faire beau** to do o.s. up
4: **se faire à** (s'habituer) to get used to; **je n'arrive pas à me faire à la nourriture/au climat** I can't get used to the food/climate
5: **se faire** +infinitif: **se faire examiner la vue/opérer** to have one's eyes tested/have an operation; **se faire couper les cheveux** to get one's hair cut; **il va se faire tuer/punir** he's going to get himself killed/get punished; **il s'est fait aider** he got somebody to help him; **il s'est fait aider par Simon** he got Simon to help him; **se faire faire un vêtement** to get a garment made for o.s.

6 (impersonnel): **comment se fait-il/faisait-il que?** how is it/was it that?

**faire-part** [fɛrpar] nm inv announcement (of birth, marriage etc)
**faisan, e** [fəzã, an] nm/f pheasant
**faisons** [fəzɔ̃] vb voir **faire**
**fait, e** [fɛ, fɛt] adj (mûr: fromage, melon) ripe ▷ nm (événement) event, occurrence; (réalité, donnée) fact; **être au ~ (de)** to be informed (of); **au ~** (à propos) by the way; **en venir au ~** to get to the point; **du ~ de ceci/qu'il a menti** because of ou on account of this/his having lied; **de ce ~** for this reason; **en ~** in fact; **prendre qn sur le ~** to catch sb in the act; **c'est bien ~ pour lui** (ou eux etc) it serves him (ou them etc) right; **fait divers** news item
**faites** [fɛt] vb voir **faire**
**falaise** [falɛz] nf cliff
**falloir** [falwar] vb impers: **il faut qu'il parte/a fallu qu'il parte** (obligation) he has to ou must leave/had to leave; **il a fallu le faire** it had to be done; **il faudrait qu'elle rentre** she should come ou go back, she ought to come ou go back; **il faut faire attention** you have to be careful; **il me faudrait 100 euros** I would need 100 euros; **il vous faut tourner à gauche après l'église** you have to turn left past the church; **nous avons ce qu'il (nous) faut** we have what we need; **il ne fallait pas** you shouldn't have (done); **comme il faut** (personne) proper; (agir) properly; **s'en falloir** vr: **il s'en est fallu de 100 euros/5 minutes** we/they etc were 100 euros short/5 minutes late (ou early); **il s'en faut de beaucoup qu'il soit** he is far from being; **il s'en est fallu de peu que cela n'arrive** it very nearly happened
**famé, e** [fame] adj: **mal ~** disreputable, of ill repute
**fameux, -euse** [famø, øz] adj (illustre) famous; (bon: repas, plat etc) first-rate, first-class; (valeur intensive) real,

downright
**familial, e, -aux** [familjal, jo] adj
family cpd
**familiarité** [familjaʀite] nf familiarity
**familier, -ère** [familje, jɛʀ] adj
(connu) familiar; (atmosphère) informal,
friendly; (Ling) informal, colloquial
▷ nm regular (visitor)
**famille** [famij] nf family; **il a de la ~ à
Paris** he has relatives in Paris
**famine** [famin] nf famine
**fanatique** [fanatik] adj fanatical
▷ nm/f fanatic
**faner** [fane]: **se faner** vi to fade
**fanfare** [fɑ̃faʀ] nf (orchestre) brass
band; (musique) fanfare
**fantaisie** [fɑ̃tezi] nf (spontanéité) fancy,
imagination; (caprice) whim ▷ adj:
**bijou ~** costume jewellery
**fantasme** [fɑ̃tasm] nm fantasy
**fantastique** [fɑ̃tastik] adj fantastic
**fantôme** [fɑ̃tom] nm ghost, phantom
**faon** [fɑ̃] nm fawn
**FAQ** sigle f (= foire aux questions) FAQ
**farce** [faʀs] nf (viande) stuffing; (blague)
(practical) joke; (Théâtre) farce; **farcir** vt
(viande) to stuff
**farder** [faʀde]: **se farder** vi to make
(o.s.) up
**farine** [faʀin] nf flour
**farouche** [faʀuʃ] adj (timide) shy, timid
**fart** [faʀt] nm (ski) wax
**fascination** [fasinasjɔ̃] nf fascination
**fasciner** [fasine] vt to fascinate
**fascisme** [faʃism] nm fascism
**fasse** etc [fas] vb voir **faire**
**fastidieux, -euse** [fastidjø, jøz] adj
tedious, tiresome
**fatal, e** [fatal] adj fatal; (inévitable)
inevitable; **fatalité** nf (destin) fate;
(coïncidence) fateful coincidence
**fatidique** [fatidik] adj fateful
**fatigant, e** [fatigɑ̃, ɑ̃t] adj tiring;
(agaçant) tiresome
**fatigue** [fatig] nf tiredness, fatigue;
**fatigué, e** adj tired; **fatiguer** vt to tire,
make tired; (fig: agacer) to annoy ▷ vi
(moteur) to labour, strain; **se fatiguer**

to get tired
**fauché, e** [foʃe] (fam) adj broke
**faucher** [foʃe] vt (herbe) to cut; (champs,
blés) to reap; (fig: véhicule) to mow
down; (fam: voler) to pinch
**faucon** [fokɔ̃] nm falcon, hawk
**faudra** [fodʀa] vb voir **falloir**
**faufiler** [fofile]: **se faufiler** vi: **se ~
dans** to edge one's way into; **se ~
parmi/entre** to thread one's way
among/between
**faune** [fon] nf (Zool) wildlife, fauna
**fausse** [fos] adj voir **faux**; **faussement**
adv (accuser) wrongly, wrongfully;
(croire) falsely
**fausser** [fose] vt (objet) to bend, buckle;
(fig) to distort; **~ compagnie à qn** to
give sb the slip
**faut** [fo] vb voir **falloir**
**faute** [fot] nf (erreur) mistake, error;
(mauvaise action) misdemeanour;
(Football etc) offence; (Tennis) fault;
**c'est de sa/ma ~** it's his ou her/my
fault; **être en ~** to be in the wrong; **~ de**
(temps, argent) for ou through lack of;
**sans ~** without fail; **faute de frappe**
typing error; **faute professionnelle**
professional misconduct no pl
**fauteuil** [fotœj] nm armchair;
(au théâtre) seat; **fauteuil roulant**
wheelchair
**fautif, -ive** [fotif, iv] adj (responsable)
at fault, in the wrong; (incorrect)
incorrect, inaccurate; **il se sentait ~**
he felt guilty
**fauve** [fov] nm wildcat ▷ adj (couleur)
fawn
**faux¹** [fo] nf scythe
**faux², fausse** [fo, fos] adj (inexact)
wrong; (voix) out of tune; (billet) fake,
forged; (sournois, postiche) false ▷ adv
(Mus) out of tune ▷ nm (copie) fake,
forgery; **faire ~ bond à qn** to let sb
down; **faire un ~ pas** to trip; (fig) to
make a faux pas; **fausse alerte** false
alarm; **fausse couche** miscarriage;
**faux frais** nmpl extras, incidental
expenses; **faux mouvement** awkward

movement; **fausse note** wrong note; **faux témoignage** (délit) perjury; **faux-filet** nm sirloin

**faveur** [favœʀ] nf favour; **traitement de ~** preferential treatment; **en ~ de** in favour of

**favorable** [favɔʀabl] adj favourable

**favori, te** [favɔʀi, it] adj, nm/f favourite

**favoriser** [favɔʀize] vt to favour

**fax** [faks] nm fax

**fécond, e** [fekɔ̃, ɔ̃d] adj fertile; **féconder** vt to fertilize

**féculent** [fekylɑ̃] nm starchy food

**fédéral, e, -aux** [federal, o] adj federal

**fée** [fe] nf fairy

**feignant, e** [fɛɲɑ̃, ɑ̃t] nm/f = **fainéant, e**

**feindre** [fɛ̃dʀ] vt to feign; **~ de faire** to pretend to do

**fêler** [fele] vt to crack; **se fêler** to crack

**félicitations** [felisitasjɔ̃] nfpl congratulations

**féliciter** [felisite] vt: **~ qn (de)** to congratulate sb (on)

**félin, e** [felɛ̃, in] nm (big) cat

**femelle** [fəmɛl] adj, nf female

**féminin, e** [feminɛ̃, in] adj feminine; (sexe) female; (équipe, vêtements etc) women's ▷ nm (Ling) feminine; **féministe** adj feminist

**femme** [fam] nf woman; (épouse) wife; **femme au foyer** housewife; **femme de chambre** chambermaid; **femme de ménage** cleaning lady

**fémur** [femyʀ] nm femur, thighbone

**fendre** [fɑ̃dʀ] vt (couper en deux) to split; (fissurer) to crack; (traverser: foule, air) to cleave through; **se fendre** vi to crack

**fenêtre** [f(ə)nɛtʀ] nf window

**fenouil** [fənuj] nm fennel

**fente** [fɑ̃t] nf (fissure) crack; (de boîte à lettres etc) slit

**fer** [fɛʀ] nm iron; **fer à cheval** horseshoe; **fer à friser** curling tongs pl; **fer (à repasser)** iron; **fer forgé** wrought iron

**ferai** etc [fəʀe] vb voir **faire**

**fer-blanc** [fɛʀblɑ̃] nm tin(plate)

**férié, e** [feʀje] adj: **jour ~** public holiday

**ferions** etc [fəʀjɔ̃] vb voir **faire**

**ferme** [fɛʀm] adj firm ▷ adv (travailler etc) hard ▷ nf (exploitation) farm; (maison) farmhouse

**fermé, e** [fɛʀme] adj closed, shut; (gaz, eau etc) off; (fig: milieu) exclusive

**fermenter** [fɛʀmɑ̃te] vi to ferment

**fermer** [fɛʀme] vt to close, shut; (cesser l'exploitation de) to close down, shut down; (eau, électricité, robinet) to turn off; (aéroport, route) to close ▷ vi to close, shut; (magasin: définitivement) to close down, shut down; **~ à clef** to lock; **se fermer** vi to close, shut

**fermeté** [fɛʀməte] nf firmness

**fermeture** [fɛʀmətyʀ] nf closing; (dispositif) catch; **heures de ~** closing times; **fermeture éclair®** ou **à glissière** zip (fastener) (BRIT), zipper (US)

**fermier** [fɛʀmje] nm farmer

**féroce** [feʀɔs] adj ferocious, fierce

**ferons** [fəʀɔ̃] vb voir **faire**

**ferrer** [feʀe] vt (cheval) to shoe

**ferroviaire** [feʀɔvjɛʀ] adj rail(way) cpd (BRIT), rail(road) cpd (US)

**ferry(-boat)** [feʀe(-bot)] nm ferry

**fertile** [fɛʀtil] adj fertile; **~ en incidents** eventful, packed with incidents

**fervent, e** [fɛʀvɑ̃, ɑ̃t] adj fervent

**fesse** [fɛs] nf buttock; **fessée** nf spanking

**festin** [fɛstɛ̃] nm feast

**festival** [fɛstival] nm festival

**festivités** [fɛstivite] nfpl festivities

**fêtard, e** [fɛtaʀ, aʀd] (fam) nm/f high liver, merry-maker

**fête** [fɛt] nf (religieuse) feast; (publique) holiday; (réception) party; (kermesse) fête, fair; (du nom) feast day, name day; **faire la ~** to live it up; **faire ~ à qn** to give sb a warm welcome; **les ~s (de fin d'année)** the festive season; **la salle des ~s** the village hall; **la ~ des Mères/**

**Pères** Mother's/Father's Day; **fête**
**foraine** (fun) fair; **fêter** vt to celebrate;
(personne) to have a celebration for

**feu, x** [fø] nm (gén) fire; (signal lumineux)
light; (de cuisinière) ring; **feux** nmpl
(Auto) (traffic) lights; **au ~!** (incendie)
fire!; **à ~ doux/vif** over a slow/brisk
heat; **à petit ~** (Culin) over a gentle
heat; (fig) slowly; **faire ~** to fire; **ne pas**
**faire long ~** not to last long; **prendre ~**
to catch fire; **mettre le ~ à** to set fire to;
**faire du ~** to make a fire; **avez-vous du**
**~?** (pour cigarette) have you (got) a light?;
**feu arrière** rear light; **feu d'artifice**
(spectacle) fireworks pl; **feu de joie**
bonfire; **feu orange/rouge/vert**
amber (BRIT) ou yellow (US)/red/green
light; **feux de brouillard** fog lights ou
lamps; **feux de croisement** dipped
(BRIT) ou dimmed (US) headlights; **feux**
**de position** sidelights; **feux de route**
headlights

**feuillage** [fœjaʒ] nm foliage, leaves pl

**feuille** [fœj] nf (d'arbre) leaf; (de papier)
sheet; **feuille de calcul** spreadsheet;
**feuille d'impôts** tax form; **feuille de**
**maladie** medical expenses claim form;
**feuille de paie** pay slip

**feuillet** [fœjɛ] nm leaf

**feuilleté, e** [fœjte] adj: **pâte ~** flaky
pastry

**feuilleter** [fœjte] vt (livre) to leaf
through

**feuilleton** [fœjtɔ̃] nm serial

**feutre** [føtʀ] nm felt; (chapeau) felt hat;
(aussi: **stylo-~**) felt-tip pen; **feutré, e**
adj (atmosphère) muffled

**fève** [fɛv] nf broad bean

**février** [fevʀije] nm February

**fiable** [fjabl] adj reliable

**fiançailles** [fjɑ̃sɑj] nfpl engagement sg

**fiancé, e** [fjɑ̃se] nm/f fiancé(e) ▷ adj:
**être ~ (à)** to be engaged (to)

**fiancer** [fjɑ̃se]: **se fiancer (avec)** vi to
become engaged (to)

**fibre** [fibʀ] nf fibre; **fibre de verre**
fibreglass, glass fibre

**ficeler** [fis(ə)le] vt to tie up

**ficelle** [fisɛl] nf string no pl; (morceau)
piece ou length of string

**fiche** [fiʃ] nf (pour fichier) (index) card;
(formulaire) form; (Élec) plug; **fiche de**
**paye** pay slip

**ficher** [fiʃe] vt (dans un fichier) to file;
(Police) to put on file; (fam: faire) to do;
(: donner) to give; (: mettre) to stick ou
shove; **fiche-(moi) le camp!** (fam)
clear off!; **fiche-moi la paix!** (fam) leave
me alone!; **se ficher de** (fam: rire de) to
make fun of; (être indifférent à) not to
care about

**fichier** [fiʃje] nm file; **~ joint** (Comput)
attachment

**fichu, e** [fiʃy] pp de **ficher** (fam) ▷ adj
(fam: fini, inutilisable) bust, done for;
(: intensif) wretched, darned ▷ nm
(foulard) (head)scarf; **mal ~** (fam)
feeling lousy

**fictif, -ive** [fiktif, iv] adj fictitious

**fiction** [fiksjɔ̃] nf fiction; (fait imaginé)
invention

**fidèle** [fidɛl] adj faithful ▷ nm/f (Rel):
**les ~s** (à l'église) the congregation sg;
**fidélité** nf (d'un conjoint) fidelity,
faithfulness; (d'un ami, client) loyalty

**fier¹** [fje] vt to trust

**fier², fière** [fjɛʀ] adj proud; **~ de** proud
of; **fierté** nf pride

**fièvre** [fjɛvʀ] nf fever; **avoir de la ~/39**
**de ~** to have a high temperature/a
temperature of 39˚C; **fiévreux, -euse**
adj feverish

**figer** [fiʒe]: **se figer** vi (huile) to congeal;
(personne) to freeze

**fignoler** [fiɲɔle] (fam) vt to polish up

**figue** [fig] nf fig; **figuier** nm fig tree

**figurant, e** [figyʀɑ̃, ɑ̃t] nm/f (Théâtre)
walk-on; (Cinéma) extra

**figure** [figyʀ] nf (visage) face; (forme,
personnage) figure; (illustration) picture,
diagram

**figuré, e** [figyʀe] adj (sens) figurative

**figurer** [figyʀe] vi to appear ▷ vt to
represent; **se figurer que** to imagine
that

**fil** [fil] nm (brin, fig: d'une histoire) thread;

(*électrique*) wire; (*d'un couteau*) edge; **au ~ des années** with the passing of the years; **au ~ de l'eau** with the stream *ou* current; **coup de ~** (*fam*) phone call; **donner/recevoir un coup de ~** to make/get *ou* receive a phone call; **fil de fer** wire; **fil de fer barbelé** barbed wire

**file** [fil] *nf* line; (*Auto*) lane; **en ~ indienne** in single file; **à la ~** (*d'affilée*) in succession; **file (d'attente)** queue (*BRIT*), line (*US*)

**filer** [file] *vt* (*tissu, toile*) to spin; (*prendre en filature*) to shadow, tail; (*fam: donner*): **~ qch à qn** to slip sb sth ▷ *vi* (*bas*) to run; (*aller vite*) to fly past; (*fam: partir*) to make *ou* be off; **~ doux** to toe the line

**filet** [filɛ] *nm* net; (*Culin*) fillet; (*d'eau, de sang*) trickle; **filet (à provisions)** string bag

**filiale** [filjal] *nf* (*Comm*) subsidiary

**filière** [filjɛʀ] *nf* (*carrière*) path; **suivre la ~** (*dans sa carrière*) to work one's way up (through the hierarchy)

**fille** [fij] *nf* girl; (*opposé à fils*) daughter; **vieille ~** old maid; **fillette** *nf* (little) girl

**filleul, e** [fijœl] *nm/f* godchild, godson/daughter

**film** [film] *nm* (*pour photo*) (roll of) film; (*œuvre*) film, picture, movie

**filtre** [filtʀ] *nm* filter; **filtrer** *vt* to filter; (*fig: candidats, visiteurs*) to screen

**fin¹** [fɛ̃] *nf* end; **fins** *nfpl* (*but*) ends; **prendre ~** to come to an end; **mettre ~ à** to put an end to; **à la ~** in the end, eventually; **en ~ de compte** in the end; **sans ~** endless; **~ juin** at the end of June; **fin prêt** quite ready

**fin², e** [fɛ̃, fin] *adj* (*papier, couche, fil*) thin; (*cheveux, visage*) fine; (*taille*) neat, slim; (*esprit, remarque*) subtle ▷ *adv* (*couper*) finely; **fines herbes** mixed herbs; **avoir la vue/l'ouïe fine** to have keen eyesight/hearing; **repas/vin fin** gourmet meal/fine wine

**final, e** [final, o] *adj* final ▷ *nm* (*Mus*) finale; **finale** *nf* final; **quarts de finale** quarter finals; **finalement** *adv* finally,

in the end; (*après tout*) after all

**finance** [finɑ̃s]: **finances** *nfpl* (*situation*) finances; (*activités*) finance *sg*; **moyennant ~** for a fee; **financer** *vt* to finance; **financier, -ière** *adj* financial

**finesse** [finɛs] *nf* thinness; (*raffinement*) fineness; (*subtilité*) subtlety

**fini, e** [fini] *adj* finished; (*Math*) finite ▷ *nm* (*d'un objet manufacturé*) finish

**finir** [finiʀ] *vt* to finish ▷ *vi* to finish, end; **~ par faire** to end up *ou* finish up doing; **~ de faire** to finish doing; (*cesser*) to stop doing; **il finit par m'agacer** he's beginning to get on my nerves; **en ~ avec** to be *ou* have done with; **il va mal ~** he will come to a bad end

**finition** [finisjɔ̃] *nf* (*résultat*) finish

**finlandais, e** [fɛ̃lɑ̃dɛ, ɛz] *adj* Finnish ▷ *nm/f*: **F~, e** Finn

**Finlande** [fɛ̃lɑ̃d] *nf*: **la ~** Finland

**finnois, e** [finwa, waz] *adj* Finnish ▷ *nm* (*Ling*) Finnish

**fioul** [fjul] *nm* fuel oil

**firme** [firm] *nf* firm

**fis** [fi] *vb voir* **faire**

**fisc** [fisk] *nm* tax authorities *pl*; **fiscal, e, -aux** *adj* tax *cpd*, fiscal; **fiscalité** *nf* tax system

**fissure** [fisyʀ] *nf* crack; **fissurer** *vt* to crack; **se fissurer** *vi* to crack

**fit** [fi] *vb voir* **faire**

**fixation** [fiksasjɔ̃] *nf* (*attache*) fastening; (*Psych*) fixation

**fixe** [fiks] *adj* fixed; (*emploi*) steady, regular ▷ *nm* (*salaire*) basic salary; (*téléphone*) landline; **à heure ~** at a set time; **menu à prix ~** set menu

**fixé, e** [fikse] *adj*: **être ~ (sur)** (*savoir à quoi s'en tenir*) to have made up one's mind (about)

**fixer** [fikse] *vt* (*attacher*): **~ qch (à/sur)** to fix *ou* fasten sth (to/onto); (*déterminer*) to fix, set; (*regarder*) to stare at; **se fixer** *vi* (*s'établir*) to settle down; **se ~ sur** (*suj: attention*) to focus on

**flacon** [flakɔ̃] *nm* bottle

**flageolet** [flaʒɔlɛ] nm (Culin) dwarf kidney bean

**flagrant, e** [flagrã, ãt] adj flagrant, blatant; **en ~ délit** in the act

**flair** [flɛʀ] nm sense of smell; (fig) intuition; **flairer** vt (humer) to sniff (at); (détecter) to scent

**flamand, e** [flamã, ãd] adj Flemish ▷ nm (Ling) Flemish ▷ nm/f: **F~, e** Fleming

**flamant** [flamã] nm flamingo

**flambant, e** [flãbã, ãt] adv: **~ neuf** brand new

**flambé, e** [flãbe] adj (Culin) flambé

**flambée** [flãbe] nf blaze; (fig: des prix) explosion

**flamber** [flãbe] vi to blaze (up)

**flamboyer** [flãbwaje] vi to blaze (up)

**flamme** [flam] nf flame; (fig) fire, fervour; **en ~s** on fire, ablaze

**flan** [flã] nm (Culin) custard tart ou pie

**flanc** [flã] nm side; (Mil) flank

**flancher** [flãʃe] (fam) vi to fail, pack up

**flanelle** [flanɛl] nf flannel

**flâner** [flɑne] vi to stroll

**flanquer** [flãke] vt to flank; (fam: mettre) to chuck, shove; (: jeter): **~ par terre/à la porte** to fling to the ground/chuck out

**flaque** [flak] nf (d'eau) puddle; (d'huile, de sang etc) pool

**flash** [flaʃ] (pl **~es**) nm (Photo) flash; **flash d'information** newsflash

**flatter** [flate] vt to flatter; **se ~ de qch** to pride o.s. on sth; **flatteur, -euse** adj flattering

**flèche** [flɛʃ] nf arrow; (de clocher) spire; **monter en ~** (fig) to soar, rocket; **partir en ~** to be off like a shot; **fléchette** nf dart

**flétrir** [fletʀiʀ]: **se flétrir** vi to wither

**fleur** [flœʀ] nf flower; (d'un arbre) blossom; **en ~** (arbre) in blossom; **à ~s** flowery

**fleuri, e** [flœʀi] adj (jardin) in flower ou bloom; (tissu, papier) flowery

**fleurir** [flœʀiʀ] vi (rose) to flower; (arbre) to blossom; (fig) to flourish ▷ vt

(tombe) to put flowers on; (chambre) to decorate with flowers

**fleuriste** [flœʀist] nm/f florist

**fleuve** [flœv] nm river

**flexible** [flɛksibl] adj flexible

**flic** [flik] (fam: péj) nm cop

**flipper** [flipœʀ] nm pinball (machine)

**flirter** [flœʀte] vi to flirt

**flocon** [flɔkɔ̃] nm flake

**flore** [flɔʀ] nf flora

**florissant, e** [flɔʀisã, ãt] adj (économie) flourishing

**flot** [flo] nm flood, stream; **flots** nmpl (de la mer) waves; **être à ~** (Navig) to be afloat; **entrer à ~s** to stream ou pour in

**flottant, e** [flɔtã, ãt] adj (vêtement) loose

**flotte** [flɔt] nf (Navig) fleet; (fam: eau) water; (: pluie) rain

**flotter** [flɔte] vi to float; (nuage, odeur) to drift; (drapeau) to fly; (vêtements) to hang loose; (fam: pleuvoir) to rain; **faire ~** to float; **flotteur** nm float

**flou, e** [flu] adj fuzzy, blurred; (fig) woolly, vague

**fluide** [flɥid] adj fluid; (circulation etc) flowing freely ▷ nm fluid

**fluor** [flyɔʀ] nm: **dentifrice au ~** fluoride toothpaste

**fluorescent, e** [flyɔʀesã, ãt] adj fluorescent

**flûte** [flyt] nf flute; (verre) flute (glass); (pain) (thin) French stick; **~!** drat it!; **flûte traversière/à bec** flute/recorder

**flux** [fly] nm incoming tide; (écoulement) flow; **le ~ et le reflux** the ebb and flow

**foc** [fɔk] nm jib

**foi** [fwa] nf faith; **digne de ~** reliable; **être de bonne/mauvaise ~** to be sincere/insincere; **ma ~ ...** well ...

**foie** [fwa] nm liver; **crise de ~** stomach upset

**foin** [fwɛ̃] nm hay; **faire du ~** (fig: fam) to kick up a row

**foire** [fwaʀ] nf fair; (fête foraine) (fun) fair; **faire la ~** (fig: fam) to whoop it up; **~ aux questions** (Internet) FAQs; **foire (exposition)** trade fair

**fois** [fwa] *nf* time; **une/deux ~**
once/twice; **2 ~ 2** 2 times 2; **une ~**
(*passé*) once; (*futur*) sometime; **une ~**
**pour toutes** once and for all; **une ~ que**
once; **des ~** (*parfois*) sometimes; **à la ~**
(*ensemble*) at once

**fol** [fɔl] *adj voir* **fou**

**folie** [fɔli] *nf* (*d'une décision, d'un acte*)
madness, folly; (*état*) madness,
insanity; **la ~ des grandeurs** delusions
of grandeur; **faire des ~s** (*en dépenses*)
to be extravagant

**folklorique** [fɔlklɔrik] *adj* folk *cpd*;
(*fam*) weird

**folle** [fɔl] *adj, nf voir* **fou**; **follement** *adv*
(*très*) madly, wildly

**foncé, e** [fɔ̃se] *adj* dark

**foncer** [fɔ̃se] *vi* to go darker; (*fam:*
*aller vite*) to tear *ou* belt along; **~ sur** to
charge at

**fonction** [fɔ̃ksjɔ̃] *nf* function; (*emploi,*
*poste*) post, position; **fonctions** *nfpl*
(*professionnelles*) duties; **voiture de ~**
company car; **en ~ de** (*par rapport à*)
according to; **faire ~ de** to serve as;
**la ~ publique** the state *ou* civil (BRIT)
service; **fonctionnaire** *nm/f* state
employee, local authority employee;
(*dans l'administration*) ≈ civil servant;
**fonctionner** *vi* to work, function

**fond** [fɔ̃] *nm* (*d'un récipient, trou*) bottom;
(*d'une salle, scène*) back; (*d'un tableau,*
*décor*) background; (*opposé à la forme*)
content; (*Sport*) **le ~** long distance
(running); **au ~ de** at the bottom of;
at the back of; **à ~** (*connaître, soutenir*)
thoroughly; (*appuyer, visser*) right down
*ou* home; **à ~ (de train)** (*fam*) full tilt;
**dans le ~, au ~** (*en somme*) basically,
really; **de ~ en comble** from top to
bottom; **fond de teint** foundation
(cream); *voir aussi* **fonds**

**fondamental, e, -aux** [fɔ̃damɑ̃tal, o]
*adj* fundamental

**fondant, e** [fɔ̃dɑ̃, ɑ̃t] *adj* (*neige*)
melting; (*poire*) that melts in the mouth

**fondation** [fɔ̃dasjɔ̃] *nf* founding;
(*établissement*) foundation; **fondations**
*nfpl* (*d'une maison*) foundations

**fondé, e** [fɔ̃de] *adj* (*accusation etc*) well-
founded; **être ~ à** to have grounds for
*ou* good reason to

**fondement** [fɔ̃dmɑ̃] *nm*: **sans ~**
(*rumeur etc*) groundless, unfounded

**fonder** [fɔ̃de] *vt* to found; (*fig*) to base;
**se fonder sur** (*suj: personne*) to base
o.s. on

**fonderie** [fɔ̃dri] *nf* smelting works *sg*

**fondre** [fɔ̃dr] *vt* (*aussi:* **faire ~**) to melt;
(*dans l'eau*) to dissolve; (*fig: mélanger*)
to merge, blend ▷ *vi* (*à la chaleur*) to
melt; (*dans l'eau*) to dissolve; (*fig*) to
melt away; (*se précipiter*): **~ sur** to
swoop down on; **~ en larmes** to burst
into tears

**fonds** [fɔ̃] *nm* (*Comm*): **~ (de**
**commerce)** business ▷ *nmpl* (*argent*)
funds

**fondu, e** [fɔ̃dy] *adj* (*beurre, neige*)
melted; (*métal*) molten; **fondue** *nf*
(*Culin*) fondue

**font** [fɔ̃] *vb voir* **faire**

**fontaine** [fɔ̃tɛn] *nf* fountain; (*source*)
spring

**fonte** [fɔ̃t] *nf* melting; (*métal*) cast iron;
**la ~ des neiges** the (spring) thaw

**foot** [fut] (*fam*) *nm* football

**football** [futbol] *nm* football, soccer;
**footballeur** *nm* footballer

**footing** [futiŋ] *nm* jogging; **faire du ~**
to go jogging

**forain, e** [fɔrɛ̃, ɛn] *adj* fairground *cpd*
▷ *nm* (*marchand*) stallholder; (*acteur*)
fairground entertainer

**forçat** [fɔrsa] *nm* convict

**force** [fɔrs] *nf* strength; (*Physique,*
*Mécanique*) force; **forces** *nfpl* (*physiques*)
strength *sg*; (*Mil*) forces; **à ~ d'insister**
by dint of insisting; as he (*ou* I *etc*) kept
on insisting; **de ~** forcibly, by force;
**dans la ~ de l'âge** in the prime of life;
**les forces de l'ordre** the police *no pl*

**forcé, e** [fɔrse] *adj* forced; **c'est ~**
(*fam*) it's inevitable; **forcément**
*adv* inevitably; **pas forcément** not
necessarily

**forcer** [fɔʀse] vt to force; (voix) to strain ▷ vi (Sport) to overtax o.s.; **~ la dose** (fam) to overdo it; **se ~ (à faire)** to force o.s. (to do)

**forestier, -ère** [fɔʀɛstje, jɛʀ] adj forest cpd

**forêt** [fɔʀɛ] nf forest

**forfait** [fɔʀfɛ] nm (Comm) all-in deal ou price; **déclarer ~** to withdraw; **forfaitaire** adj inclusive

**forge** [fɔʀʒ] nf forge, smithy; **forgeron** nm (black)smith

**formaliser** [fɔʀmalize]: **se formaliser** vi: **se ~ (de)** to take offence (at)

**formalité** [fɔʀmalite] nf formality; **simple ~** mere formality

**format** [fɔʀma] nm size; **formater** vt (disque) to format

**formation** [fɔʀmasjɔ̃] nf (développement) forming; (apprentissage) training; **formation permanente** ou **continue** continuing education

**forme** [fɔʀm] nf (gén) form; (d'un objet) shape, form; **formes** nfpl (bonnes manières) proprieties; (d'une femme) figure sg; **en ~ de poire** pear-shaped, in the shape of a pear; **être en ~** (Sport etc) to be on form; **en bonne et due ~** in due form

**formel, le** [fɔʀmɛl] adj (catégorique) definite, positive; **formellement** adv (absolument) positively; **formellement interdit** strictly forbidden

**former** [fɔʀme] vt to form; (éduquer) to train; **se former** vi to form

**formidable** [fɔʀmidabl] adj tremendous

**formulaire** [fɔʀmylɛʀ] nm form

**formule** [fɔʀmyl] nf (gén) formula; (expression) phrase; **formule de politesse** polite phrase; (en fin de lettre) letter ending

**fort, e** [fɔʀ, fɔʀt] adj strong; (intensité, rendement) high, great; (corpulent) stout; (doué) good, able ▷ adv (serrer, frapper) hard; (parler) loud(ly); (beaucoup) greatly, very much; (très) very ▷ nm (édifice) fort; (point fort) strong point,

forte; **forte tête** rebel; **forteresse** nf stronghold

**fortifiant** [fɔʀtifjɑ̃] nm tonic

**fortune** [fɔʀtyn] nf fortune; **faire ~** to make one's fortune; **de ~** makeshift; **fortuné, e** adj wealthy

**forum** [fɔʀɔm] nm forum; **~ de discussion** (Internet) message board

**fosse** [fos] nf (grand trou) pit; (tombe) grave

**fossé** [fose] nm ditch; (fig) gulf, gap

**fossette** [fosɛt] nf dimple

**fossile** [fosil] nm fossil

**fou (fol), folle** [fu, fɔl] adj mad; (déréglé etc) wild, erratic; (fam: extrême, très grand) terrific, tremendous ▷ nm/f madman(-woman) ▷ nm (du roi) jester; **être fou de** to be mad ou crazy about; **avoir le fou rire** to have the giggles

**foudre** [fudʀ] nf: **la ~** lightning

**foudroyant, e** [fudʀwajɑ̃, ɑ̃t] adj (progrès) lightning cpd; (succès) stunning; (maladie, poison) violent

**fouet** [fwɛ] nm whip; (Culin) whisk; **de plein ~** (se heurter) head on; **fouetter** vt to whip; (crème) to whisk

**fougère** [fuʒɛʀ] nf fern

**fougue** [fug] nf ardour, spirit; **fougueux, -euse** adj fiery

**fouille** [fuj] nf search; **fouilles** nfpl (archéologiques) excavations; **fouiller** vt to search; (creuser) to dig ▷ vi to rummage; **fouillis** nm jumble, muddle

**foulard** [fulaʀ] nm scarf

**foule** [ful] nf crowd; **la ~** crowds pl; **une ~ de** masses of

**foulée** [fule] nf stride

**fouler** [fule] vt to press; (sol) to tread upon; **se ~ la cheville** to sprain one's ankle; **ne pas se ~** not to overexert o.s.; **il ne se foule pas** he doesn't put himself out; **foulure** nf sprain

**four** [fuʀ] nm oven; (de potier) kiln; (Théâtre: échec) flop

**fourche** [fuʀʃ] nf pitchfork

**fourchette** [fuʀʃɛt] nf fork; (Statistique) bracket, margin

**fourgon** [fuʀgɔ̃] nm van; (Rail)

wag(g)on; **fourgonnette** nf (small) van

**fourmi** [fuʀmi] nf ant; **avoir des ~s dans les jambes/mains** to have pins and needles in one's legs/hands; **fourmilière** nf ant-hill; **fourmiller** vi to swarm

**fourneau, x** [fuʀno] nm stove

**fourni, e** [fuʀni] adj (barbe, cheveux) thick; (magasin): **bien ~ (en)** well stocked (with)

**fournir** [fuʀniʀ] vt to supply; (preuve, exemple) to provide, supply; (effort) to put in; **~ qch à qn** to supply sth to sb, supply ou provide sb with sth; **fournisseur, -euse** nm/f supplier; **fournisseur d'accès à Internet** (Internet) service provider, ISP; **fourniture** nf supply(ing); **fournitures scolaires** school stationery

**fourrage** [fuʀaʒ] nm fodder

**fourré, e** [fuʀe] adj (bonbon etc) filled; (manteau etc) fur-lined ▷ nm thicket

**fourrer** [fuʀe] (fam) vt to stick, shove; **se fourrer dans/sous** to get into/under

**fourrière** [fuʀjɛʀ] nf pound

**fourrure** [fuʀyʀ] nf fur; (sur l'animal) coat

**foutre** [futʀ] (fam!) vt = **ficher**; **foutu, e** (fam!) adj = **fichu, e**

**foyer** [fwaje] nm (maison) home; (famille) family; (de cheminée) hearth; (de jeunes etc) (social) club; (résidence) hostel; (salon) foyer; **lunettes à double ~** bi-focals

**fracassant, e** [fʀakasɑ̃, ɑ̃t] adj (succès) thundering

**fraction** [fʀaksjɔ̃] nf fraction

**fracture** [fʀaktyʀ] nf fracture; **fracture du crâne** fractured skull; **fracturer** vt (coffre, serrure) to break open; (os, membre) to fracture; **se fracturer le crâne** to fracture one's skull

**fragile** [fʀaʒil] adj fragile, delicate; (fig) frail; **fragilité** nf fragility

**fragment** [fʀagmɑ̃] nm (d'un objet) fragment, piece

**fraîche** [fʀɛʃ] adj voir **frais**; **fraîcheur** nf coolness; (d'un aliment) freshness; **fraîchir** vi to get cooler; (vent) to freshen

**frais, fraîche** [fʀɛ, fʀɛʃ] adj fresh; (froid) cool ▷ adv (récemment) newly, fresh(ly) ▷ nm: **mettre au ~** to put in a cool place ▷ nmpl (gén) expenses; (Comm) costs; **il fait ~** it's cool; **servir ~** serve chilled; **prendre le ~** to take a breath of cool air; **faire des ~** to go to a lot of expense; **frais de scolarité** school fees (BRIT), tuition (US); **frais généraux** overheads

**fraise** [fʀɛz] nf strawberry; **fraise des bois** wild strawberry

**framboise** [fʀɑ̃bwaz] nf raspberry

**franc, franche** [fʀɑ̃, fʀɑ̃ʃ] adj (personne) frank, straightforward; (visage) open; (net: refus) clear; (: coupure) clean; (intensif) downright ▷ nm franc

**français, e** [fʀɑ̃sɛ, ɛz] adj French ▷ nm/f: **F~, e** Frenchman(-woman) ▷ nm (Ling) French

**France** [fʀɑ̃s] nf: **la ~** France; **~ 2, ~ 3** public-sector television channels

● **FRANCE TÉLÉVISION**
●
● **France 2** and **France 3** are public-
● sector television channels. France
● 2 is a national general interest and
● entertainment channel; France
● 3 provides regional news and
● information as well as programmes
● for the national network.

**franche** [fʀɑ̃ʃ] adj voir **franc**; **franchement** adv frankly; (nettement) definitely; (tout à fait: mauvais etc) downright

**franchir** [fʀɑ̃ʃiʀ] vt (obstacle) to clear, get over; (seuil, ligne, rivière) to cross; (distance) to cover

**franchise** [fʀɑ̃ʃiz] nf frankness; (douanière) exemption; (Assurances) excess

**franc-maçon** [fʀɑ̃masɔ̃] nm
freemason

**franco** [fʀɑ̃ko] adv (Comm): **~ (de port)**
postage paid

**francophone** [fʀɑ̃kɔfɔn] adj French-
speaking

**franc-parler** [fʀɑ̃paʀle] nm inv
outspokenness; **avoir son ~** to speak
one's mind

**frange** [fʀɑ̃ʒ] nf fringe

**frangipane** [fʀɑ̃ʒipan] nf almond
paste

**frappant, e** [fʀapɑ̃, ɑ̃t] adj striking

**frappé, e** [fʀape] adj iced

**frapper** [fʀape] vt to hit, strike;
(étonner) to strike; **~ dans ses mains** to
clap one's hands; **frappé de stupeur**
dumbfounded

**fraternel, le** [fʀatɛʀnɛl] adj brotherly,
fraternal; **fraternité** nf brotherhood

**fraude** [fʀod] nf fraud; (Scol) cheating;
**passer qch en ~** to smuggle sth in (ou
out); **fraude fiscale** tax evasion

**frayeur** [fʀejœʀ] nf fright

**fredonner** [fʀədɔne] vt to hum

**freezer** [fʀizœʀ] nm freezing
compartment

**frein** [fʀɛ̃] nm brake; **mettre un ~
à** (fig) to curb, check; **frein à main**
handbrake; **freiner** vi to brake ▷ vt
(progrès etc) to check

**frêle** [fʀɛl] adj frail, fragile

**frelon** [fʀəlɔ̃] nm hornet

**frémir** [fʀemir] vi (de peur, d'horreur) to
shudder; (de colère) to shake; (feuillage)
to quiver

**frêne** [fʀɛn] nm ash

**fréquemment** [fʀekamɑ̃] adv
frequently

**fréquent, e** [fʀekɑ̃, ɑ̃t] adj frequent

**fréquentation** [fʀekɑ̃tasjɔ̃] nf
frequenting; **fréquentations** nfpl
(relations) company sg; **avoir de
mauvaises ~s** to be in with the wrong
crowd, keep bad company

**fréquenté, e** [fʀekɑ̃te] adj: **très ~**
(very) busy; **mal ~** patronized by
disreputable elements

**fréquenter** [fʀekɑ̃te] vt (lieu)
to frequent; (personne) to see; **se
fréquenter** to see each other

**frère** [fʀɛʀ] nm brother

**fresque** [fʀɛsk] nf (Art) fresco

**fret** [fʀɛ(t)] nm freight

**friand, e** [fʀijɑ̃, fʀijɑ̃d] adj: **~ de** very
fond of ▷ nm: **~ au fromage** cheese puff

**friandise** [fʀijɑ̃diz] nf sweet

**fric** [fʀik] (fam) nm cash, bread

**friche** [fʀiʃ]: **en ~** adj, adv (lying) fallow

**friction** [fʀiksjɔ̃] nf (massage) rub, rub-
down; (Tech, fig) friction

**frigidaire®** [fʀiʒidɛʀ] nm refrigerator

**frigo** [fʀigo] (fam) nm fridge

**frigorifique** [fʀigɔʀifik] adj
refrigerating

**frileux, -euse** [fʀilø, øz] adj sensitive
to (the) cold

**frimer** [fʀime] (fam) vi to show off

**fringale** [fʀɛ̃gal] (fam) nf: **avoir la ~** to
be ravenous

**fringues** [fʀɛ̃g] (fam) nfpl clothes

**fripé, e** [fʀipe] adj crumpled

**frire** [fʀiʀ] vt, vi: **faire ~** to fry

**frisé, e** [fʀize] adj (cheveux) curly;
(personne) curly-haired

**frisson** [fʀisɔ̃] nm (de froid) shiver; (de
peur) shudder; **frissonner** vi (de fièvre,
froid) to shiver; (d'horreur) to shudder

**frit, e** [fʀi, fʀit] pp de **frire**; **frite** nf:
**(pommes) frites** chips (BRIT), French
fries; **friteuse** nf chip pan; **friteuse
électrique** deep fat fryer; **friture** nf
(huile) (deep) fat; (plat): **friture (de
poissons)** fried fish

**froid, e** [fʀwa, fʀwad] adj, nm cold; **il
fait ~** it's cold; **avoir/prendre ~** to be/
catch cold; **être en ~ avec** to be on bad
terms with; **froidement** adv (accueillir)
coldly; (décider) coolly

**froisser** [fʀwase] vt to crumple (up),
crease; (fig) to hurt, offend; **se froisser**
vi to crumple, crease; (personne) to
take offence; **se ~ un muscle** to strain
a muscle

**frôler** [fʀole] vt to brush against; (suj:
projectile) to skim past; (fig) to come

very close to

**fromage** [fʀɔmaʒ] nm cheese; **fromage blanc** soft white cheese

**froment** [fʀɔmɑ̃] nm wheat

**froncer** [fʀɔ̃se] vt to gather; **~ les sourcils** to frown

**front** [fʀɔ̃] nm forehead, brow; (Mil) front; **de ~** (se heurter) head-on; (rouler) together (i.e. 2 or 3 abreast); (simultanément) at once; **faire ~ à** to face up to

**frontalier, -ère** [fʀɔ̃talje, jɛʀ] adj border cpd, frontier cpd; **(travailleurs) ~s** people who commute across the border

**frontière** [fʀɔ̃tjɛʀ] nf frontier, border

**frotter** [fʀɔte] vi to rub, scrape ▷ vt to rub; (pommes de terre, plancher) to scrub; **~ une allumette** to strike a match

**fruit** [fʀɥi] nm fruit gen no pl; **fruits de mer** seafood(s); **fruits secs** dried fruit sg; **fruité, e** adj fruity; **fruitier, -ère** adj: **arbre fruitier** fruit tree

**frustrer** [fʀystʀe] vt to frustrate

**fuel(-oil)** [fjul(ɔjl)] nm fuel oil; (domestique) heating oil

**fugace** [fygas] adj fleeting

**fugitif, -ive** [fyʒitif, iv] adj (fugace) fleeting ▷ nm/f fugitive

**fugue** [fyg] nf: **faire une ~** to run away, abscond

**fuir** [fɥiʀ] vt to flee from; (éviter) to shun ▷ vi to run away; (gaz, robinet) to leak

**fuite** [fɥit] nf flight; (écoulement, divulgation) leak; **être en ~** to be on the run; **mettre en ~** to put to flight

**fulgurant, e** [fylgyʀɑ̃, ɑ̃t] adj lightning cpd, dazzling

**fumé, e** [fyme] adj (Culin) smoked; (verre) tinted; **fumée** nf smoke

**fumer** [fyme] vi to smoke; (soupe) to steam ▷ vt to smoke

**fûmes** [fym] vb voir **être**

**fumeur, -euse** [fymœʀ, øz] nm/f smoker

**fumier** [fymje] nm manure

**funérailles** [fyneʀɑj] nfpl funeral sg

**fur** [fyʀ]: **au ~ et à mesure** adv as one goes along; **au ~ et à mesure que** as

**furet** [fyʀɛ] nm ferret

**fureter** [fyʀ(ə)te] (péj) vi to nose about

**fureur** [fyʀœʀ] nf fury; **être en ~** to be infuriated; **faire ~** to be all the rage

**furie** [fyʀi] nf fury; (femme) shrew, vixen; **en ~** (mer) raging; **furieux, -euse** adj furious

**furoncle** [fyʀɔ̃kl] nm boil

**furtif, -ive** [fyʀtif, iv] adj furtive

**fus** [fy] vb voir **être**

**fusain** [fyzɛ̃] nm (Art) charcoal

**fuseau, x** [fyzo] nm (pour filer) spindle; (pantalon) (ski) pants; **fuseau horaire** time zone

**fusée** [fyze] nf rocket

**fusible** [fyzibl] nm (Élec: fil) fuse wire; (: fiche) fuse

**fusil** [fyzi] nm (de guerre, à canon rayé) rifle, gun; (de chasse, à canon lisse) shotgun, gun; **fusillade** nf gunfire no pl, shooting no pl; **fusiller** vt to shoot; **fusiller qn du regard** to look daggers at sb

**fusionner** [fyzjɔne] vi to merge

**fût** [fy] vb voir **être** ▷ nm (tonneau) barrel, cask

**futé, e** [fyte] adj crafty; **Bison ~®** TV and radio traffic monitoring service

**futile** [fytil] adj futile; frivolous

**futur, e** [fytyʀ] adj, nm future

**fuyard, e** [fɥijaʀ, aʀd] nm/f runaway

# g

**Gabon** [gabɔ̃] nm: **le ~** Gabon

**gâcher** [gaʃe] vt (gâter) to spoil; (gaspiller) to waste; **gâchis** nm waste no pl

**gaffe** [gaf] nf blunder; **faire ~** (fam) to be careful

**gage** [gaʒ] nm (dans un jeu) forfeit; (fig: de fidélité, d'amour) token; **gages** nmpl (salaire) wages; **mettre en ~** to pawn

**gagnant, e** [gaɲɑ̃, ɑ̃t] adj: **billet/ numéro ~** winning ticket/number ▷ nm/f winner

**gagne-pain** [gaɲpɛ̃] nm inv job

**gagner** [gaɲe] vt to win; (somme d'argent, revenu) to earn; (aller vers, atteindre) to reach; (envahir: sommeil, peur) to overcome; (: mal) to spread to ▷ vi to win; (fig) to gain; **~ du temps/de la place** to gain time/save space; **~ sa vie** to earn one's living

**gai, e** [ge] adj cheerful; (un peu ivre) merry; **gaiement** adv cheerfully; **gaieté** nf cheerfulness; **de gaieté de cœur** with a light heart

**gain** [gɛ̃] nm (revenu) earnings pl; (bénéfice: gén pl) profits pl

**gala** [gala] nm official reception; **de ~** (soirée etc) gala

**galant, e** [galɑ̃, ɑ̃t] adj (courtois) courteous, gentlemanly; (entreprenant) flirtatious, gallant; (scène, rendez-vous) romantic

**galerie** [galʀi] nf gallery; (Théâtre) circle; (de voiture) roof rack; (fig: spectateurs) audience; **galerie de peinture** (private) art gallery; **galerie marchande** shopping arcade

**galet** [galɛ] nm pebble

**galette** [galɛt] nf flat cake; **galette des Rois** cake eaten on Twelfth Night

- **GALETTE DES ROIS**
-
- A **galette des Rois** is a cake eaten on
- Twelfth Night containing a figurine.
- The person who finds it is the king
- (or queen) and gets a paper crown.
- They then choose someone else to be
- their queen (or king).

**galipette** [galipɛt] nf somersault

**Galles** [gal] nfpl: **le pays de ~** Wales; **gallois, e** adj Welsh ▷ nm/f: **Gallois, e** Welshman(-woman) ▷ nm (Ling) Welsh

**galon** [galɔ̃] nm (Mil) stripe; (décoratif) piece of braid

**galop** [galo] nm gallop; **galoper** vi to gallop

**gambader** [gɑ̃bade] vi (animal, enfant) to leap about

**gamin, e** [gamɛ̃, in] nm/f kid ▷ adj childish

**gamme** [gam] nf (Mus) scale; (fig) range

**gang** [gɑ̃g] nm (de criminels) gang

**gant** [gɑ̃] nm glove; **gant de toilette** face flannel (BRIT), face cloth

**garage** [gaʀaʒ] nm garage; **garagiste** nm/f garage owner; (employé) garage mechanic

**garantie** [gaʀɑ̃ti] nf guarantee; **(bon de) ~** guarantee ou warranty slip

**garantir** [gaʀɑ̃tiʀ] vt to guarantee; **~ à**

**qn que** to assure sb that
**garçon** [gaʀsɔ̃] nm boy; (*célibataire*):
**vieux ~** bachelor; **garçon (de café)**
(*serveur*) waiter; **garçon de courses**
messenger
**garde** [gaʀd(ə)] nm (*de prisonnier*)
guard; (*de domaine etc*) warden; (*soldat,
sentinelle*) guardsman ▷ nf (*soldats*)
guard; **de ~** on duty; **monter la ~** to
stand guard; **mettre en ~** to warn;
**prendre ~ (à)** to be careful (of); **garde
champêtre** nm rural policeman; **garde
du corps** nm bodyguard; **garde à vue**
nf (*Jur*) ≈ police custody; **garde-boue**
nm inv mudguard; **garde-chasse** nm
gamekeeper
**garder** [gaʀde] vt (*conserver*) to keep;
(*surveiller: enfants*) to look after;
(*: immeuble, lieu, prisonnier*) to guard;
**se garder** vi (*aliment: se conserver*) to
keep; **se ~ de faire** to be careful not
to do; **~ le lit/la chambre** to stay in
bed/indoors; **pêche/chasse gardée**
private fishing/hunting (ground)
**garderie** [gaʀdəʀi] nf day nursery,
crèche
**garde-robe** [gaʀdəʀɔb] nf wardrobe
**gardien, ne** [gaʀdjɛ̃, jɛn] nm/f
(*garde*) guard; (*de prison*) warder; (*de
domaine, réserve*) warden; (*de musée etc*)
attendant; (*de phare, cimetière*) keeper;
(*d'immeuble*) caretaker; (*fig*) guardian;
**gardien de but** goalkeeper; **gardien
de la paix** policeman; **gardien de nuit**
night watchman
**gare¹** [gaʀ] nf station; **gare routière**
bus station
**gare²** [gaʀ] excl: **~ à ...!** mind ...!; **~ à toi!**
watch out!
**garer** [gaʀe] vt to park; **se garer** vi
to park
**garni, e** [gaʀni] adj (*plat*) served with
vegetables (*and chips or rice etc*)
**garniture** [gaʀnityʀ] nf (*Culin*)
vegetables pl; **garniture de frein**
brake lining
**gars** [ga] (*fam*) nm guy
**Gascogne** [gaskɔɲ] nf Gascony; **le**

**golfe de ~** the Bay of Biscay
**gas-oil** [gazɔjl] nm diesel (oil)
**gaspiller** [gaspije] vt to waste
**gastronome** [gastʀɔnɔm]
nm/f gourmet; **gastronomique** adj
gastronomic
**gâteau, x** [gɑto] nm cake; **gâteau
sec** biscuit
**gâter** [gɑte] vt to spoil; **se gâter** vi
(*dent, fruit*) to go bad; (*temps, situation*)
to change for the worse
**gâteux, -euse** [gɑtø, øz] adj senile
**gauche** [goʃ] adj left, left-hand;
(*maladroit*) awkward, clumsy ▷ nf (*Pol*)
left (wing); **la bras ~** the left arm; **le
côté ~** the left-hand side; **à ~** on the
left; (*direction*) (to the) left; **gaucher,
-ère** adj left-handed; **gauchiste** nm/f
leftist
**gaufre** [gofʀ] nf waffle
**gaufrette** [gofʀɛt] nf wafer
**gaulois, e** [golwa, waz] adj Gallic
▷ nm/f: **G~, e** Gaul
**gaz** [gaz] nm inv gas; **ça sent le ~** I can
smell gas, there's a smell of gas
**gaze** [gaz] nf gauze
**gazette** [gazɛt] nf news sheet
**gazeux, -euse** [gazø, øz] adj (*boisson*)
fizzy; (*eau*) sparkling
**gazoduc** [gazodyk] nm gas pipeline
**gazon** [gazɔ̃] nm (*herbe*) grass; (*pelouse*)
lawn
**geai** [ʒɛ] nm jay
**géant, e** [ʒeɑ̃, ɑ̃t] adj gigantic; (*Comm*)
giant-size ▷ nm/f giant
**geindre** [ʒɛ̃dʀ] vi to groan, moan
**gel** [ʒɛl] nm frost
**gélatine** [ʒelatin] nf gelatine
**gelée** [ʒ(ə)le] nf jelly; (*gel*) frost
**geler** [ʒ(ə)le] vt, vi to freeze; **il gèle** it's
freezing
**gélule** [ʒelyl] nf (*Méd*) capsule
**Gémeaux** [ʒemo] nmpl: **les ~** Gemini
**gémir** [ʒemiʀ] vi to groan, moan
**gênant, e** [ʒɛnɑ̃, ɑ̃t] adj (*irritant*)
annoying; (*embarrassant*) embarrassing
**gencive** [ʒɑ̃siv] nf gum
**gendarme** [ʒɑ̃daʀm] nm gendarme;

**gendarmerie** nf military police force in countryside and small towns; their police station or barracks
**gendre** [ʒɑ̃dʀ] nm son-in-law
**gêné, e** [ʒene] adj embarrassed
**gêner** [ʒene] vt (incommoder) to bother; (encombrer) to be in the way; (embarrasser): ~ **qn** to make sb feel ill-at-ease; **se gêner** to put o.s. out; **ne vous gênez pas!** don't mind me!
**général, e, -aux** [ʒeneʀal, o] adj, nm general; **en ~** usually, in general; **généralement** adv generally; **généraliser** vt, vi to generalize; **se généraliser** vi to become widespread; **généraliste** nm/f general practitioner, G.P.
**génération** [ʒeneʀasjɔ̃] nf generation
**généreux, -euse** [ʒeneʀø, øz] adj generous
**générique** [ʒeneʀik] nm (Cinéma) credits pl
**générosité** [ʒeneʀozite] nf generosity
**genêt** [ʒ(ə)nɛ] nm broom no pl (shrub)
**génétique** [ʒenetik] adj genetic
**Genève** [ʒ(ə)nɛv] n Geneva
**génial, e, -aux** [ʒenjal, jo] adj of genius; (fam: formidable) fantastic, brilliant
**génie** [ʒeni] nm genius; (Mil): **le ~** the Engineers pl; **génie civil** civil engineering
**genièvre** [ʒ(ə)njɛvʀ] nm juniper
**génisse** [ʒenis] nf heifer
**génital, e, -aux** [ʒenital, o] adj genital; **les parties ~es** the genitals
**génoise** [ʒenwaz] nf sponge cake
**genou, x** [ʒ(ə)nu] nm knee; **à ~x** on one's knees; **se mettre à ~x** to kneel down
**genre** [ʒɑ̃ʀ] nm kind, type, sort; (Ling) gender; **avoir bon ~** to look a nice sort; **avoir mauvais ~** to be coarse-looking; **ce n'est pas son ~** it's not like him
**gens** [ʒɑ̃] nmpl (f in some phrases) people pl
**gentil, le** [ʒɑ̃ti, ij] adj kind; (enfant: sage) good; (endroit etc) nice;

**gentillesse** nf kindness; **gentiment** adv kindly
**géographie** [ʒeɔgʀafi] nf geography
**géologie** [ʒeɔlɔʒi] nf geology
**géomètre** [ʒeɔmɛtʀ] nm/f (arpenteur) (land) surveyor
**géométrie** [ʒeɔmetʀi] nf geometry; **géométrique** adj geometric
**géranium** [ʒeʀanjɔm] nm geranium
**gérant, e** [ʒeʀɑ̃, ɑ̃t] nm/f manager(-eress); **gérant d'immeuble** (managing) agent
**gerbe** [ʒɛʀb] nf (de fleurs) spray; (de blé) sheaf
**gercé, e** [ʒɛʀse] adj chapped
**gerçure** [ʒɛʀsyʀ] nf crack
**gérer** [ʒeʀe] vt to manage
**germain, e** [ʒɛʀmɛ̃, ɛn] adj: **cousin ~** first cousin
**germe** [ʒɛʀm] nm germ; **germer** vi to sprout; (semence) to germinate
**geste** [ʒɛst] nm gesture
**gestion** [ʒɛstjɔ̃] nf management
**Ghana** [gana] nm: **le ~** Ghana
**gibier** [ʒibje] nm (animaux) game
**gicler** [ʒikle] vi to spurt, squirt
**gifle** [ʒifl] nf slap (in the face); **gifler** vt to slap (in the face)
**gigantesque** [ʒigɑ̃tɛsk] adj gigantic
**gigot** [ʒigo] nm leg (of mutton ou lamb)
**gigoter** [ʒigote] vi to wriggle (about)
**gilet** [ʒilɛ] nm waistcoat; (pull) cardigan; **gilet de sauvetage** life jacket
**gin** [dʒin] nm gin; **~-tonic** gin and tonic
**gingembre** [ʒɛ̃ʒɑ̃bʀ] nm ginger
**girafe** [ʒiʀaf] nf giraffe
**giratoire** [ʒiʀatwaʀ] adj: **sens ~** roundabout
**girofle** [ʒiʀɔfl] nf: **clou de ~** clove
**girouette** [ʒiʀwɛt] nf weather vane ou cock
**gitan, e** [ʒitɑ̃, an] nm/f gipsy
**gîte** [ʒit] nm (maison) home; (abri) shelter; **gîte (rural)** (country) holiday cottage (BRIT), gîte (self-catering accommodation in the country)
**givre** [ʒivʀ] nm (hoar) frost; **givré, e** adj

covered in frost; (*fam: fou*) nuts; **orange givrée** orange sorbet (*served in peel*)

**glace** [glas] *nf* ice; (*crème glacée*) ice cream; (*miroir*) mirror; (*de voiture*) window

**glacé, e** [glase] *adj* (*mains, vent, pluie*) freezing; (*lac*) frozen; (*boisson*) iced

**glacer** [glase] *vt* to freeze; (*gâteau*) to ice; (*fig*): **~ qn** (*intimider*) to chill sb; (*paralyser*) to make sb's blood run cold

**glacial, e** [glasjal, jo] *adj* icy

**glacier** [glasje] *nm* (*Géo*) glacier; (*marchand*) ice-cream maker

**glacière** [glasjɛʀ] *nf* icebox

**glaçon** [glasɔ̃] *nm* icicle; (*pour boisson*) ice cube

**glaïeul** [glajœl] *nm* gladiolus

**glaise** [glɛz] *nf* clay

**gland** [glã] *nm* acorn; (*décoration*) tassel

**glande** [glãd] *nf* gland

**glissade** [glisad] *nf* (*par jeu*) slide; (*chute*) slip; **faire des ~s sur la glace** to slide on the ice

**glissant, e** [glisã, ãt] *adj* slippery

**glissement** [glismã] *nm*: **glissement de terrain** landslide

**glisser** [glise] *vi* (*avancer*) to glide *ou* slide along; (*coulisser, tomber*) to slide; (*déraper*) to slip; (*être glissant*) to be slippery ▷ *vt* to slip; **se glisser dans/ entre** to slip into/between

**global, e, -aux** [global, o] *adj* overall

**globe** [glɔb] *nm* globe

**globule** [glɔbyl] *nm* (*du sang*): **~ blanc/ rouge** white/red corpuscle

**gloire** [glwaʀ] *nf* glory

**glousser** [gluse] *vi* to cluck; (*rire*) to chuckle

**glouton, ne** [glutɔ̃, ɔn] *adj* gluttonous

**gluant, e** [glyã, ãt] *adj* sticky, gummy

**glucose** [glykoz] *nm* glucose

**glycine** [glisin] *nf* wisteria

**GO** *sigle* (= *grandes ondes*) LW

**goal** [gol] *nm* goalkeeper

**gobelet** [gɔblɛ] *nm* (*en étain, verre, argent*) tumbler; (*d'enfant, de pique-nique*) beaker; (*à dés*) cup

**goéland** [gɔelã] *nm* (sea)gull

**goélette** [gɔelɛt] *nf* schooner

**goinfre** [gwɛ̃fʀ] *nm* glutton

**golf** [gɔlf] *nm* golf; (*terrain*) golf course; **golf miniature** crazy (*BRIT*) *ou* miniature golf

**golfe** [gɔlf] *nm* gulf; (*petit*) bay

**gomme** [gɔm] *nf* (*à effacer*) rubber (*BRIT*), eraser; **gommer** *vt* to rub out (*BRIT*), erase

**gonflé, e** [gɔ̃fle] *adj* swollen; **il est ~** (*fam: courageux*) he's got some nerve; (*impertinent*) he's got a nerve

**gonfler** [gɔ̃fle] *vt* (*pneu, ballon: en soufflant*) to blow up; (: *avec une pompe*) to pump up; (*nombre, importance*) to inflate ▷ *vi* to swell (up); (*Culin: pâte*) to rise

**gonzesse** [gɔ̃zɛs] (*fam*) *nf* chick, bird (*BRIT*)

**gorge** [gɔʀʒ] *nf* (*Anat*) throat; (*vallée*) gorge; **gorgée** (*petite*) sip; (*grande*) gulp

**gorille** [gɔʀij] *nm* gorilla; (*fam*) bodyguard

**gosse** [gɔs] (*fam*) *nm/f* kid

**goudron** [gudʀɔ̃] *nm* tar; **goudronner** *vt* to tar(mac) (*BRIT*), asphalt (*US*)

**gouffre** [gufʀ] *nm* abyss, gulf

**goulot** [gulo] *nm* neck; **boire au ~** to drink from the bottle

**goulu, e** [guly] *adj* greedy

**gourde** [guʀd] *nf* (*récipient*) flask; (*fam*) (*clumsy*) clot *ou* oaf ▷ *adj* oafish

**gourdin** [guʀdɛ̃] *nm* club, bludgeon

**gourmand, e** [guʀmã, ãd] *adj* greedy; **gourmandise** *nf* greed; (*bonbon*) sweet

**gousse** [gus] *nf*: **gousse d'ail** clove of garlic

**goût** [gu] *nm* taste; **avoir bon ~** to taste good; **de bon ~** tasteful; **de mauvais ~** tasteless; **prendre ~ à** to develop a taste *ou* a liking for

**goûter** [gute] *vt* (*essayer*) to taste; (*apprécier*) to enjoy ▷ *vi* to have (afternoon) tea ▷ *nm* (afternoon) tea; **je peux ~?** can I have a taste?

**goutte** [gut] *nf* drop; (*Méd*) gout; (*alcool*) brandy; **tomber ~ à ~** to drip;

une **~ de whisky** a drop of whisky;
**goutte-à-goutte** nm (Méd) drip
**gouttière** [gutjɛʀ] nf gutter
**gouvernail** [guvɛʀnaj] nm rudder;
(barre) helm, tiller
**gouvernement** [guvɛʀnəmɑ̃] nm
government
**gouverner** [guvɛʀne] vt to govern
**grâce** [gʀɑs] nf (charme, Rel) grace;
(faveur) favour; (Jur) pardon; **faire ~ à qn
de qch** to spare sb sth; **demander ~** to
beg for mercy; **~ à** thanks to; **gracieux,
-euse** adj graceful
**grade** [gʀad] nm rank; **monter en ~** to
be promoted
**gradin** [gʀadɛ̃] nm tier; step; **gradins**
nmpl (de stade) terracing sg
**gradué, e** [gʀadɥe] adj: **verre ~**
measuring jug
**graduel, le** [gʀadɥɛl] adj gradual
**graduer** [gʀadɥe] vt (effort etc) to
increase gradually; (règle, verre) to
graduate
**graffiti** [gʀafiti] nmpl graffiti
**grain** [gʀɛ̃] nm (gén) grain; (Navig)
squall; **grain de beauté** beauty spot;
**grain de café** coffee bean; **grain de
poivre** peppercorn
**graine** [gʀɛn] nf seed
**graissage** [gʀesaʒ] nm lubrication,
greasing
**graisse** [gʀes] nf fat; (lubrifiant) grease;
**graisser** vt to lubricate, grease;
(tacher) to make greasy; **graisseux,
-euse** adj greasy
**grammaire** [gʀa(m)mɛʀ] nf grammar
**gramme** [gʀam] nm gramme
**grand, e** [gʀɑ̃, gʀɑ̃d] adj (haut) tall;
(gros, vaste, large) big, large; (long)
long; (plus âgé) big; (adulte) grown-up;
(important, brillant) great ▷ adv: **~
ouvert** wide open; **au ~ air** in the open
(air); **les grands blessés** the severely
injured; **grand ensemble** housing
scheme; **grand magasin** department
store; **grande personne** grown-up;
**grande surface** hypermarket; **grandes
écoles** prestigious schools at university

level; **grandes lignes** (Rail) main lines;
**grandes vacances** summer holidays
(BRIT) ou vacation (US); **grand-chose**
nm/f inv: **pas grand-chose** not
much; **Grande-Bretagne** nf (Great)
Britain; **grandeur** nf (dimension) size;
**grandeur nature** life-size; **grandiose**
adj imposing; **grandir** vi to grow ▷ vt:
**grandir qn** (suj: vêtement, chaussure)
to make sb look taller; **grand-mère** nf
grandmother; **grand-peine: à grand-
peine** adv with difficulty; **grand-père**
nm grandfather; **grands-parents** nmpl
grandparents
**grange** [gʀɑ̃ʒ] nf barn
**granit** [gʀanit] nm granite
**graphique** [gʀafik] adj graphic ▷ nm
graph
**grappe** [gʀap] nf cluster; **grappe de
raisin** bunch of grapes
**gras, se** [gʀa, gʀɑs] adj (viande, soupe)
fatty; (personne) fat; (surface, main)
greasy; (plaisanterie) coarse; (Typo) bold
▷ nm (Culin) fat; **faire la ~se matinée**
to have a lie-in (BRIT), sleep late (US);
**grassement** adv: **grassement payé**
handsomely paid
**gratifiant, e** [gʀatifjɑ̃, jɑ̃t] adj
gratifying, rewarding
**gratin** [gʀatɛ̃] nm (plat) cheese-topped
dish; (croûte) cheese topping; (fam:
élite) upper crust; **gratiné, e** adj (Culin)
au gratin
**gratis** [gʀatis] adv free
**gratitude** [gʀatityd] nf gratitude
**gratte-ciel** [gʀatsjɛl] nm inv
skyscraper
**gratter** [gʀate] vt (avec un outil) to
scrape; (enlever: avec un outil) to scrape
off; (: avec un ongle) to scratch; (enlever
avec un ongle) to scratch off ▷ vi (irriter)
to be scratchy; (démanger) to itch; **se
gratter** to scratch (o.s.)
**gratuit, e** [gʀatɥi, ɥit] adj (entrée,
billet) free; (fig) gratuitous
**grave** [gʀav] adj (maladie, accident)
serious, bad; (sujet, problème) serious,
grave; (air) grave, solemn; (voix, son)

deep, low-pitched; **gravement** adv
seriously; (parler, regarder) gravely
**graver** [gʀave] vt (plaque, nom) to
engrave; (CD, DVD) to burn
**graveur** [gʀavœʀ] nm engraver;
**graveur de CD/DVD** CD/DVD writer
**gravier** [gʀavje] nm gravel no pl;
**gravillons** nmpl loose chippings ou
gravel sg
**gravir** [gʀaviʀ] vt to climb (up)
**gravité** [gʀavite] nf (de maladie,
d'accident) seriousness; (de sujet,
problème) gravity
**graviter** [gʀavite] vi to revolve
**gravure** [gʀavyʀ] nf engraving;
(reproduction) print
**gré** [gʀe] nm: **à son ~** to one's liking;
**de bon ~** willingly; **contre le ~ de qn**
against sb's will; **de son (plein) ~** of
one's own free will; **bon ~ mal ~** like it
or not; **de ~ ou de force** whether one
likes it or not; **savoir ~ à qn de qch** to
be grateful to sb for sth
**grec, grecque** [gʀɛk] adj Greek;
(classique: vase etc) Grecian ▷ nm/f: **G~,**
**Grecque** Greek ▷ nm (Ling) Greek
**Grèce** [gʀɛs] nf: **la ~** Greece
**greffe** [gʀɛf] nf (Bot, Méd: de tissu) graft;
(Méd: d'organe) transplant; **greffer** vt
(Bot, Méd: tissu) to graft; (Méd: organe)
to transplant
**grêle** [gʀɛl] adj (very) thin ▷ nf hail;
**grêler** vb impers: **il grêle** it's hailing;
**grêlon** nm hailstone
**grelot** [gʀəlo] nm little bell
**grelotter** [gʀəlɔte] vi to shiver
**grenade** [gʀənad] nf (explosive)
grenade; (Bot) pomegranate;
**grenadine** nf grenadine
**grenier** [gʀənje] nm attic; (de ferme) loft
**grenouille** [gʀənuj] nf frog
**grès** [gʀɛ] nm sandstone; (poterie)
stoneware
**grève** [gʀɛv] nf (d'ouvriers) strike; (plage)
shore; **se mettre en/faire ~** to go on/
be on strike; **grève de la faim** hunger
strike; **grève sauvage** wildcat strike
**gréviste** [gʀevist] nm/f striker

**grièvement** [gʀijɛvmɑ̃] adv seriously
**griffe** [gʀif] nf claw; (de couturier) label;
**griffer** vt to scratch
**grignoter** [gʀiɲɔte] vt (personne) to
nibble at; (souris) to gnaw at ▷ vi to
nibble
**gril** [gʀil] nm steak ou grill pan; **faire**
**cuire au ~** to grill; **grillade** nf (viande
etc) grill
**grillage** [gʀijaʒ] nm (treillis) wire
netting; (clôture) wire fencing
**grille** [gʀij] nf (clôture) wire fence;
(portail) (metal) gate; (d'égout) (metal)
grate; (fig) grid
**grille-pain** [gʀijpɛ̃] nm inv toaster
**griller** [gʀije] vt (pain) to toast; (viande)
to grill; (fig: ampoule etc) to blow; **faire ~**
to toast; to grill; (châtaignes) to roast; **~**
**un feu rouge** to jump the lights
**grillon** [gʀijɔ̃] nm cricket
**grimace** [gʀimas] nf grimace; (pour
faire rire): **faire des ~s** to pull ou make
faces
**grimper** [gʀɛ̃pe] vi, vt to climb
**grincer** [gʀɛ̃se] vi (objet métallique) to
grate; (plancher, porte) to creak; **~ des**
**dents** to grind one's teeth
**grincheux, -euse** [gʀɛ̃ʃø, øz] adj
grumpy
**grippe** [gʀip] nf flu, influenza; **grippe**
**aviaire** bird flu; **grippé, e** adj: **être**
**grippé** to have flu
**gris, e** [gʀi, gʀiz] adj grey; (ivre) tipsy
**grisaille** [gʀizaj] nf greyness, dullness
**griser** [gʀize] vt to intoxicate
**grive** [gʀiv] nf thrush
**Groenland** [gʀɔɛnlɑ̃d] nm Greenland
**grogner** [gʀɔɲe] vi to growl; (fig) to
grumble; **grognon, ne** adj grumpy
**grommeler** [gʀɔm(ə)le] vi to mutter
to o.s.
**gronder** [gʀɔ̃de] vi to rumble; (fig:
révolte) to be brewing ▷ vt to scold; **se**
**faire ~** to get a telling-off
**gros, se** [gʀo, gʀos] adj big, large;
(obèse) fat; (travaux, dégâts) extensive;
(épais) thick; (rhume, averse) heavy
▷ adv: **risquer/gagner ~** to risk/win

a lot ▷ *nm/f* fat man/woman ▷ *nm* (*Comm*): **le ~** the wholesale business; **le ~ de** the bulk of; **prix de gros** wholesale price; **par ~ temps/grosse mer** in rough weather/heavy seas; **en ~** roughly; (*Comm*) wholesale; **gros lot** jackpot; **gros mot** swearword; **gros plan** (*Photo*) close-up; **gros sel** cooking salt; **gros titre** headline; **grosse caisse** big drum

**groseille** [gʀozɛj] *nf*: **~ (rouge/blanche)** red/white currant; **groseille à maquereau** gooseberry

**grosse** [gʀos] *adj voir* **gros**; **grossesse** *nf* pregnancy; **grosseur** *nf* size; (*tumeur*) lump

**grossier, -ière** [gʀosje, jɛʀ] *adj* coarse; (*insolent*) rude; (*dessin*) rough; (*travail*) roughly done; (*imitation, instrument*) crude; (*évident: erreur*) gross; **grossièrement** *adv* (*sommairement*) roughly; (*vulgairement*) coarsely; **grossièreté** *nf* rudeness; (*mot*): **dire des grossièretés** to use coarse language

**grossir** [gʀosiʀ] *vi* (*personne*) to put on weight ▷ *vt* (*exagérer*) to exaggerate; (*au microscope*) to magnify; (*suj: vêtement*): **~ qn** to make sb look fatter

**grossiste** [gʀosist] *nm/f* wholesaler

**grotesque** [gʀotɛsk] *adj* (*extravagant*) grotesque; (*ridicule*) ludicrous

**grotte** [gʀot] *nf* cave

**groupe** [gʀup] *nm* group; **groupe de parole** support group; **groupe sanguin** blood group; **groupe scolaire** school complex; **grouper** *vt* to group; **se grouper** *vi* to gather

**grue** [gʀy] *nf* crane

**GSM** [ʒeɛsɛm] *nm, adj* GSM

**guenon** [gɔnɔ̃] *nf* female monkey

**guépard** [gepaʀ] *nm* cheetah

**guêpe** [gɛp] *nf* wasp

**guère** [gɛʀ] *adv* (*avec adjectif, adverbe*): **ne ... ~** hardly; (*avec verbe: pas beaucoup*): **ne ... ~** *tournure négative* +much; (*pas souvent*) hardly ever; (*pas longtemps*) *tournure négative* +(very) long; **il n'y a**

**~ que/de** there's hardly anybody (*ou* anything) but/hardly any; **ce n'est ~ difficile** it's hardly difficult; **nous n'avons ~ de temps** we have hardly any time

**guérilla** [geʀija] *nf* guerrilla warfare

**guérillero** [geʀijeʀo] *nm* guerrilla

**guérir** [geʀiʀ] *vt* (*personne, maladie*) to cure; (*membre, plaie*) to heal ▷ *vi* (*malade, maladie*) to be cured; (*blessure*) to heal; **guérison** *nf* (*de maladie*) curing; (*de membre, plaie*) healing; (*de malade*) recovery; **guérisseur, -euse** *nm/f* healer

**guerre** [gɛʀ] *nf* war; **en ~** at war; **faire la ~ à** to wage war against; **guerre civile/mondiale** civil/world war; **guerrier, -ière** *adj* warlike ▷ *nm/f* warrior

**guet** [gɛ] *nm*: **faire le ~** to be on the watch *ou* look-out; **guet-apens** [getapɑ̃] *nm* ambush; **guetter** *vt* (*épier*) to watch (intently); (*attendre*) to watch (out) for; (*hostilement*) to be lying in wait for

**gueule** [gœl] *nf* (*d'animal*) mouth; (*fam: figure*) face; (: *bouche*) mouth; **ta ~!** (*fam*) shut up!; **avoir la ~ de bois** (*fam*) to have a hangover, be hung over; **gueuler** (*fam*) *vi* to bawl

**gui** [gi] *nm* mistletoe

**guichet** [giʃɛ] *nm* (*de bureau, banque*) counter; **les ~s** (*à la gare, au théâtre*) the ticket office *sg*

**guide** [gid] *nm* (*personne*) guide; (*livre*) guide (book) ▷ *nf* (*éclaireuse*) girl guide; **guider** *vt* to guide

**guidon** [gidɔ̃] *nm* handlebars *pl*

**guignol** [giɲɔl] *nm* ≈ Punch and Judy show; (*fig*) clown

**guillemets** [gijmɛ] *nmpl*: **entre ~** in inverted commas

**guindé, e** [gɛ̃de] *adj* (*personne, air*) stiff, starchy; (*style*) stilted

**Guinée** [gine] *nf* Guinea

**guirlande** [giʀlɑ̃d] *nf* (*fleurs*) garland; **guirlande de Noël** tinsel garland

**guise** [giz] *nf*: **à votre ~** as you wish *ou*

please; **en ~ de** by way of

**guitare** [gitar] nf guitar

**Guyane** [gɥijan] nf: **la ~ (française)** French Guiana

**gym** [ʒim] nf (exercices) gym; **gymnase** nm gym(nasium); **gymnaste** nm/f gymnast; **gymnastique** nf gymnastics sg; (au réveil etc) keep-fit exercises pl

**gynécologie** [ʒinekɔlɔʒi] nf gynaecology; **gynécologique** adj gynaecological; **gynécologue** nm/f gynaecologist

**habile** [abil] adj skilful; (malin) clever; **habileté** [abilte] nf skill, skilfulness; cleverness

**habillé, e** [abije] adj dressed; (chic) dressy

**habiller** [abije] vt to dress; (fournir en vêtements) to clothe; (couvrir) to cover; **s'habiller** vi to dress (o.s.); (se déguiser, mettre des vêtements chic) to dress up

**habit** [abi] nm outfit; **habits** nmpl (vêtements) clothes; **habit (de soirée)** evening dress; (pour homme) tails pl

**habitant, e** [abitɑ̃, ɑ̃t] nm/f inhabitant; (d'une maison) occupant; **loger chez l'~** to stay with the locals

**habitation** [abitasjɔ̃] nf house; **habitations à loyer modéré** (block of) council flats

**habiter** [abite] vt to live in ▷ vi: **~ à/dans** to live in; **où habitez-vous?** where do you live?

**habitude** [abityd] nf habit; **avoir l'~ de qch** to be used to sth; **avoir l'~ de faire** to be in the habit of doing; (expérience)

to be used to doing; **d'~** usually;
**comme d'~** as usual
**habitué, e** [abitɥe] nm/f (de maison)
regular visitor; (de café) regular
(customer)
**habituel, le** [abitɥɛl] adj usual
**habituer** [abitɥe] vt: **~ qn à** to get sb
used to; **s'habituer à** to get used to
**'hache** [aʃ] nf axe
**'hacher** ['aʃe] vt (viande) to mince;
(persil) to chop; **'hachis** nm mince no pl;
**hachis Parmentier** ≈ shepherd's pie
**'haie** ['ɛ] nf hedge; (Sport) hurdle
**'haillons** ['ajõ] nmpl rags
**'haine** ['ɛn] nf hatred
**'haïr** ['aiʀ] vt to detest, hate
**'hâlé, e** ['ale] adj (sun)tanned,
sunburnt
**haleine** [alɛn] nf breath; **hors d'~** out
of breath; **tenir en ~** (attention) to hold
spellbound; (incertitude) to keep in
suspense; **de longue ~** long-term
**'haleter** ['alte] vt to pant
**'hall** ['ol] nm hall
**'halle** ['al] nf (covered) market; **halles**
nfpl (d'une grande ville) central food
market sg
**hallucination** [alysinasjõ] nf
hallucination
**'halte** ['alt] nf stop, break; (endroit)
stopping place ▷ excl stop!; **faire halte**
to stop
**haltère** [altɛʀ] nm dumbbell, barbell;
**haltères** nmpl: **(poids et) ~s** (activité)
weightlifting sg; **haltérophilie** nf
weightlifting
**'hamac** ['amak] nm hammock
**'hameau, x** ['amo] nm hamlet
**hameçon** [amsõ] nm (fish) hook
**'hanche** ['ɑ̃ʃ] nf hip
**'handball** ['ɑ̃dbal] nm handball
**'handicapé, e** ['ɑ̃dikape] adj disabled,
handicapped ▷ nm/f handicapped
person; **handicapé mental/physique**
mentally/physically handicapped
person; **'handicapé moteur** person
with a movement disorder
**'hangar** ['ɑ̃gaʀ] nm shed; (Aviat) hangar

**'hanneton** ['antõ] nm cockchafer
**'hanter** ['ɑ̃te] vt to haunt
**'hantise** ['ɑ̃tiz] nf obsessive fear
**'harceler** ['aʀsəle] vt to harass;
**harceler qn de questions** to plague sb
with questions
**'hardi, e** ['aʀdi] adj bold, daring
**'hareng** ['aʀɑ̃] nm herring; **hareng
saur** kipper, smoked herring
**'hargne** ['aʀɲ] nf aggressiveness;
**'hargneux, -euse** adj aggressive
**'haricot** ['aʀiko] nm bean; **'haricot
blanc** haricot bean; **'haricot vert**
green bean; **'haricot rouge** kidney
bean
**harmonica** [aʀmɔnika] nm mouth
organ
**harmonie** [aʀmɔni] nf harmony;
**harmonieux, -euse** adj harmonious;
(couleurs, couple) well-matched
**'harpe** ['aʀp] nf harp
**'hasard** ['azaʀ] nm: **le hasard** chance,
fate; **un hasard** a coincidence; **au
hasard** (aller) aimlessly; (choisir) at
random; **par hasard** by chance; **à tout
hasard** (en cas de besoin) just in case; (en
espérant trouver ce qu'on cherche) on the
off chance (BRIT)
**'hâte** ['at] nf haste; **à la hâte** hurriedly,
hastily; **en hâte** posthaste, with
all possible speed; **avoir hâte de** to
be eager ou anxious to; **'hâter** vt to
hasten; **se hâter** vi to hurry; **'hâtif,
-ive** adj (travail) hurried; (décision,
jugement) hasty
**'hausse** ['os] nf rise, increase; **être en
hausse** to be going up; **'hausser** vt to
raise; **hausser les épaules** to shrug
(one's shoulders)
**'haut, e** ['o, 'ot] adj high; (grand) tall
▷ adv high ▷ nm top (part); **de 3 m
de haut** 3 m high, 3 m in height; **des
hauts et des bas** ups and downs; **en
haut lieu** in high places; **à haute voix,
(tout) haut** aloud, out loud; **du haut
de** from the top of; **de haut en bas**
from top to bottom; **plus haut** higher
up, further up; (dans un texte) above;

(*parler*) louder; **en haut** (*être/aller*) at/to
the top; (*dans une maison*) upstairs;
**en haut de** at the top of; **'haut débit**
broadband

**'hautain, e** [otɛ̃, ɛn] *adj* haughty

**'hautbois** ['obwɑ] *nm* oboe

**'hauteur** ['otœʀ] *nf* height; **à la
hauteur de** (*accident*) near; (*fig: tâche,
situation*) equal to; **à la hauteur** (*fig*)
up to it

**'haut-parleur** *nm* (loud)speaker

**Hawaï** [awaj] *n*: **les îles ~** Hawaii

**'Haye** ['ɛ] *n*: **la Haye** the Hague

**hebdomadaire** [ɛbdɔmadɛʀ] *adj,
nm* weekly

**hébergement** [ebɛʀʒəmɑ̃] *nm*
accommodation

**héberger** [ebɛʀʒe] *vt* (*touristes*) to
accommodate, lodge; (*amis*) to put up;
(*réfugiés*) to take in

**hébergeur** [ebɛʀʒœʀ] *nm* (*Internet*)
host

**hébreu, x** [ebʀø] *adj m, nm* Hebrew

**Hébrides** [ebʀid] *nf*: **les ~** the Hebrides

**hectare** [ɛktaʀ] *nm* hectare

**'hein** ['ɛ̃] *excl* eh?

**'hélas** ['elɑs] *excl* alas! ▷ *adv*
unfortunately

**'héler** [ele] *vt* to hail

**hélice** [elis] *nf* propeller

**hélicoptère** [elikɔptɛʀ] *nm* helicopter

**helvétique** [ɛlvetik] *adj* Swiss

**hématome** [ematom] *nm* nasty
bruise

**hémisphère** [emisfɛʀ] *nm*: **l'~
nord/sud** the northern/southern
hemisphere

**hémorragie** [emɔʀaʒi] *nf* bleeding *no
pl*, haemorrhage

**hémorroïdes** [em`id] *nfpl* piles,
haemorrhoids

**'hennir** ['eniʀ] *vi* to neigh, whinny

**hépatite** [epatit] *nf* hepatitis

**herbe** [ɛʀb] *nf* grass; (*Culin, Méd*) herb;
**~s de Provence** mixed herbs; **en ~**
unripe; (*fig*) budding; **herbicide** *nm*
weed-killer; **herboriste** *nm/f* herbalist

**héréditaire** [eʀeditɛʀ] *adj* hereditary

**'hérisson** ['eʀisɔ̃] *nm* hedgehog

**héritage** [eʀitaʒ] *nm* inheritance;
(*coutumes, système*) heritage, legacy

**hériter** [eʀite] *vi*: **~ de qch (de qn)** to
inherit sth (from sb); **héritier, -ière**
*nm/f* heir(-ess)

**hermétique** [ɛʀmetik] *adj* airtight;
watertight; (*fig: obscur*) abstruse;
(: *impénétrable*) impenetrable

**hermine** [ɛʀmin] *nf* ermine

**'hernie** ['ɛʀni] *nf* hernia

**héroïne** [eʀɔin] *nf* heroine; (*drogue*)
heroin

**héroïque** [eʀɔik] *adj* heroic

**'héron** ['eʀɔ̃] *nm* heron

**'héros** ['eʀo] *nm* hero

**hésitant, e** [ezitɑ̃, ɑ̃t] *adj* hesitant

**hésitation** [ezitasjɔ̃] *nf* hesitation

**hésiter** [ezite] *vi*: **~ (à faire)** to hesitate
(to do)

**hétérosexuel, le** [eteʀɔsɛkɥɛl] *adj*
heterosexual

**'hêtre** ['ɛtʀ] *nm* beech

**heure** [œʀ] *nf* hour; (*Scol*) period;
(*moment*) time; **c'est l'~** it's time;
**quelle ~ est-il?** what time is it?; **2 ~s
(du matin)** 2 o'clock (in the morning);
**être à l'~** to be on time; (*montre*) to
be right; **mettre à l'~** to set right; **à
une ~ avancée (de la nuit)** at a late
hour (of the night); **de bonne ~** early;
**à toute ~** at any time; **24 ~s sur 24**
round the clock, 24 hours a day; **à l'~
qu'il est** at this time (of day); by now;
**sur l'~** at once; **à quelle ~ ouvre le
musée/magasin?** what time does
the museum/shop open?; **heures de
bureau** office hours; **heure de pointe**
rush hour; (*téléphone*) peak period;
**heures supplémentaires** overtime *sg*

**heureusement** [œʀøzmɑ̃] *adv* (*par
bonheur*) fortunately, luckily

**heureux, -euse** [œʀø, øz] *adj* happy;
(*chanceux*) lucky, fortunate

**'heurt** ['œʀ] *nm* (*choc*) collision; (*conflit*)
clash

**'heurter** ['œʀte] *vt* (*mur*) to strike, hit;
(*personne*) to collide with

**hexagone** [ɛgzagɔn] nm hexagon; **l'H~** (la France) France (because of its shape)
**hiberner** [ibɛrne] vi to hibernate
**'hibou, x** ['ibu] nm owl
**'hideux, -euse** ['idø, øz] adj hideous
**hier** [jɛr] adv yesterday; **~ matin/midi** yesterday morning/lunchtime; **~ soir** last night, yesterday evening; **toute la journée d'~** all day yesterday; **toute la matinée d'~** all yesterday morning
**'hiérarchie** ['jerarʃi] nf hierarchy
**hindou, e** [ɛ̃du] adj Hindu ▷ nm/f: **H~, e** Hindu
**hippique** [ipik] adj equestrian, horse cpd; **un club ~** a riding centre; **un concours ~** a horse show; **hippisme** nm (horse)riding
**hippodrome** [ipɔdrom] nm racecourse
**hippopotame** [ipɔpɔtam] nm hippopotamus
**hirondelle** [irɔ̃dɛl] nf swallow
**'hisser** ['ise] vt to hoist, haul up
**histoire** [istwar] nf (science, événements) history; (anecdote, récit, mensonge) story; (affaire) business no pl; **histoires** nfpl (chichis) fuss no pl; (ennuis) trouble sg; **historique** adj historical; (important) historic ▷ nm: **faire l'historique de** to give the background to
**'hit-parade** ['itparad] nm: **le hit-parade** the charts
**hiver** [ivɛr] nm winter; **hivernal, e, -aux** adj winter cpd; (glacial) wintry; **hiverner** vi to winter
**HLM** nm ou f (= habitation à loyer modéré) council flat; **des ~** council housing
**'hobby** ['ɔbi] nm hobby
**'hocher** ['ɔʃe] vt: **hocher la tête** to nod; (signe négatif ou dubitatif) to shake one's head
**'hockey** ['ɔkɛ] nm: **hockey (sur glace/gazon)** (ice/field) hockey
**'hold-up** ['ɔldœp] nm inv hold-up
**'hollandais, e** ['ɔlɑ̃dɛ, ɛz] adj Dutch ▷ nm (Ling) Dutch ▷ nm/f: **Hollandais, e** Dutchman(-woman)

**'Hollande** ['ɔlɑ̃d] nf: **la Hollande** Holland
**'homard** ['ɔmar] nm lobster
**homéopathique** [ɔmeɔpatik] adj homoeopathic
**homicide** [ɔmisid] nm murder; **homicide involontaire** manslaughter
**hommage** [ɔmaʒ] nm tribute; **rendre ~ à** to pay tribute to
**homme** [ɔm] nm man; **homme d'affaires** businessman; **homme d'État** statesman; **homme de main** hired man; **homme de paille** stooge; **l'homme de la rue** the man on the street
**homo...**: **homogène** adj homogeneous; **homologue** nm/f counterpart; **homologué, e** adj (Sport) ratified; (tarif) authorized; **homonyme** nm (Ling) homonym; (d'une personne) namesake; **homosexuel, le** adj homosexual
**'Hong Kong** ['ɔ̃gkɔ̃g] n Hong Kong
**'Hongrie** ['ɔ̃gri] nf: **la Hongrie** Hungary; **'hongrois, e** adj Hungarian ▷ nm/f: **Hongrois, e** Hungarian ▷ nm (Ling) Hungarian
**honnête** [ɔnɛt] adj (intègre) honest; (juste, satisfaisant) fair; **honnêtement** adv honestly; **honnêteté** nf honesty
**honneur** [ɔnœr] nm honour; (mérite) credit; **en l'~ de** in honour of; (événement) on the occasion of; **faire ~ à** (engagements) to honour; (famille) to be a credit to; (fig: repas etc) to do justice to
**honorable** [ɔnɔrabl] adj worthy, honourable; (suffisant) decent
**honoraire** [ɔnɔrɛr] adj honorary; **professeur ~** professor emeritus; **honoraires** nmpl fees
**honorer** [ɔnɔre] vt to honour; (estimer) to hold in high regard; (faire honneur à) to do credit to
**'honte** ['ɔ̃t] nf shame; **avoir honte de** to be ashamed of; **faire honte à qn** to make sb (feel) ashamed; **'honteux, -euse** adj ashamed; (conduite, acte) shameful, disgraceful

**hôpital, -aux** [ɔpital, o] *nm* hospital; **où est l'~ le plus proche?** where is the nearest hospital?

'**hoquet** ['ɔkɛ] *nm*: **avoir le hoquet** to have (the) hiccoughs

**horaire** [ɔRɛR] *adj* hourly ▷ *nm* timetable, schedule; **horaires** *nmpl* (*d'employé*) hours; **horaire souple** flexitime

**horizon** [ɔRizɔ̃] *nm* horizon

**horizontal, e, -aux** [ɔRizɔ̃tal, o] *adj* horizontal

**horloge** [ɔRlɔʒ] *nf* clock; **l'~ parlante** the speaking clock; **horloger, -ère** *nm/f* watchmaker; clockmaker

'**hormis** ['ɔRmi] *prép* save

**horoscope** [`skɔp] *nm* horoscope

**horreur** [ɔRœR] *nf* horror; **quelle ~!** how awful!; **avoir ~ de** to loathe *ou* detest; **horrible** *adj* horrible; **horrifier** *vt* to horrify

'**hors** ['ɔR] *prép*: **hors de** out of; **hors pair** outstanding; **hors de propos** inopportune; **être hors de soi** to be beside o.s.; '**hors d'usage** out of service; '**hors-bord** *nm inv* speedboat (*with outboard motor*); '**hors-d'œuvre** *nm inv* hors d'œuvre; **hors-la-loi** *nm inv* outlaw; '**hors-service** *adj inv* out of order; '**hors-taxe** *adj* (*boutique, articles*) duty-free

**hortensia** [ɔRtɑ̃sja] *nm* hydrangea

**hospice** [ɔspis] *nm* (*de vieillards*) home

**hospitalier, -ière** [ɔspitalje, jɛR] *adj* (*accueillant*) hospitable; (*Méd: service, centre*) hospital *cpd*

**hospitaliser** [ɔspitalize] *vt* to take/send to hospital, hospitalize

**hospitalité** [ɔspitalite] *nf* hospitality

**hostie** [ɔsti] *nf* host (*Rel*)

**hostile** [ɔstil] *adj* hostile; **hostilité** *nf* hostility

**hôte** [ot] *nm* (*maître de maison*) host; (*invité*) guest

**hôtel** [otɛl] *nm* hotel; **aller à l'~** to stay in a hotel; **hôtel de ville** town hall; **hôtel (particulier)** (private) mansion; **hôtellerie** *nf* hotel business

● **HÔTELS**
●
● There are six categories of hotel
● in France, from zero ('non classé')
● to four stars and luxury four stars
● ('quatre étoiles luxe'). Prices include
● VAT but not breakfast. In some
● towns, guests pay a small additional
● tourist tax, the 'taxe de séjour'.

**hôtesse** [otɛs] *nf* hostess; **hôtesse (de l'air)** stewardess, air hostess (BRIT)

'**houblon** ['ublɔ̃] *nm* (*Bot*) hop; (*pour la bière*) hops *pl*

'**houille** ['uj] *nf* coal; '**houille blanche** hydroelectric power

'**houle** ['ul] *nf* swell; '**houleux, -euse** *adj* stormy

'**hourra** ['uRa] *excl* hurrah!

'**housse** ['us] *nf* cover

'**houx** ['u] *nm* holly

'**hublot** ['yblo] *nm* porthole

'**huche** ['yʃ] *nf*: **huche à pain** bread bin

'**huer** ['ɥe] *vt* to boo

**huile** [ɥil] *nf* oil

**huissier** [ɥisje] *nm* usher; (*Jur*) ≈ bailiff

'**huit** ['ɥi(t)] *num* eight; **samedi en huit** a week on Saturday; **dans huit jours** in a week; '**huitaine** *nf*: **une huitaine (de jours)** a week or so; '**huitième** *num* eighth

**huître** [ɥitR] *nf* oyster

**humain, e** [ymɛ̃, ɛn] *adj* human; (*compatissant*) humane ▷ *nm* human (being); **humanitaire** *adj* humanitarian; **humanité** *nf* humanity

**humble** [œ̃bl] *adj* humble

'**humer** ['yme] *vt* (*plat*) to smell; (*parfum*) to inhale

**humeur** [ymœR] *nf* mood; **de bonne/mauvaise ~** in a good/bad mood

**humide** [ymid] *adj* damp; (*main, yeux*) moist; (*climat, chaleur*) humid; (*saison, route*) wet

**humilier** [ymilje] *vt* to humiliate

**humilité** [ymilite] *nf* humility, humbleness

**humoristique** [ymɔRistik] *adj*

humorous

**humour** [ymuʀ] *nm* humour; **avoir de l'~** to have a sense of humour; **humour noir** black humour

**'huppé, e** ['ype] *(fam) adj* posh

**'hurlement** ['yʀləmɑ̃] *nm* howling *no pl*, howl, yelling *no pl*, yell

**'hurler** ['yʀle] *vi* to howl, yell

**'hutte** ['yt] *nf* hut

**hydratant, e** [idʀatɑ̃, ɑ̃t] *adj (crème)* moisturizing

**hydraulique** [idʀolik] *adj* hydraulic

**hydravion** [idʀavjɔ̃] *nm* seaplane

**hydrogène** [idʀɔʒɛn] *nm* hydrogen

**hydroglisseur** [idʀɔglisœʀ] *nm* hydroplane

**hyène** [jɛn] *nf* hyena

**hygiène** [iʒjɛn] *nf* hygiene

**hygiénique** [iʒenik] *adj* hygienic

**hymne** [imn] *nm* hymn

**hyperlien** [ipɛʀljɛ̃] *nm* hyperlink

**hypermarché** [ipɛʀmaʀʃe] *nm* hypermarket

**hypermétrope** [ipɛʀmetʀɔp] *adj* long-sighted

**hypertension** [ipɛʀtɑ̃sjɔ̃] *nf* high blood pressure

**hypnose** [ipnoz] *nf* hypnosis; **hypnotiser** *vt* to hypnotize

**hypocrisie** [ipɔkʀizi] *nf* hypocrisy; **hypocrite** *adj* hypocritical

**hypothèque** [ipɔtɛk] *nf* mortgage

**hypothèse** [ipɔtɛz] *nf* hypothesis

**hystérique** [isteʀik] *adj* hysterical

**iceberg** [ajsbɛʀg] *nm* iceberg

**ici** [isi] *adv* here; **jusqu'~** as far as this; *(temps)* so far; **d'~ demain** by tomorrow; **d'~ là** by then, in the meantime; **d'~ peu** before long

**icône** [ikon] *nf* icon

**idéal, e, -aux** [ideal, o] *adj* ideal ▷ *nm* ideal; **idéaliste** *adj* idealistic ▷ *nm/f* idealist

**idée** [ide] *nf* idea; **avoir dans l'~ que** to have an idea that; **se faire des ~s** to imagine things, get ideas into one's head; **avoir des ~s noires** to have black *ou* dark thoughts; **idées reçues** received wisdom *sg*

**identifier** [idɑ̃tifje] *vt* to identify; **s'identifier** *vi*: **s'~ avec** *ou* **à qn/qch** *(héros etc)* to identify with sb/sth

**identique** [idɑ̃tik] *adj*: **~ (à)** identical (to)

**identité** [idɑ̃tite] *nf* identity

**idiot, e** [idjo, idjɔt] *adj* idiotic ▷ *nm/f* idiot

**idole** [idɔl] *nf* idol

**if** [if] nm yew

**ignoble** [iɲɔbl] adj vile

**ignorant, e** [iɲɔrã, ãt] adj ignorant; ~ **de** ignorant of, not aware of

**ignorer** [iɲɔre] vt not to know; (personne) to ignore

**il** [il] pron he; (animal, chose, en tournure impersonnelle) it; **il fait froid** it's cold; **Pierre est-il arrivé?** has Pierre arrived?; **il a gagné** he won; voir **avoir**

**île** [il] nf island; **l'île Maurice** Mauritius; **les îles anglo-normandes** the Channel Islands; **les îles britanniques** the British Isles

**illégal, e, -aux** [i(l)legal, o] adj illegal

**illimité, e** [i(l)limite] adj unlimited

**illisible** [i(l)lizibl] adj illegible; (roman) unreadable

**illogique** [i(l)lɔʒik] adj illogical

**illuminer** [i(l)lymine] vt to light up; (monument, rue: pour une fête) to illuminate; (: au moyen de projecteurs) to floodlight

**illusion** [i(l)lyzjɔ̃] nf illusion; **se faire des ~s** to delude o.s.; **faire ~** to delude ou fool people

**illustration** [i(l)lystrasjɔ̃] nf illustration

**illustré, e** [i(l)lystre] adj illustrated ▷ nm comic

**illustrer** [i(l)lystre] vt to illustrate; **s'illustrer** to become famous, win fame

**ils** [il] pron they

**image** [imaʒ] nf (gén) picture; (métaphore) image; **image de marque** brand image; (fig) public image; **imagé, e** adj (texte) full of imagery; (langage) colourful

**imaginaire** [imaʒiner] adj imaginary

**imagination** [imaʒinasjɔ̃] nf imagination; **avoir de l'~** to be imaginative

**imaginer** [imaʒine] vt to imagine; (inventer: expédient) to devise, think up; **s'imaginer** vt (se figurer: scène etc) to imagine, picture; **s'~ que** to imagine that

**imbécile** [ɛ̃besil] adj idiotic ▷ nm/f idiot

**imbu, e** [ɛ̃by] adj: ~ **de** full of

**imitateur, -trice** [imitatœr, tris] nm/f (gén) imitator; (Music-Hall) impersonator

**imitation** [imitasjɔ̃] nf imitation; (de personnalité) impersonation

**imiter** [imite] vt to imitate; (contrefaire) to forge; (ressembler à) to look like

**immangeable** [ɛ̃mãʒabl] adj inedible

**immatriculation** [imatrikylasjɔ̃] nf registration

● **IMMATRICULATION**
●
● The last two numbers on vehicle
● licence plates show which
● 'département' of France the vehicle
● is registered in. For example, a car
● registered in Paris has the number 75
● on its licence plates.

**immatriculer** [imatrikyle] vt to register; **faire/se faire ~** to register

**immédiat, e** [imedja, jat] adj immediate ▷ nm: **dans l'~** for the time being; **immédiatement** adv immediately

**immense** [i(m)mãs] adj immense

**immerger** [imɛrʒe] vt to immerse, submerge

**immeuble** [imœbl] nm building; (à usage d'habitation) block of flats

**immigration** [imigrasjɔ̃] nf immigration

**immigré, e** [imigre] nm/f immigrant

**imminent, e** [iminã, ãt] adj imminent

**immobile** [i(m)mɔbil] adj still, motionless

**immobilier, -ière** [imɔbilje, jɛr] adj property cpd ▷ nm: **l'~** the property business

**immobiliser** [imɔbilize] vt (gén) to immobilize; (circulation, véhicule, affaires) to bring to a standstill; **s'immobiliser** (personne) to stand still; (machine, véhicule) to come to a halt

**immoral, e, -aux** [i(m)mɔʀal, o] *adj* immoral

**immortel, le** [imɔʀtɛl] *adj* immortal

**immunisé, e** [im(m)ynize] *adj*: **~ contre** immune to

**immunité** [imynite] *nf* immunity

**impact** [ɛ̃pakt] *nm* impact

**impair, e** [ɛ̃pɛʀ] *adj* odd ▷ *nm* faux pas, blunder

**impardonnable** [ɛ̃paʀdɔnabl] *adj* unpardonable, unforgivable

**imparfait, e** [ɛ̃paʀfɛ, ɛt] *adj* imperfect

**impartial, e, -aux** [ɛ̃paʀsjal, jo] *adj* impartial, unbiased

**impasse** [ɛ̃pɑs] *nf* dead end, cul-de-sac; *(fig)* deadlock

**impassible** [ɛ̃pasibl] *adj* impassive

**impatience** [ɛ̃pasjɑ̃s] *nf* impatience

**impatient, e** [ɛ̃pasjɑ̃, jɑ̃t] *adj* impatient; **impatienter**: **s'impatienter** *vi* to get impatient

**impeccable** [ɛ̃pekabl] *adj* (*parfait*) perfect; (*propre*) impeccable; (*fam*) smashing

**impensable** [ɛ̃pɑ̃sabl] *adj* (*événement hypothétique*) unthinkable; (*événement qui a eu lieu*) unbelievable

**impératif, -ive** [ɛ̃peʀatif, iv] *adj* imperative ▷ *nm* (*Ling*) imperative; **impératifs** *nmpl* (*exigences: d'une fonction, d'une charge*) requirements; (: *de la mode*) demands

**impératrice** [ɛ̃peʀatʀis] *nf* empress

**imperceptible** [ɛ̃pɛʀsɛptibl] *adj* imperceptible

**impérial, e, -aux** [ɛ̃peʀjal, jo] *adj* imperial

**impérieux, -euse** [ɛ̃peʀjø, jøz] *adj* (*caractère, ton*) imperious; (*obligation, besoin*) pressing, urgent

**impérissable** [ɛ̃peʀisabl] *adj* undying

**imperméable** [ɛ̃pɛʀmeabl] *adj* waterproof; (*fig*): **~ à** impervious to ▷ *nm* raincoat

**impertinent, e** [ɛ̃pɛʀtinɑ̃, ɑ̃t] *adj* impertinent

**impitoyable** [ɛ̃pitwajabl] *adj* pitiless, merciless

**implanter** [ɛ̃plɑ̃te]: **s'implanter** *vi* to be set up

**impliquer** [ɛ̃plike] *vt* to imply; **~ qn (dans)** to implicate sb (in)

**impoli, e** [ɛ̃pɔli] *adj* impolite, rude

**impopulaire** [ɛ̃pɔpylɛʀ] *adj* unpopular

**importance** [ɛ̃pɔʀtɑ̃s] *nf* importance; (*de somme*) size; (*de retard, dégâts*) extent; **sans ~** unimportant

**important, e** [ɛ̃pɔʀtɑ̃, ɑ̃t] *adj* important; (*en quantité: somme, retard*) considerable, sizeable; (: *dégâts*) extensive; (*péj: airs, ton*) self-important ▷ *nm*: **l'~** the important thing

**importateur, -trice** [ɛ̃pɔʀtatœʀ, tʀis] *nm/f* importer

**importation** [ɛ̃pɔʀtasjɔ̃] *nf* importation; (*produit*) import

**importer** [ɛ̃pɔʀte] *vt* (*Comm*) to import; (*maladies, plantes*) to introduce ▷ *vi* (*être important*) to matter; **il importe qu'il fasse** it is important that he should do; **peu m'importe** (*je n'ai pas de préférence*) I don't mind; (*je m'en moque*) I don't care; **peu importe (que)** it doesn't matter (if); *voir aussi* **n'importe**

**importun, e** [ɛ̃pɔʀtœ̃, yn] *adj* irksome, importunate; (*arrivée, visite*) inopportune, ill-timed ▷ *nm* intruder; **importuner** *vt* to bother

**imposant, e** [ɛ̃pozɑ̃, ɑ̃t] *adj* imposing

**imposer** [ɛ̃poze] *vt* (*taxer*) to tax; **s'imposer** (*être nécessaire*) to be imperative; **~ qch à qn** to impose sth on sb; **en ~ à** to impress; **s'~ comme** to emerge as; **s'~ par** to win recognition through

**impossible** [ɛ̃pɔsibl] *adj* impossible; **il m'est ~ de le faire** it is impossible for me to do it, I can't possibly do it; **faire l'~** to do one's utmost

**imposteur** [ɛ̃pɔstœʀ] *nm* impostor

**impôt** [ɛ̃po] *nm* tax; **impôt foncier** land tax; **impôt sur le chiffre d'affaires** corporation (*BRIT*) *ou* corporate (*US*) tax; **impôt sur le revenu** income tax; **impôts locaux** rates, local taxes (*US*),

≈ council tax (BRIT)

**impotent, e** [ɛ̃pɔtɑ̃, ɑ̃t] adj disabled

**impraticable** [ɛ̃pratikabl] adj (projet) impracticable, unworkable; (piste) impassable

**imprécis, e** [ɛ̃presi, iz] adj imprecise

**imprégner** [ɛ̃preɲe] vt (tissu) to impregnate; (lieu, air) to fill; **s'imprégner de** (fig) to absorb

**imprenable** [ɛ̃prənabl] adj (forteresse) impregnable; **vue ~** unimpeded outlook

**impression** [ɛ̃presjɔ̃] nf impression; (d'un ouvrage, tissu) printing; **faire bonne/mauvaise ~** to make a good/ bad impression; **impressionnant, e** adj (imposant) impressive; (bouleversant) upsetting; **impressionner** vt (frapper) to impress; (bouleverser) to upset

**imprévisible** [ɛ̃previzibl] adj unforeseeable

**imprévu, e** [ɛ̃prevy] adj unforeseen, unexpected ▷ nm (incident) unexpected incident; **des vacances pleines d'~** holidays full of surprises; **en cas d'~** if anything unexpected happens; **sauf ~** unless anything unexpected crops up

**imprimante** [ɛ̃primɑ̃t] nf printer; **imprimante (à) laser** laser printer

**imprimé** [ɛ̃prime] nm (formulaire) printed form; (Postes) printed matter no pl; (tissu) printed fabric; **~ à fleur** floral print

**imprimer** [ɛ̃prime] vt to print; (publier) to publish; **imprimerie** nf printing; (établissement) printing works sg; **imprimeur** nm printer

**impropre** [ɛ̃prɔpr] adj inappropriate; **~ à** unfit for

**improviser** [ɛ̃prɔvize] vt, vi to improvise

**improviste** [ɛ̃prɔvist]: **à l'~** adv unexpectedly, without warning

**imprudence** [ɛ̃prydɑ̃s] nf (d'une personne, d'une action) carelessness no pl; (d'une remarque) imprudence no pl; **commettre une ~** to do something foolish

**imprudent, e** [ɛ̃prydɑ̃, ɑ̃t] adj (conducteur, geste, action) careless; (remarque) unwise, imprudent; (projet) foolhardy

**impuissant, e** [ɛ̃pɥisɑ̃, ɑ̃t] adj helpless; (sans effet) ineffectual; (sexuellement) impotent

**impulsif, -ive** [ɛ̃pylsif, iv] adj impulsive

**impulsion** [ɛ̃pylsjɔ̃] nf (Élec, instinct) impulse; (élan, influence) impetus

**inabordable** [inabɔrdabl] adj (cher) prohibitive

**inacceptable** [inaksɛptabl] adj unacceptable

**inaccessible** [inaksesibl] adj inaccessible; **~ à** impervious to

**inachevé, e** [inaʃ(ə)ve] adj unfinished

**inactif, -ive** [inaktif, iv] adj inactive; (remède) ineffective; (Bourse: marché) slack

**inadapté, e** [inadapte] adj (gén): **~ à** not adapted to, unsuited to; (Psych) maladjusted

**inadéquat, e** [inadekwa(t), kwat] adj inadequate

**inadmissible** [inadmisibl] adj inadmissible

**inadvertance** [inadvɛrtɑ̃s]: **par ~** adv inadvertently

**inanimé, e** [inanime] adj (matière) inanimate; (évanoui) unconscious; (sans vie) lifeless

**inanition** [inanisjɔ̃] nf: **tomber d'~** to faint with hunger (and exhaustion)

**inaperçu, e** [inapɛrsy] adj: **passer ~** to go unnoticed

**inapte** [inapt] adj: **~ à** incapable of; (Mil) unfit for

**inattendu, e** [inatɑ̃dy] adj unexpected

**inattentif, -ive** [inatɑ̃tif, iv] adj inattentive; **~ à** (dangers, détails) heedless of; **inattention** nf lack of attention; **une faute** ou **une erreur d'inattention** a careless mistake

**inaugurer** [inogyre] vt (monument) to unveil; (exposition, usine) to open; (fig) to inaugurate

**inavouable** [inavwabl] *adj* shameful; (*bénéfices*) undisclosable

**incalculable** [ɛ̃kalkylabl] *adj* incalculable

**incapable** [ɛ̃kapabl] *adj* incapable; **~ de faire** incapable of doing; (*empêché*) unable to do

**incapacité** [ɛ̃kapasite] *nf* (*incompétence*) incapability; (*impossibilité*) incapacity; **dans l'~ de faire** unable to do

**incarcérer** [ɛ̃kaʀseʀe] *vt* to incarcerate, imprison

**incassable** [ɛ̃kasabl] *adj* unbreakable

**incendie** [ɛ̃sɑ̃di] *nm* fire; **incendie criminel** arson *no pl*; **incendie de forêt** forest fire; **incendier** *vt* (*mettre le feu à*) to set fire to, set alight; (*brûler complètement*) to burn down

**incertain, e** [ɛ̃sɛʀtɛ̃, ɛn] *adj* uncertain; (*temps*) unsettled; (*imprécis: contours*) indistinct, blurred; **incertitude** *nf* uncertainty

**incessamment** [ɛ̃sesamɑ̃] *adv* very shortly

**incident** [ɛ̃sidɑ̃] *nm* incident; **incident de parcours** minor hitch *ou* setback; **incident technique** technical difficulties *pl*

**incinérer** [ɛ̃sineʀe] *vt* (*ordures*) to incinerate; (*mort*) to cremate

**incisive** [ɛ̃siziv] *nf* incisor

**inciter** [ɛ̃site] *vt*: **~ qn à (faire) qch** to encourage sb to do sth; (*à la révolte etc*) to incite sb to do sth

**incivilité** [ɛ̃sivilite] *nf* (*grossièreté*) incivility; **incivilités** *nfpl* antisocial behaviour *sg*

**inclinable** [ɛ̃klinabl] *adj*: **siège à dossier ~** reclining seat

**inclination** [ɛ̃klinasjɔ̃] *nf* (*penchant*) inclination

**incliner** [ɛ̃kline] *vt* (*pencher*) to tilt ▷ *vi*: **~ à qch/à faire** to incline towards sth/doing; **s'incliner** *vr* (*se pencher*) to bow; **s'~ devant** (*par respect*) to pay one's respects

**inclure** [ɛ̃klyʀ] *vt* to include; (*joindre à un envoi*) to enclose

**inclus, e** [ɛ̃kly, -yz] *pp de* **inclure** ▷ *adj* included; (*joint à un envoi*) enclosed ▷ *adv*: **est-ce que le service est ~?** is service included?; **jusqu'au 10 mars ~** until 10th March inclusive

**incognito** [ɛ̃kɔɲito] *adv* incognito ▷ *nm*: **garder l'~** to remain incognito

**incohérent, e** [ɛ̃kɔeʀɑ̃, ɑ̃t] *adj* (*comportement*) inconsistent; (*geste, langage, texte*) incoherent

**incollable** [ɛ̃kɔlabl] *adj* (*riz*) non-stick; **il est ~** (*fam*) he's got all the answers

**incolore** [ɛ̃kɔlɔʀ] *adj* colourless

**incommoder** [ɛ̃kɔmɔde] *vt* (*chaleur, odeur*): **~ qn** to bother sb

**incomparable** [ɛ̃kɔ̃paʀabl] *adj* incomparable

**incompatible** [ɛ̃kɔ̃patibl] *adj* incompatible

**incompétent, e** [ɛ̃kɔ̃petɑ̃, ɑ̃t] *adj* incompetent

**incomplet, -ète** [ɛ̃kɔ̃plɛ, ɛt] *adj* incomplete

**incompréhensible** [ɛ̃kɔ̃pʀeɑ̃sibl] *adj* incomprehensible

**incompris, e** [ɛ̃kɔ̃pʀi, iz] *adj* misunderstood

**inconcevable** [ɛ̃kɔ̃s(ə)vabl] *adj* inconceivable

**inconfortable** [ɛ̃kɔ̃fɔʀtabl(ə)] *adj* uncomfortable

**incongru, e** [ɛ̃kɔ̃gʀy] *adj* unseemly

**inconnu, e** [ɛ̃kɔny] *adj* unknown ▷ *nm/f* stranger ▷ *nm*: **l'~** the unknown; **inconnue** *nf* unknown factor

**inconsciemment** [ɛ̃kɔ̃sjamɑ̃] *adv* unconsciously

**inconscient, e** [ɛ̃kɔ̃sjɑ̃, jɑ̃t] *adj* unconscious; (*irréfléchi*) thoughtless, reckless; (*sentiment*) subconscious ▷ *nm* (*Psych*): **l'~** the unconscious; **~ de** unaware of

**inconsidéré, e** [ɛ̃kɔ̃sideʀe] *adj* ill-considered

**inconsistant, e** [ɛ̃kɔ̃sistɑ̃, ɑ̃t] *adj* (*fig*) flimsy, weak

**inconsolable** [ɛ̃kɔ̃sɔlabl] *adj*
inconsolable

**incontestable** [ɛ̃kɔ̃tɛstabl] *adj*
indisputable

**incontinent, e** [ɛ̃kɔ̃tinɑ̃, ɑ̃t] *adj*
incontinent

**incontournable** [ɛ̃kɔ̃turnabl] *adj*
unavoidable

**incontrôlable** [ɛ̃kɔ̃trolabl]
*adj* unverifiable; (*irrépressible*)
uncontrollable

**inconvénient** [ɛ̃kɔ̃venjɑ̃] *nm*
disadvantage, drawback; **si vous n'y
voyez pas d'~** if you have no objections

**incorporer** [ɛ̃kɔrpɔre] *vt*: **~ (à)** to
mix in (with); **~ (dans)** (*paragraphe
etc*) to incorporate (in); (*Mil: appeler*)
to recruit (into); **il a très bien su s'~
à notre groupe** he was very easily
incorporated into our group

**incorrect, e** [ɛ̃kɔrɛkt] *adj* (*impropre,
inconvenant*) improper; (*défectueux*)
faulty; (*inexact*) incorrect; (*impoli*)
impolite; (*déloyal*) underhand

**incorrigible** [ɛ̃kɔriʒibl] *adj*
incorrigible

**incrédule** [ɛ̃kredyl] *adj* incredulous;
(*Rel*) unbelieving

**incroyable** [ɛ̃krwajabl] *adj* incredible

**incruster** [ɛ̃kryste] *vt* (*Art*) to inlay;
**s'incruster** *vi* (*invité*) to take root

**inculpé, e** [ɛ̃kylpe] *nm/f* accused

**inculper** [ɛ̃kylpe] *vt*: **~ (de)** to charge
(with)

**inculquer** [ɛ̃kylke] *vt*: **~ qch à** to
inculcate sth in *ou* instil sth into

**Inde** [ɛ̃d] *nf*: **l'~** India

**indécent, e** [ɛ̃desɑ̃, ɑ̃t] *adj* indecent

**indécis, e** [ɛ̃desi, iz] *adj* (*par nature*)
indecisive; (*temporairement*) undecided

**indéfendable** [ɛ̃defɑ̃dabl] *adj*
indefensible

**indéfini, e** [ɛ̃defini] *adj* (*imprécis,
incertain*) undefined; (*illimité, Ling*)
indefinite; **indéfiniment** *adv*
indefinitely; **indéfinissable** *adj*
indefinable

**indélébile** [ɛ̃delebil] *adj* indelible

**indélicat, e** [ɛ̃delika, at] *adj* tactless

**indemne** [ɛ̃dɛmn] *adj* unharmed;
**indemniser** *vt*: **indemniser qn (de)** to
compensate sb (for)

**indemnité** [ɛ̃dɛmnite] *nf*
(*dédommagement*) compensation *no pl*;
(*allocation*) allowance; **indemnité de
licenciement** redundancy payment

**indépendamment** [ɛ̃depɑ̃damɑ̃]
*adv* independently; **~ de** (*abstraction
faite de*) irrespective of; (*en plus de*) over
and above

**indépendance** [ɛ̃depɑ̃dɑ̃s] *nf*
independence

**indépendant, e** [ɛ̃depɑ̃dɑ̃, ɑ̃t] *adj*
independent; **~ de** independent of;
**travailleur ~** self-employed worker

**indescriptible** [ɛ̃dɛskriptibl] *adj*
indescribable

**indésirable** [ɛ̃dezirabl] *adj*
undesirable

**indestructible** [ɛ̃dɛstryktibl] *adj*
indestructible

**indéterminé, e** [ɛ̃detɛrmine] *adj*
(*date, cause, nature*) unspecified; (*forme,
longueur, quantité*) indeterminate

**index** [ɛ̃dɛks] *nm* (*doigt*) index finger;
(*d'un livre etc*) index; **mettre à l'~** to
blacklist

**indicateur** [ɛ̃dikatœr] *nm* (*Police*)
informer; (*Tech*) gauge, indicator ▷ *adj*:
**panneau ~** signpost; **indicateur des
chemins de fer** railway timetable;
**indicateur de rues** street directory

**indicatif, -ive** [ɛ̃dikatif, iv] *adj*: **à titre
~** for (your) information ▷ *nm* (*Ling*)
indicative; (*Radio*) theme *ou* signature
tune; (*Tél*) dialling code (BRIT), area
code (US); **quel est l'~ de ...** what's the
code for ...?

**indication** [ɛ̃dikasjɔ̃] *nf* indication;
(*renseignement*) information *no
pl*; **indications** *nfpl* (*directives*)
instructions

**indice** [ɛ̃dis] *nm* (*marque, signe*)
indication, sign; (*Police: lors d'une
enquête*) clue; (*Jur: présomption*) piece
of evidence; (*Science, Écon, Tech*) index;

**~ de protection** (sun protection) factor
**indicible** [ɛ̃disibl] *adj* inexpressible
**indien, ne** [ɛ̃djɛ̃, jɛn] *adj* Indian
 ▷ *nm/f*: **l~, ne** Indian
**indifféremment** [ɛ̃diferamɑ̃] *adv*
 (*sans distinction*) equally (well)
**indifférence** [ɛ̃diferɑ̃s] *nf* indifference
**indifférent, e** [ɛ̃diferɑ̃, ɑ̃t] *adj* (*peu
 intéressé*) indifferent; **ça m'est ~** it
 doesn't matter to me; **elle m'est ~e**
 I am indifferent to her
**indigène** [ɛ̃diʒɛn] *adj* native,
 indigenous; (*des gens du pays*) local
 ▷ *nm/f* native
**indigeste** [ɛ̃diʒɛst] *adj* indigestible
**indigestion** [ɛ̃diʒɛstjɔ̃] *nf* indigestion
 *no pl*; **avoir une ~** to have indigestion
**indigne** [ɛ̃diɲ] *adj* unworthy
**indigner** [ɛ̃diɲe] *vt*: **s'~ de qch** to get
 annoyed about sth; **s'~ contre qn** to
 get annoyed with sb
**indiqué, e** [ɛ̃dike] *adj* (*date, lieu*)
 agreed; (*traitement*) appropriate;
 (*conseillé*) advisable
**indiquer** [ɛ̃dike] *vt* (*suj: pendule, aiguille*)
 to show; (*: étiquette, panneau*) to show,
 indicate; (*renseigner sur*) to point out,
 tell; (*déterminer: date, lieu*) to give, state;
 (*signaler, dénoter*) to indicate, point
 to; **~ qch/qn à qn** (*montrer du doigt*) to
 point sth/sb out to sb; (*faire connaître:
 médecin, restaurant*) to tell sb of sth/sb;
 **pourriez-vous m'~ les toilettes/
 l'heure?** could you direct me to the
 toilets/tell me the time?
**indiscipliné, e** [ɛ̃disipline] *adj*
 undisciplined
**indiscret, -ète** [ɛ̃diskʀɛ, ɛt] *adj*
 indiscreet
**indiscutable** [ɛ̃diskytabl] *adj*
 indisputable
**indispensable** [ɛ̃dispɑ̃sabl] *adj*
 indispensable, essential
**indisposé, e** [ɛ̃dispoze] *adj* indisposed
**indistinct, e** [ɛ̃distɛ̃(kt), ɛ̃kt] *adj*
 indistinct; **indistinctement** *adv* (*voir,
 prononcer*) indistinctly; (*sans distinction*)
 indiscriminately

**individu** [ɛ̃dividy] *nm* individual;
 **individuel, le** *adj* (*gén*) individual;
 (*responsabilité, propriété, liberté*)
 personal; **chambre individuelle** single
 room; **maison individuelle** detached
 house
**indolore** [ɛ̃dɔlɔʀ] *adj* painless
**Indonésie** [ɛ̃dɔnezi] *nf* Indonesia
**indu, e** [ɛ̃dy] *adj*: **à une heure ~e** at
 some ungodly hour
**indulgent, e** [ɛ̃dylʒɑ̃, ɑ̃t] *adj* (*parent,
 regard*) indulgent; (*juge, examinateur*)
 lenient
**industrialisé, e** [ɛ̃dystʀijalize] *adj*
 industrialized
**industrie** [ɛ̃dystʀi] *nf* industry;
 **industriel, le** *adj* industrial ▷ *nm*
 industrialist
**inébranlable** [inebʀɑ̃labl] *adj* (*masse,
 colonne*) solid; (*personne, certitude, foi*)
 unshakeable
**inédit, e** [inedi, it] *adj* (*correspondance,
 livre*) hitherto unpublished; (*spectacle,
 moyen*) novel, original; (*film*) unreleased
**inefficace** [inefikas] *adj* (*remède,
 moyen*) ineffective; (*machine, employé*)
 inefficient
**inégal, e, -aux** [inegal, o] *adj*
 unequal; (*irrégulier*) uneven; **inégalable**
 *adj* matchless; **inégalé, e** *adj* (*record*)
 unequalled; (*beauté*) unrivalled;
 **inégalité** *nf* inequality
**inépuisable** [inepɥizabl] *adj*
 inexhaustible
**inerte** [inɛʀt] *adj* (*immobile*) lifeless;
 (*sans réaction*) passive
**inespéré, e** [inɛspeʀe] *adj*
 unexpected, unhoped-for
**inestimable** [inɛstimabl] *adj*
 priceless; (*fig: bienfait*) invaluable
**inévitable** [inevitabl] *adj*
 unavoidable; (*fatal, habituel*) inevitable
**inexact, e** [inɛgza(kt), akt] *adj*
 inaccurate
**inexcusable** [inɛkskyzabl] *adj*
 unforgivable
**inexplicable** [inɛksplikabl] *adj*
 inexplicable

**in extremis** [inɛkstremis] adv at the last minute ▷ adj last-minute

**infaillible** [ɛ̃fajibl] adj infallible

**infarctus** [ɛ̃faʀktys] nm: **~ (du myocarde)** coronary (thrombosis)

**infatigable** [ɛ̃fatigabl] adj tireless

**infect, e** [ɛ̃fɛkt] adj revolting; (personne) obnoxious; (temps) foul

**infecter** [ɛ̃fɛkte] vt (atmosphère, eau) to contaminate; (Méd) to infect; **s'infecter** to become infected ou septic; **infection** nf infection; (puanteur) stench

**inférieur, e** [ɛ̃feʀjœʀ] adj lower; (en qualité, intelligence) inferior; **~ à** (somme, quantité) less ou smaller than; (moins bon que) inferior to

**infernal, e, -aux** [ɛ̃fɛʀnal, o] adj (insupportable: chaleur, rythme) infernal; (: enfant) horrid; (satanique, effrayant) diabolical

**infidèle** [ɛ̃fidɛl] adj unfaithful

**infiltrer** [ɛ̃filtʀe]: **s'infiltrer** vr: **s'~ dans** to get into; (liquide) to seep through; (fig: groupe, ennemi) to infiltrate

**infime** [ɛ̃fim] adj minute, tiny

**infini, e** [ɛ̃fini] adj infinite ▷ nm infinity; **à l'~** endlessly; **infiniment** adv infinitely; **infinité** nf: **une infinité de** an infinite number of

**infinitif** [ɛ̃finitif] nm infinitive

**infirme** [ɛ̃fiʀm] adj disabled ▷ nm/f disabled person

**infirmerie** [ɛ̃fiʀməʀi] nf medical room

**infirmier, -ière** [ɛ̃fiʀmje] nm/f nurse; **infirmière chef** sister

**infirmité** [ɛ̃fiʀmite] nf disability

**inflammable** [ɛ̃flamabl] adj (in)flammable

**inflation** [ɛ̃flasjɔ̃] nf inflation

**influençable** [ɛ̃flyɑ̃sabl] adj easily influenced

**influence** [ɛ̃flyɑ̃s] nf influence; **influencer** vt to influence; **influent, e** adj influential

**informaticien, ne** [ɛ̃fɔʀmatisjɛ̃, jɛn] nm/f computer scientist

**information** [ɛ̃fɔʀmasjɔ̃] nf (renseignement) piece of information; (Presse, TV: nouvelle) item of news; (diffusion de renseignements, Inform) information; (Jur) inquiry, investigation; **informations** nfpl (TV) news sg

**informatique** [ɛ̃fɔʀmatik] nf (technique) data processing; (science) computer science ▷ adj computer cpd; **informatiser** vt to computerize

**informer** [ɛ̃fɔʀme] vt: **~ qn (de)** to inform sb (of); **s'informer** vr: **s'~ (de/si)** to inquire ou find out (about/ whether); **s'~ sur** to inform o.s. about

**infos** [ɛ̃fo] nfpl: **les ~** the news sg

**infraction** [ɛ̃fʀaksjɔ̃] nf offence; **~ à** violation ou breach of; **être en ~** to be in breach of the law

**infranchissable** [ɛ̃fʀɑ̃ʃisabl] adj impassable; (fig) insuperable

**infrarouge** [ɛ̃fʀaʀuʒ] adj infrared

**infrastructure** [ɛ̃fʀastʀyktyʀ] nf (Aviat, Mil) ground installations pl; (Écon: touristique etc) infrastructure

**infuser** [ɛ̃fyze] vt, vi (thé) to brew; (tisane) to infuse; **infusion** nf (tisane) herb tea

**ingénier** [ɛ̃ʒenje]: **s'ingénier** vi: **s'~ à faire** to strive to do

**ingénierie** [ɛ̃ʒeniʀi] nf engineering

**ingénieur** [ɛ̃ʒenjœʀ] nm engineer; **ingénieur du son** sound engineer

**ingénieux, -euse** [ɛ̃ʒenjø, jøz] adj ingenious, clever

**ingrat, e** [ɛ̃gʀa, at] adj (personne) ungrateful; (travail, sujet) thankless; (visage) unprepossessing

**ingrédient** [ɛ̃gʀedjɑ̃] nm ingredient

**inhabité, e** [inabite] adj uninhabited

**inhabituel, le** [inabituɛl] adj unusual

**inhibition** [inibisjɔ̃] nf inhibition

**inhumain, e** [inymɛ̃, ɛn] adj inhuman

**inimaginable** [inimaʒinabl] adj unimaginable

**ininterrompu, e** [inɛ̃teʀɔ̃py] adj (file, série) unbroken; (flot, vacarme) uninterrupted, non-stop; (effort)

unremitting, continuous; (*suite, ligne*)
unbroken

**initial, e, -aux** [inisjal, jo] *adj* initial;
**initiales** *nfpl* (*d'un nom, sigle etc*) initials

**initiation** [inisjasjɔ̃] *nf*: ~ **à**
introduction to

**initiative** [inisjativ] *nf* initiative

**initier** [inisje] *vt*: ~ **qn à** to initiate
sb into; (*faire découvrir: art, jeu*) to
introduce sb to

**injecter** [ɛ̃ʒɛkte] *vt* to inject; **injection**
*nf* injection; **à injection** (*Auto*) fuel
injection *cpd*

**injure** [ɛ̃ʒyʀ] *nf* insult, abuse *no pl*;
**injurier** *vt* to insult, abuse; **injurieux,
-euse** *adj* abusive, insulting

**injuste** [ɛ̃ʒyst] *adj* unjust, unfair;
**injustice** *nf* injustice

**inlassable** [ɛ̃lɑsabl] *adj* tireless

**inné, e** [i(n)ne] *adj* innate, inborn

**innocent, e** [inɔsɑ̃, ɑ̃t] *adj* innocent;
**innocenter** *vt* to clear, prove innocent

**innombrable** [i(n)nɔ̃bʀabl] *adj*
innumerable

**innover** [inɔve] *vi* to break new ground

**inoccupé, e** [inɔkype] *adj* unoccupied

**inodore** [inɔdɔʀ] *adj* (*gaz*) odourless;
(*fleur*) scentless

**inoffensif, -ive** [inɔfɑ̃sif, iv] *adj*
harmless, innocuous

**inondation** [inɔ̃dasjɔ̃] *nf* flood

**inonder** [inɔ̃de] *vt* to flood; ~ **de** to
flood with

**inopportun, e** [inɔpɔʀtœ̃, yn] *adj*
ill-timed, untimely

**inoubliable** [inublijabl] *adj*
unforgettable

**inouï, e** [inwi] *adj* unheard-of,
extraordinary

**inox** [inɔks] *nm* stainless steel

**inquiet, -ète** [ɛ̃kjɛ, ɛ̃kjɛt] *adj*
anxious; **inquiétant, e** *adj* worrying,
disturbing; **inquiéter** *vt* to worry;
**s'inquiéter** to worry; **s'inquiéter de** to
worry about; (*s'enquérir de*) to inquire
about; **inquiétude** *nf* anxiety

**insaisissable** [ɛ̃sezisabl] *adj* (*fugitif,
ennemi*) elusive; (*différence, nuance*)

imperceptible

**insalubre** [ɛ̃salybʀ] *adj* insalubrious

**insatisfait, e** [ɛ̃satisfɛ, ɛt] *adj* (*non
comblé*) unsatisfied; (*mécontent*)
dissatisfied

**inscription** [ɛ̃skʀipsjɔ̃] *nf* inscription;
(*immatriculation*) enrolment

**inscrire** [ɛ̃skʀiʀ] *vt* (*marquer: sur son
calepin etc*) to note ou write down; (: *sur
un mur, une affiche etc*) to write; (: *dans
la pierre, le métal*) to inscribe; (*mettre:
sur une liste, un budget etc*) to put down;
**s'inscrire** (*pour une excursion etc*) to put
one's name down; **s'~ (à)** (*club, parti*) to
join; (*université*) to register ou enrol (at);
(*examen, concours*) to register (for); ~ **qn
à** (*club, parti*) to enrol sb at

**insecte** [ɛ̃sɛkt] *nm* insect; **insecticide**
*nm* insecticide

**insensé, e** [ɛ̃sɑ̃se] *adj* mad

**insensible** [ɛ̃sɑ̃sibl] *adj* (*nerf, membre*)
numb; (*dur, indifférent*) insensitive

**inséparable** [ɛ̃sepaʀabl] *adj*
inseparable ▷ *nm*: ~**s** (*oiseaux*) lovebirds

**insigne** [ɛ̃siɲ] *nm* (*d'un parti, club*)
badge; (*d'une fonction*) insignia ▷ *adj*
distinguished

**insignifiant, e** [ɛ̃siɲifjɑ̃, jɑ̃t] *adj*
insignificant; trivial

**insinuer** [ɛ̃sinɥe] *vt* to insinuate;
**s'insinuer dans** (*fig*) to worm one's
way into

**insipide** [ɛ̃sipid] *adj* insipid

**insister** [ɛ̃siste] *vi* to insist; (*continuer à
sonner*) to keep on trying; ~ **sur** (*détail,
sujet*) to lay stress on

**insolation** [ɛ̃sɔlasjɔ̃] *nf* (*Méd*)
sunstroke *no pl*

**insolent, e** [ɛ̃sɔlɑ̃, ɑ̃t] *adj* insolent

**insolite** [ɛ̃sɔlit] *adj* strange, unusual

**insomnie** [ɛ̃sɔmni] *nf* insomnia *no
pl*; **avoir des ~s** to sleep badly, not be
able to sleep

**insouciant, e** [ɛ̃susjɑ̃, jɑ̃t] *adj*
carefree; ~ **du danger** heedless of
(the) danger

**insoupçonnable** [ɛ̃supsɔnabl]
*adj* unsuspected; (*personne*) above

suspicion

**insoupçonné, e** [ɛ̃supsɔne] *adj*
unsuspected

**insoutenable** [ɛ̃sut(ə)nabl] *adj*
(*argument*) untenable; (*chaleur*)
unbearable

**inspecter** [ɛ̃spɛkte] *vt* to inspect;
**inspecteur, -trice** *nm/f* inspector;
**inspecteur d'Académie** (regional)
director of education; **inspecteur
des finances** ≈ tax inspector (BRIT),
≈ Internal Revenue Service agent
(US); **inspecteur (de police)** (police)
inspector; **inspection** *nf* inspection

**inspirer** [ɛ̃spire] *vt* (*gén*) to inspire ▷ *vi*
(*aspirer*) to breathe in; **s'inspirer** *vr*: **s'~
de** to be inspired by

**instable** [ɛ̃stabl] *adj* unstable; (*meuble,
équilibre*) unsteady; (*temps*) unsettled

**installation** [ɛ̃stalasjɔ̃] *nf* (*mise en
place*) installation; **installations** *nfpl*
(*de sport, dans un camping*) facilities;
**l'installation électrique** wiring

**installer** [ɛ̃stale] *vt* (*loger, placer*) to put;
(*meuble, gaz, électricité*) to put in; (*rideau,
étagère, tente*) to put up; (*appartement*)
to fit out; **s'installer** (*s'établir: artisan,
dentiste etc*) to set o.s. up; (*se loger*) to
settle; (*emménager*) to settle in; (*sur
un siège, à un emplacement*) to settle
(down); (*fig: maladie, grève*) to take a
firm hold

**instance** [ɛ̃stɑ̃s] *nf* (*Admin: autorité*)
authority; **affaire en ~** matter pending;
**être en ~ de divorce** to be awaiting
a divorce

**instant** [ɛ̃stɑ̃] *nm* moment, instant;
**dans un ~** in a moment; **à l'~** this
instant; **je l'ai vu à l'~** I've just this
minute seen him, I saw him a moment
ago; **pour l'~** for the moment, for the
time being

**instantané, e** [ɛ̃stɑ̃tane] *adj* (*lait, café*)
instant; (*explosion, mort*) instantaneous
▷ *nm* snapshot

**instar** [ɛ̃staʀ]: **à l'~ de** *prép* following
the example of, like

**instaurer** [ɛ̃stɔʀe] *vt* to institute;

(*couvre-feu*) to impose; **s'instaurer** *vr*
(*paix*) to be established; (*doute*) to set in

**instinct** [ɛ̃stɛ̃] *nm* instinct;
**instinctivement** *adv* instinctively

**instituer** [ɛ̃stitɥe] *vt* to establish

**institut** [ɛ̃stity] *nm* institute; **institut
de beauté** beauty salon; **Institut
universitaire de technologie**
≈ polytechnic

**instituteur, -trice** [ɛ̃stitytœʀ, tʀis]
*nm/f* (primary school) teacher

**institution** [ɛ̃stitysjɔ̃] *nf* institution;
(*collège*) private school; **institutions**
*nfpl* (*structures politiques et sociales*)
institutions

**instructif, -ive** [ɛ̃stʀyktif, iv] *adj*
instructive

**instruction** [ɛ̃stʀyksjɔ̃] *nf*
(*enseignement, savoir*) education;
(*Jur*) (preliminary) investigation and
hearing; **instructions** *nfpl* (*ordres, mode
d'emploi*) instructions; **instruction
civique** civics *sg*

**instruire** [ɛ̃stʀɥiʀ] *vt* (*élèves*) to teach;
(*recrues*) to train; (*Jur: affaire*) to conduct
the investigation for; **s'instruire** to
educate o.s.; **instruit, e** *adj* educated

**instrument** [ɛ̃stʀymɑ̃] *nm*
instrument; **instrument à cordes/à
vent** stringed/wind instrument;
**instrument de mesure** measuring
instrument; **instrument de musique**
musical instrument; **instrument de
travail** (working) tool

**insu** [ɛ̃sy] *nm*: **à l'~ de qn** without sb
knowing (it)

**insuffisant, e** [ɛ̃syfizɑ̃, ɑ̃t] *adj* (*en
quantité*) insufficient; (*en qualité*)
inadequate; (*sur une copie*) poor

**insulaire** [ɛ̃sylɛʀ] *adj* island *cpd*;
(*attitude*) insular

**insuline** [ɛ̃sylin] *nf* insulin

**insulte** [ɛ̃sylt] *nf* insult; **insulter** *vt*
to insult

**insupportable** [ɛ̃sypɔʀtabl] *adj*
unbearable

**insurmontable** [ɛ̃syʀmɔ̃tabl] *adj*
(*difficulté*) insuperable; (*aversion*)

unconquerable

**intact, e** [ɛ̃takt] adj intact

**intarissable** [ɛ̃taʀisabl] adj inexhaustible

**intégral, e, -aux** [ɛ̃tegʀal, o] adj complete; **texte ~** unabridged version; **bronzage ~** all-over suntan; **intégralement** adv in full; **intégralité** nf whole; **dans son intégralité** in full; **intégrant, e** adj: **faire partie intégrante de** to be an integral part of

**intègre** [ɛ̃tɛgʀ] adj upright

**intégrer** [ɛ̃tegʀe] : **s'intégrer** vr: **s'~ à ou dans qch** to become integrated into sth; **bien s'~** to fit in

**intégrisme** [ɛ̃tegʀism] nm fundamentalism

**intellectuel, le** [ɛ̃telɛktɥɛl] adj intellectual ▷ nm/f intellectual; (péj) highbrow

**intelligence** [ɛ̃teliʒɑ̃s] nf intelligence; (compréhension): **l'~ de** the understanding of; (complicité): **regard d'~** glance of complicity; (accord): **vivre en bonne ~ avec qn** to be on good terms with sb

**intelligent, e** [ɛ̃teliʒɑ̃, ɑ̃t] adj intelligent

**intelligible** [ɛ̃teliʒibl] adj intelligible

**intempéries** [ɛ̃tɑ̃peʀi] nfpl bad weather sg

**intenable** [ɛ̃t(ə)nabl] adj (chaleur) unbearable

**intendant, e** [ɛ̃tɑ̃dɑ̃] nm/f (Mil) quartermaster; (Scol) bursar

**intense** [ɛ̃tɑ̃s] adj intense; **intensif, -ive** adj intensive; **un cours intensif** a crash course

**intenter** [ɛ̃tɑ̃te] vt: **~ un procès contre ou à** to start proceedings against

**intention** [ɛ̃tɑ̃sjɔ̃] nf intention; (Jur) intent; **avoir l'~ de faire** to intend to do; **à l'~ de** for; (renseignement) for the benefit of; (film, ouvrage) aimed at; **à cette ~** with this aim in view; **intentionné, e** adj: **bien intentionné** well-meaning ou -intentioned; **mal intentionné** ill-intentioned

**interactif, -ive** [ɛ̃teʀaktif, iv] adj (Comput) interactive

**intercepter** [ɛ̃teʀsepte] vt to intercept; (lumière, chaleur) to cut off

**interchangeable** [ɛ̃teʀʃɑ̃ʒabl] adj interchangeable

**interdiction** [ɛ̃teʀdiksjɔ̃] nf ban; **interdiction de fumer** no smoking

**interdire** [ɛ̃teʀdiʀ] vt to forbid; (Admin) to ban, prohibit; (: journal, livre) to ban; **~ à qn de faire** to forbid sb to do; (suj: empêchement) to prevent sb from doing

**interdit, e** [ɛ̃teʀdi, it] pp de **interdire** ▷ adj (stupéfait) taken aback; **film ~ aux moins de 18/12 ans** ≈ 18-/12A-rated film; **"stationnement ~"** "no parking"

**intéressant, e** [ɛ̃teʀesɑ̃, ɑ̃t] adj interesting; (avantageux) attractive

**intéressé, e** [ɛ̃teʀese] adj (parties) involved, concerned; (amitié, motifs) self-interested

**intéresser** [ɛ̃teʀese] vt (captiver) to interest; (toucher) to be of interest to; (Admin: concerner) to affect, concern; **s'intéresser** vr: **s'~ à** to be interested in

**intérêt** [ɛ̃teʀe] nm interest; (égoïsme) self-interest; **tu as ~ à accepter** it's in your interest to accept; **tu as ~ à te dépêcher** you'd better hurry

**intérieur, e** [ɛ̃teʀjœʀ] adj (mur, escalier, poche) inside; (commerce, politique) domestic; (cour, calme, vie) inner; (navigation) inland ▷ nm: **l'~** (d'une maison, d'un récipient etc) the inside; (d'un pays, aussi: décor, mobilier) the interior; **à l'~ (de)** inside; **ministère de l'I~e** ≈ Home Office (BRIT), ≈ Department of the Interior (US); **intérieurement** adv inwardly

**intérim** [ɛ̃teʀim] nm interim period; **faire de l'~** to temp; **assurer l'~ (de)** to deputize (for); **par ~** interim

**intérimaire** [ɛ̃teʀimɛʀ] adj (directeur, ministre) acting; (secrétaire, personnel) temporary ▷ nm/f (secrétaire) temporary secretary, temp (BRIT)

**interlocuteur, -trice** [ɛ̃teʀlɔkytœʀ, tʀis] nm/f speaker; **son ~** the person he was speaking to

**intermédiaire** [ɛ̃tɛʀmedjɛʀ] *adj* intermediate; (*solution*) temporary ▷ *nm/f* intermediary; (*Comm*) middleman; **sans ~** directly; **par l'~ de** through

**interminable** [ɛ̃tɛʀminabl] *adj* endless

**intermittence** [ɛ̃tɛʀmitɑ̃s] *nf*: **par ~** sporadically, intermittently

**internat** [ɛ̃tɛʀna] *nm* boarding school

**international, e, -aux** [ɛ̃tɛʀnasjɔnal, o] *adj, nm/f* international

**internaute** [ɛ̃tɛʀnot] *nm/f* Internet user

**interne** [ɛ̃tɛʀn] *adj* internal ▷ *nm/f* (*Scol*) boarder; (*Méd*) houseman

**Internet** [ɛ̃tɛʀnɛt] *nm*: **l'~** the Internet

**interpeller** [ɛ̃tɛʀpəle] *vt* (*appeler*) to call out to; (*apostropher*) to shout at; (*Police, Pol*) to question; (*concerner*) to concern

**interphone** [ɛ̃tɛʀfɔn] *nm* intercom; (*d'immeuble*) entry phone

**interposer** [ɛ̃tɛʀpoze] *vt*: **s'interposer** to intervene; **par personnes interposées** through a third party

**interprète** [ɛ̃tɛʀpʀɛt] *nm/f* interpreter; (*porte-parole*) spokesperson; **pourriez-vous nous servir d' ~?** could you act as our interpreter?

**interpréter** [ɛ̃tɛʀpʀete] *vt* to interpret; (*jouer*) to play; (*chanter*) to sing

**interrogatif, -ive** [ɛ̃tɛʀɔgatif, iv] *adj* (*Ling*) interrogative

**interrogation** [ɛ̃tɛʀɔgasjɔ̃] *nf* question; (*action*) questioning; **~ écrite/orale** (*Scol*) written/oral test

**interrogatoire** [ɛ̃tɛʀɔgatwaʀ] *nm* (*Police*) questioning *no pl*; (*Jur, aussi fig*) cross-examination

**interroger** [ɛ̃tɛʀɔʒe] *vt* to question; (*Inform*) to consult; (*Scol*) to test

**interrompre** [ɛ̃tɛʀɔ̃pʀ] *vt* (*gén*) to interrupt; (*négociations*) to break off;

(*match*) to stop; **s'interrompre** to break off; **interrupteur** *nm* switch; **interruption** *nf* interruption; (*pause*) break; **sans interruption** without stopping; **interruption (volontaire) de grossesse** termination (of pregnancy)

**intersection** [ɛ̃tɛʀsɛksjɔ̃] *nf* intersection

**intervalle** [ɛ̃tɛʀval] *nm* (*espace*) space; (*de temps*) interval; **dans l'~** in the meantime; **à deux jours d'~** two days apart

**intervenir** [ɛ̃tɛʀvəniʀ] *vi* (*gén*) to intervene; **~ auprès de qn** to intervene with sb; **intervention** *nf* intervention; (*discours*) speech; **intervention chirurgicale** (*Méd*) (surgical) operation

**interview** [ɛ̃tɛʀvju] *nf* interview

**intestin** [ɛ̃tɛstɛ̃] *nm* intestine

**intime** [ɛ̃tim] *adj* intimate; (*vie*) private; (*conviction*) inmost; (*dîner, cérémonie*) quiet ▷ *nm/f* close friend; **un journal ~** a diary

**intimider** [ɛ̃timide] *vt* to intimidate

**intimité** [ɛ̃timite] *nf*: **dans l'~** in private; (*sans formalités*) with only a few friends, quietly

**intolérable** [ɛ̃tɔleʀabl] *adj* intolerable

**intox** [ɛ̃tɔks] (*fam*) *nf* brainwashing

**intoxication** [ɛ̃tɔksikasjɔ̃] *nf*: **intoxication alimentaire** food poisoning

**intoxiquer** [ɛ̃tɔksike] *vt* to poison; (*fig*) to brainwash

**intraitable** [ɛ̃tʀɛtabl] *adj* inflexible, uncompromising

**intransigeant, e** [ɛ̃tʀɑ̃ziʒɑ̃, ɑ̃t] *adj* intransigent

**intrépide** [ɛ̃tʀepid] *adj* dauntless

**intrigue** [ɛ̃tʀig] *nf* (*scénario*) plot; **intriguer** *vt* to puzzle, intrigue

**introduction** [ɛ̃tʀɔdyksjɔ̃] *nf* introduction

**introduire** [ɛ̃tʀɔdɥiʀ] *vt* to introduce; (*visiteur*) to show in; (*aiguille, clef*): **~ qch dans** to insert *ou* introduce sth into; **s'introduire** *vr* (*techniques, usages*) to be introduced; **s'~ (dans)** to get in(to); (*dans un groupe*) to get o.s. accepted (into)

**introuvable** [ɛ̃truvabl] *adj* which cannot be found; (*Comm*) unobtainable

**intrus, e** [ɛ̃try, yz] *nm/f* intruder

**intuition** [ɛ̃tɥisjɔ̃] *nf* intuition

**inusable** [inyzabl] *adj* hard-wearing

**inutile** [inytil] *adj* useless; (*superflu*) unnecessary; **inutilement** *adv* unnecessarily; **inutilisable** *adj* unusable

**invalide** [ɛ̃valid] *adj* disabled ▷ *nm*: **~ de guerre** disabled ex-serviceman

**invariable** [ɛ̃varjabl] *adj* invariable

**invasion** [ɛ̃vazjɔ̃] *nf* invasion

**inventaire** [ɛ̃vɑ̃tɛr] *nm* inventory; (*Comm: liste*) stocklist; (: *opération*) stocktaking *no pl*

**inventer** [ɛ̃vɑ̃te] *vt* to invent; (*subterfuge*) to devise, invent; (*histoire, excuse*) to make up, invent; **inventeur** *nm* inventor; **inventif, -ive** *adj* inventive; **invention** *nf* invention

**inverse** [ɛ̃vɛrs] *adj* opposite ▷ *nm*: **l'~** the opposite; **dans l'ordre ~** in the reverse order; **en sens ~** in (*ou* from) the opposite direction; **dans le sens ~ des aiguilles d'une montre** anticlockwise; **tu t'es trompé, c'est l'~** you've got it wrong, it's the other way round; **inversement** *adv* conversely; **inverser** *vt* to invert, reverse; (*Élec*) to reverse

**investir** [ɛ̃vɛstir] *vt* to invest; **~ qn de** (*d'une fonction, d'un pouvoir*) to vest *ou* invest sb with; **s'investir** *vr*: **s'~ dans** (*Psych*) to put a lot into; **investissement** *nm* investment

**invisible** [ɛ̃vizibl] *adj* invisible

**invitation** [ɛ̃vitasjɔ̃] *nf* invitation

**invité, e** [ɛ̃vite] *nm/f* guest

**inviter** [ɛ̃vite] *vt* to invite; **~ qn à faire qch** to invite sb to do sth

**invivable** [ɛ̃vivabl] *adj* unbearable

**involontaire** [ɛ̃vɔlɔ̃tɛr] *adj* (*mouvement*) involuntary; (*insulte*) unintentional; (*complice*) unwitting

**invoquer** [ɛ̃vɔke] *vt* (*Dieu, muse*) to call

upon, invoke; (*prétexte*) to put forward (as an excuse); (*loi, texte*) to refer to

**invraisemblable** [ɛ̃vrɛsɑ̃blabl] *adj* (*fait, nouvelle*) unlikely, improbable; (*insolence, habit*) incredible

**iode** [jɔd] *nm* iodine

**irai** *etc* [ire] *vb voir* **aller**

**Irak** [irak] *nm* Iraq; **irakien, ne** *adj* Iraqi ▷ *nm/f*: **Irakien, ne** Iraqi

**Iran** [irɑ̃] *nm* Iran; **iranien, ne** *adj* Iranian ▷ *nm/f*: **Iranien, ne** Iranian

**irions** *etc* [irjɔ̃] *vb voir* **aller**

**iris** [iris] *nm* iris

**irlandais, e** [irlɑ̃dɛ, ɛz] *adj* Irish ▷ *nm/f*: **I~, e** Irishman(-woman)

**Irlande** [irlɑ̃d] *nf* Ireland; **la République d'~** the Irish Republic; **la mer d'~** the Irish Sea; **Irlande du Nord** Northern Ireland

**ironie** [irɔni] *nf* irony; **ironique** *adj* ironical; **ironiser** *vi* to be ironical

**irons** *etc* [irɔ̃] *vb voir* **aller**

**irradier** [iradje] *vt* to irradiate

**irraisonné, e** [irɛzɔne] *adj* irrational

**irrationnel, le** [irasjɔnɛl] *adj* irrational

**irréalisable** [irealizabl] *adj* unrealizable; (*projet*) impracticable

**irrécupérable** [irekyperabl] *adj* beyond repair; (*personne*) beyond redemption

**irréel, le** [ireɛl] *adj* unreal

**irréfléchi, e** [irefleʃi] *adj* thoughtless

**irrégularité** [iregylarite] *nf* irregularity; (*de travail, d'effort, de qualité*) unevenness *no pl*

**irrégulier, -ière** [iregylje, jɛr] *adj* irregular; (*travail, effort, qualité*) uneven; (*élève, athlète*) erratic

**irrémédiable** [iremedjabl] *adj* irreparable

**irremplaçable** [irɑ̃plasabl] *adj* irreplaceable

**irréparable** [ireparabl] *adj* (*objet*) beyond repair; (*dommage etc*) irreparable

**irréprochable** [ireprɔʃabl] *adj* irreproachable, beyond reproach;

(*tenue*) impeccable

**irrésistible** [iʀezistibl] *adj* irresistible; (*besoin, désir, preuve, logique*) compelling; (*amusant*) hilarious

**irrésolu, e** [iʀezɔly] *adj* (*personne*) irresolute; (*problème*) unresolved

**irrespectueux, -euse** [iʀɛspɛktɥø, øz] *adj* disrespectful

**irresponsable** [iʀɛspɔ̃sabl] *adj* irresponsible

**irriguer** [iʀige] *vt* to irrigate

**irritable** [iʀitabl] *adj* irritable

**irriter** [iʀite] *vt* to irritate

**irruption** [iʀypsjɔ̃] *nf*: **faire ~ (chez qn)** to burst in (on sb)

**Islam** [islam] *nm*: **l'~** Islam; **islamique** *adj* Islamic; **islamophobie** *nf* Islamophobia

**Islande** [islɑ̃d] *nf* Iceland

**isolant, e** [izɔlɑ̃, ɑ̃t] *adj* insulating; (*insonorisant*) soundproofing

**isolation** [izɔlasjɔ̃] *nf* insulation; **~ acoustique** soundproofing

**isolé, e** [izɔle] *adj* isolated; (*contre le froid*) insulated

**isoler** [izɔle] *vt* to isolate; (*prisonnier*) to put in solitary confinement; (*ville*) to cut off, isolate; (*contre le froid*) to insulate; **s'isoler** *vi* to isolate o.s.

**Israël** [isʀaɛl] *nm* Israel; **israélien, ne** *adj* Israeli ▷ *nm/f*: **Israélien, ne** Israeli; **israélite** *adj* Jewish ▷ *nm/f*: **Israélite** Jew (Jewess)

**issu, e** [isy] *adj*: **~ de** (*né de*) descended from; (*résultant de*) stemming from; **issue** *nf* (*ouverture, sortie*) exit; (*solution*) way out, solution; (*dénouement*) outcome; **à l'issue de** at the conclusion *ou* close of; **voie sans issue** dead end; **issue de secours** emergency exit

**Italie** [itali] *nf* Italy; **italien, ne** *adj* Italian ▷ *nm/f*: **Italien, ne** Italian ▷ *nm* (*Ling*) Italian

**italique** [italik] *nm*: **en ~** in italics

**itinéraire** [itineʀɛʀ] *nm* itinerary, route; **itinéraire bis** alternative route

**IUT** *sigle m* = **Institut universitaire de technologie**

**IVG** *sigle f* (= *interruption volontaire de grossesse*) abortion

**ivoire** [ivwaʀ] *nm* ivory

**ivre** [ivʀ] *adj* drunk; **~ de** (*colère, bonheur*) wild with; **ivrogne** *nm/f* drunkard

# j

**j'** [ʒ] *pron voir* **je**

**jacinthe** [ʒasɛ̃t] *nf* hyacinth

**jadis** [ʒadis] *adv* long ago

**jaillir** [ʒajiʀ] *vi* (*liquide*) to spurt out; (*cris, réponses*) to burst forth

**jais** [ʒɛ] *nm* jet; **(d'un noir) de ~** jet-black

**jalousie** [ʒaluzi] *nf* jealousy; (*store*) slatted blind

**jaloux, -ouse** [ʒalu, uz] *adj* jealous; **être ~ de** to be jealous of

**jamaïquain, e** [ʒamaikɛ̃, -ɛn] *adj* Jamaican ▷ *nm/f*: **J~, e** Jamaican

**Jamaïque** [ʒamaik] *nf*: **la ~** Jamaica

**jamais** [ʒamɛ] *adv* never; (*sans négation*) ever; **ne ... ~** never; **je ne suis ~ allé en Espagne** I've never been to Spain; **si ~ vous passez dans la région, venez nous voir** if you happen to be/if you're ever in this area, come and see us; **à ~** for ever

**jambe** [ʒɑ̃b] *nf* leg

**jambon** [ʒɑ̃bɔ̃] *nm* ham

**jante** [ʒɑ̃t] *nf* (wheel) rim

**janvier** [ʒɑ̃vje] *nm* January

**Japon** [ʒapɔ̃] *nm* Japan; **japonais, e** *adj* Japanese ▷ *nm/f*: **Japonais, e** Japanese ▷ *nm* (*Ling*) Japanese

**jardin** [ʒaʀdɛ̃] *nm* garden; **jardin d'enfants** nursery school; **jardinage** *nm* gardening; **jardiner** *vi* to do some gardening; **jardinier, -ière** *nm/f* gardener; **jardinière** *nf* planter; (*de fenêtre*) window box; **jardinière de légumes** (*Culin*) mixed vegetables

**jargon** [ʒaʀgɔ̃] *nm* (*baragouin*) gibberish; (*langue professionnelle*) jargon

**jarret** [ʒaʀɛ] *nm* back of knee; (*Culin*) knuckle, shin

**jauge** [ʒoʒ] *nf* (*instrument*) gauge; **jauge (de niveau) d'huile** (*Auto*) dipstick

**jaune** [ʒon] *adj, nm* yellow ▷ *adv* (*fam*): **rire ~** to laugh on the other side of one's face; **jaune d'œuf** (egg) yolk; **jaunir** *vi, vt* to turn yellow; **jaunisse** *nf* jaundice

**Javel** [ʒavɛl] *nf voir* **eau**

**javelot** [ʒavlo] *nm* javelin

**je, j'** [ʒə] *pron* I

**jean** [dʒin] *nm* jeans *pl*

**Jésus-Christ** [ʒezykʀi(st)] *n* Jesus Christ; **600 avant/après ~** *ou* **J.-C.** 600 B.C./A.D.

**jet** [ʒɛ] *nm* (*lancer: action*) throwing *no pl*; (: *résultat*) throw; (*jaillissement: d'eaux*) jet; (: *de sang*) spurt; **jet d'eau** spray

**jetable** [ʒ(ə)tabl] *adj* disposable

**jetée** [ʒəte] *nf* jetty; (*grande*) pier

**jeter** [ʒ(ə)te] *vt* (*gén*) to throw; (*se défaire de*) to throw away *ou* out; **~ qch à qn** to throw sth to sb; (*de façon agressive*) to throw sth at sb; **~ un coup d'œil (à)** to take a look (at); **~ un sort à qn** to cast a spell on sb; **se ~ sur qn** to rush at sb; **se ~ dans** (*suj: fleuve*) to flow into

**jeton** [ʒ(ə)tɔ̃] *nm* (*au jeu*) counter

**jette** *etc* [ʒɛt] *vb voir* **jeter**

**jeu, x** [ʒø] *nm* (*divertissement, Tech: d'une pièce*) play; (*Tennis: partie, Football etc: façon de jouer*) game; (*Théâtre etc*) acting; (*série d'objets, jouet*) set; (*Cartes*) hand; (*au casino*): **le ~** gambling; **remettre en ~** (*Football*) to throw in; **être en ~** (*fig*) to be at stake; **entrer/mettre en ~** (fig) to come/bring into play; **jeu de cartes** pack of cards; **jeu d'échecs** chess set; **jeu de hasard** game of chance; **jeu de mots** pun; **jeu de société** board game; **jeu télévisé** television quiz; **jeu vidéo** video game

**jeudi** [ʒødi] nm Thursday

**jeun** [ʒœ̃]: **à ~** adv on an empty stomach; **être à ~** to have eaten nothing; **rester à ~** not to eat anything

**jeune** [ʒœn] adj young; **jeunes** nmpl: **les ~s** young people; **jeune fille** girl; **jeune homme** young man; **jeunes gens** young people

**jeûne** [ʒøn] nm fast

**jeunesse** [ʒœnɛs] nf youth; (aspect) youthfulness

**joaillier, -ière** [ʒɔaje, -jɛʀ] nm/f jeweller

**jogging** [dʒɔɡiŋ] nm jogging; (survêtement) tracksuit; **faire du ~** to go jogging

**joie** [ʒwa] nf joy

**joindre** [ʒwɛ̃dʀ] vt to join; (à une lettre): **~ qch à** to enclose sth with; (contacter) to contact, get in touch with; **se ~ à qn** to join sb; **se ~ à qch** to join in sth

**joint, e** [ʒwɛ̃, ɛ̃t] adj: **pièce ~e** (de lettre) enclosure; (de mail) attachment ▷ nm joint; (ligne) join; **joint de culasse** cylinder head gasket

**joli, e** [ʒɔli] adj pretty, attractive; **une ~e somme/situation** a tidy sum/a nice little job; **c'est du ~!** (ironique) that's very nice!; **c'est bien ~, mais ...** that's all very well but ...

**jonc** [ʒɔ̃] nm (bul)rush

**jonction** [ʒɔ̃ksjɔ̃] nf junction

**jongleur, -euse** [ʒɔ̃ɡlœʀ, øz] nm/f juggler

**jonquille** [ʒɔ̃kij] nf daffodil

**Jordanie** [ʒɔʀdani] nf: **la ~** Jordan

**joue** [ʒu] nf cheek

**jouer** [ʒwe] vt to play; (somme d'argent, réputation) to stake, wager; (simuler: sentiment) to affect, feign ▷ vi to play; (Théâtre, Cinéma) to act; (au casino) to gamble; (bois, porte: se voiler) to warp; (clef, pièce: avoir du jeu) to be loose; **~ sur** (miser) to gamble on; **~ de** (Mus) to play; **~ à** (jeu, sport, roulette) to play; **~ un tour à qn** to play a trick on sb; **~ serré** to play a close game; **~ la comédie** to put on an act; **à toi/nous de ~** it's your/our go ou turn; **bien joué!** well done!; **on joue Hamlet au théâtre X** Hamlet is on at the X theatre

**jouet** [ʒwɛ] nm toy; **être le ~ de** (illusion etc) to be the victim of

**joueur, -euse** [ʒwœʀ, øz] nm/f player; **être beau/mauvais ~** to be a good/bad loser

**jouir** [ʒwiʀ] vi (sexe: fam) to come ▷ vt: **~ de** to enjoy

**jour** [ʒuʀ] nm day; (opposé à la nuit) day, daytime; (clarté) daylight; (fig: aspect) light; (ouverture) gap; **de ~** (crème, service) day cpd; **travailler de ~** to work during the day; **voyager de ~** to travel by day; **au ~ le ~** from day to day; **de nos ~s** these days; **du ~ au lendemain** overnight; **il fait ~** it's daylight; **au grand ~** (fig) in the open; **mettre au ~** to disclose; **mettre à ~** to update; **donner le ~ à** to give birth to; **voir le ~** to be born; **le ~ J** D-day; **jour férié** public holiday; **jour ouvrable** working day

**journal, -aux** [ʒuʀnal, o] nm (news)paper; (spécialisé) journal; (intime) diary; **journal de bord** log; **journal parlé/télévisé** radio/ television news sg

**journalier, -ière** [ʒuʀnalje, jɛʀ] adj daily; (banal) everyday

**journalisme** [ʒuʀnalism] nm journalism; **journaliste** nm/f journalist

**journée** [ʒuʀne] nf day; **faire la ~ continue** to work over lunch

**joyau, x** [ʒwajo] nm gem, jewel

**joyeux, -euse** [ʒwajø, øz] adj joyful, merry; **~ Noël!** merry Christmas!; **~ anniversaire!** happy birthday!

**jubiler** [ʒybile] vi to be jubilant, exult

**judas** [ʒyda] nm (trou) spy-hole

**judiciaire** [ʒydisjɛʀ] *adj* judicial
**judicieux, -euse** [ʒydisjø, jøz] *adj* judicious
**judo** [ʒydo] *nm* judo
**juge** [ʒyʒ] *nm* judge; **juge d'instruction** examining (BRIT) ou committing (US) magistrate; **juge de paix** justice of the peace
**jugé** [ʒyʒe]: **au ~** *adv* by guesswork
**jugement** [ʒyʒmɑ̃] *nm* judgment; (*Jur: au pénal*) sentence; (: *au civil*) decision
**juger** [ʒyʒe] *vt* to judge; (*estimer*) to consider; **~ qn/qch satisfaisant** to consider sb/sth (to be) satisfactory; **~ bon de faire** to see fit to do
**juif, -ive** [ʒɥif, ʒɥiv] *adj* Jewish ▷ *nm/f*: **J~, ive** Jew (Jewess)
**juillet** [ʒɥijɛ] *nm* July

○ ● **14 JUILLET**
○
○ ● **Le 14 juillet** is a national holiday
○ ● in France and commemorates the
○ ● storming of the Bastille during the
○ ● French Revolution. Throughout
○ ● the country there are celebrations,
○ ● which feature parades, music,
○ ● dancing and firework displays. In
○ ● Paris a military parade along the
○ ● Champs-Élysées is attended by the
○ ● President.

**juin** [ʒɥɛ̃] *nm* June
**jumeau, -elle, x** [ʒymo, ɛl] *adj, nm/f* twin
**jumeler** [ʒym(ə)le] *vt* to twin
**jumelle** [ʒymɛl] *adj, nf voir* **jumeau**; **jumelles** *nfpl* (*appareil*) binoculars
**jument** [ʒymɑ̃] *nf* mare
**jungle** [ʒɔ̃gl] *nf* jungle
**jupe** [ʒyp] *nf* skirt
**jupon** [ʒypɔ̃] *nm* waist slip
**juré, e** [ʒyʀe] *nm/f* juror ▷ *adj*: **ennemi ~** sworn enemy
**jurer** [ʒyʀe] *vt* (*obéissance etc*) to swear, vow ▷ *vi* (*dire des jurons*) to swear, curse; (*dissoner*): **~ (avec)** to clash (with); **~ de faire/que** to swear to do/that; **~ de**

**qch** (*s'en porter garant*) to swear to sth
**juridique** [ʒyʀidik] *adj* legal
**juron** [ʒyʀɔ̃] *nm* curse, swearword
**jury** [ʒyʀi] *nm* jury; (*Art, Sport*) panel of judges; (*Scol*) board of examiners
**jus** [ʒy] *nm* juice; (*de viande*) gravy, (meat) juice; **jus de fruit** fruit juice
**jusque** [ʒysk]: **jusqu'à** *prép* (*endroit*) as far as, (up) to; (*moment*) until, till; (*limite*) up to; **~ sur/dans** up to; (*y compris*) even on/in; **jusqu'à ce que** until; **jusqu'à présent** ou **maintenant** so far; **jusqu'où?** how far?
**justaucorps** [ʒystokɔʀ] *nm* leotard
**juste** [ʒyst] *adj* (*équitable*) just, fair; (*légitime*) just; (*exact*) right; (*pertinent*) apt; (*étroit*) tight; (*insuffisant*) on the short side ▷ *adv* rightly, correctly; (*chanter*) in tune; (*exactement, seulement*) just; **~ assez/au-dessus** just enough/above; **au ~** exactly; **le ~ milieu** the happy medium; **c'était ~** it was a close thing; **pouvoir tout ~ faire** to be only just able to do; **justement** *adv* justly; (*précisément*) just, precisely; **justesse** *nf* (*précision*) accuracy; (*d'une remarque*) aptness; (*d'une opinion*) soundness; **de justesse** only just
**justice** [ʒystis] *nf* (*équité*) fairness, justice; (*Admin*) justice; **rendre ~ à qn** to do sb justice
**justificatif, -ive** [ʒystifikatif, iv] *adj* (*document*) supporting; **pièce justificative** written proof
**justifier** [ʒystifje] *vt* to justify; **~ de** to prove
**juteux, -euse** [ʒytø, øz] *adj* juicy
**juvénile** [ʒyvenil] *adj* youthful

**K** [kɑ] *nm* (*Inform*) K
**kaki** [kaki] *adj inv* khaki
**kangourou** [kɑ̃guʀu] *nm* kangaroo
**karaté** [kaʀate] *nm* karate
**kascher** [kaʃɛʀ] *adj* kosher
**kayak** [kajak] *nm* canoe, kayak; **faire du ~** to go canoeing
**képi** [kepi] *nm* kepi
**kermesse** [kɛʀmɛs] *nf* fair; (*fête de charité*) bazaar, (charity) fête
**kidnapper** [kidnape] *vt* to kidnap
**kilo** [kilo] *nm* = **kilogramme**
**kilo...**: **kilogramme** *nm* kilogramme; **kilométrage** *nm* number of kilometres travelled, ≈ mileage; **kilomètre** *nm* kilometre; **kilométrique** *adj* (*distance*) in kilometres
**kinésithérapeute** [kineziteʀapøt] *nm/f* physiotherapist
**kiosque** [kjɔsk] *nm* kiosk, stall
**kir** [kiʀ] *nm* kir (*white wine with blackcurrant liqueur*)
**kit** [kit] *nm* kit; **~ piéton** *ou* **mains libres** hands-free kit; **en ~** in kit form

**kiwi** [kiwi] *nm* kiwi
**klaxon** [klaksɔn] *nm* horn; **klaxonner** *vi, vt* to hoot (*BRIT*), honk (*US*)
**km** *abr* = **kilomètre**
**km/h** *abr* (= *kilomètres/heure*) ≈ mph
**K.-O.** (*fam*) *adj inv* shattered, knackered
**Kosovo** [kɔsɔvo] *nm* Kosovo
**Koweit, Kuweit** [kɔwɛt] *nm*: **le ~** Kuwait
**k-way®** [kawɛ] *nm* (*lightweight nylon*) cagoule
**kyste** [kist] *nm* cyst

**l'** [l] *art déf voir* **le**

**la** [la] *art déf voir* **le** ▷ *nm* (*Mus*) A; (*en chantant la gamme*) la

**là** [la] *adv* there; (*ici*) here; (*dans le temps*) then; **elle n'est pas là** she isn't here; **c'est là que** this is where; **là où** where; **de là** (*fig*) hence; **par là** (*fig*) by that; *voir aussi* **-ci**; **ce**; **celui**; **là-bas** *adv* there

**laboratoire** [labɔratwar] *nm* laboratory; **laboratoire de langues** language laboratory

**laborieux, -euse** [labɔrjø, jøz] *adj* (*tâche*) laborious

**labourer** *vt* to plough

**labyrinthe** [labirɛ̃t] *nm* labyrinth, maze

**lac** [lak] *nm* lake

**lacet** [lasɛ] *nm* (*de chaussure*) lace; (*de route*) sharp bend; (*piège*) snare

**lâche** [lɑʃ] *adj* (*poltron*) cowardly; (*desserré*) loose, slack ▷ *nm/f* coward

**lâcher** [lɑʃe] *vt* to let go of; (*ce qui tombe, abandonner*) to drop; (*oiseau, animal: libérer*) to release, set free; (*fig: mot,*

*remarque*) to let slip, come out with ▷ *vi* (*freins*) to fail; ~ **les amarres** (*Navig*) to cast off (the moorings); ~ **prise** to let go

**lacrymogène** [lakrimɔʒɛn] *adj*: **gaz ~** teargas

**lacune** [lakyn] *nf* gap

**là-dedans** [ladədɑ̃] *adv* inside (there), in it; (*fig*) in that

**là-dessous** [ladsu] *adv* underneath, under there; (*fig*) behind that

**là-dessus** [ladsy] *adv* on there; (*fig: sur ces mots*) at that point; (: *à ce sujet*) about that

**lagune** [lagyn] *nf* lagoon

**là-haut** [lao] *adv* up there

**laid, e** [lɛ, lɛd] *adj* ugly; **laideur** *nf* ugliness *no pl*

**lainage** [lɛnaʒ] *nm* (*vêtement*) woollen garment; (*étoffe*) woollen material

**laine** [lɛn] *nf* wool

**laïque** [laik] *adj* lay, civil; (*Scol*) state *cpd* ▷ *nm/f* layman(-woman)

**laisse** [lɛs] *nf* (*de chien*) lead, leash; **tenir en ~** to keep on a lead *ou* leash

**laisser** [lese] *vt* to leave ▷ *vb aux*: ~ **qn faire** to let sb do; **se ~ aller** to let o.s. go; **laisse-toi faire** let me (*ou* him *etc*) do it; **laisser-aller** *nm* carelessness, slovenliness; **laissez-passer** *nm inv* pass

**lait** [lɛ] *nm* milk; **frère/sœur de ~** foster brother/sister; **lait concentré/ condensé** condensed/evaporated milk; **lait écrémé/entier** skimmed/ full-cream (*brit*) *ou* whole milk; **laitage** *nm* dairy product; **laiterie** *nf* dairy; **laitier, -ière** *adj* dairy *cpd* ▷ *nm/f* milkman (dairywoman)

**laiton** [lɛtɔ̃] *nm* brass

**laitue** [lety] *nf* lettuce

**lambeau, x** [lɑ̃bo] *nm* scrap; **en ~x** in tatters, tattered

**lame** [lam] *nf* blade; (*vague*) wave; (*lamelle*) strip; **lame de fond** ground swell *no pl*; **lame de rasoir** razor blade; **lamelle** *nf* thin strip *ou* blade

**lamentable** [lamɑ̃tabl] *adj* appalling

**lamenter** [lamɑ̃te] *vb*: **se ~ (sur)** to

moan (over)

**lampadaire** [lɑ̃padɛʀ] *nm* (*de salon*) standard lamp; (*dans la rue*) street lamp

**lampe** [lɑ̃p] *nf* lamp; (*Tech*) valve; **lampe à bronzer** sun lamp; **lampe à pétrole** oil lamp; **lampe de poche** torch (BRIT), flashlight (US); **lampe halogène** halogen lamp

**lance** [lɑ̃s] *nf* spear; **lance d'incendie** fire hose

**lancée** [lɑ̃se] *nf*: **être/continuer sur sa ~** to be under way/keep going

**lancement** [lɑ̃smɑ̃] *nm* launching

**lance-pierres** [lɑ̃spjɛʀ] *nm inv* catapult

**lancer** [lɑ̃se] *nm* (*Sport*) throwing *no pl*, throw ▷ *vt* to throw; (*émettre, projeter*) to throw out, send out; (*produit, fusée, bateau, artiste*) to launch; (*injure*) to hurl, fling; **se lancer** *vi* (*prendre de l'élan*) to build up speed; (*se précipiter*): **se ~ sur** *ou* **contre** to rush at; **se ~ dans** (*discussion*) to launch into; (*aventure*) to embark on; **~ qch à qn** to throw sth to sb; (*de façon agressive*) to throw sth at sb; **~ un cri** *ou* **un appel** to shout *ou* call out; **lancer du poids** putting the shot

**landau** [lɑ̃do] *nm* pram (BRIT), baby carriage (US)

**lande** [lɑ̃d] *nf* moor

**langage** [lɑ̃ɡaʒ] *nm* language

**langouste** [lɑ̃ɡust] *nf* crayfish *inv*; **langoustine** *nf* Dublin Bay prawn

**langue** [lɑ̃ɡ] *nf* (*Anat, Culin*) tongue; (*Ling*) language; **tirer la ~ (à)** to stick out one's tongue (at); **de ~ française** French-speaking; **quelles ~s parlez-vous?** what languages do you speak?; **langue maternelle** native language, mother tongue; **langues vivantes** modern languages

**langueur** [lɑ̃ɡœʀ] *nf* languidness

**languir** [lɑ̃ɡiʀ] *vi* to languish; (*conversation*) to flag; **faire ~ qn** to keep sb waiting

**lanière** [lanjɛʀ] *nf* (*de fouet*) lash; (*de sac, bretelle*) strap

**lanterne** [lɑ̃tɛʀn] *nf* (*portable*) lantern; (*électrique*) light, lamp; (*de voiture*) (side)light

**laper** [lape] *vt* to lap up

**lapidaire** [lapidɛʀ] *adj* (*fig*) terse

**lapin** [lapɛ̃] *nm* rabbit; (*peau*) rabbitskin; (*fourrure*) cony; **poser un ~ à qn** (*fam*) to stand sb up

**Laponie** [laponi] *nf* Lapland

**laps** [laps] *nm*: **~ de temps** space of time, time *no pl*

**laque** [lak] *nf* (*vernis*) lacquer; (*pour cheveux*) hair spray

**laquelle** [lakɛl] *pron voir* **lequel**

**larcin** [larsɛ̃] *nm* theft

**lard** [laʀ] *nm* (*bacon*) (streaky) bacon; (*graisse*) fat

**lardon** [lardɔ̃] *nm*: **~s** chopped bacon

**large** [larʒ] *adj* wide, broad; (*fig*) generous ▷ *adv*: **calculer/voir ~** to allow extra/think big ▷ *nm* (*largeur*): **5 m de ~** 5 m wide *ou* in width; (*mer*): **le ~** the open sea; **au ~ de** off; **large d'esprit** broad-minded; **largement** *adv* widely; (*de loin*) greatly; (*au moins*) easily; (*généreusement*) generously; **c'est largement suffisant** that's ample; **largesse** *nf* generosity; **largesses** *nfpl* (*dons*) liberalities; **largeur** *nf* (*qu'on mesure*) width; (*impression visuelle*) wideness, width; (*d'esprit*) broadness

**larguer** [larɡe] *vt* to drop; **~ les amarres** to cast off (the moorings)

**larme** [larm] *nf* tear; (*fam: goutte*) drop; **en ~s** in tears; **larmoyer** *vi* (*yeux*) to water; (*se plaindre*) to whimper

**larvé, e** [larve] *adj* (*fig*) latent

**laryngite** [larɛ̃ʒit] *nf* laryngitis

**las, lasse** [lɑ, lɑs] *adj* weary

**laser** [lazɛʀ] *nm*: **(rayon) ~** laser (beam); **chaîne** *ou* **platine ~** laser disc (player); **disque ~** laser disc

**lasse** [lɑs] *adj voir* **las**

**lasser** [lɑse] *vt* to weary, tire; **se lasser de** *vt* to grow weary *ou* tired of

**latéral, e, -aux** [lateral, o] *adj* side *cpd*, lateral

**latin, e** [latɛ̃, in] *adj* Latin ▷ *nm/f*: **L~, e** Latin ▷ *nm* (*Ling*) Latin

**latitude** [latityd] nf latitude
**lauréat, e** [lɔʀea, at] nm/f winner
**laurier** [lɔʀje] nm (Bot) laurel; **feuille de ~** (Culin) bay leaf
**lavable** [lavabl] adj washable
**lavabo** [lavabo] nm washbasin; **lavabos** nmpl (toilettes) toilet sg
**lavage** [lavaʒ] nm washing no pl, wash; **lavage de cerveau** brainwashing no pl
**lavande** [lavɑ̃d] nf lavender
**lave** [lav] nf lava no pl
**lave-linge** [lavlɛ̃ʒ] nm inv washing machine
**laver** [lave] vt to wash; (tache) to wash off; **se laver** vi to have a wash, wash; **se ~ les mains/dents** to wash one's hands/clean one's teeth; **~ la vaisselle/le linge** to wash the dishes/clothes; **~ qn de** (accusation) to clear sb of; **laverie** nf: **laverie (automatique)** launderette; **lavette** nf dish cloth; (fam) drip; **laveur, -euse** nm/f cleaner; **lave-vaisselle** nm inv dishwasher; **lavoir** nm wash house; (évier) sink
**laxatif, -ive** [laksatif, iv] adj, nm laxative
**layette** [lɛjɛt] nf baby clothes

 **MOT-CLÉ**

**le** [lə], **la**, **l'** (pl **les**) art déf **1** the; **le livre/la pomme/l'arbre** the book/the apple/the tree; **les étudiants** the students
**2** (noms abstraits): **le courage/l'amour/la jeunesse** courage/love/youth
**3** (indiquant la possession): **se casser la jambe** etc to break one's leg etc; **levez la main** put your hand up; **avoir les yeux gris/le nez rouge** to have grey eyes/a red nose
**4** (temps): **le matin/soir** in the morning/evening; mornings/evenings; **le jeudi** etc (d'habitude) on Thursdays etc; (ce jeudi-là etc) on (the) Thursday
**5** (distribution) a, an; **10 euros le mètre/kilo** 10 euros a ou per metre/kilo; **le tiers/quart de** a third/quarter of
▷ pron **1** (personne: mâle) him; (: femelle) her; (: pluriel) them; **je le/la/les vois** I can see him/her/them
**2** (animal, chose: singulier) it; (: pluriel) them; **je le (ou la) vois** I can see it; **je les vois** I can see them
**3** (remplaçant une phrase): **je ne le savais pas** I didn't know (about it); **il était riche et ne l'est plus** he was once rich but no longer is

**lécher** [leʃe] vt to lick; (laper: lait, eau) to lick ou lap up; **se ~ les doigts/lèvres** to lick one's fingers/lips; **lèche-vitrines** nm: **faire du lèche-vitrines** to go window-shopping
**leçon** [l(ə)sɔ̃] nf lesson; **faire la ~ à** (fig) to give a lecture to; **leçons de conduite** driving lessons; **leçons particulières** private lessons ou tuition sg (BRIT)
**lecteur, -trice** [lɛktœʀ, tʀis] nm/f reader; (d'université) foreign language assistant ▷ nm (Tech): **~ de cassettes/CD/DVD** cassette/CD/DVD player; **lecteur de disquette(s)** disk drive; **lecteur MP3** MP3 player
**lecture** [lɛktyʀ] nf reading
⏐ Attention à ne pas traduire lecture par le mot anglais lecture.
**ledit** [lədi], **ladite** (mpl **lesdits**, fpl **lesdites**) dét the aforesaid
**légal, e, -aux** [legal, o] adj legal; **légaliser** vt to legalize; **légalité** nf law
**légendaire** [leʒɑ̃dɛʀ] adj legendary
**légende** [leʒɑ̃d] nf (mythe) legend; (de carte, plan) key; (de dessin) caption
**léger, -ère** [leʒe, ɛʀ] adj light; (bruit, retard) slight; (personne: superficiel) thoughtless; (: volage) free and easy; **à la légère** (parler, agir) rashly, thoughtlessly; **légèrement** adv (s'habiller, bouger) lightly; (un peu) slightly; **manger légèrement** to eat a light meal; **légèreté** nf lightness; (d'une remarque) flippancy

**législatif, -ive** [leʒislatif, iv] *adj*
legislative; **législatives** *nfpl* general
election *sg*

**légitime** [leʒitim] *adj* (*Jur*) lawful,
legitimate; (*fig*) rightful, legitimate; **en
état de ~ défense** in self-defence

**legs** [lɛg] *nm* legacy

**léguer** [lege] *vt*: **~ qch à qn** (*Jur*) to
bequeath sth to sb

**légume** [legym] *nm* vegetable;
**légumes secs** pulses; **légumes verts**
green vegetables, greens

**lendemain** [lɑ̃dmɛ̃] *nm*: **le ~** the next
*ou* following day; **le ~ matin/soir** the
next *ou* following morning/evening; **le
~ de** the day after

**lent, e** [lɑ̃, lɑ̃t] *adj* slow; **lentement** *adv*
slowly; **lenteur** *nf* slowness *no pl*

**lentille** [lɑ̃tij] *nf* (*Optique*) lens *sg*;
(*Culin*) lentil; **lentilles de contact**
contact lenses

**léopard** [leɔpaR] *nm* leopard

**lèpre** [lɛpR] *nf* leprosy

 **MOT-CLÉ**

**lequel, laquelle** [ləkɛl, lakɛl] (*mpl*
**lesquels**, *fpl* **lesquelles**) (*à + lequel =*
**auquel**, *de + lequel =* **duquel** *etc*) *pron*
**1** (*interrogatif*) which, which one; **lequel
des deux?** which one?
**2** (*relatif: personne: sujet*) who; (: *objet,
après préposition*) whom; (: *chose*) which
▷ *adj*: **auquel cas** in which case

**les** [le] *dét voir* **le**
**lesbienne** [lɛsbjɛn] *nf* lesbian
**léser** [leze] *vt* to wrong
**lésiner** [lezine] *vi*: **ne pas ~ sur les
moyens** (*pour mariage etc*) to push the
boat out
**lésion** [lezjɔ̃] *nf* lesion, damage *no pl*
**lessive** [lesiv] *nf* (*poudre*) washing
powder; (*linge*) washing *no pl*, wash;
**lessiver** *vt* to wash; (*fam: fatiguer*) to
tire out, exhaust
**lest** [lɛst] *nm* ballast
**leste** [lɛst] *adj* sprightly, nimble

**lettre** [lɛtR] *nf* letter; **lettres** *nfpl*
(*littérature*) literature *sg*; (*Scol*) arts
(subjects); **à la ~** literally; **en toutes ~s**
in full; **lettre piégée** letter bomb

**leucémie** [løsemi] *nf* leukaemia

 **MOT-CLÉ**

**leur** [lœR] *adj possessif* their; **leur
maison** their house; **leurs amis** their
friends
▷ *pron* **1** (*objet indirect*) (to) them; **je leur
ai dit la vérité** I told them the truth;
**je le leur ai donné** I gave it to them, I
gave them it
**2** (*possessif*): **le(la) leur, les leurs** theirs

**levain** [ləvɛ̃] *nm* leaven
**levé, e** [ləve] *adj*: **être ~** to be up; **levée**
*nf* (*Postes*) collection
**lever** [l(ə)ve] *vt* (*vitre, bras etc*) to raise;
(*soulever de terre, supprimer: interdiction,
siège*) to lift; (*impôts, armée*) to levy ▷ *vi*
to rise ▷ *nm*: **au ~** on getting up; **se
lever** *vi* to get up; (*soleil*) to rise; (*jour*)
to break; (*brouillard*) to lift; **ça va se ~**
(*temps*) it's going to clear up; **lever de
soleil** sunrise; **lever du jour** daybreak
**levier** [ləvje] *nm* lever
**lèvre** [lɛvR] *nf* lip
**lévrier** [levRije] *nm* greyhound
**levure** [l(ə)vyR] *nf* yeast; **levure
chimique** baking powder
**lexique** [lɛksik] *nm* vocabulary;
(*glossaire*) lexicon
**lézard** [lezaR] *nm* lizard
**lézarde** [lezaRd] *nf* crack
**liaison** [ljezɔ̃] *nf* (*rapport*) connection;
(*transport*) link; (*amoureuse*) affair;
(*Phonétique*) liaison; **entrer/être en ~
avec** to get/be in contact with
**liane** [ljan] *nf* creeper
**liasse** [ljas] *nf* wad, bundle
**Liban** [libɑ̃] *nm*: **le ~** (the) Lebanon
**libeller** [libele] *vt* (*chèque, mandat*): **~
(au nom de)** to make out (to); (*lettre*)
to word
**libellule** [libelyl] *nf* dragonfly

**libéral, e, -aux** [liberal, o] adj,
nm/f liberal; **profession ~e** (liberal)
profession

**libérer** [libere] vt (délivrer) to free,
liberate; (relâcher: prisonnier) to
discharge, release; (: d'inhibitions) to
liberate; (gaz) to release; **se libérer** vi
(de rendez-vous) to get out of previous
engagements

**liberté** [liberte] nf freedom; (loisir) free
time; **libertés** nfpl (privautés) liberties;
**mettre/être en ~** to set/be free; **en ~
provisoire/surveillée/conditionnelle**
on bail/probation/parole

**libraire** [librer] nm/f bookseller

**librairie** [libreri] nf bookshop

  Attention à ne pas traduire *librairie*
  par *library*.

**libre** [libr] adj free; (route, voie) clear;
(place, salle) free; (ligne) not engaged;
(Scol) non-state; **~ de qch/de faire** free
from sth/to do; **la place est ~?** is this
seat free?; **libre arbitre** free will; **libre-
échange** nm free trade; **libre-service**
nm self-service store

**Libye** [libi] nf: **la ~** Libya

**licence** [lisɑ̃s] nf (permis) permit;
(diplôme) degree; (liberté) liberty;
**licencié, e** nm/f (Scol): **licencié
ès lettres/en droit** ≈ Bachelor of
Arts/Law

**licenciement** [lisɑ̃simɑ̃] nm
redundancy

**licencier** [lisɑ̃sje] vt (débaucher) to
make redundant, lay off; (renvoyer)
to dismiss

**licite** [lisit] adj lawful

**lie** [li] nf dregs pl, sediment

**lié, e** [lje] adj: **très ~ avec** very friendly
with ou close to

**Liechtenstein** [liʃtɛnstain] nm: **le ~**
Liechtenstein

**liège** [ljɛʒ] nm cork

**lien** [ljɛ̃] nm (corde, fig: affectif) bond;
(rapport) link, connection; **lien de
parenté** family tie; **lien hypertexte**
hyperlink

**lier** [lje] vt (attacher) to tie up; (joindre)

to link up; (fig: unir, engager) to bind;
**~ conversation (avec)** to strike up a
conversation (with); **~ connaissance
avec** to get to know

**lierre** [ljɛr] nm ivy

**lieu, x** [ljø] nm place; **lieux** nmpl
(locaux) premises; (endroit: d'un accident
etc) scene sg; **en ~ sûr** in a safe place; **en
premier ~** in the first place; **en dernier
~** lastly; **avoir ~** to take place; **tenir ~
de** to serve as; **donner ~ à** to give rise
to; **au ~ de** instead of; **arriver/être sur
les ~x** to arrive at/be on the scene; **lieu
commun** cliché; **lieu-dit** (pl lieux-dits)
nm locality

**lieutenant** [ljøt(ə)nɑ̃] nm lieutenant

**lièvre** [ljɛvr] nm hare

**ligament** [ligamɑ̃] nm ligament

**ligne** [liɲ] nf (gén) line; (Transports:
liaison) service; (: trajet) route;
(silhouette) figure; **garder la ~** to keep
one's figure; **entrer en ~ de compte** to
come into it; **en ~** (Inform) online; **~ fixe**
(Tél) land line (phone)

**lignée** [liɲe] nf line, lineage

**ligoter** [ligɔte] vt to tie up

**ligue** [lig] nf league

**lilas** [lila] nm lilac

**limace** [limas] nf slug

**limande** [limɑ̃d] nf dab

**lime** [lim] nf file; **lime à ongles** nail file;
**limer** vt to file

**limitation** [limitasjɔ̃] nf: **limitation
de vitesse** speed limit

**limite** [limit] nf (de terrain) boundary;
(partie ou point extrême) limit; **à la ~** (au
pire) if the worst comes (ou came) to the
worst; **vitesse/charge ~** maximum
speed/load; **cas ~** borderline
case; **date ~** deadline; **date ~ de
vente/consommation** sell-by/best-
before date; **limiter** vt (restreindre) to
limit, restrict; (délimiter) to border;
**limitrophe** adj border cpd

**limoger** [limɔʒe] vt to dismiss

**limon** [limɔ̃] nm silt

**limonade** [limɔnad] nf lemonade

**lin** [lɛ̃] nm (tissu) linen

**linceul** [lɛ̃sœl] nm shroud

**linge** [lɛ̃ʒ] nm (serviettes etc) linen; (lessive) washing; (aussi: **~ de corps**) underwear; **lingerie** nf lingerie, underwear

**lingot** [lɛ̃go] nm ingot

**linguistique** [lɛ̃gɥistik] adj linguistic ▷ nf linguistics sg

**lion, ne** [ljɔ̃, ljɔn] nm/f lion (lioness); (signe): **le L~** Leo; **lionceau, x** nm lion cub

**liqueur** [likœʀ] nf liqueur

**liquidation** [likidasjɔ̃] nf (vente) sale

**liquide** [likid] adj liquid ▷ nm liquid; (Comm): **en ~** in ready money ou cash; **je n'ai pas de ~** I haven't got any cash; **liquider** vt to liquidate; (Comm: articles) to clear, sell off

**lire** [liʀ] nf (monnaie) lira ▷ vt, vi to read

**lis** [lis] nm = **lys**

**Lisbonne** [lizbɔn] n Lisbon

**lisible** [lizibl] adj legible

**lisière** [lizjɛʀ] nf (de forêt) edge

**lisons** [lizɔ̃] vb voir **lire**

**lisse** [lis] adj smooth

**liste** [list] nf list; **faire la ~ de** to list; **liste de mariage** wedding (present) list; **liste électorale** electoral roll; **listing** nm (Inform) printout

**lit** [li] nm bed; **petit ~, ~ à une place** single bed; **grand ~, ~ à deux places** double bed; **faire son ~** to make one's bed; **aller/se mettre au ~** to go to/get into bed; **lit de camp** campbed; **lit d'enfant** (BRIT), crib (US)

**literie** [litʀi] nf bedding, bedclothes pl

**litige** [litiʒ] nm dispute

**litre** [litʀ] nm litre

**littéraire** [liteʀɛʀ] adj literary ▷ nm/f arts student; **elle est très ~** she's very literary

**littéral, e, -aux** [liteʀal, o] adj literal

**littérature** [liteʀatyʀ] nf literature

**littoral, -aux** [litɔʀal, o] nm coast

**livide** [livid] adj livid, pallid

**livraison** [livʀɛzɔ̃] nf delivery

**livre** [livʀ] nm book ▷ nf (monnaie) pound; (poids) half a kilo, ≈ pound; **livre de poche** paperback

**livré, e** [livʀe] adj: **~ à soi-même** left to o.s. ou one's own devices

**livrer** [livʀe] vt (Comm) to deliver; (otage, coupable) to hand over; (secret, information) to give away; **se livrer à** (se confier) to confide in; (se rendre, s'abandonner) to give o.s. up to; (faire: pratiques, actes) to indulge in; (enquête) to carry out

**livret** [livʀɛ] nm booklet; (d'opéra) libretto; **livret de caisse d'épargne** (savings) bank-book; **livret de famille** (official) family record book; **livret scolaire** (school) report book

**livreur, -euse** [livʀœʀ, øz] nm/f delivery boy ou man/girl ou woman

**local, e, -aux** [lɔkal] adj local ▷ nm (salle) premises pl; voir aussi **locaux**; **localité** nf locality

**locataire** [lɔkatɛʀ] nm/f tenant; (de chambre) lodger

**location** [lɔkasjɔ̃] nf (par le locataire, le loueur) renting; (par le propriétaire) renting out, letting; (Théâtre) booking office; **"~ de voitures"** "car rental"; **habiter en ~** to live in rented accommodation; **prendre une ~ (pour les vacances)** to rent a house etc (for the holidays)

> Attention à ne pas traduire **location** par le mot anglais **location**.

**locomotive** [lɔkɔmɔtiv] nf locomotive, engine

**locution** [lɔkysjɔ̃] nf phrase

**loge** [lɔʒ] nf (Théâtre: d'artiste) dressing room; (: de spectateurs) box; (de concierge, franc-maçon) lodge

**logement** [lɔʒmɑ̃] nm accommodation no pl (BRIT), accommodations pl (US); (appartement) flat (BRIT), apartment (US); (Pol, Admin): **le ~** housing no pl

**loger** [lɔʒe] vt to accommodate ▷ vi to live; **être logé, nourri** to have board and lodging; **se loger** vr: **trouver à se ~** to find somewhere to live; **se ~ dans** (suj: balle, flèche) to lodge itself in;

**logeur, -euse** *nm/f* landlord(-lady)

**logiciel** [lɔʒisjɛl] *nm* software

**logique** [lɔʒik] *adj* logical ▷ *nf* logic

**logo** [lɔgo] *nm* logo

**loi** [lwa] *nf* law; **faire la ~** to lay down the law

**loin** [lwɛ̃] *adv* far; (*dans le temps: futur*) a long way off; (: *passé*) a long time ago; **plus ~** further; **~ de** far from; **c'est ~ d'ici?** is it far from here?; **au ~** far off; **de ~** from a distance; (*fig: de beaucoup*) by far

**lointain, e** [lwɛ̃tɛ̃, ɛn] *adj* faraway, distant; (*dans le futur, passé*) distant; (*cause, parent*) remote, distant ▷ *nm*: **dans le ~** in the distance

**loir** [lwaʀ] *nm* dormouse

**Loire** [lwaʀ] *nf*: **la ~** the (River) Loire

**loisir** [lwaziʀ] *nm*: **heures de ~** spare time; **loisirs** *nmpl* (*temps libre*) leisure *sg*; (*activités*) leisure activities; **avoir le ~ de faire** to have the time *ou* opportunity to do; **à ~** at leisure

**londonien, ne** [lɔ̃dɔnjɛ̃, jɛn] *adj* London *cpd*, of London ▷ *nm/f*: **L~, ne** Londoner

**Londres** [lɔ̃dʀ] *n* London

**long, longue** [lɔ̃, lɔ̃g] *adj* long ▷ *adv*: **en savoir ~** to know a great deal ▷ *nm*: **de 3 m de ~** 3 m long, 3 m in length; **ne pas faire ~ feu** not to last long; **(tout) le ~ de** (all) along; **tout au ~ de** (*année, vie*) throughout; **de ~ en large** (*marcher*) to and fro, up and down; *voir aussi* **longue**

**longer** [lɔ̃ʒe] *vt* to go (*ou* walk *ou* drive) along(side); (*suj: mur, route*) to border

**longiligne** [lɔ̃ʒiliɲ] *adj* long-limbed

**longitude** [lɔ̃ʒityd] *nf* longitude

**longtemps** [lɔ̃tɑ̃] *adv* (for) a long time, (for) long; **avant ~** before long; **pour** *ou* **pendant ~** for a long time; **mettre ~ à faire** to take a long time to do; **il en a pour ~?** will he be long?

**longue** [lɔ̃g] *adj voir* **long** ▷ *nf*: **à la ~** in the end; **longuement** *adv* (*longtemps*) for a long time; (*en détail*) at length

**longueur** [lɔ̃gœʀ] *nf* length;

**longueurs** *nfpl* (*fig: d'un film etc*) tedious parts; **en ~** lengthwise; **tirer en ~** to drag on; **à ~ de journée** all day long

**loquet** [lɔkɛ] *nm* latch

**lorgner** [lɔʀɲe] *vt* to eye; (*fig*) to have one's eye on

**lors** [lɔʀ]: **~ de** *prép* at the time of; during

**lorsque** [lɔʀsk] *conj* when, as

**losange** [lɔzɑ̃ʒ] *nm* diamond

**lot** [lo] *nm* (*part*) share; (*de loterie*) prize; (*fig: destin*) fate, lot; (*Comm, Inform*) batch; **le gros ~** the jackpot

**loterie** [lɔtʀi] *nf* lottery

**lotion** [losjɔ̃] *nf* lotion; **lotion après rasage** aftershave (lotion)

**lotissement** [lɔtismɑ̃] *nm* housing development; (*parcelle*) plot, lot

**loto** [lɔto] *nm* lotto

**lotte** [lɔt] *nf* monkfish

**louanges** [lwɑ̃ʒ] *nfpl* praise *sg*

**loubard** [lubaʀ] (*fam*) *nm* lout

**louche** [luʃ] *adj* shady, fishy, dubious ▷ *nf* ladle; **loucher** *vi* to squint

**louer** [lwe] *vt* (*maison: suj: propriétaire*) to let, rent (out); (: *locataire*) to rent; (*voiture etc: entreprise*) to hire out (BRIT), rent (out); (: *locataire*) to hire, rent; (*réserver*) to book; (*faire l'éloge de*) to praise; **"à ~"** "to let" (BRIT), "for rent" (US); **je voudrais ~ une voiture** I'd like to hire (BRIT) *ou* rent (US) a car

**loup** [lu] *nm* wolf; **jeune ~** young go-getter

**loupe** [lup] *nf* magnifying glass; **à la ~** in minute detail

**louper** [lupe] (*fam*) *vt* (*manquer*) to miss; (*examen*) to flunk

**lourd, e** [luʀ, luʀd] *adj, adv* heavy; **c'est trop ~** it's too heavy; **~ de** (*conséquences, menaces*) charged with; **il fait ~** the weather is close, it's sultry; **lourdaud, e** (*péj*) *adj* clumsy; **lourdement** *adv* heavily

**loutre** [lutʀ] *nf* otter

**louveteau, x** [luv(ə)to] *nm* wolf-cub; (*scout*) cub (scout)

**louvoyer** [luvwaje] *vi* (*fig*) to hedge,

evade the issue

**loyal, e, -aux** [lwajal, o] *adj (fidèle)*
loyal, faithful; *(fair-play)* fair; **loyauté** *nf*
loyalty, faithfulness; fairness

**loyer** [lwaje] *nm* rent

**lu, e** [ly] *pp de* lire

**lubie** [lybi] *nf* whim, craze

**lubrifiant** [lybrifjɑ̃] *nm* lubricant

**lubrifier** [lybrifje] *vt* to lubricate

**lubrique** [lybrik] *adj* lecherous

**lucarne** [lykarn] *nf* skylight

**lucide** [lysid] *adj* lucid; *(accidenté)*
conscious

**lucratif, -ive** [lykratif, iv] *adj*
lucrative, profitable; **à but non ~** non
profit-making

**lueur** [lɥœr] *nf (pâle)* (faint) light;
*(chatoyante)* glimmer *no pl*; *(fig)*
glimmer; gleam

**luge** [lyʒ] *nf* sledge (BRIT), sled (US)

**lugubre** [lygybr] *adj* gloomy, dismal

 **MOT-CLÉ**

**lui** [lɥi] *pron* **1** *(objet indirect: mâle)* (to)
him; (: *femelle*) (to) her; (: *chose, animal*)
(to) it; **je lui ai parlé** I have spoken
to him *(ou* to her); **il lui a offert un
cadeau** he gave him *(ou* her) a present
**2** *(après préposition, comparatif: personne)*
him; (: *chose, animal*) it; **elle est
contente de lui** she is pleased with
him; **je la connais mieux que lui** I
know her better than he does; I know
her better than him; **ce livre est à lui**
this book is his, this is his book; **c'est à
lui de jouer** it's his turn *ou* go
**3** *(sujet, forme emphatique)* he; **lui, il est
à Paris** HE is in Paris; **c'est lui qui l'a
fait** HE did it
**4** *(objet, forme emphatique)* him; **c'est lui
que j'attends** I'm waiting for HIM
**5: lui-même** himself; itself

**luire** [lɥir] *vi* to shine; *(en rougeoyant)*
to glow

**lumière** [lymjɛr] *nf* light; **mettre en
~** *(fig)* to highlight; **lumière du jour**
daylight

**luminaire** [lyminɛr] *nm* lamp, light

**lumineux, -euse** [lyminø, øz] *adj*
luminous; *(éclairé)* illuminated; *(ciel,
couleur)* bright; *(rayon)* of light, light *cpd*;
*(fig: regard)* radiant

**lunatique** [lynatik] *adj* whimsical,
temperamental

**lundi** [lœ̃di] *nm* Monday; **on est ~** it's
Monday; **le(s) ~(s)** on Mondays; **"à ~"**
"see you on Monday"; **lundi de Pâques**
Easter Monday

**lune** [lyn] *nf* moon; **lune de miel**
honeymoon

**lunette** [lynɛt] *nf*: **~s** *nfpl* glasses,
spectacles; *(protectrices)* goggles;
**lunette arrière** *(Auto)* rear window;
**lunettes de soleil** sunglasses;
**lunettes noires** dark glasses

**lustre** [lystr] *nm (de plafond)*
chandelier; *(fig: éclat)* lustre; **lustrer**
*vt* to shine

**luth** [lyt] *nm* lute

**lutin** [lytɛ̃] *nm* imp, goblin

**lutte** [lyt] *nf (conflit)* struggle; *(sport)*
wrestling; **lutter** *vi* to fight, struggle

**luxe** [lyks] *nm* luxury; **de ~** luxury *cpd*

**Luxembourg** [lyksɑ̃bur] *nm*: **le ~**
Luxembourg

**luxer** [lykse] *vt*: **se ~ l'épaule** to
dislocate one's shoulder

**luxueux, -euse** [lyksɥø, øz] *adj*
luxurious

**lycée** [lise] *nm* ≈ secondary school;
**lycéen, ne** *nm/f* secondary school
pupil

**Lyon** [ljɔ̃] *n* Lyons

**lyophilisé, e** [ljɔfilize] *adj (café)*
freeze-dried

**lyrique** [lirik] *adj* lyrical; *(Opéra)* lyric;
**artiste ~** opera singer

**lys** [lis] *nm* lily

**M** *abr* = **Monsieur**

**m'** [m] *pron voir* **me**

**ma** [ma] *adj voir* **mon**

**macaron** [makaʀɔ̃] *nm* (*gâteau*) macaroon; (*insigne*) (round) badge

**macaronis** [makaʀɔni] *nmpl* macaroni *sg*; **~ au fromage** *ou* **en gratin** macaroni cheese (*BRIT*), macaroni and cheese (*US*)

**macédoine** [masedwan] *nf:* **~ de fruits** fruit salad; **~ de légumes** mixed vegetables; **la M~** Macedonia

**macérer** [maseʀe] *vi, vt* to macerate; (*dans du vinaigre*) to pickle

**mâcher** [maʃe] *vt* to chew; **ne pas ~ ses mots** not to mince one's words

**machin** [maʃɛ̃] (*fam*) *nm* thing (umajig); (*personne*): **M~(e)** *nm(f)* what's-his(*ou* her)-name

**machinal, e, -aux** [maʃinal, o] *adj* mechanical, automatic

**machination** [maʃinasjɔ̃] *nf* frame-up

**machine** [maʃin] *nf* machine; (*locomotive*) engine; **machine à laver/ coudre** washing/sewing machine; **machine à sous** fruit machine

**mâchoire** [maʃwaʀ] *nf* jaw

**mâchonner** [maʃɔne] *vt* to chew (at)

**maçon** [masɔ̃] *nm* builder; (*poseur de briques*) bricklayer; **maçonnerie** *nf* (*murs*) brickwork; (*pierres*) masonry, stonework

**Madagascar** [madagaskaʀ] *nf* Madagascar

**Madame** [madam] (*pl* **Mesdames**) *nf:* **~ Dupont** Mrs Dupont; **occupez-vous de ~/Monsieur/Mademoiselle** please serve this lady/gentleman/(young) lady; **bonjour ~/Monsieur/Mademoiselle** good morning; (*ton déférent*) good morning Madam/Sir/Madam; (*le nom est connu*) good morning Mrs/Mr/Miss X; **~/Monsieur/Mademoiselle!** (*pour appeler*) Madam/Sir/Miss!; **~/Monsieur/Mademoiselle** (*sur lettre*) Dear Madam/Sir/Madam; **chère ~/ cher Monsieur/chère Mademoiselle** Dear Mrs/Mr/Miss X; **Mesdames** Ladies; **mesdames, mesdemoiselles, messieurs** ladies and gentlemen

**madeleine** [madlɛn] *nf* madeleine, small sponge cake

**Mademoiselle** [madmwazɛl] (*pl* **Mesdemoiselles**) *nf* Miss; *voir aussi* **Madame**

**madère** [madɛʀ] *nm* Madeira (wine)

**Madrid** [madʀid] *n* Madrid

**magasin** [magazɛ̃] *nm* (*boutique*) shop; (*entrepôt*) warehouse; **en ~** (*Comm*) in stock

● **MAGASINS**

● French shops are usually open from
● 9am to noon and from 2pm to 7pm.
● Most shops are closed on Sunday
● and some do not open on Monday. In
● bigger towns and shopping centres,
● most shops are open throughout
● the day.

**magazine** [magazin] *nm* magazine

**Maghreb** [magʀɛb] nm: **le ~** North Africa; **maghrébin, e** adj North African ▷ nm/f: **Maghrébin, e** North African

**magicien, ne** [maʒisjɛ̃, jɛn] nm/f magician

**magie** [maʒi] nf magic; **magique** adj magic; (enchanteur) magical

**magistral, e, -aux** [maʒistʀal, o] adj (œuvre, adresse) masterly; (ton) authoritative; **cours ~** lecture

**magistrat** [maʒistʀa] nm magistrate

**magnétique** [maɲetik] adj magnetic

**magnétophone** [maɲetɔfɔn] nm tape recorder; **magnétophone à cassettes** cassette recorder

**magnétoscope** [maɲetɔskɔp] nm video-tape recorder

**magnifique** [maɲifik] adj magnificent

**magret** [magʀɛ] nm: **~ de canard** duck steaklet

**mai** [mɛ] nm May

● **MAI**
●
● **Le premier mai** is a public holiday
● in France and commemorates the
● trades union demonstrations in the
● United States in 1886 when workers
● demanded the right to an eight-hour
● working day. Sprigs of lily of the
● valley are traditionally exchanged.
● **Le 8 mai** is also a public holiday and
● commemorates the surrender of
● the German army to Eisenhower
● on 7 May, 1945. It is marked by
● parades of ex-servicemen and ex-
● servicewomen in most towns.

**maigre** [mɛgʀ] adj (very) thin, skinny; (viande) lean; (fromage) low-fat; (végétation) thin, sparse; (fig) poor, meagre, skimpy; **jours ~s** days of abstinence, fish days; **maigreur** nf thinness; **maigrir** vi to get thinner, lose weight; **maigrir de 2 kilos** to lose 2 kilos

**mail** [mɛl] nm e-mail

**maille** [maj] nf stitch; **maille à l'endroit/l'envers** plain/purl stitch

**maillet** [majɛ] nm mallet

**maillon** [majɔ̃] nm link

**maillot** [majo] nm (aussi: **~ de corps**) vest; (de sportif) jersey; **maillot de bain** swimming ou bathing (BRIT) costume, swimsuit; (d'homme) (swimming ou bathing (BRIT)) trunks pl

**main** [mɛ̃] nf hand; **à la ~** (tenir, avoir) in one's hand; (faire, tricoter etc) by hand; **se donner la ~** to hold hands; **donner** ou **tendre la ~ à qn** to hold out one's hand to sb; **se serrer la ~** to shake hands; **serrer la ~ à qn** to shake hands with sb; **sous la ~** to ou at hand; **haut les ~s!** hands up!; **attaque à ~ armée** armed attack; **à remettre en ~s propres** to be delivered personally; **mettre la dernière ~ à** to put the finishing touches to; **se faire/perdre la ~** to get one's hand in/lose one's touch; **avoir qch bien en ~** to have (got) the hang of sth; **main-d'œuvre** nf manpower, labour; **mainmise** nf (fig): **mainmise sur** complete hold on; **mains libres** adj inv (téléphone, kit) hands-free

**maint, e** [mɛ̃, mɛ̃t] adj many a; **~s** many; **à ~es reprises** time and (time) again

**maintenant** [mɛ̃t(ə)nɑ̃] adv now; (actuellement) nowadays

**maintenir** [mɛ̃t(ə)niʀ] vt (retenir, soutenir) to support; (contenir: foule etc) to hold back; (conserver, affirmer) to maintain; **se maintenir** vi (prix) to keep steady; (amélioration) to persist

**maintien** [mɛ̃tjɛ̃] nm (sauvegarde) maintenance; (attitude) bearing

**maire** [mɛʀ] nm mayor; **mairie** nf (bâtiment) town hall; (administration) town council

**mais** [mɛ] conj but; **~ non!** of course not!; **~ enfin** but after all; (indignation) look here!

**maïs** [mais] nm maize (BRIT), corn (US)

**maison** [mɛzɔ̃] nf house; (chez-soi)

home; (*Comm*) firm ▷ *adj inv* (*Culin*) home-made; (*fig*) in-house, own; **à la ~** at home; (*direction*) home; **maison de repos** convalescent home; **maison de retraite** old people's home; **maison close** *ou* **de passe** brothel; **maison de santé** mental home; **maison des jeunes** ≈ youth club; **maison mère** parent company

**maître, -esse** [mɛtʀ, mɛtʀɛs] *nm/f* master (mistress); (*Scol*) teacher, schoolmaster(-mistress) ▷ *nm* (*peintre etc*) master; (*titre*): **M~** Maître, *term of address gen for a barrister* ▷ *adj* (*principal, essentiel*) main; **être ~ de** (*soi, situation*) to be in control of; **une ~sse femme** a managing woman; **maître chanteur** blackmailer; **maître d'école** schoolmaster; **maître d'hôtel** (*domestique*) butler; (*d'hôtel*) head waiter; **maître nageur** lifeguard; **maîtresse** *nf* (*amante*) mistress; **maîtresse (d'école)** teacher, (school)mistress; **maîtresse de maison** hostess; (*ménagère*) housewife

**maîtrise** [mɛtʀiz] *nf* (*aussi*: **~ de soi**) self-control, self-possession; (*habileté*) skill, mastery; (*suprématie*) mastery, command; (*diplôme*) ≈ master's degree; **maîtriser** *vt* (*cheval, incendie*) to (bring under) control; (*sujet*) to master; (*émotion*) to control, master; **se maîtriser** to control o.s.

**majestueux, -euse** [maʒɛstɥø, øz] *adj* majestic

**majeur, e** [maʒœʀ] *adj* (*important*) major; (*Jur*) of age ▷ *nm* (*doigt*) middle finger; **en ~e partie** for the most part; **la ~e partie de** most of

**majorer** [maʒɔʀe] *vt* to increase

**majoritaire** [maʒɔʀitɛʀ] *adj* majority *cpd*

**majorité** [maʒɔʀite] *nf* (*gén*) majority; (*parti*) party in power; **en ~** mainly; **avoir la ~** to have the majority

**majuscule** [maʒyskyl] *adj, nf*: **(lettre) ~** capital (letter)

**mal** [mal, mo] (*pl* **maux**) *nm* (*opposé*

au bien*) evil; (*tort, dommage*) harm; (*douleur physique*) pain, ache; (*maladie*) illness, sickness *no pl* ▷ *adv* badly ▷ *adj* bad, wrong; **être ~** to be uncomfortable; **être ~ avec qn** to be on bad terms with sb; **il a ~ compris** he misunderstood; **se sentir** *ou* **se trouver ~** to feel ill *ou* unwell; **dire/penser du ~ de** to speak/think ill of; **ne voir aucun ~ à** to see no harm in, see nothing wrong in; **faire ~ à qn** to hurt sb; **se faire ~** to hurt o.s.; **avoir du ~ à faire qch** to have trouble doing sth; **se donner du ~ pour faire qch** to go to a lot of trouble to do sth; **ça fait ~** it hurts; **j'ai ~ au dos** my back hurts; **avoir ~ à la tête/à la gorge/aux dents** to have a headache/a sore throat/toothache; **avoir le ~ du pays** to be homesick; *voir aussi* **cœur**; **maux**; **mal de mer** seasickness; **mal en point** in a bad state

**malade** [malad] *adj* ill, sick; (*poitrine, jambe*) bad; (*plante*) diseased ▷ *nm/f* invalid, sick person; (*à l'hôpital etc*) patient; **tomber ~** to fall ill; **être ~ du cœur** to have heart trouble *ou* a bad heart; **malade mental** mentally ill person; **maladie** *nf* (*spécifique*) disease, illness; (*mauvaise santé*) illness, sickness; **maladif, -ive** *adj* sickly; (*curiosité, besoin*) pathological

**maladresse** [maladʀɛs] *nf* clumsiness *no pl*; (*gaffe*) blunder

**maladroit, e** [maladʀwa, wat] *adj* clumsy

**malaise** [malɛz] *nm* (*Méd*) feeling of faintness; (*fig*) uneasiness, malaise; **avoir un ~** to feel faint

**Malaisie** [malɛzi] *nf*: **la ~** Malaysia

**malaria** [malaʀja] *nf* malaria

**malaxer** [malakse] *vt* (*pétrir*) to knead; (*mélanger*) to mix

**malbouffe** [malbuf] (*fam*) *nf*: **la ~** junk food

**malchance** [malʃɑ̃s] *nf* misfortune, ill luck *no pl*; **par ~** unfortunately; **malchanceux, -euse** *adj* unlucky

**mâle** [mɑl] adj (aussi Élec, Tech) male; (viril: voix, traits) manly ▷ nm male

**malédiction** [malediksjɔ̃] nf curse

**mal...: malentendant, e** nm/f: **les malentendants** the hard of hearing; **malentendu** nm misunderstanding; **il y a eu un malentendu** there's been a misunderstanding; **malfaçon** nf fault; **malfaisant, e** adj evil, harmful; **malfaiteur** nm lawbreaker, criminal; (voleur) burglar, thief; **malfamé, e** adj disreputable

**malgache** [malgaʃ] adj Madagascan, Malagasy ▷ nm/f: **M~** Madagascan, Malagasy ▷ nm (Ling) Malagasy

**malgré** [malgʀe] prép in spite of, despite; **~ tout** all the same

**malheur** [malœʀ] nm (situation) adversity, misfortune; (événement) misfortune; (: très grave) disaster, tragedy; **faire un ~** to be a smash hit; **malheureusement** adv unfortunately; **malheureux, -euse** adj (triste) unhappy, miserable; (infortuné, regrettable) unfortunate; (malchanceux) unlucky; (insignifiant) wretched ▷ nm/f poor soul

**malhonnête** [malɔnɛt] adj dishonest; **malhonnêteté** nf dishonesty

**malice** [malis] nf mischievousness; (méchanceté): **par ~** out of malice ou spite; **sans ~** guileless; **malicieux, -euse** adj mischievous

⬛ Attention à ne pas traduire malicieux par malicious.

**malin, -igne** [malɛ̃, maliɲ] adj (futé: f gén: aussi: **maline**) smart, shrewd; (Méd) malignant

**malingre** [malɛ̃gʀ] adj puny

**malle** [mal] nf trunk; **mallette** nf (small) suitcase; (porte-documents) attaché case

**malmener** [malməne] vt to manhandle; (fig) to give a rough handling to

**malodorant, e** [malɔdɔʀɑ̃, ɑ̃t] adj foul- ou ill-smelling

**malpoli, e** [malpɔli] adj impolite

**malsain, e** [malsɛ̃, ɛn] adj unhealthy

**malt** [malt] nm malt

**Malte** [malt] nf Malta

**maltraiter** [maltʀɛte] vt to manhandle, ill-treat

**malveillance** [malvɛjɑ̃s] nf (animosité) ill will; (intention de nuire) malevolence

**malversation** [malvɛʀsasjɔ̃] nf embezzlement

**maman** [mamɑ̃] nf mum(my), mother

**mamelle** [mamɛl] nf teat

**mamelon** [mam(ə)lɔ̃] nm (Anat) nipple

**mamie** [mami] (fam) nf granny

**mammifère** [mamifɛʀ] nm mammal

**mammouth** [mamut] nm mammoth

**manche** [mɑ̃ʃ] nf (de vêtement) sleeve; (d'un jeu, tournoi) round; (Géo): **la M~** the Channel ▷ nm (d'outil, casserole) handle; (de pelle, pioche etc) shaft; **à ~s courtes/longues** short-/long-sleeved; **manche à balai** broomstick; (Inform, Aviat) joystick m inv

**manchette** [mɑ̃ʃɛt] nf (de chemise) cuff; (coup) forearm blow; (titre) headline

**manchot** [mɑ̃ʃo] nm one-armed man; armless man; (Zool) penguin

**mandarine** [mɑ̃daʀin] nf mandarin (orange), tangerine

**mandat** [mɑ̃da] nm (postal) postal ou money order; (d'un député etc) mandate; (procuration) power of attorney, proxy; (Police) warrant; **mandat d'arrêt** warrant for arrest; **mandat de perquisition** search warrant; **mandataire** nm/f (représentant) representative; (Jur) proxy

**manège** [manɛʒ] nm riding school; (à la foire) roundabout, merry-go-round; (fig) game, ploy

**manette** [manɛt] nf lever, tap; **manette de jeu** joystick

**mangeable** [mɑ̃ʒabl] adj edible, eatable

**mangeoire** [mɑ̃ʒwaʀ] nf trough, manger

**manger** [mɑ̃ʒe] vt to eat; (ronger: suj: rouille etc) to eat into ou away ▷ vi to eat; **donner à ~** (enfant) to feed; **est-**

**ce qu'on peut ~ quelque chose?** can we have something to eat?

**mangue** [mɑ̃g] *nf* mango

**maniable** [manjabl] *adj* (*outil*) handy; (*voiture, voilier*) easy to handle

**maniaque** [manjak] *adj* finicky, fussy ▷ *nm/f* (*méticuleux*) fusspot; (*fou*) maniac

**manie** [mani] *nf* (*tic*) odd habit; (*obsession*) mania; **avoir la ~ de** to be obsessive about

**manier** [manje] *vt* to handle

**manière** [manjɛʀ] *nf* (*façon*) way, manner; **manières** *nfpl* (*attitude*) manners; (*chichis*) fuss *sg*; **de ~ à** so as to; **de cette ~** in this way *ou* manner; **d'une certaine ~** in a way; **de toute ~** in any case; **d'une ~ générale** generally speaking, as a general rule

**maniéré, e** [manjeʀe] *adj* affected

**manifestant, e** [manifɛstɑ̃, ɑ̃t] *nm/f* demonstrator

**manifestation** [manifɛstasjɔ̃] *nf* (*de joie, mécontentement*) expression, demonstration; (*symptôme*) outward sign; (*culturelle etc*) event; (*Pol*) demonstration

**manifeste** [manifɛst] *adj* obvious, evident ▷ *nm* manifesto; **manifester** *vt* (*volonté, intentions*) to show, indicate; (*joie, peur*) to express, show ▷ *vi* to demonstrate; **se manifester** *vi* (*émotion*) to show *ou* express itself; (*difficultés*) to arise; (*symptômes*) to appear

**manigancer** [manigɑ̃se] *vt* to plot

**manipulation** [manipylasjɔ̃] *nf* handling; (*Pol, génétique*) manipulation

**manipuler** [manipyle] *vt* to handle; (*fig*) to manipulate

**manivelle** [manivɛl] *nf* crank

**mannequin** [mankɛ̃] *nm* (*Couture*) dummy; (*Mode*) model

**manœuvre** [manœvʀ] *nf* (*gén*) manoeuvre (*BRIT*), maneuver (*US*) ▷ *nm* labourer; **manœuvrer** *vt* to manoeuvre (*BRIT*), maneuver (*US*); (*levier, machine*) to operate ▷ *vi* to manoeuvre

**manoir** [manwaʀ] *nm* manor *ou* country house

**manque** [mɑ̃k] *nm* (*insuffisance*): **~ de** lack of; (*vide*) emptiness, gap; (*Méd*) withdrawal; **être en état de ~** to suffer withdrawal symptoms

**manqué, e** [mɑ̃ke] *adj* failed; **garçon ~** tomboy

**manquer** [mɑ̃ke] *vi* (*faire défaut*) to be lacking; (*être absent*) to be missing; (*échouer*) to fail ▷ *vt* to miss ▷ *vb impers*: **il (nous) manque encore 10 euros** we are still 10 euros short; **il manque des pages (au livre)** there are some pages missing (from the book); **il/cela me manque** I miss him/this; **~ à** (*règles etc*) to be in breach of, fail to observe; **~ de** to lack; **je ne ~ai pas de le lui dire** I'll be sure to tell him; **il a manqué (de) se tuer** he very nearly got killed

**mansarde** [mɑ̃saʀd] *nf* attic; **mansardé, e** *adj*: **chambre mansardée** attic room

**manteau, x** [mɑ̃to] *nm* coat

**manucure** [manykyʀ] *nf* manicurist

**manuel, le** [manɥɛl] *adj* manual ▷ *nm* (*ouvrage*) manual, handbook

**manufacture** [manyfaktyʀ] *nf* factory; **manufacturé, e** *adj* manufactured

**manuscrit, e** [manyskʀi, it] *adj* handwritten ▷ *nm* manuscript

**manutention** [manytɑ̃sjɔ̃] *nf* (*Comm*) handling

**mappemonde** [mapmɔ̃d] *nf* (*plane*) map of the world; (*sphère*) globe

**maquereau, x** [makʀo] *nm* (*Zool*) mackerel *inv*; (*fam*) pimp

**maquette** [makɛt] *nf* (*à échelle réduite*) (scale) model; (*d'une page illustrée*) paste-up

**maquillage** [makijaʒ] *nm* making up; (*crème etc*) make-up

**maquiller** [makije] *vt* (*personne, visage*) to make up; (*truquer: passeport, statistique*) to fake; (*: voiture volée*) to do over (*respray etc*); **se maquiller** *vi* to make up (one's face)

**maquis** [maki] nm (Géo) scrub; (Mil) maquis, underground fighting no pl

**maraîcher, -ère** [mareʃe, ɛʀ] adj: **cultures maraîchères** market gardening sg ▷ nm/f market gardener

**marais** [maʀɛ] nm marsh, swamp

**marasme** [maʀasm] nm stagnation, slump

**marathon** [maʀatɔ̃] nm marathon

**marbre** [maʀbʀ] nm marble

**marc** [maʀ] nm (de raisin, pommes) marc

**marchand, e** [maʀʃɑ̃, ɑ̃d] nm/f shopkeeper, tradesman(-woman); (au marché) stallholder; (de vins, charbon) merchant ▷ adj: **prix/valeur ~(e)** market price/value; **marchand de fruits** fruiterer (BRIT), fruit seller (US); **marchand de journaux** newsagent; **marchand de légumes** greengrocer (BRIT), produce dealer (US); **marchand de poissons** fishmonger (BRIT), fish seller (US); **marchander** vi to bargain, haggle; **marchandise** nf goods pl, merchandise no pl

**marche** [maʀʃ] nf (d'escalier) step; (activité) walking; (promenade, trajet, allure) walk; (démarche) walk, gait; (Mil etc, Mus) march; (fonctionnement) running; (des événements) course; **dans le sens de la ~** (Rail) facing the engine; **en ~** (monter etc) while the vehicle is moving ou in motion; **mettre en ~** to start; **se mettre en ~** (personne) to get moving; (machine) to start; **être en état de ~** to be in working order; **marche à suivre** (correct) procedure; **marche arrière** reverse (gear); **faire marche arrière** to reverse; (fig) to backtrack, back-pedal

**marché** [maʀʃe] nm market; (transaction) bargain, deal; **faire du ~ noir** to buy and sell on the black market; **marché aux puces** flea market

**marcher** [maʀʃe] vi to walk; (Mil) to march; (aller: voiture, train, affaires) to go; (prospérer) to go well; (fonctionner) to

work, run; (fam: consentir) to go along, agree; (: croire naïvement) to be taken in; **faire ~ qn** (taquiner) to pull sb's leg; (tromper) to lead sb up the garden path; **comment est-ce que ça marche?** how does this work?; **marcheur, -euse** nm/f walker

**mardi** [maʀdi] nm Tuesday; **Mardi gras** Shrove Tuesday

**mare** [maʀ] nf pond; (flaque) pool

**marécage** [maʀekaʒ] nm marsh, swamp; **marécageux, -euse** adj marshy

**maréchal, -aux** [maʀeʃal, o] nm marshal

**marée** [maʀe] nf tide; (poissons) fresh (sea) fish; **marée haute/basse** high/low tide; **marée noire** oil slick

**marelle** [maʀɛl] nf: **(jouer à) la ~** (to play) hopscotch

**margarine** [maʀgaʀin] nf margarine

**marge** [maʀʒ] nf margin; **en ~ de** (fig) on the fringe of; **marge bénéficiaire** profit margin

**marginal, e, -aux** [maʀʒinal, o] nm/f (original) eccentric; (déshérité) dropout

**marguerite** [maʀgəʀit] nf marguerite, (oxeye) daisy; (d'imprimante) daisy-wheel

**mari** [maʀi] nm husband

**mariage** [maʀjaʒ] nm marriage; (noce) wedding; **mariage civil/religieux** registry office (BRIT) ou civil wedding/church wedding

**marié, e** [maʀje] adj married ▷ nm (bride)groom; **les ~s** the bride and groom; **les (jeunes) ~s** the newly-weds

**marier** [maʀje] vt to marry; (fig) to blend; **se ~ (avec)** to marry, get married to

**marin, e** [maʀɛ̃, in] adj sea cpd, marine ▷ nm sailor

**marine** [maʀin] adj voir **marin** ▷ adj inv navy (blue) ▷ nm (Mil) marine ▷ nf navy; **marine marchande** merchant navy

**mariner** [maʀine] vt: **faire ~** to marinade

**marionnette** [maʀjɔnɛt] nf puppet

**maritalement** [maʀitalmɑ̃] adv:
**vivre ~** to live as husband and wife

**maritime** [maʀitim] adj sea cpd,
maritime

**mark** [maʀk] nm mark

**marmelade** [maʀməlad] nf stewed
fruit, compote; **marmelade d'oranges**
marmalade

**marmite** [maʀmit] nf (cooking-)pot

**marmonner** [maʀmɔne] vt, vi to
mumble, mutter

**marmotter** [maʀmɔte] vt to mumble

**Maroc** [maʀɔk] nm: **le ~** Morocco;
**marocain, e** [maʀɔkɛ̃, ɛn] adj
Moroccan ▷ nm/f: **Marocain, e**
Moroccan

**maroquinerie** [maʀɔkinʀi] nf
(articles) fine leather goods pl; (boutique)
shop selling fine leather goods

**marquant, e** [maʀkɑ̃, ɑ̃t] adj
outstanding

**marque** [maʀk] nf mark; (Comm: de
nourriture) brand; (: de voiture, produits
manufacturés) make; (de disques) label;
**de ~** (produits) high-class; (visiteur
etc) distinguished, well-known; **une
grande ~ de vin** a well-known brand of
wine; **marque de fabrique** trademark;
**marque déposée** registered
trademark

**marquer** [maʀke] vt to mark; (inscrire)
to write down; (bétail) to brand; (Sport:
but etc) to score; (: joueur) to mark;
(accentuer: taille etc) to emphasize;
(manifester: refus, intérêt) to show
▷ vi (événement) to stand out, be
outstanding; (Sport) to score; **~ les
points** to keep the score

**marqueterie** [maʀkɛtʀi] nf inlaid
work, marquetry

**marquis** [maʀki] nm marquis,
marquess

**marraine** [maʀɛn] nf godmother

**marrant, e** [maʀɑ̃, ɑ̃t] (fam) adj funny

**marre** [maʀ] (fam) adv: **en avoir ~ de** to
be fed up with

**marrer** [maʀe]: **se ~** (fam) vi to have a

(good) laugh

**marron** [maʀɔ̃] nm (fruit) chestnut
▷ adj inv brown; **marrons glacés**
candied chestnuts; **marronnier** nm
chestnut (tree)

**mars** [maʀs] nm March

**Marseille** [maʀsɛj] n Marseilles

**marteau, x** [maʀto] nm hammer; **être
~** (fam) to be nuts; **marteau-piqueur**
nm pneumatic drill

**marteler** [maʀtəle] vt to hammer

**martien, ne** [maʀsjɛ̃, jɛn] adj
Martian, of ou from Mars

**martyr, e** [maʀtiʀ] nm/f martyr ▷ adj:
**enfants ~s** battered children; **martyre**
nm martyrdom; (fig: sens affaibli) agony,
torture; **martyriser** vt (Rel) to martyr;
(fig) to bully; (enfant) to batter, beat

**marxiste** [maʀksist] adj, nm/f Marxist

**mascara** [maskaʀa] nm mascara

**masculin, e** [maskylɛ̃, in] adj
masculine; (sexe, population) male;
(équipe, vêtements) men's; (viril) manly
▷ nm masculine

**masochiste** [mazɔʃist] adj
masochistic

**masque** [mask] nm mask; **masque de
beauté** face pack ou mask; **masque
de plongée** diving mask; **masquer** vt
(cacher: paysage, porte) to hide, conceal;
(dissimuler: vérité, projet) to mask,
obscure

**massacre** [masakʀ] nm massacre,
slaughter; **massacrer** vt to massacre,
slaughter; (fam: texte etc) to murder

**massage** [masaʒ] nm massage

**masse** [mas] nf mass; (Élec) earth;
(maillet) sledgehammer; (péj): **la ~** the
masses pl; **une ~ de**, **des ~s de** (fam) masses ou
loads of; **en ~** adv (acheter) in bulk;
(en foule) en masse ▷ adj (exécutions,
production) mass cpd

**masser** [mase] vt (assembler: gens) to
gather; (pétrir) to massage; **se masser**
vi (foule) to gather; **masseur, -euse**
nm/f masseur(-euse)

**massif, -ive** [masif, iv] adj (porte)
solid, massive; (visage) heavy, large;

(*bois, or*) solid; (*dose*) massive; (*déportations etc*) mass cpd ▷ nm (*montagneux*) massif; (*de fleurs*) clump, bank; **le M~ Central** the Massif Central

**massue** [masy] nf club, bludgeon

**mastic** [mastik] nm (*pour vitres*) putty; (*pour fentes*) filler

**mastiquer** [mastike] vt (*aliment*) to chew, masticate

**mat, e** [mat] adj (*couleur, métal*) mat(t); (*bruit, son*) dull ▷ adj inv (*Échecs*): **être ~** to be checkmate

**mât** [mɑ] nm (*Navig*) mast; (*poteau*) pole, post

**match** [matʃ] nm match; **faire ~ nul** to draw; **match aller** first leg; **match retour** second leg, return match

**matelas** [mat(ə)la] nm mattress; **matelas pneumatique** air bed ou mattress

**matelot** [mat(ə)lo] nm sailor, seaman

**mater** [mate] vt (*personne*) to bring to heel, subdue; (*révolte*) to put down

**matérialiser** [materjalize]: **se matérialiser** vi to materialize

**matérialiste** [materjalist] adj materialistic

**matériau** [materjo] nm material; **matériaux** nmpl material(s)

**matériel, le** [materjɛl] adj material ▷ nm equipment no pl; (*de camping etc*) gear no pl; (*Inform*) hardware

**maternel, le** [matɛrnɛl] adj (*amour, geste*) motherly, maternal; (*grand-père, oncle*) maternal; **maternelle** nf (*aussi*: **école maternelle**) (state) nursery school

**maternité** [matɛrnite] nf (*établissement*) maternity hospital; (*état de mère*) motherhood, maternity; (*grossesse*) pregnancy; **congé de ~** maternity leave

**mathématique** [matematik] adj mathematical; **mathématiques** nfpl (*science*) mathematics sg

**maths** [mat] (*fam*) nfpl maths

**matière** [matjɛr] nf matter; (*Comm, Tech*) material, matter no pl; (*fig: d'un* *livre etc*) subject matter, material; (*Scol*) subject; **en ~ de** as regards; **matières grasses** fat content sg; **matières premières** raw materials

**Matignon** [matiɲɔ̃] nm: (**l'hôtel**) **~** the French Prime Minister's residence

**matin** [matɛ̃] nm, adv morning; **le ~** (*pendant le matin*) in the morning; **demain/hier/dimanche ~** tomorrow/yesterday/Sunday morning; **tous les ~s** every morning; **une heure du ~** one o'clock in the morning; **du ~ au soir** from morning till night; **de bon** ou **grand ~** early in the morning; **matinal, e, -aux** adj (*toilette, gymnastique*) morning cpd; **être matinal** (*personne*) to be up early; to be an early riser; **matinée** nf morning; (*spectacle*) matinée

**matou** [matu] nm tom(cat)

**matraque** [matrak] nf (*de policier*) truncheon (BRIT), billy (US)

**matricule** [matrikyl] nm (*Mil*) regimental number; (*Admin*) reference number

**matrimonial, e, -aux** [matrimɔnjal, jo] adj marital, marriage cpd

**maudit, e** [modi, -it] (*fam*) adj (*satané*) blasted, confounded

**maugréer** [mogree] vi to grumble

**maussade** [mosad] adj sullen; (*temps*) gloomy

**mauvais, e** [mɔvɛ, ɛz] adj bad; (*faux*): **le ~ numéro/moment** the wrong number/moment; (*méchant, malveillant*) malicious, spiteful ▷ adv: **il fait ~** the weather is bad; **sentir ~** to have a nasty smell, smell nasty; **la mer est ~e** the sea is rough; **mauvais joueur** bad loser; **mauvaise herbe** weed; **mauvaise langue** gossip, scandalmonger (BRIT); **mauvaise plaisanterie** nasty trick

**mauve** [mov] adj mauve

**maux** [mo] nmpl de **mal**

**maximum** [maksimɔm] adj, nm maximum; **au ~** (*le plus possible*) as much as one can; (*tout au plus*) at the (very) most *ou* maximum; **faire le ~** to do one's level best

**mayonnaise** [majɔnɛz] *nf* mayonnaise

**mazout** [mazut] *nm* (fuel) oil

**me, m'** [m(ə)] *pron* (*direct: téléphoner, attendre etc*) me; (*indirect: parler, donner etc*) (to) me; (*réfléchi*) myself

**mec** [mɛk] (*fam*) *nm* bloke, guy

**mécanicien, ne** [mekanisjɛ̃, jɛn] *nm/f* mechanic; (*Rail*) (train *ou* engine) driver; **pouvez-vous nous envoyer un ~?** can you send a mechanic?

**mécanique** [mekanik] *adj* mechanical ▷ *nf* (*science*) mechanics *sg*; (*mécanisme*) mechanism; **ennui ~** engine trouble *no pl*

**mécanisme** [mekanism] *nm* mechanism

**méchamment** [meʃamɑ̃] *adv* nastily, maliciously, spitefully

**méchanceté** [meʃɑ̃ste] *nf* nastiness, maliciousness; **dire des ~s à qn** to say spiteful things to sb

**méchant, e** [meʃɑ̃, ɑ̃t] *adj* nasty, malicious, spiteful; (*enfant: pas sage*) naughty; (*animal*) vicious

**mèche** [mɛʃ] *nf* (*de cheveux*) lock; (*de lampe, bougie*) wick; (*d'un explosif*) fuse; **se faire faire des ~s** to have highlights put in one's hair; **de ~ avec** in league with

**méchoui** [meʃwi] *nm* barbecue of a whole roast sheep

**méconnaissable** [mekɔnɛsabl] *adj* unrecognizable

**méconnaître** [mekɔnɛtʀ] *vt* (*ignorer*) to be unaware of; (*mésestimer*) to misjudge

**mécontent, e** [mekɔ̃tɑ̃, ɑ̃t] *adj*: **~ (de)** discontented *ou* dissatisfied *ou* displeased (with); (*contrarié*) annoyed (at); **mécontentement** *nm* dissatisfaction, discontent, displeasure; (*irritation*) annoyance

**Mecque** [mɛk] *nf*: **la ~** Mecca

**médaille** [medaj] *nf* medal

**médaillon** [medajɔ̃] *nm* (*bijou*) locket

**médecin** [med(ə)sɛ̃] *nm* doctor

**médecine** [med(ə)sin] *nf* medicine

**média** [medja] *nmpl*: **les ~** the media; **médiatique** *adj* media *cpd*

**médical, e, -aux** [medikal, o] *adj* medical; **passer une visite ~e** to have a medical

**médicament** [medikamɑ̃] *nm* medicine, drug

**médiéval, e, -aux** [medjeval, o] *adj* medieval

**médiocre** [medjɔkʀ] *adj* mediocre, poor

**méditer** [medite] *vi* to meditate

**Méditerranée** [mediteʀane] *nf*: **la (mer) ~** the Mediterranean (Sea); **méditerranéen, ne** *adj* Mediterranean ▷ *nm/f*: **Méditerranéen, ne** native *ou* inhabitant of a Mediterranean country

**méduse** [medyz] *nf* jellyfish

**méfait** [mefɛ] *nm* (*faute*) misdemeanour, wrongdoing; **méfaits** *nmpl* (*ravages*) ravages, damage *sg*

**méfiance** [mefjɑ̃s] *nf* mistrust, distrust

**méfiant, e** [mefjɑ̃, jɑ̃t] *adj* mistrustful, distrustful

**méfier** [mefje]: **se méfier** *vi* to be wary; to be careful; **se ~ de** to mistrust, distrust, be wary of

**mégaoctet** [megaɔkte] *nm* megabyte

**mégarde** [megaʀd] *nf*: **par ~** (*accidentellement*) accidentally; (*par erreur*) by mistake

**mégère** [meʒɛʀ] *nf* shrew

**mégot** [mego] (*fam*) *nm* cigarette end

**meilleur, e** [mejœʀ] *adj, adv* better ▷ *nm*: **le ~** the best; **le ~ des deux** the better of the two; **il fait ~ qu'hier** it's better weather than yesterday; **meilleur marché** (*inv*) cheaper

**mél** [mɛl] *nm* e-mail

**mélancolie** [melɑ̃kɔli] *nf* melancholy, gloom; **mélancolique** *adj* melancholic, melancholy

**mélange** [melɑ̃ʒ] *nm* mixture;

**mélanger** vt to mix; (vins, couleurs) to blend; (mettre en désordre) to mix up, muddle (up)

**mêlée** [mele] nf mêlée, scramble; (Rugby) scrum(mage)

**mêler** [mele] vt (unir) to mix; (embrouiller) to muddle (up), mix up; **se mêler** vi to mix, mingle; **se ~ à** (personne: se joindre) to join; (: s'associer à) to mix with; **se ~ de** (suj: personne) to meddle with, interfere in; **mêle-toi de ce qui te regarde** ou **de tes affaires!** mind your own business!

**mélodie** [melɔdi] nf melody; **mélodieux, -euse** adj melodious

**melon** [m(ə)lɔ̃] nm (Bot) (honeydew) melon; (aussi: **chapeau ~**) bowler (hat)

**membre** [mɑ̃bʀ] nm (Anat) limb; (personne, pays, élément) member ▷ adj member cpd

**mémé** [meme] (fam) nf granny

 **MOT-CLÉ**

**même** [mɛm] adj **1** (avant le nom) same; **en même temps** at the same time; **ils ont les mêmes goûts** they have the same ou similar tastes

**2** (après le nom: renforcement): **il est la loyauté même** he is loyalty itself; **ce sont ses paroles mêmes** they are his very words

▷ pron: **le(la) même** the same one

▷ adv **1** (renforcement): **il n'a même pas pleuré** he didn't even cry; **même lui l'a dit** even HE said it; **ici même** at this very place; **même si** even if

**2**: **à même**: **à même la bouteille** straight from the bottle; **à même la peau** next to the skin; **être à même de faire** to be in a position to do, be able to do

**3**: **de même**: **faire de même** to do likewise; **lui de même** so does (ou did ou is) he; **de même que** just as; **il en va de même pour** the same goes for

**mémoire** [memwaʀ] nf memory ▷ nm

(Scol) dissertation, paper; **mémoires** nmpl (souvenirs) memoirs; **à la ~ de** to the ou in memory of; **de ~** from memory; **mémoire morte** read-only memory, ROM; **mémoire vive** random access memory, RAM

**mémorable** [memɔʀabl] adj memorable, unforgettable

**menace** [mənas] nf threat; **menacer** vt to threaten

**ménage** [menaʒ] nm (travail) housework; (couple) (married) couple; (famille, Admin) household; **faire le ~** to do the housework; **ménagement** nm care and attention; **ménager, -ère** adj household cpd, domestic ▷ vt (traiter: personne) to handle with tact; (utiliser) to use sparingly; (prendre soin de) to take (great) care of, look after; (organiser) to arrange; **ménagère** nf housewife

**mendiant, e** [mɑ̃djɑ̃, jɑ̃t] nm/f beggar

**mendier** [mɑ̃dje] vi to beg ▷ vt to beg (for)

**mener** [m(ə)ne] vt to lead; (enquête) to conduct; (affaires) to manage ▷ vi: **~ à/dans** (emmener) to take to/into; **~ qch à bien** to see sth through (to a successful conclusion), complete sth successfully

**meneur, -euse** [mənœʀ, øz] nm/f leader; (péj) agitator

**méningite** [menɛ̃ʒit] nf meningitis no pl

**ménopause** [menɔpoz] nf menopause

**menottes** [mənɔt] nfpl handcuffs

**mensonge** [mɑ̃sɔ̃ʒ] nm lie; (action) lying no pl; **mensonger, -ère** adj false

**mensualité** [mɑ̃sɥalite] nf (traite) monthly payment

**mensuel, le** [mɑ̃sɥɛl] adj monthly

**mensurations** [mɑ̃syʀasjɔ̃] nfpl measurements

**mental, e, -aux** [mɑ̃tal, o] adj mental; **mentalité** nf mentality

**menteur, -euse** [mɑ̃tœʀ, øz] nm/f liar

**menthe** [mɑ̃t] nf mint

**mention** [mɑ̃sjɔ̃] nf (annotation) note,

comment; (*Scol*) grade; **~ bien** ≈ grade
B, ≈ good pass; (*Université*) ≈ upper 2nd
class pass (BRIT), ≈ pass with (high)
honors (US); (*Admin*): **"rayer les ~s
inutiles"** "delete as appropriate";
**mentionner** vt to mention

**mentir** [mɑ̃tir] vi to lie

**menton** [mɑ̃tɔ̃] nm chin

**menu, e** [məny] adj (*personne*) slim,
slight; (*frais, difficulté*) minor ▷ adv
(*couper, hacher*) very fine ▷ nm menu;
**~ touristique/gastronomique**
economy/gourmet's menu

**menuiserie** [mənɥizri] nf (*métier*)
joinery, carpentry; (*passe-temps*)
woodwork; **menuisier** nm joiner,
carpenter

**méprendre** [meprɑ̃dr]: **se méprendre**
vi: **se ~ sur** to be mistaken (about)

**mépris** [mepri] nm (*dédain*) contempt,
scorn; **au ~ de** regardless of, in defiance
of; **méprisable** adj contemptible,
despicable; **méprisant, e** adj scornful;
**méprise** nf mistake, error; **mépriser**
vt to scorn, despise; (*gloire, danger*) to
scorn, spurn

**mer** [mɛr] nf sea; (*marée*) tide; **en ~** at
sea; **en haute** ou **pleine ~** off shore, on
the open sea; **la ~ du Nord/Rouge/
Noire/Morte** the North/Red/Black/
Dead Sea

**mercenaire** [mɛrsənɛr] nm
mercenary, hired soldier

**mercerie** [mɛrsəri] nf (*boutique*)
haberdasher's shop (BRIT), notions
store (US)

**merci** [mɛrsi] excl thank you ▷ nf: **à la
~ de qn/qch** at sb's mercy/the mercy of
sth; **~ beaucoup** thank you very much;
**~ de** thank you for; **sans ~** merciless(ly)

**mercredi** [mɛrkrədi] nm Wednesday;
**~ des Cendres** Ash Wednesday; voir
aussi **lundi**

**mercure** [mɛrkyr] nm mercury

**merde** [mɛrd] (*fam!*) nf shit (!) ▷ excl
(bloody) hell (!)

**mère** [mɛr] nf mother; **mère
célibataire** single parent, unmarried

mother; **mère de famille** housewife,
mother

**merguez** [mɛrgɛz] nf merguez
sausage (*type of spicy sausage from N
Africa*)

**méridional, e, -aux** [meridjɔnal, o]
adj southern ▷ nm/f Southerner

**meringue** [mərɛ̃g] nf meringue

**mérite** [merit] nm merit; **avoir du ~ (à
faire qch)** to deserve credit (for doing
sth); **mériter** vt to deserve

**merle** [mɛrl] nm blackbird

**merveille** [mɛrvɛj] nf marvel, wonder;
**faire ~** to work wonders; **à ~** perfectly,
wonderfully; **merveilleux, -euse** adj
marvellous, wonderful

**mes** [me] adj voir **mon**

**mésange** [mezɑ̃ʒ] nf tit(mouse)

**mésaventure** [mezavɑ̃tyr] nf
misadventure, misfortune

**Mesdames** [medam] nfpl de **Madame**

**Mesdemoiselles** [medmwazɛl] nfpl
de **Mademoiselle**

**mesquin, e** [mɛskɛ̃, in] adj mean,
petty; **mesquinerie** nf meanness;
(*procédé*) mean trick

**message** [mesaʒ] nm message; **est-ce
que je peux laisser un ~?** can I leave
a message?; **~ SMS** text message;
**messager, -ère** nm/f messenger;
**messagerie** nf (*Internet*): **messagerie
électronique** e-mail; **messagerie
vocale** (*service*) voice mail; **messagerie
instantanée** instant messenger

**messe** [mɛs] nf mass; **aller à la ~** to
go to mass

**Messieurs** [mesjø] nmpl de **Monsieur**

**mesure** [m(ə)zyr] nf (*évaluation,
dimension*) measurement; (*récipient*)
measure; (*Mus: cadence*) time, tempo;
(: *division*) bar; (*retenue*) moderation;
(*disposition*) measure, step; **sur ~**
(*costume*) made-to-measure; **dans la ~
où** insofar as, inasmuch as; **à ~ que** as;
**être en ~ de** to be in a position to; **dans
une certaine ~** to a certain extent

**mesurer** [məzyre] vt to measure;
(*juger*) to weigh up, assess; (*modérer: ses*

*paroles etc*) to moderate

**métal, -aux** [metal, o] *nm* metal;
**métallique** *adj* metallic

**météo** [meteo] *nf* (*bulletin*) weather
report

**météorologie** [mete`lɔʒi] *nf*
meteorology

**méthode** [metɔd] *nf* method; (*livre,
ouvrage*) manual, tutor

**méticuleux, -euse** [metikylø, øz] *adj*
meticulous

**métier** [metje] *nm* (*profession: gén*)
job; (: *manuel*) trade; (*artisanal*) craft;
(*technique, expérience*) (acquired) skill *ou*
technique; (*aussi*: **~ à tisser**) (weaving)
loom

**métis, se** [metis] *adj, nm/f* half-caste,
half-breed

**métrage** [metraʒ] *nm*: **long/moyen/
court ~** full-length/medium-length/
short film

**mètre** [mɛtr] *nm* metre; (*règle*) (metre)
rule; (*ruban*) tape measure; **métrique**
*adj* metric

**métro** [metro] *nm* underground (BRIT),
subway

**métropole** [metrɔpɔl] *nf* (*capitale*)
metropolis; (*pays*) home country

**mets** [mɛ] *nm* dish

**metteur** [metœr] *nm*: **~ en scène**
(*Théâtre*) producer; (*Cinéma*) director

 **MOT-CLÉ**

**mettre** [mɛtr] *vt* **1** (*placer*) to put;
**mettre en bouteille/en sac** to bottle/
put in bags *ou* sacks
**2** (*vêtements: revêtir*) to put on; (: *porter*)
to wear; **mets ton gilet** put your
cardigan on; **je ne mets plus mon
manteau** I no longer wear my coat
**3** (*faire fonctionner: chauffage, électricité*)
to put on; (: *réveil, minuteur*) to set;
(*installer: gaz, eau*) to put in, lay on;
**mettre en marche** to start up
**4** (*consacrer*): **mettre du temps à faire
qch** to take time to do sth *ou* over sth
**5** (*noter, écrire*) to say, put (down);

**qu'est-ce qu'il a mis sur la carte?**
what did he say *ou* write on the card?;
**mettez au pluriel ...** put ... into the
plural
**6** (*supposer*): **mettons que ...** let's
suppose *ou* say that ...
**7**: **y mettre du sien** to pull one's weight
**se mettre** *vi* **1** (*se placer*): **vous pouvez
vous mettre là** you can sit (*ou* stand)
there; **où ça se met?** where does it
go?; **se mettre au lit** to get into bed;
**se mettre au piano** to sit down at the
piano; **se mettre de l'encre sur les
doigts** to get ink on one's fingers
**2** (*s'habiller*): **se mettre en maillot de
bain** to get into *ou* put on a swimsuit;
**n'avoir rien à se mettre** to have
nothing to wear
**3**: **se mettre à** to begin, start; **se
mettre à faire** to begin *ou* start doing
*ou* to do; **se mettre au piano** to start
learning the piano; **se mettre au
régime** to go on a diet; **se mettre
au travail/à l'étude** to get down to
work/one's studies

**meuble** [mœbl] *nm* piece of furniture;
**des ~s** furniture; **meublé** *nm* furnished
flatlet (BRIT) *ou* room; **meubler** *vt* to
furnish

**meuf** [mœf] *nf* (*fam*) woman

**meugler** [møgle] *vi* to low, moo

**meule** [møl] *nf* (*de foin, blé*) stack; (*de
fromage*) round; (*à broyer*) millstone

**meunier** [mønje] *nm* miller

**meurs** *etc* [mœr] *vb voir* **mourir**

**meurtre** [mœrtr] *nm* murder;
**meurtrier, -ière** *adj* (*arme etc*) deadly;
(*fureur, instincts*) murderous ▷ *nm/f*
murderer(-eress)

**meurtrir** [mœrtrir] *vt* to bruise; (*fig*)
to wound

**meus** *etc* [mœ] *vb voir* **mouvoir**

**meute** [møt] *nf* pack

**mexicain, e** [mɛksikɛ̃, ɛn] *adj*
Mexican ▷ *nm/f*: **M~, e** Mexican

**Mexico** [mɛksiko] *n* Mexico City

**Mexique** [mɛksik] *nm*: **le ~** Mexico

**mi** [mi] nm (Mus) E; (en chantant la gamme) mi ▷ préfixe: **mi...** half(-); mid-; **à la mi-janvier** in mid-January; **à mi-jambes/corps** (up ou down) to the knees/waist; **à mi-hauteur** halfway up

**miauler** [mjole] vi to mew

**miche** [miʃ] nf round ou cob loaf

**mi-chemin** [miʃmɛ̃]: **à ~** adv halfway, midway

**mi-clos, e** [miklo, kloz] adj half-closed

**micro** [mikro] nm mike, microphone; (Inform) micro

**microbe** [mikrob] nm germ, microbe

**micro...**: **micro-onde** nf: **four à micro-ondes** microwave oven; **micro-ordinateur** nm microcomputer; **microscope** nm microscope; **microscopique** adj microscopic

**midi** [midi] nm midday, noon; (moment du déjeuner) lunchtime; (sud) south; **à ~** at 12 (o'clock) ou midday ou noon; **le M~** the South (of France), the Midi

**mie** [mi] nf crumb (of the loaf)

**miel** [mjɛl] nm honey; **mielleux, -euse** adj (personne) unctuous, syrupy

**mien, ne** [mjɛ̃, mjɛn] pron: **le(la) ~(ne), les ~(ne)s** mine; **les ~s** my family

**miette** [mjɛt] nf (de pain, gâteau) crumb; (fig: de la conversation etc) scrap; **en ~s** in pieces ou bits

 **MOT-CLÉ**

**mieux** [mjø] adv **1** (d'une meilleure façon): **mieux (que)** better (than); **elle travaille/mange mieux** she works/eats better; **aimer mieux** to prefer; **elle va mieux** she is better; **de mieux en mieux** better and better

**2** (de la meilleure façon) best; **ce que je connais le mieux** what I know best; **les livres les mieux faits** the best-made books

▷ adj **1** (plus à l'aise, en meilleure forme) better; **se sentir mieux** to feel better

**2** (plus satisfaisant) better; **c'est mieux ainsi** it's better like this; **c'est le mieux**

**des deux** it's the better of the two; **le(la) mieux, les mieux** the best; **demandez-lui, c'est le mieux** ask him, it's the best thing

**3** (plus joli) better-looking; **il est mieux que son frère** (plus beau) he's better-looking than his brother; (plus gentil) he's nicer than his brother; **il est mieux sans moustache** he looks better without a moustache

**4**: **au mieux** at best; **au mieux avec** on the best of terms with; **pour le mieux** for the best

▷ nm **1** (progrès) improvement

**2**: **de mon/ton mieux** as best I/you can (ou could); **faire de son mieux** to do one's best

**mignon, ne** [miɲɔ̃, ɔn] adj sweet, cute

**migraine** [migrɛn] nf headache; (Méd) migraine

**mijoter** [miʒɔte] vt to simmer; (préparer avec soin) to cook lovingly; (fam: tramer) to plot, cook up ▷ vi to simmer

**milieu, x** [miljø] nm (centre) middle; (Bio, Géo) environment; (entourage social) milieu; (provenance) background; (pègre): **le ~** the underworld; **au ~ de** in the middle of; **au beau** ou **en plein ~ (de)** right in the middle (of); **un juste ~** a happy medium

**militaire** [militɛr] adj military, army cpd ▷ nm serviceman

**militant, e** [militɑ̃, ɑ̃t] adj, nm/f militant

**militer** [milite] vi to be a militant

**mille** [mil] num a ou one thousand ▷ nm (mesure): **~ (marin)** nautical mile; **mettre dans le ~** (fig) to be bang on target; **millefeuille** nm cream ou vanilla slice; **millénaire** nm millennium ▷ adj thousand-year-old; (fig) ancient; **mille-pattes** nm inv centipede

**millet** [mijɛ] nm millet

**milliard** [miljar] nm milliard, thousand million (BRIT), billion (US); **milliardaire** nm/f multimillionaire

(BRIT), billionaire (US)
**millier** [milje] nm thousand; **un ~ (de)**
a thousand or so, about a thousand;
**par ~s** in (their) thousands, by the
thousand
**milligramme** [miligram] nm
milligramme
**millimètre** [milimɛtʀ] nm millimetre
**million** [miljɔ̃] nm million; **deux ~s
de** two million; **millionnaire** nm/f
millionaire
**mime** [mim] nm/f (acteur) mime(r)
▷ nm (art) mime, miming; **mimer** vt to
mime; (singer) to mimic, take off
**minable** [minabl] adj (décrépit)
shabby (-looking); (médiocre) pathetic
**mince** [mɛ̃s] adj thin; (personne, taille)
slim, slender; (fig: profit, connaissances)
slight, small, weak ▷ excl: **~ alors!** drat
it!, darn it! (US); **minceur** nf thinness;
(d'une personne) slimness, slenderness;
**mincir** vi to get slimmer
**mine** [min] nf (physionomie) expression,
look; (allure) exterior, appearance;
(de crayon) lead; (gisement, explosif, fig:
source) mine; **avoir bonne ~** (personne)
to look well; (ironique) to look an utter
idiot; **avoir mauvaise ~** to look unwell
ou poorly; **faire ~ de faire** to make a
pretence of doing; **~ de rien** although
you wouldn't think so
**miner** [mine] vt (saper) to undermine,
erode; (Mil) to mine
**minerai** [minʀɛ] nm ore
**minéral, e, -aux** [mineral, o] adj,
nm mineral
**minéralogique** [mineralɔʒik] adj:
**plaque ~** number (BRIT) ou license (US)
plate; **numéro ~** registration (BRIT) ou
license (US) number
**minet, te** [minɛ, ɛt] nm/f (chat) pussy-
cat; (péj) young trendy
**mineur, e** [minœʀ] adj minor ▷ nm/f
(Jur) minor, person under age ▷ nm
(travailleur) miner
**miniature** [minjatyʀ] adj, nf
miniature
**minibus** [minibys] nm minibus

**minier, -ière** [minje, jɛʀ] adj mining
**mini-jupe** [miniʒyp] nf mini-skirt
**minime** [minim] adj minor, minimal
**minimessage** [minimesaʒ] nm text
message
**minimiser** [minimize] vt to minimize;
(fig) to play down
**minimum** [minimɔm] adj, nm
minimum; **au ~** (au moins) at the
very least
**ministère** [ministɛʀ] nm (aussi Rel)
ministry; (cabinet) government
**ministre** [ministʀ] nm (aussi Rel)
minister; **ministre d'État** senior
minister ou secretary
**Minitel®** [minitel] nm videotext
terminal and service

**minoritaire** [minɔʀitɛʀ] adj minority
**minorité** [minɔʀite] nf minority; **être
en ~** to be in the ou a minority
**minuit** [minɥi] nm midnight
**minuscule** [minyskyl] adj minute,
tiny ▷ nf: **(lettre) ~** small letter
**minute** [minyt] nf minute; **à la ~** (just)
this instant; (faire) there and then;
**minuter** vt to time; **minuterie** nf
time switch
**minutieux, -euse** [minysjø, jøz]
adj (personne) meticulous; (travail)

minutely detailed

**mirabelle** [miʀabɛl] nf (cherry) plum

**miracle** [miʀɑkl] nm miracle

**mirage** [miʀaʒ] nm mirage

**mire** [miʀ] nf: **point de ~** (fig) focal point

**miroir** [miʀwaʀ] nm mirror

**miroiter** [miʀwate] vi to sparkle, shimmer; **faire ~ qch à qn** to paint sth in glowing colours for sb, dangle sth in front of sb's eyes

**mis, e** [mi, miz] pp de **mettre** ▷ adj: **bien ~** well-dressed

**mise** [miz] nf (argent: au jeu) stake; (tenue) clothing, attire; **être de ~** to be acceptable ou in season; **mise à jour** updating; **mise au point** (fig) clarification; **mise de fonds** capital outlay; **mise en plis** set; **mise en scène** production

**miser** [mize] vt (enjeu) to stake, bet; **~ sur** (cheval, numéro) to bet on; (fig) to bank ou count on

**misérable** [mizeʀabl] adj (lamentable, malheureux) pitiful, wretched; (pauvre) poverty-stricken; (insignifiant, mesquin) miserable ▷ nm/f wretch

**misère** [mizɛʀ] nf (extreme) poverty, destitution; **misères** nfpl (malheurs) woes, miseries; (ennuis) little troubles; **salaire de ~** starvation wage

**missile** [misil] nm missile

**mission** [misjɔ̃] nf mission; **partir en ~** (Admin, Pol) to go on an assignment; **missionnaire** nm/f missionary

**mité, e** [mite] adj moth-eaten

**mi-temps** [mitɑ̃] nf inv (Sport: période) half; (: pause) half-time; **à ~** part-time

**miteux, -euse** [mitø, øz] adj (lieu) seedy

**mitigé, e** [mitiʒe] adj: **sentiments ~s** mixed feelings

**mitoyen, ne** [mitwajɛ̃, jɛn] adj (mur) common, party cpd; **maisons ~nes** semi-detached houses; (plus de deux) terraced (BRIT) ou row (US) houses

**mitrailler** [mitʀaje] vt to machine-gun; (fig) to pelt, bombard; (: photographier) to take shot after shot of; **mitraillette** nf submachine gun; **mitrailleuse** nf machine gun

**mi-voix** [mivwa]: **à ~** adv in a low ou hushed voice

**mixage** [miksaʒ] nm (Cinéma) (sound) mixing

**mixer** [miksœʀ] nm (food) mixer

**mixte** [mikst] adj (gén) mixed; (Scol) mixed, coeducational; **cuisinière ~** combined gas and electric cooker (BRIT) ou stove (US)

**mixture** [mikstyʀ] nf mixture; (fig) concoction

**Mlle** (pl ~s) abr = **Mademoiselle**

**MM** abr = **Messieurs**

**Mme** (pl ~s) abr = **Madame**

**mobile** [mɔbil] adj mobile; (pièce de machine) moving ▷ nm (motif) motive; (œuvre d'art) mobile; **(téléphone) ~** mobile (phone)

**mobilier, -ière** [mɔbilje, jɛʀ] nm furniture

**mobiliser** [mɔbilize] vt to mobilize

**mocassin** [mɔkasɛ̃] nm moccasin

**moche** [mɔʃ] (fam) adj (laid) ugly; (mauvais) rotten

**modalité** [mɔdalite] nf form, mode

**mode** [mɔd] nf fashion ▷ nm (manière) form, mode; (Ling) mood; (Mus, Inform) mode; **à la ~** fashionable, in fashion; **mode d'emploi** directions pl (for use); **mode de paiement** method of payment; **mode de vie** lifestyle

**modèle** [mɔdɛl] adj, nm model; (qui pose: de peintre) sitter; **modèle déposé** registered design; **modèle réduit** small-scale model; **modeler** vt to model

**modem** [mɔdɛm] nm modem

**modéré, e** [mɔdeʀe] adj, nm/f moderate

**modérer** [mɔdeʀe] vt to moderate; **se modérer** vi to restrain o.s.

**moderne** [mɔdɛʀn] adj modern ▷ nm (style) modern style; (meubles) modern furniture; **moderniser** vt to modernize

**modeste** [mɔdɛst] adj modest;

**modestie** *nf* modesty

**modifier** [mɔdifje] *vt* to modify, alter; **se modifier** *vi* to alter

**modique** [mɔdik] *adj* modest

**module** [mɔdyl] *nm* module

**moelle** [mwal] *nf* marrow

**moelleux, -euse** [mwalø, øz] *adj* soft; *(gâteau)* light and moist

**mœurs** [mœʀ] *nfpl (conduite)* morals; *(manières)* manners; *(pratiques sociales, mode de vie)* habits

**moi** [mwa] *pron* me; *(emphatique)*: ~, **je ...** for my part, I ..., I myself ...; **c'est ~ qui l'ai fait** I did it, it was me who did it; **apporte-le-~** bring it to me; **à ~** mine; *(dans un jeu)* my turn; **moi-même** *pron* myself; *(emphatique)* I myself

**moindre** [mwɛ̃dʀ] *adj* lesser; lower; **le(la) ~, les ~s** the least, the slightest; **merci — c'est la ~ des choses!** thank you — it's a pleasure!

**moine** [mwan] *nm* monk, friar

**moineau, x** [mwano] *nm* sparrow

 **MOT-CLÉ**

**moins** [mwɛ̃] *adv* **1** *(comparatif)*: **moins (que)** less (than); **moins grand que** less tall than, not as tall as; **il a 3 ans de moins que moi** he's 3 years younger than me; **moins je travaille, mieux je me porte** the less I work, the better I feel

**2** *(superlatif)*: **le moins** (the) least; **c'est ce que j'aime le moins** it's what I like (the) least; **le(la) moins doué(e)** the least gifted; **au moins, du moins** at least; **pour le moins** at the very least

**3**: **moins de** *(quantité)* less (than); *(nombre)* fewer (than); **moins de sable/d'eau** less sand/water; **moins de livres/gens** fewer books/people; **moins de 2 ans** less than 2 years; **moins de midi** not yet midday

**4**: **de moins, en moins**: **100 euros/3 jours de moins** 100 euros/3 days less; **3 livres en moins** 3 books fewer; **de l'argent en moins**

less money; **le soleil en moins** but for the sun, minus the sun; **de moins en moins** less and less

**5**: **à moins de, à moins que** unless; **à moins de faire** unless we do *(ou* he does *etc)*; **à moins que tu ne fasses** unless you do; **à moins d'un accident** barring any accident

▷ *prép*: **4 moins 2** 4 minus 2; **il est moins 5** it's 5 to; **il fait moins 5** it's 5 (degrees) below (freezing), it's minus 5

**mois** [mwa] *nm* month

**moisi** [mwazi] *nm* mould, mildew; **odeur de ~** musty smell; **moisir** *vi* to go mouldy; **moisissure** *nf* mould *no pl*

**moisson** [mwasɔ̃] *nf* harvest; **moissonner** *vt* to harvest, reap; **moissonneuse** *nf (machine)* harvester

**moite** [mwat] *adj* sweaty, sticky

**moitié** [mwatje] *nf* half; **la ~** half; **la ~ de** half (of); **la ~ du temps** half the time; **à la ~ de** halfway through; **à ~** *(avant le verbe)* half; *(avant l'adjectif)* half-; **à ~ prix** (at) half-price

**molaire** [mɔlɛʀ] *nf* molar

**molester** [mɔlɛste] *vt* to manhandle, maul (about)

**molle** [mɔl] *adj voir* **mou**; **mollement** *adv (péj: travailler)* sluggishly; *(protester)* feebly

**mollet** [mɔlɛ] *nm* calf ▷ *adj m*: **œuf ~** soft-boiled egg

**molletonné, e** [mɔltɔne] *adj* fleece-lined

**mollir** [mɔliʀ] *vi (fléchir)* to relent; *(substance)* to go soft

**mollusque** [mɔlysk] *nm* mollusc

**môme** [mom] *nm/f (enfant)* brat

**moment** [mɔmɑ̃] *nm* moment; **ce n'est pas le ~** this is not the (right) time; **au même ~** at the same time; *(instant)* at the same moment; **pour un bon ~** for a good while; **pour le ~** for the moment, for the time being; **au ~ de** at the time of; **au ~ où** just as; **à tout ~** *(peut arriver etc)* at any time *ou* moment; *(constamment)* constantly, continually;

**en ce ~** at the moment; at present; **sur
le ~** at the time; **par ~s** now and then,
at times; **d'un ~ à l'autre** any time
(now); **du ~ où** ou **que** seeing that,
since; **momentané, e** adj temporary,
momentary; **momentanément** adv
(court instant) for a short while

**momie** [mɔmi] nf mummy

**mon, ma** [mɔ̃, ma] (pl **mes**) adj my

**Monaco** [mɔnako] nm Monaco

**monarchie** [mɔnaʀʃi] nf monarchy

**monastère** [mɔnastɛʀ] nm
monastery

**mondain, e** [mɔ̃dɛ̃, ɛn] adj (vie)
society cpd

**monde** [mɔ̃d] nm world; (haute
société): **le ~** (high) society; **il y a du
~** (beaucoup de gens) there are a lot of
people; (quelques personnes) there are
some people; **beaucoup/peu de ~**
many/few people; **mettre au ~** to
bring into the world; **pas le moins du
~** not in the least; **mondial, e, -aux**
adj (population) world cpd; (influence)
world-wide; **mondialement** adv
throughout the world; **mondialisation**
nf globalization

**monégasque** [mɔnegask] adj
Monegasque, of ou from Monaco
▷ nm/f: **M~** Monegasque, person from
ou inhabitant of Monaco

**monétaire** [mɔnetɛʀ] adj monetary

**moniteur, -trice** [mɔnitœʀ, tʀis]
nm/f (Sport) instructor(-tress); (de
colonie de vacances) supervisor ▷ nm
(écran)

**monnaie** [mɔnɛ] nf (Écon, gén: moyen
d'échange) currency; (petites pièces):
**avoir de la ~** to have (some) change;
**une pièce de ~** a coin; **faire de la ~** to
get (some) change; **avoir/faire la ~ de
20 euros** to have change of/get change
for 20 euros; **rendre à qn la ~ (sur 20
euros)** to give sb the change (out of ou
from 20 euros); **gardez la ~** keep the
change; **désolé, je n'ai pas de ~** sorry,
I don't have any change; **avez-vous de
la ~?** do you have any change?

**monologue** [mɔnɔlɔg] nm
monologue, soliloquy; **monologuer** vi
to soliloquize

**monopole** [mɔnɔpɔl] nm monopoly

**monotone** [mɔnɔtɔn] adj
monotonous

**Monsieur** [məsjø] (pl **Messieurs**) titre
Mr ▷ nm (homme quelconque): **un/le
monsieur** a/the gentleman; **~, ...**
(en tête de lettre) Dear Sir, ...; voir aussi
**Madame**

**monstre** [mɔ̃stʀ] nm monster
▷ adj (fam: colossal) monstrous; **un
travail ~** a fantastic amount of work;
**monstrueux, -euse** adj monstrous

**mont** [mɔ̃] nm: **par ~s et par vaux** up
hill and down dale; **le Mont Blanc**
Mont Blanc

**montage** [mɔ̃taʒ] nm (assemblage:
d'appareil) assembly; (Photo)
photomontage; (Cinéma) editing

**montagnard, e** [mɔ̃taɲaʀ, aʀd] adj
mountain cpd ▷ nm/f mountain-
dweller

**montagne** [mɔ̃taɲ] nf (cime)
mountain; (région): **la ~** the mountains
pl; **montagnes russes** big dipper sg,
switchback sg; **montagneux, -euse**
adj mountainous; (basse montagne) hilly

**montant, e** [mɔ̃tɑ̃, ɑ̃t] adj rising;
**pull à col ~** high-necked jumper ▷ nm
(somme, total) (sum) total, (total)
amount; (de fenêtre) upright; (de lit) post

**monte-charge** [mɔ̃tʃaʀʒ] nm inv
goods lift, hoist

**montée** [mɔ̃te] nf (des prix, hostilités)
rise; (escalade) climb; (côte) hill; **au
milieu de la ~** halfway up

**monter** [mɔ̃te] vt (escalier, côte) to go
(ou come) up; (valise, paquet) to take
(ou bring) up; (étagère) to raise; (tente,
échafaudage) to put up; (machine) to
assemble; (Cinéma) to edit; (Théâtre)
to put on, stage; (société etc) to set up
▷ vi to go (ou come) up; (prix, niveau,
température) to go up, rise; (passager)
to get on; **~ à cheval** (faire du cheval) to
ride (a horse); **~ sur** to climb up onto; **~**

**sur** ou **à un arbre/une échelle** to climb (up) a tree/ladder; **se monter à** (frais etc) to add up to, come to

**montgolfière** [mɔ̃gɔlfjɛʀ] nf hot-air balloon

**montre** [mɔ̃tʀ] nf watch; **contre la ~** (Sport) against the clock

**Montréal** [mɔ̃ʀeal] n Montreal

**montrer** [mɔ̃tʀe] vt to show; **~ qch à qn** to show sb sth; **pouvez-vous me ~ où c'est?** can you show me where it is?

**monture** [mɔ̃tyʀ] nf (cheval) mount; (de lunettes) frame; (d'une bague) setting

**monument** [mɔnymɑ̃] nm monument; **monument aux morts** war memorial

**moquer** [mɔke]: **se moquer de** vt to make fun of, laugh at; (fam: se désintéresser de) not to care about; (tromper): **se ~ de qn** to take sb for a ride

**moquette** [mɔkɛt] nf fitted carpet

**moqueur, -euse** [mɔkœʀ, øz] adj mocking

**moral, e, -aux** [mɔʀal, o] adj moral ▷ nm morale; **avoir le ~** (fam) to be in good spirits; **avoir le ~ à zéro** (fam) to be really down; **morale** nf (mœurs) morals pl; (valeurs) moral standards pl, morality; (d'une fable etc) moral; **faire la morale à** to lecture, preach at; **moralité** nf morality; (de fable) moral

**morceau, x** [mɔʀso] nm piece, bit; (d'une œuvre) passage, extract; (Mus) piece; (Culin: de viande) cut; (de sucre) lump; **mettre en ~x** to pull to pieces ou bits; **manger un ~** to have a bite (to eat)

**morceler** [mɔʀsəle] vt to break up, divide up

**mordant, e** [mɔʀdɑ̃, ɑ̃t] adj (ton, remarque) scathing, cutting; (ironie, froid) biting ▷ nm (style) bite, punch

**mordiller** [mɔʀdije] vt to nibble at, chew at

**mordre** [mɔʀdʀ] vt to bite ▷ vi (poisson) to bite; **~ sur** (fig) to go over into, overlap into; **~ à l'hameçon** to bite, rise to the bait

**mordu, e** [mɔʀdy] (fam) nm/f enthusiast; **un ~ de jazz** a jazz fanatic

**morfondre** [mɔʀfɔ̃dʀ]: **se morfondre** vi to mope

**morgue** [mɔʀg] nf (arrogance) haughtiness; (lieu: de la police) morgue; (: à l'hôpital) mortuary

**morne** [mɔʀn] adj dismal, dreary

**morose** [mɔʀoz] adj sullen, morose

**mors** [mɔʀ] nm bit

**morse** [mɔʀs] nm (Zool) walrus; (Tél) Morse (code)

**morsure** [mɔʀsyʀ] nf bite

**mort¹** [mɔʀ] nf death

**mort², e** [mɔʀ, mɔʀt] pp de **mourir** ▷ adj dead ▷ nm/f (défunt) dead man ou woman; (victime): **il y a eu plusieurs ~s** several people were killed, there were several killed; **~ de peur/fatigue** frightened to death/dead tired

**mortalité** [mɔʀtalite] nf mortality, death rate

**mortel, le** [mɔʀtɛl] adj (poison etc) deadly, fatal; (accident, blessure) fatal; (silence, ennemi) deadly; (péché) mortal; (fam: ennuyeux) deadly boring

**mort-né, e** [mɔʀne] adj (enfant) stillborn

**mortuaire** [mɔʀtɥɛʀ] adj: **avis ~** death announcement

**morue** [mɔʀy] nf (Zool) cod inv

**mosaïque** [mɔzaik] nf mosaic

**Moscou** [mɔsku] n Moscow

**mosquée** [mɔske] nf mosque

**mot** [mo] nm word; (message) line, note; **~ à ~** word for word; **mot de passe** password; **mots croisés** crossword (puzzle) sg

**motard** [mɔtaʀ] nm biker; (policier) motorcycle cop

**motel** [mɔtɛl] nm motel

**moteur, -trice** [mɔtœʀ, tʀis] adj (Anat, Physiol) motor; (Tech) driving; (Auto): **à 4 roues motrices** 4-wheel drive ▷ nm engine, motor; **à ~** power-driven, motor cpd; **moteur de recherche** search engine

**motif** [mɔtif] nm (cause) motive;

(*décoratif*) design, pattern, motif; **sans ~** groundless

**motivation** [mɔtivasjɔ̃] *nf* motivation

**motiver** [mɔtive] *vt* to motivate; (*justifier*) to justify, account for

**moto** [mɔto] *nf* (motor)bike; **motocycliste** *nm/f* motorcyclist

**motorisé, e** [mɔtɔʀize] *adj* (*personne*) having transport *ou* a car

**motrice** [mɔtʀis] *adj voir* **moteur**

**motte** [mɔt] *nf*: **~ de terre** lump of earth, clod (of earth); **motte de beurre** lump of butter

**mou (mol), molle** [mu, mɔl] *adj* soft; (*personne*) lethargic; (*protestations*) weak ▷ *nm*: **avoir du mou** to be slack

**mouche** [muʃ] *nf* fly

**moucher** [muʃe]: **se moucher** *vi* to blow one's nose

**moucheron** [muʃʀɔ̃] *nm* midge

**mouchoir** [muʃwaʀ] *nm* handkerchief, hanky; **mouchoir en papier** tissue, paper hanky

**moudre** [mudʀ] *vt* to grind

**moue** [mu] *nf* pout; **faire la ~** to pout; (*fig*) to pull a face

**mouette** [mwɛt] *nf* (sea)gull

**moufle** [mufl] *nf* (*gant*) mitt(en)

**mouillé, e** [muje] *adj* wet

**mouiller** [muje] *vt* (*humecter*) to wet, moisten; (*tremper*): **~ qn/qch** to make sb/sth wet ▷ *vi* (*Navig*) to lie *ou* be at anchor; **se mouiller** to get wet; (*fam: prendre des risques*) to commit o.s.

**moulant, e** [mulɑ̃, ɑ̃t] *adj* figure-hugging

**moule** [mul] *nf* mussel ▷ *nm* (*Culin*) mould; **moule à gâteaux** *nm* cake tin (BRIT) *ou* pan (US)

**mouler** [mule] *vt* (*suj: vêtement*) to hug, fit closely round

**moulin** [mulɛ̃] *nm* mill; **moulin à café** coffee mill; **moulin à eau** watermill; **moulin à légumes** (vegetable) shredder; **moulin à paroles** (*fig*) chatterbox; **moulin à poivre** pepper mill; **moulin à vent** windmill

**moulinet** [mulinɛ] *nm* (*de canne à pêche*) reel; (*mouvement*): **faire des ~s avec qch** to whirl sth around

**moulinette®** [mulinɛt] *nf* (vegetable) shredder

**moulu, e** [muly] *pp de* **moudre**

**mourant, e** [muʀɑ̃, ɑ̃t] *adj* dying

**mourir** [muʀiʀ] *vi* to die; (*civilisation*) to die out; **~ de froid/faim** to die of exposure/hunger; **~ de faim/d'ennui** (*fig*) to be starving/be bored to death; **~ d'envie de faire** to be dying to do

**mousse** [mus] *nf* (*Bot*) moss; (*de savon*) lather; (*écume: sur eau, bière*) froth, foam; (*Culin*) mousse ▷ *nm* (*Navig*) ship's boy; **mousse à raser** shaving foam

**mousseline** [muslin] *nf* muslin; **pommes ~** mashed potatoes

**mousser** [muse] *vi* (*bière, détergent*) to foam; (*savon*) to lather; **mousseux, -euse** *adj* frothy ▷ *nm*: **(vin) mousseux** sparkling wine

**mousson** [musɔ̃] *nf* monsoon

**moustache** [mustaʃ] *nf* moustache; **moustaches** *nfpl* (*du chat*) whiskers *pl*; **moustachu, e** *adj* with a moustache

**moustiquaire** [mustikɛʀ] *nf* mosquito net

**moustique** [mustik] *nm* mosquito

**moutarde** [mutaʀd] *nf* mustard

**mouton** [mutɔ̃] *nm* sheep *inv*; (*peau*) sheepskin; (*Culin*) mutton

**mouvement** [muvmɑ̃] *nm* movement; (*fig: impulsion*) gesture; **avoir un bon ~** to make a nice gesture; **en ~** in motion; on the move; **mouvementé, e** *adj* (*vie, poursuite*) eventful; (*réunion*) turbulent

**mouvoir** [muvwaʀ]: **se mouvoir** *vi* to move

**moyen, ne** [mwajɛ̃, jɛn] *adj* average; (*tailles, prix*) medium; (*de grandeur moyenne*) medium-sized ▷ *nm* (*façon*) means *sg*, way; **moyens** *nmpl* (*capacités*) means; **très ~** (*résultats*) pretty poor; **je n'en ai pas les ~s** I can't afford it; **au ~ de** by means of; **par tous les ~s** by every possible means, every possible way; **par ses propres ~s** all by oneself; **moyen âge** Middle Ages pl; **moyen de transport** means of transport

**moyennant** [mwajɛnɑ̃] prép (somme) for; (service, conditions) in return for; (travail, effort) with

**moyenne** [mwajɛn] nf average; (Math) mean; (Scol) pass mark; **en ~** (an) average; **moyenne d'âge** average age

**Moyen-Orient** [mwajɛnɔʀjɑ̃] nm: **le ~** the Middle East

**moyeu, x** [mwajø] nm hub

**MST** sigle f (= maladie sexuellement transmissible) STD

**mû, mue** [my] pp de **mouvoir**

**muer** [mɥe] vi (oiseau, mammifère) to moult; (serpent) to slough; (jeune garçon): **il mue** his voice is breaking

**muet, te** [mɥe, mɥɛt] adj dumb; (fig): **~ d'admiration** etc speechless with admiration etc; (Cinéma) silent ▷ nm/f mute

**mufle** [myfl] nm muzzle; (fam: goujat) boor

**mugir** [myʒiʀ] vi (taureau) to bellow; (vache) to low; (fig) to howl

**muguet** [mygɛ] nm lily of the valley

**mule** [myl] nf (Zool) (she-)mule

**mulet** [mylɛ] nm (Zool) (he-)mule

**multinationale** [myltinasjɔnal] nf multinational

**multiple** [myltipl] adj multiple, numerous; (varié) many, manifold; **multiplication** nf multiplication; **multiplier** vt to multiply; **se multiplier** vi to multiply

**municipal, e, -aux** [mynisipal, o] adj (élections, stade) municipal; (conseil) town cpd; **piscine/bibliothèque ~e** public swimming pool/library; **municipalité** nf (ville) municipality; (conseil) town council

**munir** [myniʀ] vt: **~ qch de** to equip sth with; **se ~ de** to arm o.s. with

**munitions** [mynisjɔ̃] nfpl ammunition sg

**mur** [myʀ] nm wall; **mur du son** sound barrier

**mûr, e** [myʀ] adj ripe; (personne) mature

**muraille** [myʀɑj] nf (high) wall

**mural, e, -aux** [myʀal, o] adj wall cpd; (art) mural

**mûre** [myʀ] nf blackberry

**muret** [myʀɛ] nm low wall

**mûrir** [myʀiʀ] vi (fruit, blé) to ripen; (abcès) to come to a head; (fig: idée, personne) to mature ▷ vt (projet) to nurture; (personne) to (make) mature

**murmure** [myʀmyʀ] nm murmur; **murmurer** vi to murmur

**muscade** [myskad] nf (aussi: **noix (de) ~**) nutmeg

**muscat** [myska] nm (raisins) muscat grape; (vin) muscatel (wine)

**muscle** [myskl] nm muscle; **musclé, e** adj muscular; (fig) strong-arm

**museau, x** [myzo] nm muzzle; (Culin) brawn

**musée** [myze] nm museum; (de peinture) art gallery

**museler** [myz(ə)le] vt to muzzle; **muselière** nf muzzle

**musette** [myzɛt] nf (sac) lunchbag

**musical, e, -aux** [myzikal, o] adj musical

**music-hall** [myzikol] nm (salle) variety theatre; (genre) variety

**musicien, ne** [myzisjɛ̃, jɛn] adj musical ▷ nm/f musician

**musique** [myzik] nf music

● **FÊTE DE LA MUSIQUE**

●
● The **Fête de la Musique** is a music
● festival which takes place every year
● on 21 June. Throughout France, local
● musicians perform free of charge in
● parks, streets and squares.

**musulman, e** [myzylmɑ̃, an] adj, nm/f Moslem, Muslim

**mutation** [mytasjɔ̃] nf (Admin) transfer

**muter** [myte] vt to transfer, move

**mutilé, e** [mytile] nm/f disabled

person (*through loss of limbs*)
**mutiler** [mytile] *vt* to mutilate, maim
**mutin, e** [mytɛ̃, in] *adj* (*air, ton*)
mischievous, impish ▷ *nm/f* (*Mil,
Navig*) mutineer; **mutinerie** *nf* mutiny
**mutisme** [mytism] *nm* silence
**mutuel, le** [mytɥɛl] *adj* mutual;
**mutuelle** *nf* voluntary insurance
premiums for back-up health cover
**myope** [mjɔp] *adj* short-sighted
**myosotis** [mjɔzɔtis] *nm* forget-
me-not
**myrtille** [miʀtij] *nf* bilberry
**mystère** [mistɛʀ] *nm* mystery;
**mystérieux, -euse** *adj* mysterious
**mystifier** [mistifje] *vt* to fool
**mythe** [mit] *nm* myth
**mythologie** [mitɔlɔʒi] *nf* mythology

**n'** [n] *adv voir* **ne**
**nacre** [nakʀ] *nf* mother of pearl
**nage** [naʒ] *nf* swimming; (*manière*) style
of swimming, stroke; **traverser/
s'éloigner à la ~** to swim across/away;
**en ~** bathed in sweat; **nageoire** *nf* fin;
**nager** *vi* to swim; **nageur, -euse** *nm/f*
swimmer
**naïf, -ïve** [naif, naiv] *adj* naïve
**nain, e** [nɛ̃, nɛn] *nm/f* dwarf
**naissance** [nɛsɑ̃s] *nf* birth; **donner ~ à**
to give birth to; (*fig*) to give rise to; **lieu
de ~** place of birth
**naître** [nɛtʀ] *vi* to be born; (*fig*): **~ de** to
arise from, be born out of; **il est né en
1960** he was born in 1960; **faire ~** (*fig*) to
give rise to, arouse
**naïveté** [naivte] *nf* naïvety
**nana** [nana] (*fam*) *nf* (*fille*) chick, bird
(*BRIT*)
**nappe** [nap] *nf* tablecloth; (*de pétrole,
gaz*) layer; **napperon** *nm* table-mat
**naquit** *etc* [naki] *vb voir* **naître**
**narguer** [naʀge] *vt* to taunt

**narine** [naʀin] nf nostril

**natal, e** [natal] adj native; **natalité** nf birth rate

**natation** [natasjɔ̃] nf swimming

**natif, -ive** [natif, iv] adj native

**nation** [nasjɔ̃] nf nation; **national, e, -aux** adj national; **nationale** nf: **(route) nationale** ≈ A road (BRIT), ≈ state highway (US); **nationaliser** vt to nationalize; **nationalisme** nm nationalism; **nationalité** nf nationality

**natte** [nat] nf (cheveux) plait; (tapis) mat

**naturaliser** [natyʀalize] vt to naturalize

**nature** [natyʀ] nf nature ▷ adj, adv (Culin) plain, without seasoning or sweetening; (café, thé) black, without sugar; (yaourt) natural; **payer en ~** to pay in kind; **nature morte** still life; **naturel, le** adj (gén, aussi enfant) natural ▷ nm (absence d'affectation) naturalness; (caractère) disposition, nature; **naturellement** adv naturally; (bien sûr) of course

**naufrage** [nofʀaʒ] nm (ship)wreck; **faire ~** to be shipwrecked

**nausée** [noze] nf nausea; **avoir la ~** to feel sick

**nautique** [notik] adj nautical, water cpd; **sports ~s** water sports

**naval, e** [naval] adj naval; (industrie) shipbuilding

**navet** [nave] nm turnip; (péj: film) rubbishy film

**navette** [navɛt] nf shuttle; **faire la ~ (entre)** to go to and fro ou shuttle (between)

**navigateur** [navigatœʀ] nm (Navig) seafarer; (Inform) browser

**navigation** [navigasjɔ̃] nf navigation, sailing

**naviguer** [navige] vi to navigate, sail; **~ sur Internet** to browse the Internet

**navire** [naviʀ] nm ship

**navrer** [navʀe] vt to upset, distress; **je suis navré** I'm so sorry

**ne, n'** [n(ə)] adv voir **pas; plus; jamais** etc; (sans valeur négative: non traduit): **c'est plus loin que je ne le croyais** it's further than I thought

**né, e** [ne] pp (voir **naître**): **né en 1960** born in 1960; **née Scott** née Scott

**néanmoins** [neɑ̃mwɛ̃] adv nevertheless

**néant** [neɑ̃] nm nothingness; **réduire à ~** to bring to nought; (espoir) to dash

**nécessaire** [neseseʀ] adj necessary ▷ nm necessary; (sac) kit; **je vais faire le ~** I'll see to it; **nécessaire de couture** sewing kit; **nécessaire de toilette** toilet bag; **nécessité** nf necessity; **nécessiter** vt to require

**nectar** [nɛktaʀ] nm nectar

**néerlandais, e** [neɛʀlɑ̃dɛ, ɛz] adj Dutch

**nef** [nɛf] nf (d'église) nave

**néfaste** [nefast] adj (nuisible) harmful; (funeste) ill-fated

**négatif, -ive** [negatif, iv] adj negative ▷ nm (Photo) negative

**négligé, e** [negliʒe] adj (en désordre) slovenly ▷ nm (tenue) negligee

**négligeable** [negliʒabl] adj negligible

**négligent, e** [negliʒɑ̃, ɑ̃t] adj careless, negligent

**négliger** [negliʒe] vt (tenue) to be careless about; (avis, précautions) to disregard; (épouse, jardin) to neglect; **~ de faire** to fail to do, not bother to do

**négociant, e** [negɔsjɑ̃, jɑ̃t] nm/f merchant

**négociation** [negɔsjasjɔ̃] nf negotiation

**négocier** [negɔsje] vi, vt to negotiate

**nègre** [nɛgʀ] (péj) nm (écrivain) ghost (writer)

**neige** [nɛʒ] nf snow; **neiger** vi to snow

**nénuphar** [nenyfaʀ] nm water-lily

**néon** [neɔ̃] nm neon

**néo-zélandais, e** [neozelɑ̃dɛ, ɛz] adj New Zealand cpd ▷ nm/f: **Néo-Zélandais, e** New Zealander

**Népal** [nepal] nm: **le ~** Nepal

**nerf** [nɛʀ] nm nerve; **être sur les ~s**

to be all keyed up; **nerveux, -euse**
adj nervous; (irritable) touchy, nervy;
(voiture) nippy, responsive; **nervosité**
nf excitability, tenseness; (irritabilité
passagère) irritability, nerviness

**n'est-ce pas?** [nɛspɑ] adv isn't it?,
won't you? etc, selon le verbe qui précède

**Net** [nɛt] nm (Internet): **le ~** the Net

**net, nette** [nɛt] adj (sans équivoque,
distinct) clear; (évident: amélioration,
différence) marked, distinct; (propre)
neat, clean; (Comm: prix, salaire) net
▷ adv (refuser) flatly ▷ nm: **mettre au ~**
to copy out; **s'arrêter ~** to stop dead;
**nettement** adv clearly, distinctly;
(incontestablement) decidedly; **netteté**
nf clearness

**nettoyage** [netwajaʒ] nm cleaning;
**nettoyage à sec** dry cleaning

**nettoyer** [netwaje] vt to clean

**neuf¹** [nœf] num nine

**neuf², neuve** [nœf, nœv] adj new;
**remettre à ~** to do up (as good as new),
refurbish; **quoi de ~?** what's new?

**neutre** [nøtʀ] adj neutral; (Ling) neuter

**neuve** [nœv] adj voir **neuf²**

**neuvième** [nœvjɛm] num ninth

**neveu, x** [n(ə)vø] nm nephew

**New York** [njujoʀk] n New York

**nez** [ne] nm nose; **~ à ~ avec** face to face
with; **avoir du ~** to have flair

**ni** [ni] conj: **ni ... ni** neither ... nor; **je
n'aime ni les lentilles ni les épinards**
I like neither lentils nor spinach; **il n'a
dit ni oui ni non** he didn't say either yes
or no; **elles ne sont venues ni l'une
ni l'autre** neither of them came; **il n'a
rien vu ni entendu** he didn't see or
hear anything

**niche** [niʃ] nf (du chien) kennel; (de mur)
recess, niche; **nicher** vi to nest

**nid** [ni] nm nest; **nid de poule** pothole

**nièce** [njɛs] nf niece

**nier** [nje] vt to deny

**Nil** [nil] nm: **le ~** the Nile

**n'importe** [nɛ̃poʀt] adv: **n'importe
qui/quoi/où** anybody/anything/
anywhere; **n'importe quand** any time;

**n'importe quel/quelle** any; **n'importe
lequel/laquelle** any (one); **n'importe
comment** (sans soin) carelessly

**niveau, x** [nivo] nm level; (des élèves,
études) standard; **niveau de vie**
standard of living

**niveler** [niv(ə)le] vt to level

**noble** [nɔbl] adj noble; **noblesse** nf
nobility; (d'une action etc) nobleness

**noce** [nɔs] nf wedding; (gens) wedding
party (ou guests pl); **faire la ~** (fam) to
go on a binge; **noces d'argent/d'or/de
diamant** silver/golden/diamond
wedding (anniversary)

**nocif, -ive** [nɔsif, iv] adj harmful

**nocturne** [nɔktyʀn] adj nocturnal ▷ nf
late-night opening

**Noël** [nɔɛl] nm Christmas

**nœud** [nø] nm knot; (ruban) bow; **nœud
papillon** bow tie

**noir, e** [nwaʀ] adj black; (obscur, sombre)
dark ▷ nm/f black man/woman ▷ nm:
**dans le ~** in the dark; **travail au ~**
moonlighting; **travailler au ~** to work
on the side; **noircir** vt, vi to blacken;
**noire** nf (Mus) crotchet (BRIT), quarter
note (US)

**noisette** [nwazɛt] nf hazelnut

**noix** [nwa] nf walnut; (Culin): **une ~ de
beurre** a knob of butter; **à la ~** (fam)
worthless; **noix de cajou** cashew nut;
**noix de coco** coconut; **noix muscade**
nutmeg

**nom** [nɔ̃] nm name; (Ling) noun; **nom
de famille** surname; **nom de jeune
fille** maiden name

**nomade** [nɔmad] nm/f nomad

**nombre** [nɔ̃bʀ] nm number; **venir en
~** to come in large numbers; **depuis ~
d'années** for many years; **au ~ de
mes amis** among my friends;
**nombreux, -euse** adj many,
numerous; (avec nom sg: foule etc)
large; **peu nombreux** few; **de
nombreux cas** many cases

**nombril** [nɔ̃bʀi(l)] nm navel

**nommer** [nɔme] vt to name; (élire) to
appoint, nominate; **se nommer**; **il se**

**nomme Pascal** his name's Pascal, he's called Pascal

**non** [nɔ̃] adv (réponse) no; (avec loin, sans, seulement) not; **~ (pas) que** not that; **moi ~ plus** neither do I, I don't either; **c'est bon ~?** (exprimant le doute) it's good, isn't it?; **je pense que ~** I don't think so

**non alcoolisé, e** [nɔ̃alkɔlize] adj non alcoholic

**nonchalant, e** [nɔ̃ʃalɑ̃, ɑ̃t] adj nonchalant

**non-fumeur, -euse** [nɔ̃fymœʀ, øz] nm/f non-smoker

**non-sens** [nɔ̃sɑ̃s] nm absurdity

**nord** [nɔʀ] nm North ▷ adj northern; north; **au ~** (situation) in the north; (direction) to the north; **au ~ de** (to the) north of; **nord-africain, e** adj North-African ▷ nm/f: **Nord-Africain, e** North African; **nord-est** nm North-East; **nord-ouest** nm North-West

**normal, e, -aux** [nɔʀmal, o] adj normal; **c'est tout à fait ~** it's perfectly natural; **vous trouvez ça ~?** does it seem right to you?; **normale** nf: **la normale** the norm, the average; **normalement** adv (en général) normally

**normand, e** [nɔʀmɑ̃, ɑ̃d] adj of Normandy ▷ nm/f: **N~, e** (de Normandie) Norman

**Normandie** [nɔʀmɑ̃di] nf Normandy

**norme** [nɔʀm] nf norm; (Tech) standard

**Norvège** [nɔʀvɛʒ] nf Norway; **norvégien, ne** adj Norwegian ▷ nm/f: **Norvégien, ne** Norwegian ▷ nm (Ling) Norwegian

**nos** [no] adj voir **notre**

**nostalgie** [nɔstalʒi] nf nostalgia; **nostalgique** adj nostalgic

**notable** [nɔtabl] adj (fait) notable, noteworthy; (marqué) noticeable, marked ▷ nm prominent citizen

**notaire** [nɔtɛʀ] nm solicitor

**notamment** [nɔtamɑ̃] adv in particular, among others

**note** [nɔt] nf (écrite, Mus) note; (Scol) mark (BRIT), grade; (facture) bill; **note de service** memorandum

**noter** [nɔte] vt (écrire) to write down; (remarquer) to note, notice; (devoir) to mark, grade

**notice** [nɔtis] nf summary, short article; (brochure) leaflet, instruction book

**notifier** [nɔtifje] vt: **~ qch à qn** to notify sb of sth, notify sth to sb

**notion** [nosjɔ̃] nf notion, idea

**notoire** [nɔtwaʀ] adj widely known; (en mal) notorious

**notre** [nɔtʀ] (pl **nos**) adj our

**nôtre** [nɔtʀ] pron: **le ~, la ~, les ~s** ours ▷ adj ours; **les ~s** ours; (alliés etc) our own people; **soyez des ~s** join us

**nouer** [nwe] vt to tie, knot; (fig: alliance etc) to strike up

**noueux, -euse** [nwø, øz] adj gnarled

**nourrice** [nuʀis] nf (gardienne) child-minder

**nourrir** [nuʀiʀ] vt to feed; (fig: espoir) to harbour, nurse; **nourrissant, e** adj nourishing, nutritious; **nourrisson** nm (unweaned) infant; **nourriture** nf food

**nous** [nu] pron (sujet) we; (objet) us; **nous-mêmes** pron ourselves

**nouveau (nouvel), -elle, x** [nuvo, nuvɛl] adj new ▷ nm: **y a-t-il du nouveau?** is there anything new on this? ▷ nm/f new pupil (ou employee); **de nouveau, à nouveau** again; **nouveau venu, nouvelle venue** newcomer; **nouveaux mariés** newly-weds; **nouveau-né, e** nm/f newborn baby; **nouveauté** nf novelty; (objet) new thing ou article

**nouvel** [nuvɛl] adj voir **nouveau**; **Nouvel An** New Year

**nouvelle** [nuvɛl] adj voir **nouveau** ▷ nf (piece of) news sg; (Littérature) short story; **les ~s** (Presse, TV) the news; **je suis sans ~s de lui** I haven't heard from him; **Nouvelle-Calédonie** nf New Caledonia; **Nouvelle-Zélande** nf New Zealand

**novembre** [nɔvɑ̃bʀ] *nm* November

● **NOVEMBRE**
●
● **Le 11 novembre** is a public holiday in
● France commemorating the signing
● of the armistice, near Compiègne, at
● the end of World War I.

**noyade** [nwajad] *nf* drowning *no pl*
**noyau, x** [nwajo] *nm* (*de fruit*) stone;
(*Bio, Physique*) nucleus; (*fig: centre*) core
**noyer** [nwaje] *nm* walnut (tree); (*bois*)
walnut ▷ *vt* to drown; (*moteur*) to flood;
**se noyer** *vi* to be drowned, drown;
(*suicide*) to drown o.s.
**nu, e** [ny] *adj* naked; (*membres*) naked,
bare; (*pieds, mains, chambre, fil électrique*)
bare ▷ *nm* (*Art*) nude; **tout nu** stark
naked; **se mettre nu** to strip
**nuage** [nɥaʒ] *nm* cloud; **nuageux,**
**-euse** *adj* cloudy
**nuance** [nɥɑ̃s] *nf* (*de couleur, sens*)
shade; **il y a une ~ (entre)** there's a
slight difference (between); **nuancer**
*vt* (*opinion*) to bring some reservations
*ou* qualifications to
**nucléaire** [nykleɛʀ] *adj* nuclear ▷ *nm*:
**le ~** nuclear energy
**nudiste** [nydist] *nm/f* nudist
**nuée** [nɥe] *nf*: **une ~ de** a cloud *ou* host
*ou* swarm of
**nuire** [nɥiʀ] *vi* to be harmful; **~ à** to
harm, do damage to; **nuisible** *adj*
harmful; **animal nuisible** pest
**nuit** [nɥi] *nf* night; **il fait ~** it's dark;
**cette ~** (*hier*) last night; (*aujourd'hui*)
tonight; **de ~** (*vol, service*) night *cpd*;
**nuit blanche** sleepless night
**nul, nulle** [nyl] *adj* (*aucun*) no; (*minime*)
nil, non-existent; (*non valable*) null; (*péj*):
**être ~ (en)** to be useless *ou* hopeless
(at) ▷ *pron* none, no one; **match** *ou*
**résultat ~** draw; **~le part** nowhere;
**nullement** *adv* by no means
**numérique** [nymeʀik] *adj* numerical;
(*affichage, son, télévision*) digital
**numéro** [nymeʀo] *nm* number;

(*spectacle*) act, turn; (*Presse*) issue,
number; **numéro de téléphone**
(tele)phone number; **numéro vert**
≈ freefone® number (BRIT), ≈ toll-free
number (US); **numéroter** *vt* to number
**nuque** [nyk] *nf* nape of the neck
**nu-tête** [nytɛt] *adj inv, adv* bareheaded
**nutritif, -ive** [nytʀitif, iv] *adj* (*besoins,
valeur*) nutritional; (*nourrissant*)
nutritious
**nylon** [nilɔ̃] *nm* nylon

**oasis** [ɔazis] *nf* oasis
**obéir** [ɔbeiʀ] *vi* to obey; **~ à** to obey;
**obéissance** *nf* obedience;
**obéissant, e** *adj* obedient
**obèse** [ɔbɛz] *adj* obese; **obésité** *nf*
obesity
**objecter** [ɔbʒɛkte] *vt*: **~ que** to object
that; **objecteur** *nm*: **objecteur de
conscience** conscientious objector
**objectif, -ive** [ɔbʒɛktif, iv] *adj*
objective ▷ *nm* objective; (*Photo*) lens
*sg*, objective
**objection** [ɔbʒɛksjɔ̃] *nf* objection
**objectivité** [ɔbʒɛktivite] *nf* objectivity
**objet** [ɔbʒɛ] *nm* object; (*d'une discussion,
recherche*) subject; **être** *ou* **faire l'~
de** (*discussion*) to be the subject of;
(*soins*) to be given *ou* shown; **sans ~**
purposeless; (*craintes*) groundless;
**(bureau des) ~s trouvés** lost property
*sg* (*BRIT*), lost-and-found *sg* (*US*); **objet
d'art** objet d'art; **objets de valeur**
valuables; **objets personnels** personal
items

**obligation** [ɔbligasjɔ̃] *nf* obligation;
(*Comm*) bond, debenture; **obligatoire**
*adj* compulsory, obligatory;
**obligatoirement** *adv* necessarily;
(*fam: sans aucun doute*) inevitably
**obliger** [ɔbliʒe] *vt* (*contraindre*): **~ qn à
faire** to force *ou* oblige sb to do; **je suis
bien obligé (de le faire)** I have to (do it)
**oblique** [ɔblik] *adj* oblique; **en ~**
diagonally
**oblitérer** [ɔblitere] *vt* (*timbre-poste*)
to cancel
**obnubiler** [ɔbnybile] *vt* to obsess
**obscène** [ɔpsɛn] *adj* obscene
**obscur, e** [ɔpskyʀ] *adj* dark; (*méconnu*)
obscure; **obscurcir** *vt* to darken; (*fig*)
to obscure; **s'obscurcir** *vi* to grow
dark; **obscurité** *nf* darkness; **dans
l'obscurité** in the dark, in darkness
**obsédé, e** [ɔpsede] *nm/f*: **un ~ de jazz** a
jazz fanatic; **obsédé sexuel** sex maniac
**obséder** [ɔpsede] *vt* to obsess, haunt
**obsèques** [ɔpsɛk] *nfpl* funeral *sg*
**observateur, -trice** [ɔpsɛʀvatœʀ,
tʀis] *adj* observant, perceptive ▷ *nm/f*
observer
**observation** [ɔpsɛʀvasjɔ̃] *nf*
observation; (*d'un règlement etc*)
observance; (*reproche*) reproof; **être en
~** (*Méd*) to be under observation
**observatoire** [ɔpsɛʀvatwaʀ] *nm*
observatory
**observer** [ɔpsɛʀve] *vt* (*regarder*) to
observe, watch; (*scientifiquement; aussi
règlement etc*) to observe; (*surveiller*) to
watch; (*remarquer*) to observe, notice;
**faire ~ qch à qn** (*dire*) to point out
sth to sb
**obsession** [ɔpsesjɔ̃] *nf* obsession
**obstacle** [ɔpstakl] *nm* obstacle;
(*Équitation*) jump, hurdle; **faire ~ à**
(*projet*) to hinder, put obstacles in
the path of
**obstiné, e** [ɔpstine] *adj* obstinate
**obstiner** [ɔpstine]: **s'obstiner** *vi* to
insist, dig one's heels in; **s'~ à faire** to
persist (obstinately) in doing
**obstruer** [ɔpstʀye] *vt* to block,

obstruct

**obtenir** [ɔptǝniʀ] *vt* to obtain, get;
(*résultat*) to achieve, obtain; **~ de
pouvoir faire** to obtain permission
to do

**obturateur** [ɔptyʀatœʀ] *nm* (*Photo*)
shutter

**obus** [ɔby] *nm* shell

**occasion** [ɔkazjɔ̃] *nf* (*aubaine,
possibilité*) opportunity; (*circonstance*)
occasion; (*Comm: article non neuf*)
secondhand buy; (*: acquisition
avantageuse*) bargain; **à plusieurs ~s**
on several occasions; **à l'~** sometimes,
on occasions; **d'~** secondhand;
**occasionnel, le** *adj* (*non régulier*)
occasional

**occasionner** [ɔkazjɔne] *vt* to cause

**occident** [ɔksidɑ̃] *nm:* **l'O~** the West;
**occidental, e, -aux** *adj* western; (*Pol*)
Western ▷ *nm/f* Westerner

**occupation** [ɔkypasjɔ̃] *nf* occupation

**occupé, e** [ɔkype] *adj* (*personne*) busy;
(*place, sièges*) taken; (*toilettes*) engaged;
(*Mil, Pol*) occupied; **la ligne est ~e** the
line's engaged (*BRIT*) *ou* busy (*US*)

**occuper** [ɔkype] *vt* to occupy; (*poste*) to
hold; **s'occuper de** (*être responsable de*)
to be in charge of; (*se charger de: affaire*)
to take charge of, deal with; (*: clients
etc*) to attend to; **s'~ (à qch)** to occupy
o.s. *ou* keep o.s. busy (with sth)

**occurrence** [ɔkyʀɑ̃s] *nf:* **en l'~** in
this case

**océan** [ɔseɑ̃] *nm* ocean

**octet** [ɔktɛ] *nm* byte

**octobre** [ɔktɔbʀ] *nm* October

**oculiste** [ɔkylist] *nm/f* eye specialist

**odeur** [ɔdœʀ] *nf* smell

**odieux, -euse** [ɔdjø, jøz] *adj* hateful

**odorant, e** [ɔdɔʀɑ̃, ɑ̃t] *adj* sweet-
smelling, fragrant

**odorat** [ɔdɔʀa] *nm* (sense of) smell

**œil** [œj] *nm* (*pl* **yeux**) eye; **avoir un ~ au
beurre noir** *ou* **poché** to have a black
eye; **à l'~** (*fam*) for free; **à l'~ nu** with
the naked eye; **ouvrir l'~** (*fig*) to keep
one's eyes open *ou* an eye out; **fermer
les yeux (sur)** (*fig*) to turn a blind eye
(to); **les yeux fermés** (*aussi fig*) with
one's eyes shut

**œillères** [œjɛʀ] *nfpl* blinkers (*BRIT*),
blinders (*US*)

**œillet** [œjɛ] *nm* (*Bot*) carnation

**œuf** [œf, *pl* ø] *nm* egg; **œuf à la coque**
boiled egg; **œuf au plat** fried egg; **œuf
dur** hard-boiled egg; **œuf de Pâques**
Easter egg; **œufs brouillés** scrambled
eggs

**œuvre** [œvʀ] *nf* (*tâche*) task,
undertaking; (*livre, tableau etc*) work;
(*ensemble de la production artistique*)
works *pl* ▷ *nm* (*Constr*): **le gros ~** the
shell; **mettre en ~** (*moyens*) to make use
of; **œuvre de bienfaisance** charity;
**œuvre d'art** work of art

**offense** [ɔfɑ̃s] *nf* insult; **offenser** *vt* to
offend, hurt; **s'offenser de qch** to take
offence (*BRIT*) *ou* offense (*US*) at sth

**offert, e** [ɔfɛʀ, ɛʀt] *pp de* **offrir**

**office** [ɔfis] *nm* (*agence*) bureau, agency;
(*Rel*) service ▷ *nm ou nf* (*pièce*) pantry;
**faire ~ de** to act as; **d'~** automatically;
**office du tourisme** tourist bureau

**officiel, le** [ɔfisjɛl] *adj, nm/f* official

**officier** [ɔfisje] *nm* officer

**officieux, -euse** [ɔfisjø, jøz] *adj*
unofficial

**offrande** [ɔfʀɑ̃d] *nf* offering

**offre** [ɔfʀ] *nf* offer; (*aux enchères*) bid;
(*Admin: soumission*) tender; (*Écon*): **l'~
et la demande** supply and demand;
**"~s d'emploi"** "situations vacant";
**offre d'emploi** job advertised; **offre
publique d'achat** takeover bid

**offrir** [ɔfʀiʀ] *vt:* **~ (à qn)** to offer (to sb);
(*faire cadeau de*) to give (to sb); **s'offrir**
*vt* (*vacances, voiture*) to treat o.s. to; **~ (à
qn) de faire qch** to offer to do sth (for
sb); **~ à boire à qn** (*chez soi*) to offer sb
a drink; **je vous offre un verre** I'll buy
you a drink

**OGM** *sigle m* (= *organisme génétiquement
modifié*) GMO

**oie** [wa] *nf* (*Zool*) goose

**oignon** [ɔɲɔ̃] *nm* onion; (*de tulipe*

*etc*) bulb

**oiseau, x** [wazo] *nm* bird; **oiseau de proie** bird of prey

**oisif, -ive** [wazif, iv] *adj* idle

**oléoduc** [ɔleɔdyk] *nm* (oil) pipeline

**olive** [ɔliv] *nf* (*Bot*) olive; **olivier** *nm* olive (tree)

**OLP** *sigle f* (= *Organisation de libération de la Palestine*) PLO

**olympique** [ɔlɛ̃pik] *adj* Olympic

**ombragé, e** [ɔ̃braʒe] *adj* shaded, shady

**ombre** [ɔ̃br] *nf* (*espace non ensoleillé*) shade; (*ombre portée, tache*) shadow; **à l'~** in the shade; **dans l'~** (*fig*) in the dark; **ombre à paupières** eyeshadow

**omelette** [ɔmlɛt] *nf* omelette; **omelette norvégienne** baked Alaska

**omettre** [ɔmɛtr] *vt* to omit, leave out

**omoplate** [ɔmɔplat] *nf* shoulder blade

---

**O** MOT-CLÉ

**on** [ɔ̃] *pron* **1** (*indéterminé*) you, one; **on peut le faire ainsi** you *ou* one can do it like this, it can be done like this
**2** (*quelqu'un*): **on les a attaqués** they were attacked; **on vous demande au téléphone** there's a phone call for you, you're wanted on the phone
**3** (*nous*) we; **on va y aller demain** we're going tomorrow
**4** (*les gens*) they; **autrefois, on croyait ...** they used to believe ...
**5**: **on ne peut plus** *adv*: **on ne peut plus stupide** as stupid as can be

---

**oncle** [ɔ̃kl] *nm* uncle

**onctueux, -euse** [ɔ̃ktɥø, øz] *adj* creamy, smooth

**onde** [ɔ̃d] *nf* wave; **~s courtes/ moyennes** short/medium wave *sg*; **grandes ~s** long wave *sg*

**ondée** [ɔ̃de] *nf* shower

**on-dit** [ɔ̃di] *nm inv* rumour

**onduler** [ɔ̃dyle] *vi* to undulate; (*cheveux*) to wave

**onéreux, -euse** [ɔnerø, øz] *adj* costly

**ongle** [ɔ̃gl] *nm* nail

**ont** [ɔ̃] *vb voir* **avoir**

**ONU** *sigle f* (= *Organisation des Nations Unies*) UN

**onze** [ɔ̃z] *num* eleven; **onzième** *num* eleventh

**OPA** *sigle f* = **offre publique d'achat**

**opaque** [ɔpak] *adj* opaque

**opéra** [ɔpera] *nm* opera; (*édifice*) opera house

**opérateur, -trice** [ɔperatœr, tris] *nm/f* operator; **opérateur (de prise de vues)** cameraman

**opération** [ɔperasjɔ̃] *nf* operation; (*Comm*) dealing

**opératoire** [ɔperatwar] *adj* (*choc etc*) post-operative

**opérer** [ɔpere] *vt* (*personne*) to operate on; (*faire, exécuter*) to carry out, make ▷ *vi* (*remède: faire effet*) to act, work; (*Méd*) to operate; **s'opérer** *vi* (*avoir lieu*) to occur, take place; **se faire ~** to have an operation

**opérette** [ɔperɛt] *nf* operetta, light opera

**opinion** [ɔpinjɔ̃] *nf* opinion; **l'opinion (publique)** public opinion

**opportun, e** [ɔpɔrtœ̃, yn] *adj* timely, opportune; **opportuniste** *nm/f* opportunist

**opposant, e** [ɔpozɑ̃, ɑ̃t] *nm/f* opponent

**opposé, e** [ɔpoze] *adj* (*direction*) opposite; (*faction*) opposing; (*opinions, intérêts*) conflicting; (*contre*): **~ à** opposed to, against ▷ *nm*: **l'~** the other *ou* opposite side (*ou* direction); (*contraire*) the opposite; **à l'~** (*fig*) on the other hand; **à l'~ de** (*fig*) contrary to, unlike

**opposer** [ɔpoze] *vt* (*personnes, équipes*) to oppose; (*couleurs*) to contrast; **s'opposer** *vi* (*équipes*) to confront each other; (*opinions*) to conflict; (*couleurs, styles*) to contrast; **s'~ à** (*interdire*) to oppose; **~ qch à** (*comme obstacle, défense*) to set sth against; (*comme objection*) to put sth forward against

**opposition** [ɔpozisjɔ̃] nf opposition; **par ~ à** as opposed to; **entrer en ~ avec** to come into conflict with; **faire ~ à un chèque** to stop a cheque

**oppressant, e** [ɔpresɑ̃, ɑ̃t] adj oppressive

**oppresser** [ɔprese] vt to oppress; **oppression** nf oppression

**opprimer** [ɔprime] vt to oppress

**opter** [ɔpte] vi: **~ pour** to opt for

**opticien, ne** [ɔptisjɛ̃, jɛn] nm/f optician

**optimisme** [ɔptimism] nm optimism; **optimiste** nm/f optimist ▷ adj optimistic

**option** [ɔpsjɔ̃] nf option; **matière à ~** (Scol) optional subject

**optique** [ɔptik] adj (nerf) optic; (verres) optical ▷ nf (fig: manière de voir) perspective

**or** [ɔr] nm gold ▷ conj now, but; **en or** (objet) gold cpd; **une affaire en or** a real bargain; **il croyait gagner et il a perdu** he was sure he would win and yet he lost

**orage** [ɔraʒ] nm (thunder)storm; **orageux, -euse** adj stormy

**oral, e, -aux** [ɔral, o] adj, nm oral; **par voie ~e** (Méd) orally

**orange** [ɔrɑ̃ʒ] nf orange ▷ adj inv orange; **orangé, e** adj orangey, orange-coloured; **orangeade** nf orangeade; **oranger** nm orange tree

**orateur** [ɔratœr] nm speaker

**orbite** [ɔrbit] nf (Anat) (eye-)socket; (Physique) orbit

**Orcades** [ɔrkad] nfpl: **les ~** the Orkneys, the Orkney Islands

**orchestre** [ɔrkɛstr] nm orchestra; (de jazz) band; (places) stalls pl (BRIT), orchestra (US)

**orchidée** [ɔrkide] nf orchid

**ordinaire** [ɔrdinɛr] adj ordinary; (qualité) standard; (péj: commun) common ▷ nm ordinary; (menus) everyday fare ▷ nf (essence) ≈ two-star (petrol) (BRIT), ≈ regular gas (US); **d'~** usually, normally; **comme à l'~** as usual

**ordinateur** [ɔrdinatœr] nm computer; **ordinateur individuel** ou **personnel** personal computer; **ordinateur portable** laptop (computer)

**ordonnance** [ɔrdɔnɑ̃s] nf (Méd) prescription; (Mil) orderly, batman (BRIT); **pouvez-vous me faire une ~?** can you write me a prescription?

**ordonné, e** [ɔrdɔne] adj tidy, orderly

**ordonner** [ɔrdɔne] vt (agencer) to organize, arrange; (donner un ordre): **~ à qn de faire** to order sb to do; (Rel) to ordain; (Méd) to prescribe

**ordre** [ɔrdr] nm order; (propreté et soin) orderliness, tidiness; (nature): **d'~ pratique** of a practical nature; **ordres** nmpl (Rel) holy orders; **mettre en ~** to tidy (up), put in order; **par ~ alphabétique/d'importance** in alphabetical order/in order of importance; **à l'~ de qn** payable to sb; **être aux ~s de qn/sous les ~s de qn** to be at sb's disposal/under sb's command; **jusqu'à nouvel ~** until further notice; **de premier ~** first-rate; **ordre du jour** (d'une réunion) agenda; **à l'ordre du jour** (fig) topical; **ordre publique** law and order

**ordure** [ɔrdyr] nf filth no pl; **ordures** nfpl (balayures, déchets) rubbish sg, refuse sg; **ordures ménagères** household refuse

**oreille** [ɔrɛj] nf ear; **avoir de l'~** to have a good ear (for music)

**oreiller** [ɔreje] nm pillow

**oreillons** [ɔrejɔ̃] nmpl mumps sg

**ores** [ɔr]: **d'~ et déjà** adv already

**orfèvrerie** [ɔrfɛvrəri] nf goldsmith's (ou silversmith's) trade; (ouvrage) gold (ou silver) plate

**organe** [ɔrgan] nm organ; (porte-parole) representative, mouthpiece

**organigramme** [ɔrganigram] nm (tableau hiérarchique) organization chart; (schéma) flow chart

**organique** [ɔrganik] adj organic

**organisateur, -trice** [ɔrganizatœr,

tris] *nm/f* organizer

**organisation** [ɔʀganizasjɔ̃] *nf*
organization; **Organisation des
Nations Unies** United Nations
(Organization)

**organiser** [ɔʀganize] *vt* to organize;
(*mettre sur pied: service etc*) to set up;
**s'organiser** to get organized

**organisme** [ɔʀganism] *nm* (*Bio*)
organism; (*corps, Admin*) body

**organiste** [ɔʀganist] *nm/f* organist

**orgasme** [ɔʀgasm] *nm* orgasm, climax

**orge** [ɔʀʒ] *nf* barley

**orgue** [ɔʀg] *nm* organ

**orgueil** [ɔʀgœj] *nm* pride; **orgueilleux,
-euse** *adj* proud

**oriental, e, -aux** [ɔʀjɑ̃tal, -o] *adj*
(*langue, produit*) oriental; (*frontière*)
eastern

**orientation** [ɔʀjɑ̃tasjɔ̃] *nf* (*de
recherches*) orientation; (*d'une maison
etc*) aspect; (*d'un journal*) leanings *pl*;
**avoir le sens de l'~** to have a (good)
sense of direction; **orientation
professionnelle** careers advisory
service

**orienté, e** [ɔʀjɑ̃te] *adj* (*fig: article,
journal*) slanted; **bien/mal ~**
(*appartement*) well/badly positioned; **~
au sud** facing south, with a southern
aspect

**orienter** [ɔʀjɑ̃te] *vt* (*tourner: antenne*)
to direct, turn; (*personne, recherches*)
to direct; (*fig: élève*) to orientate;
**s'orienter** (*se repérer*) to find one's
bearings; **s'~ vers** (*fig*) to turn towards

**origan** [ɔʀigɑ̃] *nm* oregano

**originaire** [ɔʀiʒinɛʀ] *adj*: **être ~ de** to
be a native of

**original, e, -aux** [ɔʀiʒinal, o] *adj*
original; (*bizarre*) eccentric ▷ *nm/f*
eccentric ▷ *nm* (*document etc, Art*)
original

**origine** [ɔʀiʒin] *nf* origin; **origines** *nfpl*
(*d'une personne*) origins; **d'~** (*pays*) of
origin; **d'~ suédoise** of Swedish origin;
(*pneus etc*) original; **à l'~** originally;
**originel, le** *adj* original

**orme** [ɔʀm] *nm* elm

**ornement** [ɔʀnəmɑ̃] *nm* ornament

**orner** [ɔʀne] *vt* to decorate, adorn

**ornière** [ɔʀnjɛʀ] *nf* rut

**orphelin, e** [ɔʀfəlɛ̃, in] *adj* orphan(ed)
▷ *nm/f* orphan; **orphelin de
mère/de père** motherless/fatherless;
**orphelinat** *nm* orphanage

**orteil** [ɔʀtɛj] *nm* toe; **gros ~** big toe

**orthographe** [ɔʀtɔgʀaf] *nf* spelling

**ortie** [ɔʀti] *nf* (*stinging*) nettle

**os** [ɔs] *nm* bone; **os à moelle**
marrowbone

**osciller** [ɔsile] *vi* (*au vent etc*) to rock;
(*fig*): **~ entre** to waver *ou* fluctuate
between

**osé, e** [oze] *adj* daring, bold

**oseille** [ozɛj] *nf* sorrel

**oser** [oze] *vi, vt* to dare; **~ faire** to dare
(to) do

**osier** [ozje] *nm* willow; **d'~, en ~**
wicker(work)

**osseux, -euse** [ɔsø, øz] *adj* bony;
(*tissu, maladie, greffe*) bone *cpd*

**otage** [ɔtaʒ] *nm* hostage; **prendre qn
comme ~** to take sb hostage

**OTAN** *sigle f* (= *Organisation du traité de
l'Atlantique Nord*) NATO

**otarie** [ɔtaʀi] *nf* sea-lion

**ôter** [ote] *vt* to remove; (*soustraire*)
to take away; **~ qch à qn** to take sth
(away) from sb; **~ qch de** to remove
sth from

**otite** [ɔtit] *nf* ear infection

**ou** [u] *conj* or; **ou ... ou** either ... or;
**ou bien** or (else)

 **MOT-CLÉ**

**où** [u] *pron relatif* **1** (*position, situation*)
where, that (*souvent omis*); **la chambre
où il était** the room (that) he was in,
the room where he was; **la ville où
je l'ai rencontré** the town where I
met him; **la pièce d'où il est sorti** the
room he came out of; **le village d'où
je viens** the village I come from; **les
villes par où il est passé** the towns he

went through
**2** (*temps, état*) that (*souvent omis*); **le jour où il est parti** the day (that) he left; **au prix où c'est** at the price it is
▷ *adv* **1** (*interrogation*) where; **où est-il/va-t-il?** where is he/is he going?; **par où?** which way?; **d'où vient que …?** how come …?
**2** (*position*) where; **je sais où il est** I know where he is; **où que l'on aille** wherever you go

**ouate** ['wat] *nf* cotton wool (BRIT), cotton (US)
**oubli** [ubli] *nm* (*acte*): **l'~ de** forgetting; (*trou de mémoire*) lapse of memory; (*négligence*) omission, oversight; **tomber dans l'~** to sink into oblivion
**oublier** [ublije] *vt* to forget; (*laisser quelque part: chapeau etc*) to leave behind; (*ne pas voir: erreurs etc*) to miss; **j'ai oublié ma clé/mon passeport** I've forgotten my key/passport
**ouest** [wɛst] *nm* west ▷ *adj inv* west; (*région*) western; **à l'~** in the west; (*direction*) (to the) west, westwards; **à l'~ de** (to the) west of
**ouf** ['uf] *excl* phew!
**oui** ['wi] *adv* yes
**ouï-dire** ['widiʀ]: **par ~** *adv* by hearsay
**ouïe** [wi] *nf* hearing; **ouïes** *nfpl* (*de poisson*) gills
**ouragan** [uʀagɑ̃] *nm* hurricane
**ourlet** [uʀlɛ] *nm* hem
**ours** [uʀs] *nm* bear; **ours blanc/brun** polar/brown bear; **ours (en peluche)** teddy (bear)
**oursin** [uʀsɛ̃] *nm* sea urchin
**ourson** [uʀsɔ̃] *nm* (bear-)cub
**ouste** [ust] *excl* hop it!
**outil** [uti] *nm* tool; **outiller** *vt* to equip
**outrage** [utʀaʒ] *nm* insult; **outrage à la pudeur** indecent conduct *no pl*
**outrance** [utʀɑ̃s]: **à ~** *adv* excessively, to excess
**outre** [utʀ] *prép* besides ▷ *adv*: **passer ~ à** to disregard, take no notice of; **en ~** besides, moreover; **~ mesure** to excess;

(*manger, boire*) immoderately; **outre-Atlantique** *adv* across the Atlantic; **outre-mer** *adv* overseas
**ouvert, e** [uvɛʀ, ɛʀt] *pp de* **ouvrir** ▷ *adj* open; (*robinet, gaz etc*) on; **ouvertement** *adv* openly; **ouverture** *nf* opening; (*Mus*) overture; **heures d'ouverture** (*Comm*) opening hours; **ouverture d'esprit** open-mindedness
**ouvrable** [uvʀabl] *adj*: **jour ~** working day, weekday
**ouvrage** [uvʀaʒ] *nm* (*tâche, de tricot etc*) work *no pl*; (*texte, livre*) work
**ouvre-boîte(s)** [uvʀəbwat] *nm inv* tin (BRIT) *ou* can opener
**ouvre-bouteille(s)** [uvʀəbutɛj] *nm inv* bottle-opener
**ouvreuse** [uvʀøz] *nf* usherette
**ouvrier, -ière** [uvʀije, ijɛʀ] *nm/f* worker ▷ *adj* working-class; (*conflit*) industrial; (*mouvement*) labour *cpd*; **classe ouvrière** working class
**ouvrir** [uvʀiʀ] *vt* (*gén*) to open; (*brèche, passage, Méd: abcès*) to open up; (*commencer l'exploitation de, créer*) to open (up); (*eau, électricité, chauffage, robinet*) to turn on ▷ *vi* to open; to open up; **s'ouvrir** *vi* to open; **s'~ à qn** to open one's heart to sb; **est-ce ouvert au public?** is it open to the public?; **quand est-ce que le musée est ouvert?** when is the museum open?; **à quelle heure ouvrez-vous?** what time do you open?; **~ l'appétit à qn** to whet sb's appetite
**ovaire** [ovɛʀ] *nm* ovary
**ovale** [oval] *adj* oval
**OVNI** [ovni] *sigle m* (= *objet volant non identifié*) UFO
**oxyder** [okside]: **s'oxyder** *vi* to become oxidized
**oxygène** [oksiʒɛn] *nm* oxygen
**oxygéné, e** [oksiʒene] *adj*: **eau ~e** hydrogen peroxide
**ozone** [ozon] *nf* ozone; **la couche d'~** the ozone layer

# p

**pacifique** [pasifik] *adj* peaceful ▷ *nm*: **le P~, l'océan P~** the Pacific (Ocean)
**pack** [pak] *nm* pack
**pacotille** [pakɔtij] *nf* cheap junk
**PACS** *sigle m* (= *pacte civil de solidarité*) contract of civil partnership; **pacser**: **se pacser** *vi* to sign a contract of civil partnership
**pacte** [pakt] *nm* pact, treaty
**pagaille** [pagaj] *nf* mess, shambles *sg*
**page** [paʒ] *nf* page ▷ *nm* page (boy); **à la ~** (*fig*) up-to-date; **page d'accueil** (*Inform*) home page; **page Web** (*Inform*) web page
**paiement** [pɛmɑ̃] *nm* payment
**païen, ne** [pajɛ̃, pajɛn] *adj, nm/f* pagan, heathen
**paillasson** [pajasɔ̃] *nm* doormat
**paille** [paj] *nf* straw
**pain** [pɛ̃] *nm* (*substance*) bread; (*unité*) loaf (of bread); (*morceau*): **~ de savon** *etc* bar of soap *etc*; **pain au chocolat** chocolate-filled pastry; **pain aux raisins** currant bun; **pain bis/complet** brown/wholemeal (BRIT) *ou* wholewheat (US) bread; **pain d'épice** ≈ gingerbread; **pain de mie** sandwich loaf; **pain grillé** toast

**pair, e** [pɛR] *adj* (*nombre*) even ▷ *nm* peer; **aller de ~** to go hand in hand *ou* together; **jeune fille au ~** au pair; **paire** *nf* pair
**paisible** [pezibl] *adj* peaceful, quiet
**paix** [pɛ] *nf* peace; **faire/avoir la ~** to make/have peace; **fiche-lui la ~!** (*fam*) leave him alone!
**Pakistan** [pakistɑ̃] *nm*: **le ~** Pakistan
**palais** [palɛ] *nm* palace; (*Anat*) palate
**pâle** [pɑl] *adj* pale; **bleu ~** pale blue
**Palestine** [palɛstin] *nf*: **la ~** Palestine
**palette** [palɛt] *nf* (*de peintre*) palette; (*produits*) range
**pâleur** [pɑlœR] *nf* paleness
**palier** [palje] *nm* (*d'escalier*) landing; (*fig*) level, plateau; **par ~s** in stages
**pâlir** [palir] *vi* to turn *ou* go pale; (*couleur*) to fade
**pallier** [palje] *vt* to offset, make up for
**palme** [palm] *nf* (*de plongeur*) flipper; **palmé, e** *adj* (*pattes*) webbed
**palmier** [palmje] *nm* palm tree; (*gâteau*) heart-shaped biscuit made of flaky pastry
**pâlot, te** [pɑlo, ɔt] *adj* pale, peaky
**palourde** [palurd] *nf* clam
**palper** [palpe] *vt* to feel, finger
**palpitant, e** [palpitɑ̃, ɑ̃t] *adj* thrilling
**palpiter** [palpite] *vi* (*cœur, pouls*) to beat; (: *plus fort*) to pound, throb
**paludisme** [palydism] *nm* malaria
**pamphlet** [pɑ̃flɛ] *nm* lampoon, satirical tract
**pamplemousse** [pɑ̃pləmus] *nm* grapefruit
**pan** [pɑ̃] *nm* section, piece ▷ *excl* bang!
**panache** [panaʃ] *nm* plume; (*fig*) spirit, panache
**panaché, e** [panaʃe] *adj*: **glace ~e** mixed-flavour ice cream ▷ *nm* (*bière*) shandy
**pancarte** [pɑ̃kart] *nf* sign, notice
**pancréas** [pɑ̃kreas] *nm* pancreas

**pané, e** [pane] *adj* fried in breadcrumbs

**panier** [panje] *nm* basket; **mettre au ~** to chuck away; **panier à provisions** shopping basket; **panier-repas** *nm* packed lunch

**panique** [panik] *nf, adj* panic; **paniquer** *vi* to panic

**panne** [pan] *nf* breakdown; **être/ tomber en ~** to have broken down/ break down; **être en ~ d'essence** *ou* **sèche** to have run out of petrol (BRIT) *ou* gas (US); **ma voiture est en ~** my car has broken down; **panne d'électricité** *ou* **de courant** power cut *ou* failure

**panneau, x** [pano] *nm* (*écriteau*) sign, notice; **panneau d'affichage** notice board; **panneau de signalisation** roadsign; **panneau indicateur** signpost

**panoplie** [panɔpli] *nf* (*jouet*) outfit; (*fig*) array

**panorama** [panɔrama] *nm* panorama

**panse** [pɑ̃s] *nf* paunch

**pansement** [pɑ̃smɑ̃] *nm* dressing, bandage; **pansement adhésif** sticking plaster

**pantacourt** [pɑ̃takuʀ] *nm* three-quarter length trousers *pl*

**pantalon** [pɑ̃talɔ̃] *nm* trousers *pl*, pair of trousers; **pantalon de ski** ski pants *pl*

**panthère** [pɑ̃tɛʀ] *nf* panther

**pantin** [pɑ̃tɛ̃] *nm* puppet

**pantoufle** [pɑ̃tufl] *nf* slipper

**paon** [pɑ̃] *nm* peacock

**papa** [papa] *nm* dad(dy)

**pape** [pap] *nm* pope

**paperasse** [papʀas] *nf* (*péj*) bumf *no pl*, papers *pl*; **paperasserie** (*péj*) *nf* paperwork *no pl*; (*tracasserie*) red tape *no pl*

**papeterie** [papetʀi] *nf* (*magasin*) stationer's (shop)

**papi** *nm* (*fam*) granddad

**papier** [papje] *nm* paper; (*article*) article; **papiers** *nmpl* (*aussi:* **~s d'identité**) (identity) papers; **papier à lettres** writing paper, notepaper;

**papier (d')aluminium** aluminium (BRIT) *ou* aluminum (US) foil, tinfoil; **papier calque** tracing paper; **papier de verre** sandpaper; **papier hygiénique** *ou* **(de) toilette** toilet paper; **papier journal** newspaper; **papier peint** wallpaper

**papillon** [papijɔ̃] *nm* butterfly; (*fam: contravention*) (parking) ticket; **papillon de nuit** moth

**papillote** [papijɔt] *nf*: **en ~** cooked in tinfoil

**papoter** [papɔte] *vi* to chatter

**paquebot** [pak(ə)bo] *nm* liner

**pâquerette** [pɑkʀɛt] *nf* daisy

**Pâques** [pɑk] *nm, nfpl* Easter

● **PÂQUES**
●
● In France, Easter eggs are said to
● be brought by the Easter bells or
● **cloches de Pâques** which fly from
● Rome and drop them in people's
● gardens.

**paquet** [pakɛ] *nm* packet; (*colis*) parcel; (*fig: tas*): **~ de** pile *ou* heap of; **un ~ de cigarettes, s'il vous plaît** a packet of cigarettes, please; **paquet-cadeau** *nm*: **pouvez-vous me faire un paquet-cadeau, s'il vous plaît?** can you gift-wrap it for me, please?

**par** [paʀ] *prép* by; **finir** *etc* **~** to end *etc* with; **~ amour** out of love; **passer ~ Lyon/la côte** to go via *ou* through Lyons/along the coast; **~ la fenêtre** (*jeter, regarder*) out of the window; **3 ~ jour/personne** 3 a *ou* per day/person; **2 ~ 2** in twos; **~ ici** this way; (*dans le coin*) round here; **~-ci, ~-là** here and there; **~ temps de pluie** in wet weather

**parabolique** [paʀabɔlik] *adj*: **antenne ~** parabolic *ou* dish aerial

**parachute** [paʀaʃyt] *nm* parachute; **parachutiste** *nm/f* parachutist; (*Mil*) paratrooper

**parade** [paʀad] *nf* (*spectacle, défilé*) parade; (*Escrime, Boxe*) parry

**paradis** [paʀadi] *nm* heaven, paradise

**paradoxe** [paʀadɔks] *nm* paradox

**paraffine** [paʀafin] *nf* paraffin

**parages** [paʀaʒ] *nmpl*: **dans les ~ (de)** in the area *ou* vicinity (of)

**paragraphe** [paʀagʀaf] *nm* paragraph

**paraître** [paʀɛtʀ] *vb +attrib* to seem, look, appear ▷ *vi* to appear; *(être visible)* to show; *(Presse, Édition)* to be published, come out, appear ▷ *vb impers*: **il paraît que** it seems *ou* appears that, they say that

**parallèle** [paʀalɛl] *adj* parallel; *(non officiel)* unofficial ▷ *nm (comparaison)*: **faire un ~ entre** to draw a parallel between ▷ *nf* parallel (line)

**paralyser** [paʀalize] *vt* to paralyse

**paramédical, e, -aux** [paʀamedikal, o] *adj*: **personnel ~** paramedics *pl*, paramedical workers *pl*

**paraphrase** [paʀafʀaz] *nf* paraphrase

**parapluie** [paʀaplɥi] *nm* umbrella

**parasite** [paʀazit] *nm* parasite; **parasites** *nmpl (Tél)* interference *sg*

**parasol** [paʀasɔl] *nm* parasol, sunshade

**paratonnerre** [paʀatɔnɛʀ] *nm* lightning conductor

**parc** [paʀk] *nm* (public) park, gardens *pl*; *(de château etc)* grounds *pl*; *(d'enfant)* playpen; **parc à thème** theme park; **parc d'attractions** amusement park; **parc de stationnement** car park

**parcelle** [paʀsɛl] *nf* fragment, scrap; *(de terrain)* plot, parcel

**parce que** [paʀsk(ə)] *conj* because

**parchemin** [paʀʃəmɛ̃] *nm* parchment

**parc(o)mètre** [paʀkmɛtʀ] *nm* parking meter

**parcourir** [paʀkuʀiʀ] *vt (trajet, distance)* to cover; *(article, livre)* to skim *ou* glance through; *(lieu)* to go all over, travel up and down; *(suj: frisson)* to run through

**parcours** [paʀkuʀ] *nm (trajet)* journey; *(itinéraire)* route

**par-dessous** [paʀd(ə)su] *prép, adv* under(neath)

**pardessus** [paʀdəsy] *nm* overcoat

**par-dessus** [paʀd(ə)sy] *prép* over (the top of) ▷ *adv* over (the top); **~ le marché** on top of all that; **~ tout** above all; **en avoir ~ la tête** to have had enough

**par-devant** [paʀd(ə)vɑ̃] *adv (passer)* round the front

**pardon** [paʀdɔ̃] *nm* forgiveness *no pl* ▷ *excl* sorry!; *(pour interpeller etc)* excuse me!; **demander ~ à qn (de)** to apologize to sb (for); **je vous demande ~** I'm sorry; *(pour interpeller)* excuse me; **pardonner** *vt* to forgive; **pardonner qch à qn** to forgive sb for sth

**pare...**: **pare-brise** *nm inv* windscreen (BRIT), windshield (US); **pare-chocs** *nm inv* bumper; **pare-feu** *nm inv (de foyer)* fireguard; *(Inform)* firewall

**pareil, le** [paʀɛj] *adj (identique)* the same, alike; *(similaire)* similar; *(tel)*: **un courage/livre ~** such courage/a book, courage/a book like this; **de ~s livres** such books; **faire ~** to do the same (thing); **~ à** the same as; *(similaire)* similar to; **sans ~** unparalleled, unequalled

**parent, e** [paʀɑ̃, ɑ̃t] *nm/f*: **un(e) ~(e)** a relative *ou* relation; **parents** *nmpl (père et mère)* parents; **parenté** *nf (lien)* relationship

**parenthèse** [paʀɑ̃tɛz] *nf (ponctuation)* bracket, parenthesis; *(digression)* parenthesis, digression; **entre ~s** in brackets; *(fig)* incidentally

**paresse** [paʀɛs] *nf* laziness; **paresseux, -euse** *adj* lazy

**parfait, e** [paʀfɛ, ɛt] *adj* perfect ▷ *nm (Ling)* perfect (tense); **parfaitement** *adv* perfectly ▷ *excl* (most) certainly

**parfois** [paʀfwa] *adv* sometimes

**parfum** [paʀfœ̃] *nm (produit)* perfume, scent; *(odeur: de fleur)* scent, fragrance; *(goût)* flavour; **quels ~s avez-vous?** what flavours do you have?; **parfumé, e** *adj (fleur, fruit)* fragrant; *(femme)* perfumed; **parfumé au café** coffee-flavoured; **parfumer** vt (suj: odeur, bouquet) to perfume; (crème, gâteau) to flavour; **parfumerie** nf (produits) perfumes pl; (boutique) perfume shop

**pari** [paʀi] nm bet; **parier** vt to bet

**Paris** [paʀi] n Paris; **parisien, ne** adj Parisian; (Géo, Admin) Paris cpd ▷ nm/f: **Parisien, ne** Parisian

**parité** [paʀite] nf (Pol): ~ **hommes-femmes** balanced representation of men and women

**parjure** [paʀʒyʀ] nm perjury

**parking** [paʀkiŋ] nm (lieu) car park

■ Attention à ne pas traduire **parking** par le mot anglais **parking**.

**parlant, e** [paʀlɑ̃, ɑ̃t] adj (regard) eloquent; (Cinéma) talking

**parlement** [paʀləmɑ̃] nm parliament; **parlementaire** adj parliamentary ▷ nm/f member of parliament

**parler** [paʀle] vi to talk, speak, talk; (avouer) to talk; ~ **(à qn) de** to talk ou speak (to sb) about; ~ **le/en français** to speak French/in French; ~ **affaires** to talk business; **sans** ~ **de** (fig) not to mention, to say nothing of; **tu parles!** (fam: bien sûr) you bet!; **parlez-vous français?** do you speak French?; **je ne parle pas anglais** I don't speak English; **est-ce que je peux** ~ **à ...?** can I speak to ...?

**parloir** [paʀlwaʀ] nm (de prison, d'hôpital) visiting room

**parmi** [paʀmi] prép among(st)

**paroi** [paʀwa] nf wall; (cloison) partition

**paroisse** [paʀwas] nf parish

**parole** [paʀɔl] nf (faculté): **la** ~ speech; (mot, promesse) word; **paroles** nfpl (Mus) words, lyrics; **tenir** ~ to keep one's word; **prendre la** ~ to speak; **demander la** ~ to ask for permission to speak; **je te crois sur** ~ I'll take your word for it

**parquet** [paʀkɛ] nm (parquet) floor; (Jur): **le** ~ the Public Prosecutor's department

**parrain** [paʀɛ̃] nm godfather;

**parrainer** vt (suj: entreprise) to sponsor

**pars** [paʀ] vb voir **partir**

**parsemer** [paʀsəme] vt (suj: feuilles, papiers) to be scattered over; ~ **qch de** to scatter sth with

**part** [paʀ] nf (qui revient à qn) share; (fraction, partie) part; **à** ~ adv (séparément) separately; (de côté) aside ▷ prép apart from, except for; **prendre** ~ **à** (débat etc) to take part in; (soucis, douleur de qn) to share in; **faire** ~ **de qch à qn** to announce sth to sb, inform sb of sth; **pour ma** ~ as for me, as far as I'm concerned; **à** ~ **entière** full; **de la** ~ **de** (au nom de) on behalf of; (donné par) from; **de toute(s)** ~**(s)** from all sides ou quarters; **de** ~ **et d'autre** on both sides, on either side; **d'une** ~ ... **d'autre** ~ on the one hand ... on the other hand; **d'autre** ~ (de plus) moreover; **faire la** ~ **des choses** to make allowances

**partage** [paʀtaʒ] nm (fractionnement) dividing up; (répartition) sharing (out) no pl, share-out

**partager** [paʀtaʒe] vt to share; (distribuer, répartir) to share (out); (morceler, diviser) to divide (up); **se partager** vt (héritage etc) to share between themselves (ou ourselves)

**partenaire** [paʀtənɛʀ] nm/f partner

**parterre** [paʀtɛʀ] nm (de fleurs) (flower) bed; (Théâtre) stalls pl

**parti** [paʀti] nm (Pol) party; (décision) course of action; (personne à marier) match; **tirer** ~ **de** to take advantage of, turn to good account; **prendre** ~ **(pour/contre)** to take sides ou a stand (for/against); **parti pris** bias

**partial, e, -aux** [paʀsjal, jo] adj biased, partial

**participant, e** [paʀtisipɑ̃, ɑ̃t] nm/f participant; (à un concours) entrant

**participation** [paʀtisipasjɔ̃] nf participation; (financière) contribution

**participer** [paʀtisipe]: ~ **à** vt (course, réunion) to take part in; (frais etc) to contribute to; (chagrin, succès de qn) to share (in)

**particularité** [partikylarite] nf
(distinctive) characteristic
**particulier, -ière** [partikylje, jɛr]
adj (spécifique) particular; (spécial)
special, particular; (personnel, privé)
private; (étrange) peculiar, odd ▷ nm
(individu: Admin) private individual; **~ à**
peculiar to; **en ~** (surtout) in particular,
particularly; (en privé) in private;
**particulièrement** adv particularly
**partie** [parti] nf (gén) part; (Jur etc:
protagonistes) party; (de cartes, tennis etc)
game; **une ~ de pêche** a fishing party
ou trip; **en ~** partly, in part; **faire ~ de**
(suj: chose) to be part of; **prendre qn à ~**
to take sb to task; **en grande ~** largely,
in the main; **partie civile** (Jur) party
claiming damages in a criminal case
**partiel, le** [parsjɛl] adj partial ▷ nm
(Scol) class exam
**partir** [partir] vi (gén) to go; (quitter)
to go, leave; (tache) to go, come out; **~**
**de** (lieu: quitter) to leave: (: commencer
à) to start from; **~ pour/à** (lieu, pays
etc) to leave for/go off to; **à ~ de** from;
**le train/le bus part à quelle heure?**
what time does the train/bus leave?
**partisan, e** [partizã, an] nm/f
partisan ▷ adj: **être ~ de qch/de faire**
to be in favour of sth/doing
**partition** [partisjɔ̃] nf (Mus) score
**partout** [partu] adv everywhere; **~**
**où il allait** everywhere ou wherever
he went
**paru** [pary] pp de **paraître**
**parution** [parysjɔ̃] nf publication
**parvenir** [parvənir]: **~ à** vt (atteindre)
to reach; (réussir): **~ à faire** to manage
to do, succeed in doing; **faire ~ qch à**
**qn** to have sth sent to sb
**pas¹** [pa] nm (enjambée, Danse) step;
(allure, mesure) pace; (bruit) (foot)step;
(trace) footprint; **~ à ~** step by step;
**au ~** at walking pace; **marcher à**
**grands ~** to stride along; **~ de loup**
stealthily; **faire les cent ~** to pace up
and down; **faire le premier ~** to make
the first move; **sur le ~ de la porte** on

the doorstep

 **MOT-CLÉ**

**pas²** [pa] adv **1** (en corrélation avec
ne, non etc) not; **il ne pleure pas**
(habituellement) he does not ou doesn't
cry; (maintenant) he's not ou isn't crying;
**il n'a pas pleuré/ne pleurera pas** he
did not ou didn't/will not ou won't cry;
**ils n'ont pas de voiture/d'enfants**
they don't have ou haven't got a car/any
children; **il m'a dit de ne pas le faire**
he told me not to do it; **non pas que ...**
not that ...
**2** (employé sans ne etc): **pas moi** not
me, I don't (ou can't etc); **elle travaille,**
**(mais) lui pas** ou **pas lui** she works but
he doesn't ou does not; **une pomme**
**pas mûre** an unripe apple; **pas du**
**tout** not at all; **pas de sucre, merci**
no sugar, thanks; **ceci est à vous ou**
**pas?** is this yours or not?, is this yours
or isn't it?
**3**: **pas mal** (joli: personne, maison) not
bad; **pas mal fait** not badly done ou
made; **comment ça va? — pas mal**
how are things? — not bad; **pas mal de**
quite a lot of

**passage** [pasaʒ] nm (fait de passer)
voir **passer**; (lieu, prix de la traversée,
extrait) passage; (chemin) way; **de ~**
(touristes) passing through; **passage à**
**niveau** level crossing; **passage clouté**
pedestrian crossing; **passage interdit**
no entry; **passage souterrain** subway
(BRIT), underpass
**passager, -ère** [pasaʒe, ɛr] adj
passing ▷ nm/f passenger
**passant, e** [pasã, ãt] adj (rue, endroit)
busy ▷ nm/f passer-by; **en ~** in passing
**passe** [pas] nf (Sport, Navig) pass; **être**
**en ~ de faire** to be on the way to doing;
**être dans une mauvaise ~** to be going
through a rough patch
**passé, e** [pase] adj (révolu) past; (dernier:
semaine etc) last; (couleur) faded ▷ prép

after ▷ *nm* past; (*Ling*) past (tense); **~ de
mode** out of fashion; **passé composé**
perfect (tense); **passé simple** past
historic (tense)

**passe-partout** [pɑspaʀtu] *nm
inv* master *ou* skeleton key ▷ *adj inv*
all-purpose

**passeport** [pɑspɔʀ] *nm* passport

**passer** [pɑse] *vi* (*aller*) to go; (*voiture,
piétons: défiler*) to pass (by), go by;
(*facteur, laitier etc*) to come, call; (*pour
rendre visite*) to call *ou* drop in; (*film,
émission*) to be on; (*temps, jours*) to pass,
go by; (*couleur*) to fade; (*mode*) to die
out; (*douleur*) to pass, to go away; (*Scol*):
**~ dans la classe supérieure** to go up
to the next class ▷ *vt* (*frontière, rivière
etc*) to cross; (*douane*) to go through;
(*examen*) to sit, take; (*visite médicale
etc*) to have; (*journée, temps*) to spend;
(*enfiler: vêtement*) to slip on; (*film, pièce*)
to show, put on; (*disque*) to play, put on;
(*commande*) to agree on; **se passer** *vi*
(*avoir lieu:
scène, action*) to take place; (*se dérouler:
entretien etc*) to go; (*s'écouler: semaine
etc*) to pass, go by; (*arriver*) **que s'est-il
passé?** what happened?; **~ qch à qn** (*sel
etc*) to pass sth to sb; (*prêter*) to lend sb
sth; (*lettre, message*) to pass sth on to sb;
(*tolérer*) to let sb get away with sth; **~
par** to go through; **~ avant qch/qn** (*fig*)
to come before sth/sb; **~ un coup de
fil à qn** (*fam*) to give sb a ring; **laisser
~** (*air, lumière, personne*) to let through;
(*occasion*) to let slip, miss; (*erreur*) to
overlook; **~ à la radio/télévision** to be
on the radio/on television; **~ à table**
to sit down to eat; **~ au salon** to go
into the sitting-room; **~ son tour** to
miss one's turn; **~ la seconde** (*Auto*)
to change into second; **~ le balai/
l'aspirateur** to sweep up/hoover; **je
vous passe M. Dupont** (*je vous mets
en communication avec lui*) I'm putting
you through to Mr Dupont; (*je lui passe
l'appareil*) here is Mr Dupont, I'll hand
you over to Mr Dupont; **se ~ de** to go *ou*
do without

**passerelle** [pɑsʀɛl] *nf* footbridge; (*de
navire, avion*) gangway

**passe-temps** [pɑstɑ̃] *nm inv* pastime

**passif, -ive** [pɑsif, iv] *adj* passive

**passion** [pɑsjɔ̃] *nf* passion;
**passionnant, e** *adj* fascinating;
**passionné, e** *adj* (*personne*) passionate;
(*récit*) impassioned; **être passionné
de** to have a passion for; **passionner** *vt*
(*personne*) to fascinate, grip

**passoire** [pɑswaʀ] *nf* sieve; (*à légumes*)
colander; (*à thé*) strainer

**pastèque** [pɑstɛk] *nf* watermelon

**pasteur** [pɑstœʀ] *nm* (*protestant*)
minister, pastor

**pastille** [pɑstij] *nf* (*à sucer*) lozenge,
pastille

**patate** [patat] *nf* (*fam: pomme de terre*)
spud; **patate douce** sweet potato

**patauger** [patoʒe] *vi* to splash about

**pâte** [pɑt] *nf* (*à tarte*) pastry; (*à pain*)
dough; (*à frire*) batter; **pâtes** *nfpl*
(*macaroni etc*) pasta *sg*; **pâte à modeler**
modelling clay, Plasticine® (*BRIT*);
**pâte brisée** shortcrust pastry; **pâte
d'amandes** almond paste, marzipan;
**pâte de fruits** crystallized fruit *no pl*;
**pâte feuilletée** puff *ou* flaky pastry

**pâté** [pɑte] *nm* (*charcuterie*) pâté; (*tache*)
ink blot; **pâté de maisons** block (of
houses); **pâté (de sable)** sandpie; **pâté
en croûte** ≈ pork pie

**pâtée** [pɑte] *nf* mash, feed

**patente** [patɑ̃t] *nf* (*Comm*) trading
licence

**paternel, le** [patɛʀnɛl] *adj* (*amour,
soins*) fatherly; (*ligne, autorité*) paternal

**pâteux, -euse** [pɑtø, øz] *adj* pasty;
(*langue*) coated

**pathétique** [patetik] *adj* moving

**patience** [pasjɑ̃s] *nf* patience

**patient, e** [pasjɑ̃, jɑ̃t] *adj, nm/f*
patient; **patienter** *vi* to wait

**patin** [patɛ̃] *nm* skate; (*sport*) skating;
**patins (à glace)** (ice) skates; **patins à
roulettes** roller skates

**patinage** [patinaʒ] *nm* skating

**patiner** [patine] vi to skate; (roue, voiture) to spin; **se patiner** vi (meuble, cuir) to acquire a sheen; **patineur, -euse** nm/f skater; **patinoire** nf skating rink, (ice) rink

**pâtir** [patiʁ]: **~ de** vt to suffer because of

**pâtisserie** [patisʁi] nf (boutique) cake shop; (gâteau) cake, pastry; (à la maison) pastry- ou cake-making, baking; **pâtissier, -ière** nm/f pastrycook

**patois** [patwa] nm dialect, patois

**patrie** [patʁi] nf homeland

**patrimoine** [patʁimwan] nm (culture) heritage

● **JOURNÉES DU PATRIMOINE**
●
● Once a year, important public
● buildings are open to the public for
● a weekend. During these **Journées**
● **du Patrimoine**, there are guided
● visits and talks based on a particular
● theme.

**patriotique** [patʁijɔtik] adj patriotic

**patron, ne** [patʁɔ̃, ɔn] nm/f boss; (Rel) patron saint ▷ nm (Couture) pattern; **patronat** nm employers pl; **patronner** vt to sponsor, support

**patrouille** [patʁuj] nf patrol

**patte** [pat] nf (jambe) leg; (pied: de chien, chat) paw; (: d'oiseau) foot

**pâturage** [patyʁaʒ] nm pasture

**paume** [pom] nf palm

**paumé, e** [pome] (fam) nm/f drop-out

**paupière** [popjɛʁ] nf eyelid

**pause** [poz] nf (arrêt) break; (en parlant, Mus) pause

**pauvre** [povʁ] adj poor; **les pauvres** nmpl the poor; **pauvreté** nf (état) poverty

**pavé, e** [pave] adj (cour) paved; (chaussée) cobbled ▷ nm (bloc) paving stone; cobblestone

**pavillon** [pavijɔ̃] nm (de banlieue) small (detached) house; pavilion; (drapeau) flag

**payant, e** [pɛjɑ̃, ɑ̃t] adj (spectateurs etc) paying; (fig: entreprise) profitable; (effort) which pays off; **c'est ~** you have to pay, there is a charge

**paye** [pɛj] nf pay, wages pl

**payer** [peje] vt (créancier, employé, loyer) to pay; (achat, réparations, fig: faute) to pay for ▷ vi to pay; (métier) to be well-paid; (tactique etc) to pay off; **il me l'a fait ~ 10 euros** he charged me 10 euros for it; **~ qch à qn** to buy sth for sb, buy sb sth; **se ~ la tête de qn** (fam) to take the mickey out of sb; **est-ce que je peux ~ par carte de crédit?** can I pay by credit card?

**pays** [pei] nm country; (région) region; **du ~** local

**paysage** [peizaʒ] nm landscape

**paysan, ne** [peizɑ̃, an] nm/f farmer; (péj) peasant ▷ adj (agricole) farming; (rural) country

**Pays-Bas** [peiba] nmpl: **les ~** the Netherlands

**PC** nm (Inform) PC

**PDA** sigle m (= personal digital assistant) PDA

**PDG** sigle m = **président directeur général**

**péage** [peaʒ] nm toll; (endroit) tollgate

**peau, x** [po] nf skin; **gants de ~** fine leather gloves; **être bien/mal dans sa ~** to be quite at ease/ill-at-ease; **peau de chamois** (chiffon) chamois leather, shammy

**pêche** [pɛʃ] nf (fruit) peach; (sport, activité) fishing; (poissons pêchés) catch; **pêche à la ligne** (en rivière) angling

**péché** [peʃe] nm sin

**pécher** [peʃe] vi (Rel) to sin

**pêcher** [peʃe] nm peach tree ▷ vi to go fishing ▷ vt (attraper) to catch; (être pêcheur de) to fish for

**pécheur, -eresse** [peʃœʁ, peʃʁɛs] nm/f sinner

**pêcheur** [peʃœʁ] nm fisherman; (à la ligne) angler

**pédagogie** [pedagɔʒi] nf educational methods pl, pedagogy; **pédagogique**

*adj* educational
**pédale** [pedal] *nf* pedal
**pédalo** [pedalo] *nm* pedal-boat
**pédant, e** [pedã, ãt] *(péj) adj* pedantic
**pédestre** [pedɛstʀ] *adj*: **randonnée ~**
ramble; **sentier ~** pedestrian footpath
**pédiatre** [pedjatʀ] *nm/f* paediatrician,
child specialist
**pédicure** [pedikyʀ] *nm/f* chiropodist
**pègre** [pɛgʀ] *nf* underworld
**peigne** [pɛɲ] *nm* comb; **peigner** *vt* to
comb (the hair of); **se peigner** *vi* to
comb one's hair; **peignoir** *nm* dressing
gown; **peignoir de bain** bathrobe
**peindre** [pɛ̃dʀ] *vt* to paint; *(fig)* to
portray, depict
**peine** [pɛn] *nf (affliction)* sorrow,
sadness *no pl; (mal, effort)* trouble *no
pl; (difficulté)* difficulty; *(Jur)*
sentence; **avoir de la ~** to be sad;
**faire de la ~ à qn** to distress *ou* upset
sb; **prendre la ~ de faire** to go to the
trouble of doing; **se donner de la ~** to
make an effort; **ce n'est pas la ~ de
faire** there's no point in doing, it's not
worth doing; **à ~** scarcely, barely; **à ~
... que** hardly ... than, no sooner ... than;
**peine capitale** capital punishment;
**peine de mort** death sentence *ou*
penalty; **peiner** *vi (personne)* to work
hard; *(moteur, voiture)* to labour ▷ *vt* to
grieve, sadden
**peintre** [pɛ̃tʀ] *nm* painter; **peintre en
bâtiment** painter (and decorator)
**peinture** [pɛ̃tyʀ] *nf* painting; *(matière)*
paint; *(surfaces peintes: aussi: ~s)*
paintwork; **"~ fraîche"** "wet paint"
**péjoratif, -ive** [peʒɔʀatif, iv] *adj*
pejorative, derogatory
**Pékin** [pekɛ̃] *n* Beijing
**pêle-mêle** [pɛlmɛl] *adv* higgledy-
piggledy
**peler** [pəle] *vt, vi* to peel
**pèlerin** [pɛlʀɛ̃] *nm* pilgrim
**pèlerinage** [pɛlʀinaʒ] *nm* pilgrimage
**pelle** [pɛl] *nf* shovel; *(d'enfant, de
terrassier)* spade
**pellicule** [pelikyl] *nf* film; **pellicules**

*nfpl (Méd)* dandruff *sg*; **je voudrais une
~ de 36 poses** I'd like a 36-exposure film
**pelote** [p(ə)lɔt] *nf (de fil, laine)* ball;
**pelote basque** pelota
**peloton** [p(ə)lɔtɔ̃] *nm* group, squad;
*(Cyclisme)* pack
**pelotonner** [p(ə)lɔtɔne]: **se
pelotonner** *vi* to curl (o.s.) up
**pelouse** [p(ə)luz] *nf* lawn
**peluche** [p(ə)lyʃ] *nf*: **(animal en) ~**
fluffy animal, soft toy; **chien/lapin en
~** fluffy dog/rabbit
**pelure** [p(ə)lyʀ] *nf* peeling, peel *no pl*
**pénal, e, -aux** [penal, o] *adj* penal;
**pénalité** *nf* penalty
**penchant** [pãʃã] *nm (tendance)*
tendency, propensity; *(faible)* liking,
fondness
**pencher** [pãʃe] *vi* to tilt, lean over ▷ *vt*
to tilt; **se pencher** *vi* to lean over; *(se
baisser)* to bend down; **se ~ sur** *(fig:
problème)* to look into; **~ pour** to be
inclined to favour
**pendant** [pãdã] *prép (au cours de)*
during; *(indique la durée)* for; **~ que** while
**pendentif** [pãdãtif] *nm* pendant
**penderie** [pãdʀi] *nf* wardrobe
**pendre** [pãdʀ] *vt, vi* to hang; **se ~** *(se
suicider)* to hang o.s.; **~ qch à** *(mur)* to
hang sth (up) on; *(plafond)* to hang sth
(up) from
**pendule** [pãdyl] *nf* clock ▷ *nm*
pendulum
**pénétrer** [penetʀe] *vi, vt* to penetrate;
**~ dans** to enter
**pénible** [penibl] *adj (travail)* hard;
*(sujet)* painful; *(personne)* tiresome;
**péniblement** *adv* with difficulty
**péniche** [peniʃ] *nf* barge
**pénicilline** [penisilin] *nf* penicillin
**péninsule** [penɛ̃syl] *nf* peninsula
**pénis** [penis] *nm* penis
**pénitence** [penitãs] *nf (peine)*
penance; *(repentir)* penitence;
**pénitencier** *nm* penitentiary
**pénombre** [penɔ̃bʀ] *nf (faible clarté)*
half-light; *(obscurité)* darkness
**pensée** [pãse] *nf* thought; *(démarche,*

*doctrine*) thinking *no pl*; (*fleur*) pansy; **en ~** in one's mind

**penser** [pɑ̃se] *vi, vt* to think; **~ à** (*ami, vacances*) to think of *ou* about; (*réfléchir à: problème, offre*) to think about *ou* over; (*prévoir*) to think of; **faire ~ à** to remind one of; **~ faire qch** to be thinking of doing sth, intend to do sth; **pensif, -ive** *adj* pensive, thoughtful

**pension** [pɑ̃sjɔ̃] *nf* (*allocation*) pension; (*prix du logement*) board and lodgings, bed and board; (*école*) boarding school; **pension alimentaire** (*de divorcée*) maintenance allowance, alimony; **pension complète** full board; **pension de famille** boarding house, guesthouse; **pensionnaire** *nm/f* (*Scol*) boarder; **pensionnat** *nm* boarding school

**pente** [pɑ̃t] *nf* slope; **en ~** sloping

**Pentecôte** [pɑ̃tkot] *nf*: **la ~** Whitsun (*BRIT*), Pentecost

**pénurie** [penyʀi] *nf* shortage

**pépé** [pepe] (*fam*) *nm* grandad

**pépin** [pepɛ̃] *nm* (*Bot: graine*) pip; (*ennui*) snag, hitch

**pépinière** [pepinjɛʀ] *nf* nursery

**perçant, e** [pɛʀsɑ̃, ɑ̃t] *adj* (*cri*) piercing, shrill; (*regard*) piercing

**percepteur, -trice** [pɛʀsɛptœʀ, tʀis] *nm/f* tax collector

**perception** [pɛʀsɛpsjɔ̃] *nf* perception; (*bureau*) tax office

**percer** [pɛʀse] *vt* to pierce; (*ouverture etc*) to make; (*mystère, énigme*) to penetrate ▷ *vi* to break through; **perceuse** *nf* drill

**percevoir** [pɛʀsəvwaʀ] *vt* (*distinguer*) to perceive, detect; (*taxe, impôt*) to collect; (*revenu, indemnité*) to receive

**perche** [pɛʀʃ] *nf* (*bâton*) pole

**percher** [pɛʀʃe] *vt, vi* to perch; **se percher** *vi* to perch; **perchoir** *nm* perch

**perçois** *etc* [pɛʀswa] *vb voir* **percevoir**

**perçu, e** [pɛʀsy] *pp de* **percevoir**

**percussion** [pɛʀkysjɔ̃] *nf* percussion

**percuter** [pɛʀkyte] *vt* to strike; (*suj:*

*véhicule*) to crash into

**perdant, e** [pɛʀdɑ̃, ɑ̃t] *nm/f* loser

**perdre** [pɛʀdʀ] *vt* to lose; (*gaspiller: temps, argent*) to waste; (*personne: moralement etc*) to ruin ▷ *vi* to lose; (*sur une vente etc*) to lose out; **se perdre** *vi* (*s'égarer*) to get lost, lose one's way; (*denrées*) to go to waste; **j'ai perdu mon portefeuille/passeport** I've lost my wallet/passport; **je me suis perdu** (*et je le suis encore*) I'm lost; (*et je ne le suis plus*) I got lost

**perdrix** [pɛʀdʀi] *nf* partridge

**perdu, e** [pɛʀdy] *pp de* **perdre** ▷ *adj* (*isolé*) out-of-the-way; (*Comm: emballage*) non-returnable; (*malade*): **il est ~** there's no hope left for him; **à vos moments ~s** in your spare time

**père** [pɛʀ] *nm* father; **père de famille** father; **le père Noël** Father Christmas

**perfection** [pɛʀfɛksjɔ̃] *nf* perfection; **à la ~** to perfection; **perfectionné, e** *adj* sophisticated; **perfectionner** *vt* to improve, perfect; **se perfectionner en anglais** to improve one's English

**perforer** [pɛʀfɔʀe] *vt* (*poinçonner*) to punch

**performant, e** [pɛʀfɔʀmɑ̃, ɑ̃t] *adj*: **très ~** high-performance *cpd*

**perfusion** [pɛʀfyzjɔ̃] *nf*: **faire une ~ à qn** to put sb on a drip

**péril** [peʀil] *nm* peril

**périmé, e** [peʀime] *adj* (*Admin*) out-of-date, expired

**périmètre** [peʀimɛtʀ] *nm* perimeter

**période** [peʀjɔd] *nf* period; **périodique** *adj* periodic ▷ *nm* periodical; **garniture** *ou* **serviette périodique** sanitary towel (*BRIT*) *ou* napkin (*US*)

**périphérique** [peʀifeʀik] *adj* (*quartiers*) outlying ▷ *nm* (*Auto*): **boulevard ~** ring road (*BRIT*), beltway (*US*)

**périr** [peʀiʀ] *vi* to die, perish

**périssable** [peʀisabl] *adj* perishable

**perle** [pɛʀl] *nf* pearl; (*de plastique, métal, sueur*) bead

**permanence** [pɛʀmanɑ̃s] *nf*

permanence; (*local*) (*duty*) office;
**assurer une ~** (*service public, bureaux*)
to operate *ou* maintain a basic service;
**être de ~** to be on call *ou* duty; **en ~**
continuously
**permanent, e** [pɛʀmanɑ̃, ɑ̃t] *adj*
permanent; (*spectacle*) continuous;
**permanente** *nf* perm
**perméable** [pɛʀmeabl] *adj* (*terrain*)
permeable; **~ à** (*fig*) receptive *ou* open to
**permettre** [pɛʀmɛtʀ] *vt* to allow,
permit; **~ à qn de faire/qch** to allow
sb to do/sth; **se ~ de faire** to take the
liberty of doing
**permis** [pɛʀmi] *nm* permit, licence;
**permis de conduire** driving licence
(*BRIT*), driver's license (*US*); **permis de
construire** planning permission (*BRIT*),
building permit (*US*); **permis de séjour**
residence permit; **permis de travail**
work permit
**permission** [pɛʀmisjɔ̃] *nf* permission;
(*Mil*) leave; **avoir la ~ de faire** to have
permission to do; **en ~** on leave
**Pérou** [peʀu] *nm* Peru
**perpétuel, le** [pɛʀpetɥɛl] *adj*
perpetual; **perpétuité** *nf*: **à perpétuité**
for life; **être condamné à perpétuité**
to receive a life sentence
**perplexe** [pɛʀplɛks] *adj* perplexed,
puzzled
**perquisitionner** [pɛʀkizisjɔne] *vi* to
carry out a search
**perron** [peʀɔ̃] *nm* steps *pl* (*leading to
entrance*)
**perroquet** [peʀɔkɛ] *nm* parrot
**perruche** [peʀyʃ] *nf* budgerigar (*BRIT*),
budgie (*BRIT*), parakeet (*US*)
**perruque** [peʀyk] *nf* wig
**persécuter** [pɛʀsekyte] *vt* to
persecute
**persévérer** [pɛʀsevere] *vi* to
persevere
**persil** [pɛʀsi] *nm* parsley
**Persique** [pɛʀsik] *adj*: **le golfe ~** the
(Persian) Gulf
**persistant, e** [pɛʀsistɑ̃, ɑ̃t] *adj*
persistent

**persister** [pɛʀsiste] *vi* to persist; **~ à
faire qch** to persist in doing sth
**personnage** [pɛʀsɔnaʒ] *nm* (*individu*)
character, individual; (*célébrité*)
important person; (*de roman, film*)
character; (*Peinture*) figure
**personnalité** [pɛʀsɔnalite] *nf*
personality; (*personnage*) prominent
figure
**personne** [pɛʀsɔn] *nf* person ▷ *pron*
nobody, no one; (*avec négation en
anglais*) anybody, anyone; **personne
âgée** elderly person; **personnel, le** *adj*
personal; (*égoïste*) selfish ▷ *nm* staff,
personnel; **personnellement** *adv*
personally
**perspective** [pɛʀspɛktiv] *nf* (*Art*)
perspective; (*vue*) view; (*point de vue*)
viewpoint, angle; (*chose envisagée*)
prospect; **en ~** in prospect
**perspicace** [pɛʀspikas] *adj* clear-
sighted, gifted with (*ou* showing)
insight; **perspicacité** *nf* clear-
sightedness
**persuader** [pɛʀsɥade] *vt*: **~ qn (de
faire)** to persuade sb (to do); **persuasif,
-ive** *adj* persuasive
**perte** [pɛʀt] *nf* loss; (*de temps*) waste;
(*fig: morale*) ruin; **à ~ de vue** as far as the
eye can (*ou* could) see; **pertes blanches**
(vaginal) discharge *sg*
**pertinent, e** [pɛʀtinɑ̃, ɑ̃t] *adj* apt,
relevant
**perturbation** [pɛʀtyʀbasjɔ̃] *nf*:
**perturbation (atmosphérique)**
atmospheric disturbance
**perturber** [pɛʀtyʀbe] *vt* to disrupt;
(*Psych*) to perturb, disturb
**pervers, e** [pɛʀvɛʀ, ɛʀs] *adj* perverted
**pervertir** [pɛʀvɛʀtiʀ] *vt* to pervert
**pesant, e** [pəzɑ̃, ɑ̃t] *adj* heavy; (*fig:
présence*) burdensome
**pèse-personne** [pɛzpɛʀsɔn] *nm*
(bathroom) scales *pl*
**peser** [pəze] *vt* to weigh ▷ *vi* to weigh;
(*fig: avoir de l'importance*) to carry
weight; **~ lourd** to be heavy
**pessimiste** [pesimist] *adj* pessimistic

▷ *nm/f* pessimist
**peste** [pɛst] *nf* plague
**pétale** [petal] *nm* petal
**pétanque** [petãk] *nf* type of bowls

● **PÉTANQUE**
●
● **Pétanque** is a version of the game
● of 'boules', played on a variety of
● hard surfaces. Standing with their
● feet together, players throw steel
● bowls at a wooden jack. **Pétanque**
● originated in the South of France
● and is still very much associated
● with that area.

**pétard** [petaʀ] *nm* banger (BRIT),
firecracker
**péter** [pete] *vi* (*fam: casser*) to bust;
(*fam!*) to fart (*!*)
**pétillant, e** [petijã, ãt] *adj* (*eau etc*)
sparkling
**pétiller** [petije] *vi* (*feu*) to crackle;
(*champagne*) to bubble; (*yeux*) to sparkle
**petit, e** [p(ə)ti, it] *adj* small; (*avec
nuance affective*) little; (*voyage*) short,
little; (*bruit etc*) faint, slight ▷ *nm/f*
(*petit enfant*) little boy/girl, child; **petits**
*nmpl* (*d'un animal*) young *no pl*; **faire des
~s** to have kittens (*ou* puppies *etc*); **la
classe des ~s** the infant class; **les tout-
~s** the little ones, the tiny tots (*fam*); **~ à
~** bit by bit, gradually; **petit(e) ami(e)**
boyfriend/girlfriend; **petit déjeuner**
breakfast; **le petit déjeuner est à
quelle heure?** what time is breakfast?;
**petit four** petit four; **petit pain** (bread)
roll; **les petites annonces** the small
ads; **petits pois** (garden) peas; **petite-
fille** *nf* granddaughter; **petit-fils** *nm*
grandson
**pétition** [petisjɔ̃] *nf* petition
**petits-enfants** [pətizɑ̃fɑ̃] *nmpl*
grandchildren
**pétrin** [petʀɛ̃] *nm* (*fig*): **dans le ~** (*fam*)
in a jam *ou* fix
**pétrir** [petʀiʀ] *vt* to knead
**pétrole** [petʀɔl] *nm* oil; (*pour lampe,*
*réchaud etc*) paraffin (oil); **pétrolier,
-ière** *nm* oil tanker

▮ Attention à ne pas traduire *pétrole*
par le mot anglais *petrol*.

 **MOT-CLÉ**

**peu** [pø] *adv* **1** (*modifiant verbe, adjectif,
adverbe*): **il boit peu** he doesn't drink
(very) much; **il est peu bavard** he's
not very talkative; **peu avant/après**
shortly before/afterwards
**2** (*modifiant nom*): **peu de: peu de
gens/d'arbres** few *ou* not (very) many
people/trees; **il a peu d'espoir** he
hasn't (got) much hope, he has little
hope; **pour peu de temps** for (only) a
short while
**3**: **peu à peu** little by little; **à peu près**
just about, more or less; **à peu près
10 kg/10 euros** approximately 10
kg/10 euros
▷ *nm* **1**: **le peu de gens qui** the few
people who; **le peu de sable qui** what
little sand, the little sand which
**2**: **un peu** a little; **un petit peu** a little
bit; **un peu d'espoir** a little hope;
**elle est un peu bavarde** she's quite
*ou* rather talkative; **un peu plus de**
slightly more than; **un peu moins de**
slightly less than; (*avec pluriel*) slightly
fewer than
▷ *pron*: **peu le savent** few know (it); **de
peu** (only) just

**peuple** [pœpl] *nm* people; **peupler** *vt*
(*pays, région*) to populate; (*étang*) to
stock; (*suj: hommes, poissons*) to inhabit
**peuplier** [pøplije] *nm* poplar (tree)
**peur** [pœʀ] *nf* fear; **avoir ~ (de/de
faire/que)** to be frightened *ou* afraid
(of/of doing/that); **faire ~ à** to
frighten; **de ~ de/que** for fear of/that;
**peureux, -euse** *adj* fearful, timorous
**peut** [pø] *vb voir* **pouvoir**
**peut-être** [pøtɛtʀ] *adv* perhaps,
maybe; **~ que** perhaps, maybe; **~ bien
qu'il fera/est** he may well do/be

**phare** [faʀ] nm (en mer) lighthouse; (de véhicule) headlight

**pharmacie** [faʀmasi] nf (magasin) chemist's (BRIT), pharmacy; (de salle de bain) medicine cabinet; **pharmacien, ne** nm/f pharmacist, chemist (BRIT)

**phénomène** [fenɔmɛn] nm phenomenon

**philosophe** [filɔzɔf] nm/f philosopher ▷ adj philosophical

**philosophie** [filɔzɔfi] nf philosophy

**phobie** [fɔbi] nf phobia

**phoque** [fɔk] nm seal

**phosphorescent, e** [fɔsfɔʀesɑ̃, ɑ̃t] adj luminous

**photo** [foto] nf photo(graph); **prendre en ~** to take a photo of; **pourriez-vous nous prendre en ~, s'il vous plaît?** would you take a picture of us, please?; **faire de la ~** to take photos; **photo d'identité** passport photograph; **photocopie** nf photocopy; **photocopier** vt to photocopy; **photocopieuse** nf photocopier; **photographe** nm/f photographer; **photographie** nf (technique) photography; (cliché) photograph; **photographier** vt to photograph

**phrase** [fʀaz] nf sentence

**physicien, ne** [fizisjɛ̃, jɛn] nm/f physicist

**physique** [fizik] adj physical ▷ nm physique ▷ nf physics sg; **au ~** physically; **physiquement** adv physically

**pianiste** [pjanist] nm/f pianist

**piano** [pjano] nm piano; **pianoter** vi to tinkle away (at the piano)

**pic** [pik] nm (instrument) pick(axe); (montagne) peak; (Zool) woodpecker; **à ~** vertically; (fig: tomber, arriver) just at the right time

**pichet** [piʃɛ] nm jug

**picorer** [pikɔʀe] vt to peck

**pie** [pi] nf magpie

**pièce** [pjɛs] nf (d'un logement) room; (Théâtre) play; (de machine) part; (de monnaie) coin; (document) document; (fragment, de collection) piece; **dix euros ~** ten euros each; **vendre à la ~** to sell separately; **travailler à la ~** to do piecework; **un maillot une ~** a one-piece swimsuit; **un deux-~s cuisine** a two-room(ed) flat (BRIT) ou apartment (US) with kitchen; **pièce à conviction** exhibit; **pièce d'eau** ornamental lake ou pond; **pièce de rechange** spare (part); **pièce d'identité**: **avez-vous une pièce d'identité?** have you got any (means of) identification?; **pièce jointe** (Comput) attachment; **pièce montée** tiered cake; **pièces détachées** spares, (spare) parts; **pièces justificatives** supporting documents

**pied** [pje] nm foot; (de table) leg; (de lampe) base; **~s nus** ou **nu-~s** barefoot; **à ~** on foot; **au ~ de la lettre** literally; **avoir ~** to be able to touch the bottom, not to be out of one's depth; **avoir le ~ marin** to be a good sailor; **sur ~** (debout, rétabli) up and about; **mettre sur ~** (entreprise) to set up; **c'est le ~** (fam) it's brilliant; **mettre les ~s dans le plat** (fam) to put one's foot in it; **il se débrouille comme un ~** (fam) he's completely useless; **pied-noir** nm Algerian-born Frenchman

**piège** [pjɛʒ] nm trap; **prendre au ~** to trap; **piéger** vt (avec une bombe) to booby-trap; **lettre/voiture piégée** letter-/car-bomb

**piercing** [pjɛʀsiŋ] nm body piercing

**pierre** [pjɛʀ] nf stone; **pierre tombale** tombstone; **pierreries** nfpl gems, precious stones

**piétiner** [pjetine] vi (trépigner) to stamp (one's foot); (fig) to be at a standstill ▷ vt to trample on

**piéton, ne** [pjetɔ̃, ɔn] nm/f pedestrian; **piétonnier, -ière** adj: **rue** ou **zone piétonnière** pedestrian precinct

**pieu, x** [pjø] nm post; (pointu) stake

**pieuvre** [pjœvʀ] nf octopus

**pieux, -euse** [pjø, pjøz] adj pious

**pigeon** [piʒɔ̃] nm pigeon

**piger** [piʒe] (fam) vi, vt to understand

**pigiste** [piʒist] nm/f freelance(r)

**pignon** [piɲɔ̃] nm (de mur) gable

**pile** [pil] nf (tas) pile; (Élec) battery
  ▷ adv (fam: s'arrêter etc) dead; **à deux
  heures ~** at two on the dot; **jouer à ~
  ou face** to toss up (for it); **~ ou face?**
  heads or tails

**piler** [pile] vt to crush, pound

**pilier** [pilje] nm pillar

**piller** [pije] vt to pillage, plunder, loot

**pilote** [pilɔt] nm pilot; (de voiture) driver
  ▷ adj pilot cpd; **pilote de course** racing
  driver; **pilote de ligne** airline pilot;
  **piloter** vt (avion) to pilot, fly; (voiture)
  to drive

**pilule** [pilyl] nf pill; **prendre la ~** to be
  on the pill

**piment** [pimɑ̃] nm (aussi: **~ rouge**)
  chilli; (fig) spice, piquancy; **~ doux**
  pepper, capsicum; **pimenté, e** adj
  (plat) hot, spicy

**pin** [pɛ̃] nm pine

**pinard** [pinaʀ] (fam) nm (cheap) wine,
  plonk (BRIT)

**pince** [pɛ̃s] nf (outil) pliers pl; (de homard,
  crabe) pincer, claw; (Couture: pli) dart;
  **pince à épiler** tweezers pl; **pince à
  linge** clothes peg (BRIT) ou pin (US)

**pincé, e** [pɛ̃se] adj (air) stiff

**pinceau, x** [pɛ̃so] nm (paint)brush

**pincer** [pɛ̃se] vt to pinch; (fam) to nab

**pinède** [pinɛd] nf pinewood, pine forest

**pingouin** [pɛ̃gwɛ̃] nm penguin

**ping-pong®** [piŋpɔ̃g] nm table tennis

**pinson** [pɛ̃sɔ̃] nm chaffinch

**pintade** [pɛ̃tad] nf guinea-fowl

**pion** [pjɔ̃] nm (Échecs) pawn; (Dames)
  piece; (Scol) supervisor

**pionnier** [pjɔnje] nm pioneer

**pipe** [pip] nf pipe; **fumer la ~** to smoke
  a pipe

**piquant, e** [pikɑ̃, ɑ̃t] adj (barbe, rosier
  etc) prickly; (saveur, sauce) hot, pungent;
  (détail) titillating; (froid) biting ▷ nm
  (épine) thorn, prickle; (fig) spiciness,
  spice

**pique** [pik] nf pike; (fig) cutting remark
  ▷ nm (Cartes) spades pl

**pique-nique** [piknik] nm picnic;
  **pique-niquer** vi to have a picnic

**piquer** [pike] vt (suj: guêpe, fumée, orties)
  to sting; (: moustique) to bite; (: barbe) to
  prick; (: froid) to bite; (Méd) to give a jab
  to; (: chien, chat) to put to sleep; (intérêt)
  to arouse; (fam: voler) to pinch ▷ vi
  (avion) to go into a dive

**piquet** [pikɛ] nm (pieu) post, stake; (de
  tente) peg

**piqûre** [pikyʀ] nf (d'épingle) prick;
  (d'ortie) sting; (de moustique) bite; (Méd)
  injection, shot (US); **faire une ~ à qn** to
  give sb an injection

**pirate** [piʀat] nm, adj pirate; **pirate de
  l'air** hijacker

**pire** [piʀ] adj worse; (superlatif): **le(la)
  ~ ...** the worst ... ▷ nm: **le ~ (de)** the
  worst (of); **au ~** at (the very) worst

**pis** [pi] nm (de vache) udder ▷ adj, adv
  worse; **de mal en ~** from bad to worse

**piscine** [pisin] nf (swimming) pool;
  **piscine couverte** indoor (swimming)
  pool

**pissenlit** [pisɑ̃li] nm dandelion

**pistache** [pistaʃ] nf pistachio (nut)

**piste** [pist] nf (d'un animal, sentier) track,
  trail; (indice) lead; (de stade) track; (de
  cirque) ring; (de danse) floor; (de patinage)
  rink; (de ski) run; (Aviat) runway; **piste
  cyclable** cycle track

**pistolet** [pistɔlɛ] nm (arme) pistol,
  gun; (à peinture) spray gun; **pistolet-
  mitrailleur** nm submachine gun

**piston** [pistɔ̃] nm (Tech) piston; **avoir
  du ~** (fam) to have friends in the right
  places; **pistonner** vt (candidat) to pull
  strings for

**piteux, -euse** [pitø, øz] adj pitiful,
  sorry (avant le nom); **en ~ état** in a
  sorry state

**pitié** [pitje] nf pity; **il me fait ~** I feel
  sorry for him; **avoir ~ de** (compassion)
  to pity, feel sorry for; (merci) to have pity
  ou mercy on

**pitoyable** [pitwajabl] adj pitiful

**pittoresque** [pitɔʀɛsk] adj

picturesque

**PJ** sigle f (= police judiciaire) ≈ CID (BRIT), ≈ FBI (US)

**placard** [plakaʀ] nm (armoire) cupboard; (affiche) poster, notice

**place** [plas] nf (emplacement, classement) place; (de ville, village) square; (espace libre) room, space; (de parking) space; (siège: de train, cinéma, voiture) seat; (emploi) job; **en ~** (mettre) in its place; **sur ~** on the spot; **faire ~ à** to give way to; **ça prend de la ~** it takes up a lot of room ou space; **à la ~ de** in place of, instead of; **à votre ~ ...** if I were you ...; **je voudrais réserver deux ~s** I'd like to book two seats; **la ~ est prise?** is this seat taken?; **se mettre à la ~ de qn** to put o.s. in sb's place ou in sb's shoes

**placé, e** [plase] adj: **haut ~** (fig) high-ranking; **être bien/mal ~** (spectateur) to have a good/a poor seat; (concurrent) to be in a good/bad position; **il est bien ~ pour le savoir** he is in a position to know

**placement** [plasmɑ̃] nm (Finance) investment; **agence** ou **bureau de ~** employment agency

**placer** [plase] vt to place; (convive, spectateur) to seat; (argent) to place, invest; **se ~ au premier rang** to go and stand (ou sit) in the first row

**plafond** [plafɔ̃] nm ceiling

**plage** [plaʒ] nf beach; **plage arrière** (Auto) parcel ou back shelf

**plaider** [plede] vi (avocat) to plead ▷ vt to plead; **~ pour** (fig) to speak for; **plaidoyer** nm (Jur) speech for the defence; (fig) plea

**plaie** [plɛ] nf wound

**plaignant, e** [plɛɲɑ̃, ɑ̃t] nm/f plaintiff

**plaindre** [plɛ̃dʀ] vt to pity, feel sorry for; **se plaindre** vi (gémir) to moan; (protester): **se ~ (à qn) (de)** to complain (to sb) (about); (souffrir): **se ~ de** to complain of

**plaine** [plɛn] nf plain

**plain-pied** [plɛ̃pje] adv: **de ~ (avec)** on the same level (as)

**plainte** [plɛ̃t] nf (gémissement) moan, groan; (doléance) complaint; **porter ~** to lodge a complaint

**plaire** [plɛʀ] vi to be a success, be successful; **ça plaît beaucoup aux jeunes** it's very popular with young people; **~ à**: **cela me plaît** I like it; **se ~ quelque part** to like being somewhere ou like it somewhere; **s'il vous plaît** please

**plaisance** [plɛzɑ̃s] nf (aussi: **navigation de ~**) (pleasure) sailing, yachting

**plaisant, e** [plɛzɑ̃, ɑ̃t] adj pleasant; (histoire, anecdote) amusing

**plaisanter** [plɛzɑ̃te] vi to joke; **plaisanterie** nf joke

**plaisir** [plɛziʀ] nm pleasure; **faire ~ à qn** (délibérément) to be nice to sb, please sb; **ça me fait ~** I like (doing) it; **j'espère que ça te fera ~** I hope you'll like it; **pour le ~** for pleasure

**plaît** [plɛ] vb voir **plaire**

**plan, e** [plɑ̃, an] adj flat ▷ nm plan; (fig) level, plane; (Cinéma) shot; **au premier/second ~** in the foreground/ middle distance; **à l'arrière ~** in the background; **plan d'eau** lake

**planche** [plɑ̃ʃ] nf (pièce de bois) plank, (wooden) board; (illustration) plate; **planche à repasser** ironing board; **planche (à roulettes)** skateboard; **planche (à voile)** (sport) windsurfing

**plancher** [plɑ̃ʃe] nm floor; floorboards pl ▷ vi (fam) to work hard

**planer** [plane] vi (plane) to glide; (fam: rêveur) to have one's head in the clouds; **~ sur** (fig: danger) to hang over

**planète** [planɛt] nf planet

**planeur** [planœʀ] nm glider

**planifier** [planifje] vt to plan

**planning** [planiŋ] nm programme, schedule; **planning familial** family planning

**plant** [plɑ̃] nm seedling, young plant

**plante** [plɑ̃t] nf plant; **la plante du pied** the sole (of the foot); **plante verte** ou **d'appartement** house plant

**planter** [plɑ̃te] vt (plante) to plant; (enfoncer) to hammer ou drive in; (tente) to put up, pitch; (fam: personne) to dump; **se planter** (fam: se tromper) to get it wrong

**plaque** [plak] nf plate; (de verglas, d'eczéma) patch; (avec inscription) plaque; **plaque chauffante** hotplate; **plaque de chocolat** bar of chocolate; **plaque tournante** (fig) centre

**plaqué, e** [plake] adj: ~ or/argent gold-/silver-plated

**plaquer** [plake] vt (Rugby) to bring down; (fam: laisser tomber) to drop

**plaquette** [plaket] nf (de chocolat) bar; (beurre) pack(et); **plaquette de frein** brake pad

**plastique** [plastik] adj, nm plastic; **plastiquer** vt to blow up (with a plastic bomb)

**plat, e** [pla, -at] adj flat; (cheveux) straight; (style) flat, dull ▷ nm (récipient, Culin) dish; (d'un repas) course; **à ~ ventre** face down; **à ~** (pneu, batterie) flat; (fam: personne) dead beat; **plat cuisiné** pre-cooked meal; **plat de résistance** main course; **plat du jour** dish of the day

**platane** [platan] nm plane tree

**plateau, x** [plato] nm (support) tray; (Géo) plateau; (Cinéma) set; **plateau à fromages** cheese board

**plate-bande** [platbɑ̃d] nf flower bed

**plate-forme** [platfɔrm] nf platform; **plate-forme de forage/pétrolière** drilling/oil rig

**platine** [platin] nm platinum ▷ nf (d'un tourne-disque) turntable; **platine laser** compact disc ou CD player

**plâtre** [plɑtr] nm (matériau) plaster; (statue) plaster statue; (Méd) (plaster) cast; **avoir un bras dans le ~** to have an arm in plaster

**plein, e** [plɛ̃, plɛn] adj full ▷ nm: **faire le ~ (d'essence)** to fill up (with petrol); **à ~es mains** (ramasser) in handfuls; **à ~ temps** full-time; **en ~ air** in the open air; **en ~ soleil** in direct sunlight; **en ~e**

nuit/rue in the middle of the night/street; **en ~ jour** in broad daylight; **le ~, s'il vous plaît** fill it up, please

**pleurer** [plœre] vi to cry; (yeux) to water ▷ vt to mourn (for); **~ sur** to lament (over), to bemoan

**pleurnicher** [plœrniʃe] vi to snivel, whine

**pleurs** [plœr] nmpl: **en ~** in tears

**pleut** [plø] vb voir **pleuvoir**

**pleuvoir** [pløvwar] vb impers to rain ▷ vi (coups) to rain down; (critiques, invitations) to shower down; **il pleut** it's raining; **il pleut des cordes** it's pouring (down), it's raining cats and dogs

**pli** [pli] nm fold; (de jupe) pleat; (de pantalon) crease

**pliant, e** [plijɑ̃, plijɑ̃t] adj folding

**plier** [plije] vt to fold; (pour ranger) to fold up; (genou, bras) to bend ▷ vi to bend; (fig) to yield; **se ~ à** to submit to

**plisser** [plise] vt (jupe) to put pleats in; (yeux) to screw up; (front) to crease

**plomb** [plɔ̃] nm (métal) lead; (d'une cartouche) (lead) shot; (Pêche) sinker; (Élec) fuse; **sans ~** (essence etc) unleaded

**plomberie** [plɔ̃bri] nf plumbing

**plombier** [plɔ̃bje] nm plumber

**plonge** [plɔ̃ʒ] nf washing-up

**plongeant, e** [plɔ̃ʒɑ̃, ɑ̃t] adj (vue) from above; (décolleté) plunging

**plongée** [plɔ̃ʒe] nf (Sport) diving no pl; (sans scaphandre) skin diving; **~ sous-marine** diving

**plongeoir** [plɔ̃ʒwar] nm diving board

**plongeon** [plɔ̃ʒɔ̃] nm dive

**plonger** [plɔ̃ʒe] vi to dive ▷ vt: **~ qch dans** to plunge sth into; **se ~ dans** (études, lecture) to bury ou immerse o.s. in; **plongeur** nm diver

**plu** [ply] pp de **plaire**; de **pleuvoir**

**pluie** [plɥi] nf rain

**plume** [plym] nf feather; (pour écrire) (pen) nib; (fig) pen

**plupart** [plypar] nf: **la ~** pron the majority, most (of them); **la ~ des** most, the majority of; **la ~ du temps/d'entre nous** most of the time/of us;

**pour la ~** for the most part, mostly
**pluriel** [plyʀjɛl] *nm* plural
**plus¹** [ply] *vb voir* **plaire**

⬤ **MOT-CLÉ**

**plus²** [ply] *adv* **1** (*forme négative*): **ne ... plus** no more, no longer; **je n'ai plus d'argent** I've got no more money *ou* no money left; **il ne travaille plus** he's no longer working, he doesn't work any more
**2** [ply, plyz + *voyelle*] (*comparatif*) more, ...+er; (*superlatif*): **le plus** the most, the ...+est; **plus grand/intelligent (que)** bigger/more intelligent (than); **le plus grand/intelligent** the biggest/ most intelligent; **tout au plus** at the very most
**3** [plys, plyz + *voyelle*] (*davantage*) more; **il travaille plus (que)** he works more (than); **plus il travaille, plus il est heureux** the more he works, the happier he is; **plus de 10 personnes/3 heures** more than *ou* over 10 people/3 hours; **3 heures de plus que** 3 hours more than; **de plus** what's more, moreover; **il a 3 ans de plus que moi** he's 3 years older than me; **3 kilos en plus** 3 kilos more; **en plus de** in addition to; **de plus en plus** more and more; **plus ou moins** more or less; **ni plus ni moins** no more, no less
▷ *prép* [plys]: **4 plus 2** 4 plus 2

**plusieurs** [plyzjœʀ] *dét, pron* several; **ils sont ~** there are several of them
**plus-value** [plyvaly] *nf* (*bénéfice*) surplus
**plutôt** [plyto] *adv* rather; **je préfère ~ celui-ci** I'd rather have this one; **~ que (de) faire** rather than *ou* instead of doing
**pluvieux, -euse** [plyvjø, jøz] *adj* rainy, wet
**PME** *sigle f* (= *petite(s) et moyenne(s) entreprise(s)*) small business(es)
**PMU** *sigle m* (= *Pari mutuel urbain*) system

of betting on horses; (*café*) betting agency
**PNB** *sigle m* (= *produit national brut*) GNP
**pneu** [pnø] *nm* tyre (BRIT), tire (US); **j'ai un ~ crevé** I've got a flat tyre
**pneumonie** [pnømɔni] *nf* pneumonia
**poche** [pɔʃ] *nf* pocket; (*sous les yeux*) bag, pouch; **argent de ~** pocket money
**pochette** [pɔʃɛt] *nf* (*d'aiguilles etc*) case; (*mouchoir*) breast pocket handkerchief; (*sac à main*) clutch bag; **pochette de disque** record sleeve
**poêle** [pwal] *nm* stove ▷ *nf*: **~ (à frire)** frying pan
**poème** [pɔɛm] *nm* poem
**poésie** [pɔezi] *nf* (*poème*) poem; (*art*): **la ~** poetry
**poète** [pɔɛt] *nm* poet
**poids** [pwa] *nm* weight; (*Sport*) shot; **vendre au ~** to sell by weight; **perdre/prendre du ~** to lose/put on weight; **poids lourd** (*camion*) lorry (BRIT), truck (US)
**poignant, e** [pwaɲā, āt] *adj* poignant
**poignard** [pwaɲaʀ] *nm* dagger; **poignarder** *vt* to stab, knife
**poigne** [pwaɲ] *nf* grip; **avoir de la ~** (*fig*) to rule with a firm hand
**poignée** [pwaɲe] *nf* (*de sel etc, fig*) handful; (*de couvercle, porte*) handle; **poignée de main** handshake
**poignet** [pwaɲɛ] *nm* (*Anat*) wrist; (*de chemise*) cuff
**poil** [pwal] *nm* (*Anat*) hair; (*de pinceau, brosse*) bristle; (*de tapis*) strand; (*pelage*) coat; **à ~** (*fam*) starkers; **au ~** (*fam*) hunky-dory; **poilu, e** *adj* hairy
**poinçonner** [pwɛ̃sɔne] *vt* (*bijou*) to hallmark; (*billet*) to punch
**poing** [pwɛ̃] *nm* fist; **coup de ~** punch
**point** [pwɛ̃] *nm* point; (*endroit*) spot; (*marque, signe*) dot; (: *de ponctuation*) full stop, period (US); (*Couture, Tricot*) stitch ▷ *adv* = **pas²**; **faire le ~** (*fig*) to take stock (of the situation); **sur le ~ de faire** (just) about to do; **à tel ~ que** so much so that; **mettre au ~** (*procédé*) to develop; (*affaire*) to settle; **à ~** (*Culin: viande*) medium; **à ~ (nommé)**

just at the right time; **deux ~s** colon; **point de côté** stitch (pain); **point d'exclamation/d'interrogation** exclamation/question mark; **point de repère** landmark; (dans le temps) point of reference; **point de vente** retail outlet; **point de vue** viewpoint; (fig: opinion) point of view; **point faible** weak spot; **point final** full stop, period (us); **point mort: au point mort** (Auto) in neutral; **points de suspension** suspension points

**pointe** [pwɛ̃t] nf point; (clou) tack; (fig): **une ~ de** a hint of; **être à la ~ de** (fig) to be in the forefront of; **sur la ~ des pieds** on tiptoe; **en ~** pointed, tapered; **de ~** (technique etc) leading; **heures de ~** peak hours

**pointer** [pwɛ̃te] vt (diriger: canon, doigt): **~ qch** to point at sth ▷ vi (employé) to clock in

**pointillé** [pwɛ̃tije] nm (trait) dotted line

**pointilleux, -euse** [pwɛ̃tijø, øz] adj particular, pernickety

**pointu, e** [pwɛ̃ty] adj pointed; (voix) shrill; (analyse) precise

**pointure** [pwɛ̃tyr] nf size

**point-virgule** [pwɛ̃virgyl] nm semi-colon

**poire** [pwar] nf pear; (fam: péj) mug

**poireau, x** [pwaro] nm leek

**poirier** [pwarje] nm pear tree

**pois** [pwa] nm (Bot) pea; (sur une étoffe) dot, spot; **~ chiche** chickpea; **à ~** (cravate etc) spotted, polka-dot cpd

**poison** [pwazɔ̃] nm poison

**poisseux, -euse** [pwasø, øz] adj sticky

**poisson** [pwasɔ̃] nm fish gén inv; (Astrol): **P~s** Pisces; **~ d'avril** April fool; (blague) April Fool's Day trick; see note; **poisson rouge** goldfish; **poissonnerie** nf fish-shop; **poissonnier, -ière** nm/f fishmonger (BRIT), fish merchant (US)

● **POISSON D'AVRIL**
●
● The traditional April Fools' Day prank
● in France involves attaching a cut-
● out paper fish, known as a 'poisson
● d'avril', to the back of one's victim,
● without being caught.

**poitrine** [pwatrin] nf chest; (seins) bust, bosom; (Culin) breast

**poivre** [pwavr] nm pepper

**poivron** [pwavrɔ̃] nm pepper, capsicum

**polaire** [pɔlɛr] adj polar

**pôle** [pol] nm (Géo, Élec) pole; **le ~ Nord/ Sud** the North/South Pole

**poli, e** [pɔli] adj polite; (lisse) smooth

**police** [pɔlis] nf police; **police judiciaire** ≈ Criminal Investigation Department (BRIT), ≈ Federal Bureau of Investigation (US); **police secours** ≈ emergency services pl (BRIT), ≈ paramedics pl (US); **policier, -ière** adj police cpd ▷ nm policeman; (aussi: **roman policier**) detective novel

**polir** [pɔlir] vt to polish

**politesse** [pɔlitɛs] nf politeness

**politicien, ne** [pɔlitisjɛ̃, jɛn] (péj) nm/f politician

**politique** [pɔlitik] adj political ▷ nf politics sg; (mesures, méthode) policies pl

**politiquement** [pɔlitikmɑ̃] adv politically; **~ correct** politically correct

**pollen** [pɔlɛn] nm pollen

**polluant, e** [pɔlɥɑ̃, ɑ̃t] adj polluting ▷ nm (produit): **~ pollutant**; **non ~** non-polluting

**polluer** [pɔlɥe] vt to pollute; **pollution** nf pollution

**polo** [pɔlo] nm (chemise) polo shirt

**Pologne** [pɔlɔɲ] nf: **la ~** Poland; **polonais, e** adj Polish ▷ nm/f: **Polonais, e** Pole ▷ nm (Ling) Polish

**poltron, ne** [pɔltrɔ̃, ɔn] adj cowardly

**polycopier** [pɔlikɔpje] vt to duplicate

**Polynésie** [pɔlinezi] nf: **la ~** Polynesia; **la ~ française** French Polynesia

**polyvalent, e** [pɔlivalɑ̃, ɑ̃t] adj (rôle) varied; (salle) multi-purpose

**pommade** [pɔmad] nf ointment, cream

**pomme** [pɔm] nf apple; **tomber**

**dans les ~s** (*fam*) to pass out; **pomme d'Adam** Adam's apple; **pomme de pin** pine *ou* fir cone; **pomme de terre** potato
**pommette** [pɔmɛt] *nf* cheekbone
**pommier** [pɔmje] *nm* apple tree
**pompe** [pɔ̃p] *nf* pump; (*faste*) pomp (and ceremony); **pompe (à essence)** petrol pump; **pompes funèbres** funeral parlour *sg*, undertaker's *sg*; **pomper** *vt* to pump; (*aspirer*) to pump up; (*absorber*) to soak up
**pompeux, -euse** [pɔ̃pø, øz] *adj* pompous
**pompier** [pɔ̃pje] *nm* fireman
**pompiste** [pɔ̃pist] *nm/f* petrol (BRIT) *ou* gas (US) pump attendant
**poncer** [pɔ̃se] *vt* to sand (down)
**ponctuation** [pɔ̃ktɥasjɔ̃] *nf* punctuation
**ponctuel, le** [pɔ̃ktɥɛl] *adj* punctual
**pondéré, e** [pɔ̃dere] *adj* level-headed, composed
**pondre** [pɔ̃dʀ] *vt* to lay
**poney** [pɔnɛ] *nm* pony
**pont** [pɔ̃] *nm* bridge; (*Navig*) deck; **faire le ~** to take the extra day off; *see note*; **pont suspendu** suspension bridge; **pont-levis** *nm* drawbridge

● PONT
●
● The expression 'faire le pont' refers
● to the practice of taking a Monday
● or Friday off to make a long weekend
● if a public holiday falls on a Tuesday
● or Thursday. The French commonly
● take an extra day off work to give
● four consecutive days' holiday at
● 'l'Ascension', 'le 14 juillet' and 'le
● 15 août'.

**pop** [pɔp] *adj inv* pop
**populaire** [pɔpylɛʀ] *adj* popular; (*manifestation*) mass *cpd*; (*milieux, quartier*) working-class; (*expression*) vernacular
**popularité** [pɔpylaʀite] *nf* popularity

**population** [pɔpylasjɔ̃] *nf* population
**populeux, -euse** [pɔpylø, øz] *adj* densely populated
**porc** [pɔʀ] *nm* pig; (*Culin*) pork
**porcelaine** [pɔʀsəlɛn] *nf* porcelain, china; piece of china(ware)
**porc-épic** [pɔʀkepik] *nm* porcupine
**porche** [pɔʀʃ] *nm* porch
**porcherie** [pɔʀʃəʀi] *nf* pigsty
**pore** [pɔʀ] *nm* pore
**porno** [pɔʀno] *adj* porno ▷ *nm* porn
**port** [pɔʀ] *nm* harbour, port; (*ville*) port; (*de l'uniforme etc*) wearing; (*pour lettre*) postage; (*pour colis, aussi: posture*) carriage; **port d'arme** (*Jur*) carrying of a firearm; **port payé** postage paid
**portable** [pɔʀtabl] *adj* (*portatif*) portable; (*téléphone*) mobile ▷ *nm* (*Comput*) laptop (computer); (*téléphone*) mobile (phone)
**portail** [pɔʀtaj] *nm* gate
**portant, e** [pɔʀtɑ̃, ɑ̃t] *adj*: **bien/mal ~** in good/poor health
**portatif, -ive** [pɔʀtatif, iv] *adj* portable
**porte** [pɔʀt] *nf* door; (*de ville, jardin*) gate; **mettre à la ~** to throw out; **porte-avions** *nm inv* aircraft carrier; **porte-bagages** *nm inv* luggage rack; **porte-bonheur** *nm inv* lucky charm; **porte-clefs** *nm inv* key ring; **porte-documents** *nm inv* attaché *ou* document case
**porté, e** [pɔʀte] *adj*: **être ~ à faire** to be inclined to do; **être ~ sur qch** to be keen on sth; **portée** *nf* (*d'une arme*) range; (*fig: effet*) impact, import; (: *capacité*) scope, capability; (*de chatte etc*) litter; (*Mus*) stave, staff; **à/hors de portée (de)** within/out of reach (of); **à portée de (la) main** within (arm's) reach; **à la portée de qn** (*fig*) at sb's level, within sb's capabilities
**porte...**: **portefeuille** *nm* wallet; **portemanteau, x** *nm* (*cintre*) coat hanger; (*au mur*) coat rack; **porte-monnaie** *nm inv* purse; **porte-parole** *nm inv* spokesman

**porter** [pɔʀte] vt to carry; (sur soi: vêtement, barbe, bague) to wear; (fig: responsabilité etc) to bear, carry; (inscription, nom, fruits) to bear; (coup) to deal; (attention) to turn; (apporter): **~ qch à qn** to take sth to sb ▷ vi (voix) to carry; (coup, argument) to hit home; **se porter** vi (se sentir): **~ bien/mal** to be well/unwell; **~ sur** (recherches) to be concerned with; **se faire ~ malade** to report sick

**porteur, -euse** [pɔʀtœʀ, øz] nm/f (de bagages) porter; (de chèque) bearer

**porte-voix** [pɔʀtəvwa] nm inv megaphone

**portier** [pɔʀtje] nm doorman

**portière** [pɔʀtjɛʀ] nf door

**portion** [pɔʀsjɔ̃] nf (part) portion, share; (partie) portion, section

**porto** [pɔʀto] nm port (wine)

**portrait** [pɔʀtʀɛ] nm (peinture) portrait; (photo) photograph; **portrait-robot** nm Identikit® ou photo-fit® picture

**portuaire** [pɔʀtɥɛʀ] adj port cpd, harbour cpd

**portugais, e** [pɔʀtɥgɛ, ɛz] adj Portuguese ▷ nm/f: **P~, e** Portuguese ▷ nm (Ling) Portuguese

**Portugal** [pɔʀtɥgal] nm: **le ~** Portugal

**pose** [poz] nf (de moquette) laying; (attitude, d'un modèle) pose; (Photo) exposure

**posé, e** [poze] adj serious

**poser** [poze] vt to put; (installer: moquette, carrelage) to lay; (rideaux, papier peint) to hang; (question) to ask; (principe, conditions) to lay ou set down; (difficulté) to pose; (formuler: problème) to formulate ▷ vi (modèle) to pose; **se poser** vi (oiseau, avion) to land; (question) to arise; **~ qch (sur)** (déposer) to put sth down (on); **~ qch sur/quelque part** (placer) to put sth on/somewhere; **~ sa candidature à un poste** to apply for a post

**positif, -ive** [pozitif, iv] adj positive

**position** [pozisjɔ̃] nf position; **prendre ~** (fig) to take a stand

**posologie** [pozɔlɔʒi] nf dosage

**posséder** [pɔsede] vt to own, possess; (qualité, talent) to have, possess; (sexuellement) to possess; **possession** nf ownership no pl, possession; **prendre possession de qch** to take possession of sth

**possibilité** [pɔsibilite] nf possibility; **possibilités** nfpl (potentiel) potential sg

**possible** [pɔsibl] adj possible; (projet, entreprise) feasible ▷ nm: **faire son ~** to do all one can, do one's utmost; **le plus/moins de livres ~** as many/few books as possible; **le plus vite ~** as quickly as possible; **aussitôt/dès que ~** as soon as possible

**postal, e, -aux** [pɔstal, o] adj postal

**poste¹** [pɔst] nf (service) post, postal service; (administration, bureau) post office; **mettre à la ~** to post; **poste restante** poste restante (BRIT), general delivery (US)

**poste²** [pɔst] nm (fonction, Mil) post; (Tél) extension; (de radio etc) set; **poste (de police)** police station; **poste de secours** first-aid post; **poste d'essence** filling station; **poste d'incendie** fire point; **poste de pilotage** cockpit, flight deck

**poster** [pɔste] vt to post; **où est-ce que je peux ~ ces cartes postales?** where can I post these cards?

**postérieur, e** [pɔsteʀjœʀ] adj (date) later; (partie) back ▷ nm (fam) behind

**postuler** [pɔstyle] vi: **~ à** ou **pour un emploi** to apply for a job

**pot** [po] nm (en verre) jar; (en terre) pot; (en plastique, carton) carton; (en métal) tin; (fam: chance) luck; **avoir du ~** (fam) to be lucky; **boire** ou **prendre un ~** (fam) to have a drink; **petit ~ (pour bébé)** (jar of) baby food; **~ catalytique** catalytic converter; **pot d'échappement** exhaust pipe

**potable** [pɔtabl] adj: **eau (non) ~** (non-)drinking water

**potage** [pɔtaʒ] nm soup; **potager,**

**-ère** adj: **(jardin) potager** kitchen ou vegetable garden

**pot-au-feu** [pɔtofø] nm inv (beef) stew

**pot-de-vin** [pɔdvɛ̃] nm bribe

**pote** [pɔt] (fam) nm pal

**poteau, x** [pɔto] nm post; **poteau indicateur** signpost

**potelé, e** [pɔt(ə)le] adj plump, chubby

**potentiel, le** [pɔtɑ̃sjɛl] adj, nm potential

**poterie** [pɔtʀi] nf pottery; (objet) piece of pottery

**potier, -ière** [pɔtje, jɛʀ] nm/f potter

**potiron** [pɔtiʀɔ̃] nm pumpkin

**pou, x** [pu] nm louse

**poubelle** [pubɛl] nf (dust)bin

**pouce** [pus] nm thumb

**poudre** [pudʀ] nf powder; (fard) (face) powder; (explosif) gunpowder; **en ~**: **café en ~** instant coffee; **lait en ~** dried ou powdered milk; **poudreuse** nf powder snow; **poudrier** nm (powder) compact

**pouffer** [pufe] vi: **~ (de rire)** to burst out laughing

**poulailler** [pulaje] nm henhouse

**poulain** [pulɛ̃] nm foal; (fig) protégé

**poule** [pul] nf hen; (Culin) (boiling) fowl; **poule mouillée** coward

**poulet** [pulɛ] nm chicken; (fam) cop

**poulie** [puli] nf pulley

**pouls** [pu] nm pulse; **prendre le ~ de qn** to feel sb's pulse

**poumon** [pumɔ̃] nm lung

**poupée** [pupe] nf doll

**pour** [puʀ] prép for ▷ nm: **le ~ et le contre** the pros and cons; **~ faire** (so as) to do, in order to do; **~ avoir fait** for having done; **~ que** so that, in order that; **fermé ~ (cause de) travaux** closed for refurbishment ou alterations; **c'est ~ ça que ...** that's why ...; **~ quoi faire?** what for?; **~ 20 euros d'essence** 20 euros' worth of petrol; **~ cent** per cent; **~ ce qui est de** as for

**pourboire** [puʀbwaʀ] nm tip; **combien de ~ est-ce qu'il faut laisser?** how much should I tip?

**pourcentage** [puʀsɑ̃taʒ] nm percentage

**pourchasser** [puʀʃase] vt to pursue

**pourparlers** [puʀpaʀle] nmpl talks, negotiations

**pourpre** [puʀpʀ] adj crimson

**pourquoi** [puʀkwa] adv, conj why ▷ nm inv: **le ~ (de)** the reason (for)

**pourrai** etc [puʀe] vb voir **pouvoir**

**pourri, e** [puʀi] adj rotten

**pourrir** [puʀiʀ] vi to rot; (fruit) to go rotten ou bad ▷ vt to rot; (fig) to spoil thoroughly; **pourriture** nf rot

**poursuite** [puʀsɥit] nf pursuit, chase; **poursuites** nfpl (Jur) legal proceedings

**poursuivre** [puʀsɥivʀ] vt to pursue, chase (after); (obséder) to haunt; (Jur) to bring proceedings against, prosecute; (: au civil) to sue; (but) to strive towards; (continuer: études etc) to carry on with, continue; **se poursuivre** vi to go on, continue

**pourtant** [puʀtɑ̃] adv yet; **c'est ~ facile** (and) yet it's easy

**pourtour** [puʀtuʀ] nm perimeter

**pourvoir** [puʀvwaʀ] vt: **~ qch/qn de** to equip sth/sb with ▷ vi: **~ à** to provide for; **pourvu, e** adj: **pourvu de** equipped with; **pourvu que** (si) provided that, so long as; (espérons que) let's hope (that)

**pousse** [pus] nf growth; (bourgeon) shoot

**poussée** [puse] nf thrust; (d'acné) eruption; (fig: prix) upsurge

**pousser** [puse] vt to push; (émettre: cri, soupir) to give; (stimuler: élève) to urge on; (poursuivre: études, discussion) to carry on (further) ▷ vi to push; (croître) to grow; **se pousser** vi to move over; **~ qn à** (inciter) to urge ou press sb to; (acculer) to drive sb to; **faire ~** (plante) to grow

**poussette** [pusɛt] nf push chair (BRIT), stroller (US)

**poussière** [pusjɛʀ] nf dust; **poussiéreux, -euse** adj dusty

**poussin** [pusɛ̃] nm chick
**poutre** [putʀ] nf beam

O MOT-CLÉ

**pouvoir** [puvwaʀ] nm power; (Pol:
dirigeants): **le pouvoir** those in power;
**les pouvoirs publics** the authorities;
**pouvoir d'achat** purchasing power
▷ vb semi-aux **1** (être en état de) can,
be able to; **je ne peux pas le réparer**
I can't ou I'm not able to repair it;
**déçu de ne pas pouvoir le faire**
disappointed not to be able to do it
**2** (avoir la permission) can, may, be
allowed to; **vous pouvez aller au
cinéma** you can ou may go to the
pictures
**3** (probabilité, hypothèse) may, might,
could; **il a pu avoir un accident** he
may ou might ou could have had an
accident; **il aurait pu le dire!** he might
ou could have said (so)!
▷ vb impers may, might, could; **il peut
arriver que** it may ou might ou could
happen that; **il pourrait pleuvoir** it
might rain
▷ vt can, be able to; **j'ai fait tout ce que
j'ai pu** I did all I could; **je n'en peux plus**
(épuisé) I'm exhausted; (à bout) I can't
take any more
▷ vi: **se pouvoir: il se peut que** it may
ou might be that; **cela se pourrait**
that's quite possible

**prairie** [pʀeʀi] nf meadow
**praline** [pʀalin] nf sugared almond
**praticable** [pʀatikabl] adj passable,
practicable
**pratiquant, e** [pʀatikɑ̃, ɑ̃t] nm/f
(regular) churchgoer
**pratique** [pʀatik] nf practice ▷ adj
practical; **pratiquement** adv (pour ainsi
dire) practically, virtually; **pratiquer**
vt to practise; (l'équitation, la pêche)
to go in for; (le golf, football) to play;
(intervention, opération) to carry out
**pré** [pʀe] nm meadow

**préalable** [pʀealabl] adj preliminary;
**au ~** beforehand
**préambule** [pʀeɑ̃byl] nm preamble;
(fig) prelude; **sans ~** straight away
**préau** [pʀeo] nm (Scol) covered
playground
**préavis** [pʀeavi] nm notice
**précaution** [pʀekosjɔ̃] nf precaution;
**avec ~** cautiously; **par ~** as a
precaution
**précédemment** [pʀesedamɑ̃] adv
before, previously
**précédent, e** [pʀesedɑ̃, ɑ̃t] adj
previous ▷ nm precedent; **sans ~**
unprecedented; **le jour ~** the day
before, the previous day
**précéder** [pʀesede] vt to precede
**prêcher** [pʀeʃe] vt to preach
**précieux, -euse** [pʀesjø, jøz] adj
precious; (aide, conseil) invaluable
**précipice** [pʀesipis] nm drop, chasm
**précipitamment** [pʀesipitamɑ̃] adv
hurriedly, hastily
**précipitation** [pʀesipitasjɔ̃] nf (hâte)
haste
**précipité, e** [pʀesipite] adj hurried,
hasty
**précipiter** [pʀesipite] vt (hâter: départ)
to hasten; (faire tomber): **~ qn/qch du
haut de** to throw ou hurl sb/sth off ou
from; **se précipiter** vi to speed up; **se ~
sur/vers** to rush at/towards
**précis, e** [pʀesi, iz] adj precise;
(mesures) accurate, precise; **à 4 heures
~es** at 4 o'clock sharp; **précisément**
adv precisely; **préciser** vt (expliquer)
to be more specific about, clarify;
(spécifier) to state, specify; **se préciser**
vi to become clear(er); **précision**
nf precision; (détail) point ou detail;
**demander des précisions** to ask for
further explanation
**précoce** [pʀekɔs] adj early; (enfant)
precocious
**préconçu, e** [pʀekɔ̃sy] adj
preconceived
**préconiser** [pʀekɔnize] vt to advocate
**prédécesseur** [pʀedesesœʀ] nm

predecessor
**prédilection** [pʀedilɛksjɔ̃] *nf*: **avoir une ~ pour** to be partial to
**prédire** [pʀediʀ] *vt* to predict
**prédominer** [pʀedɔmine] *vi* to predominate
**préface** [pʀefas] *nf* preface
**préfecture** [pʀefɛktyʀ] *nf* prefecture; **préfecture de police** police headquarters *pl*
**préférable** [pʀefeʀabl] *adj* preferable
**préféré, e** [pʀefeʀe] *adj, nm/f* favourite
**préférence** [pʀefeʀɑ̃s] *nf* preference; **de ~** preferably
**préférer** [pʀefeʀe] *vt*: **~ qn/qch (à)** to prefer sb/sth (to), like sb/sth better (than); **~ faire** to prefer to do; **je préférerais du thé** I would rather have tea, I'd prefer tea
**préfet** [pʀefɛ] *nm* prefect
**préhistorique** [pʀeistɔʀik] *adj* prehistoric
**préjudice** [pʀeʒydis] *nm* (*matériel*) loss; (*moral*) harm *no pl*; **porter ~ à** to harm, be detrimental to; **au ~ de** at the expense of
**préjugé** [pʀeʒyʒe] *nm* prejudice; **avoir un ~ contre** to be prejudiced *ou* biased against
**prélasser** [pʀelɑse]: **se prélasser** *vi* to lounge
**prélèvement** [pʀelɛvmɑ̃] *nm* (*montant*) deduction; **faire un ~ de sang** to take a blood sample
**prélever** [pʀel(ə)ve] *vt* (*échantillon*) to take; **~ (sur)** (*montant*) to deduct (from); (*argent: sur son compte*) to withdraw (from)
**prématuré, e** [pʀematyʀe] *adj* premature ▷ *nm* premature baby
**premier, -ière** [pʀəmje, jɛʀ] *adj* first; (*rang*) front; (*fig: objectif*) basic; **le ~ venu** the first person to come along; **de ~ ordre** first-rate; **Premier ministre** Prime Minister; **première** *nf* (*Scol*) year 12 (BRIT), eleventh grade (US); (*Aviat, Rail etc*) first class; **premièrement** *adv* firstly

**prémonition** [pʀemɔnisjɔ̃] *nf* premonition
**prenant, e** [pʀənɑ̃, ɑ̃t] *adj* absorbing, engrossing
**prénatal, e** [pʀenatal] *adj* (*Méd*) antenatal
**prendre** [pʀɑ̃dʀ] *vt* to take; (*repas*) to have; (*se procurer*) to get; (*malfaiteur, poisson*) to catch; (*passager*) to pick up; (*personnel*) to take on; (*traiter: personne*) to handle; (*voix, ton*) to put on; (*ôter*): **~ qch à** to take sth from; (*coincer*): **se ~ les doigts dans** to get one's fingers caught in ▷ *vi* (*liquide, ciment*) to set; (*greffe, vaccin*) to take; (*feu: foyer*) to go; (*se diriger*): **~ à gauche** to turn (to the) left; **~ froid** to catch cold; **se ~ pour** to think one is; **s'en ~ à** to attack; **se ~ d'amitié pour** to befriend; **s'y ~** (*procéder*) to set about it
**preneur** [pʀənœʀ] *nm*: **être/trouver ~** to be willing to buy/find a buyer
**prénom** [pʀenɔ̃] *nm* first *ou* Christian name
**préoccupation** [pʀeɔkypasjɔ̃] *nf* (*souci*) concern; (*idée fixe*) preoccupation
**préoccuper** [pʀeɔkype] *vt* (*inquiéter*) to worry; (*absorber*) to preoccupy; **se ~ de** to be concerned with
**préparatifs** [pʀepaʀatif] *nmpl* preparations
**préparation** [pʀepaʀasjɔ̃] *nf* preparation
**préparer** [pʀepaʀe] *vt* to prepare; (*café, thé*) to make; (*examen*) to prepare for; (*voyage, entreprise*) to plan; **se préparer** *vi* (*orage, tragédie*) to brew, be in the air; **~ qch à qn** (*surprise etc*) to have sth in store for sb; **se ~ (à qch/faire)** to prepare (o.s.) *ou* get ready (for sth/to do)
**prépondérant, e** [pʀepɔ̃deʀɑ̃, ɑ̃t] *adj* major, dominating
**préposé, e** [pʀepoze] *nm/f* employee; (*facteur*) postman
**préposition** [pʀepozisjɔ̃] *nf* preposition

**près** [prɛ] *adv* near, close; **~ de** near (to), close to; (*environ*) nearly, almost; **de ~** closely; **à 5 kg ~** to within about 5 kg; **il n'est pas à 10 minutes ~** he can spare 10 minutes; **est-ce qu'il y a une banque ~ d'ici?** is there a bank nearby?

**présage** [preza3] *nm* omen

**presbyte** [prɛsbit] *adj* long-sighted

**presbytère** [prɛsbiter] *nm* presbytery

**prescription** [prɛskripsjɔ̃] *nf* prescription

**prescrire** [prɛskrir] *vt* to prescribe

**présence** [prezɑ̃s] *nf* presence; (*au bureau, à l'école*) attendance

**présent, e** [prezɑ̃, ɑ̃t] *adj, nm* present; **à ~ (que)** now (that)

**présentation** [prezɑ̃tasjɔ̃] *nf* presentation; (*de nouveau venu*) introduction; (*allure*) appearance; **faire les ~s** to do the introductions

**présenter** [prezɑ̃te] *vt* to present; (*excuses, condoléances*) to offer; (*invité, conférencier*): **~ qn (à)** to introduce sb (to) ▷ *vi*: **~ bien** to have a pleasing appearance; **se présenter** *vi* (*occasion*) to arise; **se ~ à** (*examen*) to sit; (*élection*) to stand at, run for; **je vous présente Nadine** this is Nadine, could I introduce you to Nadine?

**préservatif** [prezɛrvatif] *nm* condom, sheath

**préserver** [prezɛrve] *vt*: **~ de** (*protéger*) to protect from

**président** [prezidɑ̃] *nm* (*Pol*) president; (*d'une assemblée, Comm*) chairman; **président directeur général** chairman and managing director; **présidentielles** *nfpl* presidential elections

**présider** [prezide] *vt* to preside over; (*dîner*) to be the guest of honour at

**presque** [prɛsk] *adv* almost, nearly; **~ personne** hardly anyone; **~ rien** hardly anything; **~ pas** hardly (at all); **~ pas (de)** hardly any

**presqu'île** [prɛskil] *nf* peninsula

**pressant, e** [presɑ̃, ɑ̃t] *adj* urgent

**presse** [prɛs] *nf* press; (*affluence*):

**heures de ~** busy times

**pressé, e** [prese] *adj* in a hurry; (*travail*) urgent; **orange ~e** freshly-squeezed orange juice

**pressentiment** [presɑ̃timɑ̃] *nm* foreboding, premonition

**pressentir** [presɑ̃tir] *vt* to sense

**presse-papiers** [prɛspapje] *nm inv* paperweight

**presser** [prese] *vt* (*fruit, éponge*) to squeeze; (*bouton*) to press; (*allure*) to speed up; (*inciter*): **~ qn de faire** to urge *ou* press sb to do ▷ *vi* to be urgent; **se presser** *vi* (*se hâter*) to hurry (up); **se ~ contre qn** to squeeze up against sb; **le temps presse** there's not much time; **rien ne presse** there's no hurry

**pressing** [presiŋ] *nm* (*magasin*) dry-cleaner's

**pression** [presjɔ̃] *nf* pressure; (*bouton*) press stud; (*fam: bière*) draught beer; **faire ~ sur** to put pressure on; **sous ~** pressurized, under pressure; (*fig*) under pressure; **pression artérielle** blood pressure

**prestataire** [prɛstater] *nm/f* supplier

**prestation** [prɛstasjɔ̃] *nf* (*allocation*) benefit; (*d'une entreprise*) service provided; (*d'un artiste*) performance

**prestidigitateur, -trice** [prɛstidiʒitatœr, tris] *nm/f* conjurer

**prestige** [prɛstiʒ] *nm* prestige; **prestigieux, -euse** *adj* prestigious

**présumer** [prezyme] *vt*: **~ que** to presume *ou* assume that

**prêt, e** [prɛ, prɛt] *adj* ready ▷ *nm* (*somme*) loan; **quand est-ce que mes photos seront ~es?** when will my photos be ready?; **prêt-à-porter** *nm* ready-to-wear *ou* off-the-peg (BRIT) clothes *pl*

**prétendre** [pretɑ̃dr] *vt* (*affirmer*): **~ que** to claim that; (*avoir l'intention de*): **~ faire qch** to mean *ou* intend to do sth; **prétendu, e** *adj* (*supposé*) so-called

▌ Attention à ne pas traduire *prétendre* par to pretend.

**prétentieux, -euse** [pretɑ̃sjø, jøz]

*adj* pretentious

**prétention** [pretɑ̃sjɔ̃] *nf* claim; (*vanité*) pretentiousness

**prêter** [prete] *vt* (*livres, argent*): **~ qch (à)** to lend sth (to); (*supposer*): **~ à qn** (*caractère, propos*) to attribute to sb; **pouvez-vous me ~ de l'argent?** can you lend me some money?

**prétexte** [pretɛkst] *nm* pretext, excuse; **sous aucun ~** on no account; **prétexter** *vt* to give as a pretext *ou* an excuse

**prêtre** [pretR] *nm* priest

**preuve** [prœv] *nf* proof; (*indice*) proof, evidence *no pl*; **faire ~ de** to show; **faire ses ~s** to prove o.s. (*ou* itself)

**prévaloir** [prevalwar] *vi* to prevail

**prévenant, e** [prev(ə)nɑ̃, ɑ̃t] *adj* thoughtful, kind

**prévenir** [prev(ə)niR] *vt* (*éviter*: *catastrophe etc*) to avoid, prevent; (*anticiper*: *désirs, besoins*) to anticipate; **~ qn (de)** (*avertir*) to warn sb (about); (*informer*) to tell *ou* inform sb (about)

**préventif, -ive** [prevɑ̃tif, iv] *adj* preventive

**prévention** [prevɑ̃sjɔ̃] *nf* prevention; **prévention routière** road safety

**prévenu, e** [prev(ə)ny] *nm/f* (*Jur*) defendant, accused

**prévision** [previzjɔ̃] *nf*: **~s** predictions; (*Écon*) forecast *sg*; **en ~ de** in anticipation of; **prévisions météorologiques** weather forecast *sg*

**prévoir** [prevwar] *vt* (*anticiper*) to foresee; (*s'attendre à*) to expect, reckon on; (*organiser*: *voyage etc*) to plan; (*envisager*) to allow; **comme prévu** as planned; **prévoyant, e** *adj* gifted with (*ou* showing) foresight; **prévu, e** *pp de* **prévoir**

**prier** [prije] *vi* to pray ▷ *vt* (*Dieu*) to pray to; (*implorer*) to beg; (*demander*): **~ qn de faire** to ask sb to do; **se faire ~** to need coaxing *ou* persuading; **je vous en prie** (*allez-y*) please do; (*de rien*) don't mention it; **prière** *nf* prayer; **"prière de ..."** "please ..."

**primaire** [primer] *adj* primary ▷ *nm* (*Scol*) primary education

**prime** [prim] *nf* (*bonus*) bonus; (*subvention*) premium; (*Comm*: *cadeau*) free gift; (*Assurances, Bourse*) premium ▷ *adj*: **de ~ abord** at first glance; **primer** *vt* (*récompenser*) to award a prize to ▷ *vi* to dominate; to be most important

**primevère** [primver] *nf* primrose

**primitif, -ive** [primitif, iv] *adj* primitive; (*originel*) original

**prince** [prɛ̃s] *nm* prince; **princesse** *nf* princess

**principal, e, -aux** [prɛ̃sipal, o] *adj* principal, main ▷ *nm* (*Scol*) principal, head(master); (*essentiel*) main thing

**principe** [prɛ̃sip] *nm* principle; **par ~** on principle; **en ~** (*habituellement*) as a rule; (*théoriquement*) in principle

**printemps** [prɛ̃tɑ̃] *nm* spring

**priorité** [prijɔrite] *nf* priority; (*Auto*) right of way; **priorité à droite** right of way to vehicles coming from the right

**pris, e** [pri, priz] *pp de* **prendre** ▷ *adj* (*place*) taken; (*mains*) full; (*personne*) busy; **avoir le nez/la gorge ~(e)** to have a stuffy nose/a hoarse throat; **être ~ de panique** to be panic-stricken

**prise** [priz] *nf* (*d'une ville*) capture; (*Pêche, Chasse*) catch; (*point d'appui ou pour empoigner*) hold; (*Élec: fiche*) plug; (: *femelle*) socket; **être aux ~s avec** to be grappling with; **prise de courant** power point; **prise de sang** blood test; **prise multiple** adaptor

**priser** [prize] *vt* (*estimer*) to prize, value

**prison** [prizɔ̃] *nf* prison; **aller/être en ~** to go to/be in prison *ou* jail; **prisonnier, -ière** *nm/f* prisoner ▷ *adj* captive

**privé, e** [prive] *adj* private; (*en punition*): **tu es ~ de télé!** no TV for you! ▷ *nm* (*Comm*) private sector; **en ~** in private

**priver** [prive] *vt*: **~ qn de** to deprive sb of; **se priver de** to go *ou* do without

**privilège** [privilɛʒ] *nm* privilege

**prix** [pri] *nm* price; (*récompense, Scol*) prize; **hors de ~** exorbitantly priced;

**à aucun ~** not at any price; **à tout ~** at all costs

**probable** [pʀɔbabl] *adj* likely, probable; **probablement** *adv* probably

**problème** [pʀɔblɛm] *nm* problem

**procédé** [pʀɔsede] *nm* (*méthode*) process; (*comportement*) behaviour *no pl*

**procéder** [pʀɔsede] *vi* to proceed; (*moralement*) to behave; **~ à** to carry out

**procès** [pʀɔsɛ] *nm* trial; (*poursuites*) proceedings *pl*; **être en ~ avec** to be involved in a lawsuit with

**processus** [pʀɔsesys] *nm* process

**procès-verbal, -aux** [pʀɔsɛvɛʀbal, o] *nm* (*de réunion*) minutes *pl*; (*aussi*: **P.-V.**) parking ticket

**prochain, e** [pʀɔʃɛ̃, ɛn] *adj* next; (*proche*: *départ, arrivée*) impending ▷ *nm* fellow man; **la ~e fois/semaine ~e** next time/week; **prochainement** *adv* soon, shortly

**proche** [pʀɔʃ] *adj* nearby; (*dans le temps*) imminent; (*parent, ami*) close; **proches** *nmpl* (*parents*) close relatives; **être ~ (de)** to be near, be close (to)

**proclamer** [pʀɔklame] *vt* to proclaim

**procuration** [pʀɔkyʀasjɔ̃] *nf* proxy

**procurer** [pʀɔkyʀe] *vt*: **~ qch à qn** (*fournir*) to obtain sth for sb; (*causer*: *plaisir etc*) to bring sb sth; **se procurer** *vt* to get; **procureur** *nm* public prosecutor

**prodige** [pʀɔdiʒ] *nm* marvel, wonder; (*personne*) prodigy; **prodiguer** *vt* (*soins, attentions*): **prodiguer qch à qn** to give sb sth

**producteur, -trice** [pʀɔdyktœʀ, tʀis] *nm/f* producer

**productif, -ive** [pʀɔdyktif, iv] *adj* productive

**production** [pʀɔdyksjɔ̃] *nf* production; (*rendement*) output

**productivité** [pʀɔdyktivite] *nf* productivity

**produire** [pʀɔdɥiʀ] *vt* to produce; **se produire** *vi* (*événement*) to happen, occur; (*acteur*) to perform, appear

**produit** [pʀɔdɥi] *nm* product;

**produit chimique** chemical; **produits agricoles** farm produce *sg*; **produits de beauté** beauty products, cosmetics; **produits d'entretien** cleaning products

**prof** [pʀɔf] (*fam*) *nm* teacher

**proférer** [pʀɔfeʀe] *vt* to utter

**professeur, e** [pʀɔfesœʀ] *nm/f* teacher; (*de faculté*) (university) lecturer; (: *titulaire d'une chaire*) professor

**profession** [pʀɔfesjɔ̃] *nf* occupation; **~ libérale** (liberal) profession; **sans ~** unemployed; **professionnel, le** *adj*, *nm/f* professional

**profil** [pʀɔfil] *nm* profile; **de ~** in profile

**profit** [pʀɔfi] *nm* (*avantage*) benefit, advantage; (*Comm, Finance*) profit; **au ~ de** in aid of; **tirer ~ de** to profit from; **profitable** *adj* (*utile*) beneficial; (*lucratif*) profitable; **profiter** *vi*: **profiter de** (*situation, occasion*) to take advantage of; (*vacances, jeunesse etc*) to make the most of

**profond, e** [pʀɔfɔ̃, ɔ̃d] *adj* deep; (*sentiment, intérêt*) profound; **profondément** *adv* deeply; **il dort profondément** he is sound asleep; **profondeur** *nf* depth; **l'eau a quelle profondeur?** how deep is the water?

**programme** [pʀɔgʀam] *nm* programme; (*Scol*) syllabus, curriculum; (*Inform*) program; **programmer** *vt* (*émission*) to schedule; (*Inform*) to program; **programmeur, -euse** *nm/f* programmer

**progrès** [pʀɔgʀɛ] *nm* progress *no pl*; **faire des ~** to make progress; **progresser** *vi* to progress; **progressif, -ive** *adj* progressive

**proie** [pʀwa] *nf* prey *no pl*

**projecteur** [pʀɔʒɛktœʀ] *nm* (*pour film*) projector; (*de théâtre, cirque*) spotlight

**projectile** [pʀɔʒɛktil] *nm* missile

**projection** [pʀɔʒɛksjɔ̃] *nf* projection; (*séance*) showing

**projet** [pʀɔʒɛ] *nm* plan; (*ébauche*) draft; **projet de loi** bill; **projeter** *vt* (*envisager*) to plan; (*film, photos*) to project; (*ombre, lueur*) to throw, cast; (*jeter*) to throw up (*ou* off *ou* out)

**prolétaire** [pʀɔletɛʀ] *adj, nmf* proletarian

**prolongement** [pʀɔlɔ̃ʒmɑ̃] *nm* extension; **dans le ~ de** running on from

**prolonger** [pʀɔlɔ̃ʒe] *vt* (*débat, séjour*) to prolong; (*délai, billet, rue*) to extend; **se prolonger** *vi* to go on

**promenade** [pʀɔm(ə)nad] *nf* walk (*ou* drive *ou* ride); **faire une ~** to go for a walk; **une ~ en voiture/à vélo** a drive-/(bicycle) ride

**promener** [pʀɔm(ə)ne] *vt* (*chien*) to take out for a walk; (*doigts, regard*): **~ qch sur** to run sth over; **se promener** *vi* to go for (*ou* be out for) a walk

**promesse** [pʀɔmɛs] *nf* promise

**promettre** [pʀɔmɛtʀ] *vt* to promise ▷ *vi* to be *ou* look promising; **~ à qn de faire** to promise sb that one will do

**promiscuité** [pʀɔmiskɥite] *nf* (*chambre*) lack of privacy

**promontoire** [pʀɔmɔ̃twaʀ] *nm* headland

**promoteur, -trice** [pʀɔmɔtœʀ, tʀis] *nm/f*: **promoteur (immobilier)** property developer (BRIT), real estate promoter (US)

**promotion** [pʀɔmosjɔ̃] *nf* promotion; **en ~** on special offer

**promouvoir** [pʀɔmuvwaʀ] *vt* to promote

**prompt, e** [pʀɔ̃(pt), pʀɔ̃(p)t] *adj* swift, rapid

**prôner** [pʀone] *vt* (*préconiser*) to advocate

**pronom** [pʀɔnɔ̃] *nm* pronoun

**prononcer** [pʀɔnɔ̃se] *vt* to pronounce; (*dire*) to utter; (*discours*) to deliver; **se prononcer** *vi* to be pronounced; **comment est-ce que ça se prononce?** how do you pronounce *ou* say it?; **se ~ (sur)** (*se décider*) to reach a decision (on *ou* about), give a verdict (on); **prononciation** *nf* pronunciation

**pronostic** [pʀɔnɔstik] *nm* (*Méd*) prognosis; (*fig: aussi:* **~s**) forecast

**propagande** [pʀɔpagɑ̃d] *nf* propaganda

**propager** [pʀɔpaʒe] *vt* to spread; **se propager** *vi* to spread

**prophète** [pʀɔfɛt] *nm* prophet

**prophétie** [pʀɔfesi] *nf* prophecy

**propice** [pʀɔpis] *adj* favourable

**proportion** [pʀɔpɔʀsjɔ̃] *nf* proportion; **toute(s) ~(s) gardée(s)** making due allowance(s)

**propos** [pʀɔpo] *nm* (*intention*) intention, aim; (*sujet*): **à quel ~?** what about? ▷ *nmpl* (*paroles*) talk *no pl*, remarks; **à ~ de** about, regarding; **à tout ~** for the slightest thing *ou* reason; **à ~** by the way; (*opportunément*) at the right moment

**proposer** [pʀɔpoze] *vt* to propose; **~ qch (à qn)** (*suggérer*) to suggest sth (to sb), propose sth (to sb); (*offrir*) to offer (sb) sth; **se ~ (pour faire)** to offer one's services (to do); **proposition** (*suggestion*) *nf* proposal, suggestion; (*Ling*) clause

**propre** [pʀɔpʀ] *adj* clean; (*net*) neat, tidy; (*possessif*) own; (*sens*) literal; (*particulier*): **~ à** peculiar to; (*approprié*): **~ à** suitable for ▷ *nm*: **recopier au ~** to make a fair copy of; **proprement** *adv* (*avec propreté*) cleanly; **le village proprement dit** the village itself; **à proprement parler** strictly speaking; **propreté** *nf* cleanliness

**propriétaire** [pʀɔpʀijetɛʀ] *nm/f* owner; (*pour le locataire*) landlord(-lady)

**propriété** [pʀɔpʀijete] *nf* property; (*droit*) ownership

**propulser** [pʀɔpylse] *vt* to propel

**prose** [pʀoz] *nf* (*style*) prose

**prospecter** [pʀɔspɛkte] *vt* to prospect; (*Comm*) to canvass

**prospectus** [pʀɔspɛktys] *nm* leaflet

**prospère** [pʀɔspɛʀ] *adj* prosperous; **prospérer** *vi* to prosper

**prosterner** [pʀɔstɛʀne]: **se prosterner** *vi* to bow low, prostrate o.s.

**prostituée** [pʀɔstitɥe] *nf* prostitute

**prostitution** [pʀɔstitysjɔ̃] *nf*
prostitution

**protecteur, -trice** [pʀɔtɛktœʀ, tʀis]
*adj* protective; (*air, ton: péj*) patronizing
▷ *nm/f* protector

**protection** [pʀɔtɛksjɔ̃] *nf* protection;
(*d'un personnage influent: aide*) patronage

**protéger** [pʀɔteʒe] *vt* to protect; **se ~
de/contre** to protect o.s. from

**protège-slip** [pʀɔtɛʒslip] *nm* panty
liner

**protéine** [pʀɔtein] *nf* protein

**protestant, e** [pʀɔtɛstɑ̃, ɑ̃t] *adj, nm/f*
Protestant

**protestation** [pʀɔtɛstasjɔ̃] *nf* (*plainte*)
protest

**protester** [pʀɔteste] *vi*: **~ (contre)** to
protest (against *ou* about); **~ de** (*son
innocence*) to protest

**prothèse** [pʀɔtɛz] *nf*: **prothèse
dentaire** denture

**protocole** [pʀɔtɔkɔl] *nm* (*fig*) etiquette

**proue** [pʀu] *nf* bow(s *pl*), prow

**prouesse** [pʀuɛs] *nf* feat

**prouver** [pʀuve] *vt* to prove

**provenance** [pʀɔv(ə)nɑ̃s] *nf* origin;
**avion en ~ de** plane (arriving) from

**provenir** [pʀɔv(ə)niʀ]: **~ de** *vt* to
come from

**proverbe** [pʀɔvɛʀb] *nm* proverb

**province** [pʀɔvɛ̃s] *nf* province

**proviseur** [pʀɔvizœʀ] *nm*
≈ head(teacher) (*BRIT*), ≈ principal (*US*)

**provision** [pʀɔvizjɔ̃] *nf* (*réserve*)
stock, supply; **provisions** *nfpl* (*vivres*)
provisions, food *no pl*

**provisoire** [pʀɔvizwaʀ] *adj*
temporary; **provisoirement** *adv*
temporarily

**provocant, e** [pʀɔvɔkɑ̃, ɑ̃t] *adj*
provocative

**provoquer** [pʀɔvɔke] *vt* (*défier*) to
provoke; (*causer*) to cause, bring about;
(*inciter*): **~ qn à** to incite sb to

**proxénète** [pʀɔksenɛt] *nm* procurer

**proximité** [pʀɔksimite] *nf* nearness,

closeness; (*dans le temps*) imminence,
closeness; **à ~** near *ou* close by; **à ~ de**
near (to), close to

**prudemment** [pʀydamɑ̃] *adv*
carefully; wisely, sensibly

**prudence** [pʀydɑ̃s] *nf* carefulness;
**avec ~** carefully; **par ~** as a precaution

**prudent, e** [pʀydɑ̃, ɑ̃t] *adj* (*pas
téméraire*) careful; (*: en général*) safety-
conscious; (*sage, conseillé*) wise,
sensible; **c'est plus ~** it's wiser

**prune** [pʀyn] *nf* plum

**pruneau, x** [pʀyno] *nm* prune

**prunier** [pʀynje] *nm* plum tree

**PS** *sigle m* = **parti socialiste**

**pseudonyme** [psødɔnim] *nm* (*gén*)
fictitious name; (*d'écrivain*) pseudonym,
pen name

**psychanalyse** [psikanaliz] *nf*
psychoanalysis

**psychiatre** [psikjatʀ] *nm/f*
psychiatrist; **psychiatrique** *adj*
psychiatric

**psychique** [psiʃik] *adj* psychological

**psychologie** [psikɔlɔʒi] *nf*
psychology; **psychologique** *adj*
psychological; **psychologue** *nm/f*
psychologist

**pu** [py] *pp de* **pouvoir**

**puanteur** [pɥɑ̃tœʀ] *nf* stink, stench

**pub** [pyb] *nf* (*fam: annonce*) ad, advert;
(*pratique*) advertising

**public, -ique** [pyblik] *adj* public;
(*école, instruction*) state *cpd* ▷ *nm* public;
(*assistance*) audience; **en ~** in public

**publicitaire** [pyblisitɛʀ] *adj*
advertising *cpd*; (*film*) publicity *cpd*

**publicité** [pyblisite] *nf* (*méthode,
profession*) advertising; (*annonce*)
advertisement; (*révélations*) publicity

**publier** [pyblije] *vt* to publish

**publipostage** [pyblipɔstaʒ] *nm*
mailing *m*

**publique** [pyblik] *adj voir* **public**

**puce** [pys] *nf* flea; (*Inform*) chip; **carte
à ~** smart card; **(marché aux) ~s** flea
market *sg*

**pudeur** [pydœʀ] *nf* modesty; **pudique**

*adj* (*chaste*) modest; (*discret*) discreet

**puer** [pye] (*péj*) *vi* to stink

**puéricultrice** [pyerikyltris] *nf* p(a)ediatric nurse

**puéril, e** [pyeril] *adj* childish

**puis** [pyi] *vb voir* **pouvoir** ▷ *adv* then

**puiser** [pyize] *vt*: ~ **(dans)** to draw (from)

**puisque** [pyisk] *conj* since

**puissance** [pyisɑ̃s] *nf* power; **en** ~ *adj* potential

**puissant, e** [pyisɑ̃, ɑ̃t] *adj* powerful

**puits** [pyi] *nm* well

**pull(-over)** [pyl(ɔvɛr)] *nm* sweater

**pulluler** [pylyle] *vi* to swarm

**pulpe** [pylp] *nf* pulp

**pulvériser** [pylverize] *vt* to pulverize; (*liquide*) to spray

**punaise** [pynɛz] *nf* (*Zool*) bug; (*clou*) drawing pin (*BRIT*), thumbtack (*US*)

**punch** [pɔ̃ʃ] *nm* (*boisson*) punch

**punir** [pynir] *vt* to punish; **punition** *nf* punishment

**pupille** [pypij] *nf* (*Anat*) pupil ▷ *nm/f* (*enfant*) ward

**pupitre** [pypitr] *nm* (*Scol*) desk

**pur, e** [pyr] *adj* pure; (*vin*) undiluted; (*whisky*) neat; **en ~e perte** to no avail; **c'est de la folie ~e** it's sheer madness

**purée** [pyre] *nf*: ~ **(de pommes de terre)** mashed potatoes *pl*; **purée de marrons** chestnut purée

**purement** [pyrmɑ̃] *adv* purely

**purgatoire** [pyrgatwar] *nm* purgatory

**purger** [pyrʒe] *vt* (*Méd, Pol*) to purge; (*Jur: peine*) to serve

**pur-sang** [pyrsɑ̃] *nm inv* thoroughbred

**pus** [py] *nm* pus

**putain** [pytɛ̃] (*fam!*) *nf* whore (!)

**puzzle** [pœzl] *nm* jigsaw (puzzle)

**P.-V.** [peve] *sigle m* = **procès-verbal**

**pyjama** [piʒama] *nm* pyjamas *pl* (*BRIT*), pajamas *pl* (*US*)

**pyramide** [piramid] *nf* pyramid

**Pyrénées** [pirene] *nfpl*: **les ~** the Pyrenees

**QI** *sigle m* (= *quotient intellectuel*) IQ

**quadragénaire** [k(w)adraʒenɛr] *nm/f* man/woman in his/her forties

**quadruple** [k(w)adrypl] *nm*: **le ~ de** four times as much as

**quai** [ke] *nm* (*de port*) quay; (*de gare*) platform; **être à ~** (*navire*) to be alongside; **de quel ~ part le train pour Paris?** which platform does the Paris train go from?

**qualification** [kalifikasjɔ̃] *nf* (*aptitude*) qualification

**qualifier** [kalifje] *vt* to qualify; **se qualifier** *vi* to qualify; **~ qch/qn de** to describe sth/sb as

**qualité** [kalite] *nf* quality

**quand** [kɑ̃] *conj, adv* when; **~ je serai riche** when I'm rich; **~ même** all the same; **~ même, il exagère!** really, he overdoes it!; **~ bien même** even though

**quant** [kɑ̃]: **~ à** *prép* (*pour ce qui est de*) as for, as to; (*au sujet de*) regarding

**quantité** [kɑ̃tite] *nf* quantity, amount; (*grand nombre*): **une** *ou* **des ~(s) de** a

great deal of

**quarantaine** [kaʀɑ̃tɛn] nf (Méd) quarantine; **avoir la ~** (âge) to be around forty; **une ~ (de)** forty or so, about forty

**quarante** [kaʀɑ̃t] num forty

**quart** [kaʀ] nm (fraction) quarter; (surveillance) watch; **un ~ de vin** a quarter litre of wine; **le ~ de** a quarter of; **quart d'heure** quarter of an hour; **quarts de finale** quarter finals

**quartier** [kaʀtje] nm (de ville) district, area; (de bœuf) quarter; (de fruit) piece; **cinéma de ~** local cinema; **avoir ~ libre** (fig) to be free; **quartier général** headquarters pl

**quartz** [kwaʀts] nm quartz

**quasi** [kazi] adv almost, nearly; **quasiment** adv almost, nearly; **quasiment jamais** hardly ever

**quatorze** [katɔʀz] num fourteen

**quatorzième** [katɔʀzjɛm] num fourteenth

**quatre** [katʀ] num four; **à ~ pattes** on all fours; **se mettre en ~ pour qn** to go out of one's way for sb; **~ à ~** (monter, descendre) four at a time; **quatre-vingt-dix** num ninety; **quatre-vingts** num eighty; **quatrième** num fourth ▷ nf (Scol) year 9 (BRIT), eighth grade (US)

**quatuor** [kwatɥɔʀ] nm quartet(te)

 **MOT-CLÉ**

**que** [kə] conj 1 (introduisant complétive) that; **il sait que tu es là** he knows (that) you're here; **je veux que tu acceptes** I want you to accept; **il a dit que oui** he said he would (out it was etc)
2 (reprise d'autres conjonctions): **quand il rentrera et qu'il aura mangé** when he gets back and (when) he has eaten; **si vous y allez et que vous ...** if you go there and if you ...
3 (en tête de phrase: hypothèse, souhait etc): **qu'il le veuille ou non** whether he likes it or not; **qu'il fasse ce qu'il voudra!** let him do as he pleases!

4 (après comparatif) than, as; voir aussi **plus**; **aussi**; **autant** etc
5 (seulement): **ne ... que** only; **il ne boit que de l'eau** he only drinks water
6 (temps): **il y a 4 ans qu'il est parti** it is 4 years since he left, he left 4 years ago
▷ adv (exclamation): **qu'il** ou **qu'est-ce qu'il est bête/court vite!** he's so silly!/he runs so fast!; **que de livres!** what a lot of books!
▷ pron 1 (relatif: personne) whom; (: chose) that, which; **l'homme que je vois** the man (whom) I see; **le livre que tu vois** the book (that ou which) you see; **un jour que j'étais ...** a day when I was ...
2 (interrogatif) what; **que fais-tu?, qu'est-ce que tu fais?** what are you doing?; **qu'est-ce que c'est?** what is it?, what's that?; **que faire?** what can one do?

**Québec** [kebɛk] n: **le ~** Quebec; **québecois, e** adj Quebec ▷ nm/f: **Québecois, e** Quebecker ▷ nm (Ling) Quebec French

 **MOT-CLÉ**

**quel, quelle** [kɛl] adj 1 (interrogatif: personne) who; (: chose) what; **quel est cet homme?** who is this man?; **quel est ce livre?** what is this book?; **quel livre/homme?** what book/man?; (parmi un certain choix) which book/man?; **quels acteurs préférez-vous?** which actors do you prefer?; **dans quels pays êtes-vous allé?** which ou what countries did you go to?
2 (exclamatif): **quelle surprise!** what a surprise!
3: **quel que soit le coupable** whoever is guilty; **quel que soit votre avis** whatever your opinion

**quelconque** [kɛlkɔ̃k] adj (indéfini): **un ami/prétexte ~** some friend/pretext or other; (*médiocre: repas*) indifferent, poor; (*laid: personne*) plain-looking

 **MOT-CLÉ**

**quelque** [kɛlk] *adj* **1** (*au singulier*) some; (*au pluriel*) a few, some; (*tournure interrogative*) any; **quelque espoir** some hope; **il a quelques amis** he has a few *ou* some friends; **a-t-il quelques amis?** does he have any friends?; **les quelques livres qui** the few books which; **20 kg et quelque(s)** a bit over 20 kg
**2**: **quelque ... que**: **quelque livre qu'il choisisse** whatever (*ou* whichever) book he chooses
**3**: **quelque chose** something; (*tournure interrogative*) anything; **quelque chose d'autre** something else; anything else; **quelque part** somewhere; anywhere; **en quelque sorte** as it were
▷ *adv* **1** (*environ*): **quelque 100 mètres** some 100 metres
**2**: **quelque peu** rather, somewhat

**quelquefois** [kɛlkəfwa] *adv* sometimes
**quelques-uns, -unes** [kɛlkəzœ̃, yn] *pron* a few, some
**quelqu'un** [kɛlkœ̃] *pron* someone, somebody; (*+ tournure interrogative*) anyone, anybody; **quelqu'un d'autre** someone *ou* somebody else; (*+ tournure interrogative*) anybody else
**qu'en dira-t-on** [kɑ̃diratɔ̃] *nm inv*: **le qu'en dira-t-on** gossip, what people say
**querelle** [kəʀɛl] *nf* quarrel; **quereller**: **se quereller** *vi* to quarrel
**qu'est-ce que** [kɛskə] *vb + conj voir* **que**
**qu'est-ce qui** [kɛski] *vb + conj voir* **qui**
**question** [kɛstjɔ̃] *nf* question; (*fig*) matter, issue; **il a été ~ de** we (*ou* they) spoke about; **de quoi est-il ~?** what is it about?; **il n'en est pas ~** there's no question of it; **en ~** in question; **hors de ~** out of the question; **remettre**

**en ~** to question; **questionnaire** *nm* questionnaire; **questionner** *vt* to question
**quête** [kɛt] *nf* collection; (*recherche*) quest, search; **faire la ~** (*à l'église*) to take the collection; (*artiste*) to pass the hat round
**quetsche** [kwɛtʃ] *nf* kind of dark-red plum
**queue** [kø] *nf* tail; (*fig: du classement*) bottom; (: *de poêle*) handle; (: *de fruit, feuille*) stalk; (: *de train, colonne, file*) rear; **faire la ~** to queue (up) (BRIT), line up (US); **queue de cheval** ponytail; **queue de poisson** (*Auto*): **faire une queue de poisson à qn** to cut in front of sb

 **MOT-CLÉ**

**qui** [ki] *pron* **1** (*interrogatif: personne*) who; (: *chose*) **qu'est-ce qui est sur la table?** what is on the table?; **qui est-ce qui?** who?; **qui est-ce que?** who?; **à qui est ce sac?** whose bag is this?; **à qui parlais-tu?** who were you talking to?, to whom were you talking?; **chez qui allez-vous?** whose house are you going to?
**2** (*relatif: personne*) who; (*+prép*) whom; **l'ami de qui je vous ai parlé** the friend I told you about; **la dame chez qui je suis allé** the lady whose house I went to
**3** (*sans antécédent*): **amenez qui vous voulez** bring who you like; **qui que ce soit** whoever it may be

**quiconque** [kikɔ̃k] *pron* (*celui qui*) whoever, anyone who; (*n'importe qui*) anyone, anybody
**quille** [kij] *nf*: (*jeu de*) **~s** skittles *sg* (BRIT), bowling (US)
**quincaillerie** [kɛ̃kajʀi] *nf* (*ustensiles*) hardware; (*magasin*) hardware shop
**quinquagénaire** [kɛ̃kaʒenɛʀ] *nm/f* man/woman in his/her fifties
**quinquennat** [kɛ̃kena] *nm* five year term of office (of French President)

**quinte** [kɛ̃t] *nf:* **~ (de toux)** coughing fit

**quintuple** [kɛ̃typl] *nm:* **le ~ de** five times as much as

**quinzaine** [kɛ̃zɛn] *nf:* **une ~ (de)** about fifteen, fifteen or so; **une ~ (de jours)** a fortnight (*BRIT*), two weeks

**quinze** [kɛ̃z] *num* fifteen; **dans ~ jours** in a fortnight('s time), in two weeks(' time)

**quinzième** [kɛ̃zjɛm] *num* fifteenth

**quiproquo** [kipʀɔko] *nm* misunderstanding

**quittance** [kitɑ̃s] *nf* (*reçu*) receipt

**quitte** [kit] *adj:* **être ~ envers qn** to be no longer in sb's debt; (*fig*) to be quits with sb; **~ à faire** even if it means doing

**quitter** [kite] *vt* to leave; (*vêtement*) to take off; **se quitter** *vi* (*couples, interlocuteurs*) to part; **ne quittez pas** (*au téléphone*) hold the line

**qui-vive** [kiviv] *nm:* **être sur le ~** to be on the alert

 **MOT-CLÉ**

**quoi** [kwa] *pron interrog* **1** what; **quoi de neuf?** what's new?; **quoi?** (*qu'est-ce que tu dis?*) what?
**2** (*avec prép*): **à quoi tu penses?** what are you thinking about?; **de quoi parlez-vous?** what are you talking about?; **à quoi bon?** what's the use?
▷ *pron rel:* **as-tu de quoi écrire?** do you have anything to write with?; **il n'y a pas de quoi** (please) don't mention it; **il n'y a pas de quoi rire** there's nothing to laugh about
▷ *pron* (*locutions*): **quoi qu'il arrive** whatever happens; **quoi qu'il en soit** be that as it may; **quoi que ce soit** anything at all
▷ *excl* what!

**quoique** [kwak] *conj* (al)though

**quotidien, ne** [kɔtidjɛ̃, jɛn] *adj* daily; (*banal*) everyday ▷ *nm* (*journal*) daily (paper); **quotidiennement** *adv* daily

**r.** *abr* = **route; rue**

**rab** [ʀab] (*fam*) *nm* (*nourriture*) extra; **est-ce qu'il y a du ~?** are there any seconds?

**rabâcher** [ʀabɑʃe] *vt* to keep on repeating

**rabais** [ʀabɛ] *nm* reduction, discount; **rabaisser** *vt* (*dénigrer*) to belittle; (*rabattre: prix*) to reduce

**Rabat** [ʀaba(t)] *n* Rabat

**rabattre** [ʀabatʀ] *vt* (*couvercle, siège*) to pull down; (*déduire*) to reduce; **se rabattre** *vi* (*se refermer: couvercle*) to fall shut; (*véhicule, coureur*) to cut in; **se ~ sur** to fall back on

**rabbin** [ʀabɛ̃] *nm* rabbi

**rabougri, e** [ʀabugʀi] *adj* stunted

**raccommoder** [ʀakɔmɔde] *vt* to mend, repair

**raccompagner** [ʀakɔ̃paɲe] *vt* to take *ou* see back

**raccord** [ʀakɔʀ] *nm* link; (*retouche*) touch up; **raccorder** *vt* to join (up), link up; (*suj: pont etc*) to connect, link

**raccourci** [ʀakuʀsi] nm short cut

**raccourcir** [ʀakuʀsiʀ] vt to shorten
▷ vi (jours) to grow shorter, draw in

**raccrocher** [ʀakʀɔʃe] vt (tableau) to
hang back up; (récepteur) to put down
▷ vi (Tél) to hang up, ring off

**race** [ʀas] nf race; (d'animaux, fig) breed;
**de ~** purebred, pedigree

**rachat** [ʀaʃa] nm buying; (du même
objet) buying back

**racheter** [ʀaʃ(ə)te] vt (article perdu) to
buy another; (après avoir vendu) to buy
back; (d'occasion) to buy; (Comm: part,
firme) to buy up; (davantage): **~ du lait/3
œufs** to buy more milk/another 3 eggs
ou 3 more eggs; **se racheter** vi (fig) to
make amends

**racial, e, -aux** [ʀasjal, jo] adj racial

**racine** [ʀasin] nf root; **racine carrée/
cubique** square/cube root

**racisme** [ʀasism] nm racism

**raciste** [ʀasist] adj, nm/f racist

**racket** [ʀaket] nm racketeering no pl

**raclée** [ʀɑkle] (fam) nf hiding,
thrashing

**racler** [ʀɑkle] vt (surface) to scrape; **se ~
la gorge** to clear one's throat

**racontars** [ʀakɔ̃taʀ] nmpl story, lie

**raconter** [ʀakɔ̃te] vt: **~ (à qn)** (décrire)
to relate (to sb), tell (sb) about; (dire de
mauvaise foi) to tell (sb); **~ une histoire**
to tell a story

**radar** [ʀadaʀ] nm radar

**rade** [ʀad] nf (natural) harbour; **rester
en ~** (fig) to be left stranded

**radeau, x** [ʀado] nm raft

**radiateur** [ʀadjatœʀ] nm radiator,
heater; (Auto) radiator; **radiateur
électrique** electric heater ou fire

**radiation** [ʀadjasjɔ̃] nf (Physique)
radiation

**radical, e, -aux** [ʀadikal, o] adj
radical

**radieux, -euse** [ʀadjø, jøz] adj radiant

**radin, e** [ʀadɛ̃, in] (fam) adj stingy

**radio** [ʀadjo] nf radio; (Méd) X-ray
▷ nm radio operator; **à la ~** on the
radio; **radioactif, -ive** adj radioactive;

**radiocassette** nm cassette radio,
radio cassette player; **radiographie** nf
radiography; (photo) X-ray photograph;
**radiophonique** adj radio cpd; **radio-
réveil** (pl **radios-réveils**) nm radio
alarm clock

**radis** [ʀadi] nm radish

**radoter** [ʀadɔte] vi to ramble on

**radoucir** [ʀadusiʀ]: **se radoucir** vi
(temps) to become milder; (se calmer)
to calm down

**rafale** [ʀafal] nf (vent) gust (of wind);
(tir) burst of gunfire

**raffermir** [ʀafɛʀmiʀ] vt to firm up

**raffiner** [ʀafine] vt to refine; **raffinerie**
nf refinery

**raffoler** [ʀafɔle]: **~ de** vt to be very
keen on

**rafle** [ʀafl] nf (de police) raid; **rafler** (fam)
vt to swipe, nick

**rafraîchir** [ʀafʀeʃiʀ] vt (atmosphère,
température) to cool (down); (aussi:
**mettre à ~**) to chill; (fig: rénover) to
brighten up; **se rafraîchir** vi (temps)
to grow cooler; (en se lavant) to
freshen up; (en buvant) to refresh o.s.;
**rafraîchissant, e** adj refreshing;
**rafraîchissement** nm (boisson) cool
drink; **rafraîchissements** nmpl
(boissons, fruits etc) refreshments

**rage** [ʀaʒ] nf (Méd): **la ~** rabies; (fureur)
rage, fury; **faire ~** to rage; **rage de
dents** (raging) toothache

**ragot** [ʀago] (fam) nm malicious
gossip no pl

**ragoût** [ʀagu] nm stew

**raide** [ʀɛd] adj stiff; (câble) taut, tight;
(escarpé) steep; (droit: cheveux) straight;
(fam: sans argent) flat broke; (osé)
daring, bold ▷ adv (en pente) steeply; **~
mort** stone dead; **raideur** nf (rigidité)
stiffness; **avec raideur** (répondre) stiffly,
abruptly; **raidir** vt (muscles) to stiffen;
**se raidir** vi (tissu) to stiffen; (personne)
to tense up; (: se préparer moralement) to
brace o.s.; (fig: position) to harden

**raie** [ʀɛ] nf (Zool) skate, ray; (rayure)
stripe; (des cheveux) parting

**raifort** [RɛfɔR] *nm* horseradish
**rail** [Rɑj] *nm* rail; (*chemins de fer*) railways
*pl*; **par ~** by rail
**railler** [Rɑje] *vt* to scoff at, jeer at
**rainure** [RenyR] *nf* groove
**raisin** [Rɛzɛ̃] *nm* (*aussi*: **~s**) grapes *pl*;
**raisins secs** raisins
**raison** [Rɛzɔ̃] *nf* reason; **avoir ~** to be
right; **donner ~ à qn** to agree with sb;
(*événement*) to prove sb right; **perdre
la ~** to become insane; **se faire une
~** to learn to live with it; **~ de plus** all
the more reason; **à plus forte ~** all the
more so; **en ~ de** because of; **à ~ de** at
the rate of; **sans ~** for no reason; **raison
sociale** corporate name; **raisonnable**
*adj* reasonable, sensible
**raisonnement** [Rɛzɔnmɑ̃] *nm* (*façon
de réfléchir*) reasoning; (*argumentation*)
argument
**raisonner** [Rɛzɔne] *vi* (*penser*) to
reason; (*argumenter, discuter*) to argue
▷ *vt* (*personne*) to reason with
**rajeunir** [RaʒœniR] *vt* (*suj: coiffure,
robe*): **~ qn** to make sb look younger;
(*fig: personnel*) to inject new blood into
▷ *vi* to become (ou look) younger
**rajouter** [Raʒute] *vt* to add
**rajuster** [Raʒyste] *vt* (*vêtement*) to
straighten, tidy; (*salaires*) to adjust
**ralenti** [Ralɑ̃ti] *nm*: **au ~** (*fig*) at a
slower pace; **tourner au ~** (*Auto*) to
tick over, idle
**ralentir** [Ralɑ̃tiR] *vt* to slow down
**râler** [Rɑle] *vi* to groan; (*fam*) to grouse,
moan (and groan)
**rallier** [Ralje] *vt* (*rejoindre*) to rejoin;
(*gagner à sa cause*) to win over
**rallonge** [Ralɔ̃ʒ] *nf* (*de table*) (extra) leaf
**rallonger** [Ralɔ̃ʒe] *vt* to lengthen
**rallye** [Rali] *nm* rally; (*Pol*) march
**ramassage** [Ramɑsaʒ] *nm*:
**ramassage scolaire** school bus service
**ramasser** [Ramɑse] *vt* (*objet tombé
ou par terre, fam*) to pick up; (*recueillir:
copies, ordures*) to collect; (*récolter*) to
gather; **ramassis** (*péj*) *nm* (*de voyous*)
bunch; (*d'objets*) jumble

**rambarde** [Rɑ̃baRd] *nf* guardrail
**rame** [Ram] *nf* (*aviron*) oar; (*de métro*)
train; (*de papier*) ream
**rameau, x** [Ramo] *nm* (small) branch;
**les Rameaux** (*Rel*) Palm Sunday *sg*
**ramener** [Ram(ə)ne] *vt* to bring back;
(*reconduire*) to take back; **~ qch à** (*réduire
à*) to reduce sth to
**ramer** [Rame] *vi* to row
**ramollir** [RamɔliR] *vt* to soften; **se
ramollir** *vi* to go soft
**rampe** [Rɑ̃p] *nf* (*d'escalier*) banister(s
*pl*); (*dans un garage*) ramp; (*Théâtre*): **la ~**
the footlights *pl*; **rampe de lancement**
launching pad
**ramper** [Rɑ̃pe] *vi* to crawl
**rancard** [Rɑ̃kaR] (*fam*) *nm* (*rendez-vous*)
date
**rancart** [Rɑ̃kaR] *nm*: **mettre au ~** (*fam*)
to scrap
**rance** [Rɑ̃s] *adj* rancid
**rancœur** [Rɑ̃kœR] *nf* rancour
**rançon** [Rɑ̃sɔ̃] *nf* ransom
**rancune** [Rɑ̃kyn] *nf* grudge, rancour;
**garder ~ à qn (de qch)** to bear sb
a grudge (for sth); **sans ~!** no hard
feelings!; **rancunier, -ière** *adj*
vindictive, spiteful
**randonnée** [Rɑ̃dɔne] *nf* (*pédestre*)
walk, ramble; (*: en montagne*) hike,
hiking *no pl*; **la ~** (*activité*) hiking,
walking; **une ~ à cheval** a pony trek
**rang** [Rɑ̃] *nm* (*rangée*) row; (*grade,
classement*) rank; **rangs** *nmpl* (*Mil*)
ranks; **se mettre en ~s** to get into *ou*
form rows; **au premier ~** in the first
row; (*fig*) ranking first
**rangé, e** [Rɑ̃ʒe] *adj* (*vie*) well-ordered;
(*personne*) steady
**rangée** [Rɑ̃ʒe] *nf* row
**ranger** [Rɑ̃ʒe] *vt* (*mettre de l'ordre dans*)
to tidy up; (*classer, grouper*) to order,
arrange; (*mettre à sa place*) to put away;
(*fig: classer*): **~ qn/qch parmi** to rank
sb/sth among; **se ranger** *vi* (*véhicule,
conducteur*) to pull over *ou* in; (*piéton*)
to step aside; (*s'assagir*) to settle down; **se
~ à** (*avis*) to come round to

**ranimer** [ʀanime] vt (personne) to bring round; (douleur, souvenir) to revive; (feu) to rekindle

**rapace** [ʀapas] nm bird of prey

**râpe** [ʀɑp] nf (Culin) grater; **râper** vt (Culin) to grate

**rapide** [ʀapid] adj fast; (prompt: coup d'œil, mouvement) quick ▷ nm express (train); (de cours d'eau) rapid; **rapidement** adv fast; quickly

**rapiécer** [ʀapjese] vt to patch

**rappel** [ʀapɛl] nm (Théâtre) curtain call; (Méd: vaccination) booster; (deuxième avis) reminder; **rappeler** vt to call back; (ambassadeur, Mil) to recall; (faire se souvenir): **rappeler qch à qn** to remind sb of sth; **se rappeler** vt (se souvenir de) to remember, recall; **pouvez-vous rappeler plus tard?** can you call back later?

**rapport** [ʀapɔʀ] nm (lien, analogie) connection; (compte rendu) report; (profit) yield, return; **rapports** nmpl (entre personnes, pays) relations; **avoir ~ à** to have something to do with; **être/se mettre en ~ avec qn** to be/get in touch with sb; **par ~ à** in relation to; **rapports (sexuels)** (sexual) intercourse sg; **rapport qualité-prix** value (for money)

**rapporter** [ʀapɔʀte] vt (rendre, ramener) to bring back; (bénéfice) to yield, bring in; (mentionner, répéter) to report ▷ vi (investissement) to give a good return ou yield; (activité) to be very profitable; **se ~ à** to relate to

**rapprochement** [ʀapʀɔʃmɑ̃] nm (de nations) reconciliation; (rapport) parallel

**rapprocher** [ʀapʀɔʃe] vt (deux objets) to bring closer together; (fig: ennemis, partis etc) to bring together; (comparer) to establish a parallel between; (chaise d'une table): **~ qch (de)** to bring sth closer (to); **se rapprocher** vi to draw closer ou nearer; **se ~ de** to come closer to; (présenter une analogie avec) to be close to

**raquette** [ʀakɛt] nf (de tennis) racket;

(de ping-pong) bat

**rare** [ʀɑʀ] adj rare; **se faire ~** to become scarce; **rarement** adv rarely, seldom

**ras, e** [ʀɑ, ʀɑz] adj (poil, herbe) short; (tête) close-cropped ▷ adv short; **en ~e campagne** in open country; **à ~ bords** to the brim; **en avoir ~ le bol** (fam) to be fed up

**raser** [ʀɑze] vt (barbe, cheveux) to shave off; (menton, personne) to shave; (fam: ennuyer) to bore; (démolir) to raze (to the ground); (frôler) to graze, skim; **se raser** vi to shave; (fam) to be bored (to tears); **rasoir** nm razor

**rassasier** [ʀasazje] vt: **être rassasié** to have eaten one's fill

**rassemblement** [ʀasɑ̃bləmɑ̃] nm (groupe) gathering; (Pol) union

**rassembler** [ʀasɑ̃ble] vt (réunir) to assemble, gather; (documents, notes) to gather together, collect; **se rassembler** vi to gather

**rassurer** [ʀasyʀe] vt to reassure; **se rassurer** vi to reassure o.s.; **rassure-toi** don't worry

**rat** [ʀa] nm rat

**rate** [ʀat] nf spleen

**raté, e** [ʀate] adj (tentative) unsuccessful, failed ▷ nm/f (fam: personne) failure

**râteau, x** [ʀɑto] nm rake

**rater** [ʀate] vi (affaire, projet etc) to go wrong, fail ▷ vt (fam: cible, train, occasion) to miss; (plat) to spoil; (fam: examen) to fail; **nous avons raté notre train** we missed our train

**ration** [ʀasjɔ̃] nf ration

**RATP** sigle f (= Régie autonome des transports parisiens) Paris transport authority

**rattacher** [ʀataʃe] vt (animal, cheveux) to tie up again; (fig: relier): **~ qch à** to link sth with

**rattraper** [ʀatʀape] vt (fugitif) to recapture; (empêcher de tomber) to catch (hold of); (atteindre, rejoindre) to catch up with; (réparer: erreur) to make up for; **se rattraper** vi to make up for it; **se ~**

**(à)** (se raccrocher) to stop o.s. falling (by catching hold of)

**rature** [RatyR] nf deletion, erasure

**rauque** [Rok] adj (voix) hoarse

**ravages** [Rava3] nmpl: **faire des ~** to wreak havoc

**ravi, e** [Ravi] adj: **être ~ de/que** to be delighted with/that

**ravin** [Ravɛ̃] nm gully, ravine

**ravir** [RaviR] vt (enchanter) to delight; **à ~** adv beautifully

**raviser** [Ravize]: **se raviser** vi to change one's mind

**ravissant, e** [Ravisɑ̃, ɑ̃t] adj delightful

**ravisseur, -euse** [RavisœR, øz] nm/f abductor, kidnapper

**ravitailler** [Ravitaje] vt (en vivres, munitions) to provide with fresh supplies; (avion) to refuel; **se ~ (en)** to get fresh supplies (of)

**raviver** [Ravive] vt (feu, douleur) to revive; (couleurs) to brighten up

**rayé, e** [Reje] adj (à rayures) striped

**rayer** [Reje] vt (érafler) to scratch; (barrer) to cross out; (d'une liste) to cross off

**rayon** [Rejɔ̃] nm (de soleil etc) ray; (Géom) radius; (de roue) spoke; (étagère) shelf; (de grand magasin) department; **dans un ~ de** within a radius of; **rayon de soleil** sunbeam; **rayons X** X-rays

**rayonnement** [Rejɔnmɑ̃] nm (fig: d'une culture) influence

**rayonner** [Rejɔne] vi (fig) to shine forth; (personne: de joie, de beauté) to be radiant; (touriste) to go touring (from one base)

**rayure** [RejyR] nf (motif) stripe; (éraflure) scratch; **à ~s** striped

**raz-de-marée** [RɑdmaRe] nm inv tidal wave

**ré** [Re] nm (Mus) D; (en chantant la gamme) re

**réaction** [Reaksjɔ̃] nf reaction

**réadapter** [Readapte]: **se réadapter (à)** vi to readjust (to)

**réagir** [Rea3iR] vi to react

**réalisateur, -trice** [RealizatœR, tRis]

nm/f (TV, Cinéma) director

**réalisation** [Realizasjɔ̃] nf realization; (cinéma) production; **en cours de ~** under way

**réaliser** [Realize] vt (projet, opération) to carry out, realize; (rêve, souhait) to realize, fulfil; (exploit) to achieve; (film) to produce; (se rendre compte de) to realize; **se réaliser** vi to be realized

**réaliste** [Realist] adj realistic

**réalité** [Realite] nf reality; **en ~** in (actual) fact; **dans la ~** in reality

**réanimation** [Reanimasjɔ̃] nf resuscitation; **service de ~** intensive care unit

**rébarbatif, -ive** [RebaRbatif, iv] adj forbidding

**rebattu, e** [R(ə)baty] adj hackneyed

**rebelle** [Rəbɛl] nm/f rebel ▷ adj (troupes) rebel; (enfant) rebellious; (mèche etc) unruly

**rebeller** [R(ə)bele]: **se rebeller** vi to rebel

**rebondir** [R(ə)bɔ̃diR] vi (ballon: au sol) to bounce; (: contre un mur) to rebound; (fig) to get moving again

**rebord** [R(ə)bɔR] nm edge; **le ~ de la fenêtre** the windowsill

**rebours** [R(ə)buR]: **à ~** adv the wrong way

**rebrousser** [R(ə)bRuse] vt: **~ chemin** to turn back

**rebuter** [Rəbyte] vt to put off

**récalcitrant, e** [Rekalsitrɑ̃, ɑ̃t] adj refractory

**récapituler** [Rekapityle] vt to recapitulate, sum up

**receler** [R(ə)səle] vt (produit d'un vol) to receive; (fig) to conceal; **receleur, -euse** nm/f receiver

**récemment** [Resamɑ̃] adv recently

**recensement** [R(ə)sɑ̃smɑ̃] nm (population) census

**recenser** [R(ə)sɑ̃se] vt (population) to take a census of; (inventorier) to list

**récent, e** [Resɑ̃, ɑ̃t] adj recent

**récépissé** [Resepise] nm receipt

**récepteur** [ReseptœR] nm receiver

**réception** [Resɛpsjɔ̃] nf receiving no pl; (accueil) reception, welcome; (bureau) reception desk; (réunion mondaine) reception, party; **réceptionniste** nm/f receptionist

**recette** [R(ə)sɛt] nf recipe; (Comm) takings pl; **recettes** nfpl (Comm: rentrées) receipts; **faire ~** (spectacle, exposition) to be a winner

**recevoir** [R(ə)səvwaR] vt to receive; (client, patient) to see; **être reçu** (à un examen) to pass

**rechange** [R(ə)ʃɑ̃ʒ]: **de ~** adj (pièces, roue) spare; (fig: solution) alternative; **des vêtements de ~** a change of clothes

**recharge** [R(ə)ʃaRʒ] nf refill; **rechargeable** adj (stylo etc) refillable; **recharger** vt (stylo) to refill; (batterie) to recharge

**réchaud** [Reʃo] nm (portable) stove

**réchauffer** [Reʃofe] vt (plat) to reheat; (mains, personne) to warm; **se réchauffer** vi (température) to get warmer; (personne) to warm o.s. (up)

**rêche** [Rɛʃ] adj rough

**recherche** [R(ə)ʃɛRʃ] nf (action) search; (raffinement) studied elegance; (scientifique etc): **la ~** research; **recherches** nfpl (de la police) investigations; (scientifiques) research sg; **la ~ de** the search for; **être à la ~ de qch** to be looking for sth

**recherché, e** [R(ə)ʃɛRʃe] adj (rare, demandé) much sought-after; (raffiné: style) mannered; (: tenue) elegant

**rechercher** [R(ə)ʃɛRʃe] vt (objet égaré, personne) to look for; (causes, nouveau procédé) to try to find; (bonheur, compliments) to seek

**rechute** [R(ə)ʃyt] nf (Méd) relapse

**récidiver** [Residive] vi to commit a subsequent offence; (fig) to do it again

**récif** [Resif] nm reef

**récipient** [Resipjɑ̃] nm container

**réciproque** [ResipRɔk] adj reciprocal

**récit** [Resi] nm story; **récital** nm recital; **réciter** vt to recite

**réclamation** [Reklamasjɔ̃] nf complaint; **(service des) ~s** complaints department

**réclame** [Reklam] nf ad, advert(isement); **en ~** on special offer; **réclamer** vt to ask for; (revendiquer) to claim, demand ▷ vi to complain

**réclusion** [Reklyzjɔ̃] nf imprisonment

**recoin** [Rəkwɛ̃] nm nook, corner

**reçois** etc [Rəswa] vb voir **recevoir**

**récolte** [Rekɔlt] nf harvesting, gathering; (produits) harvest, crop; **récolter** vt to harvest, gather (in); (fig) to collect

**recommandé** [R(ə)kɔmɑ̃de] nm (Postes): **en ~** by registered mail

**recommander** [R(ə)kɔmɑ̃de] vt to recommend; (Postes) to register

**recommencer** [R(ə)kɔmɑ̃se] vt (reprendre: lutte, séance) to resume, start again; (refaire: travail, explications) to start afresh, start (over) again ▷ vi to start again; (récidiver) to do it again

**récompense** [Rekɔ̃pɑ̃s] nf reward; (prix) award; **récompenser** vt: **récompenser qn (de** ou **pour)** to reward sb (for)

**réconcilier** [Rekɔ̃silje] vt to reconcile; **se réconcilier (avec)** to make up (with)

**reconduire** [R(ə)kɔ̃dɥiR] vt (raccompagner) to take ou see back; (renouveler) to renew

**réconfort** [Rekɔ̃fɔR] nm comfort; **réconforter** vt (consoler) to comfort

**reconnaissance** [R(ə)kɔnɛsɑ̃s] nf (gratitude) gratitude, gratefulness; (action de reconnaître) recognition; (Mil) reconnaissance, recce; **reconnaissant, e** adj grateful; **je vous serais reconnaissant de bien vouloir ...** I would be most grateful if you would (kindly) ...

**reconnaître** [R(ə)kɔnɛtR] vt to recognize; (Mil: lieu) to reconnoitre; (Jur: enfant, torts) to acknowledge; **~ que** to admit ou acknowledge that; **~ qn/qch à** (l'identifier grâce à) to recognize sb/sth by; **reconnu, e** adj (indiscuté, connu) recognized

**reconstituer** [R(ə)kɔ̃stitɥe] vt (événement, accident) to reconstruct; (fresque, vase brisé) to piece together, reconstitute

**reconstruire** [R(ə)kɔ̃stRɥiR] vt to rebuild

**reconvertir** [R(ə)kɔ̃vɛRtiR]: **se reconvertir dans** vr (un métier, une branche) to go into

**record** [R(ə)kɔR] nm, adj record

**recoupement** [R(ə)kupmɑ̃] nm: **par ~** by cross-checking

**recouper** [R(ə)kupe]: **se recouper** vi (témoignages) to tie ou match up

**recourber** [R(ə)kuRbe]: **se recourber** vi to curve (up), bend (up)

**recourir** [R(ə)kuRiR]: **~ à** vt (ami, agence) to turn ou appeal to; (force, ruse, emprunt) to resort to

**recours** [R(ə)kuR] nm: **avoir ~ à** = **recourir à**; **en dernier ~** as a last resort

**recouvrer** [R(ə)kuvRe] vt (vue, santé etc) to recover, regain

**recouvrir** [R(ə)kuvRiR] vt (couvrir à nouveau) to re-cover; (couvrir entièrement, aussi fig) to cover

**récréation** [RekReasjɔ̃] nf (Scol) break

**recroqueviller** [R(ə)kRɔk(ə)vije]: **se recroqueviller** vi (personne) to huddle up

**recrudescence** [R(ə)kRydesɑ̃s] nf fresh outbreak

**recruter** [R(ə)kRyte] vt to recruit

**rectangle** [Rɛktɑ̃gl] nm rectangle; **rectangulaire** adj rectangular

**rectificatif** [Rɛktifikatif] nm correction

**rectifier** [Rɛktifje] vt (calcul, adresse, paroles) to correct; (erreur) to rectify

**rectiligne** [Rɛktiliɲ] adj straight

**recto** [Rɛkto] nm front (of a page); **~ verso** on both sides (of the page)

**reçu, e** [R(ə)sy] pp de **recevoir** ▷ adj (candidat) successful; (admis, consacré) accepted ▷ nm (Comm) receipt; **je peux**

**avoir un ~, s'il vous plaît?** can I have a receipt, please?

**recueil** [Rəkœj] nm collection;
**recueillir** vt to collect; (voix, suffrages) to win; (accueillir: réfugiés, chat) to take in; **se recueillir** vi to gather one's thoughts, meditate

**recul** [R(ə)kyl] nm (éloignement) distance; (déclin) decline; **être en ~** to be on the decline; **avec du ~** with hindsight; **avoir un mouvement de ~** to recoil; **prendre du ~** to stand back; **reculé, e** adj remote; **reculer** vi to move back, back away; (Auto) to reverse, back (up); (fig) to (be on the) decline ▷ vt to move back; (véhicule) to reverse, back (up); (date, décision) to postpone; **reculer devant** (danger, difficulté) to shrink from; **reculons: à reculons** adv backwards

**récupérer** [Rekypere] vt to recover, get back; (heures de travail) to make up; (déchets) to salvage ▷ vi to recover

**récurer** [RekyRe] vt to scour; **poudre à ~** scouring powder

**reçut** [Rəsy] vb voir **recevoir**

**recycler** [R(ə)sikle] vt (Tech) to recycle; **se recycler** vi to retrain

**rédacteur, -trice** [Redaktœr, tRis] nm/f (journaliste) writer; subeditor; (d'ouvrage de référence) editor, compiler

**rédaction** [Redaksjɔ̃] nf writing; (rédacteurs) editorial staff; (Scol: devoir) essay, composition

**redescendre** [R(ə)desɑ̃dR] vi to go back down ▷ vt (pente etc) to go down

**rédiger** [Rediʒe] vt to write; (contrat) to draw up

**redire** [R(ə)diR] vt to repeat; **trouver à ~ à** to find fault with

**redoubler** [R(ə)duble] vi (tempête, violence) to intensify; (Scol) to repeat a year; **~ de patience/prudence** to be doubly patient/careful

**redoutable** [R(ə)dutabl] adj formidable, fearsome

**redouter** [R(ə)dute] vt to dread

**redressement** [R(ə)dRɛsmɑ̃] nm

(*économique*) recovery

**redresser** [R(ə)dRese] vt (*relever*) to set upright; (*pièce tordue*) to straighten out; (*situation, économie*) to put right; **se redresser** vi (*personne*) to sit (*ou* stand) up (straight); (*économie*) to recover

**réduction** [Redyksjɔ̃] nf reduction; **y a-t-il une ~ pour les étudiants?** is there a reduction for students?

**réduire** [RedɥiR] vt to reduce; (*prix, dépenses*) to cut, reduce; **réduit** nm (*pièce*) tiny room

**rééducation** [Reedykasjɔ̃] nf (*d'un membre*) re-education; (*de délinquants, d'un blessé*) rehabilitation

**réel, le** [Reel] adj real; **réellement** adv really

**réexpédier** [Reekspedje] vt (*à l'envoyeur*) to return, send back; (*au destinataire*) to send on, forward

**refaire** [R(ə)fER] vt to do again; (*faire de nouveau: sport*) to take up again; (*réparer, restaurer*) to do up

**réfectoire** [Refektwar] nm refectory

**référence** [Referɑ̃s] nf reference; **références** nfpl (*recommandations*) reference sg

**référer** [Refere]: **se référer à** vt to refer to

**refermer** [R(ə)fERme] vt to close *ou* shut again; **se refermer** vi (*porte*) to close *ou* shut (again)

**refiler** [R(ə)file] vi (*fam*) to palm off

**réfléchi, e** [Refleʃi] adj (*caractère*) thoughtful; (*action*) well-thought-out; (*Ling*) reflexive; **c'est tout ~** my mind's made up

**réfléchir** [RefleʃiR] vt to reflect ▷ vi to think; **~ à** to think about

**reflet** [R(ə)flE] nm reflection; (*sur l'eau etc*) sheen *no pl*, glint; **refléter** vt to reflect; **se refléter** vi to be reflected

**réflexe** [Refleks] nm, adj reflex

**réflexion** [Refleksjɔ̃] nf (*de la lumière etc*) reflection; (*fait de penser*) thought; (*remarque*) remark; **~ faite, à la ~** on reflection

**réflexologie** [Refleksɔlɔʒi] nf

reflexology

**réforme** [RefɔRm] nf reform; (*Rel*): **la R~** the Reformation; **réformer** vt to reform; (*Mil*) to declare unfit for service

**refouler** [R(ə)fule] vt (*envahisseurs*) to drive back; (*larmes*) to force back; (*désir, colère*) to repress

**refrain** [R(ə)frɛ̃] nm refrain, chorus

**refréner** [Rəfrene], **réfréner** [Refrene] vt to curb, check

**réfrigérateur** [RefriʒeRatœR] nm refrigerator, fridge

**refroidir** [R(ə)fRwadiR] vt to cool; (*fig: personne*) to put off ▷ vi to cool (down); **se refroidir** vi (*temps*) to get cooler *ou* colder; (*fig: ardeur*) to cool (off); **refroidissement** nm (*grippe etc*) chill

**refuge** [R(ə)fyʒ] nm refuge; **réfugié, e** adj, nm/f refugee; **réfugier: se réfugier** vi to take refuge

**refus** [R(ə)fy] nm refusal; **ce n'est pas de ~** I won't say no, it's welcome; **refuser** vt to refuse; (*Scol: candidat*) to fail; **refuser qch à qn** to refuse sb sth; **refuser du monde** to have to turn people away; **se refuser à faire** to refuse to do

**regagner** [R(ə)ɡaɲe] vt (*faveur*) to win back; (*lieu*) to get back to

**régal** [Regal] nm treat; **régaler: se régaler** vi to have a delicious meal; (*fig*) to enjoy o.s.

**regard** [R(ə)ɡaR] nm (*coup d'œil*) look, glance; (*expression*) look (in one's eye); **au ~ de** (*loi, morale*) from the point of view of; **en ~ de** in comparison with

**regardant, e** [R(ə)ɡaRdɑ̃, ɑ̃t] adj (*économe*) tight-fisted; **peu ~ (sur)** very free (about)

**regarder** [R(ə)ɡaRde] vt to look at; (*film, télévision, match*) to watch; (*concerner*) to concern ▷ vi to look; **ne pas ~ à la dépense** to spare no expense; **~ qn/qch comme** to regard sb/sth as

**régie** [Reʒi] nf (*Comm, Industrie*) state-owned company; (*Théâtre, Cinéma*) production; (*Radio, TV*) control room

**régime** [Reʒim] nm (Pol) régime; (Méd)
diet; (Admin: carcéral, fiscal etc) system;
(de bananes, dattes) bunch; **se mettre
au/suivre un ~** to go on/be on a diet
**régiment** [Reʒimã] nm regiment
**région** [Reʒjɔ̃] nf region; **régional, e,
-aux** adj regional
**régir** [Reʒiʀ] vt to govern
**régisseur** [Reʒisœʀ] nm (d'un domaine)
steward; (Cinéma, TV) assistant
director; (Théâtre) stage manager
**registre** [Reʒistʀ] nm register
**réglage** [Reglaʒ] nm adjustment
**règle** [Regl] nf (instrument) ruler; (loi)
rule; **règles** nfpl (menstruation) period
sg; **en ~** (papiers d'identité) in order; **en ~
générale** as a (general) rule
**réglé, e** [Regle] adj (vie) well-ordered;
(arrangé) settled
**règlement** [Reglǝmã] nm (paiement)
settlement; (arrêté) regulation;
(règles, statuts) regulations pl, rules pl;
**réglementaire** adj conforming to the
regulations; (tenue) regulation cpd;
**réglementation** nf (règles)
regulations; **réglementer** vt to
regulate
**régler** [Regle] vt (conflit, facture) to
settle; (personne) to settle up with;
(mécanisme, machine) to regulate,
adjust; (thermostat etc) to set, adjust
**réglisse** [Reglis] nf liquorice
**règne** [Reɲ] nm (d'un roi etc, fig) reign; **le
~ végétal/animal** the vegetable/
animal kingdom; **régner** vi (roi) to rule,
reign; (fig) to reign
**regorger** [R(ǝ)gɔʀʒe] vi: **~ de** to
overflow with, be bursting with
**regret** [R(ǝ)gʀɛ] nm regret; **à ~** with
regret; **sans ~** with no regrets;
**regrettable** adj regrettable; **regretter**
vt to regret; (personne) to miss; **je
regrette mais ...** I'm sorry but ...
**regrouper** [R(ǝ)gʀupe] vt (grouper) to
group together; (contenir) to include,
comprise; **se regrouper** vi to gather
(together)
**régulier, -ière** [Regylje, jɛʀ] adj (gén)

regular; (vitesse, qualité) steady; (égal:
couche, ligne) even; (Transports: ligne,
service) scheduled, regular; (légal)
lawful, in order; (honnête) straight, on
the level; **régulièrement** adv regularly;
(uniformément) evenly
**rehausser** [Rǝose] vt (relever) to
heighten, raise; (fig: souligner) to set
off, enhance
**rein** [Rɛ̃] nm kidney; **reins** nmpl (dos)
back sg
**reine** [Rɛn] nf queen
**reine-claude** [Rɛnklod] nf greengage
**réinscriptible** [Reɛ̃skʀiptibl] adj (CD,
DVD) rewritable
**réinsertion** [Reɛ̃sɛʀsjɔ̃] nf
(de délinquant) reintegration,
rehabilitation
**réintégrer** [Reɛ̃tegʀe] vt (lieu) to return
to; (fonctionnaire) to reinstate
**rejaillir** [R(ǝ)ʒajiʀ] vi to splash up; **~ sur**
(fig: scandale) to rebound on; (: gloire) to
be reflected on
**rejet** [Rǝʒɛ] nm rejection; **rejeter**
vt (relancer) to throw back; (écarter)
to reject; (déverser) to throw out,
discharge; (vomir) to bring ou throw
up; **rejeter la responsabilité de qch
sur qn** to lay the responsibility for sth
at sb's door
**rejoindre** [R(ǝ)ʒwɛ̃dʀ] vt (famille,
régiment) to rejoin, return to; (lieu) to
get (back) to; (suj: route etc) to meet,
join; (rattraper) to catch up (with); **se
rejoindre** vi to meet; **je te rejoins à la
gare** I'll see ou meet you at the station
**réjouir** [Reʒwiʀ] vt to delight; **se ~ (de
qch/de faire)** to be delighted (about
sth/to do); **réjouissances** nfpl (fête)
festivities
**relâche** [Rǝlaʃ] nm ou nf: **sans ~**
without respite ou a break; **relâché, e**
adj loose, lax; **relâcher** vt (libérer)
to release; (desserrer) to loosen; **se
relâcher** vi (discipline) to become slack
ou lax; (élève etc) to slacken off
**relais** [R(ǝ)lɛ] nm (Sport): **(course de) ~**
relay (race); **prendre le ~ (de)** to take

over (from); **relais routier** ≈ transport café (BRIT), ≈ truck stop (US)

**relancer** [R(ə)lãse] vt (balle) to throw back; (moteur) to restart; (fig) to boost, revive; (harceler): **~ qn** to pester sb

**relatif, -ive** [R(ə)latif, iv] adj relative

**relation** [R(ə)lasjɔ̃] nf (rapport) relation(ship); (connaissance) acquaintance; **relations** nfpl (rapports) relations; (connaissances) connections; **être/entrer en ~(s) avec** to be/get in contact with

**relaxer** [Rəlakse]: **se relaxer** vi to relax

**relayer** [R(ə)leje] vt (collaborateur, coureur etc) to relieve; **se relayer** vi (dans une activité) to take it in turns

**reléguer** [R(ə)lege] vt to relegate

**relevé, e** [Rəl(ə)ve] adj (manches) rolled-up; (sauce) highly-seasoned ▷ nm (de compteur) reading; **relevé bancaire** ou **de compte** bank statement

**relève** [Rəlɛv] nf (personne) relief; **prendre la ~** to take over

**relever** [Rəl(ə)ve] vt (meuble) to stand up again; (personne tombée) to help up; (vitre, niveau de vie) to raise; (inf) to turn up; (style) to elevate; (plat, sauce) to season; (sentinelle, équipe) to relieve; (fautes) to pick out; (défi) to accept, take up; (noter: adresse etc) to take down, note; (: plan) to sketch; (compteur) to read; (ramasser: cahiers) to collect, take in; **se relever** vi (se remettre debout) to get up; **~ de** (maladie) to be recovering from; (être du ressort de) to be a matter for; (fig) to pertain to; **~ qn de** (fonctions) to relieve sb of; **~ la tête** to look up

**relief** [Rəljɛf] nm relief; **mettre en ~** (fig) to bring out, highlight

**relier** [Rəlje] vt to link up; (livre) to bind; **~ qch à** to link sth to

**religieux, -euse** [R(ə)liʒjø, jøz] adj religious ▷ nm monk

**religion** [R(ə)liʒjɔ̃] nf religion

**relire** [R(ə)liR] vt (à nouveau) to reread, read again; (vérifier) to read over

**reluire** [R(ə)lɥiR] vi to gleam

**remanier** [R(ə)manje] vt to reshape, recast; (Pol) to reshuffle

**remarquable** [R(ə)maRkabl] adj remarkable

**remarque** [R(ə)maRk] nf remark; (écrite) note

**remarquer** [R(ə)maRke] vt (voir) to notice; **se remarquer** vi to be noticeable; **faire ~ (à qn) que** to point out (to sb) that; **faire ~ qch (à qn)** to point sth out (to sb); **remarquez, ...** mind you ...; **se faire ~** to draw attention to o.s.

**rembourrer** [RãbuRe] vt to stuff

**remboursement** [RãbuRsəmã] nm (de dette, d'emprunt) repayment; (de frais) refund; **rembourser** vt to pay back, repay; (frais, billet etc) to refund; **se faire rembourser** to get a refund

**remède** [R(ə)mɛd] nm (médicament) medicine; (traitement, fig) remedy, cure

**remémorer** [R(ə)memɔre]: **se remémorer** vt to recall, recollect

**remerciements** [RəmɛRsimã] nmpl thanks; **(avec) tous mes ~** (with) grateful ou many thanks

**remercier** [R(ə)mɛRsje] vt to thank; (congédier) to dismiss; **~ qn de/d'avoir fait** to thank sb for/for having done

**remettre** [R(ə)mɛtR] vt (replacer) to put back; (vêtement) to put back on; (ajouter) to add; (ajourner) to postpone sth (until); **se remettre** vi: **se ~ (de)** to recover (from); **~ qch à qn** (donner: lettre, clé etc) to hand over sth to sb; (: prix, décoration) to present sb with sth; **se ~ à faire qch** to start doing sth again; **s'en ~ à** to leave it (up) to

**remise** [R(ə)miz] nf (rabais) discount; (local) shed; **remise de peine** reduction of sentence; **remise des prix** prize-giving; **remise en cause** ou **question** calling into question, challenging; **remise en jeu** (Football) throw-in

**remontant** [R(ə)mɔ̃tã] nm tonic, pick-me-up

**remonte-pente** [R(ə)mɔ̃tpãt] nm ski-lift

**remonter** [R(ə)mɔ̃te] vi to go back

up; (*prix, température*) to go up again
▷ *vt* (*pente*) to go up; (*fleuve*) to sail (*ou* swim *etc*) up; (*manches, pantalon*) to roll up; (*col*) to turn up; (*niveau, limite*) to raise; (*fig: personne*) to buck up; (*qch de démonté*) to put back together, reassemble; (*montre*) to wind up; **~ le moral à qn** to raise sb's spirits; **~ à** (*dater de*) to date *ou* go back to

**remords** [R(ə)mɔR] *nm* remorse *no pl*; **avoir des ~** to feel remorse

**remorque** [R(ə)mɔRk] *nf* trailer; **remorquer** *vt* to tow; **remorqueur** *nm* tug(boat)

**remous** [Rəmu] *nm* (*d'un navire*) (back)wash *no pl*; (*de rivière*) swirl, eddy ▷ *nmpl* (*fig*) stir *sg*

**remparts** [Rɑ̃paR] *nmpl* walls, ramparts

**remplaçant, e** [Rɑ̃plasɑ̃, ɑ̃t] *nm/f* replacement, stand-in; (*Scol*) supply teacher

**remplacement** [Rɑ̃plasmɑ̃] *nm* replacement; **faire des ~s** (*professeur*) to do supply teaching; (*secrétaire*) to temp

**remplacer** [Rɑ̃plase] *vt* to replace; **~ qch/qn par** to replace sth/sb with

**rempli, e** [Rɑ̃pli] *adj* (*emploi du temps*) full, busy; **~ de** full of, filled with

**remplir** [Rɑ̃pliR] *vt* to fill (up); (*questionnaire*) to fill out *ou* up; (*obligations, fonction, condition*) to fulfil; **se remplir** *vi* to fill up

**remporter** [Rɑ̃pɔRte] *vt* (*marchandise*) to take away; (*fig*) to win, achieve

**remuant, e** [Rəmɥɑ̃, ɑ̃t] *adj* restless

**remue-ménage** [R(ə)mymenaʒ] *nm inv* commotion

**remuer** [Rəmɥe] *vt* to move; (*café, sauce*) to stir ▷ *vi* to move; **se remuer** *vi* to move; (*fam: s'activer*) to get a move on

**rémunérer** [Remynere] *vt* to remunerate

**renard** [R(ə)naR] *nm* fox

**renchérir** [Rɑ̃feriR] *vi* (*fig*): **~ (sur)** (*en paroles*) to add something (to)

**rencontre** [Rɑ̃kɔ̃tR] *nf* meeting; (*imprévue*) encounter; **aller à la ~ de qn**

to go and meet sb; **rencontrer** *vt* to meet; (*mot, expression*) to come across; (*difficultés*) to meet with; **se rencontrer** *vi* to meet

**rendement** [Rɑ̃dmɑ̃] *nm* (*d'un travailleur, d'une machine*) output; (*d'un champ*) yield

**rendez-vous** [Rɑ̃devu] *nm* appointment; (*d'amoureux*) date; (*lieu*) meeting place; **donner ~ à qn** to arrange to meet sb; **avoir/ prendre ~ (avec)** to have/make an appointment (with); **j'ai ~ avec ...** I have an appointment with ...; **je voudrais prendre ~** I'd like to make an appointment

**rendre** [Rɑ̃dR] *vt* (*restituer*) to give back, return; (*invitation*) to return, repay; (*vomir*) to bring up; (*exprimer, traduire*) to render; (*faire devenir*): **~ qn célèbre/qch possible** to make sb famous/sth possible; **se rendre** *vi* (*capituler*) to surrender, give o.s. up; (*aller*): **se ~ quelque part** to go somewhere; **~ la monnaie à qn** to give sb his change; **se ~ compte de qch** to realize sth

**rênes** [Rɛn] *nfpl* reins

**renfermé, e** [Rɑ̃fɛrme] *adj* (*fig*) withdrawn ▷ *nm*: **sentir le ~** to smell stuffy

**renfermer** [Rɑ̃fɛrme] *vt* to contain

**renforcer** [Rɑ̃fɔRse] *vt* to reinforce; **renfort**: **renforts** *nmpl* reinforcements; **à grand renfort de** with a great deal of

**renfrogné, e** [Rɑ̃fRɔɲe] *adj* sullen

**renier** [Rənje] *vt* (*personne*) to disown, repudiate; (*foi*) to renounce

**renifler** [R(ə)nifle] *vi*, *vt* to sniff

**renne** [Rɛn] *nm* reindeer *inv*

**renom** [Rənɔ̃] *nm* reputation; (*célébrité*) renown; **renommé, e** *adj* celebrated, renowned; **renommée** *nf* fame

**renoncer** [R(ə)nɔ̃se]: **~ à** *vt* to give up; **~ à faire** to give up the idea of doing

**renouer** [Rənwe] *vt*: **~ avec** (*habitude*) to take up again

**renouveler** [R(ə)nuv(ə)le] *vt* to

renew; (*exploit, méfait*) to repeat; **se
renouveler** vi (*incident*) to recur,
happen again; **renouvellement** nm
(*remplacement*) renewal

**rénover** [ʀenɔve] vt (*immeuble*) to
renovate, do up; (*quartier*) to redevelop

**renseignement** [ʀɑ̃sɛɲmɑ̃] nm
information no pl, piece of information;
**(guichet des) ~s** information office;
**(service des) ~s** (*Tél*) directory
enquiries (BRIT), information (US)

**renseigner** [ʀɑ̃sɛɲe] vt: **~ qn (sur)**
to give information to sb (about); **se
renseigner** vi to ask for information,
make inquiries

**rentabilité** [ʀɑ̃tabilite] nf profitability

**rentable** [ʀɑ̃tabl] adj profitable

**rente** [ʀɑ̃t] nf private income; (*pension*)
pension

**rentrée** [ʀɑ̃tʀe] nf: **~ (d'argent)** cash
no pl coming in; **la ~ (des classes)** the
start of the new school year

**rentrer** [ʀɑ̃tʀe] vi (*revenir chez soi*) to
go (ou come) (back) home; (*entrer de
nouveau*) to go (ou come) back in; (*entrer*)
to go (ou come) in; (*air, clou: pénétrer*) to
go in; (*revenu*) to come in ▷ vt to bring
in; (*véhicule*) to put away; (*chemise dans
pantalon etc*) to tuck in; (*griffes*) to draw
in; **~ le ventre** to pull in one's stomach;
**~ dans** (*heurter*) to crash into; **~ dans
l'ordre** to be back to normal; **~ dans
ses frais** to recover one's expenses;
**je rentre mardi** I'm going ou coming
home on Tuesday

**renverse** [ʀɑ̃vɛʀs]: **à la ~** adv
backwards

**renverser** [ʀɑ̃vɛʀse] vt (*faire tomber:
chaise, verre*) to knock over, overturn;
(*liquide, contenu*) to spill, upset; (*piéton*)
to knock down; (*retourner*) to turn
upside down; (: *ordre des mots etc*)
to reverse; (*fig: gouvernement etc*) to
overthrow; (*fam: stupéfier*) to bowl over;
**se renverser** vi (*verre, vase*) to fall over;
(*contenu*) to spill

**renvoi** [ʀɑ̃vwa] nm (*d'employé*)
dismissal; (*d'élève*) expulsion; (*référence*)

cross-reference; (*éructation*) belch;
**renvoyer** vt to send back; (*congédier*) to
dismiss; (*élève: définitivement*) to expel;
(*lumière*) to reflect; (*ajourner*): **renvoyer
qch (à)** to put sth off ou postpone
sth (until)

**repaire** [ʀ(ə)pɛʀ] nm den

**répandre** [ʀepɑ̃dʀ] vt (*renverser*) to
spill; (*étaler, diffuser*) to spread; (*odeur*)
to give off; **se répandre** vi to spill; (*se
propager*) to spread; **répandu, e** adj
(*opinion, usage*) widespread

**réparation** [ʀepaʀasjɔ̃] nf repair

**réparer** [ʀepaʀe] vt to repair; (*fig:
offense*) to make up for, atone for;
(: *oubli, erreur*) to put right; **où est-ce
que je peux le faire ~?** where can I
get it fixed?

**repartie** [ʀepaʀti] nf retort; **avoir de
la ~** to be quick at repartee

**repartir** [ʀ(ə)paʀtiʀ] vi to leave again;
(*voyageur*) to set off again; (*fig*) to get
going again; **~ à zéro** to start from
scratch (again)

**répartir** [ʀepaʀtiʀ] vt (*pour attribuer*)
to share out; (*pour disperser, disposer*)
to divide up; (*poids*) to distribute; **se
répartir** vt (*travail, rôles*) to share out
between themselves; **répartition** nf
(*des richesses etc*) distribution

**repas** [ʀ(ə)pɑ] nm meal

**repassage** [ʀ(ə)pɑsaʒ] nm ironing

**repasser** [ʀ(ə)pɑse] vi to come (ou
go) back ▷ vt (*vêtement, tissu*) to iron;
(*examen*) to retake, resit; (*film*) to show
again; (*leçon: revoir*) to go over (again)

**repentir** [ʀəpɑ̃tiʀ] nm repentance; **se
repentir** vi to repent; **se ~ d'avoir fait
qch** (*regretter*) to regret having done sth

**répercussions** [ʀepɛʀkysjɔ̃] nfpl (*fig*)
repercussions

**répercuter** [ʀepɛʀkyte]: **se répercuter**
vi (*bruit*) to reverberate; (*fig*): **se ~ sur** to
have repercussions on

**repère** [ʀ(ə)pɛʀ] nm mark; (*monument,
événement*) landmark

**repérer** [ʀ(ə)peʀe] vt (*fam: erreur,
personne*) to spot; (: *endroit*) to locate; **se**

**repérer** vi to find one's way about

**répertoire** [ʀepɛʀtwaʀ] nm (liste) (alphabetical) list; (carnet) index notebook; (Inform) folder, directory; (d'un artiste) repertoire

**répéter** [ʀepete] vt to repeat; (préparer: leçon) to learn, go over; (Théâtre) to rehearse; **se répéter** vi (redire) to repeat o.s.; (se reproduire) to be repeated, recur; **pouvez-vous ~, s'il vous plaît?** can you repeat that, please?

**répétition** [ʀepetisjɔ̃] nf repetition; (Théâtre) rehearsal; **~ générale** (final) dress rehearsal

**répit** [ʀepi] nm respite; **sans ~** without letting up

**replier** [ʀ(ə)plije] vt (rabattre) to fold down ou over; **se replier** vi (troupes, armée) to withdraw, fall back; (sur soi-même) to withdraw into o.s.

**réplique** [ʀeplik] nf (repartie, fig) reply; (Théâtre) line; (copie) replica; **répliquer** vi to reply; (riposter) to retaliate

**répondeur** [ʀepɔ̃dœʀ] nm: **~ (automatique)** (Tél) answering machine

**répondre** [ʀepɔ̃dʀ] vi to answer, reply; (freins) to respond; **~ à** to reply to, answer; (affection, salut) to return; (provocation) to respond to; (correspondre à: besoin) to answer; (: conditions) to meet; (: description) to match; (avec impertinence): **~ à qn** to answer sb back; **~ de** to answer for

**réponse** [ʀepɔ̃s] nf answer, reply; **en ~ à** in reply to

**reportage** [ʀ(ə)pɔʀtaʒ] nm report

**reporter¹** [ʀəpɔʀtɛʀ] nm reporter

**reporter²** [ʀəpɔʀte] vt (ajourner): **~ qch (à)** to postpone sth (until); (transférer): **~ qch sur** to transfer sth to; **se reporter à** (époque) to think back to; (document) to refer to

**repos** [ʀ(ə)po] nm rest; (tranquillité) peace (and quiet); (Mil): **~!** stand at ease!; **ce n'est pas de tout ~!** it's no picnic!

**reposant, e** [ʀ(ə)pozɑ̃, ɑ̃t] adj restful

**reposer** [ʀ(ə)poze] vt (verre, livre) to put down; (délasser) to rest ▷ vi: **laisser ~** (pâte) to leave to stand; **se reposer** vi to rest; **se ~ sur qn** to rely on sb; **~ sur** (fig) to rest on

**repoussant, e** [ʀ(ə)pusɑ̃, ɑ̃t] adj repulsive

**repousser** [ʀ(ə)puse] vi to grow again ▷ vt to repel, repulse; (offre) to turn down, reject; (personne) to push back; (différer) to put back

**reprendre** [ʀ(ə)pʀɑ̃dʀ] vt (objet prêté, donné) to take back; (prisonnier, ville) to recapture; (firme, entreprise) to take over; (le travail) to resume; (emprunter: argument, idée) to take up, use; (refaire: article etc) to go over again; (vêtement) to alter; (réprimander) to tell off; (corriger) to correct; (chercher): **je viendrai te ~ à 4 h** I'll come and fetch you at 4; (se resservir de): **~ du pain/un œuf** to take (ou eat) more bread/another egg ▷ vi (classes, pluie) to start (up) again; (activités, travaux, combats) to resume, start (up) again; (affaires) to pick up; (dire): **reprit-il** he went on; **~ des forces** to recover one's strength; **~ courage** to take new heart; **~ la route** to resume one's journey, set off again; **~ haleine** ou **son souffle** to get one's breath back

**représentant, e** [ʀ(ə)pʀezɑ̃tɑ̃, ɑ̃t] nm/f representative

**représentation** [ʀ(ə)pʀezɑ̃tasjɔ̃] nf (symbole, image) representation; (spectacle) performance

**représenter** [ʀ(ə)pʀezɑ̃te] vt to represent; (donner: pièce, opéra) to perform; **se représenter** vt (se figurer) to imagine

**répression** [ʀepʀesjɔ̃] nf repression

**réprimer** [ʀepʀime] vt (émotions) to suppress; (peuple etc) to repress

**repris** [ʀ(ə)pʀi] nm: **~ de justice** ex-prisoner, ex-convict

**reprise** [ʀ(ə)pʀiz] nf (recommencement) resumption; (économique) recovery; (TV) repeat; (Comm) trade-in, part exchange; (*raccommodage*) mend; **à plusieurs ~s** on several occasions

**repriser** [ʀ(ə)pʀize] *vt* (*chaussette, lainage*) to darn; (*tissu*) to mend

**reproche** [ʀ(ə)pʀɔʃ] *nm* (*remontrance*) reproach; **faire des ~s à qn** to reproach sb; **sans ~(s)** beyond reproach; **reprocher** *vt*: **reprocher qch à qn** to reproach *ou* blame sb for sth; **reprocher qch à** (*critiquer*) to have sth against

**reproduction** [ʀ(ə)pʀɔdyksjɔ̃] *nf* reproduction

**reproduire** [ʀ(ə)pʀɔdɥiʀ] *vt* to reproduce; **se reproduire** *vi* (*Bio*) to reproduce; (*recommencer*) to recur, re-occur

**reptile** [ʀɛptil] *nm* reptile

**république** [ʀepyblik] *nf* republic

**répugnant, e** [ʀepyɲɑ̃, ɑ̃t] *adj* disgusting

**répugner** [ʀepyɲe] **~ à** *vt* : **~ à qn** to repel *ou* disgust sb; **~ à faire** to be loath *ou* reluctant to do

**réputation** [ʀepytasjɔ̃] *nf* reputation; **réputé, e** *adj* renowned

**requérir** [ʀəkeʀiʀ] *vt* (*nécessiter*) to require, call for

**requête** [ʀəkɛt] *nf* request

**requin** [ʀəkɛ̃] *nm* shark

**requis, e** [ʀəki, iz] *adj* required

**RER** *sigle m* (= *réseau express régional*) *Greater Paris high-speed train service*

**rescapé, e** [ʀɛskape] *nm/f* survivor

**rescousse** [ʀɛskus] *nf*: **aller à la ~ de qn** to go to sb's aid *ou* rescue

**réseau, x** [ʀezo] *nm* network

**réservation** [ʀezɛʀvasjɔ̃] *nf* booking, reservation; **j'ai confirmé ma ~ par fax/e-mail** I confirmed my booking by fax/e-mail

**réserve** [ʀezɛʀv] *nf* (*retenue*) reserve; (*entrepôt*) storeroom; (*restriction, d'Indiens*) reservation; (*de pêche, chasse*) preserve; **de ~** (*provisions etc*) in reserve

**réservé, e** [ʀezɛʀve] *adj* reserved; **chasse/pêche ~e** private hunting/fishing

**réserver** [ʀezɛʀve] *vt* to reserve;

(*chambre, billet etc*) to book, reserve; (*fig: destiner*) to have in store; (*garder*): **~ qch pour/à** to keep *ou* save sth for; **je voudrais ~ une chambre pour deux personnes** I'd like to book a double room; **j'ai réservé une table au nom de ...** I booked a table in the name of ...

**réservoir** [ʀezɛʀvwaʀ] *nm* tank

**résidence** [ʀezidɑ̃s] *nf* residence; **résidence secondaire** second home; **résidence universitaire** hall of residence (BRIT), dormitory (US); **résidentiel, le** *adj* residential; **résider** *vi*: **résider à/dans/en** to reside in; **résider dans** (*fig*) to lie in

**résidu** [ʀezidy] *nm* residue *no pl*

**résigner** [ʀeziɲe]: **se résigner** *vi*: **se ~ (à qch/à faire)** to resign o.s. (to sth/to doing)

**résilier** [ʀezilje] *vt* to terminate

**résistance** [ʀezistɑ̃s] *nf* resistance; (*de réchaud, bouilloire: fil*) element

**résistant, e** [ʀezistɑ̃, ɑ̃t] *adj* (*personne*) robust, tough; (*matériau*) strong, hard-wearing

**résister** [ʀeziste] *vi* to resist; **~ à** (*assaut, tentation*) to resist; (*supporter: gel etc*) to withstand; (*désobéir à*) to stand up to, oppose

**résolu, e** [ʀezɔly] *pp de* **résoudre** ▷ *adj*: **être ~ à qch/faire** to be set upon sth/doing

**résolution** [ʀezɔlysjɔ̃] *nf* (*fermeté, décision*) resolution; (*d'un problème*) solution

**résolve** *etc* [ʀezɔlv] *vb voir* **résoudre**

**résonner** [ʀezɔne] *vi* (*cloche, pas*) to reverberate, resound; (*salle*) to be resonant

**résorber** [ʀezɔʀbe]: **se résorber** *vi* (*fig: chômage*) to be reduced; (: *déficit*) to be absorbed

**résoudre** [ʀezudʀ] *vt* to solve; **se ~ à faire** to bring o.s. to do

**respect** [ʀɛspɛ] *nm* respect; **tenir en ~** to keep at bay; **présenter ses ~s à qn** to pay one's respects to sb; **respecter** *vt* to respect; **respectueux, -euse** *adj* respectful

**respiration** [ʀɛspiʀasjɔ̃] nf
breathing no pl

**respirer** [ʀɛspiʀe] vi to breathe; (fig: se
détendre) to get one's breath;
(: se rassurer) to breathe again ▷ vt to
breathe (in), inhale; (manifester: santé,
calme etc) to exude

**resplendir** [ʀɛsplɑ̃diʀ] vi to shine;
(fig): ~ **(de)** to be radiant (with)

**responsabilité** [ʀɛspɔ̃sabilite] nf
responsibility; (légale) liability

**responsable** [ʀɛspɔ̃sabl] adj
responsible ▷ nm/f (coupable) person
responsible; (personne compétente)
person in charge; (de parti, syndicat)
official; ~ **de** responsible for

**ressaisir** [ʀ(ə)seziʀ]: **se ressaisir** vi to
regain one's self-control

**ressasser** [ʀ(ə)sase] vt to keep going
over

**ressemblance** [ʀ(ə)sɑ̃blɑ̃s] nf
resemblance, similarity, likeness

**ressemblant, e** [ʀ(ə)sɑ̃blɑ̃, ɑ̃t] adj
(portrait) lifelike, true to life

**ressembler** [ʀ(ə)sɑ̃ble]: ~ **à** vt to
be like, resemble; (visuellement) to
look like; **se ressembler** vi to be (ou
look) alike

**ressentiment** [ʀ(ə)sɑ̃timɑ̃] nm
resentment

**ressentir** [ʀ(ə)sɑ̃tiʀ] vt to feel; **se ~ de**
to feel (ou show) the effects of

**resserrer** [ʀ(ə)seʀe] vt (nœud, boulon)
to tighten (up); (fig: liens) to strengthen

**resservir** [ʀ(ə)sɛʀviʀ] vi to do ou serve
again; ~ **qn (d'un plat)** to give sb a
second helping (of a dish); **se ~ de** (plat)
to take a second helping of; (outil etc)
to use again

**ressort** [ʀəsɔʀ] nm (pièce) spring;
(énergie) spirit; (recours): **en dernier ~** as
a last resort; (compétence): **être du ~ de**
to fall within the competence of

**ressortir** [ʀəsɔʀtiʀ] vi to go (ou come)
out (again); (contraster) to stand out;
~ **de** to emerge from; **faire ~** (fig:
souligner) to bring out

**ressortissant, e** [ʀ(ə)sɔʀtisɑ̃, ɑ̃t]
nm/f national

**ressources** [ʀ(ə)suʀs] nfpl (moyens)
resources

**ressusciter** [ʀesysite] vt (fig) to revive,
bring back ▷ vi to rise (from the dead)

**restant, e** [ʀɛstɑ̃, ɑ̃t] adj remaining
▷ nm: **le ~ (de)** the remainder (of); **un ~
de** (de trop) some left-over

**restaurant** [ʀɛstɔʀɑ̃] nm restaurant;
**pouvez-vous m'indiquer un bon
~?** can you recommend a good
restaurant?

**restauration** [ʀɛstɔʀasjɔ̃] nf
restoration; (hôtellerie) catering;
**restauration rapide** fast food

**restaurer** [ʀɛstɔʀe] vt to restore; **se
restaurer** vi to have something to eat

**reste** [ʀɛst] nm (restant): **le ~ (de)** the
rest (of); (de trop): **un ~ (de)** some
left-over; **restes** nmpl (nourriture) left-
overs; (d'une cité etc, dépouille mortelle)
remains; **du ~, au ~** besides, moreover

**rester** [ʀɛste] vi to stay, remain;
(subsister) to remain, be left; (durer)
to last, live on ▷ vb impers: **il reste du
pain/2 œufs** there's some bread/there
are 2 eggs left (over); **restons-en là** let's
leave it at that; **il me reste assez de
temps** I have enough time left; **il ne me
reste plus qu'à ...** I've just got to ...

**restituer** [ʀɛstitɥe] vt (objet, somme): ~
**qch (à qn)** to return sth (to sb)

**restreindre** [ʀɛstʀɛ̃dʀ] vt to restrict,
limit

**restriction** [ʀɛstʀiksjɔ̃] nf restriction

**résultat** [ʀezylta] nm result; **résultats**
nmpl (d'examen, d'élection) results pl

**résulter** [ʀezylte]: ~ **de** vt to result
from, be the result of

**résumé** [ʀezyme] nm summary,
résumé; **en ~** in brief; (pour conclure)
to sum up

**résumer** [ʀezyme] vt (texte) to
summarize; (récapituler) to sum up
▌ Attention à ne pas traduire **résumer**
par **to resume**.

**résurrection** [ʀezyʀɛksjɔ̃] nf

resurrection

**rétablir** [ʀetabliʀ] vt to restore, re-establish; **se rétablir** vi (guérir) to recover; (silence, calme) to return, be restored; **rétablissement** nm restoring; (guérison) recovery

**retaper** [ʀ(ə)tape] (fam) vt (maison, voiture etc) to do up; (revigorer) to buck up

**retard** [ʀ(ə)taʀ] nm (d'une personne attendue) lateness no pl; (sur l'horaire, un programme) delay; (fig: scolaire, mental etc) backwardness; **en ~ (de 2 heures)** (2 hours) late; **avoir du ~** to be late; (sur un programme) to be behind (schedule); **prendre du ~** (train, avion) to be delayed; **sans ~** without delay; **désolé d'être en ~** sorry I'm late; **le vol a deux heures de ~** the flight is two hours late

**retardataire** [ʀ(ə)taʀdatɛʀ] nm/f latecomer

**retardement** [ʀ(ə)taʀdəmɑ̃]: **à ~** adj delayed action cpd; **bombe à ~** time bomb

**retarder** [ʀ(ə)taʀde] vt to delay; (montre) to put back ▷ vi (montre) to be slow; **~ qn (d'une heure)** (sur un horaire) to delay sb (an hour); **~ qch (de 2 jours)** (départ, date) to put sth back (2 days)

**retenir** [ʀət(ə)niʀ] vt (garder, retarder) to keep, detain; (maintenir: objet qui glisse, fig: colère, larmes) to hold back; (se rappeler) to retain; (réserver) to reserve; (accepter: proposition etc) to accept; (fig: empêcher d'agir): **~ qn (de faire)** to hold sb back (from doing); (prélever): **~ qch (sur)** to deduct sth (from); **se retenir** vi (se raccrocher): **se ~ à** to hold onto; (se contenir): **se ~ de faire** to restrain o.s. from doing; **~ son souffle** to hold one's breath

**retentir** [ʀ(ə)tɑ̃tiʀ] vi to ring out; **retentissant, e** adj resounding

**retenue** [ʀət(ə)ny] nf (prélèvement) deduction; (Scol) detention; (modération) (self-)restraint

**réticence** [ʀetisɑ̃s] nf hesitation, reluctance no pl; **réticent, e** adj

hesitant, reluctant

**rétine** [ʀetin] nf retina

**retiré, e** [ʀ(ə)tiʀe] adj (vie) secluded; (lieu) remote

**retirer** [ʀ(ə)tiʀe] vt (vêtement, lunettes) to take off, remove; (argent, plainte) to withdraw; (reprendre: bagages, billets) to collect; (extraire): **~ qch de** to take sth out of, remove sth from

**retomber** [ʀ(ə)tɔ̃be] vi (à nouveau) to fall again; (atterrir: après un saut etc) to land; (échoir): **~ sur qn** to fall on sb

**rétorquer** [ʀetɔʀke] vt: **~ (à qn) que** to retort (to sb) that

**retouche** [ʀ(ə)tuʃ] nf (sur vêtement) alteration; **retoucher** vt (photographie) to touch up; (texte, vêtement) to alter

**retour** [ʀ(ə)tuʀ] nm return; **au ~** (en route) on the way back; **à mon ~** when I get/got back; **être de ~ (de)** to be back (from); **par ~ du courrier** by return of post; **quand serons-nous de ~?** when do we get back?

**retourner** [ʀ(ə)tuʀne] vt (dans l'autre sens: matelas, crêpe etc) to turn (over); (: sac, vêtement) to turn inside out; (fam: bouleverser) to shake; (renvoyer, restituer): **~ qch à qn** to return sth to sb ▷ vi (aller, revenir): **~ quelque part/à** to go back ou return somewhere/to; **se retourner** vi (tourner la tête) to turn round; **~ à** (état, activité) to return to, go back to; **se ~ contre** (fig) to turn against

**retrait** [ʀ(ə)tʀɛ] nm (d'argent) withdrawal; **~** set back; **retrait du permis (de conduire)** disqualification from driving (BRIT), revocation of driver's license (US)

**retraite** [ʀ(ə)tʀɛt] nf (d'un employé) retirement; (revenu) pension; (d'une armée, Rel) retreat; **prendre sa ~** to retire; **retraite anticipée** early retirement; **retraité, e** adj retired ▷ nm/f pensioner

**retrancher** [ʀ(ə)tʀɑ̃ʃe] vt (nombre, somme): **~ qch de** to take ou deduct sth from; **se ~ derrière/dans** to take refuge behind/in

**rétrécir** [ʀetʀesiʀ] vt (vêtement) to take in ▷ vi to shrink; **se rétrécir** (route, vallée) to narrow

**rétro** [ʀetʀo] adj inv: **la mode ~** the nostalgia vogue

**rétroprojecteur** [ʀetʀopʀɔʒɛktœʀ] nm overhead projector

**rétrospective** [ʀetʀɔspɛktiv] nf (Art) retrospective; (Cinéma) season, retrospective; **rétrospectivement** adv in retrospect

**retrousser** [ʀ(ə)tʀuse] vt to roll up

**retrouvailles** [ʀ(ə)tʀuvaj] nfpl reunion sg

**retrouver** [ʀ(ə)tʀuve] vt (fugitif, objet perdu) to find; (calme, santé) to regain; (revoir) to see again; (rejoindre) to meet (again), join; **se retrouver** vi to meet; (s'orienter) to find one's way; **se ~ quelque part** to find o.s. somewhere; **s'y ~** (y voir clair) to make sense of it; (rentrer dans ses frais) to break even; **je ne retrouve plus mon portefeuille** I can't find my wallet (BRIT) ou billfold (US)

**rétroviseur** [ʀetʀɔvizœʀ] nm (rear-view) mirror

**réunion** [ʀeynjɔ̃] nf (séance) meeting

**réunir** [ʀeyniʀ] vt (rassembler) to gather together; (inviter: amis, famille) to have round, have in; (cumuler: qualités etc) to combine; (rapprocher: ennemis) to bring together (again), reunite; (rattacher: parties) to join (together); **se réunir** vi (se rencontrer) to meet

**réussi, e** [ʀeysi] adj successful

**réussir** [ʀeysiʀ] vi to succeed, be successful; (à un examen) to pass ▷ vt to make a success of; **~ à faire** to succeed in doing; **~ à qn** (être bénéfique à) to agree with sb; **réussite** nf success; (Cartes) patience

**revaloir** [ʀ(ə)valwaʀ] vt: **je vous revaudrai cela** I'll repay you some day; (en mal) I'll pay you back for this

**revanche** [ʀ(ə)vɑ̃ʃ] nf revenge; (sport) revenge match; **en ~** on the other hand

**rêve** [ʀɛv] nm dream; **de ~** dream cpd;

**faire un ~** to have a dream

**réveil** [ʀevɛj] nm waking up no pl; (fig) awakening; (pendule) alarm (clock); **au ~** on waking (up); **réveiller** vt (personne) to wake up; (fig) to awaken, revive; **se réveiller** vi to wake up; **pouvez-vous me réveiller à 7 heures, s'il vous plaît?** could I have an alarm call at 7am, please?

**réveillon** [ʀevɛjɔ̃] nm Christmas Eve; (de la Saint-Sylvestre) New Year's Eve; **réveillonner** vi to celebrate Christmas Eve (ou New Year's Eve)

**révélateur, -trice** [ʀevelatœʀ, tʀis] adj: **~ (de qch)** revealing (sth)

**révéler** [ʀevele] vt to reveal; **se révéler** vi to be revealed, reveal itself ▷ vb +attrib: **se ~ difficile/aisé** to prove difficult/easy

**revenant, e** [ʀ(ə)vənɑ̃, ɑ̃t] nm/f ghost

**revendeur, -euse** [ʀ(ə)vɑ̃dœʀ, øz] nm/f (détaillant) retailer; (de drogue) (drug-)dealer

**revendication** [ʀ(ə)vɑ̃dikasjɔ̃] nf claim, demand

**revendiquer** [ʀ(ə)vɑ̃dike] vt to claim, demand; (responsabilité) to claim

**revendre** [ʀ(ə)vɑ̃dʀ] vt (d'occasion) to resell; (détailler) to sell; **à ~** (en abondance) to spare

**revenir** [ʀəv(ə)niʀ] vi to come back; (coûter): **~ cher/à 100 euros (à qn)** to cost (sb) a lot/100 euros; **~ à** (reprendre: études, projet) to return to, go back to; (équivaloir à) to amount to; **~ à qn** (part, honneur) to go to sb, be sb's; (souvenir, nom) to come back to sb; **~ sur** (question, sujet) to go back over; (engagement) to go back on; **~ à soi** to come round; **n'en pas ~: je n'en reviens pas** I can't get over it; **~ sur ses pas** to retrace one's steps; **cela revient à dire que/au même** it amounts to saying that/the same thing; **faire ~** (Culin) to brown

**revenu** [ʀəv(ə)ny] nm income; **revenus** nmpl income sg

**rêver** [ʀeve] vi, vt to dream; **~ de/à** to dream of

**réverbère** [ʀevɛʀbɛʀ] nm street lamp ou light; **réverbérer** vt to reflect

**revers** [ʀ(ə)vɛʀ] nm (de feuille, main) back; (d'étoffe) wrong side; (de pièce, médaille) back, reverse; (Tennis, Ping-Pong) backhand; (de veste) lapel; (fig: échec) setback

**revêtement** [ʀ(ə)vɛtmɑ̃] nm (des sols) flooring; (de chaussée) surface

**revêtir** [ʀ(ə)vetiʀ] vt (habit) to don, put on; (prendre: importance, apparence) to take on; **~ qch de** to cover sth with

**rêveur, -euse** [ʀevœʀ, øz] adj dreamy ▷ nm/f dreamer

**revient** [ʀəvjɛ̃] vb voir **revenir**

**revigorer** [ʀ(ə)vigɔʀe] vt (air frais) to invigorate, brace up; (repas, boisson) to revive, buck up

**revirement** [ʀ(ə)viʀmɑ̃] nm change of mind; (d'une situation) reversal

**réviser** [ʀevize] vt to revise; (machine) to overhaul, service

**révision** [ʀevizjɔ̃] nf revision; (de voiture) servicing no pl

**revivre** [ʀ(ə)vivʀ] vi (reprendre des forces) to come alive again ▷ vt (épreuve, moment) to relive

**revoir** [ʀəvwaʀ] vt to see again; (réviser) to revise ▷ nm: **au ~** goodbye

**révoltant, e** [ʀevɔltɑ̃, ɑ̃t] adj revolting, appalling

**révolte** [ʀevɔlt] nf rebellion, revolt

**révolter** [ʀevɔlte] vt to revolt; **se révolter (contre)** to rebel (against)

**révolu, e** [ʀevɔly] adj past; (Admin): **âgé de 18 ans ~s** over 18 years of age

**révolution** [ʀevɔlysjɔ̃] nf revolution; **révolutionnaire** adj, nm/f revolutionary

**revolver** [ʀevɔlvɛʀ] nm gun; (à barillet) revolver

**révoquer** [ʀevɔke] vt (fonctionnaire) to dismiss; (arrêt, contrat) to revoke

**revue** [ʀ(ə)vy] nf review; (périodique) review, magazine; (de music-hall) variety show; **passer en ~** (mentalement) to go through

**rez-de-chaussée** [ʀed(ə)ʃose] nm inv ground floor

**RF** sigle f = **République française**

**Rhin** [ʀɛ̃] nm Rhine

**rhinocéros** [ʀinɔseʀɔs] nm rhinoceros

**Rhône** [ʀon] nm Rhone

**rhubarbe** [ʀybaʀb] nf rhubarb

**rhum** [ʀɔm] nm rum

**rhumatisme** [ʀymatism] nm rheumatism no pl

**rhume** [ʀym] nm cold; **rhume de cerveau** head cold; **le rhume des foins** hay fever

**ricaner** [ʀikane] vi (avec méchanceté) to snigger; (bêtement) to giggle

**riche** [ʀiʃ] adj rich; (personne, pays) rich, wealthy; **~ en** rich in; **richesse** nf wealth; (fig: de sol, musée etc) richness; **richesses** nfpl (ressources, argent) wealth sg; (fig: trésors) treasures

**ricochet** [ʀikɔʃɛ] nm: **faire des ~s** to skip stones

**ride** [ʀid] nf wrinkle

**rideau, x** [ʀido] nm curtain; **rideau de fer** (boutique) metal shutter(s)

**rider** [ʀide] vt to wrinkle; **se rider** vi to become wrinkled

**ridicule** [ʀidikyl] adj ridiculous ▷ nm: **le ~** ridicule; **ridiculiser** vt to ridicule; **se ridiculiser** vi to make a fool of o.s.

 **MOT-CLÉ**

**rien** [ʀjɛ̃] pron **1**: **(ne) ... rien** nothing, tournure négative + anything; **qu'est-ce que vous avez? — rien** what have you got? — nothing; **il n'a rien dit/fait** he said/did nothing; he hasn't said/done anything; **n'avoir peur de rien** to be afraid ou frightened of nothing, not to be afraid ou frightened of anything; **il n'a rien** (n'est pas blessé) he's all right; **ça ne fait rien** it doesn't matter; **de rien!** not at all!

**2**: **rien de**: **rien d'intéressant** nothing interesting; **rien d'autre** nothing else; **rien du tout** nothing at all

**3**: **rien que** just, only; nothing but; **rien que pour lui faire plaisir** only ou just to please him; **rien que la vérité** nothing but the truth; **rien que cela** that alone ▷ *nm*: **un petit rien** (*cadeau*) a little something; **des riens** trivia *pl*; **un rien de** a hint of; **en un rien de temps** in no time at all

**rieur, -euse** [R(i)jœR, R(i)jøz] *adj* cheerful

**rigide** [Riʒid] *adj* stiff; (*fig*) rigid; strict

**rigoler** [Rigɔle] *vi* (*fam: rire*) to laugh; (*s'amuser*) to have (some) fun; (*plaisanter*) to be joking *ou* kidding; **rigolo, -ote** (*fam*) *adj* funny ▷ *nm/f* comic; (*péj*) fraud, phoney

**rigoureusement** [RiguRøzmɑ̃] *adv* (*vrai*) absolutely; (*interdit*) strictly

**rigoureux, -euse** [RiguRø, øz] *adj* rigorous; (*hiver*) hard, harsh

**rigueur** [RigœR] *nf* rigour; **"tenue de soirée de ~"** "formal dress only"; **à la ~** at a pinch; **tenir ~ à qn de qch** to hold sth against sb

**rillettes** [Rijet] *nfpl* potted meat (*made from pork or goose*)

**rime** [Rim] *nf* rhyme

**rinçage** [Rɛ̃saʒ] *nm* rinsing (out); (*opération*) rinse

**rincer** [Rɛ̃se] *vt* to rinse; (*récipient*) to rinse out

**ringard, e** [Rɛ̃gaR, aRd] (*fam*) *adj* old-fashioned

**riposter** [Ripɔste] *vi* to retaliate ▷ *vt*: **~ que** to retort that

**rire** [RiR] *vi* to laugh; (*se divertir*) to have fun ▷ *nm* laugh; **le ~** laughter; **~ de** to laugh at; **pour ~** (*pas sérieusement*) for a joke *ou* a laugh

**risible** [Rizibl] *adj* laughable

**risque** [Risk] *nm* risk; **le ~** danger; **à ses ~s et périls** at his own risk; **risqué, e** *adj* risky; (*plaisanterie*) risqué, daring; **risquer** *vt* to risk; (*allusion, question*) to venture, hazard; **ça ne risque rien** it's quite safe; **risquer de: il risque de se tuer** he could get himself killed; **ce qui risque de se produire** what might *ou* could well happen; **il ne risque pas**

**de recommencer** there's no chance of him doing that again; **se risquer à faire** (*tenter*) to venture *ou* dare to do

**rissoler** [Risɔle] *vi, vt*: **(faire) ~** to brown

**ristourne** [RistuRn] *nf* discount

**rite** [Rit] *nm* rite; (*fig*) ritual

**rivage** [Rivaʒ] *nm* shore

**rival, e, -aux** [Rival, o] *adj, nm/f* rival; **rivaliser** *vi*: **rivaliser avec** (*personne*) to rival, vie with; **rivalité** *nf* rivalry

**rive** [Riv] *nf* shore; (*de fleuve*) bank; **riverain, e** *nm/f* riverside (*ou* lakeside) resident; (*d'une route*) local resident

**rivière** [RivjeR] *nf* river

**riz** [Ri] *nm* rice; **rizière** *nf* paddy-field, ricefield

**RMI** *sigle m* (= *revenu minimum d'insertion*) ≈ income support (BRIT), ≈ welfare (US)

**RN** *sigle f* = **route nationale**

**robe** [Rɔb] *nf* dress; (*de juge*) robe; (*pelage*) coat; **robe de chambre** dressing gown; **robe de mariée** wedding dress; **robe de soirée** evening dress

**robinet** [Rɔbinɛ] *nm* tap (BRIT), faucet (US)

**robot** [Rɔbo] *nm* robot; **robot de cuisine** food processor

**robuste** [Rɔbyst] *adj* robust, sturdy; **robustesse** *nf* robustness, sturdiness

**roc** [Rɔk] *nm* rock

**rocade** [Rɔkad] *nf* bypass

**rocaille** [Rɔkaj] *nf* loose stones *pl*; (*jardin*) rockery, rock garden

**roche** [Rɔʃ] *nf* rock

**rocher** [Rɔʃe] *nm* rock

**rocheux, -euse** [Rɔʃø, øz] *adj* rocky

**rodage** [Rɔdaʒ] *nm*: **en ~** running in

**rôder** [Rode] *vi* to roam about; (*de façon suspecte*) to lurk (about *ou* around); **rôdeur, -euse** *nm/f* prowler

**rogne** [Rɔɲ] (*fam*) *nf*: **être en ~** to be in a temper

**rogner** [Rɔɲe] *vt* to clip; **~ sur** (*fig*) to cut down *ou* back on

**rognons** [Rɔɲɔ̃] *nmpl* (*Culin*) kidneys

**roi** [Rwa] *nm* king; **la fête des Rois, les**

**Rois** Twelfth Night

**rôle** [ʀol] nm role, part

**rollers** [ʀɔlœʀ] nmpl Rollerblades®

**romain, e** [ʀɔmɛ̃, ɛn] adj Roman
▷ nm/f: **R~, e** Roman

**roman, e** [ʀɔmɑ̃, an] adj (Archit)
Romanesque ▷ nm novel; **roman
policier** detective story

**romancer** [ʀɔmɑ̃se] vt (agrémenter) to
romanticize; **romancier, -ière** nm/f
novelist; **romanesque** adj (amours,
aventures) storybook cpd; (sentimental:
personne) romantic

**roman-feuilleton** [ʀɔmɑ̃fœjtɔ̃] nm
serialized novel

**romanichel, le** [ʀɔmaniʃɛl] (péj)
nm/f gipsy

**romantique** [ʀɔmɑ̃tik] adj romantic

**romarin** [ʀɔmaʀɛ̃] nm rosemary

**Rome** [ʀɔm] n Rome

**rompre** [ʀɔ̃pʀ] vt to break; (entretien,
fiançailles) to break off ▷ vi (fiancés) to
break it off; **se rompre** vi to break;
**rompu, e** adj (fourbu) exhausted

**ronces** [ʀɔ̃s] nfpl brambles

**ronchonner** [ʀɔ̃ʃɔne] (fam) vi to
grouse, grouch

**rond, e** [ʀɔ̃, ʀɔ̃d] adj round; (joues,
mollets) well-rounded; (fam: ivre) tight
▷ nm (cercle) ring; (fam: sou): **je n'ai
plus un ~** I haven't a penny left; **en ~**
(s'asseoir, danser) in a ring; **ronde** nf
(gén: de surveillance) rounds pl, patrol;
(danse) round (dance); (Mus) semibreve
(BRIT), whole note (US); **à la ronde**
(alentour): **à 10 km à la ronde** for 10 km
round; **rondelet, te** adj plump

**rondelle** [ʀɔ̃dɛl] nf (tranche) slice,
round; (Tech) washer

**rond-point** [ʀɔ̃pwɛ̃] nm roundabout

**ronflement** [ʀɔ̃fləmɑ̃] nm snore,
snoring

**ronfler** [ʀɔ̃fle] vi to snore; (moteur,
poêle) to hum

**ronger** [ʀɔ̃ʒe] vt to gnaw (at); (suj: vers,
rouille) to eat into; **se ~ les ongles** to
bite one's nails; **se ~ les sangs** to worry
o.s. sick; **rongeur** nm rodent

**ronronner** [ʀɔ̃ʀɔne] vi to purr

**rosbif** [ʀɔsbif] nm: **du ~** roasting beef;
(cuit) roast beef

**rose** [ʀoz] nf rose ▷ adj pink; **rose
bonbon** adj inv candy pink

**rosé, e** [ʀoze] adj pinkish; (vin) **~** rosé

**roseau, x** [ʀozo] nm reed

**rosée** [ʀoze] nf dew

**rosier** [ʀozje] nm rosebush, rose tree

**rossignol** [ʀɔsiɲɔl] nm (Zool)
nightingale

**rotation** [ʀɔtasjɔ̃] nf rotation

**roter** [ʀɔte] (fam) vi to burp, belch

**rôti** [ʀoti] nm: **du ~** roasting meat; (cuit)
roast meat; **un ~ de bœuf/porc** a joint
of beef/pork

**rotin** [ʀɔtɛ̃] nm rattan (cane); **fauteuil
en ~** cane (arm)chair

**rôtir** [ʀotiʀ] vi, vt (aussi: **faire ~**)
to roast; **rôtisserie** nf (restaurant)
steakhouse; (traiteur) roast meat shop;
**rôtissoire** nf (roasting) spit

**rotule** [ʀɔtyl] nf kneecap

**rouage** [ʀwaʒ] nm cog(wheel),
gearwheel; **les ~s de l'État** the wheels
of State

**roue** [ʀu] nf wheel; **roue de secours**
spare wheel

**rouer** [ʀwe] vt: **~ qn de coups** to give
sb a thrashing

**rouge** [ʀuʒ] adj, nm/f red ▷ nm red;
(vin) **~** red wine; **sur la liste ~** ex-
directory (BRIT), unlisted (US); **passer
au ~** (signal) to go red; (automobiliste)
to go through a red light; **rouge à joue**
blusher; **rouge (à lèvres)** lipstick;
**rouge-gorge** nm robin (redbreast)

**rougeole** [ʀuʒɔl] nf measles sg

**rougeoyer** [ʀuʒwaje] vi to glow red

**rouget** [ʀuʒɛ] nm mullet

**rougeur** [ʀuʒœʀ] nf redness; (Méd:
tache) red blotch

**rougir** [ʀuʒiʀ] vi to turn red; (de honte,
timidité) to blush, flush; (de plaisir, colère)
to flush

**rouille** [ʀuj] nf rust; **rouillé, e** adj rusty;
**rouiller** vt to rust ▷ vi to rust, go rusty

**roulant, e** [ʀulɑ̃, ɑ̃t] adj (meuble) on

wheels; (*tapis etc*) moving; **escalier ~** escalator

**rouleau, x** [ʀulo] *nm* roll; (*à mise en plis, à peinture, vague*) roller; **rouleau à pâtisserie** rolling pin

**roulement** [ʀulmɑ̃] *nm* (*rotation*) rotation; (*bruit*) rumbling *no pl*, rumble; **travailler par ~** to work on a rota (BRIT) *ou* rotation (US) basis; **roulement (à billes)** ball bearings *pl*; **roulement de tambour** drum roll

**rouler** [ʀule] *vt* to roll; (*papier, tapis*) to roll up; (*Culin: pâte*) to roll out; (*fam: duper*) to do, con ▷ *vi* (*bille, boule*) to roll; (*voiture, train*) to go, run; (*automobiliste*) to drive; (*bateau*) to roll; **se ~ dans** (*boue*) to roll in; (*couverture*) to roll o.s. (up) in

**roulette** [ʀulɛt] *nf* (*de table, fauteuil*) castor; (*de dentiste*) drill; (*jeu*) roulette; **à ~s** on castors; **ça a marché comme sur des ~s** (*fam*) it went off very smoothly

**roulis** [ʀuli] *nm* roll(ing)

**roulotte** [ʀulɔt] *nf* caravan

**roumain, e** [ʀumɛ̃, ɛn] *adj* Rumanian ▷ *nm/f*: **R~, e** Rumanian

**Roumanie** [ʀumani] *nf* Rumania

**rouquin, e** [ʀukɛ̃, in] (*péj*) *nm/f* redhead

**rouspéter** [ʀuspete] (*fam*) *vi* to moan

**rousse** [ʀus] *adj voir* **roux**

**roussir** [ʀusiʀ] *vt* to scorch ▷ *vi* (*Culin*): **faire ~** to brown

**route** [ʀut] *nf* road; (*fig: chemin*) way; (*itinéraire, parcours*) route; (*fig: voie*) road, path; **il y a 3h de ~** it's a 3-hour ride *ou* journey; **en ~** on the way; **en ~!** let's go!; **mettre en ~** to start up; **se mettre en ~** to set off; **quelle ~ dois-je prendre pour aller à ...?** which road do I take for ...?; **route nationale** ≈ A road (BRIT), ≈ state highway (US); **routier, -ière** *adj cpd* ▷ *nm* (*camionneur*) (long-distance) lorry (BRIT) *ou* truck (US) driver; (*restaurant*) ≈ transport café (BRIT), ≈ truck stop (US)

**routine** [ʀutin] *nf* routine; **routinier, -ière** (*péj*) *adj* (*activité*) humdrum;

(*personne*) addicted to routine

**rouvrir** [ʀuvʀiʀ] *vt, vi* to reopen, open again; **se rouvrir** *vi* to reopen, open again

**roux, rousse** [ʀu, ʀus] *adj* red; (*personne*) red-haired ▷ *nm/f* redhead

**royal, e, -aux** [ʀwajal, o] *adj* royal; (*cadeau etc*) fit for a king

**royaume** [ʀwajom] *nm* kingdom; (*fig*) realm; **le Royaume-Uni** the United Kingdom

**royauté** [ʀwajote] *nf* (*régime*) monarchy

**ruban** [ʀybɑ̃] *nm* ribbon; **ruban adhésif** adhesive tape

**rubéole** [ʀybeɔl] *nf* German measles *sg*, rubella

**rubis** [ʀybi] *nm* ruby

**rubrique** [ʀybʀik] *nf* (*titre, catégorie*) heading; (*Presse: article*) column

**ruche** [ʀyʃ] *nf* hive

**rude** [ʀyd] *adj* (*au toucher*) rough; (*métier, tâche*) hard, tough; (*climat*) severe, harsh; (*bourru*) harsh, rough; (*fruste: manières*) rugged, tough; (*fam: fameux*) jolly good; **rudement** (*fam*) *adv* (*très*) terribly

**rudimentaire** [ʀydimɑ̃tɛʀ] *adj* rudimentary, basic

**rudiments** [ʀydimɑ̃] *nmpl*: **avoir des ~ d'anglais** to have a smattering of English

**rue** [ʀy] *nf* street

**ruée** [ʀɥe] *nf* rush

**ruelle** [ʀɥɛl] *nf* alley(-way)

**ruer** [ʀɥe] *vi* (*cheval*) to kick out; **se ruer** *vi*: **se ~ sur** to pounce on; **se ~ vers/dans/hors de** to rush *ou* dash towards/into/out of

**rugby** [ʀygbi] *nm* rugby (football)

**rugir** [ʀyʒiʀ] *vi* to roar

**rugueux, -euse** [ʀygø, øz] *adj* rough

**ruine** [ʀɥin] *nf* ruin; **ruiner** *vt* to ruin; **ruineux, -euse** *adj* ruinous

**ruisseau, x** [ʀɥiso] *nm* stream, brook

**ruisseler** [ʀɥis(ə)le] *vi* to stream

**rumeur** [ʀymœʀ] *nf* (*nouvelle*) rumour; (*bruit confus*) rumbling

**ruminer** [ʀymine] *vt* (*herbe*) to ruminate; (*fig*) to ruminate on *ou* over, chew over

**rupture** [ʀyptyʀ] *nf* (*séparation, désunion*) break-up, split; (*de négociations etc*) breakdown; (*de contrat*) breach; (*dans continuité*) break

**rural, e, -aux** [ʀyʀal, o] *adj* rural, country *cpd*

**ruse** [ʀyz] *nf*: **la ~** cunning, craftiness; (*pour tromper*) trickery; **une ~** a trick, a ruse; **rusé, e** *adj* cunning, crafty

**russe** [ʀys] *adj* Russian ▷ *nm/f*: **R~** Russian ▷ *nm* (*Ling*) Russian

**Russie** [ʀysi] *nf*: **la ~** Russia

**rustine®** [ʀystin] *nf* rubber repair patch (*for bicycle tyre*)

**rustique** [ʀystik] *adj* rustic

**rythme** [ʀitm] *nm* rhythm; (*vitesse*) rate; (: *de la vie*) pace, tempo; **rythmé, e** *adj* rhythmic(al)

# S

**s'** [s] *pron voir* **se**

**sa** [sa] *adj voir* **son¹**

**sable** [sabl] *nm* sand

**sablé** [sable] *nm* shortbread biscuit

**sabler** [sable] *vt* (*contre le verglas*) to grit; **~ le champagne** to drink champagne

**sabot** [sabo] *nm* clog; (*de cheval*) hoof; **sabot de frein** brake shoe

**saboter** [sabɔte] *vt* to sabotage; (*bâcler*) to make a mess of, botch

**sac** [sak] *nm* bag; (*à charbon etc*) sack; **mettre à ~** to sack; **sac à dos** rucksack; **sac à main** handbag; **sac de couchage** sleeping bag; **sac de voyage** travelling bag

**saccadé, e** [sakade] *adj* jerky; (*respiration*) spasmodic

**saccager** [sakaʒe] *vt* (*piller*) to sack; (*dévaster*) to create havoc in

**saccharine** [sakaʀin] *nf* saccharin

**sachet** [saʃɛ] *nm* (small) bag; (*de sucre, café*) sachet; **du potage en ~** packet soup; **sachet de thé** tea bag

**sacoche** [sakɔʃ] *nf* (*gén*) bag; (*de bicyclette*) saddlebag

**sacré, e** [sakʀe] *adj* sacred; (*fam: satané*) blasted; (: *fameux*): **un ~ toupet** a heck of a cheek

**sacrement** [sakʀəmɑ̃] *nm* sacrament

**sacrifice** [sakʀifis] *nm* sacrifice; **sacrifier** *vt* to sacrifice

**sacristie** [sakʀisti] *nf* (*catholique*) sacristy; (*protestante*) vestry

**sadique** [sadik] *adj* sadistic

**safran** [safʀɑ̃] *nm* saffron

**sage** [saʒ] *adj* wise; (*enfant*) good

**sage-femme** [saʒfam] *nf* midwife

**sagesse** [saʒɛs] *nf* wisdom

**Sagittaire** [saʒitɛʀ] *nm*: **le ~** Sagittarius

**Sahara** [saaʀa] *nm*: **le ~** the Sahara (desert)

**saignant, e** [sɛɲɑ̃, ɑ̃t] *adj* (*viande*) rare

**saigner** [seɲe] *vi* to bleed ▷ *vt* to bleed; (*animal*) to kill (by bleeding); **~ du nez** to have a nosebleed

**saillir** [sajiʀ] *vi* to project, stick out; (*veine, muscle*) to bulge

**sain, e** [sɛ̃, sɛn] *adj* healthy; **~ et sauf** safe and sound, unharmed; **~ d'esprit** sound in mind, sane

**saindoux** [sɛ̃du] *nm* lard

**saint, e** [sɛ̃, sɛ̃t] *adj* holy ▷ *nm/f* saint; **le Saint Esprit** the Holy Spirit *ou* Ghost; **la Sainte Vierge** the Blessed Virgin; **la Saint-Sylvestre** New Year's Eve; **sainteté** *nf* holiness

**sais** *etc* [sɛ] *vb voir* **savoir**

**saisie** [sezi] *nf* seizure; **saisie (de données)** (data) capture

**saisir** [seziʀ] *vt* to take hold of, grab; (*fig: occasion*) to seize; (*comprendre*) to grasp; (*entendre*) to get, catch; (*données*) to capture; (*Culin*) to fry quickly; (*Jur: biens, publication*) to seize; **saisissant, e** *adj* startling, striking

**saison** [sɛzɔ̃] *nf* season; **haute/basse/morte ~** high/low/slack season; **saisonnier, -ière** *adj* seasonal

**salade** [salad] *nf* (*Bot*) lettuce *etc*; (*Culin*) (green) salad; (*fam: confusion*) tangle, muddle; **salade composée** mixed salad; **salade de fruits** fruit salad; **saladier** *nm* (salad) bowl

**salaire** [salɛʀ] *nm* (*annuel, mensuel*) salary; (*hebdomadaire, journalier*) pay, wages *pl*; **salaire minimum interprofessionnel de croissance** index-linked guaranteed minimum wage

**salarié, e** [salaʀje] *nm/f* salaried employee; wage-earner

**salaud** [salo] (*fam!*) *nm* sod (*!*), bastard (*!*)

**sale** [sal] *adj* dirty, filthy; (*fam: mauvais*) nasty

**salé, e** [sale] *adj* (*mer, goût*) salty; (*Culin: amandes, beurre etc*) salted; (: *gâteaux*) savoury; (*fam: grivois*) spicy; (: *facture*) steep

**saler** [sale] *vt* to salt

**saleté** [salte] *nf* (*état*) dirtiness; (*crasse*) dirt, filth; (*tache etc*) dirt *no pl*; (*fam: méchanceté*) dirty trick; (: *camelote*) rubbish *no pl*; (: *obscénité*) filthy thing (to say)

**salière** [saljɛʀ] *nf* saltcellar

**salir** [saliʀ] *vt* to (make) dirty; (*fig: quelqu'un*) to soil the reputation of; **se salir** *vi* to get dirty; **salissant, e** *adj* (*tissu*) which shows the dirt; (*travail*) dirty, messy

**salle** [sal] *nf* room; (*d'hôpital*) ward; (*de restaurant*) dining room; (*d'un cinéma*) auditorium; (: *public*) audience; **salle à manger** dining room; **salle d'attente** waiting room; **salle de bain(s)** bathroom; **salle de classe** classroom; **salle de concert** concert hall; **salle d'eau** shower-room; **salle d'embarquement** (*à l'aéroport*) departure lounge; **salle de jeux** (*pour enfants*) playroom; **salle de séjour** living room; **salle des ventes** saleroom

**salon** [salɔ̃] *nm* lounge, sitting room; (*mobilier*) lounge suite; (*exposition*) exhibition, show; **salon de coiffure** hairdressing salon; **salon de thé** tearoom

**salope** [salɔp] (*fam!*) *nf* bitch (*!*);

**saloperie** [*fam!*] *nf* (*action*) dirty trick; (*chose sans valeur*) rubbish *no pl*
**salopette** [salɔpɛt] *nf* dungarees *pl*; (*d'ouvrier*) overall(s)
**salsifis** [salsifi] *nm* salsify
**salubre** [salybʀ] *adj* healthy, salubrious
**saluer** [salɥe] *vt* (*pour dire bonjour, fig*) to greet; (*pour dire au revoir*) to take one's leave; (*Mil*) to salute
**salut** [saly] *nm* (*geste*) wave; (*parole*) greeting; (*Mil*) salute; (*sauvegarde*) safety; (*Rel*) salvation ▷ *excl* (*fam: bonjour*) hi (there); (: *au revoir*) see you, bye
**salutations** [salytasjɔ̃] *nfpl* greetings; **Veuillez agréer, Monsieur, mes ~ distinguées** yours faithfully
**samedi** [samdi] *nm* Saturday
**SAMU** [samy] *sigle m* (= *service d'assistance médicale d'urgence*) ≈ ambulance (service) (*BRIT*), ≈ paramedics *pl* (*US*)
**sanction** [sɑ̃ksjɔ̃] *nf* sanction; **sanctionner** *vt* (*loi, usage*) to sanction; (*punir*) to punish
**sandale** [sɑ̃dal] *nf* sandal
**sandwich** [sɑ̃dwi(t)ʃ] *nm* sandwich; **je voudrais un ~ au jambon/fromage** I'd like a ham/cheese sandwich
**sang** [sɑ̃] *nm* blood; **en ~** covered in blood; **se faire du mauvais ~** to fret, get in a state; **sang-froid** *nm* calm, sangfroid; **de sang-froid** in cold blood; **sanglant, e** *adj* bloody
**sangle** [sɑ̃gl] *nf* strap
**sanglier** [sɑ̃glije] *nm* (wild) boar
**sanglot** [sɑ̃glo] *nm* sob; **sangloter** *vi* to sob
**sangsue** [sɑ̃sy] *nf* leech
**sanguin, e** [sɑ̃gɛ̃, in] *adj* blood *cpd*
**sanitaire** [sanitɛʀ] *adj* health *cpd*; **sanitaires** *nmpl* (*lieu*) bathroom *sg*
**sans** [sɑ̃] *prép* without; **un pull ~ manches** a sleeveless jumper; **~ faute** without fail; **~ arrêt** without a break; **~ ça** (*fam*) otherwise; **~ qu'il s'en aperçoive** without him

*ou* his noticing; **sans-abri** *nmpl* homeless; **sans-emploi** *nm/f inv* unemployed person; **les sans-emploi** the unemployed; **sans-gêne** *adj inv* inconsiderate
**santé** [sɑ̃te] *nf* health; **en bonne ~** in good health; **boire à la ~ de qn** to drink (to) sb's health; **à ta/votre ~!** cheers!
**saoudien, ne** [saudjɛ̃, jɛn] *adj* Saudi Arabian ▷ *nm/f*: **S~, ne** Saudi Arabian
**saoul, e** [su, sul] *adj* = **soûl**
**saper** [sape] *vt* to undermine, sap
**sapeur-pompier** [sapœʀpɔ̃pje] *nm* fireman
**saphir** [safiʀ] *nm* sapphire
**sapin** [sapɛ̃] *nm* fir (tree); (*bois*) fir; **sapin de Noël** Christmas tree
**sarcastique** [saʀkastik] *adj* sarcastic
**Sardaigne** [saʀdɛɲ] *nf*: **la ~** Sardinia
**sardine** [saʀdin] *nf* sardine
**SARL** *sigle f* (= *société à responsabilité limitée*) ≈ plc (*BRIT*), ≈ Inc. (*US*)
**sarrasin** [saʀazɛ̃] *nm* buckwheat
**satané, e** [satane] (*fam*) *adj* confounded
**satellite** [satelit] *nm* satellite
**satin** [satɛ̃] *nm* satin
**satire** [satiʀ] *nf* satire; **satirique** *adj* satirical
**satisfaction** [satisfaksjɔ̃] *nf* satisfaction
**satisfaire** [satisfɛʀ] *vt* to satisfy; **~ à** (*conditions*) to meet; **satisfaisant, e** *adj* (*acceptable*) satisfactory; **satisfait, e** *adj* satisfied; **satisfait de** happy *ou* satisfied with
**saturer** [satyʀe] *vt* to saturate
**sauce** [sos] *nf* sauce; (*avec un rôti*) gravy; **sauce tomate** tomato sauce; **saucière** *nf* sauceboat
**saucisse** [sosis] *nf* sausage
**saucisson** [sosisɔ̃] *nm* (slicing) sausage
**sauf, sauve** [sof, sov] *adj* unharmed, unhurt; (*fig: honneur*) intact, saved ▷ *prép* except; **laisser la vie sauve à qn** to spare sb's life; **~ si** (*à moins que*) unless; **~ erreur** if I'm not mistaken;

**~ avis contraire** unless you hear to the contrary

**sauge** [soʒ] nf sage

**saugrenu, e** [sogʀəny] adj preposterous

**saule** [sol] nm willow (tree)

**saumon** [somɔ̃] nm salmon inv

**saupoudrer** [sopudʀe] vt: **~ qch de** to sprinkle sth with

**saur** [sɔʀ] adj m: **hareng ~** smoked herring, kipper

**saut** [so] nm jump; (discipline sportive) jumping; **faire un ~ chez qn** to pop over to sb's (place); **saut à l'élastique** bungee jumping; **saut à la perche** pole vaulting; **saut en hauteur/longueur** high/long jump; **saut périlleux** somersault

**sauter** [sote] vi to jump, leap; (exploser) to blow up, explode; (: fusibles) to blow; (se détacher) to pop out (ou off) ▷ vt to jump (over), leap (over); (fig: omettre) to skip, miss (out); **faire ~** to blow up; (Culin) to sauté; **~ à la corde** to skip; **~ au cou de qn** to fly into sb's arms; **~ sur une occasion** to jump at an opportunity; **~ aux yeux** to be (quite) obvious

**sauterelle** [sotʀɛl] nf grasshopper

**sautiller** [sotije] vi (oiseau) to hop; (enfant) to skip

**sauvage** [sovaʒ] adj (gén) wild; (peuplade) savage; (farouche: personne) unsociable; (barbare) wild, savage; (non officiel) unauthorized, unofficial; **faire du camping ~** to camp in the wild ▷ nm/f savage; (timide) unsociable type

**sauve** [sov] adj f voir **sauf**

**sauvegarde** [sovgaʀd] nf safeguard; (Inform) backup; **sauvegarder** vt to safeguard; (Inform: enregistrer) to save; (: copier) to back up

**sauve-qui-peut** [sovkipø] excl run for your life!

**sauver** [sove] vt to save; (porter secours à) to rescue; (récupérer) to salvage, rescue; **se sauver** vi (s'enfuir) to run away; (fam: partir) to be off; **sauvetage**

nm rescue; **sauveteur** nm rescuer; **sauvette: à la sauvette** adv (se marier etc) hastily, hurriedly; **sauveur** nm saviour (BRIT), savior (US)

**savant, e** [savɑ̃, ɑ̃t] adj scholarly, learned ▷ nm scientist

**saveur** [savœʀ] nf flavour; (fig) savour

**savoir** [savwaʀ] vt to know; (être capable de): **il sait nager** he can swim ▷ nm knowledge; **se savoir** vi (être connu) to be known; **je ne sais pas** I don't know; **je ne sais pas parler français** I don't speak French; **savez-vous où je peux ...?** do you know where I can ...?; **je n'en sais rien** I (really) don't know; **à ~** that is, namely; **faire ~ qch à qn** to let sb know sth; **pas que je sache** not as far as I know

**savon** [savɔ̃] nm (produit) soap; (morceau) bar of soap; (fam): **passer un ~ à qn** to give sb a good dressing-down; **savonner** vt to soap; **savonnette** nf bar of soap

**savourer** [savuʀe] vt to savour; **savoureux, -euse** adj tasty; (fig: anecdote) spicy, juicy

**saxo(phone)** [saksɔ(fɔn)] nm sax(ophone)

**scabreux, -euse** [skabʀø, øz] adj risky; (indécent) improper, shocking

**scandale** [skɑ̃dal] nm scandal; **faire un ~** (scène) to make a scene; (Jur) to create a disturbance; **faire ~** to scandalize people; **scandaleux, -euse** adj scandalous, outrageous

**scandinave** [skɑ̃dinav] adj Scandinavian ▷ nm/f: **S~** Scandinavian

**Scandinavie** [skɑ̃dinavi] nf Scandinavia

**scarabée** [skaʀabe] nm beetle

**scarlatine** [skaʀlatin] nf scarlet fever

**scarole** [skaʀɔl] nf endive

**sceau, x** [so] nm seal

**sceller** [sele] vt to seal

**scénario** [senaʀjo] nm scenario

**scène** [sɛn] nf (gén) scene; (estrade, fig: théâtre) stage; **entrer en ~** to come on stage; **mettre en ~** (Théâtre) to stage;

(*Cinéma*) to direct; **faire une ~ (à qn)** to make a scene (with sb); **scène de ménage** domestic scene

**sceptique** [sɛptik] *adj* sceptical

**schéma** [ʃema] *nm* (*diagramme*) diagram, sketch; **schématique** *adj* diagrammatic(al), schematic; (*fig*) oversimplified

**sciatique** [sjatik] *nf* sciatica

**scie** [si] *nf* saw

**sciemment** [sjamɑ̃] *adv* knowingly

**science** [sjɑ̃s] *nf* science; (*savoir*) knowledge; **sciences humaines/ sociales** social sciences; **sciences naturelles** (*Scol*) natural science *sg*, biology *sg*; **sciences po** political science *ou* studies *pl*; **science-fiction** *nf* science fiction; **scientifique** *adj* scientific ▷ *nm/f* scientist; (*étudiant*) science student

**scier** [sje] *vt* to saw; (*retrancher*) to saw off; **scierie** *nf* sawmill

**scintiller** [sɛ̃tije] *vi* to sparkle; (*étoile*) to twinkle

**sciure** [sjyʀ] *nf*: **~ (de bois)** sawdust

**sclérose** [skleʀoz] *nf*: **sclérose en plaques** multiple sclerosis

**scolaire** [skɔlɛʀ] *adj* school *cpd*; **scolariser** *vt* to provide with schooling/schools; **scolarité** *nf* schooling

**scooter** [skutœʀ] *nm* (motor) scooter

**score** [skɔʀ] *nm* score

**scorpion** [skɔʀpjɔ̃] *nm* (*signe*): **le S~** Scorpio

**scotch** [skɔtʃ] *nm* (*whisky*) scotch, whisky; **S~®** (*adhésif*) Sellotape® (BRIT), Scotch® tape (US)

**scout, e** [skut] *adj, nm* scout

**script** [skʀipt] *nm* (*écriture*) printing; (*Cinéma*) (shooting) script

**scrupule** [skʀypyl] *nm* scruple

**scruter** [skʀyte] *vt* to scrutinize; (*l'obscurité*) to peer into

**scrutin** [skʀytɛ̃] *nm* (*vote*) ballot; (*ensemble des opérations*) poll

**sculpter** [skylte] *vt* to sculpt; (*bois*) to carve; **sculpteur** *nm* sculptor

**sculpture** *nf* sculpture

**SDF** *sigle m*: **sans domicile fixe** homeless person; **les ~** the homeless

 **MOT-CLÉ**

**se** [sə], **s'** *pron* **1** (*emploi réfléchi*) oneself; (: *masc*) himself; (: *fém*) herself; (: *sujet non humain*) itself; (: *pl*) themselves; **se savonner** to soap o.s.

**2** (*réciproque*) one another, each other; **ils s'aiment** they love one another *ou* each other

**3** (*passif*): **cela se répare facilement** it is easily repaired

**4** (*possessif*): **se casser la jambe/se laver les mains** to break one's leg/ wash one's hands

**séance** [seɑ̃s] *nf* (*d'assemblée*) meeting, session; (*de tribunal*) sitting, session; (*musicale, Cinéma, Théâtre*) performance

**seau, x** [so] *nm* bucket, pail

**sec, sèche** [sɛk, sɛʃ] *adj* dry; (*raisins, figues*) dried; (*cœur: insensible*) hard, cold ▷ *nm*: **tenir au ~** to keep in a dry place ▷ *adv* hard; **je le bois ~** I drink it straight *ou* neat; **à ~** (*puits*) dried up

**sécateur** [sekatœʀ] *nm* secateurs *pl* (BRIT), shears *pl*

**sèche** [sɛʃ] *adj f voir* **sec**; **sèche-cheveux** *nm inv* hair-drier; **sèche-linge** *nm inv* tumble dryer; **sèchement** *adv* (*répondre*) drily

**sécher** [seʃe] *vt* to dry; (*dessécher: peau, blé*) to dry (out); (: *étang*) to dry up; (*fam: cours*) to skip ▷ *vi* to dry; to dry out; to dry up; (*fam: candidat*) to be stumped; **se sécher** (*après le bain*) to dry o.s.; **sécheresse** *nf* dryness; (*absence de pluie*) drought; **séchoir** *nm* drier

**second, e** [s(ə)gɔ̃, ɔ̃d] *adj* second ▷ *nm* (*assistant*) second in command; (*Navig*) first mate ▷ *nf* (*Scol*) year 11 (BRIT), tenth grade (US); (*Aviat, Rail etc*) second class; **voyager en ~e** to travel second-class; **secondaire** *adj* secondary; **seconde²** *nf* second; **seconder** *vt* to assist

**secouer** [s(ə)kwe] *vt* to shake;
(*passagers*) to rock; (*traumatiser*) to
shake (up)

**secourir** [s(ə)kuʀiʀ] *vt* (*venir en aide à*)
to assist, aid; **secourisme** *nm* first aid;
**secouriste** *nm/f* first-aid worker

**secours** [s(ə)kuʀ] *nm* help, aid,
assistance ▷ *nmpl* aid *sg*; **au ~!** help!;
**appeler au ~** to shout *ou* call for help;
**porter ~ à qn** to give sb assistance,
help sb; **les premiers ~** first aid *sg*

● **ÉQUIPES DE SECOURS**
●
● Emergency phone numbers can
● be dialled free from public phones.
● For the police ('la police') dial 17; for
● medical services ('le SAMU') dial
● 15; for the fire brigade ('les sapeurs
● pompiers'), dial 18.

**secousse** [s(ə)kus] *nf* jolt, bump;
(*électrique*) shock; (*fig: psychologique*)
jolt, shock

**secret, -ète** [səkʀɛ, ɛt] *adj* secret;
(*fig: renfermé*) reticent, reserved
▷ *nm* secret; (*discrétion absolue*): **le ~**
secrecy; **en ~** in secret, secretly; **secret
professionel** professional secrecy

**secrétaire** [s(ə)kʀetɛʀ] *nm/f* secretary
▷ *nm* (*meuble*) writing desk; **secrétaire
de direction** private *ou* personal
secretary; **secrétaire d'État** junior
minister; **secrétariat** *nm* (*profession*)
secretarial work; (*bureau*) office;
(: *d'organisation internationale*)
secretariat

**secteur** [sɛktœʀ] *nm* sector; (*zone*)
area; (*Élec*): **branché sur ~** plugged into
the mains (supply)

**section** [sɛksjɔ̃] *nf* section; (*de parcours
d'autobus*) fare stage; (*Mil: unité*)
platoon; **sectionner** *vt* to sever

**sécu** [seky] *abr f* = **sécurité sociale**

**sécurité** [sekyʀite] *nf* (*absence de
danger*) safety; (*absence de troubles*)
security; **système de ~** security
system; **être en ~** to be safe; **la sécurité**

**routière** road safety; **la sécurité
sociale** ≈ (the) Social Security (BRIT),
≈ Welfare (US)

**sédentaire** [sedɑ̃tɛʀ] *adj* sedentary

**séduction** [sedyksjɔ̃] *nf* seduction;
(*charme, attrait*) appeal, charm

**séduire** [seduiʀ] *vt* to charm; (*femme:
abuser de*) to seduce; **séduisant, e** *adj*
(*femme*) seductive; (*homme, offre*) very
attractive

**ségrégation** [segʀegasjɔ̃] *nf*
segregation

**seigle** [sɛgl] *nm* rye

**seigneur** [sɛɲœʀ] *nm* lord

**sein** [sɛ̃] *nm* breast; (*entrailles*) womb;
**au ~ de** (*équipe, institution*) within

**séisme** [seism] *nm* earthquake

**seize** [sɛz] *num* sixteen; **seizième** *num*
sixteenth

**séjour** [seʒuʀ] *nm* stay; (*pièce*) living
room; **séjourner** *vi* to stay

**sel** [sɛl] *nm* salt; (*fig: piquant*) spice

**sélection** [selɛksjɔ̃] *nf* selection;
**sélectionner** *vt* to select

**self-service** [sɛlfsɛʀvis] *adj, nm*
self-service

**selle** [sɛl] *nf* saddle; **selles** *nfpl* (*Méd*)
stools; **seller** *vt* to saddle

**selon** [s(ə)lɔ̃] *prép* according to; (*en se
conformant à*) in accordance with; **~ que**
according to whether; **~ moi** as I see it

**semaine** [s(ə)mɛn] *nf* week; **en ~**
during the week, on weekdays

**semblable** [sɑ̃blabl] *adj* similar; (*de
ce genre*): **de ~s mésaventures** such
mishaps ▷ *nm* fellow creature *ou* man;
**~ à** similar to, like

**semblant** [sɑ̃blɑ̃] *nm*: **un ~ de ...** a
semblance of ...; **faire ~ (de faire)** to
pretend (to do)

**sembler** [sɑ̃ble] *vb* +*attrib* to seem ▷ *vb
impers*: **il semble (bien) que/inutile
de** it (really) seems *ou* appears that/
useless to; **il me semble que** it seems
to me that; **comme bon lui semble**
as he sees fit

**semelle** [s(ə)mɛl] *nf* sole; (*intérieure*)
insole, inner sole

**semer** [s(ə)me] *vt* to sow; (*fig: éparpiller*) to scatter; (: *confusion*) to spread; (*fam: poursuivants*) to lose, shake off; **semé de** (*difficultés*) riddled with

**semestre** [s(ə)mɛstʀ] *nm* half-year; (*Scol*) semester

**séminaire** [seminɛʀ] *nm* seminar

**semi-remorque** [səmiʀəmɔʀk] *nm* articulated lorry (BRIT), semi(trailer) (US)

**semoule** [s(ə)mul] *nf* semolina

**sénat** [sena] *nm* senate; **sénateur** *nm* senator

**Sénégal** [senegal] *nm*: **le ~** Senegal

**sens** [sɑ̃s] *nm* (*Physiol*,) sense; (*signification*) meaning, sense; (*direction*) direction; **à mon ~** to my mind; **dans le ~ des aiguilles d'une montre** clockwise; **dans le ~ contraire des aiguilles d'une montre** anticlockwise; **dans le mauvais ~** (*aller*) the wrong way, in the wrong direction; **le bon ~** common sense; **sens dessus dessous** upside down; **sens interdit/unique** one-way street

**sensation** [sɑ̃sasjɔ̃] *nf* sensation; **à ~** (*péj*) sensational; **faire ~** to cause *ou* create a sensation; **sensationnel, le** *adj* (*fam*) fantastic, terrific

**sensé, e** [sɑ̃se] *adj* sensible

**sensibiliser** [sɑ̃sibilize] *vt*: **~ qn à** to make sb sensitive to

**sensibilité** [sɑ̃sibilite] *nf* sensitivity

**sensible** [sɑ̃sibl] *adj* sensitive; (*aux sens*) perceptible; (*appréciable: différence, progrès*) appreciable, noticeable; **~ à** sensitive to; **sensiblement** *adv* (*à peu près*): **ils sont sensiblement du même âge** they are approximately the same age; **sensiblerie** *nf* sentimentality

▌ Attention à ne pas traduire *sensible* par le mot anglais *sensible*.

**sensuel, le** [sɑ̃sɥɛl] *adj* (*personne*) sensual; (*musique*) sensuous

**sentence** [sɑ̃tɑ̃s] *nf* (*jugement*) sentence

**sentier** [sɑ̃tje] *nm* path

**sentiment** [sɑ̃timɑ̃] *nm* feeling; **recevez mes ~s respectueux** (*personne nommée*) yours sincerely; (*personne non nommée*) yours faithfully; **sentimental, e, -aux** *adj* sentimental; (*vie, aventure*) love *cpd*

**sentinelle** [sɑ̃tinɛl] *nf* sentry

**sentir** [sɑ̃tiʀ] *vt* (*par l'odorat*) to smell; (*par le goût*) to taste; (*au toucher, fig*) to feel; (*répandre une odeur de*) to smell of; (: *ressemblance*) to smell like ▷ *vi* to smell; **~ mauvais** to smell bad; **se ~ bien** to feel good; **se ~ mal** (*être indisposé*) to feel unwell *ou* ill; **se ~ le courage/la force de faire** to feel brave/strong enough to do; **il ne peut pas le ~** (*fam*) he can't stand him; **je ne me sens pas bien** I don't feel well

**séparation** [separasjɔ̃] *nf* separation; (*cloison*) division, partition

**séparé, e** [separe] *adj* (*distinct*) separate; (*époux*) separated; **séparément** *adv* separately

**séparer** [separe] *vt* to separate; (*désunir*) to drive apart; (*détacher*): **~ qch de** to pull sth (off) from; **se séparer** *vi* (*époux, amis*) to separate, part; (*se diviser: route etc*) to divide; **se ~ de** (*époux*) to separate *ou* part from; (*employé, objet personnel*) to part with

**sept** [sɛt] *num* seven; **septante** (BELGIQUE, SUISSE) *adj inv* seventy

**septembre** [sɛptɑ̃bʀ] *nm* September

**septicémie** [sɛptisemi] *nf* blood poisoning, septicaemia

**septième** [sɛtjɛm] *num* seventh

**séquelles** [sekɛl] *nfpl* after-effects; (*fig*) aftermath *sg*

**serbe** [sɛʀb(ə)] *adj* Serbian

**Serbie** [sɛʀbi] *nf*: **la ~** Serbia

**serein, e** [səʀɛ̃, ɛn] *adj* serene

**sergent** [sɛʀʒɑ̃] *nm* sergeant

**série** [seʀi] *nf* series *inv*; (*de clés, casseroles, outils*) set; (*catégorie: Sport*) rank; **en ~** in quick succession; (*Comm*) mass *cpd*; **de ~** (*voiture*) standard; **hors ~** (*Comm*) custom-built; **série noire** (*crime*) thriller

**sérieusement** [seʀjøzmɑ̃] *adv* seriously

**sérieux, -euse** [seʀjø, jøz] adj serious; (élève, employé) reliable, responsible; (client, maison) reliable, dependable ▷ nm seriousness; (d'une entreprise etc) reliability; **garder son ~** to keep a straight face; **prendre qch/qn au ~** to take sth/sb seriously

**serin** [s(ə)ʀɛ̃] nm canary

**seringue** [s(ə)ʀɛ̃g] nf syringe

**serment** [seʀmɑ̃] nm (juré) oath; (promesse) pledge, vow

**sermon** [seʀmɔ̃] nm sermon

**séropositif, -ive** [seʀopozitif, iv] adj (Méd) HIV positive

**serpent** [seʀpɑ̃] nm snake; **serpenter** vi to wind

**serpillière** [seʀpijeʀ] nf floorcloth

**serre** [seʀ] nf (Agr) greenhouse; **serres** nfpl (griffes) claws, talons

**serré, e** [seʀe] adj (habits) tight; (fig: lutte, match) tight, close-fought; (passagers etc) (tightly) packed; (réseau) dense; **avoir le cœur ~** to have a heavy heart

**serrer** [seʀe] vt (tenir) to grip ou hold tight; (comprimer, coincer) to squeeze; (poings, mâchoires) to clench; (suj: vêtement) to be too tight for; (ceinture, nœud, vis) to tighten ▷ vi: **- à droite** to keep ou get over to the right

**serrure** [seʀyʀ] nf lock; **serrurier** nm locksmith

**sert** etc [seʀ] vb voir **servir**

**servante** [seʀvɑ̃t] nf (maid)servant

**serveur, -euse** [seʀvœʀ, øz] nm/f waiter (waitress)

**serviable** [seʀvjabl] adj obliging, willing to help

**service** [seʀvis] nm service; (assortiment de vaisselle) set, service; (bureau: de la vente etc) department, section; (travail) duty; **premier ~** (série de repas) first sitting; **être de ~** to be on duty; **faire le ~** to serve; **rendre un ~ à qn** to do sb a favour; (objet: s'avérer utile) to come in useful ou handy for sb; **mettre en ~** to put into service ou operation; **~ compris/non compris**

service included/not included; **hors ~** out of order; **service après vente** after sales service; **service d'ordre** police (ou stewards) in charge of maintaining order; **service militaire** military service; see note; **services secrets** secret service sg

● **SERVICE MILITAIRE**
●
● Until 1997, French men over the age
● of 18 who were passed as fit, and
● who were not in full-time higher
● education, were required to do
● ten months' "service militaire".
● Conscientious objectors were
● required to do two years' community
● service.
● Since 1997, military service has been
● suspended in France. However, all
● sixteen-year-olds, both male and
● female, are required to register for
● a compulsory one-day training
● course, the "JAPD" ("journée d'appel
● de préparation à la défense"), which
● covers basic information on the
● principles and organization of
● defence in France, and also advises
● on career opportunities in the
● military and in the voluntary sector.
● Young people must attend the
● training day before their eighteenth
● birthday.

**serviette** [seʀvjɛt] nf (de table) (table) napkin, serviette; (de toilette) towel; (porte-documents) briefcase; **serviette hygiénique** sanitary towel

**servir** [seʀviʀ] vt to serve; (au restaurant) to wait on; (au magasin) to serve, attend to ▷ vi (Tennis) to serve; (Cartes) to deal; **se servir** vi (prendre d'un plat) to help o.s.; **vous êtes servi?** are you being served?; **~ à qn** (diplôme, livre) to be of use to sb; **~ à qch/faire** (outil etc) to be used for sth/doing; **ça ne sert à rien** it's no use; **~ (à qn) de** to serve as (for sb); **se ~ de** (plat) to help o.s. to;

(*voiture, outil, relations*) to use; **sers-toi!**
help yourself!
**serviteur** [sɛʀvitœʀ] *nm* servant
**ses** [se] *adj voir* **son'**
**seuil** [sœj] *nm* doorstep; (*fig*) threshold
**seul, e** [sœl] *adj* (*sans compagnie*) alone;
(*unique*): **un ~ livre** only one book, a
single book ▷ *adv* (*vivre*): alone, on one's
own ▷ *nm, nf*: **il en reste un(e) ~(e)**
there's only one left; **le ~ livre** the only
book; **parler tout ~** to talk to oneself;
**faire qch (tout) ~** to do sth (all) on
one's own *ou* (all) by oneself; **à lui
(tout) ~** single-handed, on his own; **se
sentir ~** to feel lonely; **seulement** *adv*
only; **non seulement ... mais aussi** *ou*
**encore** not only ... but also
**sève** [sɛv] *nf* sap
**sévère** [sevɛʀ] *adj* severe
**sexe** [sɛks] *nm* sex; (*organes génitaux*)
genitals, sex organs; **sexuel, le** *adj*
sexual
**shampooing** [ʃɑ̃pwɛ̃] *nm* shampoo
**Shetland** [ʃɛtlɑ̃d] *n*: **les îles ~** the
Shetland Islands, Shetland
**short** [ʃɔʀt] *nm* (pair of) shorts *pl*

🔘 **MOT-CLÉ**

**si** [si] *adv* **1** (*oui*) yes; **"Paul n'est pas
venu" — "si!"** "Paul hasn't come"
— "yes, he has!"; **je vous assure que si**
I assure you he did *ou* she is *etc*
**2** (*tellement*) so; **si gentil/rapidement**
so kind/fast; **si bien que** so
much so that; **si rapide qu'il soit**
however fast he may be
▷ *conj* if; **si tu veux** if you want; **je me
demande si** I wonder if *ou* whether; **si
seulement** if only
▷ *nm* (*Mus*) B; (*en chantant la gamme*) ti

**Sicile** [sisil] *nf*: **la ~** Sicily
**SIDA** [sida] *sigle m* (= *syndrome immuno-
déficitaire acquis*) AIDS *sg*
**sidéré, e** [sidere] *adj* staggered
**sidérurgie** [sideryʀʒi] *nf* steel
industry

**siècle** [sjɛkl] *nm* century
**siège** [sjɛʒ] *nm* seat; (*d'entreprise*) head
office; (*d'organisation*) headquarters
*pl*; (*Mil*) siege; **siège social** registered
office; **siéger** *vi* to sit
**sien, ne** [sjɛ̃, sjɛn] *pron*: **le(la) ~(ne),
les ~(ne)s** (*homme*) his; (*femme*) hers;
(*chose, animal*) its
**sieste** [sjɛst] *nf* (afternoon) snooze *ou*
nap; **faire la ~** to have a snooze *ou* nap
**sifflement** [sifləmɑ̃] *nm*: **un ~** a
whistle
**siffler** [sifle] *vi* (*gén*) to whistle; (*en
respirant*) to wheeze; (*serpent, vapeur*)
to hiss ▷ *vt* (*chanson*) to whistle; (*chien
etc*) to whistle for; (*fille*) to whistle at;
(*pièce, orateur*) to hiss, boo; (*fin du match,
départ*) to blow one's whistle for; (*fam:
verre*) to guzzle
**sifflet** [sifle] *nm* whistle; **coup de ~**
whistle
**siffloter** [sifləte] *vi, vt* to whistle
**sigle** [sigl] *nm* acronym
**signal, -aux** [siɲal, o] *nm* signal;
(*indice, écriteau*) sign; **donner le ~ de**
to give the signal for; **signal d'alarme**
alarm signal; **signalement** *nm*
description, particulars *pl*
**signaler** [siɲale] *vt* to indicate;
(*personne: faire un signe*) to signal; (*vol,
perte*) to report; (*faire remarquer*): **~ qch
à qn/(à qn) que** to point out sth to
sb/(to sb) that; **je voudrais ~ un vol** I'd
like to report a theft
**signature** [siɲatyʀ] *nf* signature;
(*action*) signing
**signe** [siɲ] *nm* sign; (*Typo*) mark; **faire
un ~ de la main** to give a sign with
one's hand; **faire ~ à qn** (*fig*: contacter)
to get in touch with sb; **faire ~ à qn
d'entrer** to motion (to) sb to come in;
**signer** *vt* to sign; **se signer** *vi* to cross
o.s.; **où dois-je signer?** where do I sign?
**significatif, -ive** [siɲifikatif, iv] *adj*
significant
**signification** [siɲifikasjɔ̃] *nf* meaning
**signifier** [siɲifje] *vt* (*vouloir dire*) to
mean; (*faire connaître*): **~ qch (à qn)** to

make sth known (to sb)

**silence** [silɑ̃s] nm silence; (Mus) rest; **garder le ~** to keep silent, say nothing; **silencieux, -euse** adj quiet, silent ▷ nm silencer

**silhouette** [silwɛt] nf outline, silhouette; (allure) figure

**sillage** [sijaʒ] nm wake

**sillon** [sijɔ̃] nm furrow; (de disque) groove; **sillonner** vt to criss-cross

**simagrées** [simagʀe] nfpl fuss sg

**similaire** [similɛʀ] adj similar; **similicuir** nm imitation leather; **similitude** nf similarity

**simple** [sɛ̃pl] adj simple; (non multiple) single ▷ nm: **~ messieurs/dames** men's/ladies' singles sg ▷ nm/f: **~ d'esprit** simpleton

**simplicité** [sɛ̃plisite] nf simplicity; **en toute ~** quite simply

**simplifier** [sɛ̃plifje] vt to simplify

**simuler** [simyle] vt to sham, simulate

**simultané, e** [simyltane] adj simultaneous

**sincère** [sɛ̃sɛʀ] adj sincere; **sincèrement** adv sincerely; (pour parler franchement) honestly, really; **sincérité** nf sincerity

**Singapour** [sɛ̃gapuʀ] nm Singapore

**singe** [sɛ̃ʒ] nm monkey; (de grande taille) ape; **singer** vt to ape, mimic; **singeries** nfpl antics

**singulariser** [sɛ̃gylaʀize]: **se singulariser** vi to call attention to o.s.

**singularité** [sɛ̃gylaʀite] nf peculiarity

**singulier, -ière** [sɛ̃gylje, jɛʀ] adj remarkable, singular ▷ nm singular

**sinistre** [sinistʀ] adj sinister ▷ nm (incendie) blaze; (catastrophe) disaster; (Assurances) damage (giving rise to a claim); **sinistré, e** adj disaster-stricken ▷ nm/f disaster victim

**sinon** [sinɔ̃] conj (autrement, sans quoi) otherwise, or else; (sauf) except, other than; (si ce n'est) if not

**sinueux, -euse** [sinɥø, øz] adj winding

**sinus** [sinys] nm (Anat) sinus; (Géom)

sine; **sinusite** nf sinusitis

**sirène** [siʀɛn] nf siren; **sirène d'alarme** fire alarm; (en temps de guerre) air-raid siren

**sirop** [siʀo] nm (à diluer: de fruit etc) syrup; (pharmaceutique) syrup, mixture; **~ pour la toux** cough mixture

**siroter** [siʀote] vt to sip

**sismique** [sismik] adj seismic

**site** [sit] nm (paysage, environnement) setting; (d'une ville etc: emplacement) site; **site (pittoresque)** beauty spot; **sites touristiques** places of interest; **site Web** (Inform) website

**sitôt** [sito] adv: **~ parti** as soon as he etc had left; **~ que** as soon as; **pas de ~** not for a long time

**situation** [sitɥasjɔ̃] nf situation; (d'un édifice, d'une ville) position, location; **situation de famille** marital status

**situé, e** [sitɥe] adj situated

**situer** [sitɥe] vt to site, situate; (en pensée) to set, place; **se situer** vi to be situated

**six** [sis] num six; **sixième** num sixth ▷ nf (Scol) year 7 (BRIT), sixth grade (US)

**skaï®** [skaj] nm Leatherette®

**ski** [ski] nm (objet) ski; (sport) skiing; **faire du ~** to ski; **ski de fond** cross-country skiing; **ski nautique** water-skiing; **ski de piste** downhill skiing; **ski de randonnée** cross-country skiing; **skier** vi to ski; **skieur, -euse** nm/f skier

**slip** [slip] nm (sous-vêtement) pants pl, briefs pl; (de bain: d'homme) trunks pl; (: du bikini) (bikini) briefs pl

**slogan** [slɔgɑ̃] nm slogan

**Slovaquie** [slɔvaki] nf: **la ~** Slovakia

**SMIC** [smik] sigle m = **salaire minimum interprofessionnel de croissance**

**smoking** [smɔkiŋ] nm dinner ou evening suit

**SMS** sigle m (= short message service) (service) SMS; (message) text message

**SNCF** sigle f (= Société nationale des chemins de fer français) French railways

**snob** [snɔb] adj snobbish ▷ nm/f snob; **snobisme** nm snobbery, snobbishness

**sobre** [sɔbʀ] adj (personne) temperate, abstemious; (élégance, style) sober

**sobriquet** [sɔbʀikɛ] nm nickname

**social, e, -aux** [sɔsjal, jo] adj social

**socialisme** [sɔsjalism] nm socialism; **socialiste** nm/f socialist

**société** [sɔsjete] nf society; (sportive) club; (Comm) company; **la ~ de consommation** the consumer society; **société anonyme** ≈ limited (BRIT) ou incorporated (US) company

**sociologie** [sɔsjɔlɔʒi] nf sociology

**socle** [sɔkl] nm (de colonne, statue) plinth, pedestal; (de lampe) base

**socquette** [sɔkɛt] nf ankle sock

**sœur** [sœʀ] nf sister; (religieuse) nun, sister

**soi** [swa] pron oneself; **en ~** (intrinsèquement) in itself; **cela va de ~** that ou it goes without saying; **soi-disant** adj inv so-called ▷ adv supposedly

**soie** [swa] nf silk; **soierie** nf (tissu) silk

**soif** [swaf] nf thirst; **avoir ~** to be thirsty; **donner ~ à qn** to make sb thirsty

**soigné, e** [swaɲe] adj (tenue) well-groomed, neat; (travail) careful, meticulous

**soigner** [swaɲe] vt (malade, maladie: suj: docteur) to treat; (suj: infirmière, mère) to nurse, look after; (travail, détails) to take care over; (jardin, invités) to look after; **soigneux, -euse** adj (propre) tidy, neat; (appliqué) painstaking, careful

**soi-même** [swamɛm] pron oneself

**soin** [swɛ̃] nm (application) care; (propreté, ordre) tidiness, neatness; **soins** nmpl (à un malade, blessé) treatment sg, medical attention sg; (hygiène) care sg; **prendre ~ de** to take care of, look after; **prendre ~ de faire** to take care to do; **les premiers ~s** first aid sg

**soir** [swaʀ] nm evening; **ce ~** this evening, tonight; **à ce ~!** see you this evening (ou tonight)!; **sept/dix heures du ~** seven in the evening/ten at night; **demain ~** tomorrow evening, tomorrow night; **soirée** nf evening; (réception) party

**soit¹** [swa] vb voir **être** ▷ conj (à savoir) namely; (ou): **~ ... ~** either ... or; **~ que ... ~ que** ou **ou que** whether ... or whether

**soit²** [swat] adv so be it, very well

**soixantaine** [swasɑ̃tɛn] nf: **une ~ (de)** sixty or so, about sixty; **avoir la ~ (âge)** to be around sixty

**soixante** [swasɑ̃t] num sixty; **soixante-dix** num seventy

**soja** [sɔʒa] nm soya; (graines) soya beans pl; **germes de ~** beansprouts

**sol** [sɔl] nm ground; (de logement) floor; (Agr) soil; (Mus) G; (: en chantant la gamme) so(h)

**solaire** [sɔlɛʀ] adj (énergie etc) solar; (crème etc) sun cpd

**soldat** [sɔlda] nm soldier

**solde** [sɔld] nf pay ▷ nm (Comm) balance; **soldes** nm ou f pl (articles) sale goods; (vente) sales; **en ~** at sale price; **solder** vt (marchandise) to sell at sale price, sell off

**sole** [sɔl] nf sole inv (fish)

**soleil** [sɔlɛj] nm sun; (lumière) sun(light); (temps ensoleillé) sun(shine); **il fait du ~** it's sunny; **au ~** in the sun

**solennel, le** [sɔlanɛl] adj solemn

**solfège** [sɔlfɛʒ] nm musical theory

**solidaire** [sɔlidɛʀ] adj: **être ~s** to show solidarity, stand ou stick together; **être ~ de** (collègues) to stand by; **solidarité** nf solidarity; **par solidarité (avec)** in sympathy (with)

**solide** [sɔlid] adj solid; (mur, maison, meuble) solid, sturdy; (connaissances, argument) sound; (personne, estomac) robust, sturdy ▷ nm solid

**soliste** [sɔlist] nm/f soloist

**solitaire** [sɔlitɛʀ] adj (sans compagnie) solitary, lonely; (lieu) lonely ▷ nm/f (ermite) recluse; (fig: ours) loner

**solitude** [sɔlityd] nf loneliness; (tranquillité) solitude

**solliciter** [sɔlisite] vt (personne) to appeal to; (emploi, faveur) to seek

**sollicitude** [sɔlisityd] nf concern
**soluble** [sɔlybl] adj soluble
**solution** [sɔlysjɔ̃] nf solution; **solution de facilité** easy way out
**solvable** [sɔlvabl] adj solvent
**sombre** [sɔ̃bʀ] adj dark; (fig) gloomy; **sombrer** vi (bateau) to sink; **sombrer dans** (misère, désespoir) to sink into
**sommaire** [sɔmɛʀ] adj (simple) basic; (expéditif) summary ▷ nm summary
**somme** [sɔm] nf (Math) sum; (quantité) amount; (argent) sum, amount ▷ nm: **faire un ~** to have a (short) nap; **en ~** all in all; **~ toute** all in all
**sommeil** [sɔmɛj] nm sleep; **avoir ~** to be sleepy; **sommeiller** vi to doze
**sommet** [sɔmɛ] nm top; (d'une montagne) summit, top; (fig: de la perfection, gloire) height
**sommier** [sɔmje] nm (bed) base
**somnambule** [sɔmnɑ̃byl] nm/f sleepwalker
**somnifère** [sɔmnifɛʀ] nm sleeping drug no pl (ou pill)
**somnoler** [sɔmnɔle] vi to doze
**somptueux, -euse** [sɔ̃ptɥø, øz] adj sumptuous
**son¹, sa** [sɔ̃, sa] (pl ses) adj (antécédent humain: mâle) his; (: femelle) her; (: valeur indéfinie) one's, his/her; (antécédent non humain) its
**son²** [sɔ̃] nm sound; (de blé) bran
**sondage** [sɔ̃daʒ] nm: **sondage (d'opinion)** (opinion) poll
**sonde** [sɔ̃d] nf (Navig) lead ou sounding line; (Méd) probe; (Tech: de forage) borer, driller
**sonder** [sɔ̃de] vt (Navig) to sound; (Tech) to bore, drill; (fig: personne) to sound out; **~ le terrain** (fig) to test the ground
**songe** [sɔ̃ʒ] nm dream; **songer** vi: **songer à** (penser à) to think over; (envisager) to consider, think of; **songer que** to think that; **songeur, -euse** adj pensive
**sonnant, e** [sɔnɑ̃, ɑ̃t] adj: **à 8 heures ~es** on the stroke of 8
**sonné, e** [sɔne] adj (fam) cracked; **il est**

**midi ~** it's gone twelve
**sonner** [sɔne] vi to ring ▷ vt (cloche) to ring; (glas, tocsin) to sound; (portier, infirmière) to ring for; **~ faux** (instrument) to sound out of tune; (rire) to ring false
**sonnerie** [sɔnʀi] nf (son) ringing; (sonnette) bell; (de portable) ringtone; **sonnerie d'alarme** alarm bell
**sonnette** [sɔnɛt] nf bell; **sonnette d'alarme** alarm bell
**sonore** [sɔnɔʀ] adj (voix) sonorous, ringing; (salle) resonant; (film, signal) sound cpd; **sonorisation** nf (équipement: de salle de conférences) public address system, P.A. system; (: de discothèque) sound system; **sonorité** nf (de piano, violon) tone; (d'une salle) acoustics pl
**sophistiqué, e** [sɔfistike] adj sophisticated
**sorbet** [sɔʀbɛ] nm water ice, sorbet
**sorcier** [sɔʀsje] nm sorcerer
**sordide** [sɔʀdid] adj (lieu) squalid; (action) sordid
**sort** [sɔʀ] nm (destinée) fate; (condition) lot; (magique) curse, spell; **tirer au ~** to draw lots
**sorte** [sɔʀt] nf sort, kind; **de la ~** in that way; **de (telle) ~ que** so that; **en quelque ~** in a way; **faire en ~ que** to see to it that; **quelle ~ de ...?** what kind of ...?
**sortie** [sɔʀti] nf (issue) way out, exit; (remarque drôle) sally; (promenade) outing; (le soir: au restaurant etc) night out; (Comm: d'un disque) release; (: d'un livre) publication; (: d'un modèle) launching; **où est la ~?** where's the exit?; **sortie de bain** (vêtement) bathrobe
**sortilège** [sɔʀtilɛʒ] nm (magic) spell
**sortir** [sɔʀtiʀ] vi (gén) to come out; (partir, se promener, aller au spectacle) to go out; (numéro gagnant) to come up ▷ vt (gén) to take out; (produit, modèle) to bring out; (fam: dire) to come out with; **~ avec qn** to be going out with sb; **s'en ~** (malade) to pull through;

(d'une difficulté etc) to get through; **~ de** (endroit) to go (ou come) out of, leave; (provenir de) to come from; (compétence) to be outside

**sosie** [sɔzi] nm double

**sot, sotte** [so, sɔt] adj silly, foolish ▷ nm/f fool; **sottise** nf (caractère) silliness, foolishness; (action) silly ou foolish thing

**sou** [su] nm: **près de ses ~s** tight-fisted; **sans le ~** penniless

**soubresaut** [subrəso] nm start; (cahot) jolt

**souche** [suʃ] nf (d'arbre) stump; (de carnet) counterfoil (BRIT), stub

**souci** [susi] nm (inquiétude) worry; (préoccupation) concern; (Bot) marigold; **se faire du ~** to worry; **soucier**: **se soucier de** vt to care about; **soucieux, -euse** adj concerned, worried

**soucoupe** [sukup] nf saucer; **soucoupe volante** flying saucer

**soudain, e** [sudɛ̃, ɛn] adj (douleur, mort) sudden ▷ adv suddenly, all of a sudden

**Soudan** [sudɑ̃] nm: **le ~** Sudan

**soude** [sud] nf soda

**souder** [sude] vt (avec fil à souder) to solder; (par soudure autogène) to weld; (fig) to bind together

**soudure** [sudyʀ] nf soldering; welding; (joint) soldered joint; weld

**souffle** [sufl] nm (en expirant) breath; (en soufflant) puff, blow; (respiration) breathing; (d'explosion, de ventilateur) blast; (du vent) blowing; **être à bout de ~** to be out of breath; **un ~ d'air** a breath of air

**soufflé, e** [sufle] adj (fam: stupéfié) staggered ▷ nm (Culin) soufflé

**souffler** [sufle] vi (gén) to blow; (haleter) to puff (and blow) ▷ vt (feu, bougie) to blow out; (chasser: poussière etc) to blow away; (Tech: verre) to blow; (dire): **~ qch à qn** to whisper sth to sb

**souffrance** [sufʀɑ̃s] nf suffering; **en ~** (affaire) pending

**souffrant, e** [sufʀɑ̃, ɑ̃t] adj unwell

**souffre-douleur** [sufʀədulœʀ] nm inv

butt, underdog

**souffrir** [sufʀiʀ] vi to suffer, be in pain ▷ vt to suffer, endure; (supporter) to bear, stand; **~ de** (maladie, froid) to suffer from; **elle ne peut pas le ~** she can't stand ou bear him

**soufre** [sufʀ] nm sulphur

**souhait** [swɛ] nm wish; **tous nos ~s pour la nouvelle année** (our) best wishes for the New Year; **à vos ~s!** bless you!; **souhaitable** adj desirable

**souhaiter** [swete] vt to wish for; **~ la bonne année à qn** to wish sb a happy New Year; **~ que** to hope that

**soûl, e** [su, sul] adj drunk ▷ nm: **tout son ~** to one's heart's content

**soulagement** [sulaʒmɑ̃] nm relief

**soulager** [sulaʒe] vt to relieve

**soûler** [sule] vt: **~ qn** to get sb drunk; (suj: boisson) to make sb drunk; (fig) to make sb's head spin ou reel; **se soûler** vi to get drunk

**soulever** [sul(ə)ve] vt to lift; (poussière) to send up; (enthousiasme) to arouse; (question, débat) to raise; **se soulever** vi (peuple) to rise up; (personne couchée) to lift o.s. up

**soulier** [sulje] nm shoe

**souligner** [suliɲe] vt to underline; (fig) to emphasize, stress

**soumettre** [sumɛtʀ] vt (pays) to subject, subjugate; (rebelle) to put down, subdue; **~ qch à qn** (projet etc) to submit sth to sb; **se soumettre (à)** to submit (to)

**soumis, e** [sumi, iz] adj submissive; **soumission** nf submission

**soupçon** [supsɔ̃] nm suspicion; (petite quantité): **un ~ de** a hint ou touch of; **soupçonner** vt to suspect; **soupçonneux, -euse** adj suspicious

**soupe** [sup] nf soup

**souper** [supe] vi to have supper ▷ nm supper

**soupeser** [supəze] vt to weigh in one's hand(s); (fig) to weigh up

**soupière** [supjɛʀ] nf (soup) tureen

**soupir** [supiʀ] nm sigh; **pousser un**

**~ de soulagement** to heave a sigh
of relief
**soupirer** [supiʀe] vi to sigh
**souple** [supl] adj supple; (fig: règlement,
caractère) flexible; (: démarche, taille)
lithe, supple; **souplesse** nf suppleness;
(de caractère) flexibility
**source** [suʀs] nf (point d'eau) spring;
(d'un cours d'eau, fig) source; **de bonne ~**
on good authority
**sourcil** [suʀsi] nm (eye)brow;
**sourciller** vi: **sans sourciller** without
turning a hair ou batting an eyelid
**sourd, e** [suʀ, suʀd] adj deaf; (bruit)
muffled; (douleur) dull ▷ nm/f deaf
person; **faire la ~e oreille** to turn a
deaf ear; **sourdine** nf (Mus) mute; **en
sourdine** softly, quietly; **sourd-muet,
sourde-muette** adj deaf-and-dumb
▷ nm/f deaf-mute
**souriant, e** [suʀjɑ̃, jɑ̃t] adj cheerful
**sourire** [suʀiʀ] nm smile ▷ vi to smile;
**~ à qn** to smile at sb; (fig: plaire à) to
appeal to sb; (suj: chance) to smile on sb;
**garder le ~** to keep smiling
**souris** [suʀi] nf mouse
**sournois, e** [suʀnwa, waz] adj
deceitful, underhand
**sous** [su] prép under; **~ la pluie** in the
rain; **~ terre** underground; **~ peu**
shortly, before long; **sous-bois** nm inv
undergrowth
**souscrire** [suskʀiʀ]: **~ à** vt to
subscribe to
**sous...**: **sous-directeur, -trice** nm/f
assistant manager(-manageress);
**sous-entendre** vt to imply, infer;
**sous-entendu, e** adj implied ▷ nm
innuendo, insinuation; **sous-estimer**
vt to underestimate; **sous-jacent, e**
adj underlying; **sous-louer** vt to
sublet; **sous-marin, e** adj (flore,
faune) submarine; (pêche) underwater
▷ nm submarine; **sous-pull** nm thin
poloneck jersey; **soussigné, e** adj: **je
soussigné** I the undersigned; **sous-sol**
nm basement; **sous-titre** nm subtitle
**soustraction** [sustʀaksjɔ̃] nf

subtraction
**soustraire** [sustʀɛʀ] vt to subtract,
take away; (dérober): **~ qch à qn** to
remove sth from sb; **se soustraire à**
(autorité etc) to elude, escape from
**sous...**: **sous-traitant** nm sub-
contractor; **sous-traiter** vt to
sub-contract; **sous-vêtements** nmpl
underwear sg
**soutane** [sutan] nf cassock, soutane
**soute** [sut] nf hold
**soutenir** [sut(ə)niʀ] vt to support;
(assaut, choc) to stand up to, withstand;
(intérêt, effort) to keep up; (assurer): **~
que** to maintain that; **soutenu, e**
(efforts) sustained, unflagging; (style)
elevated
**souterrain, e** [suteʀɛ̃, ɛn] adj
underground ▷ nm underground
passage
**soutien** [sutjɛ̃] nm support; **soutien-
gorge** nm bra
**soutirer** [sutiʀe] vt: **~ qch à qn** to
squeeze ou get sth out of sb
**souvenir** [suv(ə)niʀ] nm (réminiscence)
memory; (objet) souvenir ▷ vb:
**se ~ de** to remember; **se ~ que** to
remember that; **en ~ de** in memory
ou remembrance of; **avec mes
affectueux/meilleurs ~s, ...** with love
from, .../regards, ...
**souvent** [suvɑ̃] adv often; **peu ~**
seldom, infrequently
**souverain, e** [suv(ə)ʀɛ̃, ɛn] nm/f
sovereign, monarch
**soyeux, -euse** [swajø, øz] adj silky
**spacieux, -euse** [spasjø, jøz] adj
spacious, roomy
**spaghettis** [spageti] nmpl spaghetti sg
**sparadrap** [spaʀadʀa] nm sticking
plaster (BRIT), Bandaid® (US)
**spatial, e, -aux** [spasjal, jo] adj (Aviat)
space cpd
**speaker, ine** [spikœʀ, kʀin] nm/f
announcer
**spécial, e, -aux** [spesjal, jo]
adj special; (bizarre) peculiar;
**spécialement** adv especially,

particularly; (*tout exprès*) specially;
**spécialiser: se spécialiser** vi to
specialize; **spécialiste** nm/f specialist;
**spécialité** nf speciality; (*branche*)
special field

**spécifier** [spesifje] vt to specify, state

**spécimen** [spesimɛn] nm specimen

**spectacle** [spɛktakl] nm (*scène*)
sight; (*représentation*) show; (*industrie*)
show business; **spectaculaire** adj
spectacular

**spectateur, -trice** [spɛktatœr,
tris] nm/f (*Cinéma etc*) member of
the audience; (*Sport*) spectator; (*d'un
événement*) onlooker, witness

**spéculer** [spekyle] vi to speculate

**spéléologie** [speleolɔʒi] nf potholing

**sperme** [spɛrm] nm semen, sperm

**sphère** [sfɛr] nf sphere

**spirale** [spiral] nf spiral

**spirituel, le** [spirituɛl] adj spiritual;
(*fin, piquant*) witty

**splendide** [splɑ̃did] adj splendid

**spontané, e** [spɔ̃tane] adj
spontaneous; **spontanéité** nf
spontaneity

**sport** [spɔr] nm sport ▷ adj inv
(*vêtement*) casual; **faire du ~** to do sport;
**sports d'hiver** winter sports; **sportif,
-ive** adj (*journal, association, épreuve*)
sports cpd; (*allure, démarche*) athletic;
(*attitude, esprit*) sporting

**spot** [spɔt] nm (*lampe*) spot(light);
(*annonce*) **spot (publicitaire)**
commercial (break)

**square** [skwar] nm public garden(s)

**squelette** [skəlɛt] nm skeleton;
**squelettique** adj scrawny

**SRAS** [sras] sigle m (= *syndrome
respiratoire aigu sévère*) SARS

**Sri Lanka** [srilɑ̃ka] nm: **le ~** Sri Lanka

**stabiliser** [stabilize] vt to stabilize

**stable** [stabl] adj stable, steady

**stade** [stad] nm (*Sport*) stadium; (*phase,
niveau*) stage

**stage** [staʒ] nm (*cours*) training course;
**~ de formation (professionnelle)**
vocational (training) course; **~ de**

**perfectionnement** advanced training
course; **stagiaire** nm/f, adj trainee
▌ Attention à ne pas traduire *stage*
par le mot anglais *stage*.

**stagner** [stagne] vi to stagnate

**stand** [stɑ̃d] nm (*d'exposition*) stand; (*de
foire*) stall; **stand de tir** (*à la foire, Sport*)
shooting range

**standard** [stɑ̃dar] adj inv standard
▷ nm switchboard; **standardiste** nm/f
switchboard operator

**standing** [stɑ̃diŋ] nm standing; **de
grand ~** luxury

**starter** [starter] nm (*Auto*) choke

**station** [stasjɔ̃] nf station; (*de
bus*) stop; (*de villégiature*) resort;
**station de ski** ski resort; **station
de taxis** taxi rank (BRIT) ou stand
(US); **stationnement** nm parking;
**stationner** vi to park; **station-service**
nf service station

**statistique** [statistik] nf (*science*)
statistics sg; (*rapport, étude*) statistic
▷ adj statistical

**statue** [staty] nf statue

**statu quo** [statykwo] nm status quo

**statut** [staty] nm status; **statuts** nmpl
(*Jur, Admin*) statutes; **statutaire** adj
statutory

**Sté** abr = **société**

**steak** [stɛk] nm steak; **~ haché**
hamburger

**sténo(graphie)** [stenɔ(grafi)] nf
shorthand

**stérile** [steril] adj sterile

**stérilet** [sterilɛ] nm coil, loop

**stériliser** [sterilize] vt to sterilize

**stimulant** [stimylɑ̃] nm (*fig*) stimulus,
incentive; (*physique*) stimulant

**stimuler** [stimyle] vt to stimulate

**stipuler** [stipyle] vt to stipulate

**stock** [stɔk] nm stock; **stocker** vt to
stock

**stop** [stɔp] nm (*Auto: écriteau*) stop sign;
(: *feu arrière*) brake-light; **faire du ~**
(*fam*) to hitch(hike); **stopper** vt, vi to
stop, halt

**store** [stɔr] nm blind; (*de magasin*)

shade, awning

**strabisme** [strabism] *nm* squinting

**strapontin** [strapɔ̃tɛ̃] *nm* jump *ou* foldaway seat

**stratégie** [strateʒi] *nf* strategy; **stratégique** *adj* strategic

**stress** [strɛs] *nm* stress; **stressant, e** *adj* stressful; **stresser** *vt*: **stresser qn** to make sb (feel) tense

**strict, e** [strikt] *adj* strict; (*tenue, décor*) severe, plain; **le ~ nécessaire/ minimum** the bare essentials/ minimum

**strident, e** [stridã, ãt] *adj* shrill, strident

**strophe** [strɔf] *nf* verse, stanza

**structure** [stryktyr] *nf* structure; **~s d'accueil** reception facilities

**studieux, -euse** [stydjø, jøz] *adj* studious

**studio** [stydjo] *nm* (*logement*) (one-roomed) flatlet (*BRIT*) *ou* apartment (*US*); (*d'artiste, TV etc*) studio

**stupéfait, e** [stypefɛ, ɛt] *adj* astonished

**stupéfiant, e** [stypefjã, jãt] *adj* (*étonnant*) stunning, astounding ▷ *nm* (*Méd*) drug, narcotic

**stupéfier** [stypefje] *vt* (*étonner*) to stun, astonish

**stupeur** [stypœr] *nf* astonishment

**stupide** [stypid] *adj* stupid; **stupidité** *nf* stupidity; (*parole, acte*) stupid thing (to do *ou* say)

**style** [stil] *nm* style

**stylé, e** [stile] *adj* well-trained

**styliste** [stilist] *nm/f* designer

**stylo** [stilo] *nm*: **~ (à encre)** (fountain) pen; **stylo (à) bille** ball-point pen

**su, e** [sy] *pp de* **savoir** ▷ *nm*: **au su de** with the knowledge of

**suave** [sɥav] *adj* sweet

**subalterne** [sybaltɛrn] *adj* (*employé, officier*) junior; (*rôle*) subordinate, subsidiary ▷ *nm/f* subordinate

**subconscient** [sypkɔ̃sjã] *nm* subconscious

**subir** [sybir] *vt* (*affront, dégâts*) to suffer;

(*opération, châtiment*) to undergo

**subit, e** [sybi, it] *adj* sudden; **subitement** *adv* suddenly, all of a sudden

**subjectif, -ive** [sybʒɛktif, iv] *adj* subjective

**subjonctif** [sybʒɔ̃ktif] *nm* subjunctive

**subjuguer** [sybʒyge] *vt* to captivate

**submerger** [sybmɛrʒe] *vt* to submerge; (*fig*) to overwhelm

**subordonné, e** [sybɔrdɔne] *adj, nm/f* subordinate

**subrepticement** [sybrɛptismã] *adv* surreptitiously

**subside** [sybzid] *nm* grant

**subsidiaire** [sybzidjɛr] *adj*: **question ~** deciding question

**subsister** [sybziste] *vi* (*rester*) to remain, subsist; (*survivre*) to live on

**substance** [sypstãs] *nf* substance

**substituer** [sypstitɥe] *vt*: **~ qn/qch à** to substitute sb/sth for; **se ~ à qn** (*évincer*) to substitute o.s. for sb

**substitut** [sypstity] *nm* (*succédané*) substitute

**subterfuge** [syptɛrfyʒ] *nm* subterfuge

**subtil, e** [syptil] *adj* subtle

**subvenir** [sybvənir]: **~ à** *vt* to meet

**subvention** [sybvãsjɔ̃] *nf* subsidy, grant; **subventionner** *vt* to subsidize

**suc** [syk] *nm* (*Bot*) sap; (*de viande, fruit*) juice

**succéder** [syksede]: **~ à** *vt* to succeed; **se succéder** *vi* (*accidents, années*) to follow one another

**succès** [syksɛ] *nm* success; **avoir du ~** to be a success, be successful; **à ~** successful; **succès de librairie** bestseller

**successeur** [syksesœr] *nm* successor

**successif, -ive** [syksesif, iv] *adj* successive

**succession** [syksesjɔ̃] *nf* (*série, Pol*) succession; (*Jur: patrimoine*) estate, inheritance

**succomber** [sykɔ̃be] *vi* to die, succumb; (*fig*): **~ à** to succumb to

**succulent, e** [sykylã, ãt] *adj* (*repas,*

*mets*) delicious

**succursale** [sykyʀsal] *nf* branch

**sucer** [syse] *vt* to suck; **sucette** *nf* (*bonbon*) lollipop; (*de bébé*) dummy (BRIT), pacifier (US)

**sucre** [sykʀ] *nm* (*substance*) sugar; (*morceau*) lump of sugar, sugar lump *ou* cube; **sucre d'orge** barley sugar; **sucre en morceaux/cristallisé/en poudre** lump/granulated/caster sugar; **sucre glace** icing sugar (BRIT), confectioner's sugar (US); **sucré, e** *adj* (*produit alimentaire*) sweetened; (*au goût*) sweet; **sucrer** *vt* (*thé, café*) to sweeten, put sugar in; **sucreries** *nfpl* (*bonbons*) sweets, sweet things; **sucrier** *nm* (*récipient*) sugar bowl

**sud** [syd] *nm*: **le ~** the south ▷ *adj inv* south; (*côté*) south, southern; **au ~** (*situation*) in the south; (*direction*) to the south; **au ~ de** (to the) south of; **sud-africain, e** *adj* South African ▷ *nm/f*: **Sud-Africain, e** South African; **sud-américain, e** *adj* South American ▷ *nm/f*: **Sud-Américain, e** South American; **sud-est** *nm, adj inv* south-east; **sud-ouest** *nm, adj inv* south-west

**Suède** [sɥɛd] *nf*: **la ~** Sweden; **suédois, e** *adj* Swedish ▷ *nm/f*: **Suédois, e** Swede ▷ *nm* (*Ling*) Swedish

**suer** [sɥe] *vi* to sweat; (*suinter*) to ooze; **sueur** *nf* sweat; **en sueur** sweating, in a sweat; **donner des sueurs froides à qn** to put sb in(to) a cold sweat

**suffire** [syfiʀ] *vi*: **~ (à qn/ pour qch/pour faire)** to be enough *ou* sufficient (for sb/for sth/to do); **il suffit d'une négligence ...** it only takes one act of carelessness ...; **il suffit qu'on oublie pour que ...** one only needs to forget for ...; **ça suffit!** that's enough!

**suffisamment** [syfizamɑ̃] *adv* sufficiently, enough; **~ de** sufficient, enough

**suffisant, e** [syfizɑ̃, ɑ̃t] *adj* sufficient; (*résultats*) satisfactory; (*vaniteux*) self-important, bumptious

**suffixe** [syfiks] *nm* suffix

**suffoquer** [syfɔke] *vt* to choke, suffocate; (*stupéfier*) to stagger, astound ▷ *vi* to choke, suffocate

**suffrage** [syfʀaʒ] *nm* (Pol: *voix*) vote

**suggérer** [sygʒeʀe] *vt* to suggest; **suggestion** *nf* suggestion

**suicide** [sɥisid] *nm* suicide; **suicider**: **se suicider** *vi* to commit suicide

**suie** [sɥi] *nf* soot

**suisse** [sɥis] *adj* Swiss ▷ *nm*: **S~** Swiss *pl inv* ▷ *nf*: **la S~** Switzerland; **la S~ romande/allemande** French-speaking/German-speaking Switzerland

**suite** [sɥit] *nf* (*continuation: d'énumération etc*) rest, remainder; (: *de feuilleton*) continuation; (: *film etc sur le même thème*) sequel; (*série*) series, succession; (*conséquence*) result; (*ordre, liaison logique*) coherence; (*appartement, Mus*) suite; (*escorte*) retinue, suite; **suites** *nfpl* (*d'une maladie etc*) effects; **prendre la ~ de** (*directeur etc*) to succeed, take over from; **donner ~ à** (*requête, projet*) to follow up; **faire ~ à** to follow; **(faisant) ~ à votre lettre du ...** further to your letter of the ...; **de ~** (*d'affilée*) in succession; (*immédiatement*) at once; **par la ~** afterwards, subsequently; **à la ~** one after the other; **à la ~ de** (*derrière*) behind; (*en conséquence de*) following

**suivant, e** [sɥivɑ̃, ɑ̃t] *adj* next, following ▷ *prép* (*selon*) according to; **au ~!** next!

**suivi, e** [sɥivi] *adj* (*effort, qualité*) consistent; (*cohérent*) coherent; **très/ peu ~** (*cours*) well-/poorly-attended

**suivre** [sɥivʀ] *vt* (*gén*) to follow; (Scol: *cours*) to attend; (*comprendre*) to keep up with; (Comm: *article*) to continue to stock ▷ *vi* to follow; (*élève: assimiler*) to keep up; **se suivre** *vi* (*accidents etc*) to follow one after the other; **faire ~** (*lettre*) to forward; **"à ~"** "to be continued"

**sujet, te** [syʒɛ, ɛt] *adj*: **être ~ à** (*vertige etc*) to be liable *ou* subject to ▷ *nm/f*

(*d'un souverain*) subject ▷ *nm* subject;
**au ~ de** about; **sujet de conversation**
topic *ou* subject of conversation;
**sujet d'examen** (*Scol*) examination
question

**super** [sypɛʀ] (*fam*) *adj inv* terrific,
great, fantastic, super

**superbe** [sypɛʀb] *adj* magnificent,
superb

**superficie** [sypɛʀfisi] *nf* (surface) area

**superficiel, le** [sypɛʀfisjɛl] *adj*
superficial

**superflu, e** [sypɛʀfly] *adj* superfluous

**supérieur, e** [sypeʀjœʀ] *adj* (*lèvre,
étages, classes*) upper; (*plus élevé:
température, niveau, enseignement*): **~ (à)**
higher (than); (*meilleur: qualité, produit*):
**~ (à)** superior (to); (*excellent, hautain*)
superior ▷ *nm*, *nf* superior; **supériorité**
*nf* superiority

**supermarché** [sypɛʀmaʀʃe] *nm*
supermarket

**superposer** [sypɛʀpoze] *vt* (*faire
chevaucher*) to superimpose; **lits
superposés** bunk beds

**superpuissance** [sypɛʀpɥisɑ̃s] *nf*
super-power

**superstitieux, -euse** [sypɛʀstisjø,
jøz] *adj* superstitious

**superviser** [sypɛʀvize] *vt* to
supervise

**supplanter** [syplɑ̃te] *vt* to supplant

**suppléant, e** [sypleɑ̃, -ɑ̃t] *adj*
(*professeur*) supply *cpd*; (*juge,
fonctionnaire*) deputy *cpd* ▷ *nm/f*
(*professeur*) supply teacher

**suppléer** [syplee] *vt* (*ajouter: mot
manquant etc*) to supply, provide;
(*compenser: lacune*) to fill in; **~ à** to
make up for

**supplément** [syplemɑ̃] *nm*
supplement; (*de frites etc*) extra portion;
**un ~ de travail** extra *ou* additional
work; **payer un ~** to pay an additional
charge; **le vin est en ~** wine is extra;
**supplémentaire** *adj* additional,
further; (*train, bus*) relief *cpd*, extra

**supplications** [syplikasjɔ̃] *nfpl* pleas,

entreaties

**supplice** [syplis] *nm* torture *no pl*

**supplier** [syplije] *vt* to implore,
beseech

**support** [sypɔʀ] *nm* support;
(*publicitaire*) medium; (*audio-visuel*) aid

**supportable** [sypɔʀtabl] *adj* (*douleur*)
bearable

**supporter¹** [sypɔʀtɛʀ] *nm* supporter,
fan

**supporter²** [sypɔʀte] *vt* (*conséquences,
épreuve*) to bear, endure; (*défauts,
personne*) to put up with; (*suj: chose:
chaleur etc*) to withstand; (: *personne:
chaleur, vin*) to be able to take

 Attention à ne pas traduire
*supporter* par *to support*.

**supposer** [sypoze] *vt* to suppose;
(*impliquer*) to presuppose; **à ~ que**
supposing (that)

**suppositoire** [sypozitwaʀ] *nm*
suppository

**suppression** [sypʀesjɔ̃] *nf* (*voir
supprimer*) cancellation; removal;
deletion

**supprimer** [sypʀime] *vt* (*congés,
service d'autobus etc*) to cancel; (*emplois,
privilèges, témoin gênant*) to do away
with; (*cloison, cause, anxiété*) to remove;
(*clause, mot*) to delete

**suprême** [sypʀɛm] *adj* supreme

---

⬤ **MOT-CLÉ**

**sur** [syʀ] *prép* **1** (*position*) on; (*par-dessus*)
over; (*au-dessus*) above; **pose-le sur
la table** put it on the table; **je n'ai
pas d'argent sur moi** I haven't any
money on me

**2** (*direction*) towards; **en allant sur
Paris** going towards Paris; **sur votre
droite** on *ou* to your right

**3** (*à propos de*) on, about; **un livre/une
conférence sur Balzac** a book/lecture
on *ou* about Balzac

**4** (*proportion*) out of; **un sur 10** one in
10; (*Scol*) one out of 10

**5** (*mesures*) by; **4 m sur 2** 4 m by 2

**6** (*succession*): **avoir accident sur accident** to have one accident after the other

**sûr, e** [syʀ] *adj* sure, certain; (*digne de confiance*) reliable; (*sans danger*) safe; (*diagnostic, goût*) reliable; **le plus ~ est de** the safest thing is to; **sûr de soi** self-assured, self-confident

**surcharge** [syʀʃaʀʒ] *nf* (*de passagers, marchandises*) excess load; **surcharger** *vt* to overload

**surcroît** [syʀkʀwa] *nm*: **un ~ de** additional +*nom*; **par ou de ~** moreover; **en ~** in addition

**surdité** [syʀdite] *nf* deafness

**sûrement** [syʀmɑ̃] *adv* (*certainement*) certainly; (*sans risques*) safely

**surenchère** [syʀɑ̃ʃɛʀ] *nf* (*aux enchères*) higher bid; **surenchérir** *vi* to bid higher; (*fig*) to try and outbid each other

**surestimer** [syʀɛstime] *vt* to overestimate

**sûreté** [syʀte] *nf* (*sécurité*) safety; (*exactitude: de renseignements etc*) reliability; (*d'un geste*) steadiness; **mettre en ~** to put in a safe place; **pour plus de ~** as an extra precaution, to be on the safe side

**surf** [sœʀf] *nm* surfing

**surface** [syʀfas] *nf* surface; (*superficie*) surface area; **une grande ~** a supermarket; **faire ~** to surface; **en ~** near the surface; (*fig*) superficially

**surfait, e** [syʀfɛ, ɛt] *adj* overrated

**surfer** [syʀfe] *vi*: **~ sur Internet** to surf *ou* browse the Internet

**surgelé, e** [syʀʒəle] *adj* (deep-)frozen ▷ *nm*: **les ~s** (deep-)frozen food

**surgir** [syʀʒiʀ] *vi* to appear suddenly; (*fig: problème, conflit*) to arise

**sur...**: **surhumain, e** *adj* superhuman; **sur-le-champ** *adv* immediately; **surlendemain** *nm*: **le surlendemain (soir)** two days later (in the evening); **le surlendemain de** two days after; **surmenage** *nm* overwork(ing);

**surmener**: **se surmener** *vi* to overwork

**surmonter** [syʀmɔ̃te] *vt* (*vaincre*) to overcome; (*être au-dessus de*) to top

**surnaturel, le** [syʀnatyʀɛl] *adj, nm* supernatural

**surnom** [syʀnɔ̃] *nm* nickname

**surnombre** [syʀnɔ̃bʀ] *nm*: **être en ~** to be too many (*ou* one too many)

**surpeuplé, e** [syʀpœple] *adj* overpopulated

**surplace** [syʀplas] *nm*: **faire du ~** to mark time

**surplomber** [syʀplɔ̃be] *vt, vi* to overhang

**surplus** [syʀply] *nm* (*Comm*) surplus; (*reste*): **~ de bois** wood left over

**surprenant, e** [syʀpʀənɑ̃, ɑ̃t] *adj* amazing

**surprendre** [syʀpʀɑ̃dʀ] *vt* (*étonner*) to surprise; (*tomber sur: intrus etc*) to catch; (*entendre*) to overhear

**surpris, e** [syʀpʀi, iz] *adj*: **~ (de/que)** surprised (at/that); **surprise** *nf* surprise; **faire une surprise à qn** to give sb a surprise; **surprise-partie** *nf* party

**sursaut** [syʀso] *nm* start, jump; **~ de** (*énergie, indignation*) sudden fit *ou* burst of; **en ~** with a start; **sursauter** *vi* to (give a) start, jump

**sursis** [syʀsi] *nm* (*Jur: gén*) suspended sentence; (*fig*) reprieve

**surtout** [syʀtu] *adv* (*avant tout, d'abord*) above all; (*spécialement, particulièrement*) especially; **~, ne dites rien!** whatever you do don't say anything!; **~ pas!** certainly *ou* definitely not!; **~ que ...** especially as ...

**surveillance** [syʀvejɑ̃s] *nf* watch; (*Police, Mil*) surveillance; **sous ~ médicale** under medical supervision

**surveillant, e** [syʀvejɑ̃, ɑ̃t] *nm/f* (*de prison*) warder; (*Scol*) monitor

**surveiller** [syʀveje] *vt* (*enfant, élèves, bagages*) to watch, keep an eye on; (*prisonnier, suspect*) to keep (a) watch on; (*territoire, bâtiment*) to (keep) watch over; (*travaux, cuisson*) to supervise; (*Scol: examen*) to invigilate; **~ son langage/sa ligne** to watch one's language/figure

**survenir** [syʀvəniʀ] *vi* (*incident, retards*) to occur, arise; (*événement*) to take place

**survêtement** [syʀvɛtmɑ̃] *nm* tracksuit

**survie** [syʀvi] *nf* survival; **survivant, e** *nm/f* survivor; **survivre** *vi* to survive; **survivre à** (*accident etc*) to survive

**survoler** [syʀvɔle] *vt* to fly over; (*fig: livre*) to skim through

**survolté, e** [syʀvɔlte] *adj* (*fig*) worked up

**sus** [sy(s)]: **en ~ de** *prép* in addition to, over and above; **en ~** in addition

**susceptible** [sysɛptibl] *adj* touchy, sensitive; **~ de faire** (*hypothèse*) liable to do

**susciter** [sysite] *vt* (*admiration*) to arouse; (*ennuis*) **~ (à qn)** to create (for sb)

**suspect, e** [syspɛ(kt), ɛkt] *adj* suspicious; (*témoignage, opinions*) suspect ▷ *nm/f* suspect; **suspecter** *vt* to suspect; (*honnêteté de qn*) to question, have one's suspicions about

**suspendre** [syspɑ̃dʀ] *vt* (*accrocher: vêtement*): **~ qch (à)** to hang sth up (on); (*interrompre, démettre*) to suspend

**suspendu, e** [syspɑ̃dy] *adj* (*accroché*): **~ à** hanging on (*ou* from); (*perché*): **~ au-dessus de** suspended over

**suspens** [syspɑ̃]: **en ~** *adv* (*affaire*) in abeyance; **tenir en ~** to keep in suspense

**suspense** [syspɛns, syspɑ̃s] *nm* suspense

**suspension** [syspɑ̃sjɔ̃] *nf* suspension; (*lustre*) light fitting *ou* fitment

**suture** [sytyʀ] *nf* (*Méd*): **point de ~** stitch

**svelte** [svɛlt] *adj* slender, svelte

**SVP** *abr* (= *s'il vous plaît*) please

**sweat** [swit] *nm* (*fam*) sweatshirt

**sweat-shirt** [switʃœʀt] (*pl* **~s**) *nm* sweatshirt

**syllabe** [si(l)lab] *nf* syllable

**symbole** [sɛ̃bɔl] *nm* symbol; **symbolique** *adj* symbolic(al); (*geste, offrande*) token *cpd*; **symboliser** *vt* to symbolize

**symétrique** [simetʀik] *adj* symmetrical

**sympa** [sɛ̃pa] (*fam*) *adj inv* nice; **sois ~, prête-le moi** be a pal and lend it to me

**sympathie** [sɛ̃pati] *nf* (*inclination*) liking; (*affinité*) friendship; (*condoléances*) sympathy; **j'ai beaucoup de ~ pour lui** I like him a lot; **sympathique** *adj* nice, friendly

> Attention à ne pas traduire *sympathique* par *sympathetic*.

**sympathisant, e** [sɛ̃patizɑ̃, ɑ̃t] *nm/f* sympathizer

**sympathiser** [sɛ̃patize] *vi* (*voisins etc: s'entendre*) to get on (BRIT) *ou* along (US) (well)

**symphonie** [sɛ̃fɔni] *nf* symphony

**symptôme** [sɛ̃ptom] *nm* symptom

**synagogue** [sinagɔg] *nf* synagogue

**syncope** [sɛ̃kɔp] *nf* (*Méd*) blackout; **tomber en ~** to faint, pass out

**syndic** [sɛ̃dik] *nm* (*d'immeuble*) managing agent

**syndical, e, -aux** [sɛ̃dikal, o] *adj* (trade) union *cpd*; **syndicaliste** *nm/f* trade unionist

**syndicat** [sɛ̃dika] *nm* (*d'ouvriers, employés*) (trade) union; **syndicat d'initiative** tourist office; **syndiqué, e** *adj* belonging to a (trade) union; **syndiquer**: **se syndiquer** *vi* to form a trade union; (*adhérer*) to join a trade union

**synonyme** [sinɔnim] *adj* synonymous ▷ *nm* synonym; **~ de** synonymous with

**syntaxe** [sɛ̃taks] *nf* syntax

**synthèse** [sɛ̃tɛz] *nf* synthesis

**synthétique** [sɛ̃tetik] *adj* synthetic

**Syrie** [siʀi] *nf*: **la ~** Syria

**systématique** [sistematik] *adj* systematic

**système** [sistɛm] *nm* system; **le ~ D** resourcefulness

**t'** [t] *pron voir* **te**

**ta** [ta] *adj voir* **ton'**

**tabac** [taba] *nm* tobacco; *(magasin)* tobacconist's (shop)

**tabagisme** [tabaʒism] *nm*: **tabagisme passif** passive smoking

**table** [tabl] *nf* table; **à ~!** dinner *etc* is ready!; **se mettre à ~** to sit down to eat; **mettre la ~** to lay the table; **une ~ pour 4, s'il vous plaît** a table for 4, please; **table à repasser** ironing board; **table de cuisson** hob; **table de nuit ou de chevet** bedside table; **table des matières** (table of) contents *pl*; **table d'orientation** viewpoint indicator; **table roulante** trolley *(BRIT)*, tea wagon *(US)*

**tableau, x** [tablo] *nm (peinture)* painting; *(reproduction, fig)* picture; *(panneau)* board; *(schéma)* table, chart; **tableau d'affichage** notice board; **tableau de bord** dashboard; *(Aviat)* instrument panel; **tableau noir** blackboard

**tablette** [tablɛt] *nf (planche)* shelf; **tablette de chocolat** bar of chocolate

**tablier** [tablije] *nm* apron

**tabou** [tabu] *nm* taboo

**tabouret** [taburɛ] *nm* stool

**tac** [tak] *nm*: **il m'a répondu du ~ au ~** he answered me right back

**tache** [taʃ] *nf (saleté)* stain, mark; *(Art, de couleur, lumière)* spot; **tache de rousseur** freckle

**tâche** [taʃ] *nf* task

**tacher** [taʃe] *vt* to stain, mark

**tâcher** [taʃe] *vi*: **~ de faire** to try *ou* endeavour to do

**tacheté, e** [taʃte] *adj* spotted

**tact** [takt] *nm* tact; **avoir du ~** to be tactful

**tactique** [taktik] *adj* tactical ▷ *nf (technique)* tactics *sg*; *(plan)* tactic

**taie** [tɛ] *nf*: **~ (d'oreiller)** pillowslip, pillowcase

**taille** [taj] *nf* cutting; *(d'arbre etc)* pruning; *(milieu du corps)* waist; *(hauteur)* height; *(grandeur)* size; **de ~ à faire** capable of doing; **de ~** sizeable; **taille-crayon(s)** *nm* pencil sharpener

**tailler** [taje] *vt (pierre, diamant)* to cut; *(arbre, plante)* to prune; *(vêtement)* to cut out; *(crayon)* to sharpen

**tailleur** [tajœr] *nm (couturier)* tailor; *(vêtement)* suit; **en ~** *(assis)* cross-legged

**taillis** [taji] *nm* copse

**taire** [tɛr] *vi*: **faire ~ qn** to make sb be quiet; **se taire** *vi* to be silent *ou* quiet; **taisez-vous!** be quiet!

**Taiwan** [tajwan] *nf* Taiwan

**talc** [talk] *nm* talc, talcum powder

**talent** [talɑ̃] *nm* talent

**talkie-walkie** [tokiwoki] *nm* walkie-talkie

**talon** [talɔ̃] *nm* heel; *(de chèque, billet)* stub, counterfoil *(BRIT)*; **talons plats/aiguilles** flat/stiletto heels

**talus** [taly] *nm* embankment

**tambour** [tɑ̃bur] *nm (Mus, aussi Tech)* drum; *(musicien)* drummer; *(porte)* revolving door(s *pl*); **tambourin** *nm* tambourine

**Tamise** [tamiz] *nf*: **la ~** the Thames
**tamisé, e** [tamize] *adj* (*fig*) subdued, soft
**tampon** [tɑ̃pɔ̃] *nm* (*de coton, d'ouate*) wad, pad; (*amortisseur*) buffer; (*bouchon*) plug, stopper; (*cachet, timbre*) stamp; (**mémoire**) ~ (*Inform*) buffer; **tampon (hygiénique)** tampon; **tamponner** *vt* (*timbres*) to stamp; (*heurter*) to crash *ou* ram into; **tamponneuse** *adj f*: **autos tamponneuses** dodgems
**tandem** [tɑ̃dɛm] *nm* tandem
**tandis** [tɑ̃di]: **~ que** *conj* while
**tanguer** [tɑ̃ge] *vi* to pitch (and toss)
**tant** [tɑ̃] *adv* so much; **~ de** (*sable, eau*) so much; (*gens, livres*) so many; **~ que** as long as; (*autant que*) as much as; **~ mieux** that's great; (*avec une certaine réserve*) so much the better; **~ pis** too bad; (*conciliant*) never mind; **~ bien que mal** as well as can be expected
**tante** [tɑ̃t] *nf* aunt
**tantôt** [tɑ̃to] *adv* (*parfois*): **~ ... ~** now ... now; (*cet après-midi*) this afternoon
**taon** [tɑ̃] *nm* horsefly
**tapage** [tapaʒ] *nm* uproar, din
**tapageur, -euse** [tapaʒœʀ, øz] *adj* noisy; (*voyant*) loud, flashy
**tape** [tap] *nf* slap
**tape-à-l'œil** [tapalœj] *adj inv* flashy, showy
**taper** [tape] *vt* (*porte*) to bang, slam; (*enfant*) to slap; (*dactylographier*) to type (out); (*fam: emprunter*): **~ qn de 10 euros** to touch sb for 10 euros ▷ *vi* (*soleil*) to beat down; **se taper** *vt* (*repas*) to put away; (*fam: corvée*) to get landed with; **~ sur qn** to thump sb; (*fig*) to run sb down; **~ sur un clou** to hit a nail; **~ sur la table** to bang on the table; **~ à** (*porte etc*) to knock on; **~ dans** (*se servir*) to dig into; **~ des mains/pieds** to clap one's hands/stamp one's feet; **~ (à la machine)** to type
**tapi, e** [tapi] *adj* (*blotti*) crouching; (*caché*) hidden away
**tapis** [tapi] *nm* carpet; (*petit*) rug; **tapis de sol** (*de tente*) groundsheet;

**tapis de souris** (*Inform*) mouse mat; **tapis roulant** (*pour piétons*) moving walkway; (*pour bagages*) carousel
**tapisser** [tapise] *vt* (*avec du papier peint*) to paper; (*recouvrir*): **~ qch (de)** to cover sth (with); **tapisserie** *nf* (*tenture, broderie*) tapestry; (*papier peint*) wallpaper; **tapissier-décorateur** *nm* interior decorator
**tapoter** [tapɔte] *vt* (*joue, main*) to pat; (*objet*) to tap
**taquiner** [takine] *vt* to tease
**tard** [taʀ] *adv* late; **plus ~** later (on); **au plus ~** at the latest; **sur le ~** late in life; **il est trop ~** it's too late
**tarder** [taʀde] *vi* (*chose*) to be a long time coming; (*personne*): **~ à faire** to delay doing; **il me tarde d'être** I am longing to be; **sans (plus) ~** without (further) delay
**tardif, -ive** [taʀdif, iv] *adj* late
**tarif** [taʀif] *nm*: **~ des consommations** price list; **~s postaux/douaniers** postal/customs rates; **~ des taxis** taxi fares; **~ plein/réduit** (*train*) full/reduced fare; (*téléphone*) peak/off-peak rate
**tarir** [taʀiʀ] *vi* to dry up, run dry
**tarte** [taʀt] *nf* tart; **~ aux fraises** strawberry tart; **~ Tatin** ≈ apple upside-down tart
**tartine** [taʀtin] *nf* slice of bread; **tartine de miel** slice of bread and honey; **tartiner** *vt* to spread; **fromage à tartiner** cheese spread
**tartre** [taʀtʀ] *nm* (*des dents*) tartar; (*de bouilloire*) fur, scale
**tas** [tɑ] *nm* heap, pile; (*fig*): **un ~ de** heaps of, lots of; **en ~** in a heap *ou* pile; **formé sur le ~** trained on the job
**tasse** [tɑs] *nf* cup; **tasse à café** coffee cup
**tassé, e** [tɑse] *adj*: **bien ~** (*café etc*) strong
**tasser** [tɑse] *vt* (*terre, neige*) to pack down; (*entasser*): **~ qch dans** to cram sth into; **se tasser** *vi* (*se serrer*) to squeeze up; (*s'affaisser*) to settle; (*fig*) to

settle down
**tâter** [tate] vt to feel; (fig) to try out; **se tâter** (hésiter) to be in two minds; **~ de** (prison etc) to have a taste of
**tatillon, ne** [tatijɔ̃, ɔn] adj pernickety
**tâtonnement** [tatɔnmɑ̃] nm: **par ~s** (fig) by trial and error
**tâtonner** [tatɔne] vi to grope one's way along
**tâtons** [tatɔ̃]: **à ~** adv: **chercher/ avancer à ~** to grope around for/grope one's way forward
**tatouage** [tatwaʒ] nm tattoo
**tatouer** [tatwe] vt to tattoo
**taudis** [todi] nm hovel, slum
**taule** [tol] (fam) nf nick (fam), prison
**taupe** [top] nf mole
**taureau, x** [tɔʀo] nm bull; (signe): **le T~** Taurus
**taux** [to] nm rate; (d'alcool) level; **taux d'intérêt** interest rate
**taxe** [taks] nf tax; (douanière) duty; **toutes ~s comprises** inclusive of tax; **la boutique hors ~s** the duty-free shop; **taxe à la valeur ajoutée** value-added tax; **taxe de séjour** tourist tax
**taxer** [takse] vt (personne) to tax; (produit) to put a tax on, tax
**taxi** [taksi] nm taxi; (chauffeur: fam) taxi driver; **pouvez-vous m'appeler un ~, s'il vous plaît?** can you call me a taxi, please?
**Tchécoslovaquie** [tʃekɔslɔvaki] nf Czechoslovakia; **tchèque** adj Czech ▷ nm/f: **Tchèque** Czech ▷ nm (Ling) Czech; **la République tchèque** the Czech Republic
**Tchétchénie** [tʃetʃeni] nf: **la ~** Chechnya
**te, t'** [tə] pron you; (réfléchi) yourself
**technicien, ne** [tɛknisjɛ̃, jɛn] nm/f technician
**technico-commercial, e, -aux** [tɛknikokɔmɛʀsjal, jo] adj: **agent ~** sales technician
**technique** [tɛknik] adj technical ▷ nf technique; **techniquement** adv technically

**techno** [tɛkno] nf (Mus) techno (music)
**technologie** [tɛknɔlɔʒi] nf technology; **technologique** adj technological
**teck** [tɛk] nm teak
**tee-shirt** [tiʃœʀt] nm T-shirt, tee-shirt
**teindre** [tɛ̃dʀ] vt to dye; **se ~ les cheveux** to dye one's hair; **teint, e** adj dyed ▷ nm (du visage) complexion; (momentané) colour ▷ nf shade; **grand teint** colourfast
**teinté, e** [tɛ̃te] adj: **~ de** (fig) tinged with
**teinter** [tɛ̃te] vt (verre, papier) to tint; (bois) to stain
**teinture** [tɛ̃tyʀ] nf dye; **teinture d'iode** tincture of iodine; **teinturerie** nf dry cleaner's; **teinturier** nm dry cleaner
**tel, telle** [tɛl] adj (pareil) such; (comme): **~ un/des ...** like a/like ...; (indéfini) such-and-such a; (intensif): **un ~/de ~s ...** such (a)/such ...; **rien de ~** nothing like it; **~ que** like, such as; **~ quel** as it is ou stands (ou was etc); **venez ~ jour** come on such-and-such a day
**télé** [tele] (fam) nf TV; **à la ~** on TV ou telly
**télé...: télécabine** nf (benne) cable car; **télécarte** nf phonecard; **téléchargeable** adj downloadable; **téléchargement** nm (action) downloading; (fichier) download; **télécharger** vt to download; **télécommande** nf remote control; **télécopieur** nm fax machine; **télédistribution** nf cable TV; **télégramme** nm telegram; **télégraphier** vt to telegraph, cable; **téléguider** vt to radio-control; **télématique** nf telematics sg; **téléobjectif** nm telephoto lens sg; **télépathie** nf telepathy; **téléphérique** nm cable car
**téléphone** [telefɔn] nm telephone; **avoir le ~** to be on the (tele)phone; **au ~** on the phone; **téléphoner** vi to make a phone call; **téléphoner à** to phone,

call up; **est-ce que je peux téléphoner d'ici?** can I make a call from here?; **téléphonique** adj (tele)phone cpd
**télé...: téléréalité** nf reality TV
**télescope** [teleskɔp] nm telescope
**télescoper** [teleskɔpe] vt to smash up; **se télescoper** (véhicules) to concertina
**télé...: télescripteur** nm teleprinter; **télésiège** nm chairlift; **téléski** nm ski-tow; **téléspectateur, -trice** nm/f (television) viewer; **télétravail** nm telecommuting; **télévente** nf telesales; **téléviseur** nm television set; **télévision** nf television; **à la télévision** on television; **télévision numérique** digital TV; **télévision par câble/satellite** cable/satellite television
**télex** [teleks] nm telex
**telle** [tɛl] adj voir **tel; tellement** adv (tant) so much; (si) so; **tellement de** (sable, eau) so much; (gens, livres) so many; **il s'est endormi tellement il était fatigué** he was so tired (that) he fell asleep; **pas tellement** not (all) that much; not (all) that +adjectif
**téméraire** [temerɛr] adj reckless, rash
**témoignage** [temwaɲaʒ] nm (Jur: déclaration) testimony no pl, evidence no pl; (rapport, récit) account; (fig: d'affection etc: cadeau) token, mark; (: geste) expression
**témoigner** [temwaɲe] vt (intérêt, gratitude) to show ▷ vi (Jur) to testify, give evidence; **~ de** to bear witness to, testify to
**témoin** [temwɛ̃] nm witness ▷ adj: **appartement ~** show flat (BRIT); **être ~ de** to witness; **témoin oculaire** eyewitness
**tempe** [tɑ̃p] nf temple
**tempérament** [tɑ̃peramɑ̃] nm temperament, disposition; **à ~** (vente) on deferred (payment) terms; (achat) by instalments, hire purchase cpd
**température** [tɑ̃peratyr] nf temperature; **avoir** ou **faire de la ~** to be running ou have a temperature

**tempête** [tɑ̃pɛt] nf storm; **tempête de sable/neige** sand/snowstorm
**temple** [tɑ̃pl] nm temple; (protestant) church
**temporaire** [tɑ̃pɔrɛr] adj temporary
**temps** [tɑ̃] nm (atmosphérique) weather; (durée) time; (époque) time, times pl; (Ling) tense; (Mus) beat; (Tech) stroke; **un ~ de chien** (fam) rotten weather; **quel ~ fait-il?** what's the weather like?; **il fait beau/mauvais** the weather is fine/bad; **avoir le ~/tout son ~** to have time/plenty of time; **en ~ de paix/ guerre** in peacetime/wartime; **en ~ utile** ou **voulu** in due time ou course; **ces derniers ~** lately; **dans quelque ~** in a (little) while; **de ~ en ~, de ~ à autre** from time to time; **à ~** (partir, arriver) in time; **à ~ complet, à plein ~** full-time; **à ~ partiel, à mi-~** part-time; **dans le ~** at one time; **temps d'arrêt** pause, halt; **temps libre** free ou spare time; **temps mort** (Comm) slack period
**tenable** [t(ə)nabl] adj bearable
**tenace** [tənas] adj persistent
**tenant, e** [tənɑ̃, ɑ̃t] nm/f (Sport): **~ du titre** title-holder
**tendance** [tɑ̃dɑ̃s] nf tendency; (opinions) leanings pl, sympathies pl; (évolution) trend; **avoir ~ à** to have a tendency to, tend to
**tendeur** [tɑ̃dœr] nm (attache) elastic strap
**tendre** [tɑ̃dr] adj tender; (bois, roche, couleur) soft ▷ vt (élastique, peau) to stretch; (corde) to tighten; (muscle) to tense; (fig: piège) to set, lay; (donner): **~ qch à qn** to hold sth out to sb; (offrir) to offer sb sth; **se tendre** vi (corde) to tighten; (relations) to become strained; **~ à qch/à faire** to tend towards sth/to do; **~ l'oreille** to prick up one's ears; **~ la main/le bras** to hold out one's hand/ stretch out one's arm; **tendrement** adv tenderly; **tendresse** nf tenderness
**tendu, e** [tɑ̃dy] pp de **tendre** ▷ adj (corde) tight; (muscles) tensed; (relations) strained

**ténèbres** [tenɛbr] *nfpl* darkness *sg*

**teneur** [tənœr] *nf* content; (*d'une lettre*) terms *pl*, content

**tenir** [t(ə)niʀ] *vt* to hold; (*magasin, hôtel*) to run; (*promesse*) to keep ▷ *vi* to hold; (*neige, gel*) to last; **se tenir** *vi* (*avoir lieu*) to be held, take place; (*être: personne*) to stand; **~ à** (*personne, objet*) to be attached to; (*réputation*) to care about; **~ à faire** to be determined to do; **~ de** (*ressembler à*) to take after; **ça ne tient qu'à lui** it is entirely up to him; **~ qn pour** to regard sb as; **~ qch de qn** (*histoire*) to have heard *ou* learnt sth from sb; (*qualité, défaut*) to have inherited *ou* got sth from sb; **~ dans** to fit into; **~ compte de qch** to take sth into account; **~ les comptes** to keep the books; **~ bon** to stand fast; **~ le coup** to hold out; **~ au chaud** (*café, plat*) to keep hot; **un manteau qui tient chaud** a warm coat; **tiens/tenez, voilà le stylo** there's the pen!; **tiens, voilà Alain!** look, here's Alain!; **tiens?** (*surprise*) really?; **se ~ droit** to stand (*ou* sit) up straight; **bien se ~** to behave well; **se ~ à qch** to hold on to sth; **s'en ~ à qch** to confine o.s. to sth

**tennis** [tenis] *nm* tennis; (*court*) tennis court ▷ *nm ou f pl* (*aussi:* **chaussures de ~**) tennis *ou* gym shoes; **tennis de table** table tennis; **tennisman** *nm* tennis player

**tension** [tɑ̃sjɔ̃] *nf* tension; (*Méd*) blood pressure; **avoir de la ~** to have high blood pressure

**tentation** [tɑ̃tasjɔ̃] *nf* temptation

**tentative** [tɑ̃tativ] *nf* attempt

**tente** [tɑ̃t] *nf* tent

**tenter** [tɑ̃te] *vt* (*éprouver, attirer*) to tempt; (*essayer*): **~ qch/de faire** to attempt *ou* try sth/to do; **~ sa chance** to try one's luck

**tenture** [tɑ̃tyʀ] *nf* hanging

**tenu, e** [t(ə)ny] *pp de* **tenir** ▷ *adj* (*maison, comptes*): **bien ~** well-kept; (*obligé*): **~ de faire** obliged to do ▷ *nf* (*vêtements*) clothes *pl*; (*comportement*)

(good) manners *pl*, good behaviour; (*d'une maison*) upkeep; **en petite ~e** scantily dressed *ou* clad

**ter** [tɛʀ] *adj*: **16 ~** 16b *ou* B

**terme** [tɛʀm] *nm* term; (*fin*) end; **à court/long ~** *adj* short-/long-term ▷ *adv* in the short/long term; **avant ~** (*Méd*) prematurely; **mettre un ~ à** to put an end *ou* a stop to; **en bons ~s** on good terms

**terminaison** [tɛʀminɛzɔ̃] *nf* (*Ling*) ending

**terminal, -aux** [tɛʀminal, o] *nm* terminal; **terminale** *nf* (*Scol*) ≈ year 13 (*BRIT*), ≈ twelfth grade (*US*)

**terminer** [tɛʀmine] *vt* to finish; **se terminer** *vi* to end; **quand est-ce que le spectacle se termine?** when does the show finish?

**terne** [tɛʀn] *adj* dull

**ternir** [tɛʀniʀ] *vt* to dull; (*fig*) to sully, tarnish; **se ternir** *vi* to become dull

**terrain** [teʀɛ̃] *nm* (*sol, fig*) ground; (*Comm: étendue de terre*) land *no pl*; (*parcelle*) plot (of land); (*à bâtir*) site; **sur le ~** (*fig*) on the field; **terrain d'aviation** airfield; **terrain de camping** campsite; **terrain de football/rugby** football/ rugby pitch (*BRIT*) *ou* field (*US*); **terrain de golf** golf course; **terrain de jeu** games field; (*pour les petits*) playground; **terrain de sport** sports ground; **terrain vague** waste ground *no pl*

**terrasse** [teʀas] *nf* terrace; **à la ~** (*café*) outside; **terrasser** *vt* (*adversaire*) to floor; (*suj: maladie etc*) to strike down

**terre** [tɛʀ] *nf* (*gén, aussi* Élec) earth; (*substance*) soil, earth; (*opposé à mer*) land *no pl*; (*contrée*) land; **terres** *nfpl* (*terrains*) lands, land *sg*; **en ~** (*pipe, poterie*) clay *cpd*; **à ~ ou par ~** (*mettre, être, s'asseoir*) on the ground (*ou* floor); (*jeter, tomber*) to the ground, down; **terre à terre** *adj inv* (*considération, personne*) down-to-earth; **terre cuite** terracotta; **la terre ferme** dry land; **terre glaise** clay

**terreau** [teʀo] *nm* compost

**terre-plein** [tɛʀplɛ̃] nm platform; (sur chaussée) central reservation

**terrestre** [teʀɛstʀ] adj (surface) earth's, of the earth; (Bot, Zool, Mil) land cpd; (Rel) earthly

**terreur** [teʀœʀ] nf terror no pl

**terrible** [teʀibl] adj terrible, dreadful; (fam) terrific; **pas ~** nothing special

**terrien, ne** [teʀjɛ̃, jɛn] adj: **propriétaire ~** landowner ▷ nm/f (non martien etc) earthling

**terrier** [teʀje] nm burrow, hole; (chien) terrier

**terrifier** [teʀifje] vt to terrify

**terrine** [teʀin] nf (récipient) terrine; (Culin) pâté

**territoire** [teʀitwaʀ] nm territory

**terroriser** [teʀɔʀize] vt to terrorize

**terrorisme** [teʀɔʀism] nm terrorism; **terroriste** nm/f terrorist

**tertiaire** [tɛʀsjɛʀ] adj tertiary ▷ nm (Écon) service industries pl

**tes** [te] adj voir **ton¹**

**test** [tɛst] nm test

**testament** [tɛstamɑ̃] nm (Jur) will; (Rel) Testament; (fig) legacy

**tester** [tɛste] vt to test

**testicule** [tɛstikyl] nm testicle

**tétanos** [tetanos] nm tetanus

**têtard** [tɛtaʀ] nm tadpole

**tête** [tɛt] nf head; (cheveux) hair no pl; (visage) face; **de ~** (comme adj: wagon etc) front cpd; (comme adv: calculer) in one's head, mentally; **perdre la ~** (fig: s'affoler) to lose one's head; (: devenir fou) to go off one's head; **tenir ~ à qn** to stand up to sb; **la ~ en bas** with one's head down; **la ~ la première** (tomber) headfirst; **faire une ~** (Football) to head the ball; **faire la ~** (fig) to sulk; **en ~** at the front; (Sport) in the lead; **à la ~ de** at the head of; **à ~ reposée** in a more leisurely moment; **n'en faire qu'à sa ~** to do as one pleases; **en avoir par-dessus la ~** to be fed up; **en ~ à ~** in private, alone together; **de la ~ aux pieds** from head to toe; **tête de lecture** (playback) head; **tête de liste** (Pol) chief candidate; **tête**

de mort skull and crossbones; **tête de série** (Tennis) seeded player, seed; **tête de Turc** (fig) whipping boy (BRIT), butt; **tête-à-queue** nm inv: **faire un tête-à-queue** to spin round

**téter** [tete] vt: **~ (sa mère)** to suck at one's mother's breast, feed

**tétine** [tetin] nf teat; (sucette) dummy (BRIT), pacifier (US)

**têtu, e** [tety] adj stubborn, pigheaded

**texte** [tɛkst] nm text; (morceau choisi) passage

**textile** [tɛkstil] adj textile cpd ▷ nm textile; **le ~** the textile industry

**Texto®** [tɛksto] nm text message

**texture** [tɛkstyʀ] nf texture

**TGV** sigle m (= train à grande vitesse) high-speed train

**thaïlandais, e** [tajlɑ̃dɛ, ɛz] adj Thai ▷ nm/f: **T~, e** Thai

**Thaïlande** [tailɑ̃d] nf Thailand

**thé** [te] nm tea; **~ au citron** lemon tea; **~ au lait** tea with milk; **prendre le ~** to have tea; **faire le ~** to make the tea

**théâtral, e, -aux** [teatʀal, o] adj theatrical

**théâtre** [teatʀ] nm theatre; (péj: simulation) playacting; (fig: lieu): **le ~ de** the scene of; **faire du ~** to act

**théière** [tejɛʀ] nf teapot

**thème** [tɛm] nm theme; (Scol: traduction) prose (composition)

**théologie** [teɔlɔʒi] nf theology

**théorie** [teɔʀi] nf theory; **théorique** adj theoretical

**thérapie** [teʀapi] nf therapy

**thermal, e, -aux** [tɛʀmal, o] adj: **station ~e** spa; **cure ~e** water cure

**thermomètre** [tɛʀmɔmɛtʀ] nm thermometer

**thermos®** [tɛʀmos] nm ou nf: **(bouteille) thermos** vacuum ou Thermos® flask

**thermostat** [tɛʀmɔsta] nm thermostat

**thèse** [tɛz] nf thesis

**thon** [tɔ̃] nm tuna (fish)

**thym** [tɛ̃] nm thyme

**Tibet** [tibɛ] nm: **le ~** Tibet

**tibia** [tibja] nm shinbone, tibia; (partie antérieure de la jambe) shin

**TIC** sigle fpl (= technologies de l'information et de la communication) ICT sg

**tic** [tik] nm tic, (nervous) twitch; (de langage etc) mannerism

**ticket** [tikɛ] nm ticket; **ticket de caisse** receipt; **je peux avoir un ticket de caisse, s'il vous plaît?** can I have a receipt, please?

**tiède** [tjɛd] adj lukewarm; (vent, air) mild, warm; **tiédir** vi to cool; (se réchauffer) to grow warmer

**tien, ne** [tjɛ̃, tjɛn] pron: **le(la) ~(ne), les ~(ne)s** yours; **à la ~ne!** cheers!

**tiens** [tjɛ̃] vb, excl voir **tenir**

**tiercé** [tjɛRse] nm system of forecast betting giving first 3 horses

**tiers, tierce** [tjɛR, tjɛRs] adj third ▷ nm (Jur) third party; (fraction) third; **le tiers monde** the Third World

**tige** [tiʒ] nf stem; (baguette) rod

**tignasse** [tiɲas] (péj) nf mop of hair

**tigre** [tigR] nm tiger; **tigré, e** adj (rayé) striped; (tacheté) spotted; (chat) tabby; **tigresse** nf tigress

**tilleul** [tijœl] nm lime (tree), linden (tree); (boisson) lime(-blossom) tea

**timbre** [tɛ̃bR] nm (tampon) stamp; (aussi: **~-poste**) (postage) stamp; (Mus: de voix, instrument) timbre, tone

**timbré, e** [tɛ̃bRe] (fam) adj cracked

**timide** [timid] adj shy; (timoré) timid; **timidement** adv shyly; timidly; **timidité** nf shyness; timidity

**tintamarre** [tɛ̃tamaR] nm din, uproar

**tinter** [tɛ̃te] vi to ring, chime; (argent, clefs) to jingle

**tique** [tik] nf (parasite) tick

**tir** [tiR] nm (sport) shooting; (fait ou manière de tirer) firing no pl; (rafale) fire; (stand) shooting gallery; **tir à l'arc** archery

**tirage** [tiRaʒ] nm (action) printing; (Photo) print; (de journal) circulation; (de livre: nombre d'exemplaires) (print) run; (: édition) edition; (de loterie) draw; **par ~**

**au sort** by drawing lots

**tire** [tiR] nf: **vol à la ~** pickpocketing

**tiré, e** [tiRe] adj (traits) drawn; **~ par les cheveux** far-fetched

**tire-bouchon** [tiRbuʃɔ̃] nm corkscrew

**tirelire** [tiRliR] nf moneybox

**tirer** [tiRe] vt (gén) to pull; (trait, rideau, carte, conclusion, chèque) to draw; (langue) to stick out; (en faisant feu: balle, coup) to fire; (: animal) to shoot; (journal, livre, photo) to print; (Football: corner etc) to take ▷ vi (faire feu) to fire; (faire du tir, Football) to shoot; **se tirer** vi (fam) to push off; **s'en ~** (éviter le pire) to get off; (survivre) to pull through; (se débrouiller) to manage; **~ qch de** (extraire) to take ou pull sth out of; **~ qn de** (embarras etc) to help ou get sb out of; **~ sur** (corde) to pull on ou at; (faire feu sur) to shoot ou fire at; (pipe) to draw on; (approcher de: couleur) to verge ou border on; **~ à l'arc/la carabine** to shoot with a bow and arrow/with a rifle; **~ à sa fin** to be drawing to a close; **~ qch au clair** to clear sth up; **~ au sort** to draw lots; **~ parti de** to take advantage of; **~ profit de** to profit from; **~ les cartes** to read ou tell the cards

**tiret** [tiRɛ] nm dash

**tireur** [tiRœR] nm gunman; **tireur d'élite** marksman

**tiroir** [tiRwaR] nm drawer; **tiroir-caisse** nm till

**tisane** [tizan] nf herb tea

**tisser** [tise] vt to weave

**tissu** [tisy] nm fabric, material, cloth no pl; (Anat, Bio) tissue; **tissu-éponge** nm (terry) towelling no pl

**titre** [titR] nm (gén) title; (de journal) headline; (diplôme) qualification; (Comm) security; **en ~** (champion) official; **à juste ~** rightly; **à quel ~?** on what grounds?; **à aucun ~** on no account; **au même ~ (que)** in the same way (as); **à ~ d'information** for (your) information; **à ~ gracieux** free of charge; **à ~ d'essai** on a trial basis; **à ~ privé** in a private capacity;

**titre de propriété** title deed; **titre de transport** ticket

**tituber** [titybe] vi to stagger (along)

**titulaire** [titylɛʀ] adj (Admin) with tenure ▷ nm/f (de permis) holder; **être ~ de** (diplôme, permis) to hold

**toast** [tost] nm slice ou piece of toast; (de bienvenue) (welcoming) toast; **porter un ~ à qn** to propose ou drink a toast to sb

**toboggan** [tɔbɔgɑ̃] nm slide; (Auto) flyover

**toc** [tɔk] excl: **~, ~** knock knock ▷ nm: **en ~** fake

**tocsin** [tɔksɛ̃] nm alarm (bell)

**tohu-bohu** [tɔybɔy] nm hubbub

**toi** [twa] pron you

**toile** [twal] nf (tableau) canvas; **de** ou **en ~** (pantalon) cotton; (sac) canvas; **la T~** (Internet) the Web; **toile cirée** oilcloth; **toile d'araignée** cobweb; **toile de fond** (fig) backdrop

**toilette** [twalɛt] nf (habits) outfit; **toilettes** nfpl (w.-c.) toilet sg; **faire sa ~** to have a wash, get washed; **articles de ~** toiletries; **où sont les ~s?** where's the toilet?

**toi-même** [twamɛm] pron yourself

**toit** [twa] nm roof; **toit ouvrant** sunroof

**toiture** [twatyʀ] nf roof

**Tokyo** [tɔkjo] n Tokyo

**tôle** [tol] nf (plaque) steel ou iron sheet; **tôle ondulée** corrugated iron

**tolérable** [tɔleʀabl] adj tolerable

**tolérant, e** [tɔleʀɑ̃, ɑ̃t] adj tolerant

**tolérer** [tɔleʀe] vt to tolerate; (Admin: hors taxe etc) to allow

**tollé** [tɔ(l)le] nm outcry

**tomate** [tɔmat] nf tomato; **~s farcies** stuffed tomatoes

**tombe** [tɔ̃b] nf (sépulture) grave; (avec monument) tomb

**tombeau, x** [tɔ̃bo] nm tomb

**tombée** [tɔ̃be] nf: **à la ~ de la nuit** at nightfall

**tomber** [tɔ̃be] vi to fall; (fièvre, vent) to drop; **laisser ~** (objet) to drop; (personne) to let down; (activité) to give up; **laisse ~!** forget it!; **faire ~** to knock over; **~ sur** (rencontrer) to bump into; **~ de fatigue/sommeil** to drop from exhaustion/be falling asleep on one's feet; **ça tombe bien** that's come at the right time; **il est bien tombé** he's been lucky; **~ à l'eau** (projet) to fall through; **~ en panne** to break down

**tombola** [tɔ̃bɔla] nf raffle

**tome** [tɔm] nm volume

**ton¹, ta** [tɔ̃, ta] (pl tes) adj your

**ton²** [tɔ̃] nm (gén) tone; (couleur) shade, tone; **de bon ~** in good taste

**tonalité** [tɔnalite] nf (au téléphone) dialling tone

**tondeuse** [tɔ̃døz] nf (à gazon) (lawn)mower; (du coiffeur) clippers pl; (pour les moutons) shears pl

**tondre** [tɔ̃dʀ] vt (pelouse, herbe) to mow; (haie) to cut, clip; (mouton, toison) to shear; (cheveux) to crop

**tongs** [tɔ̃g] nfpl flip-flops

**tonifier** [tɔnifje] vt (peau, organisme) to tone up

**tonique** [tɔnik] adj fortifying ▷ nm tonic

**tonne** [tɔn] nf metric ton, tonne

**tonneau, x** [tɔno] nm (à vin, cidre) barrel; **faire des ~x** (voiture, avion) to roll over

**tonnelle** [tɔnɛl] nf bower, arbour

**tonner** [tɔne] vi to thunder; **il tonne** it is thundering, there's some thunder

**tonnerre** [tɔnɛʀ] nm thunder

**tonus** [tɔnys] nm energy

**top** [tɔp] nm: **au 3ème ~** at the 3rd stroke ▷ adj: **~ secret** top secret

**topinambour** [tɔpinɑ̃buʀ] nm Jerusalem artichoke

**torche** [tɔʀʃ] nf torch

**torchon** [tɔʀʃɔ̃] nm cloth; (à vaisselle) tea towel ou cloth

**tordre** [tɔʀdʀ] vt (chiffon) to wring; (barre, fig: visage) to twist; **se tordre** vi: **se ~ le poignet/la cheville** to twist one's wrist/ankle; **se ~ de douleur/rire** to be doubled up with pain/laughter;

**tordu, e** adj bent; (fig) crazy

**tornade** [tɔʀnad] nf tornado

**torrent** [tɔʀɑ̃] nm mountain stream

**torsade** [tɔʀsad] nf: **un pull à ~s** a cable sweater

**torse** [tɔʀs] nm chest; (Anat, Sculpture) torso; **~ nu** stripped to the waist

**tort** [tɔʀ] nm (défaut) fault; **torts** nmpl (Jur) fault sg; **avoir ~** to be wrong; **être dans son ~** to be in the wrong; **donner ~ à qn** to lay the blame on sb; **causer du ~ à qn** to harm sb; **à ~** wrongly; **à ~ et à travers** wildly

**torticolis** [tɔʀtikɔli] nm stiff neck

**tortiller** [tɔʀtije] vt to twist; (moustache) to twirl; **se tortiller** vi to wriggle; (en dansant) to wiggle

**tortionnaire** [tɔʀsjɔnɛʀ] nm torturer

**tortue** [tɔʀty] nf tortoise; (d'eau douce) terrapin; (d'eau de mer) turtle

**tortueux, -euse** [tɔʀtɥø, øz] adj (rue) twisting; (fig) tortuous

**torture** [tɔʀtyʀ] nf torture; **torturer** vt to torture; (fig) to torment

**tôt** [to] adv early; **~ ou tard** sooner or later; **si ~** so early; (déjà) so soon; **plus ~** earlier; **au plus ~** at the earliest

**total, e, -aux** [tɔtal, o] adj, nm total; **au ~** in total; (fig) on the whole; **faire le ~** to work out the total; **totalement** adv totally; **totaliser** vt to total; **totalitaire** adj totalitarian; **totalité** nf: **la totalité de** all (of); the whole +sg; **en totalité** entirely

**toubib** [tubib] (fam) nm doctor

**touchant, e** [tuʃɑ̃, ɑ̃t] adj touching

**touche** [tuʃ] nf (de piano, de machine à écrire) key; (de téléphone) button; (Peinture etc) stroke, touch; (fig: de nostalgie) touch; (Football: aussi: **remise en ~**) throw-in; (aussi: **ligne de ~**) touch-line; **touche dièse** (de téléphone, clavier) hash key

**toucher** [tuʃe] nm touch ▷ vt to touch; (palper) to feel; (atteindre: d'un coup de feu etc) to hit; (concerner) to concern, affect; (contacter) to reach, contact; (recevoir: récompense) to receive, get; (: salaire) to draw, get; (: chèque) to cash; **se toucher** (être en contact) to touch; **au ~** to the touch; **~ à** to touch; (concerner) to have to do with, concern; **je vais lui en ~ un mot** I'll have a word with him about it; **~ au but** (fig) to near one's goal; **~ à sa fin** to be drawing to a close

**touffe** [tuf] nf tuft

**touffu, e** [tufy] adj thick, dense

**toujours** [tuʒuʀ] adv always; (encore) still; (constamment) forever; **~ plus** more and more; **pour ~** forever; **~ est-il que** the fact remains that; **essaie ~** (you can) try anyway

**toupie** [tupi] nf (spinning) top

**tour**[1] [tuʀ] nf tower; (immeuble) high-rise block (BRIT ou building (US); (Échecs) castle, rook; **tour de contrôle** nf control tower; **la tour Eiffel** the Eiffel Tower

**tour**[2] [tuʀ] nm (excursion) trip; (à pied) stroll, walk; (en voiture) run, ride; (Sport: aussi: **~ de piste**) lap; (d'être servi ou de jouer etc) turn; (de roue etc) revolution; (Pol: aussi: **~ de scrutin**) ballot; (ruse, de prestidigitation) trick; (de potier) wheel; (à bois, métaux) lathe; (circonférence): **de 3 m de ~** 3 m round, with a circumference ou girth of 3 m; **faire le ~ de** to go round; (à pied) to walk round; **c'est au ~ de Renée** it's Renée's turn; **à ~ de rôle, à ~** in turn; **tour de chant** nm song recital; **tour de force** tour de force; **tour de garde** nm spell of duty; **tour d'horizon** nm (fig) general survey; **tour de taille/tête** nm waist/head measurement; **un 33 tours** an LP; **un 45 tours** a single

**tourbe** [tuʀb] nf peat

**tourbillon** [tuʀbijɔ̃] nm whirlwind; (d'eau) whirlpool; (fig) whirl, swirl; **tourbillonner** vi to whirl (round)

**tourelle** [tuʀɛl] nf turret

**tourisme** [tuʀism] nm tourism; **agence de ~** tourist agency; **faire du ~** to go touring; (en ville) to go sightseeing; **touriste** nm/f tourist; **touristique** adj tourist cpd; (région) touristic

**tourment** [tuʁmɑ̃] *nm* torment;
**tourmenter** *vt* to torment; **se
tourmenter** to fret, worry o.s.

**tournage** [tuʁnaʒ] *nm* (*Cinéma*)
shooting

**tournant** [tuʁnɑ̃] *nm* (*de route*) bend;
(*fig*) turning point

**tournée** [tuʁne] *nf* (*du facteur etc*)
round; (*d'artiste, politicien*) tour; (*au café*)
round (of drinks)

**tourner** [tuʁne] *vt* to turn; (*sauce,
mélange*) to stir; (*Cinéma: faire les prises
de vues*) to shoot; (: *produire*) to make
▷ *vi* to turn; (*moteur*) to run; (*taximètre*)
to tick away; (*lait etc*) to turn (sour); **se
tourner** *vi* to turn round; **tournez à
gauche/droite au prochain carrefour**
turn left/right at the next junction;
**mal ~** to go wrong; **~ autour de** to go
round; (*péj*) to hang round; **~ à/en** to
turn into; **~ qn en ridicule** to ridicule
sb; **~ le dos à** (*mouvement*) to turn one's
back on; (*position*) to have one's back
to; **~ de l'œil** to pass out; **se ~ vers** to
turn towards; (*fig*) to turn to; **se ~ les
pouces** to twiddle one's thumbs

**tournesol** [tuʁnəsɔl] *nm* sunflower

**tournevis** [tuʁnəvis] *nm* screwdriver

**tournoi** [tuʁnwa] *nm* tournament

**tournure** [tuʁnyʁ] *nf* (*Ling*) turn of
phrase; (*évolution*): **la ~ de qch** the way
sth is developing; **tournure d'esprit**
turn *ou* cast of mind

**tourte** [tuʁt] *nf* pie

**tourterelle** [tuʁtəʁɛl] *nf* turtledove

**tous** [tu] *adj, pron voir* **tout**

**Toussaint** [tusɛ̃] *nf*: **la ~** All Saints' Day

**tousser** [tuse] *vi* to cough

○ **MOT-CLÉ**

**tout, e** [tu, tut] (*mpl* **tous**, *fpl* **toutes**)
*adj* **1** (*avec article singulier*) all; **tout le
lait** all the milk; **toute la nuit** all night,
the whole night; **tout le livre** the whole
book; **tout un pain** a whole loaf; **tout
le temps** all the time; the whole time;
**tout le monde** everybody; **c'est tout
le contraire** it's quite the opposite
**2** (*avec article pluriel*) every, all; **tous les
livres** all the books; **toutes les nuits**
every night; **toutes les fois** every time;
**toutes les trois/deux semaines** every
third/other *ou* second week, every
three/two weeks; **tous les deux** both
*ou* each of us (*ou* them *ou* you); **toutes
les trois** all three of us (*ou* them *ou* you)
**3** (*sans article*): **à tout âge** at any age;
**pour toute nourriture, il avait ...** his
only food was ...
▷ *pron* everything, all; **il a tout fait**
he's done everything; **je les vois tous**
I can see them all *ou* all of them; **nous y
sommes tous allés** all of us went, we
all went; **c'est tout** that's all; **en tout** in
all; **tout ce qu'il sait** all he knows
▷ *nm* whole; **le tout** all of it (*ou* them);
**le tout est de ...** the main thing is to ...;
**pas du tout** not at all
▷ *adv* **1** (*très, complètement*) very; **tout
près** very near; **le tout premier** the
very first; **tout seul** all alone; **le livre
tout entier** the whole book; **tout
en haut** right at the top; **tout droit**
straight ahead
**2**: **tout en** while; **tout en travaillant**
while working, as he *etc* works *ou* worked
**3**: **tout d'abord** first of all; **tout à coup**
suddenly; **tout à fait** absolutely; **tout
à l'heure** a short while ago; (*futur*) in a
short while, shortly; **à tout à l'heure!**
see you later!; **tout de même** all the
same; **tout de suite** immediately,
straight away; **tout simplement**
quite simply

**toutefois** [tutfwa] *adv* however

**toutes** [tut] *adj, pron voir* **tout**

**tout-terrain** [tuterɛ̃] *adj*: **vélo ~**
mountain bike; **véhicule ~** four-wheel
drive

**toux** [tu] *nf* cough

**toxicomane** [tɔksikɔman] *nm/f*
drug addict

**toxique** [tɔksik] *adj* toxic

**trac** [tʀak] *nm (au théâtre, en public)*
stage fright; *(aux examens)* nerves *pl*;
**avoir le ~** *(au théâtre, en public)* to have
stage fright; *(aux examens)* to be feeling
nervous

**tracasser** [tʀakase] *vt* to worry,
bother; **se tracasser** to worry

**trace** [tʀas] *nf (empreintes)* tracks *pl*;
*(marques, aussi fig)* mark; *(quantité
infime, indice, vestige)* trace; **traces de
pas** footprints

**tracer** [tʀase] *vt* to draw; *(piste)* to
open up

**tract** [tʀakt] *nm* tract, pamphlet

**tracteur** [tʀaktœʀ] *nm* tractor

**traction** [tʀaksjɔ̃] *nf*: **~ avant/arrière**
front-wheel/rear-wheel drive

**tradition** [tʀadisjɔ̃] *nf* tradition;
**traditionnel, le** *adj* traditional

**traducteur, -trice** [tʀadyktœʀ, tʀis]
*nm/f* translator

**traduction** [tʀadyksjɔ̃] *nf* translation

**traduire** [tʀadɥiʀ] *vt* to translate;
*(exprimer)* to convey; **~ qn en justice**
to bring sb before the courts; **pouvez-
vous me ~ ceci?** can you translate
this for me?

**trafic** [tʀafik] *nm* traffic; **trafic
d'armes** arms dealing; **trafiquant, e**
*nm/f* trafficker; *(d'armes)* dealer;
**trafiquer** *(péj) vt (vin)* to doctor;
*(moteur, document)* to tamper with

**tragédie** [tʀaʒedi] *nf* tragedy;
**tragique** *adj* tragic

**trahir** [tʀaiʀ] *vt* to betray; **trahison** *nf*
betrayal; *(Jur)* treason

**train** [tʀɛ̃] *nm (Rail)* train; *(allure)* pace;
**être en ~ de faire qch** to be doing
sth; **c'est bien le ~ pour ...?** is this
the train for ...?; **train d'atterrissage**

undercarriage; **train de vie** lifestyle;
**train électrique** *(jouet)* (electric)
train set

**traîne** [tʀɛn] *nf (de robe)* train; **être à la
~** to lag behind

**traîneau, x** [tʀɛno] *nm* sleigh, sledge

**traîner** [tʀene] *vt (remorque)* to pull;
*(enfant, chien)* to drag *ou* trail along ▷ *vi
(robe, manteau)* to trail; *(être en désordre)*
to lie around; *(aller lentement)* to dawdle
(along); *(vagabonder, agir lentement)*
to hang about; *(durer)* to drag on; **se
traîner** *vi*: **se ~ par terre** to crawl
(on the ground); **~ les pieds** to drag
one's feet

**train-train** [tʀɛ̃tʀɛ̃] *nm* humdrum
routine

**traire** [tʀɛʀ] *vt* to milk

**trait** [tʀɛ] *nm (ligne)* line; *(de dessin)*
stroke; *(caractéristique)* feature, trait;
**traits** *nmpl (du visage)* features; **d'un
~** *(boire)* in one gulp; **de ~** *(animal)*
draught; **avoir ~ à** to concern; **trait
d'union** hyphen

**traitant, e** [tʀɛtɑ̃, ɑ̃t] *adj (shampooing)*
medicated; **votre médecin ~** your
usual *ou* family doctor

**traite** [tʀɛt] *nf (Comm)* draft; *(Agr)*
milking; **d'une ~** without stopping

**traité** [tʀete] *nm* treaty

**traitement** [tʀɛtmɑ̃] *nm* treatment;
*(salaire)* salary; **traitement de
données** data processing; **traitement
de texte** word processing; *(logiciel)*
word processing package

**traiter** [tʀete] *vt* to treat; *(qualifier)*: **~
qn d'idiot** to call sb a fool ▷ *vi* to deal; **~
de** to deal with

**traiteur** [tʀɛtœʀ] *nm* caterer

**traître, -esse** [tʀɛtʀ, tʀɛtʀɛs] *adj
(dangereux)* treacherous ▷ *nm* traitor

**trajectoire** [tʀaʒɛktwaʀ] *nf* path

**trajet** [tʀaʒɛ] *nm (parcours, voyage)*
journey; *(itinéraire)* route; *(distance à
parcourir)* distance; **il y a une heure de
~** the journey takes one hour

**trampoline** [tʀɑ̃pɔlin] *nm* trampoline

**tramway** [tʀamwɛ] *nm* tram(way);

(*voiture*) tram(car) (BRIT), streetcar (US)

**tranchant, e** [tʀɑ̃ʃɑ̃, ɑ̃t] *adj* sharp; (*fig*) peremptory ▷ *nm* (*d'un couteau*) cutting edge; (*de la main*) edge; **à double ~** double-edged

**tranche** [tʀɑ̃ʃ] *nf* (*morceau*) slice; (*arête*) edge; **~ d'âge/de salaires** age/wage bracket

**tranché, e** [tʀɑ̃ʃe] *adj* (*couleurs*) distinct; (*opinions*) clear-cut

**trancher** [tʀɑ̃ʃe] *vt* to cut, sever ▷ *vi* to take a decision; **~ avec** to contrast sharply with

**tranquille** [tʀɑ̃kil] *adj* quiet; (*rassuré*) easy in one's mind, with one's mind at rest; **se tenir ~** (*enfant*) to be quiet; **laisse-moi/laisse-ça ~** leave me/it alone; **avoir la conscience ~** to have a clear conscience; **tranquillisant** *nm* tranquillizer; **tranquillité** *nf* peace (and quiet); (*d'esprit*) peace of mind

**transférer** [tʀɑ̃sfeʀe] *vt* to transfer; **transfert** *nm* transfer

**transformation** [tʀɑ̃sfɔʀmasjɔ̃] *nf* change, alteration; (*radicale*) transformation; (*Rugby*) conversion; **transformations** *nfpl* (*travaux*) alterations

**transformer** [tʀɑ̃sfɔʀme] *vt* to change; (*radicalement*) to transform; (*vêtement*) to alter; (*matière première, appartement, Rugby*) to convert; **(se) ~ en** to turn into

**transfusion** [tʀɑ̃sfyzjɔ̃] *nf*: **~ sanguine** blood transfusion

**transgénique** [tʀɑ̃sʒenik] *adj* transgenic

**transgresser** [tʀɑ̃sgʀese] *vt* to contravene

**transi, e** [tʀɑ̃zi] *adj* numb (with cold), chilled to the bone

**transiger** [tʀɑ̃ziʒe] *vi* to compromise

**transit** [tʀɑ̃zit] *nm* transit; **transiter** *vi* to pass in transit

**transition** [tʀɑ̃zisjɔ̃] *nf* transition; **transitoire** *adj* transitional

**transmettre** [tʀɑ̃smɛtʀ] *vt* (*passer*): **~ qch à qn** to pass sth on to sb;

(*Tech, Tél, Méd*) to transmit; (*TV, Radio: retransmettre*) to broadcast; **transmission** *nf* transmission

**transparent, e** [tʀɑ̃spaʀɑ̃, ɑ̃t] *adj* transparent

**transpercer** [tʀɑ̃spɛʀse] *vt* (*froid, pluie*) to go through, pierce; (*balle*) to go through

**transpiration** [tʀɑ̃spiʀasjɔ̃] *nf* perspiration

**transpirer** [tʀɑ̃spiʀe] *vi* to perspire

**transplanter** [tʀɑ̃splɑ̃te] *vt* (*Méd, Bot*) to transplant

**transport** [tʀɑ̃spɔʀ] *nm* transport; **transports en commun** public transport *sg*; **transporter** *vt* to carry, move; (*Comm*) to transport, convey; **transporteur** *nm* haulage contractor (BRIT), trucker (US)

**transvaser** [tʀɑ̃svɑze] *vt* to decant

**transversal, e, -aux** [tʀɑ̃svɛʀsal, o] *adj* (*rue*) which runs across; **coupe ~e** cross section

**trapèze** [tʀapɛz] *nm* (*au cirque*) trapeze

**trappe** [tʀap] *nf* trap door

**trapu, e** [tʀapy] *adj* squat, stocky

**traquenard** [tʀaknaʀ] *nm* trap

**traquer** [tʀake] *vt* to track down; (*harceler*) to hound

**traumatiser** [tʀomatize] *vt* to traumatize

**travail, -aux** [tʀavaj] *nm* (*gén*) work; (*tâche, métier*) work *no pl*, job; (*Écon, Méd*) labour; **être sans ~** (*employé*) to be unemployed; *voir aussi* **travaux**; **travail (au) noir** moonlighting

**travailler** [tʀavaje] *vi* to work; (*bois*) to warp ▷ *vt* (*bois, métal*) to work; (*objet d'art, discipline*) to work on; **cela travaille** it is on his mind; **travailleur, -euse** *adj* hard-working ▷ *nm/f* worker; **travailleur social** social worker; **travailliste** *adj* ≈ Labour *cpd*

**travaux** [tʀavo] *nmpl* (*de réparation, agricoles etc*) work *sg*; (*sur route*) roadworks *pl*; (*de construction*) building (work); **travaux des champs** farmwork *sg*; **travaux dirigés** (*Scol*) tutorial sg; **travaux forcés** hard labour no pl; **travaux manuels** (Scol) handicrafts; **travaux ménagers** housework no pl; **travaux pratiques** (Scol) practical work; (en laboratoire) lab work

**travers** [tʀavɛʀ] nm fault, failing; **en ~ (de)** across; **au ~ (de)/à ~** through; **de ~** (nez, bouche) crooked; (chapeau) askew; **comprendre de ~** to misunderstand; **regarder de ~** (fig) to look askance at

**traverse** [tʀavɛʀs] nf (de voie ferrée) sleeper; **chemin de ~** shortcut

**traversée** [tʀavɛʀse] nf crossing; **combien de temps dure la ~?** how long does the crossing take?

**traverser** [tʀavɛʀse] vt (gén) to cross; (ville, tunnel, aussi: percer, fig) to go through; (suj: ligne, trait) to run across

**traversin** [tʀavɛʀsɛ̃] nm bolster

**travesti** [tʀavɛsti] nm transvestite

**trébucher** [tʀebyʃe] vi: **~ (sur)** to stumble (over), trip (against)

**trèfle** [tʀɛfl] nm (Bot) clover; (Cartes: couleur) clubs pl; (: carte) club; **~ à quatre feuilles** four-leaf clover

**treize** [tʀɛz] num thirteen; **treizième** num thirteenth

**tréma** [tʀema] nm diaeresis

**tremblement** [tʀɑ̃bləmɑ̃] nm: **tremblement de terre** earthquake

**trembler** [tʀɑ̃ble] vi to tremble, shake; **~ de** (froid, fièvre) to shiver ou tremble with; (peur) to shake ou tremble with; **~ pour qn** to fear for sb

**trémousser** [tʀemuse]: **se trémousser** vi to jig about, wriggle about

**trempé, e** [tʀɑ̃pe] adj soaking (wet), drenched; (Tech) tempered

**tremper** [tʀɑ̃pe] vt to soak, drench; (aussi: **faire ~, mettre à ~**) to soak; (plonger): **~ qch dans** to dip sth in(to) ▷ vi to soak; (fig): **~ dans** to be involved ou have a hand in; **se tremper** vi to have a quick dip

**tremplin** [tʀɑ̃plɛ̃] nm springboard; (Ski) ski-jump

**trentaine** [tʀɑ̃tɛn] nf: **une ~ (de)** thirty or so, about thirty; **avoir la ~** (âge) to be around thirty

**trente** [tʀɑ̃t] num thirty; **être sur son ~ et un** to be wearing one's Sunday best; **trentième** num thirtieth

**trépidant, e** [tʀepidɑ̃, ɑ̃t] adj (fig: rythme) pulsating; (: vie) hectic

**trépigner** [tʀepiɲe] vi to stamp (one's feet)

**très** [tʀɛ] adv very; much +pp, highly +pp

**trésor** [tʀezɔʀ] nm treasure; **Trésor (public)** public revenue; **trésorerie** nf (gestion) accounts pl; (bureaux) accounts department; **difficultés de trésorerie** cash problems, shortage of cash ou funds; **trésorier, -ière** nm/f treasurer

**tressaillir** [tʀesajiʀ] vi to shiver, shudder

**tressauter** [tʀesote] vi to start, jump

**tresse** [tʀɛs] nf braid, plait; **tresser** vt (cheveux) to braid, plait; (fil, jonc) to plait; (corbeille) to weave; (corde) to twist

**tréteau, x** [tʀeto] nm trestle

**treuil** [tʀœj] nm winch

**trêve** [tʀɛv] nf (Mil, Pol) truce; (fig) respite; **~ de ...** enough of this ...

**tri** [tʀi] nm: **faire le ~ (de)** to sort out; **le (bureau de) ~** (Postes) the sorting office

**triangle** [tʀijɑ̃gl] nm triangle; **triangulaire** adj triangular

**tribord** [tʀibɔʀ] nm: **à ~** to starboard, on the starboard side

**tribu** [tʀiby] nf tribe

**tribunal, -aux** [tʀibynal, o] nm (Jur) court; (Mil) tribunal

**tribune** [tʀibyn] nf (estrade) platform, rostrum; (débat) forum; (d'église, de tribunal) gallery; (de stade) stand

**tribut** [tʀiby] nm tribute

**tributaire** [tʀibytɛʀ] adj: **être ~ de** to be dependent on

**tricher** [tʀiʃe] vi to cheat; **tricheur, -euse** nm/f cheat(er)

**tricolore** [tʀikɔlɔʀ] adj three-coloured; (français) red, white and blue

**tricot** [tʀiko] nm (technique, ouvrage) knitting no pl; (vêtement) jersey, sweater; **~ de peau** vest; **tricoter** vt to knit

**tricycle** [tʀisikl] nm tricycle

**trier** [tʀije] vt to sort out; (Postes, fruits) to sort

**trimestre** [tʀimɛstʀ] nm (Scol) term; (Comm) quarter; **trimestriel, le** adj quarterly; (Scol) end-of-term

**trinquer** [tʀɛ̃ke] vi to clink glasses

**triomphe** [tʀijɔ̃f] nm triumph; **triompher** vi to triumph, win; **triompher de** to triumph over, overcome

**tripes** [tʀip] nfpl (Culin) tripe sg

**triple** [tʀipl] adj triple ▷ nm: **le ~ (de)** (comparaison) three times as much (as); **en ~ exemplaire** in triplicate; **tripler** vi, vt to triple, treble

**triplés, -ées** [tʀiple] nm/fpl triplets

**tripoter** [tʀipɔte] vt to fiddle with

**triste** [tʀist] adj sad; (couleur, temps, journée) dreary; (péj): **~ personnage/ affaire** sorry individual/affair; **tristesse** nf sadness

**trivial, e, -aux** [tʀivjal, jo] adj coarse, crude; (commun) mundane

**troc** [tʀɔk] nm barter

**trognon** [tʀɔɲɔ̃] nm (de fruit) core; (de légume) stalk

**trois** [tʀwa] num three; **troisième** num third ▷ nf (Scol) year 10 (BRIT), ninth grade (US); **le troisième âge** (période de vie) one's retirement years; (personnes âgées) senior citizens pl

**trombe** [tʀɔ̃b] nf: **des ~s d'eau** a downpour; **en ~** like a whirlwind

**trombone** [tʀɔ̃bɔn] nm (Mus) trombone; (de bureau) paper clip

**trompe** [tʀɔ̃p] nf (d'éléphant) trunk; (Mus) trumpet, horn

**tromper** [tʀɔ̃pe] vt to deceive; (vigilance, poursuivants) to elude; **se tromper** vi to make a mistake, be mistaken; **se ~ de voiture/jour** to take the wrong car/get the day wrong; **se ~ de 3 cm/20 euros** to be out by 3 cm/20

euros; **je me suis trompé de route** I took the wrong road

**trompette** [tʀɔ̃pɛt] nf trumpet; **en ~ (nez)** turned-up

**trompeur, -euse** [tʀɔ̃pœʀ, øz] adj deceptive

**tronc** [tʀɔ̃] nm (Bot, Anat) trunk; (d'église) collection box

**tronçon** [tʀɔ̃sɔ̃] nm section; **tronçonner** vt to saw up; **tronçonneuse** nf chainsaw

**trône** [tʀon] nm throne

**trop** [tʀo] adv (+vb) too much; (+adjectif, adverbe) too; **~ (nombreux)** too many; **~ peu (nombreux)** too few; **~ (souvent)** too often; **~ (longtemps)** (for) too long; **~ de** (nombre) too many; (quantité) too much; **de ~, en ~**: **des livres en ~** a few books too many; **du lait en ~** too much milk; **3 livres/3 euros de ~** 3 books too many/3 euros too much; **ça coûte ~ cher** it's too expensive

**tropical, e, -aux** [tʀɔpikal, o] adj tropical

**tropique** [tʀɔpik] nm tropic

**trop-plein** [tʀoplɛ̃] nm (tuyau) overflow ou outlet (pipe); (liquide) overflow

**troquer** [tʀɔke] vt: **~ qch contre** to barter ou trade sth for; (fig) to swap sth for

**trot** [tʀo] nm trot; **trotter** vi to trot

**trottinette** [tʀɔtinɛt] nf (child's) scooter

**trottoir** [tʀɔtwaʀ] nm pavement (BRIT), sidewalk (US); **faire le ~** (péj) to walk the streets; **trottoir roulant** moving walkway, travellator

**trou** [tʀu] nm hole; (fig) gap; (Comm) deficit; **trou d'air** air pocket; **trou de mémoire** blank, lapse of memory

**troublant, e** [tʀublɑ̃, ɑ̃t] adj disturbing

**trouble** [tʀubl] adj (liquide) cloudy; (image, photo) blurred; (affaire) shady, murky ▷ adv: **voir ~** to have blurred vision ▷ nm agitation; **troubles** nmpl (Pol) disturbances, troubles, unrest sg;

(*Méd*) trouble *sg*, disorders; **trouble-fête** *nm* spoilsport

**troubler** [tʀuble] *vt* to disturb; (*liquide*) to make cloudy; (*intriguer*) to bother; **se troubler** *vi* (*personne*) to become flustered *ou* confused

**trouer** [tʀue] *vt* to make a hole (*ou* holes) in

**trouille** [tʀuj] (*fam*) *nf*: **avoir la ~** to be scared to death

**troupe** [tʀup] *nf* troop; **troupe (de théâtre)** (theatrical) company

**troupeau, x** [tʀupo] *nm* (*de moutons*) flock; (*de vaches*) herd

**trousse** [tʀus] *nf* case, kit; (*d'écolier*) pencil case; **aux ~s de** (*fig*) on the heels *ou* tail of; **trousse à outils** toolkit; **trousse de toilette** toilet bag

**trousseau, x** [tʀuso] *nm* (*de mariée*) trousseau; **trousseau de clefs** bunch of keys

**trouvaille** [tʀuvaj] *nf* find

**trouver** [tʀuve] *vt* to find; (*rendre visite*): **aller/venir ~ qn** to go/come and see sb; **se trouver** *vi* (*être*) to be; **je trouve que** I find *ou* think that; **~ à boire/critiquer** to find something to drink/criticize; **se ~ mal** to pass out

**truand** [tʀyɑ̃] *nm* (*astuce*) gangster; **truander** *vt*: **se faire truander** to be swindled

**truc** [tʀyk] *nm* (*astuce*) way, trick; (*de cinéma, prestidigitateur*) trick, effect; (*chose*) thing, thingumajig; **avoir le ~** to have the knack; **c'est pas mon ~** (*fam*) it's not really my thing

**truffe** [tʀyf] *nf* truffle; (*nez*) nose

**truffé, e** [tʀyfe] *adj* (*Culin*) garnished with truffles; **~ de** (*fig: citations*) peppered with; (*: fautes*) riddled with; (*: pièges*) bristling with

**truie** [tʀɥi] *nf* sow

**truite** [tʀɥit] *nf* trout *inv*

**truquage** [tʀykaʒ] *nm* special effects *pl*

**truquer** [tʀyke] *vt* (*élections, serrure, dés*) to fix

**TSVP** *sigle* (= *tournez svp*) PTO

**TTC** *sigle* (= *toutes taxes comprises*) inclusive of tax

**tu¹** [ty] *pron* you; **dire tu à qn** to use the "tu" form to sb

**tu², e** [ty] *pp de* **taire**

**tuba** [tyba] *nm* (*Mus*) tuba; (*Sport*) snorkel

**tube** [tyb] *nm* tube; (*chanson*) hit

**tuberculose** [tybɛʀkyloz] *nf* tuberculosis

**tuer** [tɥe] *vt* to kill; **se tuer** *vi* to be killed; (*suicide*) to kill o.s.; **se ~ au travail** (*fig*) to work o.s. to death; **tuerie** *nf* slaughter *no pl*

**tue-tête** [tytɛt]: **à ~** *adv* at the top of one's voice

**tueur** [tɥœʀ] *nm* killer; **tueur à gages** hired killer

**tuile** [tɥil] *nf* tile; (*fam*) spot of bad luck, blow

**tulipe** [tylip] *nf* tulip

**tuméfié, e** [tymefje] *adj* puffed-up, swollen

**tumeur** [tymœʀ] *nf* growth, tumour

**tumulte** [tymylt] *nm* commotion; **tumultueux, -euse** *adj* stormy, turbulent

**tunique** [tynik] *nf* tunic

**Tunis** [tynis] *n* Tunis

**Tunisie** [tynizi] *nf*: **la ~** Tunisia; **tunisien, ne** *adj* Tunisian ▷ *nm/f*: **Tunisien, ne** Tunisian

**tunnel** [tynɛl] *nm* tunnel; **le ~ sous la Manche** the Channel Tunnel

**turbulent, e** [tyʀbylɑ̃, ɑ̃t] *adj* boisterous, unruly

**turc, turque** [tyʀk] *adj* Turkish ▷ *nm/f*: **T~, Turque** Turk/Turkish woman ▷ *nm* (*Ling*) Turkish

**turf** [tyʀf] *nm* racing; **turfiste** *nm/f* racegoer

**Turquie** [tyʀki] *nf*: **la ~** Turkey

**turquoise** [tyʀkwaz] *nf* turquoise ▷ *adj inv* turquoise

**tutelle** [tytɛl] *nf* (*Jur*) guardianship; (*Pol*) trusteeship; **sous la ~ de** (*fig*) under the supervision of

**tuteur** [tytœʀ] *nm* (*Jur*) guardian; (*de plante*) stake, support

**tutoyer** [tytwaje] *vt*: **~ qn** to address

sb as "tu"

**tuyau, x** [tɥijo] *nm* pipe; *(flexible)* tube;
*(fam)* tip; **tuyau d'arrosage** hosepipe;
**tuyau d'échappement** exhaust pipe;
**tuyauterie** *nf* piping *no pl*

**TVA** *sigle f* (= *taxe à la valeur ajoutée*) VAT

**tympan** [tɛ̃pɑ̃] *nm* (*Anat*) eardrum

**type** [tip] *nm* type; *(fam)* chap, guy ▷ *adj*
typical, classic

**typé, e** [tipe] *adj* ethnic

**typique** [tipik] *adj* typical

**tyran** [tiʀɑ̃] *nm* tyrant; **tyrannique** *adj*
tyrannical

**tzigane** [dzigan] *adj* gipsy, tzigane

**ulcère** [ylsɛʀ] *nm* ulcer

**ultérieur, e** [ylteʀjœʀ] *adj* later,
subsequent; **remis à une date**
**~e** postponed to a later date;
**ultérieurement** *adv* later,
subsequently

**ultime** [yltim] *adj* final

 **MOT-CLÉ**

**un, une** [œ̃, yn] *art indéf* a; (*devant*
*voyelle*) an; **un garçon/vieillard** a
boy/an old man; **une fille** a girl
▷ *pron* one; **l'un des meilleurs** one of
the best; **l'un ..., l'autre** (the) one ...,
the other; **les uns ..., les autres**
some ..., others; **l'un et l'autre** both
(of them); **l'un ou l'autre** either (of
them); **l'un l'autre** each other; **les**
**uns les autres** one another; **pas un**
**seul** not a single one; **un par un** one
by one
▷ *num* one; **un pamplemousse**
**seulement** one grapefruit only, just

one grapefruit
▷ *nf*: **la une** (*Presse*) the front page

**unanime** [ynanim] *adj* unanimous;
**unanimité** *nf*: **à l'unanimité**
unanimously

**uni, e** [yni] *adj* (*ton, tissu*) plain; (*surface*)
smooth, even; (*famille*) close(-knit);
(*pays*) united

**unifier** [ynifje] *vt* to unite, unify

**uniforme** [yniform] *adj* uniform;
(*surface, ton*) even ▷ *nm* uniform;
**uniformiser** *vt* (*systèmes*) to
standardize

**union** [ynjɔ̃] *nf* union; **union de
consommateurs** consumers'
association; **union libre**: **vivre en
union libre** (*en concubinage*) to cohabit;
**Union européenne** European Union;
**Union soviétique** Soviet Union

**unique** [ynik] *adj* (*seul*) only;
(*exceptionnel*) unique; (*le même*): **un
prix/système ~** a single price/system;
**fils/fille ~** only son/daughter,
only child; **sens ~** one-way street;
**uniquement** *adv* only, solely; (*juste*)
only, merely

**unir** [ynir] *vt* (*nations*) to unite; (*en
mariage*) to unite, join together; **s'unir**
*vi* to unite; (*en mariage*) to be joined
together

**unitaire** [yniter] *adj*: **prix ~** unit price

**unité** [ynite] *nf* unit; (*harmonie,
cohésion*) unity

**univers** [yniver] *nm* universe;
**universel, le** *adj* universal

**universitaire** [yniversiter] *adj*
university *cpd*; (*diplôme, études*)
academic, university *cpd* ▷ *nm/f*
academic

**université** [yniversite] *nf* university

**urbain, e** [yrbɛ̃, ɛn] *adj* urban, city
*cpd*, town *cpd*; **urbanisme** *nm* town
planning

**urgence** [yrʒɑ̃s] *nf* urgency; (*Méd etc*)
emergency; **d'~** *adj* emergency *cpd*
▷ *adv* as a matter of urgency; **(service
des) ~s** casualty

**urgent, e** [yrʒɑ̃, ɑ̃t] *adj* urgent

**urine** [yrin] *nf* urine; **urinoir** *nm*
(public) urinal

**urne** [yrn] *nf* (*électorale*) ballot box;
(*vase*) urn

**urticaire** [yrtiker] *nf* nettle rash

**us** [ys] *nmpl*: **us et coutumes** (habits
and) customs

**usage** [yzaʒ] *nm* (*emploi, utilisation*) use;
(*coutume*) custom; **à l'~** with use; **à l'~
de** (*pour*) for (use of); **en ~** in use; **hors
d'~** out of service; **à ~ interne** (*Méd*) to
be taken (internally); **à ~ externe** (*Méd*)
for external use only; **usagé, e** *adj* (*usé*)
worn; **usager, -ère** *nm/f* user

**usé, e** [yze] *adj* worn; (*banal: argument
etc*) hackneyed

**user** [yze] *vt* (*outil*) to wear down;
(*vêtement*) to wear out; (*matière*) to wear
away; (*consommer: charbon etc*) to use;
**s'user** *vi* (*tissu, vêtement*) to wear out;
**~ de** (*moyen, procédé*) to use, employ;
(*droit*) to exercise

**usine** [yzin] *nf* factory

**usité, e** [yzite] *adj* common

**ustensile** [ystɑ̃sil] *nm* implement;
**ustensile de cuisine** kitchen utensil

**usuel, le** [yzɥɛl] *adj* everyday, common

**usure** [yzyr] *nf* wear

**utérus** [yterys] *nm* uterus, womb

**utile** [ytil] *adj* useful

**utilisation** [ytilizasjɔ̃] *nf* use

**utiliser** [ytilize] *vt* to use

**utilitaire** [ytiliter] *adj* utilitarian

**utilité** [ytilite] *nf* usefulness *no pl*; **de
peu d'~** of little use *ou* help

**utopie** [ytɔpi] *nf* utopia

**V**

**va** [va] *vb voir* **aller**

**vacance** [vakɑ̃s] *nf* (*Admin*) vacancy; **vacances** *nfpl* holiday(s *pl* (BRIT)), vacation *sg* (US); **les grandes ~s** the summer holidays; **prendre des/ses ~s** to take a holiday/one's holiday(s); **aller en ~s** to go on holiday; **je suis ici en ~s** I'm here on holiday; **vacancier, -ière** *nm/f* holiday-maker

**vacant, e** [vakɑ̃, ɑ̃t] *adj* vacant

**vacarme** [vakaʀm] *nm* (*bruit*) racket

**vaccin** [vaksɛ̃] *nm* vaccine; (*opération*) vaccination; **vaccination** *nf* vaccination; **vacciner** *vt* to vaccinate; **être vacciné contre qch** (*fam*) to be cured of sth

**vache** [vaʃ] *nf* (*Zool*) cow; (*cuir*) cowhide ▷ *adj* (*fam*) rotten, mean; **vachement** (*fam*) *adv* (*très*) really; (*pleuvoir, travailler*) a hell of a lot; **vacherie** *nf* (*action*) dirty trick; (*remarque*) nasty remark

**vaciller** [vasije] *vi* to sway, wobble; (*bougie, lumière*) to flicker; (*fig*) to be failing, falter

**va-et-vient** [vaevjɛ̃] *nm inv* (*de personnes, véhicules*) comings and goings *pl*, to-ings and fro-ings *pl*

**vagabond** [vagabɔ̃] *nm* (*rôdeur*) tramp, vagrant; (*voyageur*) wanderer; **vagabonder** *vi* to roam, wander

**vagin** [vaʒɛ̃] *nm* vagina

**vague** [vag] *nf* wave ▷ *adj* vague; (*regard*) faraway; (*manteau, robe*) loose(-fitting); (*quelconque*): **un ~ bureau/cousin** some office/cousin or other; **vague de fond** ground swell; **vague de froid** cold spell

**vaillant, e** [vajɑ̃, ɑ̃t] *adj* (*courageux*) gallant; (*robuste*) hale and hearty

**vain, e** [vɛ̃, vɛn] *adj* vain; **en ~** in vain

**vaincre** [vɛ̃kʀ] *vt* to defeat; (*fig*) to conquer, overcome; **vaincu, e** *nm/f* defeated party; **vainqueur** *nm* victor; (*Sport*) winner

**vaisseau, x** [vɛso] *nm* (*Anat*) vessel; (*Navig*) ship, vessel; **vaisseau spatial** spaceship

**vaisselier** [vɛsəlje] *nm* dresser

**vaisselle** [vɛsɛl] *nf* (*service*) crockery; (*plats etc à laver*) (dirty) dishes *pl*; **faire la ~** to do the washing-up (BRIT) *ou* the dishes

**valable** [valabl] *adj* valid; (*acceptable*) decent, worthwhile

**valet** [valɛ] *nm* manservant; (*Cartes*) jack

**valeur** [valœʀ] *nf* (*gén*) value; (*mérite*) worth, merit; (*Comm: titre*) security; **valeurs** *nfpl* (*morales*) values; (*objet décoratif*) **en ~** to highlight; (*objet décoratif*) to show off to advantage; **avoir de la ~** to be valuable; **sans ~** worthless; **prendre de la ~** to go up *ou* gain in value

**valide** [valid] *adj* (*en bonne santé*) fit; (*valable*) valid; **valider** *vt* to validate

**valise** [valiz] *nf* (suit)case; **faire ses ~s** to pack one's bags

**vallée** [vale] *nf* valley

**vallon** [valɔ̃] *nm* small valley

**valoir** [valwaʀ] *vi* (*être valable*) to hold, apply ▷ *vt* (*prix, valeur, effort*) to be worth; (*causer*): **~ qch à qn** to earn sb sth; **se valoir** *vi* to be of equal merit; (*péj*) to be two of a kind; **faire ~** (*droits, prérogatives*) to assert; **se faire ~** to make the most of o.s.; **à ~ sur** to be deducted from; **vaille que vaille** somehow or other; **cela ne me dit rien qui vaille** I don't like the look of it at all; **ce climat ne me vaut rien** this climate doesn't suit me; **~ le coup** *ou* **la peine** to be worth the trouble *ou* worth it; **~ mieux: il vaut mieux se taire** it's better to say nothing; **ça ne vaut rien** it's worthless; **que vaut ce candidat?** how good is this applicant?

**valse** [vals] *nf* waltz

**vandalisme** [vãdalism] *nm* vandalism

**vanille** [vanij] *nf* vanilla

**vanité** [vanite] *nf* vanity; **vaniteux, -euse** *adj* vain, conceited

**vanne** [van] *nf* gate; (*fig*) joke

**vannerie** [vanʀi] *nf* basketwork

**vantard, e** [vãtaʀ, aʀd] *adj* boastful

**vanter** [vãte] *vt* to speak highly of, praise; **se vanter** *vi* to boast, brag; **se ~ de** to pride o.s. on; (*péj*) to boast of

**vapeur** [vapœʀ] *nf* steam; (*émanation*) vapour, fumes *pl*; **vapeurs** *nfpl* (*bouffées*) vapours; **à ~** steam-powered, steam *cpd*; **cuit à la ~** steamed; **vaporeux, -euse** *adj* (*flou*) hazy, misty; (*léger*) filmy; **vaporisateur** *nm* spray; **vaporiser** *vt* (*parfum etc*) to spray

**varappe** [vaʀap] *nf* rock climbing

**vareuse** [vaʀøz] *nf* (*blouson*) pea jacket; (*d'uniforme*) tunic

**variable** [vaʀjabl] *adj* variable; (*temps, humeur*) changeable; (*divers: résultats*) varied, various

**varice** [vaʀis] *nf* varicose vein

**varicelle** [vaʀisɛl] *nf* chickenpox

**varié, e** [vaʀje] *adj* varied; (*divers*) various; **hors d'œuvre ~s** selection of hors d'œuvres

**varier** [vaʀje] *vi* to vary; (*temps, humeur*) to change ▷ *vt* to vary; **variété** *nf* variety; **variétés** *nfpl*: **spectacle/émission de variétés** variety show

**variole** [vaʀjɔl] *nf* smallpox

**Varsovie** [vaʀsɔvi] *n* Warsaw

**vas** [va] *vb voir* **aller**; **~-y!** [vazi] go on!

**vase** [vaz] *nm* vase ▷ *nf* silt, mud; **vaseux, -euse** *adj* silty, muddy; (*fig: confus*) woolly, hazy; (*: fatigué*) woozy

**vasistas** [vazistas] *nm* fanlight

**vaste** [vast] *adj* vast, immense

**vautour** [votuʀ] *nm* vulture

**vautrer** [votʀe] *vb*: **se ~ dans/sur** to wallow in/sprawl on

**va-vite** [vavit]: **à la ~** *adv* in a rush *ou* hurry

**VDQS** *sigle* (= *vin délimité de qualité supérieure*) *label guaranteeing the quality of wine*

**veau, x** [vo] *nm* (*Zool*) calf; (*Culin*) veal; (*peau*) calfskin

**vécu, e** [veky] *pp de* **vivre**

**vedette** [vədɛt] *nf* (*artiste etc*) star; (*canot*) motor boat; (*police*) launch

**végétal, e, -aux** [veʒetal, o] *adj* vegetable ▷ *nm* vegetable, plant; **végétalien, ne** *adj, nm/f* vegan

**végétarien, ne** [veʒetaʀjɛ̃, jɛn] *adj, nm/f* vegetarian; **avez-vous des plats ~s?** do you have any vegetarian dishes?

**végétation** [veʒetasjɔ̃] *nf* vegetation; **végétations** *nfpl* (*Méd*) adenoids

**véhicule** [veikyl] *nm* vehicle; **véhicule utilitaire** commercial vehicle

**veille** [vɛj] *nf* (*état*) wakefulness; (*jour*): **la ~ (de)** the day before; **la ~ au soir** the previous evening; **à la ~ de** on the eve of; **la ~ de Noël** Christmas Eve; **la ~ du jour de l'An** New Year's Eve

**veillée** [veje] *nf* (*soirée*) evening; (*réunion*) evening gathering; **veillée (funèbre)** wake

**veiller** [veje] *vi* to stay up ▷ *vt* (*malade, mort*) to watch over, sit up with; **~ à** to attend to, see to; **~ à ce que** to make sure that; **~ sur** to watch over; **veilleur** *nm*: **veilleur de nuit** night watchman; **veilleuse** *nf* (*lampe*) night light; (*Auto*) sidelight; (*flamme*) pilot light

**veinard, e** [venaʀ, aʀd] *nm/f* lucky devil

**veine** [vɛn] *nf* (*Anat, du bois etc*) vein; (*filon*) vein, seam; (*fam: chance*): **avoir de la ~** to be lucky

**véliplanchiste** [veliplɑ̃ʃist] *nm/f* windsurfer

**vélo** [velo] *nm* bike, cycle; **faire du ~** to go cycling; **vélomoteur** *nm* moped

**velours** [v(ə)luʀ] *nm* velvet; **velours côtelé** corduroy; **velouté, e** *adj* velvety ▷ *nm*: **velouté de tomates** cream of tomato soup

**velu, e** [vəly] *adj* hairy

**vendange** [vɑ̃dɑ̃ʒ] *nf* (*aussi*: ~**s**) grape harvest; **vendanger** *vi* to harvest the grapes

**vendeur, -euse** [vɑ̃dœʀ, øz] *nm/f* shop assistant ▷ *nm* (*Jur*) vendor, seller

**vendre** [vɑ̃dʀ] *vt* to sell; **~ qch à qn** to sell sb sth; **"à ~"** "for sale"

**vendredi** [vɑ̃dʀədi] *nm* Friday; **vendredi saint** Good Friday

**vénéneux, -euse** [venenø, øz] *adj* poisonous

**vénérien, ne** [veneʀjɛ̃, jɛn] *adj* venereal

**vengeance** [vɑ̃ʒɑ̃s] *nf* vengeance *no pl*, revenge *no pl*

**venger** [vɑ̃ʒe] *vt* to avenge; **se venger** *vi* to avenge o.s.; **se ~ de qch** to avenge o.s. for sth, take one's revenge for sth; **se ~ de qn** to take revenge on sb; **se ~ sur** to take revenge on

**venimeux, -euse** [vənimø, øz] *adj* poisonous, venomous; (*fig: haineux*) venomous, vicious

**venin** [vənɛ̃] *nm* venom, poison

**venir** [v(ə)niʀ] *vi* to come; **~ de** to come from; **~ de faire: je viens d'y aller/de le voir** I've just been there/seen him; **s'il vient à pleuvoir** if it should rain; **j'en viens à croire que** I have come to believe that; **où veux-tu en ~?** what are you getting at?; **faire ~** (*docteur, plombier*) to call (out)

**vent** [vɑ̃] *nm* wind; **il y a du ~** it's windy; **c'est du ~** it's all hot air; **dans le ~** (*fam*) trendy

**vente** [vɑ̃t] *nf* sale; **la ~** (*activité*) selling; (*secteur*) sales *pl*; **mettre en ~** (*produit*) to put on sale; (*maison, objet personnel*) to put up for sale; **vente aux enchères** auction sale; **vente de charité** jumble sale

**venteux, -euse** [vɑ̃tø, øz] *adj* windy

**ventilateur** [vɑ̃tilatœʀ] *nm* fan

**ventiler** [vɑ̃tile] *vt* to ventilate

**ventouse** [vɑ̃tuz] *nf* (*de caoutchouc*) suction pad

**ventre** [vɑ̃tʀ] *nm* (*Anat*) stomach; (*légèrement péj*) belly; (*utérus*) womb; **avoir mal au ~** to have stomach ache (BRIT) *ou* a stomach ache (US)

**venu, e** [v(ə)ny] *pp de* **venir** ▷ *adj*: **bien ~** timely; **mal ~** out of place; **être mal ~ à** *ou* **de faire** to have no grounds for doing, be in no position to do

**ver** [vɛʀ] *nm* worm; (*des fruits etc*) maggot; (*du bois*) woodworm *no pl*; *voir aussi* **vers**; **ver à soie** silkworm; **ver de terre** earthworm; **ver luisant** glow-worm; **ver solitaire** tapeworm

**verbe** [vɛʀb] *nm* verb

**verdâtre** [vɛʀdatʀ] *adj* greenish

**verdict** [vɛʀdik(t)] *nm* verdict

**verdir** [vɛʀdiʀ] *vi, vt* to turn green; **verdure** *nf* greenery

**véreux, -euse** [veʀø, øz] *adj* worm-eaten; (*malhonnête*) shady, corrupt

**verge** [vɛʀʒ] *nf* (*Anat*) penis

**verger** [vɛʀʒe] *nm* orchard

**verglacé, e** [vɛʀglase] *adj* icy, iced-over

**verglas** [vɛʀglɑ] *nm* (black) ice

**véridique** [veʀidik] *adj* truthful

**vérification** [veʀifikasjɔ̃] *nf* (*action*) checking *no pl*; (*contrôle*) check

**vérifier** [veʀifje] *vt* to check; (*corroborer*) to confirm, bear out

**véritable** [veʀitabl] *adj* real; (*ami, amour*) true; **un ~ désastre** an absolute disaster

**vérité** [veʀite] *nf* truth; **en ~** really, actually

**verlan** [vɛʀlɑ̃] *nm* (*fam*) (back) slang

**vermeil, le** [vɛʀmɛj] *adj* ruby red

**vermine** [vɛʀmin] *nf* vermin *pl*

**vermoulu, e** [vɛʁmuly] adj worm-eaten

**verni, e** [vɛʁni] adj (fam) lucky; **cuir ~** patent leather

**vernir** [vɛʁniʁ] vt (bois, tableau, ongles) to varnish; (poterie) to glaze; **vernis** nm (enduit) varnish; glaze; (fig) veneer; **vernis à ongles** nail polish ou varnish; **vernissage** nm (d'une exposition) preview

**vérole** [veʁɔl] nf (variole) smallpox

**verre** [vɛʁ] nm glass; (de lunettes) lens sg; **boire** ou **prendre un ~** to have a drink; **verres de contact** contact lenses; **verrière** nf (paroi vitrée) glass wall; (toit vitré) glass roof

**verrou** [veʁu] nm (targette) bolt; **mettre qn sous les ~s** to put sb behind bars; **verrouillage** nm locking; **verrouillage centralisé** central locking; **verrouiller** vt (porte) to bolt; (ordinateur) to lock

**verrue** [veʁy] nf wart

**vers** [vɛʁ] nm line ▷ nmpl (poésie) verse sg ▷ prép (en direction de) toward(s); (près de) around (about); (temporel) about, around

**versant** [vɛʁsɑ̃] nm slopes pl, side

**versatile** [vɛʁsatil] adj fickle, changeable

**verse** [vɛʁs]: **à ~** adv: **il pleut à ~** it's pouring (with rain)

**Verseau** [vɛʁso] nm: **le ~** Aquarius

**versement** [vɛʁsəmɑ̃] nm payment; **en 3 ~s** in 3 instalments

**verser** [vɛʁse] vt (liquide, grains) to pour; (larmes, sang) to shed; (argent) to pay; **~ qch sur un compte** to pay sth into an account

**version** [vɛʁsjɔ̃] nf version; (Scol) translation (into the mother tongue); **film en ~ originale** film in the original language

**verso** [vɛʁso] nm back; **voir au ~** see over(leaf)

**vert, e** [vɛʁ, vɛʁt] adj green; (vin) young; (vigoureux) sprightly ▷ nm green; **les V~s** (Pol) the Greens

**vertèbre** [vɛʁtɛbʁ] nf vertebra

**vertement** [vɛʁtəmɑ̃] adv (réprimander) sharply

**vertical, e, -aux** [vɛʁtikal, o] adj vertical; **verticale** nf vertical; **à la verticale** vertically; **verticalement** adv vertically

**vertige** [vɛʁtiʒ] nm (peur du vide) vertigo; (étourdissement) dizzy spell; (fig) fever; **vertigineux, -euse** adj breathtaking

**vertu** [vɛʁty] nf virtue; **en ~ de** in accordance with; **vertueux, -euse** adj virtuous

**verve** [vɛʁv] nf witty eloquence; **être en ~** to be in brilliant form

**verveine** [vɛʁvɛn] nf (Bot) verbena, vervain; (infusion) verbena tea

**vésicule** [vezikyl] nf vesicle; **vésicule biliaire** gall-bladder

**vessie** [vesi] nf bladder

**veste** [vɛst] nf jacket; **veste droite/croisée** single-/double-breasted jacket

**vestiaire** [vɛstjɛʁ] nm (au théâtre etc) cloakroom; (de stade etc) changing-room (BRIT), locker-room (US)

**vestibule** [vɛstibyl] nm hall

**vestige** [vɛstiʒ] nm relic; (fig) vestige; **vestiges** nmpl (de ville) remains

**vestimentaire** [vɛstimɑ̃tɛʁ] adj (détail) of dress; (élégance) sartorial; **dépenses ~s** clothing expenditure

**veston** [vɛstɔ̃] nm jacket

**vêtement** [vɛtmɑ̃] nm garment, item of clothing; **vêtements** nmpl clothes

**vétérinaire** [veteʁinɛʁ] nm/f vet, veterinary surgeon

**vêtir** [vetiʁ] vt to clothe, dress

**vêtu, e** [vety] pp de **vêtir** ▷ adj: **~ de** dressed in, wearing

**vétuste** [vetyst] adj ancient, timeworn

**veuf, veuve** [vœf, vœv] adj widowed ▷ nm widower

**veuve** [vœv] nf widow

**vexant, e** [vɛksɑ̃, ɑ̃t] adj (contrariant) annoying; (blessant) hurtful

**vexation** [vɛksasjɔ̃] nf humiliation

**vexer** [vɛkse] vt: ~ **qn** to hurt sb's feelings; **se vexer** vi to be offended

**viable** [vjabl] adj viable; (*économie, industrie etc*) sustainable

**viande** [vjɑ̃d] nf meat; **je ne mange pas de ~** I don't eat meat

**vibrer** [vibʀe] vi to vibrate; (*son, voix*) to be vibrant; (*fig*) to be stirred; **faire ~** (cause to) vibrate; (*fig*) to stir, thrill

**vice** [vis] nm vice; (*défaut*) fault ▷ préfixe: **~...** vice-; **vice de forme** legal flaw ou irregularity

**vicié, e** [visje] adj (*air*) polluted, tainted; (*Jur*) invalidated

**vicieux, -euse** [visjø, jøz] adj (*pervers*) lecherous; (*rétif*) unruly ▷ nm/f lecher

**vicinal, e, -aux** [visinal, o] adj: **chemin ~** by-road, byway

**victime** [viktim] nf victim; (*d'accident*) casualty

**victoire** [viktwaʀ] nf victory

**victuailles** [viktɥaj] nfpl provisions

**vidange** [vidɑ̃ʒ] nf (*d'un fossé, réservoir*) emptying; (*Auto*) oil change; (*de lavabo: bonde*) waste outlet; **vidanges** nfpl (*matières*) sewage sg; **vidanger** vt to empty

**vide** [vid] adj empty ▷ nm (*Physique*) vacuum; (*espace*) (empty) space, gap; (*futilité, néant*) void; **avoir peur du ~** to be afraid of heights; **emballé sous ~** vacuum packed; **à ~** (*sans occupants*) empty; (*sans charge*) unladen

**vidéo** [video] nf video ▷ adj: **cassette ~** video cassette; **jeu ~** video game; **vidéoclip** nm music video; **vidéoconférence** nf videoconference

**vide-ordures** [vidɔʀdyʀ] nm inv (rubbish) chute

**vider** [vide] vt to empty; (*Culin: volaille, poisson*) to gut, clean out; **se vider** vi to empty; **~ les lieux** to quit ou vacate the premises; **videur** nm (*de boîte de nuit*) bouncer, doorman

**vie** [vi] nf life; **être en ~** to be alive; **sans ~** lifeless; **à ~** for life; **que faites-vous dans la ~?** what do you do?

**vieil** [vjɛj] adj m voir **vieux**; **vieillard**

nm old man; **vieille** adj, nf voir **vieux**; **vieilleries** nfpl old things; **vieillesse** nf old age; **vieillir** vi (*prendre de l'âge*) to grow old; (*population, vin*) to age; (*doctrine, auteur*) to become dated ▷ vt to age; **vieillissement** nm growing old; ageing

**Vienne** [vjɛn] nf Vienna

**viens** [vjɛ̃] vb voir **venir**

**vierge** [vjɛʀʒ] adj virgin; (*page*) clean, blank ▷ nf virgin; (*signe*): **la V~** Virgo

**Vietnam, Viet-Nam** [vjɛtnam] nm Vietnam; **vietnamien, ne** adj Vietnamese ▷ nm/f: **Vietnamien, ne** Vietnamese

**vieux, vieil, vieille** [vjø, vjɛj] adj old ▷ nm/f old man (woman); **les vieux** nmpl old people; **un petit ~** a little old man; **mon ~/ma vieille** (*fam*) old man/girl; **prendre un coup de ~** to put years on; **vieux garçon** bachelor; **vieux jeu** adj inv old-fashioned

**vif, vive** [vif, viv] adj (*animé*) lively; (*alerte, brusque, aigu*) sharp; (*lumière, couleur*) bright; (*air*) crisp; (*vent, émotion*) keen; (*fort: regret, déception*) great, deep; (*vivant*): **brûlé ~** burnt alive; **de vive voix** personally; **avoir l'esprit ~** to be quick-witted; **piquer qn au ~** to cut sb to the quick; **à ~** (*plaie*) open; **avoir les nerfs à ~** to be on edge

**vigne** [viɲ] nf (*plante*) vine; (*plantation*) vineyard; **vigneron** nm wine grower

**vignette** [viɲɛt] nf (*Admin*) ≈ (road) tax disc (BRIT), ≈ license plate sticker (US); (*de médicament*) price label (*used for reimbursement*)

**vignoble** [viɲɔbl] nm (*plantation*) vineyard; (*vignes d'une région*) vineyards pl

**vigoureux, -euse** [viguʀø, øz] adj vigorous, robust

**vigueur** [vigœʀ] nf vigour; **entrer en ~** to come into force; **en ~** current

**vilain, e** [vilɛ̃, ɛn] adj (*laid*) ugly; (*affaire, blessure*) nasty; (*pas sage: enfant*) naughty; **vilain mot** naughty ou bad word

**villa** [villa] nf (detached) house; **~ en multipropriété** time-share villa
**village** [vilaʒ] nm village; **villageois, e** adj village cpd ▷ nm/f villager
**ville** [vil] nf town; (importante): city; (administration): **la ~** the (town) council, the local authority; **ville d'eaux** spa; **ville nouvelle** new town
**vin** [vɛ̃] nm wine; **avoir le ~ gai** to get happy after a few drinks; **vin d'honneur** reception (with wine and snacks); **vin de pays** local wine; **vin ordinaire** ou **de table** table wine
**vinaigre** [vinɛgʁ] nm vinegar; **vinaigrette** nf vinaigrette, French dressing
**vindicatif, -ive** [vɛ̃dikatif, iv] adj vindictive
**vingt** [vɛ̃] num twenty; **~-quatre heures sur ~-quatre** twenty-four hours a day, round the clock; **vingtaine** nf: **une vingtaine (de)** about twenty, twenty or so; **vingtième** num twentieth
**vinicole** [vinikɔl] adj wine cpd, wine-growing
**vinyle** [vinil] nm vinyl
**viol** [vjɔl] nm (d'une femme) rape; (d'un lieu sacré) violation
**violacé, e** [vjɔlase] adj purplish, mauvish
**violemment** [vjɔlamɑ̃] adv violently
**violence** [vjɔlɑ̃s] nf violence
**violent, e** [vjɔlɑ̃, ɑ̃t] adj violent; (remède) drastic
**violer** [vjɔle] vt (femme) to rape; (sépulture, loi, traité) to violate
**violet, te** [vjɔlɛ, ɛt] adj, nm purple, mauve; **violette** nf (fleur) violet
**violon** [vjɔlɔ̃] nm violin; (fam: prison) lock-up; **violon d'Ingres** hobby; **violoncelle** nm cello; **violoniste** nm/f violinist
**vipère** [vipɛʁ] nf viper, adder
**virage** [viʁaʒ] nm (d'un véhicule) turn; (d'une route, piste) bend
**virée** [viʁe] nf trip; (à pied) walk; (longue) walking tour; (dans les cafés) tour

**virement** [viʁmɑ̃] nm (Comm) transfer
**virer** [viʁe] vt (Comm): **~ qch (sur)** to transfer sth (into); (fam: expulser): **~ qn** to kick sb out ▷ vi to turn; (Chimie): **~ au bleu/rouge** to turn blue/red; **~ de bord** to tack
**virevolter** [viʁvɔlte] vi to twirl around
**virgule** [viʁgyl] nf comma; (Math) point
**viril, e** [viʁil] adj (propre à l'homme) masculine; (énergique, courageux) manly, virile
**virtuel, le** [viʁtɥɛl] adj potential; (théorique) virtual
**virtuose** [viʁtɥoz] nm/f (Mus) virtuoso; (gén) master
**virus** [viʁys] nm virus
**vis¹** [vi] vb voir **voir**; **vivre**
**vis²** [vis] nf screw
**visa** [viza] nm (sceau) stamp; (validation de passeport) visa
**visage** [vizaʒ] nm face
**vis-à-vis** [vizavi] prép: **~ de qn** to(wards) sb; **~** facing each other
**visées** [vize] nfpl (intentions) designs
**viser** [vize] vi to aim ▷ vt to aim at; (concerner) to be aimed ou directed at; (apposer un visa sur) to stamp, visa; **~ à qch/faire** to aim at sth/at doing ou to do
**visibilité** [vizibilite] nf visibility
**visible** [vizibl] adj visible; (disponible): **est-il ~?** can he see me?, will he see visitors?
**visière** [vizjɛʁ] nf (de casquette) peak; (qui s'attache) eyeshade
**vision** [vizjɔ̃] nf vision; (sens) (eye)sight, vision; (fait de voir): **la ~ de** the sight of; **visionneuse** nf viewer
**visiophone** [vizjɔfɔn] nm videophone
**visite** [vizit] nf visit; **~ médicale** medical examination; **~ accompagnée** ou **guidée** guided tour; **la ~ guidée commence à quelle heure?** what time does the guided tour start?; **faire une ~ à qn** to call on sb, pay sb a visit; **rendre ~ à qn** to visit sb, pay sb a visit; **être en ~ (chez qn)** to be visiting (sb); **avoir**

de la ~ to have visitors; **heures de ~**
(*hôpital, prison*) visiting hours
**visiter** [vizite] *vt* to visit; **visiteur,**
**-euse** *nm/f* visitor
**vison** [vizɔ̃] *nm* mink
**visser** [vise] *vt*: **~ qch** (*fixer, serrer*) to
screw sth on
**visuel, le** [vizɥɛl] *adj* visual
**vital, e, -aux** [vital, o] *adj* vital
**vitamine** [vitamin] *nf* vitamin
**vite** [vit] *adv* (*rapidement*) quickly, fast;
(*sans délai*) quickly; (*sous peu*) soon; **~!**
quick!; **faire ~** to be quick; **le temps**
**passe ~** time flies
**vitesse** [vitɛs] *nf* speed; (*Auto: dispositif*)
gear; **prendre de la ~** to pick up *ou*
gather speed; **à toute ~** at full *ou* top
speed; **en ~** (*rapidement*) quickly; (*en*
*hâte*) in a hurry

● **LIMITE DE VITESSE**
●
● The speed limit in France is 50 km/h
● in built-up areas, 90 km/h on main
● roads, and 130 km/h on motorways
● (110 km/h when it is raining).

**viticulteur** [vitikyltœʀ] *nm* wine
grower
**vitrage** [vitʀaʒ] *nm*: **double ~** double
glazing
**vitrail, -aux** [vitʀaj, o] *nm* stained-
glass window
**vitre** [vitʀ] *nf* (*window*) pane; (*de*
*portière, voiture*) window; **vitré, e** *adj*
glass *cpd*
**vitrine** [vitʀin] *nf* (*shop*) window;
(*petite armoire*) display cabinet; **en ~** in
the window
**vivable** [vivabl] *adj* (*personne*) livable-
with; (*maison*) fit to live in
**vivace** [vivas] *adj* (*arbre, plante*) hardy;
(*fig*) indestructible, inveterate
**vivacité** [vivasite] *nf* liveliness,
vivacity
**vivant, e** [vivɑ̃, ɑ̃t] *adj* (*qui vit*) living,
alive; (*animé*) lively; (*preuve, exemple*)
living ▷ *nm*: **du ~ de qn** in sb's lifetime;

**les ~s** the living
**vive** [viv] *adj voir* **vif** ▷ *vb voir* **vivre**
▷ *excl*: **~ le roi!** long live the king!;
**vivement** *adv* deeply ▷ *excl*: **vivement**
**les vacances!** roll on the holidays!
**vivier** [vivje] *nm* (*étang*) fish tank;
(*réservoir*) fishpond
**vivifiant, e** [vivifjɑ̃, jɑ̃t] *adj*
invigorating
**vivoter** [vivɔte] *vi* (*personne*) to scrape
a living, get by; (*fig: affaire etc*) to
struggle along
**vivre** [vivʀ] *vi, vt* to live; (*période*) to live
through; **vivres** *nmpl* provisions, food
supplies; **~ de** to live on; **il vit encore**
he is still alive; **se laisser ~** to take life
as it comes; **se plus ~** (*être anxieux*) to
live on one's nerves; **il a vécu** (*eu une vie*
*aventureuse*) he has seen life; **être facile**
**à ~** to be easy to get on with; **faire ~ qn**
(*pourvoir à sa subsistance*) to provide (a
living) for sb
**vlan** [vlɑ̃] *excl* wham!, bang!
**VO** [veo] *nf*: **film en VO** film in the
original version; **en VO sous-titrée** in
the original version with subtitles
**vocabulaire** [vɔkabylɛʀ] *nm*
vocabulary
**vocation** [vɔkasjɔ̃] *nf* vocation, calling
**vœu, x** [vø] *nm* wish; (*promesse*) vow;
**faire ~ de** to take a vow of; **tous nos ~x**
**de bonne année, meilleurs ~x** best
wishes for the New Year
**vogue** [vɔg] *nf* fashion, vogue; **en ~** in
fashion, in vogue
**voici** [vwasi] *prép* (*pour introduire,*
*désigner*) here is +*sg*, here are +*pl*; **et**
**~ que ...** and now it (*ou* he) ...; *voir*
*aussi* **voilà**
**voie** [vwa] *nf* way; (*Rail*) track, line;
(*Auto*) lane; **être en bonne ~** to be
going well; **mettre qn sur la ~** to
put sb on the right track; **pays en**
**~ de développement** developing
country; **être en ~ d'achèvement/de**
**rénovation** to be nearing completion/
in the process of renovation; **par ~**
**buccale** *ou* **orale** orally; **route à ~**

unique single-track road; **route à 2/3 ~s** 2-/3-lane road; **voie de garage** (Rail) siding; **voie express** expressway; **voie ferrée** track; railway line (BRIT), railroad (US); **la voie lactée** the Milky Way; **la voie publique** the public highway

**voilà** [vwala] prép (en désignant) there is +sg, there are +pl; **les ~ ou voici** here ou there they are; **en ~ ou voici un** here's one, there's one; **voici mon frère et ~ ma sœur** this is my brother and that's my sister; **~ ou voici deux ans** two years ago; **~ ou voici deux ans que** it's two years since; **et ~!** there we are!; **~ tout** that's all; **~ ou voici** (en offrant etc) there ou here you are; **tiens! ~ Paul** look! there's Paul

**voile** [vwal] nm veil; (tissu léger) net ▷ nf sail; (sport) sailing; **voiler** vt to veil; (fausser: roue) to buckle; (: bois) to warp; **se voiler** vi (lune, regard) to mist over; (voix) to become husky; (roue, disque) to buckle; (planche) to warp; **voilier** nm sailing ship; (de plaisance) sailing boat; **voilure** nf (de voilier) sails pl

**voir** [vwar] vi, vt to see; **se voir** vi (être visible) to show; (se fréquenter) to see each other; (se produire) to happen; **cela se voit** (c'est visible) that's obvious, it shows; **faire ~ qch à qn** to show sb sth; **en faire ~ à qn** (fig) to give sb a hard time; **ne pas pouvoir ~ qn** not to be able to stand sb; **voyons!** let's see now; (indignation etc) come on!; **ça n'a rien à ~ avec lui** that has nothing to do with him

**voire** [vwar] adv even

**voisin, e** [vwazɛ̃, in] adj (proche) neighbouring; (contigu) next; (ressemblant) connected ▷ nm/f neighbour; **voisinage** nm (proximité) proximity; (environs) vicinity; (quartier, voisins) neighbourhood

**voiture** [vwatyr] nf car; (wagon) coach, carriage; **voiture de course** racing car; **voiture de sport** sports car

**voix** [vwa] nf voice; (Pol) vote; **à haute ~** aloud; **à ~ basse** in a low voice; **à 2/4 ~** (Mus) in 2/4 parts; **avoir ~ au chapitre** to have a say in the matter

**vol** [vɔl] nm (d'oiseau, d'avion) flight; (larcin) theft; **~ régulier** scheduled flight; **à ~ d'oiseau** as the crow flies; **au ~: attraper qch au ~** to catch sth as it flies past; **en ~** in flight; **je voudrais signaler un ~** I'd like to report a theft; **vol à main armée** armed robbery; **vol à voile** gliding; **vol libre** hang-gliding

**volage** [vɔlaʒ] adj fickle

**volaille** [vɔlaj] nf (oiseaux) poultry pl; (viande) poultry no pl; (oiseau) fowl

**volant, e** [vɔlɑ̃, ɑ̃t] adj voir **feuille** etc ▷ nm (d'automobile) (steering) wheel; (de commande) wheel; (objet lancé) shuttlecock; (bande de tissu) flounce

**volcan** [vɔlkɑ̃] nm volcano

**volée** [vɔle] nf (Tennis) volley; **à la ~: rattraper à la ~** to catch in mid-air; **à toute ~** (sonner les cloches) vigorously; (lancer un projectile) with full force

**voler** [vɔle] vi (avion, oiseau, fig) to fly; (voleur) to steal ▷ vt (objet) to steal; (personne) to rob; **~ qch à qn** to steal sth from sb; **on m'a volé mon portefeuille** my wallet (BRIT) ou billfold (US) has been stolen; **il ne l'a pas volé!** he asked for it!

**volet** [vɔlɛ] nm (de fenêtre) shutter; (de feuillet, document) section

**voleur, -euse** [vɔlœr, øz] nm/f thief ▷ adj thieving; **"au ~!"** "stop thief!"

**volontaire** [vɔlɔ̃tɛr] adj (acte, enrôlement, prisonnier) voluntary; (oubli) intentional; (caractère, personne: décidé) self-willed ▷ nm/f volunteer

**volonté** [vɔlɔ̃te] nf (faculté de vouloir) will; (énergie, fermeté) will(power); (souhait, désir) wish; **à ~** as much as one likes; **bonne ~** goodwill, willingness; **mauvaise ~** lack of goodwill, unwillingness

**volontiers** [vɔlɔ̃tje] adv (avec plaisir) willingly, gladly; (habituellement, souvent) readily, willingly; **voulez-vous boire quelque chose? — ~!** would you like something to drink? — yes, please!

**volt** [vɔlt] *nm* volt

**volte-face** [vɔltəfas] *nf inv*: **faire ~** to turn round

**voltige** [vɔltiʒ] *nf* (Équitation) trick riding; (au cirque) acrobatics sg; **voltiger** *vi* to flutter (about)

**volubile** [vɔlybil] *adj* voluble

**volume** [vɔlym] *nm* volume; (Géom: solide) solid; **volumineux, -euse** *adj* voluminous, bulky

**volupté** [vɔlypte] *nf* sensual delight ou pleasure

**vomi** [vɔmi] *nm* vomit; **vomir** *vi* to vomit, be sick ▷ *vt* to vomit, bring up; (fig) to belch out, spew out; (exécrer) to loathe, abhor

**vorace** [vɔʀas] *adj* voracious

**vos** [vo] *adj voir* **votre**

**vote** [vɔt] *nm* vote; **vote par correspondance/procuration** postal/proxy vote; **voter** *vi* to vote ▷ *vt* (projet de loi) to vote for; (loi, réforme) to pass

**votre** [vɔtʀ] (*pl* **vos**) *adj* your

**vôtre** [votʀ] *pron*: **le ~, la ~, les ~s** yours; **les ~s** (fig) your family ou folks; **à la ~** (toast) your (good) health!

**vouer** [vwe] *vt*: **~ sa vie à** (étude, cause etc) to devote one's life to; **~ une amitié éternelle à qn** to vow undying friendship to sb

 **MOT-CLÉ**

**vouloir** [vulwaʀ] *nm*: **le bon vouloir de qn** sb's goodwill; sb's pleasure ▷ *vt* **1** (exiger, désirer) to want; **vouloir faire/que qn fasse** to want to do/sb to do; **voulez-vous du thé?** would you like ou do you want some tea?; **que me veut-il?** what does he want with me?; **sans le vouloir** (involontairement) without meaning to, unintentionally; **je voudrais ceci/faire** I would ou I'd like this/to do; **le hasard a voulu que ...** as fate would have it ...; **la tradition veut que ...** it is a tradition that ...

**2** (consentir): **je veux bien** (bonne volonté) I'll be happy to; (concession) fair enough, that's fine; **je peux le faire, si vous voulez** I can do it if you like; **oui, si on veut** (en quelque sorte) yes, if you like; **veuillez attendre** please wait; **veuillez agréer ...** (formule épistolaire: personne nommée) yours sincerely; (personne non nommée) yours faithfully

**3**: **en vouloir à qn** to bear sb a grudge; **s'en vouloir (de)** to be annoyed with o.s. (for); **il en veut à mon argent** he's after my money

**4**: **vouloir de**: **l'entreprise ne veut plus de lui** the firm doesn't want him any more; **elle ne veut pas de son aide** she doesn't want his help

**5**: **vouloir dire** to mean

**voulu, e** [vuly] *adj* (requis) required, requisite; (délibéré) deliberate, intentional; *voir aussi* **vouloir**

**vous** [vu] *pron* you; (objet indirect) (to) you; (réfléchi: sg) yourself; (: pl) yourselves; (réciproque) each other ▷ *nm*: **employer le ~** (vouvoyer) to use the "vous" form; **~-même** yourself; **~-mêmes** yourselves

**vouvoyer** [vuvwaje] *vt*: **~ qn** to address sb as "vous"

**voyage** [vwajaʒ] *nm* journey, trip; (fait de voyager): **le ~** travel(ling); **partir/être en ~** to go off/be away on a journey ou trip; **faire bon ~** to have a good journey; **votre ~ s'est bien passé?** how was your journey?; **voyage d'affaires/d'agrément** business/pleasure trip; **voyage de noces** honeymoon; **nous sommes en voyage de noces** we're on honeymoon; **voyage organisé** package tour

**voyager** [vwajaʒe] *vi* to travel; **voyageur, -euse** *nm/f* traveller; (passager) passenger; **voyageur de commerce** sales representative, commercial traveller

**voyant, e** [vwajã, ãt] *adj* (couleur) loud, gaudy ▷ *nm* (signal) (warning) light

**voyelle** [vwajɛl] *nf* vowel

**voyou** [vwaju] *nm* hooligan

**vrac** [vʀak]: **en ~** *adv* (*au détail*) loose; (*en gros*) in bulk; (*en désordre*) in a jumble

**vrai, e** [vʀɛ] *adj* (*véridique: récit, faits*) true; (*non factice, authentique*) real; **à ~ dire** to tell the truth; **vraiment** *adv* really; **vraisemblable** *adj* likely; (*excuse*) convincing; **vraisemblablement** *adj* probably; **vraisemblance** *nf* likelihood; (*romanesque*) verisimilitude

**vrombir** [vʀɔ̃biʀ] *vi* to hum

**VRP** *sigle m* (= *voyageur, représentant, placier*) sales rep (*fam*)

**VTT** *sigle m* (= *vélo tout-terrain*) mountain bike

**vu, e** [vy] *pp de* **voir** ▷ *adj*: **bien/mal vu** (*fig: personne*) popular/unpopular; (: *chose*) approved/disapproved of ▷ *prép* (*en raison de*) in view of: **vu que** in view of the fact that

**vue** [vy] *nf* (*fait de voir*): **la ~ de** the sight of; (*sens, faculté*) (eye)sight; (*panorama, image, photo*) view; **vues** *nfpl* (*idées*) views; (*dessein*) designs; **hors de ~** out of sight; **avoir en ~** to have in mind; **tirer à ~** to shoot on sight; **à ~ d'œil** visibly; **à première ~** at first sight; **de ~** by sight; **perdre de ~** to lose sight of; **en ~** (*visible*) in sight; (*célèbre*) in the public eye; **en ~ de faire** with a view to doing; **perdre la ~** to lose one's (eye)sight; **avoir ~ sur** (*suj: fenêtre*) to have a view of; **vue d'ensemble** overall view

**vulgaire** [vylgɛʀ] *adj* (*grossier*) vulgar, coarse; (*ordinaire*) commonplace, mundane; (*péj: quelconque*): **de ~s touristes** common tourists; (*Bot, Zool: non latin*) common; **vulgariser** *vt* to popularize

**vulnérable** [vylneʀabl] *adj* vulnerable

**wagon** [vagɔ̃] *nm* (*de voyageurs*) carriage; (*de marchandises*) truck, wagon; **wagon-lit** *nm* sleeper, sleeping car; **wagon-restaurant** *nm* restaurant *ou* dining car

**wallon, ne** [walɔ̃, ɔn] *adj* Walloon ▷ *nm* (*Ling*) Walloon ▷ *nm/f*: **W~, ne** Walloon

**watt** [wat] *nm* watt

**w-c** *sigle mpl* (= *water-closet(s)*) toilet

**Web** [wɛb] *nm inv*: **le ~** the (World Wide) Web; **webmaster** [-mastœʀ], **webmestre** [-mɛstʀ] *nm/f* webmaster

**week-end** [wikɛnd] *nm* weekend

**western** [wɛstɛʀn] *nm* western

**whisky** [wiski] (*pl* **whiskies**) *nm* whisky

# X Y

**xénophobe** [gzenɔfɔb] *adj*
xenophobic ▷ *nm/f* xenophobe
**xérès** [gzeʀɛs] *nm* sherry
**xylophone** [gzilɔfɔn] *nm* xylophone

**y** [i] *adv* (*à cet endroit*) there; (*dessus*) on
it (*ou* them); (*dedans*) in it (*ou* them)
▷ *pron* (about *ou* on *ou* of) it (*d'après le
verbe employé*); **j'y pense** I'm thinking
about it; **ça y est!** that's it!; *voir aussi*
**aller**; **avoir**
**yacht** [jɔt] *nm* yacht
**yaourt** [jauʀt] *nm* yoghourt; **~ nature/
aux fruits** plain/fruit yogurt
**yeux** [jø] *nmpl de* **œil**
**yoga** [jɔga] *nm* yoga
**yoghourt** [jɔguʀt] *nm* = **yaourt**
**yougoslave** [jugɔslav] (*Histoire*) *adj*
Yugoslav(ian) ▷ *nm/f*: **Y~** Yugoslav
**Yougoslavie** [jugɔslavi] *nf* (*Histoire*)
Yugoslavia; **l'ex-~** the former
Yugoslavia

# Z

≈ restricted parking area; **zone industrielle** industrial estate

**zoo** [zo(o)] *nm* zoo

**zoologie** [zɔɔlɔʒi] *nf* zoology; **zoologique** *adj* zoological

**zut** [zyt] *excl* dash (it)! (BRIT), nuts! (US)

**zapper** [zape] *vi* to zap

**zapping** [zapiŋ] *nm*: **faire du ~** to flick through the channels

**zèbre** [zɛbʀ(ə)] *nm* (*Zool*) zebra; **zébré, e** *adj* striped, streaked

**zèle** [zɛl] *nm* zeal; **faire du ~** (*péj*) to be over-zealous; **zélé, e** *adj* zealous

**zéro** [zeʀo] *nm* zero, nought (BRIT); **au-dessous de ~** below zero (Centigrade) *ou* freezing; **partir de ~** to start from scratch; **trois (buts) à ~** 3 (goals to) nil

**zeste** [zɛst] *nm* peel, zest

**zézayer** [zezeje] *vi* to have a lisp

**zigzag** [zigzag] *nm* zigzag; **zigzaguer** *vi* to zigzag

**Zimbabwe** [zimbabwe] *nm*: **le ~** Zimbabwe

**zinc** [zɛ̃g] *nm* (*Chimie*) zinc

**zipper** [zipe] *vt* (*Inform*) to zip

**zizi** [zizi] *nm* (*langage enfantin*) willy

**zodiaque** [zɔdjak] *nm* zodiac

**zona** [zona] *nm* shingles *sg*

**zone** [zon] *nf* zone, area; (*fam: quartiers pauvres*): **la ~** the slums; **zone bleue**

# VERB TABLES

## Introduction

The **Verb Tables** in the following section contain 29 tables of French verbs (some regular and some irregular) in alphabetical order. Each table shows you the following forms: **Present**, **Perfect**, **Future**, **Subjunctive**, **Imperfect**, **Conditional**, **Imperative** and the **Present** and **Past Participles**.

In order to help you use the verbs shown in Verb Tables correctly, there are also a number of example phrases at the bottom of each page to show the verb as it is used in context.

In French there are both **regular** verbs (their forms follow the normal rules) and **irregular** verbs (their forms do not follow the normal rules). The regular verbs in these tables are:

**donner** (regular -**er** verb, Verb Table 11)
**finir** (regular -**ir** verb, Verb Table 16)
**attendre** (regular -**re** verb, Verb Table 3)

The irregular verbs are shown in full.

For a further list of French irregular verb forms see pages xv–xvi.

# ▶ **aller** (to go)

## PRESENT

| | |
|---|---|
| je | vais |
| tu | vas |
| il/elle/on | va |
| nous | allons |
| vous | allez |
| ils/elles | vont |

## PRESENT SUBJUNCTIVE

| | |
|---|---|
| j' | aille |
| tu | ailles |
| il/elle/on | aille |
| nous | allions |
| vous | alliez |
| ils/elles | aillent |

## PERFECT

| | |
|---|---|
| je | suis allé(e) |
| tu | es allé(e) |
| il/elle/on | est allé(e) |
| nous | sommes allé(e)s |
| vous | êtes allé(e)(s) |
| ils/elles | sont allé(e)s |

## IMPERFECT

| | |
|---|---|
| j' | allais |
| tu | allais |
| il/elle/on | allait |
| nous | allions |
| vous | alliez |
| ils/elles | allaient |

## FUTURE

| | |
|---|---|
| j' | irai |
| tu | iras |
| il/elle/on | ira |
| nous | irons |
| vous | irez |
| ils/elles | iront |

## CONDITIONAL

| | |
|---|---|
| j' | irais |
| tu | irais |
| il/elle/on | irait |
| nous | irions |
| vous | iriez |
| ils/elles | iraient |

## IMPERATIVE

va / allons / allez

## PAST PARTICIPLE

allé

## PRESENT PARTICIPLE

allant

---

### EXAMPLE PHRASES

*Vous **allez** au cinéma?* Are you going to the cinema?
*Je **suis allé** à Londres.* I went to London.
*Est-ce que tu **es** déjà **allé** en Allemagne?* Have you ever been to Germany?

---

**je/j'** = I **tu** = you **il** = he/it **elle** = she/it **on** = we/one **nous** = we **vous** = you **ils/elles** = they

# ▶ **attendre** (to wait)

**PRESENT**

| | |
|---|---|
| j' | attends |
| tu | attends |
| il/elle/on | attend |
| nous | attendons |
| vous | attendez |
| ils/elles | attendent |

**PRESENT SUBJUNCTIVE**

| | |
|---|---|
| j' | attende |
| tu | attendes |
| il/elle/on | attende |
| nous | attendions |
| vous | attendiez |
| ils/elles | attendent |

**PERFECT**

| | |
|---|---|
| j' | ai attendu |
| tu | as attendu |
| il/elle/on | a attendu |
| nous | avons attendu |
| vous | avez attendu |
| ils/elles | ont attendu |

**IMPERFECT**

| | |
|---|---|
| j' | attendais |
| tu | attendais |
| il/elle/on | attendait |
| nous | attendions |
| vous | attendiez |
| ils/elles | attendaient |

**FUTURE**

| | |
|---|---|
| j' | attendrai |
| tu | attendras |
| il/elle/on | attendra |
| nous | attendrons |
| vous | attendrez |
| ils/elles | attendront |

**CONDITIONAL**

| | |
|---|---|
| j' | attendrais |
| tu | attendrais |
| il/elle/on | attendrait |
| nous | attendrions |
| vous | attendriez |
| ils/elles | attendraient |

**IMPERATIVE**

attends / attendons / attendez

**PAST PARTICIPLE**

attendu

**PRESENT PARTICIPLE**

attendant

---

### EXAMPLE PHRASES

**Attends**-moi! Wait for me!
Tu **attends** depuis longtemps? Have you been waiting long?
Je l'**ai attendu** à la poste. I waited for him at the post office.
Je m'**attends** à ce qu'il soit en retard. I expect he'll be late.

▶ **avoir** (to have)

**PRESENT**

|  |  |
|---|---|
| j' | ai |
| tu | as |
| il/elle/on | a |
| nous | avons |
| vous | avez |
| ils/elles | ont |

**PRESENT SUBJUNCTIVE**

|  |  |
|---|---|
| j' | aie |
| tu | aies |
| il/elle/on | ait |
| nous | ayons |
| vous | ayez |
| ils/elles | aient |

**PERFECT**

|  |  |
|---|---|
| j' | ai eu |
| tu | as eu |
| il/elle/on | a eu |
| nous | avons eu |
| vous | avez eu |
| ils/elles | ont eu |

**IMPERFECT**

|  |  |
|---|---|
| j' | avais |
| tu | avais |
| il/elle/on | avait |
| nous | avions |
| vous | aviez |
| ils/elles | avaient |

**FUTURE**

|  |  |
|---|---|
| j' | aurai |
| tu | auras |
| il/elle/on | aura |
| nous | aurons |
| vous | aurez |
| ils/elles | auront |

**CONDITIONAL**

|  |  |
|---|---|
| j' | aurais |
| tu | aurais |
| il/elle/on | aurait |
| nous | aurions |
| vous | auriez |
| ils/elles | auraient |

**IMPERATIVE**

aie / ayons / ayez

**PAST PARTICIPLE**

eu

**PRESENT PARTICIPLE**

ayant

---

*EXAMPLE PHRASES*

*Il **a** les yeux bleus.* He's got blue eyes.
*Quel âge **as**-tu?* How old are you?
*Il **a eu** un accident.* He's had an accident.
*J'**avais** faim.* I was hungry.
*Il y **a** beaucoup de monde.* There are lots of people.

---

**je/j'** = I  **tu** = you  **il** = he/it  **elle** = she/it  **on** = we/one  **nous** = we  **vous** = you  **ils/elles** = they

# ▶ **boire** (to drink)

## PRESENT

| | |
|---|---|
| je | bois |
| tu | bois |
| il/elle/on | boit |
| nous | buvons |
| vous | buvez |
| ils/elles | boivent |

## PRESENT SUBJUNCTIVE

| | |
|---|---|
| je | boive |
| tu | boives |
| il/elle/on | boive |
| nous | buvions |
| vous | buviez |
| ils/elles | boivent |

## PERFECT

| | |
|---|---|
| j' | ai bu |
| tu | as bu |
| il/elle/on | a bu |
| nous | avons bu |
| vous | avez bu |
| ils/elles | ont bu |

## IMPERFECT

| | |
|---|---|
| je | buvais |
| tu | buvais |
| il/elle/on | buvait |
| nous | buvions |
| vous | buviez |
| ils/elles | buvaient |

## FUTURE

| | |
|---|---|
| je | boirai |
| tu | boiras |
| il/elle/on | boira |
| nous | boirons |
| vous | boirez |
| ils/elles | boiront |

## CONDITIONAL

| | |
|---|---|
| je | boirais |
| tu | boirais |
| il/elle/on | boirait |
| nous | boirions |
| vous | boiriez |
| ils/elles | boiraient |

## IMPERATIVE

bois / buvons / buvez

## PAST PARTICIPLE

bu

## PRESENT PARTICIPLE

buvant

---

### EXAMPLE PHRASES

*Qu'est-ce que tu veux **boire**?* What would you like to drink?
*Il ne **boit** jamais d'alcool.* He never drinks alcohol.
*J'**ai bu** un litre d'eau.* I drank a litre of water.

---

**je/j'** = I **tu** = you **il** = he/it **elle** = she/it **on** = we/one **nous** = we **vous** = you **ils/elles** = they

## ▶ **connaître** (to know)

### PRESENT

| | |
|---|---|
| je | connais |
| tu | connais |
| il/elle/on | connaît |
| nous | connaissons |
| vous | connaissez |
| ils/elles | connaissent |

### PRESENT SUBJUNCTIVE

| | |
|---|---|
| je | connaisse |
| tu | connaisses |
| il/elle/on | connaisse |
| nous | connaissions |
| vous | connaissiez |
| ils/elles | connaissent |

### PERFECT

| | |
|---|---|
| j' | ai connu |
| tu | as connu |
| il/elle/on | a connu |
| nous | avons connu |
| vous | avez connu |
| ils/elles | ont connu |

### IMPERFECT

| | |
|---|---|
| je | connaissais |
| tu | connaissais |
| il/elle/on | connaissait |
| nous | connaissions |
| vous | connaissiez |
| ils/elles | connaissaient |

### FUTURE

| | |
|---|---|
| je | connaîtrai |
| tu | connaîtras |
| il/elle/on | connaîtra |
| nous | connaîtrons |
| vous | connaîtrez |
| ils/elles | connaîtront |

### CONDITIONAL

| | |
|---|---|
| je | connaîtrais |
| tu | connaîtrais |
| il/elle/on | connaîtrait |
| nous | connaîtrions |
| vous | connaîtriez |
| ils/elles | connaîtraient |

### IMPERATIVE

connais / connaissons / connaissez

### PAST PARTICIPLE

connu

### PRESENT PARTICIPLE

connaissant

---

### EXAMPLE PHRASES

*Je ne **connais** pas du tout cette région.* I don't know the area at all.
*Vous **connaissez** M Amiot?* Do you know Mr Amiot?
*Il n'**a** pas **connu** son grand-père.* He never knew his granddad.
*Ils **se sont connus** à Rouen.* They first met in Rouen.

---

**je/j'** = I **tu** = you **il** = he/it **elle** = she/it **on** = we/one **nous** = we **vous** = you **ils/elles** = they

# ▶ **courir** (to run)

## PRESENT

| | |
|---|---|
| je | cours |
| tu | cours |
| il/elle/on | court |
| nous | courons |
| vous | courez |
| ils/elles | courent |

## PRESENT SUBJUNCTIVE

| | |
|---|---|
| je | coure |
| tu | coures |
| il/elle/on | coure |
| nous | courions |
| vous | couriez |
| ils/elles | courent |

## PERFECT

| | |
|---|---|
| j' | ai couru |
| tu | as couru |
| il/elle/on | a couru |
| nous | avons couru |
| vous | avez couru |
| ils/elles | ont couru |

## IMPERFECT

| | |
|---|---|
| je | courais |
| tu | courais |
| il/elle/on | courait |
| nous | courions |
| vous | couriez |
| ils/elles | couraient |

## FUTURE

| | |
|---|---|
| je | courrai |
| tu | courras |
| il/elle/on | courra |
| nous | courrons |
| vous | courrez |
| ils/elles | courront |

## CONDITIONAL

| | |
|---|---|
| je | courrais |
| tu | courrais |
| il/elle/on | courrait |
| nous | courrions |
| vous | courriez |
| ils/elles | courraient |

## IMPERATIVE

cours / courons / courez

## PAST PARTICIPLE

couru

## PRESENT PARTICIPLE

courant

---

### *EXAMPLE PHRASES*

*Je ne **cours** pas très vite.* I can't run very fast.
*Elle est sortie en **courant**.* She ran out.
*Ne **courez** pas dans le couloir.* Don't run in the corridor.
*J'**ai couru** jusqu'à l'école.* I ran all the way to school.

---

**je/j'** = I   **tu** = you   **il** = he/it   **elle** = she/it   **on** = we/one   **nous** = we   **vous** = you   **ils/elles** = they

# ▶ **croire** (to believe)

## PRESENT

|  |  |
|---|---|
| je | crois |
| tu | crois |
| il/elle/on | croit |
| nous | croyons |
| vous | croyez |
| ils/elles | croient |

## PRESENT SUBJUNCTIVE

|  |  |
|---|---|
| je | croie |
| tu | croies |
| il/elle/on | croie |
| nous | croyions |
| vous | croyiez |
| ils/elles | croient |

## PERFECT

|  |  |
|---|---|
| j' | ai cru |
| tu | as cru |
| il/elle/on | a cru |
| nous | avons cru |
| vous | avez cru |
| ils/elles | ont cru |

## IMPERFECT

|  |  |
|---|---|
| je | croyais |
| tu | croyais |
| il/elle/on | croyait |
| nous | croyions |
| vous | croyiez |
| ils/elles | croyaient |

## FUTURE

|  |  |
|---|---|
| je | croirai |
| tu | croiras |
| il/elle/on | croira |
| nous | croirons |
| vous | croirez |
| ils/elles | croiront |

## CONDITIONAL

|  |  |
|---|---|
| je | croirais |
| tu | croirais |
| il/elle/on | croirait |
| nous | croirions |
| vous | croiriez |
| ils/elles | croiraient |

## IMPERATIVE

crois / croyons / croyez

## PAST PARTICIPLE

cru

## PRESENT PARTICIPLE

croyant

---

### *EXAMPLE PHRASES*

*Je ne te **crois** pas.* I don't believe you.
*J'**ai cru** que tu n'allais pas venir.* I thought you weren't going to come.
*Elle **croyait** encore au père Noël.* She still believed in Santa.

# ▶ **devoir** (to have to; to owe)

## PRESENT

| | |
|---|---|
| je | dois |
| tu | dois |
| il/elle/on | doit |
| nous | devons |
| vous | devez |
| ils/elles | doivent |

## PRESENT SUBJUNCTIVE

| | |
|---|---|
| je | doive |
| tu | doives |
| il/elle/on | doive |
| nous | devions |
| vous | deviez |
| ils/elles | doivent |

## PERFECT

| | |
|---|---|
| j' | ai dû |
| tu | as dû |
| il/elle/on | a dû |
| nous | avons dû |
| vous | avez dû |
| ils/elles | ont dû |

## IMPERFECT

| | |
|---|---|
| je | devais |
| tu | devais |
| il/elle/on | devait |
| nous | devions |
| vous | deviez |
| ils/elles | devaient |

## FUTURE

| | |
|---|---|
| je | devrai |
| tu | devras |
| il/elle/on | devra |
| nous | devrons |
| vous | devrez |
| ils/elles | devront |

## CONDITIONAL

| | |
|---|---|
| je | devrais |
| tu | devrais |
| il/elle/on | devrait |
| nous | devrions |
| vous | devriez |
| ils/elles | devraient |

## IMPERATIVE

dois / devons / devez

## PAST PARTICIPLE

dû (*NB*: due, dus, dues)

## PRESENT PARTICIPLE

devant

---

### *EXAMPLE PHRASES*

*Je **dois** aller faire les courses ce matin.* I have to do the shopping this morning.
*À quelle heure est-ce que tu **dois** partir?* What time do you have to leave?
*Il **a dû** faire ses devoirs hier soir.* He had to do his homework last night.
*Il **devait** prendre le train pour aller travailler.* He had to go to work by train.

---

**je/j'** = I  **tu** = you  **il** = he/it  **elle** = she/it  **on** = we/one  **nous** = we  **vous** = you  **ils/elles** = they

# ▶ **dire** (to say)

| PRESENT | | PRESENT SUBJUNCTIVE | |
|---|---|---|---|
| je | dis | je | dise |
| tu | dis | tu | dises |
| il/elle/on | dit | il/elle/on | dise |
| nous | disons | nous | disions |
| vous | dites | vous | disiez |
| ils/elles | disent | ils/elles | disent |

| PERFECT | | IMPERFECT | |
|---|---|---|---|
| j' | ai dit | je | disais |
| tu | as dit | tu | disais |
| il/elle/on | a dit | il/elle/on | disait |
| nous | avons dit | nous | disions |
| vous | avez dit | vous | disiez |
| ils/elles | ont dit | ils/elles | disaient |

| FUTURE | | CONDITIONAL | |
|---|---|---|---|
| je | dirai | je | dirais |
| tu | diras | tu | dirais |
| il/elle/on | dira | il/elle/on | dirait |
| nous | dirons | nous | dirions |
| vous | direz | vous | diriez |
| ils/elles | diront | ils/elles | diraient |

**IMPERATIVE**

dis / disons / dites

**PAST PARTICIPLE**

dit

**PRESENT PARTICIPLE**

disant

---

### EXAMPLE PHRASES

*Qu'est-ce qu'elle **dit**?* What is she saying?
*"Bonjour!", **a-t-il dit**.* "Hello!" he said.
*Ils m'**ont dit** que le film était nul.* They told me that the film was rubbish.
*Comment ça **se dit** en anglais?* How do you say that in English?

**je/j'** = I   **tu** = you   **il** = he/it   **elle** = she/it   **on** = we/one   **nous** = we   **vous** = you   **ils/elles** = they

# ▶ **donner** (to give)

## PRESENT

|  |  |
|---|---|
| je | donne |
| tu | donnes |
| il/elle/on | donne |
| nous | donnons |
| vous | donnez |
| ils/elles | donnent |

## PRESENT SUBJUNCTIVE

|  |  |
|---|---|
| je | donne |
| tu | donnes |
| il/elle/on | donne |
| nous | donnions |
| vous | donniez |
| ils/elles | donnent |

## PERFECT

|  |  |
|---|---|
| j' | ai donné |
| tu | as donné |
| il/elle/on | a donné |
| nous | avons donné |
| vous | avez donné |
| ils/elles | ont donné |

## IMPERFECT

|  |  |
|---|---|
| je | donnais |
| tu | donnais |
| il/elle/on | donnait |
| nous | donnions |
| vous | donniez |
| ils/elles | donnaient |

## FUTURE

|  |  |
|---|---|
| je | donnerai |
| tu | donneras |
| il/elle/on | donnera |
| nous | donnerons |
| vous | donnerez |
| ils/elles | donneront |

## CONDITIONAL

|  |  |
|---|---|
| je | donnerais |
| tu | donnerais |
| il/elle/on | donnerait |
| nous | donnerions |
| vous | donneriez |
| ils/elles | donneraient |

## IMPERATIVE

donne / donnons / donnez

## PAST PARTICIPLE

donné

## PRESENT PARTICIPLE

donnant

---

### EXAMPLE PHRASES

*Donne-moi la main.* Give me your hand.
*Est-ce que je t'ai donné mon adresse?* Did I give you my address?
*L'appartement donne sur la place.* The flat overlooks the square.

---

**je/j'** = I  **tu** = you  **il** = he/it  **elle** = she/it  **on** = we/one  **nous** = we  **vous** = you  **ils/elles** = they

# ▶ **écrire** (to write)

## PRESENT

|  |  |
|---|---|
| j' | écris |
| tu | écris |
| il/elle/on | écrit |
| nous | écrivons |
| vous | écrivez |
| ils/elles | écrivent |

## PRESENT SUBJUNCTIVE

|  |  |
|---|---|
| j' | écrive |
| tu | écrives |
| il/elle/on | écrive |
| nous | écrivions |
| vous | écriviez |
| ils/elles | écrivent |

## PERFECT

|  |  |
|---|---|
| j' | ai écrit |
| tu | as écrit |
| il/elle/on | a écrit |
| nous | avons écrit |
| vous | avez écrit |
| ils/elles | ont écrit |

## IMPERFECT

|  |  |
|---|---|
| j' | écrivais |
| tu | écrivais |
| il/elle/on | écrivait |
| nous | écrivions |
| vous | écriviez |
| ils/elles | écrivaient |

## FUTURE

|  |  |
|---|---|
| j' | écrirai |
| tu | écriras |
| il/elle/on | écrira |
| nous | écrirons |
| vous | écrirez |
| ils/elles | écriront |

## CONDITIONAL

|  |  |
|---|---|
| j' | écrirais |
| tu | écrirais |
| il/elle/on | écrirait |
| nous | écririons |
| vous | écririez |
| ils/elles | écriraient |

## IMPERATIVE

écris / écrivons / écrivez

## PAST PARTICIPLE

écrit

## PRESENT PARTICIPLE

écrivant

---

### EXAMPLE PHRASES

*Tu **as écrit** à ta correspondante récemment?* Have you written to your penfriend lately?
*Elle **écrit** des romans.* She writes novels.
*Comment ça **s'écrit**, "brouillard"?* How do you spell "brouillard"?

---

**je/j'** = I **tu** = you **il** = he/it **elle** = she/it **on** = we/one **nous** = we **vous** = you **ils/elles** = they

## ▶ **être** (to be)

### PRESENT

| | |
|---|---|
| je | suis |
| tu | es |
| il/elle/on | est |
| nous | sommes |
| vous | êtes |
| ils/elles | sont |

### PRESENT SUBJUNCTIVE

| | |
|---|---|
| je | sois |
| tu | sois |
| il/elle/on | soit |
| nous | soyons |
| vous | soyez |
| ils/elles | soient |

### PERFECT

| | |
|---|---|
| j' | ai été |
| tu | as été |
| il/elle/on | a été |
| nous | avons été |
| vous | avez été |
| ils/elles | ont été |

### IMPERFECT

| | |
|---|---|
| j' | étais |
| tu | étais |
| il/elle/on | était |
| nous | étions |
| vous | étiez |
| ils/elles | étaient |

### FUTURE

| | |
|---|---|
| je | serai |
| tu | seras |
| il/elle/on | sera |
| nous | serons |
| vous | serez |
| ils/elles | seront |

### CONDITIONAL

| | |
|---|---|
| je | serais |
| tu | serais |
| il/elle/on | serait |
| nous | serions |
| vous | seriez |
| ils/elles | seraient |

### IMPERATIVE

sois / soyons / soyez

### PAST PARTICIPLE

été

### PRESENT PARTICIPLE

étant

---

### EXAMPLE PHRASES

*Mon père **est** professeur.* My father's a teacher.
*Quelle heure **est**-il? – Il **est** dix heures.* What time is it? – It's 10 o'clock.
*Ils ne **sont** pas encore arrivés.* They haven't arrived yet.

---

**je/j'** = I  **tu** = you  **il** = he/it  **elle** = she/it  **on** = we/one  **nous** = we  **vous** = you  **ils/elles** = they

## ▶ **faire** (to do; to make)

| PRESENT | | PRESENT SUBJUNCTIVE | |
|---|---|---|---|
| je | fais | je | fasse |
| tu | fais | tu | fasses |
| il/elle/on | fait | il/elle/on | fasse |
| nous | faisons | nous | fassions |
| vous | faites | vous | fassiez |
| ils/elles | font | ils/elles | fassent |

| PERFECT | | IMPERFECT | |
|---|---|---|---|
| j' | ai fait | je | faisais |
| tu | as fait | tu | faisais |
| il/elle/on | a fait | il/elle/on | faisait |
| nous | avons fait | nous | faisions |
| vous | avez fait | vous | faisiez |
| ils/elles | ont fait | ils/elles | faisaient |

| FUTURE | | CONDITIONAL | |
|---|---|---|---|
| je | ferai | je | ferais |
| tu | feras | tu | ferais |
| il/elle/on | fera | il/elle/on | ferait |
| nous | ferons | nous | ferions |
| vous | ferez | vous | feriez |
| ils/elles | feront | ils/elles | feraient |

**IMPERATIVE**

fais / faisons / faites

**PAST PARTICIPLE**

fait

**PRESENT PARTICIPLE**

faisant

---

### EXAMPLE PHRASES

*Qu'est-ce que tu **fais**?* What are you doing?
*Qu'est-ce qu'il **a fait**?* What has he done? *or* What did he do?
*J'**ai fait** un gâteau.* I've made a cake *or* I made a cake.
*Il **s'est fait** couper les cheveux.* He's had his hair cut.

---

**je/j'** = I **tu** = you **il** = he/it **elle** = she/it **on** = we/one **nous** = we **vous** = you **ils/elles** = they

## ▶ **falloir** (to be necessary)

**PRESENT**

il faut

**PRESENT SUBJUNCTIVE**

il faille

**PERFECT**

il a fallu

**IMPERFECT**

il fallait

**FUTURE**

il faudra

**CONDITIONAL**

il faudrait

**IMPERATIVE**

*not used*

**PAST PARTICIPLE**

fallu

**PRESENT PARTICIPLE**

*not used*

---

### EXAMPLE PHRASES

*Il **faut** se dépêcher!* We have to hurry up!
*Il me **fallait** de l'argent.* I needed money.
*Il **faudra** que tu sois là à 8 heures.* You'll have to be there at 8.

# ▶ **finir** (to finish)

## PRESENT

| | |
|---:|:---|
| je | finis |
| tu | finis |
| il/elle/on | finit |
| nous | finissons |
| vous | finissez |
| ils/elles | finissent |

## PRESENT SUBJUNCTIVE

| | |
|---:|:---|
| je | finisse |
| tu | finisses |
| il/elle/on | finisse |
| nous | finissions |
| vous | finissiez |
| ils/elles | finissent |

## PERFECT

| | |
|---:|:---|
| j' | ai fini |
| tu | as fini |
| il/elle/on | a fini |
| nous | avons fini |
| vous | avez fini |
| ils/elles | ont fini |

## IMPERFECT

| | |
|---:|:---|
| je | finissais |
| tu | finissais |
| il/elle/on | finissait |
| nous | finissions |
| vous | finissiez |
| ils/elles | finissaient |

## FUTURE

| | |
|---:|:---|
| je | finirai |
| tu | finiras |
| il/elle/on | finira |
| nous | finirons |
| vous | finirez |
| ils/elles | finiront |

## CONDITIONAL

| | |
|---:|:---|
| je | finirais |
| tu | finirais |
| il/elle/on | finirait |
| nous | finirions |
| vous | finiriez |
| ils/elles | finiraient |

## IMPERATIVE

finis / finissons / finissez

## PAST PARTICIPLE

fini

## PRESENT PARTICIPLE

finissant

---

### *EXAMPLE PHRASES*

*Finis ta soupe!* Finish your soup!
*J'ai fini!* I've finished!
*Je finirai mes devoirs demain.* I'll finish my homework tomorrow.

---

**je/j'** = I **tu** = you **il** = he/it **elle** = she/it **on** = we/one **nous** = we **vous** = you **ils/elles** = they

# ▶ **se laver** (to wash oneself)

**PRESENT**

| | |
|---|---|
| je | me lave |
| tu | te laves |
| il/elle/on | se lave |
| nous | nous lavons |
| vous | vous lavez |
| ils/elles | se lavent |

**PRESENT SUBJUNCTIVE**

| | |
|---|---|
| je | me lave |
| tu | te laves |
| il/elle/on | se lave |
| nous | nous lavions |
| vous | vous laviez |
| ils/elles | se lavent |

**PERFECT**

| | |
|---|---|
| je | me suis lavé(e) |
| tu | t'es lavé(e) |
| il/elle/on | s'est lavé(e) |
| nous | nous sommes lavé(e)s |
| vous | vous êtes lavé(e)(s) |
| ils/elles | se sont lavé(e)s |

**IMPERFECT**

| | |
|---|---|
| je | me lavais |
| tu | te lavais |
| il/elle/on | se lavait |
| nous | nous lavions |
| vous | vous laviez |
| ils/elles | se lavient |

**FUTURE**

| | |
|---|---|
| je | me laverai |
| tu | te laveras |
| il/elle/on | se lavera |
| nous | nous laverons |
| vous | vous laverez |
| ils/elles | se laveront |

**CONDITIONAL**

| | |
|---|---|
| je | me laverais |
| tu | te laverais |
| il/elle/on | se laverait |
| nous | nous laverions |
| vous | vous laveriez |
| ils/elles | se laveraient |

**IMPERATIVE**

lave-toi / lavons-nous / lavez-vous

**PAST PARTICIPLE**

lavé(e)

**PRESENT PARTICIPLE**

se lavant

---

### EXAMPLE PHRASES

*Lave-toi* vite, tu vas être en retard. Have a quick wash, you're going to be late.

*Lavez-vous* les mains avant de vous mettre à table. Wash your hands before you sit at the table.

Nous nous sommes *lavé* les dents puis nous sommes allés nous coucher. We cleaned our teeth and went to bed.

---

**je/j'** = I **tu** = you **il** = he/it **elle** = she/it **on** = we/one **nous** = we **vous** = you **ils/elles** = they

## ▶ **mettre** (to put)

### PRESENT

| | |
|---|---|
| je | mets |
| tu | mets |
| il/elle/on | met |
| nous | mettons |
| vous | mettez |
| ils/elles | mettent |

### PRESENT SUBJUNCTIVE

| | |
|---|---|
| je | mette |
| tu | mettes |
| il/elle/on | mette |
| nous | mettions |
| vous | mettiez |
| ils/elles | mettent |

### PERFECT

| | |
|---|---|
| j' | ai mis |
| tu | as mis |
| il/elle/on | a mis |
| nous | avons mis |
| vous | avez mis |
| ils/elles | ont mis |

### IMPERFECT

| | |
|---|---|
| je | mettais |
| tu | mettais |
| il/elle/on | mettait |
| nous | mettions |
| vous | mettiez |
| ils/elles | mettaient |

### FUTURE

| | |
|---|---|
| je | mettrai |
| tu | mettras |
| il/elle/on | mettra |
| nous | mettrons |
| vous | mettrez |
| ils/elles | mettront |

### CONDITIONAL

| | |
|---|---|
| je | mettrais |
| tu | mettrais |
| il/elle/on | mettrait |
| nous | mettrions |
| vous | mettriez |
| ils/elles | mettraient |

### IMPERATIVE

mets / mettons / mettez

### PAST PARTICIPLE

mis

### PRESENT PARTICIPLE

mettant

---

### *EXAMPLE PHRASES*

*Mets* ton manteau! Put your coat on!
*Où est-ce que tu **as mis** les clés?* Where have you put the keys?
*J'ai mis le livre sur la table.* I put the book on the table.
*Elle s'est mise à pleurer.* She started crying.

---

**je/j'** = I  **tu** = you  **il** = he/it  **elle** = she/it  **on** = we/one  **nous** = we  **vous** = you  **ils/elles** = they

# ▶ **mourir** (to die)

## PRESENT

| | |
|---|---|
| je | meurs |
| tu | meurs |
| il/elle/on | meurt |
| nous | mourons |
| vous | mourez |
| ils/elles | meurent |

## PRESENT SUBJUNCTIVE

| | |
|---|---|
| je | meure |
| tu | meures |
| il/elle/on | meure |
| nous | mourions |
| vous | mouriez |
| ils/elles | meurent |

## PERFECT

| | |
|---|---|
| je | suis mort(e) |
| tu | es mort(e) |
| il/elle/on | est mort(e) |
| nous | sommes mort(e)s |
| vous | êtes mort(e)(s) |
| ils/elles | sont mort(e)s |

## IMPERFECT

| | |
|---|---|
| je | mourais |
| tu | mourais |
| il/elle/on | mourait |
| nous | mourions |
| vous | mouriez |
| ils/elles | mouraient |

## FUTURE

| | |
|---|---|
| je | mourrai |
| tu | mourras |
| il/elle/on | mourra |
| nous | mourrons |
| vous | mourrez |
| ils/elles | mourront |

## CONDITIONAL

| | |
|---|---|
| je | mourrais |
| tu | mourrais |
| il/elle/on | mourrait |
| nous | mourrions |
| vous | mourriez |
| ils/elles | mourraient |

## IMPERATIVE

meurs / mourons / mourez

## PAST PARTICIPLE

mort

## PRESENT PARTICIPLE

mourant

---

### EXAMPLE PHRASES

*Elle **est morte** en 1998.* She died in 1998.
*Ils **sont morts**.* They're dead.
*On **meurt** de froid ici!* We're freezing to death in here!

---

**je/j'** = I   **tu** = you   **il** = he/it   **elle** = she/it   **on** = we/one   **nous** = we   **vous** = you   **ils/elles** = they

# ▶ **naître** (to be born)

## PRESENT

| | |
|---|---|
| je | nais |
| tu | nais |
| il/elle/on | naît |
| nous | naissons |
| vous | naissez |
| ils/elles | naissent |

## PRESENT SUBJUNCTIVE

| | |
|---|---|
| je | naisse |
| tu | naisses |
| il/elle/on | naisse |
| nous | naissions |
| vous | naissiez |
| ils/elles | naissent |

## PERFECT

| | |
|---|---|
| je | suis né(e) |
| tu | es né(e) |
| il/elle/on | est né(e) |
| nous | sommes né(e)s |
| vous | êtes né(e)(s) |
| ils/elles | sont né(e)s |

## IMPERFECT

| | |
|---|---|
| je | naissais |
| tu | naissais |
| il/elle/on | naissait |
| nous | naissions |
| vous | naissiez |
| ils/elles | naissaient |

## FUTURE

| | |
|---|---|
| je | naîtrai |
| tu | naîtras |
| il/elle/on | naîtra |
| nous | naîtrons |
| vous | naîtrez |
| ils/elles | naîtront |

## CONDITIONAL

| | |
|---|---|
| je | naîtrais |
| tu | naîtrais |
| il/elle/on | naîtrait |
| nous | naîtrions |
| vous | naîtriez |
| ils/elles | naîtraient |

## IMPERATIVE

nais / naissons / naissez

## PAST PARTICIPLE

né

## PRESENT PARTICIPLE

naissant

---

### EXAMPLE PHRASES

*Je **suis née** le 12 février.* I was born on 12 February.
*Le bébé de Delphine **naîtra** en mars.* Delphine is going to have a baby in March.
*Quand est-ce que tu **es né**?* When were you born?

# ▶ **ouvrir** (to open)

## PRESENT

| | |
|---|---|
| j' | ouvre |
| tu | ouvres |
| il/elle/on | ouvre |
| nous | ouvrons |
| vous | ouvrez |
| ils/elles | ouvrent |

## PRESENT SUBJUNCTIVE

| | |
|---|---|
| j' | ouvre |
| tu | ouvres |
| il/elle/on | ouvre |
| nous | ouvrions |
| vous | ouvriez |
| ils/elles | ouvrent |

## PERFECT

| | |
|---|---|
| j' | ai ouvert |
| tu | as ouvert |
| il/elle/on | a ouvert |
| nous | avons ouvert |
| vous | avez ouvert |
| ils/elles | ont ouvert |

## IMPERFECT

| | |
|---|---|
| j' | ouvrais |
| tu | ouvrais |
| il/elle/on | ouvrait |
| nous | ouvrions |
| vous | ouvriez |
| ils/elles | ouvraient |

## FUTURE

| | |
|---|---|
| j' | ouvrirai |
| tu | ouvriras |
| il/elle/on | ouvrira |
| nous | ouvrirons |
| vous | ouvrirez |
| ils/elles | ouvriront |

## CONDITIONAL

| | |
|---|---|
| j' | ouvrirais |
| tu | ouvrirais |
| il/elle/on | ouvrirait |
| nous | ouvririons |
| vous | ouvririez |
| ils/elles | ouvriraient |

## IMPERATIVE

ouvre / ouvrons / ouvrez

## PAST PARTICIPLE

ouvert

## PRESENT PARTICIPLE

ouvrant

---

### EXAMPLE PHRASES

*Elle **a ouvert** la porte.* She opened the door.
*Est-ce que tu pourrais **ouvrir** la fenêtre?* Could you open the window?
*Je me suis coupé en **ouvrant** une boîte de conserve.* I cut myself opening a tin.
*La porte **s'est ouverte**.* The door opened.

---

**je/j'** = I  **tu** = you  **il** = he/it  **elle** = she/it  **on** = we/one  **nous** = we  **vous** = you  **ils/elles** = they

# ▶ **pouvoir** (to be able)

## PRESENT

| | |
|---|---|
| je | peux |
| tu | peux |
| il/elle/on | peut |
| nous | pouvons |
| vous | pouvez |
| ils/elles | peuvent |

## PRESENT SUBJUNCTIVE

| | |
|---|---|
| je | puisse |
| tu | puisses |
| il/elle/on | puisse |
| nous | puissions |
| vous | puissiez |
| ils/elles | puissent |

## PERFECT

| | |
|---|---|
| j' | ai pu |
| tu | as pu |
| il/elle/on | a pu |
| nous | avons pu |
| vous | avez pu |
| ils/elles | ont pu |

## IMPERFECT

| | |
|---|---|
| je | pouvais |
| tu | pouvais |
| il/elle/on | pouvait |
| nous | pouvions |
| vous | pouviez |
| ils/elles | pouvaient |

## FUTURE

| | |
|---|---|
| je | pourrai |
| tu | pourras |
| il/elle/on | pourra |
| nous | pourrons |
| vous | pourrez |
| ils/elles | pourront |

## CONDITIONAL

| | |
|---|---|
| je | pourrais |
| tu | pourrais |
| il/elle/on | pourrait |
| nous | pourrions |
| vous | pourriez |
| ils/elles | pourraient |

## IMPERATIVE

*not used*

## PAST PARTICIPLE

pu

## PRESENT PARTICIPLE

pouvant

---

### *EXAMPLE PHRASES*

*Je **peux** t'aider, si tu veux.* I can help you if you like.
*J'ai fait tout ce que j'**ai pu**.* I did all I could.
*Je ne **pourrai** pas venir samedi.* I won't be able to come on Saturday.

---

**je/j'** = I  **tu** = you  **il** = he/it  **elle** = she/it  **on** = we/one  **nous** = we  **vous** = you  **ils/elles** = they

# ▶ **prendre** (to take)

## PRESENT

| | |
|---|---|
| je | prends |
| tu | prends |
| il/elle/on | prend |
| nous | prenons |
| vous | prenez |
| ils/elles | prennent |

## PRESENT SUBJUNCTIVE

| | |
|---|---|
| je | prenne |
| tu | prennes |
| il/elle/on | prenne |
| nous | prenions |
| vous | preniez |
| ils/elles | prennent |

## PERFECT

| | |
|---|---|
| j' | ai pris |
| tu | as pris |
| il/elle/on | a pris |
| nous | avons pris |
| vous | avez pris |
| ils/elles | ont pris |

## IMPERFECT

| | |
|---|---|
| je | prenais |
| tu | prenais |
| il/elle/on | prenait |
| nous | prenions |
| vous | preniez |
| ils/elles | prenaient |

## FUTURE

| | |
|---|---|
| je | prendrai |
| tu | prendras |
| il/elle/on | prendra |
| nous | prendrons |
| vous | prendrez |
| ils/elles | prendront |

## CONDITIONAL

| | |
|---|---|
| je | prendrais |
| tu | prendrais |
| il/elle/on | prendrait |
| nous | prendrions |
| vous | prendriez |
| ils/elles | prendraient |

## IMPERATIVE

prends / prenons / prenez

## PAST PARTICIPLE

pris

## PRESENT PARTICIPLE

prenant

---

### EXAMPLE PHRASES

*J'**ai pris** plein de photos.* I took lots of pictures.
*N'oublie pas de **prendre** ton passeport.* Don't forget to take your passport.
*Il **prendra** le train de 8h20.* He'll take the 8.20 train.
*Pour qui est-ce qu'il **se prend**?* Who does he think he is?

---

**je/j'** = I  **tu** = you  **il** = he/it  **elle** = she/it  **on** = we/one  **nous** = we  **vous** = you  **ils/elles** = they

## ▶ **savoir** (to know)

### PRESENT

| | |
|---|---|
| je | sais |
| tu | sais |
| il/elle/on | sait |
| nous | savons |
| vous | savez |
| ils/elles | savent |

### PRESENT SUBJUNCTIVE

| | |
|---|---|
| je | sache |
| tu | saches |
| il/elle/on | sache |
| nous | sachions |
| vous | sachiez |
| ils/elles | sachent |

### PERFECT

| | |
|---|---|
| j' | ai su |
| tu | as su |
| il/elle/on | a su |
| nous | avons su |
| vous | avez su |
| ils/elles | ont su |

### IMPERFECT

| | |
|---|---|
| je | savais |
| tu | savais |
| il/elle/on | savait |
| nous | savions |
| vous | saviez |
| ils/elles | savaient |

### FUTURE

| | |
|---|---|
| je | saurai |
| tu | sauras |
| il/elle/on | saura |
| nous | saurons |
| vous | saurez |
| ils/elles | sauront |

### CONDITIONAL

| | |
|---|---|
| je | saurais |
| tu | saurais |
| il/elle/on | saurait |
| nous | saurions |
| vous | sauriez |
| ils/elles | sauraient |

### IMPERATIVE

sache / sachons / sachez

### PAST PARTICIPLE

su

### PRESENT PARTICIPLE

sachant

---

### EXAMPLE PHRASES

*Tu **sais** ce que tu vas faire l'année prochaine?* Do you know what you're doing next year?
*Je ne **sais** pas.* I don't know.
*Elle ne **sait** pas nager.* She can't swim.
*Tu **savais** que son père était pakistanais?* Did you know her father was Pakistani?

---

**je/j**' = I  **tu** = you  **il** = he/it  **elle** = she/it  **on** = we/one  **nous** = we  **vous** = you  **ils/elles** = they

# ▶ **sortir** (to go out)

## PRESENT

| | |
|---|---|
| je | sors |
| tu | sors |
| il/elle/on | sort |
| nous | sortons |
| vous | sortez |
| ils/elles | sortent |

## PRESENT SUBJUNCTIVE

| | |
|---|---|
| je | sorte |
| tu | sortes |
| il/elle/on | sorte |
| nous | sortions |
| vous | sortiez |
| ils/elles | sortent |

## PERFECT

| | |
|---|---|
| je | suis sorti(e) |
| tu | es sorti(e) |
| il/elle/on | est sorti(e) |
| nous | sommes sorti(e)s |
| vous | êtes sorti(e)(s) |
| ils/elles | sont sorti(e)s |

## IMPERFECT

| | |
|---|---|
| je | sortais |
| tu | sortais |
| il/elle/on | sortait |
| nous | sortions |
| vous | sortiez |
| ils/elles | sortaient |

## FUTURE

| | |
|---|---|
| je | sortirai |
| tu | sortiras |
| il/elle/on | sortira |
| nous | sortirons |
| vous | sortirez |
| ils/elles | sortiront |

## CONDITIONAL

| | |
|---|---|
| je | sortirais |
| tu | sortirais |
| il/elle/on | sortirait |
| nous | sortirions |
| vous | sortiriez |
| ils/elles | sortiraient |

## IMPERATIVE

sors / sortons / sortez

## PAST PARTICIPLE

sorti

## PRESENT PARTICIPLE

sortant

---

### EXAMPLE PHRASES

*Je ne suis pas **sortie** ce week-end.* I didn't go out this weekend.
*Aurélie **sort** avec Bruno.* Aurélie is going out with Bruno.
*Elle **est sortie** de l'hôpital hier.* She came out of hospital yesterday.
*Je n'ai pas **sorti** le chien parce qu'il pleuvait.* I didn't take the dog out for a walk because it was raining.

ℹ️ Note that **sortir** takes **avoir** in the perfect tense when it is used with a direct object.

**je/j'** = I  **tu** = you  **il** = he/it  **elle** = she/it  **on** = we/one  **nous** = we  **vous** = you  **ils/elles** = they

## ▶ **tenir** (to hold)

### PRESENT

|  |  |
|---|---|
| je | tiens |
| tu | tiens |
| il/elle/on | tient |
| nous | tenons |
| vous | tenez |
| ils/elles | tiennent |

### PRESENT SUBJUNCTIVE

|  |  |
|---|---|
| je | tienne |
| tu | tiennes |
| il/elle/on | tienne |
| nous | tenions |
| vous | teniez |
| ils/elles | tiennent |

### PERFECT

|  |  |
|---|---|
| j' | ai tenu |
| tu | as tenu |
| il/elle/on | a tenu |
| nous | avons tenu |
| vous | avez tenu |
| ils/elles | ont tenu |

### IMPERFECT

|  |  |
|---|---|
| je | tenais |
| tu | tenais |
| il/elle/on | tenait |
| nous | tenions |
| vous | teniez |
| ils/elles | tenaient |

### FUTURE

|  |  |
|---|---|
| je | tiendrai |
| tu | tiendras |
| il/elle/on | tiendra |
| nous | tiendrons |
| vous | tiendrez |
| ils/elles | tiendront |

### CONDITIONAL

|  |  |
|---|---|
| je | tiendrais |
| tu | tiendrais |
| il/elle/on | tiendrait |
| nous | tiendrions |
| vous | tiendriez |
| ils/elles | tiendraient |

### IMPERATIVE

tiens / tenons / tenez

### PAST PARTICIPLE

tenu

### PRESENT PARTICIPLE

tenant

---

### *EXAMPLE PHRASES*

**Tiens**-*moi la main*. Hold my hand.
*Elle* **tenait** *beaucoup à son chat*. She was really attached to her cat.
**Tiens**, *prends mon stylo*. Here, have my pen.
**Tiens-toi** *droit!* Sit up straight!

---

**je/j** = I **tu** = you **il** = he/it **elle** = she/it **on** = we/one **nous** = we **vous** = you **ils/elles** = they

# ▶ **venir** (to come)

## PRESENT

| | |
|---|---|
| je | viens |
| tu | viens |
| il/elle/on | vient |
| nous | venons |
| vous | venez |
| ils/elles | viennent |

## PRESENT SUBJUNCTIVE

| | |
|---|---|
| je | vienne |
| tu | viennes |
| il/elle/on | vienne |
| nous | venions |
| vous | veniez |
| ils/elles | viennent |

## PERFECT

| | |
|---|---|
| je | suis venu(e) |
| tu | es venu(e) |
| il/elle/on | est venu(e) |
| nous | sommes venu(e)s |
| vous | êtes venu(e)(s) |
| ils/elles | sont venu(e)s |

## IMPERFECT

| | |
|---|---|
| je | venais |
| tu | venais |
| il/elle/on | venait |
| nous | venions |
| vous | veniez |
| ils/elles | venaient |

## FUTURE

| | |
|---|---|
| je | viendrai |
| tu | viendras |
| il/elle/on | viendra |
| nous | viendrons |
| vous | viendrez |
| ils/elles | viendront |

## CONDITIONAL

| | |
|---|---|
| je | viendrais |
| tu | viendrais |
| il/elle/on | viendrait |
| nous | viendrions |
| vous | viendriez |
| ils/elles | viendraient |

## IMPERATIVE

viens / venons / venez

## PAST PARTICIPLE

venu

## PRESENT PARTICIPLE

venant

---

### EXAMPLE PHRASES

*Elle ne **viendra** pas cette année.* She won't be coming this year.
*Fatou et Malik **viennent** du Sénégal.* Fatou and Malik come from Senegal.
*Je **viens** de manger.* I've just eaten.

## ▶ **vivre** (to live)

### PRESENT

|  |  |
|---|---|
| je | vis |
| tu | vis |
| il/elle/on | vit |
| nous | vivons |
| vous | vivez |
| ils/elles | vivent |

### PRESENT SUBJUNCTIVE

|  |  |
|---|---|
| je | vive |
| tu | vives |
| il/elle/on | vive |
| nous | vivions |
| vous | viviez |
| ils/elles | vivent |

### PERFECT

|  |  |
|---|---|
| j' | ai vécu |
| tu | as vécu |
| il/elle/on | a vécu |
| nous | avons vécu |
| vous | avez vécu |
| ils/elles | ont vécu |

### IMPERFECT

|  |  |
|---|---|
| je | vivais |
| tu | vivais |
| il/elle/on | vivait |
| nous | vivions |
| vous | viviez |
| ils/elles | vivaient |

### FUTURE

|  |  |
|---|---|
| je | vivrai |
| tu | vivras |
| il/elle/on | vivra |
| nous | vivrons |
| vous | vivrez |
| ils/elles | vivront |

### CONDITIONAL

|  |  |
|---|---|
| je | vivrais |
| tu | vivrais |
| il/elle/on | vivrait |
| nous | vivrions |
| vous | vivriez |
| ils/elles | vivraient |

### IMPERATIVE

vis / vivons / vivez

### PAST PARTICIPLE

vécu

### PRESENT PARTICIPLE

vivant

---

### EXAMPLE PHRASES

*Ma sœur **vit** en Espagne.* My sister lives in Spain.
*Il **a vécu** dix ans à Lyon.* He lived in Lyons for 10 years.
*Les gorilles **vivent** surtout dans la forêt.* Gorillas mostly live in the forest.

---

## ▶ **voir** (to see)

### PRESENT

| | |
|---|---|
| je | vois |
| tu | vois |
| il/elle/on | voit |
| nous | voyons |
| vous | voyez |
| ils/elles | voient |

### PRESENT SUBJUNCTIVE

| | |
|---|---|
| je | voie |
| tu | voies |
| il/elle/on | voie |
| nous | voyions |
| vous | voyiez |
| ils/elles | voient |

### PERFECT

| | |
|---|---|
| j' | ai vu |
| tu | as vu |
| il/elle/on | a vu |
| nous | avons vu |
| vous | avez vu |
| ils/elles | ont vu |

### IMPERFECT

| | |
|---|---|
| je | voyais |
| tu | voyais |
| il/elle/on | voyait |
| nous | voyions |
| vous | voyiez |
| ils/elles | voyaient |

### FUTURE

| | |
|---|---|
| je | verrai |
| tu | verras |
| il/elle/on | verra |
| nous | verrons |
| vous | verrez |
| ils/elles | verront |

### CONDITIONAL

| | |
|---|---|
| je | verrais |
| tu | verrais |
| il/elle/on | verrait |
| nous | verrions |
| vous | verriez |
| ils/elles | verraient |

### IMPERATIVE

vois / voyons / voyez

### PAST PARTICIPLE

vu

### PRESENT PARTICIPLE

voyant

---

### EXAMPLE PHRASES

*Venez me **voir** quand vous serez à Paris.* Come and see me when you're in Paris.
*Je ne **vois** rien sans mes lunettes.* I can't see anything without my glasses.
*Est-ce que tu l'**as vu**?* Did you see him? or Have you seen him?
*Est-ce que cette tache **se voit**?* Does that stain show?

# ▶ **vouloir** (to want)

## PRESENT

|           |         |
|-----------|---------|
| je        | veux    |
| tu        | veux    |
| il/elle/on | veut    |
| nous      | voulons |
| vous      | voulez  |
| ils/elles | veulent |

## PRESENT SUBJUNCTIVE

|           |          |
|-----------|----------|
| je        | veuille  |
| tu        | veuilles |
| il/elle/on | veuille  |
| nous      | voulions |
| vous      | vouliez  |
| ils/elles | veuillent |

## PERFECT

|           |            |
|-----------|------------|
| j'        | ai voulu   |
| tu        | as voulu   |
| il/elle/on | a voulu    |
| nous      | avons voulu |
| vous      | avez voulu |
| ils/elles | ont voulu  |

## IMPERFECT

|           |           |
|-----------|-----------|
| je        | voulais   |
| tu        | voulais   |
| il/elle/on | voulait   |
| nous      | voulions  |
| vous      | vouliez   |
| ils/elles | voulaient |

## FUTURE

|           |          |
|-----------|----------|
| je        | voudrai  |
| tu        | voudras  |
| il/elle/on | voudra   |
| nous      | voudrons |
| vous      | voudrez  |
| ils/elles | voudront |

## CONDITIONAL

|           |            |
|-----------|------------|
| je        | voudrais   |
| tu        | voudrais   |
| il/elle/on | voudrait   |
| nous      | voudrions  |
| vous      | voudriez   |
| ils/elles | voudraient |

## IMPERATIVE

veuille / veuillons / veuillez

## PAST PARTICIPLE

voulu

## PRESENT PARTICIPLE

voulant

---

## EXAMPLE PHRASES

*Elle **veut** un vélo pour Noël.* She wants a bike for Christmas.
*Ils **voulaient** aller au cinéma.* They wanted to go to the cinema.
*Tu **voudrais** une tasse de thé?* Would you like a cup of tea?

---

**A** [eɪ] *n* (*Mus*) la *m*

**KEYWORD**

**a** [eɪ, ə] (*before vowel or silent h* **an**) *indef art* **1** un(e); **a book** un livre; **an apple** une pomme; **she's a doctor** elle est médecin

**2** (*instead of the number "one"*) un(e); **a year ago** il y a un an; **a hundred/thousand** *etc* **pounds** cent/mille *etc* livres

**3** (*in expressing ratios, prices etc*): **3 a day/week** 3 par jour/semaine; **10 km an hour** 10 km à l'heure; **£5 a person** 5£ par personne; **30p a kilo** 30p le kilo

**A2** *n* (*BRIT: Scol*) deuxième partie de l'examen équivalent au baccalauréat
**A.A.** *n abbr* (*BRIT: = Automobile Association*) ≈ ACF *m*; (*= Alcoholics Anonymous*) AA
**A.A.A.** *n abbr* (*= American Automobile Association*) ≈ ACF *m*

**aback** [ə'bæk] *adv*: **to be taken ~** être décontenancé(e)
**abandon** [ə'bændən] *vt* abandonner
**abattoir** ['æbətwɑːʳ] *n* (*BRIT*) abattoir *m*
**abbey** ['æbɪ] *n* abbaye *f*
**abbreviation** [əbriːvɪ'eɪʃən] *n* abréviation *f*
**abdomen** ['æbdəmən] *n* abdomen *m*
**abduct** [æb'dʌkt] *vt* enlever
**abide** [ə'baɪd] *vt* souffrir, supporter; **I can't ~ it/him** je ne le supporte pas; **abide by** *vt fus* observer, respecter
**ability** [ə'bɪlɪtɪ] *n* compétence *f*; capacité *f*; (*skill*) talent *m*
**able** ['eɪbl] *adj* compétent(e); **to be ~ to do sth** pouvoir faire qch, être capable de faire qch
**abnormal** [æb'nɔːməl] *adj* anormal(e)
**aboard** [ə'bɔːd] *adv* à bord ▷ *prep* à bord de; (*train*) dans
**abolish** [ə'bɔlɪʃ] *vt* abolir
**abolition** [æbə'lɪʃən] *n* abolition *f*
**abort** [ə'bɔːt] *vt* (*Med*) faire avorter; (*Comput, fig*) abandonner; **abortion** [ə'bɔːʃən] *n* avortement *m*; **to have an abortion** se faire avorter

**KEYWORD**

**about** [ə'baut] *adv* **1** (*approximately*) environ, à peu près; **about a hundred/thousand** *etc* environ cent/mille *etc*, une centaine (de)/un millier (de) *etc*; **it takes about 10 hours** ça prend environ or à peu près 10 heures; **at about 2 o'clock** vers 2 heures; **I've just about finished** j'ai presque fini
**2** (*referring to place*) çà et là, de-ci de-là; **to run about** courir çà et là; **to walk about** se promener, aller et venir; **they left all their things lying about** ils ont laissé traîner toutes leurs affaires
**3**: **to be about to do sth** être sur le point de faire qch
▷ *prep* **1** (*relating to*) au sujet de, à propos de; **a book about London** un livre sur Londres; **what is it about?** de

quoi s'agit-il?; **we talked about it** nous
en avons parlé; **what** or **how about
doing this?** et si nous faisions ceci?
**2** (referring to place) dans; **to walk
about the town** se promener dans
la ville

**above** [əˈbʌv] adv au-dessus ▷ prep
au-dessus de; (more than) plus de;
**mentioned ~** mentionné ci-dessus; **~
all** par-dessus tout, surtout
**abroad** [əˈbrɔːd] adv à l'étranger
**abrupt** [əˈbrʌpt] adj (steep, blunt)
abrupt(e); (sudden, gruff) brusque
**abscess** [ˈæbsɪs] n abcès m
**absence** [ˈæbsəns] n absence f
**absent** [ˈæbsənt] adj absent(e);
**absent-minded** adj distrait(e)
**absolute** [ˈæbsəluːt] adj absolu(e);
**absolutely** [æbsəˈluːtlɪ] adv
absolument
**absorb** [əbˈzɔːb] vt absorber; **to be
~ed in a book** être plongé(e) dans
un livre; **absorbent cotton** n (US)
coton m hydrophile; **absorbing**
adj absorbant(e); (book, film etc)
captivant(e)
**abstain** [əbˈsteɪn] vi: **to ~ (from)**
s'abstenir (de)
**abstract** [ˈæbstrækt] adj abstrait(e)
**absurd** [əbˈsəːd] adj absurde
**abundance** [əˈbʌndəns] n abondance f
**abundant** [əˈbʌndənt] adj
abondant(e)
**abuse** n [əˈbjuːs] (insults) insultes
fpl, injures fpl; (ill-treatment) mauvais
traitements mpl; (of power etc) abus
m ▷ vt [əˈbjuːz] (insult) insulter;
(ill-treat) malmener; (power etc) abuser
de; **abusive** adj grossier(-ière),
injurieux(-euse)
**abysmal** [əˈbɪzməl] adj exécrable;
(ignorance etc) sans bornes
**academic** [ækəˈdemɪk] adj
universitaire; (person: scholarly)
intellectuel(-le); (pej: issue)
oiseux(-euse), purement théorique ▷ n
universitaire m/f; **academic year** n

(University) année f universitaire; (Scol)
année scolaire
**academy** [əˈkædəmɪ] n (learned body)
académie f; (school) collège m; **~ of
music** conservatoire m
**accelerate** [ækˈseləreɪt] vt, vi
accélérer; **acceleration** [ækseləˈreɪʃən]
n accélération f; **accelerator** n (BRIT)
accélérateur m
**accent** [ˈæksent] n accent m
**accept** [əkˈsept] vt accepter;
**acceptable** adj acceptable;
**acceptance** n acceptation f
**access** [ˈækses] n accès m; **to have ~
to** (information, library etc) avoir accès
à, pouvoir utiliser or consulter; (person)
avoir accès auprès de; **accessible**
[ækˈsesəbl] adj accessible
**accessory** [ækˈsesərɪ] n accessoire m;
**~ to** (Law) accessoire à
**accident** [ˈæksɪdənt] n accident
m; (chance) hasard m; **I've had
an ~** j'ai eu un accident; **by ~** (by
chance) par hasard; (not deliberately)
accidentellement; **accidental**
[æksɪˈdentl] adj accidentel(le);
**accidentally** [æksɪˈdentəlɪ] adv
accidentellement; **Accident and
Emergency Department** n (BRIT)
service m des urgences; **accident
insurance** n assurance f accident
**acclaim** [əˈkleɪm] vt acclamer ▷ n
acclamations fpl
**accommodate** [əˈkɔmədeɪt] vt loger,
recevoir; (oblige, help) obliger; (car etc)
contenir
**accommodation** (US
**accommodations**) [əkɔməˈdeɪʃən(z)]
n(pl) logement m
**accompaniment** [əˈkʌmpənɪmənt] n
accompagnement m
**accompany** [əˈkʌmpənɪ] vt
accompagner
**accomplice** [əˈkʌmplɪs] n complice
m/f
**accomplish** [əˈkʌmplɪʃ] vt accomplir;
**accomplishment** n (skill: gen pl) talent
m; (completion) accomplissement m;

(*achievement*) réussite *f*

**accord** [ə'kɔːd] *n* accord *m* ▷ *vt* accorder; **of his own ~** de son plein gré; **accordance** *n*: **in accordance with** conformément à; **according**: **according to** *prep* selon; **accordingly** *adv* (*appropriately*) en conséquence; (*as a result*) par conséquent

**account** [ə'kaunt] *n* (*Comm*) compte *m*; (*report*) compte rendu, récit *m*; **accounts** *npl* (*Comm: records*) comptabilité *f*, comptes; **of no ~** sans importance; **on ~** en acompte; **to buy sth on ~** acheter qch à crédit; **on no ~** en aucun cas; **on ~ of** à cause de; **to take into ~, take ~ of** tenir compte de; **account for** *vt fus* (*explain*) expliquer, rendre compte de; (*represent*) représenter; **accountable** *adj*: **accountable (to)** responsable (devant); **accountant** *n* comptable *m/f*; **account number** *n* numéro *m* de compte

**accumulate** [ə'kjuːmjuleɪt] *vt* accumuler, amasser ▷ *vi* s'accumuler, s'amasser

**accuracy** ['ækjurəsɪ] *n* exactitude *f*, précision *f*

**accurate** ['ækjurɪt] *adj* exact(e), précis(e); (*device*) précis; **accurately** *adv* avec précision

**accusation** [ækju'zeɪʃən] *n* accusation *f*

**accuse** [ə'kjuːz] *vt*: **to ~ sb (of sth)** accuser qn (de qch); **accused** *n* (*Law*) accusé(e)

**accustomed** [ə'kʌstəmd] *adj*: **~ to** habitué(e) or accoutumé(e) à

**ace** [eɪs] *n* as *m*

**ache** [eɪk] *n* mal *m*, douleur *f* ▷ *vi* (*be sore*) faire mal, être douloureux(-euse); **my head ~s** j'ai mal à la tête

**achieve** [ə'tʃiːv] *vt* (*aim*) atteindre; (*victory, success*) remporter, obtenir; **achievement** *n* exploit *m*, réussite *f*; (*of aims*) réalisation *f*

**acid** ['æsɪd] *adj, n* acide (*m*)

**acknowledge** [ək'nɔlɪdʒ] *vt* (*also: ~*

**receipt of**) accuser réception de; (*fact*) reconnaître; **acknowledgement** *n* (*of letter*) accusé *m* de réception

**acne** ['æknɪ] *n* acné *m*

**acorn** ['eɪkɔːn] *n* gland *m*

**acoustic** [ə'kuːstɪk] *adj* acoustique

**acquaintance** [ə'kweɪntəns] *n* connaissance *f*

**acquire** [ə'kwaɪəʳ] *vt* acquérir; **acquisition** [ækwɪ'zɪʃən] *n* acquisition *f*

**acquit** [ə'kwɪt] *vt* acquitter; **to ~ o.s. well** s'en tirer très honorablement

**acre** ['eɪkəʳ] *n* acre *f* (= 4047 m²)

**acronym** ['ækrənɪm] *n* acronyme *m*

**across** [ə'krɔs] *prep* (*on the other side*) de l'autre côté de; (*crosswise*) en travers de ▷ *adv* de l'autre côté; en travers; **to run/swim ~** traverser en courant/à la nage; **~ from** en face de

**acrylic** [ə'krɪlɪk] *adj, n* acrylique (*m*)

**act** [ækt] *n* acte *m*, action *f*; (*Theat: part of play*) acte; (: *of performer*) numéro *m*; (*Law*) loi *f* ▷ *vi* agir; (*Theat*) jouer; (*pretend*) jouer la comédie ▷ *vt* (*role*) jouer, tenir; **to catch sb in the ~** prendre qn sur le fait or en flagrant délit; **to ~ as** servir de; **act up** (*inf*) ▷ *vi* (*person*) se conduire mal; (*knee, back, injury*) jouer des tours; (*machine*) être capricieux(-ieuse); **acting** *adj* suppléant(e), par intérim ▷ *n* (*activity*): **to do some acting** faire du théâtre (or du cinéma)

**action** ['ækʃən] *n* action *f*; (*Mil*) combat(s) *m(pl)*; (*Law*) procès *m*, action en justice; **out of ~** hors de combat; (*machine etc*) hors d'usage; **to take ~** agir, prendre des mesures; **action replay** *n* (BRIT TV) ralenti *m*

**activate** ['æktɪveɪt] *vt* (*mechanism*) actionner, faire fonctionner

**active** ['æktɪv] *adj* actif(-ive); (*volcano*) en activité; **actively** *adv* activement; (*discourage*) vivement

**activist** ['æktɪvɪst] *n* activiste *m/f*

**activity** [æk'tɪvɪtɪ] *n* activité *f*; **activity holiday** *n* vacances actives

**actor** ['æktə<sup>r</sup>] n acteur m

**actress** ['æktrɪs] n actrice f

**actual** ['æktjuəl] adj réel(le), véritable; (emphatic use) lui-même (elle-même)

▌ Be careful not to translate **actual** by the French word **actuel**.

**actually** ['æktjuəlɪ] adv réellement, véritablement; (in fact) en fait

▌ Be careful not to translate **actually** by the French word **actuellement**.

**acupuncture** ['ækjupʌŋktʃə<sup>r</sup>] n acuponcture f

**acute** [ə'kju:t] adj aigu(ë); (mind, observer) pénétrant(e)

**A.D.** adv abbr (= Anno Domini) ap. J.-C.

**ad** [æd] n abbr = **advertisement**

**adamant** ['ædəmənt] adj inflexible

**adapt** [ə'dæpt] vt adapter ▷ vi: **to ~ (to)** s'adapter (à); **adapter, adaptor** n (Elec) adaptateur m; (for several plugs) prise f multiple

**add** [æd] vt ajouter; (figures: also: **to ~ up**) additionner ▷ vi (fig): **it doesn't ~ up** cela ne rime à rien; **add up to** vt fus (Math) s'élever à; (fig: mean) signifier

**addict** ['ædɪkt] n toxicomane m/f; (fig) fanatique m/f; **addicted** [ə'dɪktɪd] adj: **to be addicted to** (drink, drugs) être adonné(e) à; (fig: football etc) être un(e) fanatique de; **addiction** [ə'dɪkʃən] n (Med) dépendance f; **addictive** [ə'dɪktɪv] adj qui crée une dépendance

**addition** [ə'dɪʃən] n (adding up) addition f; (thing added) ajout m; **in ~** de plus, de surcroît; **in ~ to** en plus de; **additional** adj supplémentaire

**additive** ['ædɪtɪv] n additif m

**address** [ə'drɛs] n adresse f; (talk) discours m, allocution f ▷ vt adresser; (speak to) s'adresser à; **my ~ is ...** mon adresse, c'est ...; **address book** n carnet m d'adresses

**adequate** ['ædɪkwɪt] adj (enough) suffisant(e); (satisfactory) satisfaisant(e)

**adhere** [əd'hɪə<sup>r</sup>] vi: **to ~ to** adhérer à; (fig: rule, decision) se tenir à

**adhesive** [əd'hi:zɪv] n adhésif m;

**adhesive tape** n (BRIT) ruban m adhésif; (US Med) sparadrap m

**adjacent** [ə'dʒeɪsənt] adj adjacent(e), contigu(ë); **~ to** adjacent à

**adjective** ['ædʒɛktɪv] n adjectif m

**adjoining** [ə'dʒɔɪnɪŋ] adj voisin(e), adjacent(e), attenant(e)

**adjourn** [ə'dʒə:n] vt ajourner ▷ vi suspendre la séance; lever la séance; clore la session

**adjust** [ə'dʒʌst] vt (machine) ajuster, régler; (prices, wages) rajuster ▷ vi: **to ~ (to)** s'adapter (à); **adjustable** adj réglable; **adjustment** n (of machine) ajustage m, réglage m; (of prices, wages) rajustement m; (of person) adaptation f

**administer** [əd'mɪnɪstə<sup>r</sup>] vt administrer; **administration** [ədmɪnɪs'treɪʃən] n (management) administration f; (government) gouvernement m; **administrative** [əd'mɪnɪstrətɪv] adj administratif(-ive)

**administrator** [əd'mɪnɪstreɪtə<sup>r</sup>] n administrateur(-trice)

**admiral** ['ædmərəl] n amiral m

**admiration** [ædmə'reɪʃən] n admiration f

**admire** [əd'maɪə<sup>r</sup>] vt admirer; **admirer** n (fan) admirateur(-trice)

**admission** [əd'mɪʃən] n admission f; (to exhibition, night club etc) entrée f; (confession) aveu m

**admit** [əd'mɪt] vt laisser entrer; admettre; (agree) reconnaître, admettre; (crime) reconnaître avoir commis; **"children not ~ted"** "entrée interdite aux enfants"; **admit to** vt fus reconnaître, avouer; **admittance** n admission f, (droit m d')entrée f; **admittedly** adv il faut en convenir

**adolescent** [ædəu'lɛsnt] adj, n adolescent(e)

**adopt** [ə'dɔpt] vt adopter; **adopted** adj adoptif(-ive), adopté(e); **adoption** [ə'dɔpʃən] n adoption f

**adore** [ə'dɔ:<sup>r</sup>] vt adorer

**adorn** [ə'dɔ:n] vt orner

**Adriatic (Sea)** [eɪdrɪ'ætɪk-] n, adj:
**the Adriatic (Sea)** la mer Adriatique,
l'Adriatique f

**adrift** [ə'drɪft] adv à la dérive

**adult** ['ædʌlt] n adulte m/f ▷ adj
(grown-up) adulte; (for adults) pour
adultes; **adult education** n éducation
f des adultes

**adultery** [ə'dʌltərɪ] n adultère m

**advance** [əd'vɑ:ns] n avance f ▷ vt
avancer ▷ vi s'avancer; **in ~** en avance,
d'avance; **to make ~s to sb** (gen) faire
des propositions à qn; (amorously) faire
des avances à qn; **~ booking** location f;
**~ notice**, **~ warning** préavis m; (verbal)
avertissement m; **do I need to book in
~?** est-ce qu'il faut réserver à l'avance?;
**advanced** adj avancé(e); (Scol: studies)
supérieur(e)

**advantage** [əd'vɑ:ntɪdʒ] n (also Tennis)
avantage m; **to take ~ of** (person)
exploiter; (opportunity) profiter de

**advent** ['ædvənt] n avènement m,
venue f; **A~** (Rel) avent m

**adventure** [əd'vɛntʃər] n aventure f;
**adventurous** [əd'vɛntʃərəs] adj
aventureux(-euse)

**adverb** ['ædvə:b] n adverbe m

**adversary** ['ædvəsərɪ] n adversaire
m/f

**adverse** ['ædvə:s] adj adverse; (effect)
négatif(-ive); (weather, publicity)
mauvais(e); (wind) contraire

**advert** ['ædvə:t] n abbr (BRIT)
= **advertisement**

**advertise** ['ædvətaɪz] vi faire de la
publicité or de la réclame; (in classified
ads etc) mettre une annonce ▷ vt faire
de la publicité or de la réclame pour; (in
classified ads etc) mettre une annonce
pour vendre; **to ~ for** (staff) recruter
par (voie d')annonce; **advertisement**
[əd'və:tɪsmənt] n (Comm) publicité
f, réclame f; (in classified ads etc)
annonce f; **advertiser** n annonceur m;
**advertising** n publicité f

**advice** [əd'vaɪs] n conseils mpl;
(notification) avis m; **a piece of ~** un

conseil; **to take legal ~** consulter
un avocat

**advisable** [əd'vaɪzəbl] adj
recommandable, indiqué(e)

**advise** [əd'vaɪz] vt **to ~ sb
of sth** aviser or informer qn de qch; **to
~ against sth/doing sth** déconseiller
qch/conseiller de ne pas faire qch;
**adviser, advisor** n conseiller(-ère);
**advisory** adj consultatif(-ive)

**advocate** n ['ædvəkɪt] (lawyer)
avocat (plaidant); (upholder) défenseur
m, avocat(e) ▷ vt ['ædvəkeɪt]
recommander, prôner; **to be an ~ of**
être partisan(e) de

**Aegean** [iː'dʒiːən] n, adj: **the ~ (Sea)** la
mer Égée, l'Égée f

**aerial** ['ɛərɪəl] n antenne f ▷ adj
aérien(ne)

**aerobics** [ɛə'rəubɪks] n aérobic m

**aeroplane** ['ɛərəpleɪn] n (BRIT) avion m

**aerosol** ['ɛərəsɔl] n aérosol m

**affair** [ə'fɛər] n affaire f; (also: **love ~**)
liaison f; aventure f

**affect** [ə'fɛkt] vt affecter; (subj: disease)
atteindre; **affected** adj affecté(e);
**affection** n affection f; **affectionate**
adj affectueux(-euse)

**afflict** [ə'flɪkt] vt affliger

**affluent** ['æfluənt] adj (person, family,
surroundings) aisé(e), riche; **the ~
society** la société d'abondance

**afford** [ə'fɔːd] vt (behaviour) se
permettre; (provide) fournir, procurer;
**can we ~ a car?** avons-nous de quoi
acheter or les moyens d'acheter une
voiture?; **affordable** adj abordable

**Afghanistan** [æf'gænɪstæn] n
Afghanistan m

**afraid** [ə'freɪd] adj effrayé(e); **to be ~
of** or **to** avoir peur de; **I am ~ that** je
crains que + sub; **I'm ~ so/not** oui/non,
malheureusement

**Africa** ['æfrɪkə] n Afrique f; **African** adj
africain(e) ▷ n Africain(e); **African-
American** adj afro-américain(e) ▷ n
Afro-Américain(e)

**after** ['ɑːftər] prep, adv après ▷ conj

après que; **it's quarter ~ two** (us) il est deux heures et quart; **~ having done/~ he left** après avoir fait/ après son départ; **to name sb ~ sb** donner à qn le nom de qn; **to ask ~ sb** demander des nouvelles de qn; **what/who are you ~?** que/qui cherchez-vous?; **~ you!** après vous!; **~ all** après tout; **after-effects** npl (of disaster, radiation, drink etc) répercussions fpl; (of illness) séquelles fpl, suites fpl; **aftermath** n conséquences fpl; **afternoon** n après-midi m or f; **after-shave (lotion)** n lotion f après-rasage; **aftersun (lotion/cream)** n après-soleil m inv; **afterwards** (us **afterward**) adv après

**again** [əˈgɛn] adv de nouveau, encore (une fois); **to do sth ~** refaire qch; **~ and ~** à plusieurs reprises

**against** [əˈgɛnst] prep contre; (compared to) par rapport à

**age** [eɪdʒ] n âge m ▷ vt, vi vieillir; **he is 20 years of ~** il a 20 ans; **to come of ~** atteindre sa majorité; **it's been ~s since I saw you** ça fait une éternité que je ne t'ai pas vu; **~d 10** âgé(e) de 10 ans; **age group** n tranche f d'âge; **age limit** n limite f d'âge

**agency** [ˈeɪdʒənsɪ] n agence f

**agenda** [əˈdʒɛndə] n ordre m du jour

> Be careful not to translate *agenda* by the French word *agenda*.

**agent** [ˈeɪdʒənt] n agent m; (firm) concessionnaire m

**aggravate** [ˈægrəveɪt] vt (situation) aggraver; (annoy) exaspérer, agacer

**aggression** [əˈgrɛʃən] n agression f

**aggressive** [əˈgrɛsɪv] adj agressif(-ive)

**agile** [ˈædʒaɪl] adj agile

**agitated** [ˈædʒɪteɪtɪd] adj inquiet(-ète)

**AGM** n abbr (= annual general meeting) AG f

**ago** [əˈgəu] adv: **2 days ~** il y a 2 jours; **not long ~** il n'y a pas longtemps; **how long ~?** il y a combien de temps (de cela)?

**agony** [ˈægənɪ] n (pain) douleur f atroce; (distress) angoisse f; **to be in ~**

souffrir le martyre

**agree** [əˈgriː] vt (price) convenir de ▷ vi: **to ~ with** (person) être d'accord avec; (statements etc) concorder avec; (Ling) s'accorder avec; **to ~ to do** accepter de or consentir à faire; **to ~ to sth** consentir à qch; **to ~ that** (admit) convenir or reconnaître que; **garlic doesn't ~ with me** je ne supporte pas l'ail; **agreeable** adj (pleasant) agréable; (willing) consentant(e), d'accord; **agreed** adj (time, place) convenu(e); **agreement** n accord m; **in agreement** d'accord

**agricultural** [ægrɪˈkʌltʃərəl] adj agricole

**agriculture** [ˈægrɪkʌltʃər] n agriculture f

**ahead** [əˈhɛd] adv en avant; devant; **go right** or **straight ~** (direction) allez tout droit; **go ~!** (permission) allez-y!; **~ of** devant; (fig: schedule etc) en avance sur; **~ of time** en avance

**aid** [eɪd] n aide f; (device) appareil m ▷ vt aider; **in ~ of** en faveur de

**aide** [eɪd] n (person) assistant(e)

**AIDS** [eɪdz] n abbr (= acquired immune (or immuno-)deficiency syndrome) SIDA m

**ailing** [ˈeɪlɪŋ] adj (person) souffreteux(euse); (economy) malade

**ailment** [ˈeɪlmənt] n affection f

**aim** [eɪm] vt: **to ~ sth (at)** (gun, camera) braquer or pointer qch (sur); (missile) lancer qch (à or contre or en direction de); (remark, blow) destiner or adresser qch (à) ▷ vi (also: **to take ~**) viser ▷ n (objective) but m; (skill): **his ~ is bad** il vise mal; **to ~ at** viser; (fig) viser (à); **to ~ to do** avoir l'intention de faire

**ain't** [eɪnt] (inf) = **am not**; **aren't**; **isn't**

**air** [ɛər] n air m ▷ vt aérer; (idea, grievance, views) mettre sur le tapis ▷ cpd (currents, attack etc) aérien(ne); **to throw sth into the ~** (ball etc) jeter qch en l'air; **by ~** par avion; **to be on the ~** (Radio, TV: programme) être diffusé(e); (: station) émettre; **airbag** n airbag m; **airbed** n (BRIT) matelas *m* pneumatique; **airborne** *adj* (*plane*) en vol; **as soon as the plane was airborne** dès que l'avion eut décollé; **air-conditioned** *adj* climatisé(e), à air conditionné; **air conditioning** *n* climatisation *f*; **aircraft** *n inv* avion *m*; **airfield** *n* terrain *m* d'aviation; **Air Force** *n* Armée *f* de l'air; **air hostess** *n* (BRIT) hôtesse *f* de l'air; **airing cupboard** *n* (BRIT) placard qui contient la chaudière et dans lequel on met le linge à sécher; **airlift** *n* pont aérien; **airline** *n* ligne aérienne, compagnie aérienne; **airliner** *n* avion *m* de ligne; **airmail** *n*: **by airmail** par avion; **airplane** *n* (US) avion *m*; **airport** *n* aéroport *m*; **air raid** *n* attaque aérienne; **airsick** *adj*: **to be airsick** avoir le mal de l'air; **airspace** *n* espace *m* aérien; **airstrip** *n* terrain *m* d'atterrissage; **air terminal** *n* aérogare *f*; **airtight** *adj* hermétique; **air-traffic controller** *n* aiguilleur *m* du ciel; **airy** *adj* bien aéré(e); (*manners*) dégagé(e)

**aisle** [aɪl] *n* (*of church*: *central*) allée *f* centrale; (: *side*) nef *f* latérale, bas-côté *m*; (*in theatre*, *supermarket*) allée; (*on plane*) couloir *m*; **aisle seat** *n* place *f* côté couloir

**ajar** [əˈdʒɑːʳ] *adj* entrouvert(e)

**à la carte** [ælæˈkɑːt] *adv* à la carte

**alarm** [əˈlɑːm] *n* alarme *f* ▷ *vt* alarmer; **alarm call** *n* coup *m* de fil pour réveiller; **could I have an alarm call at 7 am, please?** pouvez-vous me réveiller à 7 heures, s'il vous plaît?; **alarm clock** *n* réveille-matin *m inv*, réveil *m*; **alarmed** *adj* (*frightened*) alarmé(e); (*protected by an alarm*) protégé(e) par un système d'alarme; **alarming** *adj* alarmant(e)

**Albania** [ælˈbeɪnɪə] *n* Albanie *f*

**albeit** [ɔːlˈbiːɪt] *conj* bien que + *sub*, encore que + *sub*

**album** [ˈælbəm] *n* album *m*

**alcohol** [ˈælkəhɒl] *n* alcool *m*; **alcohol-free** *adj* sans alcool; **alcoholic** [ælkəˈhɒlɪk] *adj*, *n* alcoolique (*m/f*)

**alcove** [ˈælkəuv] *n* alcôve *f*

**ale** [eɪl] *n* bière *f*

**alert** [əˈlɜːt] *adj* alerte, vif (vive); (*watchful*) vigilant(e) ▷ *n* alerte *f* ▷ *vt* alerter; **on the ~** sur le qui-vive; (*Mil*) en état d'alerte

**algebra** [ˈældʒɪbrə] *n* algèbre *m*

**Algeria** [ælˈdʒɪərɪə] *n* Algérie *f*

**Algerian** [ælˈdʒɪərɪən] *adj* algérien(ne) ▷ *n* Algérien(ne)

**Algiers** [ælˈdʒɪəz] *n* Alger

**alias** [ˈeɪlɪəs] *adv* alias ▷ *n* faux nom, nom d'emprunt

**alibi** [ˈælɪbaɪ] *n* alibi *m*

**alien** [ˈeɪlɪən] *n* (*from abroad*) étranger(-ère); (*from outer space*) extraterrestre ▷ *adj*: **~ (to)** étranger(-ère) (à); **alienate** *vt* aliéner; (*subj*: *person*) s'aliéner

**alight** [əˈlaɪt] *adj* en feu ▷ *vi* mettre pied à terre; (*passenger*) descendre; (*bird*) se poser

**align** [əˈlaɪn] *vt* aligner

**alike** [əˈlaɪk] *adj* semblable, pareil(le) ▷ *adv* de même; **to look ~** se ressembler

**alive** [əˈlaɪv] *adj* vivant(e); (*active*) plein(e) de vie

🔵 **KEYWORD**

**all** [ɔːl] *adj* (*singular*) tout(e); (*plural*) tous (toutes); **all day** toute la journée; **all night** toute la nuit; **all men** tous les hommes; **all five** tous les cinq; **all the books** tous les livres; **all his life** toute sa vie

▷ *pron* **1** tout; **I ate it all, I ate all of it** j'ai tout mangé; **all of us went** nous y sommes tous allés; **all of the boys went** tous les garçons y sont allés; **is that all?** c'est tout?; (*in shop*) ce sera tout?

**2** (*in phrases*): **above all** surtout, par-dessus tout; **after all** après tout; **at all**: **not at all** (*in answer to question*) pas du tout; (*in answer to thanks*) je vous en prie!; **I'm not at all tired** je ne suis pas du tout fatigué(e); **anything at all will**

**do** n'importe quoi fera l'affaire; **all in all** tout bien considéré, en fin de compte ▷ adv: **all alone** tout(e) seul(e); **it's not as hard as all that** ce n'est pas si difficile que ça; **all the more/the better** d'autant plus/mieux; **all but** presque, pratiquement; **the score is 2 all** le score est de 2 partout

**Allah** [ˈælə] n Allah m
**allegation** [ælɪˈɡeɪʃən] n allégation f
**alleged** [əˈlɛdʒd] adj prétendu(e);
**allegedly** adv à ce que l'on prétend, paraît-il
**allegiance** [əˈliːdʒəns] n fidélité f, obéissance f
**allergic** [əˈləːdʒɪk] adj: **~ to** allergique à; **I'm ~ to penicillin** je suis allergique à la pénicilline
**allergy** [ˈælədʒɪ] n allergie f
**alleviate** [əˈliːvɪeɪt] vt soulager, adoucir
**alley** [ˈælɪ] n ruelle f
**alliance** [əˈlaɪəns] n alliance f
**allied** [ˈælaɪd] adj allié(e)
**alligator** [ˈælɪɡeɪtər] n alligator m
**all-in** [ˈɔːlɪn] adj, adv (BRIT: charge) tout compris
**allocate** [ˈæləkeɪt] vt (share out) répartir, distribuer; **to ~ sth to** (duties) assigner or attribuer qch à; (sum, time) allouer qch à
**allot** [əˈlɔt] vt (share out) répartir, distribuer; **to ~ sth to** (time) allouer qch à; (duties) assigner qch à
**all-out** [ˈɔːlaut] adj (effort etc) total(e)
**allow** [əˈlau] vt (practice, behaviour) permettre, autoriser; (sum to spend etc) accorder, allouer; (sum, time estimated) compter, prévoir; (claim, goal) admettre; (concede): **to ~ that** convenir que; **to ~ sb to do** permettre à qn de faire; autoriser qn à faire; **he is ~ed to ...** on lui permet de ...; **allow for** vt fus tenir compte de; **allowance** n (money received) allocation f; (: from parent etc) subside m; (: for expenses) indemnité f; (US: pocket money) argent m

de poche; (Tax) somme f déductible du revenu imposable, abattement m; **to make allowances for** (person) essayer de comprendre; (thing) tenir compte de
**all right** adv (feel, work) bien; (as answer) d'accord
**ally** n [ˈælaɪ] allié m ▷ vt [əˈlaɪ]: **to ~ o.s. with** s'allier avec
**almighty** [ɔːlˈmaɪtɪ] adj tout(e)-puissant(e); (tremendous) énorme
**almond** [ˈɑːmənd] n amande f
**almost** [ˈɔːlməust] adv presque
**alone** [əˈləun] adj, adv seul(e); **to leave sb ~** laisser qn tranquille; **to leave sth ~** ne pas toucher à qch; **let ~ ...** sans parler de ...; encore moins ...
**along** [əˈlɔŋ] prep le long de ▷ adv: **is he coming ~ with us?** vient-il avec nous?; **he was hopping/limping ~** il venait or avançait en sautillant/boitant; **~ with** avec, en plus de; (person) en compagnie de; **all ~** (all the time) depuis le début; **alongside** prep (along) le long de; (beside) à côté de ▷ adv bord à bord; côte à côte
**aloof** [əˈluːf] adj distant(e) ▷ adv: **to stand ~** se tenir à l'écart or à distance
**aloud** [əˈlaud] adv à haute voix
**alphabet** [ˈælfəbɛt] n alphabet m
**Alps** [ælps] npl: **the ~** les Alpes fpl
**already** [ɔːlˈrɛdɪ] adv déjà
**alright** [ˈɔːlˈraɪt] adv (BRIT) = **all right**
**also** [ˈɔːlsəu] adv aussi
**altar** [ˈɔltər] n autel m
**alter** [ˈɔltər] vt, vi changer; **alteration** [ɔltəˈreɪʃən] n changement m, modification f; **alterations** npl (Sewing) retouches fpl; (Archit) modifications fpl
**alternate** adj [ɔlˈtəːnɪt] alterné(e), alternant(e), alternatif(-ive); (US) = **alternative** ▷ vi [ˈɔltəːneɪt] alterner; **to ~ with** alterner avec; **on ~ days** un jour sur deux, tous les deux jours
**alternative** [ɔlˈtəːnətɪv] adj (solution, plan) autre, de remplacement; (lifestyle) parallèle ▷ n (choice) alternative f; (other possibility) autre possibilité f;

**~ medicine** médecine alternative, médecine douce; **alternatively** adv: **alternatively one could ...** une autre or l'autre solution serait de ...

**although** [ɔːlˈðəu] conj bien que + sub

**altitude** [ˈæltɪtjuːd] n altitude f

**altogether** [ɔːltəˈɡeðəʳ] adv entièrement, tout à fait; (on the whole) tout compte fait; (in all) en tout

**aluminium** [æljuˈmɪnɪəm] (BRIT **aluminum**) [əˈluːmɪnəm] (US) n aluminium m

**always** [ˈɔːlweɪz] adv toujours

**Alzheimer's (disease)** [ˈæltshaɪməz-] n maladie f d'Alzheimer

**am** [æm] vb see **be**

**a.m.** adv abbr (= ante meridiem) du matin

**amalgamate** [əˈmælɡəmeɪt] vt, vi fusionner

**amass** [əˈmæs] vt amasser

**amateur** [ˈæmətəʳ] n amateur m

**amaze** [əˈmeɪz] vt stupéfier; **to be ~d (at)** être stupéfait(e) (de); **amazed** adj stupéfait(e); **amazement** n surprise f, étonnement m; **amazing** adj étonnant(e), incroyable; (bargain, offer) exceptionnel(le)

**Amazon** [ˈæməzən] n (Geo) Amazone f

**ambassador** [æmˈbæsədəʳ] n ambassadeur m

**amber** [ˈæmbəʳ] n ambre m; **at ~** (BRIT Aut) à l'orange

**ambiguous** [æmˈbɪɡjuəs] adj ambigu(ë)

**ambition** [æmˈbɪʃən] n ambition f; **ambitious** [æmˈbɪʃəs] adj ambitieux(-euse)

**ambulance** [ˈæmbjuləns] n ambulance f; **call an ~!** appelez une ambulance!

**ambush** [ˈæmbuʃ] n embuscade f ▷ vt tendre une embuscade à

**amen** [ˈɑːˈmɛn] excl amen

**amend** [əˈmɛnd] vt (law) amender; (text) corriger; **to make ~s** réparer ses torts, faire amende honorable; **amendment** n (to law) amendement m; (to text) correction f

**amenities** [əˈmiːnɪtɪz] npl aménagements mpl, équipements mpl

**America** [əˈmɛrɪkə] n Amérique f; **American** adj américain(e) ▷ n Américain(e); **American football** (BRIT) football m américain

**amicable** [ˈæmɪkəbl] adj amical(e); (Law) à l'amiable

**amid(st)** [əˈmɪd(st)] prep parmi, au milieu de

**ammunition** [æmjuˈnɪʃən] n munitions fpl

**amnesty** [ˈæmnɪstɪ] n amnistie f

**among(st)** [əˈmʌŋ(st)] prep parmi, entre

**amount** [əˈmaunt] n (sum of money) somme f; (total) montant m; (quantity) quantité f; nombre m ▷ vi: **to ~ to** (total) s'élever à; (be same as) équivaloir à, revenir à

**amp(ère)** [ˈæmp(ɛəʳ)] n ampère m

**ample** [ˈæmpl] adj ample, spacieux(-euse); (enough): **this is ~** c'est largement suffisant; **to have ~ time/ room** avoir bien assez de temps/place

**amplifier** [ˈæmplɪfaɪəʳ] n amplificateur m

**amputate** [ˈæmpjuteɪt] vt amputer

**Amtrak** [ˈæmtræk] (US) n société mixte de transports ferroviaires interurbains pour voyageurs

**amuse** [əˈmjuːz] vt amuser; **amusement** n amusement m; (pastime) distraction f; **amusement arcade** n salle f de jeu; **amusement park** n parc m d'attractions

**amusing** [əˈmjuːzɪŋ] adj amusant(e), divertissant(e)

**an** [æn, ən, n] indef art see **a**

**anaemia** [əˈniːmɪə] (US **anemia**) n anémie f

**anaemic** [əˈniːmɪk] (US **anemic**) adj anémique

**anaesthetic** [ænɪsˈθɛtɪk] (US **anesthetic**) n anesthésique m

**analog(ue)** [ˈænələɡ] adj (watch, computer) analogique

**analogy** [əˈnælədʒɪ] n analogie f

**analyse** ['ænəlaɪz] (us **analyze**) vt
analyser; **analysis** (pl **analyses**)
[ə'næləsɪs, -siːz] n analyse f; **analyst**
['ænəlɪst] n (political analyst etc)
analyste m/f; (us) psychanalyste m/f

**analyze** ['ænəlaɪz] vt (us) = **analyse**

**anarchy** ['ænəkɪ] n anarchie f

**anatomy** [ə'nætəmɪ] n anatomie f

**ancestor** ['ænsɪstəʳ] n ancêtre m,
aïeul m

**anchor** ['æŋkəʳ] n ancre f ▷ vi (also:
**to drop ~**) jeter l'ancre, mouiller ▷ vt
mettre à l'ancre; (fig): **to ~ sth to**
fixer qch à

**anchovy** ['æntʃəvɪ] n anchois m

**ancient** ['eɪnʃənt] adj ancien(ne),
antique; (person) d'un âge vénérable;
(car) antédiluvien(ne)

**and** [ænd] conj et; **~ so on** et ainsi de
suite; **try ~ come** tâchez de venir;
**come ~ sit here** venez vous asseoir ici;
**he talked ~ talked** il a parlé pendant
des heures; **better ~ better** de mieux
en mieux; **more ~ more** de plus en plus

**Andorra** [æn'dɔːrə] n (principauté f
d')Andorre f

**anemia** etc [ə'niːmɪə] (us) = **anaemia**
etc

**anesthetic** [ænɪs'θetɪk] (us)
= **anaesthetic**

**angel** ['eɪndʒəl] n ange m

**anger** ['æŋgəʳ] n colère f

**angina** [æn'dʒaɪnə] n angine f de
poitrine

**angle** ['æŋgl] n angle m; **from their ~** de
leur point de vue

**angler** ['æŋgləʳ] n pêcheur(-euse) à
la ligne

**Anglican** ['æŋglɪkən] adj, n anglican(e)

**angling** ['æŋglɪŋ] n pêche f à la ligne

**angrily** ['æŋgrɪlɪ] adv avec colère

**angry** ['æŋgrɪ] adj en colère,
furieux(-euse); (wound) enflamé(e); **to
be ~ with sb/at sth** être furieux contre
qn/de qch; **to get ~** se fâcher, se mettre
en colère

**anguish** ['æŋgwɪʃ] n angoisse f

**animal** ['ænɪməl] n animal m ▷ adj

animal(e)

**animated** ['ænɪmeɪtɪd] adj animé(e)

**animation** [ænɪ'meɪʃən] n (of person)
entrain m; (of street, Cine) animation f

**aniseed** ['ænɪsiːd] n anis m

**ankle** ['æŋkl] n cheville f

**annex** ['æneks] n (BRIT: also: **~e**) annexe
f ▷ vt [ə'neks] annexer

**anniversary** [ænɪ'vəːsərɪ] n
anniversaire m

**announce** [ə'nauns] vt annoncer;
(birth, death) faire part de;
**announcement** n annonce f; (for births
etc: in newspaper) avis m de faire-part;
(: letter, card) faire-part m; **announcer**
n (Radio, TV: between programmes)
speaker(ine); (: in a programme)
présentateur(-trice)

**annoy** [ə'nɔɪ] vt agacer, ennuyer,
contrarier; **don't get ~ed!** ne vous
fâchez pas!; **annoying** adj agaçant(e),
contrariant(e)

**annual** ['ænjuəl] adj annuel(le) ▷ n
(Bot) plante annuelle; (book) album m;
**annually** adv annuellement

**annum** ['ænəm] n see **per**

**anonymous** [ə'nɔnɪməs] adj
anonyme

**anorak** ['ænəræk] n anorak m

**anorexia** [ænə'reksɪə] n (also: **~
nervosa**) anorexie f

**anorexic** [ænə'reksɪk] adj, n
anorexique (m/f)

**another** [ə'nʌðəʳ] adj: **~ book** (one more)
un autre livre, encore un livre, un livre
de plus; (a different one) un autre livre
▷ pron un(e) autre, encore un(e), un(e)
de plus; see also **one**

**answer** ['ɑːnsəʳ] n réponse f; (to
problem) solution f ▷ vi répondre ▷ vt
(reply to) répondre à; (problem) résoudre;
(prayer) exaucer; **in ~ to your letter**
suite à or en réponse à votre lettre; **to
~ the phone** répondre (au téléphone);
**to ~ the bell** or **the door** aller or venir
ouvrir (la porte); **answer back** vi
répondre, répliquer; **answerphone** n
(esp BRIT) répondeur m (téléphonique)

**ant** [ænt] n fourmi f
**Antarctic** [ænt'ɑ:ktɪk] n: **the ~**
l'Antarctique m
**antelope** ['æntɪləup] n antilope f
**antenatal** ['æntɪ'neɪtl] adj prénatal(e)
**antenna** (pl **~e**) [æn'tɛnə, -ni:] n
antenne f
**anthem** ['ænθəm] n: **national ~** hymne
national
**anthology** [æn'θɒlədʒɪ] n anthologie f
**anthrax** ['ænθræks] n anthrax m
**anthropology** [ænθrə'pɒlədʒɪ] n
anthropologie f
**anti** ['æntɪ] prefix anti-; **antibiotic**
['æntɪbaɪ'ɔtɪk] n antibiotique m;
**antibody** ['æntɪbɒdɪ] n anticorps m
**anticipate** [æn'tɪsɪpeɪt] vt s'attendre
à, prévoir; (wishes, request) aller au
devant de, devancer; **anticipation**
[æntɪsɪ'peɪʃən] n attente f
**anticlimax** ['æntɪ'klaɪmæks] n
déception f
**anticlockwise** ['æntɪ'klɒkwaɪz] (BRIT)
adv dans le sens inverse des aiguilles
d'une montre
**antics** ['æntɪks] npl singeries fpl
**anti**: **antidote** ['æntɪdəut] n antidote
m, contrepoison m; **antifreeze**
['æntɪfri:z] n antigel m; **anti-**
**globalization** n antimondialisation f;
**antihistamine** [æntɪ'hɪstəmɪn] n
antihistaminique m; **antiperspirant**
[æntɪ'pə:spɪrənt] n déodorant m
**antique** [æn'ti:k] n (ornament) objet m
d'art ancien; (furniture) meuble ancien
▷ adj ancien(ne); **antique shop** n
magasin m d'antiquités
**antiseptic** [æntɪ'sɛptɪk] adj, n
antiseptique (m)
**antisocial** ['æntɪ'səuʃəl] adj (unfriendly)
peu liant(e), insociable; (against society)
antisocial(e)
**antlers** ['æntləz] npl bois mpl, ramure f
**anxiety** [æŋ'zaɪətɪ] n anxiété f;
(keenness): **~ to do** grand désir or
impatience f de faire
**anxious** ['æŋkʃəs] adj (très)
inquiet(-ète); (always worried)

anxieux(-euse); (worrying)
angoissant(e); (keen): **~ to do/that** qui
tient beaucoup à faire/à ce que + sub;
impatient(e) de faire/que + sub

 **KEYWORD**

**any** ['ɛnɪ] adj **1** (in questions etc: singular)
du, de l', de la; (: plural) des; **do you have**
**any butter/children/ink?** avez-vous
du beurre/des enfants/de l'encre?
**2** (with negative) de, d'; **I don't have any**
**money/books** je n'ai pas d'argent/de
livres
**3** (no matter which) n'importe quel(le);
(each and every) tout(e), chaque; **choose**
**any book you like** vous pouvez choisir
n'importe quel livre; **any teacher**
**you ask will tell you** n'importe quel
professeur vous le dira
**4** (in phrases): **in any case** de toute
façon; **any day now** d'un jour à l'autre;
**at any moment** à tout moment, d'un
instant à l'autre; **any rate** en tout
cas; **any time** n'importe quand; **he**
**might come (at) any time** il pourrait
venir n'importe quand; **come (at) any**
**time** venez quand vous voulez
▷ pron **1** (in questions etc) en; **have you**
**got any?** est-ce que vous en avez?; **can**
**any of you sing?** est-ce que parmi vous
il y en a qui savent chanter?
**2** (with negative) en; **I don't have any**
**(of them)** je n'en ai pas, je n'en ai aucun
**3** (no matter which one(s)) n'importe
lequel (or laquelle); (anybody) n'importe
qui; **take any of those books (you**
**like)** vous pouvez prendre n'importe
lequel de ces livres
▷ adv **1** (in questions etc): **do you**
**want any more soup/sandwiches?**
voulez-vous encore de la soupe/des
sandwichs?; **are you feeling any**
**better?** est-ce que vous vous sentez
mieux?
**2** (with negative): **I can't hear him**
**any more** je ne l'entends plus; **don't**
**wait any longer** n'attendez pas plus

longtemps; **anybody** pron n'importe qui; (in interrogative sentences) quelqu'un; (in negative sentences): **I don't see anybody** je ne vois personne; **if anybody should phone ...** si quelqu'un téléphone ...; **anyhow** adv quoi qu'il en soit; (haphazardly) n'importe comment; **do it anyhow you like** faites-le comme vous voulez; **she leaves things just anyhow** elle laisse tout traîner; **I shall go anyhow** j'irai de toute façon; **anyone** pron = **anybody**; **anything** pron (no matter what) n'importe quoi; (in questions) quelque chose; (with negative) ne ... rien; **can you see anything?** tu vois quelque chose?; **if anything happens to me ...** s'il m'arrive quoi que ce soit ...; **you can say anything you like** vous pouvez dire ce que vous voulez; **anything will do** n'importe quoi fera l'affaire; **he'll eat anything** il mange de tout; **anytime** adv (at any moment) d'un moment à l'autre; (whenever) n'importe quand; **anyway** adv de toute façon; **anyway, I couldn't come even if I wanted to** de toute façon, je ne pouvais pas venir même si je le voulais; **I shall go anyway** j'irai quand même; **why are you phoning, anyway?** au fait, pourquoi tu me téléphones?; **anywhere** adv n'importe où; (in interrogative sentences) quelque part; (in negative sentences): **I can't see him anywhere** je ne le vois nulle part; **can you see him anywhere?** tu le vois quelque part?; **put the books down anywhere** pose les livres n'importe où; **anywhere in the world** (no matter where) n'importe où dans le monde

**apart** [ə'pɑːt] adv (to one side) à part; de côté; à l'écart; (separately) séparément; **to take/pull ~** démonter; **10 miles/a long way ~** à 10 miles/très éloignés l'un de l'autre; **~ from** prep à part, excepté

**apartment** [ə'pɑːtmənt] n (US) appartement m, logement m; (room) chambre f; **apartment building** n (US) immeuble m; maison divisée en appartements

**apathy** ['æpəθɪ] n apathie f, indifférence f

**ape** [eɪp] n (grand) singe ▷ vt singer

**aperitif** [ə'pɛrɪtɪf] n apéritif m

**aperture** ['æpətʃjuər'] n orifice m, ouverture f; (Phot) ouverture (du diaphragme)

**APEX** ['eɪpɛks] n abbr (Aviat: = advance purchase excursion) APEX m

**apologize** [ə'pɒlədʒaɪz] vi: **to ~ (for sth to sb)** s'excuser (de qch auprès de qn), présenter ses excuses (à qn pour qch)

**apology** [ə'pɒlədʒɪ] n excuses fpl

**apostrophe** [ə'pɒstrəfɪ] n apostrophe f

**appal** [ə'pɔːl] (US **appall**) vt consterner, atterrer; horrifier; **appalling** adj épouvantable; (stupidity) consternant(e)

**apparatus** [æpə'reɪtəs] n appareil m, dispositif m; (in gymnasium) agrès mpl

**apparent** [ə'pærənt] adj apparent(e); **apparently** adv apparemment

**appeal** [ə'piːl] vi (Law) faire or interjeter appel ▷ n (Law) appel m; (request) appel; prière f; (charm) attrait m, charme m; **to ~ for** demander (instamment); implorer; **to ~ to** (beg) faire appel à; (be attractive) plaire à; **it doesn't ~ to me** cela ne m'attire pas; **appealing** adj (attractive) attrayant(e)

**appear** [ə'pɪər'] vi apparaître, se montrer; (Law) comparaître; (publication) paraître, sortir, être publié(e); (seem) paraître, sembler; **it would ~ that** il semble que; **to ~ in Hamlet** jouer dans Hamlet; **to ~ on TV** passer à la télé; **appearance** n apparition f; parution f; (look, aspect) apparence f, aspect m

**appendices** [ə'pɛndɪsiːz] npl of **appendix**

**appendicitis** [əpɛndɪ'saɪtɪs] n appendicite f

**appendix** (pl **appendices**) [ə'pɛndɪks,

-si:z] n appendice m
**appetite** ['æpɪtaɪt] n appétit m
**appetizer** ['æpɪtaɪzə'] n (food) amuse-
gueule m; (drink) apéritif m
**applaud** [ə'plɔ:d] vt, vi applaudir
**applause** [ə'plɔ:z] n
applaudissements mpl
**apple** ['æpl] n pomme f; **apple pie** n
tarte f aux pommes
**appliance** [ə'plaɪəns] n appareil m
**applicable** [ə'plɪkəbl] adj applicable;
**to be ~ to** (relevant) valoir pour
**applicant** ['æplɪkənt] n: **~ (for)**
candidat(e) (à)
**application** [æplɪ'keɪʃən] n
application f; (for a job, a grant etc)
demande f; candidature f; **application
form** n formulaire m de demande
**apply** [ə'plaɪ] vt: **to ~ (to)** (paint,
ointment) appliquer (sur); (law,
etc) appliquer (à) ▷ vi: **to ~ to** (ask)
s'adresser à; (be suitable for, relevant to)
s'appliquer à; **to ~ (for)** (permit, grant)
faire une demande (en vue d'obtenir);
(job) poser sa candidature (pour), faire
une demande d'emploi (concernant);
**to ~ o.s. to** s'appliquer à
**appoint** [ə'pɔɪnt] vt (to post) nommer,
engager; (date, place) fixer, désigner;
**appointment** n (to post) nomination
f; (job) poste m; (arrangement to
meet) rendez-vous m; **to have an
appointment** avoir un rendez-vous;
**to make an appointment (with)**
prendre rendez-vous (avec); **I'd like to
make an appointment** je voudrais
prendre rendez-vous
**appraisal** [ə'preɪzl] n évaluation f
**appreciate** [ə'pri:ʃɪeɪt] vt (like)
apprécier, faire cas de; (be grateful
for) être reconnaissant(e) de; (be
aware of) comprendre, se rendre
compte de ▷ vi (Finance) prendre
de la valeur; **appreciation**
[əpri:ʃɪ'eɪʃən] n appréciation f;
(gratitude) reconnaissance f; (Finance)
hausse f, valorisation f
**apprehension** [æprɪ'hɛnʃən] n

appréhension f, inquiétude f
**apprehensive** [æprɪ'hɛnsɪv] adj
inquiet(-ète), appréhensif(-ive)
**apprentice** [ə'prɛntɪs] n apprenti m
**approach** [ə'prəutʃ] vi approcher ▷ vt
(come near) approcher de; (ask, apply to)
s'adresser à; (subject, passer-by) aborder
▷ n approche f; accès m, abord m;
démarche f (intellectuelle)
**appropriate** adj [ə'prəuprɪɪt] (tool etc)
qui convient, approprié(e); (moment,
remark) opportun(e) ▷ vt [ə'prəuprɪeɪt]
(take) s'approprier
**approval** [ə'pru:vəl] n approbation f;
**on ~** (Comm) à l'examen
**approve** [ə'pru:v] vt approuver;
**approve of** vt fus (thing) approuver;
(person): **they don't ~ of her** ils n'ont
pas bonne opinion d'elle
**approximate** [ə'prɔksɪmɪt] adj
approximatif(-ive); **approximately** adv
approximativement
**Apr.** abbr = **April**
**apricot** ['eɪprɪkɔt] n abricot m
**April** ['eɪprəl] n avril m; **April Fools' Day**
n le premier avril

● **APRIL FOOLS' DAY**
●
● **April Fools' Day** est le 1er avril, à
● l'occasion duquel on fait des farces
● de toutes sortes. Les victimes de
● ces farces sont les "April fools".
● Traditionnellement, on n'est censé
● faire des farces que jusqu'à midi.

**apron** ['eɪprən] n tablier m
**apt** [æpt] adj (suitable) approprié(e);
(likely): **~ to do** susceptible de faire;
ayant tendance à faire
**aquarium** [ə'kwɛərɪəm] n aquarium m
**Aquarius** [ə'kwɛərɪəs] n le Verseau
**Arab** ['ærəb] n Arabe m/f ▷ adj arabe
**Arabia** [ə'reɪbɪə] n Arabie f; **Arabian**
adj arabe; **Arabic** ['ærəbɪk] adj, n
arabe (m)
**arbitrary** ['ɑ:bɪtrərɪ] adj arbitraire
**arbitration** [ɑ:bɪ'treɪʃən] n

arbitrage *m*

**arc** [ɑːk] *n* arc *m*

**arcade** [ɑːˈkeɪd] *n* arcade *f*; (*passage with shops*) passage *m*, galerie *f*; (*with games*) salle *f* de jeu

**arch** [ɑːtʃ] *n* arche *f*; (*of foot*) cambrure *f*, voûte *f* plantaire ▷ *vt* arquer, cambrer

**archaeology** [ɑːkɪˈɔlədʒɪ] (*us* **archeology**) *n* archéologie *f*

**archbishop** [ɑːtʃˈbɪʃəp] *n* archevêque *m*

**archeology** [ɑːkɪˈɔlədʒɪ] (*us*) = **archaeology**

**architect** [ˈɑːkɪtɛkt] *n* architecte *m*; **architectural** [ɑːkɪˈtɛktʃərəl] *adj* architectural(e); **architecture** *n* architecture *f*

**archive** [ˈɑːkaɪv] *n* (*often pl*) archives *fpl*

**Arctic** [ˈɑːktɪk] *adj* arctique ▷ *n*: **the ~** l'Arctique *m*

**are** [ɑːʳ] *vb see* **be**

**area** [ˈɛərɪə] *n* (*Geom*) superficie *f*; (*zone*) région *f*; (: *smaller*) secteur *m*; (*in room*) coin *m*; (*knowledge, research*) domaine *m*; **area code** (*us*) *n* (*Tel*) indicatif *m* de zone

**arena** [əˈriːnə] *n* arène *f*

**aren't** [ɑːnt] = **are not**

**Argentina** [ɑːdʒənˈtiːnə] *n* Argentine *f*; **Argentinian** [ɑːdʒənˈtɪnɪən] *adj* argentin(e) ▷ *n* Argentin(e)

**arguably** [ˈɑːɡjuəblɪ] *adv*: **it is ~ ...** on peut soutenir que c'est ...

**argue** [ˈɑːɡjuː] *vi* (*quarrel*) se disputer; (*reason*) argumenter; **to ~ that** objecter *or* alléguer que, donner comme argument que

**argument** [ˈɑːɡjumənt] *n* (*quarrel*) dispute *f*, discussion *f*; (*reasons*) argument *m*

**Aries** [ˈɛərɪz] *n* le Bélier

**arise** (*pt* **arose**, *pp* **~n**) [əˈraɪz, əˈrəuz, əˈrɪzn] *vi* survenir, se présenter

**arithmetic** [əˈrɪθmətɪk] *n* arithmétique *f*

**arm** [ɑːm] *n* bras *m* ▷ *vt* armer; **arms** *npl* (*weapons, Heraldry*) armes *fpl*; **~ in ~** bras dessus bras dessous; **armchair**

[ˈɑːmtʃɛəʳ] *n* fauteuil *m*

**armed** [ɑːmd] *adj* armé(e); **armed forces** *npl*: **the armed forces** les forces armées; **armed robbery** *n* vol *m* à main armée

**armour** (*us* **armor**) [ˈɑːməʳ] *n* armure *f*; (*Mil*: *tanks*) blindés *mpl*

**armpit** [ˈɑːmpɪt] *n* aisselle *f*

**armrest** [ˈɑːmrɛst] *n* accoudoir *m*

**army** [ˈɑːmɪ] *n* armée *f*

**A road** *n* (*BRIT*) ≈ route nationale

**aroma** [əˈrəumə] *n* arôme *m*; **aromatherapy** *n* aromathérapie *f*

**arose** [əˈrəuz] *pt of* **arise**

**around** [əˈraund] *adv* (tout) autour; (*nearby*) dans les parages ▷ *prep* autour de; (*near*) près de; (*fig*: *about*) environ; (: *date, time*) vers; **is he ~?** est-il dans les parages *or* là?

**arouse** [əˈrauz] *vt* (*sleeper*) éveiller; (*curiosity, passions*) éveiller, susciter; (*anger*) exciter

**arrange** [əˈreɪndʒ] *vt* arranger; **to ~ to do sth** prévoir de faire qch; **arrangement** *n* arrangement *m*; **arrangements** *npl* (*plans etc*) arrangements *mpl*, dispositions *fpl*

**array** [əˈreɪ] *n* (*of objects*) déploiement *m*, étalage *m*

**arrears** [əˈrɪəz] *npl* arriéré *m*; **to be in ~ with one's rent** devoir un arriéré de loyer

**arrest** [əˈrɛst] *vt* arrêter; (*sb's attention*) retenir, attirer ▷ *n* arrestation *f*; **under ~** en état d'arrestation

**arrival** [əˈraɪvl] *n* arrivée *f*; **new ~** nouveau venu/nouvelle venue; (*baby*) nouveau-né(e)

**arrive** [əˈraɪv] *vi* arriver; **arrive at** *vt fus* (*decision, solution*) parvenir à

**arrogance** [ˈærəgəns] *n* arrogance *f*

**arrogant** [ˈærəgənt] *adj* arrogant(e)

**arrow** [ˈærəu] *n* flèche *f*

**arse** [ɑːs] *n* (*BRIT inf!*) cul *m* (!)

**arson** [ˈɑːsn] *n* incendie criminel

**art** [ɑːt] *n* art *m*; **Arts** *npl* (*Scol*) les lettres *fpl*; **art college** *n* école *f* des beaux-arts

**artery** ['ɑːtərɪ] n artère f
**art gallery** n musée m d'art; (saleroom) galerie f de peinture
**arthritis** [ɑːˈθraɪtɪs] n arthrite f
**artichoke** ['ɑːtɪtʃəʊk] n artichaut m; **Jerusalem ~** topinambour m
**article** ['ɑːtɪkl] n article m
**articulate** adj [ɑːˈtɪkjʊlɪt] (person) qui s'exprime clairement et aisément; (speech) bien articulé(e), prononcé(e) clairement ▷ vb [ɑːˈtɪkjʊleɪt] ▷ vi articuler, parler distinctement ▷ vt articuler
**artificial** [ɑːtɪˈfɪʃəl] adj artificiel(le)
**artist** ['ɑːtɪst] n artiste m/f; **artistic** [ɑːˈtɪstɪk] adj artistique
**art school** n ≈ école f des beaux-arts

 **KEYWORD**

**as** [æz] conj **1** (time: moment) comme, alors que; à mesure que; **he came in as I was leaving** il est arrivé comme je partais; **as the years went by** à mesure que les années passaient; **as from tomorrow** à partir de demain
**2** (since, because) comme, puisque; **he left early as he had to be home by 10** comme il or puisqu'il devait être de retour avant 10h, il est parti de bonne heure
**3** (referring to manner, way) comme; **do as you wish** faites comme vous voudrez; **as she said** comme elle disait ▷ adv **1** (in comparisons): **as big as** aussi grand que; **twice as big as** deux fois plus grand que; **as much** or **many as** autant que; **as much money/many books as** autant d'argent/de livres que; **as soon as** dès que
**2** (concerning): **as for** or **to that** quant à cela, pour ce qui est de cela
**3**: **as if** or **though** comme si; **he looked as if he was ill** il avait l'air d'être malade; see also **long**; **such**; **well** ▷ prep (in the capacity of) en tant que, en qualité de; **he works as a driver** il travaille comme chauffeur; **as**

**chairman of the company, he ...** en tant que président de la société, il ...; **he gave me it as a present** il me l'a offert, il m'en a fait cadeau

**a.s.a.p.** abbr = **as soon as possible**
**asbestos** [æzˈbɛstəs] n asbeste m, amiante m
**ascent** [əˈsɛnt] n (climb) ascension f
**ash** [æʃ] n (dust) cendre f; (also: **~ tree**) frêne m
**ashamed** [əˈʃeɪmd] adj honteux(-euse), confus(e); **to be ~ of** avoir honte de
**ashore** [əˈʃɔːʳ] adv à terre
**ashtray** ['æʃtreɪ] n cendrier m
**Ash Wednesday** n mercredi m des Cendres
**Asia** ['eɪʃə] n Asie f; **Asian** n (from Asia) Asiatique m/f; (BRIT: from Indian subcontinent) Indo-Pakistanais(-e) ▷ adj asiatique; indo-pakistanais(-e)
**aside** [əˈsaɪd] adv de côté; à l'écart ▷ n aparté m
**ask** [ɑːsk] vt demander; (invite) inviter; **to ~ sb sth/to do sth** demander à qn qch/de faire qch; **to ~ sb about sth** questionner qn au sujet de qch; se renseigner auprès de qn au sujet de qch; **to ~ (sb) a question** poser une question (à qn); **to ~ sb out to dinner** inviter qn au restaurant; **ask for** vt fus demander; **it's just ~ing for trouble** or **for it** ce serait chercher des ennuis
**asleep** [əˈsliːp] adj endormi(e); **to fall ~** s'endormir
**AS level** n abbr (= Advanced Subsidiary level) première partie de l'examen équivalent au baccalauréat
**asparagus** [əsˈpærəgəs] n asperges fpl
**aspect** ['æspɛkt] n aspect m; (direction in which a building etc faces) orientation f, exposition f
**aspirations** [æspəˈreɪʃənz] npl (hopes, ambition) aspirations fpl
**aspire** [əsˈpaɪəʳ] vi: **to ~ to** aspirer à
**aspirin** ['æsprɪn] n aspirine f
**ass** [æs] n âne m; (inf) imbécile m/f; (us

*infl)* cul *m* (!)

**assassin** [ə'sæsɪn] *n* assassin *m*;
**assassinate** *vt* assassiner

**assault** [ə'sɔːlt] *n* (*Mil*) assaut *m*; (*gen:
attack*) agression *f* ▷ *vt* attaquer;
(*sexually*) violenter

**assemble** [ə'sɛmbl] *vt* assembler ▷ *vi*
s'assembler, se rassembler

**assembly** [ə'sɛmblɪ] *n* (*meeting*)
rassemblement *m*; (*parliament*)
assemblée *f*; (*construction*)
assemblage *m*

**assert** [ə'səːt] *vt* affirmer, déclarer;
(*authority*) faire valoir; (*innocence*)
protester de; **assertion** [ə'səːʃən] *n*
assertion *f*, affirmation *f*

**assess** [ə'sɛs] *vt* évaluer, estimer; (*tax,
damages*) établir or fixer le montant de;
(*person*) juger la valeur de; **assessment**
*n* évaluation *f*, estimation *f*; (*of tax*)
fixation *f*

**asset** [ə'sɛt] *n* avantage *m*, atout *m*;
(*person*) atout; **assets** *npl* (*Comm*)
capital *m*; (*moveables*) *m(pl)*; actif *m*

**assign** [ə'saɪn] *vt* (*date*) fixer, arrêter; **to
~ sth to** (*task*) assigner qch à; (*resources*)
affecter qch à; **assignment** *n* (*task*)
mission *f*; (*homework*) devoir *m*

**assist** [ə'sɪst] *vt* aider, assister;
**assistance** *n* aide *f*, assistance *f*;
**assistant** *n* assistant(e), adjoint(e);
(BRIT: *also*: **shop assistant**)
vendeur(-euse)

**associate** *adj, n* [ə'səʊʃɪɪt] associé(e)
▷ *vb* [ə'səʊʃɪeɪt] ▷ *vt* associer ▷ *vi*: **to ~
with sb** fréquenter qn

**association** [əsəʊsɪ'eɪʃən] *n*
association *f*

**assorted** [ə'sɔːtɪd] *adj* assorti(e)

**assortment** [ə'sɔːtmənt] *n*
assortiment *m*; (*of people*) mélange *m*

**assume** [ə'sjuːm] *vt* supposer;
(*responsibilities etc*) assumer; (*attitude,
name*) prendre, adopter

**assumption** [ə'sʌmpʃən] *n*
supposition *f*, hypothèse *f*; (*of power*)
assomption *f*, prise *f*

**assurance** [ə'ʃuərəns] *n* assurance *f*

**assure** [ə'ʃuəʳ] *vt* assurer

**asterisk** ['æstərɪsk] *n* astérisque *m*

**asthma** ['æsmə] *n* asthme *m*

**astonish** [ə'stɒnɪʃ] *vt* étonner,
stupéfier; **astonished** *adj* étonné(e);
**to be astonished at** être étonné(e)
de; **astonishing** *adj* étonnant(e),
stupéfiant(e); **I find it astonishing
that ...** je trouve incroyable que ... + *sub*;
**astonishment** *n* (grand) étonnement,
stupéfaction *f*

**astound** [ə'staund] *vt* stupéfier,
sidérer

**astray** [ə'streɪ] *adv*: **to go ~** s'égarer;
(*fig*) quitter le droit chemin; **to lead ~**
(*morally*) détourner du droit chemin

**astrology** [əs'trɒlədʒɪ] *n* astrologie *f*

**astronaut** ['æstrənɔːt] *n*
astronaute *m/f*

**astronomer** [əs'trɒnəməʳ] *n*
astronome *m*

**astronomical** [æstrə'nɒmɪkl] *adj*
astronomique

**astronomy** [əs'trɒnəmɪ] *n*
astronomie *f*

**astute** [əs'tjuːt] *adj* astucieux(-euse),
malin(-igne)

**asylum** [ə'saɪləm] *n* asile *m*; **asylum
seeker** [-siːkəʳ] *n* demandeur(-euse)
d'asile

 **KEYWORD**

**at** [æt] *prep* **1** (*referring to position,
direction*) à; **at the top** au sommet; **at
home/school** à la maison or chez soi/à
l'école; **at the baker's** à la boulangerie,
chez le boulanger; **to look at sth**
regarder qch

**2** (*referring to time*): **at 4 o'clock** à 4
heures; **at Christmas** à Noël; **at night**
la nuit; **at times** par moments, parfois

**3** (*referring to rates, speed etc*) à; **at £1
a kilo** une livre le kilo; **two at a time**
deux à la fois; **at 50 km/h** à 50 km/h

**4** (*referring to manner*): **at a stroke** d'un
seul coup; **at peace** en paix

**5** (*referring to activity*): **to be at work** (*in*

*the office etc*) être au travail; (*working*)
travailler; **to play at cowboys** jouer
aux cowboys; **to be good at sth** être
bon en qch
**6** (*referring to cause*): **shocked/
surprised/annoyed at sth** choqué
par/étonné de/agacé par qch; **I went
at his suggestion** j'y suis allé sur son
conseil
**7** (*symbol*) arobase *f*

**ate** [eɪt] *pt of* **eat**
**atheist** ['eɪθɪɪst] *n* athée *m/f*
**Athens** ['æθɪnz] *n* Athènes
**athlete** ['æθliːt] *n* athlète *m/f*
**athletic** [æθ'letɪk] *adj* athlétique;
**athletics** *n* athlétisme *m*
**Atlantic** [ət'læntɪk] *adj* atlantique ▷ *n*:
**the ~ (Ocean)** l'(océan *m*) Atlantique *m*
**atlas** ['ætləs] *n* atlas *m*
**A.T.M.** *n abbr* (= *Automated Telling
Machine*) guichet *m* automatique
**atmosphere** ['ætməsfɪəʳ] *n* (*air*)
atmosphère *f*; (*fig: of place etc*)
atmosphère, ambiance *f*
**atom** ['ætəm] *n* atome *m*; **atomic**
[ə'tɔmɪk] *adj* atomique; **atom(ic)
bomb** *n* bombe *f* atomique
**A to Z®** *n* (*map*) plan *m* des rues
**atrocity** [ə'trɔsɪtɪ] *n* atrocité *f*
**attach** [ə'tætʃ] *vt* (*gen*) attacher;
(*document, letter*) joindre; **to be ~ed to
sb/sth** (*to like*) être attaché à qn/qch;
**attachment** *n* (*tool*) accessoire
*m*; (*Comput*) fichier *m* joint; (*love*):
**attachment (to)** affection *f* (pour),
attachement *m* (à)
**attack** [ə'tæk] *vt* attaquer; (*task etc*)
s'attaquer à ▷ *n* attaque *f*; **heart ~** crise
*f* cardiaque; **attacker** *n* attaquant *m*;
agresseur *m*
**attain** [ə'teɪn] *vt* (*also*: **to ~ to**) parvenir
à, atteindre; (*knowledge*) acquérir
**attempt** [ə'tɛmpt] *n* tentative *f* ▷ *vt*
essayer, tenter
**attend** [ə'tɛnd] *vt* (*course*) suivre;
(*meeting, talk*) assister à; (*school, church*)
aller à, fréquenter; (*patient*) soigner,

s'occuper de; **attend to** *vt fus* (*needs,
affairs etc*) s'occuper de; (*customer*)
s'occuper de, servir; **attendance** *n*
(*being present*) présence *f*; (*people present*)
assistance *f*; **attendant** *n* employé(e);
gardien(ne) ▷ *adj* concomitant(e), qui
accompagne *or* s'ensuit

> Be careful not to translate **to attend**
> by the French word **attendre**.

**attention** [ə'tɛnʃən] *n* attention *f*
▷ *excl* (*Mil*) garde-à-vous!; **for the ~ of**
(*Admin*) à l'attention de
**attic** ['ætɪk] *n* grenier *m*, combles *mpl*
**attitude** ['ætɪtjuːd] *n* attitude *f*
**attorney** [ə'təːnɪ] *n* (*us: lawyer*)
avocat *m*; **Attorney General** *n* (*BRIT*)
≈ procureur général; (*us*) ≈ garde *m* des
Sceaux, ministre *m* de la Justice
**attract** [ə'trækt] *vt* attirer;
**attraction** [ə'trækʃən] *n* (*gen pl:
pleasant things*) attraction *f*, attrait
*m*; (*Physics*) attraction; (*fig: towards
sb, sth*) attirance *f*; **attractive** *adj*
séduisant(e), attrayant(e)
**attribute** *n* ['ætrɪbjuːt] attribut *m* ▷ *vt*
[ə'trɪbjuːt]: **to ~ sth to** attribuer qch à
**aubergine** ['əubəʒiːn] *n* aubergine *f*
**auburn** ['ɔːbən] *adj* auburn *inv*, châtain
roux *inv*
**auction** ['ɔːkʃən] *n* (*also*: **sale by ~**)
vente *f* aux enchères ▷ *vt* (*also*: **to sell
by ~**) vendre aux enchères
**audible** ['ɔːdɪbl] *adj* audible
**audience** ['ɔːdɪəns] *n* (*people*)
assistance *f*, public *m*; (*on radio*)
auditeurs *mpl*; (*at theatre*) spectateurs
*mpl*; (*interview*) audience *f*
**audit** ['ɔːdɪt] *vt* vérifier
**audition** [ɔː'dɪʃən] *n* audition *f*
**auditor** ['ɔːdɪtəʳ] *n* vérificateur *m* des
comptes
**auditorium** [ɔːdɪ'tɔːrɪəm] *n*
auditorium *m*, salle *f* de concert *or* de
spectacle
**Aug.** *abbr* = **August**
**August** ['ɔːgəst] *n* août *m*
**aunt** [ɑːnt] *n* tante *f*; **auntie, aunty** *n*
*diminutive of* **aunt**

**au pair** [ˈəuˈpɛəʳ] n (also: ~ **girl**) jeune fille f au pair

**aura** [ˈɔːrə] n atmosphère f; (of person) aura f

**austerity** [ɔsˈtɛrɪtɪ] n austérité f

**Australia** [ɔsˈtreɪlɪə] n Australie f; **Australian** adj australien(ne) ▷ n Australien(ne)

**Austria** [ˈɔstrɪə] n Autriche f; **Austrian** adj autrichien(ne) ▷ n Autrichien(ne)

**authentic** [ɔːˈθɛntɪk] adj authentique

**author** [ˈɔːθəʳ] n auteur m

**authority** [ɔːˈθɔrɪtɪ] n autorité f; (permission) autorisation (formelle); **the authorities** les autorités fpl, l'administration f

**authorize** [ˈɔːθəraɪz] vt autoriser

**auto** [ˈɔːtəu] n (us) auto f, voiture f; **autobiography** [ɔːtəbaɪˈɔgrəfɪ] n autobiographie f; **autograph** [ˈɔːtəgrɑːf] n autographe m ▷ vt signer, dédicacer; **automatic** [ɔːtəˈmætɪk] adj automatique ▷ n (gun) automatique m; (car) voiture f à transmission automatique; **automatically** adv automatiquement; **automobile** [ˈɔːtəməbiːl] n (us) automobile f; **autonomous** [ɔːˈtɔnəməs] adj autonome; **autonomy** [ɔːˈtɔnəmɪ] n autonomie f

**autumn** [ˈɔːtəm] n automne m

**auxiliary** [ɔːgˈzɪlɪərɪ] adj, n auxiliaire (m/f)

**avail** [əˈveɪl] vt: **to ~ o.s. of** user de; profiter de ▷ n: **to no ~** sans résultat, en vain, en pure perte

**availability** [əveɪləˈbɪlɪtɪ] n disponibilité f

**available** [əˈveɪləbl] adj disponible

**avalanche** [ˈævəlɑːnʃ] n avalanche f

**Ave.** abbr = **avenue**

**avenue** [ˈævənjuː] n avenue f; (fig) moyen m

**average** [ˈævərɪdʒ] n moyenne f ▷ adj moyen(ne) ▷ vt (a certain figure) atteindre or faire etc en moyenne; **on ~** en moyenne

**avert** [əˈvəːt] vt (danger) prévenir, écarter; (one's eyes) détourner

**avid** [ˈævɪd] adj avide

**avocado** [ævəˈkɑːdəu] n (BRIT: also: ~ **pear**) avocat m

**avoid** [əˈvɔɪd] vt éviter

**await** [əˈweɪt] vt attendre

**awake** [əˈweɪk] adj éveillé(e) ▷ vb (pt **awoke**, pp **awoken**) ▷ vt éveiller ▷ vi s'éveiller; **to be ~** être réveillé(e)

**award** [əˈwɔːd] n (for bravery) récompense f; (prize) prix m; (Law: damages) dommages-intérêts mpl ▷ vt (prize) décerner; (Law: damages) accorder

**aware** [əˈwɛəʳ] adj: ~ **of** (conscious) conscient(e) de; (informed) au courant de; **to become ~ of/that** prendre conscience de/que; se rendre compte de/que; **awareness** n conscience f, connaissance f

**away** [əˈweɪ] adv (au) loin; (movement): **she went ~** elle est partie ▷ adj (not in, not here) absent(e); **far ~** (au) loin; **two kilometres ~** à (une distance de) deux kilomètres, à deux kilomètres de distance; **two hours ~ by car** à deux heures de voiture or de route; **the holiday was two weeks ~** il restait deux semaines jusqu'aux vacances; **he's ~ for a week** il est parti (pour) une semaine; **to take sth ~ from sb** prendre qch à qn; **to take sth ~ from sth** (subtract) ôter qch de qch; **to work/pedal ~** travailler/pédaler à cœur joie; **to fade ~** (colour) s'estomper; (sound) s'affaiblir

**awe** [ɔː] n respect mêlé de crainte, effroi mêlé d'admiration; **awesome** [ˈɔːsəm] (us) adj (inf: excellent) génial(e)

**awful** [ˈɔːfəl] adj affreux(-euse); **an ~ lot of** énormément de; **awfully** adv (very) terriblement, vraiment

**awkward** [ˈɔːkwəd] adj (clumsy) gauche, maladroit(e); (inconvenient) peu pratique; (embarrassing) gênant

**awoke** [əˈwəuk] pt of **awake**

**awoken** [əˈwəukən] pp of **awake**

**axe** [æks] (US **ax**) n hache f ▷ vt (project
etc) abandonner; (jobs) supprimer
**axle** ['æksl] n essieu m
**ay(e)** [aɪ] excl (yes) oui
**azalea** [ə'zeɪlɪə] n azalée f

**B** [biː] n (Mus): **B** si m
**B.A.** abbr (Scol) = **Bachelor of Arts**
**baby** ['beɪbɪ] n bébé m; **baby carriage**
n (US) voiture f d'enfant; **baby-sit**
vi garder les enfants; **baby-sitter** n
baby-sitter m/f; **baby wipe** n lingette
f (pour bébé)
**bachelor** ['bætʃələ'] n célibataire m; **B~
of Arts/Science (BA/BSc)** ≈ licencié(e)
ès or en lettres/sciences
**back** [bæk] n (of person, horse) dos m; (of
hand) dos, revers m; (of house) derrière
m; (of car, train) arrière m; (of chair)
dossier m; (of page) verso m; (of crowd):
**can the people at the ~ hear me
properly?** est-ce que les gens du fond
peuvent m'entendre?; (Football) arrière
m; **~ to front** à l'envers ▷ vt (financially)
soutenir (financièrement); (candidate:
also: **~ up**) soutenir, appuyer; (horse: at
races) parier or miser sur; (car) (faire)
reculer ▷ vi reculer; (car etc) faire
marche arrière ▷ adj (in compounds) de
derrière, à l'arrière; **~ seat/wheel** (Aut)

siège m/roue f arrière inv; **~ payments/
rent** arriéré m de paiements/loyer; **~
garden/room** jardin/pièce sur l'arrière
▷ adv (not forward) en arrière; (returned):
**he's ~** il est rentré, il est de retour;
**he ran ~** il est revenu en courant;
(restitution): **throw the ball ~** renvoie
la balle; **can I have it ~?** puis-je le
ravoir?, peux-tu me le rendre?; (again):
**he called ~** il a rappelé; **back down**
vi rabattre de ses prétentions; **back
out** vi (of promise) se dédire; **back up**
vt (person) soutenir; (Comput) faire une
copie de sauvegarde de; **backache** n
mal m au dos; **backbencher** (BRIT) n
membre du parlement sans portefeuille;
**backbone** n colonne vertébrale,
épine dorsale; **back door** n porte f de
derrière; **backfire** vi (Aut) pétarader;
(plans) mal tourner; **backgammon** n
trictrac m; **background** n arrière-plan
m; (of events) situation f, conjoncture
f; (basic knowledge) éléments mpl de
base; (experience) formation f; **family
background** milieu familial; **backing**
n (fig) soutien m, appui m; **backlog** n:
**backlog of work** travail m en retard;
**backpack** n sac m à dos; **backpacker**
n randonneur(-euse); **backslash** n
barre oblique inversée; **backstage**
adv dans les coulisses; **backstroke** n
dos crawlé; **backup** adj (train, plane)
supplémentaire, de réserve; (Comput)
de sauvegarde ▷ n (support) appui m,
soutien m; (Comput: also: **backup file**)
sauvegarde f; **backward** adj (movement)
en arrière; (person, country) arriéré(e),
attardé(e); **backwards** adv (move,
go) en arrière; (read a list) à l'envers,
à rebours; (fall) à la renverse; (walk) à
reculons; **backyard** n arrière-cour f
**bacon** ['beɪkən] n bacon m, lard m
**bacteria** [bæk'tɪərɪə] npl bactéries fpl
**bad** [bæd] adj mauvais(e); (child)
vilain(e); (mistake, accident) grave;
(meat, food) gâté(e), avarié(e); **his ~ leg**
sa jambe malade; **to go ~** (meat, food) se
gâter; (milk) tourner;

**bade** [bæd] pt of bid
**badge** [bædʒ] n insigne m; (of
policeman) plaque f; (stick-on, sew-on)
badge m
**badger** ['bædʒəʳ] n blaireau m
**badly** ['bædlɪ] adv (work, dress etc)
mal; **to reflect ~ on sb** donner une
mauvaise image de qn; **~ wounded**
grièvement blessé; **he needs it ~** il en
a absolument besoin; **~ off** adj, adv
dans la gêne
**bad-mannered** ['bæd'mænəd] adj
mal élevé(e)
**badminton** ['bædmɪntən] n
badminton m
**bad-tempered** ['bæd'tɛmpəd] adj (by
nature) ayant mauvais caractère; (on one
occasion) de mauvaise humeur
**bag** [bæg] n sac m; **~s of** (inf: lots of)
des tas de; **baggage** n bagages mpl;
**baggage allowance** n franchise f
de bagages; **baggage reclaim** n (at
airport) livraison f des bagages; **baggy**
adj avachi(e), qui fait des poches;
**bagpipes** npl cornemuse f
**bail** [beɪl] n caution f ▷ vt (prisoner:
also: **grant ~ to**) mettre en liberté sous
caution; (boat: also: **~ out**) écoper; **to
be released on ~** être libéré(e) sous
caution; **bail out** vt (prisoner) payer la
caution de
**bait** [beɪt] n appât m ▷ vt appâter; (fig:
tease) tourmenter
**bake** [beɪk] vt (faire) cuire au four
▷ vi (bread etc) cuire (au four); (make
cakes etc) faire de la pâtisserie; **baked
beans** npl haricots blancs à la sauce
tomate; **baked potato** n pomme f
de terre en robe des champs; **baker** n
boulanger m; **bakery** n boulangerie f;
**baking** n (process) cuisson f; **baking
powder** n levure f (chimique)
**balance** ['bæləns] n équilibre m;
(Comm: sum) solde m; (remainder) reste
m; (scales) balance f ▷ vt mettre or
faire tenir en équilibre; (pros and cons)
peser; (budget) équilibrer; (account)
balancer; (compensate) compenser,

contrebalancer; **~ of trade/payments**
balance commerciale/des comptes or
paiements; **balanced** adj (personality,
diet) équilibré(e); (report) objectif(-ive);
**balance sheet** n bilan m

**balcony** ['bælkənɪ] n balcon m; **do you
have a room with a ~?** avez-vous une
chambre avec balcon?

**bald** [bɔːld] adj chauve; (tyre) lisse

**ball** [bɔːl] n boule f; (football) ballon m;
(for tennis, golf) balle f; (dance) bal m; **to
play ~** jouer au ballon (or à la balle);
(fig) coopérer

**ballerina** [bælə'riːnə] n ballerine f

**ballet** ['bæleɪ] n ballet m; (art)
danse f (classique); **ballet dancer** n
danseur(-euse) de ballet

**balloon** [bə'luːn] n ballon m

**ballot** ['bælət] n scrutin m

**ballpoint (pen)** ['bɔːlpɔɪnt-] n stylo
m à bille

**ballroom** ['bɔːlrum] n salle f de bal

**Baltic** [bɔːltɪk] n: **the ~ (Sea)** la (mer)
Baltique

**bamboo** [bæm'buː] n bambou m

**ban** [bæn] n interdiction f ▷ vt interdire

**banana** [bə'nɑːnə] n banane f

**band** [bænd] n bande f; (at a dance)
orchestre m; (Mil) musique f, fanfare f

**bandage** ['bændɪdʒ] n bandage m,
pansement m ▷ vt (wound, leg) mettre
un pansement or un bandage sur

**Band-Aid®** ['bændeɪd] n (US)
pansement adhésif

**B. & B.** n abbr = **bed and breakfast**

**bandit** ['bændɪt] n bandit m

**bang** [bæŋ] n détonation f; (of door)
claquement m; (blow) coup (violent)
▷ vt frapper (violemment); (door)
claquer ▷ vi détoner; claquer

**Bangladesh** [bæŋglə'dɛʃ] n
Bangladesh m

**Bangladeshi** [bæŋglə'dɛʃɪ] adj du
Bangladesh ▷ n habitant(e) du
Bangladesh

**bangle** ['bæŋgl] n bracelet m

**bangs** [bæŋz] npl (US: fringe) frange f

**banish** ['bænɪʃ] vt bannir

**banister(s)** ['bænɪstə(z)] n(pl) rampe
f (d'escalier)

**banjo** (pl **~es** or **~s**) ['bændʒəu] n
banjo m

**bank** [bæŋk] n banque f; (of river, lake)
bord m, rive f; (of earth) talus m, remblai
m ▷ vi (Aviat) virer sur l'aile; **bank on** vt
fus miser or tabler sur; **bank account**
n compte m en banque; **bank balance**
n solde m bancaire; **bank card** (BRIT)
n carte f d'identité bancaire; **bank
charges** npl (BRIT) frais mpl de banque;
**banker** n banquier m; **bank holiday**
n (BRIT) jour m férié (où les banques
sont fermées); voir encadré; **banking**
n opérations fpl bancaires; profession
f de banquier; **bank manager** n
directeur m d'agence (bancaire);
**banknote** n billet m de banque

● **BANK HOLIDAY**
●
● Le terme **bank holiday** s'applique
● au Royaume-Uni aux jours fériés
● pendant lesquels banques et
● commerces sont fermés. Les
● principaux **bank holidays** à part
● Noël et Pâques se situent au mois
● de mai et fin août, et contrairement
● aux pays de tradition catholique, ne
● coïncident pas nécessairement avec
● une fête religieuse.

**bankrupt** ['bæŋkrʌpt] adj en faillite;
**to go ~** faire faillite; **bankruptcy** n
faillite f

**bank statement** n relevé m de
compte

**banner** ['bænər] n bannière f

**bannister(s)** ['bænɪstə(z)] n(pl)
= **banister(s)**

**banquet** ['bæŋkwɪt] n banquet m,
festin m

**baptism** ['bæptɪzəm] n baptême m

**baptize** [bæp'taɪz] vt baptiser

**bar** [bɑːr] n (pub) bar m; (counter)
comptoir m, bar; (rod: of metal etc) barre
f; (of window etc) barreau m; (of chocolate)

tablette f, plaque f; (fig: obstacle)
obstacle m; (prohibition) mesure f
d'exclusion; (Mus) mesure f ▷ vt (road)
barrer; (person) exclure; (activity)
interdire; **~ of soap** savonnette
f; **behind ~s** (prisoner) derrière les
barreaux; **the B~** (Law) le barreau; **~
none** sans exception

**barbaric** [bɑː'bærɪk] adj barbare

**barbecue** ['bɑːbɪkjuː] n barbecue m

**barbed wire** ['bɑːbd-] n fil m de fer
barbelé

**barber** ['bɑːbəʳ] n coiffeur m (pour
hommes); **barber's (shop)** (us **barber
(shop)**) n salon m de coiffure (pour
hommes)

**bar code** n code m à barres, code-
barre m

**bare** [bɛəʳ] adj nu(e) ▷ vt mettre à nu,
dénuder; (teeth) montrer; **barefoot** adj,
adv nu-pieds, (les) pieds nus; **barely**
adv à peine

**bargain** ['bɑːgɪn] n (transaction)
marché m; (good buy) affaire f, occasion
f ▷ vi (haggle) marchander; (negotiate)
négocier, traiter; **into the ~** par-dessus
le marché; **bargain for** vt fus (inf): **he
got more than he ~ed for!** il en a eu
pour son argent!

**barge** [bɑːdʒ] n péniche f; **barge in** vi
(walk in) faire irruption; (interrupt talk)
intervenir mal à propos

**bark** [bɑːk] n (of tree) écorce f; (of dog)
aboiement m ▷ vi aboyer

**barley** ['bɑːlɪ] n orge f

**barmaid** ['bɑːmeɪd] n serveuse f (de
bar), barmaid f

**barman** ['bɑːmən] n serveur m (de bar),
barman m

**barn** [bɑːn] n grange f

**barometer** [bə'rɒmɪtəʳ] n baromètre m

**baron** ['bærən] n baron m; **baroness**
n baronne f

**barracks** ['bærəks] npl caserne f

**barrage** ['bærɑːʒ] n (Mil) tir m de
barrage; (dam) barrage m; (of criticism)
feu m

**barrel** ['bærəl] n tonneau m; (of gun)

canon m

**barren** ['bærən] adj stérile

**barrette** [bə'ret] (us) n barrette f

**barricade** [bærɪ'keɪd] n barricade f

**barrier** ['bærɪəʳ] n barrière f

**barring** ['bɑːrɪŋ] prep sauf

**barrister** ['bærɪstəʳ] n (BRIT) avocat m
(plaidant)

**barrow** ['bærəu] n (cart) charrette
f à bras

**bartender** ['bɑːtendəʳ] n (us) serveur
m (de bar), barman m

**base** [beɪs] n base f ▷ vt (opinion, belief):
**to ~ sth on** baser or fonder qch sur ▷ adj
vil(e), bas(se)

**baseball** ['beɪsbɔːl] n base-ball m;
**baseball cap** n casquette f de base-ball

**Basel** [bɑːl] n = **Basle**

**basement** ['beɪsmənt] n sous-sol m

**bases** ['beɪsiːz] npl of **basis**

**bash** [bæʃ] vt (inf) frapper, cogner

**basic** ['beɪsɪk] adj (precautions, rules)
élémentaire; (principles, research)
fondamental(e); (vocabulary, salary) de
base; (minimal) réduit(e) au minimum,
rudimentaire; **basically** adv (in fact) en
fait; (essentially) fondamentalement;
**basics** npl: **the basics** l'essentiel m

**basil** ['bæzl] n basilic m

**basin** ['beɪsn] n (vessel, also Geo) cuvette
f, bassin m; (BRIT: for food) bol m; (also:
**wash~**) lavabo m

**basis** (pl **bases**) ['beɪsɪs, -siːz] n base
f; **on a part-time/trial ~** à temps
partiel/à l'essai

**basket** ['bɑːskɪt] n corbeille f; (with
handle) panier m; **basketball** n
basket-ball m

**Basle** [bɑːl] n Bâle

**Basque** [bæsk] adj basque ▷ n Basque
m/f; **the ~ Country** le Pays basque

**bass** [beɪs] n (Mus) basse f

**bastard** ['bɑːstəd] n enfant naturel(le),
bâtard(e); (inf!) salaud m (!)

**bat** [bæt] n chauve-souris f; (for baseball
etc) batte f; (BRIT: for table tennis)
raquette f ▷ vt: **he didn't ~ an eyelid** il
n'a pas sourcillé or bronché

**batch** [bætʃ] n (of bread) fournée f; (of papers) liasse f; (of applicants, letters) paquet m

**bath** (pl **~s**) [bɑːθ, bɑːðz] n bain m; (bathtub) baignoire f ▷ vt baigner, donner un bain à; **to have a ~** prendre un bain; see also **baths**

**bathe** [beɪð] vi se baigner ▷ vt baigner; (wound etc) laver

**bathing** [ˈbeɪðɪŋ] n baignade f; **bathing costume** (us **bathing suit**) n maillot m (de bain)

**bath**: **bathrobe** n peignoir m de bain; **bathroom** n salle f de bains; **baths** [bɑːðz] npl (BRIT: also: **swimming baths**) piscine f; **bath towel** n serviette f de bain; **bathtub** n baignoire f

**baton** [ˈbætən] n bâton m; (Mus) baguette f; (club) matraque f

**batter** [ˈbætəʳ] vt battre ▷ n pâte f à frire; **battered** adj (hat, pan) cabossé(e); **battered wife/child** épouse/enfant maltraité(e) or martyr(e)

**battery** [ˈbætərɪ] n (for torch, radio) pile f; (Aut, Mil) batterie f; **battery farming** n élevage m en batterie

**battle** [ˈbætl] n bataille f, combat m ▷ vi se battre, lutter; **battlefield** n champ m de bataille

**bay** [beɪ] n (of sea) baie f; (BRIT: for parking) place f de stationnement; (: for loading) aire f de chargement; **B~ of Biscay** golfe m de Gascogne; **to hold sb at ~** tenir qn à distance or en échec

**bay leaf** n laurier m

**bazaar** [bəˈzɑːʳ] n (shop, market) bazar m; (sale) vente f de charité

**BBC** n abbr (= British Broadcasting Corporation) office de la radiodiffusion et télévision britannique

**B.C.** adv abbr (= before Christ) av. J.-C.

 **KEYWORD**

**be** [biː] (pt **was, were**, pp **been**) aux vb **1** (with present participle: forming continuous tenses): **what are you**

**doing?** que faites-vous?; **they're coming tomorrow** ils viennent demain; **I've been waiting for you for 2 hours** je t'attends depuis 2 heures

**2** (with pp: forming passives) être; **to be killed** être tué(e); **the box had been opened** la boîte avait été ouverte; **he was nowhere to be seen** on ne le voyait nulle part

**3** (in tag questions): **it was fun, wasn't it?** c'était drôle, n'est-ce pas?; **he's good-looking, isn't he?** il est beau, n'est-ce pas?; **she's back, is she?** elle est rentrée, n'est-ce pas or alors?

**4** (+to +infinitive): **the house is to be sold** (necessity) la maison doit être vendue; (future) la maison va être vendue; **he's not to open it** il ne doit pas l'ouvrir

▷ vb + complement **1** (gen) être; **I'm English** je suis anglais(e); **I'm tired** je suis fatigué(e); **I'm hot/cold** j'ai chaud/froid; **he's a doctor** il est médecin; **be careful/good/quiet!** faites attention/soyez sages/taisez-vous!; **2 and 2 are 4** 2 et 2 font 4

**2** (of health) aller; **how are you?** comment allez-vous?; **I'm better now** je vais mieux maintenant; **he's very ill** il est très malade

**3** (of age) avoir; **how old are you?** quel âge avez-vous?; **I'm sixteen (years old)** j'ai seize ans

**4** (cost) coûter; **how much was the meal?** combien a coûté le repas?; **that'll be £5, please** ça fera 5 livres, s'il vous plaît; **this shirt is £17** cette chemise coûte 17 livres

▷ vi **1** (exist, occur etc) être, exister; **the prettiest girl that ever was** la fille la plus jolie qui ait jamais existé; **is there a God?** y a-t-il un dieu?; **be that as it may** quoi qu'il en soit; **so be it** soit

**2** (referring to place) être, se trouver; **I won't be here tomorrow** je ne serai pas là demain

**3** (referring to movement) aller; **where have you been?** où êtes-vous allé(s)?

▷ *impers vb* **1** (*referring to time*) être; **it's 5 o'clock** il est 5 heures; **it's the 28th of April** c'est le 28 avril

**2** (*referring to distance*): **it's 10 km to the village** le village est à 10 km

**3** (*referring to the weather*) faire; **it's too hot/cold** il fait trop chaud/froid; **it's windy today** il y a du vent aujourd'hui

**4** (*emphatic*): **it's me/the postman** c'est moi/le facteur; **it was Maria who paid the bill** c'est Maria qui a payé la note

**beach** [biːtʃ] *n* plage *f* ▷ *vt* échouer

**beacon** ['biːkən] *n* (*lighthouse*) fanal *m*; (*marker*) balise *f*

**bead** [biːd] *n* perle *f*; (*of dew, sweat*) goutte *f*; **beads** *npl* (*necklace*) collier *m*

**beak** [biːk] *n* bec *m*

**beam** [biːm] *n* (*Archit*) poutre *f*; (*of light*) rayon *m* ▷ *vi* rayonner

**bean** [biːn] *n* haricot *m*; (*of coffee*) grain *m*; **beansprouts** *npl* pousses *fpl* or germes *mpl* de soja

**bear** [bɛəʳ] *n* ours *m* ▷ *vb* (*pt* **bore**, *pp* **borne**) ▷ *vt* porter; (*endure*) supporter, rapporter ▷ *vi*: **to ~ right/left** obliquer à droite/gauche, se diriger vers la droite/gauche

**beard** [bɪəd] *n* barbe *f*

**bearer** ['bɛərəʳ] *n* porteur *m*; (*of passport etc*) titulaire *m/f*

**bearing** ['bɛərɪŋ] *n* maintien *m*, allure *f*; (*connection*) rapport *m*; (*Tech*): **(ball) bearings** *npl* roulement *m* (à billes)

**beast** [biːst] *n* bête *f*; (*inf: person*) brute *f*

**beat** [biːt] *n* battement *m*; (*Mus*) temps *m*, mesure *f*; (*of policeman*) ronde *f* ▷ *vt*, *vi* (*pt* **~**, *pp* **~en**) battre; **off the ~en track** hors des chemins *or* sentiers battus; **to ~ it** (*inf*) ficher le camp; **beat up** *vt* (*inf: person*) tabasser; **beating** *n* raclée *f*

**beautiful** ['bjuːtɪful] *adj* beau (belle); **beautifully** *adv* admirablement

**beauty** ['bjuːtɪ] *n* beauté *f*; **beauty parlour** (*US* **beauty parlor**) [-'pɑːləʳ] *n* institut *m* de beauté; **beauty salon** *n* institut *m* de beauté; **beauty spot**

*n* (*on skin*) grain *m* de beauté; (*BRIT Tourism*) site naturel (d'une grande beauté)

**beaver** ['biːvəʳ] *n* castor *m*

**became** [bɪ'keɪm] *pt of* **become**

**because** [bɪ'kɔz] *conj* parce que; **~ of** *prep* à cause de

**beckon** ['bɛkən] *vt* (*also*: **~ to**) faire signe (de venir) à

**become** [bɪ'kʌm] *vi* devenir; **to ~ fat/thin** grossir/maigrir; **to ~ angry** se mettre en colère

**bed** [bɛd] *n* lit *m*; (*of flowers*) parterre *m*; (*of coal, clay*) couche *f*; (*of sea, lake*) fond *m*; **to go to ~** aller se coucher; **bed and breakfast** *n* (*terms*) chambre et petit déjeuner; (*place*) ≈ chambre *f* d'hôte; *voir encadré*; **bedclothes** *npl* couvertures *fpl* et draps *mpl*; **bedding** *n* literie *f*; **bed linen** *n* draps *mpl* de lit (et taies *fpl* d'oreillers), literie *f*; **bedroom** *n* chambre *f* (à coucher); **bedside** *n*: **at sb's bedside** au chevet de qn; **bedside lamp** *n* lampe *f* de chevet; **bedside table** *n* table *f* de chevet; **bedsit(ter)** *n* (*BRIT*) chambre meublée, studio *m*; **bedspread** *n* couvre-lit *m*, dessus-de-lit *m*; **bedtime** *n*: **it's ~** c'est l'heure de se coucher

● **BED AND BREAKFAST**
●
● Un **bed and breakfast** est une
● petite pension dans une maison
● particulière ou une ferme où l'on
● peut louer une chambre avec
● petit déjeuner compris pour un
● prix modique par rapport à ce que
● l'on paierait dans un hôtel. Ces
● établissements sont communément
● appelés "B & B", et sont signalés par
● une pancarte dans le jardin ou au-
● dessus de la porte.

**bee** [biː] *n* abeille *f*

**beech** [biːtʃ] *n* hêtre *m*

**beef** [biːf] *n* bœuf *m*; **roast ~** rosbif *m*; **beefburger** *n* hamburger *m*;

**Beefeater** n hallebardier m (de la tour de Londres)

**been** [biːn] pp of **be**

**beer** [bɪə⁺] n bière f; **beer garden** n (BRIT) jardin m d'un pub (où l'on peut emmener ses consommations)

**beet** [biːt] n (vegetable) betterave f; (US: also: **red ~**) betterave (potagère)

**beetle** ['biːtl] n scarabée m, coléoptère m

**beetroot** ['biːtruːt] n (BRIT) betterave f

**before** [bɪ'fɔː⁺] prep (of time) avant; (of space) devant ▷ conj avant que + sub; avant de ▷ adv avant; **~ going** avant de partir; **~ she goes** avant qu'elle (ne) parte; **the week ~** la semaine précédente or d'avant; **I've never seen it ~** c'est la première fois que je le vois; **beforehand** adv au préalable, à l'avance

**beg** [bɛg] vi mendier ▷ vt mendier; (forgiveness, mercy etc) demander; (entreat) supplier; **to ~ sb to do sth** supplier qn de faire qch; see also **pardon**

**began** [bɪ'gæn] pt of **begin**

**beggar** ['bɛgə⁺] n mendiant(e)

**begin** [bɪ'gɪn] (pt **began**, pp **begun**) vt, vi commencer; **to ~ doing** or **to do sth** commencer à faire qch; **beginner** n débutant(e); **beginning** n commencement m, début m

**begun** [bɪ'gʌn] pp of **begin**

**behalf** [bɪ'hɑːf] n: **on ~ of**, (US) **in ~ of** (representing) de la part de; (for benefit of) pour le compte de; **on my/his ~** de ma/sa part

**behave** [bɪ'heɪv] vi se conduire, se comporter; (well: also: **~ o.s.**) se conduire bien or comme il faut; **behaviour** (US **behavior**) n comportement m, conduite f

**behind** [bɪ'haɪnd] prep derrière; (time) en retard sur; (supporting): **to be ~ sb** soutenir qn ▷ adv derrière; en retard ▷ n derrière m; **~ the scenes** dans les coulisses; **to be ~ (schedule) with sth** être en retard dans qch

**beige** [beɪʒ] adj beige

**Beijing** ['beɪ'dʒɪŋ] n Pékin

**being** ['biːɪŋ] n être m; **to come into ~** prendre naissance

**belated** [bɪ'leɪtɪd] adj tardif(-ive)

**belch** [bɛltʃ] vi avoir un renvoi, roter ▷ vt (also: **~ out**: smoke etc) vomir, cracher

**Belgian** ['bɛldʒən] adj belge, de Belgique ▷ n Belge m/f

**Belgium** ['bɛldʒəm] n Belgique f

**belief** [bɪ'liːf] n (opinion) conviction f; (trust, faith) foi f

**believe** [bɪ'liːv] vt, vi croire, estimer; **to ~ in** (God) croire en; (ghosts, method) croire à; **believer** n (in idea, activity) partisan(e); (Rel) croyant(e)

**bell** [bɛl] n cloche f; (small) clochette f, grelot m; (on door) sonnette f; (electric) sonnerie f

**bellboy** ['bɛlbɔɪ] (US **bellhop** ['bɛlhɔp]) n groom m, chasseur m

**bellow** ['bɛləʊ] vi (bull) meugler; (person) brailler

**bell pepper** n (esp US) poivron m

**belly** ['bɛlɪ] n ventre m; **belly button** (inf) n nombril m

**belong** [bɪ'lɔŋ] vi: **to ~ to** appartenir à; (club etc) faire partie de; **this book ~s here** ce livre va ici, la place de ce livre est ici; **belongings** npl affaires fpl, possessions fpl

**beloved** [bɪ'lʌvɪd] adj (bien-)aimé(e), chéri(e)

**below** [bɪ'ləʊ] prep sous, au-dessous de ▷ adv en dessous; en contre-bas; **see ~** voir plus bas or plus loin or ci-dessous

**belt** [bɛlt] n ceinture f; (Tech) courroie f ▷ vt (thrash) donner une raclée à; **beltway** n (US Aut) route f de ceinture; (: motorway) périphérique m

**bemused** [bɪ'mjuːzd] adj médusé(e)

**bench** [bɛntʃ] n banc m; (in workshop) établi m; **the B~** (Law: judges) la magistrature, la Cour

**bend** [bɛnd] vb (pt, pp **bent**) ▷ vt courber; (leg, arm) plier ▷ vi se courber ▷ n (BRIT: in road) virage m, tournant m; (in pipe, river) coude m; **bend down** vi se baisser; **bend over** vi se pencher

**beneath** [bɪ'ni:θ] prep sous, au-dessous de; (unworthy of) indigne de ▷ adv dessous, au-dessous, en bas

**beneficial** [bɛnɪ'fɪʃəl] adj: ~ **(to)** salutaire (pour), bénéfique (à)

**benefit** ['bɛnɪfɪt] n avantage m, profit m; (allowance of money) allocation f ▷ vt faire du bien à, profiter à ▷ vi: **he'll ~ from it** cela lui fera du bien, il y gagnera or s'en trouvera bien

**Benelux** ['bɛnɪlʌks] n Bénélux m

**benign** [bɪ'naɪn] adj (person, smile) bienveillant(e), affable; (Med) bénin(-igne)

**bent** [bɛnt] pt, pp of **bend** ▷ n inclination f, penchant m ▷ adj: **to be ~ on** être résolu(e) à

**bereaved** [bɪ'ri:vd] n: **the ~** la famille du disparu

**beret** ['bɛreɪ] n béret m

**Berlin** [bə:'lɪn] n Berlin

**Bermuda** [bə:'mju:də] n Bermudes fpl

**Bern** [bə:n] n Berne

**berry** ['bɛrɪ] n baie f

**berth** [bə:θ] n (bed) couchette f; (for ship) poste m d'amarrage, mouillage m ▷ vi (in harbour) venir à quai; (at anchor) mouiller

**beside** [bɪ'saɪd] prep à côté de; (compared with) par rapport à; **that's ~ the point** ça n'a rien à voir; **to be ~ o.s. (with anger)** être hors de soi; **besides** adv en outre, de plus ▷ prep en plus de; (except) excepté

**best** [bɛst] adj meilleur(e) ▷ adv le mieux; **the ~ part of** (quantity) le plus clair de, la plus grande partie de; **at ~** au mieux; **to make the ~ of sth** s'accommoder de qch (du mieux que l'on peut); **to do one's ~** faire de son mieux; **to the ~ of my knowledge** pour autant que je sache; **to the ~ of my ability** du mieux que je pourrai; **best-before date** n date f de limite d'utilisation or de consommation; **best man** (irreg) n garçon m d'honneur; **bestseller** n best-seller m, succès m

de librairie

**bet** [bɛt] n pari m ▷ vt, vi (pt, pp ~ or ~ted) parier; **to ~ sb sth** parier qch à qn

**betray** [bɪ'treɪ] vt trahir

**better** ['bɛtər] adj meilleur(e) ▷ adv mieux ▷ vt améliorer ▷ n: **to get the ~ of** triompher de, l'emporter sur; **you had ~ do it** vous feriez mieux de le faire; **he thought ~ of it** il s'est ravisé; **to get ~** (Med) aller mieux; (improve) s'améliorer

**betting** ['bɛtɪŋ] n paris mpl; **betting shop** n (BRIT) bureau m de paris

**between** [bɪ'twi:n] prep entre ▷ adv au milieu, dans l'intervalle

**beverage** ['bɛvərɪdʒ] n boisson f (gén sans alcool)

**beware** [bɪ'wɛər] vi: **to ~ (of)** prendre garde (à); **"~ of the dog"** (attention) chien méchant"

**bewildered** [bɪ'wɪldəd] adj dérouté(e), ahuri(e)

**beyond** [bɪ'jɔnd] prep (in space, time) au-delà de; (exceeding) au-dessus de ▷ adv au-delà; ~ **doubt** hors de doute; ~ **repair** irréparable

**bias** ['baɪəs] n (prejudice) préjugé m, parti pris; (preference) prévention f; **bias(s)ed** adj partial(e), montrant un parti pris

**bib** [bɪb] n bavoir m

**Bible** ['baɪbl] n Bible f

**bicarbonate of soda** [baɪ'kɑ:bənɪt-] n bicarbonate m de soude

**biceps** ['baɪsɛps] n biceps m

**bicycle** ['baɪsɪkl] n bicyclette f; **bicycle pump** n pompe f à vélo

**bid** [bɪd] n offre f; (at auction) enchère f; (attempt) tentative f ▷ vb (pt ~ or **bade**, pp ~ or ~**den**) ▷ vi faire une enchère or offre ▷ vt faire une enchère or offre de; **to ~ sb good day** souhaiter le bonjour à qn; **bidder** n: **the highest bidder** le plus offrant

**bidet** ['bi:deɪ] n bidet m

**big** [bɪg] adj (in height: person, building, tree) grand(e); (in bulk, amount: person, parcel, book) gros(se); **bigheaded** adj

prétentieux(-euse); **big toe** n gros
orteil

**bike** [baɪk] n vélo m; **bike lane** n piste
f cyclable
**bikini** [bɪ'ki:nɪ] n bikini m
**bilateral** [baɪ'lætərl] adj bilatéral(e)
**bilingual** [baɪ'lɪŋgwəl] adj bilingue
**bill** [bɪl] n note f, facture f; (in restaurant)
addition f, note f; (Pol) projet m de loi;
(US: banknote) billet m (de banque);
(notice) affiche f; (of bird) bec m; **put it
on my ~** mettez-le sur mon compte;
**"post no ~s"** "défense d'afficher"; **to fit**
or **fill the ~** (fig) faire l'affaire; **billboard**
(US) n panneau m d'affichage; **billfold**
['bɪlfəʊld] n (US) portefeuille m
**billiards** ['bɪljədz] n (jeu m de) billard m
**billion** ['bɪljən] n (BRIT) billion m (million
de millions); (US) milliard m
**bin** [bɪn] n boîte f; (BRIT: also: **dust~**,
**litter ~**) poubelle f; (for coal) coffre m
**bind** (pt, pp **bound**) [baɪnd, baʊnd] vt
attacher; (book) relier; (oblige) obliger,
contraindre ▷ n (inf: nuisance) scie f
**binge** [bɪndʒ] n (inf): **to go on a ~** faire
la bringue
**bingo** ['bɪŋgəʊ] n sorte de jeu de loto
pratiqué dans des établissements publics
**binoculars** [bɪ'nɒkjʊləz] npl
jumelles fpl
**bio...** ['baɪə'] prefix: **biochemistry**

n biochimie f; **biodegradable**
['baɪəʊdɪ'greɪdəbl] adj biodégradable;
**biography** [baɪ'ɒgrəfɪ] n biographie f;
**biological** adj biologique; **biology**
[baɪ'ɒlədʒɪ] n biologie f; **biometric**
[baɪə'mɛtrɪk] adj biométrique
**birch** [bə:tʃ] n bouleau m
**bird** [bə:d] n oiseau m; (BRIT inf: girl)
nana f; **bird flu** n grippe f aviaire;
**bird of prey** n oiseau m de proie;
**birdwatching** n ornithologie f
(d'amateur)
**Biro®** ['baɪərəʊ] n stylo m à bille
**birth** [bə:θ] n naissance f; **to give
~ to** donner naissance à, mettre
au monde; (subj: animal) mettre
bas; **birth certificate** n acte m de
naissance; **birth control** n (policy)
limitation f des naissances; (methods)
méthode(s) contraceptive(s); **birthday**
n anniversaire m ▷ cpd (cake, card etc)
d'anniversaire; **birthmark** n envie f,
tache f de vin; **birthplace** n lieu m de
naissance
**biscuit** ['bɪskɪt] n (BRIT) biscuit m; (US)
petit pain au lait
**bishop** ['bɪʃəp] n évêque m; (Chess) fou m
**bistro** ['bi:strəʊ] n petit restaurant
m, bistrot m
**bit** [bɪt] pt of **bite** ▷ n morceau m;
(Comput) bit m, élément m binaire; (of
tool) mèche f; (of horse) mors m; **a ~ of**
un peu de; **a ~ mad/dangerous** un peu
fou/risqué; **~ by ~** petit à petit
**bitch** [bɪtʃ] n (dog) chienne f; (inf!) salope
f (!), garce f
**bite** [baɪt] vt, vi (pt **bit**, pp **bitten**)
mordre; (insect) piquer ▷ n morsure f;
(insect bite) piqûre f; (mouthful) bouchée
f; **let's have a ~ (to eat)** mangeons un
morceau; **to ~ one's nails** se ronger
les ongles
**bitten** ['bɪtn] pp of **bite**
**bitter** ['bɪtər] adj amer(-ère); (criticism)
cinglant(e); (icy: weather, wind)
glacial(e) ▷ n (BRIT: beer) bière f (à forte
teneur en houblon)
**bizarre** [bɪ'zɑ:r] adj bizarre

**black** [blæk] *adj* noir(e) ▷ *n* (*colour*)
noir *m*; (*person*): **B~** noir(e) ▷ *vt* (*BRIT
Industry*) boycotter; **to give sb a ~
eye** pocher l'œil à qn, faire un œil
au beurre noir à qn; **to be in the ~**
(*in credit*) avoir un compte créditeur;
**~ and blue** (*bruised*) couvert(e) de
bleus; **black out** *vi* (*faint*) s'évanouir;
**blackberry** *n* mûre *f*; **blackbird** *n*
merle *m*; **blackboard** *n* tableau noir;
**black coffee** *n* café noir; **blackcurrant**
*n* cassis *m*; **black ice** *n* verglas *m*;
**blackmail** *n* chantage *m* ▷ *vt* faire
chanter, soumettre au chantage; **black
market** *n* marché noir; **blackout**
*n* panne *f* d'électricité; (*in wartime*) blackout *m*; (*TV*) interruption *f* d'émission;
(*fainting*) syncope *f*; **black pepper** *n*
poivre noir; **black pudding** *n* boudin
(noir); **Black Sea** *n*: **the Black Sea** la
mer Noire

**bladder** ['blædə<sup>r</sup>] *n* vessie *f*

**blade** [bleɪd] *n* lame *f*; (*of propeller*) pale
*f*; **a ~ of grass** un brin d'herbe

**blame** [bleɪm] *n* faute *f*, blâme *m* ▷ *vt*:
**to ~ sb/sth for sth** attribuer à qn/qch
la responsabilité de qch, reprocher
qch à qn/qch; **I'm not to ~** ce n'est pas
ma faute

**bland** [blænd] *adj* (*taste, food*) doux
(douce), fade

**blank** [blæŋk] *adj* blanc (blanche);
(*look*) sans expression, dénué(e)
d'expression ▷ *n* espace *m* vide, blanc
*m*; (*cartridge*) cartouche *f* à blanc;
**his mind was a ~** il avait la tête vide

**blanket** ['blæŋkɪt] *n* couverture *f*; (*of
snow, cloud*) couche *f*

**blast** [blɑːst] *n* explosion *f*; (*shock wave*)
souffle *m*; (*of air, steam*) bouffée *f* ▷ *vt*
faire sauter *or* exploser

**blatant** ['bleɪtənt] *adj* flagrant(e),
criant(e)

**blaze** [bleɪz] *n* (*fire*) incendie *m*; (*fig*)
flamboiement *m* ▷ *vi* (*fire*) flamber; (*fig*)
flamboyer, resplendir ▷ *vt*: **to ~ a trail**
(*fig*) montrer la voie; **in a ~ of publicity**
à grand renfort de publicité

**blazer** ['bleɪzə<sup>r</sup>] *n* blazer *m*

**bleach** [bliːtʃ] *n* (*also*: **household ~**)
eau *f* de Javel ▷ *vt* (*linen*) blanchir;
**bleachers** *npl* (*US Sport*) gradins *mpl*
(*en plein soleil*)

**bleak** [bliːk] *adj* morne, désolé(e);
(*weather*) triste, maussade; (*smile*)
lugubre; (*prospect, future*) morose

**bled** [bled] *pt, pp of* **bleed**

**bleed** (*pt, pp* **bled**) [bliːd, bled] *vt*
saigner; (*brakes, radiator*) purger ▷ *vi*
saigner; **my nose is ~ing** je saigne
du nez

**blemish** ['blemɪʃ] *n* défaut *m*; (*on
reputation*) tache *f*

**blend** [blend] *n* mélange *m* ▷ *vt*
mélanger ▷ *vi* (*colours etc: also*: **~ in**) se
mélanger, se fondre, s'allier; **blender** *n*
(*Culin*) mixeur *m*

**bless** (*pt, pp* **~ed** *or* **blest**) [bles, blest]
*vt* bénir; **~ you!** (*after sneeze*) à tes
souhaits!; **blessing** *n* bénédiction *f*;
(*godsend*) bienfait *m*

**blew** [bluː] *pt of* **blow**

**blight** [blaɪt] *vt* (*hopes etc*) anéantir,
briser

**blind** [blaɪnd] *adj* aveugle ▷ *n* (*for
window*) store *m* ▷ *vt* aveugler; **the
blind** *npl* les aveugles *mpl*; **blind alley**
*n* impasse *f*; **blindfold** *n* bandeau *m*
▷ *adj, adv* les yeux bandés ▷ *vt* bander
les yeux à

**blink** [blɪŋk] *vi* cligner des yeux; (*light*)
clignoter

**bliss** [blɪs] *n* félicité *f*, bonheur *m* sans
mélange

**blister** ['blɪstə<sup>r</sup>] *n* (*on skin*) ampoule *f*,
cloque *f*; (*on paintwork*) boursouflure *f*
▷ *vi* (*paint*) se boursoufler, se cloquer

**blizzard** ['blɪzəd] *n* blizzard *m*, tempête
*f* de neige

**bloated** ['bləʊtɪd] *adj* (*face*) bouffi(e);
(*stomach, person*) gonflé(e)

**blob** [blɔb] *n* (*drop*) goutte *f*; (*stain,
spot*) tache *f*

**block** [blɔk] *n* bloc *m*; (*in pipes*)
obstruction *f*; (*toy*) cube *m*; (*of buildings*)
pâté *m* (de maisons) ▷ *vt* bloquer;

(fig) faire obstacle à; **the sink is ~ed** l'évier est bouché; **~ of flats** (BRIT) immeuble (locatif); **mental ~** blocage m; **block up** vt boucher; **blockade** [blɔ'keɪd] n blocus m ▷ vt faire le blocus de; **blockage** n obstruction f; **blockbuster** n (film, book) grand succès; **block capitals** npl majuscules fpl d'imprimerie; **block letters** npl majuscules fpl

**blog** [blɔg] n blog m, blogue m

**bloke** [bləuk] n (BRIT inf) type m

**blond(e)** [blɔnd] adj, n blond(e)

**blood** [blʌd] n sang m; **blood donor** n donneur(-euse) de sang; **blood group** n groupe sanguin; **blood poisoning** n empoisonnement m du sang; **blood pressure** n tension (artérielle); **bloodshed** n effusion f de sang, carnage m; **bloodshot** adj: **bloodshot eyes** yeux injectés de sang; **bloodstream** n sang m, système sanguin; **blood test** n analyse f de sang; **blood transfusion** n transfusion f de sang; **blood type** n groupe sanguin; **blood vessel** n vaisseau sanguin; **bloody** adj sanglant(e); (BRIT inf!): **this bloody ...** ce foutu ..., ce putain de ... (!) ▷ adv: **bloody strong/good** (BRIT: inf!) vachement or sacrément fort/bon

**bloom** [blu:m] n fleur f ▷ vi être en fleur

**blossom** ['blɔsəm] n fleur(s) f(pl) ▷ vi être en fleurs; (fig) s'épanouir

**blot** [blɔt] n tache f ▷ vt tacher; (ink) sécher

**blouse** [blauz] n (feminine garment) chemisier m, corsage m

**blow** [bləu] n coup m ▷ vb (pt blew, pp ~n) ▷ vi souffler ▷ vt (instrument) jouer de; (fuse) faire sauter; **to ~ one's nose** se moucher; **blow away** vi s'envoler ▷ vt chasser, faire s'envoler; **blow out** vi (fire, flame) s'éteindre; (tyre) éclater; (fuse) sauter; **blow up** vi exploser, sauter ▷ vt faire sauter; (tyre) gonfler; (Phot) agrandir; **blow-dry** n (hairstyle) brushing m

**blown** [bləun] pp of **blow**

**blue** [blu:] adj bleu(e); (depressed) triste; **~ film/joke** film m/histoire f pornographique; **out of the ~** (fig) à l'improviste, sans qu'on s'y attende; **bluebell** n jacinthe f des bois; **blueberry** n myrtille f, airelle f; **blue cheese** n (fromage) bleu m; **blues** npl: **the blues** (Mus) le blues; **to have the blues** (inf: feeling) avoir le cafard; **bluetit** n mésange bleue

**bluff** [blʌf] vi bluffer ▷ n bluff m; **to call sb's ~** mettre qn au défi d'exécuter ses menaces

**blunder** ['blʌndəʳ] n gaffe f, bévue f ▷ vi faire une gaffe or une bévue

**blunt** [blʌnt] adj (knife) émoussé(e), peu tranchant(e); (pencil) mal taillé(e); (person) brusque, ne mâchant pas ses mots

**blur** [bləːʳ] n (shape): **to become a ~** devenir flou ▷ vt brouiller, rendre flou(e); **blurred** adj flou(e)

**blush** [blʌʃ] vi rougir ▷ n rougeur f; **blusher** n rouge m à joues

**board** [bɔːd] n (wooden) planche f; (on wall) panneau m; (for chess etc) plateau m; (cardboard) carton m; (committee) conseil m, comité m; (in firm) conseil d'administration; (Naut, Aviat): **on ~** à bord ▷ vt (ship) monter à bord de; (train) monter dans; **full ~** (BRIT) pension complète; **half ~** (BRIT) demi-pension f; **~ and lodging** n chambre f avec pension; **to go by the ~** (hopes, principles) être abandonné(e); **board game** n jeu m de société; **boarding card** n (Aviat, Naut) carte f d'embarquement; **boarding pass** n (BRIT) = **boarding card**; **boarding school** n internat m, pensionnat m; **board room** n salle f du conseil d'administration

**boast** [bəust] vi: **to ~ (about or of)** se vanter (de)

**boat** [bəut] n bateau m; (small) canot m; barque f

**bob** [bɔb] vi (boat, cork on water: also: **~**

_up and down_) danser, se balancer
**bobby pin** ['bɔbɪ-] _n_ (_US_) pince f à cheveux
**body** ['bɔdɪ] _n_ corps _m_; (_of car_) carrosserie f; (_fig: society_) organe _m_, organisme _m_; **body-building** _n_ body-building _m_, culturisme _m_; **bodyguard** _n_ garde _m_ du corps; **bodywork** _n_ carrosserie f
**bog** [bɔg] _n_ tourbière f ▷ _vt_: **to get ~ged down (in)** (_fig_) s'enliser (dans)
**bogus** ['bəugəs] _adj_ bidon _inv_; fantôme
**boil** [bɔɪl] _vt_ (faire) bouillir ▷ _vi_ bouillir ▷ _n_ (_Med_) furoncle _m_; **to come to the** _or_ (_US_) **a ~** bouillir; **boil down to** (_fig_): **to ~ down to** se réduire _or_ ramener à; **boil over** _vi_ déborder; **boiled egg** _n_ œuf _m_ à la coque; **boiled potatoes** _n_ pommes fpl à l'anglaise _or_ à l'eau; **boiler** _n_ chaudière f; **boiling** ['bɔɪlɪŋ] _adj_: **I'm boiling (hot)** (_inf_) je crève de chaud; **boiling point** _n_ point _m_ d'ébullition
**bold** [bəuld] _adj_ hardi(e), audacieux(-euse); (_pej_) effronté(e); (_outline, colour_) franc (franche), tranché(e), marqué(e)
**bollard** ['bɔləd] _n_ (_BRIT Aut_) borne lumineuse _or_ de signalisation
**bolt** [bəult] _n_ verrou _m_; (_with nut_) boulon _m_ ▷ _adv_: **~ upright** droit(e) comme un piquet ▷ _vt_ (_door_) verrouiller; (_food_) engloutir ▷ _vi_ se sauver, filer (comme une flèche); (_horse_) s'emballer
**bomb** [bɔm] _n_ bombe f ▷ _vt_ bombarder; **bombard** [bɔm'ba:d] _vt_ bombarder; **bomber** _n_ (_Aviat_) bombardier _m_; (_terrorist_) poseur _m_ de bombes; **bomb scare** _n_ alerte f à la bombe
**bond** [bɔnd] _n_ lien _m_; (_binding promise_) engagement _m_, obligation f; (_Finance_) obligation; **bonds** _npl_ (_chains_) chaînes fpl; **in ~** (_of goods_) en entrepôt
**bone** [bəun] _n_ os _m_; (_of fish_) arête f ▷ _vt_ désosser; ôter les arêtes de
**bonfire** ['bɔnfaɪə'] _n_ feu _m_ (de joie); (_for rubbish_) feu
**bonnet** ['bɔnɪt] _n_ bonnet _m_; (_BRIT: of car_) capot _m_
**bonus** ['bəunəs] _n_ (_money_) prime f; (_advantage_) avantage _m_
**boo** [bu:] _excl_ hou!, peuh! ▷ _vt_ huer
**book** [buk] _n_ livre _m_; (_of stamps, tickets etc_) carnet _m_; (_Comm_): **books** _npl_ comptes mpl, comptabilité f ▷ _vt_ (_ticket_) prendre; (_seat, room_) réserver; (_football player_) prendre le nom de, donner un carton à; **I ~ed a table in the name of ...** j'ai réservé une table au nom de ...; **book in** _vi_ (_BRIT: at hotel_) prendre sa chambre; **book up** _vt_ réserver; **the hotel is ~ed up** l'hôtel est complet; **bookcase** _n_ bibliothèque f; **booking** _n_ (_BRIT_) réservation f; **I confirmed my booking by fax/e-mail** j'ai confirmé ma réservation par fax/e-mail; **booking office** _n_ (_BRIT_) bureau _m_ de location; **book-keeping** _n_ comptabilité f; **booklet** _n_ brochure f; **bookmaker** _n_ bookmaker _m_; **bookmark** _n_ (_for book_) marque-page _m_; (_Comput_) signet _m_; **bookseller** _n_ libraire _m/f_; **bookshelf** _n_ (_single_) étagère f (à livres); (_bookcase_) bibliothèque f; **bookshop, bookstore** _n_ librairie f
**boom** [bu:m] _n_ (_noise_) grondement _m_; (_in prices, population_) forte augmentation f; (_busy period_) boom _m_, vague f de prospérité ▷ _vi_ gronder; prospérer
**boost** [bu:st] _n_ stimulant _m_, remontant _m_ ▷ _vt_ stimuler
**boot** [bu:t] _n_ botte f; (_for hiking_) chaussure f (de marche); (_ankle boot_) bottine f; (_BRIT: of car_) coffre _m_ ▷ _vt_ (_Comput_) lancer, mettre en route; **to ~** (_in addition_) par-dessus le marché, en plus
**booth** [bu:ð] _n_ (_at fair_) baraque (foraine); (_of telephone etc_) cabine f; (_also:_ **voting ~**) isoloir _m_
**booze** [bu:z] (_inf_) _n_ boissons fpl alcooliques, alcool _m_
**border** ['bɔ:də'] _n_ bordure f; bord _m_; (_of a country_) frontière f; **borderline** _n_ (_fig_)

ligne *f* de démarcation

**bore** [bɔːʳ] *pt of* **bear** ▷ *vt* (*person*) ennuyer, raser; (*hole*) percer; (*well, tunnel*) creuser ▷ *n* (*person*) raseur(-euse); (*boring thing*) barbe *f*; (*of gun*) calibre *m*; **bored** *adj*: **to be bored** s'ennuyer; **boredom** *n* ennui *m*

**boring** ['bɔːrɪŋ] *adj* ennuyeux(-euse)

**born** [bɔːn] *adj*: **to be ~** naître; **I was ~ in 1960** je suis né en 1960

**borne** [bɔːn] *pp of* **bear**

**borough** ['bʌrə] *n* municipalité *f*

**borrow** ['bɔrəu] *vt*: **to ~ sth (from sb)** emprunter qch (à qn)

**Bosnia(-Herzegovina)** ['bɔːsnɪə(hɛrzə'gəuvi:nə)] *n* Bosnie-Herzégovine *f*; **Bosnian** ['bɔznɪən] *adj* bosniaque, bosnien(ne) ▷ *n* Bosniaque *m/f*, Bosnien(ne)

**bosom** ['buzəm] *n* poitrine *f*; (*fig*) sein *m*

**boss** [bɔs] *n* patron(ne) ▷ *vt* (*also*: **~ about, ~ around**) mener à la baguette; **bossy** *adj* autoritaire

**both** [bəuθ] *adj* les deux, l'un(e) et l'autre ▷ *pron*: **~ (of them)** les deux, tous (toutes) (les) deux, l'un(e) et l'autre; **~ of us went, we ~ went** nous y sommes allés tous les deux ▷ *adv*: **~ A and B** A et B

**bother** ['bɔðəʳ] *vt* (*worry*) tracasser; (*needle, bait*) importuner, ennuyer; (*disturb*) déranger ▷ *vi* (*also*: **~ o.s.**) se tracasser, se faire du souci ▷ *n* (*trouble*) ennuis *mpl*; **to ~ doing** prendre la peine de faire; **don't ~** ce n'est pas la peine; **it's no ~** aucun problème

**bottle** ['bɔtl] *n* bouteille *f*; (*baby's*) biberon *m*; (*of perfume, medicine*) flacon *m* ▷ *vt* mettre en bouteille(s); **bottle bank** *n* conteneur *m* (de bouteilles); **bottle-opener** *n* ouvre-bouteille *m*

**bottom** ['bɔtəm] *n* (*of container, sea etc*) fond *m*; (*buttocks*) derrière *m*; (*of page, list*) bas *m*; (*of mountain, tree, hill*) pied *m* ▷ *adj* (*shelf, step*) du bas

**bought** [bɔːt] *pt, pp of* **buy**

**boulder** ['bəuldəʳ] *n* gros rocher (*gén lisse, arrondi*)

**bounce** [bauns] *vi* (*ball*) rebondir; (*cheque*) être refusé (*étant sans provision*) ▷ *vt* faire rebondir ▷ *n* (*rebound*) rebond *m*; **bouncer** *n* (*inf: at dance, club*) videur *m*

**bound** [baund] *pt, pp of* **bind** ▷ *n* (*gen pl*) limite *f*; (*leap*) bond *m* ▷ *vi* (*leap*) bondir ▷ *vt* (*limit*) borner ▷ *adj*: **to be ~ to do sth** (*obliged*) être obligé(e) *or* avoir obligation de faire qch; **he's ~ to fail** (*likely*) il est sûr d'échouer, son échec est inévitable *or* assuré; **~ by** (*law, regulation*) engagé(e) par; **~ for** à destination de; **out of ~s** dont l'accès est interdit

**boundary** ['baundrɪ] *n* frontière *f*

**bouquet** ['bukeɪ] *n* bouquet *m*

**bourbon** ['buəbən] *n* (*us: also*: **~ whiskey**) bourbon *m*

**bout** [baut] *n* période *f*; (*of malaria etc*) accès *m*, crise *f*, attaque *f*; (*Boxing etc*) combat *m*, match *m*

**boutique** [bu:'ti:k] *n* boutique *f*

**bow¹** [bəu] *n* nœud *m*; (*weapon*) arc *m*; (*Mus*) archet *m*

**bow²** [bau] *n* (*with body*) révérence *f*, inclination *f* (du buste *or* corps); (*Naut: also*: **~s**) proue *f* ▷ *vi* faire une révérence, s'incliner

**bowels** [bauəlz] *npl* intestins *mpl*; (*fig*) entrailles *fpl*

**bowl** [bəul] *n* (*for eating*) bol *m*; (*for washing*) cuvette *f*; (*ball*) boule *f* ▷ *vi* (*Cricket*) lancer (la balle); **bowler** *n* (*Cricket*) lanceur *m* (de la balle); (*BRIT: also*: **bowler hat**) (chapeau *m*) melon *m*; **bowling** *n* (*game*) jeu *m* de boules, jeu de quilles; **bowling alley** *n* bowling *m*; **bowling green** *n* terrain *m* de boules (*gazonné et carré*); **bowls** *n* (jeu *m* de) boules *fpl*

**bow tie** [bəu-] *n* nœud *m* papillon

**box** [bɔks] *n* boîte *f*; (*also*: **cardboard ~**) carton *m*; (*Theat*) loge *f* ▷ *vt* mettre en boîte ▷ *vi* boxer, faire de la boxe; **boxer** ['bɔksəʳ] *n* (*person*) boxeur *m*; **boxer shorts** *npl* caleçon *m*; **boxing** ['bɔksɪŋ] *n* (*sport*) boxe *f*; **Boxing Day**

*n* (BRIT) le lendemain de Noël; *voir encadré*; **boxing gloves** *npl* gants *mpl* de boxe; **boxing ring** *n* ring *m*; **box junction** *n* (BRIT Aut) zone *f* (de carrefour) d'accès réglementé; **box office** *n* bureau *m* de location

● **BOXING DAY**
●
● **Boxing Day** est le lendemain de
● Noël, férié en Grande-Bretagne. Ce
● nom vient d'une coutume du XIXe
● siècle qui consistait à donner des
● cadeaux de Noël (dans des boîtes) à
● ses employés etc le 26 décembre.

**boy** [bɔɪ] *n* garçon *m*; **boy band** *n* boys band *m*

**boycott** ['bɔɪkɔt] *n* boycottage *m* ▷ *vt* boycotter

**boyfriend** ['bɔɪfrɛnd] *n* (petit) ami

**bra** [brɑː] *n* soutien-gorge *m*

**brace** [breɪs] *n* (support) attache *f*, agrafe *f*; (BRIT: also: **~s**: on teeth) appareil *m* (dentaire); (tool) vilebrequin *m* ▷ *vt* (support) consolider, soutenir; **braces** *npl* (BRIT: for trousers) bretelles *fpl*; **to ~ o.s.** (fig) se préparer mentalement

**bracelet** ['breɪslɪt] *n* bracelet *m*

**bracket** ['brækɪt] *n* (Tech) tasseau *m*, support *m*; (group) classe *f*, tranche *f*; (also: **brace ~**) accolade *f*; (also: **round ~**) parenthèse *f*; (also: **square ~**) crochet *m* ▷ *vt* mettre entre parenthèses; **in ~s** entre parenthèses *or* crochets

**brag** [bræg] *vi* se vanter

**braid** [breɪd] *n* (trimming) galon *m*; (of hair) tresse *f*, natte *f*

**brain** [breɪn] *n* cerveau *m*; **brains** *npl* (intellect, food) cervelle *f*

**braise** [breɪz] *vt* braiser

**brake** [breɪk] *n* frein *m* ▷ *vt*, *vi* freiner; **brake light** *n* feu *m* de stop

**bran** [bræn] *n* son *m*

**branch** [brɑːntʃ] *n* branche *f*; (Comm) succursale *f*; (: of bank) agence *f*; **branch off** *vi* (road) bifurquer; **branch out** *vi* diversifier ses activités

**brand** [brænd] *n* marque (commerciale) ▷ *vt* (cattle) marquer (au fer rouge); **brand name** *n* nom *m* de marque; **brand-new** *adj* tout(e) neuf (neuve), flambant neuf (neuve)

**brandy** ['brændɪ] *n* cognac *m*

**brash** [bræʃ] *adj* effronté(e)

**brass** [brɑːs] *n* cuivre *m* (jaune), laiton *m*; **the ~** (Mus) les cuivres; **brass band** *n* fanfare *f*

**brat** [bræt] *n* (pej) mioche *m/f*, môme *m/f*

**brave** [breɪv] *adj* courageux(-euse), brave ▷ *vt* braver, affronter; **bravery** *n* bravoure *f*, courage *m*

**brawl** [brɔːl] *n* rixe *f*, bagarre *f*

**Brazil** [brə'zɪl] *n* Brésil *m*; **Brazilian** *adj* brésilien(ne) ▷ *n* Brésilien(ne)

**breach** [briːtʃ] *vt* ouvrir une brèche dans ▷ *n* (gap) brèche *f*; (breaking): **~ of contract** rupture *f* de contrat; **~ of the peace** attentat *m* à l'ordre public

**bread** [brɛd] *n* pain *m*; **breadbin** *n* (BRIT) boîte *for* huche *f* à pain; **breadbox** *n* (US) boîte *for* huche *f* à pain; **breadcrumbs** *npl* miettes *fpl* de pain; (Culin) chapelure *f*, panure *f*

**breadth** [brɛtθ] *n* largeur *f*

**break** [breɪk] (pt **broke**, pp **broken**) *vt* casser, briser; (promise) rompre; (law) violer ▷ *vi* se casser, se briser; (weather) tourner; (storm) éclater; (day) se lever ▷ *n* (gap) brèche *f*; (fracture) cassure *f*; (rest) interruption *f*, arrêt *m*; (: short) pause *f*; (: at school) récréation *f*; (chance) chance *f*, occasion *f* favorable; **to ~ one's leg** *etc* se casser la jambe *etc*; **to ~ a record** battre un record; **to ~ the news to sb** annoncer la nouvelle à qn; **break down** *vt* (door etc) enfoncer; (figures, data) décomposer, analyser ▷ *vi* s'effondrer; (Med) faire une dépression (nerveuse); (Aut) tomber en panne; **my car has broken down** ma voiture est en panne; **break in** *vt* (horse etc) dresser ▷ *vi* (burglar) entrer par effraction; (interrupt) interrompre; **break into** *vt fus* (house) s'introduire *or* pénétrer par

effraction dans; **break off** vi (speaker)
s'interrompre; (branch) se rompre ▷ vt
(talks, engagement) rompre; **break
out** vi éclater, se déclarer; (prisoner)
s'évader; **to ~ out in spots** se couvrir
de boutons; **break up** vi (partnership)
cesser, prendre fin; (marriage) se
briser; (crowd, meeting) se séparer;
(ship) se disloquer; (Scol: pupils) être en
vacances; (line) couper; **the line's or
you're ~ing up** ça coupe ▷ vt fracasser,
casser; (fight etc) interrompre, faire
cesser; (marriage) désunir; **breakdown**
n (Aut) panne f; (in communications,
marriage) rupture f; (Med: also: **nervous
breakdown**) dépression (nerveuse);
(of figures) ventilation f, répartition f;
**breakdown truck** (us **breakdown
van**) n dépanneuse f
**breakfast** ['brɛkfəst] n petit déjeuner
m; **what time is ~?** le petit déjeuner est
à quelle heure?
**break**: **break-in** n cambriolage m;
**breakthrough** n percée f
**breast** [brɛst] n (of woman) sein m;
(chest) poitrine f; (of chicken, turkey)
blanc m; **breast-feed** vt, vi (irreg: like
**feed**) allaiter; **breast-stroke** n brasse f
**breath** [brɛθ] n haleine f, souffle m; **to
take a deep ~** respirer à fond; **out of ~** à
bout de souffle, essoufflé(e)
**Breathalyser®** ['brɛθəlaɪzər] (BRIT) n
alcootest m
**breathe** [bri:ð] vt, vi respirer; **breathe
in** vi inspirer ▷ vt aspirer; **breathe out**
vt, vi expirer; **breathing** n respiration f
**breath**: **breathless** adj essoufflé(e),
haletant(e); **breathtaking** adj
stupéfiant(e), à vous couper le souffle;
**breath test** n alcootest m
**bred** [brɛd] pt, pp of **breed**
**breed** [bri:d] (pt, pp **bred**) vt élever, faire
l'élevage de ▷ vi se reproduire ▷ n race
f, variété f
**breeze** [bri:z] n brise f
**breezy** ['bri:zɪ] adj (day, weather)
venteux(-euse); (manner) désinvolte;
(person) jovial(e)

**brew** [bru:] vt (tea) faire infuser; (beer)
brasser ▷ vi (fig) se préparer, couver;
**brewery** n brasserie f (fabrique)
**bribe** [braɪb] n pot-de-vin m ▷ vt
acheter; soudoyer; **bribery** n
corruption f
**bric-a-brac** ['brɪkəbræk] n bric-à-
brac m
**brick** [brɪk] n brique f; **bricklayer** n
maçon m
**bride** [braɪd] n mariée f, épouse f;
**bridegroom** n marié m, époux m;
**bridesmaid** n demoiselle f d'honneur
**bridge** [brɪdʒ] n pont m; (Naut)
passerelle f (de commandement); (of
nose) arête f; (Cards, Dentistry) bridge m
▷ vt (gap) combler
**bridle** ['braɪdl] n bride f
**brief** [bri:f] adj bref (brève) ▷ n
(Law) dossier m, cause f; (gen) tâche
f ▷ vt mettre au courant; **briefs**
npl slip m; **briefcase** n serviette f,
porte-documents m inv; **briefing** n
instructions fpl; (Press) briefing m;
**briefly** adv brièvement
**brigadier** [brɪgə'dɪər] n brigadier
général
**bright** [braɪt] adj brillant(e); (room,
weather) clair(e); (person: clever)
intelligent(e), doué(e); (: cheerful)
gai(e); (idea) génial(e); (colour) vif (vive)
**brilliant** ['brɪljənt] adj brillant(e); (light,
sunshine) éclatant(e); (inf: great) super
**brim** [brɪm] n bord m
**brine** [braɪn] n (Culin) saumure f
**bring** (pt, pp **brought**) [brɪŋ, brɔ:t] vt
(thing) apporter; (person) amener; **bring
about** vt provoquer, entraîner; **bring
back** vt rapporter; (person) ramener;
**bring down** vt (lower) abaisser; (shoot
down) abattre; (government) faire
s'effondrer; **bring in** vt (person) faire
entrer; (object) rentrer; (Pol: legislation)
introduire; (produce: income) rapporter;
**bring on** vt (illness, attack) provoquer;
(player, substitute) amener; **bring out** vt
sortir; (meaning) faire ressortir, mettre
en relief; **bring up** vt élever; (carry up)

monter; (*question*) soulever; (*food: vomit*) vomir, rendre

**brink** [brɪŋk] *n* bord *m*

**brisk** [brɪsk] *adj* vif (vive); (*abrupt*) brusque; (*trade etc*) actif(-ive)

**bristle** ['brɪsl] *n* poil *m* ▷ *vi* se hérisser

**Brit** [brɪt] *n abbr* (*inf*: = *British person*) Britannique *m/f*

**Britain** ['brɪtən] *n* (*also*: **Great ~**) la Grande-Bretagne

**British** ['brɪtɪʃ] *adj* britannique ▷ *npl*: **the ~** les Britanniques *mpl*; **British Isles** *npl*: **the British Isles** les îles *fpl* Britanniques

**Briton** ['brɪtən] *n* Britannique *m/f*

**Brittany** ['brɪtənɪ] *n* Bretagne *f*

**brittle** ['brɪtl] *adj* cassant(e), fragile

**B road** *n* (BRIT) ≈ route départementale

**broad** [brɔːd] *adj* large; (*distinction*) général(e); (*accent*) prononcé(e); **in ~ daylight** en plein jour; **broadband** *n* transmission *f* à haut débit; **broad bean** *n* fève *f*; **broadcast** *n* émission *f* ▷ *vb* (*pt, pp* **broadcast**) ▷ *vt* (*Radio*) radiodiffuser; (*TV*) téléviser ▷ *vi* émettre; **broaden** *vt* élargir; **to broaden one's mind** élargir ses horizons ▷ *vi* s'élargir; **broadly** *adv* en gros, généralement; **broad-minded** *adj* large d'esprit

**broccoli** ['brɔkəlɪ] *n* brocoli *m*

**brochure** ['brəʊʃjuəʳ] *n* prospectus *m*, dépliant *m*

**broil** [brɔɪl] (US) *vt* rôtir

**broiler** ['brɔɪləʳ] *n* (*fowl*) poulet *m* (à rôtir); (US: *grill*) gril *m*

**broke** [brəʊk] *pt of* **break** ▷ *adj* (*inf*) fauché(e)

**broken** ['brəʊkn] *pp of* **break** ▷ *adj* (*stick, leg etc*) cassé(e); (*machine: also*: **~ down**) fichu(e); **in ~ French/English** dans un français/anglais approximatif *or* hésitant

**broker** ['brəʊkəʳ] *n* courtier *m*

**bronchitis** [brɔŋ'kaɪtɪs] *n* bronchite *f*

**bronze** [brɔnz] *n* bronze *m*

**brooch** [brəʊtʃ] *n* broche *f*

**brood** [bruːd] *n* couvée *f* ▷ *vi* (*person*) méditer (sombrement), ruminer

**broom** [brum] *n* balai *m*; (*Bot*) genêt *m*

**Bros.** *abbr* (Comm: = *brothers*) Frères

**broth** [brɔθ] *n* bouillon *m* de viande et de légumes

**brothel** ['brɔθl] *n* maison close, bordel *m*

**brother** ['brʌðəʳ] *n* frère *m*; **brother-in-law** *n* beau-frère *m*

**brought** [brɔːt] *pt, pp of* **bring**

**brow** [brau] *n* front *m*; (*eyebrow*) sourcil *m*; (*of hill*) sommet *m*

**brown** [braun] *adj* brun(e), marron *inv*; (*hair*) châtain *inv*; (*tanned*) bronzé(e) ▷ *n* (*colour*) brun *m*, marron *m* ▷ *vt* brunir; (*Culin*) faire dorer, faire roussir; **brown bread** *n* pain *m* bis

**Brownie** ['braunɪ] *n* jeannette *f* éclaireuse (cadette)

**brown rice** *n* riz *m* complet

**brown sugar** *n* cassonade *f*

**browse** [brauz] *vi* (*in shop*) regarder (*sans acheter*); **to ~ through a book** feuilleter un livre; **browser** *n* (*Comput*) navigateur *m*

**bruise** [bruːz] *n* bleu *m*, ecchymose *f*, contusion *f* ▷ *vt* contusionner, meurtrir

**brunette** [bru:'nɛt] *n* (*femme*) brune

**brush** [brʌʃ] *n* brosse *f*; (*for painting*) pinceau *m*; (*for shaving*) blaireau *m*; (*quarrel*) accrochage *m*, prise *f* de bec ▷ *vt* brosser; (*also*: **~ past, ~ against**) effleurer, frôler

**Brussels** ['brʌslz] *n* Bruxelles

**Brussels sprout** [-spraut] *n* chou *m* de Bruxelles

**brutal** ['bru:tl] *adj* brutal(e)

**B.Sc.** *n abbr* = **Bachelor of Science**

**BSE** *n abbr* (= *bovine spongiform encephalopathy*) ESB *f*, BSE *f*

**bubble** ['bʌbl] *n* bulle *f* ▷ *vi* bouillonner, faire des bulles; (*sparkle, fig*) pétiller; **bubble bath** *n* bain moussant; **bubble gum** *n* chewing-gum *m*; **bubblejet printer** ['bʌblʤɛt-] *n* imprimante *f* à bulle d'encre

**buck** [bʌk] *n* mâle *m* (*d'un lapin, lièvre*,

*daim etc*); (*us inf*) dollar *m* ▷ *vi* ruer, lancer une ruade; **to pass the ~ (to sb)** se décharger de la responsabilité (sur qn)

**bucket** ['bʌkɪt] *n* seau *m*

**buckle** ['bʌkl] *n* boucle *f* ▷ *vt* (*belt etc*) boucler, attacher ▷ *vi* (*warp*) tordre, gauchir; (: *wheel*) se voiler

**bud** [bʌd] *n* bourgeon *m*; (*of flower*) bouton *m* ▷ *vi* bourgeonner; (*flower*) éclore

**Buddhism** ['budɪzəm] *n* bouddhisme *m*

**Buddhist** ['budɪst] *adj* bouddhiste ▷ *n* Bouddhiste *m/f*

**buddy** ['bʌdɪ] *n* (*us*) copain *m*

**budge** [bʌdʒ] *vt* faire bouger ▷ *vi* bouger

**budgerigar** ['bʌdʒərɪgɑːʳ] *n* perruche *f*

**budget** ['bʌdʒɪt] *n* budget *m* ▷ *vi*: **to ~ for sth** inscrire qch au budget

**budgie** ['bʌdʒɪ] *n* = **budgerigar**

**buff** [bʌf] *adj* (*couleur f*) chamois *m* ▷ *n* (*inf: enthusiast*) mordu(e)

**buffalo** (*pl* ~ *or* ~**es**) ['bʌfələu] *n* (*BRIT*) buffle *m*; (*us*) bison *m*

**buffer** ['bʌfəʳ] *n* tampon *m*; (*Comput*) mémoire *f* tampon

**buffet** *n* ['bufeɪ] (*food BRIT*: *bar*) buffet *m* ▷ *vt* ['bʌfɪt] secouer, ébranler; **buffet car** *n* (*BRIT Rail*) voiture-bar *f*

**bug** [bʌg] *n* (*bedbug etc*) punaise *f*; (*esp us*: *any insect*) insecte *m*, bestiole *f*; (*fig*: *germ*) virus *m*, microbe *m*; (*spy device*) dispositif *m* d'écoute (électronique), micro clandestin; (*Comput: of program*) erreur *f* ▷ *vt* (*room*) poser des micros dans; (*inf: annoy*) embêter

**buggy** ['bʌgɪ] *n* poussette *f*

**build** [bɪld] *n* (*of person*) carrure *f*, charpente *f* ▷ *vt* (*pt, pp* **built**) construire, bâtir; **build up** *vt* accumuler, amasser; (*business*) développer; (*reputation*) bâtir; **builder** *n* entrepreneur *m*; **building** *n* (*trade*) construction *f*; (*structure*) bâtiment *m*, construction *f*; (: *residential, offices*) immeuble *m*; **building site** *n* chantier

*m* (de construction); **building society** *n* (*BRIT*) société *f* de crédit immobilier

**built** [bɪlt] *pt, pp of* **build**; **built-in** *adj* (*cupboard*) encastré(e); (*device*) incorporé(e), intégré(e); **built-up** *adj*: **built-up area** zone urbanisée

**bulb** [bʌlb] *n* (*Bot*) bulbe *m*, oignon *m*; (*Elec*) ampoule *f*

**Bulgaria** [bʌl'geərɪə] *n* Bulgarie *f*; **Bulgarian** *adj* bulgare ▷ *n* Bulgare *m/f*

**bulge** [bʌldʒ] *n* renflement *m*, gonflement *m* ▷ *vi* faire saillie; présenter un renflement; (*pocket, file*): **to be bulging with** être plein(e) à craquer de

**bulimia** [bə'lɪmɪə] *n* boulimie *f*

**bulimic** [bju:'lɪmɪk] *adj, n* boulimique (*m/f*)

**bulk** [bʌlk] *n* masse *f*, volume *m*; **in ~** (*Comm*) en gros, en vrac; **the ~ of** la plus grande *or* grosse partie de; **bulky** *adj* volumineux(-euse), encombrant(e)

**bull** [bul] *n* taureau *m*; (*male elephant, whale*) mâle *m*

**bulldozer** ['buldəuzəʳ] *n* bulldozer *m*

**bullet** ['bulɪt] *n* balle *f* (*de fusil etc*)

**bulletin** ['bulɪtɪn] *n* bulletin *m*, communiqué *m*; (*also*: **news ~**) (bulletin d')informations *fpl*; **bulletin board** *n* (*Comput*) messagerie *f* (électronique)

**bullfight** ['bulfaɪt] *n* corrida *f*, course *f* de taureaux; **bullfighter** *n* torero *m*; **bullfighting** *n* tauromachie *f*

**bully** ['bulɪ] *n* brute *f*, tyran *m* ▷ *vt* tyranniser, rudoyer

**bum** [bʌm] *n* (*inf: BRIT: backside*) derrière *m*; (: *esp us: tramp*) vagabond(e), traîne-savates *m/f inv*; (: *idler*) glandeur *m*

**bumblebee** ['bʌmblbiː] *n* bourdon *m*

**bump** [bʌmp] *n* (*blow*) coup *m*, choc *m*; (*jolt*) cahot *m*; (*on road etc, on head*) bosse *f* ▷ *vt* heurter, cogner; (*car*) emboutir; **bump into** *vt fus* rentrer dans, tamponner; (*inf: meet*) tomber sur; **bumper** *n* pare-chocs *m inv* ▷ *adj*: **bumper crop/harvest** récolte/moisson exceptionnelle; **bumpy** *adj* (*road*) cahoteux(-euse); **it was a**

bumpy flight/ride on a été secoués dans l'avion/la voiture

**bun** [bʌn] n (cake) petit gâteau; (bread) petit pain au lait; (of hair) chignon m

**bunch** [bʌntʃ] n (of flowers) bouquet m; (of keys) trousseau m; (of bananas) régime m; (of people) groupe m; **bunches** npl (in hair) couettes fpl; **~ of grapes** grappe f de raisin

**bundle** ['bʌndl] n paquet m ▷ vt (also: **~ up**) faire un paquet de; (put): **to ~ sth/sb into** fourrer or enfourner qch/qn dans

**bungalow** ['bʌŋɡələu] n bungalow m

**bungee jumping** ['bʌndʒi:'dʒʌmpɪŋ] n saut m à l'élastique

**bunion** ['bʌnjən] n oignon m (au pied)

**bunk** [bʌŋk] n couchette f; **bunk beds** npl lits superposés

**bunker** ['bʌŋkəʳ] n (coal store) soute f à charbon; (Mil, Golf) bunker m

**bunny** ['bʌnɪ] n (also: **~ rabbit**) lapin m

**buoy** [bɔɪ] n bouée f; **buoyant** adj (ship) flottable; (carefree) gai(e), plein(e) d'entrain; (Comm: market, economy) actif(-ive)

**burden** ['bə:dn] n fardeau m, charge f ▷ vt charger; (oppress) accabler, surcharger

**bureau** (pl **~x**) ['bjuərəu, -z] n (BRIT: writing desk) bureau m, secrétaire m; (US: chest of drawers) commode f; (office) bureau, office m

**bureaucracy** [bjuə'rɔkrəsɪ] n bureaucratie f

**bureaucrat** ['bjuərəkræt] n bureaucrate m/f, rond-de-cuir m

**bureau de change** [-də'ʃɑːʒ] (pl **bureaux de change**) n bureau m de change

**bureaux** ['bjuərəuz] npl of **bureau**

**burger** ['bə:ɡəʳ] n hamburger m

**burglar** ['bə:ɡləʳ] n cambrioleur m; **burglar alarm** n sonnerie f d'alarme; **burglary** n cambriolage m

**Burgundy** ['bə:ɡəndɪ] n Bourgogne f

**burial** ['bɛrɪəl] n enterrement m

**burn** [bə:n] vt, vi (pt, pp **~ed** or **~t**) brûler

▷ n brûlure f; **burn down** vt incendier, détruire par le feu; **burn out** vt (writer etc): **to ~ o.s. out** s'user (à force de travailler); **burning** adj (building, forest) en flammes; (issue, question) brûlant(e); (ambition) dévorant(e)

**Burns' Night** [bə:nz-] n fête écossaise à la mémoire du poète Robert Burns

● **BURNS NIGHT**
●
● **Burns Night** est une fête qui a lieu
● le 25 janvier, à la mémoire du poète
● écossais Robert Burns (1759 - 1796),
● à l'occasion de laquelle les Écossais
● partout dans le monde organisent
● un souper, en général arrosé de
● whisky. Le plat principal est toujours
● le haggis, servi avec de la purée de
● pommes de terre et de la purée de
● rutabagas. On apporte le haggis au
● son des cornemuses et au cours du
● repas on lit des poèmes de Burns et
● on chante ses chansons.

**burnt** [bə:nt] pt, pp of **burn**

**burp** [bə:p] (inf) n rot m ▷ vi roter

**burrow** ['bʌrəu] n terrier m ▷ vi (rabbit) creuser un terrier; (rummage) fouiller

**burst** [bə:st] (pt, pp **~**) vt faire éclater; (river: banks etc) rompre ▷ vi éclater; (tyre) crever ▷ n explosion f; (also: **~ pipe**) fuite f (due à une rupture); **a ~ of enthusiasm/energy** un accès d'enthousiasme/d'énergie; **to ~ into flames** s'enflammer soudainement; **to ~ out laughing** éclater de rire; **to ~ into tears** fondre en larmes; **to ~ open** vi s'ouvrir violemment or soudainement; **to be ~ing with** (container) être plein(e) (à craquer) de, regorger de; (fig) être débordant(e) de; **burst into** vt fus (room etc) faire irruption dans

**bury** ['bɛrɪ] vt enterrer

**bus** (pl **~es**) [bʌs, 'bʌsɪz] n autobus m; **bus conductor** n receveur(-euse) m/f de bus

**bush** [buʃ] n buisson m; (scrub land)

brousse f; **to beat about the ~** tourner autour du pot

**business** ['bɪznɪs] n (matter, firm) affaire f; (trading) affaires fpl; (job, duty) travail m; **to be away on ~** être en déplacement d'affaires; **it's none of my ~** ce ne me regarde pas, ce ne sont pas mes affaires; **he means ~** il ne plaisante pas, il est sérieux; **business class** n (on plane) classe f affaires; **businesslike** adj sérieux(-euse), efficace; **businessman** (irreg) n homme m d'affaires; **business trip** n voyage m d'affaires; **businesswoman** (irreg) n femme f d'affaires

**busker** ['bʌskə<sup>r</sup>] n (BRIT) artiste ambulant(e)

**bus**: **bus pass** n carte f de bus; **bus shelter** n abribus m; **bus station** n gare routière; **bus-stop** n arrêt m d'autobus

**bust** [bʌst] n buste m; (measurement) tour m de poitrine ▷ adj (inf: broken) fichu(e), fini(e); **to go ~** faire faillite

**bustling** ['bʌslɪŋ] adj (town) très animé(e)

**busy** ['bɪzɪ] adj occupé(e); (shop, street) très fréquenté(e); (us: telephone, line) occupé ▷ vt: **to ~ o.s.** s'occuper; **busy signal** n (us) tonalité f occupé inv

🔘 **KEYWORD**

**but** [bʌt] conj mais; **I'd love to come, but I'm busy** j'aimerais venir mais je suis occupé; **he's not English but French** il n'est pas anglais mais français; **but that's far too expensive!** mais c'est bien trop cher!
▷ prep (apart from, except) sauf, excepté; **nothing but** rien d'autre que; **we've had nothing but trouble** nous n'avons eu que des ennuis; **no-one but him can do it** lui seul peut le faire; **who but a lunatic would do such a thing?** qui sinon un fou ferait une chose pareille?; **but for you/your help** sans toi/ton aide; **anything but that** tout sauf or

excepté ça, tout mais pas ça
▷ adv (just, only) ne ... que; **she's but a child** elle n'est qu'une enfant; **had I but known** si seulement j'avais su; **I can but try** je peux toujours essayer; **all but finished** pratiquement terminé

**butcher** ['bʊtʃə<sup>r</sup>] n boucher m ▷ vt massacrer; (cattle etc for meat) tuer; **butcher's (shop)** n boucherie f

**butler** ['bʌtlə<sup>r</sup>] n maître m d'hôtel

**butt** [bʌt] n (cask) gros tonneau; (of gun) crosse f; (of cigarette) mégot m; (BRIT fig: target) cible f ▷ vt donner un coup de tête à

**butter** ['bʌtə<sup>r</sup>] n beurre m ▷ vt beurrer; **buttercup** n bouton m d'or

**butterfly** ['bʌtəflaɪ] n papillon m; (Swimming: also: **~ stroke**) brasse f papillon

**buttocks** ['bʌtəks] npl fesses fpl

**button** ['bʌtn] n bouton m; (us: badge) pin m ▷ vt (also: **~ up**) boutonner ▷ vi se boutonner

**buy** [baɪ] (pt, pp **bought**) vt acheter ▷ n achat m; **to ~ sb sth/sth from sb** acheter qch à qn; **to ~ sb a drink** offrir un verre or à boire à qn; **can I ~ you a drink?** je vous offre un verre?; **where can I ~ some postcards?** où est-ce que je peux acheter des cartes postales?; **buy out** vt (partner) désintéresser; **buy up** vt acheter en bloc, rafler; **buyer** n acheteur(-euse) m/f

**buzz** [bʌz] n bourdonnement m; (inf: phone call): **to give sb a ~** passer un coup de fil à qn ▷ vi bourdonner; **buzzer** n timbre m électrique

🔘 **KEYWORD**

**by** [baɪ] prep **1** (referring to cause, agent) par, de; **killed by lightning** tué par la foudre; **surrounded by a fence** entouré d'une barrière; **a painting by Picasso** un tableau de Picasso
**2** (referring to method, manner, means): **by bus/car** en autobus/voiture; **by train**

par le or en train; **to pay by cheque**
payer par chèque; **by moonlight/
candlelight** à la lueur de la lune/d'une
bougie; **by saving hard, he ...** à force
d'économiser, il ...
**3** (*via, through*) par; **we came by Dover**
nous sommes venus par Douvres
**4** (*close to, past*) à côté de; **the house by
the school** la maison à côté de l'école;
**a holiday by the sea** des vacances au
bord de la mer; **she went by me** elle est
passée à côté de moi; **I go by the post
office every day** je passe devant la
poste tous les jours
**5** (*with time: not later than*) avant;
(: *during*): **by daylight** à la lumière du
jour; **by night** la nuit, de nuit; **by 4
o'clock** avant 4 heures; **by this time
tomorrow** d'ici demain à la même
heure; **by the time I got here it was
too late** lorsque je suis arrivé il était
déjà trop tard
**6** (*amount*) à; **by the kilo/metre** au
kilo/au mètre; **paid by the hour** payé
à l'heure
**7** (*Math: measure*): **to divide/multiply
by 3** diviser/multiplier par 3; **a room 3
metres by 4** une pièce de 3 mètres sur
4; **it's broader by a metre** c'est plus
large d'un mètre
**8** (*according to*) d'après, selon; **it's 3
o'clock by my watch** il est 3 heures à
ma montre; **it's all right by me** je n'ai
rien contre
**9**: (**all**) **by oneself** *etc* tout(e) seul(e)
▷ *adv* **1** *see* **go**; **pass** *etc*
**2**: **by and by** un peu plus tard, bientôt;
**by and large** dans l'ensemble

**bye(-bye)** ['baɪ('baɪ)] *excl* au revoir!,
salut!
**by-election** ['baɪɪlɛkʃən] *n* (*BRIT*)
élection (législative) partielle
**bypass** ['baɪpɑːs] *n* rocade *f*; (*Med*)
pontage *m* ▷ *vt* éviter
**byte** [baɪt] *n* (*Comput*) octet *m*

# C

**C** [siː] *n* (*Mus*): **C** do *m*
**cab** [kæb] *n* taxi *m*; (*of train, truck*)
cabine *f*
**cabaret** ['kæbəreɪ] *n* (*show*) spectacle
*m* de cabaret
**cabbage** ['kæbɪdʒ] *n* chou *m*
**cabin** ['kæbɪn] *n* (*house*) cabane *f*,
hutte *f*; (*on ship*) cabine *f*; (*on plane*)
compartiment *m*; **cabin crew** *n* (*Aviat*)
équipage *m*
**cabinet** ['kæbɪnɪt] *n* (*Pol*) cabinet *m*;
(*furniture*) petit meuble à tiroirs et
rayons; (*also*: **display ~**) vitrine *f*, petite
armoire vitrée; **cabinet minister** *n*
ministre *m* (*membre du cabinet*)
**cable** ['keɪbl] *n* câble *m* ▷ *vt*
câbler, télégraphier; **cable car** *n*
téléphérique *m*; **cable television** *n*
télévision *f* par câble
**cactus** (*pl* **cacti**) ['kæktəs, -taɪ] *n*
cactus *m*
**café** ['kæfeɪ] *n* ≈ café(-restaurant) *m*
(*sans alcool*)
**cafeteria** [kæfɪ'tɪərɪə] *n* cafétéria *f*

**caffein(e)** ['kæfi:n] n caféine f
**cage** [keɪdʒ] n cage f
**cagoule** [kə'guːl] n K-way® m
**Cairo** ['kaɪərəʊ] n le Caire
**cake** [keɪk] n gâteau m; **~ of soap**
savonnette f
**calcium** ['kælsɪəm] n calcium m
**calculate** ['kælkjʊleɪt] vt calculer;
(estimate: chances, effect) évaluer;
**calculation** [kælkjʊ'leɪʃən] n calcul m;
**calculator** n calculatrice f
**calendar** ['kæləndəʳ] n calendrier m
**calf** (pl **calves**) [kɑːf, kɑːvz] n (of cow)
veau m; (of other animals) petit m;
(also: **~skin**) veau m, vachette f; (Anat)
mollet m
**calibre** (US **caliber**) ['kælɪbəʳ] n
calibre m
**call** [kɔːl] vt appeler; (meeting)
convoquer ▷ vi appeler; (visit: also: **~
in**, **~ round**) passer ▷ n (shout) appel
m, cri m; (also: **telephone ~**) coup
m de téléphone; **to be on ~** être de
permanence; **to be ~ed** s'appeler; **can
I make a ~ from here?** est-ce que je
peux téléphoner d'ici?; **call back** vi
(return) repasser; (Tel) rappeler ▷ vt
(Tel) rappeler; **can you ~ back later?**
pouvez-vous rappeler plus tard?; **call
for** vt fus (demand) demander; (fetch)
passer prendre; **call in** vt (doctor, expert,
police) appeler, faire venir; **call off** vt
annuler; **call on** vt fus (visit) rendre
visite à, passer voir; (request): **to ~ on
sb to do** inviter qn à faire; **call out** vi
pousser un cri or des cris; **call up** vt
(Mil) appeler, mobiliser; (Tel) appeler;
**callbox** n (BRIT) cabine f téléphonique;
**call centre** (US **call center**) n centre m
d'appels; **caller** n (Tel) personne f qui
appelle; (visitor) visiteur m
**callous** ['kæləs] adj dur(e), insensible
**calm** [kɑːm] adj calme ▷ n calme m
▷ vt calmer, apaiser; **calm down** vi se
calmer, s'apaiser ▷ vt calmer, apaiser;
**calmly** ['kɑːmlɪ] adv calmement,
avec calme
**Calor gas®** ['kæləʳ-] n (BRIT) butane m,

butagaz® m
**calorie** ['kælərɪ] n calorie f
**calves** [kɑːvz] npl of **calf**
**Cambodia** [kæm'bəʊdɪə] n
Cambodge m
**camcorder** ['kæmkɔːdəʳ] n
caméscope m
**came** [keɪm] pt of **come**
**camel** ['kæməl] n chameau m
**camera** ['kæmərə] n appareil-photo m;
(Cine, TV) caméra f; **in ~** à huis clos, en
privé; **cameraman** n caméraman m;
**camera phone** n téléphone m avec
appareil photo numérique intégré
**camouflage** ['kæməflɑːʒ] n
camouflage m ▷ vt camoufler
**camp** [kæmp] n camp m ▷ vi camper
▷ adj (man) efféminé(e)
**campaign** [kæm'peɪn] n (Mil,
Pol etc) campagne f ▷ vi (also fig)
faire campagne; **campaigner** n:
**campaigner for** partisan(e) de;
**campaigner against** opposant(e) à
**camp**: **campbed** n (BRIT) lit m de camp;
**camper** n campeur(-euse); (vehicle)
camping-car m; **campground** (US) n
(terrain m de) camping m; **camping**
camping m de); **to go camping** faire du
camping; **campsite** n (terrain m de)
camping m
**campus** ['kæmpəs] n campus m
**can¹** [kæn] n (of milk, oil, water) bidon m;
(tin) boîte f (de conserve) ▷ vt mettre
en conserve

◯ **KEYWORD**

**can²** [kæn] (negative **cannot, can't**,
conditional and pt **could**) aux vb **1** (be able
to) pouvoir; **you can do it if you try**
vous pouvez le faire si vous essayez; **I
can't hear you** je ne t'entends pas
**2** (know how to) savoir; **I can swim/
play tennis/drive** je sais nager/jouer
au tennis/conduire; **can you speak
French?** parlez-vous français?
**3** (may) pouvoir; **can I use your phone?**
puis-je me servir de votre téléphone?

**4** (expressing disbelief, puzzlement etc):
**it can't be true!** ce n'est pas possible!;
**what can he want?** qu'est-ce qu'il peut
bien vouloir?

**5** (expressing possibility, suggestion etc):
**he could be in the library** il est peut-
être dans la bibliothèque; **she could
have been delayed** il se peut qu'elle ait
été retardée

**Canada** ['kænədə] n Canada m;
**Canadian** [kə'neɪdɪən] adj
canadien(ne) ▷ n Canadien(ne)
**canal** [kə'næl] n canal m
**canary** [kə'nɛərɪ] n canari m, serin m
**cancel** ['kænsəl] vt annuler; (train)
supprimer; (party, appointment)
décommander; (cross out) barrer, rayer;
(cheque) faire opposition à; **I would
like to ~ my booking** je voudrais
annuler ma réservation; **cancellation**
[kænsə'leɪʃən] n annulation f;
suppression f
**Cancer** ['kænsər] n (Astrology) le Cancer
**cancer** ['kænsər] n cancer m
**candidate** ['kændɪdeɪt] n candidat(e)
**candle** ['kændl] n bougie f; (in church)
cierge m; **candlestick** n (also: **candle
holder**) bougeoir m; (bigger, ornate)
chandelier m
**candy** ['kændɪ] n sucre candi; (US)
bonbon m; **candy bar** (US) n barre f
chocolatée; **candyfloss** n (BRIT) barbe
f à papa
**cane** [keɪn] n canne f; (for baskets, chairs
etc) rotin m ▷ vt (BRIT Scol) administrer
des coups de bâton à
**canister** ['kænɪstər] n boîte f (gén en
métal); (of gas) bombe f
**cannabis** ['kænəbɪs] n (drug)
cannabis m
**canned** ['kænd] adj (food) en boîte,
en conserve; (inf: music) enregistré(e);
(BRIT inf: drunk) bourré(e); (US inf: worker)
mis(e) à la porte
**cannon** (pl ~ or ~s) ['kænən] n (gun)
canon m
**cannot** ['kænɔt] = can not

**canoe** [kə'nu:] n pirogue f; (Sport)
canoë m; **canoeing** n (sport) canoë m
**canon** ['kænən] n (clergyman) chanoine
m; (standard) canon m
**can-opener** [-'əupnər] n ouvre-boîte m
**can't** [kɑ:nt] = can not
**canteen** [kæn'ti:n] n (eating place)
cantine f; (BRIT: of cutlery) ménagère f
**canter** ['kæntər] vi aller au petit galop
**canvas** ['kænvəs] n toile f
**canvass** ['kænvəs] vi (Pol): **to ~ for**
faire campagne pour ▷ vt (citizens,
opinions) sonder
**canyon** ['kænjən] n cañon m, gorge f
(profonde)
**cap** [kæp] n casquette f; (for swimming)
bonnet m de bain; (of pen) capuchon m;
(of bottle) capsule f; (BRIT: contraceptive:
also: **Dutch ~**) diaphragme m ▷ vt
(outdo) surpasser; (put limit on)
plafonner
**capability** [keɪpə'bɪlɪtɪ] n aptitude
f, capacité f
**capable** ['keɪpəbl] adj capable
**capacity** [kə'pæsɪtɪ] n (of container)
capacité f, contenance f; (ability)
aptitude f
**cape** [keɪp] n (garment) cape f; (Geo)
cap m
**caper** ['keɪpər] n (Culin: gen pl) câpre f;
(prank) farce f
**capital** ['kæpɪtl] n (also: **~ city**)
capitale f; (money) capital m; (also:
**~ letter**) majuscule f; **capitalism**
n capitalisme m; **capitalist** adj, n
capitaliste m/f; **capital punishment** n
peine capitale
**Capitol** ['kæpɪtl] n: **the ~** le Capitole
**Capricorn** ['kæprɪkɔːn] n le Capricorne
**capsize** [kæp'saɪz] vt faire chavirer
▷ vi chavirer
**capsule** ['kæpsjuːl] n capsule f
**captain** ['kæptɪn] n capitaine m
**caption** ['kæpʃən] n légende f
**captivity** [kæp'tɪvɪtɪ] n captivité f
**capture** ['kæptʃər] vt (prisoner, animal)
capturer; (town) prendre; (attention)
capter; (Comput) saisir ▷ n capture f; (of

*data*) saisie f de données

**car** [kɑ:ʳ] n voiture f, auto f; (*US Rail*) wagon m, voiture

**carafe** [kəˈræf] n carafe f

**caramel** [ˈkærəməl] n caramel m

**carat** [ˈkærət] n carat m

**caravan** [ˈkærəvæn] n caravane f; **caravan site** n (*BRIT*) camping m pour caravanes

**carbohydrate** [kɑ:bəuˈhaɪdreɪt] n hydrate m de carbone; (*food*) féculent m

**carbon** [ˈkɑ:bən] n carbone m; **carbon dioxide** [-daɪˈɔksaɪd] n gaz m carbonique, dioxyde m de carbone; **carbon monoxide** [-mɔˈnɔksaɪd] n oxyde m de carbone

**car boot sale** n voir encadré

- **CAR BOOT SALE**
-
- Type de brocante très populaire, où
- chacun vide sa cave ou son grenier.
- Les articles sont présentés dans
- des coffres de voitures et la vente
- a souvent lieu sur un parking ou
- dans un champ. Les brocanteurs
- d'un jour doivent s'acquitter d'une
- petite contribution pour participer
- à la vente.

**carburettor** (*US* **carburetor**) [kɑ:bjuˈretəʳ] n carburateur m

**card** [kɑ:d] n carte f; (*material*) carton m; **cardboard** n carton m; **card game** n jeu m de cartes

**cardigan** [ˈkɑ:dɪgən] n cardigan m

**cardinal** [ˈkɑ:dɪnl] adj cardinal(e); (*importance*) capital(e) ▷ n cardinal m

**cardphone** [ˈkɑ:dfəun] n téléphone m à carte (magnétique)

**care** [kɛəʳ] n soin m, attention f; (*worry*) souci m ▷ vi: **to ~ about** (*feel interest for*) se soucier de, s'intéresser à; (*person: love*) être attaché(e) à; **in sb's ~** à la garde de qn, confié à qn; **~ of** (*on letter*) chez; **to take ~ (to do)** faire attention (à faire); **to take ~ of** vt s'occuper de; **I don't ~** ça m'est bien

égal, peu m'importe; **I couldn't ~ less** cela m'est complètement égal, je m'en fiche complètement; **care for** vt fus s'occuper de; (*like*) aimer

**career** [kəˈrɪəʳ] n carrière f ▷ vi (*also: ~ along*) aller à toute allure

**care: carefree** adj sans souci, insouciant(e); **careful** adj soigneux(-euse); (*cautious*) prudent(e); **(be) careful!** (fais) attention!; **carefully** adv avec soin, soigneusement; prudemment; **caregiver** (*US*) n (*professional*) travailleur social; (*unpaid*) personne qui s'occupe d'un proche qui est malade; **careless** adj négligent(e); (*heedless*) insouciant(e); **carelessness** n manque m de soin, négligence f; insouciance f; **carer** [ˈkɛərəʳ] n (*professional*) travailleur social; (*unpaid*) personne qui s'occupe d'un proche qui est malade; **caretaker** n gardien(ne), concierge m/f

**car-ferry** [ˈkɑ:fɛrɪ] n (*on sea*) ferry(-boat) m; (*on river*) bac m

**cargo** (*pl ~es*) [ˈkɑ:gəu] n cargaison f, chargement m

**car hire** n (*BRIT*) location f de voitures

**Caribbean** [kærɪˈbi:ən] adj, n: **the ~ (Sea)** la mer des Antilles or des Caraïbes

**caring** [ˈkɛərɪŋ] adj (*person*) bienveillant(e); (*society, organization*) humanitaire

**carnation** [kɑ:ˈneɪʃən] n œillet m

**carnival** [ˈkɑ:nɪvl] n (*public celebration*) carnaval m; (*US: funfair*) fête foraine

**carol** [ˈkærəl] n: **(Christmas) ~** chant m de Noël

**carousel** [kærəˈsɛl] n (*for luggage*) carrousel m; (*US*) manège m

**car park** (*BRIT*) n parking m, parc m de stationnement

**carpenter** [ˈkɑ:pɪntəʳ] n charpentier m; (*joiner*) menuisier m

**carpet** [ˈkɑ:pɪt] n tapis m ▷ vt recouvrir (d'un tapis); **fitted ~** (*BRIT*) moquette f

**car rental** n (*US*) location f de voitures

**carriage** [ˈkærɪdʒ] n (*BRIT Rail*)

wagon m; (horse-drawn) voiture f; (of goods) transport m; (: cost) port m; **carriageway** n (BRIT: part of road) chaussée f

**carrier** ['kærɪəʳ] n transporteur m, camionneur m; (company) entreprise f de transport; (Med) porteur(-euse); **carrier bag** n (BRIT) sac m en papier or en plastique

**carrot** ['kærət] n carotte f

**carry** ['kærɪ] vt (subj: person) porter; (: vehicle) transporter; (involve: responsibilities etc) comporter, impliquer; (Med: disease) être porteur de ▷ vi (sound) porter; **to get carried away** (fig) s'emballer, s'enthousiasmer; **carry on** vi (continue) continuer ▷ vt (conduct: business) diriger; (: conversation) entretenir; (: continue: business, conversation) continuer; **to ~ on with sth/doing** continuer qch/à faire; **carry out** vt (orders) exécuter; (investigation) effectuer

**cart** [kɑːt] n charrette f ▷ vt (inf) transporter

**carton** ['kɑːtən] n (box) carton m; (of yogurt) pot m (en carton)

**cartoon** [kɑːˈtuːn] n (Press) dessin m (humoristique); (satirical) caricature f; (comic strip) bande dessinée; (Cine) dessin animé

**cartridge** ['kɑːtrɪdʒ] n (for gun, pen) cartouche f

**carve** [kɑːv] vt (meat: also: ~ up) découper; (wood, stone) tailler, sculpter; **carving** n (in wood etc) sculpture f

**car wash** n station f de lavage (de voitures)

**case** [keɪs] n cas m; (Law) affaire f, procès m; (box) caisse f, boîte f; (for glasses) étui m; (BRIT: also: **suit~**) valise f; **in ~ of** en cas de; **in ~ he** au cas où il; **just in ~** à tout hasard; **in any ~** en tout cas, de toute façon

**cash** [kæʃ] n argent m; (Comm) (argent m) liquide m ▷ vt encaisser; **to pay (in) ~** payer (en argent) comptant or en espèces; **~ with order/on delivery** (Comm) payable or paiement à la commande/livraison; **I haven't got any ~** je n'ai pas de liquide; **cashback** n (discount) remise f; (at supermarket etc) retrait m (à la caisse); **cash card** n carte f de retrait; **cash desk** n (BRIT) caisse f; **cash dispenser** n distributeur m automatique de billets

**cashew** [kæˈʃuː] n (also: ~ **nut**) noix f de cajou

**cashier** [kæˈʃɪəʳ] n caissier(-ère)

**cashmere** ['kæʃmɪəʳ] n cachemire m

**cash point** n distributeur m automatique de billets

**cash register** n caisse enregistreuse

**casino** [kəˈsiːnəu] n casino m

**casket** ['kɑːskɪt] n coffret m; (US: coffin) cercueil m

**casserole** ['kæsərəul] n (pot) cocotte f; (food) ragoût m (en cocotte)

**cassette** [kæˈsɛt] n cassette f; **cassette player** n lecteur m de cassettes

**cast** [kɑːst] (vb: pt, pp ~) vt (throw) jeter; (shadow: lit) projeter; (: fig) jeter; (glance) jeter ▷ n (Theat) distribution f; (also: **plaster ~**) plâtre m; **to ~ sb as Hamlet** attribuer à qn le rôle d'Hamlet; **to ~ one's vote** voter, exprimer son suffrage; **to ~ doubt on** jeter un doute sur; **cast off** vi (Naut) larguer les amarres; (Knitting) arrêter les mailles

**castanets** [kæstəˈnɛts] npl castagnettes fpl

**caster sugar** ['kɑːstə-] n (BRIT) sucre m semoule

**cast-iron** ['kɑːstaɪən] adj (lit) de or en fonte; (fig: will) de fer; (alibi) en béton

**castle** ['kɑːsl] n château m; (fortress) château-fort m; (Chess) tour f

**casual** ['kæʒjul] adj (by chance) de hasard, fait(e) au hasard, fortuit(e); (irregular: work etc) temporaire; (unconcerned) désinvolte; **~ wear** vêtements mpl sport inv

**casualty** ['kæʒjultɪ] n accidenté(e), blessé(e); (dead) victime f, mort(e); (BRIT: Med: department) urgences fpl

**cat** [kæt] n chat m

**Catalan** ['kætələn] *adj* catalan(e)

**catalogue** (*us* **catalog**) ['kætələɡ] *n* catalogue *m* ▷ *vt* cataloguer

**catalytic converter** [kætə'lɪtɪkkən'vɜːtə<sup>r</sup>] *n* pot *m* catalytique

**cataract** ['kætərækt] *n* (*also Med*) cataracte *f*

**catarrh** [kə'tɑː<sup>r</sup>] *n* rhume *m* chronique, catarrhe *f*

**catastrophe** [kə'tæstrəfɪ] *n* catastrophe *f*

**catch** [kætʃ] (*pt, pp* **caught**) *vt* attraper; (*person: by surprise*) prendre, surprendre; (*understand*) saisir; (*get entangled*) accrocher ▷ *vi* (*fire*) prendre; (*get entangled*) s'accrocher ▷ *n* (*fish etc*) prise *f*; (*hidden problem*) attrape *f*; (*Tech*) loquet *m*; cliquet *m*; **to ~ sb's attention** *or* **eye** attirer l'attention de qn; **to ~ fire** prendre feu; **to ~ sight of** apercevoir; **catch up** *vi* (*with work*) se rattraper, combler son retard ▷ *vt* (*also: ~ **up with**) rattraper; **catching** ['kætʃɪŋ] *adj* (*Med*) contagieux(-euse)

**category** ['kætɪɡərɪ] *n* catégorie *f*

**cater** ['keɪtə<sup>r</sup>] *vi*: **to ~ for** (*BRIT: needs*) satisfaire, pourvoir à; (*: readers, consumers*) s'adresser à, pourvoir aux besoins de; (*Comm: parties etc*) préparer des repas pour

**caterpillar** ['kætəpɪlə<sup>r</sup>] *n* chenille *f*

**cathedral** [kə'θiːdrəl] *n* cathédrale *f*

**Catholic** ['kæθəlɪk] (*Rel*) *adj* catholique ▷ *n* catholique *m/f*

**Catseye®** ['kæts'aɪ] *n* (*BRIT Aut*) (clou *m* à) catadioptre *m*

**cattle** ['kætl] *npl* bétail *m*, bestiaux *mpl*

**catwalk** ['kætwɔːk] *n* passerelle *f*; (*for models*) podium *m* (*de défilé de mode*)

**caught** [kɔːt] *pt, pp of* **catch**

**cauliflower** ['kɒlɪflauə<sup>r</sup>] *n* chou-fleur *m*

**cause** [kɔːz] *n* cause *f* ▷ *vt* causer

**caution** ['kɔːʃən] *n* prudence *f*; (*warning*) avertissement *m* ▷ *vt* avertir, donner un avertissement à; **cautious** *adj* prudent(e)

**cave** [keɪv] *n* caverne *f*, grotte *f*; **cave in** *vi* (*roof etc*) s'effondrer

**caviar(e)** ['kævɪɑː<sup>r</sup>] *n* caviar *m*

**cavity** ['kævɪtɪ] *n* cavité *f*; (*Med*) carie *f*

**cc** *abbr* (= *cubic centimetre*) cm³; (*on letter etc*) = **carbon copy**

**CCTV** *n abbr* = **closed-circuit television**

**CD** *n abbr* (= *compact disc*) CD *m*; **CD burner** *n* graveur *m* de CD; **CD player** *n* platine *f* laser; **CD-ROM** [siːdiː'rɔm] *n abbr* (= *compact disc read-only memory*) CD-ROM *m inv*; **CD writer** *n* graveur *m* de CD

**cease** [siːs] *vt, vi* cesser; **ceasefire** *n* cessez-le-feu *m*

**cedar** ['siːdə<sup>r</sup>] *n* cèdre *m*

**ceilidh** ['keɪlɪ] *n* bal *m* folklorique écossais *or* irlandais

**ceiling** ['siːlɪŋ] *n* (*also fig*) plafond *m*

**celebrate** ['sɛlɪbreɪt] *vt, vi* célébrer; **celebration** [sɛlɪ'breɪʃən] *n* célébration *f*

**celebrity** [sɪ'lɛbrɪtɪ] *n* célébrité *f*

**celery** ['sɛlərɪ] *n* céleri *m* (en branches)

**cell** [sɛl] *n* (*gen*) cellule *f*; (*Elec*) élément *m* (de pile)

**cellar** ['sɛlə<sup>r</sup>] *n* cave *f*

**cello** ['tʃɛləu] *n* violoncelle *m*

**Cellophane®** ['sɛləfeɪn] *n* cellophane® *f*

**cellphone** ['sɛlfəun] *n* téléphone *m* cellulaire

**Celsius** ['sɛlsɪəs] *adj* Celsius *inv*

**Celtic** ['kɛltɪk, 'sɛltɪk] *adj* celte, celtique

**cement** [sə'mɛnt] *n* ciment *m*

**cemetery** ['sɛmɪtrɪ] *n* cimetière *m*

**censor** ['sɛnsə<sup>r</sup>] *n* censeur *m* ▷ *vt* censurer; **censorship** *n* censure *f*

**census** ['sɛnsəs] *n* recensement *m*

**cent** [sɛnt] *n* (*unit of dollar, euro*) cent *m* (= un centième du dollar, de l'euro); *see also* **per**

**centenary** [sɛn'tiːnərɪ] (*us* **centennial**) [sɛn'tɛnɪəl]) *n* centenaire *m*

**center** ['sɛntə<sup>r</sup>] (*us*) = **centre**

**centi...** [sɛntɪ] *prefix*: **centigrade** *adj* centigrade; **centimetre** (*us*

**centimeter**) n centimètre m;
**centipede** ['sɛntɪpiːd] n mille-
pattes m inv
**central** ['sɛntrəl] adj central(e);
**Central America** n Amérique centrale;
**central heating** n chauffage central;
**central reservation** n (BRIT Aut) terre-
plein central
**centre** (US **center**) ['sɛntər] n centre m
▷ vt centrer; **centre-forward** n (Sport)
avant-centre m; **centre-half** n (Sport)
demi-centre m
**century** ['sɛntjuri] n siècle m; **in the
twentieth ~** au vingtième siècle
**CEO** n abbr (US) = **chief executive
officer**
**ceramic** [sɪ'ræmɪk] adj céramique
**cereal** ['siːrɪəl] n céréale f
**ceremony** ['sɛrɪmənɪ] n cérémonie f;
**to stand on ~** faire des façons
**certain** ['səːtən] adj certain(e);
**to make ~ of** s'assurer de; **for ~**
certainement, sûrement; **certainly**
adv certainement; **certainty** n
certitude f
**certificate** [sə'tɪfɪkɪt] n certificat m
**certify** ['səːtɪfaɪ] vt certifier; (award
diploma to) conférer un diplôme etc
à; (declare insane) déclarer malade
mental(e)
**cf.** abbr (= compare) cf., voir
**CFC** n abbr (= chlorofluorocarbon) CFC m
**chain** [tʃeɪn] n (gen) chaîne f ▷ vt
(also: ~ **up**) enchaîner, attacher (avec
une chaîne); **chain-smoke** vi fumer
cigarette sur cigarette
**chair** [tʃɛər] n chaise f; (armchair)
fauteuil m; (of university) chaire f; (of
meeting) présidence f ▷ vt (meeting)
présider; **chairlift** n télésiège m;
**chairman** n président m; **chairperson**
n président(e); **chairwoman** n
présidente f
**chalet** ['ʃæleɪ] n chalet m
**chalk** [tʃɔːk] n craie f; **chalkboard** (US)
n tableau noir
**challenge** ['tʃælɪndʒ] n défi m ▷ vt
défier; (statement, right) mettre en

question, contester; **to ~ sb to do**
mettre qn au défi de faire; **challenging**
adj (task, career) qui représente un défi
or une gageure; (tone, look) de défi,
provocateur(-trice)
**chamber** ['tʃeɪmbər] n chambre f; (BRIT
Law: gen pl) cabinet m; **~ of commerce**
chambre de commerce; **chambermaid**
n femme f de chambre
**champagne** [ʃæm'peɪn] n
champagne m
**champion** ['tʃæmpɪən] n (also of cause)
champion(ne); **championship** n
championnat m
**chance** [tʃɑːns] n (luck) hasard m;
(opportunity) occasion f, possibilité f;
(hope, likelihood) chance f; (risk) risque
m ▷ vt (risk) risquer ▷ adj fortuit(e), de
hasard; **to take a ~** prendre un risque;
**by ~** par hasard; **to ~ it** risquer le coup,
essayer
**chancellor** ['tʃɑːnsələr] n chancelier m;
**Chancellor of the Exchequer**
[-ɪks'tʃɛkər] (BRIT) n chancelier m de
l'Échiquier
**chandelier** [ʃændə'lɪər] n lustre m
**change** [tʃeɪndʒ] vt (alter, replace;
Comm: money) changer; (switch,
substitute: hands, trains, clothes,
one's name etc) changer de ▷ vi (gen)
changer; (change clothes) se changer;
(be transformed): **to ~ into** se changer
or transformer en ▷ n changement
m; (money) monnaie f; (Aut)
changer de vitesse; **to ~ one's mind**
changer d'avis; **a ~ of clothes** des
vêtements de rechange; **for a ~** pour
changer; **do you have ~ for £10?** vous
avez la monnaie de 10 livres?; **where
can I ~ some money?** où est-ce que je
peux changer de l'argent?; **keep the
~!** gardez la monnaie!; **change over**
vi (swap) échanger; (change: drivers
etc) changer; (change sides: players etc)
changer de côté; **to ~ over from sth to
sth** passer de qch à qch; **changeable**
adj (weather) variable; **change
machine** n distributeur m de monnaie;

**changing room** n (BRIT: in shop) salon m d'essayage; (: Sport) vestiaire m

**channel** ['tʃænl] n (TV) chaîne f; (waveband, groove, fig: medium) canal m; (of river, sea) chenal m ▷ vt canaliser; **the (English) C~** la Manche; **Channel Islands** npl: **the Channel Islands** les îles fpl Anglo-Normandes; **Channel Tunnel** n: **the Channel Tunnel** le tunnel sous la Manche

**chant** [tʃɑ:nt] n chant m; (Rel) psalmodie f ▷ vt chanter, scander

**chaos** ['keɪɒs] n chaos m

**chaotic** [keɪ'ɒtɪk] adj chaotique

**chap** [tʃæp] n (BRIT inf: man) type m

**chapel** ['tʃæpl] n chapelle f

**chapped** [tʃæpt] adj (skin, lips) gercé(e)

**chapter** ['tʃæptər] n chapitre m

**character** ['kærɪktər] n caractère m; (in novel, film) personnage m; (eccentric person) numéro m, phénomène m; **characteristic** ['kærɪktə'rɪstɪk] adj, n caractéristique (f); **characterize** ['kærɪktəraɪz] vt caractériser

**charcoal** ['tʃɑ:kəul] n charbon m de bois; (Art) charbon

**charge** [tʃɑ:dʒ] n (accusation) accusation f; (Law) inculpation f; (cost) prix (demandé) ▷ vt (gun, battery, Mil: enemy) charger; (customer, sum) faire payer ▷ vi foncer; **charges** npl (costs) frais mpl; (BRIT Tel): **to reverse the ~s** téléphoner en PCV; **to take ~ of** se charger de; **to be in ~ of** être responsable de, s'occuper de; **to ~ sb (with)** (Law) inculper qn (de); **charge card** n carte f de client (émise par un grand magasin); **charger** n (also: **battery charger**) chargeur m

**charismatic** [kærɪz'mætɪk] adj charismatique

**charity** ['tʃærɪtɪ] n charité f; (organization) institution f charitable or de bienfaisance, œuvre f (de charité); **charity shop** n (BRIT) boutique vendant des articles d'occasion au profit d'une organisation caritative

**charm** [tʃɑ:m] n charme m; (on bracelet) breloque f ▷ vt charmer, enchanter; **charming** adj charmant(e)

**chart** [tʃɑ:t] n tableau m, diagramme m; graphique m; (map) carte marine ▷ vt dresser or établir la carte de; (sales, progress) établir la courbe de; **charts** npl (Mus) hit-parade m; **to be in the ~s** (record, pop group) figurer au hit-parade

**charter** ['tʃɑ:tər] vt (plane) affréter ▷ n (document) charte f; **chartered accountant** n (BRIT) expert-comptable m; **charter flight** n charter m

**chase** [tʃeɪs] vt poursuivre, pourchasser; (also: **~ away**) chasser ▷ n poursuite f, chasse f

**chat** [tʃæt] vi (also: **have a ~**) bavarder, causer; (on Internet) chatter ▷ n conversation f; (BRIT inf: girl) baratiner; **chat up** vt (BRIT inf: girl) baratiner; **chat room** n (Internet) forum m de discussion; **chat show** n (BRIT) talk-show m

**chatter** ['tʃætər] vi (person) bavarder, papoter ▷ n bavardage m, papotage m; **my teeth are ~ing** je claque des dents

**chauffeur** ['ʃəufər] n chauffeur m (de maître)

**chauvinist** ['ʃəuvɪnɪst] n (also: **male ~**) phallocrate m, macho m; (nationalist) chauvin(e)

**cheap** [tʃi:p] adj bon marché inv, pas cher (chère); (reduced: ticket) à prix réduit; (: fare) réduit(e); (joke) facile, d'un goût douteux; (poor quality) à bon marché, de qualité médiocre ▷ adv à bon marché, pour pas cher; **can you recommend a ~ hotel/restaurant, please?** pourriez-vous m'indiquer un hôtel/restaurant bon marché?; **cheap day return** n billet m d'aller et retour réduit (valable pour la journée); **cheaply** adv à bon marché, à bon compte

**cheat** [tʃi:t] vi tricher; (in exam) copier ▷ vt tromper, duper; (rob): **to ~ sb out of sth** escroquer qch à qn ▷ n tricheur(-euse) m/f; escroc m; **cheat on** vt fus tromper

**Chechnya** [tʃɪtʃ'njɑ:] n Tchétchénie f

**check** [tʃɛk] vt vérifier; (*passport, ticket*) contrôler; (*halt*) enrayer; (*restrain*) maîtriser ▷ vi (*official etc*) se renseigner ▷ n vérification f; contrôle m; (*curb*) frein m; (BRIT: *bill*) addition f; (US) = **cheque**; (*pattern: gen pl*) carreaux mpl; **to ~ with sb** demander à qn; **check in** vi (*in hotel*) remplir sa fiche (d'hôtel); (*at airport*) se présenter à l'enregistrement ▷ vt (*luggage*) (faire) enregistrer; **check off** vt (*tick off*) cocher; **check out** vi (*in hotel*) régler sa note ▷ vt (*investigate: story*) vérifier; **check up** vi: **to ~ up (on sth)** vérifier (qch); **to ~ up on sb** se renseigner sur le compte de qn; **checkbook** (US) = **chequebook**; **checked** adj (*pattern, cloth*) à carreaux; **checkers** n (US) jeu m de dames; **check-in** n (*also*: **check-in desk**: *at airport*) enregistrement m; **checking account** n (US) compte courant; **checklist** n liste f de contrôle; **checkmate** n échec et mat m; **checkout** n (*in supermarket*) caisse f; **checkpoint** n contrôle m; **checkroom** (US) n consigne f; **checkup** n (*Med*) examen médical, check-up m

**cheddar** ['tʃɛdəʳ] n (*also*: **~ cheese**) cheddar m

**cheek** [tʃiːk] n joue f; (*impudence*) toupet m, culot m; **what a ~!** quel toupet!; **cheekbone** n pommette f; **cheeky** adj effronté(e), culotté(e)

**cheer** [tʃɪəʳ] vt acclamer, applaudir; (*gladden*) réjouir, réconforter ▷ vi applaudir ▷ n (*gen pl*) acclamations fpl, applaudissements mpl; bravos mpl, hourras mpl; **~s!** à la vôtre!; **cheer up** vi se dérider, reprendre courage ▷ vt remonter le moral à or de, dérider, égayer; **cheerful** adj gai(e), joyeux(-euse)

**cheerio** [tʃɪərɪ'əu] excl (BRIT) salut!, au revoir!

**cheerleader** ['tʃɪəliːdəʳ] n membre d'un groupe de majorettes qui chantent et dansent pour soutenir leur équipe pendant les matchs de football américain

**cheese** [tʃiːz] n fromage m; **cheeseburger** n cheeseburger m; **cheesecake** n tarte f au fromage

**chef** [ʃɛf] n chef (cuisinier)

**chemical** ['kɛmɪkl] adj chimique ▷ n produit m chimique

**chemist** ['kɛmɪst] n (BRIT: *pharmacist*) pharmacien(ne); (*scientist*) chimiste m/f; **chemistry** n chimie f; **chemist's (shop)** n (BRIT) pharmacie f

**cheque** (US **check**) [tʃɛk] n chèque m; **chequebook** (US **checkbook**) n chéquier m, carnet m de chèques; **cheque card** n (BRIT) carte f (d'identité) bancaire

**cherry** ['tʃɛrɪ] n cerise f; (*also*: **~ tree**) cerisier m

**chess** [tʃɛs] n échecs mpl

**chest** [tʃɛst] n poitrine f; (*box*) coffre m, caisse f

**chestnut** ['tʃɛsnʌt] n châtaigne f; (*also*: **~ tree**) châtaignier m

**chest of drawers** n commode f

**chew** [tʃuː] vt mâcher; **chewing gum** n chewing-gum m

**chic** [ʃiːk] adj chic inv, élégant(e)

**chick** [tʃɪk] n poussin m; (*inf*) pépée f

**chicken** ['tʃɪkɪn] n poulet m; (*inf: coward*) poule mouillée; **chicken out** vi (*inf*) se dégonfler; **chickenpox** n varicelle f

**chickpea** ['tʃɪkpiː] n pois m chiche

**chief** [tʃiːf] n chef m ▷ adj principal(e); **chief executive** (US **chief executive officer**) n directeur(-trice) général(e); **chiefly** adv principalement, surtout

**child** (pl **~ren**) [tʃaɪld, 'tʃɪldrən] n enfant m/f; **child abuse** n maltraitance f d'enfants; (*sexual*) abus mpl sexuels sur des enfants; **child benefit** n (BRIT) ≈ allocations familiales; **childbirth** n accouchement m; **child-care** n (*for working parents*) garde f des enfants (*pour les parents qui travaillent*); **childhood** n enfance f; **childish** adj puéril(e), enfantin(e); **child minder** n (BRIT) garde f d'enfants; **children** ['tʃɪldrən] npl of **child**

**Chile** ['tʃɪlɪ] n Chili m

**chill** [tʃɪl] n (of water) froid m; (of air) fraîcheur f; (Med) refroidissement m, coup m de froid ▷ vt (person) faire frissonner; (Culin) mettre au frais, rafraîchir; **chill out** vi (inf: esp US) se relaxer

**chil(l)i** ['tʃɪlɪ] n piment m (rouge)

**chilly** ['tʃɪlɪ] adj froid(e), glacé(e); (sensitive to cold) frileux(-euse)

**chimney** ['tʃɪmnɪ] n cheminée f

**chimpanzee** [tʃɪmpæn'ziː] n chimpanzé m

**chin** [tʃɪn] n menton m

**China** ['tʃaɪnə] n Chine f

**china** ['tʃaɪnə] n (material) porcelaine f; (crockery) (vaisselle f en) porcelaine

**Chinese** [tʃaɪ'niːz] adj chinois(e) ▷ n (pl inv) Chinois(e); (Ling) chinois m

**chip** [tʃɪp] n (gen pl: Culin: BRIT) frite f; (: US: also: **potato ~**) chip m; (of wood) copeau m; (of glass, stone) éclat m; (also: **micro~**) puce f; (in gambling) fiche f ▷ vt (cup, plate) ébrécher; **chip shop** n (BRIT) friterie f

● **CHIP SHOP**
●
● Un **chip shop**, que l'on appelle
● également un "fish-and-chip shop",
● est un magasin où l'on vend des plats
● à emporter. Les **chip shops** sont
● d'ailleurs à l'origine des "takeaways".
● On y achète en particulier du
● poisson frit et des frites, mais
● on y trouve également des plats
● traditionnels britanniques ("steak
● pies", saucisses, etc). Tous les plats
● étaient à l'origine emballés dans du
● papier journal. Dans certains de ces
● magasins, on peut s'asseoir pour
● consommer sur place.

**chiropodist** [kɪ'rɔpədɪst] n (BRIT) pédicure m/f

**chisel** ['tʃɪzl] n ciseau m

**chives** [tʃaɪvz] npl ciboulette f, civette f

**chlorine** ['klɔːriːn] n chlore m

**choc-ice** ['tʃɔkaɪs] n (BRIT) esquimau® m

**chocolate** ['tʃɔklɪt] n chocolat m

**choice** [tʃɔɪs] n choix m ▷ adj de choix

**choir** ['kwaɪə'] n chœur m, chorale f

**choke** [tʃəuk] vi étouffer ▷ vt étrangler; étouffer; (block) boucher, obstruer ▷ n (Aut) starter m

**cholesterol** [kə'lɛstərɔl] n cholestérol m

**choose** (pt **chose**, pp **chosen**) [tʃuːz, tʃəuz, 'tʃəuzn] vt choisir; **to ~ to do** décider de faire, juger bon de faire

**chop** [tʃɔp] vt (wood) couper (à la hache); (Culin: also: **~ up**) couper (fin), émincer, hacher (en morceaux) ▷ n (Culin) côtelette f; **chop down** vt (tree) abattre; **chop off** vt trancher; **chopsticks** ['tʃɔpstɪks] npl baguettes fpl

**chord** [kɔːd] n (Mus) accord m

**chore** [tʃɔː'] n travail m de routine; **household ~s** travaux mpl du ménage

**chorus** ['kɔːrəs] n chœur m; (repeated part of song, also fig) refrain m

**chose** [tʃəuz] pt of **choose**

**chosen** ['tʃəuzn] pp of **choose**

**Christ** [kraɪst] n Christ m

**christen** ['krɪsn] vt baptiser; **christening** n baptême m

**Christian** ['krɪstɪən] adj, n chrétien(ne); **Christianity** [krɪstɪ'ænɪtɪ] n christianisme m; **Christian name** n prénom m

**Christmas** ['krɪsməs] n Noël m or f; **happy** or **merry ~!** joyeux Noël!; **Christmas card** n carte f de Noël; **Christmas carol** n chant m de Noël; **Christmas Day** n le jour de Noël; **Christmas Eve** n la veille de Noël; la nuit de Noël; **Christmas pudding** n (esp BRIT) Christmas m pudding; **Christmas tree** n arbre m de Noël

**chrome** [krəum] n chrome m

**chronic** ['krɔnɪk] adj chronique

**chrysanthemum** [krɪ'sænθəməm] n chrysanthème m

**chubby** ['tʃʌbɪ] adj potelé(e),

rondelet(te)

**chuck** [tʃʌk] vt (inf) lancer, jeter; (BRIT: also: ~ **up**: job) lâcher; **chuck out** vt (inf: person) flanquer dehors or à la porte; (: rubbish etc) jeter

**chuckle** ['tʃʌkl] vi glousser

**chum** [tʃʌm] n copain (copine)

**chunk** [tʃʌŋk] n gros morceau

**church** [tʃə:tʃ] n église f; **churchyard** n cimetière m

**churn** [tʃə:n] n (for butter) baratte f; (also: **milk ~**) (grand) bidon à lait

**chute** [ʃu:t] n goulotte f; (also: **rubbish ~**) vide-ordures m inv; (BRIT: children's slide) toboggan m

**chutney** ['tʃʌtnɪ] n chutney m

**CIA** n abbr (= Central Intelligence Agency) CIA f

**CID** n abbr (= Criminal Investigation Department) ≈ P.J. f

**cider** ['saɪdə'] n cidre m

**cigar** [sɪ'gɑ:'] n cigare m

**cigarette** [sɪgə'rɛt] n cigarette f; **cigarette lighter** n briquet m

**cinema** ['sɪnəmə] n cinéma m

**cinnamon** ['sɪnəmən] n cannelle f

**circle** ['sə:kl] n cercle m; (in cinema) balcon m ▷ vi faire or décrire des cercles ▷ vt (surround) entourer, encercler; (move round) faire le tour de, tourner autour de

**circuit** ['sə:kɪt] n circuit m; (lap) tour m

**circular** ['sə:kjulə'] adj circulaire ▷ n circulaire f; (as advertisement) prospectus m

**circulate** ['sə:kjuleɪt] vi circuler ▷ vt faire circuler; **circulation** [sə:kju'leɪʃən] n circulation f; (of newspaper) tirage m

**circumstances** ['sə:kəmstənsɪz] npl circonstances fpl; (financial condition) moyens mpl, situation financière

**circus** ['sə:kəs] n cirque m

**cite** [saɪt] vt citer

**citizen** ['sɪtɪzn] n (Pol) citoyen(ne); (resident): **the ~s of this town** les habitants de cette ville; **citizenship** n citoyenneté f; (BRIT: Scol) ≈ éducation

f civique

**citrus fruits** ['sɪtrəs-] npl agrumes mpl

**city** ['sɪtɪ] n (grande) ville f; **the C~** la Cité de Londres (centre des affaires); **city centre** n centre ville m; **city technology college** n (BRIT) établissement m d'enseignement technologique (situé dans un quartier défavorisé)

**civic** ['sɪvɪk] adj civique; (authorities) municipal(e)

**civil** ['sɪvɪl] adj civil(e); (polite) poli(e), civil(e); **civilian** [sɪ'vɪlɪən] adj, n civil(e)

**civilization** [sɪvɪlaɪ'zeɪʃən] n civilisation f

**civilized** ['sɪvɪlaɪzd] adj civilisé(e); (fig) où règnent les bonnes manières

**civil**: **civil law** n code civil; (study) droit civil; **civil rights** npl droits mpl civiques; **civil servant** n fonctionnaire m/f; **Civil Service** n fonction publique, administration f; **civil war** n guerre civile

**CJD** n abbr (= Creutzfeldt-Jakob disease) MCJ f

**claim** [kleɪm] vt (rights etc) revendiquer; (compensation) réclamer; (assert) déclarer, prétendre ▷ vi (for insurance) faire une déclaration de sinistre ▷ n revendication f; prétention f; (right) droit m; **(insurance) ~** demande f d'indemnisation, déclaration f de sinistre; **claim form** n (gen) formulaire m de demande

**clam** [klæm] n palourde f

**clamp** [klæmp] n crampon m; (on workbench) valet m; (on car) sabot m de Denver ▷ vt attacher; (car) mettre un sabot à; **clamp down on** vt fus sévir contre, prendre des mesures draconiennes à l'égard de

**clan** [klæn] n clan m

**clap** [klæp] vi applaudir

**claret** ['klærət] n (vin m de) bordeaux m (rouge)

**clarify** ['klærɪfaɪ] vt clarifier

**clarinet** [klærɪ'nɛt] n clarinette f

**clarity** ['klærɪtɪ] n clarté f

**clash** [klæʃ] n (sound) choc m, fracas m; (with police) affrontement m; (fig) conflit m ▷ vi se heurter; être or entrer en conflit; (colours) jurer; (dates, events) tomber en même temps

**clasp** [klɑːsp] n (of necklace, bag) fermoir m ▷ vt serrer, étreindre

**class** [klɑːs] n (gen) classe f; (group, category) catégorie f ▷ vt classer, classifier

**classic** ['klæsɪk] adj classique ▷ n (author, work) classique m; **classical** adj classique

**classification** [klæsɪfɪ'keɪʃən] n classification f

**classify** ['klæsɪfaɪ] vt classifier, classer

**classmate** ['klɑːsmeɪt] n camarade m/f de classe

**classroom** ['klɑːsrum] n (salle f de) classe f; **classroom assistant** n assistant(-e) d'éducation

**classy** ['klɑːsɪ] (inf) adj classe (inf)

**clatter** ['klætər] n cliquetis m ▷ vi cliqueter

**clause** [klɔːz] n clause f; (Ling) proposition f

**claustrophobic** [klɔːstrə'fəubɪk] adj (person) claustrophobe; (place) où l'on se sent claustrophobe

**claw** [klɔː] n griffe f; (of bird of prey) serre f; (of lobster) pince f

**clay** [kleɪ] n argile f

**clean** [kliːn] adj propre; (clear, smooth) net(te); (record, reputation) sans tache; (joke, story) correct(e) ▷ vt nettoyer; **clean up** vt nettoyer; (fig) remettre de l'ordre dans; **cleaner** n (person) nettoyeur(-euse), femme f de ménage; (product) détachant m; **cleaner's** n (also: **dry cleaner's**) teinturier m; **cleaning** n nettoyage m

**cleanser** ['klɛnzər] n (for face) démaquillant m

**clear** [klɪər] adj clair(e); (glass, plastic) transparent(e); (road, way) libre, dégagé(e); (profit, majority) net(te); (conscience) tranquille; (skin) frais (fraîche); (sky) dégagé(e) ▷ vt (road)

dégager, déblayer; (table) débarrasser; (room etc: of people) faire évacuer; (cheque) compenser; (Law: suspect) innocenter; (obstacle) franchir or sauter sans heurter ▷ vi (weather) s'éclaircir; (fog) se dissiper ▷ adv: **~ of** à distance de, à l'écart de; **to ~ the table** débarrasser la table, desservir; **clear away** vt (things, clothes etc) enlever, retirer; **to ~ away the dishes** débarrasser la table; **clear up** vt ranger, mettre en ordre; (mystery) éclaircir, résoudre; **clearance** n (removal) déblayage m; (permission) autorisation f; **clear-cut** adj précis(e), nettement défini(e); **clearing** n (in forest) clairière f; **clearly** adv clairement; (obviously) de toute évidence; **clearway** n (BRIT) route f à stationnement interdit

**clench** [klɛntʃ] vt serrer

**clergy** ['klɜːdʒɪ] n clergé m

**clerk** [klɑːk, US klɜːrk] n (BRIT) employé(e) de bureau; (US: salesman/woman) vendeur(-euse)

**clever** ['klɛvər] adj (intelligent) intelligent(e); (skilful) habile, adroit(e); (device, arrangement) ingénieux(-euse), astucieux(-euse)

**cliché** ['kliːʃeɪ] n cliché m

**click** [klɪk] vi (Comput) cliquer ▷ vt: **to ~ one's tongue** faire claquer sa langue; **to ~ one's heels** claquer des talons; **to ~ on an icon** cliquer sur une icône

**client** ['klaɪənt] n client(e)

**cliff** [klɪf] n falaise f

**climate** ['klaɪmɪt] n climat m; **climate change** n changement m climatique

**climax** ['klaɪmæks] n apogée m, point culminant; (sexual) orgasme m

**climb** [klaɪm] vi grimper, monter; (plane) prendre de l'altitude ▷ vt (stairs) monter; (mountain) escalader; (tree) grimper à ▷ n montée f, escalade f; **to ~ over a wall** passer par dessus un mur; **climb down** vi (re)descendre; (BRIT fig) rabattre de ses prétentions; **climber** n (also: **rock climber**) grimpeur(-euse), varappeur(-euse); (*plant*) plante grimpante; **climbing** *n* (*also*: **rock climbing**) escalade *f*, varappe *f*

**clinch** [klɪntʃ] *vt* (*deal*) conclure, sceller

**cling** (*pt*, *pp* **clung**) [klɪŋ, klʌŋ] *vi*: **to ~ (to)** se cramponner (à), s'accrocher (à); (*clothes*) coller (à)

**Clingfilm®** ['klɪŋfɪlm] *n* film *m* alimentaire

**clinic** ['klɪnɪk] *n* clinique *f*; centre médical

**clip** [klɪp] *n* (*for hair*) barrette *f*; (*also*: **paper ~**) trombone *m*; (*TV*, *Cinema*) clip *m* ▷ *vt* (*also*: **~ together**: *papers*) attacher; (*hair*, *nails*) couper; (*hedge*) tailler; **clipping** *n* (*from newspaper*) coupure *f* de journal

**cloak** [kləuk] *n* grande cape ▷ *vt* (*fig*) masquer, cacher; **cloakroom** *n* (*for coats etc*) vestiaire *m*; (BRIT: W.C.) toilettes *fpl*

**clock** [klɔk] *n* (*large*) horloge *f*; (*small*) pendule *f*; **clock in** or **on** (BRIT) *vi* (*with card*) pointer (en arrivant); (*start work*) commencer à travailler; **clock off** or **out** (BRIT) *vi* (*with card*) pointer (en partant); (*leave work*) quitter le travail; **clockwise** *adv* dans le sens des aiguilles d'une montre; **clockwork** *n* rouages *mpl*, mécanisme *m*; (*of clock*) mouvement *m* (d'horlogerie) ▷ *adj* (*toy*, *train*) mécanique

**clog** [klɔg] *n* sabot *m* ▷ *vt* boucher, encrasser ▷ *vi* (*also*: **~ up**) se boucher, s'encrasser

**clone** [kləun] *n* clone *m* ▷ *vt* cloner

**close¹** [kləus] *adj* (*near*): **~ (to)** près (de), proche (de); (*contact*, *link*, *watch*) étroit(e); (*examination*) attentif(-ive), minutieux(-euse); (*contest*) très serré(e); (*weather*) lourd(e), étouffant(e) ▷ *adv* près, à proximité; **~ to** *prep* près de; **~ by**, **~ at hand** *adj*, *adv* tout(e) près; **a ~ friend** un ami intime; **to have a ~ shave** (*fig*) l'échapper belle

**close²** [kləuz] *vt* fermer ▷ *vi* (*shop etc*) fermer; (*lid*, *door etc*) se fermer; (*end*) se terminer, se conclure ▷ *n* (*end*)

conclusion *f*; **what time do you ~?** à quelle heure fermez-vous?; **close down** *vi* fermer (*définitivement*); **closed** *adj* (*shop etc*) fermé(e)

**closely** ['kləuslɪ] *adv* (*examine*, *watch*) de près

**closet** ['klɔzɪt] *n* (*cupboard*) placard *m*, réduit *m*

**close-up** ['kləusʌp] *n* gros plan

**closing time** *n* heure *f* de fermeture

**closure** ['kləuʒə'] *n* fermeture *f*

**clot** [klɔt] *n* (*of blood*, *milk*) caillot *m*; (*inf*: *person*) ballot *m* ▷ *vi* (: *external bleeding*) se coaguler

**cloth** [klɔθ] *n* (*material*) tissu *m*, étoffe *f*; (BRIT: *also*: **tea ~**) torchon *m*; lavette *f*; (*also*: **table~**) nappe *f*

**clothes** [kləuðz] *npl* vêtements *mpl*, habits *mpl*; **clothes line** *n* corde *f* (à linge); **clothes peg** (US **clothes pin**) *n* pince *f* à linge

**clothing** ['kləuðɪŋ] *n* = **clothes**

**cloud** [klaud] *n* nuage *m*; **cloud over** *vi* se couvrir; (*fig*) s'assombrir; **cloudy** *adj* nuageux(-euse), couvert(e); (*liquid*) trouble

**clove** [kləuv] *n* clou *m* de girofle; **a ~ of garlic** une gousse d'ail

**clown** [klaun] *n* clown *m* ▷ *vi* (*also*: **~ about**, **~ around**) faire le clown

**club** [klʌb] *n* (*society*) club *m*; (*weapon*) massue *f*, matraque *f*; (*also*: **golf ~**) club ▷ *vt* matraquer ▷ *vi*: **to ~ together** s'associer; **clubs** *npl* (*Cards*) trèfle *m*; **club class** *n* (*Aviat*) classe *f* club

**clue** [klu:] *n* indice *m*; (*in crosswords*) définition *f*; **I haven't a ~** je n'en ai pas la moindre idée

**clump** [klʌmp] *n*: **~ of trees** bouquet *m* d'arbres

**clumsy** ['klʌmzɪ] *adj* (*person*) gauche, maladroit(e); (*object*) malcommode, peu maniable

**clung** [klʌŋ] *pt*, *pp of* **cling**

**cluster** ['klʌstə'] *n* (petit) groupe; (*of flowers*) grappe *f* ▷ *vi* se rassembler

**clutch** [klʌtʃ] *n* (*Aut*) embrayage *m*; (*grasp*): **~es** étreinte *f*, prise *f* ▷ *vt* (*grasp*) agripper; (hold tightly) serrer fort; (hold on to) se cramponner à

**cm** abbr (= centimetre) cm

**Co.** abbr = **company, county**

**c/o** abbr (= care of) c/o, aux bons soins de

**coach** [kəʊtʃ] n (bus) autocar m; (horse-drawn) diligence f; (of train) voiture f, wagon m; (Sport: trainer) entraîneur(-euse); (school: tutor) répétiteur(-trice) ▷ vt (Sport) entraîner; (student) donner des leçons particulières à; **coach station** (BRIT) n gare routière; **coach trip** n excursion f en car

**coal** [kəʊl] n charbon m

**coalition** [kəʊə'lɪʃən] n coalition f

**coarse** [kɔːs] adj grossier(-ère), rude; (vulgar) vulgaire

**coast** [kəʊst] n côte f ▷ vi (car, cycle) descendre en roue libre; **coastal** adj côtier(-ère); **coastguard** n garde-côte m; **coastline** n côte f, littoral m

**coat** [kəʊt] n manteau m; (of animal) pelage m, poil m; (of paint) couche f ▷ vt couvrir, enduire; **coat hanger** n cintre m; **coating** n couche f, enduit m

**coax** [kəʊks] vt persuader par des cajoleries

**cob** [kɔb] n see **corn**

**cobbled** ['kɔbld] adj pavé(e)

**cobweb** ['kɔbwɛb] n toile f d'araignée

**cocaine** [kə'keɪn] n cocaïne f

**cock** [kɔk] n (rooster) coq m; (male bird) mâle m ▷ vt (gun) armer; **cockerel** n jeune coq m

**cockney** ['kɔknɪ] n cockney m/f (habitant des quartiers populaires de l'East End de Londres), ≈ faubourien(ne)

**cockpit** ['kɔkpɪt] n (in aircraft) poste m de pilotage, cockpit m

**cockroach** ['kɔkrəʊtʃ] n cafard m, cancrelat m

**cocktail** ['kɔkteɪl] n cocktail m

**cocoa** ['kəʊkəʊ] n cacao m

**coconut** ['kəʊkənʌt] n noix f de coco

**C.O.D.** abbr = **cash on delivery**

**cod** [kɔd] n morue fraîche, cabillaud m

**code** [kəʊd] n code m; (Tel: area code)

indicatif m

**coeducational** ['kəʊɛdju'keɪʃənl] adj mixte

**coffee** ['kɔfɪ] n café m; **coffee bar** n (BRIT) café m; **coffee bean** n grain m de café; **coffee break** n pause-café f; **coffee maker** n cafetière f; **coffeepot** n cafetière f; **coffee shop** n café m; **coffee table** n (petite) table basse

**coffin** ['kɔfɪn] n cercueil m

**cog** [kɔg] n (wheel) roue dentée; (tooth) dent f (d'engrenage)

**cognac** ['kɔnjæk] n cognac m

**coherent** [kəʊ'hɪərənt] adj cohérent(e)

**coil** [kɔɪl] n rouleau m, bobine f; (contraceptive) stérilet m ▷ vt enrouler

**coin** [kɔɪn] n pièce f (de monnaie) ▷ vt (word) inventer

**coincide** [kəʊɪn'saɪd] vi coïncider; **coincidence** [kəʊ'ɪnsɪdəns] n coïncidence f

**Coke®** [kəʊk] n coca m

**coke** [kəʊk] n (coal) coke m

**colander** ['kɔləndər] n passoire f (à légumes)

**cold** [kəʊld] adj froid(e) ▷ n froid m; (Med) rhume m; **it's ~** il fait froid; **to be ~** (person) avoir froid; **to catch a ~** s'enrhumer, attraper un rhume; **in ~ blood** de sang-froid; **cold cuts** (US) npl viandes froides; **cold sore** n bouton m de fièvre

**coleslaw** ['kəʊlslɔː] n sorte de salade de chou cru

**colic** ['kɔlɪk] n colique(s) f(pl)

**collaborate** [kə'læbəreɪt] vi collaborer

**collapse** [kə'læps] vi s'effondrer, s'écrouler; (Med) avoir un malaise ▷ n effondrement m, écroulement m; (of government) chute f

**collar** ['kɔlər] n (of coat, shirt) col m; (for dog) collier m; **collarbone** n clavicule f

**colleague** ['kɔliːg] n collègue m/f

**collect** [kə'lɛkt] vt rassembler; (pick up) ramasser; (as a hobby) collectionner; (BRIT: call for) (passer) prendre; (mail) faire la levée de, ramasser; (money owed)

encaisser; (*donations, subscriptions*)
recueillir ▷ vi (*people*) se rassembler;
(*dust, dirt*) s'amasser; **to call ~** (*US
Tel*) téléphoner en PCV; **collection**
[kə'lɛkʃən] n collection f; (*of mail*)
levée f; (*for money*) collecte f, quête f;
**collective** [kə'lɛktɪv] adj collectif(-ive);
**collector** n collectionneur m
**college** ['kɔlɪdʒ] n collège m; (*of
technology, agriculture etc*) institut m
**collide** [kə'laɪd] vi: **to ~ (with)** entrer en
collision (avec)
**collision** [kə'lɪʒən] n collision f,
heurt m
**cologne** [kə'ləun] n (*also:* **eau de ~**) eau
f de cologne
**colon** ['kəulən] n (*sign*) deux-points
mpl; (*Med*) côlon m
**colonel** ['kə:nl] n colonel m
**colonial** [kə'ləunɪəl] adj colonial(e)
**colony** ['kɔlənɪ] n colonie f
**colour** etc (*US* **color** etc) ['kʌlə'] n
couleur f ▷ vt colorer; (*dye*) teindre;
(*paint*) peindre; (*with crayons*) colorier;
(*news*) fausser, exagérer ▷ vi (*blush*)
rougir; **I'd like a different ~** je le
voudrais dans un autre coloris;
**colour in** vt colorier; **colour-blind** adj
daltonien(ne); **coloured** adj coloré(e);
(*photo*) en couleur; **colour film** n
(*for camera*) pellicule f (en) couleur;
**colourful** adj coloré(e), vif (vive);
(*personality*) pittoresque, haut(e) en
couleurs; **colouring** n colorant m;
(*complexion*) teint m; **colour television**
n télévision f (en) couleur
**column** ['kɔləm] n colonne f; (*fashion
column, sports column etc*) rubrique f
**coma** ['kəumə] n coma m
**comb** [kəum] n peigne m ▷ vt (*hair*)
peigner; (*area*) ratisser, passer au
peigne fin
**combat** ['kɔmbæt] n combat m ▷ vt
combattre, lutter contre
**combination** [kɔmbɪ'neɪʃən] n (*gen*)
combinaison f
**combine** vb [kəm'baɪn] ▷ vt combiner
▷ vi s'associer; (*Chem*) se combiner ▷ n
['kɔmbaɪn] (*Econ*) trust m; **to ~ sth with
sth** (*one quality with another*) joindre *ou*
allier qch à qch
**come** (*pt* **came**, *pp* **~**) [kʌm, keɪm]
vi **1** (*movement towards*) venir; **to ~
running** arriver en courant; **he's ~ here
to work** il est venu ici pour travailler; **~
with me** suivez-moi
**2** (*arrive*) arriver; **to ~ home** rentrer
(chez soi *or* à la maison); **we've just ~
from Paris** nous arrivons de Paris
**3** (*reach*): **to ~ to** (*decision etc*) parvenir
à, arriver à; **the bill came to £40** la
note s'est élevée à 40 livres
**4** (*occur*): **an idea came to me** il m'est
venu une idée
**5** (*be, become*): **to ~ loose/undone** se
défaire/desserrer; **I've ~ to like him**
j'ai fini par bien l'aimer; **come across**
vt fus rencontrer par hasard, tomber
sur; **come along** vi (*BRIT: pupil, work*)
faire des progrès, avancer; **come back**
vi revenir; **come down** vi descendre;
(*prices*) baisser; (*buildings*) s'écrouler;
(: *be demolished*) être démoli(e); **come
from** vt fus (*source*) venir de; (*place*)
venir de, être originaire de; **come in** vi
entrer; (*train*) arriver; (*fashion*) entrer
en vogue; (*on deal etc*) participer; **come
off** vi (*button*) se détacher; (*attempt*)
réussir; **come on** vi (*lights, electricity*)
s'allumer; (*central heating*) se mettre
en marche; (*pupil, work, project*) faire
des progrès, avancer; **~ on!** viens!;
allons!, allez!; **come out** vi sortir; (*sun*)
se montrer; (*book*) paraître; (*stain*)
s'enlever; (*strike*) cesser le travail, se
mettre en grève; **come round** vi (*after
faint, operation*) revenir à soi, reprendre
connaissance; **come to** vi revenir à
soi; **come up** vi monter; (*sun*) se lever;
(*problem*) se poser; (*event*) survenir; (*in
conversation*) être soulevé; **come up
with** vt fus (*money*) fournir; **he came
up with an idea** il a eu une idée, il a
proposé quelque chose
**comeback** ['kʌmbæk] n (*Theat etc*)
rentrée f

**comedian** [kə'miːdɪən] n (comic)
comique m; (Theat) comédien m
**comedy** ['kɒmɪdɪ] n comédie f;
(humour) comique m
**comet** ['kɒmɪt] n comète f
**comfort** ['kʌmfət] n confort m,
bien-être m; (solace) consolation f,
réconfort m ▷ vt consoler, réconforter;
**comfortable** adj confortable; (person)
à l'aise; (financially) aisé(e); (patient)
dont l'état est stationnaire; **comfort
station** n (us) toilettes fpl
**comic** ['kɒmɪk] adj (also: **~al**)
comique ▷ n (person) comique m;
(BRIT: magazine: for children) magazine
m de bandes dessinées or de BD;
(: for adults) illustré m; **comic book**
(us) n (for children) magazine m de
bandes dessinées or de BD; (for adults)
illustré m; **comic strip** n bande
dessinée
**comma** ['kɒmə] n virgule f
**command** [kə'mɑːnd] n ordre m,
commandement m; (Mil: authority)
commandement; (mastery) maîtrise
f ▷ vt (troops) commander; **to ~ sb
to do** donner l'ordre or commander
à qn de faire; **commander** n (Mil)
commandant m
**commemorate** [kə'mɛməreɪt] vt
commémorer
**commence** [kə'mɛns] vt, vi
commencer; **commencement** (us) n
(University) remise f des diplômes
**commend** [kə'mɛnd] vt louer;
(recommend) recommander
**comment** ['kɒmɛnt] n commentaire
m ▷ vi: **to ~ on** faire des remarques
sur; **"no ~"** "je n'ai rien à déclarer";
**commentary** ['kɒməntərɪ] n
commentaire m; (Sport) reportage m (en
direct); **commentator** ['kɒmənteɪtə']
n commentateur m; (Sport) reporter m
**commerce** ['kɒməːs] n commerce m
**commercial** [kə'məːʃəl] adj
commercial(e) ▷ n (Radio, TV) annonce
f publicitaire, spot m (publicitaire);
**commercial break** n (Radio, TV) spot m

(publicitaire)
**commission** [kə'mɪʃən] n (committee,
fee) commission f ▷ vt (work of art)
commander, charger un artiste de
l'exécution de; **out of ~** (machine) hors
service; **commissioner** n (Police) préfet
m (de police)
**commit** [kə'mɪt] vt (act) commettre;
(resources) consacrer; (to sb's care)
confier (à); **to ~ o.s. (to do)** s'engager
(à faire); **to ~ suicide** se suicider;
**commitment** n engagement m;
(obligation) responsabilité(s) (fpl)
**committee** [kə'mɪtɪ] n comité m;
commission f
**commodity** [kə'mɒdɪtɪ] n produit m,
marchandise f, article m
**common** ['kɒmən] adj (gen)
commun(e); (usual) courant(e) ▷ n
terrain communal; **commonly** adv
communément, généralement;
couramment; **commonplace** adj
banal(e), ordinaire; **Commons** npl
(BRIT Pol): **the (House of) Commons**
la chambre des Communes; **common
sense** n bon sens; **Commonwealth**
n: **the Commonwealth** le
Commonwealth
**communal** ['kɒmjuːnl] adj (life)
communautaire; (for common use)
commun(e)
**commune** n ['kɒmjuːn] (group)
communauté f ▷ vi [kə'mjuːn]: **to ~
with** (nature) communier avec
**communicate** [kə'mjuːnɪkeɪt] vt
communiquer, transmettre ▷ vi: **to ~
(with)** communiquer (avec)
**communication** [kəmjuːnɪ'keɪʃən] n
communication f
**communion** [kə'mjuːnɪən] n (also:
**Holy C~**) communion f
**communism** ['kɒmjunɪzəm] n
communisme m; **communist** adj, n
communiste m/f
**community** [kə'mjuːnɪtɪ] n
communauté f; **community centre**
(us **community center**) n foyer
socio-éducatif, centre m de loisirs;

**community service** n ≈ travail m d'intérêt général, TIG m

**commute** [kə'mju:t] vi faire le trajet journalier (de son domicile à un lieu de travail assez éloigné) ▷ vt (Law) commuer; **commuter** n banlieusard(e) (qui fait un trajet journalier pour se rendre à son travail)

**compact** adj [kəm'pækt] compact(e) ▷ n ['kɒmpækt] (also: **powder ~**) poudrier m; **compact disc** n disque compact; **compact disc player** n lecteur m de disques compacts

**companion** [kəm'pænjən] n compagnon (compagne)

**company** ['kʌmpənɪ] n compagnie f; **to keep sb ~** tenir compagnie à qn; **company car** n voiture f de fonction; **company director** n administrateur(-trice)

**comparable** ['kɒmpərəbl] adj comparable

**comparative** [kəm'pærətɪv] adj (study) comparatif(-ive); (relative) relatif(-ive); **comparatively** adv (relatively) relativement

**compare** [kəm'pɛəʳ] vt: **to ~ sth/sb with** or **to** comparer qch/qn avec or à ▷ vi: **to ~ (with)** se comparer (à); être comparable (à); **comparison** [kəm'pærɪsn] n comparaison f

**compartment** [kəm'pɑːtmənt] n (also Rail) compartiment m; **a non-smoking ~** un compartiment non-fumeurs

**compass** ['kʌmpəs] n boussole f; **compasses** npl (Math) compas m

**compassion** [kəm'pæʃən] n compassion f, humanité f

**compatible** [kəm'pætɪbl] adj compatible

**compel** [kəm'pɛl] vt contraindre, obliger; **compelling** adj (fig: argument) irrésistible

**compensate** ['kɒmpənseɪt] vt indemniser, dédommager ▷ vi: **to ~ for** compenser; **compensation** [kɒmpən'seɪʃən] n compensation

f; (money) dédommagement m, indemnité f

**compete** [kəm'pi:t] vi (take part) concourir; (vie): **to ~ (with)** rivaliser (avec), faire concurrence (à)

**competent** ['kɒmpɪtənt] adj compétent(e), capable

**competition** [kɒmpɪ'tɪʃən] n (contest) compétition f, concours m; (Econ) concurrence f

**competitive** [kəm'pɛtɪtɪv] adj (Econ) concurrentiel(le); (sports) de compétition; (person) qui a l'esprit de compétition

**competitor** [kəm'pɛtɪtəʳ] n concurrent(e)

**complacent** [kəm'pleɪsnt] adj (trop) content(e) de soi

**complain** [kəm'pleɪn] vi: **to ~ (about)** se plaindre (de); (in shop etc) réclamer (au sujet de); **complaint** n plainte f; (in shop etc) réclamation f; (Med) affection f

**complement** ['kɒmplɪmənt] n complément m; (esp of ship's crew etc) effectif complet ▷ vt (enhance) compléter; **complementary** [kɒmplɪ'mɛntərɪ] adj complémentaire

**complete** [kəm'pli:t] adj complet(-ète); (finished) achevé(e) ▷ vt achever, parachever; (set, group) compléter; (a form) remplir; **completely** adv complètement; **completion** [kəm'pli:ʃən] n achèvement m; (of contract) exécution f

**complex** ['kɒmplɛks] adj complexe ▷ n (Psych, buildings etc) complexe m

**complexion** [kəm'plɛkʃən] n (of face) teint m

**compliance** [kəm'plaɪəns] n (submission) docilité f; (agreement): **~ with** le fait de se conformer à; **in ~ with** en conformité avec, conformément à

**complicate** ['kɒmplɪkeɪt] vt compliquer; **complicated** adj compliqué(e); **complication** [kɒmplɪ'keɪʃən] n complication f

**compliment** n ['kɒmplɪmənt] compliment m ▷ vt ['kɒmplɪmɛnt]

complimenter; **complimentary**
[kɔmplɪ'mɛntərɪ] adj flatteur(-euse);
(free) à titre gracieux

**comply** [kəm'plaɪ] vi: **to ~ with** se
soumettre à, se conformer à

**component** [kəm'pəunənt] adj
composant(e), constituant(e) ▷ n
composant m, élément m

**compose** [kəm'pəuz] vt composer;
(form): **to be ~d of** se composer de; **to ~
o.s.** se calmer, se maîtriser; **composer**
n (Mus) compositeur m; **composition**
[kɔmpə'zɪʃən] n composition f

**composure** [kəm'pəuʒər] n calme m,
maîtrise f de soi

**compound** ['kɔmpaund] n (Chem,
Ling) composé m; (enclosure) enclos m,
enceinte f ▷ adj composé(e); (fracture)
compliqué(e)

**comprehension** [kɔmprɪ'hɛnʃən] n
compréhension f

**comprehensive** [kɔmprɪ'hɛnsɪv]
adj (très) complet(-ète); **~ policy**
(Insurance) assurance f tous risques;
**comprehensive (school)** n (BRIT)
école secondaire non sélective avec libre
circulation d'une section à l'autre, ≈ CES m

> Be careful not to translate
> *comprehensive* by the French word
> *compréhensif*.

**compress** vt [kəm'prɛs] comprimer;
(text, information) condenser ▷ n
['kɔmprɛs] (Med) compresse f

**comprise** [kəm'praɪz] vt (also: **be ~d
of**) comprendre; (constitute) constituer,
représenter

**compromise** ['kɔmprəmaɪz] n
compromis m ▷ vt compromettre ▷ vi
transiger, accepter un compromis

**compulsive** [kəm'pʌlsɪv] adj (Psych)
compulsif(-ive); (book, film etc)
captivant(e)

**compulsory** [kəm'pʌlsərɪ] adj
obligatoire

**computer** [kəm'pju:tər] n
ordinateur m; **computer game** n jeu
m vidéo; **computer-generated** adj
de synthèse; **computerize** vt (data)

traiter par ordinateur; (system, office)
informatiser; **computer programmer**
n programmeur(-euse); **computer
programming** n programmation f;
**computer science** n informatique f;
**computer studies** npl informatique f;
**computing** [kəm'pju:tɪŋ] n
informatique f

**con** [kɔn] vt duper; (cheat) escroquer ▷ n
escroquerie f

**conceal** [kən'si:l] vt cacher, dissimuler

**concede** [kən'si:d] vt concéder ▷ vi
céder

**conceited** [kən'si:tɪd] adj
vaniteux(-euse), suffisant(e)

**conceive** [kən'si:v] vt, vi concevoir

**concentrate** ['kɔnsəntreɪt] vi se
concentrer ▷ vt concentrer

**concentration** [kɔnsən'treɪʃən] n
concentration f

**concept** ['kɔnsɛpt] n concept m

**concern** [kən'sə:n] n affaire f;
(Comm) entreprise f, firme f; (anxiety)
inquiétude f, souci m ▷ vt (worry)
inquiéter; (involve) concerner; (relate
to) se rapporter à; **to be ~ed (about)**
s'inquiéter (de), être inquiet(-ète) (au
sujet de); **concerning** prep en ce qui
concerne, à propos de

**concert** ['kɔnsət] n concert m; **concert
hall** n salle f de concert

**concerto** [kən'tʃə:təu] n concerto m

**concession** [kən'sɛʃən] n (compromise)
concession f; (reduced price) réduction
f; **tax ~** dégrèvement fiscal; **"~s"** tarif
réduit

**concise** [kən'saɪs] adj concis(e)

**conclude** [kən'klu:d] vt conclure;
**conclusion** [kən'klu:ʒən] n
conclusion f

**concrete** ['kɔŋkri:t] n béton m ▷ adj
concret(-ète); (Constr) en béton

**concussion** [kən'kʌʃən] n (Med)
commotion (cérébrale)

**condemn** [kən'dɛm] vt condamner

**condensation** [kɔndɛn'seɪʃən] n
condensation f

**condense** [kən'dɛns] vi se condenser

▷ vt condenser

**condition** [kən'dɪʃən] n condition f; (*disease*) maladie f ▷ vt déterminer, conditionner; **on ~ that** à condition que + sub, à condition de; **conditional** [kən'dɪʃnl] adj conditionnel(le); **conditioner** n (*for hair*) baume démêlant; (*for fabrics*) assouplissant m

**condo** ['kɒndəʊ] n (*us inf*) = **condominium**

**condom** ['kɒndəm] n préservatif m

**condominium** [kɒndə'mɪnɪəm] n (*us: building*) immeuble m (en copropriété); (: *rooms*) appartement m (dans un immeuble en copropriété)

**condone** [kən'dəʊn] vt fermer les yeux sur, approuver (tacitement)

**conduct** n ['kɒndʌkt] conduite f ▷ vt [kən'dʌkt] (*manage*) mener, diriger; (*Mus*) diriger; **to ~ o.s.** se conduire, se comporter; **conducted tour** (*BRIT*) n voyage organisé; (*of building*) visite guidée; **conductor** n (*of orchestra*) chef m d'orchestre; (*on bus*) receveur m; (*us: on train*) chef m de train; (*Elec*) conducteur m

**cone** [kəʊn] n cône m; (*for ice-cream*) cornet m; (*Bot*) pomme f de pin, cône

**confectionery** [kən'fɛkʃənrɪ] n (*sweets*) confiserie f

**confer** [kən'fɜː<sup>r</sup>] vt: **to ~ sth on** conférer qch à ▷ vi conférer, s'entretenir

**conference** ['kɒnfərns] n conférence f

**confess** [kən'fɛs] vt confesser, avouer ▷ vi (*admit sth*) avouer; (*Rel*) se confesser; **confession** [kən'fɛʃən] n confession f

**confide** [kən'faɪd] vi: **to ~ in** s'ouvrir à, se confier à

**confidence** ['kɒnfɪdns] n confiance f; (*also*: **self-~**) assurance f, confiance en soi; (*secret*) confidence f; **in ~** (*speak, write*) en confidence, confidentiellement; **confident** adj (*self-assured*) sûr(e) de soi; (*sure*) sûr; **confidential** [kɒnfɪ'dɛnʃəl] adj confidentiel(le)

**confine** [kən'faɪn] vt limiter, borner; (*shut up*) confiner, enfermer; **confined** adj (*space*) restreint(e), réduit(e)

**confirm** [kən'fɜːm] vt (*report, Rel*) confirmer; (*appointment*) ratifier; **confirmation** [kɒnfə'meɪʃən] n confirmation f; ratification f

**confiscate** ['kɒnfɪskeɪt] vt confisquer

**conflict** n ['kɒnflɪkt] conflit m, lutte f ▷ vi [kən'flɪkt] (*opinions*) s'opposer, se heurter

**conform** [kən'fɔːm] vi: **to ~ (to)** se conformer (à)

**confront** [kən'frʌnt] vt (*two people*) confronter; (*enemy, danger*) affronter, faire face à; (*problem*) faire face à; **confrontation** [kɒnfrən'teɪʃən] n confrontation f

**confuse** [kən'fjuːz] vt (*person*) troubler; (*situation*) embrouiller; (*one thing with another*) confondre; **confused** adj (*person*) dérouté(e), désorienté(e); (*situation*) embrouillé(e); **confusing** adj peu clair(e), déroutant(e); **confusion** [kən'fjuːʒən] n confusion f

**congestion** [kən'dʒɛstʃən] n (*Med*) congestion f; (*fig: traffic*) encombrement m

**congratulate** [kən'grætjuleɪt] vt: **to ~ sb (on)** féliciter qn (de); **congratulations** [kəngrætju'leɪʃənz] npl: **congratulations (on)** félicitations fpl (pour) ▷ excl: **congratulations!** (toutes mes) félicitations!

**congregation** [kɒŋgrɪ'geɪʃən] n assemblée f (des fidèles)

**congress** ['kɒŋgrɛs] n congrès m; (*Pol*): **C~** Congrès m; **congressman** n membre m du Congrès; **congresswoman** n membre m du Congrès

**conifer** ['kɒnɪfə<sup>r</sup>] n conifère m

**conjugate** ['kɒndʒugeɪt] vt conjuguer

**conjugation** [kɒndʒə'geɪʃən] n conjugaison f

**conjunction** [kən'dʒʌŋkʃən] n conjonction f; **in ~ with** (conjointement) avec

**conjure** ['kʌndʒə<sup>r</sup>] vi faire des tours de

passe-passe

**connect** [kə'nɛkt] vt joindre, relier;
(Elec) connecter; (Tel: caller) mettre
en connexion; (: subscriber) brancher;
(fig) établir un rapport entre, faire un
rapprochement entre ▷ vi (train): **to ~
with** assurer la correspondance avec;
**to be ~ed with** avoir un rapport avec;
(have dealings with) avoir des rapports
avec, être en relation avec; **connecting
flight** n (vol m de) correspondance
f; **connection** [kə'nɛkʃən] n
relation f, lien m; (Elec) connexion
f; (Tel) communication f; (train etc)
correspondance f

**conquer** ['kɔŋkər] vt conquérir;
(feelings) vaincre, surmonter

**conquest** ['kɔŋkwɛst] n conquête f

**cons** [kɔnz] npl see **convenience; pro**

**conscience** ['kɔnʃəns] n conscience f

**conscientious** [kɔnʃɪ'ɛnʃəs] adj
consciencieux(-euse)

**conscious** ['kɔnʃəs] adj conscient(e);
(deliberate: insult, error) délibéré(e);
**consciousness** n conscience f; (Med)
connaissance f

**consecutive** [kən'sɛkjutɪv] adj
consécutif(-ive); **on three ~ occasions**
trois fois de suite

**consensus** [kən'sɛnsəs] n
consensus m

**consent** [kən'sɛnt] n consentement m
▷ vi: **to ~ (to)** consentir (à)

**consequence** ['kɔnsɪkwəns] n
suites fpl, conséquence f; (significance)
importance f

**consequently** ['kɔnsɪkwəntlɪ] adv
par conséquent, donc

**conservation** [kɔnsə'veɪʃən] n
préservation f, protection f; (also:
**nature ~**) défense f de l'environnement

**conservative** [kən'sə:vətɪv] adj
conservateur(-trice); (cautious)
prudent(e); **Conservative** adj, n (BRIT
Pol) conservateur(-trice)

**conservatory** [kən'sə:vətrɪ] n (room)
jardin m d'hiver; (Mus) conservatoire m

**consider** [kən'sɪdər] vt (study)

considérer, réfléchir à; (take into
account) penser à, prendre en
considération; (regard, judge)
considérer, estimer; **to ~ doing sth**
envisager de faire qch; **considerable**
adj considérable; **considerably**
adv nettement; **considerate** adj
prévenant(e), plein(e) d'égards;
**consideration** [kənsɪdə'reɪʃən] n
considération f; (reward) rétribution
f, rémunération f; **considering** prep:
**considering (that)** étant donné (que)

**consignment** [kən'saɪnmənt] n
arrivage m, envoi m

**consist** [kən'sɪst] vi: **to ~ of** consister
en, se composer de

**consistency** [kən'sɪstənsɪ] n
(thickness) consistance f; (fig)
cohérence f

**consistent** [kən'sɪstənt] adj logique,
cohérent(e)

**consolation** [kɔnsə'leɪʃən] n
consolation f

**console¹** [kən'səul] vt consoler

**console²** ['kɔnsəul] n console f

**consonant** ['kɔnsənənt] n consonne f

**conspicuous** [kən'spɪkjuəs] adj
voyant(e), qui attire l'attention

**conspiracy** [kən'spɪrəsɪ] n
conspiration f, complot m

**constable** ['kʌnstəbl] n (BRIT) ≈ agent
m de police, gendarme m; **chief ~**
≈ préfet m de police

**constant** ['kɔnstənt] adj constant(e);
incessant(e); **constantly** adv
constamment, sans cesse

**constipated** ['kɔnstɪpeɪtɪd]
adj constipé(e); **constipation**
[kɔnstɪ'peɪʃən] n constipation f

**constituency** [kən'stɪtjuənsɪ] n (Pol:
area) circonscription électorale; (:
electors) électorat m

**constitute** ['kɔnstɪtju:t] vt constituer

**constitution** [kɔnstɪ'tju:ʃən] n
constitution f

**constraint** [kən'streɪnt] n contrainte f

**construct** [kən'strʌkt] vt construire;
**construction** [kən'strʌkʃən] n

construction f; **constructive** adj
constructif(-ive)

**consul** ['kɔnsl] n consul m; **consulate**
['kɔnsjulit] n consulat m

**consult** [kən'sʌlt] vt consulter;
**consultant** n (Med) médecin
consultant n; (other specialist) consultant
m, (expert-)conseil m; **consultation**
[kɔnsəl'teɪʃən] n consultation f;
**consulting room** n (BRIT) cabinet m de
consultation

**consume** [kən'sjuːm] vt consommer;
(subj: flames, hatred, desire) consumer;
**consumer** n consommateur(-trice)

**consumption** [kən'sʌmpʃən] n
consommation f

**cont.** abbr (= continued) suite

**contact** ['kɔntækt] n contact m;
(person) connaissance f, relation f ▷ vt
se mettre en contact or en rapport
avec; **contact lenses** npl verres mpl
de contact

**contagious** [kən'teɪdʒəs] adj
contagieux(-euse)

**contain** [kən'teɪn] vt contenir;
**to ~ o.s.** se contenir, se maîtriser;
**container** n récipient m; (for shipping
etc) conteneur m

**contaminate** [kən'tæmɪneɪt] vt
contaminer

**cont'd** abbr (= continued) suite

**contemplate** ['kɔntəmpleɪt] vt
contempler; (consider) envisager

**contemporary** [kən'tempərərɪ] adj
contemporain(e); (design, wallpaper)
moderne ▷ n contemporain(e)

**contempt** [kən'tempt] n mépris m,
dédain m; **~ of court** (Law) outrage m à
l'autorité de la justice

**contend** [kən'tend] vt: **to ~ that**
soutenir or prétendre que ▷ vi: **to ~
with** (compete) rivaliser avec; (struggle)
lutter avec

**content** [kən'tent] adj content(e),
satisfait(e) ▷ vt contenter, satisfaire
▷ n ['kɔntent] contenu m; (of fat,
moisture) teneur f; **contents** npl (of
container etc) contenu m; **(table of) ~s**

table f des matières; **contented** adj
content(e), satisfait(e)

**contest** n ['kɔntest] combat m, lutte f;
(competition) concours m ▷ vt [kən'test]
contester, discuter; (compete for)
disputer; (Law) attaquer; **contestant**
[kən'testənt] n concurrent(e); (in fight)
adversaire m/f

**context** ['kɔntekst] n contexte m

**continent** ['kɔntɪnənt] n continent
m; **the C~** (BRIT) l'Europe continentale;
**continental** [kɔntɪ'nentl] adj
continental(e); **continental breakfast**
n café (or thé) complet; **continental
quilt** n (BRIT) couette f

**continual** [kən'tɪnjuəl] adj
continuel(le); **continually** adv
continuellement, sans cesse

**continue** [kən'tɪnjuː] vi continuer ▷ vt
continuer; (start again) reprendre

**continuity** [kɔntɪ'njuːɪtɪ] n continuité
f; (TV etc) enchaînement m

**continuous** [kən'tɪnjuəs] adj
continu(e), permanent(e); (Ling)
progressif(-ive); **continuous
assessment** (BRIT) n contrôle
continu; **continuously** adv (repeatedly)
continuellement; (uninterruptedly) sans
interruption

**contour** ['kɔntuə'] n contour m, profil
m; (also: **~ line**) courbe f de niveau

**contraception** [kɔntrə'sepʃən] n
contraception f

**contraceptive** [kɔntrə'septɪv]
adj contraceptif(-ive),
anticonceptionnel(le) ▷ n
contraceptif m

**contract** n ['kɔntrækt] contrat m ▷ vb
[kən'trækt] ▷ vi (become smaller) se
contracter, se resserrer ▷ vt contracter;
(Comm): **to ~ to do sth** s'engager (par
contrat) à faire qch; **contractor** n
entrepreneur m

**contradict** [kɔntrə'dɪkt] vt contredire;
**contradiction** [kɔntrə'dɪkʃən] n
contradiction f

**contrary¹** ['kɔntrərɪ] adj contraire,
opposé(e) ▷ n contraire m; **on the ~** au

contraire; **unless you hear to the ~** sauf avis contraire

**contrary²** [kən'trɛərɪ] *adj* (*perverse*) contrariant(e), entêté(e)

**contrast** *n* ['kɒntrɑːst] contraste *m* ▷ *vt* [kən'trɑːst] mettre en contraste, contraster; **in ~ to** *or* **with** contrairement à, par opposition à

**contribute** [kən'trɪbjuːt] *vi* contribuer ▷ *vt*: **to ~ £10/an article to** donner 10 livres/un article à; **to ~ to** (*gen*) contribuer à; (*newspaper*) collaborer à; (*discussion*) prendre part à; **contribution** [kɒntrɪ'bjuːʃən] *n* contribution *f*; (*BRIT: for social security*) cotisation *f*; (*to publication*) article *m*; **contributor** *n* (*to newspaper*) collaborateur(-trice); (*of money, goods*) donateur(-trice)

**control** [kən'trəul] *vt* (*process, machinery*) commander; (*temper*) maîtriser; (*disease*) enrayer ▷ *n* maîtrise *f*; (*power*) autorité *f*; **controls** *npl* (*of machine etc*) commandes *fpl*; (*on radio*) boutons *mpl* de réglage; **to be in ~ of** être maître de, maîtriser; (*in charge of*) être responsable de; **everything is under ~** j'ai (*or* il a *etc*) la situation en main; **the car went out of ~** j'ai (*or* il a *etc*) perdu le contrôle du véhicule; **control tower** *n* (*Aviat*) tour *f* de contrôle

**controversial** [kɒntrə'vəːʃl] *adj* discutable, controversé(e)

**controversy** ['kɒntrəvəːsɪ] *n* controverse *f*, polémique *f*

**convenience** [kən'viːnɪəns] *n* commodité *f*; **at your ~** quand *or* comme cela vous convient; **all modern ~s, all mod cons** (*BRIT*) avec tout le confort moderne, tout confort

**convenient** [kən'viːnɪənt] *adj* commode

**convent** ['kɒnvənt] *n* couvent *m*

**convention** [kən'vɛnʃən] *n* convention *f*; (*custom*) usage *m*; **conventional** *adj* conventionnel(le)

**conversation** [kɒnvə'seɪʃən] *n*

conversation *f*

**conversely** [kɒn'vəːslɪ] *adv* inversement, réciproquement

**conversion** [kən'vəːʃən] *n* conversion *f*; (*BRIT: of house*) transformation *f*, aménagement *m*; (*Rugby*) transformation *f*

**convert** *vt* [kən'vəːt] (*Rel, Comm*) convertir; (*alter*) transformer; (*house*) aménager ▷ *n* ['kɒnvəːt] converti(e); **convertible** *adj* convertible ▷ *n* (*voiture f*) décapotable *f*

**convey** [kən'veɪ] *vt* transporter; (*thanks*) transmettre; (*idea*) communiquer; **conveyor belt** *n* convoyeur *m* tapis roulant

**convict** *vt* [kən'vɪkt] déclarer (*or* reconnaître) coupable ▷ *n* ['kɒnvɪkt] forçat *m*, convict *m*; **conviction** [kən'vɪkʃən] *n* (*Law*) condamnation *f*; (*belief*) conviction *f*

**convince** [kən'vɪns] *vt* convaincre, persuader; **convinced** *adj*: **convinced of/that** convaincu(e) de/que; **convincing** *adj* persuasif(-ive), convaincant(e)

**convoy** ['kɒnvɔɪ] *n* convoi *m*

**cook** [kuk] *vt* (faire) cuire ▷ *vi* cuire; (*person*) faire la cuisine ▷ *n* cuisinier(-ière); **cookbook** *n* livre *m* de cuisine; **cooker** *n* cuisinière *f*; **cookery** *n* cuisine *f*; **cookery book** *n* (*BRIT*) = **cookbook**; **cookie** *n* (*US*) biscuit *m*, petit gâteau sec; **cooking** *n* cuisine *f*

**cool** [kuːl] *adj* frais (fraîche); (*not afraid*) calme; (*unfriendly*) froid(e); (*inf: trendy*) cool *inv* (*inf*); (: *great*) super *inv* (*inf*) ▷ *vt*, *vi* rafraîchir, refroidir; **cool down** *vi* refroidir; (*fig: person, situation*) se calmer; **cool off** *vi* (*become calmer*) se calmer; (*lose enthusiasm*) perdre son enthousiasme

**cop** [kɒp] *n* (*inf*) flic *m*

**cope** [kəup] *vi* s'en sortir, tenir le coup; **to ~ with** (*problem*) faire face à

**copper** ['kɒpə'] *n* cuivre *m*; (*BRIT: inf: policeman*) flic *m*

**copy** ['kɒpɪ] *n* copie *f*; (*book etc*)

exemplaire m ▷ vt copier; (*imitate*)
imiter; **copyright** n droit m d'auteur,
copyright m

**coral** ['kɔrəl] n corail m

**cord** [kɔ:d] n corde f; (*fabric*) velours
côtelé; (*Elec*) cordon m (d'alimentation),
fil m (électrique); **cords** npl (*trousers*)
pantalon m de velours côtelé; **cordless**
adj sans fil

**corduroy** ['kɔ:dərɔɪ] n velours côtelé

**core** [kɔ:ʳ] n (*of fruit*) trognon m; (*fig: of problem etc*) cœur ▷ vt enlever le
trognon or le cœur de

**coriander** [kɔrɪ'ændəʳ] n coriandre f

**cork** [kɔ:k] n (*material*) liège m; (*of bottle*) bouchon m; **corkscrew** n tire-
bouchon m

**corn** [kɔ:n] n (*BRIT: wheat*) blé m; (*US: maize*) maïs m; (*on foot*) cor m; **~ on the
cob** (*Culin*) épi m de maïs au naturel

**corned beef** ['kɔ:nd-] n corned-beef m

**corner** ['kɔ:nəʳ] n coin m; (*in road*)
tournant m, virage m; (*Football*) corner
m ▷ vt (*trap: prey*) acculer; (*fig*) coincer;
(*Comm: market*) accaparer ▷ vi prendre
un virage; **corner shop** (*BRIT*) n
magasin m du coin

**cornflakes** ['kɔ:nfleiks] npl
cornflakes mpl

**cornflour** ['kɔ:nflauəʳ] n (*BRIT*) farine f
de maïs, maïzena® f

**cornstarch** ['kɔ:nstɑ:tʃ] n (*US*) farine f
de maïs, maïzena® f

**Cornwall** ['kɔ:nwəl] n Cornouailles f

**coronary** ['kɔrənəri] n: **~ (thrombosis)**
infarctus m (du myocarde), thrombose
f coronaire

**coronation** [kɔrə'neiʃən] n
couronnement m

**coroner** ['kɔrənəʳ] n coroner m, *officier
de police judiciaire chargé de déterminer les
causes d'un décès*

**corporal** ['kɔ:pərl] n caporal m,
brigadier m ▷ adj: **~ punishment**
châtiment corporel

**corporate** ['kɔ:pərit] adj (*action,
ownership*) en commun; (*Comm*) de
la société

**corporation** [kɔ:pə'reiʃən] n (*of town*)
municipalité f, conseil municipal;
(*Comm*) société f

**corps** [kɔ:ʳ, pl kɔ:z] n corps m; **the
diplomatic ~** le corps diplomatique;
**the press ~** la presse

**corpse** [kɔ:ps] n cadavre m

**correct** [kə'rɛkt] adj (*accurate*)
correct(e), exact(e); (*proper*) correct,
convenable ▷ vt corriger; **correction**
[kə'rɛkʃən] n correction f

**correspond** [kɔris'pɔnd] vi
correspondre; **to ~ to sth** (*be
equivalent to*) correspondre à qch;
**correspondence** n correspondance f;
**correspondent** n correspondant(e);
**corresponding** adj correspondant(e)

**corridor** ['kɔridɔ:ʳ] n couloir m,
corridor m

**corrode** [kə'rəud] vt corroder, ronger
▷ vi se corroder

**corrupt** [kə'rʌpt] adj corrompu(e);
(*Comput*) altéré(e) ▷ vt corrompre;
(*Comput*) altérer; **corruption** n
corruption f; (*Comput*) altération f (de
données)

**Corsica** ['kɔ:sikə] n Corse f

**cosmetic** [kɔz'mɛtik] n produit m
de beauté, cosmétique m ▷ adj (*fig:
reforms*) symbolique, superficiel(le);
**cosmetic surgery** n chirurgie f
esthétique

**cosmopolitan** [kɔzmə'pɔlitn] adj
cosmopolite

**cost** [kɔst] n coût m ▷ vb (*pt, pp* **~**) ▷ vi
coûter ▷ vt établir or calculer le prix
de revient de; **costs** npl (*Comm*) frais
mpl; (*Law*) dépens mpl; **how much
does it ~?** combien ça coûte?; **to ~ sb
time/effort** demander du temps/un
effort à qn; **it ~ him his life/job** ça lui a
coûté la vie/son emploi; **at all ~s** coûte
que coûte, à tout prix

**co-star** ['kəustɑ:ʳ] n partenaire m/f

**costly** ['kɔstli] adj coûteux(-euse)

**cost of living** n coût m de la vie

**costume** ['kɔstju:m] n costume m;
(*BRIT: also:* **swimming ~**) maillot m

(de bain)

**cosy** (US **cozy**) ['kəuzɪ] adj (room, bed) douillet(te); **to be ~** (person) être bien (au chaud)

**cot** [kɒt] n (BRIT: child's) lit m d'enfant, petit lit; (US: campbed) lit de camp

**cottage** ['kɒtɪdʒ] n petite maison (à la campagne), cottage m; **cottage cheese** n fromage blanc (maigre)

**cotton** ['kɒtn] n coton m; (thread) fil m (de coton); **cotton on vi** (inf): **to ~ on (to sth)** piger (qch); **cotton bud** (BRIT) n coton-tige® m; **cotton candy** (US) n barbe f à papa; **cotton wool** n (BRIT) ouate f, coton m hydrophile

**couch** [kautʃ] n canapé m; divan m

**cough** [kɒf] vi tousser ▷ n toux f; **I've got a ~** j'ai la toux; **cough mixture, cough syrup** n sirop m pour la toux

**could** [kud] pt of **can²**; **couldn't** = **could not**

**council** ['kaunsl] n conseil m; **city** or **town ~** conseil municipal; **council estate** (BRIT) (quartier m or zone f de) logements loués à/par la municipalité; **council house** n (BRIT) maison f (à loyer modéré) louée par la municipalité; **councillor** (US **councilor**) n conseiller(-ère); **council tax** n (BRIT) impôts locaux

**counsel** ['kaunsl] n conseil m; (lawyer) avocat(e) ▷ vt: **to ~ (sb to do sth)** conseiller (à qn de faire qch); **counselling** (US **counseling**) n (Psych) aide psychosociale; **counsellor** (US **counselor**) n conseiller(-ère); (US Law) avocat m

**count** [kaunt] vt, vi compter ▷ n compte m; (nobleman) comte m; **count in** vt (inf): **to ~ sb in on sth** inclure qn dans qch; **count on** vt fus compter sur; **countdown** n compte m à rebours

**counter** ['kauntə<sup>r</sup>] n comptoir m; (in post office, bank) guichet m; (in game) jeton m ▷ vt aller à l'encontre de, opposer ▷ adv: **~ to** à l'encontre de; contrairement à; **counterclockwise** (US) adv en sens inverse des aiguilles

d'une montre

**counterfeit** ['kauntəfɪt] n faux m, contrefaçon f ▷ vt contrefaire ▷ adj faux (fausse)

**counterpart** ['kauntəpɑːt] n (of person) homologue m/f

**countess** ['kauntɪs] n comtesse f

**countless** ['kauntlɪs] adj innombrable

**country** ['kʌntrɪ] n pays m; (native land) patrie f; (as opposed to town) campagne f; (region) région f, pays; **country and western (music)** n musique f country; **country house** n manoir m, (petit) château; **countryside** n campagne f

**county** ['kauntɪ] n comté m

**coup** [kuː, pl kuːz] n (achievement) beau coup; (also: **~ d'état**) coup d'État

**couple** ['kʌpl] n couple m; **a ~ of** (two) deux; (a few) deux ou trois

**coupon** ['kuːpɒn] n (voucher) bon m de réduction; (detachable form) coupon m détachable, coupon-réponse m

**courage** ['kʌrɪdʒ] n courage m; **courageous** [kə'reɪdʒəs] adj courageux(-euse)

**courgette** [kuə'ʒɛt] n (BRIT) courgette f

**courier** ['kurɪə<sup>r</sup>] n messager m, courrier m; (for tourists) accompagnateur(-trice)

**course** [kɔːs] n cours m; (of ship) route f; (for golf) terrain m; (part of meal) plat m; **of ~** adv bien sûr; **(no,) of ~ not!** bien sûr que non!, évidemment que non!; **~ of treatment** (Med) traitement m

**court** [kɔːt] n cour f; (Law) cour, tribunal m; (Tennis) court m ▷ vt (woman) courtiser, faire la cour à; **to take to ~** actionner or poursuivre en justice

**courtesy** ['kəːtəsɪ] n courtoisie f, politesse f; **(by) ~ of** avec l'aimable autorisation de; **courtesy bus, courtesy coach** n navette gratuite

**court:** **court-house** ['kɔːthaus] n (US) palais m de justice; **courtroom** ['kɔːtrum] n salle f de tribunal; **courtyard** ['kɔːtjɑːd] n cour f

**cousin** ['kʌzn] n cousin(e); **first ~** cousin(e) germain(e)

**cover** ['kʌvə<sup>r</sup>] vt couvrir; (Press: report

*on*) faire un reportage sur; (*feelings, mistake*) cacher; (*include*) englober; (*discuss*) traiter ▷ *n* (*of book, Comm*) couverture *f*; (*of pan*) couvercle *m*; (*over furniture*) housse *f*; (*shelter*) abri *m*; **covers** *npl* (*on bed*) couvertures; **to take ~** se mettre à l'abri; **under ~** à l'abri; **under ~ of darkness** à la faveur de la nuit; **under separate ~** (*Comm*) sous pli séparé; **cover up** *vi*: **to ~ up for sb** (*fig*) couvrir qn; **coverage** *n* (*in media*) reportage *m*; **cover charge** *n* couvert *m* (*supplément à payer*); **cover-up** *n* tentative *f* pour étouffer une affaire

**cow** [kau] *n* vache *f* ▷ *vt* effrayer, intimider

**coward** ['kauəd] *n* lâche *m/f*; **cowardly** *adj* lâche

**cowboy** ['kaubɔɪ] *n* cow-boy *m*

**cozy** ['kəuzɪ] *adj* (*us*) = **cosy**

**crab** [kræb] *n* crabe *m*

**crack** [kræk] *n* (*split*) fente *f*, fissure *f*; (*in cup, bone*) fêlure *f*; (*in wall*) lézarde *f*; (*noise*) craquement *m*, coup (sec); (*Drugs*) crack *m* ▷ *vt* fendre, fissurer; fêler; lézarder; (*whip*) faire claquer; (*nut*) casser; (*problem*) résoudre; (*code*) déchiffrer ▷ *cpd* (*athlete*) de première classe, d'élite; **crack down on** *vt fus* (*crime*) sévir contre, réprimer; **cracked** *adj* (*cup, bone*) fêlé(e); (*broken*) cassé(e); (*wall*) lézardé(e); (*surface*) craquelé(e); (*inf*) toqué(e), timbré(e); **cracker** *n* (*also*: **Christmas cracker**) pétard *m*; (*biscuit*) biscuit (salé), craquelin *m*

**crackle** ['krækl] *vi* crépiter, grésiller

**cradle** ['kreɪdl] *n* berceau *m*

**craft** [krɑːft] *n* métier (artisanal); (*cunning*) ruse *f*, astuce *f*; (*boat: pl inv*) embarcation *f*, barque *f*; (*plane: pl inv*) appareil *m*; **craftsman** (*irreg*) *n* artisan *m* ouvrier (qualifié); **craftsmanship** *n* métier *m*, habileté *f*

**cram** [kræm] *vt* (*fill*): **to ~ sth with** bourrer qch de; (*put*): **to ~ sth into** fourrer qch dans ▷ *vi* (*for exams*) bachoter

**cramp** [kræmp] *n* crampe *f*; **I've got ~ in my leg** j'ai une crampe à la jambe; **cramped** *adj* à l'étroit, très serré(e)

**cranberry** ['krænbərɪ] *n* canneberge *f*

**crane** [kreɪn] *n* grue *f*

**crap** [kræp] *n* (*inf!: nonsense*) conneries *fpl* (!); (*: excrement*) merde *f* (!)

**crash** [kræʃ] *n* (*noise*) fracas *m*; (*of car, plane*) collision *f*; (*of business*) faillite *f* ▷ *vt* (*plane*) écraser ▷ *vi* (*plane*) s'écraser; (*two cars*) se percuter, s'emboutir; (*business*) s'effondrer; **to ~ into** se jeter or se fracasser contre; **crash course** *n* cours intensif; **crash helmet** *n* casque (protecteur)

**crate** [kreɪt] *n* cageot *m*; (*for bottles*) caisse *f*

**crave** [kreɪv] *vt, vi*: **to ~ (for)** avoir une envie irrésistible de

**crawl** [krɔːl] *vi* ramper; (*vehicle*) avancer au pas ▷ *n* (*Swimming*) crawl *m*

**crayfish** ['kreɪfɪʃ] *n* (*pl inv: freshwater*) écrevisse *f*; (*saltwater*) langoustine *f*

**crayon** ['kreɪən] *n* crayon *m* (de couleur)

**craze** [kreɪz] *n* engouement *m*

**crazy** ['kreɪzɪ] *adj* fou (folle); **to be ~ about sb/sth** (*inf*) être fou de qn/qch

**creak** [kriːk] *vi* (*hinge*) grincer; (*floor, shoes*) craquer

**cream** [kriːm] *n* crème *f* ▷ *adj* (*colour*) crème *inv*; **cream cheese** *n* fromage *m* à la crème, fromage blanc; **creamy** *adj* crémeux(-euse)

**crease** [kriːs] *n* pli *m* ▷ *vt* froisser, chiffonner ▷ *vi* se froisser, se chiffonner

**create** [kriː'eɪt] *vt* créer; **creation** [kriː'eɪʃən] *n* création *f*; **creative** *adj* créatif(-ive); **creator** *n* créateur(-trice)

**creature** ['kriːtʃə'] *n* créature *f*

**crèche** [krɛʃ] *n* garderie *f*, crèche *f*

**credentials** [krɪ'dɛnʃlz] *npl* (*references*) références *fpl*; (*identity papers*) pièce *f* d'identité

**credibility** [krɛdɪ'bɪlɪtɪ] *n* crédibilité *f*

**credible** ['krɛdɪbl] *adj* digne de foi, crédible

**credit** ['krɛdɪt] *n* crédit *m*; (*recognition*)

honneur m; (Scol) unité f de valeur ▷ vt
(Comm) créditer; (believe: also: **give ~ to**)
ajouter foi à, croire; **credits** npl (Cine)
générique m; **to be in ~** (person, bank
account) être créditeur(-trice); **to ~ sb
with** (fig) prêter or attribuer à qn; **credit
card** n carte f de crédit; **do you take
credit cards?** acceptez-vous les cartes
de crédit?

**creek** [kriːk] n (inlet) crique f, anse f; (US:
stream) ruisseau m, petit cours d'eau

**creep** (pt, pp **crept**) [kriːp, krɛpt] vi
ramper

**cremate** [krɪˈmeɪt] vt incinérer

**crematorium** (pl **crematoria**)
[krɛməˈtɔːrɪəm, -ˈtɔːrɪə] n four m
crématoire

**crept** [krɛpt] pt, pp of **creep**

**crescent** [ˈkrɛsnt] n croissant m;
(street) rue f (en arc de cercle)

**cress** [krɛs] n cresson m

**crest** [krɛst] n crête f; (of coat of arms)
timbre m

**crew** [kruː] n équipage m; (Cine) équipe
f (de tournage); **crew-neck** n col ras

**crib** [krɪb] n lit m d'enfant; (for baby)
berceau m ▷ vt (inf) copier

**cricket** [ˈkrɪkɪt] n (insect) grillon m,
cri-cri m inv; (game) cricket m; **cricketer**
n joueur m de cricket ·

**crime** [kraɪm] n crime m; **criminal**
[ˈkrɪmɪnl] adj, n criminel(le)

**crimson** [ˈkrɪmzn] adj cramoisi(e)

**cringe** [krɪndʒ] vi avoir un mouvement
de recul

**cripple** [ˈkrɪpl] n boiteux(-euse),
infirme m/f ▷ vt (person) estropier,
paralyser; (ship, plane) immobiliser;
(production, exports) paralyser

**crisis** (pl **crises**) [ˈkraɪsɪs, -siːz] n crise f

**crisp** [krɪsp] adj croquant(e); (weather)
vif (vive); (manner etc) brusque; **crisps**
(BRIT) npl (pommes fpl) chips fpl; **crispy**
adj croustillant(e)

**criterion** (pl **criteria**) [kraɪˈtɪərɪən,
-ˈtɪərɪə] n critère m

**critic** [ˈkrɪtɪk] n critique m/f; **critical**
adj critique; **criticism** [ˈkrɪtɪsɪzəm]

n critique f; **criticize** [ˈkrɪtɪsaɪz] vt
critiquer

**Croat** [ˈkrəuæt] adj, n = **Croatian**

**Croatia** [krəuˈeɪʃə] n Croatie f;
**Croatian** adj croate ▷ n Croate m/f;
(Ling) croate m

**crockery** [ˈkrɔkərɪ] n vaisselle f

**crocodile** [ˈkrɔkədaɪl] n crocodile m

**crocus** [ˈkrəukəs] n crocus m

**croissant** [ˈkrwasã] n croissant m

**crook** [kruk] n escroc m; (of shepherd)
houlette f; **crooked** [ˈkrukɪd]
adj courbé(e), tordu(e); (action)
malhonnête

**crop** [krɔp] n (produce) culture f; (amount
produced) récolte f; (riding crop) cravache
f ▷ vt (hair) tondre; **crop up** vi surgir, se
présenter, survenir

**cross** [krɔs] n croix f; (Biol) croisement
m ▷ vt (street etc) traverser; (arms, legs,
Biol) croiser; (cheque) barrer ▷ adj en
colère, fâché(e); **cross off** or **out** vt
barrer, rayer; **cross over** vi traverser;
**cross-Channel ferry** [ˈkrɔsˈtʃænl-]
n ferry m qui fait la traversée de la
Manche; **crosscountry (race)** n
cross(-country) m; **crossing** n (sea
passage) traversée f; (also: **pedestrian
crossing**) passage clouté; **how long
does the crossing take?** combien de
temps dure la traversée?; **crossing
guard** (US) n contractuel qui fait
traverser la rue aux enfants; **crossroads** n
carrefour m; **crosswalk** n (US) passage
clouté; **crossword** n mots mpl croisés

**crotch** [krɔtʃ] n (of garment) entrejambe
m; (Anat) entrecuisse m

**crouch** [krautʃ] vi s'accroupir; (hide) se
tapir; (before springing) se ramasser

**crouton** [ˈkruːtɔn] n croûton m

**crow** [krəu] n (bird) corneille f; (of cock)
chant m du coq, cocorico m ▷ vi (cock)
chanter

**crowd** [kraud] n foule f ▷ vt bourrer,
remplir ▷ vi affluer, s'attrouper,
s'entasser; **crowded** adj bondé(e),
plein(e)

**crown** [kraun] n couronne f; (of head)

sommet *m* de la tête; (*of hill*) sommet *m* ▷ *vt* (*also tooth*) couronner; **crown jewels** *npl* joyaux *mpl* de la Couronne
**crucial** ['kru:ʃl] *adj* crucial(e), décisif(-ive)
**crucifix** ['kru:sɪfɪks] *n* crucifix *m*
**crude** [kru:d] *adj* (*materials*) brut(e); non raffiné(e); (*basic*) rudimentaire, sommaire; (*vulgar*) cru(e), grossier(-ière); **crude (oil)** *n* (pétrole) brut *m*
**cruel** ['kruəl] *adj* cruel(le); **cruelty** *n* cruauté *f*
**cruise** [kru:z] *n* croisière *f* ▷ *vi* (*ship*) croiser; (*car*) rouler; (*aircraft*) voler
**crumb** [krʌm] *n* miette *f*
**crumble** ['krʌmbl] *vt* émietter ▷ *vi* (*plaster etc*) s'effriter; (*land, earth*) s'ébouler; (*building*) s'écrouler, crouler; (*fig*) s'effondrer
**crumpet** ['krʌmpɪt] *n* petite crêpe (épaisse)
**crumple** ['krʌmpl] *vt* froisser, friper
**crunch** [krʌntʃ] *vt* croquer; (*underfoot*) faire craquer, écraser; faire crisser ▷ *n* (*fig*) instant *m* or moment *m* critique, moment de vérité; **crunchy** *adj* croquant(e), croustillant(e)
**crush** [krʌʃ] *n* (*crowd*) foule *f*, cohue *f*; (*love*): **to have a ~ on sb** avoir le béguin pour qn; (*drink*): **lemon ~** citron pressé ▷ *vt* écraser; (*crumple*) froisser; (*grind, break up: garlic, ice*) piler; (*: grapes*) presser; (*hopes*) anéantir
**crust** [krʌst] *n* croûte *f*; **crusty** *adj* (*bread*) croustillant(e); (*inf: person*) revêche, bourru(e)
**crutch** [krʌtʃ] *n* béquille *f*; (*also: **crotch***) entrejambe *m*
**cry** [kraɪ] *vi* pleurer; (*shout: also:* **~ out**) crier ▷ *n* cri *m*; **cry off** *vi* (*call out, shout*) pousser un cri ▷ *vt* crier
**crystal** ['krɪstl] *n* cristal *m*
**cub** [kʌb] *n* petit *m* (*d'un animal*); (*also:* **~ scout**) louveteau *m*
**Cuba** ['kju:bə] *n* Cuba *m*
**cube** [kju:b] *n* cube *m* ▷ *vt* (*Math*) élever au cube

**cubicle** ['kju:bɪkl] *n* (*in hospital*) box *m*; (*at pool*) cabine *f*
**cuckoo** ['kuku:] *n* coucou *m*
**cucumber** ['kju:kʌmbər] *n* concombre *m*
**cuddle** ['kʌdl] *vt* câliner, caresser ▷ *vi* se blottir l'un contre l'autre
**cue** [kju:] *n* queue *f* de billard; (*Theat etc*) signal *m*
**cuff** [kʌf] *n* (*BRIT: of shirt, coat etc*) poignet *m*, manchette *f*; (*US: on trousers*) revers *m*; (*blow*) gifle *f*; **off the ~** *adv* à l'improviste; **cufflinks** *n* boutons *m* de manchette
**cuisine** [kwɪ'zi:n] *n* cuisine *f*
**cul-de-sac** ['kʌldəsæk] *n* cul-de-sac *m*, impasse *f*
**cull** [kʌl] *vt* sélectionner ▷ *n* (*of animals*) abattage sélectif
**culminate** ['kʌlmɪneɪt] *vi*: **to ~ in** finir or se terminer par; (*lead to*) mener à
**culprit** ['kʌlprɪt] *n* coupable *m/f*
**cult** [kʌlt] *n* culte *m*
**cultivate** ['kʌltɪveɪt] *vt* cultiver
**cultural** ['kʌltʃərəl] *adj* culturel(le)
**culture** ['kʌltʃər] *n* culture *f*
**cumin** ['kʌmɪn] *n* (*spice*) cumin *m*
**cunning** ['kʌnɪŋ] *n* ruse *f*, astuce *f* ▷ *adj* rusé(e), malin(-igne); (*clever: device, idea*) astucieux(-euse)
**cup** [kʌp] *n* tasse *f*; (*prize, event*) coupe *f*; (*of bra*) bonnet *m*
**cupboard** ['kʌbəd] *n* placard *m*
**cup final** *n* (*BRIT Football*) finale *f* de la coupe
**curator** [kjuə'reɪtər] *n* conservateur *m* (*d'un musée etc*)
**curb** [kə:b] *vt* refréner, mettre un frein à ▷ *n* (*fig*) frein *m*; (*US*) bord *m* du trottoir
**curdle** ['kə:dl] *vi* (se) cailler
**cure** [kjuər] *vt* guérir; (*Culin: salt*) saler; (*: smoke*) fumer; (*: dry*) sécher ▷ *n* remède *m*
**curfew** ['kə:fju:] *n* couvre-feu *m*
**curiosity** [kjuərɪ'ɔsɪtɪ] *n* curiosité *f*
**curious** ['kjuərɪəs] *adj* curieux(-euse); **I'm ~ about him** il m'intrigue
**curl** [kə:l] *n* boucle *f* (de cheveux) ▷ *vt*,

vi boucler; (*tightly*) friser; **curl up** vi s'enrouler; (*person*) se pelotonner; **curler** n bigoudi m, rouleau m; **curly** adj bouclé(e); (*tightly curled*) frisé(e)

**currant** ['kʌrnt] n raisin m de Corinthe, raisin sec; (*fruit*) groseille f

**currency** ['kʌrnsɪ] n monnaie f; **to gain ~** (*fig*) s'accréditer

**current** ['kʌrnt] n courant m ▷ adj (*common*) courant(e); (*tendency, price, event*) actuel(le); **current account** n (BRIT) compte courant; **current affairs** npl (questions fpl d')actualité f; **currently** adv actuellement

**curriculum** (pl **~s** or **curricula**) [kəˈrɪkjuləm, -lə] n programme m d'études; **curriculum vitae** [-ˈviːtaɪ] n curriculum vitae (CV) m

**curry** ['kʌrɪ] n curry m ▷ vt: **to ~ favour with** chercher à gagner la faveur or à s'attirer les bonnes grâces de; **curry powder** n poudre f de curry

**curse** [kəːs] vi jurer, blasphémer ▷ vt maudire ▷ n (*spell*) malédiction f; (*problem, scourge*) fléau m; (*swearword*) juron m

**cursor** ['kəːsəʳ] n (Comput) curseur m

**curt** [kəːt] adj brusque, sec(-sèche)

**curtain** ['kəːtn] n rideau m

**curve** [kəːv] n courbe f; (*in the road*) tournant m, virage m ▷ vi se courber; (*road*) faire une courbe; **curved** adj courbe

**cushion** ['kuʃən] n coussin m ▷ vt (*fall, shock*) amortir

**custard** ['kʌstəd] n (*for pouring*) crème anglaise

**custody** ['kʌstədɪ] n (*of child*) garde f; (*for offenders*): **to take sb into ~** placer qn en détention préventive

**custom** ['kʌstəm] n coutume f, usage m; (Comm) clientèle f

**customer** ['kʌstəməʳ] n client(e)

**customized** ['kʌstəmaɪzd] adj personnalisé(e); (*car etc*) construit(e) sur commande

**customs** ['kʌstəmz] npl douane f; **customs officer** n douanier m

**cut** [kʌt] vb (pt, pp **~**) ▷ vt couper; (*meat*) découper; (*reduce*) réduire ▷ vi couper ▷ n (*gen*) coupure f; (*of clothes*) coupe f; (*in salary etc*) réduction f; (*of meat*) morceau m; **to ~ a tooth** percer une dent; **to ~ one's finger** se couper le doigt; **to get one's hair ~** se faire couper les cheveux; **I've ~ myself** je me suis coupé; **cut back** vt (*plants*) tailler; (*production, expenditure*) réduire; **cut down** vt (*tree*) abattre; (*reduce*) réduire; **cut off** vt couper; (*fig*) isoler; **cut out** vt (*picture etc*) découper; (*remove*) supprimer; **cut up** vt découper; **cutback** n réduction f

**cute** [kjuːt] adj mignon(ne), adorable

**cutlery** ['kʌtlərɪ] n couverts mpl

**cutlet** ['kʌtlɪt] n côtelette f

**cut-price** ['kʌt'praɪs] (us **cut-rate** ['kʌt'reɪt]) adj au rabais, à prix réduit

**cutting** ['kʌtɪŋ] adj (*fig*) cinglant(e) ▷ n (BRIT: *from newspaper*) coupure f (de journal); (*from plant*) bouture f

**CV** n abbr = **curriculum vitae**

**cwt** abbr = **hundredweight(s)**

**cyberspace** ['saɪbəspeɪs] n cyberespace m

**cycle** ['saɪkl] n cycle m; (*bicycle*) bicyclette f, vélo m ▷ vi faire de la bicyclette; **cycle hire** n location f de vélos; **cycle lane, cycle path** n piste f cyclable; **cycling** n cyclisme m; **cyclist** n cycliste m/f

**cyclone** ['saɪkləun] n cyclone m

**cylinder** ['sɪlɪndəʳ] n cylindre m

**cymbals** ['sɪmblz] npl cymbales fpl

**cynical** ['sɪnɪkl] adj cynique

**Cypriot** ['sɪprɪət] adj cypriote, chypriote ▷ n Cypriote m/f, Chypriote m/f

**Cyprus** ['saɪprəs] n Chypre f

**cyst** [sɪst] n kyste m; **cystitis** [sɪs'taɪtɪs] n cystite f

**czar** [zaːʳ] n tsar m

**Czech** [tʃɛk] adj tchèque ▷ n Tchèque m/f; (Ling) tchèque m; **Czech Republic** n: **the Czech Republic** la République tchèque

**D** [di:] *n* (*Mus*): **D** ré *m*

**dab** [dæb] *vt* (*eyes, wound*) tamponner; (*paint, cream*) appliquer (par petites touches *or* rapidement)

**dad, daddy** [dæd, 'dædı] *n* papa *m*

**daffodil** ['dæfədıl] *n* jonquille *f*

**daft** [dɑ:ft] *adj* (*inf*) idiot(e), stupide

**dagger** ['dægər] *n* poignard *m*

**daily** ['deılı] *adj* quotidien(ne), journalier(-ière) ▷ *adv* tous les jours

**dairy** ['dɛərı] *n* (*shop*) crémerie *f*, laiterie *f*; (*on farm*) laiterie *f*; **dairy produce** *n* produits laitiers

**daisy** ['deızı] *n* pâquerette *f*

**dam** [dæm] *n* (*wall*) barrage *m*; (*water*) réservoir *m*, lac *m* de retenue ▷ *vt* endiguer

**damage** ['dæmıdʒ] *n* dégâts *mpl*, dommages *mpl*; (*fig*) tort *m* ▷ *vt* endommager, abîmer; (*fig*) faire du tort à; **damages** *npl* (*Law*) dommages-intérêts *mpl*

**damn** [dæm] *vt* condamner; (*curse*) maudire ▷ *n* (*inf*): **I don't give a ~** je m'en fous ▷ *adj* (*inf: also*: **~ed**): **this ~ ...** ce sacré *or* foutu ...; **~ (it)!** zut!

**damp** [dæmp] *adj* humide ▷ *n* humidité *f* ▷ *vt* (*also*: **~en**: *cloth, rag*) humecter; (: *enthusiasm etc*) refroidir

**dance** [dɑ:ns] *n* danse *f*; (*ball*) bal *m* ▷ *vi* danser; **dance floor** *n* piste *f* de danse; **dancer** *n* danseur(-euse); **dancing** *n* danse *f*

**dandelion** ['dændılaıən] *n* pissenlit *m*

**dandruff** ['dændrəf] *n* pellicules *fpl*

**D & T** *n abbr* (BRIT: *Scol*) = **design and technology**

**Dane** [deın] *n* Danois(e)

**danger** ['deındʒər] *n* danger *m*; **~!** (*on sign*) danger!; **in ~** en danger; **he was in ~ of falling** il risquait de tomber; **dangerous** *adj* dangereux(-euse)

**dangle** ['dæŋgl] *vt* balancer ▷ *vi* pendre, se balancer

**Danish** ['deınıʃ] *adj* danois(e) ▷ *n* (*Ling*) danois *m*

**dare** [dɛər] *vt*: **to ~ sb to do** défier qn *or* mettre qn au défi de faire ▷ *vi*: **to ~ (to) do sth** oser faire qch; **I ~ say he'll turn up** il est probable qu'il viendra; **daring** *adj* hardi(e), audacieux(-euse) ▷ *n* audace *f*, hardiesse *f*

**dark** [dɑ:k] *adj* (*night, room*) obscur(e), sombre; (*colour, complexion*) foncé(e), sombre ▷ *n*: **in the ~** dans le noir; **to be in the ~ about** (*fig*) ignorer tout de; **after ~** après la tombée de la nuit; **darken** *vt* obscurcir, assombrir ▷ *vi* s'obscurcir, s'assombrir; **darkness** *n* obscurité *f*; **darkroom** *n* chambre noire

**darling** ['dɑ:lıŋ] *adj*, *n* chéri(e)

**dart** [dɑ:t] *n* fléchette *f*; (*in sewing*) pince *f* ▷ *vi*: **to ~ towards** se précipiter *or* s'élancer vers; **dartboard** *n* cible *f* (de jeu de fléchettes); **darts** *n* jeu *m* de fléchettes

**dash** [dæʃ] *n* (*sign*) tiret *m*; (*small quantity*) goutte *f*, larme *f* ▷ *vt* (*throw*) jeter *or* lancer violemment; (*hopes*) anéantir ▷ *vi*: **to ~ towards** se précipiter *or* se ruer vers

**dashboard** ['dæʃbɔːd] n (Aut) tableau m de bord

**data** ['deɪtə] npl données fpl; **database** n base f de données; **data processing** n traitement m (électronique) de l'information

**date** [deɪt] n date f; (with sb) rendez-vous m; (fruit) datte f ▷ vt dater; (person) sortir avec; **~ of birth** date de naissance; **to ~** adv à ce jour; **out of ~** périmé(e); **up to ~** à la page, mis(e) à jour, moderne; **dated** adj démodé(e)

**daughter** ['dɔːtər] n fille f; **daughter-in-law** n belle-fille f, bru f

**daunting** ['dɔːntɪŋ] adj décourageant(e), intimidant(e)

**dawn** [dɔːn] n aube f, aurore f ▷ vi (day) se lever, poindre; **it ~ed on him that ...** il lui vint à l'esprit que ...

**day** [deɪ] n jour m; (as duration) journée f; (period of time, age) époque f, temps m; **the ~ before** la veille, le jour précédent; **the ~ after, the following ~** le lendemain, le jour suivant; **the ~ before yesterday** avant-hier; **the ~ after tomorrow** après-demain; **by ~** de jour; **day-care centre** ['deɪkɛə-] n (for elderly etc) centre m d'accueil de jour; (for children) garderie f, **daydream** vi rêver (tout éveillé); **daylight** n (lumière f du) jour m; **day return** n (BRIT) billet m d'aller-retour (valable pour la journée); **daytime** n jour m, journée f; **day-to-day** adj (routine, expenses) journalier(-ière); **day trip** n excursion f (d'une journée)

**dazed** [deɪzd] adj abruti(e)

**dazzle** ['dæzl] vt éblouir, aveugler; **dazzling** adj (light) aveuglant(e), éblouissant(e); (fig) éblouissant(e)

**DC** abbr (Elec) = **direct current**

**dead** [dɛd] adj mort(e); (numb) engourdi(e), insensible; (battery) à plat ▷ adv (completely) absolument, complètement; (exactly) juste; **he was shot ~** il a été tué d'un coup de revolver; **~ tired** éreinté(e), complètement fourbu(e); **to stop ~** s'arrêter pile or net;

**the line is ~** (Tel) la ligne est coupée; **dead end** n impasse f; **deadline** n date f or heure f limite; **deadly** adj mortel(le); (weapon) meurtrier(-ière); **Dead Sea** n: **the Dead Sea** la mer Morte

**deaf** [dɛf] adj sourd(e); **deafen** vt rendre sourd(e); **deafening** adj assourdissant(e)

**deal** [diːl] n affaire f, marché m ▷ vt (pt, pp **~t**) (blow) porter; (cards) donner, distribuer; **a great ~ of** beaucoup de; **deal with** vt fus (handle) s'occuper or se charger de; (be about: book etc) traiter de; **dealer** n (Comm) marchand m; (Cards) donneur m; **dealings** npl (in goods, shares) opérations fpl, transactions fpl; (relations) relations fpl, rapports mpl

**dealt** [dɛlt] pt, pp of **deal**

**dean** [diːn] n (Rel, BRIT Scol) doyen m; (US Scol) conseiller principal (conseillère principale) d'éducation

**dear** [dɪər] adj cher (chère); (expensive) cher, coûteux(-euse) ▷ n: **my ~** mon cher (ma chère) ▷ excl: **~ me!** mon Dieu!; **D~ Sir/Madam** (in letter) Monsieur/Madame; **D~ Mr/Mrs X** Cher Monsieur X (Chère Madame X); **dearly** adv (love) tendrement; (pay) cher

**death** [dɛθ] n mort f; (Admin) décès m; **death penalty** n peine f de mort; **death sentence** n condamnation f à mort

**debate** [dɪ'beɪt] n discussion f, débat m ▷ vt discuter, débattre

**debit** ['dɛbɪt] n débit m ▷ vt: **to ~ a sum to sb or to sb's account** porter une somme au débit de qn, débiter qn d'une somme; **debit card** n carte f de paiement

**debris** ['dɛbriː] n débris mpl, décombres mpl

**debt** [dɛt] n dette f; **to be in ~** avoir des dettes, être endetté(e)

**debut** ['deɪbjuː] n début(s) m(pl)

**Dec.** abbr (= December) déc

**decade** ['dɛkeɪd] n décennie f, décade f

**decaffeinated** [dɪ'kæfɪneɪtɪd] *adj*
décaféiné(e)

**decay** [dɪ'keɪ] *n* (*of building*)
délabrement *m*; (*also*: **tooth ~**) carie
*f* (dentaire) ▷ *vi* (*rot*) se décomposer,
pourrir; (: *teeth*) se carier

**deceased** [dɪ'si:st] *n*: **the ~** le (la)
défunt(e)

**deceit** [dɪ'si:t] *n* tromperie *f*,
supercherie *f*; **deceive** [dɪ'si:v] *vt*
tromper

**December** [dɪ'sɛmbə<sup>r</sup>] *n* décembre *m*

**decency** ['di:sənsɪ] *n* décence *f*

**decent** ['di:sənt] *adj* (*proper*) décent(e),
convenable

**deception** [dɪ'sɛpʃən] *n* tromperie *f*

**deceptive** [dɪ'sɛptɪv] *adj*
trompeur(-euse)

**decide** [dɪ'saɪd] *vt* (*subj: person*) décider;
(*question, argument*) trancher, régler ▷ *vi*
se décider, décider; **to ~ to do/that**
décider de faire/que; **to ~ on** décider,
se décider pour

**decimal** ['dɛsɪməl] *adj* décimal(e) ▷ *n*
décimale *f*

**decision** [dɪ'sɪʒən] *n* décision *f*

**decisive** [dɪ'saɪsɪv] *adj* décisif(-ive);
(*manner, person*) décidé(e), catégorique

**deck** [dɛk] *n* (*Naut*) pont *m*; (*of cards*) jeu
*m*; (*record deck*) platine *f*; (*of bus*): **top ~**
impériale *f*; **deckchair** *n* chaise longue

**declaration** [dɛklə'reɪʃən] *n*
déclaration *f*

**declare** [dɪ'klɛə<sup>r</sup>] *vt* déclarer

**decline** [dɪ'klaɪn] *n* (*decay*) déclin *m*;
(*lessening*) baisse *f* ▷ *vt* refuser, décliner
▷ *vi* décliner; (*business*) baisser

**decorate** ['dɛkəreɪt] *vt* (*adorn, give
a medal to*) décorer; (*paint and paper*)
peindre et tapisser; **decoration**
[dɛkə'reɪʃən] *n* (*medal etc, adornment*)
décoration *f*; **decorator** *n* peintre *m*
en bâtiment

**decrease** *n* ['di:kri:s] diminution *f*
▷ *vt, vi* [di:'kri:s] diminuer

**decree** [dɪ'kri:] *n* (*Pol, Rel*) décret *m*;
(*Law*) arrêt *m*, jugement *m*

**dedicate** ['dɛdɪkeɪt] *vt* consacrer; (*book*

*etc*) dédier; **dedicated** *adj* (*person*)
dévoué(e); (*Comput*) spécialisé(e),
dédié(e); **dedicated word processor**
station *f* de traitement de texte;
**dedication** [dɛdɪ'keɪʃən] *n* (*devotion*)
dévouement *m*; (*in book*) dédicace *f*

**deduce** [dɪ'dju:s] *vt* déduire, conclure

**deduct** [dɪ'dʌkt] *vt*: **to ~ sth (from)**
déduire qch (de), retrancher qch (de);
**deduction** [dɪ'dʌkʃən] *n* (*deducting,
deducing*) déduction *f*; (*from wage etc*)
prélèvement *m*, retenue *f*

**deed** [di:d] *n* action *f*, acte *m*; (*Law*) acte
notarié, contrat *m*

**deem** [di:m] *vt* (*formal*) juger, estimer

**deep** [di:p] *adj* profond(e); (*voice*) grave
▷ *adv*: **spectators stood 20 ~** il y avait
20 rangs de spectateurs; **4 metres ~**
de 4 mètres de profondeur; **how ~ is
the water?** l'eau a quelle profondeur?;
**deep-fry** *vt* faire frire (dans une
friteuse); **deeply** *adv* profondément;
(*regret, interested*) vivement

**deer** [dɪə<sup>r</sup>] *n* (*pl inv*): (**red**) **~** cerf *m*;
(**fallow**) **~** daim *m*; (**roe**) **~** chevreuil *m*

**default** [dɪ'fɔ:lt] *n* (*Comput: also*:
**~ value**) valeur *f* par défaut; **by ~** (*Law*)
par défaut, par contumace; (*Sport*)
par forfait

**defeat** [dɪ'fi:t] *n* défaite *f* ▷ *vt* (*team,
opponents*) battre

**defect** *n* ['di:fɛkt] défaut *m* ▷ *vi*
[dɪ'fɛkt]: **to ~ to the enemy/the West**
passer à l'ennemi/l'Ouest; **defective**
[dɪ'fɛktɪv] *adj* défectueux(-euse)

**defence** (*us* **defense**) [dɪ'fɛns] *n*
défense *f*

**defend** [dɪ'fɛnd] *vt* défendre;
**defendant** *n* défendeur(-deresse); (*in
criminal case*) accusé(e), prévenu(e);
**defender** *n* défenseur *m*

**defense** [dɪ'fɛns] (*us*) = **defence**

**defensive** [dɪ'fɛnsɪv] *adj* défensif(-ive)
▷ *n*: **on the ~** sur la défensive

**defer** [dɪ'fə:<sup>r</sup>] *vt* (*postpone*) différer,
ajourner

**defiance** [dɪ'faɪəns] *n* défi *m*; **in ~ of**
au mépris de; **defiant** [dɪ'faɪənt] *adj*

provocant(e), de défi; (*person*) rebelle, intraitable

**deficiency** [dɪˈfɪʃənsɪ] n (*lack*) insuffisance f; (: *Med*) carence f; (*flaw*) faiblesse f; **deficient** [dɪˈfɪʃənt] adj (*inadequate*) insuffisant(e); **to be deficient in** manquer de

**deficit** [ˈdɛfɪsɪt] n déficit m

**define** [dɪˈfaɪn] vt définir

**definite** [ˈdɛfɪnɪt] adj (*fixed*) défini(e), (bien) déterminé(e); (*clear, obvious*) net(te), manifeste; (*certain*) sûr(e); **he was ~ about it** il a été catégorique; **definitely** adv sans aucun doute

**definition** [dɛfɪˈnɪʃən] n définition f; (*clearness*) netteté f

**deflate** [diːˈfleɪt] vt dégonfler

**deflect** [dɪˈflɛkt] vt détourner, faire dévier

**defraud** [dɪˈfrɔːd] vt: **to ~ sb of sth** escroquer qch à qn

**defrost** [diːˈfrɒst] vt (*fridge*) dégivrer; (*frozen food*) décongeler

**defuse** [diːˈfjuːz] vt désamorcer

**defy** [dɪˈfaɪ] vt défier; (*efforts etc*) résister à; **it defies description** cela défie toute description

**degree** [dɪˈgriː] n degré m; (*Scol*) diplôme m (universitaire); **a (first) ~ in maths** (*BRIT*) une licence en maths; **by ~s** (*gradually*) par degrés; **to some ~** jusqu'à un certain point, dans une certaine mesure

**dehydrated** [diːhaɪˈdreɪtɪd] adj déshydraté(e); (*milk, eggs*) en poudre

**de-icer** [diːˈaɪsəʳ] n dégivreur m

**delay** [dɪˈleɪ] vt retarder; (*payment*) différer ▷ vi s'attarder ▷ n délai m, retard m; **to be ~ed** être en retard

**delegate** n [ˈdɛlɪgɪt] délégué(e) ▷ vt [ˈdɛlɪgeɪt] déléguer

**delete** [dɪˈliːt] vt rayer, supprimer; (*Comput*) effacer

**deli** [ˈdɛlɪ] n épicerie fine

**deliberate** adj [dɪˈlɪbərɪt] (*intentional*) délibéré(e); (*slow*) mesuré(e) ▷ vi [dɪˈlɪbəreɪt] délibérer, réfléchir; **deliberately** adv (*on purpose*) exprès,

délibérément

**delicacy** [ˈdɛlɪkəsɪ] n délicatesse f; (*choice food*) mets fin or délicat, friandise f

**delicate** [ˈdɛlɪkɪt] adj délicat(e)

**delicatessen** [dɛlɪkəˈtɛsn] n épicerie fine

**delicious** [dɪˈlɪʃəs] adj délicieux(-euse)

**delight** [dɪˈlaɪt] n (grande) joie, grand plaisir ▷ vt enchanter; **she's a ~ to work with** c'est un plaisir de travailler avec elle; **to take ~ in** prendre grand plaisir à; **delighted** adj: **delighted (at or with sth)** ravi(e) (de qch); **to be delighted to do sth/that** être enchanté(e) or ravi(e) de faire qch/que; **delightful** adj (*person*) adorable; (*meal, evening*) merveilleux(-euse)

**delinquent** [dɪˈlɪŋkwənt] adj, n délinquant(e)

**deliver** [dɪˈlɪvəʳ] vt (*mail*) distribuer; (*goods*) livrer; (*message*) remettre; (*speech*) prononcer; (*Med: baby*) mettre au monde; **delivery** n (*of mail*) distribution f; (*of goods*) livraison f; (*of speaker*) élocution f; (*Med*) accouchement m; **to take delivery of** prendre livraison de

**delusion** [dɪˈluːʒən] n illusion f

**de luxe** [dəˈlʌks] adj de luxe

**delve** [dɛlv] vi: **to ~ into** fouiller dans

**demand** [dɪˈmɑːnd] vt réclamer, exiger ▷ n exigence f; (*claim*) revendication f; (*Econ*) demande f; **in ~** demandé(e), recherché(e); **on ~** sur demande; **demanding** adj (*person*) exigeant(e); (*work*) astreignant(e)

> Be careful not to translate **to demand** by the French word **demander**.

**demise** [dɪˈmaɪz] n décès m

**demo** [ˈdɛməu] n abbr (*inf*) = **demonstration** (*protest*) manif f; (*Comput*) démonstration f

**democracy** [dɪˈmɔkrəsɪ] n démocratie f; **democrat** [ˈdɛməkræt] n démocrate m/f; **democratic** [dɛməˈkrætɪk] adj démocratique

**demolish** [dɪ'mɔlɪʃ] vt démolir
**demolition** [dɛmə'lɪʃən] n
démolition f
**demon** ['di:mən] n démon m
**demonstrate** ['dɛmənstreɪt] vt
démontrer, prouver; (show) faire
une démonstration de ▷ vi: **to
~ (for/against)** manifester (en
faveur de/contre); **demonstration**
[dɛmən'streɪʃən] n démonstration
f; (Pol etc) manifestation f;
**demonstrator** n (Pol etc)
manifestant(e)
**demote** [dɪ'məut] vt rétrograder
**den** [dɛn] n (of lion) tanière f; (room)
repaire m
**denial** [dɪ'naɪəl] n (of accusation)
démenti m; (of rights, guilt, truth)
dénégation f
**denim** ['dɛnɪm] n jean m; **denims** npl
(blue-)jeans mpl
**Denmark** ['dɛnmɑːk] n Danemark m
**denomination** [dɪnɔmɪ'neɪʃən] n
(money) valeur f; (Rel) confession f
**denounce** [dɪ'nauns] vt dénoncer
**dense** [dɛns] adj dense; (inf: stupid)
obtus(e)
**density** ['dɛnsɪtɪ] n densité f;
**single-/double-~ disk** (Comput)
disquette f (à) simple/double densité
**dent** [dɛnt] n bosse f ▷ vt (also: **make a
~ in**) cabosser
**dental** ['dɛntl] adj dentaire; **dental
floss** [-flɔs] n fil m dentaire; **dental
surgery** n cabinet m de dentiste
**dentist** ['dɛntɪst] n dentiste m/f
**dentures** ['dɛntʃəz] npl dentier msg
**deny** [dɪ'naɪ] vt nier; (refuse) refuser
**deodorant** [diː'əudərənt] n
déodorant m
**depart** [dɪ'pɑːt] vi partir; **to ~ from** (fig:
differ from) s'écarter de
**department** [dɪ'pɑːtmənt] n (Comm)
rayon m; (Scol) section f; (Pol) ministère
m, département m; **department store**
n grand magasin
**departure** [dɪ'pɑːtʃər] n départ m; (fig):
**a new ~** une nouvelle voie; **departure**

**lounge** n salle f de départ
**depend** [dɪ'pɛnd] vi: **to ~ (up)on**
dépendre de; (rely on) compter sur; **it
~s** cela dépend; **~ing on the result ...**
selon le résultat ...; **dependant** n
personne f à charge; **dependent** adj: **to
be dependent (on)** dépendre (de) ▷ n
= **dependant**
**depict** [dɪ'pɪkt] vt (in picture)
représenter; (in words) (dé)peindre,
décrire
**deport** [dɪ'pɔːt] vt déporter, expulser
**deposit** [dɪ'pɔzɪt] n (Chem, Comm, Geo)
dépôt m; (of ore, oil) gisement m; (part
payment) arrhes fpl, acompte m; (on
bottle etc) consigne f; (for hired goods
etc) cautionnement m, garantie f ▷ vt
déposer; **deposit account** n compte
m sur livret
**depot** ['dɛpəu] n dépôt m; (us: Rail)
gare f
**depreciate** [dɪ'priːʃɪeɪt] vi se déprécier,
se dévaloriser
**depress** [dɪ'prɛs] vt déprimer; (press
down) appuyer sur, abaisser; (wages etc)
faire baisser; **depressed** adj (person)
déprimé(e); (area) en déclin, touché(e)
par le sous-emploi; **depressing** adj
déprimant(e); **depression** [dɪ'prɛʃən]
n dépression f
**deprive** [dɪ'praɪv] vt: **to ~ sb of** priver
qn de; **deprived** adj déshérité(e)
**dept.** abbr (= department) dép, dépt
**depth** [dɛpθ] n profondeur f; **to be in
the ~s of despair** être au plus profond
du désespoir; **to be out of one's ~**
(BRIT: swimmer) ne plus avoir pied; (fig)
être dépassé(e), nager
**deputy** ['dɛpjutɪ] n (second in command)
adjoint(e); (Pol) député m; (us: also: ~
**sheriff**) shérif adjoint ▷ adj: **~ head**
(Scol) directeur(-trice) adjoint(e), sous-
directeur(-trice)
**derail** [dɪ'reɪl] vt: **to be ~ed** dérailler
**derelict** ['dɛrɪlɪkt] adj abandonné(e),
à l'abandon
**derive** [dɪ'raɪv] vt: **to ~ sth from** tirer
qch de; trouver qch dans ▷ vi: **to ~ from**

provenir de, dériver de

**descend** [dɪ'sɛnd] *vt, vi* descendre;
**to ~ from** descendre de, être issu(e)
de; **to ~ to** s'abaisser à; **descendant** *n*
descendant(e); **descent** *n* descente *f*;
(*origin*) origine *f*

**describe** [dɪs'kraɪb] *vt* décrire;
**description** [dɪs'krɪpʃən] *n*
description *f*; (*sort*) sorte *f*, espèce *f*

**desert** *n* ['dɛzət] désert *m* ▷ *vb*
[dɪ'zə:t] ▷ *vt* déserter, abandonner
▷ *vi* (*Mil*) déserter; **deserted** [dɪ'zə:tɪd]
*adj* désert(e)

**deserve** [dɪ'zə:v] *vt* mériter

**design** [dɪ'zaɪn] *n* (*sketch*) plan *m*,
dessin *m*; (*layout, shape*) conception *f*,
ligne *f*; (*pattern*) dessin, motif(s) *m(pl)*;
(*of dress, car*) modèle *m*; (*art*) design *m*,
stylisme *m*; (*intention*) dessein *m* ▷ *vt*
dessiner; (*plan*) concevoir; **design and
technology** *vt* (BRIT: *Scol*) technologie *f*

**designate** *vt* ['dɛzɪgneɪt] désigner
▷ *adj* ['dɛzɪgnɪt] désigné(e)

**designer** [dɪ'zaɪnə'] *n* (*Archit,
Art*) dessinateur(-trice); (*Industry*)
concepteur *m*, designer *m*; (*Fashion*)
styliste *m/f*

**desirable** [dɪ'zaɪərəbl] *adj* (*property,
location, purchase*) attrayant(e)

**desire** [dɪ'zaɪə'] *n* désir *m* ▷ *vt* désirer,
vouloir

**desk** [dɛsk] *n* (*in office*) bureau *m*;
(*for pupil*) pupitre *m*; (BRIT: *in shop,
restaurant*) caisse *f*; (*in hotel, at airport*)
réception *f*; **desk-top publishing**
['dɛsktɔp-] *n* publication assistée par
ordinateur, PAO *f*

**despair** [dɪs'pɛə'] *n* désespoir *m* ▷ *vi*: **to
~ of** désespérer de

**despatch** [dɪs'pætʃ] *n, vt* = **dispatch**

**desperate** ['dɛspərɪt] *adj* désespéré(e);
(*fugitive*) prêt(e) à tout; **to be ~ for sth/
to do sth** avoir désespérément besoin
de qch/de faire qch; **desperately** *adv*
désespérément; (*very*) terriblement,
extrêmement; **desperation**
[dɛspə'reɪʃən] *n* désespoir *m*; **in
(sheer) desperation** en désespoir

de cause

**despise** [dɪs'paɪz] *vt* mépriser

**despite** [dɪs'paɪt] *prep* malgré, en
dépit de

**dessert** [dɪ'zə:t] *n* dessert *m*;
**dessertspoon** *n* cuiller *f* à dessert

**destination** [dɛstɪ'neɪʃən] *n*
destination *f*

**destined** ['dɛstɪnd] *adj*: **~ for London** à
destination de Londres

**destiny** ['dɛstɪnɪ] *n* destinée *f*, destin *m*

**destroy** [dɪs'trɔɪ] *vt* détruire; (*injured
horse*) abattre; (*dog*) faire piquer

**destruction** [dɪs'trʌkʃən] *n*
destruction *f*

**destructive** [dɪs'trʌktɪv] *adj*
destructeur(-trice)

**detach** [dɪ'tætʃ] *vt* détacher; **detached**
*adj* (*attitude*) détaché(e); **detached
house** *n* pavillon *m* maison(nette)
(individuelle)

**detail** ['di:teɪl] *n* détail *m* ▷ *vt* raconter
en détail, énumérer; **in ~** en détail;
**detailed** *adj* détaillé(e)

**detain** [dɪ'teɪn] *vt* retenir; (*in captivity*)
détenir

**detect** [dɪ'tɛkt] *vt* déceler, percevoir;
(*Med, Police*) dépister; (*Mil, Radar,
Tech*) détecter; **detection** [dɪ'tɛkʃən]
*n* découverte *f*; **detective** *n* policier
*m*; **private detective** détective privé;
**detective story** *n* roman policier

**detention** [dɪ'tɛnʃən] *n* détention *f*;
(*Scol*) retenue *f*, consigne *f*

**deter** [dɪ'tə:'] *vt* dissuader

**detergent** [dɪ'tə:dʒənt] *n* détersif *m*,
détergent *m*

**deteriorate** [dɪ'tɪərɪəreɪt] *vi* se
détériorer, se dégrader

**determination** [dɪtə:mɪ'neɪʃən] *n*
détermination *f*

**determine** [dɪ'tə:mɪn] *vt* déterminer;
**to ~ to do** résoudre de faire, se
déterminer à faire; **determined** *adj*
(*person*) déterminé(e), décidé(e);
**determined to do** bien décidé à faire

**deterrent** [dɪ'tɛrənt] *n* effet *m* de
dissuasion; force *f* de dissuasion

**detest** [dɪ'tɛst] vt détester, avoir
horreur de

**detour** ['di:tuər] n détour m; (us Aut:
diversion) déviation f

**detract** [dɪ'trækt] vt: **to ~ from** (quality,
pleasure) diminuer; (reputation) porter
atteinte à

**detrimental** [dɛtrɪ'mɛntl] adj: **~ to**
préjudiciable or nuisible à

**devastating** ['dɛvəsteɪtɪŋ] adj
dévastateur(-trice); (news) accablant(e)

**develop** [dɪ'vɛləp] vt (gen) développer;
(disease) commencer à souffrir
de; (resources) mettre en valeur,
exploiter; (land) aménager ▷ vi se
développer; (situation, disease: evolve)
évoluer; (facts, symptoms: appear) se
manifester, se produire; **can you ~
this film?** pouvez-vous développer
cette pellicule?; **developing country**
n pays m en voie de développement;
**development** n développement m;
(of land) exploitation f; (new fact, event)
rebondissement m, fait(s) nouveau(x)

**device** [dɪ'vaɪs] n (apparatus) appareil
m, dispositif m

**devil** ['dɛvl] n diable m; démon m

**devious** ['di:viəs] adj (person)
sournois(e), dissimulé(e)

**devise** [dɪ'vaɪz] vt imaginer, concevoir

**devote** [dɪ'vəut] vt: **to ~ sth to**
consacrer qch à; **devoted** adj
dévoué(e); **to be devoted to** être
dévoué(e) or très attaché(e) à; (book
etc) être consacré(e) à; **devotion** n
dévouement m, attachement m; (Rel)
dévotion f, piété f

**devour** [dɪ'vauər] vt dévorer

**devout** [dɪ'vaut] adj pieux(-euse),
dévot(e)

**dew** [dju:] n rosée f

**diabetes** [daɪə'bi:ti:z] n diabète m

**diabetic** [daɪə'bɛtɪk] n diabétique m/f
▷ adj (person) diabétique

**diagnose** [daɪəg'nəuz] vt
diagnostiquer

**diagnosis** (pl **diagnoses**)
[daɪəg'nəusɪs, -si:z] n diagnostic m

**diagonal** [daɪ'ægənl] adj diagonal(e)
▷ n diagonale f

**diagram** ['daɪəgræm] n diagramme
m, schéma m

**dial** ['daɪəl] n cadran m ▷ vt (number)
faire, composer

**dialect** ['daɪəlɛkt] n dialecte m

**dialling code** ['daɪəlɪŋ-] (us **dial code**)
n indicatif m (téléphonique); **what's
the ~ for Paris?** quel est l'indicatif
de Paris?

**dialling tone** ['daɪəlɪŋ-] (us **dial tone**)
n tonalité f

**dialogue** (us **dialog**) ['daɪəlɔg] n
dialogue m

**diameter** [daɪ'æmɪtər] n diamètre m

**diamond** ['daɪəmənd] n diamant
m; (shape) losange m; **diamonds** npl
(Cards) carreau m

**diaper** ['daɪəpər] n (us) couche f

**diarrhoea** (us **diarrhea**) [daɪə'ri:ə] n
diarrhée f

**diary** ['daɪərɪ] n (daily account) journal
m; (book) agenda m

**dice** [daɪs] n (pl inv) dé m ▷ vt (Culin)
couper en dés or en cubes

**dictate** [dɪk'teɪt] vt dicter; **dictation**
[dɪk'teɪʃən] n dictée f

**dictator** [dɪk'teɪtər] n dictateur m

**dictionary** ['dɪkʃənrɪ] n dictionnaire m

**did** [dɪd] pt of **do**

**didn't** [dɪdnt] = **did not**

**die** [daɪ] vi mourir; **to be dying for
sth** avoir une envie folle de qch; **to be
dying to do sth** mourir d'envie de faire
qch; **die down** vi se calmer, s'apaiser;
**die out** vi disparaître, s'éteindre

**diesel** ['di:zl] n (vehicle) diesel m; (also: ~
**oil**) carburant m diesel, gas-oil m

**diet** ['daɪət] n alimentation f; (restricted
food) régime m ▷ vi (also: **be on a ~**)
suivre un régime

**differ** ['dɪfər] vi: **to ~ from sth** (be
different) être différent(e) de qch,
différer de qch; **to ~ from sb over sth**
ne pas être d'accord avec qn au sujet de
qch; **difference** n différence f; (quarrel)
différend m, désaccord m; **different**

*adj* différent(e); **differentiate**
[dɪfə'renʃɪeɪt] *vi*: **to differentiate**
**between** faire une différence entre;
**differently** *adv* différemment

**difficult** ['dɪfɪkəlt] *adj* difficile;
**difficulty** *n* difficulté *f*

**dig** [dɪg] *vt* (*pt, pp* **dug**) (*hole*) creuser;
(*garden*) bêcher ▷ *n* (*prod*) coup *m* de
coude; (*fig: remark*) coup de griffe *or* de
patte; (*Archaeology*) fouille *f*; **to ~ one's**
**nails into** enfoncer ses ongles dans;
**dig up** *vt* déterrer

**digest** [daɪ'dʒɛst] digérer ▷ *n*
['daɪdʒɛst] sommaire *m*, résumé *m*;
**digestion** [dɪ'dʒɛstʃən] digestion *f*

**digit** ['dɪdʒɪt] *n* (*number*) chiffre *m* (*de 0*
*à 9*); (*finger*) doigt *m*; **digital** *adj* (*system,*
*recording, radio*) numérique, digital(e);
(*watch*) à affichage numérique *or*
digital; **digital camera** *n* appareil
*m* photo numérique; **digital TV** *n*
télévision *f* numérique

**dignified** ['dɪgnɪfaɪd] *adj* digne

**dignity** ['dɪgnɪtɪ] *n* dignité *f*

**digs** [dɪgz] *npl* (BRIT inf) piaule *f*,
chambre meublée

**dilemma** [daɪ'lɛmə] *n* dilemme *m*

**dill** [dɪl] *n* aneth *m*

**dilute** [daɪ'luːt] *vt* diluer

**dim** [dɪm] *adj* (*light, eyesight*) faible;
(*memory, outline*) vague, indécis(e);
(*room*) sombre; (*inf: stupid*) borné(e),
obtus(e) ▷ *vt* (*light*) réduire, baisser; (us
Aut) mettre en code, baisser

**dime** [daɪm] *n* (*us*) pièce *f* de 10 cents

**dimension** [daɪ'mɛnʃən] *n*
dimension *f*

**diminish** [dɪ'mɪnɪʃ] *vt, vi* diminuer

**din** [dɪn] *n* vacarme *m*

**dine** [daɪn] *vi* dîner; **diner** *n* (*person*)
dîneur(-euse); (*us: eating place*) petit
restaurant

**dinghy** ['dɪŋgɪ] *n* youyou *m*; (*inflatable*)
canot *m* pneumatique; (*also*: **sailing ~**)
voilier *m*, dériveur *m*

**dingy** ['dɪndʒɪ] *adj* miteux(-euse),
minable

**dining car** ['daɪnɪŋ-] *n* (BRIT) voiture-

restaurant *f*, wagon-restaurant *m*

**dining room** ['daɪnɪŋ-] *n* salle *f* à
manger

**dining table** [daɪnɪŋ-] *n* table *f* de (la)
salle à manger

**dinner** ['dɪnə'] *n* (*evening meal*) dîner *m*;
(*lunch*) déjeuner *m*; (*public*) banquet *m*;
**dinner jacket** *n* smoking *m*; **dinner**
**party** *n* dîner *m*; **dinner time** *n*
(*evening*) heure *f* du dîner; (*midday*)
heure du déjeuner

**dinosaur** ['daɪnəsɔː'] *n* dinosaure *m*

**dip** [dɪp] *n* (*slope*) déclivité *f*; (*in sea*)
baignade *f*, bain *m*; (*Culin*) ≈ sauce *f*
▷ *vt* tremper, plonger; (BRIT Aut: lights)
mettre en code, baisser ▷ *vi* plonger

**diploma** [dɪ'pləumə] *n* diplôme *m*

**diplomacy** [dɪ'pləuməsɪ] *n*
diplomatie *f*

**diplomat** ['dɪpləmæt] *n* diplomate *m*;
**diplomatic** [dɪplə'mætɪk] *adj*
diplomatique

**dipstick** ['dɪpstɪk] *n* (BRIT Aut) jauge *f*
de niveau d'huile

**dire** [daɪə'] *adj* (*poverty*) extrême; (*awful*)
affreux(-euse)

**direct** [daɪ'rɛkt] *adj* direct(e) ▷ *vt* (*tell*
*way*) diriger, orienter; (*letter, remark*)
adresser; (*Cine, TV*) réaliser; (*Theat*)
mettre en scène; (*order*): **to ~ sb to do**
**sth** ordonner à qn de faire qch ▷ *adv*
directement; **can you ~ me to ...?**
pouvez-vous m'indiquer le chemin
de ...?; **direct debit** *n* (BRIT Banking)
prélèvement *m* automatique

**direction** [dɪ'rɛkʃən] *n* direction *f*;
**directions** *npl* (*to a place*) indications
*fpl*; **~s for use** mode *m* d'emploi; **sense**
**of ~** sens *m* de l'orientation

**directly** [dɪ'rɛktlɪ] *adv* (*in straight line*)
directement, tout droit; (*at once*) tout
de suite, immédiatement

**director** [dɪ'rɛktə'] *n* directeur *m*;
(*Theat*) metteur *m* en scène; (*Cine, TV*)
réalisateur(-trice)

**directory** [dɪ'rɛktərɪ] *n* annuaire
*m*; (*Comput*) répertoire *m*; **directory**
**enquiries** (*us* **directory assistance**) *n*

(*Tel: service*) renseignements *mpl*

**dirt** [dəːt] *n* saleté *f*; (*mud*) boue *f*; **dirty** *adj* sale; (*joke*) cochon(ne) ▷ *vt* salir

**disability** [dɪsə'bɪlɪtɪ] *n* invalidité *f*, infirmité *f*

**disabled** [dɪs'eɪbld] *adj* handicapé(e); (*maimed*) mutilé(e)

**disadvantage** [dɪsəd'vɑːntɪdʒ] *n* désavantage *m*, inconvénient *m*

**disagree** [dɪsə'griː] *vi* (*differ*) ne pas concorder; (*be against, think otherwise*): **to ~ (with)** ne pas être d'accord (avec); **disagreeable** *adj* désagréable; **disagreement** *n* désaccord *m*, différend *m*

**disappear** [dɪsə'pɪəʳ] *vi* disparaître; **disappearance** *n* disparition *f*

**disappoint** [dɪsə'pɔɪnt] *vt* décevoir; **disappointed** *adj* déçu(e); **disappointing** *adj* décevant(e); **disappointment** *n* déception *f*

**disapproval** [dɪsə'pruːvəl] *n* désapprobation *f*

**disapprove** [dɪsə'pruːv] *vi*: **to ~ of** désapprouver

**disarm** [dɪs'ɑːm] *vt* désarmer; **disarmament** [dɪs'ɑːməmənt] *n* désarmement *m*

**disaster** [dɪ'zɑːstəʳ] *n* catastrophe *f*, désastre *m*; **disastrous** *adj* désastreux(-euse)

**disbelief** ['dɪsbə'liːf] *n* incrédulité *f*

**disc** [dɪsk] *n* disque *m*; (*Comput*) = **disk**

**discard** [dɪs'kɑːd] *vt* (*old things*) se débarrasser de; (*fig*) écarter, renoncer à

**discharge** *vt* [dɪs'tʃɑːdʒ] (*duties*) s'acquitter de; (*waste etc*) déverser; décharger; (*patient*) renvoyer (chez lui); (*employee, soldier*) congédier, licencier ▷ *n* ['dɪstʃɑːdʒ] (*Elec, Med*) émission *f*; (*dismissal*) renvoi *m*;

**discipline** ['dɪsɪplɪn] *n* discipline *f* ▷ *vt* discipliner; (*punish*) punir

**disc jockey** *n* disque-jockey *m* (DJ)

**disclose** [dɪs'kləuz] *vt* révéler, divulguer

**disco** ['dɪskəu] *n abbr* discothèque *f*

**discoloured** [dɪs'kʌləd] (*US*

**discolored**) *adj* décoloré(e), jauni(e)

**discomfort** [dɪs'kʌmfət] *n* malaise *m*, gêne *f*; (*lack of comfort*) manque *m* de confort

**disconnect** [dɪskə'nɛkt] *vt* (*Elec, Radio*) débrancher; (*gas, water*) couper

**discontent** [dɪskən'tɛnt] *n* mécontentement *m*

**discontinue** [dɪskən'tɪnjuː] *vt* cesser, interrompre; **"~d"** (*Comm*) "fin de série"

**discount** *n* ['dɪskaunt] remise *f*, rabais *m* ▷ *vt* [dɪs'kaunt] (*report etc*) ne pas tenir compte de

**discourage** [dɪs'kʌrɪdʒ] *vt* décourager

**discover** [dɪs'kʌvəʳ] *vt* découvrir; **discovery** *n* découverte *f*

**discredit** [dɪs'krɛdɪt] *vt* (*idea*) mettre en doute; (*person*) discréditer

**discreet** [dɪ'skriːt] *adj* discret(-ète)

**discrepancy** [dɪ'skrɛpənsɪ] *n* divergence *f*, contradiction *f*

**discretion** [dɪ'skrɛʃən] *n* discrétion *f*; **at the ~ of** à la discrétion de

**discriminate** [dɪ'skrɪmɪneɪt] *vi*: **to ~ between** établir une distinction entre, faire la différence entre; **to ~ against** pratiquer une discrimination contre; **discrimination** [dɪskrɪmɪ'neɪʃən] *n* discrimination *f*; (*judgment*) discernement *m*

**discuss** [dɪ'skʌs] *vt* discuter de; (*debate*) discuter; **discussion** [dɪ'skʌʃən] *n* discussion *f*

**disease** [dɪ'ziːz] *n* maladie *f*

**disembark** [dɪsɪm'bɑːk] *vt*, *vi* débarquer

**disgrace** [dɪs'greɪs] *n* honte *f*; (*disfavour*) disgrâce *f* ▷ *vt* déshonorer, couvrir de honte; **disgraceful** *adj* scandaleux(-euse), honteux(-euse)

**disgruntled** [dɪs'grʌntld] *adj* mécontent(e)

**disguise** [dɪs'gaɪz] *n* déguisement *m* ▷ *vt* déguiser; **in ~** déguisé(e)

**disgust** [dɪs'gʌst] *n* dégoût *m*, aversion *f* ▷ *vt* dégoûter, écœurer

**disgusted** [dɪs'gʌstɪd] *adj* dégoûté(e), écœuré(e)

**disgusting** [dɪsˈɡʌstɪŋ] adj
dégoûtant(e)

**dish** [dɪʃ] n plat m; **to do** or **wash the
~es** faire la vaisselle; **dishcloth** n (for
drying) torchon m; (for washing) lavette f

**dishonest** [dɪsˈɔnɪst] adj malhonnête

**dishtowel** [ˈdɪʃtauəl] n (us) torchon m
(à vaisselle)

**dishwasher** [ˈdɪʃwɔʃəʳ] n lave-
vaisselle m

**disillusion** [dɪsɪˈluːʒən] vt désabuser,
désenchanter

**disinfectant** [dɪsɪnˈfɛktənt] n
désinfectant m

**disintegrate** [dɪsˈɪntɪɡreɪt] vi se
désintégrer

**disk** [dɪsk] n (Comput) disquette f;
**single-/double-sided ~** disquette une
face/double face; **disk drive** n lecteur
m de disquette; **diskette** n (Comput)
disquette f

**dislike** [dɪsˈlaɪk] n aversion f,
antipathie f ▷ vt ne pas aimer

**dislocate** [ˈdɪsləkeɪt] vt disloquer,
déboîter

**disloyal** [dɪsˈlɔɪəl] adj déloyal(e)

**dismal** [ˈdɪzml] adj (gloomy) lugubre,
maussade; (very bad) lamentable

**dismantle** [dɪsˈmæntl] vt démonter

**dismay** [dɪsˈmeɪ] n consternation f ▷ vt
consterner

**dismiss** [dɪsˈmɪs] vt congédier,
renvoyer; (idea) écarter; (Law) rejeter;
**dismissal** n renvoi m

**disobedient** [dɪsəˈbiːdɪənt] adj
désobéissant(e), indiscipliné(e)

**disobey** [dɪsəˈbeɪ] vt désobéir à

**disorder** [dɪsˈɔːdəʳ] n désordre
m; (rioting) désordres mpl; (Med)
troubles mpl

**disorganized** [dɪsˈɔːɡənaɪzd] adj
désorganisé(e)

**disown** [dɪsˈəun] vt renier

**dispatch** [dɪsˈpætʃ] vt expédier,
envoyer ▷ n envoi m, expédition f; (Mil,
Press) dépêche f

**dispel** [dɪsˈpɛl] vt dissiper, chasser

**dispense** [dɪsˈpɛns] vt (medicine)
préparer (et vendre); **dispense with** vt
fus se passer de; **dispenser** n (device)
distributeur m

**disperse** [dɪsˈpəːs] vt disperser ▷ vi se
disperser

**display** [dɪsˈpleɪ] n (of goods) étalage
m; affichage m; (Comput: information)
visualisation f; (: device) visuel m; (of
feeling) manifestation f ▷ vt montrer;
(goods) mettre à l'étalage, exposer;
(results, departure times) afficher; (pej)
faire étalage de

**displease** [dɪsˈpliːz] vt mécontenter,
contrarier

**disposable** [dɪsˈpəuzəbl] adj (pack etc)
jetable; (income) disponible

**disposal** [dɪsˈpəuzl] n (of rubbish)
évacuation f, destruction f; (of property
etc: by selling) vente f; (: by giving away)
cession f; **at one's ~** à sa disposition

**dispose** [dɪsˈpəuz] vi: **to ~ of** (unwanted
goods) se débarrasser de, se défaire
de; (problem) expédier; **disposition**
[dɪspəˈzɪʃən] n disposition f;
(temperament) naturel m

**disproportionate** [dɪsprəˈpɔːʃənət]
adj disproportionné(e)

**dispute** [dɪsˈpjuːt] n discussion f; (also:
**industrial ~**) conflit m ▷ vt (question)
contester; (matter) discuter

**disqualify** [dɪsˈkwɔlɪfaɪ] vt (Sport)
disqualifier; **to ~ sb for sth/from
doing** rendre qn inapte à qch/à faire

**disregard** [dɪsrɪˈɡɑːd] vt ne pas tenir
compte de

**disrupt** [dɪsˈrʌpt] vt (plans, meeting,
lesson) perturber, déranger; **disruption**
[dɪsˈrʌpʃən] n perturbation f,
dérangement m

**dissatisfaction** [dɪssætɪsˈfækʃən] n
mécontentement m, insatisfaction f

**dissatisfied** [dɪsˈsætɪsfaɪd] adj: **~
(with)** insatisfait(e) (de)

**dissect** [dɪˈsɛkt] vt disséquer

**dissent** [dɪˈsɛnt] n dissentiment m,
différence f d'opinion

**dissertation** [dɪsəˈteɪʃən] n (Scol)
mémoire m

**dissolve** [dɪ'zɔlv] vt dissoudre ▷ vi se dissoudre, fondre; **to ~ in(to) tears** fondre en larmes

**distance** ['dɪstns] n distance f; **in the ~** au loin

**distant** ['dɪstnt] adj lointain(e), éloigné(e); (manner) distant(e), froid(e)

**distil** (us **distill**) [dɪs'tɪl] vt distiller; **distillery** n distillerie f

**distinct** [dɪs'tɪŋkt] adj distinct(e); (clear) marqué(e); **as ~ from** par opposition à; **distinction** [dɪs'tɪŋkʃən] n distinction f; (in exam) mention f très bien; **distinctive** adj distinctif(-ive)

**distinguish** [dɪs'tɪŋgwɪʃ] vt distinguer; **to ~ o.s.** se distinguer; **distinguished** adj (eminent, refined) distingué(e)

**distort** [dɪs'tɔːt] vt déformer

**distract** [dɪs'trækt] vt distraire, déranger; **distracted** adj (not concentrating) distrait(e); (worried) affolé(e); **distraction** [dɪs'trækʃən] n distraction f

**distraught** [dɪs'trɔːt] adj éperdu(e)

**distress** [dɪs'trɛs] n détresse f ▷ vt affliger; **distressing** adj douloureux(-euse), pénible

**distribute** [dɪs'trɪbjuːt] vt distribuer; **distribution** [dɪstrɪ'bjuːʃən] n distribution f; **distributor** n (gen: Tech) distributeur m; (Comm) concessionnaire m/f

**district** ['dɪstrɪkt] n (of country) région f; (of town) quartier m; (Admin) district m; **district attorney** n (us) ≈ procureur m de la République

**distrust** [dɪs'trʌst] n méfiance f, doute m ▷ vt se méfier de

**disturb** [dɪs'təːb] vt troubler; (inconvenience) déranger; **disturbance** n dérangement m; (political etc) troubles mpl; **disturbed** adj (worried, upset) agité(e), troublé(e); **to be emotionally disturbed** avoir des problèmes affectifs; **disturbing** adj troublant(e), inquiétant(e)

**ditch** [dɪtʃ] n fossé m; (for irrigation) rigole f ▷ vt (inf) abandonner; (person) plaquer

**ditto** ['dɪtəu] adv idem

**dive** [daɪv] n plongeon m; (of submarine) plongée f ▷ vi plonger; **to ~ into** (bag etc) plonger la main dans; (place) se précipiter dans; **diver** n plongeur m

**diverse** [daɪ'vəːs] adj divers(e)

**diversion** [daɪ'vəːʃən] n (BRIT Aut) déviation f; (distraction, Mil) diversion f

**diversity** [daɪ'vəːsɪtɪ] n diversité f, variété f

**divert** [daɪ'vəːt] vt (BRIT: traffic) dévier; (plane) dérouter; (train, river) détourner

**divide** [dɪ'vaɪd] vt diviser; (separate) séparer ▷ vi se diviser; **divided highway** (us) n route f à quatre voies

**divine** [dɪ'vaɪn] adj divin(e)

**diving** ['daɪvɪŋ] n plongée (sous-marine); **diving board** n plongeoir m

**division** [dɪ'vɪʒən] n division f; (separation) séparation f; (Comm) service m

**divorce** [dɪ'vɔːs] n divorce m ▷ vt divorcer d'avec; **divorced** adj divorcé(e); **divorcee** [dɪvɔ'siː] n divorcé(e)

**D.I.Y.** adj, n abbr (BRIT) = **do-it-yourself**

**dizzy** ['dɪzɪ] adj: **I feel ~** la tête me tourne, j'ai la tête qui tourne

**DJ** n abbr = **disc jockey**

**DNA** n abbr (= deoxyribonucleic acid) ADN m

○ **KEYWORD**

**do** [duː] (pt **did**, pp **done**) n (inf: party etc) soirée f, fête f
▷ vb **1** (in negative constructions) non traduit; **I don't understand** je ne comprends pas
**2** (to form questions) non traduit; **didn't you know?** vous ne le saviez pas?; **what do you think?** qu'en pensez-vous?
**3** (for emphasis, in polite expressions): **people do make mistakes sometimes** on peut toujours se tromper; **she does seem rather late** je

trouve qu'elle est bien en retard; **do sit
down/help yourself** asseyez-vous/
servez-vous je vous en prie; **do take
care!** faites bien attention à vous!
**4** (used to avoid repeating vb): **she swims
better than I do** elle nage mieux que
moi; **do you agree? - yes, I do/no I
don't** vous êtes d'accord? - oui/non;
**she lives in Glasgow - so do I** elle
habite Glasgow - moi aussi; **he didn't
like it and neither did we** il n'a pas
aimé ça, et nous non plus; **who broke
it? - I did** qui l'a cassé? - c'est moi; **he
asked me to help him and I did** il
m'a demandé de l'aider, et c'est ce
que j'ai fait
**5** (in question tags): **you like him, don't
you?** vous l'aimez bien, n'est-ce pas?; **I
don't know him, do I?** je ne crois pas
le connaître
▷ vt **1** (gen: carry out, perform etc) faire;
(visit: city, museum) faire, visiter; **what
are you doing tonight?** qu'est-ce que
vous faites ce soir?; **what do you do?**
(job) que faites-vous dans la vie?; **what
can I do for you?** que puis-je faire pour
vous?; **to do the cooking/washing-
up** faire la cuisine/la vaisselle; **to do
one's teeth/hair/nails** se brosser les
dents/se coiffer/se faire les ongles
**2** (Aut etc: distance) faire; (: speed) faire
du; **we've done 200 km already** nous
avons déjà fait 200 km; **the car was
doing 100** la voiture faisait du 100 (à
l'heure); **he can do 100 in that car** il
peut faire du 100 (à l'heure) dans cette
voiture-là
▷ vi **1** (act, behave) faire; **do as I do** faites
comme moi
**2** (get on, fare) marcher; **the firm is
doing well** l'entreprise marche bien;
**he's doing well/badly at school** ça
marche bien/mal pour lui à l'école;
**how do you do?** comment allez-vous?;
(on being introduced) enchanté(e)!
**3** (suit) aller; **will it do?** est-ce que
ça ira?
**4** (be sufficient) suffire, aller; **will £10**

**do?** est-ce que 10 livres suffiront?;
**that'll do** ça suffit, ça ira; **that'll do!** (in
annoyance) ça va or suffit comme ça!; **to
make do (with)** se contenter (de)
**do up** vt (laces, dress) attacher; (buttons)
boutonner; (zip) fermer; (renovate: room)
refaire; (: house) remettre à neuf
**do with** vt fus (need): **I could do with
a drink/some help** quelque chose à
boire/un peu d'aide ne serait pas de
refus; **it could do with a wash** ça ne
lui ferait pas de mal d'être lavé; (be
connected with): **that has nothing to
do with you** cela ne vous concerne pas;
**I won't have anything to do with it** je
ne veux pas m'en mêler
**do without** vi s'en passer; **if you're
late for tea then you'll do without**
si vous êtes en retard pour le dîner il
faudra vous en passer
▷ vt fus se passer de; **I can do without
a car** je peux me passer de voiture

**dock** [dɔk] n dock m; (wharf) quai m;
(Law) banc m des accusés ▷ vi se mettre
à quai; (Space) s'arrimer; **docks** npl
(Naut) docks
**doctor** ['dɔktəʳ] n médecin m, docteur
m; (PhD etc) docteur ▷ vt (drink) frelater;
**call a ~!** appelez un docteur or un
médecin!; **Doctor of Philosophy (PhD)**
n (degree) doctorat m; (person) titulaire
m/f d'un doctorat
**document** ['dɔkjumənt] n
document m; **documentary**
[dɔkju'mɛntərɪ] adj, n
documentaire (m); **documentation**
[dɔkjumən'teɪʃən] n documentation f
**dodge** [dɔdʒ] n truc m; combine f ▷ vt
esquiver, éviter
**dodgy** ['dɔdʒɪ] adj (inf: uncertain)
douteux(-euse); (: shady) louche
**does** [dʌz] vb see **do**
**doesn't** ['dʌznt] = **does not**
**dog** [dɔg] n chien(ne) ▷ vt (follow
closely) suivre de près; (fig: memory etc)
poursuivre, harceler; **doggy bag**
['dɔgɪ-] n petit sac pour emporter les restes

**do-it-yourself** ['duːɪtjɔːˈsɛlf] n
bricolage m

**dole** [dəul] n (BRIT: payment) allocation f
de chômage; **on the ~** au chômage

**doll** [dɔl] n poupée f

**dollar** ['dɔlər] n dollar m

**dolphin** ['dɔlfɪn] n dauphin m

**dome** [dəum] n dôme m

**domestic** [dəˈmɛstɪk] adj (duty,
happiness) familial(e); (policy,
affairs, flight) intérieur(e); (animal)
domestique; **domestic appliance** n
appareil ménager

**dominant** ['dɔmɪnənt] adj
dominant(e)

**dominate** ['dɔmɪneɪt] vt dominer

**domino** ['dɔmɪnəu] (pl **-es**) n
domino m; **dominoes** n (game)
dominos mpl

**donate** [dəˈneɪt] vt faire don de,
donner; **donation** [dəˈneɪʃən] n
donation f, don m

**done** [dʌn] pp of **do**

**donkey** ['dɔŋkɪ] n âne m

**donor** ['dəunər] n (of blood etc)
donneur(-euse); (to charity)
donateur(-trice); **donor card** n carte f
de don d'organes

**don't** [dəunt] = **do not**

**donut** ['dəunʌt] (US) n = **doughnut**

**doodle** ['duːdl] vi griffonner, gribouiller

**doom** [duːm] n (fate) destin m ▷ vt: **to
be ~ed to failure** être voué(e) à l'échec

**door** [dɔːʳ] n porte f; (Rail, car) portière f;
**doorbell** n sonnette f; **door handle**
n poignée f de porte; (of car) poignée
de portière; **doorknob** n poignée f or
bouton m de porte; **doorstep** n pas
m de (la) porte, seuil m; **doorway** n
(embrasure f de) porte f

**dope** [dəup] n (inf: drug) drogue f,
(: person) andouille f ▷ vt (horse etc)
doper

**dormitory** ['dɔːmɪtrɪ] n (BRIT) dortoir
m; (US: hall of residence) résidence f
universitaire

**DOS** [dɔs] n abbr (= disk operating system)
DOS m

**dosage** ['dəusɪdʒ] n dose f; dosage m;
(on label) posologie f

**dose** [dəus] n dose f

**dot** [dɔt] n point m; (on material) pois m
▷ vt: **~ted with** parsemé(e) de; **on the
~** à l'heure tapante; **dotcom** [dɔtˈkɔm]
n point com m, pointcom m; **dotted
line** ['dɔtɪd-] n ligne pointillée; **to sign
on the dotted line** signer à l'endroit
indiqué or sur la ligne pointillée

**double** ['dʌbl] adj double ▷ adv (twice):
**to cost ~ (sth)** coûter le double
(de qch) or deux fois plus (que qch) ▷ n
double m; (Cine) doublure f ▷ vt
doubler; (fold) plier en deux ▷ vi
doubler; **on the ~, at the ~** au pas
de course; **double back** vi (person)
revenir sur ses pas; **double bass** n
contrebasse f; **double bed** n grand
lit; **double-check** vt, vi revérifier;
**double-click** vi (Comput) double-
cliquer; **double-cross** vt doubler,
trahir; **doubledecker** n autobus m à
impériale; **double glazing** n (BRIT)
double vitrage m; **double room** n
chambre f pour deux; **doubles** n
(Tennis) double m; **double yellow
lines** npl (BRIT: Aut) double bande jaune
marquant l'interdiction de stationner

**doubt** [daut] n doute m ▷ vt douter
de; **no ~** sans doute; **to ~ that** douter
que + sub; **doubtful** adj douteux(-euse);
(person) incertain(e); **doubtless** adv
sans doute, sûrement

**dough** [dəu] n pâte f; **doughnut** (US
**donut**) n beignet m

**dove** [dʌv] n colombe f

**Dover** ['dəuvəʳ] n Douvres

**down** [daun] n (fluff) duvet m ▷ adv
en bas, vers le bas; (on the ground) par
terre ▷ prep en bas de; (along) le long
de ▷ vt (inf: drink) siffler; **to walk ~** a
**hill** descendre une colline; **to run ~ the
street** descendre la rue en courant;
**~ with X!** à bas X!; **down-and-out** n
(tramp) clochard(e); **downfall** n chute
f; ruine f; **downhill** adv: **to go downhill**
descendre; (business) péricliter

**Downing Street** ['daʊnɪŋ-] n (BRIT):
**10 ~** résidence du Premier ministre

● DOWNING STREET
●
● **Downing Street** est une rue de
● Westminster (à Londres) où se
● trouvent la résidence officielle
● du Premier ministre et celle du
● ministre des Finances. Le nom
● **Downing Street** est souvent utilisé
● pour désigner le gouvernement
● britannique.

**down**: **download** vt (Comput)
télécharger; **downright** adj (lie etc)
effronté(e); (refusal) catégorique
**Down's syndrome** ['daʊnz-] n
trisomie f
**down**: **downstairs** adv (on or to
ground floor) au rez-de-chaussée; (on
or to floor below) à l'étage inférieur;
**down-to-earth** adj terre à terre inv;
**downtown** adv en ville; **down under**
adv en Australie ou Nouvelle Zélande;
**downward** ['daʊnwəd] adj, adv vers
le bas; **downwards** ['daʊnwədz] adv
vers le bas
**doz.** abbr = **dozen**
**doze** [dəʊz] vi sommeiller
**dozen** ['dʌzn] n douzaine f; **a ~ books**
une douzaine de livres; **~s of** des
centaines de
**Dr.** abbr (= doctor) Dr; (in street names)
= **drive**
**drab** [dræb] adj terne, morne
**draft** [drɑːft] n (of letter, school
work) brouillon m; (of literary work)
ébauche f; (Comm) traite f; (US: call-up)
conscription f ▷ vt faire le brouillon de;
(Mil: send) détacher; see also **draught**
**drag** [dræg] vt traîner; (river) draguer
▷ vi traîner ▷ n (inf) casse-pieds m/f;
(women's clothing): **in ~** (en) travesti; **to
~ and drop** (Comput) glisser-poser
**dragon** ['drægn] n dragon m
**dragonfly** ['drægənflaɪ] n libellule f
**drain** [dreɪn] n égout m; (on resources)

saignée f ▷ vt (land, marshes) drainer,
assécher; (vegetables) égoutter;
(reservoir etc) vider ▷ vi (water) s'écouler
**drainage** n (system) système m
d'égouts; (act) drainage m; **drainpipe** n
tuyau m d'écoulement
**drama** ['drɑːmə] n (art) théâtre m, art
m dramatique; (play) pièce f; (event)
drame m; **dramatic** [drə'mætɪk]
adj (Theat) dramatique; (impressive)
spectaculaire
**drank** [dræŋk] pt of **drink**
**drape** [dreɪp] vt draper; **drapes** npl (US)
rideaux mpl
**drastic** ['dræstɪk] adj (measures)
d'urgence, énergique; (change)
radical(e)
**draught** (US **draft**) [drɑːft] n courant m
d'air; **on ~** (beer) à la pression; **draught
beer** n bière f (à la) pression; **draughts**
n (BRIT: game) (jeu m de) dames fpl
**draw** [drɔː] (vb: pt **drew**, pp **~n**) vt tirer;
(picture) dessiner; (attract) attirer; (line,
circle) tracer; (money) retirer; (wages)
toucher ▷ vi (Sport) faire match nul ▷ n
match nul; (lottery) loterie f; (: picking
of ticket) tirage m au sort; **draw out**
vi (lengthen) s'allonger ▷ vt (money)
retirer; **draw up** vi (stop) s'arrêter
▷ vt (document) établir, dresser; (plan)
formuler, dessiner; (chair) approcher;
**drawback** n inconvénient m,
désavantage m
**drawer** [drɔːʳ] n tiroir m
**drawing** ['drɔːɪŋ] n dessin m; **drawing
pin** n (BRIT) punaise f; **drawing room**
n salon m
**drawn** [drɔːn] pp of **draw**
**dread** [dred] n épouvante f, effroi m ▷ vt
redouter, appréhender; **dreadful** adj
épouvantable, affreux(-euse)
**dream** [driːm] n rêve m ▷ vt, vi (pt,
pp **~ed** or **~t**) rêver; **dreamer** n
rêveur(-euse)
**dreamt** [dremt] pt, pp of **dream**
**dreary** ['drɪərɪ] adj triste; monotone
**drench** [drentʃ] vt tremper
**dress** [dres] n robe f; (clothing)

habillement *m*, tenue *f* ▷ *vt* habiller; (*wound*) panser ▷ *vi*: **to get ~ed** s'habiller; **dress up** *vi* s'habiller; (*in fancy dress*) se déguiser; **dress circle** *n* (BRIT) premier balcon; **dresser** *n* (*furniture*) vaisselier *m*; (: *US*) coiffeuse *f*, commode *f*; **dressing** *n* (*Med*) pansement *m*; (*Culin*) sauce *f*, assaisonnement *m*; **dressing gown** *n* (BRIT) robe *f* de chambre; **dressing room** *n* (*Theat*) loge *f*; (*Sport*) vestiaire *m*; **dressing table** *n* coiffeuse *f*; **dressmaker** *n* couturière *f*

**drew** [druː] *pt of* **draw**

**dribble** ['drɪbl] *vi* (*baby*) baver ▷ *vt* (*ball*) dribbler

**dried** [draɪd] *adj* (*fruit, beans*) sec (sèche); (*eggs, milk*) en poudre

**drier** ['draɪə<sup>r</sup>] *n* = **dryer**

**drift** [drɪft] *n* (*of current etc*) force *f*; direction *f*; (*of snow*) rafale *f*, coulée *f*; (: *on ground*) congère *f*; (*general meaning*) sens général ▷ *vi* (*boat*) aller à la dérive, dériver; (*sand, snow*) s'amonceler, s'entasser

**drill** [drɪl] *n* perceuse *f*; (*bit*) foret *m*; (*of dentist*) roulette *f*, fraise *f*; (*Mil*) exercice *m* ▷ *vt* percer; (*troops*) entraîner ▷ *vi* (*for oil*) faire un or des forage(s)

**drink** [drɪŋk] *n* boisson *f*; (*alcoholic*) verre *m* ▷ *vt*, *vi* (*pt* **drank**, *pp* **drunk**) boire; **to have a ~** boire quelque chose, boire un verre; **a ~ of water** un verre d'eau; **would you like a ~?** tu veux boire quelque chose?; **drink-driving** *n* conduite *f* en état d'ivresse; **drinker** *n* buveur(-euse); **drinking water** *n* eau *f* potable

**drip** [drɪp] *n* (*drop*) goutte *f*; (*Med: device*) goutte-à-goutte *m inv*; (: *liquid*) perfusion *f* ▷ *vi* tomber goutte à goutte; (*tap*) goutter

**drive** [draɪv] *n* promenade *f* or trajet *m* en voiture; (*also:* **~way**) allée *f*; (*energy*) dynamisme *m*, énergie *f*; (*push*) effort (concerté); campagne *f*; (*Comput: also:* **disk ~**) lecteur *m* de disquette ▷ *vb* (*pt* **drove**, *pp* **~n**) ▷ *vt* conduire; (*nail*)

enfoncer; (*push*) chasser, pousser; (*Tech: motor*) actionner; entraîner ▷ *vi* (*be at the wheel*) conduire; (*travel by car*) aller en voiture; **left-/right-hand ~** (*Aut*) conduite *f* à gauche/droite; **to ~ sb mad** rendre qn fou (folle); **drive out** *vt* (*force out*) chasser; **drive-in** *adj*, *n* (*esp US*) drive-in *m*

**driven** ['drɪvn] *pp of* **drive**

**driver** ['draɪvə<sup>r</sup>] *n* conducteur(-trice); (*of taxi, bus*) chauffeur *m*; **driver's license** *n* (*US*) permis *m* de conduire

**driveway** ['draɪvweɪ] *n* allée *f*

**driving** ['draɪvɪŋ] *n* conduite *f*; **driving instructor** *n* moniteur *m* d'auto-école; **driving lesson** *n* leçon *f* de conduite; **driving licence** *n* (BRIT) permis *m* de conduire; **driving test** *n* examen *m* du permis de conduire

**drizzle** ['drɪzl] *n* bruine *f*, crachin *m*

**droop** [druːp] *vi* (*flower*) commencer à se faner; (*shoulders, head*) tomber

**drop** [drɒp] *n* (*of liquid*) goutte *f*; (*fall*) baisse *f*; (*also:* **parachute ~**) saut *m* ▷ *vt* laisser tomber; (*voice, eyes, price*) baisser; (*passenger*) déposer ▷ *vi* tomber; **drop in** *vi* (*inf: visit*): **to ~ in (on)** faire un saut (chez), passer (chez); **drop off** *vi* (*sleep*) s'assoupir ▷ *vt* (*passenger*) déposer; **drop out** *vi* (*withdraw*) se retirer; (*student etc*) abandonner, décrocher

**drought** [draut] *n* sécheresse *f*

**drove** [drəuv] *pt of* **drive**

**drown** [draun] *vt* noyer ▷ *vi* se noyer

**drowsy** ['drauzɪ] *adj* somnolent(e)

**drug** [drʌg] *n* médicament *m*; (*narcotic*) drogue *f* ▷ *vt* droguer; **to be on ~s** se droguer; **drug addict** *n* toxicomane *m/f*; **drug dealer** *n* revendeur(-euse) de drogue; **druggist** *n* (*US*) pharmacien(ne)-droguiste; **drugstore** *n* (*US*) pharmacie-droguerie *f*, drugstore *m*

**drum** [drʌm] *n* tambour *m*; (*for oil, petrol*) bidon *m*; **drums** *npl* (*Mus*) batterie *f*; **drummer** *n* (joueur *m* de) tambour *m*

**drunk** [drʌŋk] pp of **drink** ▷ adj ivre,
soûl(e) ▷ n (also: **~ard**) ivrogne m/f;
**to get ~** se soûler; **drunken** adj ivre,
soûl(e); (rage, stupor) ivrogne, d'ivrogne

**dry** [draɪ] adj sec (sèche); (day) sans
pluie ▷ vt sécher; (clothes) faire sécher
▷ vi sécher; **dry off** vi, vt sécher; **dry up**
vi (river, supplies) se tarir; **dry-cleaner's**
n teinturerie f; **dry-cleaning** n (process)
nettoyage m à sec; **dryer** n (tumble-
dryer) sèche-linge m inv; (for hair) sèche-
cheveux m inv

**DSS** n abbr (BRIT) = **Department of
Social Security**

**DTP** n abbr (= desktop publishing) PAO f

**dual** ['djuəl] adj double; **dual
carriageway** n (BRIT) route f à quatre
voies

**dubious** ['djuːbɪəs] adj hésitant(e),
incertain(e); (reputation, company)
douteux(-euse)

**duck** [dʌk] n canard m ▷ vi se baisser
vivement, baisser subitement la tête

**due** [djuː] adj (money, payment) dû
(due); (expected) attendu(e); (fitting)
qui convient ▷ adv: **~ north** droit vers
le nord; **~ to** (because of) en raison de;
(caused by) dû à; **the train is ~ at 8 a.m.**
le train est attendu à 8 h; **she is ~ back
tomorrow** elle doit rentrer demain; **he
is ~ £10** on lui doit 10 livres; **to give sb
his** or **her ~** être juste envers qn

**duel** ['djuəl] n duel m

**duet** [djuːˈɛt] n duo m

**dug** [dʌg] pt, pp of **dig**

**duke** [djuːk] n duc m

**dull** [dʌl] adj (boring) ennuyeux(-euse);
(not bright) morne, terne; (sound,
pain) sourd(e); (weather, day) gris(e),
maussade ▷ vt (pain, grief) atténuer;
(mind, senses) engourdir

**dumb** [dʌm] adj muet(te); (stupid) bête

**dummy** ['dʌmɪ] n (tailor's model)
mannequin m; (mock-up) factice m,
maquette f; (BRIT: for baby) tétine f ▷ adj
faux (fausse), factice

**dump** [dʌmp] n (also: **rubbish ~**)
décharge (publique); (inf: place) trou m

▷ vt (put down) déposer; déverser; (get
rid of) se débarrasser de; (Comput) lister

**dumpling** ['dʌmplɪŋ] n boulette f
(de pâte)

**dune** [djuːn] n dune f

**dungarees** [dʌŋgəˈriːz] npl bleu(s)
m(pl); (for child, woman) salopette f

**dungeon** ['dʌndʒən] n cachot m

**duplex** ['djuːplɛks] n (us: also: **~
apartment**) duplex m

**duplicate** n ['djuːplɪkət] double m
▷ vt ['djuːplɪkeɪt] faire un double de;
(on machine) polycopier; **in ~** en deux
exemplaires, en double

**durable** ['djuərəbl] adj durable;
(clothes, metal) résistant(e), solide

**duration** [djuəˈreɪʃən] n durée f

**during** ['djuərɪŋ] prep pendant, au
cours de

**dusk** [dʌsk] n crépuscule m

**dust** [dʌst] n poussière f ▷ vt
(furniture) essuyer, épousseter;
(cake etc): **to ~ with** saupoudrer de;
**dustbin** n (BRIT) poubelle f; **duster**
n chiffon m; **dustman** n (BRIT: irreg)
boueux m, éboueur m; **dustpan**
n pelle f à poussière; **dusty** adj
poussiéreux(-euse)

**Dutch** [dʌtʃ] adj hollandais(e),
néerlandais(e) ▷ n (Ling) hollandais m,
néerlandais m ▷ adv: **to go ~** or **dutch**
(inf) partager les frais; **the Dutch**
npl les Hollandais, les Néerlandais;
**Dutchman** (irreg) n Hollandais m;
**Dutchwoman** (irreg) n Hollandaise f

**duty** ['djuːtɪ] n devoir m; (tax) droit m,
taxe f; **on ~** de service; (at night etc) de
garde; **off ~** libre, pas de service or de
garde; **duty-free** adj exempté(e) de
douane, hors-taxe

**duvet** ['duːveɪ] n (BRIT) couette f

**DVD** n abbr (= digital versatile or video disc)
DVD m; **DVD burner** n graveur m de
DVD; **DVD player** n lecteur m de DVD;
**DVD writer** n graveur m de DVD

**dwarf** (pl **dwarves**) [dwɔːf, dwɔːvz] n
nain(e) ▷ vt écraser

**dwell** (pt, pp **dwelt**) [dwɛl, dwɛlt] vi

demeurer; **dwell on** vt fus s'étendre sur

**dwelt** [dwɛlt] pt, pp of **dwell**

**dwindle** ['dwɪndl] vi diminuer, décroître

**dye** [daɪ] n teinture f ▷ vt teindre

**dying** ['daɪɪŋ] adj mourant(e), agonisant(e)

**dynamic** [daɪ'næmɪk] adj dynamique

**dynamite** ['daɪnəmaɪt] n dynamite f

**dyslexia** [dɪs'lɛksɪə] n dyslexie f

**dyslexic** [dɪs'lɛksɪk] adj, n dyslexique m/f

**E** [i:] n (Mus): **E** mi m

**E111** n abbr (= form E111) formulaire m E111

**each** [i:tʃ] adj chaque ▷ pron chacun(e): **~ other** l'un l'autre; **they hate ~ other** ils se détestent (mutuellement); **they have 2 books ~** ils ont 2 livres chacun; **they cost £5 ~** ils coûtent 5 livres (la) pièce

**eager** ['i:gəʳ] adj (person, buyer) empressé(e); (keen: pupil, worker) enthousiaste; **to be ~ to do sth** (impatient) brûler de faire qch; (keen) désirer vivement faire qch; **to be ~ for** (event) désirer vivement; (vengeance, affection, information) être avide de

**eagle** ['i:gl] n aigle m

**ear** [ɪəʳ] n oreille f; (of corn) épi m; **earache** n mal m aux oreilles; **eardrum** n tympan m

**earl** [ə:l] n comte m

**earlier** ['ə:lɪəʳ] adj (date etc) plus rapproché(e); (edition etc) plus ancien(ne), antérieur(e) ▷ adv plus tôt

**early** ['ə:lɪ] adv tôt, de bonne heure;

(*ahead of time*) en avance; (*near the beginning*) au début ▷ *adj* précoce, qui se manifeste (*or se fait*) tôt *or* de bonne heure; (*Christians, settlers*) premier(-ière); (*reply*) rapide; (*death*) prématuré(e); (*work*) de jeunesse; **to have an ~ night/start** se coucher/ partir tôt *or* de bonne heure; **in the ~ ~ in the spring/19th century** au début *or* commencement du printemps/ 19ème siècle; **early retirement** *n* retraite anticipée

**earmark** ['ɪəmɑːk] *vt*: **to ~ sth for** réserver *or* destiner qch à qch

**earn** [əːn] *vt* gagner; (*Comm: yield*) rapporter; **to ~ one's living** gagner sa vie

**earnest** ['əːnɪst] *adj* sérieux(-euse) ▷ *n*: **in ~** *adv* sérieusement, pour de bon

**earnings** ['əːnɪŋz] *npl* salaire *m*; gains *mpl*; (*of company etc*) profits *mpl*, bénéfices *mpl*

**ear**: **earphones** *npl* écouteurs *mpl*; **earplugs** *npl* boules *fpl* Quiès®; (*to keep out water*) protège-tympans *mpl*; **earring** *n* boucle *f* d'oreille

**earth** [əːθ] *n* (*gen, also BRIT Elec*) terre *f* ▷ *vt* (*BRIT Elec*) relier à la terre; **earthquake** *n* tremblement *m* de terre, séisme *m*

**ease** [iːz] *n* facilité *f*, aisance *f*; (*comfort*) bien-être *m* ▷ *vt* (*soothe: mind*) tranquilliser; (*reduce: pain, problem*) atténuer; (: *tension*) réduire; (*loosen*) relâcher, détendre; (*help pass*): **to ~ sth in/out** faire pénétrer/sortir qch délicatement *or* avec douceur, faciliter la pénétration/la sortie de qch; **at ~** à l'aise; (*Mil*) au repos

**easily** ['iːzɪlɪ] *adv* facilement; (*by far*) de loin

**east** [iːst] *n* est *m* ▷ *adj* (*wind*) d'est; (*side*) est *inv* ▷ *adv* à l'est, vers l'est; **the E~** l'Orient *m*; (*Pol*) les pays *mpl* de l'Est; **eastbound** *adj* en direction de l'est; (*carriageway*) est *inv*

**Easter** ['iːstə<sup>r</sup>] *n* Pâques *fpl*; **Easter egg** *n* œuf *m* de Pâques

**eastern** ['iːstən] *adj* de l'est, oriental(e)

**Easter Sunday** *n* le dimanche de Pâques

**easy** ['iːzɪ] *adj* facile; (*manner*) aisé(e) ▷ *adv*: **to take it** *or* **things ~** (*rest*) ne pas se fatiguer; (*not worry*) ne pas (trop) s'en faire; **easy-going** *adj* accommodant(e), facile à vivre

**eat** (*pt* **ate**, *pp* **~en**) [iːt, eɪt, 'iːtn] *vt, vi* manger; **can we have something to ~?** est-ce qu'on peut manger quelque chose?; **eat out** *vi* manger au restaurant

**eavesdrop** ['iːvzdrɔp] *vi*: **to ~ (on)** écouter de façon indiscrète

**e-book** ['iːbuk] *n* livre *m* électronique

**e-business** ['iːbɪznɪs] *n* (*company*) entreprise *f* électronique; (*commerce*) commerce *m* électronique

**EC** *n abbr* (= *European Community*) CE *f*

**eccentric** [ɪk'sɛntrɪk] *adj, n* excentrique *m/f*

**echo, echoes** ['ɛkəu] *n* écho *m* ▷ *vt* répéter ▷ *vi* résonner; faire écho

**eclipse** [ɪ'klɪps] *n* éclipse *f*

**eco-friendly** [iːkəu'frɛndlɪ] *adj* non nuisible à *or* qui ne nuit pas à l'environnement

**ecological** [iːkə'lɔdʒɪkəl] *adj* écologique

**ecology** [ɪ'kɔlədʒɪ] *n* écologie *f*

**e-commerce** [iːkə'məːs] *n* commerce *m* électronique

**economic** [iːkə'nɔmɪk] *adj* économique; (*profitable*) rentable; **economical** *adj* économique; (*person*) économe; **economics** *n* (*Scol*) économie *f* politique ▷ *npl* (*of project etc*) côté *m or* aspect *m* économique

**economist** [ɪ'kɔnəmɪst] *n* économiste *m/f*

**economize** [ɪ'kɔnəmaɪz] *vi* économiser, faire des économies

**economy** [ɪ'kɔnəmɪ] *n* économie *f*; **economy class** *n* (*Aviat*) classe *f* touriste; **economy class syndrome** *n* syndrome *m* de la classe économique

**ecstasy** ['ɛkstəsɪ] *n* extase *f*; (*Drugs*)

**ecstasy** m; **ecstatic** [ɛks'tætɪk] adj extatique, en extase

**eczema** ['ɛksɪmə] n eczéma m

**edge** [ɛdʒ] n bord m; (of knife etc) tranchant m, fil m ▷ vt border; **on ~** (fig) crispé(e), tendu(e)

**edgy** ['ɛdʒɪ] adj crispé(e), tendu(e)

**edible** ['ɛdɪbl] adj comestible; (meal) mangeable

**Edinburgh** ['ɛdɪnbərə] n Édimbourg

**edit** ['ɛdɪt] vt (text, book) éditer; (report) préparer; (film) monter; (magazine) diriger; (newspaper) être le rédacteur or la rédactrice en chef de; **edition** [ɪ'dɪʃən] n édition f; **editor** n (of newspaper) rédacteur(-trice), rédacteur(-trice) en chef; (of sb's work) éditeur(-trice); (also: **film editor**) monteur(-euse); **political/foreign editor** rédacteur politique/au service étranger; **editorial** [ɛdɪ'tɔːrɪəl] adj de la rédaction, éditorial(e) ▷ n éditorial m

**educate** ['ɛdjukeɪt] vt (teach) instruire; (bring up) éduquer; **educated** ['ɛdjukeɪtɪd] adj (person) cultivé(e)

**education** [ɛdju'keɪʃən] n éducation f; (studies) études fpl; (teaching) enseignement m, instruction f; **educational** adj pédagogique; (institution) scolaire; (game, toy) éducatif(-ive)

**eel** [iːl] n anguille f

**eerie** ['ɪərɪ] adj inquiétant(e), spectral(e), surnaturel(le)

**effect** [ɪ'fɛkt] n effet m ▷ vt effectuer; **effects** npl (property) effets, affaires fpl; **to take ~** (Law) entrer en vigueur, prendre effet; (drug) agir, faire son effet; **in ~** en fait; **effective** adj efficace; (actual) véritable; **effectively** adv efficacement; (in reality) effectivement, en fait

**efficiency** [ɪ'fɪʃənsɪ] n efficacité f; (of machine, car) rendement m

**efficient** [ɪ'fɪʃənt] adj efficace; (machine, car) d'un bon rendement; **efficiently** adv efficacement

**effort** ['ɛfət] n effort m; **effortless** adj sans effort, aisé(e); (achievement) facile

**e.g.** adv abbr (= exempli gratia) par exemple, p. ex.

**egg** [ɛg] n œuf m; **hard-boiled/soft-boiled ~** œuf dur/à la coque; **eggcup** n coquetier m; **egg plant** (US) n aubergine f; **eggshell** n coquille f d'œuf; **egg white** n blanc m d'œuf; **egg yolk** n jaune m d'œuf

**ego** ['iːgəu] n (self-esteem) amour-propre m; (Psych) moi m

**Egypt** ['iːdʒɪpt] n Égypte f; **Egyptian** [ɪ'dʒɪpʃən] adj égyptien(ne) ▷ n Égyptien(ne)

**Eiffel Tower** ['aɪfəl-] n tour f Eiffel

**eight** [eɪt] num huit; **eighteen** num dix-huit; **eighteenth** num dix-huitième; **eighth** num huitième; **eightieth** ['eɪtɪɪθ] num quatre-vingtième

**eighty** ['eɪtɪ] num quatre-vingt(s)

**Eire** ['ɛərə] n République f d'Irlande

**either** ['aɪðə'] adj l'un ou l'autre; (both, each) chaque ▷ pron: **~ (of them)** l'un ou l'autre ▷ adv non plus ▷ conj: **~ good or bad** soit bon soit mauvais; **on ~ side** de chaque côté; **I don't like ~** je n'aime ni l'un ni l'autre; **no, I don't ~** moi non plus; **which bike do you want? - ~ will do** quel vélo voulez-vous? - n'importe lequel; **answer with ~ yes or no** répondez par oui ou par non

**eject** [ɪ'dʒɛkt] vt (tenant etc) expulser;
(object) éjecter
**elaborate** adj [ɪ'læbərɪt]
compliqué(e), recherché(e),
minutieux(-euse) ▷ vb [ɪ'læbəreɪt] ▷ vt
élaborer ▷ vi entrer dans les détails
**elastic** [ɪ'læstɪk] adj, n élastique (m);
**elastic band** n (BRIT) élastique m
**elbow** ['ɛlbəu] n coude m
**elder** ['ɛldə'] adj aîné(e) ▷ n (tree)
sureau m; **one's ~s** ses aînés; **elderly**
adj âgé(e) ▷ npl: **the elderly** les
personnes âgées
**eldest** ['ɛldɪst] adj, n: **the ~ (child)**
l'aîné(e) (des enfants)
**elect** [ɪ'lɛkt] vt élire; (choose): **to ~ to do**
choisir de faire ▷ adj: **the president
~** le président désigné; **election** n
élection f; **electoral** adj électoral(e);
**electorate** n électorat m
**electric** [ɪ'lɛktrɪk] adj électrique;
**electrical** adj électrique; **electric
blanket** n couverture chauffante;
**electric fire** n (BRIT) radiateur m
électrique; **electrician** [ɪlɛk'trɪʃən] n
électricien m; **electricity** [ɪlɛk'trɪsɪtɪ]
n électricité f; **electric shock** n choc
m or décharge f électrique; **electrify**
[ɪ'lɛktrɪfaɪ] vt (Rail) électrifier;
(audience) électriser
**electronic** [ɪlɛk'trɔnɪk] adj
électronique; **electronic mail** n
courrier m électronique; **electronics** n
électronique f
**elegance** ['ɛlɪɡəns] n élégance f
**elegant** ['ɛlɪɡənt] adj élégant(e)
**element** ['ɛlɪmənt] n (gen) élément m;
(of heater, kettle etc) résistance f
**elementary** [ɛlɪ'mɛntərɪ] adj
élémentaire; (school, education)
primaire; **elementary school** n (US)
école f primaire
**elephant** ['ɛlɪfənt] n éléphant m
**elevate** ['ɛlɪveɪt] vt élever
**elevator** ['ɛlɪveɪtə'] n (in warehouse etc)
élévateur m, monte-charge m inv; (US:
lift) ascenseur m
**eleven** [ɪ'lɛvn] num onze; **eleventh**

num onzième
**eligible** ['ɛlɪdʒəbl] adj éligible; (for
membership) admissible; **an ~ young
man** un beau parti; **to be ~ for sth**
remplir les conditions requises
pour qch
**eliminate** [ɪ'lɪmɪneɪt] vt éliminer
**elm** [ɛlm] n orme m
**eloquent** ['ɛləkwənt] adj éloquent(e)
**else** [ɛls] adv: **something ~** quelque
chose d'autre, autre chose;
**somewhere ~** ailleurs, autre part;
**everywhere ~** partout ailleurs;
**everyone ~** tous les autres; **nothing
~** rien d'autre; **where ~?** à quel autre
endroit?; **little ~** pas grand-chose
d'autre; **elsewhere** adv ailleurs,
autre part
**elusive** [ɪ'luːsɪv] adj insaisissable
**e-mail** ['iːmeɪl] n abbr (= electronic
mail) e-mail m, courriel m ▷ vt: **to ~ sb**
envoyer un e-mail or un courriel à qn;
**e-mail address** n adresse f e-mail
**embankment** [ɪm'bæŋkmənt] n (of
road, railway) remblai m, talus m; (of
river) berge f, quai m; (dyke) digue f
**embargo, embargoes** [ɪm'baːgəu] n
(Comm, Naut) embargo m; (prohibition)
interdiction f
**embark** [ɪm'baːk] vi embarquer
▷ vt embarquer; **to ~ on** (journey etc)
commencer, entreprendre; (fig) se
lancer or s'embarquer dans
**embarrass** [ɪm'bærəs] vt embarrasser,
gêner; **embarrassed** adj gêné(e);
**embarrassing** adj gênant(e),
embarrassant(e); **embarrassment** n
embarras m, gêne f; (embarrassing thing,
person) source f d'embarras
**embassy** ['ɛmbəsɪ] n ambassade f
**embrace** [ɪm'breɪs] vt embrasser,
étreindre; (include) embrasser ▷ vi
s'embrasser, s'étreindre ▷ n étreinte f
**embroider** [ɪm'brɔɪdə'] vt broder;
**embroidery** n broderie f
**embryo** ['ɛmbrɪəu] n (also fig)
embryon m
**emerald** ['ɛmərəld] n émeraude f

**emerge** [ɪ'məːdʒ] vi apparaître; (*from room, car*) surgir; (*from sleep, imprisonment*) sortir

**emergency** [ɪ'məːdʒənsɪ] n (*crisis*) cas m d'urgence; (*Med*) urgence f; **in an ~** en cas d'urgence; **state of ~** état m d'urgence; **emergency brake** (*us*) n frein m à main; **emergency exit** n sortie f de secours; **emergency landing** n atterrissage forcé; **emergency room** n (*us: Med*) urgences fpl; **emergency services** npl: **the emergency services** (*fire, police, ambulance*) les services mpl d'urgence

**emigrate** ['ɛmɪgreɪt] vi émigrer; **emigration** [ɛmɪ'greɪʃən] n émigration f

**eminent** ['ɛmɪnənt] adj éminent(e)

**emissions** [ɪ'mɪʃənz] npl émissions fpl

**emit** [ɪ'mɪt] vt émettre

**emotion** [ɪ'məʊʃən] n sentiment m; **emotional** adj (*person*) émotif(-ive), très sensible; (*needs*) affectif(-ive); (*scene*) émouvant(e); (*tone, speech*) qui fait appel aux sentiments

**emperor** ['ɛmpərər] n empereur m

**emphasis** (pl **-ases**) ['ɛmfəsɪs, -siːz] n accent m; **to lay** or **place ~ on sth** (*fig*) mettre l'accent sur, insister sur

**emphasize** ['ɛmfəsaɪz] vt (*syllable, word, point*) appuyer or insister sur; (*feature*) souligner, accentuer

**empire** ['ɛmpaɪər] n empire m

**employ** [ɪm'plɔɪ] vt employer; **employee** [ɪmplɔɪ'iː] n employé(e); **employer** n employeur(-euse); **employment** n emploi m; **employment agency** n agence f or bureau m de placement

**empower** [ɪm'pauər] vt: **to ~ sb to do** autoriser or habiliter qn à faire

**empress** ['ɛmprɪs] n impératrice f

**emptiness** ['ɛmptɪnɪs] n vide m; (*of area*) aspect m désertique

**empty** ['ɛmptɪ] adj vide; (*street, area*) désert(e); (*threat, promise*) en l'air, vain(e) ▷ vt vider ▷ vi se vider; (*liquid*) s'écouler; **empty-handed** adj les mains vides

**EMU** n abbr (= *European Monetary Union*) UME f

**emulsion** [ɪ'mʌlʃən] n émulsion f; (*also:* **~ paint**) peinture mate

**enable** [ɪ'neɪbl] vt: **to ~ sb to do** permettre à qn de faire

**enamel** [ɪ'næməl] n émail m; (*also:* **~ paint**) (peinture f) laque f

**enchanting** [ɪn'tʃɑːntɪŋ] adj ravissant(e), enchanteur(-eresse)

**encl.** abbr (*on letters etc*: = *enclosed*) ci-joint(e); (= *enclosure*) PJ f

**enclose** [ɪn'kləʊz] vt (*land*) clôturer; (*space, object*) entourer; (*letter etc*): **to ~ (with)** joindre (à); **please find ~d** veuillez trouver ci-joint

**enclosure** [ɪn'kləʊʒər] n enceinte f

**encore** [ɔŋ'kɔːr] excl, n bis (m)

**encounter** [ɪn'kauntər] n rencontre f ▷ vt rencontrer

**encourage** [ɪn'kʌrɪdʒ] vt encourager; **encouragement** n encouragement m

**encouraging** [ɪn'kʌrɪdʒɪŋ] adj encourageant(e)

**encyclop(a)edia** [ɛnsaɪkləʊ'piːdɪə] n encyclopédie f

**end** [ɛnd] n fin f; (*of table, street, rope etc*) bout m, extrémité f ▷ vt terminer; (*also:* **bring to an ~, put an ~ to**) mettre fin à ▷ vi se terminer, finir; **in the ~** finalement; **on ~** (*object*) debout, dressé(e); **to stand on ~** (*hair*) se dresser sur la tête; **for hours on ~** pendant des heures (et des heures); **end up** vi: **to ~ up in** (*condition*) finir or se terminer par; (*place*) finir or aboutir à

**endanger** [ɪn'deɪndʒər] vt mettre en danger; **an ~ed species** une espèce en voie de disparition

**endearing** [ɪn'dɪərɪŋ] adj attachant(e)

**endeavour** (*us* **endeavor**) [ɪn'dɛvər] n effort m; (*attempt*) tentative f ▷ vt: **to ~ to do** tenter or s'efforcer de faire

**ending** ['ɛndɪŋ] n dénouement m, conclusion f; (*Ling*) terminaison f

**endless** ['ɛndlɪs] adj sans fin, interminable

**endorse** [ɪn'dɔ:s] vt (cheque) endosser; (approve) appuyer, approuver, sanctionner; **endorsement** n (approval) appui m, aval m; (BRIT: on driving licence) contravention f (portée au permis de conduire)

**endurance** [ɪn'djʊərəns] n endurance f

**endure** [ɪn'djʊər] vt (bear) supporter, endurer ▷ vi (last) durer

**enemy** ['ɛnəmɪ] adj, n ennemi(e)

**energetic** [ɛnə'dʒɛtɪk] adj énergique; (activity) très actif(-ive), qui fait se dépenser (physiquement)

**energy** ['ɛnədʒɪ] n énergie f

**enforce** [ɪn'fɔ:s] vt (law) appliquer, faire respecter

**engaged** [ɪn'geɪdʒd] adj (BRIT: busy, in use) occupé(e); (betrothed) fiancé(e); **to get ~** se fiancer; **the line's ~** la ligne est occupée; **engaged tone** n (BRIT Tel) tonalité f occupé inv

**engagement** [ɪn'geɪdʒmənt] n (undertaking) obligation f, engagement m; (appointment) rendez-vous m inv; (to marry) fiançailles fpl; **engagement ring** n bague f de fiançailles

**engaging** [ɪn'geɪdʒɪŋ] adj engageant(e), attirant(e)

**engine** ['ɛndʒɪn] n (Aut) moteur m; (Rail) locomotive f

Be careful not to translate **engine** by the French word **engin**.

**engineer** [ɛndʒɪ'nɪər] n ingénieur m; (BRIT: repairer) dépanneur m; (Navy, US Rail) mécanicien m; **engineering** n engineering m, ingénierie f; (of bridges, ships) génie m; (of machine) mécanique f

**England** ['ɪŋglənd] n Angleterre f

**English** ['ɪŋglɪʃ] adj anglais(e) ▷ n (Ling) anglais m; **the ~** npl les Anglais; **English Channel** n: **the English Channel** la Manche; **Englishman** (irreg) n Anglais m; **Englishwoman** (irreg) n Anglaise f

**engrave** [ɪn'greɪv] vt graver

**engraving** [ɪn'greɪvɪŋ] n gravure f

**enhance** [ɪn'hɑ:ns] vt rehausser, mettre en valeur

**enjoy** [ɪn'dʒɔɪ] vt aimer, prendre plaisir à; (have benefit of: health, fortune) jouir de; (: success) connaître; **to ~ o.s.** s'amuser; **enjoyable** adj agréable; **enjoyment** n plaisir m

**enlarge** [ɪn'lɑ:dʒ] vt accroître; (Phot) agrandir ▷ vi: **to ~ on** (subject) s'étendre sur; **enlargement** n (Phot) agrandissement m

**enlist** [ɪn'lɪst] vt recruter; (support) s'assurer ▷ vi s'engager

**enormous** [ɪ'nɔ:məs] adj énorme

**enough** [ɪ'nʌf] adj: **~ time/books** assez or suffisamment de temps/livres ▷ adv: **big ~** assez or suffisamment grand ▷ pron: **have you got ~?** (en) avez-vous assez?; **~ to eat** assez à manger; **that's ~, thanks** cela suffit or c'est assez, merci; **I've had ~ of him** j'en ai assez de lui; **he has not worked ~** il n'a pas assez or suffisamment travaillé, il n'a pas travaillé assez or suffisamment; **... which, funnily** or **oddly ~ ...** qui, chose curieuse

**enquire** [ɪn'kwaɪər] vt, vi = **inquire**

**enquiry** [ɪn'kwaɪərɪ] n = **inquiry**

**enrage** [ɪn'reɪdʒ] vt mettre en fureur or en rage, rendre furieux(-euse)

**enrich** [ɪn'rɪtʃ] vt enrichir

**enrol** (US **enroll**) [ɪn'rəul] vt inscrire ▷ vi s'inscrire; **enrolment** (US **enrollment**) n inscription f

**en route** [ɔn'ru:t] adv en route, en chemin

**en suite** ['ɔnswi:t] adj: **with ~ bathroom** avec salle de bains en attenante

**ensure** [ɪn'ʃuər] vt assurer, garantir

**entail** [ɪn'teɪl] vt entraîner, nécessiter

**enter** ['ɛntər] vt (room) entrer dans, pénétrer dans; (club, army) entrer à; (competition) s'inscrire à or pour; (sb for a competition) (faire) inscrire; (write down) inscrire, noter; (Comput) entrer, introduire ▷ vi entrer

**enterprise** ['ɛntəpraɪz] n (company, undertaking) entreprise f; (initiative) (esprit *m* d')initiative *f*; **free ~** libre entreprise; **private ~** entreprise privée; **enterprising** *adj* entreprenant(e), dynamique; (*scheme*) audacieux(-euse)

**entertain** [ɛntəˈteɪn] *vt* amuser, distraire; (*invite*) recevoir (à dîner); (*idea, plan*) envisager; **entertainer** *n* artiste *m/f* de variétés; **entertaining** *adj* amusant(e), distrayant(e); **entertainment** *n* (*amusement*) distraction *f*, divertissement *m*, amusement *m*; (*show*) spectacle *m*

**enthusiasm** [ɪnˈθuːzɪæzəm] *n* enthousiasme *m*

**enthusiast** [ɪnˈθuːzɪæst] *n* enthousiaste *m/f*; **enthusiastic** [ɪnθuːzɪˈæstɪk] *adj* enthousiaste; **to be enthusiastic about** être enthousiasmé(e) par

**entire** [ɪnˈtaɪəʳ] *adj* (tout) entier(-ère); **entirely** *adv* entièrement, complètement

**entitle** [ɪnˈtaɪtl] *vt*: **to ~ sb to sth** donner droit à qch à qn; **entitled** *adj* (*book*) intitulé(e); **to be entitled to do** avoir le droit de faire

**entrance** *n* [ˈɛntrns] entrée *f* ▷ *vt* [ɪnˈtrɑːns] enchanter, ravir; **where's the ~?** où est l'entrée?; **to gain ~ to** (*university etc*) être admis à; **entrance examination** *n* examen *m* d'entrée *or* d'admission; **entrance fee** *n* (*to museum etc*) prix *m* d'entrée; (*to join club etc*) droit *m* d'inscription; **entrance ramp** *n* (*us Aut*) bretelle *f* d'accès; **entrant** *n* (*in race etc*) participant(e), concurrent(e); (*BRIT: in exam*) candidat(e)

**entrepreneur** [ˈɔntrəprəˈnəːʳ] *n* entrepreneur *m*

**entrust** [ɪnˈtrʌst] *vt*: **to ~ sth to** confier qch à

**entry** [ˈɛntrɪ] *n* entrée *f*; (*in register, diary*) inscription *f*; **"no ~"** "défense d'entrer", "entrée interdite"; (*Aut*) "sens interdit"; **entry phone** *n* (*BRIT*) interphone *m* (à l'entrée d'un immeuble)

**envelope** [ˈɛnvələup] *n* enveloppe *f*

**envious** [ˈɛnvɪəs] *adj* envieux(-euse)

**environment** [ɪnˈvaɪərnmənt] *n* (*social, moral*) milieu *m*; (*natural world*): **the ~** l'environnement *m*; **environmental** [ɪnvaɪərnˈmɛntl] *adj* (*of surroundings*) du milieu; (*issue, disaster*) écologique; **environmentally** [ɪnvaɪərnˈmɛntlɪ] *adv*: **environmentally sound/friendly** qui ne nuit pas à l'environnement

**envisage** [ɪnˈvɪzɪdʒ] *vt* (*foresee*) prévoir

**envoy** [ˈɛnvɔɪ] *n* envoyé(e); (*diplomat*) ministre *m* plénipotentiaire

**envy** [ˈɛnvɪ] *n* envie *f* ▷ *vt* envier; **to ~ sb sth** envier qch à qn

**epic** [ˈɛpɪk] *n* épopée *f* ▷ *adj* épique

**epidemic** [ɛpɪˈdɛmɪk] *n* épidémie *f*

**epilepsy** [ˈɛpɪlɛpsɪ] *n* épilepsie *f*; **epileptic** *adj*, *n* épileptique *m/f*; **epileptic fit** *n* crise *f* d'épilepsie

**episode** [ˈɛpɪsəud] *n* épisode *m*

**equal** [ˈiːkwl] *adj* égal(e) ▷ *vt* égaler; **~ to** (*task*) à la hauteur de; **equality** [iːˈkwɔlɪtɪ] *n* égalité *f*; **equalize** *vt, vi* (*Sport*) égaliser; **equally** *adv* également; (*share*) en parts égales; (*treat*) de la même façon; (*pay*) autant; (*just as*) tout aussi

**equation** [ɪˈkweɪʃən] *n* (*Math*) équation *f*

**equator** [ɪˈkweɪtəʳ] *n* équateur *m*

**equip** [ɪˈkwɪp] *vt* équiper; **to ~ sb/sth with** équiper *or* munir qn/qch de; **equipment** *n* équipement *m*; (*electrical etc*) appareillage *m*, installation *f*

**equivalent** [ɪˈkwɪvəlnt] *adj* équivalent(e) ▷ *n* équivalent *m*; **to be ~ to** équivaloir à, être équivalent(e) à

**ER** *abbr* (*BRIT*: = *Elizabeth Regina*) *la reine Élisabeth*; (*us: Med*: = *emergency room*) urgences *fpl*

**era** [ˈɪərə] *n* ère *f*, époque *f*

**erase** [ɪˈreɪz] *vt* effacer; **eraser** *n* gomme *f*

**erect** [ɪˈrɛkt] *adj* droit(e) ▷ *vt* construire; (*monument*) ériger, élever; (*tent etc*) dresser; **erection** [ɪˈrɛkʃən] *n* (*Physiol*) érection *f*; (*of building*) construction f

**ERM** n abbr (= Exchange Rate Mechanism) mécanisme m des taux de change

**erode** [ɪˈrəʊd] vt éroder; (metal) ronger

**erosion** [ɪˈrəʊʒən] n érosion f

**erotic** [ɪˈrɒtɪk] adj érotique

**errand** [ˈɛrnd] n course f, commission f

**erratic** [ɪˈrætɪk] adj irrégulier(-ière), inconstant(e)

**error** [ˈɛrəʳ] n erreur f

**erupt** [ɪˈrʌpt] vi entrer en éruption; (fig) éclater; **eruption** [ɪˈrʌpʃən] n éruption f; (of anger, violence) explosion f

**escalate** [ˈɛskəleɪt] vi s'intensifier; (costs) monter en flèche

**escalator** [ˈɛskəleɪtəʳ] n escalier roulant

**escape** [ɪˈskeɪp] n évasion f, fuite f; (of gas etc) fuite f ▷ vi s'échapper, fuir; (from jail) s'évader; (fig) s'en tirer; (leak) s'échapper ▷ vt échapper à; **to ~ from** (person) échapper à; (place) s'échapper de; (fig) fuir; **his name ~s me** son nom m'échappe

**escort** vt [ɪˈskɔːt] escorter ▷ n [ˈɛskɔːt] (Mil) escorte f

**especially** [ɪˈspɛʃlɪ] adv (particularly) particulièrement; (above all) surtout

**espionage** [ˈɛspɪənɑːʒ] n espionnage m

**essay** [ˈɛseɪ] n (Scol) dissertation f; (Literature) essai m

**essence** [ˈɛsns] n essence f; (Culin) extrait m

**essential** [ɪˈsɛnʃl] adj essentiel(le); (basic) fondamental(e); **essentials** npl éléments essentiels; **essentially** adv essentiellement

**establish** [ɪˈstæblɪʃ] vt établir; (business) fonder, créer; (one's power etc) asseoir, affermir; **establishment** n établissement m; (founding) création f; (institution) établissement; **the Establishment** les pouvoirs établis; l'ordre établi

**estate** [ɪˈsteɪt] n (land) domaine m, propriété f; (Law) biens mpl, succession f; (BRIT: also: **housing ~**)

lotissement m; **estate agent** n (BRIT) agent immobilier; **estate car** n (BRIT) break m

**estimate** n [ˈɛstɪmət] estimation f; (Comm) devis m ▷ vb [ˈɛstɪmeɪt] ▷ vt estimer

**etc** abbr (= et cetera) etc

**eternal** [ɪˈtəːnl] adj éternel(le)

**eternity** [ɪˈtəːnɪtɪ] n éternité f

**ethical** [ˈɛθɪkl] adj moral(e); **ethics** [ˈɛθɪks] n éthique f ▷ npl moralité f

**Ethiopia** [iːθɪˈəʊpɪə] n Éthiopie f

**ethnic** [ˈɛθnɪk] adj ethnique; (clothes, food) folklorique, exotique, propre aux minorités ethniques non-occidentales; **ethnic minority** n minorité f ethnique

**e-ticket** [ˈiːtɪkɪt] n billet m électronique

**etiquette** [ˈɛtɪkɛt] n convenances fpl, étiquette f

**EU** n abbr (= European Union) UE f

**euro** [ˈjuərəʊ] n (currency) euro m

**Europe** [ˈjuərəp] n Europe f; **European** [juərəˈpiːən] adj européen(ne) ▷ n Européen(ne); **European Community** n Communauté européenne; **European Union** n Union européenne

**Eurostar®** [ˈjuərəustɑːʳ] n Eurostar® m

**evacuate** [ɪˈvækjueɪt] vt évacuer

**evade** [ɪˈveɪd] vt échapper à; (question etc) éluder; (duties) se dérober à

**evaluate** [ɪˈvæljueɪt] vt évaluer

**evaporate** [ɪˈvæpəreɪt] vi s'évaporer; (fig: hopes, fear) s'envoler; (anger) se dissiper

**eve** [iːv] n: **on the ~ of** à la veille de

**even** [ˈiːvn] adj (level, smooth) régulier(-ière); (equal) égal(e); (number) pair(e) ▷ adv même; **~ if** même si + indic; **~ though** alors même que + cond; **~ more** encore plus; **~ faster** encore plus vite; **~ so** quand même; **not ~** pas même; **~ he was there** même lui était là; **~ on Sundays** même le dimanche; **to get ~ with sb** prendre sa revanche sur qn

**evening** [ˈiːvnɪŋ] n soir m; (as duration,

*event*) soirée f; **in the ~** le soir; **evening class** n cours m du soir; **evening dress** n (*man's*) tenue f de soirée, smoking m; (*woman's*) robe f de soirée

**event** [ɪ'vɛnt] n événement m; (*Sport*) épreuve f; **in the ~ of** en cas de; **eventful** adj mouvementé(e)

**eventual** [ɪ'vɛntʃuəl] adj final(e)

 Be careful not to translate *eventual* by the French word *éventuel*.

**eventually** [ɪ'vɛntʃuəlɪ] adv finalement

Be careful not to translate *eventually* by the French word *éventuellement*.

**ever** ['ɛvəʳ] adv jamais; (*at all times*) toujours; (*in questions*): **why ~ not?** mais enfin, pourquoi pas?; **the best ~** le meilleur qu'on ait jamais vu; **have you ~ seen it?** l'as-tu déjà vu?, as-tu eu l'occasion or t'est-il arrivé de le voir?; **~ since** (*as adv*) depuis; (*as conj*) depuis que; **~ so pretty** si joli; **evergreen** n arbre m à feuilles persistantes

**KEYWORD**

**every** ['ɛvrɪ] adj **1** (*each*) chaque; **every one of them** tous (sans exception); **every shop in town was closed** tous les magasins en ville étaient fermés
**2** (*all possible*) tous (toutes) les; **I gave you every assistance** j'ai fait tout mon possible pour vous aider; **I have every confidence in him** j'ai entièrement or pleinement confiance en lui; **we wish you every success** nous vous souhaitons beaucoup de succès
**3** (*showing recurrence*) tous les; **every day** tous les jours, chaque jour; **every other car** une voiture sur deux; **every other/third day** tous les deux/trois jours; **every now and then** de temps en temps; **everybody = everyone**; **everyday** adj (*expression*) courant(e), d'usage courant; (*use*) courant; (*clothes, life*) de tous les jours; (*occurrence,*

*problem*) quotidien(ne); **everyone** pron tout le monde, tous pl; **everything** pron tout; **everywhere** adv partout; **everywhere you go you meet ...** où qu'on aille, on rencontre ...

**evict** [ɪ'vɪkt] vt expulser

**evidence** ['ɛvɪdns] n (*proof*) preuve(s) f(pl); (*of witness*) témoignage m; (*sign*): **to show ~ of** donner des signes de; **to give ~** témoigner, déposer

**evident** ['ɛvɪdnt] adj évident(e); **evidently** adv de toute évidence; (*apparently*) apparemment

**evil** ['i:vl] adj mauvais(e) ▷ n mal m

**evoke** [ɪ'vəuk] vt évoquer

**evolution** [i:və'lu:ʃən] n évolution f

**evolve** [ɪ'vɔlv] vt élaborer ▷ vi évoluer, se transformer

**ewe** [ju:] n brebis f

**ex** [ɛks] n (*inf*): **my ex** mon ex

**ex-** [ɛks] prefix ex-

**exact** [ɪg'zækt] adj exact(e) ▷ vt: **to ~ sth (from)** (*signature, confession*) extorquer qch (à); (*apology*) exiger qch (de); **exactly** adv exactement

**exaggerate** [ɪg'zædʒəreɪt] vt, vi exagérer; **exaggeration** [ɪgzædʒə'reɪʃən] n exagération f

**exam** [ɪg'zæm] n abbr (*Scol*) = **examination**

**examination** [ɪgzæmɪ'neɪʃən] n (*Scol, Med*) examen m; **to take** or **sit an ~** (*BRIT*) passer un examen

**examine** [ɪg'zæmɪn] vt (*gen*) examiner; (*Scol, Law: person*) interroger; **examiner** n examinateur(-trice)

**example** [ɪg'zɑ:mpl] n exemple m; **for ~** par exemple

**exasperated** [ɪg'zɑ:spəreɪtɪd] adj exaspéré(e)

**excavate** ['ɛkskəveɪt] vt (*site*) fouiller, excaver; (*object*) mettre au jour

**exceed** [ɪk'si:d] vt dépasser; (*one's powers*) outrepasser; **exceedingly** adv extrêmement

**excel** [ɪk'sɛl] vi exceller ▷ vt surpasser; **to ~ o.s.** se surpasser

**excellence** [ˈɛksələns] n excellence f
**excellent** [ˈɛksələnt] adj excellent(e)
**except** [ɪkˈsɛpt] prep (also: **~ for, ~ing**)
sauf, excepté, à l'exception de ▷ vt
excepter; **~ if/when** sauf si/quand;
**~ that** excepté que, si ce n'est que;
**exception** [ɪkˈsɛpʃən] n exception
f; **to take exception to** s'offusquer
de; **exceptional** [ɪkˈsɛpʃənl] adj
exceptionnel(le); **exceptionally**
[ɪkˈsɛpʃənəlɪ] adv exceptionnellement
**excerpt** [ˈɛksəːpt] n extrait m
**excess** [ɪkˈsɛs] n excès m; **excess**
**baggage** n excédent m de bagages;
**excessive** adj excessif(-ive)
**exchange** [ɪksˈtʃeɪndʒ] n échange m;
(also: **telephone ~**) central m ▷ vt: **to ~**
**(for)** échanger (contre); **could I ~ this,**
**please?** est-ce que je peux échanger
ceci, s'il vous plaît?; **exchange rate** n
taux m de change
**excite** [ɪkˈsaɪt] vt exciter; **excited** adj
(tout (toute) excité(e); **to get excited**
s'exciter; **excitement** n excitation f;
**exciting** adj passionnant(e)
**exclaim** [ɪkˈskleɪm] vi s'exclamer;
**exclamation** [ɛkskləˈmeɪʃən] n
exclamation f; **exclamation mark**
(us **exclamation point**) n point m
d'exclamation
**exclude** [ɪkˈskluːd] vt exclure
**excluding** [ɪkˈskluːdɪŋ] prep: **~ VAT**
TVA non comprise
**exclusion** [ɪkˈskluːʒən] n exclusion f
**exclusive** [ɪkˈskluːsɪv] adj
exclusif(-ive); (club, district) sélect(e);
(item of news) en exclusivité; **~ of VAT**
TVA non comprise; **exclusively** adv
exclusivement
**excruciating** [ɪkˈskruːʃɪeɪtɪŋ]
adj (pain) atroce, déchirant(e);
(embarrassing) pénible
**excursion** [ɪkˈskəːʃən] n excursion f
**excuse** n [ɪkˈskjuːs] excuse f ▷ vt
[ɪkˈskjuːz] (forgive) excuser; **to ~ sb**
**from** (activity) dispenser qn de; **~ me!**
excusez-moi!, pardon!; **now if you**
**will ~ me, ...** maintenant, si vous (le)

permettez ...
**ex-directory** [ˈɛksdɪˈrɛktərɪ] adj (BRIT)
sur la liste rouge
**execute** [ˈɛksɪkjuːt] vt exécuter;
**execution** [ɛksɪˈkjuːʃən] n exécution f
**executive** [ɪgˈzɛkjutɪv] n (person) cadre
m; (managing group) bureau m; (Pol)
exécutif m ▷ adj exécutif(-ive); (position,
job) de cadre
**exempt** [ɪgˈzɛmpt] adj: **~ from**
exempté(e) or dispensé(e) de ▷ vt: **to ~**
**sb from** exempter or dispenser qn de
**exercise** [ˈɛksəsaɪz] n exercice m ▷ vt
exercer; (patience etc) faire preuve de;
(dog) promener ▷ vi (also: **to take ~**)
prendre de l'exercice; **exercise book**
n cahier m
**exert** [ɪgˈzəːt] vt exercer, employer; **to**
**~ o.s.** se dépenser; **exertion** [ɪgˈzəːʃən]
n effort m
**exhale** [ɛksˈheɪl] vt exhaler ▷ vi expirer
**exhaust** [ɪgˈzɔːst] n (also: **~ fumes**)
gaz mpl d'échappement; (also: **~ pipe**)
tuyau m d'échappement ▷ vt épuiser;
**exhausted** adj épuisé(e); **exhaustion**
[ɪgˈzɔːstʃən] n épuisement m; **nervous**
**exhaustion** fatigue nerveuse
**exhibit** [ɪgˈzɪbɪt] n (Art) pièce f or objet
m exposé(e); (Law) pièce à conviction
▷ vt (Art) exposer; (courage, skill) faire
preuve de; **exhibition** [ɛksɪˈbɪʃən] n
exposition f
**exhilarating** [ɪgˈzɪləreɪtɪŋ] adj
grisant(e), stimulant(e)
**exile** [ˈɛksaɪl] n exil m; (person) exilé(e)
▷ vt exiler
**exist** [ɪgˈzɪst] vi exister; **existence** n
existence f; **existing** adj actuel(le)
**exit** [ˈɛksɪt] n sortie f ▷ vi (Comput,
Theat) sortir; **where's the ~?** où est la
sortie?; **exit ramp** n (us Aut) bretelle
f d'accès
**exotic** [ɪgˈzɔtɪk] adj exotique
**expand** [ɪkˈspænd] vt (area) agrandir;
(quantity) accroître ▷ vi (trade, etc) se
développer, s'accroître; (gas, metal)
se dilater
**expansion** [ɪkˈspænʃən] n (territorial,

*economic*) expansion f; (*of trade, influence etc*) développement m; (*of production*) accroissement m; (*of population*) croissance f; (*of gas, metal*) expansion, dilatation f

**expect** [ɪk'spɛkt] vt (*anticipate*) s'attendre à, s'attendre à ce que + sub; (*count on*) compter sur, escompter; (*require*) demander, exiger; (*suppose*) supposer; (*await: also baby*) attendre ▷ vi: **to be ~ing** (*pregnant woman*) être enceinte; **expectation** [ɛkspɛk'teɪʃən] n (*hope*) attente f, espérance(s) f(pl); (*belief*) attente

**expedition** [ɛkspə'dɪʃən] n expédition f

**expel** [ɪk'spɛl] vt chasser, expulser; (*Scol*) renvoyer, exclure

**expenditure** [ɪk'spɛndɪtʃəʳ] n (*act of spending*) dépense f; (*money spent*) dépenses fpl

**expense** [ɪk'spɛns] n (*high cost*) coût m; (*spending*) dépense f, frais mpl; **expenses** npl frais mpl; dépenses; **at the ~ of** (*fig*) aux dépens de; **expense account** n (*note f de*) frais mpl

**expensive** [ɪk'spɛnsɪv] adj cher (chère), coûteux(-euse); **it's too ~** ça coûte trop cher

**experience** [ɪk'spɪərɪəns] n expérience f ▷ vt connaître; (*feeling*) éprouver; **experienced** adj expérimenté(e)

**experiment** [ɪk'spɛrɪmənt] n expérience f ▷ vi faire une expérience; **experimental** [ɪkspɛrɪ'mɛntl] adj expérimental(e)

**expert** ['ɛkspəːt] adj expert(e) ▷ n expert m; **expertise** [ɛkspəː'tiːz] n (grande) compétence

**expire** [ɪk'spaɪəʳ] vi expirer; **expiry** n expiration f; **expiry date** n date f d'expiration; (*on label*) à utiliser avant …

**explain** [ɪk'spleɪn] vt expliquer; **explanation** [ɛksplə'neɪʃən] n explication f

**explicit** [ɪk'splɪsɪt] adj explicite; (*definite*) formel(le)

**explode** [ɪk'spləud] vi exploser

**exploit** n ['ɛksplɔɪt] exploit m ▷ vt [ɪk'splɔɪt] exploiter; **exploitation** [ɛksplɔɪ'teɪʃən] n exploitation f

**explore** [ɪk'splɔːʳ] vt explorer; (*possibilities*) étudier, examiner; **explorer** n explorateur(-trice)

**explosion** [ɪk'spləuʒən] n explosion f; **explosive** [ɪk'spləusɪv] adj explosif(-ive) ▷ n explosif m

**export** vt [ɛk'spɔːt] exporter ▷ n ['ɛkspɔːt] exportation f ▷ cpd d'exportation; **exporter** n exportateur m

**expose** [ɪk'spəuz] vt exposer; (*unmask*) démasquer, dévoiler; **exposed** adj (*land, house*) exposé(e); **exposure** [ɪk'spəuʒəʳ] n exposition f; (*publicity*) couverture f; (*Phot: speed*) (temps m de) pose f; (: *shot*) pose; **to die of exposure** (*Med*) mourir de froid

**express** [ɪk'sprɛs] adj (*definite*) formel(le), exprès(-esse); (BRIT: *letter etc*) exprès inv ▷ n (*train*) rapide m ▷ vt exprimer; **expression** [ɪk'sprɛʃən] n expression f; **expressway** n (US) voie f express (à plusieurs files)

**exquisite** [ɛk'skwɪzɪt] adj exquis(e)

**extend** [ɪk'stɛnd] vt (*visit, street*) prolonger, remettre; (*building*) agrandir; (*offer*) présenter, offrir; (*hand, arm*) tendre ▷ vi (*land*) s'étendre; **extension** n (*of visit, street*) prolongation f; (*building*) annexe f; (*telephone: in offices*) poste m; (: *in private house*) téléphone m supplémentaire; **extension cable, extension lead** n (*Elec*) rallonge f; **extensive** adj étendu(e), vaste; (*damage, alterations*) considérable; (*inquiries*) approfondi(e)

**extent** [ɪk'stɛnt] n étendue f; **to some ~** dans une certaine mesure; **to the ~ of …** au point de …; **to what ~?** dans quelle mesure?, jusqu'à quel point?; **to such an ~ that …** à tel point que …

**exterior** [ɛk'stɪərɪəʳ] adj extérieur(e) ▷ n extérieur m

**external** [ɛk'stəːnl] adj externe

**extinct** [ɪk'stɪŋkt] *adj* (*volcano*)
éteint(e); (*species*) disparu(e);
**extinction** *n* extinction *f*
**extinguish** [ɪk'stɪŋgwɪʃ] *vt* éteindre
**extra** ['ɛkstrə] *adj* supplémentaire,
de plus ▷ *adv* (*in addition*) en plus ▷ *n*
supplément *m*; (*perk*) à-coté *m*; (*Cine,
Theat*) figurant(e)
**extract** *vt* [ɪk'strækt] extraire; (*tooth*)
arracher; (*money, promise*) soutirer ▷ *n*
['ɛkstrækt] extrait *m*
**extradite** ['ɛkstrədaɪt] *vt* extrader
**extraordinary** [ɪk'strɔ:dnrɪ] *adj*
extraordinaire
**extravagance** [ɪk'strævəgəns]
*n* (*excessive spending*) prodigalités
*fpl*; (*thing bought*) folie *f*, dépense
excessive; **extravagant** *adj*
extravagant(e); (*in spending: person*)
prodigue, dépensier(-ière); (*: tastes*)
dispendieux(-euse)
**extreme** [ɪk'stri:m] *adj, n* extrême (*m*);
**extremely** *adv* extrêmement
**extremist** [ɪk'stri:mɪst] *adj, n*
extrémiste *m/f*
**extrovert** ['ɛkstrəvə:t] *n* extraverti(e)
**eye** [aɪ] *n* œil *m* ((*yeux*) *pl*); (*of needle*)
trou *m*, chas *m* ▷ *vt* examiner; **to keep
an ~ on** surveiller; **eyeball** *n* globe
*m* oculaire; **eyebrow** *n* sourcil *m*;
**eyedrops** *npl* gouttes *fpl* pour les yeux;
**eyelash** *n* cil *m*; **eyelid** *n* paupière *f*;
**eyeliner** *n* eye-liner *m*; **eyeshadow** *n*
ombre *f* à paupières; **eyesight** *n* vue *f*;
**eye witness** *n* témoin *m* oculaire

**F** [ɛf] *n* (*Mus*): **F** fa *m*
**fabric** ['fæbrɪk] *n* tissu *m*
**fabulous** ['fæbjuləs] *adj*
fabuleux(-euse); (*inf: super*) formidable,
sensationnel(le)
**face** [feɪs] *n* visage *m*, figure *f*;
(*expression*) air *m*; (*of clock*) cadran *m*;
(*of cliff*) paroi *f*; (*of mountain*) face *f*;
(*of building*) façade *f* ▷ *vt* faire face à;
(*facts etc*) accepter; **~ down** (*person*)
à plat ventre; (*card*) face en dessous;
**to lose/save ~** perdre/sauver la face;
**to pull a ~** faire une grimace; **in the
~ of** (*difficulties etc*) face à, devant; **on
the ~ of it** à première vue; **~ to ~** face
à face; **face up to** *vt fus* faire face à,
affronter; **face cloth** *n* (BRIT) gant *m*
de toilette; **face pack** *n* (BRIT) masque
*m* (de beauté)
**facial** ['feɪʃl] *adj* facial(e) ▷ *n* soin
complet du visage
**facilitate** [fə'sɪlɪteɪt] *vt* faciliter
**facilities** [fə'sɪlɪtɪz] *npl* installations
*fpl*, équipement *m*; **credit ~** facilités

de paiement
**fact** [fækt] n fait m; **in ~** en fait
**faction** ['fækʃən] n faction f
**factor** ['fæktəʳ] n facteur m; (of sun cream) indice m (de protection); **I'd like a ~ 15 suntan lotion** je voudrais une crème solaire d'indice 15
**factory** ['fæktərɪ] n usine f, fabrique f
**factual** ['fæktjuəl] adj basé(e) sur les faits
**faculty** ['fækəltɪ] n faculté f; (us: teaching staff) corps enseignant
**fad** [fæd] n (personal) manie f; (craze) engouement m
**fade** [feɪd] vi se décolorer, passer; (light, sound) s'affaiblir; (flower) se faner; **fade away** vi (sound) s'affaiblir
**fag** [fæg] (BRIT inf: cigarette) clope f
**Fahrenheit** ['fɑːrənhaɪt] n Fahrenheit m inv
**fail** [feɪl] vt (exam) échouer à; (candidate) recaler; (subj: courage, memory) faire défaut à ▷ vi échouer; (eyesight, health, light: also: **be ~ing**) baisser, s'affaiblir; (brakes) lâcher; **to ~ to do sth** (neglect) négliger de or ne pas faire qch; (be unable) ne pas arriver or parvenir à faire qch; **without ~** à coup sûr; sans faute; **failing** n défaut m ▷ prep faute de; **failing that** à défaut, sinon; **failure** ['feɪljəʳ] n échec m; (person) raté(e); (mechanical etc) défaillance f
**faint** [feɪnt] adj faible; (recollection) vague; (mark) à peine visible ▷ n évanouissement m ▷ vi s'évanouir; **to feel ~** défaillir; **faintest** adj: **I haven't the faintest idea** je n'en ai pas la moindre idée; **faintly** adv faiblement; (vaguely) vaguement
**fair** [fɛəʳ] adj équitable, juste; (hair) blond(e); (skin, complexion) pâle, blanc (blanche); (weather) beau (belle); (good enough) assez bon(ne); (sizeable) considérable ▷ adv: **to play ~** jouer franc jeu ▷ n foire f; (BRIT: funfair) fête f (foraine); **fairground** n champ m de foire; **fair-haired** adj (person) aux cheveux clairs, blond(e); **fairly** adv

(justly) équitablement; (quite) assez;
**fair trade** n commerce m équitable;
**fairway** n (Golf) fairway m
**fairy** ['fɛərɪ] n fée f; **fairy tale** n conte m de fées
**faith** [feɪθ] n foi f; (trust) confiance f; (sect) culte m, religion f; **faithful** adj fidèle; **faithfully** adv fidèlement; **yours faithfully** (BRIT: in letters) veuillez agréer l'expression de mes salutations les plus distinguées
**fake** [feɪk] n (painting etc) faux m; (person) imposteur m ▷ adj faux (fausse) ▷ vt (emotions) simuler; (painting) faire un faux de
**falcon** ['fɔːlkən] n faucon m
**fall** [fɔːl] n chute f; (decrease) baisse f; (us: autumn) automne m ▷ vi (pt **fell**, pp **~en**) tomber; (price, temperature, dollar) baisser; **falls** npl (waterfall) chute f d'eau, cascade f; **to ~ flat** vi (on one's face) tomber de tout son long, s'étaler; (joke) tomber à plat; (plan) échouer; **fall apart** vi (object) tomber en morceaux; **fall down** vi (person) tomber; (building) s'effondrer, s'écrouler; **fall for** vt fus (trick) se laisser prendre à; (person) tomber amoureux(-euse) de; **fall off** vi tomber; (diminish) baisser, diminuer; **fall out** vi (friends etc) se brouiller; (hair, teeth) tomber; **fall over** vi tomber (par terre); **fall through** vi (plan, project) tomber à l'eau
**fallen** ['fɔːlən] pp of **fall**
**fallout** ['fɔːlaut] n retombées (radioactives)
**false** [fɔːls] adj faux (fausse); **under ~ pretences** sous un faux prétexte; **false alarm** n fausse alerte; **false teeth** npl (BRIT) fausses dents, dentier m
**fame** [feɪm] n renommée f, renom m
**familiar** [fə'mɪlɪəʳ] adj familier(-ière); **to be ~ with sth** connaître qch; **familiarize** [fə'mɪlɪəraɪz] vt: **to familiarize o.s. with** se familiariser avec
**family** ['fæmɪlɪ] n famille f; **family doctor** n médecin m de famille; **family**

**planning** n planning familial
**famine** ['fæmɪn] n famine f
**famous** ['feɪməs] adj célèbre
**fan** [fæn] n (folding) éventail m;
(Elec) ventilateur m; (person) fan m,
admirateur(-trice); (Sport) supporter
m/f ▷ vt éventer; (fire, quarrel) attiser
**fanatic** [fə'nætɪk] n fanatique m/f
**fan belt** n courroie f de ventilateur
**fan club** n fan-club m
**fancy** ['fænsɪ] n (whim) fantaisie f,
envie f; (imagination) imagination
f ▷ adj (luxury) de luxe; (elaborate:
jewellery, packaging) fantaisie inv ▷ vt
(feel like, want) avoir envie de; (imagine)
imaginer; **to take a ~ to** se prendre
d'affection pour; s'enticher de; **he
fancies her** elle lui plaît; **fancy dress** n
déguisement m, travesti m
**fan heater** n (BRIT) radiateur soufflant
**fantasize** ['fæntəsaɪz] vi fantasmer
**fantastic** [fæn'tæstɪk] adj fantastique
**fantasy** ['fæntəsɪ] n imagination f,
fantaisie f; (unreality) fantasme m
**fanzine** ['fænziːn] n fanzine m
**FAQ** n abbr (= frequently asked question)
FAQ f inv, faq f inv
**far** [fɑːʳ] adj (distant) lointain(e),
éloigné(e) ▷ adv loin; **the ~ side/end**
l'autre côté/bout; **it's not ~ (from
here)** ce n'est pas loin (d'ici); **~ away**,
**~ off** au loin, dans le lointain; **~ better**
beaucoup mieux; **~ from** loin de; **by ~**
de loin, de beaucoup; **go as ~ as the
bridge** allez jusqu'au pont; **as ~ as I
know** pour autant que je sache; **how ~
is it to …?** combien y a-t-il jusqu'à …?;
**how ~ have you got with your work?**
où en êtes-vous dans votre travail?
**farce** [fɑːs] n farce f
**fare** [fɛəʳ] n (on trains, buses) prix m du
billet; (in taxi) prix de la course; (food)
table f, chère f; **half ~** demi-tarif; **full
~** plein tarif
**Far East** n: **the ~** l'Extrême-Orient m
**farewell** [fɛə'wɛl] excl, n adieu m
**farm** [fɑːm] n ferme f ▷ vt cultiver;
**farmer** n fermier(-ière); **farmhouse**

n (maison f de) ferme f; **farming** n
agriculture f; (of animals) élevage m;
**farmyard** n cour f de ferme
**far-reaching** ['fɑː'riːtʃɪŋ] adj d'une
grande portée
**fart** [fɑːt] (inf!) vi péter
**farther** ['fɑːðəʳ] adv plus loin ▷ adj plus
eloigné(e), plus lointain(e)
**farthest** ['fɑːðɪst] superlative of **far**
**fascinate** ['fæsɪneɪt] vt fasciner,
captiver; **fascinated** adj fasciné(e)
**fascinating** ['fæsɪneɪtɪŋ] adj
fascinant(e)
**fascination** [fæsɪ'neɪʃən] n
fascination f
**fascist** ['fæʃɪst] adj, n fasciste m/f
**fashion** ['fæʃən] n mode f; (manner)
façon f, manière f ▷ vt façonner; **in
~** à la mode; **out of ~** démodé(e);
**fashionable** adj à la mode; **fashion
show** n défilé m de mannequins or
de mode
**fast** [fɑːst] adj rapide; (clock): **to be ~**
avancer; (dye, colour) grand or bon teint
inv ▷ adv vite, rapidement; (stuck, held)
solidement ▷ n jeûne m ▷ vi jeûner; **~
asleep** profondément endormi
**fasten** ['fɑːsn] vt attacher, fixer;
(coat) attacher, fermer ▷ vi se fermer,
s'attacher
**fast food** n fast food m, restauration
f rapide
**fat** [fæt] adj gros(se) ▷ n graisse f; (on
meat) gras m; (for cooking) matière
grasse
**fatal** ['feɪtl] adj (mistake) fatal(e); (injury)
mortel(le); **fatality** [fə'tælɪtɪ] n (road
death etc) victime f, décès m; **fatally** adv
fatalement; (injured) mortellement
**fate** [feɪt] n destin m; (of person) sort m
**father** ['fɑːðəʳ] n père m; **Father
Christmas** n le Père Noël; **father-in-
law** n beau-père m
**fatigue** [fə'tiːg] n fatigue f
**fattening** ['fætnɪŋ] adj (food) qui
fait grossir
**fatty** ['fætɪ] adj (food) gras(se) ▷ n (inf)
gros (grosse)

**faucet** ['fɔːsɪt] n (us) robinet m
**fault** [fɔːlt] n faute f; (defect) défaut m;
(Geo) faille f ▷ vt trouver des défauts à,
prendre en défaut; **it's my ~** c'est de ma
faute; **to find ~ with** trouver à redire or
à critiquer à; **at ~** fautif(-ive), coupable;
**faulty** adj défectueux(-euse)
**fauna** ['fɔːnə] n faune f
**favour** etc (us **favor** etc) ['feɪvər]
n faveur f; (help) service m ▷ vt
(proposition) être en faveur de; (pupil
etc) favoriser; (team, horse) donner
gagnant; **to do sb a ~** rendre un service
à qn; **in ~ of** en faveur de; **to find ~
with sb** trouver grâce aux yeux de qn;
**favourable** adj favorable; **favourite**
['feɪvrɪt] adj, n favori(te)
**fawn** [fɔːn] n (deer) faon m ▷ adj (also:
**~-coloured**) fauve ▷ vi: **to ~ (up)on**
flatter servilement
**fax** [fæks] n (document) télécopie f;
(machine) télécopieur m ▷ vt envoyer
par télécopie
**FBI** n abbr (us: = Federal Bureau of
Investigation) FBI m
**fear** [fɪər] n crainte f, peur f ▷ vt
craindre; **for ~ of** de peur que + sub or
de + infinitive; **fearful** adj craintif(-ive);
(sight, noise) affreux(-euse),
épouvantable; **fearless** adj intrépide
**feasible** ['fiːzəbl] adj faisable,
réalisable
**feast** [fiːst] n festin m, banquet m; (Rel:
also: **~ day**) fête f ▷ vi festoyer
**feat** [fiːt] n exploit m, prouesse f
**feather** ['feðər] n plume f
**feature** ['fiːtʃər] n caractéristique f;
(article) chronique f, rubrique f ▷ vt
(film) avoir pour vedette(s) ▷ vi figurer
(en bonne place); **features** npl (of face)
traits mpl; **a (special) ~ on sth/sb** un
reportage sur qch/qn; **feature film** n
long métrage
**Feb.** abbr (= February) fév
**February** ['fɛbruərɪ] n février m
**fed** [fɛd] pt, pp of **feed**
**federal** ['fɛdərəl] adj fédéral(e)
**federation** [fɛdə'reɪʃən] n fédération f

**fed up** adj: **to be ~ (with)** en avoir marre
or plein le dos (de)
**fee** [fiː] n rémunération f; (of doctor,
lawyer) honoraires mpl; (of school,
college etc) frais mpl de scolarité; (for
examination) droits mpl
**feeble** ['fiːbl] adj faible; (attempt, excuse)
pauvre; (joke) piteux(-euse)
**feed** [fiːd] n (of animal) nourriture f,
pâture f; (on printer) mécanisme m
d'alimentation ▷ vt (pt, pp **fed**) (person)
nourrir; (BRIT: baby: breastfeed) allaiter;
(: with bottle) donner le biberon à;
(horse etc) donner à manger à; (machine)
alimenter; (data etc): **to ~ sth into**
enregistrer qch dans; **feedback** n
(Elec) effet m Larsen; (from person)
réactions fpl
**feel** [fiːl] n (sensation) sensation f;
(impression) impression f ▷ vt (pt, pp
**felt**) (touch) toucher; (explore) tâter,
palper; (cold, pain) sentir; (grief, anger)
ressentir, éprouver; (think, believe): **to ~
(that)** trouver que; **to ~ hungry/cold**
avoir faim/froid; **to ~ lonely/better**
se sentir seul/mieux; **I don't ~ well**
je ne me sens pas bien; **it ~s soft** c'est
doux au toucher; **to ~ like** (want) avoir
envie de; **feeling** n (physical) sensation
f; (emotion, impression) sentiment m; **to
hurt sb's feelings** froisser qn
**feet** [fiːt] npl of **foot**
**fell** [fɛl] pt of **fall** ▷ vt (tree) abattre
**fellow** ['fɛləu] n type m; (comrade)
compagnon m; (of learned
society) membre m ▷ cpd: **their ~
prisoners/students** leurs camarades
prisonniers/étudiants; **fellow citizen**
n concitoyen(ne); **fellow countryman**
n (irreg) compatriote m; **fellow men** npl
semblables mpl; **fellowship** n (society)
association f; (comradeship) amitié
f, camaraderie f; (Scol) sorte de bourse
universitaire
**felony** ['fɛlənɪ] n crime m, forfait m
**felt** [fɛlt] pt, pp of **feel** ▷ n feutre m; **felt-
tip** n (also: **felt-tip pen**) stylo-feutre m
**female** ['fiːmeɪl] n (Zool) femelle f;

(*pej: woman*) bonne femme ▷ *adj* (*Biol*) femelle; (*sex, character*) féminin(e); (*vote etc*) des femmes

**feminine** [ˈfɛmɪnɪn] *adj* féminin(e)

**feminist** [ˈfɛmɪnɪst] *n* féministe *m/f*

**fence** [fɛns] *n* barrière *f* ▷ *vi* faire de l'escrime; **fencing** *n* (*sport*) escrime *m*

**fend** [fɛnd] *vi*: **to ~ for o.s.** se débrouiller (tout seul); **fend off** *vt* (*attack etc*) parer; (*questions*) éluder

**fender** [ˈfɛndəʳ] *n* garde-feu *m inv*; (*on boat*) défense *f*; (*us: of car*) aile *f*

**fennel** [ˈfɛnl] *n* fenouil *m*

**ferment** *vi* [fəˈmɛnt] fermenter ▷ *n* [ˈfəːmɛnt] (*fig*) agitation *f*, effervescence *f*

**fern** [fəːn] *n* fougère *f*

**ferocious** [fəˈrəuʃəs] *adj* féroce

**ferret** [ˈfɛrɪt] *n* furet *m*

**ferry** [ˈfɛrɪ] *n* (*small*) bac *m*; (*large: also*: **~boat**) ferry(-boat *m*) *m* ▷ *vt* transporter

**fertile** [ˈfəːtaɪl] *adj* fertile; (*Biol*) fécond(e); **fertilize** [ˈfəːtɪlaɪz] *vt* fertiliser; (*Biol*) féconder; **fertilizer** *n* engrais *m*

**festival** [ˈfɛstɪvəl] *n* (*Rel*) fête *f*; (*Art, Mus*) festival *m*

**festive** [ˈfɛstɪv] *adj* de fête; **the ~ season** (*BRIT: Christmas*) la période des fêtes

**fetch** [fɛtʃ] *vt* aller chercher; (*BRIT: sell for*) rapporter

**fête** [feɪt] *n* fête *f*, kermesse *f*

**fetus** [ˈfiːtəs] *n* (*us*) = **foetus**

**feud** [fjuːd] *n* querelle *f*, dispute *f*

**fever** [ˈfiːvəʳ] *n* fièvre *f*; **feverish** *adj* fiévreux(-euse), fébrile

**few** [fjuː] *adj* (*not many*) peu de ▷ *pron* peu; **a ~** (*as adj*) quelques; (*as pron*) quelques-uns(-unes); **quite a ~ ...** *adj* un certain nombre de ..., pas mal de ...; **in the past ~ days** ces derniers jours; **fewer** *adj* moins de; **fewest** *adj* le moins nombreux

**fiancé** [fɪˈɑ̃ːŋseɪ] *n* fiancé *m*; **fiancée** *n* fiancée *f*

**fiasco** [fɪˈæskəu] *n* fiasco *m*

**fib** [fɪb] *n* bobard *m*

**fibre** (*us* **fiber**) [ˈfaɪbəʳ] *n* fibre *f*; **fibreglass** (*us* **Fiberglass®**) *n* fibre *f* de verre

**fickle** [ˈfɪkl] *adj* inconstant(e), volage, capricieux(-euse)

**fiction** [ˈfɪkʃən] *n* romans *mpl*, littérature *f* romanesque; (*invention*) fiction *f*; **fictional** *adj* fictif(-ive)

**fiddle** [ˈfɪdl] *n* (*Mus*) violon *m*; (*cheating*) combine *f*, escroquerie *f* ▷ *vt* (*BRIT: accounts*) falsifier, maquiller; **fiddle with** *vt fus* tripoter

**fidelity** [fɪˈdɛlɪtɪ] *n* fidélité *f*

**fidget** [ˈfɪdʒɪt] *vi* se trémousser, remuer

**field** [fiːld] *n* champ *m*; (*fig*) domaine *m*, champ; (*Sport: ground*) terrain *m*; **field marshal** *n* maréchal *m*

**fierce** [fɪəs] *adj* (*look, animal*) féroce, sauvage; (*wind, attack, person*) (très) violent(e); (*fighting, enemy*) acharné(e)

**fifteen** [fɪfˈtiːn] *num* quinze; **fifteenth** *num* quinzième

**fifth** [fɪfθ] *num* cinquième

**fiftieth** [ˈfɪftɪɪθ] *num* cinquantième

**fifty** [ˈfɪftɪ] *num* cinquante; **fifty-fifty** *adv* moitié-moitié ▷ *adj*: **to have a fifty-fifty chance (of success)** avoir une chance sur deux (de réussir)

**fig** [fɪg] *n* figue *f*

**fight** [faɪt] *n* (*between persons*) bagarre *f*; (*argument*) dispute *f*; (*Mil*) combat *m*; (*against cancer etc*) lutte *f* ▷ *vb* (*pt, pp* **fought**) ▷ *vt* se battre contre; (*cancer, alcoholism, emotion*) combattre, lutter contre; (*election*) se présenter à ▷ *vi* se battre; (*argue*) se disputer; (*fig*): **to ~ (for/against)** lutter (pour/contre); **fight back** *vi* rendre les coups; (*after illness*) reprendre le dessus ▷ *vt* (*tears*) réprimer; **fight off** *vt* repousser; (*disease, sleep, urge*) lutter contre; **fighting** *n* combats *mpl*; (*brawls*) bagarres *fpl*

**figure** [ˈfɪgəʳ] *n* (*Drawing, Geom*) figure *f*; (*number*) chiffre *m*; (*body, outline*) silhouette *f*; (*person's shape*) ligne *f*, formes *fpl*; (*person*) personnage *m*

▷ vt (us: think) supposer ▷ vi (appear) figurer; (us: make sense) s'expliquer; **figure out** vt (understand) arriver à comprendre; (plan) calculer

**file** [faɪl] n (tool) lime f; (dossier) dossier m; (folder) dossier, chemise f; (: binder) classeur m; (Comput) fichier m; (row) file f ▷ vt (nails, wood) limer; (papers) classer; (Law: claim) faire enregistrer; déposer; **filing cabinet** n classeur m (meuble)

**Filipino** [fɪlɪ'piːnəʊ] adj philippin(e) ▷ n (person) Philippin(e)

**fill** [fɪl] vt remplir; (vacancy) pourvoir à ▷ n: **to eat one's ~** manger à sa faim; **to ~ with** remplir de; **fill in** vt (hole) boucher; (form) remplir; **fill out** vt (form, receipt) remplir; **fill up** vt remplir ▷ vi (Aut) faire le plein

**fillet** ['fɪlɪt] n filet m; **fillet steak** n filet m de bœuf, tournedos m

**filling** ['fɪlɪŋ] n (Culin) garniture f, farce f; (for tooth) plombage m; **filling station** n station-service f, station f d'essence

**film** [fɪlm] n film m; (Phot) pellicule f, film; (of powder, liquid) couche f, pellicule ▷ vt (scene) filmer ▷ vi tourner; **I'd like a 36-exposure ~** je voudrais une pellicule de 36 poses; **film star** n vedette f de cinéma

**filter** ['fɪltə'] n filtre m ▷ vt filtrer; **filter lane** n (BRIT Aut: at traffic lights) voie f de dégagement; (: on motorway) voie f de sortie

**filth** [fɪlθ] n saleté f; **filthy** adj sale, dégoûtant(e); (language) ordurier(-ière), grossier(-ière)

**fin** [fɪn] n (of fish) nageoire f; (of shark) aileron m; (of diver) palme f

**final** ['faɪnl] adj final(e), dernier(-ière); (decision, answer) définitif(-ive) ▷ n (BRIT Sport) finale f; **finals** npl (Scol) examens mpl de dernière année; (us Sport) finale f; **finale** [fɪ'nɑːlɪ] n finale m; **finalist** n (Sport) finaliste m/f; **finalize** vt mettre au point; **finally** adv (eventually) enfin, finalement; (lastly) en dernier lieu

**finance** [faɪ'næns] n finance f ▷ vt financer; **finances** npl finances fpl; **financial** [faɪ'nænʃəl] adj financier(-ière); **financial year** n année f budgétaire

**find** [faɪnd] vt (pt, pp **found**) trouver; (lost object) retrouver ▷ n trouvaille f, découverte f; **to ~ sb guilty** (Law) déclarer qn coupable; **find out** vt se renseigner sur; (truth, secret) découvrir; (person) démasquer ▷ vi: **to ~ out about** (make enquiries) se renseigner sur; (by chance) apprendre; **findings** npl (Law) conclusions fpl, verdict m; (of report) constatations fpl

**fine** [faɪn] adj (weather) beau (belle); (excellent) excellent(e); (thin, subtle, not coarse) fin(e); (acceptable) bien inv ▷ adv (well) très bien; (small) fin, finement ▷ n (Law) amende f, contravention f ▷ vt (Law) condamner à une amende; donner une contravention à; **he's ~** il va bien; **the weather is ~** il fait beau; **fine arts** npl beaux-arts mpl

**finger** ['fɪŋgə'] n doigt m ▷ vt palper, toucher; **index ~** index m; **fingernail** n ongle m (de la main); **fingerprint** n empreinte digitale; **fingertip** n bout m du doigt

**finish** ['fɪnɪʃ] n fin f; (Sport) arrivée f; (polish etc) finition f ▷ vt finir, terminer ▷ vi finir, se terminer; **to ~ doing sth** finir de faire qch; **to ~ third** arriver or terminer troisième; **when does the show ~?** quand est-ce que le spectacle se termine?; **finish off** vt finir, terminer; (kill) achever; **finish up** vi, vt finir

**Finland** ['fɪnlənd] n Finlande f; **Finn** n Finnois(e), Finlandais(e); **Finnish** adj finnois(e), finlandais(e) ▷ n (Ling) finnois m

**fir** [fəː'] n sapin m

**fire** ['faɪə'] n feu m; (accidental) incendie m; (heater) radiateur m ▷ vt (discharge): **to ~ a gun** tirer un coup de feu; (fig: interest) enflammer, animer; (inf: dismiss) mettre à la porte, renvoyer ▷ vi (*shoot*) tirer, faire feu; **~!** au feu!; **on ~** en feu; **to set ~ to sth, set sth on ~** mettre le feu à qch; **fire alarm** n avertisseur m d'incendie; **firearm** n arme f à feu; **fire brigade** n (*US* **fire department**) (régiment m de sapeurs-)pompiers mpl; **fire engine** n (*BRIT*) pompe f à incendie; **fire escape** n escalier m de secours; **fire exit** n issue f or sortie f de secours; **fire extinguisher** n extincteur m; **fireman** (*irreg*) n pompier m; **fireplace** n cheminée f; **fire station** n caserne f de pompiers; **fire truck** (*US*) n = **fire engine**; **firewall** n (*Internet*) pare-feu m; **firewood** n bois m de chauffage; **fireworks** npl (*display*) feu(x) m(pl) d'artifice

**firm** [fəːm] adj ferme ▷ n compagnie f, firme f; **firmly** adv fermement

**first** [fəːst] adj premier(-ière) ▷ adv (*before other people*) le premier, la première; (*before other things*) en premier, d'abord; (*when listing reasons etc*) en premier lieu, premièrement; (*in the beginning*) au début ▷ n (*person: in race*) premier(-ière); (*BRIT Scol*) mention f très bien; (*Aut*) première f; **the ~ of January** le premier janvier; **at ~** au commencement, au début; **~ of all** tout d'abord, pour commencer; **first aid** n premiers secours or soins; **first-aid kit** n trousse f à pharmacie; **first-class** adj (*ticket etc*) de première classe; (*excellent*) excellent(e), exceptionnel(le); (*post*) en tarif prioritaire; **first-hand** adj de première main; **first lady** n (*US*) femme f du président; **firstly** adv premièrement, en premier lieu; **first name** n prénom m; **first-rate** adj excellent(e)

**fiscal** ['fɪskl] adj fiscal(e); **fiscal year** n exercice financier

**fish** [fɪʃ] n (pl inv) poisson m ▷ vt, vi pêcher; **~ and chips** poisson frit et frites; **fisherman** (*irreg*) n pêcheur m; **fish fingers** npl (*BRIT*) bâtonnets de poisson (congelés); **fishing** n pêche f; **to go fishing** aller à la pêche;

**fishing boat** n barque f de pêche; **fishing line** n ligne f (de pêche); **fishmonger** n (*BRIT*) marchand m de poisson; **fishmonger's (shop)** n (*BRIT*) poissonnerie f; **fish sticks** npl (*US*) = **fish fingers**; **fishy** adj (*inf*) suspect(e), louche

**fist** [fɪst] n poing m

**fit** [fɪt] adj (*Med, Sport*) en (bonne) forme; (*proper*) convenable; approprié(e) ▷ vt (*subj: clothes*) aller à; (*put in, attach*) installer, poser; (*equip*) équiper, garnir, munir; (*suit*) convenir à ▷ vi (*clothes*) aller; (*parts*) s'adapter; (*in space, gap*) entrer, s'adapter ▷ n (*Med*) accès m, crise f; (*of anger*) accès; (*of hysterics, jealousy*) crise; **~ to** (*ready to*) en état de; **~ for** (*worthy*) digne de; (*capable*) apte à; **to keep ~** se maintenir en forme; **this dress is a tight/good ~** cette robe est un peu juste/(me) va très bien; **a ~ of coughing** une quinte de toux; **by ~s and starts** par à-coups; **fit in** vi (*add up*) cadrer; (*integrate*) s'intégrer; (*to new situation*) s'adapter; **fitness** n (*Med*) forme f physique; **fitted** adj (*jacket, shirt*) ajusté(e); **fitted carpet** n moquette f; **fitted kitchen** n (*BRIT*) cuisine équipée; **fitted sheet** n drap-housse m; **fitting** adj approprié(e) ▷ n (*of dress*) essayage m; (*of piece of equipment*) pose f, installation f; **fitting room** n (*in shop*) cabine f d'essayage; **fittings** npl installations fpl

**five** [faɪv] num cinq; **fiver** n (*inf: BRIT*) billet m de cinq livres; (: *US*) billet de cinq dollars

**fix** [fɪks] vt (*date, amount etc*) fixer; (*sort out*) arranger; (*mend*) réparer; (*make ready: meal, drink*) préparer ▷ n: **to be in a ~** être dans le pétrin; **fix up** vt (*meeting*) arranger; **to ~ sb up with sth** faire avoir qch à qn; **fixed** adj (*prices etc*) fixe; **fixture** n installation f (fixe); (*Sport*) rencontre f (au programme)

**fizzy** ['fɪzɪ] adj pétillant(e), gazeux(-euse)

**flag** [flæg] n drapeau m; (*also:* **~stone**)

dalle f ▷ vi faiblir; fléchir; **flag down**
vt héler, faire signe (de s'arrêter) à;
**flagpole** n mât m

**flair** [fleər] n flair m

**flak** [flæk] n (Mil) tir antiaérien; (inf:
criticism) critiques fpl

**flake** [fleɪk] n (of rust, paint) écaille f; (of
snow, soap powder) flocon m ▷ vi (also: ~
off) s'écailler

**flamboyant** [flæm'bɔɪənt] adj
flamboyant(e), éclatant(e); (person)
haut(e) en couleur

**flame** [fleɪm] n flamme f

**flamingo** [flə'mɪŋgəu] n flamant
m (rose)

**flammable** ['flæməbl] adj
inflammable

**flan** [flæn] n (BRIT) tarte f

**flank** [flæŋk] n flanc m ▷ vt flanquer

**flannel** ['flænl] n (BRIT: also: **face ~**)
gant m de toilette; (fabric) flanelle f

**flap** [flæp] n (of pocket, envelope) rabat
m ▷ vt (wings) battre (de) ▷ vi (sail,
flag) claquer

**flare** [fleər] n (signal) signal lumineux;
(Mil) fusée éclairante; (in skirt etc)
évasement m; **flares** npl (trousers)
pantalon m à pattes d'éléphant; **flare
up** vi s'embraser; (fig: person) se mettre
en colère, s'emporter; (: revolt) éclater

**flash** [flæʃ] n éclair m; (also: **news ~**)
flash m (d'information); (Phot) flash
m ▷ vt (switch on) allumer (brièvement);
(direct): **to ~ sth at** braquer qch sur;
(send: message) câbler; (smile) lancer
▷ vi briller; jeter des éclairs; (light
on ambulance etc) clignoter; **a ~ of
lightning** un éclair; **in a ~** en un clin
d'œil; **to ~ one's headlights** faire un
appel de phares; **he ~ed by** or **past** il
passa (devant nous) comme un éclair;
**flashback** n flashback m, retour m en
arrière; **flashbulb** n ampoule f de flash;
**flashlight** n lampe f de poche

**flask** [flɑ:sk] n flacon m, bouteille f;
(also: **vacuum ~**) bouteille f thermos®

**flat** [flæt] adj plat(e); (tyre) dégonflé(e),
à plat; (beer) éventé(e); (battery) à plat;
(denial) catégorique; (Mus) bémol inv;
(: voice) faux (fausse) ▷ n (BRIT:
apartment) appartement m; (Aut)
crevaison f, pneu crevé; (Mus) bémol m;
**~ out** (work) sans relâche; (race) à fond;
**flatten** vt (also: **flatten out**) aplatir;
(crop) coucher; (house, city) raser

**flatter** ['flætər] vt flatter; **flattering** adj
flatteur(-euse); (clothes etc) seyant(e)

**flaunt** [flɔ:nt] vt faire étalage de

**flavour** etc (US **flavor** etc) ['fleɪvər]
n goût m, saveur f; (of ice cream etc)
parfum m ▷ vt parfumer, aromatiser;
**vanilla-~ed** à l'arôme de vanille,
vanillé(e); **what ~s do you have?** quels
parfums avez-vous?; **flavouring** n
arôme m (synthétique)

**flaw** [flɔ:] n défaut m; **flawless** adj
sans défaut

**flea** [fli:] n puce f; **flea market** n
marché m aux puces

**flee** (pt, pp **fled**) [fli:, flɛd] vt fuir, s'enfuir
de ▷ vi fuir, s'enfuir

**fleece** [fli:s] n (of sheep) toison f; (top)
(laine f) polaire f ▷ vt (inf) voler, filouter

**fleet** [fli:t] n flotte f; (of lorries, cars etc)
parc m; convoi m

**fleeting** ['fli:tɪŋ] adj fugace,
fugitif(-ive); (visit) très bref (brève)

**Flemish** ['flɛmɪʃ] adj flamand(e)
▷ n (Ling) flamand m; **the ~** npl les
Flamands

**flesh** [flɛʃ] n chair f

**flew** [flu:] pt of **fly**

**flex** [flɛks] n fil m or câble m électrique
(souple) ▷ vt (knee) fléchir; (muscles)
tendre; **flexibility** n flexibilité f;
**flexible** adj flexible; (person, schedule)
souple; **flexitime** (US **flextime**) n
horaire m variable or à la carte

**flick** [flɪk] n petit coup m; (with finger)
chiquenaude f ▷ vt donner un petit
coup à; (switch) appuyer sur; **flick
through** vt fus feuilleter

**flicker** ['flɪkər] vi (light, flame) vaciller

**flies** [flaɪz] npl of **fly**

**flight** [flaɪt] n vol m; (escape) fuite f;
(also: **~ of steps**) escalier m; **flight**

**attendant** n steward m, hôtesse f
de l'air

**flimsy** ['flɪmzɪ] adj peu solide; (clothes)
trop léger(-ère); (excuse) pauvre, mince

**flinch** [flɪntʃ] vi tressaillir; **to ~ from** se
dérober à, reculer devant

**fling** [flɪŋ] vt (pt, pp **flung**) jeter, lancer

**flint** [flɪnt] n silex m; (in lighter) pierre
f (à briquet)

**flip** [flɪp] vt (throw) donner une
chiquenaude à; (switch) appuyer sur;
(US: pancake) faire sauter; **to ~ sth over**
retourner qch

**flip-flops** ['flɪpflɒps] npl (esp BRIT)
tongs fpl

**flipper** ['flɪpə'] n (of animal) nageoire f;
(for swimmer) palme f

**flirt** [flɜ:t] vi flirter ▷ n flirteur(-euse)

**float** [fləut] n flotteur m; (in procession)
char m; (sum of money) réserve f ▷ vi
flotter

**flock** [flɒk] n (of sheep) troupeau m; (of
birds) vol m; (of people) foule f

**flood** [flʌd] n inondation f; (of letters,
refugees etc) flot m ▷ vt inonder ▷ vi
(place) être inondé; (people): **to ~ into**
envahir; **flooding** n inondation f;
**floodlight** n projecteur m

**floor** [flɔ:'] n sol m; (storey) étage m;
(of sea, valley) fond m ▷ vt (knock down)
terrasser; (baffle) désorienter; **ground
~**, (US) **first ~** rez-de-chaussée m; **first
~**, (US) **second ~** premier étage; **what ~
is it on?** c'est à quel étage?; **floorboard**
n planche f (du plancher); **flooring** n
sol m; (wooden) plancher m; (covering)
revêtement m de sol; **floor show** n
spectacle m de variétés

**flop** [flɒp] n fiasco m ▷ vi (fail) faire
fiasco; (fall) s'affaler, s'effondrer; **floppy**
adj lâche, flottant(e) ▷ n (Comput: also:
**floppy disk**) disquette f

**flora** ['flɔ:rə] n flore f

**floral** ['flɔ:rl] adj floral(e); (dress) à fleurs

**florist** ['flɒrɪst] n fleuriste m/f; **florist's
(shop)** n magasin m or boutique f de
fleuriste

**flotation** [fləu'teɪʃən] n (of shares)

émission f; (of company) lancement m
(en Bourse)

**flour** ['flauə'] n farine f

**flourish** ['flʌrɪʃ] vi prospérer ▷ n
(gesture) moulinet m

**flow** [fləu] n (of water, traffic etc)
écoulement m; (tide, influx) flux m;
(of blood, Elec) circulation f; (of river)
courant m ▷ vi couler; (traffic) s'écouler;
(robes, hair) flotter

**flower** ['flauə'] n fleur f ▷ vi fleurir;
**flower bed** n plate-bande f; **flowerpot**
n pot m (à fleurs)

**flown** [fləun] pp of **fly**

**fl. oz.** abbr = **fluid ounce**

**flu** [flu:] n grippe f

**fluctuate** ['flʌktjueɪt] vi varier,
fluctuer

**fluent** ['flu:ənt] adj (speech, style)
coulant(e), aisé(e); **he speaks ~
French**, **he's ~ in French** il parle le
français couramment

**fluff** [flʌf] n duvet m; (on jacket, carpet)
peluche f; **fluffy** adj duveteux(-euse);
(toy) en peluche

**fluid** ['flu:ɪd] n fluide m; (in diet) liquide
m ▷ adj fluide; **fluid ounce** n (BRIT) =
0.028 l; 0.05 pints

**fluke** [flu:k] n coup m de veine

**flung** [flʌŋ] pt, pp of **fling**

**fluorescent** [fluə'rɛsnt] adj
fluorescent(e)

**fluoride** ['fluəraɪd] n fluor m

**flurry** ['flʌrɪ] n (of snow) rafale f,
bourrasque f; **a ~ of activity** un
affairement soudain

**flush** [flʌʃ] n (on face) rougeur f; (fig: of
youth etc) éclat m ▷ vt nettoyer à grande
eau ▷ vi rougir ▷ adj (level): **~ with** au
ras de, de niveau avec; **to ~ the toilet**
tirer la chasse (d'eau)

**flute** [flu:t] n flûte f

**flutter** ['flʌtə'] n (of panic, excitement)
agitation f; (of wings) battement m ▷ vi
(bird) battre des ailes, voleter

**fly** [flaɪ] n (insect) mouche f; (on trousers:
also: **flies**) braguette f ▷ vb (pt **flew**, pp
**flown**) ▷ vt (plane) piloter; (passengers,

*cargo*) transporter (par avion); (*distance*) parcourir ▷ vi voler; (*passengers*) aller en avion; (*escape*) s'enfuir, fuir; (*flag*) se déployer; **fly away, fly off** vi s'envoler; **fly-drive** n formule f avion plus voiture; **flying** n (*activity*) aviation f; (*action*) vol m ▷ adj: **flying visit** visite f éclair inv; **with flying colours** haut la main; **flying saucer** n soucoupe volante; **flyover** n (BRIT: *overpass*) pont routier

**FM** abbr (Radio: = *frequency modulation*) FM

**foal** [fəul] n poulain m

**foam** [fəum] n écume f; (*on beer*) mousse f; (*also:* ~ **rubber**) caoutchouc m mousse ▷ vi (*liquid*) écumer; (*soapy water*) mousser

**focus** ['fəukəs] n (*pl* ~**es**) foyer m; (*of interest*) centre m ▷ vt (*field glasses etc*) mettre au point ▷ vi: **to** ~ (**on**) (*with camera*) régler la mise au point (sur); (*with eyes*) fixer son regard (sur); (*fig: concentrate*) se concentrer; **out of/in** ~ (*picture*) flou(e)/net(te); (*camera*) pas au point/au point

**foetus** (US **fetus**) ['fiːtəs] n fœtus m

**fog** [fɔg] n brouillard m; **foggy** adj: **it's foggy** il y a du brouillard; **fog lamp** (US **fog light**) n (Aut) phare m anti-brouillard

**foil** [fɔil] vt déjouer, contrecarrer ▷ n feuille f de métal; (*kitchen foil*) papier m d'alu(minium); **to act as a** ~ **to** (*fig*) servir de repoussoir or de faire-valoir à

**fold** [fəuld] n (*bend, crease*) pli m; (Agr) parc m à moutons; (*fig*) bercail m ▷ vt plier; **to** ~ **one's arms** croiser les bras; **fold up** vi (*map etc*) se plier, se replier; (*business*) fermer boutique ▷ vt (*map etc*) plier, replier; **folder** n (*for papers*) chemise f; (: *binder*) classeur m; (Comput) dossier m; **folding** adj (*chair, bed*) pliant(e)

**foliage** ['fəulɪɪdʒ] n feuillage m

**folk** [fəuk] npl gens mpl ▷ cpd folklorique; **folks** npl (*inf: parents*) famille f, parents mpl; **folklore**

['fəuklɔːʳ] n folklore m; **folk music** n musique f folklorique; (*contemporary*) musique folk, folk m; **folk song** n chanson f folklorique; (*contemporary*) chanson folk inv

**follow** ['fɔləu] vt suivre ▷ vi suivre; (*result*) s'ensuivre; **to** ~ **suit** (*fig*) faire de même; **follow up** vt (*letter, offer*) donner suite à; (*case*) suivre; **follower** n disciple m/f, partisan(e); **following** adj suivant(e) ▷ n partisans mpl, disciples mpl; **follow-up** n suite f; (*on file, case*) suivi m

**fond** [fɔnd] adj (*memory, look*) tendre, affectueux(-euse); (*hopes, dreams*) un peu fou (folle); **to be** ~ **of** aimer beaucoup

**food** [fuːd] n nourriture f; **food mixer** n mixeur m; **food poisoning** n intoxication f alimentaire; **food processor** n robot m de cuisine; **food stamp** n (US) bon m de nourriture (*pour indigents*)

**fool** [fuːl] n idiot(e); (Culin) mousse f de fruits ▷ vt berner, duper; **fool about, fool around** vi (*pej: waste time*) traînailler, glandouiller; (: *behave foolishly*) faire l'idiot ou l'imbécile; **foolish** adj idiot(e), stupide; (*rash*) imprudent(e); **foolproof** adj (*plan etc*) infaillible

**foot** (*pl* **feet**) [fut, fiːt] n pied m; (*of animal*) patte f; (*measure*) pied (= 30.48 cm; 12 *inches*) ▷ vt (*bill*) payer; **on** ~ à pied; **footage** n (Cine: *length*) = métrage m; (: *material*) séquences fpl; **foot-and-mouth (disease)** [futənd'mauθ-] n fièvre aphteuse; **football** n (*ball*) ballon m (de football); (*sport: BRIT*) football m; (: US) football américain; **footballer** n (BRIT) = **football player**; **football match** n (BRIT) match m de foot(ball); **football player** n footballeur(-euse), joueur(-euse) de football; (US) joueur(-euse) de football américain; **footbridge** n passerelle f; **foothills** npl contreforts mpl; **foothold** n prise f (de pied); **footing** n (*fig*) position f; **to lose**

one's footing perdre pied; **footnote** n note f (en bas de page); **footpath** n sentier m; **footprint** n trace f (de pied); **footstep** n pas m; **footwear** n chaussures fpl

 **KEYWORD**

**for** [fɔːʳ] prep **1** (indicating destination, intention, purpose) pour; **the train for London** le train pour (or à destination de) Londres; **he left for Rome** il est parti pour Rome; **he went for the paper** il est allé chercher le journal; **is this for me?** c'est pour moi?; **it's time for lunch** c'est l'heure du déjeuner; **what's it for?** ça sert à quoi?; **what for?** (why) pourquoi?; (to what end) pour quoi faire?, à quoi bon?; **for sale** à vendre; **to pray for peace** prier pour la paix **2** (on behalf of, representing) pour; **the MP for Hove** le député de Hove; **to work for sb/sth** travailler pour qn/qch; **I'll ask him for you** je vais lui demander pour toi; **G for George** G comme Georges **3** (because of) pour; **for this reason** pour cette raison; **for fear of being criticized** de peur d'être critiqué **4** (with regard to) pour; **it's cold for July** il fait froid pour juillet; **a gift for languages** un don pour les langues **5** (in exchange for): **I sold it for £5** je l'ai vendu 5 livres; **to pay 50 pence for a ticket** payer un billet 50 pence **6** (in favour of) pour; **are you for or against us?** êtes-vous pour ou contre nous?; **I'm all for it** je suis tout à fait pour; **vote for X** votez pour X **7** (referring to distance) pendant, sur; **there are roadworks for 5 km** il y a des travaux sur or pendant 5 km; **we walked for miles** nous avons marché pendant des kilomètres **8** (referring to time) pendant; depuis; pour; **he was away for 2 years** il a été absent pendant 2 ans; **she will be away for a month** elle sera absente

(pendant) un mois; **it hasn't rained for 3 weeks** ça fait 3 semaines qu'il ne pleut pas, il ne pleut pas depuis 3 semaines; **I have known her for years** je la connais depuis des années; **can you do it for tomorrow?** est-ce que tu peux le faire pour demain? **9** (with infinitive clauses): **it is not for me to decide** ce n'est pas à moi de décider; **it would be best for you to leave** le mieux serait que vous partiez; **there is still time for you to do it** vous avez encore le temps de le faire; **for this to be possible ...** pour que cela soit possible ... **10** (in spite of): **for all that** malgré cela, néanmoins; **for all his work/efforts** malgré tout son travail/tous ses efforts; **for all his complaints, he's very fond of her** il a beau se plaindre, il l'aime beaucoup

▷ conj (since, as: rather formal) car

**forbid** (pt forbad(e), pp ~den) [fəˈbɪd, -ˈbæd, -ˈbɪdn] vt défendre, interdire; **to ~ sb to do** défendre or interdire à qn de faire; **forbidden** adj défendu(e)

**force** [fɔːs] n force f ▷ vt forcer; (push) pousser (de force); **to ~ o.s. to do** se forcer à faire; **in ~** (being used: rule, law, prices) en vigueur; (in large numbers) en force; **forced** adj forcé(e); **forceful** adj énergique

**ford** [fɔːd] n gué m

**fore** [fɔːʳ] n: **to the ~** en évidence; **forearm** n avant-bras m inv; **forecast** n prévision f; (also: **weather forecast**) prévisions fpl météorologiques, météo f ▷ vt (irreg: like **cast**) prévoir; **forecourt** n (of garage) devant m; **forefinger** n index m; **forefront** n: **in the forefront of** au premier rang or plan de; **foreground** n premier plan; **forehead** [ˈfɔrɪd] n front m

**foreign** [ˈfɔrɪn] adj étranger(-ère); (trade) extérieur(e); (travel) à l'étranger; **foreign currency** n devises étrangères; **foreigner** n étranger(-ère);

**foreign exchange** n (system) change m; (money) devises fpl; **Foreign Office** n (BRIT) ministère m des Affaires étrangères; **Foreign Secretary** n (BRIT) ministre m des Affaires étrangères

**fore**: **foreman** (irreg) n (in construction) contremaître m; **foremost** adj le (la) plus en vue, premier(-ière) ▷ adv: **first and foremost** avant tout, tout d'abord; **forename** n prénom m

**forensic** [fə'rɛnsɪk] adj: **~ medicine** médecine légale

**foresee** (pt foresaw, pp **~n**) [fɔ:'si:, -'sɔ:, -'si:n] vt prévoir; **foreseeable** adj prévisible

**forest** ['fɔrɪst] n forêt f; **forestry** n sylviculture f

**forever** [fə'rɛvəʳ] adv pour toujours; (fig: endlessly) continuellement

**foreword** ['fɔ:wə:d] n avant-propos m inv

**forfeit** ['fɔ:fɪt] vt perdre

**forgave** [fə'geɪv] pt of **forgive**

**forge** [fɔ:dʒ] n forge f ▷ vt (signature) contrefaire; (wrought iron) forger; **to ~ money** (BRIT) fabriquer de la fausse monnaie; **forger** n faussaire m; **forgery** n faux m, contrefaçon f

**forget** (pt forgot, pp **forgotten**) [fə'gɛt, -'gɔt, -'gɔtn] vt, vi oublier; **I've forgotten my key/passport** j'ai oublié ma clé/mon passeport; **forgetful** adj distrait(e), étourdi(e)

**forgive** (pt forgave, pp **~n**) [fə'gɪv, -'geɪv, -'gɪvn] vt pardonner; **to ~ sb for sth/for doing sth** pardonner qch à qn/de faire qch

**forgot** [fə'gɔt] pt of **forget**

**forgotten** [fə'gɔtn] pp of **forget**

**fork** [fɔ:k] n (for eating) fourchette f; (for gardening) fourche f; (of roads) bifurcation f ▷ vi (road) bifurquer

**forlorn** [fə'lɔ:n] adj (deserted) abandonné(e); (hope, attempt) désespéré(e)

**form** [fɔ:m] n forme f; (Scol) classe f; (questionnaire) formulaire m ▷ vt former; (habit) contracter; **to ~ part**

of sth faire partie de qch; **on top ~** en pleine forme

**formal** ['fɔ:məl] adj (offer, receipt) en bonne et due forme; (person) cérémonieux(-euse); (occasion, dinner) officiel(le); (garden) à la française; (clothes) de soirée; **formality** [fɔ:'mælɪtɪ] n formalité f

**format** ['fɔ:mæt] n format m ▷ vt (Comput) formater

**formation** [fɔ:'meɪʃən] n formation f

**former** ['fɔ:məʳ] adj ancien(ne); (before n) précédent(e); **the ~ ... the latter** le premier ... le second, celui-là ... celui-ci; **formerly** adv autrefois

**formidable** ['fɔ:mɪdəbl] adj redoutable

**formula** ['fɔ:mjulə] n formule f

**fort** [fɔ:t] n fort m

**forthcoming** [fɔ:θ'kʌmɪŋ] adj qui va paraître or avoir lieu prochainement; (character) ouvert(e), communicatif(-ive); (available) disponible

**fortieth** ['fɔ:tɪɪθ] num quarantième

**fortify** ['fɔ:tɪfaɪ] vt (city) fortifier; (person) remonter

**fortnight** ['fɔ:tnaɪt] n (BRIT) quinzaine f, quinze jours mpl; **fortnightly** adj bimensuel(le) ▷ adv tous les quinze jours

**fortress** ['fɔ:trɪs] n forteresse f

**fortunate** ['fɔ:tʃənɪt] adj heureux(-euse); (person) chanceux(-euse); **it is ~ that** c'est une chance que, il est heureux que; **fortunately** adv heureusement, par bonheur

**fortune** ['fɔ:tʃən] n chance f; (wealth) fortune f; **fortune-teller** n diseuse f de bonne aventure

**forty** ['fɔ:tɪ] num quarante

**forum** ['fɔ:rəm] n forum m, tribune f

**forward** ['fɔ:wəd] adj (movement, position) en avant, vers l'avant; (not shy) effronté(e); (in time) en avance ▷ adv (also: **~s**) en avant ▷ n (Sport) avant m ▷ vt (letter) faire suivre; (parcel, goods) expédier; (fig) promouvoir, favoriser; **to move ~** avancer; **forwarding address** n adresse f de réexpédition

**forward slash** n barre f oblique

**fossil** ['fɔsl] adj, n fossile m

**foster** ['fɔstə'] vt (encourage) encourager, favoriser; (child) élever (sans adopter); **foster child** n enfant élevé dans une famille d'accueil

**foster parent** n parent qui élève un enfant sans l'adopter

**fought** [fɔːt] pt, pp of **fight**

**foul** [faul] adj (weather, smell, food) infect(e); (language) ordurier(-ière) ▷ n (Football) faute f ▷ vt (dirty) salir, encrasser; **he's got a ~ temper** il a un caractère de chien; **foul play** n (Law) acte criminel

**found** [faund] pt, pp of **find** ▷ vt (establish) fonder; **foundation** [faun'deɪʃən] n (act) fondation f; (base) fondement m; (also: **foundation cream**) fond m de teint; **foundations** npl (of building) fondations fpl

**founder** ['faundə'] n fondateur m ▷ vi couler, sombrer

**fountain** ['fauntɪn] n fontaine f; **fountain pen** n stylo m (à encre)

**four** [fɔː'] num quatre; **on all ~s** à quatre pattes; **four-letter word** n obscénité f, gros mot; **four-poster** n (also: **four-poster bed**) lit m à baldaquin; **fourteen** num quatorze; **fourteenth** num quatorzième; **fourth** num quatrième ▷ n (Aut: also: **fourth gear**) quatrième f; **four-wheel drive** n (Aut: car) voiture f à quatre roues motrices

**fowl** [faul] n volaille f

**fox** [fɔks] n renard m ▷ vt mystifier

**foyer** ['fɔɪeɪ] n (in hotel) vestibule m; (Theat) foyer m

**fraction** ['frækʃən] n fraction f

**fracture** ['fræktʃə'] n fracture f ▷ vt fracturer

**fragile** ['frædʒaɪl] adj fragile

**fragment** ['frægmənt] n fragment m

**fragrance** ['freɪgrəns] n parfum m

**frail** [freɪl] adj fragile, délicat(e); (person) frêle

**frame** [freɪm] n (of building) charpente f; (of human, animal) charpente f; (of picture) cadre m; (of door, window) encadrement m, chambranle m; (of spectacles: also: **~s**) monture f ▷ vt (picture) encadrer; **~ of mind** disposition f d'esprit; **framework** n structure f

**France** [frɑːns] n la France

**franchise** ['fræntʃaɪz] n (Pol) droit m de vote; (Comm) franchise f

**frank** [fræŋk] adj franc (franche) ▷ vt (letter) affranchir; **frankly** adv franchement

**frantic** ['fræntɪk] adj (hectic) frénétique; (distraught) hors de soi

**fraud** [frɔːd] n supercherie f, fraude f, tromperie f; (person) imposteur m

**fraught** [frɔːt] adj (tense: person) très tendu(e); (: situation) pénible; **~ with** (difficulties etc) chargé(e) de, plein(e) de

**fray** [freɪ] vt effilocher ▷ vi s'effilocher

**freak** [friːk] n (eccentric person) phénomène m; (unusual event) hasard m extraordinaire; (pej: fanatic): **health food ~** fana m/f or obsédé(e) de l'alimentation saine ▷ adj (storm) exceptionnel(le); (accident) bizarre

**freckle** ['frekl] n tache f de rousseur

**free** [friː] adj libre; (gratis) gratuit(e) ▷ vt (prisoner etc) libérer; (jammed object or person) dégager; **is this seat ~?** la place est libre?; **~ (of charge)** gratuitement; **freedom** n liberté f; **Freefone®** n numéro vert; **free gift** n prime f; **free kick** n (Sport) coup franc; **freelance** adj (journalist etc) indépendant(e), free-lance inv ▷ adv en free-lance; **freely** adv librement; (liberally) libéralement; **Freepost®** n (BRIT) port payé; **free-range** adj (egg) de ferme; (chicken) fermier; **freeway** n (US) autoroute f; **free will** n libre arbitre m; **of one's own free will** de son plein gré

**freeze** [friːz] vb (pt **froze**, pp **frozen**) ▷ vi geler ▷ vt geler; (food) congeler; (prices, salaries) bloquer, geler ▷ n gel m;

(*of prices, salaries*) blocage *m*; **freezer** *n* congélateur *m*; **freezing** *adj*: **freezing (cold)** (*room etc*) glacial(e); (*person, hands*) gelé(e), glacé(e) ▷ *n*: **3 degrees below freezing** 3 degrés au-dessous de zéro; **it's freezing** il fait un froid glacial; **freezing point** *n* point *m* de congélation

**freight** [freit] *n* (*goods*) fret *m*, cargaison *f*; (*money charged*) fret, prix *m* du transport; **freight train** *n* (*us*) train *m* de marchandises

**French** [frentʃ] *adj* français(e) ▷ *n* (*Ling*) français *m*; **the ~** *npl* les Français; **what's the ~ (word) for ...?** comment dit-on ... en français?; **French bean** *n* (*BRIT*) haricot vert; **French bread** *n* pain *m* français; **French dressing** *n* (*Culin*) vinaigrette *f*; **French fried potatoes** (*us* **French fries**) *npl* (pommes de terre *fpl*) frites *fpl*; **Frenchman** (*irreg*) *n* Français *m*; **French stick** *n* = baguette *f*; **French window** *n* porte-fenêtre *f*; **Frenchwoman** (*irreg*) *n* Française *f*

**frenzy** ['frenzi] *n* frénésie *f*

**frequency** ['friːkwənsɪ] *n* fréquence *f*

**frequent** *adj* ['friːkwənt] fréquent(e) ▷ *vt* [frɪˈkwɛnt] fréquenter; **frequently** ['friːkwəntlɪ] *adv* fréquemment

**fresh** [frɛʃ] *adj* frais (fraîche); (*new*) nouveau (nouvelle); (*cheeky*) familier(-ière), culotté(e); **freshen** *vi* (*wind, air*) fraîchir; **freshen up** *vi* faire un brin de toilette; **fresher** *n* (*BRIT University*: *inf*) bizuth *m*, étudiant(e) de première année; **freshly** *adv* nouvellement, récemment; **freshman** (*us*: *irreg*) *n* = **fresher**; **freshwater** *adj* (*fish*) d'eau douce

**fret** [frɛt] *vi* s'agiter, se tracasser

**Fri** *abbr* (= *Friday*) ve

**friction** ['frɪkʃən] *n* friction *f*, frottement *m*

**Friday** ['fraɪdɪ] *n* vendredi *m*

**fridge** [frɪdʒ] *n* (*BRIT*) frigo *m*, frigidaire® *m*

**fried** [fraɪd] *adj* frit(e); **~ egg** œuf *m* sur le plat

**friend** [frɛnd] *n* ami(e); **friendly** *adj* amical(e); (*kind*) sympathique, gentil(le); (*place*) accueillant(e); (*Pol*: *country*) ami(e) ▷ *n* (*also*: **friendly match**) match amical; **friendship** *n* amitié *f*

**fries** [fraɪz] (*esp us*) *npl* = **French fried potatoes**

**frigate** ['frɪgɪt] *n* frégate *f*

**fright** [fraɪt] *n* peur *f*, effroi *m*; **to give sb a ~** faire peur à qn; **to take ~** prendre peur, s'effrayer; **frighten** *vt* effrayer, faire peur à; **frightened** *adj*: **to be frightened (of)** avoir peur (de); **frightening** *adj* effrayant(e); **frightful** *adj* affreux(-euse)

**frill** [frɪl] *n* (*of dress*) volant *m*; (*of shirt*) jabot *m*

**fringe** [frɪndʒ] *n* (*BRIT*: *of hair*) frange *f*; (*edge*: *of forest etc*) bordure *f*

**Frisbee®** ['frɪzbɪ] *n* Frisbee® *m*

**fritter** ['frɪtər] *n* beignet *m*

**frivolous** ['frɪvələs] *adj* frivole

**fro** [frəu] *see* **to**

**frock** [frɔk] *n* robe *f*

**frog** [frɔg] *n* grenouille *f*; **frogman** (*irreg*) *n* homme-grenouille *m*

○ **KEYWORD**

**from** [frɔm] *prep* **1** (*indicating starting place, origin etc*) de; **where do you come from?**, **where are you from?** d'où venez-vous?; **where has he come from?** d'où arrive-t-il?; **from London to Paris** de Londres à Paris; **to escape from sb/sth** échapper à qn/qch; **a letter/telephone call from my sister** une lettre/un appel de ma sœur; **to drink from the bottle** boire à (même) la bouteille; **tell him from me that ...** dites-lui de ma part que ...

**2** (*indicating time*) (à partir) de; **from one o'clock to** *or* **until** *or* **till two** d'une heure à deux heures; **from January (on)** à partir de janvier

**3** (*indicating distance*) de; **the hotel is one kilometre from the beach** l'hôtel est à un kilomètre de la plage
**4** (*indicating price, number etc*) de; **prices range from £10 to £50** les prix varient entre 10 livres et 50 livres; **the interest rate was increased from 9% to 10%** le taux d'intérêt est passé de 9% à 10%
**5** (*indicating difference*) de; **he can't tell red from green** il ne peut pas distinguer le rouge du vert; **to be different from sb/sth** être différent de qn/qch
**6** (*because of, on the basis of*): **from what he says** d'après ce qu'il dit; **weak from hunger** affaibli par la faim

**front** [frʌnt] *n* (*of house, dress*) devant *m*; (*of coach, train*) avant *m*; (*promenade: also:* **sea ~**) bord *m* de mer; (*Mil, Pol, Meteorology*) front *m*; (*fig: appearances*) contenance *f*, façade *f* ▷ *adj* de devant; (*seat, wheel*) avant *inv* ▷ *vi*: **in ~ (of)** devant; **front door** *n* porte *f* d'entrée; (*of car*) portière *f* avant; **frontier** ['frʌntɪər] *n* frontière *f*; **front page** *n* première page; **front-wheel drive** *n* traction *f* avant
**frost** [frɔst] *n* gel *m*, gelée *f*; (*also:* **hoar~**) givre *m*; **frostbite** *n* gelures *fpl*; **frosting** *n* (*esp us: on cake*) glaçage *m*; **frosty** *adj* (*window*) couvert(e) de givre; (*weather, welcome*) glacial(e)
**froth** [frɔθ] *n* mousse *f*; écume *f*
**frown** [fraun] *n* froncement *m* de sourcils ▷ *vi* froncer les sourcils
**froze** [frəuz] *pt of* **freeze**
**frozen** ['frəuzn] *pp of* **freeze** ▷ *adj* (*food*) congelé(e); (*very cold: person: Comm: assets*) gelé(e)
**fruit** [fruːt] *n* (*pl inv*) fruit *m*; **fruit juice** *n* jus *m* de fruit; **fruit machine** *n* (BRIT) machine *f* à sous; **fruit salad** *n* salade *f* de fruits
**frustrate** [frʌs'treɪt] *vt* frustrer; **frustrated** *adj* frustré(e)
**fry** (*pt, pp* **fried**) [fraɪ, -d] *vt* (faire) frire;

small ~ le menu fretin; **frying pan** *n* poêle *f* (à frire)
**ft.** *abbr* = **foot; feet**
**fudge** [fʌdʒ] *n* (*Culin*) sorte de confiserie à base de sucre, de beurre et de lait
**fuel** [fjuəl] *n* (*for heating*) combustible *m*; (*for engine*) carburant *m*; **fuel tank** *n* (*in vehicle*) réservoir *m* de or à carburant
**fulfil** (*us* **fulfill**) [ful'fɪl] *vt* (*function, condition*) remplir; (*order*) exécuter; (*wish, desire*) satisfaire, réaliser
**full** [ful] *adj* plein(e); (*details, hotel, bus*) complet(-ète); (*busy: day*) chargé(e); (*skirt*) ample, large ▷ *adv*: **to know ~ well** savoir fort bien que; **I'm ~ (up)** j'ai bien mangé; **~ employment/ fare** plein emploi/tarif; **a ~ two hours** deux bonnes heures; **at ~ speed** à toute vitesse; **in ~** (*reproduce, quote, pay*) intégralement; (*write name etc*) en toutes lettres; **full-length** *adj* (*portrait*) en pied; (*coat*) long(ue); **full-length film** long métrage; **full moon** *n* pleine lune; **full-scale** *adj* (*model*) grandeur nature *inv*; (*search, retreat*) complet(-ète), total(e); **full stop** *n* point *m*; **full-time** *adj, adv* (*work*) à plein temps; **fully** *adv* entièrement, complètement; (*at least*)
**fumble** ['fʌmbl] *vi* fouiller, tâtonner; **fumble with** *vt fus* tripoter
**fume** [fjuːm] *vi* (*rage*) rager; **fumes** *npl* vapeurs *fpl*, émanations *fpl*, gaz *mpl*
**fun** [fʌn] *n* amusement *m*, divertissement *m*; **to have ~** s'amuser; **for ~** pour rire; **to make ~ of** se moquer de
**function** ['fʌŋkʃən] *n* fonction *f*; (*reception, dinner*) cérémonie *f*, soirée officielle ▷ *vi* fonctionner
**fund** [fʌnd] *n* caisse *f*, fonds *m*; (*source, store*) source *f*, mine *f*; **funds** *npl* (*money*) fonds *mpl*
**fundamental** [fʌndə'mɛntl] *adj* fondamental(e)
**funeral** ['fjuːnərəl] *n* enterrement *m*, obsèques *fpl* (*more formal occasion*); **funeral director** *n* entrepreneur *m*

des pompes funèbres; **funeral parlour**
[-'pɑːləʳ] n (BRIT) dépôt m mortuaire
**funfair** ['fʌnfɛəʳ] n (BRIT) fête (foraine)
**fungus** (pl **fungi**) ['fʌŋgəs, -gaɪ] n
champignon m; (mould) moisissure f
**funnel** ['fʌnl] n entonnoir m; (of ship)
cheminée f
**funny** ['fʌnɪ] adj amusant(e), drôle;
(strange) curieux(-euse), bizarre
**fur** [fəːʳ] n fourrure f; (BRIT: in kettle
etc) (dépôt m de) tartre m; **fur coat** n
manteau m de fourrure
**furious** ['fjuərɪəs] adj furieux(-euse);
(effort) acharné(e)
**furnish** ['fəːnɪʃ] vt meubler; (supply)
fournir; **furnishings** npl mobilier m,
articles mpl d'ameublement
**furniture** ['fəːnɪtʃəʳ] n meubles mpl,
mobilier m; **piece of ~** meuble m
**furry** ['fəːrɪ] adj (animal) à fourrure; (toy)
en peluche
**further** ['fəːðəʳ] adj supplémentaire,
autre; nouveau (nouvelle) ▷ adv plus
loin; (more) davantage; (moreover) de
plus ▷ vt faire avancer or progresser,
promouvoir; **further education**
n enseignement m postscolaire
(recyclage, formation professionnelle);
**furthermore** adv de plus, en outre
**furthest** ['fəːðɪst] superlative of **far**
**fury** ['fjuərɪ] n fureur f
**fuse** (US **fuze**) [fjuːz] n fusible m; (for
bomb etc) amorce f, détonateur m ▷ vt,
vi (metal) fondre; (BRIT: Elec): **to ~ the
lights** faire sauter les fusibles or les
plombs; **fuse box** n boîte f à fusibles
**fusion** ['fjuːʒən] n fusion f
**fuss** [fʌs] n (anxiety, excitement) chichis
mpl, façons fpl; (commotion) tapage m;
(complaining, trouble) histoire(s) f(pl);
**to make a ~** faire des façons (or des
histoires); **to make a ~ of sb** dorloter
qn; **fussy** adj (person) tatillon(ne),
difficile, chichiteux(-euse); (dress, style)
tarabiscoté(e)
**future** ['fjuːtʃəʳ] adj futur(e) ▷ n avenir
m; (Ling) futur m; **futures** npl (Comm)
opérations fpl à terme; **in (the) ~** à

l'avenir
**fuze** [fjuːz] n, vt, vi (US) = **fuse**
**fuzzy** ['fʌzɪ] adj (Phot) flou(e); (hair)
crépu(e)

# g

**G** [dʒiː] n (Mus): **G** sol m
**g.** abbr (= gram) g
**gadget** ['gædʒɪt] n gadget m
**Gaelic** ['geɪlɪk] adj, n (Ling) gaélique (m)
**gag** [gæg] n (on mouth) bâillon m; (joke) gag m ▷ vt (prisoner etc) bâillonner
**gain** [geɪn] n (improvement) gain m; (profit) gain, profit m ▷ vt gagner ▷ vi (watch) avancer; **to ~ from/by** gagner de/à; **to ~ on sb** (catch up) rattraper qn; **to ~3lbs (in weight)** prendre 3 livres; **to ~ ground** gagner du terrain
**gal.** abbr = **gallon**
**gala** ['gɑːlə] n gala m
**galaxy** ['gæləksɪ] n galaxie f
**gale** [geɪl] n coup m de vent
**gall bladder** ['gɔːl-] n vésicule f biliaire
**gallery** ['gælərɪ] n (also: **art ~**) musée m; (: private) galerie; (: in theatre) dernier balcon
**gallon** ['gæln] n gallon m (BRIT = 4.543 l; US = 3.785 l)
**gallop** ['gæləp] n galop m ▷ vi galoper
**gallstone** ['gɔːlstəun] n calcul m

(biliaire)
**gamble** ['gæmbl] n pari m, risque calculé ▷ vt, vi jouer; **to ~ on** (fig) miser sur; **gambler** n joueur m; **gambling** n jeu m
**game** [geɪm] n jeu m; (event) match m; (of tennis, chess, cards) partie f; (Hunting) gibier m ▷ adj (willing): **to be ~ (for)** être prêt(e) (à or pour); **big ~** gros gibier; **games** npl (Scol) sport m; (sport event) jeux; **games console** ['geɪmz-] n console f de jeux vidéo; **game show** n jeu télévisé
**gammon** ['gæmən] n (bacon) quartier m de lard fumé; (ham) jambon fumé or salé
**gang** [gæŋ] n bande f; (of workmen) équipe f
**gangster** ['gæŋstəʳ] n gangster m, bandit m
**gap** [gæp] n trou m; (in time) intervalle m; (difference): **~ (between)** écart m (entre)
**gape** [geɪp] vi (person) être or rester bouche bée; (hole, shirt) être ouvert(e)
**gap year** n année que certains étudiants prennent pour voyager ou pour travailler avant d'entrer à l'université
**garage** ['gærɑːʒ] n garage m; **garage sale** n vide-grenier m
**garbage** ['gɑːbɪdʒ] n (US: rubbish) ordures fpl, détritus mpl; (inf: nonsense) âneries fpl; **garbage can** n (US) poubelle f, boîte f à ordures; **garbage collector** n (US) éboueur m
**garden** ['gɑːdn] n jardin m; **gardens** npl (public) jardin public; (private) parc m; **garden centre** (BRIT) n pépinière f, jardinerie f; **gardener** n jardinier m; **gardening** n jardinage m
**garlic** ['gɑːlɪk] n ail m
**garment** ['gɑːmənt] n vêtement m
**garnish** ['gɑːnɪʃ] (Culin) vt garnir ▷ n décoration f
**garrison** ['gærɪsn] n garnison f
**gas** [gæs] n gaz m; (US: gasoline) essence f ▷ vt asphyxier; **I can smell ~** ça sent le gaz; **gas cooker** n (BRIT) cuisinière f à

gaz; **gas cylinder** n bouteille f de gaz; **gas fire** n (BRIT) radiateur m à gaz

**gasket** ['gæskɪt] n (Aut) joint m de culasse

**gasoline** ['gæsəliːn] n (US) essence f

**gasp** [gɑːsp] n halètement m; (of shock etc): **she gave a small ~ of pain** la douleur lui coupa le souffle ▷ vi haleter; (fig) avoir le souffle coupé

**gas: gas pedal** n (US) accélérateur m; **gas station** n (US) station-service f; **gas tank** n (US Aut) réservoir m d'essence

**gate** [geɪt] n (of garden) portail m; (of field, at level crossing) barrière f; (of building, town, at airport) porte f

**gateau** (pl ~x) ['gætəu, -z] n gros gâteau à la crème

**gatecrash** ['geɪtkræʃ] vt s'introduire sans invitation dans

**gateway** ['geɪtweɪ] n porte f

**gather** ['gæðər] vt (flowers, fruit) cueillir; (pick up) ramasser; (assemble: objects) rassembler; (: people) réunir; (: information) recueillir; (understand) comprendre; (Sewing) froncer ▷ vi (assemble) se rassembler; **to ~ speed** prendre de la vitesse; **gathering** n rassemblement m

**gauge** [geɪdʒ] n (instrument) jauge f ▷ vt jauger; (fig) juger de

**gave** [geɪv] pt of **give**

**gay** [geɪ] adj (homosexual) homosexuel(le); (colour) gai, vif (vive)

**gaze** [geɪz] n regard m fixe ▷ vi: **to ~ at** vt fixer du regard

**GB** abbr = **Great Britain**

**GCSE** n abbr (BRIT: = General Certificate of Secondary Education) examen passé à l'âge de 16 ans sanctionnant les connaissances de l'élève

**gear** [gɪər] n matériel m, équipement m; (Tech) engrenage m; (Aut) vitesse f ▷ vt (fig: adapt) adapter; **top** or (US) **high/low ~** quatrième (or cinquième)/ première vitesse; **in ~** en prise; **gear up** vi: **to ~ up (to do)** se préparer (à faire); **gear box** n boîte f de vitesse; **gear**

**lever** n levier m de vitesse; **gear shift** (US) n = **gear lever**; **gear stick** (BRIT) n = **gear lever**

**geese** [giːs] npl of **goose**

**gel** [dʒɛl] n gelée f

**gem** [dʒɛm] n pierre précieuse

**Gemini** ['dʒɛmɪnaɪ] n les Gémeaux mpl

**gender** ['dʒɛndər] n genre m; (person's sex) sexe m

**gene** [dʒiːn] n (Biol) gène m

**general** ['dʒɛnərl] n général m ▷ adj général(e); **in ~** en général; **general anaesthetic** (US **general anesthetic**) n anesthésie générale; **general election** n élection(s) législative(s); **generalize** vi généraliser; **generally** adv généralement; **general practitioner** n généraliste m/f; **general store** n épicerie f

**generate** ['dʒɛnəreɪt] vt engendrer; (electricity) produire

**generation** [dʒɛnə'reɪʃən] n génération f; (of electricity etc) production f

**generator** ['dʒɛnəreɪtər] n générateur m

**generosity** [dʒɛnə'rɔsɪtɪ] n générosité f

**generous** ['dʒɛnərəs] adj généreux(-euse); (copious) copieux(-euse)

**genetic** [dʒɪ'nɛtɪk] adj génétique; **~ engineering** ingénierie m génétique; **~ fingerprinting** système m d'empreinte génétique; **genetically modified** adj (food etc) génétiquement modifié(e); **genetics** n génétique f

**Geneva** [dʒɪ'niːvə] n Genève

**genitals** ['dʒɛnɪtlz] npl organes génitaux

**genius** ['dʒiːnɪəs] n génie m

**gent** [dʒɛnt] n abbr (BRIT inf) = **gentleman**

**gentle** ['dʒɛntl] adj doux (douce); (breeze, touch) léger(-ère)

**gentleman** (irreg) ['dʒɛntlmən] n monsieur m; (well-bred man) gentleman m

**gently** ['dʒɛntlɪ] *adv* doucement

**gents** [dʒɛnts] *n* W.-C. *mpl* (pour hommes)

**genuine** ['dʒɛnjuɪn] *adj* véritable, authentique; (*person, emotion*) sincère; **genuinely** *adv* sincèrement, vraiment

**geographic(al)** [dʒɪə'græfɪk(l)] *adj* géographique

**geography** [dʒɪ'ɔgrəfɪ] *n* géographie *f*

**geology** [dʒɪ'ɔlədʒɪ] *n* géologie *f*

**geometry** [dʒɪ'ɔmətrɪ] *n* géométrie *f*

**geranium** [dʒɪ'reɪnɪəm] *n* géranium *m*

**geriatric** [dʒɛrɪ'ætrɪk] *adj* gériatrique
▷ *n* patient/e *f* gériatrique

**germ** [dʒəːm] *n* (*Med*) microbe *m*

**German** ['dʒəːmən] *adj* allemand(e)
▷ *n* Allemand(e); (*Ling*) allemand *m*;
**German measles** *n* rubéole *f*

**Germany** ['dʒəːmənɪ] *n* Allemagne *f*

**gesture** ['dʒɛstjər] *n* geste *m*

 **KEYWORD**

**get** [gɛt] (*pt, pp* **got**, *pp* **gotten** (*US*)) *vi*
**1** (*become, be*) devenir; **to get old/tired** devenir vieux/fatigué, vieillir/se fatiguer; **to get drunk** s'enivrer; **to get dirty** se salir; **to get married** se marier; **when do I get paid?** quand est-ce que je serai payé?; **it's getting late** il se fait tard

**2** (*go*): **to get to/from** aller à/de; **to get home** rentrer chez soi; **how did you get here?** comment es-tu arrivé ici?

**3** (*begin*) commencer *or* se mettre à; **to get to know sb** apprendre à connaître qn; **I'm getting to like him** je commence à l'apprécier; **let's get going** *or* **started** allons-y

**4** (*modal aux vb*): **you've got to do it** il faut que vous le fassiez; **I've got to tell the police** je dois le dire à la police
▷ *vt* **1**: **to get sth done** (*do*) faire qch; (*have done*) faire faire qch; **to get sth/sb ready** préparer qch/qn; **to get one's hair cut** se faire couper les cheveux; **to get the car going** *or* **to go** (faire) démarrer la voiture; **to get sb to do sth** faire faire qch à qn

**2** (*obtain: money, permission, results*) obtenir, avoir; (*buy*) acheter; (*find: job, flat*) trouver; (*fetch: person, doctor, object*) aller chercher; **to get sth for sb** procurer qch à qn; **get me Mr Jones, please** (*on phone*) passez-moi Mr Jones, s'il vous plaît; **can I get you a drink?** est-ce que je peux vous servir à boire?

**3** (*receive: present, letter*) recevoir, avoir; (*acquire: reputation*) avoir; (*prize*) obtenir; **what did you get for your birthday?** qu'est-ce que tu as eu pour ton anniversaire?; **how much did you get for the painting?** combien avez-vous vendu le tableau?

**4** (*catch*) prendre, saisir, attraper; (*hit: target etc*) atteindre; **to get sb by the arm/throat** prendre *or* saisir *or* attraper qn par le bras/à la gorge; **get him!** arrête-le!; **the bullet got him in the leg** il a pris la balle dans la jambe

**5** (*take, move*): **to get sth to sb** faire parvenir qch à qn; **do you think we'll get it through the door?** on arrivera à le faire passer par la porte?

**6** (*catch, take: plane, bus etc*) prendre; **where do I get the train for Birmingham?** où prend-on le train pour Birmingham?

**7** (*understand*) comprendre, saisir; (*hear*) entendre; **I've got it!** j'ai compris!; **I don't get your meaning** je ne vois *or* comprends pas ce que vous voulez dire; **I didn't get your name** je n'ai pas entendu votre nom

**8** (*have, possess*): **to have got** avoir; **how many have you got?** vous en avez combien?

**9** (*illness*) avoir; **I've got a cold** j'ai le rhume; **she got pneumonia and died** elle a fait une pneumonie et elle en est morte

**get away** *vi* partir, s'en aller; (*escape*) s'échapper

**get away with** *vt fus* (*punishment*) en être quitte pour; (*crime etc*) se faire pardonner

**get back** vi (*return*) rentrer
▷ vt récupérer, recouvrer; **when do
we get back?** quand serons-nous de
retour?
**get in** vi entrer; (*arrive home*) rentrer;
(*train*) arriver
**get into** vt fus entrer dans; (*car, train
etc*) monter dans; (*clothes*) mettre,
enfiler, endosser; **to get into bed/a
rage** se mettre au lit/en colère
**get off** vi (*from train etc*) descendre;
(*depart: person, car*) s'en aller
▷ vt (*remove: clothes, stain*) enlever
▷ vt fus (*train, bus*) descendre de; **where
do I get off?** où est-ce que je dois
descendre?
**get on** vi (*at exam etc*) se débrouiller;
(*agree*): **to get on (with)** s'entendre
(avec); **how are you getting on?**
comment ça va?
▷ vt fus monter dans; (*horse*) monter sur
**get out** vi sortir; (*of vehicle*) descendre
▷ vt sortir
**get out of** vt fus sortir de; (*duty etc*)
échapper à, se soustraire à
**get over** vt fus (*illness*) se remettre de
**get through** vi (*Tel*) avoir la
communication; **to get through to sb**
atteindre qn
**get up** vi (*rise*) se lever
▷ vt fus monter

**getaway** ['gɛtəweɪ] n fuite f
**Ghana** ['gɑːnə] n Ghana m
**ghastly** ['gɑːstlɪ] adj atroce, horrible
**ghetto** ['gɛtəu] n ghetto m
**ghost** [gəust] n fantôme m, revenant m
**giant** ['dʒaɪənt] n géant(e) ▷ adj
géant(e), énorme
**gift** [gɪft] n cadeau m; (*donation, talent*)
don m; **gifted** adj doué(e); **gift shop**
(*us* **gift store**) n boutique f de cadeaux;
**gift token, gift voucher** n chèque-
cadeau m
**gig** [gɪg] n (*inf: concert*) concert m
**gigabyte** ['dʒɪgəbaɪt] n gigaoctet m
**gigantic** [dʒaɪ'gæntɪk] adj
gigantesque

**giggle** ['gɪgl] vi pouffer, ricaner
sottement
**gills** [gɪlz] npl (*of fish*) ouïes fpl,
branchies fpl
**gilt** [gɪlt] n dorure f ▷ adj doré(e)
**gimmick** ['gɪmɪk] n truc m
**gin** [dʒɪn] n gin m
**ginger** ['dʒɪndʒə*r*] n gingembre m
**gipsy** ['dʒɪpsɪ] n = **gypsy**
**giraffe** [dʒɪ'rɑːf] n girafe f
**girl** [gəːl] n fille f, fillette f; (*young
unmarried woman*) jeune fille; (*daughter*)
fille; **an English ~** une jeune Anglaise;
**girl band** n girls band m; **girlfriend**
n (*of girl*) amie f; (*of boy*) petite amie;
**Girl Guide** n (*brit*) éclaireuse f; (*Roman
Catholic*) guide f; **Girl Scout** n (*us*)
= **Girl Guide**
**gist** [dʒɪst] n essentiel m
**give** [gɪv] vb (*pt* **gave**, *pp* **~n**) ▷ vt
donner ▷ vi (*break*) céder; (*stretch:
fabric*) se prêter; **to ~ sb sth, ~ sth to
sb** donner qch à qn; (*gift*) offrir qch à
qn; (*message*) transmettre qch à qn; **to
~ sb a call/kiss** appeler/embrasser
qn; **to ~ a cry/sigh** pousser un cri/un
soupir; **give away** vt donner; (*give
free*) faire cadeau de; (*betray*) donner,
trahir; (*disclose*) révéler; **give back** vt
rendre; **give in** vi céder ▷ vt donner;
**give out** vt (*food etc*) distribuer; **give
up** vi renoncer ▷ vt renoncer à; **to ~
up smoking** arrêter de fumer; **to ~ o.s.
up** se rendre
**given** ['gɪvn] pp of **give** ▷ adj (*fixed:
time, amount*) donné(e), déterminé(e)
▷ conj: **~ the circumstances ...** étant
donné les circonstances ..., vu les
circonstances ...; **~ that ...** étant
donné que ...
**glacier** ['glæsɪə*r*] n glacier m
**glad** [glæd] adj content(e); **gladly**
['glædlɪ] adv volontiers
**glamorous** ['glæmərəs] adj (*person*)
séduisant(e); (*job*) prestigieux(-euse)
**glamour** (*us* **glamor**) ['glæmə*r*] n éclat
m, prestige m
**glance** [glɑːns] n coup m d'œil ▷ vi: **to ~**

**at** jeter un coup d'œil à

**gland** [glænd] n glande f

**glare** [glɛəʳ] n (of anger) regard furieux; (of light) lumière éblouissante; (of publicity) feux mpl ▷ vi briller d'un éclat aveuglant; **to ~ at** lancer un regard or des regards furieux à; **glaring** adj (mistake) criant(e), qui saute aux yeux

**glass** [glɑːs] n verre m; **glasses** npl (spectacles) lunettes fpl

**glaze** [gleɪz] vt (door) vitrer; (pottery) vernir ▷ n vernis m

**gleam** [gliːm] vi luire, briller

**glen** [glɛn] n vallée f

**glide** [glaɪd] vi glisser; (Aviat, bird) planer; **glider** n (Aviat) planeur m

**glimmer** ['glɪməʳ] n lueur f

**glimpse** [glɪmps] n vision passagère, aperçu m ▷ vt entrevoir, apercevoir

**glint** [glɪnt] vi étinceler

**glisten** ['glɪsn] vi briller, luire

**glitter** ['glɪtəʳ] vi scintiller, briller

**global** ['gləubl] adj (world-wide) mondial(e); (overall) global(e); **globalization** n mondialisation f; **global warming** n réchauffement m de la planète

**globe** [gləub] n globe m

**gloom** [gluːm] n obscurité f; (sadness) tristesse f, mélancolie f; **gloomy** adj (person) morose; (place, outlook) sombre

**glorious** ['glɔːrɪəs] adj glorieux(-euse); (beautiful) splendide

**glory** ['glɔːrɪ] n gloire f; splendeur f

**gloss** [glɔs] n (shine) brillant m, vernis m; (also: ~ **paint**) peinture brillante or laquée

**glossary** ['glɔsərɪ] n glossaire m, lexique m

**glossy** ['glɔsɪ] adj brillant(e), luisant(e) ▷ n (also: ~ **magazine**) revue f de luxe

**glove** [glʌv] n gant m; **glove compartment** n (Aut) boîte f à gants, vide-poches m inv

**glow** [gləu] vi rougeoyer; (face) rayonner; (eyes) briller

**glucose** ['gluːkəus] n glucose m

**glue** [gluː] n colle f ▷ vt coller

**GM** abbr (= genetically modified) génétiquement modifié(e)

**gm** abbr (= gram) g

**GMO** n abbr (= genetically modified organism) OGM m

**GMT** abbr (= Greenwich Mean Time) GMT

**gnaw** [nɔː] vt ronger

**go** [gəu] vb (pt **went**, pp **gone**) ▷ vi aller; (depart) partir, s'en aller; (work) marcher; (break) céder; (time) passer; (be sold): **to go for £10** se vendre 10 livres; (become): **to go pale/mouldy** pâlir/moisir ▷ n (pl **goes**): **to have a go (at)** essayer (de faire); **to be on the go** être en mouvement; **whose go is it?** à qui est-ce de jouer?; **he's going to do it** il va le faire, il est sur le point de le faire; **to go for a walk** aller se promener; **to go dancing/shopping** aller danser/faire les courses; **to go and see sb, go to see sb** aller voir qn; **how did it go?** comment est-ce que ça s'est passé?; **to go round the back/by the shop** passer par derrière/devant le magasin; **... to go** (us: food) ... à emporter; **go ahead** vi (take place) avoir lieu; (get going) y aller; **go away** vi partir, s'en aller; **go back** vi rentrer; revenir; (go again) retourner; **go by** vi (years, time) passer, s'écouler ▷ vt fus s'en tenir à; (believe) en croire; **go down** vi descendre; (number, price, amount) baisser; (ship) couler; (sun) se coucher ▷ vt fus descendre; **go for** vt fus (fetch) aller chercher; (like) aimer; (attack) s'en prendre à; attaquer; **go in** vi entrer; **go into** vt fus entrer dans; (investigate) étudier, examiner; (embark on) se lancer dans; **go off** vi partir, s'en aller; (food) se gâter; (milk) tourner; (bomb) sauter; (alarm clock) sonner; (alarm) se déclencher; (lights etc) s'éteindre; (event) se dérouler ▷ vt fus ne plus aimer; **the gun went off** le coup est parti; **go on** vi continuer; (happen) se passer; (lights) s'allumer ▷ vt fus: **to go on doing** continuer à faire; **go out** vi sortir; (fire, light) s'éteindre;

(*tide*) descendre; **to go out with sb** sortir avec qn; **go over** *vi, vt fus* (*check*) revoir, vérifier; **go past** *vt fus*: **to go past sth** passer devant qch; **go round** *vi* (*circulate: news, rumour*) circuler; (*revolve*) tourner; (*suffice*) suffire (pour tout le monde); (*visit*): **to go round to sb's** passer chez qn; aller chez qn; (*make a detour*): **to go round (by)** faire un détour (par); **go through** *vt fus* (*town etc*) traverser; (*search through*) fouiller; (*suffer*) subir; **go up** *vi* monter; (*price*) augmenter ▷ *vt fus* gravir; **go with** *vt fus* aller avec; **go without** *vt fus* se passer de

**go-ahead** ['gəʊəhɛd] *adj* dynamique, entreprenant(e) ▷ *n* feu vert

**goal** [gəʊl] *n* but *m*; **goalkeeper** *n* gardien *m* de but; **goal-post** *n* poteau *m* de but

**goat** [gəʊt] *n* chèvre *f*

**gobble** ['gɔbl] *vt* (*also:* **~ down**, **~ up**) engloutir

**god** [gɔd] *n* dieu *m*; **G~** Dieu; **godchild** *n* filleul(e); **goddaughter** *n* filleule *f*; **goddess** *n* déesse *f*; **godfather** *n* parrain *m*; **godmother** *n* marraine *f*; **godson** *n* filleul *m*

**goggles** ['gɔglz] *npl* (*for skiing etc*) lunettes (protectrices); (*for swimming*) lunettes de piscine

**going** ['gəʊɪŋ] *n* (*conditions*) état *m* du terrain ▷ *adj*: **the ~ rate** le tarif (en vigueur)

**gold** [gəʊld] *n or m* ▷ *adj* en or; (*reserves*) d'or; **golden** *adj* (*made of gold*) en or; (*gold in colour*) doré(e); **goldfish** *n* poisson *m* rouge; **goldmine** *n* mine *f* d'or; **gold-plated** *adj* plaqué(e) or *inv*

**golf** [gɔlf] *n* golf *m*; **golf ball** *n* balle *f* de golf; (*on typewriter*) boule *f*; **golf club** *n* club *m* de golf; (*stick*) club *m*, crosse *f* de golf; **golf course** *n* terrain *m* de golf; **golfer** *n* joueur(-euse) de golf

**gone** [gɔn] *pp of* **go**

**gong** [gɔŋ] *n* gong *m*

**good** [gʊd] *adj* bon(ne); (*kind*) gentil(le); (*child*) sage; (*weather*) beau (belle) ▷ *n*

bien *m*; **goods** *npl* marchandise *f*, articles *mpl*; **~!** bon!, très bien!; **to be ~ at** être bon en; **to be ~ for** être bon pour; **it's no ~ complaining** cela ne sert à rien de se plaindre; **to make ~** (*deficit*) combler; (*losses*) compenser; **for ~** (*for ever*) pour de bon, une fois pour toutes; **would you be ~ enough to …?** auriez-vous la bonté *or* l'amabilité de …?; **is this any ~?** (*will it do?*) est-ce que ceci fera l'affaire?; (*what's it like?*) qu'est-ce que ça vaut?; **a ~ deal (of)** beaucoup (de); **a ~ many** beaucoup (de); **~ morning/afternoon!** bonjour!; **~ evening!** bonsoir!; **~ night!** bonsoir!; (*on going to bed*) bonne nuit!; **goodbye** *excl* au revoir!; **to say goodbye to sb** dire au revoir à qn; **Good Friday** *n* Vendredi saint; **good-looking** *adj* beau (belle), bien *inv*; **good-natured** *adj* (*person*) qui a un bon naturel; **goodness** *n* (*of person*) bonté *f*; **for goodness sake!** je vous en prie!; **goodness gracious!** mon Dieu!; **goods train** *n* (BRIT) train *m* de marchandises; **goodwill** *n* bonne volonté

**goose** (*pl* **geese**) [guːs, giːs] *n* oie *f*

**gooseberry** ['gʊzbərɪ] *n* groseille *f* à maquereau; **to play ~** (BRIT) tenir la chandelle

**goose bumps**, **goose pimples** *npl* chair *f* de poule

**gorge** [gɔːdʒ] *n* gorge *f* ▷ *vt*: **to ~ o.s. (on)** se gorger (de)

**gorgeous** ['gɔːdʒəs] *adj* splendide, superbe

**gorilla** [gə'rɪlə] *n* gorille *m*

**gosh** (*inf*) [gɔʃ] *excl* mince alors!

**gospel** ['gɔspl] *n* évangile *m*

**gossip** ['gɔsɪp] *n* (*chat*) bavardages *mpl*; (*malicious*) commérage *m*, cancans *mpl*; (*person*) commère *f* ▷ *vi* bavarder; cancaner, faire des commérages; **gossip column** *n* (*Press*) échos *mpl*

**got** [gɔt] *pt, pp of* **get**

**gotten** ['gɔtn] *pp of* **get**

**gourmet** ['gʊəmeɪ] *n* gourmet *m*,

gastronome m/f

**govern** ['gʌvən] vt gouverner;
(influence) déterminer; **government**
n gouvernement m; (BRIT: ministers)
ministère m; **governor** n (of colony,
state, bank) gouverneur m; (of school,
hospital etc) administrateur(-trice);
(BRIT: of prison) directeur(-trice)

**gown** [gaun] n robe f; (of teacher, BRIT:
of judge) toge f

**G.P.** n abbr (Med) = **general practitioner**

**grab** [græb] vt saisir, empoigner ▷ vi: **to
~ at** essayer de saisir

**grace** [greɪs] n grâce f ▷ vt (honour)
honorer; (adorn) orner; **5 days' ~**
un répit de 5 jours; **graceful** adj
gracieux(-euse), élégant(e); **gracious**
['greɪʃəs] adj bienveillant(e)

**grade** [greɪd] n (Comm: quality) qualité
f; (size) calibre m; (type) catégorie
f; (in hierarchy) grade m, échelon m;
(Scol) note f; (us: school class) classe
f; (: gradient) pente f ▷ vt classer; (by
size) calibrer; **grade crossing** n (us)
passage m à niveau; **grade school** n
(us) école f primaire

**gradient** ['greɪdɪənt] n inclinaison
f, pente f

**gradual** ['grædjuəl] adj graduel(le),
progressif(-ive); **gradually** adv peu à
peu, graduellement

**graduate** n ['grædjuɪt] diplômé(e)
d'université; (us: of high school)
diplômé(e) de fin d'études ▷ vi
['grædjueɪt] obtenir un diplôme
d'université (or de fin d'études);
**graduation** [grædju'eɪʃən] n
cérémonie f de remise des diplômes

**graffiti** [grə'fiːtɪ] npl graffiti mpl

**graft** [grɑːft] n (Agr, Med) greffe f;
(bribery) corruption f ▷ vt greffer; **hard
~** (BRIT: inf) boulot acharné

**grain** [greɪn] n (single piece) grain m; (no
pl: cereals) céréales fpl; (us: corn) blé m

**gram** [græm] n gramme m

**grammar** ['græmə'] n grammaire f;
**grammar school** n (BRIT) ≈ lycée m

**gramme** [græm] n = **gram**

**gran** (inf) [græn] n (BRIT) mamie f (inf),
mémé f (inf)

**grand** [grænd] adj magnifique,
splendide; (gesture etc) noble; **grandad**
(inf) n = **granddad**; **grandchild** (pl
**~ren**) n petit-fils m, petite-fille f;
**grandchildren** npl petits-enfants;
**granddad** n (inf) papy m (inf), papi
m (inf), pépé m (inf); **granddaughter**
n petite-fille f; **grandfather** n
grand-père m; **grandma** n (inf)
= **gran**; **grandmother** n grand-
mère f; **grandpa** n (inf) = **granddad**;
**grandparents** npl grands-parents mpl;
**grand piano** n piano m à queue; **Grand
Prix** ['grɑ̃ː'priː] n (Aut) grand prix
automobile; **grandson** n petit-fils m

**granite** ['grænɪt] n granit m

**granny** ['grænɪ] n (inf) = **gran**

**grant** [grɑːnt] vt accorder; (a request)
accéder à; (admit) concéder ▷ n (Scol)
bourse f; (Admin) subside m, subvention
f; **to take sth for ~ed** considérer qch
comme acquis; **to take sb for ~ed**
considérer qn comme faisant partie
du décor

**grape** [greɪp] n raisin m

**grapefruit** ['greɪpfruːt] n
pamplemousse m

**graph** [grɑːf] n graphique m, courbe f;
**graphic** ['græfɪk] adj graphique; (vivid)
vivant(e); **graphics** n (art) arts mpl
graphiques; (process) graphisme m
▷ npl (drawings) illustrations fpl

**grasp** [grɑːsp] vt saisir ▷ n (grip) prise f;
(fig) compréhension f, connaissance f

**grass** [grɑːs] n herbe f; (lawn) gazon m;
**grasshopper** n sauterelle f

**grate** [greɪt] n grille f de cheminée ▷ vi
grincer ▷ vt (Culin) râper

**grateful** ['greɪtful] adj
reconnaissant(e)

**grater** ['greɪtə'] n râpe f

**gratitude** ['grætɪtjuːd] n gratitude f

**grave** [greɪv] n tombe f ▷ adj grave,
sérieux(-euse)

**gravel** ['grævl] n gravier m

**gravestone** ['greɪvstəun] n pierre

tombale

**graveyard** ['greɪvjɑːd] n cimetière m

**gravity** ['grævɪtɪ] n (Physics) gravité f; pesanteur f; (seriousness) gravité

**gravy** ['greɪvɪ] n jus m (de viande), sauce f (au jus de viande)

**gray** [greɪ] adj (US) = **grey**

**graze** [greɪz] vi paître, brouter ▷ vt (touch lightly) frôler, effleurer; (scrape) écorcher ▷ n écorchure f

**grease** [griːs] n (fat) graisse f; (lubricant) lubrifiant m ▷ vt graisser; lubrifier; **greasy** adj gras(se), graisseux(-euse); (hands, clothes) graisseux

**great** [greɪt] adj grand(e); (heat, pain etc) très fort(e), intense; (inf) formidable; **Great Britain** n Grande-Bretagne f; **great-grandfather** n arrière-grand-père m; **great-grandmother** n arrière-grand-mère f; **greatly** adv très, grandement; (with verbs) beaucoup

**Greece** [griːs] n Grèce f

**greed** [griːd] n (also: **~iness**) avidité f; (for food) gourmandise f; **greedy** adj avide; (for food) gourmand(e)

**Greek** [griːk] adj grec (grecque) ▷ n Grec (Grecque); (Ling) grec m

**green** [griːn] adj vert(e); (inexperienced) (bien) jeune, naïf(-ïve); (ecological: product etc) écologique ▷ n (colour) vert m; (on golf course) green m; (stretch of grass) pelouse f; **greens** npl (vegetables) légumes verts; **green card** n (Aut) carte verte; (US: work permit) permis m de travail; **greengage** n reine-claude f; **greengrocer** n (BRIT) marchand m de fruits et légumes; **greengrocer's (shop)** n magasin m de fruits et légumes; **greenhouse** n serre f; **greenhouse effect** n: **the greenhouse effect** l'effet m de serre

**Greenland** ['griːnlənd] n Groenland m

**green salad** n salade verte

**greet** [griːt] vt accueillir; **greeting** n salutation f; **Christmas/birthday greetings** souhaits mpl de Noël/de bon anniversaire; **greeting(s) card** n carte f de vœux

**grew** [gruː] pt of **grow**

**grey** (US **gray**) [greɪ] adj gris(e); (dismal) sombre; **grey-haired** adj aux cheveux gris; **greyhound** n lévrier m

**grid** [grɪd] n grille f; (Elec) réseau m; **gridlock** n (traffic jam) embouteillage m

**grief** [griːf] n chagrin m, douleur f

**grievance** ['griːvəns] n doléance f, grief m; (cause for complaint) grief

**grieve** [griːv] vi avoir du chagrin; se désoler ▷ vt faire de la peine à, affliger; **to ~ for sb** pleurer qn

**grill** [grɪl] n (on cooker) gril m; (also: **mixed ~**) grillade(s) f(pl) ▷ vt griller; (inf: question) cuisiner

**grille** [grɪl] n grillage m; (Aut) calandre f

**grim** [grɪm] adj sinistre, lugubre; (serious, stern) sévère

**grime** [graɪm] n crasse f

**grin** [grɪn] n large sourire m ▷ vi sourire

**grind** [graɪnd] vb (pt, pp **ground**) ▷ vt écraser; (coffee, pepper etc) moudre; (US: meat) hacher ▷ n (work) corvée f

**grip** [grɪp] n (handclasp) poigne f; (control) prise f; (handle) poignée f; (holdall) sac m de voyage ▷ vt saisir, empoigner; (viewer, reader) captiver; **to come to ~s with** se colleter avec, en venir aux prises avec; **to ~ the road** (Aut) adhérer à la route; **gripping** adj prenant(e), palpitant(e)

**grit** [grɪt] n gravillon m; (courage) cran m ▷ vt (road) sabler; **to ~ one's teeth** serrer les dents

**grits** [grɪts] npl (US) gruau m de maïs

**groan** [grəun] n (of pain) gémissement m ▷ vi gémir

**grocer** ['grəusər] n épicier m; **groceries** npl provisions fpl; **grocer's (shop)**, **grocery** n épicerie f

**groin** [grɔɪn] n aine f

**groom** [gruːm] n (for horses) palefrenier m; (also: **bride~**) marié m ▷ vt (horse) panser; (fig): **to ~ sb for** former qn pour

**groove** [gruːv] n sillon m, rainure f

**grope** [grəup] vi tâtonner; **to ~ for** chercher à tâtons

**gross** [grəus] *adj* grossier(-ière);
(*Comm*) brut(e); **grossly** *adv* (*greatly*)
très, grandement

**grotesque** [grə'tɛsk] *adj* grotesque

**ground** [graund] *pt, pp of* **grind** ▷ *n*
sol *m*, terre *f*; (*land*) terrain *m*, terres *fpl*;
(*Sport*) terrain; (*reason: gen pl*) raison
*f*; (*us: also:* **~ wire**) terre *f* ▷ *vt* (*plane*)
empêcher de décoller, retenir au sol;
(*us Elec*) équiper d'une prise de terre;
**grounds** *npl* (*gardens etc*) parc *m*,
domaine *m*; (*of coffee*) marc *m*; **on the
~, to the ~** par terre; **to gain/lose ~**
gagner/perdre du terrain; **ground
floor** *n* (*BRIT*) rez-de-chaussée *m*;
**groundsheet** *n* (*BRIT*) tapis *m* de sol;
**groundwork** *n* préparation *f*

**group** [gru:p] *n* groupe *m* ▷ *vt* (*also:*
**~ together**) grouper ▷ *vi* (*also:* **~
together**) se grouper

**grouse** [graus] *n* (*pl inv: bird*) grouse *f*
(*sorte de coq de bruyère*) ▷ *vi* (*complain*)
rouspéter, râler

**grovel** ['grɔvl] *vi* (*fig*): **to ~ (before)**
ramper (devant)

**grow** (*pt* **grew**, *pp* **~n**) [grəu, gru:,
grəun] *vi* (*plant*) pousser, croître; (*person*) grandir; (*increase*) augmenter,
se développer; (*become*) devenir; **to ~
rich/weak** s'enrichir/s'affaiblir ▷ *vt*
cultiver, faire pousser; (*hair, beard*)
laisser pousser; **grow on** *vt fus*: **that
painting is ~ing on me** je finirai par
aimer ce tableau; **grow up** *vi* grandir

**growl** [graul] *vi* grogner

**grown** [grəun] *pp of* **grow**; **grown-up** *n*
adulte *m/f*, grande personne *f*

**growth** [grəuθ] *n* croissance *f*,
développement *m*; (*what has grown*)
pousse *f*; poussée *f*; (*Med*) grosseur *f*,
tumeur *f*

**grub** [grʌb] *n* larve *f*; (*inf: food*) bouffe *f*

**grubby** ['grʌbi] *adj* crasseux(-euse)

**grudge** [grʌdʒ] *n* rancune *f* ▷ *vt*: **to ~ sb
sth** (*in giving*) donner qch à qn à contre-
cœur; (*resent*) reprocher qch à qn; **to
bear sb a ~ (for)** garder rancune or en
vouloir à qn (de)

**gruelling** (*us* **grueling**) ['gruəlɪŋ] *adj*
exténuant(e)

**gruesome** ['gru:səm] *adj* horrible

**grumble** ['grʌmbl] *vi* rouspéter,
ronchonner

**grumpy** ['grʌmpi] *adj* grincheux(-euse)

**grunt** [grʌnt] *vi* grogner

**guarantee** [gærən'ti:] *n* garantie *f*
▷ *vt* garantir

**guard** [gɑːd] *n* garde *f*; (*one man*) garde
*m*; (*BRIT Rail*) chef *m* de train; (*safety
device: on machine*) dispositif *m* de
sûreté; (*also:* **fire~**) garde-feu *m inv* ▷ *vt*
garder, surveiller; (*protect*): **to ~ sb/sth
(against** *or* **from**) protéger qn/qch
(contre); **to be on one's ~** (*fig*) être sur
ses gardes; **guardian** *n* gardien(ne); (*of
minor*) tuteur(-trice)

**guerrilla** [gə'rɪlə] *n* guérillero *m*

**guess** [gɛs] *vi* deviner ▷ *vt* deviner;
(*estimate*) évaluer; (*us*) croire, penser
▷ *n* supposition *f*, hypothèse *f*; **to take**
*or* **have a ~** essayer de deviner

**guest** [gɛst] *n* invité(e); (*in hotel*)
client(e); **guest house** *n* pension *f*;
**guest room** *n* chambre *f* d'amis

**guidance** ['gaɪdəns] *n* (*advice*)
conseils *mpl*

**guide** [gaɪd] *n* (*person*) guide *m/f*; (*book*)
guide *m*; (*also:* **Girl G~**) éclaireuse *f*;
(*Roman Catholic*) guide *f* ▷ *vt* guider; **is
there an English-speaking ~?** est-ce
que l'un des guides parle anglais?;
**guidebook** *n* guide *m*; **guide dog** *n*
chien *m* d'aveugle; **guided tour** *n* visite
guidée; **what time does the guided
tour start?** la visite guidée commence
à quelle heure?; **guidelines** *npl* (*advice*)
instructions générales, conseils *mpl*

**guild** [gɪld] *n* (*History*) corporation *f*;
(*sharing interests*) cercle *m*, association *f*

**guilt** [gɪlt] *n* culpabilité *f*; **guilty** *adj*
coupable

**guinea pig** ['gɪnɪ-] *n* cobaye *m*

**guitar** [gɪ'tɑːr] *n* guitare *f*; **guitarist** *n*
guitariste *m/f*

**gulf** [gʌlf] *n* golfe *m*; (*abyss*) gouffre *m*

**gull** [gʌl] *n* mouette *f*

**gulp** [gʌlp] *vi* avaler sa salive; (*from emotion*) avoir la gorge serrée, s'étrangler ▷ *vt* (*also:* **~ down**) avaler

**gum** [gʌm] *n* (*Anat*) gencive *f*; (*glue*) colle *f*; (*also:* **chewing-~**) chewing-gum *m* ▷ *vt* coller

**gun** [gʌn] *n* (*small*) revolver *m*, pistolet *m*; (*rifle*) fusil *m*, carabine *f*; (*cannon*) canon *m*; **gunfire** *n* fusillade *f*; **gunman** (*irreg*) *n* bandit armé; **gunpoint** *n*: **at gunpoint** sous la menace du pistolet (*or* fusil); **gunpowder** *n* poudre f à canon; **gunshot** *n* coup *m* de feu

**gush** [gʌʃ] *vi* jaillir; (*fig*) se répandre en effusions

**gust** [gʌst] *n* (*of wind*) rafale *f*

**gut** [gʌt] *n* intestin *m*, boyau *m*; **guts** *npl* (*Anat*) boyaux *mpl*; (*inf: courage*) cran *m*

**gutter** ['gʌtəʳ] *n* (*of roof*) gouttière *f*; (*in street*) caniveau *m*

**guy** [gaɪ] *n* (*inf: man*) type *m*; (*also:* **~rope**) corde *f*; (*figure*) effigie de Guy Fawkes

**Guy Fawkes' Night** [gaɪ'fɔːks-] *n* voir encadré

● **GUY FAWKES' NIGHT**

● **Guy Fawkes' Night**, que l'on
● appelle également "bonfire night",
● commémore l'échec du complot (le
● "Gunpowder Plot") contre James Ist
● et son parlement le 5 novembre 1605.
● L'un des conspirateurs, Guy Fawkes,
● avait été surpris dans les caves du
● parlement alors qu'il s'apprêtait à y
● mettre le feu. Chaque année pour le
● 5 novembre, les enfants préparent à
● l'avance une effigie de Guy Fawkes
● et ils demandent aux passants "un
● penny pour le guy" avec lequel ils
● pourront s'acheter des fusées de feu
● d'artifice. Beaucoup de gens font
● encore un feu dans leur jardin sur
● lequel ils brûlent le "guy".

**gym** [dʒɪm] *n* (*also:* **~nasium**) gymnase *m*; (*also:* **~nastics**) gym *f*; **gymnasium** *n* gymnase *m*; **gymnast** *n* gymnaste *m/f*; **gymnastics** *n, npl* gymnastique *f*; **gym shoes** *npl* chaussures *fpl* de gym(nastique)

**gynaecologist** (*us* **gynecologist**) [gaɪnɪ'kɔlədʒɪst] *n* gynécologue *m/f*

**gypsy** ['dʒɪpsɪ] *n* gitan(e), bohémien(ne)

# h

**haberdashery** [hæbə'dæʃərɪ] n (BRIT)
mercerie f
**habit** ['hæbɪt] n habitude f; (costume:
Rel) habit m
**habitat** ['hæbɪtæt] n habitat m
**hack** [hæk] vt hacher, tailler ▷ n (pej:
writer) nègre m; **hacker** n (Comput)
pirate m (informatique)
**had** [hæd] pt, pp of **have**
**haddock** (pl ~ or ~**s**) ['hædək] n églefin
m; **smoked ~** haddock m
**hadn't** ['hædnt] = **had not**
**haemorrhage** (US **hemorrhage**)
['hɛmərɪdʒ] n hémorragie f
**haemorrhoids** (US **hemorrhoids**)
['hɛmərɔɪdz] npl hémorroïdes fpl
**haggle** ['hægl] vi marchander
**Hague** [heɪg] n: **The ~** La Haye
**hail** [heɪl] n grêle f ▷ vt (call) héler;
(greet) acclamer ▷ vi grêler; **hailstone**
n grêlon m
**hair** [hɛəʳ] n cheveux mpl; (on body)
poils mpl; (of animal) pelage m; (single
hair: on head) cheveu m; (: on body, of
animal) poil m; **to do one's ~** se coiffer;
**hairband** n (elasticated) bandeau m;
(plastic) serre-tête m; **hairbrush** n
brosse f à cheveux; **haircut** n coupe
f (de cheveux); **hairdo** n coiffure f;
**hairdresser** n coiffeur(-euse);
**hairdresser's** n salon m de coiffure,
coiffeur m; **hair dryer** n sèche-cheveux
m, séchoir m; **hair gel** n gel m pour
cheveux; **hair spray** n laque f (pour les
cheveux); **hairstyle** n coiffure f; **hairy**
adj poilu(e), chevelu(e); (inf: frightening)
effrayant(e)
**hake** (pl ~ or ~**s**) [heɪk] n colin m,
merlu m
**half** [hɑːf] n (pl **halves**) moitié f; (of
beer: also: ~ **pint**) ≈ demi m; (Rail, bus:
also: ~ **fare**) demi-tarif m; (Sport: of
match) mi-temps f ▷ adj demi(e) ▷ adv
(à) moitié, à demi; ~ **an hour** une
demi-heure; ~ **a dozen** une demi-
douzaine; ~ **a pound** une demi-livre,
≈ 250 g; **two and a** ~ deux et demi; **to
cut sth in** ~ couper qch en deux; **half
board** n (BRIT: in hotel) demi-pension f;
**half-brother** n demi-frère m; **half
day** n demi-journée f; **half fare** n
demi-tarif m; **half-hearted** adj tiède,
sans enthousiasme; **half-hour** n demi-
heure f; **half-price** adj à moitié prix
▷ adv (also: **at half-price**) à moitié
prix; **half term** n (BRIT Scol) vacances
fpl (de demi-trimestre); **half-time** n
mi-temps f; **halfway** adv à mi-
chemin; **halfway through sth** au
milieu de qch
**hall** [hɔːl] n salle f; (entrance way: big)
hall m; (small) entrée f; (US: corridor)
couloir m; (mansion) château m,
manoir m
**hallmark** ['hɔːlmɑːk] n poinçon m;
(fig) marque f
**hallo** [hə'ləʊ] excl = **hello**
**hall of residence** n (BRIT) pavillon m
or résidence f universitaire
**Halloween, Hallowe'en**
['hæləʊ'iːn] n veille f de la Toussaint;
voir encadré

● **HALLOWEEN**
●
●
● Selon la tradition, **Halloween** est la
● nuit des fantômes et des sorcières.
● En Écosse et aux États-Unis surtout
● (et de plus en plus en Angleterre) les
● enfants, pour fêter **Halloween**, se
● déguisent ce soir-là et ils vont ainsi
● de porte en porte en demandant de
● petits cadeaux (du chocolat, une
● pomme etc).

**hallucination** [həluːsɪˈneɪʃən] n
hallucination f

**hallway** [ˈhɔːlweɪ] n (entrance)
vestibule m; (corridor) couloir m

**halo** [ˈheɪləu] n (of saint etc) auréole f

**halt** [hɔːlt] n halte f, arrêt m ▷ vt faire
arrêter; (progress etc) interrompre ▷ vi
faire halte, s'arrêter

**halve** [hɑːv] vt (apple etc) partager or
diviser en deux; (reduce by half) réduire
de moitié

**halves** [hɑːvz] npl of **half**

**ham** [hæm] n jambon m

**hamburger** [ˈhæmbəːgəʳ] n
hamburger m

**hamlet** [ˈhæmlɪt] n hameau m

**hammer** [ˈhæməʳ] n marteau m ▷ vt
(nail) enfoncer; (fig) éreinter, démolir
▷ vi (at door) frapper à coups redoublés;
**to ~ a point home to sb** faire rentrer
qch dans la tête de qn

**hammock** [ˈhæmək] n hamac m

**hamper** [ˈhæmpəʳ] vt gêner ▷ n panier
m (d'osier)

**hamster** [ˈhæmstəʳ] n hamster m

**hamstring** [ˈhæmstrɪŋ] n (Anat)
tendon m du jarret

**hand** [hænd] n main f; (of clock) aiguille
f; (handwriting) écriture f; (at cards) jeu
m; (worker) ouvrier(-ière) m/f ▷ vt passer,
donner; **to give sb a ~** donner un coup
de main à qn; **at ~** à portée de la main;
**in ~** (situation) en main; (work) en cours;
**to be on ~** (person) être disponible;
(emergency services) se tenir prêt(e) (à
intervenir); **to ~** (information etc) sous

la main, à portée de la main; **on the
one ~ ..., on the other ~** d'une part ...,
d'autre part; (tradition, heirloom) transmettre; (us:
sentence, verdict) prononcer; **hand in**
vt remettre; **hand out** vt distribuer;
**hand over** vt remettre; (powers etc)
transmettre; **handbag** n sac m à main;
**hand baggage** n = **hand luggage**;
**handbook** n manuel m; **handbrake**
n frein m à main; **handcuffs** npl
menottes fpl; **handful** n poignée f

**handicap** [ˈhændɪkæp] n handicap m
▷ vt handicaper; **mentally/physically
~ped** handicapé(e) mentalement/
physiquement

**handkerchief** [ˈhæŋkətʃɪf] n
mouchoir m

**handle** [ˈhændl] n (of door etc) poignée
f; (of cup etc) anse f; (of knife etc) manche
m; (of saucepan) queue f; (for winding)
manivelle f ▷ vt toucher, manier;
(deal with) s'occuper de; (treat: people)
prendre; **"~ with care"** "fragile"; **to fly
off the ~** s'énerver; **handlebar(s)** n(pl)
guidon m

**hand**: **hand luggage** n bagages mpl
à main; **handmade** adj fait(e) à la
main; **handout** n (money) aide f, don
m; (leaflet) prospectus m; (at lecture)
polycopié m; **hands-free** adj (phone)
mains libres inv ▷ n (also: **hands-free
kit**) kit m mains libres inv

**handsome** [ˈhænsəm] adj beau (belle);
(profit) considérable

**handwriting** [ˈhændraɪtɪŋ] n
écriture f

**handy** [ˈhændɪ] adj (person) adroit(e);
(close at hand) sous la main; (convenient)
pratique

**hang** (pt, pp hung) [hæŋ, hʌŋ] vt
accrocher; (criminal: pt, pp **~ed**) pendre
▷ vi pendre; (hair, drapery) tomber
▷ n: **to get the ~ of (doing) sth** (inf)
attraper le coup pour faire qch; **hang
about, hang around** vi traîner; **hang
down** vi pendre; **hang on** vi (wait)
attendre; **hang out** vt (washing)

étendre (dehors) ▷ vi (inf: live) habiter, percher; (: spend time) traîner; **hang round** vi = **hang around**; **hang up** vi (Tel) raccrocher ▷ vt (coat, painting etc) accrocher, suspendre

**hanger** ['hæŋər] n cintre m, portemanteau m

**hang-gliding** ['hæŋglaɪdɪŋ] n vol m libre or sur aile delta

**hangover** ['hæŋəuvər] n (after drinking) gueule f de bois

**hankie, hanky** ['hæŋkɪ] n abbr = **handkerchief**

**happen** ['hæpən] vi arriver, se passer, se produire; **what's ~ing?** que se passe-t-il?; **she ~ed to be free** il s'est trouvé (or se trouvait) qu'elle était libre; **as it ~s** justement

**happily** ['hæpɪlɪ] adv heureusement; (cheerfully) joyeusement

**happiness** ['hæpɪnɪs] n bonheur m

**happy** ['hæpɪ] adj heureux(-euse); **~ with** (arrangements etc) satisfait(e) de; **to be ~ to do** faire volontiers; **~ birthday!** bon anniversaire!

**harass** ['hærəs] vt accabler, tourmenter; **harassment** n tracasseries fpl

**harbour** (US harbor) ['hɑ:bər] n port m ▷ vt héberger, abriter; (hopes, suspicions) entretenir

**hard** [hɑ:d] adj dur(e); (question, problem) difficile; (facts, evidence) concret(-ète) ▷ adv (work) dur; (think, try) sérieusement; **to look ~ at** regarder fixement; (thing) regarder de près; **no ~ feelings!** sans rancune!; **to be ~ of hearing** être dur(e) d'oreille; **to be ~ done by** être traité(e) injustement; **hardback** n livre relié; **hardboard** n Isorel® m; **hard disk** n (Comput) disque dur; **harden** vt durcir; (fig) endurcir ▷ vi (substance) durcir

**hardly** ['hɑ:dlɪ] adv (scarcely) à peine; (harshly) durement; **~ anywhere/ever** presque nulle part/jamais

**hard**: **hardship** n (difficulties) épreuves fpl; (deprivation) privations fpl; **hard**

**shoulder** n (BRIT Aut) accotement stabilisé; **hard-up** adj (inf) fauché(e); **hardware** n quincaillerie f; (Comput, Mil) matériel m; **hardware shop** (US **hardware store**) n quincaillerie f; **hard-working** adj travailleur(-euse), consciencieux(-euse)

**hardy** ['hɑ:dɪ] adj robuste; (plant) résistant(e) au gel

**hare** [hɛər] n lièvre m

**harm** [hɑ:m] n mal m; (wrong) tort m ▷ vt (person) faire du mal or du tort à; (thing) endommager; **out of ~'s way** à l'abri du danger, en lieu sûr; **harmful** adj nuisible; **harmless** adj inoffensif(-ive)

**harmony** ['hɑ:mənɪ] n harmonie f

**harness** ['hɑ:nɪs] n harnais m ▷ vt (horse) harnacher; (resources) exploiter

**harp** [hɑ:p] n harpe f ▷ vi: **to ~ on about** revenir toujours sur

**harsh** [hɑ:ʃ] adj (hard) dur(e); (severe) sévère; (unpleasant: sound) discordant(e); (: light) cru(e)

**harvest** ['hɑ:vɪst] n (of corn) moisson f; (of fruit) récolte f; (of grapes) vendange f ▷ vt moissonner; récolter; vendanger

**has** [hæz] vb see **have**

**hasn't** ['hæznt] = **has not**

**hassle** ['hæsl] n (inf: fuss) histoire(s) f(pl)

**haste** [heɪst] n hâte f, précipitation f; **hasten** ['heɪsn] vt hâter, accélérer ▷ vi se hâter, s'empresser; **hastily** adv à la hâte; (leave) précipitamment; **hasty** adj (decision, action) hâtif(-ive); (departure, escape) précipité(e)

**hat** [hæt] n chapeau m

**hatch** [hætʃ] n (Naut: also: **~way**) écoutille f; (BRIT: also: **service ~**) passe-plats m inv ▷ vi éclore

**hatchback** ['hætʃbæk] n (Aut) modèle m avec hayon arrière

**hate** [heɪt] vt haïr, détester ▷ n haine f; **hatred** ['heɪtrɪd] n haine f

**haul** [hɔ:l] vt traîner, tirer ▷ n (of fish) prise f; (of stolen goods etc) butin m

**haunt** [hɔ:nt] vt (subj: ghost, fear)

hanter; (: *person*) fréquenter ▷ *n*
repaire *m*; **haunted** *adj* (*castle etc*)
hanté(e); (*look*) égaré(e), hagard(e)

 **KEYWORD**

**have** [hæv] (*pt, pp* **had**) *aux vb* **1** (*gen*)
avoir; être; **to have eaten/slept** avoir
mangé/dormi; **to have arrived/gone**
être arrivé(e)/allé(e); **having finished**
*or* **when he had finished, he left**
quand il a eu fini, il est parti; **we'd
already eaten** nous avions déjà mangé
**2** (*in tag questions*): **you've done it,
haven't you?** vous l'avez fait, n'est-ce
pas?
**3** (*in short answers and questions*): **no I
haven't!/yes we have!** mais non!/
mais si!; **so I have!** ah oui!, oui c'est
vrai!; **I've been there before, have
you?** j'y suis déjà allé, et vous?
▷ *modal aux vb* (*be obliged*): **to have
(got) to do sth** devoir faire qch, être
obligé(e) de faire qch; **she has (got)
to do it** elle doit le faire, il faut qu'elle
le fasse; **you haven't to tell her** vous
n'êtes pas obligé de le lui dire; (*must not*)
ne le lui dites surtout pas; **do you have
to book?** il faut réserver?
▷ *vt* **1** (*possess*) avoir; **he has (got) blue
eyes/dark hair** il a les yeux bleus/les
cheveux bruns
**2** (*referring to meals etc*): **to have
breakfast** prendre le petit déjeuner; **to
have dinner/lunch** dîner/déjeuner; **to
have a drink** prendre un verre; **to have
a cigarette** fumer une cigarette
**3** (*receive*) avoir, recevoir; (*obtain*) avoir;
**may I have your address?** puis-je
avoir votre adresse?; **you can have it
for £5** vous pouvez l'avoir pour 5 livres;
**I must have it for tomorrow** il me
le faut pour demain; **to have a baby**
avoir un bébé
**4** (*maintain, allow*): **I won't have it!** ça
ne se passera pas comme ça!; **we can't
have that** nous ne tolérerons pas ça
**5** (*by sb else*): **to have sth done** faire

faire qch; **to have one's hair cut** se
faire couper les cheveux; **to have sb do
sth** faire faire qch à qn
**6** (*experience, suffer*) avoir; **to have a
cold/flu** avoir un rhume/la grippe;
**to have an operation** se faire opérer;
**she had her bag stolen** elle s'est fait
voler son sac
**7** (*+noun*): **to have a swim/walk** nager/
se promener; **to have a bath/shower**
prendre un bain/une douche; **let's
have a look** regardons; **to have a
meeting** se réunir; **to have a party**
organiser une fête; **let me have a try**
laissez-moi essayer

**haven** ['heɪvn] *n* port *m*; (*fig*) havre *m*
**haven't** ['hævnt] = **have not**
**havoc** ['hævək] *n* ravages *mpl*
**Hawaii** [hə'waɪː] *n* (*îles fpl*) Hawaï *m*
**hawk** [hɔːk] *n* faucon *m*
**hawthorn** ['hɔːθɔːn] *n* aubépine *f*
**hay** [heɪ] *n* foin *m*; **hay fever** *n* rhume *m*
des foins; **haystack** *n* meule *f* de foin
**hazard** ['hæzəd] *n* (*risk*) danger *m*,
risque *m* ▷ *vt* risquer, hasarder;
**hazardous** *adj* hasardeux(-euse),
risqué(e); **hazard warning lights** *npl*
(*Aut*) feux *mpl* de détresse
**haze** [heɪz] *n* brume *f*
**hazel** ['heɪzl] *n* (*tree*) noisetier *m*
▷ *adj* (*eyes*) noisette *inv*; **hazelnut** *n*
noisette *f*
**hazy** ['heɪzɪ] *adj* brumeux(-euse);
(*idea*) vague
**he** [hiː] *pron* il; **it is he who ...** c'est lui
qui ...; **here he is** le voici

**head** [hɛd] *n* tête *f*; (*leader*) chef *m*; (*of
school*) directeur(-trice); (*of secondary
school*) proviseur *m* ▷ *vt* (*list*) être
en tête de; (*group, company*) être à
la tête de; **~s or tails** pile ou face; **~
first** la tête la première; **~ over heels
in love** follement *or* éperdument
amoureux(-euse); **to ~ the ball** faire
une tête; **head for** *vt fus* se diriger vers;
(*disaster*) aller à; **head off** *vt* (*threat,
danger*) détourner; **headache** *n* mal *m*

de tête; **to have a headache** avoir mal à la tête; **heading** n titre m; (*subject title*) rubrique f; **headlamp** (BRIT) n = **headlight**; **headlight** n phare m; **headline** n titre m; **head office** n siège m, bureau m central; **headphones** npl casque m (à écouteurs); **headquarters** npl (*of business*) bureau or siège central; (*Mil*) quartier général; **headroom** n (*in car*) hauteur f de plafond; (*under bridge*) hauteur limite; **headscarf** n foulard m; **headset** n = **headphones**; **headteacher** n directeur(-trice); (*of secondary school*) proviseur m; **head waiter** n maître m d'hôtel

**heal** [hiːl] vt, vi guérir

**health** [hɛlθ] n santé f; **health care** n services médicaux; **health centre** n (BRIT) centre m de santé; **health food** n aliment(s) naturel(s); **Health Service** n: **the Health Service** (BRIT) ≈ la Sécurité Sociale; **healthy** adj (*person*) en bonne santé; (*climate, food, attitude etc*) sain(e)

**heap** [hiːp] n tas m ▷ vt (*also*: **~ up**) entasser, amonceler; **she ~ed her plate with cakes** elle a chargé son assiette de gâteaux; **~s (of)** (*inf*: lots) des tas (de)

**hear** (*pt, pp* **~d**) [hɪəʳ, həːd] vt entendre; (*news*) apprendre ▷ vi entendre; **to ~ about** entendre parler de; (*have news of*) avoir des nouvelles de; **to ~ from sb** recevoir des nouvelles de qn

**heard** [həːd] pt, pp of **hear**

**hearing** [ˈhɪərɪŋ] n (*sense*) ouïe f; (*of witnesses*) audition f; (*of a case*) audience f; **hearing aid** n appareil m acoustique

**hearse** [həːs] n corbillard m

**heart** [hɑːt] n cœur m; **hearts** npl (*Cards*) cœur m; **at ~** au fond; **by ~** (*learn, know*) par cœur; **to lose/take ~** perdre/prendre courage; **heart attack** n crise f cardiaque; **heartbeat** n battement m de cœur; **heartbroken** adj: **to be heartbroken** avoir beaucoup de chagrin; **heartburn** n brûlures fpl d'estomac; **heart disease** n maladie

f cardiaque

**hearth** [hɑːθ] n foyer m, cheminée f

**heartless** [ˈhɑːtlɪs] adj (*person*) sans cœur, insensible; (*treatment*) cruel(le)

**hearty** [ˈhɑːtɪ] adj chaleureux(-euse); (*appetite*) solide; (*dislike*) cordial(e); (*meal*) copieux(-euse)

**heat** [hiːt] n chaleur f; (*Sport: also*: **qualifying ~**) éliminatoire f ▷ vt chauffer; **heat up** vi (*liquid*) chauffer; (*room*) se réchauffer ▷ vt réchauffer; **heated** adj chauffé(e); (*fig*) passionné(e), échauffé(e), excité(e); **heater** n appareil m de chauffage; radiateur m; (*in car*) chauffage m; (*water heater*) chauffe-eau m

**heather** [ˈhɛðəʳ] n bruyère f

**heating** [ˈhiːtɪŋ] n chauffage m

**heatwave** [ˈhiːtweɪv] n vague f de chaleur

**heaven** [ˈhɛvn] n ciel m, paradis m; (*fig*) paradis; **heavenly** adj céleste, divin(e)

**heavily** [ˈhɛvɪlɪ] adv lourdement; (*drink, smoke*) beaucoup; (*sleep, sigh*) profondément

**heavy** [ˈhɛvɪ] adj lourd(e); (*work, rain, user, eater*) gros(se); (*drinker, smoker*) grand(e); (*schedule, week*) chargé(e)

**Hebrew** [ˈhiːbruː] adj hébraïque ▷ n (*Ling*) hébreu m

**Hebrides** [ˈhɛbrɪdiːz] npl: **the ~** les Hébrides fpl

**hectare** [ˈhɛktɑːʳ] n (BRIT) hectare m

**hectic** [ˈhɛktɪk] adj (*schedule*) très chargé(e); (*day*) mouvementé(e); (*lifestyle*) trépidant(e)

**he'd** [hiːd] = **he would**; **he had**

**hedge** [hɛdʒ] n haie f ▷ vi se dérober ▷ vt: **to ~ one's bets** (*fig*) se couvrir

**hedgehog** [ˈhɛdʒhɔg] n hérisson m

**heed** [hiːd] vt (*also*: **take ~ of**) tenir compte de, prendre garde à

**heel** [hiːl] n talon m ▷ vt retalonner

**hefty** [ˈhɛftɪ] adj (*person*) costaud(e); (*parcel*) lourd(e); (*piece, price*) gros(se)

**height** [haɪt] n (*of person*) taille f, grandeur f; (*of object*) hauteur f; (*of plane, mountain*) altitude f; (*high ground*) hauteur, éminence f; (fig: of glory, fame, power) sommet m; (: of luxury, stupidity) comble m; **at the ~ of summer** au cœur de l'été; **heighten** vt hausser, surélever; (fig) augmenter

**heir** [ɛəʳ] n héritier m; **heiress** n héritière f

**held** [hɛld] pt, pp of **hold**

**helicopter** ['hɛlɪkɔptəʳ] n hélicoptère m

**hell** [hɛl] n enfer m; **oh ~!** (inf) merde!

**he'll** [hi:l] = **he will**; **he shall**

**hello** [hə'ləu] excl bonjour!; (to attract attention) hé!; (surprise) tiens!

**helmet** ['hɛlmɪt] n casque m

**help** [hɛlp] n aide f; (cleaner etc) femme f de ménage ▷ vt, vi aider; **~!** au secours!; **~ yourself** servez-vous; **can you ~ me?** pouvez-vous m'aider?; **can I ~ you?** (in shop) vous désirez?; **he can't ~ it** il n'y peut rien; **help out** vi aider ▷ vt: **to ~ sb out** aider qn; **helper** n aide m/f, assistant(e); **helpful** adj serviable, obligeant(e); (useful) utile; **helping** n portion f; **helpless** adj impuissant(e); (baby) sans défense; **helpline** n service m d'assistance téléphonique; (free) ≈ numéro vert

**hem** [hɛm] n ourlet m ▷ vt ourler

**hemisphere** ['hɛmɪsfɪəʳ] n hémisphère m

**hemorrhage** ['hɛmərɪdʒ] n (us) = **haemorrhage**

**hemorrhoids** ['hɛmərɔɪdz] npl (us) = **haemorrhoids**

**hen** [hɛn] n poule f; (female bird) femelle f

**hence** [hɛns] adv (therefore) d'où, de là; **2 years ~** d'ici 2 ans

**hen night, hen party** n soirée f entre filles (avant le mariage de l'une d'elles)

**hepatitis** [hɛpə'taɪtɪs] n hépatite f

**her** [həːʳ] pron (direct) la, l' + vowel or h mute; (indirect) lui; (stressed, after prep) elle ▷ adj son (sa), ses pl; see also **me**; **my**

**herb** [həːb] n herbe f; **herbal** adj à base de plantes; **herbal tea** n tisane f

**herd** [həːd] n troupeau m

**here** [hɪəʳ] adv ici; (time) alors ▷ excl tiens!, tenez!; **~!** (present) présent!; **~ is**, **~ are** voici; **~ he/she is** le (la) voici

**hereditary** [hɪ'rɛdɪtrɪ] adj héréditaire

**heritage** ['hɛrɪtɪdʒ] n héritage m, patrimoine m

**hernia** ['həːnɪə] n hernie f

**hero** (pl **~es**) ['hɪərəu] n héros m; **heroic** [hɪ'rəuɪk] adj héroïque

**heroin** ['hɛrəuɪn] n héroïne f (drogue)

**heroine** ['hɛrəuɪn] n héroïne f (femme)

**heron** ['hɛrən] n héron m

**herring** ['hɛrɪŋ] n hareng m

**hers** [həːz] pron le (la) sien(ne), les siens (siennes); see also **mine¹**

**herself** [həː'sɛlf] pron (reflexive) se; (emphatic) elle-même; (after prep) elle; see also **oneself**

**he's** [hi:z] = **he is**; **he has**

**hesitant** ['hɛzɪtənt] adj hésitant(e), indécis(e)

**hesitate** ['hɛzɪteɪt] vi: **to ~ (about/to do)** hésiter (sur/à faire); **hesitation** [hɛzɪ'teɪʃən] n hésitation f

**heterosexual** ['hɛtərəu'sɛksjuəl] adj, n hétérosexuel(le)

**hexagon** ['hɛksəgən] n hexagone m

**hey** [heɪ] excl hé!

**heyday** ['heɪdeɪ] n: **the ~ of** l'âge m d'or de, les beaux jours de

**HGV** n abbr = **heavy goods vehicle**

**hi** [haɪ] excl salut!; (to attract attention) hé!

**hibernate** ['haɪbəneɪt] vi hiberner

**hiccough, hiccup** ['hɪkʌp] vi hoqueter ▷ n: **to have (the) ~s** avoir le hoquet

**hid** [hɪd] pt of **hide**

**hidden** ['hɪdn] pp of **hide** ▷ adj: **~ agenda** intentions non déclarées

**hide** [haɪd] n (skin) peau f ▷ vb (pt **hid**, pp **hidden**) ▷ vt cacher ▷ vi: **to ~ (from sb)** se cacher (de qn)

**hideous** ['hɪdɪəs] adj hideux(-euse), atroce

**hiding** ['haɪdɪŋ] n (beating) correction f, volée f de coups; **to be in ~** (concealed) se tenir caché(e)

**hi-fi** ['haɪfaɪ] adj, n abbr (= high fidelity) hi-fi f inv

**high** [haɪ] adj haut(e); (speed, respect, number) grand(e); (price) élevé(e); (wind) fort(e), violent(e); (voice) aigu(ë) ▷ adv haut, en haut; **20 m** ~ haut(e) de 20 m; ~ **in the air** haut dans le ciel; **highchair** n (child's) chaise haute; **high-class** adj (neighbourhood, hotel) chic inv, de grand standing; **higher education** n études supérieures; **high heels** npl talons hauts, hauts talons; **high jump** n (Sport) saut m en hauteur; **highlands** ['haɪləndz] npl région montagneuse; **the Highlands** (in Scotland) les Highlands mpl; **highlight** n (fig: of event) point culminant ▷ vt (emphasize) faire ressortir, souligner; **highlights** npl (in hair) reflets mpl; **highlighter** n (pen) surligneur (lumineux); **highly** adv extrêmement, très; (unlikely) fort; (recommended, skilled, qualified) hautement; **to speak highly of** dire beaucoup de bien de; **highness** n: **His/Her Highness** son Altesse f; **high-rise** n (also: **high-rise block, high-rise building**) tour f (d'habitation); **high school** n lycée m; (US) établissement m d'enseignement supérieur; **high season** n (BRIT) haute saison; **high street** n (BRIT) grand-rue f; **high-tech** (inf) adj de pointe; **highway** n (BRIT) route f; (US) route nationale; **Highway Code** n (BRIT) code m de la route

**hijack** ['haɪdʒæk] vt détourner (par la force); **hijacker** n auteur m d'un détournement d'avion, pirate m de l'air

**hike** [haɪk] vi faire des excursions à pied ▷ n excursion f à pied, randonnée f; **hiker** n promeneur(-euse), excursionniste m/f; **hiking** n excursions fpl à pied, randonnée f

**hilarious** [hɪ'lɛərɪəs] adj (behaviour, event) désopilant(e)

**hill** [hɪl] n colline f; (fairly high) montagne f; (on road) côte f; **hillside** (flanc m de) coteau m; **hill walking** n

randonnée f de basse montagne; **hilly** adj vallonné(e), montagneux(-euse)

**him** [hɪm] pron (direct) le, l' + vowel or h mute; (stressed, indirect, after prep) lui; see also **me**; **himself** pron (reflexive) se; (emphatic) lui-même; (after prep) lui; see also **oneself**

**hind** [haɪnd] adj de derrière

**hinder** ['hɪndə<sup>r</sup>] vt gêner; (delay) retarder

**hindsight** ['haɪndsaɪt] n: **with (the benefit of)** ~ avec du recul, rétrospectivement

**Hindu** ['hɪnduː] n Hindou(e); **Hinduism** n (Rel) hindouisme m

**hinge** [hɪndʒ] n charnière f ▷ vi (fig): **to** ~ **on** dépendre de

**hint** [hɪnt] n allusion f; (advice) conseil m; (clue) indication f ▷ vt: **to** ~ **that** insinuer que ▷ vi: **to** ~ **at** faire une allusion à

**hip** [hɪp] n hanche f

**hippie, hippy** ['hɪpɪ] n hippie m/f

**hippo** ['hɪpəʊ] (pl ~**s**) n hippopotame m

**hippopotamus** [hɪpə'pɒtəməs] (pl ~**es** or **hippopotami**) n hippopotame m

**hippy** ['hɪpɪ] n = **hippie**

**hire** ['haɪə<sup>r</sup>] vt (BRIT: car, equipment) louer; (worker) embaucher, engager ▷ n location f; **for** ~ à louer; (taxi) libre; **I'd like to** ~ **a car** je voudrais louer une voiture; **hire(d) car** n (BRIT) voiture f de location; **hire purchase** n (BRIT) achat m (or vente f) à tempérament or crédit

**his** [hɪz] pron le (la) sien(ne), les siens (siennes) ▷ adj son (sa), ses pl; see also **mine¹**; **my**

**Hispanic** [hɪs'pænɪk] adj (in US) hispano-américain(e) ▷ n Hispano-Américain(e)

**hiss** [hɪs] vi siffler

**historian** [hɪ'stɔːrɪən] n historien(ne)

**historic(al)** [hɪ'stɒrɪk(l)] adj historique

**history** ['hɪstərɪ] n histoire f

**hit** [hɪt] vt (pt, pp ~) frapper; (reach: target) atteindre, toucher; (collide with: car) entrer en collision avec, heurter;

(fig: affect) toucher ▷ n coup m; (success) succès m; (song) tube m; (to website) visite f; (on search engine) résultat m de recherche; **to ~ it off with sb** bien s'entendre avec qn; **hit back** vi: **to ~ back at sb** prendre sa revanche sur qn

**hitch** [hɪtʃ] vt (fasten) accrocher, attacher; (also: **~ up**) remonter d'une saccade ▷ vi faire de l'autostop ▷ n (difficulty) anicroche f, contretemps m; **to ~ a lift** faire du stop; **hitch-hike** vi faire de l'auto-stop; **hitch-hiker** n auto-stoppeur(-euse); **hitch-hiking** n auto-stop m, stop m (inf)

**hi-tech** ['haɪtɛk] adj de pointe

**hitman** ['hɪtmæn] (irreg) n (inf) tueur m à gages

**HIV** n abbr (= human immunodeficiency virus) HIV m, VIH m; **~-negative/positive** séronégatif(-ive)/positif(-ive)

**hive** [haɪv] n ruche f

**hoard** [hɔːd] n (of food) provisions fpl, réserves fpl; (of money) trésor m ▷ vt amasser

**hoarse** [hɔːs] adj enroué(e)

**hoax** [həʊks] n canular m

**hob** [hɒb] n plaque chauffante

**hobble** ['hɒbl] vi boitiller

**hobby** ['hɒbɪ] n passe-temps favori

**hobo** ['həʊbəʊ] n (US) vagabond m

**hockey** ['hɒkɪ] n hockey m; **hockey stick** n crosse f de hockey

**hog** [hɒg] n porc (châtré) m ▷ vt (fig) accaparer; **to go the whole ~** aller jusqu'au bout

**Hogmanay** [hɒgmə'neɪ] n réveillon m du jour de l'An, Saint-Sylvestre f; voir encadré

**hoist** [hɔɪst] n palan m ▷ vt hisser

**hold** [həʊld] (pt, pp **held**) vt tenir; (contain) contenir; (meeting) tenir; (keep back) retenir; (believe) considérer; (possess) avoir ▷ vi (withstand pressure) tenir (bon); (be valid) valoir; (on telephone) attendre ▷ n prise f; (find) influence f; (Naut) cale f; **to catch** or **get (a) ~ of** saisir; **to get ~ of** (find) trouver; **~ the line!** (Tel) ne quittez pas!; **to ~ one's own** (fig) (bien) se défendre; **hold back** vt retenir; (secret) cacher; **hold on** vi tenir bon; (wait) attendre; **~ on!** (Tel) ne quittez pas!; **to ~ on to sth** (grasp) se crampronner à qch; (keep) conserver or garder qch; **hold out** vt offrir ▷ vi (resist): **to ~ out (against)** résister (devant), tenir bon (devant); **hold up** vt (raise) lever; (support) soutenir; (delay) retarder; (: traffic) ralentir; (rob) braquer; **holdall** n (BRIT) fourre-tout m inv; **holder** n (container) support m; (of ticket, record) détenteur(-trice); (of office, title, passport etc) titulaire m/f

**hole** [həʊl] n trou m

**holiday** ['hɒlədɪ] n (BRIT: vacation) vacances fpl; (day off) jour m de congé; (public) jour férié; **to be on ~** être en vacances; **I'm here on ~** je suis ici en vacances; **holiday camp** n (also: **holiday centre**) camp m de vacances; **holiday job** n (BRIT) boulot m (inf) de vacances; **holiday-maker** n (BRIT) vacancier(-ière); **holiday resort** n centre m de villégiature or de vacances

**Holland** ['hɒlənd] n Hollande f

**hollow** ['hɒləʊ] adj creux(-euse); (fig) faux (fausse) ▷ n creux m; (in land) dépression f (de terrain), cuvette f ▷ vt: **to ~ out** creuser, évider

**holly** ['hɒlɪ] n houx m

**Hollywood** ['hɒlɪwʊd] n Hollywood

**holocaust** ['hɔləkɔːst] n holocauste m

**holy** ['həʊlɪ] adj saint(e); (bread, water) bénit(e); (ground) sacré(e)

**home** [həʊm] n foyer m, maison f; (country) pays natal, patrie f; (institution) maison ▷ adj de famille; (Econ, Pol) national(e), intérieur(e); (Sport: team) qui reçoit; (: match, win) sur leur (or notre) terrain ▷ adv chez soi, à la maison; au pays natal; (right in: nail etc) à fond; **at ~** chez soi, à la maison; **to go** (or **come**) **~** rentrer (chez soi), rentrer à la maison (or au pays); **make yourself at ~** faites comme chez vous; **home address** n domicile permanent; **homeland** n patrie f; **homeless** adj sans foyer, sans abri; **homely** adj (plain) simple, sans prétention; (welcoming) accueillant(e); **home-made** adj fait(e) à la maison; **home match** n match m à domicile; **Home Office** n (BRIT) ministère m de l'Intérieur; **home owner** n propriétaire occupant; **home page** n (Comput) page f d'accueil; **Home Secretary** n (BRIT) ministre m de l'Intérieur; **homesick** adj: **to be homesick** avoir le mal du pays; (missing one's family) s'ennuyer de sa famille; **home town** n ville natale; **homework** n devoirs mpl

**homicide** ['hɔmɪsaɪd] n (US) homicide m

**homoeopathic** (US **homeopathic**) [həʊmɪɔ'pəθɪk] adj (medicine) homéopathique; (doctor) homéopathe

**homoeopathy** (US **homeopathy**) [həʊmɪ'ɔpəθɪ] n homéopathie f

**homosexual** [hɔməʊ'sɛksjʊəl] adj, n homosexuel(le)

**honest** ['ɔnɪst] adj honnête; (sincere) franc (franche); **honestly** adv honnêtement; franchement; **honesty** n honnêteté f

**honey** ['hʌnɪ] n miel m; **honeymoon** n lune f de miel, voyage m de noces; **we're on honeymoon** nous sommes en voyage de noces; **honeysuckle** n chèvrefeuille m

**Hong Kong** ['hɔŋ'kɔŋ] n Hong Kong

**honorary** ['ɔnərərɪ] adj honoraire; (duty, title) honorifique; **~ degree** diplôme m honoris causa

**honour** (US **honor**) ['ɔnər] vt honorer ▷ n honneur m; **to graduate with ~s** obtenir sa licence avec mention; **honourable** (US **honorable**) adj honorable; **honours degree** n (Scol) ≈ licence f avec mention

**hood** [hʊd] n capuchon m; (of cooker) hotte f; (BRIT Aut) capote f; (US Aut) capot m; **hoodie** ['hʊdɪ] n (top) sweat m à capuche

**hoof** (pl **~s** or **hooves**) [huːf, huːvz] n sabot m

**hook** [hʊk] n crochet m; (on dress) agrafe f; (for fishing) hameçon m ▷ vt accrocher; **off the ~** (Tel) décroché

**hooligan** ['huːlɪgən] n voyou m

**hoop** [huːp] n cerceau m

**hooray** [huː'reɪ] excl = **hurray**

**hoot** [huːt] vi (BRIT Aut) klaxonner; (siren) mugir; (owl) hululer

**Hoover®** ['huːvər] n (BRIT) aspirateur m ▷ vt: **to hoover** (room) passer l'aspirateur dans; (carpet) passer l'aspirateur sur

**hooves** [huːvz] npl of **hoof**

**hop** [hɔp] vi sauter; (on one foot) sauter à cloche-pied; (bird) sautiller

**hope** [həʊp] vt, vi espérer ▷ n espoir m; **I ~ so** je l'espère; **I ~ not** j'espère que non; **hopeful** adj (person) plein(e) d'espoir; (situation) prometteur(-euse), encourageant(e); **hopefully** adv (expectantly) avec espoir, avec optimisme; (one hopes) avec un peu de chance; **hopeless** adj désespéré(e); (useless) nul(le)

**hops** [hɔps] npl houblon m

**horizon** [hə'raɪzn] n horizon m; **horizontal** [hɔrɪ'zɔntl] adj horizontal(e)

**hormone** ['hɔːməʊn] n hormone f

**horn** [hɔːn] n corne f; (Mus) cor m; (Aut) klaxon m

**horoscope** ['hɔrəskəʊp] n

horoscope m

**horrendous** [həˈrɛndəs] adj horrible, affreux(-euse)

**horrible** [ˈhɔrɪbl] adj horrible, affreux(-euse)

**horrid** [ˈhɔrɪd] adj (person) détestable; (weather, place, smell) épouvantable

**horrific** [hɔˈrɪfɪk] adj horrible

**horrifying** [ˈhɔrɪfaɪɪŋ] adj horrifiant(e)

**horror** [ˈhɔrəʳ] n horreur f; **horror film** n film m d'épouvante

**hors d'œuvre** [ɔːˈdəːvrə] n hors d'œuvre m

**horse** [hɔːs] n cheval m; **horseback**: **on horseback** adj, adv à cheval; **horse chestnut** n (nut) marron m (d'Inde); (tree) marronnier m (d'Inde); **horsepower** n puissance f (en chevaux); (unit) cheval-vapeur m (CV); **horse-racing** n courses fpl de chevaux; **horseradish** n raifort m; **horse riding** n (BRIT) équitation f

**hose** [həuz] n (also: ~pipe) tuyau m; (also: garden ~) tuyau d'arrosage; **hosepipe** n tuyau m; (in garden) tuyau d'arrosage

**hospital** [ˈhɔspɪtl] n hôpital m; **in** ~ à l'hôpital; **where's the nearest ~?** où est l'hôpital le plus proche?

**hospitality** [hɔspɪˈtælɪtɪ] n hospitalité f

**host** [həust] n hôte m; (TV, Radio) présentateur(-trice), animateur(-trice); (large number): **a ~ of** une foule de; (Rel) hostie f

**hostage** [ˈhɔstɪdʒ] n otage m

**hostel** [ˈhɔstl] n foyer m; (also: **youth ~**) auberge f de jeunesse

**hostess** [ˈhəustɪs] n hôtesse f; (BRIT: also: **air ~**) hôtesse de l'air; (TV, Radio) animatrice f

**hostile** [ˈhɔstaɪl] adj hostile

**hostility** [hɔˈstɪlɪtɪ] n hostilité f

**hot** [hɔt] adj chaud(e); (as opposed to only warm) très chaud; (spicy) fort(e); (fig: contest) acharné(e); (topic) brûlant(e); (temper) violent(e), passionné(e); **to be ~** (person) avoir chaud; (thing) être (très) chaud; (weather) faire chaud; **hot dog** n hot-dog m

**hotel** [həuˈtɛl] n hôtel m

**hot-water bottle** [hɔtˈwɔːtə-] n bouillotte f

**hound** [haund] vt poursuivre avec acharnement ▷ n chien courant

**hour** [ˈauəʳ] n heure f; **hourly** adj toutes les heures; (rate) horaire

**house** n [haus] maison f; (Pol) chambre f; (Theat) salle f; auditoire m ▷ vt [hauz] (person) loger, héberger; **on the ~** (fig) aux frais de la maison; **household** n (Admin etc) ménage m; (people) famille f, maisonnée f; **householder** n propriétaire m/f; (head of house) chef m de famille; **housekeeper** n gouvernante f; **housekeeping** n (work) ménage m; **housewife** (irreg) n ménagère f, femme f au foyer; **house wine** n cuvée f maison or du patron; **housework** n (travaux mpl du) ménage m

**housing** [ˈhauzɪŋ] n logement m; **housing development** (BRIT **housing estate**) n (blocks of flats) cité f; (houses) lotissement m

**hover** [ˈhɔvəʳ] vi planer; **hovercraft** n aéroglisseur m, hovercraft m

**how** [hau] adv comment; **~ are you?** comment allez-vous?; **~ do you do?** bonjour; (on being introduced) enchanté(e); **~ long have you been here?** depuis combien de temps êtes-vous là?; **~ lovely/awful!** que or comme c'est joli/affreux!; **~ much time/many people?** combien de temps/gens?; **~ much does it cost?** ça coûte combien?; **~ old are you?** quel âge avez-vous?; **~ tall is he?** combien mesure-t-il?; **~ is school?** ça va à l'école?; **~ was the film?** comment était le film?

**however** [hauˈɛvəʳ] conj pourtant, cependant ▷ adv: **~ I do it** de quelque manière que je m'y prenne; **~ cold it is** même s'il fait très froid; **~ did you do it?** comment y êtes-vous donc arrivé?

**howl** [haul] n hurlement m ▷ vi hurler;

(wind) mugir

**H.P.** n abbr (BRIT) = **hire purchase**

**h.p.** abbr (Aut) = **horsepower**

**HQ** n abbr (= headquarters) QG m

**hr(s)** abbr (= hour(s)) h

**HTML** n abbr (= hypertext markup language) HTML m

**hubcap** ['hʌbkæp] n (Aut) enjoliveur m

**huddle** ['hʌdl] vi: **to ~ together** se blottir les uns contre les autres

**huff** [hʌf] n: **in a ~** fâché(e)

**hug** [hʌg] vt serrer dans ses bras; (shore, kerb) serrer ▷ n: **to give sb a ~** serrer qn dans ses bras

**huge** [hjuːdʒ] adj énorme, immense

**hull** [hʌl] n (of ship) coque f

**hum** [hʌm] vt (tune) fredonner ▷ vi fredonner; (insect) bourdonner; (plane, tool) vrombir

**human** ['hjuːmən] adj humain(e) ▷ n (also: **~ being**) être humain

**humane** [hjuːˈmeɪn] adj humain(e), humanitaire

**humanitarian** [hjuːmænɪˈtɛərɪən] adj humanitaire

**humanity** [hjuːˈmænɪtɪ] n humanité f

**human rights** npl droits mpl de l'homme

**humble** ['hʌmbl] adj humble, modeste

**humid** ['hjuːmɪd] adj humide; **humidity** [hjuːˈmɪdɪtɪ] n humidité f

**humiliate** [hjuːˈmɪlɪeɪt] vt humilier

**humiliating** [hjuːˈmɪlɪeɪtɪŋ] adj humiliant(e)

**humiliation** [hjuːmɪlɪˈeɪʃən] n humiliation f

**hummus** ['huməs] n houm(m)ous m

**humorous** ['hjuːmərəs] adj humoristique

**humour** (US **humor**) ['hjuːməʳ] n humour m; (mood) humeur f ▷ vt (person) faire plaisir à; se prêter aux caprices de

**hump** [hʌmp] n bosse f

**hunch** [hʌntʃ] n (premonition) intuition f

**hundred** ['hʌndrəd] num cent; **~s of** des centaines de; **hundredth** [-ɪdθ]

num centième

**hung** [hʌŋ] pt, pp of **hang**

**Hungarian** [hʌŋˈgɛərɪən] adj hongrois(e) ▷ n Hongrois(e); (Ling) hongrois m

**Hungary** ['hʌŋgərɪ] n Hongrie f

**hunger** ['hʌŋgəʳ] n faim f ▷ vi: **to ~ for** avoir faim de, désirer ardemment

**hungry** ['hʌŋgrɪ] adj affamé(e); **to be ~** avoir faim; **~ for** (fig) avide de

**hunt** [hʌnt] vt (seek) chercher; (Sport) chasser ▷ vi (search): **to ~ for** chercher (partout); (Sport) chasser ▷ n (Sport) chasse f; **hunter** n chasseur m; **hunting** n chasse f

**hurdle** ['həːdl] n (Sport) haie f; (fig) obstacle m

**hurl** [həːl] vt lancer (avec violence); (abuse, insults) lancer

**hurrah, hurray** [hu'rɑː, hu'reɪ] excl hourra!

**hurricane** ['hʌrɪkən] n ouragan m

**hurry** ['hʌrɪ] n hâte f, précipitation f ▷ vi se presser, se dépêcher ▷ vt (person) faire presser, faire se dépêcher; (work) presser; **to be in a ~** être pressé(e); **to do sth in a ~** faire qch en vitesse; **hurry up** vi se dépêcher

**hurt** [həːt] (pt, pp **~**) vt (cause pain to) faire mal à; (injure, fig) blesser ▷ vi faire mal ▷ adj blessé(e); **my arm ~s** j'ai mal au bras; **to ~ o.s.** se faire mal

**husband** ['hʌzbənd] n mari m

**hush** [hʌʃ] n calme m, silence m ▷ vt faire taire; **~!** chut!

**husky** ['hʌskɪ] adj (voice) rauque ▷ n chien m esquimau or de traîneau

**hut** [hʌt] n hutte f; (shed) cabane f

**hyacinth** ['haɪəsɪnθ] n jacinthe f

**hydrangea** [haɪˈdreɪndʒə] n hortensia m

**hydrofoil** ['haɪdrəfɔɪl] n hydrofoil m

**hydrogen** ['haɪdrədʒən] n hydrogène m

**hygiene** ['haɪdʒiːn] n hygiène f; **hygienic** [haɪˈdʒiːnɪk] adj hygiénique

**hymn** [hɪm] n hymne m; cantique m

**hype** [haɪp] n (inf) matraquage m

publicitaire *or* médiatique

**hypermarket** ['haɪpəmɑːkɪt] (BRIT) *n*
hypermarché *m*

**hyphen** ['haɪfn] *n* trait *m* d'union

**hypnotize** ['hɪpnətaɪz] *vt* hypnotiser

**hypocrite** ['hɪpəkrɪt] *n* hypocrite *m/f*

**hypocritical** [hɪpə'krɪtɪkl] *adj*
hypocrite

**hypothesis** (*pl* **hypotheses**)
[haɪ'pɔθɪsɪs, -siːz] *n* hypothèse *f*

**hysterical** [hɪ'stɛrɪkl] *adj* hystérique;
(*funny*) hilarant(e)

**hysterics** [hɪ'stɛrɪks] *npl*: **to be in/
have ~** (*anger, panic*) avoir une crise de
nerfs; (*laughter*) attraper un fou rire

**I** [aɪ] *pron* je; (*before vowel*) j'; (*stressed*)
moi

**ice** [aɪs] *n* glace *f*; (*on road*) verglas *m*
▷ *vt* (*cake*) glacer ▷ *vi* (*also*: **~ over**)
geler; (*also*: **~ up**) se givrer; **iceberg**
*n* iceberg *m*; **ice cream** *n* glace *f*; **ice
cube** *n* glaçon *m*; **ice hockey** *n* hockey
*m* sur glace

**Iceland** ['aɪslənd] *n* Islande *f*; **Icelander**
*n* Islandais(e); **Icelandic** [aɪs'lændɪk]
*adj* islandais(e) ▷ *n* (*Ling*) islandais *m*

**ice**: **ice lolly** *n* (BRIT) esquimau *m*;
**ice rink** *n* patinoire *f*; **ice skating** *n*
patinage *m* (sur glace)

**icing** ['aɪsɪŋ] *n* (*Culin*) glaçage *m*; **icing
sugar** *n* (BRIT) sucre *m* glace

**icon** ['aɪkɔn] *n* icône *f*

**ICT** *n abbr* (BRIT: *Scol*: = *information and
communications technology*) TIC *fpl*

**icy** ['aɪsɪ] *adj* glacé(e); (*road*) verglacé(e);
(*weather, temperature*) glacial(e)

**I'd** [aɪd] = **I would**; **I had**

**ID card** *n* carte *f* d'identité

**idea** [aɪ'dɪə] *n* idée *f*

**ideal** [aɪˈdɪəl] n idéal m ▷ adj idéal(e);
  **ideally** [aɪˈdɪəlɪ] adv (preferably) dans
  l'idéal; (perfectly): **he is ideally suited
  to the job** il est parfait pour ce poste
**identical** [aɪˈdɛntɪkl] adj identique
**identification** [aɪdɛntɪfɪˈkeɪʃən] n
  identification f; **means of ~** pièce f
  d'identité
**identify** [aɪˈdɛntɪfaɪ] vt identifier
**identity** [aɪˈdɛntɪtɪ] n identité f;
  **identity card** n carte f d'identité;
  **identity theft** n usurpation f
  d'identité
**ideology** [aɪdɪˈɔlədʒɪ] n idéologie f
**idiom** [ˈɪdɪəm] n (phrase) expression f
  idiomatique; (style) style m
**idiot** [ˈɪdɪət] n idiot(e), imbécile m/f
**idle** [ˈaɪdl] adj (doing nothing) sans
  occupation, désœuvré(e); (lazy)
  oisif(-ive), paresseux(-euse);
  (unemployed) au chômage; (machinery)
  au repos; (question, pleasures) vain(e),
  futile ▷ vi (engine) tourner au ralenti
**idol** [ˈaɪdl] n idole f
**idyllic** [ɪˈdɪlɪk] adj idyllique
**i.e.** abbr (= id est: that is) c. à d., c'est-
  à-dire
**if** [ɪf] conj si; **if necessary** si nécessaire,
  le cas échéant; **if so** si c'est le cas; **if not**
  sinon; **if only I could!** si seulement je
  pouvais!; see also **as**; **even**
**ignite** [ɪgˈnaɪt] vt mettre le feu à,
  enflammer ▷ vi s'enflammer
**ignition** [ɪgˈnɪʃən] n (Aut) allumage m;
  **to switch on/off the ~** mettre/couper
  le contact
**ignorance** [ˈɪgnərəns] n ignorance f
**ignorant** [ˈɪgnərənt] adj ignorant(e);
  **to be ~ of** (subject) ne rien connaître en;
  (events) ne pas être au courant de
**ignore** [ɪgˈnɔːʳ] vt ne tenir aucun
  compte de; (mistake) ne pas relever;
  (person: pretend to not see) faire
  semblant de ne pas reconnaître; (: pay
  no attention to) ignorer
**ill** [ɪl] adj (sick) malade; (bad) mauvais(e)
  ▷ n mal m ▷ adv: **to speak/think ~
  of sb** dire/penser du mal de qn; **to be**

**taken ~** tomber malade
**I'll** [aɪl] = I will; I shall
**illegal** [ɪˈliːgl] adj illégal(e)
**illegible** [ɪˈlɛdʒɪbl] adj illisible
**illegitimate** [ɪlɪˈdʒɪtɪmət] adj
  illégitime
**ill health** n mauvaise santé
**illiterate** [ɪˈlɪtərət] adj illettré(e)
**illness** [ˈɪlnɪs] n maladie f
**illuminate** [ɪˈluːmɪneɪt] vt (room,
  street) éclairer; (for special effect)
  illuminer
**illusion** [ɪˈluːʒən] n illusion f
**illustrate** [ˈɪləstreɪt] vt illustrer
**illustration** [ɪləˈstreɪʃən] n
  illustration f
**I'm** [aɪm] = I am
**image** [ˈɪmɪdʒ] n image f; (public face)
  image de marque
**imaginary** [ɪˈmædʒɪnərɪ] adj
  imaginaire
**imagination** [ɪmædʒɪˈneɪʃən] n
  imagination f
**imaginative** [ɪˈmædʒɪnətɪv] adj
  imaginatif(-ive); (person) plein(e)
  d'imagination
**imagine** [ɪˈmædʒɪn] vt s'imaginer;
  (suppose) imaginer, supposer
**imbalance** [ɪmˈbæləns] n
  déséquilibre m
**imitate** [ˈɪmɪteɪt] vt imiter; **imitation**
  [ɪmɪˈteɪʃən] n imitation f
**immaculate** [ɪˈmækjulət] adj
  impeccable; (Rel) immaculé(e)
**immature** [ɪməˈtjuəʳ] adj (fruit) qui
  n'est pas mûr(e); (person) qui manque
  de maturité
**immediate** [ɪˈmiːdɪət] adj
  immédiat(e); **immediately** adv (at
  once) immédiatement; **immediately
  next to** juste à côté de
**immense** [ɪˈmɛns] adj immense,
  énorme; **immensely** adv (+adj)
  extrêmement; (+vb) énormément
**immerse** [ɪˈməːs] vt immerger,
  plonger; **to be ~d in** (fig) être plongé
  dans
**immigrant** [ˈɪmɪgrənt] n

immigrant(e); (*already established*)
immigré(e); **immigration** [ɪmɪˈɡreɪʃən]
*n* immigration *f*

**imminent** [ˈɪmɪnənt] *adj* imminent(e)

**immoral** [ɪˈmɒrl] *adj* immoral(e)

**immortal** [ɪˈmɔːtl] *adj, n* immortel(le)

**immune** [ɪˈmjuːn] *adj*: ~ **(to)**
immunisé(e) (contre); **immune
system** *n* système *m* immunitaire

**immunize** [ˈɪmjunaɪz] *vt* immuniser

**impact** [ˈɪmpækt] *n* choc *m*, impact *m*;
(*fig*) impact

**impair** [ɪmˈpɛər] *vt* détériorer,
diminuer

**impartial** [ɪmˈpɑːʃl] *adj* impartial(e)

**impatience** [ɪmˈpeɪʃəns] *n*
impatience *f*

**impatient** [ɪmˈpeɪʃənt] *adj*
impatient(e); **to get** *or* **grow ~**
s'impatienter

**impeccable** [ɪmˈpɛkəbl] *adj*
impeccable, parfait(e)

**impending** [ɪmˈpɛndɪŋ] *adj*
imminent(e)

**imperative** [ɪmˈpɛrətɪv] *adj* (*need*)
urgent(e), pressant(e); (*tone*)
impérieux(-euse) ▷ *n* (*Ling*) impératif *m*

**imperfect** [ɪmˈpəːfɪkt] *adj*
imparfait(e); (*goods etc*)
défectueux(-euse) ▷ *n* (*Ling: also:* ~
**tense**) imparfait *m*

**imperial** [ɪmˈpɪərɪəl] *adj* impérial(e);
(*BRIT: measure*) légal(e)

**impersonal** [ɪmˈpəːsənl] *adj*
impersonnel(le)

**impersonate** [ɪmˈpəːsəneɪt] *vt* se
faire passer pour; (*Theat*) imiter

**impetus** [ˈɪmpətəs] *n* impulsion *f*; (*of
runner*) élan *m*

**implant** [ɪmˈplɑːnt] *vt* (*Med*) implanter;
(*fig: idea, principle*) inculquer

**implement** *n* [ˈɪmplɪmənt] outil *m*,
instrument *m*; (*for cooking*) ustensile *m*
▷ *vt* [ˈɪmplɪmɛnt] exécuter

**implicate** [ˈɪmplɪkeɪt] *vt* impliquer,
compromettre

**implication** [ɪmplɪˈkeɪʃən] *n*
implication *f*; **by ~** indirectement

**implicit** [ɪmˈplɪsɪt] *adj* implicite;
(*complete*) absolu(e), sans réserve

**imply** [ɪmˈplaɪ] *vt* (*hint*) suggérer,
laisser entendre; (*mean*) indiquer,
supposer

**impolite** [ɪmpəˈlaɪt] *adj* impoli(e)

**import** *vt* [ɪmˈpɔːt] importer ▷ *n*
[ˈɪmpɔːt] (*Comm*) importation *f*;
(*meaning*) portée *f*, signification *f*

**importance** [ɪmˈpɔːtns] *n*
importance *f*

**important** [ɪmˈpɔːtnt] *adj*
important(e); **it's not ~** c'est sans
importance, ce n'est pas important

**importer** [ɪmˈpɔːtər] *n*
importateur(-trice)

**impose** [ɪmˈpəuz] *vt* imposer ▷ *vi*:
**to ~ on sb** abuser de la gentillesse
de qn; **imposing** *adj* imposant(e),
impressionnant(e)

**impossible** [ɪmˈpɔsɪbl] *adj* impossible

**impotent** [ˈɪmpətnt] *adj*
impuissant(e)

**impoverished** [ɪmˈpɔvərɪʃt] *adj*
pauvre, appauvri(e)

**impractical** [ɪmˈpræktɪkl] *adj* pas
pratique; (*person*) qui manque d'esprit
pratique

**impress** [ɪmˈprɛs] *vt* impressionner,
faire impression sur; (*mark*) imprimer,
marquer; **to ~ sth on sb** faire bien
comprendre qch à qn

**impression** [ɪmˈprɛʃən] *n* impression
*f*; (*of stamp, seal*) empreinte *f*; (*imitation*)
imitation *f*; **to be under the ~ that**
avoir l'impression que

**impressive** [ɪmˈprɛsɪv] *adj*
impressionnant(e)

**imprison** [ɪmˈprɪzn] *vt* emprisonner,
mettre en prison; **imprisonment**
*n* emprisonnement *m*; (*period*):
**to sentence sb to 10 years'
imprisonment** condamner qn à 10
ans de prison

**improbable** [ɪmˈprɔbəbl] *adj*
improbable; (*excuse*) peu plausible

**improper** [ɪmˈprɔpər] *adj* (*unsuitable*)
déplacé(e), de mauvais goût; (*indecent*)

indécent(e); (*dishonest*) malhonnête

**improve** [ɪm'pruːv] *vt* améliorer ▷ *vi*
s'améliorer; (*pupil etc*) faire des progrès;
**improvement** *n* amélioration *f*; (*of
pupil etc*) progrès *m*

**improvise** ['ɪmprəvaɪz] *vt*, *vi*
improviser

**impulse** ['ɪmpʌls] *n* impulsion *f*;
**on ~** impulsivement, sur un coup
de tête; **impulsive** [ɪm'pʌlsɪv] *adj*
impulsif(-ive)

 **KEYWORD**

**in** [ɪn] *prep* **1** (*indicating place, position*)
dans; **in the house/the fridge** dans la
maison/le frigo; **in the garden** dans
le *or* au jardin; **in town** en ville; **in the
country** à la campagne; **in school** à
l'école; **in here/there** ici/là
**2** (*with place names: of town, region,
country*): **in London** à Londres; **in
England** en Angleterre; **in Japan**
au Japon; **in the United States** aux
États-Unis
**3** (*indicating time: during*): **in spring**
au printemps; **in summer** en été;
**in May/2005** en mai/2005; **in the
afternoon** (dans) l'après-midi; **at 4
o'clock in the afternoon** à 4 heures de
l'après-midi
**4** (*indicating time: in the space of*) en;
(: *future*) dans; **I did it in 3 hours/days**
je l'ai fait en 3 heures/jours; **I'll see you
in 2 weeks** *or* **in 2 weeks' time** je te
verrai dans 2 semaines
**5** (*indicating manner etc*) à; **in a
loud/soft voice** à voix haute/basse;
**in pencil** au crayon; **in writing** par
écrit; **in French** en français; **the boy
in the blue shirt** le garçon à *or* avec la
chemise bleue
**6** (*indicating circumstances*): **in the sun**
au soleil; **in the shade** à l'ombre; **in the
rain** sous la pluie; **a change in policy**
un changement de politique
**7** (*indicating mood, state*): **in tears** en
larmes; **in anger** sous le coup de la

colère; **in despair** au désespoir; **in
good condition** en bon état; **to live in
luxury** vivre dans le luxe
**8** (*with ratios, numbers*): **1 in 10
households, 1 household in 10** 1
ménage sur 10; **20 pence in the pound**
20 pence par livre sterling; **they lined
up in twos** ils se mirent en rangs (deux)
par deux; **in hundreds** par centaines
**9** (*referring to people, works*) chez; **the
disease is common in children** c'est
une maladie courante chez les enfants;
**in (the works of) Dickens** chez
Dickens, dans (l'œuvre de) Dickens
**10** (*indicating profession etc*) dans; **to be
in teaching** être dans l'enseignement
**11** (*after superlative*) de; **the best pupil
in the class** le meilleur élève de la
classe
**12** (*with present participle*): **in saying
this** en disant ceci
▷ *adv*: **to be in** (*person: at home, work*)
être là; (*train, ship, plane*) être arrivé(e);
(*in fashion*) être à la mode; **to ask sb in**
inviter qn à entrer; **to run/limp** *etc* **in**
entrer en courant/boitant *etc*
▷ *n*: **the ins and outs (of)** (*of
proposal, situation etc*) les tenants et
aboutissants (de)

**inability** [ɪnə'bɪlɪtɪ] *n* incapacité *f*; **~ to
pay** incapacité de payer

**inaccurate** [ɪn'ækjurət] *adj*
inexact(e); (*person*) qui manque de
précision

**inadequate** [ɪn'ædɪkwət] *adj*
insuffisant(e), inadéquat(e)

**inadvertently** [ɪnəd'vəːtntlɪ] *adv* par
mégarde

**inappropriate** [ɪnə'prəuprɪət] *adj*
inopportun(e), mal à propos; (*word,
expression*) impropre

**inaugurate** [ɪ'nɔːgjureɪt] *vt*
inaugurer; (*president, official*) investir de
ses fonctions

**Inc.** *abbr* = **incorporated**

**incapable** [ɪn'keɪpəbl] *adj*: **~ (of)**
incapable (de)

**incense** n ['ɪnsɛns] encens m ▷ vt
[ɪn'sɛns] (anger) mettre en colère
**incentive** [ɪn'sɛntɪv] n
encouragement m, raison f de se
donner de la peine
**inch** [ɪntʃ] n pouce m (=25 mm; 12 in a
foot); **within an ~ of** à deux doigts de;
**he wouldn't give an ~** (fig) il n'a pas
voulu céder d'un pouce
**incidence** ['ɪnsɪdns] n (of crime, disease)
fréquence f
**incident** ['ɪnsɪdnt] n incident m
**incidentally** [ɪnsɪ'dɛntəlɪ] adv (by the
way) à propos
**inclination** [ɪnklɪ'neɪʃən] n
inclination f; (desire) envie f
**incline** n ['ɪnklaɪn] pente f, plan
incliné ▷ vb [ɪn'klaɪn] ▷ vt incliner ▷ vi
(surface) s'incliner; **to be ~d to do** (have
a tendency to do) avoir tendance à faire
**include** [ɪn'kluːd] vt inclure,
comprendre; **service is/is not ~d** le
service est compris/n'est pas compris;
**including** prep y compris; **inclusion**
n inclusion f; **inclusive** adj inclus(e),
compris(e); **inclusive of tax** taxes
comprises
**income** ['ɪnkʌm] n revenu m; (from
property etc) rentes fpl; **income
support** n (BRIT) ≈ revenu m minimum
d'insertion, RMI m; **income tax** n
impôt m sur le revenu
**incoming** ['ɪnkʌmɪŋ] adj (passengers,
mail) à l'arrivée; (government, tenant)
nouveau (nouvelle)
**incompatible** [ɪnkəm'pætɪbl] adj
incompatible
**incompetence** [ɪn'kɔmpɪtns] n
incompétence f, incapacité f
**incompetent** [ɪn'kɔmpɪtnt] adj
incompétent(e), incapable
**incomplete** [ɪnkəm'pliːt] adj
incomplet(-ète)
**inconsistent** [ɪnkən'sɪstnt] adj
qui manque de constance; (work)
irrégulier(-ière); (statement) peu
cohérent(e); **~ with** en contradiction
avec

**inconvenience** [ɪnkən'viːnjəns] n
inconvénient m; (trouble) dérangement
m ▷ vt déranger
**inconvenient** [ɪnkən'viːnjənt]
adj malcommode; (time, place) mal
choisi(e), qui ne convient pas; (visitor)
importun(e)
**incorporate** [ɪn'kɔːpəreɪt] vt
incorporer; (contain) contenir
**incorrect** [ɪnkə'rɛkt] adj incorrect(e);
(opinion, statement) inexact(e)
**increase** n ['ɪnkriːs] augmentation
f ▷ vi, vt [ɪn'kriːs] augmenter;
**increasingly** adv de plus en plus
**incredible** [ɪn'krɛdɪbl] adj incroyable;
**incredibly** adv incroyablement
**incur** [ɪn'kəːr] vt (expenses) encourir;
(anger, risk) s'exposer à; (debt)
contracter; (loss) subir
**indecent** [ɪn'diːsnt] adj indécent(e),
inconvenant(e)
**indeed** [ɪn'diːd] adv (confirming,
agreeing) en effet, effectivement; (for
emphasis) vraiment; (furthermore)
d'ailleurs; **yes ~!** certainement!
**indefinitely** [ɪn'dɛfɪnɪtlɪ] adv (wait)
indéfiniment
**independence** [ɪndɪ'pɛndns] n
indépendance f; **Independence Day**
n (US) fête de l'Indépendance américaine;
voir encadré

● **INDEPENDENCE DAY**
●
● L'**Independence Day** est la fête
● nationale aux États-Unis, le 4
● juillet. Il commémore l'adoption
● de la déclaration d'Indépendance,
● en 1776, écrite par Thomas Jefferson
● et proclamant la séparation des 13
● colonies américaines de la Grande-
● Bretagne.

**independent** [ɪndɪ'pɛndnt]
adj indépendant(e); (radio) libre;
**independent school** n (BRIT) école
privée
**index** ['ɪndɛks] n (pl **~es**) (in book)

index m; (: *in library etc*) catalogue m (*pl* **indices**) (*ratio, sign*) indice m

**India** ['ɪndɪə] n Inde f; **Indian** adj indien(ne) ▷ n Indien(ne); **(American) Indian** Indien(ne) (d'Amérique)

**indicate** ['ɪndɪkeɪt] vt indiquer ▷ vi (*BRIT Aut*): **to ~ left/right** mettre son clignotant à gauche/à droite; **indication** [ɪndɪ'keɪʃən] n indication f, signe m; **indicative** [ɪn'dɪkətɪv] adj: **to be indicative of sth** être symptomatique de qch ▷ n (*Ling*) indicatif m; **indicator** n (*sign*) indicateur m; (*Aut*) clignotant m

**indices** ['ɪndɪsiːz] npl of **index**

**indict** [ɪn'daɪt] vt accuser; **indictment** n accusation f

**indifference** [ɪn'dɪfrəns] n indifférence f

**indifferent** [ɪn'dɪfrənt] adj indifférent(e); (*poor*) médiocre, quelconque

**indigenous** [ɪn'dɪdʒɪnəs] adj indigène

**indigestion** [ɪndɪ'dʒɛstʃən] n indigestion f, mauvaise digestion

**indignant** [ɪn'dɪgnənt] adj: **~ (at sth/ with sb)** indigné(e) (de qch/contre qn)

**indirect** [ɪndɪ'rɛkt] adj indirect(e)

**indispensable** [ɪndɪ'spɛnsəbl] adj indispensable

**individual** [ɪndɪ'vɪdjuəl] n individu m ▷ adj individuel(le); (*characteristic*) particulier(-ière), original(e); **individually** adv individuellement

**Indonesia** [ɪndə'niːzɪə] n Indonésie f

**indoor** ['ɪndɔːr] adj d'intérieur; (*plant*) d'appartement; (*swimming pool*) couvert(e); (*sport, games*) pratiqué(e) en salle; **indoors** [ɪn'dɔːz] adv à l'intérieur

**induce** [ɪn'djuːs] vt (*persuade*) persuader; (*bring about*) provoquer; (*labour*) déclencher

**indulge** [ɪn'dʌldʒ] vt (*whim*) céder à, satisfaire; (*child*) gâter ▷ vi: **to ~ in sth** (*luxury*) s'offrir qch, se permettre qch; (*fantasies etc*) se livrer à qch; **indulgent** adj indulgent(e)

**industrial** [ɪn'dʌstrɪəl] adj

industriel(le); (*injury*) du travail; (*dispute*) ouvrier(-ière); **industrial estate** n (*BRIT*) zone industrielle; **industrialist** n industriel m; **industrial park** n (*US*) zone industrielle

**industry** ['ɪndəstrɪ] n industrie f; (*diligence*) zèle m, application f

**inefficient** [ɪnɪ'fɪʃənt] adj inefficace

**inequality** [ɪnɪ'kwɔlɪtɪ] n inégalité f

**inevitable** [ɪn'ɛvɪtəbl] adj inévitable; **inevitably** adv inévitablement, fatalement

**inexpensive** [ɪnɪk'spɛnsɪv] adj bon marché inv

**inexperienced** [ɪnɪk'spɪərɪənst] adj inexpérimenté(e)

**inexplicable** [ɪnɪk'splɪkəbl] adj inexplicable

**infamous** ['ɪnfəməs] adj infâme, abominable

**infant** ['ɪnfənt] n (*baby*) nourrisson m; (*young child*) petit(e) enfant

**infantry** ['ɪnfəntrɪ] n infanterie f

**infant school** n (*BRIT*) classes fpl préparatoires (*entre 5 et 7 ans*)

**infect** [ɪn'fɛkt] vt (*wound*) infecter; (*person, blood*) contaminer; **infection** [ɪn'fɛkʃən] n infection f; (*contagion*) contagion f; **infectious** [ɪn'fɛkʃəs] adj infectieux(-euse); (*also fig*) contagieux(-euse)

**infer** [ɪn'fəːr] vt: **to ~ (from)** conclure (de), déduire (de)

**inferior** [ɪn'fɪərɪər] adj inférieur(e); (*goods*) de qualité inférieure ▷ n inférieur(e); (*in rank*) subalterne m/f

**infertile** [ɪn'fəːtaɪl] adj stérile

**infertility** [ɪnfəː'tɪlɪtɪ] n infertilité f, stérilité f

**infested** [ɪn'fɛstɪd] adj: **~ (with)** infesté(e) (de)

**infinite** ['ɪnfɪnɪt] adj infini(e); (*time, money*) illimité(e); **infinitely** adv infiniment

**infirmary** [ɪn'fəːmərɪ] n hôpital m; (*in school, factory*) infirmerie f

**inflamed** [ɪn'fleɪmd] adj enflammé(e)

**inflammation** [ɪnflə'meɪʃən] n

inflammation f

**inflatable** [ɪnˈfleɪtəbl] *adj* gonflable

**inflate** [ɪnˈfleɪt] *vt* (*tyre, balloon*) gonfler; (*fig: exaggerate*) grossir; (*: increase*) gonfler; **inflation** [ɪnˈfleɪʃən] *n* (*Econ*) inflation f

**inflexible** [ɪnˈflɛksɪbl] *adj* inflexible, rigide

**inflict** [ɪnˈflɪkt] *vt*: **to ~ on** infliger à

**influence** [ˈɪnfluəns] *n* influence f ▷ *vt* influencer; **under the ~ of alcohol** en état d'ébriété; **influential** [ɪnfluˈɛnʃl] *adj* influent(e)

**influenza** [ɪnfluˈɛnzə] *n* grippe f

**influx** [ˈɪnflʌks] *n* afflux m

**info** (*inf*) [ˈɪnfəu] *n* (= *information*) renseignements *mpl*

**inform** [ɪnˈfɔːm] *vt*: **to ~ sb (of)** informer or avertir qn (de) ▷ *vi*: **to ~ on sb** dénoncer qn, informer contre qn

**informal** [ɪnˈfɔːml] *adj* (*person, manner, party*) simple; (*visit, discussion*) dénué(e) de formalités; (*announcement, invitation*) non officiel(le); (*colloquial*) familier(-ère)

**information** [ɪnfəˈmeɪʃən] *n* information(s) f(pl); renseignements *mpl*; (*knowledge*) connaissances *fpl*; **a piece of ~** un renseignement; **information office** *n* bureau *m* de renseignements; **information technology** *n* informatique f

**informative** [ɪnˈfɔːmətɪv] *adj* instructif(-ive)

**infra-red** [ɪnfrəˈrɛd] *adj* infrarouge

**infrastructure** [ˈɪnfrəstrʌktʃəʳ] *n* infrastructure f

**infrequent** [ɪnˈfriːkwənt] *adj* peu fréquent(e), rare

**infuriate** [ɪnˈfjuərɪeɪt] *vt* mettre en fureur

**infuriating** [ɪnˈfjuərɪeɪtɪŋ] *adj* exaspérant(e)

**ingenious** [ɪnˈdʒiːnjəs] *adj* ingénieux(-euse)

**ingredient** [ɪnˈgriːdɪənt] *n* ingrédient *m*; (*fig*) élément *m*

**inhabit** [ɪnˈhæbɪt] *vt* habiter

**inhabitant** *n* habitant(e)

**inhale** [ɪnˈheɪl] *vt* inhaler; (*perfume*) respirer; (*smoke*) avaler ▷ *vi* (*breathe in*) aspirer; (*in smoking*) avaler la fumée; **inhaler** *n* inhalateur *m*

**inherent** [ɪnˈhɪərənt] *adj*: **~ (in or to)** inhérent(e) (à)

**inherit** [ɪnˈhɛrɪt] *vt* hériter (de); **inheritance** *n* héritage *m*

**inhibit** [ɪnˈhɪbɪt] *vt* (*Psych*) inhiber; (*growth*) freiner; **inhibition** [ɪnhɪˈbɪʃən] *n* inhibition f

**initial** [ɪˈnɪʃl] *adj* initial(e) ▷ *n* initiale f ▷ *vt* parafer; **initials** *npl* initiales *fpl*; (*as signature*) parafe *m*; **initially** *adv* initialement, au début

**initiate** [ɪˈnɪʃɪeɪt] *vt* (*start*) entreprendre; amorcer; (*enterprise*) lancer; (*person*) initier; **to ~ proceedings against sb** (*Law*) intenter une action à qn, engager des poursuites contre qn

**initiative** [ɪˈnɪʃətɪv] *n* initiative f

**inject** [ɪnˈdʒɛkt] *vt* injecter; (*person*): **to ~ sb with sth** faire une piqûre de qch à qn; **injection** [ɪnˈdʒɛkʃən] *n* injection f, piqûre f

**injure** [ˈɪndʒəʳ] *vt* blesser; (*damage: reputation etc*) compromettre; **to ~ o.s.** se blesser; **injured** *adj* (*person, leg etc*) blessé(e); **injury** *n* blessure f; (*wrong*) tort *m*

**injustice** [ɪnˈdʒʌstɪs] *n* injustice f

**ink** [ɪŋk] *n* encre f; **ink-jet printer** [ˈɪŋkdʒɛt-] *n* imprimante f à jet d'encre

**inland** *adj* [ˈɪnlənd] intérieur(e) ▷ *adv* [ɪnˈlænd] à l'intérieur, dans les terres; **Inland Revenue** *n* (*BRIT*) fisc *m*

**in-laws** [ˈɪnlɔːz] *npl* beaux-parents *mpl*; belle famille

**inmate** [ˈɪnmeɪt] *n* (*in prison*) détenu(e); (*in asylum*) interné(e)

**inn** [ɪn] *n* auberge f

**inner** [ˈɪnəʳ] *adj* intérieur(e); **inner-city** *adj* (*schools, problems*) de quartiers déshérités

**inning** [ˈɪnɪŋ] *n* (*US: Baseball*) tour *m* de batte; **innings** *npl* (*Cricket*) tour de batte

**innocence** ['məsns] n innocence f

**innocent** ['məsnt] adj innocent(e)

**innovation** [ɪnəu'veɪʃən] n
innovation f

**innovative** ['ɪnəu'veɪtɪv] adj
novateur(-trice); (product) innovant(e)

**in-patient** ['ɪnpeɪʃənt] n malade
hospitalisé(e)

**input** ['ɪnput] n (contribution)
contribution f; (resources) ressources
fpl; (Comput) entrée f (de données);
(: data) données fpl ▷ vt (Comput)
introduire, entrer

**inquest** ['ɪnkwest] n enquête
(criminelle); (coroner's) enquête
judiciaire

**inquire** [ɪn'kwaɪər] vi demander
▷ vt demander; **to ~ about**
s'informer de, se renseigner sur; **to ~
when/where/whether** demander
quand/où/si; **inquiry** n demande f
de renseignements; (Law) enquête
f, investigation f; **"inquiries"**
"renseignements"

**ins.** abbr = **inches**

**insane** [ɪn'seɪn] adj fou (folle); (Med)
aliéné(e)

**insanity** [ɪn'sænɪtɪ] n folie f; (Med)
aliénation (mentale)

**insect** ['ɪnsekt] n insecte m; **insect
repellent** n crème f anti-insectes

**insecure** [ɪnsɪ'kjuər] adj (person)
anxieux(-euse); (job) précaire; (building
etc) peu sûr(e)

**insecurity** [ɪnsɪ'kjuərɪtɪ] n insécurité f

**insensitive** [ɪn'sensɪtɪv] adj insensible

**insert** vt [ɪn'səːt] insérer ▷ n
['ɪnsəːt] insertion f

**inside** ['ɪn'saɪd] n intérieur m ▷ adj
intérieur(e) ▷ adv à l'intérieur, dedans
▷ prep à l'intérieur de; (of time): **~ 10
minutes** en moins de 10 minutes; **to go
~** rentrer; **inside lane** n (Aut: in Britain)
voie f de gauche; (: in US, Europe) voie
f de droite; **inside out** adv à l'envers;
(know) à fond; **to turn sth inside out**
retourner qch

**insight** ['ɪnsaɪt] n perspicacité f;
(glimpse, idea) aperçu m

**insignificant** [ɪnsɪg'nɪfɪknt] adj
insignifiant(e)

**insincere** [ɪnsɪn'sɪər] adj hypocrite

**insist** [ɪn'sɪst] vi insister; **to ~ on doing**
insister pour faire; **to ~ on sth** exiger
qch; **to ~ that** insister pour que + sub;
(claim) maintenir or soutenir que;
**insistent** adj insistant(e), pressant(e);
(noise, action) ininterrompu(e)

**insomnia** [ɪn'sɔmnɪə] n insomnie f

**inspect** [ɪn'spekt] vt inspecter;
(BRIT: ticket) contrôler; **inspection**
[ɪn'spekʃən] n inspection f; (BRIT:
of tickets) contrôle m; **inspector** n
inspecteur(-trice); (BRIT: on buses,
trains) contrôleur(-euse)

**inspiration** [ɪnspə'reɪʃən] n
inspiration f; **inspire** [ɪn'spaɪər] vt
inspirer; **inspiring** adj inspirant(e)

**instability** [ɪnstə'bɪlɪtɪ] n instabilité f

**install** (US **instal**) [ɪn'stɔːl] vt
installer; **installation** [ɪnstə'leɪʃən] n
installation f

**instalment** (US **installment**)
[ɪn'stɔːlmənt] n (payment) acompte
m, versement partiel; (of TV serial etc)
épisode m; **in ~s** (pay) à tempérament;
(receive) en plusieurs fois

**instance** ['ɪnstəns] n exemple m; **for ~**
par exemple; **in the first ~** tout d'abord,
en premier lieu

**instant** ['ɪnstənt] n instant m ▷ adj
immédiat(e), urgent(e); (coffee, food)
instantané(e), en poudre; **instantly**
adv immédiatement, tout de suite;
**instant messaging** n messagerie f
instantanée

**instead** [ɪn'sted] adv au lieu de cela; **~
of** au lieu de; **~ of sb** à la place de qn

**instinct** ['ɪnstɪŋkt] n instinct m;
**instinctive** adj instinctif(-ive)

**institute** ['ɪnstɪtjuːt] n institut m
▷ vt instituer, établir; (inquiry) ouvrir;
(proceedings) entamer

**institution** [ɪnstɪ'tjuːʃən] n
institution f; (school) établissement

*m* (scolaire); (*for care*) établissement (psychiatrique *etc*)

**instruct** [ɪnˈstrʌkt] *vt*: **to ~ sb in sth** enseigner qch à qn; **to ~ sb to do** charger qn *or* ordonner à qn de faire; **instruction** [ɪnˈstrʌkʃən] *n* instruction *f*; **instructions** *npl* (*orders*) directives *fpl*; **instructions for use** mode *m* d'emploi; **instructor** *n* professeur *m*; (*for skiing, driving*) moniteur *m*

**instrument** [ˈɪnstrʊmənt] *n* instrument *m*; **instrumental** [ɪnstrʊˈmɛntl] *adj* (*Mus*) instrumental(e); **to be instrumental in sth/in doing sth** contribuer à qch/à faire qch

**insufficient** [ɪnsəˈfɪʃənt] *adj* insuffisant(e)

**insulate** [ˈɪnsjʊleɪt] *vt* isoler; (*against sound*) insonoriser; **insulation** [ɪnsjʊˈleɪʃən] *n* isolation *f*; (*against sound*) insonorisation *f*

**insulin** [ˈɪnsjʊlɪn] *n* insuline *f*

**insult** *n* [ˈɪnsʌlt] insulte *f*, affront *m* ▷ *vt* [ɪnˈsʌlt] insulter, faire un affront à; **insulting** *adj* insultant(e), injurieux(-euse)

**insurance** [ɪnˈʃʊərəns] *n* assurance *f*; **fire/life ~** assurance-incendie/-vie; **insurance company** *n* compagnie *f* *or* société *f* d'assurances; **insurance policy** *n* police *f* d'assurance

**insure** [ɪnˈʃʊəʳ] *vt* assurer; **to ~ (o.s.) against** (*fig*) parer à

**intact** [ɪnˈtækt] *adj* intact(e)

**intake** [ˈɪnteɪk] *n* (*Tech*) admission *f*; (*consumption*) consommation *f*; (*BRIT Scol*) **an ~ of 200 a year** 200 admissions par an

**integral** [ˈɪntɪɡrəl] *adj* (*whole*) intégral(e); (*part*) intégrant(e)

**integrate** [ˈɪntɪɡreɪt] *vt* intégrer ▷ *vi* s'intégrer

**integrity** [ɪnˈtɛɡrɪtɪ] *n* intégrité *f*

**intellect** [ˈɪntəlɛkt] *n* intelligence *f*; **intellectual** [ɪntəˈlɛktjʊəl] *adj, n* intellectuel(le)

**intelligence** [ɪnˈtɛlɪdʒəns] *n*

intelligence *f*; (*Mil etc*) informations *fpl*, renseignements *mpl*

**intelligent** [ɪnˈtɛlɪdʒənt] *adj* intelligent(e)

**intend** [ɪnˈtɛnd] *vt* (*gift etc*): **to ~ sth for** destiner qch à; **to ~ to do** avoir l'intention de faire

**intense** [ɪnˈtɛns] *adj* intense; (*person*) véhément(e)

**intensify** [ɪnˈtɛnsɪfaɪ] *vt* intensifier

**intensity** [ɪnˈtɛnsɪtɪ] *n* intensité *f*

**intensive** [ɪnˈtɛnsɪv] *adj* intensif(-ive); **intensive care** *n*: **to be in intensive care** être en réanimation; **intensive care unit** *n* service *m* de réanimation

**intent** [ɪnˈtɛnt] *n* intention *f* ▷ *adj* attentif(-ive), absorbé(e); **to all ~s and purposes** en fait, pratiquement; **to be ~ on doing sth** être (bien) décidé à faire qch

**intention** [ɪnˈtɛnʃən] *n* intention *f*; **intentional** *adj* intentionnel(le), délibéré(e)

**interact** [ɪntərˈækt] *vi* avoir une action réciproque; (*people*) communiquer; **interaction** [ɪntərˈækʃən] *n* interaction *f*; **interactive** *adj* (*Comput*) interactif, conversationnel(le)

**intercept** [ɪntəˈsɛpt] *vt* intercepter; (*person*) arrêter au passage

**interchange** *n* [ˈɪntətʃeɪndʒ] (*exchange*) échange *m*; (*on motorway*) échangeur *m*

**intercourse** [ˈɪntəkɔːs] *n*: **sexual ~** rapports sexuels

**interest** [ˈɪntrɪst] *n* intérêt *m*; (*Comm: stake, share*) participation *f*, intérêts *mpl* ▷ *vt* intéresser; **interested** *adj* intéressé(e); **to be interested in sth** s'intéresser à qch; **I'm interested in going** ça m'intéresse d'y aller; **interesting** *adj* intéressant(e); **interest rate** *n* taux *m* d'intérêt

**interface** [ˈɪntəfeɪs] *n* (*Comput*) interface *f*

**interfere** [ɪntəˈfɪəʳ] *vi*: **to ~ in** (*quarrel*) s'immiscer dans; (*other people's business*) se mêler de; **to ~ with** (*object*) tripoter,

toucher à; (plans) contrecarrer; (duty)
être en conflit avec; **interference**
n (gen) ingérence f; (Radio, TV)
parasites mpl

**interim** ['ɪntərɪm] adj provisoire; (post)
intérimaire ▷ n: **in the ~** dans l'intérim

**interior** [ɪn'tɪərɪə'] n intérieur m ▷ adj
intérieur(e); (minister, department)
de l'intérieur; **interior design** n
architecture f d'intérieur

**intermediate** [ɪntə'miːdɪət] adj
intermédiaire; (Scol: course, level)
moyen(ne)

**intermission** [ɪntə'mɪʃən] n pause f;
(Theat, Cine) entracte m

**intern** vt [ɪn'tə:n] interner ▷ n
['ɪntə:n] (US) interne m/f

**internal** [ɪn'tə:nl] adj interne; (dispute,
reform etc) intérieur(e); **Internal
Revenue Service** n (US) fisc m

**international** [ɪntə'næʃənl] adj
international(e) ▷ n (BRIT Sport)
international m

**Internet** [ɪntə'nɛt] n: **the ~** l'Internet m;
**Internet café** n cybercafé m; **Internet
Service Provider** n fournisseur m
d'accès à Internet; **Internet user** n
internaute m/f

**interpret** [ɪn'tə:prɪt] vt interpréter
▷ vi servir d'interprète; **interpretation**
[ɪntə:prɪ'teɪʃən] n interprétation f;
**interpreter** n interprète m/f; **could
you act as an interpreter for us?**
pourriez-vous nous servir d'interprète?

**interrogate** [ɪn'tɛrəugeɪt] vt
interroger; (suspect etc) soumettre
à un interrogatoire; **interrogation**
[ɪntɛrəu'geɪʃən] n interrogation f; (by
police) interrogatoire m

**interrogative** [ɪntə'rɔgətɪv] adj
interrogateur(-trice) ▷ n (Ling)
interrogatif m

**interrupt** [ɪntə'rʌpt] vt, vi interrompre;
**interruption** [ɪntə'rʌpʃən] n
interruption f

**intersection** [ɪntə'sɛkʃən] n (of roads)
croisement m

**interstate** ['ɪntəsteɪt] (US) n

autoroute f (qui relie plusieurs États)

**interval** ['ɪntəvl] n intervalle m; (BRIT:
Theat) entracte m; (: Sport) mi-temps f;
**at ~s** par intervalles

**intervene** [ɪntə'viːn] vi (time) s'écouler
(entre-temps); (event) survenir; (person)
intervenir

**interview** ['ɪntəvjuː] n (Radio, TV
etc) interview f; (for job) entrevue f
▷ vt interviewer; avoir une entrevue
avec; **interviewer** n (Radio, TV etc)
interviewer m

**intimate** adj ['ɪntɪmət] intime;
(friendship) profond(e); (knowledge)
approfondi(e) ▷ vt ['ɪntɪmeɪt]
suggérer, laisser entendre; (announce)
faire savoir

**intimidate** [ɪn'tɪmɪdeɪt] vt intimider

**intimidating** [ɪn'tɪmɪdeɪtɪŋ] adj
intimidant(e)

**into** ['ɪntu] prep dans; **~ pieces/French**
en morceaux/français

**intolerant** [ɪn'tɔlərnt] adj: **~ (of)**
intolérant(e)

**intranet** [ɪn'trənet] n intranet m

**intransitive** [ɪn'trænsɪtɪv] adj
intransitif(-ive)

**intricate** ['ɪntrɪkət] adj complexe,
compliqué(e)

**intrigue** [ɪn'tri:g] n intrigue f ▷ vt
intriguer; **intriguing** adj fascinant(e)

**introduce** [ɪntrə'djuːs] vt introduire;
(TV show etc) présenter; **to ~ sb (to sb)**
présenter qn (à qn); **to ~ sb to** (pastime,
technique) initier qn à; **introduction**
[ɪntrə'dʌkʃən] n introduction f;
(of person) présentation f; (to new
experience) initiation f; **introductory**
[ɪntrə'dʌktərɪ] adj préliminaire,
introductif(-ive)

**intrude** [ɪn'truːd] vi (person) être
importun(e); **to ~ on** or **into**
(conversation etc) s'immiscer dans;
**intruder** n intrus(e)

**intuition** [ɪntju:'ɪʃən] n intuition f

**inundate** ['ɪnʌndeɪt] vt: **to ~ with**
inonder de

**invade** [ɪn'veɪd] vt envahir

**invalid** n ['invəlid] malade m/f; (with disability) invalide m/f ▷ adj [in'vælid] (not valid) invalide, non valide

**invaluable** [in'væljuəbl] adj inestimable, inappréciable

**invariably** [in'vɛəriəblɪ] adv invariablement; **she is ~ late** elle est toujours en retard

**invasion** [in'veiʒən] n invasion f

**invent** [in'vɛnt] vt inventer; **invention** [in'vɛnʃən] n invention f; **inventor** n inventeur(-trice)

**inventory** ['invəntrɪ] n inventaire m

**inverted commas** [in'və:tid-] npl (BRIT) guillemets mpl

**invest** [in'vɛst] vt investir ▷ vi: **to ~ in** placer de l'argent or investir dans; (fig: acquire) s'offrir, faire l'acquisition de

**investigate** [in'vɛstigeit] vt étudier, examiner; (crime) faire une enquête sur; **investigation** [invɛsti'geiʃən] n (of crime) enquête f, investigation f

**investigator** [in'vɛstigeitər] n investigateur(-trice); **private ~** détective privé

**investment** [in'vɛstmənt] n investissement m, placement m

**investor** [in'vɛstər] n épargnant(e); (shareholder) actionnaire m/f

**invisible** [in'vizibl] adj invisible

**invitation** [invi'teiʃən] n invitation f

**invite** [in'vait] vt inviter; (opinions etc) demander; **inviting** adj engageant(e), attrayant(e)

**invoice** ['invɔis] n facture f ▷ vt facturer

**involve** [in'vɔlv] vt (entail) impliquer; (concern) concerner; (require) nécessiter; **to ~ sb in** (theft etc) impliquer qn dans; (activity, meeting) faire participer qn à; **involved** adj (complicated) complexe; **to be involved in** (take part) participer à; **involvement** n (personal role) rôle m; (participation) participation f; (enthusiasm) enthousiasme m

**inward** ['inwəd] adj (movement) vers l'intérieur; (thought, feeling) profond(e), intime ▷ adv = **inwards**; **inwards** adv vers l'intérieur

**IQ** n abbr (= intelligence quotient) Q.I. m

**IRA** n abbr (= Irish Republican Army) IRA f

**Iran** [i'rɑːn] n Iran m; **Iranian** [i'reiniən] adj iranien(ne) ▷ n Iranien(ne)

**Iraq** [i'rɑːk] n Irak m; **Iraqi** adj irakien(ne) ▷ n Irakien(ne)

**Ireland** ['aiələnd] n Irlande f

**iris, irises** ['airis, -iz] n iris m

**Irish** ['airiʃ] adj irlandais(e) ▷ npl: **the ~** les Irlandais; **Irishman** (irreg) n Irlandais m; **Irishwoman** (irreg) n Irlandaise f

**iron** ['aiən] n fer m; (for clothes) fer m à repasser ▷ adj de or en fer ▷ vt (clothes) repasser

**ironic(al)** [ai'rɔnik(l)] adj ironique; **ironically** adv ironiquement

**ironing** ['aiənin] n (activity) repassage m; (clothes: ironed) linge repassé; (: to be ironed) linge à repasser; **ironing board** n planche f à repasser

**irony** ['airəni] n ironie f

**irrational** [i'ræʃənl] adj irrationnel(le); (person) qui n'est pas rationnel

**irregular** [i'rɛgjulər] adj irrégulier(-ière); (surface) inégal(e); (action, event) peu orthodoxe

**irrelevant** [i'rɛləvənt] adj sans rapport, hors de propos

**irresistible** [iri'zistibl] adj irrésistible

**irresponsible** [iri'spɔnsibl] adj (act) irréfléchi(e); (person) qui n'a pas le sens des responsabilités

**irrigation** [iri'geiʃən] n irrigation f

**irritable** ['iritəbl] adj irritable

**irritate** ['iriteit] vt irriter; **irritating** adj irritant(e); **irritation** [iri'teiʃən] n irritation f

**IRS** n abbr (US) = **Internal Revenue Service**

**is** [iz] vb see **be**

**ISDN** n abbr (= Integrated Services Digital Network) RNIS m

**Islam** ['izlɑːm] n Islam m; **Islamic** [iz'lɑːmik] adj islamique

**island** ['ailənd] n île f; (also: **traffic ~**) refuge m (pour piétons); **islander** n

habitant(e) d'une île, insulaire *m/f*
**isle** [aɪl] *n* île *f*
**isn't** ['ɪznt] = **is not**
**isolated** ['aɪsəleɪtɪd] *adj* isolé(e)
**isolation** [aɪsə'leɪʃən] *n* isolement *m*
**ISP** *n abbr* = **Internet Service Provider**
**Israel** ['ɪzreɪl] *n* Israël *m*; **Israeli** [ɪz'reɪlɪ]
*adj* israélien(ne) ▷ *n* Israélien(ne)
**issue** ['ɪʃuː] *n* question *f*, problème *m*;
(*of banknotes*) émission *f*; (*of newspaper*)
numéro *m*; (*of book*) publication *f*,
parution *f* ▷ *vt* (*rations, equipment*)
distribuer; (*orders*) donner; (*statement*)
publier, faire; (*certificate, passport*)
délivrer; (*banknotes, cheques, stamps*)
émettre, mettre en circulation; **at ~** en
jeu, en cause; **to take ~ with sb (over
sth)** exprimer son désaccord avec qn
(sur qch)
**IT** *n abbr* = **information technology**

 **KEYWORD**

**it** [ɪt] *pron* **1** (*specific: subject*) il (elle);
(: *direct object*) le (la, l'); (: *indirect object*)
lui; **it's on the table** c'est or il (*or*
elle) est sur la table; **I can't find it** je
n'arrive pas à le trouver; **give it to me**
donne-le-moi
**2** (*after prep*): **about/from/of it** en; **I
spoke to him about it** je lui en ai parlé;
**what did you learn from it?** qu'est-ce
que vous en avez retiré?; **I'm proud
of it** j'en suis fier; **in/to it** y; **put the
book in it** mettez-y le livre; **he agreed
to it** il y a consenti; **did you go to it?**
(*party, concert etc*) est-ce que vous y
êtes allé(s)?
**3** (*impersonal*) il; ce, cela, ça; **it's raining**
il pleut; **it's Friday tomorrow** demain,
c'est vendredi *or* nous sommes,
vendredi; **it's 6 o'clock** il est 6 heures;
**how far is it? — it's 10 miles** c'est si loin?
— c'est à 10 miles; **who is it? — it's me**
qui est-ce? — c'est moi

**Italian** [ɪ'tæljən] *adj* italien(ne) ▷ *n*
Italien(ne); (*Ling*) italien *m*

**italics** [ɪ'tælɪks] *npl* italique *m*
**Italy** ['ɪtəlɪ] *n* Italie *f*
**itch** [ɪtʃ] *n* démangeaison *f* ▷ *vi* (*person*)
éprouver des démangeaisons; (*part
of body*) démanger; **I'm ~ing to do**
l'envie me démange de faire; **itchy**
*adj*: **my back is itchy** j'ai le dos qui me
démange
**it'd** ['ɪtd] = **it would**; **it had**
**item** ['aɪtəm] *n* (*gen*) article *m*; (*on
agenda*) question *f*, point *m*; (*also*: **news
~**) nouvelle *f*
**itinerary** [aɪ'tɪnərərɪ] *n* itinéraire *m*
**it'll** ['ɪtl] = **it will**; **it shall**
**its** [ɪts] *adj* son (sa), ses *pl*
**it's** [ɪts] = **it is**; **it has**
**itself** [ɪt'self] *pron* (*reflexive*) se;
(*emphatic*) lui-même (elle-même)
**ITV** *n abbr* (BRIT: = *Independent Television*)
chaîne de télévision commerciale
**I've** [aɪv] = **I have**
**ivory** ['aɪvərɪ] *n* ivoire *m*
**ivy** ['aɪvɪ] *n* lierre *m*

**J**

**jab** [dʒæb] vt: **to ~ sth into** enfoncer or planter qch dans ▷ n (Med: inf) piqûre f
**jack** [dʒæk] n (Aut) cric m; (Cards) valet m
**jacket** ['dʒækɪt] n veste f, veston m; (of book) couverture f, jaquette f; **jacket potato** n pomme f de terre en robe des champs
**jackpot** ['dʒækpɒt] n gros lot
**Jacuzzi®** [dʒə'ku:zɪ] n jacuzzi® m
**jagged** ['dʒægɪd] adj dentelé(e)
**jail** [dʒeɪl] n prison f ▷ vt emprisonner, mettre en prison; **jail sentence** n peine f de prison
**jam** [dʒæm] n confiture f; (also: **traffic ~**) embouteillage m ▷ vt (passage etc) encombrer, obstruer; (mechanism, drawer etc) bloquer, coincer; (Radio) brouiller ▷ vi (mechanism, sliding part) se coincer, se bloquer; (gun) s'enrayer; **to be in a ~** (inf) être dans le pétrin; **to ~ sth into** (stuff) entasser or comprimer qch dans; (thrust) enfoncer qch dans
**Jamaica** [dʒə'meɪkə] n Jamaïque f
**jammed** [dʒæmd] adj (window etc)

coincé(e)
**Jan** abbr (=January) janv
**janitor** ['dʒænɪtər] n (caretaker) concierge m
**January** ['dʒænjuərɪ] n janvier m
**Japan** [dʒə'pæn] n Japon m; **Japanese** [dʒæpə'ni:z] adj japonais(e) ▷ n (pl inv) Japonais(e); (Ling) japonais m
**jar** [dʒɑ:r] n (stone, earthenware) pot m; (glass) bocal m ▷ vi (sound) produire un son grinçant or discordant; (colours etc) détonner, jurer
**jargon** ['dʒɑ:gən] n jargon m
**javelin** ['dʒævlɪn] n javelot m
**jaw** [dʒɔ:] n mâchoire f
**jazz** [dʒæz] n jazz m
**jealous** ['dʒɛləs] adj jaloux(-ouse); **jealousy** n jalousie f
**jeans** [dʒi:nz] npl jean m
**Jello®** ['dʒɛləu] (us) n gelée f
**jelly** ['dʒɛlɪ] n (dessert) gelée f; (us: jam) confiture f; **jellyfish** n méduse f
**jeopardize** ['dʒɛpədaɪz] vt mettre en danger or péril
**jerk** [dʒə:k] n secousse f, saccade f; (of muscle) spasme m; (inf) pauvre type m ▷ vt (shake) donner une secousse à; (pull) tirer brusquement ▷ vi (vehicles) cahoter
**jersey** ['dʒə:zɪ] n tricot m; (fabric) jersey m
**Jesus** ['dʒi:zəs] n Jésus
**jet** [dʒɛt] n (of gas, liquid) jet m; (Aviat) avion m à réaction, jet m; **jet lag** n décalage m horaire; **jet-ski** vi faire du jet-ski or scooter des mers
**jetty** ['dʒɛtɪ] n jetée f, digue f
**Jew** [dʒu:] n Juif m
**jewel** ['dʒu:əl] n bijou m, joyau m; (in watch) rubis m; **jeweller** (us **jeweler**) n bijoutier(-ière), joaillier m; **jeweller's (shop)** (us **jewelry store**) n bijouterie f, joaillerie f; **jewellery** (us **jewelry**) n bijoux mpl
**Jewish** ['dʒu:ɪʃ] adj juif (juive)
**jigsaw** ['dʒɪgsɔ:] n (also: **~ puzzle**) puzzle m
**job** [dʒɔb] n (chore, task) travail m, tâche

f; (*employment*) emploi *m*, poste *m*, place f; **it's a good ~ that ...** c'est heureux *or* c'est une chance que ... + *sub*; **just the ~!** (c'est) juste *or* exactement ce qu'il faut!; **job centre** (BRIT) *n* ≈ ANPE f, ≈ Agence nationale pour l'emploi; **jobless** *adj* sans travail, au chômage

**jockey** ['dʒɒkɪ] *n* jockey *m* ▷ *vi*: **to ~ for position** manœuvrer pour être bien placé

**jog** [dʒɒg] *vt* secouer ▷ *vi* (*Sport*) faire du jogging; **to ~ sb's memory** rafraîchir la mémoire de qn; **jogging** *n* jogging *m*

**join** [dʒɔɪn] *vt* (*put together*) unir, assembler; (*become member of*) s'inscrire à; (*meet*) rejoindre, retrouver; (*queue*) se joindre à ▷ *vi* (*roads, rivers*) se rejoindre, se rencontrer ▷ *n* raccord *m*; **join in** *vi* se mettre de la partie ▷ *vt fus* se mêler à; **join up** *vi* (*meet*) se rejoindre; (*Mil*) s'engager

**joiner** ['dʒɔɪnə'] (BRIT) *n* menuisier *m*

**joint** [dʒɔɪnt] *n* (*Tech*) jointure f, joint *m*; (*Anat*) articulation f, jointure; (BRIT *Culin*) rôti *m*; (*inf: place*) boîte f; (*of cannabis*) joint ▷ *adj* commun(e); (*committee*) mixte, paritaire; (*winner*) ex aequo; **joint account** *n* compte joint; **jointly** *adv* ensemble, en commun

**joke** [dʒəʊk] *n* plaisanterie f; (*also*: **practical ~**) farce f ▷ *vi* plaisanter; **to play a ~ on** jouer un tour à, faire une farce à; **joker** *n* (*Cards*) joker *m*

**jolly** ['dʒɒlɪ] *adj* gai(e), enjoué(e); (*enjoyable*) amusant(e), plaisant(e) ▷ *adv* (BRIT *inf*) rudement, drôlement

**jolt** [dʒəʊlt] *n* cahot *m*, secousse f; (*shock*) choc *m* ▷ *vt* cahoter, secouer

**Jordan** ['dʒɔːdən] *n* (*country*) Jordanie f

**journal** ['dʒəːnl] *n* journal *m*; **journalism** *n* journalisme *m*; **journalist** *n* journaliste *m/f*

**journey** ['dʒəːnɪ] *n* voyage *m*; (*distance covered*) trajet *m*; **the ~ takes two hours** le trajet dure deux heures; **how was your ~?** votre voyage s'est bien passé?

**joy** [dʒɔɪ] *n* joie f; **joyrider** *n*

voleur(-euse) de voiture (*qui fait une virée dans le véhicule volé*); **joy stick** *n* (*Aviat*) manche *m* à balai; (*Comput*) manche à balai, manette f (de jeu)

**Jr** *abbr* = **junior**

**judge** [dʒʌdʒ] *n* juge *m* ▷ *vt* juger; (*estimate: weight, size etc*) apprécier; (*consider*) estimer

**judo** ['dʒuːdəʊ] *n* judo *m*

**jug** [dʒʌg] *n* pot *m*, cruche f

**juggle** ['dʒʌgl] *vi* jongler; **juggler** *n* jongleur *m*

**juice** [dʒuːs] *n* jus *m*; **juicy** *adj* juteux(-euse)

**Jul** *abbr* (= *July*) juil

**July** [dʒuːˈlaɪ] *n* juillet *m*

**jumble** ['dʒʌmbl] *n* fouillis *m* ▷ *vt* (*also*: **~ up, ~ together**) mélanger, brouiller; **jumble sale** *n* (BRIT) vente f de charité

● **JUMBLE SALE**
●
● Les **jumble sales** ont lieu dans les
● églises, salles des fêtes ou halls
● d'écoles, et l'on y vend des articles
● de toutes sortes, en général bon
● marché et surtout d'occasion, pour
● collecter des fonds pour une œuvre
● de charité, une école (par exemple,
● pour acheter un ordinateur), ou
● encore une église (pour réparer un
● toit etc).

**jumbo** ['dʒʌmbəʊ] *adj* (*also*: **~ jet**) (avion) gros porteur (à réaction)

**jump** [dʒʌmp] *vi* sauter, bondir; (*with fear etc*) sursauter; (*increase*) monter en flèche ▷ *vt* sauter, franchir ▷ *n* saut *m*, bond *m*; (*with fear etc*) sursaut *m*; (*fence*) obstacle *m*; **to ~ the queue** (BRIT) passer avant son tour

**jumper** ['dʒʌmpə'] *n* (BRIT: *pullover*) pull-over *m*; (US: *pinafore dress*) robe-chasuble f

**jump leads** (US **jumper cables**) *npl* câbles *mpl* de démarrage

**Jun.** *abbr* = **June**; **junior**

**junction** ['dʒʌŋkʃən] *n* (BRIT:

of roads) carrefour m; (of rails)
embranchement m
**June** [dʒuːn] n juin m
**jungle** [ˈdʒʌŋgl] n jungle f
**junior** [ˈdʒuːnɪəʳ] adj, n: **he's ~ to me
(by 2 years), he's my ~ (by 2 years)**
il est mon cadet (de 2 ans), il est plus
jeune que moi (de 2 ans); **he's ~ to me**
(seniority) il est en dessous de moi (dans
la hiérarchie), j'ai plus d'ancienneté que
lui; **junior high school** n (us) ≈ collège
m d'enseignement secondaire; see also
**high school; junior school** n (BRIT)
école f primaire, cours moyen
**junk** [dʒʌŋk] n (rubbish) camelote f;
(cheap goods) bric-à-brac m inv; **junk
food** n snacks vite prêts (sans valeur
nutritive)
**junkie** [ˈdʒʌŋkɪ] n (inf) junkie m,
drogué(e)
**junk mail** n prospectus mpl; (Comput)
messages mpl publicitaires
**Jupiter** [ˈdʒuːpɪtəʳ] n (planet) Jupiter f
**jurisdiction** [dʒuərɪsˈdɪkʃən] n
juridiction f; **it falls** or **comes within/
outside our ~** cela est/n'est pas de
notre compétence or ressort
**jury** [ˈdʒuərɪ] n jury m
**just** [dʒʌst] adj juste ▷ adv: **he's ~ done
it/left** il vient de le faire/partir; **~
right/two o'clock** exactement or juste
ce qu'il faut/deux heures; **we were ~
going** nous partions; **I was ~ about to
phone** j'allais téléphoner; **~ as he was
leaving** au moment or à l'instant précis
où il partait; **~ before/enough/here**
juste avant/assez/là; **it's ~ me/a
mistake** ce n'est que moi/(rien) qu'une
erreur; **~ missed/caught** manqué/
attrapé de justesse; **~ listen to this!**
écoutez un peu ça!; **she's ~ as clever
as you** elle est tout aussi intelligente
que vous; **it's ~ as well that you ...**
heureusement que vous ...; **~ a
minute!, ~ one moment!** un instant
(s'il vous plaît)!
**justice** [ˈdʒʌstɪs] n justice f; (us: judge)
juge m de la Cour suprême

**justification** [dʒʌstɪfɪˈkeɪʃən] n
justification f
**justify** [ˈdʒʌstɪfaɪ] vt justifier
**jut** [dʒʌt] vi (also: ~ out) dépasser,
faire saillie
**juvenile** [ˈdʒuːvənaɪl] adj juvénile;
(court, books) pour enfants ▷ n
adolescent(e)

**K, k** [keɪ] *abbr* (= *one thousand*) K;
(= *kilobyte*) Ko
**kangaroo** [kæŋgəˈruː] *n* kangourou *m*
**karaoke** [kɑːrəˈəʊki] *n* karaoké *m*
**karate** [kəˈrɑːtɪ] *n* karaté *m*
**kebab** [kəˈbæb] *n* kébab *m*
**keel** [kiːl] *n* quille *f*; **on an even ~**
(*fig*) à flot
**keen** [kiːn] *adj* (*eager*) plein(e)
d'enthousiasme; (*interest, desire,
competition*) vif (vive); (*eye, intelligence*)
pénétrant(e); (*edge*) effilé(e); **to be ~ to
do** *or* **on doing sth** désirer vivement
faire qch, tenir beaucoup à faire qch;
**to be ~ on sth/sb** aimer beaucoup
qch/qn
**keep** [kiːp] (*pt, pp* **kept**) *vt* (*retain,
preserve*) garder; (*hold back*) retenir;
(*shop, accounts, promise, diary*) tenir;
(*support*) entretenir; (*chickens, bees,
pigs etc*) élever ▷ *vi* (*food*) se conserver;
(*remain: in a certain state or place*)
rester ▷ *n* (*of castle*) donjon *m*; (*food
etc*): **enough for his ~** assez pour

(*assurer*) sa subsistance; **to ~ doing
sth** (*continue*) continuer à faire qch;
(*repeatedly*) ne pas arrêter de faire
qch; **to ~ sb from doing/sth from
happening** empêcher qn de faire *or* que
qn (ne) fasse/que qch (n')arrive; **to ~ sb
happy/a place tidy** faire que qn soit
content/qu'un endroit reste propre; **to
~ sth to o.s.** garder qch pour soi, tenir
qch secret; **to ~ sth from sb** cacher qch
à qn; **to ~ time** (*clock*) être à l'heure,
ne pas retarder; **for ~s** (*inf*) pour de
bon, pour toujours; **keep away** *vt*: **to
~ sth/sb away from sb** tenir qch/qn
éloigné de qn ▷ *vi*: **to ~ away (from)**
ne pas s'approcher (de); **keep back** *vt*
(*crowds, tears, money*) retenir; (*conceal:
information*): **to ~ sth back from sb**
cacher qch à qn ▷ *vi* rester en arrière;
**keep off** *vt* (*dog, person*) éloigner ▷ *vi*: **if
the rain ~s off** s'il ne pleut pas; **~ your
hands off!** pas touche! (*inf*); **"~ off the
grass"** "pelouse interdite"; **keep on** *vi*
continuer; **to ~ on doing** continuer à
faire; **don't ~ on about it!** arrête (d'en
parler)!; **keep out** *vt* empêcher d'entrer
▷ *vi* (*stay out*) rester en dehors; **"~ out"**
"défense d'entrer"; **keep up** *vi* (*fig: in
comprehension*) suivre ▷ *vt* continuer,
maintenir; **to ~ up with sb** (*in work
etc*) se maintenir au même niveau
que qn; (*in race etc*) aller aussi vite que
qn; **keeper** *n* gardien(ne); **keep-fit** *n*
gymnastique *f* (d'entretien); **keeping**
*n* (*care*) garde *f*; **in keeping with** en
harmonie avec
**kennel** ['kɛnl] *n* niche *f*; **kennels** *npl*
(*for boarding*) chenil *m*
**Kenya** ['kɛnjə] *n* Kenya *m*
**kept** [kɛpt] *pt, pp of* **keep**
**kerb** [kəːb] *n* (BRIT) bordure *f* du trottoir
**kerosene** ['kɛrəsiːn] *n* kérosène *m*
**ketchup** ['kɛtʃəp] *n* ketchup *m*
**kettle** ['kɛtl] *n* bouilloire *f*
**key** [kiː] *n* (*gen, Mus*) clé *f*; (*of piano,
typewriter*) touche *f*; (*on map*) légende
*f* ▷ *adj* (*factor, role, area*) clé *inv* ▷ *vt*
(*also: ~ in: text*) saisir; **can I have my**

**~?** je peux avoir ma clé?; **a ~ issue** un problème fondamental; **keyboard** n clavier m; **keyhole** n trou m de la serrure; **keyring** n porte-clés m

**kg** abbr (= kilogram) K

**khaki** ['kɑːkɪ] adj, n kaki m

**kick** [kɪk] vt donner un coup de pied à ▷ vi (horse) ruer ▷ n coup m de pied; (inf: thrill): **he does it for ~s** il le fait parce que ça l'excite, il le fait pour le plaisir; **to ~ the habit** (inf) arrêter; **kick off** vi (Sport) donner le coup d'envoi; **kick-off** n (Sport) coup m d'envoi

**kid** [kɪd] n (inf: child) gamin(e), gosse m/f; (animal, leather) chevreau m ▷ vi (inf) plaisanter, blaguer

**kidnap** ['kɪdnæp] vt enlever, kidnapper; **kidnapping** n enlèvement m

**kidney** ['kɪdnɪ] n (Anat) rein m; (Culin) rognon m; **kidney bean** n haricot m rouge

**kill** [kɪl] vt tuer ▷ n mise f à mort; **to ~ time** tuer le temps; **killer** n tueur(-euse); (murderer) meurtrier(-ière); **killing** n meurtre m; (of group of people) tuerie f, massacre m; (inf): **to make a killing** se remplir les poches, réussir un beau coup

**kiln** [kɪln] n four m

**kilo** ['kiːləʊ] n kilo m; **kilobyte** n (Comput) kilo-octet m; **kilogram(me)** n kilogramme m; **kilometre** (US **kilometer**) ['kɪləmiːtəʳ] n kilomètre m; **kilowatt** n kilowatt m

**kilt** [kɪlt] n kilt m

**kin** [kɪn] n see **next-of-kin**

**kind** [kaɪnd] adj gentil(le), aimable ▷ n sorte f, espèce f; (species) genre m; **to be two of a ~** se ressembler; **in ~** (Comm) en nature; **~ of** (inf: rather) plutôt; **a ~ of** une sorte de; **what ~ of ...?** quelle sorte de ...?

**kindergarten** ['kɪndəgɑːtn] n jardin m d'enfants

**kindly** ['kaɪndlɪ] adj bienveillant(e), plein(e) de gentillesse ▷ adv avec bonté; **will you ~ ...** auriez-vous la bonté or l'obligeance de ...

**kindness** ['kaɪndnɪs] n (quality) bonté f, gentillesse f

**king** [kɪŋ] n roi m; **kingdom** n royaume m; **kingfisher** n martin-pêcheur m; **king-size(d) bed** n grand lit (de 1,95 m de large)

**kiosk** ['kiːɒsk] n kiosque m; (BRIT: also: **telephone ~**) cabine f (téléphonique)

**kipper** ['kɪpəʳ] n hareng fumé et salé

**kiss** [kɪs] n baiser m ▷ vt embrasser; **to ~ (each other)** s'embrasser; **kiss of life** n (BRIT) bouche à bouche m

**kit** [kɪt] n équipement m, matériel m; (set of tools etc) trousse f; (for assembly) kit m

**kitchen** ['kɪtʃɪn] n cuisine f

**kite** [kaɪt] n (toy) cerf-volant m

**kitten** ['kɪtn] n petit chat, chaton m

**kitty** ['kɪtɪ] n (money) cagnotte f

**kiwi** ['kiːwiː] n (also: **~ fruit**) kiwi m

**km** abbr (= kilometre) km

**km/h** abbr (= kilometres per hour) km/h

**knack** [næk] n: **to have the ~ (of doing)** avoir le coup (pour faire)

**knee** [niː] n genou m; **kneecap** n rotule f

**kneel** (pt, pp knelt) [niːl, nɛlt] vi (also: **~ down**) s'agenouiller

**knelt** [nɛlt] pt, pp of **kneel**

**knew** [njuː] pt of **know**

**knickers** ['nɪkəz] npl (BRIT) culotte f (de femme)

**knife** [naɪf] n (pl knives) couteau m ▷ vt poignarder, frapper d'un coup de couteau

**knight** [naɪt] n chevalier m; (Chess) cavalier m

**knit** [nɪt] vt tricoter ▷ vi tricoter; (broken bones) se ressouder; **to ~ one's brows** froncer les sourcils; **knitting** n tricot m; **knitting needle** n aiguille f à tricoter; **knitwear** n tricots mpl, lainages mpl

**knives** [naɪvz] npl of **knife**

**knob** [nɒb] n bouton m; (BRIT): **a ~ of butter** une noix de beurre

**knock** [nɒk] vt frapper; (bump into) heurter; (fig: col) dénigrer ▷ vi (at

door etc): **to ~ at/on** frapper à/sur ▷ n
coup m; **knock down** vt renverser;
(price) réduire; **knock off** vi (inf: finish)
s'arrêter (de travailler) ▷ vt (vase,
object) faire tomber; (inf: steal) piquer;
(fig: from price etc): **to ~ off £10** faire
une remise de 10 livres; **knock out**
vt assommer; (Boxing) mettre k.-o.;
(in competition) éliminer; **knock over**
vt (object) faire tomber; (pedestrian)
renverser; **knockout** n (Boxing) knockout m, K.-O. m; **knockout competition**
(BRIT) compétition f avec épreuves
éliminatoires

**knot** [nɔt] n (gen) nœud m ▷ vt nouer
**know** [nəʊ] vt (pt **knew**, pp **~n**) savoir;
(person, place) connaître; **to ~ that**
savoir que; **to ~ how to do** savoir faire;
**to ~ how to swim** savoir nager; **to ~
about/of sth** (event) être au courant
de qch; (subject) connaître qch; **I don't
~** je ne sais pas; **do you ~ where I
can ...?** savez-vous où je peux ...?;
**know-all** n (BRIT pej) je-sais-tout
m/f; **know-how** n savoir-faire m,
technique f, compétence f; **knowing**
adj (look etc) entendu(e); **knowingly**
adv (on purpose) sciemment; (smile, look)
d'un air entendu; **know-it-all** n (US)
= **know-all**
**knowledge** ['nɔlɪdʒ] n connaissance
f; (learning) connaissances, savoir
m; **without my ~** à mon insu;
**knowledgeable** adj bien informé(e)
**known** [nəʊn] pp of **know** ▷ adj (thief,
facts) notoire; (expert) célèbre
**knuckle** ['nʌkl] n articulation f (des
phalanges), jointure f
**koala** [kəʊ'ɑːlə] n (also: **~ bear**) koala m
**Koran** [kɔ'rɑːn] n Coran m
**Korea** [kə'rɪə] n Corée f; **Korean** adj
coréen(ne) ▷ n Coréen(ne)
**kosher** ['kəʊʃər] adj kascher inv
**Kosovar, Kosovan** ['kɔsəvɑːr,
'kɔsəvən] adj kosovar(e)
**Kosovo** ['kɔsɔvəʊ] n Kosovo m
**Kuwait** [ku'weit] n Koweït m

**L** abbr (BRIT Aut: = learner) signale un
conducteur débutant
**l.** abbr (= litre) l
**lab** [læb] n abbr (= laboratory) labo m
**label** ['leɪbl] n étiquette f; (brand: of
record) marque f ▷ vt étiqueter
**labor** etc ['leɪbər] (US) = **labour** etc
**laboratory** [lə'bɔrətərɪ] n laboratoire m
**Labor Day** n (US, CANADA) fête f du
travail (le premier lundi de septembre)

● **LABOR DAY**

● La fête du Travail aux États-Unis et au
● Canada est fixée au premier lundi de
● septembre. Instituée par le Congrès
● en 1894 après avoir été réclamée par
● les mouvements ouvriers pendant
● douze ans, elle a perdu une grande
● partie de son caractère politique
● pour devenir un jour férié assez
● ordinaire et l'occasion de partir pour
● un long week-end avant la rentrée
● des classes.

**labor union** n (us) syndicat m
**Labour** ['leɪbəʳ] n (BRIT Pol: also:
**the ~ Party**) le parti travailliste, les
travaillistes mpl
**labour** (us labor) ['leɪbəʳ] n (work)
travail m; (workforce) main-d'œuvre f
▷ vi: **to ~ (at)** travailler dur (à), peiner
(sur) ▷ vt: **to ~ a point** insister sur un
point; **in ~** (Med) en travail; **labourer** n
manœuvre m; **farm labourer** ouvrier
m agricole
**lace** [leɪs] n dentelle f; (of shoe etc) lacet
m ▷ vt (shoe: also: **~ up**) lacer
**lack** [læk] n manque m ▷ vt manquer
de; **through** or **for ~ of** faute de, par
manque de; **to be ~ing** manquer, faire
défaut; **to be ~ing in** manquer de
**lacquer** ['lækəʳ] n laque f
**lacy** ['leɪsɪ] adj (of lace) en dentelle; (like
lace) comme de la dentelle
**lad** [læd] n garçon m, gars m
**ladder** ['lædəʳ] n échelle f; (BRIT:
in tights) maille filée ▷ vt, vi (BRIT:
tights) filer
**ladle** ['leɪdl] n louche f
**lady** ['leɪdɪ] n dame f; **"ladies and
gentlemen ..."** "Mesdames (et)
Messieurs ..."; **young ~** jeune fille f;
(married) jeune femme f; **the ladies'
(room)** les toilettes fpl des dames;
**ladybird** (us **ladybug**) n coccinelle f
**lag** [læg] n retard m ▷ vi (also: **~ behind**)
rester en arrière, traîner; (fig) rester à la
traîne ▷ vt (pipes) calorifuger
**lager** ['lɑːgəʳ] n bière blonde
**lagoon** [lə'guːn] n lagune f
**laid** [leɪd] pt, pp of **lay**; **laid back** adj (inf)
relaxe, décontracté(e)
**lain** [leɪn] pp of **lie**
**lake** [leɪk] n lac m
**lamb** [læm] n agneau m
**lame** [leɪm] adj (also fig) boiteux(-euse)
**lament** [lə'mɛnt] n lamentation f ▷ vt
pleurer, se lamenter sur
**lamp** [læmp] n lampe f; **lamppost**
n (BRIT) réverbère m; **lampshade** n
abat-jour m inv
**land** [lænd] n (as opposed to sea)

terre f (ferme); (country) pays m; (soil)
terre; (piece of land) terrain m; (estate)
terre(s), domaine(s) m(pl) ▷ vi (from
ship) débarquer; (Aviat) atterrir; (fig:
fall) (re)tomber ▷ vt (passengers,
goods) débarquer; (obtain) décrocher;
**to ~ sb with sth** (inf) coller qch à qn;
**landing** n (from ship) débarquement
m; (Aviat) atterrissage m; (of staircase)
palier m; **landing card** n carte f
de débarquement; **landlady** n
propriétaire, logeuse f; (of pub)
patronne f; **landlord** n propriétaire
m, logeur m; (of pub etc) patron m;
**landmark** n (point m de) repère m;
**to be a landmark** (fig) faire date or
époque; **landowner** n propriétaire
foncier or terrien; **landscape**
n paysage m; **landslide** n (Geo)
glissement m (de terrain); (fig: Pol) raz-
de-marée (électoral)
**lane** [leɪn] n (in country) chemin m; (Aut:
of road) voie f; (: line of traffic) file f; (in
race) couloir m
**language** ['læŋgwɪdʒ] n langue f; (way
one speaks) langage m; **what ~s do you
speak?** quelles langues parlez-vous?;
**bad ~** grossièretés fpl, langage grossier;
**language laboratory** n laboratoire m
de langues; **language school** n école
f de langue
**lantern** ['læntn] n lanterne f
**lap** [læp] n (of track) tour m (de piste); (of
body): **in** or **on one's ~** sur les genoux
▷ vt (also: **~ up**) laper ▷ vi (waves)
clapoter
**lapel** [lə'pɛl] n revers m
**lapse** [læps] n défaillance f; (in
behaviour) écart m (de conduite) ▷ vi
(Law) cesser d'être en vigueur; (contract)
expirer; **to ~ into bad habits** prendre
de mauvaises habitudes; **~ of time** laps
m de temps, intervalle m
**laptop (computer)** ['læptɔp-] n
portable m
**lard** [lɑːd] n saindoux m
**larder** ['lɑːdəʳ] n garde-manger m inv
**large** [lɑːdʒ] adj grand(e); (person,

*animal*) gros (grosse); **at ~** (*free*) en liberté; (*generally*) en général; pour la plupart; *see also* **by**; **largely** *adv* en grande partie; (*principally*) surtout; **large-scale** *adj* (*map, drawing etc*) à grande échelle; (*fig*) important(e)

**lark** [lɑːk] *n* (*bird*) alouette *f*; (*joke*) blague *f*, farce *f*

**laryngitis** [lærɪnˈdʒaɪtɪs] *n* laryngite *f*

**lasagne** [ləˈzænjə] *n* lasagne *f*

**laser** [ˈleɪzəʳ] *n* laser *m*; **laser printer** *n* imprimante *f* laser

**lash** [læʃ] *n* coup *m* de fouet; (*also:* **eye~**) cil *m* ▷ *vt* fouetter; (*tie*) attacher; **lash out** *vi*: **to ~ out (at** *or* **against sb/sth)** attaquer violemment (qn/qch)

**lass** [læs] (*BRIT*) *n* (jeune) fille *f*

**last** [lɑːst] *adj* dernier(-ière) ▷ *adv* en dernier; (*most recently*) la dernière fois; (*finally*) finalement ▷ *vi* durer; **~ week** la semaine dernière; **~ night** (*evening*) hier soir; (*night*) la nuit dernière; **at ~** enfin; **~ but one** avant-dernier(-ière); **lastly** *adv* en dernier lieu, pour finir; **last-minute** *adj* de dernière minute

**latch** [lætʃ] *n* loquet *m*; **latch onto** *vt fus* (*cling to: person, group*) s'accrocher à; (*idea*) se mettre en tête

**late** [leɪt] *adj* (*not on time*) en retard; (*far on in day etc*) tardif(-ive); (*: edition, delivery*) dernier(-ière); (*dead*) défunt(e) ▷ *adv* tard; (*behind time, schedule*) en retard; **to be 10 minutes ~** avoir 10 minutes de retard; **sorry I'm ~** désolé d'être en retard; **it's too ~** il est trop tard; **of ~** dernièrement; **in ~ May** vers la fin (du mois) de mai, fin mai; **the ~ Mr X** feu M. X; **latecomer** *n* retardataire *m/f*; **lately** *adv* récemment; **later** *adj* (*date etc*) ultérieur(e); (*version etc*) plus récent(e) ▷ *adv* plus tard; **latest** [ˈleɪtɪst] *adj* tout(e) dernier(-ière); **at the latest** au plus tard

**lather** [ˈlɑːðəʳ] *n* mousse *f* (de savon) ▷ *vt* savonner

**Latin** [ˈlætɪn] *n* latin *m* ▷ *adj* latin(e); **Latin America** *n* Amérique latine;

**Latin American** *adj* latino-américain(e), d'Amérique latine ▷ *n* Latino-Américain(e)

**latitude** [ˈlætɪtjuːd] *n* (*also fig*) latitude *f*

**latter** [ˈlætəʳ] *adj* deuxième, dernier(-ière) ▷ *n*: **the ~** ce dernier, celui-ci

**laugh** [lɑːf] *n* rire *m* ▷ *vi* rire; **(to do sth) for a ~** (faire qch) pour rire; **laugh at** *vt fus* se moquer de; (*joke*) rire de; **laughter** *n* rire *m*; (*of several people*) rires *mpl*

**launch** [lɔːntʃ] *n* lancement *m*; (*also:* **motor ~**) vedette *f* ▷ *vt* (*ship, rocket, plan*) lancer; **launch into** *vt fus* se lancer dans

**launder** [ˈlɔːndəʳ] *vt* laver; (*fig: money*) blanchir

**Launderette®** [lɔːnˈdrɛt] (*BRIT*) (*US* **Laundromat®** [ˈlɔːndrəmæt]) *n* laverie *f* (automatique)

**laundry** [ˈlɔːndrɪ] *n* (*clothes*) linge *m*; (*business*) blanchisserie *f*; (*room*) buanderie *f*; **to do the ~** faire la lessive

**lava** [ˈlɑːvə] *n* lave *f*

**lavatory** [ˈlævətərɪ] *n* toilettes *fpl*

**lavender** [ˈlævəndəʳ] *n* lavande *f*

**lavish** [ˈlævɪʃ] *adj* (*amount*) copieux(-euse); (*person: giving freely*): **~ with** prodigue de ▷ *vt*: **to ~ sth on sb** prodiguer qch à qn; (*money*) dépenser qch sans compter pour qn

**law** [lɔː] *n* loi *f*; (*science*) droit *m*; **lawful** *adj* légal(e), permis(e); **lawless** *adj* (*action*) illégal(e); (*place*) sans loi

**lawn** [lɔːn] *n* pelouse *f*; **lawnmower** *n* tondeuse *f* à gazon

**lawsuit** [ˈlɔːsuːt] *n* procès *m*

**lawyer** [ˈlɔːjəʳ] *n* (*consultant, with company*) juriste *m*; (*for sales, wills etc*) ≈ notaire *m*; (*partner, in court*) ≈ avocat *m*

**lax** [læks] *adj* relâché(e)

**laxative** [ˈlæksətɪv] *n* laxatif *m*

**lay** [leɪ] *pt of* **lie** ▷ *adj* laïque; (*not expert*) profane ▷ *vt* (*pt, pp* **laid**) poser, mettre; (*eggs*) pondre; (*trap*) tendre; (*plans*) élaborer; **to ~ the table** mettre la table;

**lay down** vt poser; (*rules etc*) établir; **to ~ down the law** (*fig*) faire la loi; **lay off** vt (*workers*) licencier; (*provide: meal etc*) fournir; **lay out** vt (*design*) dessiner, concevoir; (*display*) disposer; (*spend*) dépenser; **lay-by** n (BRIT) aire f de stationnement (sur le bas-côté)

**layer** ['leɪə'] n couche f

**layman** ['leɪmən] (*irreg*) n (*Rel*) laïque m; (*non-expert*) profane m

**layout** ['leɪaut] n disposition f, plan m, agencement m; (*Press*) mise f en page

**lazy** ['leɪzɪ] adj paresseux(-euse)

**lb.** abbr (*weight*) = **pound**

**lead**[1] [liːd] n (*front position*) tête f; (*distance, time ahead*) avance f; (*clue*) piste f; (*Elec*) fil m; (*for dog*) laisse f; (*Theat*) rôle principal ▷ vb (*pt, pp* **led**) ▷ vt (*guide*) mener, conduire; (*be leader of*) être à la tête de ▷ vi (*Sport*) mener, être en tête; **to ~ to** (*road, pipe*) mener à, conduire à; (*result in*) conduire à; aboutir à; **to be in the ~** (*Sport: in race*) mener, être en tête; (: *in match*) mener (à la marque); **to ~ sb to do sth** amener qn à faire qch; **to ~ the way** montrer le chemin; **lead up to** vt conduire à; (*in conversation*) en venir à

**lead**[2] [lɛd] n (*metal*) plomb m; (*in pencil*) mine f

**leader** ['liːdə'] n (*of team*) chef m; (*of party etc*) dirigeant(e), leader m; (*Sport: in league*) leader m; (: *in race*) coureur m de tête; **leadership** n (*position*) direction f; **under the leadership of ...** sous la direction de ...; **qualities of leadership** qualités fpl de chef or de meneur

**lead-free** ['lɛdfriː] adj sans plomb

**leading** ['liːdɪŋ] adj de premier plan; (*main*) principal(e); (*in race*) de tête

**lead singer** [liːd-] n (*in pop group*) (chanteur m) vedette f

**leaf** (*pl* **leaves**) [liːf, liːvz] n feuille f; (*of table*) rallonge f; **to turn over a new ~** (*fig*) changer de conduite or d'existence; **leaf through** vt (*book*) feuilleter

**leaflet** ['liːflɪt] n prospectus m, brochure f; (*Pol, Rel*) tract m

**league** [liːg] n ligue f; (*Football*) championnat m; **to be in ~ with** avoir partie liée avec, être de mèche avec

**leak** [liːk] n (*out: also fig*) fuite f ▷ vi (*pipe, liquid etc*) fuir; (*shoes*) prendre l'eau; (*ship*) faire eau ▷ vt (*liquid*) répandre; (*information*) divulguer

**lean** [liːn] adj maigre ▷ vb (*pt, pp* **~ed** or **~t**) ▷ vt: **to ~ sth on** appuyer qch sur ▷ vi (*slope*) pencher; (*rest*): **to ~ against** s'appuyer contre; être appuyé(e) contre; **to ~ on** s'appuyer sur; **lean forward** vi se pencher en avant; **lean over** vi se pencher; **leaning** n: **leaning (towards)** penchant m (pour)

**leant** [lɛnt] pt, pp of **lean**

**leap** [liːp] n bond m, saut m ▷ vi (*pt, pp* **~ed** or **~t**) bondir, sauter

**leapt** [lɛpt] pt, pp of **leap**

**leap year** n année f bissextile

**learn** (*pt, pp* **~ed** or **~t**) [ləːn, -t] vt, vi apprendre; **to ~ (how) to do sth** apprendre à faire qch; **to ~ about sth** (*Scol*) étudier qch; (*hear, read*) apprendre qch; **learner** n débutant(e); (BRIT: *also*: **learner driver**) (conducteur(-trice)) débutant(e); **learning** n savoir m

**learnt** [ləːnt] pp of **learn**

**lease** [liːs] n bail m ▷ vt louer à bail

**leash** [liːʃ] n laisse f

**least** [liːst] adj: **the ~** (+ *noun*) le (la) plus petit(e), le (la) moindre; (*smallest amount of*) le moins de ▷ pron: **(the) ~** le moins ▷ adv (+ *verb*) le moins; (+ *adj*): **the ~** le (la) moins; (**the ~ money** le moins d'argent; **the ~ expensive** le (la) moins cher (chère); **the ~ possible effort** le moins d'effort possible; **at ~** au moins; (*or rather*) du moins; **you could at ~ have written** tu aurais au moins pu écrire; **not in the ~** pas le moins du monde

**leather** ['lɛðə'] n cuir m

**leave** [liːv] (*vb: pt, pp* **left**) vt laisser; (*go away from*) quitter; (*forget*) oublier ▷ vi partir, s'en aller ▷ n (*time off*) congé m; (*Mil, also: consent*) permission f; **what time does the train/bus ~?** le train/le

bus part à quelle heure?; **to ~ sth to
sb** (money etc) laisser qch à qn; **to be
left** rester; **there's some milk left
over** il reste du lait; **~ it to me!** laissez-
moi faire!, je m'en occupe!; **on ~** en
permission; **leave behind** vt (also fig)
laisser; (forget) laisser, oublier; **leave
out** vt oublier, omettre

**leaves** [liːvz] npl of **leaf**

**Lebanon** ['lɛbənən] n Liban m

**lecture** ['lɛktʃər] n conférence f;
(Scol) cours (magistral) ▷ vi donner
des cours; enseigner ▷ vt (scold)
sermonner, réprimander; **to give
a ~ (on)** faire une conférence (sur),
faire un cours (sur); **lecture hall** n
amphithéâtre m; **lecturer** n (speaker)
conférencier(-ière); (BRIT: at university)
professeur m (d'université), prof m/f de
fac (inf); **lecture theatre** n = **lecture
hall**

> Be careful not to translate **lecture**
> by the French word **lecture**.

**led** [lɛd] pt, pp of **lead¹**

**ledge** [lɛdʒ] n (of window, on wall) rebord
m; (of mountain) saillie f, corniche f

**leek** [liːk] n poireau m

**left** [lɛft] pt, pp of **leave** ▷ adj gauche
▷ adv à gauche ▷ n gauche f; **there
are two ~** il en reste deux; **on the
~, to the ~** à gauche; **the L~** (Pol) la
gauche; **left-hand** adj: **the left-hand
side** la gauche; **left-hand drive**
n (BRIT: vehicle) véhicule m avec la
conduite à gauche; **left-handed**
adj gaucher(-ère); (scissors etc) pour
gauchers; **left-luggage locker** n (BRIT)
(casier m à) consigne f automatique;
**left-luggage (office)** n (BRIT)
consigne f; **left-overs** npl restes mpl;
**left-wing** adj (Pol) de gauche

**leg** [lɛg] n jambe f; (of animal) patte f;
(of furniture) pied m; (Culin: of chicken)
cuisse f; (of journey) étape f; **1st/2nd ~**
(Sport) match m aller/retour; **~ of lamb**
(Culin) gigot m d'agneau

**legacy** ['lɛgəsɪ] n (also fig) héritage
m, legs m

**legal** ['liːgl] adj (permitted by law)
légal(e); (relating to law) juridique; **legal
holiday** (US) n jour férié; **legalize** vt
légaliser; **legally** adv légalement

**legend** ['lɛdʒənd] n légende f;
**legendary** ['lɛdʒəndərɪ] adj légendaire

**leggings** ['lɛgɪŋz] npl caleçon m

**legible** ['lɛdʒəbl] adj lisible

**legislation** [lɛdʒɪs'leɪʃən] n
législation f

**legislative** ['lɛdʒɪslətɪv] adj
législatif(-ive)

**legitimate** [lɪ'dʒɪtɪmət] adj légitime

**leisure** ['lɛʒər] n (free time) temps libre,
loisirs mpl; **at ~ (tout)** à loisir; **at your ~**
(later) à tête reposée; **leisure centre** n
(BRIT) centre m de loisirs; **leisurely** adj
tranquille, fait(e) sans se presser

**lemon** ['lɛmən] n citron m; **lemonade**
n (fizzy) limonade f; **lemon tea** n thé
m au citron

**lend** (pt, pp **lent**) [lɛnd, lɛnt] vt: **to ~ sth
(to sb)** prêter qch (à qn); **could you ~
me some money?** pourriez-vous me
prêter de l'argent?

**length** [lɛŋθ] n longueur f; (section: of
road, pipe etc) morceau m, bout m; **~ of
time** durée f; **it is 2 metres in ~** cela fait
2 mètres de long; **at ~** (at last) enfin, à la
fin; (lengthily) longuement; **lengthen**
vt allonger, prolonger ▷ vi s'allonger;
**lengthways** adv dans le sens de la
longueur, en long; **lengthy** adj (très)
long (longue)

**lens** [lɛnz] n lentille f; (of spectacles)
verre m; (of camera) objectif m

**Lent** [lɛnt] n carême m

**lent** [lɛnt] pt, pp of **lend**

**lentil** ['lɛntl] n lentille f

**Leo** ['liːəu] n le Lion

**leopard** ['lɛpəd] n léopard m

**leotard** ['liːətɑːd] n justaucorps m

**leprosy** ['lɛprəsɪ] n lèpre f

**lesbian** ['lɛzbɪən] n lesbienne f ▷ adj
lesbien(ne)

**less** [lɛs] adj moins de ▷ pron, adv moins
▷ prep: **~ tax/10% discount** avant
impôt/moins 10% de remise; **~ than**

**that/you** moins que cela/vous; **~ than half** moins de la moitié; **~ than ever** moins que jamais; **~ and ~** de moins en moins; **the ~ he works ...** moins il travaille ...; **lessen** vi diminuer, s'amoindrir, s'atténuer ▷ vt diminuer, réduire, atténuer; **lesser** ['lɛsə<sup>r</sup>] adj moindre; **to a lesser extent** or **degree** à un degré moindre

**lesson** ['lɛsn] n leçon f; **to teach sb a ~** (fig) donner une bonne leçon à qn

**let** (pt, pp ~~) [lɛt] vt laisser; (BRIT: lease) louer; **to ~ sb do sth** laisser qn faire qch; **to ~ sb know sth** faire savoir qch à qn, prévenir qn de qch; **to ~ go** lâcher prise; **to ~ go of sth, to ~ sth go** lâcher qch; **~'s go** allons-y; **~ him come** qu'il vienne; **"to ~"** (BRIT) "à louer"; **let down** vt (lower) baisser; (BRIT: tyre) dégonfler; (disappoint) décevoir; **let in** vt laisser entrer; (visitor etc) faire entrer; **let off** vt (allow to leave) laisser partir; (not punish) ne pas punir; (firework etc) faire partir; (bomb) faire exploser; **let out** vt laisser sortir; (scream) laisser échapper; (BRIT: rent out) louer

**lethal** ['liːθl] adj mortel(le), fatal(e); (weapon) meurtrier(-ère)

**letter** ['lɛtə<sup>r</sup>] n lettre f; **letterbox** n (BRIT) boîte f aux or à lettres

**lettuce** ['lɛtɪs] n laitue f, salade f

**leukaemia** (US **leukemia**) [luːˈkiːmɪə] n leucémie f

**level** ['lɛvl] adj (flat) plat(e), plan(e), uni(e); (horizontal) horizontal(e) ▷ n niveau m ▷ vt niveler, aplanir; **"A" ~s** npl (BRIT) ≈ baccalauréat m; **to be ~ with** être au même niveau que; **to draw ~ with** (runner, car) arriver à la hauteur de, rattraper; **on the ~** (fig: honest) régulier(-ière); **level crossing** n (BRIT) passage m à niveau

**lever** ['liːvə<sup>r</sup>] n levier m; **leverage** n (influence): **leverage (on** or **with)** prise f (sur)

**levy** ['lɛvɪ] n taxe f, impôt m ▷ vt (tax) lever; (fine) infliger

**liability** [laɪəˈbɪlətɪ] n responsabilité f;

(handicap) handicap m

**liable** ['laɪəbl] adj (subject): **~ to** sujet(te) à, passible de; (responsible): **~ (for)** responsable (de); (likely): **~ to do** susceptible de faire

**liaise** [liːˈeɪz] vi: **to ~ with** assurer la liaison avec

**liar** ['laɪə<sup>r</sup>] n menteur(-euse)

**libel** ['laɪbl] n diffamation f; (document) écrit m diffamatoire ▷ vt diffamer

**liberal** ['lɪbərl] adj libéral(e); (generous): **~ with** prodigue de, généreux(-euse) avec ▷ n: **L~** (Pol) libéral(e); **Liberal Democrat** n (BRIT) libéral(e)-démocrate m/f

**liberate** ['lɪbəreɪt] vt libérer

**liberation** [lɪbəˈreɪʃən] n libération f

**liberty** ['lɪbətɪ] n liberté f; **to be at ~** (criminal) être en liberté; **at ~ to do** libre de faire; **to take the ~ of** prendre la liberté de, se permettre de

**Libra** ['liːbrə] n la Balance

**librarian** [laɪˈbrɛərɪən] n bibliothécaire m/f

**library** ['laɪbrərɪ] n bibliothèque f

> Be careful not to translate *library* by the French word *librairie*.

**Libya** ['lɪbɪə] n Libye f

**lice** [laɪs] npl of **louse**

**licence** (US **license**) ['laɪsns] n autorisation f, permis m; (Comm) licence f; (Radio, TV) redevance f; (also: **driving ~**, US: also: **driver's license**) permis m (de conduire)

**license** ['laɪsns] n (US) = **licence**; **licensed** adj (for alcohol) patenté(e) pour la vente des spiritueux, qui a une patente de débit de boissons; (car) muni(e) de la vignette; **license plate** n (US Aut) plaque f minéralogique; **licensing hours** (BRIT) npl heures fpl d'ouvertures (des pubs)

**lick** [lɪk] vt lécher; (inf: defeat) écraser, flanquer une piquette or raclée à; **to ~ one's lips** (fig) se frotter les mains

**lid** [lɪd] n couvercle m; (eyelid) paupière f

**lie** [laɪ] n mensonge m ▷ vi (pt, pp ~d) (tell lies) mentir; (pt **lay**, pp **lain**) (rest) être étendu(e) or allongé(e) or couché(e); (object: be situated) se trouver, être; **to ~ low** (fig) se cacher, rester caché(e); **to tell ~s** mentir; **lie about, lie around** vi (things) traîner; (BRIT: person) traînasser, flemmarder; **lie down** vi se coucher, s'étendre

**Liechtenstein** ['lɪktənstaɪn] n Liechtenstein m

**lie-in** ['laɪɪn] n (BRIT): **to have a ~** faire la grasse matinée

**lieutenant** [lɛf'tɛnənt, US lu:'tɛnənt] n lieutenant m

**life** (pl **lives**) [laɪf, laɪvz] n vie f; **to come to ~** (fig) s'animer; **life assurance** n (BRIT) = **life insurance**; **lifeboat** n canot m or chaloupe f de sauvetage; **lifeguard** n surveillant m de baignade; **life insurance** n assurance-vie f; **life jacket** n gilet m or ceinture f de sauvetage; **lifelike** adj qui semble vrai(e) or vivant(e), ressemblant(e); (painting) réaliste; **life preserver** n (US) gilet m or ceinture f de sauvetage; **life sentence** n condamnation f à vie or à perpétuité; **lifestyle** n style m de vie; **lifetime** n: **in his lifetime** du vivant

**lift** [lɪft] vt soulever, lever; (end) supprimer, lever ▷ vi (fog) se lever ▷ n (BRIT: elevator) ascenseur m; **to give sb a ~** (BRIT) emmener or prendre qn en voiture; **can you give me a ~ to the station?** pouvez-vous m'emmener à la gare?; **lift up** vt soulever; **lift-off** n décollage m

**light** [laɪt] n lumière f; (lamp) lampe f; (Aut: rear light) feu m; (: headlamp) phare m; (for cigarette etc): **have you got a ~?** avez-vous du feu? ▷ vt (pt, pp **~ed** or **lit**) (candle, cigarette, fire) allumer; (room) éclairer ▷ adj (room, colour) clair(e); (not heavy, also fig) léger(-ère); (not strenuous) peu fatigant(e); **lights** npl (traffic lights) feux mpl; **to come to ~** être dévoilé(e) or découvert(e); **in the ~ of** à la lumière de; étant donné; **light up** vi s'allumer; (face) s'éclairer; (smoke) allumer une cigarette or une pipe etc ▷ vt (illuminate)

éclairer, illuminer; **light bulb** n ampoule f; **lighten** vt (light up) éclairer; (make lighter) éclaircir; (make less heavy) alléger; **lighter** n (also: cigarette lighter) briquet m; **light-hearted** adj gai(e), joyeux(-euse), enjoué(e); **lighthouse** n phare m; **lighting** n éclairage m; (in theatre) éclairages; **lightly** adv légèrement; **to get off lightly** s'en tirer à bon compte

**lightning** ['laɪtnɪŋ] n foudre f; (flash) éclair m

**lightweight** ['laɪtweɪt] adj (suit) léger(-ère) ▷ n (Boxing) poids léger

**like** [laɪk] vt aimer (bien) ▷ prep comme ▷ adj semblable, pareil(le) ▷ n: **the ~** (pej) (d')autres du même genre or acabit; **his ~s and dislikes** ses goûts mpl or préférences fpl; **I would ~, I'd ~** je voudrais, j'aimerais; **would you ~ a coffee?** voulez-vous du café?; **to be/look ~ sb/sth** ressembler à qn/qch; **what's he ~?** comment est-il?; **what does it look ~?** de quoi est-ce que ça a l'air?; **what does it taste ~?** quel goût est-ce que ça a?; **that's just ~ him** c'est bien de lui, ça lui ressemble; **do it ~ this** fais-le comme ceci; **it's nothing ~ ...** ce n'est pas du tout comme ...; **likeable** adj sympathique, agréable

**likelihood** ['laɪklɪhud] n probabilité f

**likely** ['laɪklɪ] adj (result, outcome) probable; (excuse) plausible; **he's ~ to leave** il va sûrement partir, il risque fort de partir; **not ~!** (inf) pas de danger!

**likewise** ['laɪkwaɪz] adv de même, pareillement

**liking** ['laɪkɪŋ] n (for person) affection f; (for thing) penchant m, goût m; **to be to sb's ~** être au goût de qn, plaire à qn

**lilac** ['laɪlək] n lilas m

**Lilo®** ['laɪləu] n matelas m pneumatique

**lily** ['lɪlɪ] n lis m; **~ of the valley** muguet m

**limb** [lɪm] n membre m

**limbo** ['lɪmbəu] n: **to be in ~** (fig) être tombé(e) dans l'oubli

**lime** [laɪm] n (tree) tilleul m; (fruit) citron vert, lime f; (Geo) chaux f

**limelight** ['laɪmlaɪt] n: **in the ~** (fig) en vedette, au premier plan

**limestone** ['laɪmstəun] n pierre f à chaux; (Geo) calcaire m

**limit** ['lɪmɪt] n limite f ▷ vt limiter; **limited** adj limité(e), restreint(e); **to be limited to** se limiter à, ne concerner que

**limousine** ['lɪməziːn] n limousine f

**limp** [lɪmp] n: **to have a ~** boiter ▷ vi boiter ▷ adj mou (molle)

**line** [laɪn] n (gen) ligne f; (stroke) trait m; (wrinkle) ride f; (rope) corde f; (wire) fil m; (of poem) vers m; (row, series) rangée f; (of people) file f, queue f; (railway track) voie f; (Comm: series of goods) article(s) m(pl), ligne de produits; (work) métier m ▷ vt: **to ~ (with)** (clothes) doubler (de); (box) garnir or tapisser (de); (subj: trees, crowd) border; **to stand in ~** (us) faire la queue; **in his ~ of business** dans sa partie, dans son rayon; **to be in ~ for sth** (fig) être en lice pour qch; **in ~ with** en accord avec, en conformité avec; **in a ~** aligné(e); **line up** vi s'aligner, se mettre en rang(s); (in queue) faire la queue ▷ vt aligner; (event) prévoir; (find) trouver; **to have sb/sth ~d up** avoir qn/qch en vue or de prévu(e)

**linear** ['lɪnɪər] adj linéaire

**linen** ['lɪnɪn] n linge m (de corps or de maison); (cloth) lin m

**liner** ['laɪnər] n (ship) paquebot m de ligne; (for bin) sac-poubelle m

**line-up** ['laɪnʌp] n (us: queue) file f; (also: **police ~**) parade f d'identification; (Sport) composition f de l'équipe f

**linger** ['lɪŋgər] vi s'attarder; traîner; (smell, tradition) persister

**lingerie** ['lænʒəriː] n lingerie f

**linguist** ['lɪŋgwɪst] n linguiste m/f; **to be a good ~** être doué(e) pour les langues; **linguistic** adj linguistique

**lining** ['laɪnɪŋ] n doublure f; (of brakes) garniture f

**link** [lɪŋk] n (connection) lien m, rapport m; (Internet) lien m; (of a chain) maillon m ▷ vt relier, lier, unir; **links** npl (Golf) (terrain m de) golf m; **link up** vt relier ▷ vi (people) se rejoindre; (companies etc) s'associer

**lion** ['laɪən] n lion m; **lioness** n lionne f

**lip** [lɪp] n lèvre f; (of cup etc) rebord m; **lipread** vi lire sur les lèvres; **lip salve** [-sælv] n pommade f pour les lèvres, pommade rosat; **lipstick** n rouge m à lèvres

**liqueur** [lɪˈkjuər] n liqueur f

**liquid** ['lɪkwɪd] n liquide m ▷ adj liquide; **liquidizer** ['lɪkwɪdaɪzər] n (Brit Culin) mixer m

**liquor** ['lɪkər] n spiritueux m, alcool m; **liquor store** n (us) magasin m de vins et spiritueux

**Lisbon** ['lɪzbən] n Lisbonne

**lisp** [lɪsp] n zézaiement m ▷ vi zézayer

**list** [lɪst] n liste f ▷ vt (write down) inscrire; (make list of) faire la liste de; (enumerate) énumérer

**listen** ['lɪsn] vi écouter; **to ~ to** écouter; **listener** n auditeur(-trice)

**lit** [lɪt] pt, pp of **light**

**liter** ['liːtər] n (us) = **litre**

**literacy** ['lɪtərəsɪ] n degré m d'alphabétisation, fait m de savoir lire et écrire

**literal** ['lɪtərl] adj littéral(e); **literally** adv littéralement; (really) réellement

**literary** ['lɪtərərɪ] adj littéraire

**literate** ['lɪtərət] adj qui sait lire et écrire; (educated) instruit(e)

**literature** ['lɪtrɪtʃər] n littérature f; (brochures etc) copie f publicitaire, prospectus mpl

**litre** (us **liter**) ['liːtər] n litre m

**litter** ['lɪtər] n (rubbish) détritus mpl; (dirtier) ordures fpl; (young animals) portée f; **litter bin** n (Brit) poubelle f; **littered** adj: **littered with** (scattered) jonché(e) de

**little** ['lɪtl] adj (small) petit(e); (not much): **~ milk** peu de lait ▷ adv peu; **a ~** un peu (de); **a ~ milk** un peu de lait; **a ~ bit** un peu; **as ~ as possible**

le moins possible; **~ by ~** petit à petit, peu à peu; **little finger** n auriculaire m, petit doigt

**live**[1] [laɪv] adj (animal) vivant(e), en vie; (wire) sous tension; (broadcast) (transmis(e)) en direct; (unexploded) non explosé(e)

**live**[2] [lɪv] vi vivre; (reside) vivre, habiter; **to ~ in London** habiter (à) Londres; **where do you ~?** où habitez-vous?; **live together** vivre ensemble, cohabiter; **live up to** vt fus se montrer à la hauteur de

**livelihood** ['laɪvlɪhud] n moyens mpl d'existence

**lively** ['laɪvlɪ] adj vif (vive), plein(e) d'entrain; (place, book) vivant(e)

**liven up** ['laɪvn-] vt (room etc) égayer; (discussion, evening) animer ▷ vi s'animer

**liver** ['lɪvəʳ] n foie m

**lives** [laɪvz] npl of **life**

**livestock** ['laɪvstɔk] n cheptel m, bétail m

**living** ['lɪvɪŋ] adj vivant(e), en vie ▷ n: **to earn** or **make a ~** gagner sa vie; **living room** n salle f de séjour

**lizard** ['lɪzəd] n lézard m

**load** [ləud] n (weight) poids m; (thing carried) chargement m, charge f; (Elec, Tech) charge f ▷ vt (also: **~ up**): **to ~ (with)** (lorry, ship) charger (de); (gun, camera) charger (avec); (Comput) charger; **a ~ of**, **~s of** (fig) un or des tas de, des masses de; **to talk a ~ of rubbish** (inf) dire des bêtises; **loaded** adj (dice) pipé(e); (question) insidieux(-euse); (inf: rich) bourré(e) de fric

**loaf** (pl **loaves**) [ləuf, ləuvz] n pain m, miche f ▷ vi (also: **~ about**, **~ around**) fainéanter, traîner

**loan** [ləun] n prêt m ▷ vt prêter; **on ~** prêté(e), en prêt

**loathe** [ləuð] vt détester, avoir en horreur

**loaves** [ləuvz] npl of **loaf**

**lobby** ['lɔbɪ] n hall m, entrée f; (Pol) groupe m de pression, lobby m ▷ vt faire pression sur

**lobster** ['lɔbstəʳ] n homard m

**local** ['ləukl] adj local(e) ▷ n (BRIT: pub) pub m or café m du coin; **the locals** npl les gens mpl du pays or du coin; **local anaesthetic** n anesthésie locale; **local authority** n collectivité locale, municipalité f; **local government** n administration locale or municipale; **locally** ['ləukəlɪ] adv localement; dans les environs or la région

**locate** [ləu'keɪt] vt (find) trouver, repérer; (situate) situer; **to be ~d in** être situé e or en

**location** [ləu'keɪʃən] n emplacement m; **on ~** (Cine) en extérieur

▌ Be careful not to translate *location* by the French word *location*.

**loch** [lɔx] n lac m, loch m

**lock** [lɔk] n (of door, box) serrure f; (of canal) écluse f; (of hair) mèche f, boucle f ▷ vt (with key) fermer à clé ▷ vi (door etc) fermer à clé; (wheels) se bloquer; **lock in** vt enfermer; **lock out** vt enfermer dehors; (on purpose) mettre à la porte; **lock up** vt (person) enfermer; (house) fermer à clé ▷ vi tout fermer (à clé)

**locker** ['lɔkəʳ] n casier m; (in station) consigne f automatique; **locker-room** (US) n (Sport) vestiaire m

**locksmith** ['lɔksmɪθ] n serrurier m

**locomotive** [ləukə'məutɪv] n locomotive f

**locum** ['ləukəm] n (Med) suppléant(e) de médecin etc

**lodge** [lɔdʒ] n pavillon m (de gardien); (also: **hunting ~**) pavillon de chasse ▷ vi (person): **to ~ with** être logé(e) chez, être en pension chez; (bullet) se loger ▷ vt (appeal etc) présenter; déposer; **to ~ a complaint** porter plainte; **lodger** n locataire m/f; (with room and meals) pensionnaire m/f

**lodging** ['lɔdʒɪŋ] n logement m

**loft** [lɔft] n grenier m; (apartment) grenier aménagé (en appartement) (gén dans ancien entrepôt ou fabrique)

**log** [lɒg] n (of wood) bûche f; (Naut) livre m or journal m de bord; (of car) ≈ carte grise ▷ vt enregistrer; **log in, log on** vi (Comput) ouvrir une session, entrer dans le système; **log off, log out** vi (Comput) clore une session, sortir du système

**logic** [ˈlɒdʒɪk] n logique f; **logical** adj logique

**logo** [ˈləʊgəʊ] n logo m

**Loire** [lwaː] n: **the (River)** ~ la Loire

**lollipop** [ˈlɒlɪpɒp] n sucette f; **lollipop man/lady** (BRIT: irreg) n contractuel qui fait traverser la rue aux enfants

**lolly** [ˈlɒlɪ] n (inf: ice) esquimau m; (: lollipop) sucette f

**London** [ˈlʌndən] n Londres; **Londoner** n Londonien(ne)

**lone** [ləʊn] adj solitaire

**loneliness** [ˈləʊnlɪnɪs] n solitude f, isolement m

**lonely** [ˈləʊnlɪ] adj seul(e); (childhood etc) solitaire; (place) solitaire, isolé(e)

**long** [lɒŋ] adj long (longue) ▷ adv longtemps ▷ vi: **to ~ for sth/to do sth** avoir très envie de qch/de faire qch, attendre qch avec impatience/ attendre avec impatience de faire qch; **how ~ is this river/course?** quelle est la longueur de ce fleuve/la durée de ce cours?; **6 metres** ~ (long) de 6 mètres; **6 months** ~ qui dure 6 mois, de 6 mois; **all night** ~ toute la nuit; **he no ~er comes** il ne vient plus; **I can't stand it any ~er** je ne peux plus le supporter; **~ before** longtemps avant; **before** ~ (+ future) avant peu, dans peu de temps; (+ past) peu de temps après; **don't be ~!** fais vite!, dépêche-toi!; **I shan't be ~** je n'en ai pas pour longtemps; **at ~ last** enfin; **so** or **as ~ as** à condition que + sub; **long-distance** adj (race) de fond; (call) interurbain(e); **long-haul** adj (flight) long-courrier; **longing** n désir m, envie f; (nostalgia) nostalgie f ▷ adj plein(e) d'envie or de nostalgie

**longitude** [ˈlɒŋgɪtjuːd] n longitude f

**long**: **long jump** n saut m en longueur;

**long-life** adj (batteries etc) longue durée inv; (milk) longue conservation; **long-sighted** adj (BRIT) presbyte; (fig) prévoyant(e); **long-standing** adj de longue date; **long-term** adj à long terme

**loo** [luː] n (BRIT inf) w.-c mpl, petit coin

**look** [lʊk] vi regarder; (seem) sembler, paraître, avoir l'air; (building etc): **to ~ south/on to the sea** donner au sud/ sur la mer ▷ n regard m; (appearance) air m, allure f, aspect m; **looks** npl (good looks) physique m, beauté f; **to ~ like** ressembler à; **to have a ~** regarder; **to have a ~ at sth** jeter un coup d'œil à qch; **~ (here)!** (annoyance) écoutez!; **look after** vt fus s'occuper de; (luggage etc: watch over) garder, surveiller; **look around** vi regarder autour de soi; **look at** vt fus regarder; (problem etc) examiner; **look back** vi: **to ~ back at sth/sb** se retourner pour regarder qch/qn; **to ~ back on** (event, period) évoquer, repenser à; **look down on** vt fus (fig) regarder de haut, dédaigner; **look for** vt fus chercher; **we're ~ing for a hotel/restaurant** nous cherchons un hôtel/restaurant; **look forward to** vt fus attendre avec impatience; **~ing forward to hearing from you** (in letter) dans l'attente de vous lire; **look into** vt fus (matter, possibility) examiner, étudier; **look out** vi (beware): **to ~ out (for)** prendre garde (à), faire attention (à); **~ out!** attention!; **look out for** vt fus (seek) être à la recherche de; (try to spot) guetter; **look round** vt fus (house, shop) faire le tour de ▷ vi (turn) regarder derrière soi, se retourner; **look through** vt fus (papers, book) examiner; (: briefly) parcourir; **look up** vi lever les yeux; (improve) s'améliorer ▷ vt (word) chercher; **look up to** vt fus avoir du respect pour; **lookout** n (tower etc) poste m de guet; (person) guetteur m; **to be on the lookout (for)** guetter

**loom** [luːm] n vi (also: ~ **up**) surgir; (event) paraître imminent(e); (threaten) menacer

**loony** ['luːnɪ] *adj, n* (*inf*) timbré(e), cinglé(e) *m/f*

**loop** [luːp] *n* boucle *f* ▷ *vt*: **to ~ sth round sth** passer qch autour de qch; **loophole** *n* (*fig*) porte *f* de sortie; échappatoire *f*

**loose** [luːs] *adj* (*knot, screw*) desserré(e); (*clothes*) vague, ample, lâche; (*hair*) dénoué(e), épars(e); (*not firmly fixed*) pas solide; (*morals, discipline*) relâché(e); (*translation*) approximatif(-ive) ▷ *n*: **to be on the ~** être en liberté; **~ connection** (*Elec*) mauvais contact; **to be at a ~ end** *or* (*US*) **at ~ ends** (*fig*) ne pas trop savoir quoi faire; **loosely** *adv* sans serrer; (*imprecisely*) approximativement; **loosen** *vt* desserrer, relâcher, défaire

**loot** [luːt] *n* butin *m* ▷ *vt* piller

**lop-sided** ['lɔp'saɪdɪd] *adj* de travers, asymétrique

**lord** [lɔːd] *n* seigneur *m*; **L~ Smith** lord Smith; **the L~** (*Rel*) le Seigneur; **my L~** (*to noble*) Monsieur le comte/le baron; (*to judge*) Monsieur le juge; (*to bishop*) Monseigneur; **good L~!** mon Dieu!; **Lords** *npl* (*BRIT: Pol*): **the (House of) Lords** (*BRIT*) la Chambre des Lords

**lorry** ['lɔrɪ] *n* (*BRIT*) camion *m*; **lorry driver** *n* (*BRIT*) camionneur *m*, routier *m*

**lose** (*pt, pp* **lost**) [luːz, lɔst] *vt* perdre ▷ *vi* perdre; **I've lost my wallet/passport** j'ai perdu mon portefeuille/passeport; **to ~ (time)** (*clock*) retarder; **lose out** *vi* être perdant(e); **loser** *n* perdant(e)

**loss** [lɔs] *n* perte *f*; **to make a ~** enregistrer une perte; **to be at a ~** être perplexe *or* embarrassé(e)

**lost** [lɔst] *pt, pp of* **lose** ▷ *adj* perdu(e); **to get ~** *vi* se perdre; **I'm ~** je me suis perdu; **~ and found property** *n* (*US*) objets trouvés; **~ and found** *n* (*US*) (bureau *m* des) objets trouvés; **lost property** *n* (*BRIT*) objets trouvés; **lost property office** *or* **department** (bureau *m* des) objets trouvés

**lot** [lɔt] *n* (*at auctions, set*) lot *m*; (*destiny*) sort *m*, destinée *f*; **the ~** (*everything*) le tout; (*everyone*) tous *mpl*, toutes *fpl*; **a ~** beaucoup; **a ~ of** beaucoup de; **~s of** des tas de; **to draw ~s (for sth)** tirer (qch) au sort

**lotion** ['ləuʃən] *n* lotion *f*

**lottery** ['lɔtərɪ] *n* loterie *f*

**loud** [laud] *adj* bruyant(e), sonore; (*voice*) fort(e); (*condemnation etc*) vigoureux(-euse); (*gaudy*) voyant(e), tapageur(-euse) ▷ *adv* (*speak etc*) fort; **out ~** tout haut; **loudly** *adv* fort, bruyamment; **loudspeaker** *n* haut-parleur *m*

**lounge** [laundʒ] *n* salon *m*; (*of airport*) salle *f*; (*BRIT: also*: **~ bar**) (salle de) café *m* *or* bar *m* ▷ *vi* (*also*: **~ about** *or* **around**) se prélasser, paresser

**louse** (*pl* **lice**) [laus, laɪs] *n* pou *m*

**lousy** ['lauzɪ] (*inf*) *adj* (*bad quality*) infect(e), moche; **I feel ~** je suis mal fichu(e)

**love** [lʌv] *n* amour *m* ▷ *vt* aimer; (*caringly, kindly*) aimer beaucoup; **I ~ chocolate** j'adore le chocolat; **to ~ to do** aimer beaucoup *or* adorer faire; **"15 ~"** (*Tennis*) "15 à rien *or* zéro"; **to be/fall in ~ with** être/tomber amoureux(-euse) de; **to make ~** faire l'amour; **~ from Anne, ~,** Anne affectueusement, Anne; **I ~ you** je t'aime; **love affair** *n* liaison (amoureuse); **love life** *n* vie sentimentale

**lovely** ['lʌvlɪ] *adj* (*pretty*) ravissant(e); (*friend, wife*) charmant(e); (*holiday, surprise*) très agréable, merveilleux(-euse)

**lover** ['lʌvə<sup>r</sup>] *n* amant *m*; (*person in love*) amoureux(-euse); (*amateur*): **a ~ of** un(e) ami(e) de, un(e) amoureux(-euse) de

**loving** ['lʌvɪŋ] *adj* affectueux(-euse), tendre, aimant(e)

**low** [ləu] *adj* bas (basse); (*quality*) mauvais(e), inférieur(e) ▷ *adv* bas ▷ *n* (*Meteorology*) dépression *f*; **to feel ~** se sentir déprimé(e); **he's very ~** (ill) il est bien bas or très affaibli; **to turn (down) ~** vt baisser; **to be ~ on** (supplies etc) être à court de; **to reach a new** or **an all-time ~** tomber au niveau le plus bas; **low-alcohol** adj à faible teneur en alcool, peu alcoolisé(e); **low-calorie** adj hypocalorique

**lower** ['ləuə'] adj inférieur(e) ▷ vt baisser; (resistance) diminuer; **to ~ o.s. to** s'abaisser à

**low-fat** ['ləu'fæt] adj maigre

**loyal** ['lɔɪəl] adj loyal(e), fidèle; **loyalty** n loyauté f, fidélité f; **loyalty card** n carte f de fidélité

**L.P.** n abbr = **long-playing record**

**L-plates** ['ɛlpleɪts] npl (BRIT) plaques fpl (obligatoires) d'apprenti conducteur

**Lt** abbr (= lieutenant) Lt.

**Ltd** abbr (Comm: company: = limited) ≈ S.A.

**luck** [lʌk] n chance f; **bad ~** malchance f, malheur m; **good ~!** bonne chance!; **bad** or **hard** or **tough ~!** pas de chance!; **luckily** adv heureusement, par bonheur; **lucky** adj (person) qui a de la chance; (coincidence) heureux(-euse); (number etc) qui porte bonheur

**lucrative** ['lu:krətɪv] adj lucratif(-ive), rentable, qui rapporte

**ludicrous** ['lu:dɪkrəs] adj ridicule, absurde

**luggage** ['lʌgɪdʒ] n bagages mpl; **our ~ hasn't arrived** nos bagages ne sont pas arrivés; **could you send someone to collect our ~?** pourriez-vous envoyer quelqu'un chercher nos bagages?; **luggage rack** n (in train) porte-bagages m inv; (: on car) galerie f

**lukewarm** ['lu:kwɔ:m] adj tiède

**lull** [lʌl] n accalmie f; (in conversation) pause f ▷ vt: **to ~ sb to sleep** bercer qn pour qu'il s'endorme; **to be ~ed into a false sense of security** s'endormir dans une fausse sécurité

**lullaby** ['lʌləbaɪ] n berceuse f

**lumber** ['lʌmbə'] n (wood) bois m de charpente; (junk) bric-à-brac m inv ▷ vt (BRIT inf): **to ~ sb with sth/sb** coller or

refiler qch/qn à qn

**luminous** ['lu:mɪnəs] adj lumineux(-euse)

**lump** [lʌmp] n morceau m; (in sauce) grumeau m; (swelling) grosseur f ▷ vt (also: **~ together**) réunir, mettre en tas; **lump sum** n somme globale or forfaitaire; **lumpy** adj (sauce) qui a des grumeaux; (bed) défoncé(e), peu confortable

**lunatic** ['lu:nətɪk] n fou (folle), dément(e) ▷ adj fou (folle), dément(e)

**lunch** [lʌntʃ] n déjeuner m ▷ vi déjeuner; **lunch break, lunch hour** n pause f de midi, heure f du déjeuner; **lunchtime** n: **it's lunchtime** c'est l'heure du déjeuner

**lung** [lʌŋ] n poumon m

**lure** [luə'] n (attraction) attrait m, charme m; (in hunting) appât m, leurre m ▷ vt attirer or persuader par la ruse

**lurk** [lə:k] vi se tapir, se cacher

**lush** [lʌʃ] adj luxuriant(e)

**lust** [lʌst] n (sexual) désir (sexuel); (Rel) luxure f; (fig): **~ for** soif f de

**Luxembourg** ['lʌksəmbə:g] n Luxembourg m

**luxurious** [lʌg'zjuərɪəs] adj luxueux(-euse)

**luxury** ['lʌkʃərɪ] n luxe m ▷ cpd de luxe

**Lycra®** ['laɪkrə] n Lycra® m

**lying** ['laɪɪŋ] n mensonge(s) m(pl) ▷ adj (statement, story) mensonger(-ère), faux (fausse); (person) menteur(-euse)

**Lyons** ['ljɔ̃] n Lyon

**lyrics** ['lɪrɪks] npl (of song) paroles fpl

**m**

**m.** *abbr* (= *metre*) m; (= *million*) M; (= *mile*) mi

**M.A.** *n abbr* (*Scol*) = **Master of Arts**

**ma** [mɑ:] (*inf*) *n* maman *f*

**mac** [mæk] *n* (*BRIT*) imper(méable *m*) *m*

**macaroni** [mækə'rəʊnɪ] *n* macaronis *mpl*

**Macedonia** [mæsɪ'dəʊnɪə] *n* Macédoine *f*; **Macedonian** [mæsɪ'dəʊnɪən] *adj* macédonien(ne) ▷ *n* Macédonien(ne); (*Ling*) macédonien *m*

**machine** [mə'ʃi:n] *n* machine *f* ▷ *vt* (*dress etc*) coudre à la machine; (*Tech*) usiner; **machine gun** *n* mitrailleuse *f*; **machinery** *n* machinerie *f*, machines *fpl*; (*fig*) mécanisme(s) *m(pl)*; **machine washable** *adj* (*garment*) lavable en machine

**macho** ['mætʃəʊ] *adj* macho *inv*

**mackerel** ['mækrl] *n* (*pl inv*) maquereau *m*

**mackintosh** ['mækɪntɔʃ] *n* (*BRIT*) imperméable *m*

**mad** [mæd] *adj* fou (folle); (*foolish*) insensé(e); (*angry*) furieux(-euse); **to be ~ (keen) about** or **on sth** (*inf*) être follement passionné de qch, être fou de qch

**Madagascar** [mædə'gæskəʳ] *n* Madagascar *m*

**madam** ['mædəm] *n* madame *f*

**mad cow disease** *n* maladie *f* des vaches folles

**made** [meɪd] *pt, pp of* **make**; **made-to-measure** *adj* (*BRIT*) fait(e) sur mesure; **made-up** ['meɪdʌp] *adj* (*story*) inventé(e), fabriqué(e)

**madly** ['mædlɪ] *adv* follement; **~ in love** éperdument amoureux(-euse)

**madman** ['mædmən] (*irreg*) *n* fou *m*, aliéné *m*

**madness** ['mædnɪs] *n* folie *f*

**Madrid** [mə'drɪd] *n* Madrid

**Mafia** ['mæfɪə] *n* maf(f)ia *f*

**mag** [mæg] *n abbr* (*BRIT inf*: = *magazine*) magazine *m*

**magazine** [mægə'zi:n] *n* (*Press*) magazine *m*, revue *f*; (*Radio, TV*) magazine

**maggot** ['mægət] *n* ver *m*, asticot *m*

**magic** ['mædʒɪk] *n* magie *f* ▷ *adj* magique; **magical** *adj* magique; (*experience, evening*) merveilleux(-euse); **magician** [mə'dʒɪʃən] *n* magicien(ne)

**magistrate** ['mædʒɪstreɪt] *n* magistrat *m*; juge *m*

**magnet** ['mægnɪt] *n* aimant *m*; **magnetic** [mæg'nɛtɪk] *adj* magnétique

**magnificent** [mæg'nɪfɪsnt] *adj* superbe, magnifique; (*splendid*: *robe, building*) somptueux(-euse), magnifique

**magnify** ['mægnɪfaɪ] *vt* grossir; (*sound*) amplifier; **magnifying glass** *n* loupe *f*

**magpie** ['mægpaɪ] *n* pie *f*

**mahogany** [mə'hɔgənɪ] *n* acajou *m*

**maid** [meɪd] *n* bonne *f*; (*in hotel*) femme *f* de chambre; **old ~** (*pej*) vieille fille

**maiden name** *n* nom *m* de jeune fille

**mail** [meɪl] n poste f; (letters) courrier m ▷ vt envoyer (par la poste); **by ~** par la poste; **mailbox** n (us: also Comput) boîte f aux lettres; **mailing list** n liste f d'adresses; **mailman** (irreg) n (us) facteur m; **mail-order** n vente f or achat m par correspondance

**main** [meɪn] adj principal(e) ▷ n (pipe) conduite principale, canalisation f; **the ~s** (Elec) le secteur; **the ~ thing** l'essentiel m; **in the ~** dans l'ensemble; **main course** n (Culin) plat m de résistance; **mainland** n continent m; **mainly** adv principalement, surtout; **main road** n grand axe, route nationale; **mainstream** n (fig) courant principal; **main street** n rue f principale

**maintain** [meɪnˈteɪn] vt entretenir; (continue) maintenir, préserver; (affirm) soutenir; **maintenance** [ˈmeɪntənəns] n entretien m; (Law: alimony) pension f alimentaire

**maisonette** [meɪzəˈnɛt] n (BRIT) appartement m en duplex

**maize** [meɪz] n (BRIT) maïs m

**majesty** [ˈmædʒɪstɪ] n majesté f; (title): **Your M~** Votre Majesté

**major** [ˈmeɪdʒəʳ] n (Mil) commandant m ▷ adj (important) important(e); (most important) principal(e); (Mus) majeur(e) ▷ vi (us Scol): **to ~ (in)** se spécialiser (en)

**Majorca** [məˈjɔːkə] n Majorque f

**majority** [məˈdʒɔrɪtɪ] n majorité f

**make** [meɪk] vt (pt, pp made) faire; (manufacture) faire, fabriquer; (earn) gagner; (decision) prendre; (friend) se faire; (speech) faire, prononcer; (cause to be): **to ~ sb sad** etc rendre qn triste etc; (force): **to ~ sb do sth** obliger qn à faire qch, faire faire qch à qn; (equal): **2 and 2 ~ 4** 2 et 2 font 4 ▷ n (manufacture) fabrication f; (brand) marque f; **to ~ the bed** faire le lit; **to ~ a fool of sb** (ridicule) ridiculiser qn; (trick) avoir or duper qn; **to ~ a profit** faire un or des bénéfice(s); **to ~ a loss** essuyer une perte; **to ~ it** (in time etc) y arriver; (succeed) réussir;

**what time do you ~ it?** quelle heure avez-vous?; **I ~ it £249** d'après mes calculs ça fait 249 livres; **to be made of** être en; **to ~ do with** se contenter de; se débrouiller avec; **make off** vi filer; **make out** vt (write out: cheque) faire; (decipher) déchiffrer; (understand) comprendre; (see) distinguer; (claim, imply) prétendre, vouloir faire croire; **make up** vt (invent) inventer, imaginer; (constitute) constituer; (parcel, bed) faire ▷ vi se réconcilier; (with cosmetics) se maquiller, se farder; **to be made up of** se composer de; **make up for** vt fus compenser; (lost time) rattraper; **makeover** [ˈmeɪkəʊvəʳ] n (by beautician) soins mpl de maquillage; (change of image) changement m d'image; **maker** n fabricant m; (of film, programme) réalisateur(-trice); **makeshift** adj provisoire, improvisé(e); **make-up** n maquillage m

**making** [ˈmeɪkɪŋ] n (fig): **in the ~** en formation or gestation; **to have the ~s of** (actor, athlete) avoir l'étoffe de

**malaria** [məˈlɛərɪə] n malaria f, paludisme m

**Malaysia** [məˈleɪzɪə] n Malaisie f

**male** [meɪl] n (Biol, Elec) mâle m ▷ adj (sex, attitude) masculin(e); (animal) mâle; (child etc) du sexe masculin

**malicious** [məˈlɪʃəs] adj méchant(e), malveillant(e)

> Be careful not to translate *malicious* by the French word *malicieux*.

**malignant** [məˈlɪgnənt] adj (Med) malin(-igne)

**mall** [mɔːl] n (also: **shopping ~**) centre commercial

**mallet** [ˈmælɪt] n maillet m

**malnutrition** [mælnjuːˈtrɪʃən] n malnutrition f

**malpractice** [mælˈpræktɪs] n faute professionnelle; négligence f

**malt** [mɔːlt] n malt m ▷ cpd (whisky) pur malt

**Malta** ['mɔːltə] n Malte f; **Maltese**
[mɔːl'tiːz] adj maltais(e) ▷ n (pl inv)
Maltais(e)
**mammal** ['mæml] n mammifère m
**mammoth** ['mæməθ] n mammouth m
▷ adj géant(e), monstre
**man** (pl **men**) [mæn, mɛn] n homme
m; (Sport) joueur m; (Chess) pièce f ▷ vt
(Naut: ship) garnir d'hommes; (machine)
assurer le fonctionnement de; (Mil: gun)
servir; (: post) être de service à; **an old ~**
un vieillard; **~ and wife** mari et femme
**manage** ['mænɪdʒ] vi se débrouiller;
(succeed) y arriver, réussir ▷ vt (business)
gérer; (team, operation) diriger;
(control: ship) manier, manœuvrer;
(: person) savoir s'y prendre avec; **to**
**~ to do** se débrouiller pour faire;
(succeed) réussir à faire; **manageable**
adj maniable; (task etc) faisable;
(number) raisonnable; **management**
n (running) administration f, direction
f; (people in charge: of business, firm)
dirigeants mpl, cadres mpl; (: of hotel,
shop, theatre) direction f; **manager** n
(of business) directeur m; (of institution
etc) administrateur m; (of department,
unit) responsable m/f, chef m; (of hotel
etc) gérant m; (Sport) manager m; (of
artist) impresario m; **manageress**
n directrice f; (of hotel etc) gérante f;
**managerial** [mænɪ'dʒɪərɪəl] adj
directorial(e); (skills) de cadre, de
gestion; **managing director** n
directeur général
**mandarin** ['mændərɪn] n (also: **~**
**orange**) mandarine f
**mandate** ['mændeɪt] n mandat m
**mandatory** ['mændətərɪ] adj
obligatoire
**mane** [meɪn] n crinière f
**maneuver** [mə'nuːvər] (US)
= **manoeuvre**
**mangetout** ['mɒnʒ'tuː] n mangetout m inv
**mango** (pl **~es**) ['mæŋɡəu] n mangue f
**man**: **manhole** n trou m d'homme;
**manhood** n (age) âge m d'homme;

(manliness) virilité f
**mania** ['meɪnɪə] n manie f; **maniac**
['meɪnɪæk] n maniaque m/f; (fig)
fou (folle)
**manic** ['mænɪk] adj maniaque
**manicure** ['mænɪkjuər] n manucure f
**manifest** ['mænɪfɛst] vt manifester
▷ adj manifeste, évident(e)
**manifesto** [mænɪ'fɛstəu] n (Pol)
manifeste m
**manipulate** [mə'nɪpjuleɪt] vt
manipuler; (system, situation) exploiter
**man**: **mankind** [mæn'kaɪnd] n
humanité f, genre humain; **manly** adj
viril(e); **man-made** adj artificiel(le);
(fibre) synthétique
**manner** ['mænər] n manière f, façon f;
(behaviour) attitude f, comportement
m; **manners** npl (good) **~s** (bonnes)
manières; **bad ~s** mauvaises manières;
**all ~ of** toutes sortes de
**manoeuvre** (US **maneuver**)
[mə'nuːvər] vt (move) manœuvrer;
(manipulate: person) manipuler;
(: situation) exploiter ▷ n manœuvre f
**manpower** ['mænpauər] n main-
d'œuvre f
**mansion** ['mænʃən] n château m,
manoir m
**manslaughter** ['mænslɔːtər] n
homicide m involontaire
**mantelpiece** ['mæntlpiːs] n
cheminée f
**manual** ['mænjuəl] adj manuel(le)
▷ n manuel m
**manufacture** [mænju'fæktʃər]
vt fabriquer ▷ n fabrication f;
**manufacturer** n fabricant m
**manure** [mə'njuər] n fumier m;
(artificial) engrais m
**manuscript** ['mænjuskrɪpt] n
manuscrit m
**many** ['mɛnɪ] adj beaucoup de,
nombreux(-euses) ▷ pron beaucoup,
un grand nombre; **a great ~** un grand
nombre (de); **~ a ...** bien des ..., plus
d'un(e) ...
**map** [mæp] n carte f; (of town) plan

*m*; **can you show it to me on the ~?**
pouvez-vous me l'indiquer sur la carte?;
**map out** *vt* tracer; (*fig: task*) planifier
**maple** ['meɪpl] *n* érable *m*
**Mar** *abbr* = **March**
**mar** [mɑːʳ] *vt* gâcher, gâter
**marathon** ['mærəθən] *n* marathon *m*
**marble** ['mɑːbl] *n* marbre *m*; (*toy*) bille *f*
**March** [mɑːtʃ] *n* mars *m*
**march** [mɑːtʃ] *vi* marcher au pas;
(*demonstrators*) défiler ▷ *n* marche *f*;
(*demonstration*) manifestation *f*
**mare** [mɛəʳ] *n* jument *f*
**margarine** [mɑːdʒə'riːn] *n* margarine *f*
**margin** ['mɑːdʒɪn] *n* marge *f*; **marginal**
*adj* marginal(e); **marginal seat** (*Pol*)
siège disputé; **marginally** *adv* très
légèrement, sensiblement
**marigold** ['mærɪgəuld] *n* souci *m*
**marijuana** [mærɪ'wɑːnə] *n*
marijuana *f*
**marina** [mə'riːnə] *n* marina *f*
**marinade** *n* [mærɪ'neɪd] marinade *f*
**marinate** ['mærɪneɪt] *vt* (faire)
mariner
**marine** [mə'riːn] *adj* marin(e) ▷ *n*
fusilier marin; (*us*) marine *m*
**marital** ['mærɪtl] *adj* matrimonial(e);
**marital status** *n* situation *f* de famille
**maritime** ['mærɪtaɪm] *adj* maritime
**marjoram** ['mɑːdʒərəm] *n*
marjolaine *f*
**mark** [mɑːk] *n* marque *f*; (*of skid
etc*) trace *f*; (*brit Scol*) note *f*; (*oven
temperature*): **(gas) ~ 4** thermostat *m* 4
▷ *vt* (*also Sport: player*) marquer; (*stain*)
tacher; (*brit Scol*) corriger, noter; **to
~ time** marquer le pas; **marked** *adj*
(*obvious*) marqué(e), net(te); **marker** *n*
(*sign*) jalon *m*; (*bookmark*) signet *m*
**market** ['mɑːkɪt] *n* marché *m* ▷ *vt*
(*Comm*) commercialiser; **marketing**
*n* marketing *m*; **marketplace** *n* place *f*
du marché; (*Comm*) marché *m*; **market
research** *n* étude *f* de marché
**marmalade** ['mɑːməleɪd] *n* confiture
*f* d'oranges
**maroon** [mə'ruːn] *vt*: **to be ~ed** être

abandonné(e); (*fig*) être bloqué(e) ▷ *adj*
(*colour*) bordeaux *inv*
**marquee** [mɑː'kiː] *n* chapiteau *m*
**marriage** ['mærɪdʒ] *n* mariage *m*;
**marriage certificate** *n* extrait *m*
d'acte de mariage
**married** ['mærɪd] *adj* marié(e); (*life,
love*) conjugal(e)
**marrow** ['mærəu] *n* (*of bone*) moelle *f*;
(*vegetable*) courge *f*
**marry** ['mærɪ] *vt* épouser, se marier
avec; (*subj: father, priest etc*) marier ▷ *vi*
(*also*: **get married**) se marier
**Mars** [mɑːz] *n* (*planet*) Mars *f*
**Marseilles** [mɑː'seɪ] *n* Marseille
**marsh** [mɑːʃ] *n* marais *m*, marécage *m*
**marshal** ['mɑːʃl] *n* maréchal *m*; (*us: fire,
police*) ≈ capitaine *m*; (*for demonstration,
meeting*) membre *m* du service d'ordre
▷ *vt* rassembler
**martyr** ['mɑːtəʳ] *n* martyr(e)
**marvel** ['mɑːvl] *n* merveille *f* ▷ *vi*: **to ~
(at)** s'émerveiller (de); **marvellous** (*us*
**marvelous**) *adj* merveilleux(-euse)
**Marxism** ['mɑːksɪzəm] *n* marxisme *m*
**Marxist** ['mɑːksɪst] *adj*, *n* marxiste
(*m/f*)
**marzipan** ['mɑːzɪpæn] *n* pâte *f*
d'amandes
**mascara** [mæs'kɑːrə] *n* mascara *m*
**mascot** ['mæskət] *n* mascotte *f*
**masculine** ['mæskjulɪn] *adj*
masculin(e) ▷ *n* masculin *m*
**mash** [mæʃ] *vt* (*Culin*) faire une purée
de; **mashed potato(es)** *n(pl)* purée *f* de
pommes de terre
**mask** [mɑːsk] *n* masque *m* ▷ *vt*
masquer
**mason** ['meɪsn] *n* (*also*: **stone~**)
maçon *m*; (*also*: **free~**) franc-maçon *m*;
**masonry** *n* maçonnerie *f*
**mass** [mæs] *n* multitude *f*, masse
*f*; (*Physics*) masse *f*; (*Rel*) messe *f*
▷ *cpd* (*communication*) de masse;
(*unemployment*) massif(-ive) ▷ *vi* se
masser; **masses** *npl*: **the ~es** les
masses; **~es of** (*inf*) des tas de
**massacre** ['mæsəkəʳ] *n* massacre *m*

**massage** ['mæsɑːʒ] n massage m
▷ vt masser
**massive** ['mæsɪv] adj énorme,
massif(-ive)
**mass media** npl mass-media mpl
**mass-produce** ['mæsprə'djuːs] vt
fabriquer en série
**mast** [mɑːst] n mât m; (Radio, TV)
pylône m
**master** ['mɑːstər] n maître m; (in
secondary school) professeur m; (in
primary school) instituteur m; (title for
boys): **M~ X** Monsieur X ▷ vt maîtriser;
(learn) apprendre à fond; **M~ of Arts/
Science (MA/MSc)** n ≈ titulaire m/f
d'une maîtrise (en lettres/science); **M~
of Arts/Science degree (MA/MSc)**
n ≈ maîtrise f; **mastermind** n esprit
supérieur ▷ vt diriger, être le cerveau
de; **masterpiece** n chef-d'œuvre m
**masturbate** ['mæstəbeɪt] vi se
masturber
**mat** [mæt] n petit tapis; (also: **door-**
**mat**) paillasson m; (also: **table~**) set m de
table ▷ adj = **matt**
**match** [mætʃ] n allumette f; (game)
match m, partie f; (fig) égal(e) ▷ vt (also:
**~ up**) assortir; (go well with) aller bien
avec, s'assortir à; (equal) égaler, valoir
▷ vi être assorti(e); **to be a good ~** être
bien assorti(e); **matchbox** n boîte f
d'allumettes; **matching** adj assorti(e)
**mate** [meɪt] n (inf) copain (copine);
(animal) partenaire m/f, mâle (femelle);
(in merchant navy) second m ▷ vi
s'accoupler
**material** [mə'tɪərɪəl] n (substance)
matière f, matériau m; (cloth) tissu m,
étoffe f; (information, data) données fpl
▷ adj matériel(le); (relevant: evidence)
pertinent(e); **materials** npl (equipment)
matériaux mpl
**materialize** [mə'tɪərɪəlaɪz] vi se
matérialiser, se réaliser
**maternal** [mə'tɜːnl] adj maternel(le)
**maternity** [mə'tɜːnɪtɪ] n maternité f;
**maternity hospital** n maternité f;
**maternity leave** n congé m de

maternité
**math** [mæθ] n (US: = mathematics)
maths fpl
**mathematical** [mæθə'mætɪkl] adj
mathématique
**mathematician** [mæθəmə'tɪʃən] n
mathématicien(ne)
**mathematics** [mæθə'mætɪks] n
mathématiques fpl
**maths** [mæθs] n abbr (BRIT:
= mathematics) maths fpl
**matinée** ['mætɪneɪ] n matinée f
**matron** ['meɪtrən] n (in hospital)
infirmière-chef f; (in school) infirmière f
**matt** [mæt] adj mat(e)
**matter** ['mætər] n question f; (Physics)
matière f, substance f; (Med: pus) pus
m ▷ vi importer; **matters** npl (affairs,
situation) la situation; **it doesn't ~** cela
n'a pas d'importance; (I don't mind) cela
ne fait rien; **what's the ~?** qu'est-ce
qu'il y a?, qu'est-ce qui ne va pas?; **no ~
what** quoi qu'il arrive; **as a ~ of course**
tout naturellement; **as a ~ of fact** en
fait; **reading ~** (BRIT) de quoi lire, de
la lecture
**mattress** ['mætrɪs] n matelas m
**mature** [mə'tjuər] adj mûr(e); (cheese)
fait(e); (wine) arrive(e) à maturité ▷ vi
mûrir; (cheese, wine) se faire; **mature
student** n étudiant(e) plus âgé(e) que la
moyenne; **maturity** n maturité f
**maul** [mɔːl] vt lacérer
**mauve** [məuv] adj mauve
**max** abbr = **maximum**
**maximize** ['mæksɪmaɪz] vt (profits etc,
chances) maximiser
**maximum** ['mæksɪməm] (pl **maxima**)
adj maximum ▷ n maximum m
**May** [meɪ] n mai m
**may** [meɪ] (conditional **might**) vi
(indicating possibility): **he ~ come** il se
peut qu'il vienne; (be allowed to): **~ I
smoke?** puis-je fumer?; (wishes): **~ God
bless you!** (que) Dieu vous bénisse!;
**you ~ as well go** vous feriez aussi
bien d'y aller
**maybe** ['meɪbiː] adv peut-être; **~**

**he'll ...** peut-être qu'il ...
**May Day** n le Premier mai
**mayhem** ['meɪhɛm] n grabuge m
**mayonnaise** [meɪə'neɪz] n
mayonnaise f
**mayor** [mɛəʳ] n maire m; **mayoress** n
(female mayor) maire m; (wife of mayor)
épouse f du maire
**maze** [meɪz] n labyrinthe m, dédale m
**MD** n abbr (Comm) = **managing director**
**me** [miː] pron me, m' + vowel or h mute;
(stressed, after prep) moi; **it's me** c'est
moi; **he heard me** il m'a entendu; **give
me a book** donnez-moi un livre; **it's for
me** c'est pour moi
**meadow** ['mɛdəʊ] n prairie f, pré m
**meagre** (US **meager**) ['miːgəʳ] adj
maigre
**meal** [miːl] n repas m; (flour) farine f;
**mealtime** n heure f du repas
**mean** [miːn] adj (with money) avare,
radin(e); (unkind) mesquin(e),
méchant(e); (shabby) misérable;
(average) moyen(ne) ▷ vt (pt, pp ~t)
(signify) signifier, vouloir dire; (refer to)
faire allusion à, parler de; (intend): **to
~ to do** avoir l'intention de faire ▷ n
moyenne f; **means** npl (way, money)
moyens mpl; **by ~s of** (instrument) au
moyen de; **by all ~s** je vous en prie; **to
be ~t for** être destiné(e) à; **do you ~ it?**
vous êtes sérieux?; **what do you ~?** que
voulez-vous dire?
**meaning** ['miːnɪŋ] n signification
f, sens m; **meaningful** adj
significatif(-ive); (relationship) valable;
**meaningless** adj dénué(e) de sens
**meant** [mɛnt] pt, pp of **mean**
**meantime** ['miːntaɪm] adv (also: **in
the ~**) pendant ce temps
**meanwhile** ['miːnwaɪl] adv
= **meantime**
**measles** ['miːzlz] n rougeole f
**measure** ['mɛʒəʳ] vt, vi mesurer ▷ n
mesure f; (ruler) règle (graduée)
**measurements** ['mɛʒəməntz] npl
mesures fpl; **chest/hip ~** tour m de
poitrine/hanches

**meat** [miːt] n viande f; **I don't eat ~** je
ne mange pas de viande; **cold ~s** (BRIT)
viandes froides; **meatball** n boulette
f de viande
**Mecca** ['mɛkə] n la Mecque
**mechanic** [mɪ'kænɪk] n mécanicien
m; **can you send a ~?** pouvez-vous
nous envoyer un mécanicien?;
**mechanical** adj mécanique
**mechanism** ['mɛkənɪzəm] n
mécanisme m
**medal** ['mɛdl] n médaille f; **medallist**
(US **medalist**) n (Sport) médaillé(e)
**meddle** ['mɛdl] vi: **to ~ in** se mêler de,
s'occuper de; **to ~ with** toucher à
**media** ['miːdɪə] npl media mpl ▷ npl
of **medium**
**mediaeval** [mɛdɪ'iːvl] adj = **medieval**
**mediate** ['miːdɪeɪt] vi servir
d'intermédiaire
**medical** ['mɛdɪkl] adj médical(e) ▷ n
(also: **~ examination**) visite médicale;
(private) examen médical; **medical
certificate** n certificat médical
**medicated** ['mɛdɪkeɪtɪd] adj
traitant(e), médicamenteux(-euse)
**medication** [mɛdɪ'keɪʃən] n (drugs etc)
médication f
**medicine** ['mɛdsɪn] n médecine f;
(drug) médicament m
**medieval** [mɛdɪ'iːvl] adj médiéval(e)
**mediocre** [miːdɪ'əʊkəʳ] adj médiocre
**meditate** ['mɛdɪteɪt] vi: **to ~ (on)**
méditer (sur)
**meditation** [mɛdɪ'teɪʃən] n
méditation f
**Mediterranean** [mɛdɪtə'reɪnɪən]
adj méditerranéen(ne); **the ~ (Sea)** la
(mer) Méditerranée
**medium** ['miːdɪəm] adj moyen(ne)
▷ n (pl **media**: means) moyen m; (pl **~s**:
person) médium m; **the happy ~** le juste
milieu; **medium-sized** adj de taille
moyenne; **medium wave** n (Radio)
ondes moyennes, petites ondes
**meek** [miːk] adj doux (douce), humble
**meet** (pt, pp **met**) [miːt, mɛt] vt
rencontrer; (by arrangement) retrouver,

rejoindre; (for the first time) faire la connaissance de; (go and fetch): **I'll ~ you at the station** j'irai te chercher à la gare; (opponent, danger, problem) faire face à; (requirements) satisfaire à, répondre à ▷ vi (friends) se rencontrer; se retrouver; (in session) se réunir; (join: lines, roads) se joindre; **nice ~ing you** ravi d'avoir fait votre connaissance; **meet up** vi: **to ~ up with sb** rencontrer qn; **meet with** vt fus (difficulty) rencontrer; **to ~ with success** être couronné(e) de succès; **meeting** n (of group of people) réunion f; (between individuals) rendez-vous m; **she's at** or **in a meeting** (Comm) elle est en réunion; **meeting place** n lieu m de (la) réunion; (for appointment) lieu de rendez-vous

**megabyte** ['mɛɡəbaɪt] n (Comput) méga-octet m

**megaphone** ['mɛɡəfəʊn] n porte-voix m inv

**megapixel** ['mɛɡəpɪksl] n mégapixel m

**melancholy** ['mɛlənkəlɪ] n mélancolie f ▷ adj mélancolique

**melody** ['mɛlədɪ] n mélodie f

**melon** ['mɛlən] n melon m

**melt** [mɛlt] vi fondre ▷ vt faire fondre

**member** ['mɛmbə<sup>r</sup>] n membre m; **Member of Congress** (US) n membre m du Congrès, ≈ député m; **Member of Parliament (MP)** n (BRIT) député m; **Member of the European Parliament (MEP)** n Eurodéputé m; **Member of the House of Representatives (MHR)** n (US) membre m de la Chambre des représentants; **Member of the Scottish Parliament (MSP)** n (BRIT) député m au Parlement écossais; **membership** n (becoming a member) adhésion f; admission f; (the members) membres mpl, adhérents mpl; **membership card** n carte f de membre

**memento** [mə'mɛntəʊ] n souvenir m

**memo** ['mɛməʊ] n note f (de service)

**memorable** ['mɛmərəbl] adj mémorable

**memorandum** (pl **memoranda**) [mɛmə'rændəm, -də] n note f (de service)

**memorial** [mɪ'mɔːrɪəl] n mémorial m ▷ adj commémoratif(-ive)

**memorize** ['mɛməraɪz] vt apprendre or retenir par cœur

**memory** ['mɛmərɪ] n (also Comput) mémoire f; (recollection) souvenir m; **in ~ of** à la mémoire de; **memory card** n (for digital camera) carte f mémoire

**men** [mɛn] npl of **man**

**menace** ['mɛnɪs] n menace f; (inf: nuisance) peste f, plaie f ▷ vt menacer

**mend** [mɛnd] vt réparer; (darn) raccommoder, repriser ▷ n: **on the ~** en voie de guérison; **to ~ one's ways** s'amender

**meningitis** [mɛnɪn'dʒaɪtɪs] n méningite f

**menopause** ['mɛnəʊpɔːz] n ménopause f

**men's room** (US) n: **the men's room** les toilettes fpl pour hommes

**menstruation** [mɛnstru'eɪʃən] n menstruation f

**menswear** ['mɛnzwɛə<sup>r</sup>] n vêtements mpl d'hommes

**mental** ['mɛntl] adj mental(e); **mental hospital** n hôpital m psychiatrique; **mentality** [mɛn'tælɪtɪ] n mentalité f; **mentally** adv: **to be mentally handicapped** être handicapé(e) mental(e); **the mentally ill** les malades mentaux

**menthol** ['mɛnθɒl] n menthol m

**mention** ['mɛnʃən] n mention f ▷ vt mentionner, faire mention de; **don't ~ it!** je vous en prie, il n'y a pas de quoi!

**menu** ['mɛnjuː] n (set menu, Comput) menu m; (list of dishes) carte f; **could we see the ~?** est-ce qu'on peut voir la carte?

**MEP** n abbr = **Member of the European Parliament**

**mercenary** ['mɜːsɪnərɪ] adj (person) intéressé(e), mercenaire ▷ n mercenaire m

**merchandise** ['mə:tʃəndaɪz] n
marchandises fpl

**merchant** ['mə:tʃənt] n négociant
m, marchand m; **merchant bank** n
(BRIT) banque f d'affaires; **merchant
navy** (US **merchant marine**) n marine
marchande

**merciless** ['mə:sɪlɪs] adj impitoyable,
sans pitié

**mercury** ['mə:kjurɪ] n mercure m

**mercy** ['mə:sɪ] n pitié f, merci f; (Rel)
miséricorde f; **at the ~ of** à la merci de

**mere** [mɪə'] adj simple; (chance) pur(e);
**a ~ two hours** seulement deux heures;
**merely** adv simplement, purement

**merge** [mə:dʒ] vt unir; (Comput)
fusionner, interclasser ▷ vi (colours,
shapes, sounds) se mêler; (roads) se
joindre; (Comm) fusionner; **merger** n
(Comm) fusion f

**meringue** [mə'ræŋ] n meringue f

**merit** ['mɛrɪt] n mérite m, valeur f ▷ vt
mériter

**mermaid** ['mə:meɪd] n sirène f

**merry** ['mɛrɪ] adj gai(e); **M~
Christmas!** joyeux Noël!; **merry-go-
round** n manège m

**mesh** [mɛʃ] n mailles fpl

**mess** [mɛs] n désordre m, fouillis m,
pagaille f; (muddle: of life) gâchis m;
(: of economy) pagaille f; (dirt) saleté f;
(Mil) mess m, cantine f; **to be (in) a
~** être en désordre; **to be/get o.s. in a
~** (fig) être/se mettre dans le pétrin;
**mess about** or **around** (inf) vi perdre
son temps; **mess up** vt (dirty) salir;
(spoil) gâcher; **mess with** (inf) vt fus
(challenge, confront) se frotter à; (interfere
with) toucher à

**message** ['mɛsɪdʒ] n message m; **can I
leave a ~?** est-ce que je peux laisser un
message?; **are there any ~s for me?**
est-ce que j'ai des messages?

**messenger** ['mɛsɪndʒə'] n messager m

**Messrs, Messrs.** ['mɛsəz] abbr (on
letters: = messieurs) MM

**messy** ['mɛsɪ] adj (dirty) sale; (untidy)
en désordre

**met** [mɛt] pt, pp of **meet**

**metabolism** [mɛ'tæbəlɪzəm] n
métabolisme m

**metal** ['mɛtl] n métal m ▷ cpd en métal;
**metallic** [mɛ'tælɪk] adj métallique

**metaphor** ['mɛtəfə'] n métaphore f

**meteor** ['mi:tɪə'] n météore m;
**meteorite** ['mi:tɪəraɪt] n météorite
m or f

**meteorology** [mi:tɪə'rɔlədʒɪ] n
météorologie f

**meter** ['mi:tə'] n (instrument) compteur
m; (also: **parking ~**) parc(o)mètre m; (US:
unit) = **metre** ▷ vt (US Post) affranchir
à la machine

**method** ['mɛθəd] n méthode f;
**methodical** [mɪ'θɔdɪkl] adj
méthodique

**methylated spirit** ['mɛθɪleɪtɪd-] n
(BRIT: also: **meths**) alcool m à brûler

**meticulous** [mɛ'tɪkjuləs] adj
méticuleux(-euse)

**metre** (US **meter**) ['mi:tə'] n mètre m

**metric** ['mɛtrɪk] adj métrique

**metro** ['mɛtrəu] n métro m

**metropolitan** [mɛtrə'pɔlɪtən] adj
métropolitain(e); **the M~ Police** (BRIT)
la police londonienne

**Mexican** ['mɛksɪkən] adj mexicain(e)
▷ n Mexicain(e)

**Mexico** ['mɛksɪkəu] n Mexique m

**mg** abbr (= milligram) mg

**mice** [maɪs] npl of **mouse**

**micro...** [maɪkrəu] prefix: **microchip**
n (Elec) puce f; **microphone** n
microphone m; **microscope** n
microscope m; **microwave** n (also:
**microwave oven**) four m à micro-
ondes

**mid** [mɪd] adj: **~ May** la mi-mai; **~
afternoon** le milieu de l'après-midi; **in
~ air** en plein ciel; **he's in his ~ thirties**
il a dans les trente-cinq ans; **midday**
n midi m

**middle** ['mɪdl] n milieu m; (waist)
ceinture f, taille f ▷ adj du milieu;
(average) moyen(ne); **in the ~ of the
night** au milieu de la nuit; **middle-**

**aged** adj d'un certain âge, ni vieux ni jeune; **Middle Ages** npl: **the Middle Ages** le moyen âge; **middle-class** adj bourgeois(e); **middle class(es)** n(pl): **the middle class(es)** ≈ les classes moyennes; **Middle East** n: **the Middle East** le Proche-Orient, le Moyen-Orient; **middle name** n second prénom; **middle school** n (US) école pour les enfants de 12 à 14 ans, ≈ collège m; (BRIT) école pour les enfants de 8 à 14 ans

**midge** [mɪdʒ] n moucheron m

**midget** ['mɪdʒɪt] n nain(e)

**midnight** ['mɪdnaɪt] n minuit m

**midst** [mɪdst] n: **in the ~ of** au milieu de

**midsummer** [mɪd'sʌmər] n milieu m de l'été

**midway** [mɪd'weɪ] adj, adv: **~ (between)** à mi-chemin (entre); **~ through ...** au milieu de ..., en plein(e) ...

**midweek** [mɪd'wiːk] adv au milieu de la semaine, en pleine semaine

**midwife** (pl **midwives**) ['mɪdwaɪf, -vz] n sage-femme f

**midwinter** [mɪd'wɪntər] n milieu m de l'hiver

**might** [maɪt] vb see **may** ▷ n puissance f, force f; **mighty** adj puissant(e)

**migraine** ['miːgreɪn] n migraine f

**migrant** ['maɪgrənt] n (bird, animal) migrateur m; (person) migrant(e) ▷ adj migrateur(-trice); migrant(e); (worker) saisonnier(-ière)

**migrate** [maɪ'greɪt] vi migrer

**migration** [maɪ'greɪʃən] n migration f

**mike** [maɪk] n abbr (= microphone) micro m

**mild** [maɪld] adj doux (douce); (reproach, infection) léger(-ère); (illness) bénin(-igne); (interest) modéré(e); (taste) peu relevé(e); **mildly** ['maɪldlɪ] adv doucement; légèrement; **to put it mildly** (inf) c'est le moins qu'on puisse dire

**mile** [maɪl] n mil(l)e m (= 1609 m); **mileage** n distance f en milles, ≈ kilométrage m; **mileometer**

[maɪ'lɒmɪtər] n compteur m kilométrique; **milestone** n borne f; (fig) jalon m

**military** ['mɪlɪtərɪ] adj militaire

**militia** [mɪ'lɪʃə] n milice f

**milk** [mɪlk] n lait m ▷ vt (cow) traire; (fig: person) dépouiller, plumer; (: situation) exploiter à fond; **milk chocolate** n chocolat m au lait; **milkman** (irreg) n laitier m; **milky** adj (drink) au lait; (colour) laiteux(-euse)

**mill** [mɪl] n moulin m; (factory) usine f, fabrique f; (spinning mill) filature f; (flour mill) minoterie f ▷ vt moudre, broyer ▷ vi (also: **~ about**) grouiller

**millennium** (pl **~s** or **millennia**) [mɪ'lenɪəm, -'lenɪə] n millénaire m

**milli...** ['mɪlɪ] prefix milli...; **milligram(me)** n milligramme m; **millilitre** (US **milliliter**) ['mɪlɪliːtər] n millilitre m; **millimetre** (US **millimeter**) n millimètre m

**million** ['mɪljən] n million m; **a ~ pounds** un million de livres sterling; **millionaire** [mɪljə'nɛər] n millionnaire m; **millionth** [-θ] num millionième

**milometer** [maɪ'lɒmɪtər] n = **mileometer**

**mime** [maɪm] n mime m ▷ vt, vi mimer

**mimic** ['mɪmɪk] n imitateur(-trice) ▷ vt, vi imiter, contrefaire

**min.** abbr (= minute(s)) mn.; (= minimum) min.

**mince** [mɪns] vt hacher ▷ n (BRIT Culin) viande hachée, hachis m; **mincemeat** n hachis de fruits secs utilisés en pâtisserie; (US) viande hachée, hachis m; **mince pie** n sorte de tarte aux fruits secs

**mind** [maɪnd] n esprit m ▷ vt (attend to, look after) s'occuper de; (be careful) faire attention à; (object to): **I don't ~ the noise** je ne crains pas le bruit, le bruit ne me dérange pas; **it is on my ~** cela me préoccupe; **to change one's ~** changer d'avis; **to my ~** à mon avis, selon moi; **to bear sth in ~** tenir compte de qch; **to have sb/sth**

in ~ avoir qn/qch en tête; **to make
up one's ~** se décider; **do you ~ if …?**
est-ce que cela vous gêne si …?; **I don't
~** cela ne me dérange pas; (*don't care*)
ça m'est égal; **~ you, …** remarquez, …;
**never ~** peu importe, ça ne fait rien;
(*don't worry*) ne vous en faîtes pas; **"~
the step"** "attention à la marche";
**mindless** *adj* irréfléchi(e); (*violence,
crime*) insensé(e); (*boring: job*) idiot(e)

**mine¹** [maɪn] *pron* le (la) mien(ne), les
miens (miennes); **a friend of ~** un de
mes amis, un ami à moi; **this book is ~**
ce livre est à moi

**mine²** [maɪn] *n* mine *f* ▷ *vt* (*coal*)
extraire; (*ship, beach*) miner; **minefield**
*n* champ *m* de mines; **miner** *n*
mineur *m*

**mineral** ['mɪnərəl] *adj* minéral(e)
▷ *n* minéral *m*; **mineral water** *n* eau
minérale

**mingle** ['mɪŋgl] *vi*: **to ~ with** se mêler à

**miniature** ['mɪnətʃəʳ] *adj* (en)
miniature ▷ *n* miniature *f*

**minibar** ['mɪnɪbɑːʳ] *n* minibar *m*

**minibus** ['mɪnɪbʌs] *n* minibus *m*

**minicab** ['mɪnɪkæb] *n* (BRIT) taxi *m*
indépendant

**minimal** ['mɪnɪml] *adj* minimal(e)

**minimize** ['mɪnɪmaɪz] *vt* (*reduce*)
réduire au minimum; (*play down*)
minimiser

**minimum** ['mɪnɪməm] *n* (*pl* **minima**)
minimum *m* ▷ *adj* minimum

**mining** ['maɪnɪŋ] *n* exploitation
minière

**miniskirt** ['mɪnɪskəːt] *n* mini-jupe *f*

**minister** ['mɪnɪstəʳ] *n* (BRIT Pol)
ministre *m*; (Rel) pasteur *m*

**ministry** ['mɪnɪstrɪ] *n* (BRIT Pol)
ministère *m*; (Rel): **to go into the ~**
devenir pasteur

**minor** ['maɪnəʳ] *adj* petit(e), de peu
d'importance; (Mus, poet, problem)
mineur(e) ▷ *n* (Law) mineur(e)

**minority** [maɪ'nɔrɪtɪ] *n* minorité *f*

**mint** [mɪnt] *n* (*plant*) menthe *f*; (*sweet*)
bonbon *m* à la menthe ▷ *vt* (*coins*)

battre; **the (Royal) M~**, **the (US)
M~** ≈ l'hôtel *m* de la Monnaie; **in ~
condition** à l'état de neuf

**minus** ['maɪnəs] *n* (*also*: **~ sign**) signe *m*
moins ▷ *prep* moins; **12 ~ 6 equals 6** 12
moins 6 égal 6; **~ 24°C** moins 24°C

**minute¹** *n* ['mɪnɪt] minute *f*; **minutes**
*npl* (*of meeting*) procès-verbal *m*,
compte rendu; **wait a ~!** (attendez)
un instant!; **at the last ~** à la dernière
minute

**minute²** *adj* [maɪ'njuːt] minuscule;
(*detailed*) minutieux(-euse); **in ~ detail**
par le menu

**miracle** ['mɪrəkl] *n* miracle *m*

**miraculous** [mɪ'rækjuləs] *adj*
miraculeux(-euse)

**mirage** ['mɪrɑːʒ] *n* mirage *m*

**mirror** ['mɪrəʳ] *n* miroir *m*, glace *f*; (*in
car*) rétroviseur *m*

**misbehave** [mɪsbɪ'heɪv] *vi* mal se
conduire

**misc.** *abbr* = **miscellaneous**

**miscarriage** ['mɪskærɪdʒ] *n* (Med)
fausse couche; **~ of justice** erreur *f*
judiciaire

**miscellaneous** [mɪsɪ'leɪnɪəs] *adj*
(*items, expenses*) divers(es); (*selection*)
varié(e)

**mischief** ['mɪstʃɪf] *n* (*naughtiness*)
sottises *fpl*; (*playfulness*) espièglerie
*f*; (*harm*) mal *m*, dommage *m*;
(*maliciousness*) méchanceté *f*;
**mischievous** ['mɪstʃɪvəs] *adj* (*playful,
naughty*) coquin(e), espiègle

**misconception** ['mɪskən'sɛpʃən] *n*
idée fausse

**misconduct** [mɪs'kɔndʌkt] *n*
inconduite *f*; **professional ~** faute
professionnelle

**miser** ['maɪzəʳ] *n* avare *m/f*

**miserable** ['mɪzərəbl] *adj* (*person,
expression*) malheureux(-euse);
(*conditions*) misérable; (*weather*)
maussade; (*offer, donation*) minable;
(*failure*) pitoyable

**misery** ['mɪzərɪ] *n* (*unhappiness*)
tristesse *f*; (*pain*) souffrances *fpl*;

(*wretchedness*) misère f

**misfortune** [mɪsˈfɔːtʃən] n malchance f, malheur m

**misgiving** [mɪsˈgɪvɪŋ] n (*apprehension*) craintes fpl; **to have ~s about sth** avoir des doutes quant à qch

**misguided** [mɪsˈgaɪdɪd] adj malavisé(e)

**mishap** [ˈmɪshæp] n mésaventure f

**misinterpret** [mɪsɪnˈtəːprɪt] vt mal interpréter

**misjudge** [mɪsˈdʒʌdʒ] vt méjuger, se méprendre sur le compte de

**mislay** [mɪsˈleɪ] vt (*irreg: like* **lay**) égarer

**mislead** [mɪsˈliːd] vt (*irreg: like* **lead**) induire en erreur; **misleading** adj trompeur(-euse)

**misplace** [mɪsˈpleɪs] vt égarer; **to be ~d** (*trust etc*) être mal placé(e)

**misprint** [ˈmɪsprɪnt] n faute f d'impression

**misrepresent** [mɪsrɛprɪˈzɛnt] vt présenter sous un faux jour

**Miss** [mɪs] n Mademoiselle

**miss** [mɪs] vt (*fail to get, attend, see*) manquer, rater; (*regret the absence of*): **I ~ him/it** il/cela me manque ▷ vi manquer ▷ n (*shot*) coup manqué; **we ~ed our train** nous avons raté notre train; **you can't ~ it** vous ne pouvez pas vous tromper; **miss out** vt (BRIT) oublier; **miss out on** vt fus (*fun, party*) rater, manquer; (*chance, bargain*) laisser passer

**missile** [ˈmɪsaɪl] n (*Aviat*) missile m; (*object thrown*) projectile m

**missing** [ˈmɪsɪŋ] adj manquant(e); (*after escape, disaster: person*) disparu(e); **to go ~** disparaître; **~ in action** (*Mil*) porté(e) disparu(e)

**mission** [ˈmɪʃən] n mission f; **on a ~ to sb** en mission auprès de qn; **missionary** n missionnaire m/f

**misspell** [ˈmɪsˈspɛl] vt (*irreg: like* **spell**) mal orthographier

**mist** [mɪst] n brume f ▷ vi (*also:* **~ over**, **~ up**) devenir brumeux(-euse); (BRIT: *windows*) s'embuer

**mistake** [mɪsˈteɪk] n erreur f, faute

f ▷ vt (*irreg: like* **take**) (*meaning*) mal comprendre; (*intentions*) se méprendre sur; **to ~ for** prendre pour; **by ~** par erreur, par inadvertance; **to make a ~** (*in writing*) faire une faute; (*in calculating etc*) faire une erreur; **there must be some ~** il doit y avoir une erreur, se tromper; **mistaken** pp of **mistake** ▷ adj (*idea etc*) erroné(e); **to be mistaken** faire erreur, se tromper

**mister** [ˈmɪstər] n (*inf*) Monsieur m; *see* **Mr**

**mistletoe** [ˈmɪsltəu] n gui m

**mistook** [mɪsˈtuk] pt of **mistake**

**mistress** [ˈmɪstrɪs] n maîtresse f; (BRIT: *in primary school*) institutrice f; (: *in secondary school*) professeur m

**mistrust** [mɪsˈtrʌst] vt se méfier de

**misty** [ˈmɪstɪ] adj brumeux(-euse); (*glasses, window*) embué(e)

**misunderstand** [mɪsʌndəˈstænd] vt, vi (*irreg: like* **stand**) mal comprendre; **misunderstanding** n méprise f, malentendu m; **there's been a misunderstanding** il y a eu un malentendu

**misunderstood** [mɪsʌndəˈstud] pt, pp of **misunderstand** ▷ adj (*person*) incompris(e)

**misuse** n [mɪsˈjuːs] mauvais emploi; (*of power*) abus m ▷ vt [mɪsˈjuːz] mal employer; abuser de

**mitt(en)** [ˈmɪt(n)] n moufle f; (*fingerless*) mitaine f

**mix** [mɪks] vt mélanger; (*sauce, drink etc*) préparer ▷ vi se mélanger; (*socialize*): **he doesn't ~ well** il est peu sociable ▷ n mélange m; **to ~ sth with sth** mélanger qch à qch; **cake ~** préparation f pour gâteau; **mix up** vt mélanger; (*confuse*) confondre; **to be ~ed up in sth** être mêlé(e) à qch or impliqué(e) dans qch; **mixed** adj (*feelings, reactions*) contradictoires; (*school, marriage*) mixte; **mixed grill** n (BRIT) assortiment m de grillades; **mixed salad** n salade f de crudités; **mixed-up** adj (*person*) désorienté(e), embrouillé(e); **mixer**

*n* (*for food*) batteur *m*, mixeur *m*;
(*drink*) boisson gazeuse (*servant à
couper un alcool*); (*person*): **he is a good
mixer** il est très sociable; **mixture**
*n* assortiment *m*, mélange *m*; (*Med*)
préparation *f*; **mix-up** *n*: **there was a
mix-up** il y a eu confusion

**ml** *abbr* (= *millilitre(s)*) ml

**mm** *abbr* (= *millimetre*) mm

**moan** [məʊn] *n* gémissement *m* ▷ *vi*
gémir; (*inf: complain*): **to ~ (about)** se
plaindre (de)

**moat** [məʊt] *n* fossé *m*, douves *fpl*

**mob** [mɒb] *n* foule *f*; (*disorderly*) cohue
*f* ▷ *vt* assaillir

**mobile** [ˈməʊbaɪl] *adj* mobile ▷ *n* (*Art*)
mobile *m*; **mobile home** *n* caravane *f*;
**mobile phone** *n* téléphone portatif

**mobility** [məʊˈbɪlɪtɪ] *n* mobilité *f*

**mobilize** [ˈməʊbɪlaɪz] *vt*, *vi* mobiliser

**mock** [mɒk] *vt* ridiculiser; (*laugh at*)
se moquer de ▷ *adj* faux (fausse);
**mocks** *npl* (*BRIT: Scol*) examens blancs;
**mockery** *n* moquerie *f*, raillerie *f*

**mod cons** [ˈmɒdˈkɒnz] *npl abbr*
(*BRIT*) = **modern conveniences**; *see*
**convenience**

**mode** [məʊd] *n* mode *m*; (*of transport*)
moyen *m*

**model** [ˈmɒdl] *n* modèle *m*; (*person:
for fashion*) mannequin *m*; (: *for artist*)
modèle ▷ *vt* (*with clay etc*) modeler ▷ *vi*
travailler comme mannequin ▷ *adj*
(*railway: toy*) modèle réduit *inv*; (*child,
factory*) modèle; **to ~ clothes** présenter
des vêtements; **to ~ o.s. on** imiter

**modem** [ˈməʊdɛm] *n* modem *m*

**moderate** *adj* [ˈmɒdərət] modéré(e);
(*amount, change*) peu important(e)
▷ *vb* [ˈmɒdəreɪt] ▷ *vi* se modérer, se
calmer ▷ *vt* modérer; **moderation**
[mɒdəˈreɪʃən] *n* modération *f*, mesure
*f*; **in ~** à dose raisonnable, pris(e) or
pratiqué(e) modérément

**modern** [ˈmɒdən] *adj* moderne;
**modernize** *vt* moderniser; **modern
languages** *npl* langues vivantes

**modest** [ˈmɒdɪst] *adj* modeste;

**modesty** *n* modestie *f*

**modification** [mɒdɪfɪˈkeɪʃən] *n*
modification *f*

**modify** [ˈmɒdɪfaɪ] *vt* modifier

**module** [ˈmɒdjuːl] *n* module *m*

**mohair** [ˈməʊhɛəʳ] *n* mohair *m*

**Mohammed** [məˈhæməd] *n*
Mahomet *m*

**moist** [mɔɪst] *adj* humide, moite;
**moisture** [ˈmɔɪstʃəʳ] *n* humidité
*f*; (*on glass*) buée *f*; **moisturizer**
[ˈmɔɪstʃəraɪzəʳ] *n* crème hydratante

**mold** *etc* [məʊld] (*US*) = **mould** *etc*

**mole** [məʊl] *n* (*animal, spy*) taupe *f*;
(*spot*) grain *m* de beauté

**molecule** [ˈmɒlɪkjuːl] *n* molécule *f*

**molest** [məʊˈlɛst] *vt* (*assault sexually*)
attenter à la pudeur de

**molten** [ˈməʊltən] *adj* fondu(e); (*rock*)
en fusion

**mom** [mɒm] *n* (*US*) = **mum**

**moment** [ˈməʊmənt] *n* moment *m*,
instant *m*; **at the ~** en ce moment;
**momentarily** [ˈməʊməntrɪlɪ] *adv*
momentanément; (*US: soon*) bientôt;
**momentary** *adj* momentané(e),
passager(-ère); **momentous**
[məʊˈmɛntəs] *adj* important(e),
capital(e)

**momentum** [məʊˈmɛntəm] *n* élan
*m*, vitesse acquise; (*fig*) dynamique *f*;
**to gather ~** prendre de la vitesse; (*fig*)
gagner du terrain

**mommy** [ˈmɒmɪ] *n* (*US: mother*)
maman *f*

**Mon** *abbr* (= *Monday*) l.

**Monaco** [ˈmɒnəkəʊ] *n* Monaco *f*

**monarch** [ˈmɒnək] *n* monarque *m*;
**monarchy** *n* monarchie *f*

**monastery** [ˈmɒnəstərɪ] *n*
monastère *m*

**Monday** [ˈmʌndɪ] *n* lundi *m*

**monetary** [ˈmʌnɪtərɪ] *adj* monétaire

**money** [ˈmʌnɪ] *n* argent *m*; **to
make ~** (*person*) gagner de l'argent;
(*business*) rapporter; **money belt** *n*
ceinture-portefeuille *f*; **money order**
*n* mandat *m*

**mongrel** ['mʌŋgrəl] n (dog) bâtard m

**monitor** ['mɒnɪtə<sup>r</sup>] n (TV, Comput) écran m, moniteur m ▷ vt contrôler; (foreign station) être à l'écoute de; (progress) suivre de près

**monk** [mʌŋk] n moine m

**monkey** ['mʌŋkɪ] n singe m

**monologue** ['mɒnəlɒg] n monologue m

**monopoly** [mə'nɒpəlɪ] n monopole m

**monosodium glutamate** [mɒnə'səudɪəm 'glu:təmeɪt] n glutamate m de sodium

**monotonous** [mə'nɒtənəs] adj monotone

**monsoon** [mɒn'su:n] n mousson f

**monster** ['mɒnstə<sup>r</sup>] n monstre m

**month** [mʌnθ] n mois m; **monthly** adj mensuel(le) ▷ adv mensuellement

**Montreal** [mɒntrɪ'ɔ:l] n Montréal

**monument** ['mɒnjumənt] n monument m

**mood** [mu:d] n humeur f, disposition f; **to be in a good/bad ~** être de bonne/mauvaise humeur; **moody** adj (variable) d'humeur changeante, lunatique; (sullen) morose, maussade

**moon** [mu:n] n lune f; **moonlight** n clair m de lune

**moor** [muə<sup>r</sup>] n lande f ▷ vt (ship) amarrer ▷ vi mouiller

**moose** [mu:s] n (pl inv) élan m

**mop** [mɒp] n balai m à laver; (for dishes) lavette f à vaisselle ▷ vt éponger, essuyer; **~ of hair** tignasse f; **mop up** vt éponger

**mope** [məup] vi avoir le cafard, se morfondre

**moped** ['məupɛd] n cyclomoteur m

**moral** ['mɒrl] adj moral(e) ▷ n morale f; **morals** npl moralité f

**morale** [mɔ'rɑ:l] n moral m

**morality** [mə'rælɪtɪ] n moralité f

**morbid** ['mɔ:bɪd] adj morbide

**KEYWORD**

**more** [mɔ:<sup>r</sup>] adj **1** (greater in number etc) plus (de), davantage (de); **more**

**people/work (than)** plus de gens/de travail (que)

**2** (additional) encore (de); **do you want (some) more tea?** voulez-vous encore du thé?; **is there any more wine?** reste-t-il du vin?; **I have no** or **I don't have any more money** je n'ai plus d'argent; **it'll take a few more weeks** ça prendra encore quelques semaines ▷ pron plus, davantage; **more than 10** plus de 10; **it cost more than we expected** cela a coûté plus que prévu; **I want more** j'en veux plus or davantage; **is there any more?** est-ce qu'il en reste?; **there's no more** il n'y en a plus; **a little more** un peu plus; **many/much more** beaucoup plus, bien davantage ▷ adv plus; **more dangerous/easily (than)** plus dangereux/facilement (que); **more and more expensive** de plus en plus cher; **more or less** plus ou moins; **more than ever** plus que jamais; **once more** encore une fois, une fois de plus

**moreover** [mɔ:'rəuvə<sup>r</sup>] adv de plus

**morgue** [mɔ:g] n morgue f

**morning** ['mɔ:nɪŋ] n matin m; (as duration) matinée f ▷ cpd matinal(e); (paper) du matin; **in the ~** le matin; **7 o'clock in the ~** 7 heures du matin; **morning sickness** n nausées matinales

**Moroccan** [mə'rɔkən] adj marocain(e) ▷ n Marocain(e)

**Morocco** [mə'rɔkəu] n Maroc m

**moron** ['mɔ:rɒn] n idiot(e), minus m/f

**morphine** ['mɔ:fi:n] n morphine f

**morris dancing** ['mɒrɪs-] n (BRIT) danses folkloriques anglaises

**MORRIS DANCING**

• Le **Morris dancing** est une
• danse folklorique anglaise
• traditionnellement réservée aux
• hommes. Habillés tout en blanc
• et portant des clochettes, ils

- exécutent différentes figures avec
- des mouchoirs et de longs bâtons.
- Cette danse est très populaire dans
- les fêtes de village.

**Morse** [mɔːs] n (also: ~ code) morse m
**mortal** ['mɔːtl] adj, n mortel(le)
**mortar** ['mɔːtəʳ] n mortier m
**mortgage** ['mɔːgɪdʒ] n hypothèque f;
(loan) prêt m (or crédit m) hypothécaire
▷ vt hypothéquer
**mortician** [mɔː'tɪʃən] n (US)
entrepreneur m de pompes funèbres
**mortified** ['mɔːtɪfaɪd] adj mort(e)
de honte
**mortuary** ['mɔːtjuərɪ] n morgue f
**mosaic** [məu'zeɪɪk] n mosaïque f
**Moscow** ['mɔskəu] n Moscou
**Moslem** ['mɔzləm] adj, n = **Muslim**
**mosque** [mɔsk] n mosquée f
**mosquito** (pl ~es) [mɔs'kiːtəu] n
moustique m
**moss** [mɔs] n mousse f
**most** [məust] adj (majority of) la plupart
de; (greatest amount of) le plus de ▷ pron
la plupart ▷ adv le plus; (very) très,
extrêmement; **the ~** le plus; **~ fish** la
plupart des poissons; **the ~ beautiful
woman in the world** la plus belle
femme du monde; **~ of** (with plural) la
plupart de; (with singular) la plus grande
partie de; **~ of them** la plupart d'entre
eux; **~ of the time** la plupart du temps;
**I saw ~** (a lot but not all) j'en ai vu la
plupart; (more than anyone else) c'est
moi qui en ai vu le plus; **at the (very)
~** au plus; **to make the ~ of** profiter
au maximum de; **mostly** adv (chiefly)
surtout, principalement; (usually)
généralement
**MOT** n abbr (BRIT) = **Ministry of
Transport**; **the ~ (test)** visite technique
(annuelle) obligatoire des véhicules à
moteur
**motel** [məu'tɛl] n motel m
**moth** [mɔθ] n papillon m de nuit; (in
clothes) mite f
**mother** ['mʌðəʳ] n mère f ▷ vt (pamper,

protect) dorloter; **motherhood** n
maternité f; **mother-in-law** n belle-
mère f; **mother-of-pearl** n nacre f;
**Mother's Day** n fête f des Mères;
**mother-to-be** n future maman;
**mother tongue** n langue maternelle
**motif** [məu'tiːf] n motif m
**motion** ['məuʃən] n mouvement m;
(gesture) geste m; (at meeting) motion
f ▷ vt, vi: **to ~ (to) sb to do** faire signe à
qn de faire; **motionless** adj immobile,
sans mouvement; **motion picture**
n film m
**motivate** ['məutɪveɪt] vt motiver
**motivation** [məutɪ'veɪʃən] n
motivation f
**motive** ['məutɪv] n motif m, mobile m
**motor** ['məutəʳ] n moteur m; (BRIT inf:
vehicle) auto f; **motorbike** n moto f;
**motorboat** n bateau m à moteur;
**motorcar** n (BRIT) automobile f;
**motorcycle** n moto f; **motorcyclist**
n motocycliste m/f; **motoring** (BRIT)
n tourisme m automobile; **motorist**
n automobiliste m/f; **motor racing** n
(BRIT) course f automobile; **motorway**
n (BRIT) autoroute f
**motto** (pl ~es) ['mɔtəu] n devise f
**mould** (US **mold**) [məuld] n moule
m; (mildew) moisissure f ▷ vt mouler,
modeler; (fig) façonner; **mouldy** adj
moisi(e); (smell) de moisi
**mound** [maund] n monticule m,
tertre m
**mount** [maunt] n (hill) mont m,
montagne f; (horse) monture f; (for
picture) carton m de montage ▷ vt
monter; (horse) monter à; (bike) monter
sur; (picture) monter sur carton ▷ vi
(inflation, tension) augmenter; **mount
up** vi s'élever, monter; (bills, problems,
savings) s'accumuler
**mountain** ['mauntɪn] n montagne
f ▷ cpd de (la) montagne; **mountain
bike** n VTT m, vélo m tout terrain;
**mountaineer** n alpiniste m/f;
**mountaineering** n alpinisme m;
**mountainous** adj montagneux(-euse);

**mountain range** n chaîne f de montagnes

**mourn** [mɔ:n] vt pleurer ▷ vi: **to ~ for sb** pleurer qn; **to ~ for sth** se lamenter sur qch; **mourner** n parent(e) or ami(e) du défunt; personne f en deuil or venue rendre hommage au défunt; **mourning** n deuil m; **in mourning** en deuil

**mouse** (pl **mice**) [maus, maɪs] n (also Comput) souris f; **mouse mat** n (Comput) tapis m de souris

**moussaka** [muˈsɑːkə] n moussaka f

**mousse** [muːs] n mousse f

**moustache** (us **mustache**) [məsˈtɑːʃ] n moustache(s) f(pl)

**mouth** [mauθ, pl -ðz] n bouche f; (of dog, cat) gueule f; (of river) embouchure f; (of hole, cave) ouverture f; **mouthful** n bouchée f; **mouth organ** n harmonica m; **mouthpiece** n (of musical instrument) bec m, embouchure f; (spokesperson) porte-parole m inv; **mouthwash** n eau f dentifrice

**move** [muːv] n (movement) mouvement m; (in game) coup m; (: turn to play) tour m; (change of house) déménagement m; (change of job) changement m d'emploi ▷ vt déplacer, bouger; (emotionally) émouvoir; (Pol: resolution etc) proposer ▷ vi (gen) bouger, remuer; (traffic) circuler; (also: ~ **house**) déménager; (in game) jouer; **can you ~ your car, please?** pouvez-vous déplacer votre voiture, s'il vous plaît?; **to ~ sb to do sth** pousser or inciter qn à faire qch; **to get a ~ on** se dépêcher, se remuer; **move back** vi revenir, retourner; **move in** vi (to a house) emménager; (police, soldiers) intervenir; **move off** vi s'éloigner, s'en aller; **move on** vi se remettre en route; **move out** vi (of house) déménager; **move over** vi se pousser, se déplacer; **move up** vi avancer; (employee) avoir de l'avancement; (pupil) passer dans la classe supérieure; **movement** n mouvement m

**movie** [ˈmuːvɪ] n film m; **movies** npl: **the ~s** le cinéma; **movie theater** (us) n cinéma m

**moving** [ˈmuːvɪŋ] adj en mouvement; (touching) émouvant(e)

**mow** (pt **~ed**, pp **~ed** or **~n**) [məu, -d, -n] vt faucher; (lawn) tondre; **mower** n (also: **lawnmower**) tondeuse f à gazon

**Mozambique** [məuzəmˈbiːk] n Mozambique m

**MP** n abbr (BRIT) = **Member of Parliament**

**MP3** n mp3 m; **MP3 player** n lecteur m mp3

**mpg** n abbr = miles per gallon (30 mpg = 9,4 l. aux 100 km)

**m.p.h.** abbr = miles per hour (60 mph = 96 km/h)

**Mr** (us **Mr.**) [ˈmɪstər] n: **Mr X** Monsieur X, M. X

**Mrs** (us **Mrs.**) [ˈmɪsɪz] n: **~ X** Madame X, Mme X

**Ms** (us **Ms.**) [mɪz] n (Miss or Mrs): **Ms X** Madame X, Mme X

**MSP** n abbr (= Member of the Scottish Parliament) député m au Parlement écossais

**Mt** abbr (Geo: = mount) Mt

**much** [mʌtʃ] adj beaucoup de ▷ adv, n or pron beaucoup; **we don't have ~ time** nous n'avons pas beaucoup de temps; **how ~ is it?** combien est-ce que ça coûte?; **it's not ~** ce n'est pas beaucoup; **too ~** trop (de); **so ~** tant (de); **I like it very/so ~** j'aime beaucoup/tellement ça; **as ~ as** autant de; **that's ~ better** c'est beaucoup mieux

**muck** [mʌk] n (mud) boue f; (dirt) ordures fpl; **muck up** vt (inf: ruin) gâcher, esquinter; (: dirty) salir; (: exam, interview) se planter à; **mucky** adj (dirty) boueux(-euse), sale

**mucus** [ˈmjuːkəs] n mucus m

**mud** [mʌd] n boue f

**muddle** [ˈmʌdl] n (mess) pagaille f, fouillis m; (mix-up) confusion f ▷ vt (also: ~ **up**) brouiller, embrouiller; **to get in a ~** (while explaining etc) s'embrouiller

**muddy** ['mʌdɪ] *adj* boueux(-euse)

**mudguard** ['mʌdgɑːd] *n* garde-boue *m inv*

**muesli** ['mjuːzlɪ] *n* muesli *m*

**muffin** ['mʌfɪn] *n* (*roll*) petit pain rond et plat; (*cake*) petit gâteau au chocolat ou aux fruits

**muffled** ['mʌfld] *adj* étouffé(e), voilé(e)

**muffler** ['mʌflər] *n* (*scarf*) cache-nez *m inv*; (*us Aut*) silencieux *m*

**mug** [mʌg] *n* (*cup*) tasse *f* (*sans soucoupe*); (: *for beer*) chope *f*; (*inf: face*) bouille *f*; (: *fool*) poire *f* ▷ *vt* (*assault*) agresser; **mugger** ['mʌgər] *n* agresseur *m*; **mugging** *n* agression *f*

**muggy** ['mʌgɪ] *adj* lourd(e), moite

**mule** [mjuːl] *n* mule *f*

**multicoloured** (*us* **multicolored**) ['mʌltɪkʌləd] *adj* multicolore

**multimedia** ['mʌltɪˈmiːdɪə] *adj* multimédia *inv*

**multinational** [mʌltɪˈnæʃənl] *n* multinationale *f* ▷ *adj* multinational(e)

**multiple** ['mʌltɪpl] *adj* multiple ▷ *n* multiple *m*; **multiple choice (test)** *n* QCM *m*, questionnaire *m* à choix multiple; **multiple sclerosis** [-sklɪˈrəʊsɪs] *n* sclérose *f* en plaques

**multiplex (cinema)** ['mʌltɪplɛks-] *n* (cinéma *m*) multisalles *m*

**multiplication** [mʌltɪplɪˈkeɪʃən] *n* multiplication *f*

**multiply** ['mʌltɪplaɪ] *vt* multiplier ▷ *vi* se multiplier

**multistorey** ['mʌltɪˈstɔːrɪ] *adj* (*BRIT: building*) à étages; (: *car park*) à étages *or* niveaux multiples

**mum** [mʌm] *n* (*BRIT*) maman *f* ▷ *adj*: **to keep ~** ne pas souffler mot

**mumble** ['mʌmbl] *vt*, *vi* marmotter, marmonner

**mummy** ['mʌmɪ] *n* (*BRIT: mother*) maman *f*; (*embalmed*) momie *f*

**mumps** [mʌmps] *n* oreillons *mpl*

**munch** [mʌntʃ] *vt*, *vi* mâcher

**municipal** [mjuːˈnɪsɪpl] *adj* municipal(e)

**mural** ['mjuərl] *n* peinture murale

**murder** ['məːdər] *n* meurtre *m*, assassinat *m* ▷ *vt* assassiner; **murderer** *n* meurtrier *m*, assassin *m*

**murky** ['məːkɪ] *adj* sombre, ténébreux(-euse); (*water*) trouble

**murmur** ['məːmər] *n* murmure *m* ▷ *vt*, *vi* murmurer

**muscle** ['mʌsl] *n* muscle *m*; (*fig*) force *f*; **muscular** ['mʌskjulər] *adj* musculaire; (*person, arm*) musclé(e)

**museum** [mjuːˈzɪəm] *n* musée *m*

**mushroom** ['mʌʃrum] *n* champignon *m* ▷ *vi* (*fig*) pousser comme un (*or* des) champignon(s)

**music** ['mjuːzɪk] *n* musique *f*; **musical** *adj* musical(e); (*person*) musicien(ne) ▷ *n* (*show*) comédie musicale; **musical instrument** *n* instrument *m* de musique; **musician** [mjuːˈzɪʃən] *n* musicien(ne)

**Muslim** ['mʌzlɪm] *adj*, *n* musulman(e)

**muslin** ['mʌzlɪn] *n* mousseline *f*

**mussel** ['mʌsl] *n* moule *f*

**must** [mʌst] *aux vb* (*obligation*): **I ~ do it** je dois le faire, il faut que je le fasse; (*probability*): **he ~ be there by now** il doit y être maintenant, il y est probablement maintenant; (*suggestion, invitation*): **you ~ come and see me** il faut que vous veniez me voir ▷ *n* nécessité *f*, impératif *m*; **it's a ~** c'est indispensable; **I ~ have made a mistake** j'ai dû me tromper

**mustache** ['mʌstæʃ] *n* (*us*) = **moustache**

**mustard** ['mʌstəd] *n* moutarde *f*

**mustn't** ['mʌsnt] = **must not**

**mute** [mjuːt] *adj*, *n* muet(te)

**mutilate** ['mjuːtɪleɪt] *vt* mutiler

**mutiny** ['mjuːtɪnɪ] *n* mutinerie *f* ▷ *vi* se mutiner

**mutter** ['mʌtər] *vt*, *vi* marmonner, marmotter

**mutton** ['mʌtn] *n* mouton *m*

**mutual** ['mjuːtʃuəl] *adj* mutuel(le), réciproque; (*benefit, interest*) commun(e)

**muzzle** ['mʌzl] n museau m; (protective device) muselière f; (of gun) gueule f ▷ vt museler

**my** [maɪ] adj mon (ma), mes pl; **my house/car/gloves** ma maison/ma voiture/mes gants; **I've washed my hair/cut my finger** je me suis lavé les cheveux/coupé le doigt; **is this my pen or yours?** c'est mon stylo ou c'est le vôtre?

**myself** [maɪ'sɛlf] pron (reflexive) me; (emphatic) moi-même; (after prep) moi; see also **oneself**

**mysterious** [mɪs'tɪərɪəs] adj mystérieux(-euse)

**mystery** ['mɪstərɪ] n mystère m

**mystical** ['mɪstɪkl] adj mystique

**mystify** ['mɪstɪfaɪ] vt (deliberately) mystifier; (puzzle) ébahir

**myth** [mɪθ] n mythe m; **mythology** [mɪ'θɔlədʒɪ] n mythologie f

# n

**n/a** abbr (= not applicable) n.a.

**nag** [næg] vt (scold) être toujours après, reprendre sans arrêt

**nail** [neɪl] n (human) ongle m; (metal) clou m ▷ vt clouer; **to ~ sth to sth** clouer qch à qch; **to ~ sb down to a date/price** contraindre qn à accepter or donner une date/un prix; **nailbrush** n brosse f à ongles; **nailfile** n lime f à ongles; **nail polish** n vernis m à ongles; **nail polish remover** n dissolvant m; **nail scissors** npl ciseaux mpl à ongles; **nail varnish** n (BRIT) = nail polish

**naïve** [naɪ'iːv] adj naïf(-ïve)

**naked** ['neɪkɪd] adj nu(e)

**name** [neɪm] n nom m; (reputation) réputation f ▷ vt nommer; (identify: accomplice etc) citer; (price, date) fixer, donner; **by ~** par son nom; de nom; **in the ~ of** au nom de; **what's your ~?** comment vous appelez-vous?, quel est votre nom?; **namely** adv à savoir

**nanny** ['nænɪ] n bonne f d'enfants

**nap** [næp] n (sleep) (petit) somme

**napkin** ['næpkɪn] n serviette f (de
table)

**nappy** ['næpɪ] n (BRIT) couche f

**narcotics** [nɑːˈkɒtɪkz] npl (illegal drugs)
stupéfiants mpl

**narrative** ['nærətɪv] n récit m ▷ adj
narratif(-ive)

**narrator** [nəˈreɪtər] n narrateur(-trice)

**narrow** ['nærəʊ] adj étroit(e); (fig)
restreint(e), limité(e) ▷ vi (road)
devenir plus étroit, se rétrécir; (gap,
difference) se réduire; **to have a ~
escape** l'échapper belle; **narrow
down** vt restreindre; **narrowly** adv: **he
narrowly missed injury/the tree** il a
failli se blesser/rentrer dans l'arbre; **he
only narrowly missed the target** il a
manqué la cible de peu or de justesse;
**narrow-minded** adj à l'esprit étroit,
borné(e); (attitude) borné(e)

**nasal** ['neɪzl] adj nasal(e)

**nasty** ['nɑːstɪ] adj (person: malicious)
méchant(e); (: rude) très désagréable;
(smell) dégoûtant(e); (wound, situation)
mauvais(e), vilain(e)

**nation** ['neɪʃən] n nation f

**national** ['næʃənl] adj national(e)
▷ n (abroad) ressortissant(e); (when
home) national(e); **national anthem**
n hymne national; **national dress** n
costume national; **National Health
Service** n (BRIT) service national de
santé, ≈ Sécurité Sociale; **National
Insurance** n (BRIT) ≈ Sécurité Sociale;
**nationalist** adj, n nationaliste
m/f; **nationality** [næʃəˈnælɪtɪ]
n nationalité f; **nationalize** vt
nationaliser; **national park** n parc
national; **National Trust** n (BRIT)
≈ Caisse f nationale des monuments
historiques et des sites

- **NATIONAL TRUST**
-
- Le **National Trust** est un organisme
- indépendant, à but non lucratif,
- dont la mission est de protéger et
- de mettre en valeur les monuments

- et les sites britanniques en raison
- de leur intérêt historique ou de leur
- beauté naturelle.

**nationwide** ['neɪʃənwaɪd] adj
s'étendant à l'ensemble du pays;
(problem) à l'échelle du pays entier

**native** ['neɪtɪv] n habitant(e) du
pays, autochtone m/f ▷ adj du pays,
indigène; (country) natal(e); (language)
maternel(le); (ability) inné(e); **Native
American** ▷ n Indien(ne) d'Amérique
▷ adj amérindien(ne); **native speaker**
n locuteur natif

**NATO** ['neɪtəʊ] n abbr (= North Atlantic
Treaty Organization) OTAN f

**natural** ['nætʃrəl] adj naturel(le);
**natural gas** n gaz naturel; **natural
history** n histoire naturelle; **naturally**
adv naturellement; **natural resources**
npl ressources naturelles

**nature** ['neɪtʃər] n nature f; **by ~** par
tempérament, de nature; **nature
reserve** n (BRIT) réserve naturelle

**naughty** ['nɔːtɪ] adj (child) vilain(e),
pas sage

**nausea** ['nɔːsɪə] n nausée f

**naval** ['neɪvl] adj naval(e)

**navel** ['neɪvl] n nombril m

**navigate** ['nævɪgeɪt] vt (steer)
diriger, piloter ▷ vi naviguer; (Aut)
indiquer la route à suivre; **navigation**
[nævɪˈgeɪʃən] n navigation f

**navy** ['neɪvɪ] n marine f

**navy-blue** ['neɪvɪ'bluː] adj bleu
marine inv

**Nazi** ['nɑːtsɪ] n Nazi(e)

**NB** abbr (= nota bene) NB

**near** [nɪər] adj proche ▷ adv près ▷ prep
(also: **~ to**) près de ▷ vt approcher de;
**in the ~ future** dans un proche avenir;
**nearby** [nɪəˈbaɪ] adj proche ▷ adv tout
près, à proximité; **nearly** adv presque;
**I nearly fell** j'ai failli tomber; **it's not
nearly big enough** ce n'est vraiment
pas assez grand, c'est loin d'être assez
grand; **near-sighted** adj myope

**neat** [niːt] adj (person, work) soigné(e);

(*room etc*) bien tenu(e) *or* rangé(e);
(*solution, plan*) habile; (*spirits*) pur(e);
**neatly** *adv* avec soin *or* ordre; (*skilfully*)
habilement
**necessarily** ['nɛsɪsrɪlɪ] *adv*
nécessairement; **not ~** pas
nécessairement *or* forcément
**necessary** ['nɛsɪsrɪ] *adj* nécessaire; **if ~**
si besoin est, le cas échéant
**necessity** [nɪ'sɛsɪtɪ] *n* nécessité *f*;
chose nécessaire *or* essentielle
**neck** [nɛk] *n* cou *m*; (*of horse, garment*)
encolure *f*; (*of bottle*) goulot *m*; **~ and ~** à
égalité; **necklace** ['nɛklɪs] *n* collier *m*;
**necktie** ['nɛktaɪ] *n* (*esp us*) cravate *f*
**nectarine** ['nɛktərɪn] *n* brugnon *m*,
nectarine *f*
**need** [niːd] *n* besoin *m* ▷ *vt* avoir besoin
de; **to ~ to do** devoir faire; avoir besoin
de faire; **you don't ~ to go** vous n'avez
pas besoin *or* vous n'êtes pas obligé de
partir; **a signature is ~ed** il faut
une signature; **there's no ~ to do ....**
il n'y a pas lieu de faire ..., il n'est pas
nécessaire de faire ...
**needle** ['niːdl] *n* aiguille *f* ▷ *vt* (*inf*)
asticoter, tourmenter
**needless** ['niːdlɪs] *adj* inutile; **~ to
say, ...** inutile de dire que ...
**needlework** ['niːdlwəːk] *n* (*activity*)
travaux *mpl* d'aiguille; (*object*)
ouvrage *m*
**needn't** ['niːdnt] = **need not**
**needy** ['niːdɪ] *adj* nécessiteux(-euse)
**negative** ['nɛgətɪv] *n* (*Phot, Elec*)
négatif *m*; (*Ling*) terme *m* de négation
▷ *adj* négatif(-ive)
**neglect** [nɪ'glɛkt] *vt* négliger; (*garden*)
ne pas entretenir; (*duty*) manquer à
▷ *n* (*of person, duty, garden*) le fait de
négliger; **(state of) ~** abandon *m*; **to ~
to do sth** négliger *or* omettre de faire
qch; **to ~ one's appearance** se négliger
**negotiate** [nɪ'gəʊʃɪeɪt] *vi* négocier ▷ *vt*
négocier; (*obstacle*) franchir, négocier;
**to ~ with sb for sth** négocier avec qn
en vue d'obtenir qch
**negotiation** [nɪgəʊʃɪ'eɪʃən] *n*

négociation *f*, pourparlers *mpl*
**negotiator** [nɪ'gəʊʃɪeɪtə<sup>r</sup>] *n*
négociateur(-trice)
**neighbour** (*us* **neighbor** *etc*) ['neɪbə<sup>r</sup>]
*n* voisin(e); **neighbourhood** *n* (*place*)
quartier *m*; (*people*) voisinage *m*;
**neighbouring** *adj* voisin(e),
avoisinant(e)
**neither** ['naɪðə<sup>r</sup>] *adj, pron* aucun(e)
(des deux), ni l'un(e) ni l'autre ▷ *conj*:
**~ do I** moi non plus ▷ *adv*: **~ good nor
bad** ni bon ni mauvais; **~ of them** ni
l'un ni l'autre
**neon** ['niːɔn] *n* néon *m*
**Nepal** [nɪ'pɔːl] *n* Népal *m*
**nephew** ['nɛvjuː] *n* neveu *m*
**nerve** [nəːv] *n* nerf *m*; (*bravery*) sang-
froid *m*, courage *m*; (*cheek*) aplomb *m*,
toupet *m*; **nerves** *npl* (*nervousness*)
nervosité *f*; **he gets on my ~s** il
m'énerve
**nervous** ['nəːvəs] *adj* nerveux(-euse);
(*anxious*) inquiet(-ète), plein(e)
d'appréhension; (*timid*) intimidé(e);
**nervous breakdown** *n* dépression
nerveuse
**nest** [nɛst] *n* nid *m* ▷ *vi* (se) nicher,
faire son nid
**Net** [nɛt] *n* (*Comput*): **the ~** (*Internet*)
le Net
**net** [nɛt] *n* filet *m*; (*fabric*) tulle *f* ▷ *adj*
net(te) ▷ *vt* (*fish etc*) prendre au filet;
**netball** *n* netball *m*
**Netherlands** ['nɛðələndz] *npl*: **the ~**
les Pays-Bas *mpl*
**nett** [nɛt] *adj* = **net**
**nettle** ['nɛtl] *n* ortie *f*
**network** ['nɛtwəːk] *n* réseau *m*
**neurotic** [njuə'rɔtɪk] *adj* névrosé(e)
**neuter** ['njuːtə<sup>r</sup>] *adj* neutre ▷ *vt* (*cat etc*)
châtrer, couper
**neutral** ['njuːtrəl] *adj* neutre ▷ *n* (*Aut*)
point mort
**never** ['nɛvə<sup>r</sup>] *adv* (ne ...) jamais; **I ~
went** je n'y suis pas allé; **I've ~ been to
Spain** je ne suis jamais allé en Espagne;
**~ again** plus jamais; **~ in my life** jamais
de ma vie; *see also* **mind**; **never-ending**

*adj* interminable; **nevertheless**
[nɛvəðə'lɛs] *adv* néanmoins, malgré
tout

**new** [njuː] *adj* nouveau (nouvelle);
(*brand new*) neuf (neuve); **New Age** *n*
New Age *m*; **newborn** *adj* nouveau-
né(e); **newcomer** ['njuːkʌmə<sup>r</sup>] *n*
nouveau venu (nouvelle venue); **newly**
*adv* nouvellement, récemment

**news** [njuːz] *n* nouvelle(s) *f(pl)*; (*Radio*,
*TV*) informations *fpl*, actualités *fpl*;
**a piece of ~** une nouvelle; **news
agency** *n* agence *f* de presse;
**newsagent** *n* (*BRIT*) marchand *m*
de journaux; **newscaster** *n* (*Radio*,
*TV*) présentateur(-trice); **news
dealer** *n* (*US*) marchand *m* de
journaux; **newsletter** *n* bulletin *m*;
**newspaper** *n* journal *m*; **newsreader**
*n* = **newscaster**

**newt** [njuːt] *n* triton *m*

**New Year** *n* Nouvel An; **Happy ~!**
Bonne Année!; **New Year's Day** *n*
le jour de l'An; **New Year's Eve** *n* la
Saint-Sylvestre

**New York** [-'jɔːk] *n* New York

**New Zealand** [-'ziːlənd] *n* Nouvelle-
Zélande *f*; **New Zealander** *n* Néo-
Zélandais(e) *m*

**next** [nɛkst] *adj* (*in time*) prochain(e);
(*seat, room*) voisin(e), d'à côté; (*meeting,
bus stop*) suivant(e) ▷ *adv* la fois
suivante; la prochaine fois; (*afterwards*)
ensuite; **~ to** *prep* à côté de; **~ to
nothing** presque rien; **~ time** *adv* la
prochaine fois; **the ~ day** le lendemain,
le jour suivant *or* d'après; **~ year** l'année
prochaine; **~ please!** (*at doctor's etc*) au
suivant!; **the week after ~** dans deux
semaines; **next door** *adv* à côté ▷ *adj*
(*neighbour*) d'à côté; **next-of-kin** *n*
parent *m* le plus proche

**NHS** *n abbr* (*BRIT*) = **National Health
Service**

**nibble** ['nɪbl] *vt* grignoter

**nice** [naɪs] *adj* (*holiday, trip, taste*)
agréable; (*flat, picture*) joli(e); (*person*)
gentil(le); (*distinction, point*) subtil(e);

**nicely** *adv* agréablement; joliment;
gentiment; subtilement

**niche** [niːʃ] *n* (*Archit*) niche *f*

**nick** [nɪk] *n* (*indentation*) encoche *f*;
(*wound*) entaille *f*; (*BRIT inf*): **in good
~** en bon état ▷ *vt* (*cut*): **to ~ o.s.** se
couper; (*inf: steal*) faucher, piquer; **in
the ~ of time** juste à temps

**nickel** ['nɪkl] *n* nickel *m*; (*US*) pièce *f*
de 5 cents

**nickname** ['nɪkneɪm] *n* surnom *m* ▷ *vt*
surnommer

**nicotine** ['nɪkətiːn] *n* nicotine *f*

**niece** [niːs] *n* nièce *f*

**Nigeria** [naɪ'dʒɪərɪə] *n* Nigéria *m or f*

**night** [naɪt] *n* nuit *f*; (*evening*) soir
*m*; **at ~** la nuit; **by ~** de nuit; **last ~**
(*evening*) hier soir; (*night-time*) la nuit
dernière; **night club** *n* boîte *f* de
nuit; **nightdress** *n* chemise *f* de nuit;
**nightie** ['naɪtɪ] *n* chemise *f* de nuit;
**nightlife** *n* vie *f* nocturne; **nightly**
*adj* (*news*) du soir; (*by night*) nocturne
▷ *adv* (*every evening*) tous les soirs; (*every
night*) toutes les nuits; **nightmare** *n*
cauchemar *m*; **night school** *n* cours
*mpl* du soir; **night shift** *n* équipe *f* de
nuit; **night-time** *n* nuit *f*

**nil** [nɪl] *n* (*BRIT Sport*) zéro *m*

**nine** [naɪn] *num* neuf; **nineteen** *num*
dix-neuf; **nineteenth** [naɪn'tiːnθ] *num*
dix-neuvième; **ninetieth** ['naɪntɪɪθ]
*num* quatre-vingt-dixième; **ninety**
*num* quatre-vingt-dix

**ninth** [naɪnθ] *num* neuvième

**nip** [nɪp] *vt* pincer ▷ *vi* (*BRIT inf*): **to
~ out/down/up** sortir/descendre/
monter en vitesse

**nipple** ['nɪpl] *n* (*Anat*) mamelon *m*, bout
*m* du sein

**nitrogen** ['naɪtrədʒən] *n* azote *m*

 **KEYWORD**

**no** [nəu] (*pl* **noes**) *adv* (*opposite of "yes"*)
non; **are you coming? — no (I'm not)**
est-ce que vous venez? — non; **would
you like some more? — no thank you**

vous en voulez encore? — non merci
▷ adj (not any) (ne ...) pas de, (ne ...)
aucun(e); **I have no money/books** je
n'ai pas d'argent/de livres; **no student
would have done it** aucun étudiant ne
l'aurait fait; **"no smoking"** "défense de
fumer"; **"no dogs"** "les chiens ne sont
pas admis"
▷ n non m

**nobility** [nəu'bɪlɪtɪ] n noblesse f
**noble** ['nəubl] adj noble
**nobody** ['nəubədɪ] pron (ne ...)
personne
**nod** [nɔd] vi faire un signe de (la) tête
(affirmatif ou amical); (sleep) somnoler
▷ vt: **to ~ one's head** faire un signe de
(la) tête; (in agreement) faire signe que
oui ▷ n signe m de (la) tête; **nod off** vi
s'assoupir
**noise** [nɔɪz] n bruit m; **I can't sleep for
the ~** je n'arrive pas à dormir à cause du
bruit; **noisy** adj bruyant(e)
**nominal** ['nɔmɪnl] adj (rent, fee)
symbolique; (value) nominal(e)
**nominate** ['nɔmɪneɪt] vt (propose)
proposer; (appoint) nommer;
**nomination** [nɔmɪ'neɪʃən] n
nomination f; **nominee** [nɔmɪ'niː] n
candidat agréé; personne nommée
**none** [nʌn] pron aucun(e); **~ of you**
aucun d'entre vous, personne parmi
vous; **I have ~ left** je n'en ai plus; **he's
~ the worse for it** il ne s'en porte pas
plus mal
**nonetheless** ['nʌnðə'lɛs] adv
néanmoins
**non-fiction** [nɔn'fɪkʃən] n littérature f
non-romanesque
**nonsense** ['nɔnsəns] n absurdités fpl,
idioties fpl; **~!** ne dites pas d'idioties!
**non**: **non-smoker** n non-fumeur m;
**non-smoking** adj non-fumeur; **non-
stick** adj qui n'attache pas
**noodles** ['nuːdlz] npl nouilles fpl
**noon** [nuːn] n midi m
**no-one** ['nəuwʌn] pron = **nobody**
**nor** [nɔːʳ] conj = **neither** ▷ adv see

**neither**
**norm** [nɔːm] n norme f
**normal** ['nɔːml] adj normal(e);
**normally** adv normalement
**Normandy** ['nɔːməndɪ] n Normandie f
**north** [nɔːθ] n nord m ▷ adj nord inv;
(wind) du nord ▷ adv au or vers le nord;
**North Africa** n Afrique f du Nord;
**North African** adj nord-africain(e),
d'Afrique du Nord ▷ n Nord-Africain(e);
**North America** n Amérique f du Nord;
**North American** n Nord-Américain(e)
▷ adj nord-américain(e), d'Amérique
du Nord; **northbound** ['nɔːθbaund]
adj (traffic) en direction du nord;
(carriageway) nord inv; **north-east** n
nord-est m; **northeastern** adj (du)
nord-est inv; **northern** ['nɔːðən] adj
du nord, septentrional(e); **Northern
Ireland** n Irlande f du Nord; **North
Korea** n Corée f du Nord; **North
Pole** n: **the North Pole** le pôle Nord;
**North Sea** n: **the North Sea** la mer
du Nord; **north-west** n nord-ouest m;
**northwestern** ['nɔːθ'westən] adj (du)
nord-ouest inv
**Norway** ['nɔːweɪ] n Norvège f;
**Norwegian** [nɔː'wiːdʒən] adj
norvégien(ne) ▷ n Norvégien(ne);
(Ling) norvégien m
**nose** [nəuz] n nez m; (of dog, cat)
museau m; (fig) flair m; **nose about,
nose around** vi fouiner or fureter
(partout); **nosebleed** n saignement m
de nez; **nosey** adj (inf) curieux(-euse)
**nostalgia** [nɔs'tældʒɪə] n nostalgie f
**nostalgic** [nɔs'tældʒɪk] adj
nostalgique
**nostril** ['nɔstrɪl] n narine f; (of horse)
naseau m
**nosy** ['nəuzɪ] (inf) adj = **nosey**
**not** [nɔt] adv (ne ...) pas; **he is ~** or **isn't
here** il n'est pas ici; **you must ~** or
**mustn't do that** tu ne dois pas faire
ça; **I hope ~** j'espère que non; **~ at
all** pas du tout; (after thanks) de rien;
**it's too late, isn't it?** c'est trop tard,
n'est-ce pas?; **~ yet/now** pas encore/

maintenant; *see also* **only**

**notable** ['nəutəbl] *adj* notable; **notably** *adv* (*particularly*) en particulier; (*markedly*) spécialement

**notch** [nɔtʃ] *n* encoche *f*

**note** [nəut] *n* note *f*; (*letter*) mot *m*; (*banknote*) billet *m* ▷ *vt* (*also*: **~ down**) noter; (*notice*) constater; **notebook** *n* carnet *m*; (*for shorthand etc*) bloc-notes *m*; **noted** ['nəutɪd] *adj* réputé(e); **notepad** *n* bloc-notes *m*; **notepaper** *n* papier *m* à lettres

**nothing** ['nʌθɪŋ] *n* rien *m*; **he does ~** il ne fait rien; **~ new** rien de nouveau; **for ~** (*free*) pour rien, gratuitement; (*in vain*) pour rien; **~ at all** rien du tout; **~ much** pas grand-chose

**notice** ['nəutɪs] *n* (*announcement, warning*) avis *m* ▷ *vt* remarquer, s'apercevoir de; **advance ~** préavis *m*; **at short ~** dans un délai très court; **until further ~** jusqu'à nouvel ordre; **to give ~, hand in one's ~** (*employee*) donner sa démission, démissionner; **to take ~ of** prêter attention à; **to bring sth to sb's ~** porter qch à la connaissance de qn; **noticeable** *adj* visible

**notice board** *n* (BRIT) panneau *m* d'affichage

**notify** ['nəutɪfaɪ] *vt*: **to ~ sb of sth** avertir qn de qch

**notion** ['nəuʃən] *n* idée *f*; (*concept*) notion *f*; **notions** *npl* (US: *haberdashery*) mercerie *f*

**notorious** [nəu'tɔːrɪəs] *adj* notoire (*souvent en mal*)

**notwithstanding** [nɔtwɪθ'stændɪŋ] *adv* néanmoins ▷ *prep* en dépit de

**nought** [nɔːt] *n* zéro *m*

**noun** [naun] *n* nom *m*

**nourish** ['nʌrɪʃ] *vt* nourrir; **nourishment** *n* nourriture *f*

**Nov.** *abbr* (= *November*) nov

**novel** ['nɔvl] *n* roman *m* ▷ *adj* nouveau (nouvelle), original(e); **novelist** *n* romancier *m*; **novelty** *n* nouveauté *f*

**November** [nəu'vɛmbər] *n*

novembre *m*

**novice** ['nɔvɪs] *n* novice *m/f*

**now** [nau] *adv* maintenant ▷ *conj*: **~ (that)** maintenant (que); **right ~** tout de suite; **by ~** à l'heure qu'il est; **just ~**: **that's the fashion just ~** c'est la mode en ce moment *or* maintenant; **~ and then, ~ and again** de temps en temps; **from ~ on** dorénavant; **nowadays** ['nauədeɪz] *adv* de nos jours

**nowhere** ['nəuwɛər] *adv* (ne ...) nulle part

**nozzle** ['nɔzl] *n* (*of hose*) jet *m*, lance *f*; (*of vacuum cleaner*) suceur *m*

**nr** *abbr* (BRIT) = **near**

**nuclear** ['njuːklɪər] *adj* nucléaire

**nucleus** (*pl* **nuclei**) ['njuːklɪəs, 'njuːklɪaɪ] *n* noyau *m*

**nude** [njuːd] *adj* nu(e) ▷ *n* (*Art*) nu *m*; **in the ~** (tout(e)) nu(e)

**nudge** [nʌdʒ] *vt* donner un (petit) coup de coude à

**nudist** ['njuːdɪst] *n* nudiste *m/f*

**nudity** ['njuːdɪtɪ] *n* nudité *f*

**nuisance** ['njuːsns] *n*: **it's a ~** c'est (très) ennuyeux *or* gênant; **he's a ~** il est assommant *or* casse-pieds; **what a ~!** quelle barbe!

**numb** [nʌm] *adj* engourdi(e); (*with fear*) paralysé(e)

**number** ['nʌmbər] *n* nombre *m*; (*numeral*) chiffre *m*; (*of house, car, telephone, newspaper*) numéro *m* ▷ *vt* numéroter; (*amount to*) compter; **a ~ of** un certain nombre de; **they were seven in ~** ils étaient (au nombre de) sept; **to be ~ed among** compter parmi; **number plate** *n* (BRIT Aut) plaque *f* minéralogique *or* d'immatriculation; **Number Ten** *n* (BRIT: 10 Downing Street) *résidence du Premier ministre*

**numerical** [njuː'mɛrɪkl] *adj* numérique

**numerous** ['njuːmərəs] *adj* nombreux(-euse)

**nun** [nʌn] *n* religieuse *f*, sœur *f*

**nurse** [nəːs] *n* infirmière *f*; (*also*: **~maid**) bonne *f* d'enfants ▷ *vt* (*patient, cold*) soigner

**nursery** ['nə:sərɪ] *n* (*room*) nursery *f*; (*institution*) crèche *f*, garderie *f*; (*for plants*) pépinière *f*; **nursery rhyme** *n* comptine *f*, chansonnette *f* pour enfants; **nursery school** *n* école maternelle; **nursery slope** *n* (BRIT Ski) piste *f* pour débutants

**nursing** ['nə:sɪŋ] *n* (*profession*) profession *f* d'infirmière; (*care*) soins *mpl*; **nursing home** *n* clinique *f*; (*for convalescence*) maison *f* de convalescence *or* de repos; (*for old people*) maison de retraite

**nurture** ['nə:tʃə*] *vt* élever

**nut** [nʌt] *n* (*of metal*) écrou *m*; (*fruit: walnut*) noix *f*; (: *hazelnut*) noisette *f*; (: *peanut*) cacahuète *f* (*terme générique en anglais*)

**nutmeg** ['nʌtmɛg] *n* (noix *f*) muscade *f*

**nutrient** ['nju:trɪənt] *n* substance nutritive

**nutrition** [nju:'trɪʃən] *n* nutrition *f*, alimentation *f*

**nutritious** [nju:'trɪʃəs] *adj* nutritif(-ive), nourrissant(e)

**nuts** [nʌts] (*inf*) *adj* dingue

**NVQ** *n abbr* (BRIT) = **National Vocational Qualification**

**nylon** ['naɪlɔn] *n* nylon *m* ▷ *adj* de *or* en nylon

# O

**oak** [əuk] *n* chêne *m* ▷ *cpd* de *or* en (bois de) chêne

**O.A.P.** *n abbr* (BRIT) = **old age pensioner**

**oar** [ɔ:*] *n* aviron *m*, rame *f*

**oasis** (*pl* **oases**) [əu'eɪsɪs, əu'eɪsi:z] *n* oasis *f*

**oath** [əuθ] *n* serment *m*; (*swear word*) juron *m*; **on** (BRIT) *or* **under ~** sous serment; assermenté(e)

**oatmeal** ['əutmi:l] *n* flocons *mpl* d'avoine

**oats** [əuts] *n* avoine *f*

**obedience** [ə'bi:dɪəns] *n* obéissance *f*

**obedient** [ə'bi:dɪənt] *adj* obéissant(e)

**obese** [əu'bi:s] *adj* obèse

**obesity** [əu'bi:sɪtɪ] *n* obésité *f*

**obey** [ə'beɪ] *vt* obéir à; (*instructions, regulations*) se conformer à ▷ *vi* obéir

**obituary** [ə'bɪtjuərɪ] *n* nécrologie *f*

**object** *n* ['ɔbdʒɪkt] objet *m*; (*purpose*) but *m*, objet; (*Ling*) complément *m* d'objet ▷ *vi* [əb'dʒɛkt]: **to ~ to** (*attitude*) désapprouver; (*proposal*) protester contre, élever une objection contre; **I ~!** je proteste!; **he ~ed that ...** il a fait valoir or a objecté que ...; **money is no ~** l'argent n'est pas un problème; **objection** [əb'dʒɛkʃən] n objection f; **if you have no objection** si vous n'y voyez pas d'inconvénient; **objective** n objectif m ▷ adj objectif(-ive)

**obligation** [ɔblɪ'geɪʃən] n obligation f, devoir m; (debt) dette f (de reconnaissance)

**obligatory** [ə'blɪgətərɪ] adj obligatoire

**oblige** [ə'blaɪdʒ] vt (force): **to ~ sb to do** obliger or forcer qn à faire; (do a favour) rendre service à, obliger; **to be ~d to sb for sth** être obligé(e) à qn de qch

**oblique** [ə'bliːk] adj oblique; (allusion) indirect(e)

**obliterate** [ə'blɪtəreɪt] vt effacer

**oblivious** [ə'blɪvɪəs] adj: **~ of** oublieux(-euse) de

**oblong** ['ɔblɔŋ] adj oblong(ue) ▷ n rectangle m

**obnoxious** [əb'nɔkʃəs] adj odieux(-euse); (smell) nauséabond(e)

**oboe** ['əubəu] n hautbois m

**obscene** [əb'siːn] adj obscène

**obscure** [əb'skjuər] adj obscur(e) ▷ vt obscurcir; (hide: sun) cacher

**observant** [əb'zəːvnt] adj observateur(-trice)

**observation** [ɔbzə'veɪʃən] n observation f; (by police etc) surveillance f

**observatory** [əb'zəːvətrɪ] n observatoire m

**observe** [əb'zəːv] vt observer; (remark) faire observer or remarquer; **observer** n observateur(-trice)

**obsess** [əb'sɛs] vt obséder; **obsession** [əb'sɛʃən] n obsession f; **obsessive** adj obsédant(e)

**obsolete** ['ɔbsəliːt] adj dépassé(e), périmé(e)

**obstacle** ['ɔbstəkl] n obstacle m

**obstinate** ['ɔbstɪnɪt] adj obstiné(e); (pain, cold) persistant(e)

**obstruct** [əb'strʌkt] vt (block) boucher, obstruer; (hinder) entraver; **obstruction** [əb'strʌkʃən] n obstruction f; (to plan, progress) obstacle m

**obtain** [əb'teɪn] vt obtenir

**obvious** ['ɔbvɪəs] adj évident(e), manifeste; **obviously** adv manifestement; (of course): **obviously!** bien sûr!; **obviously not!** évidemment pas!, bien sûr que non!

**occasion** [ə'keɪʒən] n occasion f; (event) événement m; **occasional** adj pris(e) (or fait(e) etc) de temps en temps; (worker, spending) occasionnel(le); **occasionally** adv de temps en temps, quelquefois

**occult** [ɔ'kʌlt] adj occulte ▷ n: **the ~** le surnaturel

**occupant** ['ɔkjupənt] n occupant m

**occupation** [ɔkju'peɪʃən] n occupation f; (job) métier m, profession f

**occupy** ['ɔkjupaɪ] vt occuper; **to ~ o.s. with** or **by doing** s'occuper à faire

**occur** [ə'kəːr] vi se produire; (difficulty, opportunity) se présenter; (phenomenon, error) se rencontrer; **to ~ to sb** venir à l'esprit de qn; **occurrence** [ə'kʌrəns] n (existence) présence f, existence f; (event) cas m, fait m

**ocean** ['əuʃən] n océan m

**o'clock** [ə'klɔk] adv: **it is 5 o'clock** il est 5 heures

**Oct.** abbr (= October) oct

**October** [ɔk'təubər] n octobre m

**octopus** ['ɔktəpəs] n pieuvre f

**odd** [ɔd] adj (strange) bizarre, curieux(-euse); (number) impair(e); (not of a set) dépareillé(e); **60-~** 60 et quelques; **at ~ times** de temps en temps; **the ~ one out** l'exception f; **oddly** adv bizarrement, curieusement; **odds** npl (in betting) cote f; **it makes no odds** cela n'a pas d'importance; **odds and ends** de petites choses; **at odds** en désaccord

**odometer** [ɔ'dɔmɪtər] n (us) odomètre m

**odour** (*US* **odor**) ['əʊdə<sup>r</sup>] *n* odeur *f*

○ **KEYWORD**

**of** [ɔv, əv] *prep* **1** (*gen*) de; **a friend of ours** un de nos amis; **a boy of 10** un garçon de 10 ans; **that was kind of you** c'était gentil de votre part

**2** (*expressing quantity, amount, dates etc*) de; **a kilo of flour** un kilo de farine; **how much of this do you need?** combien vous en faut-il?; **there were three of them** (*people*) ils étaient 3; (*objects*) il y en avait 3; **three of us went** 3 d'entre nous y sont allé(e)s; **the 5th of July** le 5 juillet; **a quarter of 4** (*US*) 4 heures moins le quart

**3** (*from, out of*) en, de; **a statue of marble** une statue de *or* en marbre; **made of wood** (fait) en bois

**off** [ɔf] *adj, adv* (*engine*) coupé(e); (*light, TV*) éteint(e); (*tap*) fermé(e); (BRIT: *food*) mauvais(e), avancé(e); (: *milk*) tourné(e); (*absent*) absent(e); (*cancelled*) annulé(e); (*removed*): **the lid was ~** le couvercle était retiré *or* n'était pas mis; (*away*): **to run/drive ~** partir en courant/en voiture ▷ *prep* de; **to be ~** (*to leave*) partir, s'en aller; **to be ~ sick** être absent pour cause de maladie; **a day ~** un jour de congé; **to have an ~ day** n'être pas en forme; **he had his coat ~** il avait enlevé son manteau; **10% ~** (*Comm*) 10% de rabais; **5 km ~ (the road)** à 5 km (de la route); **~ the coast** au large de la côte; **it's a long way ~** c'est loin (d'ici); **I'm ~ meat** je ne mange plus de viande; **je n'aime plus la viande**; **on the ~-chance** à tout hasard; **~ and on, on and ~** de temps à autre

**offence** (*US* **offense**) [ə'fɛns] *n* (*crime*) délit *m*, infraction *f*; **to take ~ at** se vexer de, s'offenser de

**offend** [ə'fɛnd] *vt* (*person*) offenser, blesser; **offender** *n* délinquant(e); (*against regulations*) contrevenant(e)

**offense** [ə'fɛns] *n* (*US*) = **offence**

**offensive** [ə'fɛnsɪv] *adj* offensant(e), choquant(e); (*smell etc*) très déplaisant(e); (*weapon*) offensif(-ive) ▷ *n* (*Mil*) offensive *f*

**offer** ['ɔfə<sup>r</sup>] *n* offre *f*, proposition *f* ▷ *vt* offrir, proposer; **"on ~"** (*Comm*) "en promotion"

**offhand** [ɔf'hænd] *adj* désinvolte ▷ *adv* spontanément

**office** ['ɔfɪs] *n* (*place*) bureau *m*; (*position*) charge *f*, fonction *f*; **doctor's ~** (*US*) cabinet (médical); **to take ~** entrer en fonctions; **office block** (*US* **office building**) *n* immeuble *m* de bureaux; **office hours** *npl* heures *fpl* de bureau; (*US Med*) heures de consultation

**officer** ['ɔfɪsə<sup>r</sup>] *n* (*Mil etc*) officier *m*; (*also*: **police ~**) agent *m* (de police); (*of organization*) membre *m* du bureau directeur

**office worker** *n* employé(e) de bureau

**official** [ə'fɪʃl] *adj* (*authorized*) officiel(le) ▷ *n* officiel *m*; (*civil servant*) fonctionnaire *m/f*; (*of railways, post office, town hall*) employé(e)

**off**: **off-licence** *n* (BRIT: *shop*) débit *m* de vins et de spiritueux; **off-line** *adj* (*Comput*) (en mode) autonome; (: *switched off*) non connecté(e); **off-peak** *adj* aux heures creuses; (*electricity, ticket*) au tarif heures creuses; **off-putting** *adj* (BRIT: *remark*) rébarbatif(-ive); (*person*) rebutant(e), peu engageant(e); **off-season** *adj, adv* hors-saison *inv*

**offset** ['ɔfsɛt] *vt* (*irreg: like* **set**) (*counteract*) contrebalancer, compenser

**offshore** [ɔf'ʃɔ:<sup>r</sup>] *adj* (*breeze*) de terre; (*island*) proche du littoral; (*fishing*) côtier(-ière)

**offside** ['ɔf'saɪd] *adj* (*Sport*) hors jeu; (*Aut: in Britain*) de droite; (: *in US, Europe*) de gauche

**offspring** ['ɔfsprɪŋ] *n* progéniture *f*

**often** ['ɔfn] *adv* souvent; **how ~ do you go?** vous y allez tous les combien?; **every so ~** de temps en temps, de temps à autre

**oh** [əu] *excl* ô!, oh!, ah!

**oil** [ɔil] *n* huile *f*; (*petroleum*) pétrole *m*; (*for central heating*) mazout *m* ▷ *vt* (*machine*) graisser; **oil filter** *n* (*Aut*) filtre *m* à huile; **oil painting** *n* peinture *f* à l'huile; **oil refinery** *n* raffinerie *f* de pétrole; **oil rig** *n* derrick *m*; (*at sea*) plate-forme pétrolière; **oil slick** *n* nappe *f* de mazout; **oil tanker** *n* (*ship*) pétrolier *m*; (*truck*) camion-citerne *m*; **oil well** *n* puits *m* de pétrole; **oily** *adj* huileux(-euse); (*food*) gras(se)

**ointment** ['ɔintmənt] *n* onguent *m*

**O.K., okay** ['əu'kei] (*inf*) *excl* d'accord! ▷ *vt* approuver, donner son accord à ▷ *adj* (*not bad*) pas mal; **is it O.K.?, are you O.K.?** ça va?

**old** [əuld] *adj* vieux (vieille); (*person*) vieux, âgé(e); (*former*) ancien(ne), vieux; **how ~ are you?** quel âge avez-vous?; **he's 10 years ~** il a 10 ans, il est âgé de 10 ans; **~er brother/sister** frère/sœur aîné(e); **old age** *n* vieillesse *f*; **old-age pension** *n* (*BRIT*) (pension *f* de) retraite *f* (*de la sécurité sociale*); **old-age pensioner** *n* (*BRIT*) retraité(e); **old-fashioned** *adj* démodé(e); (*person*) vieux jeu *inv*; **old people's home** *n* (*esp BRIT*) maison *f* de retraite

**olive** ['ɔliv] *n* (*fruit*) olive *f*; (*tree*) olivier *m* ▷ *adj* (*also:* **~-green**) (vert) olive *inv*; **olive oil** *n* huile *f* d'olive

**Olympic** [əu'limpik] *adj* olympique; **the ~ Games, the ~s** les Jeux *mpl* olympiques

**omelet(te)** ['ɔmlit] *n* omelette *f*

**omen** ['əumən] *n* présage *m*

**ominous** ['ɔminəs] *adj* menaçant(e), inquiétant(e); (*event*) de mauvais augure

**omit** [əu'mit] *vt* omettre

**KEYWORD**

**on** [ɔn] *prep* **1** (*indicating position*) sur; **on the table** sur la table; **on the wall** sur le *or* au mur; **on the left** à gauche
**2** (*indicating means, method, condition etc*): **on foot** à pied; **on the train/plane** (*be*) dans le train/l'avion; (*go*) en train/avion; **on the telephone/radio/television** au téléphone/à la radio/à la télévision; **to be on drugs** se droguer; **on holiday** (*BRIT*), **on vacation** (*US*) en vacances
**3** (*referring to time*): **on Friday** vendredi; **on Fridays** le vendredi; **on June 20th** le 20 juin; **a week on Friday** vendredi en huit; **on arrival** à l'arrivée; **on seeing this** en voyant cela
**4** (*about, concerning*) sur, de; **a book on Balzac/physics** un livre sur Balzac/de physique
▷ *adv* **1** (*referring to dress*): **to have one's coat on** avoir (mis) son manteau; **to put one's coat on** mettre son manteau; **what's she got on?** qu'est-ce qu'elle porte?
**2** (*referring to covering*): **screw the lid on tightly** vissez bien le couvercle
**3** (*further, continuously*): **to walk** *etc* **on** continuer à marcher *etc*; **from that day on** depuis ce jour
▷ *adj* **1** (*in operation: machine*) en marche; (: *radio, TV, light*) allumé(e); (: *tap, gas*) ouvert(e); (: *brakes*) mis(e); **is the meeting still on?** (*not cancelled*) est-ce que la réunion a bien lieu?; (*in progress*) la réunion dure-t-elle encore?; **when is this film on?** quand passe ce film?
**2** (*inf*): **that's not on!** (*not acceptable*) cela ne se fait pas!; (*not possible*) pas question!

**once** [wʌns] *adv* une fois; (*formerly*) autrefois ▷ *conj* une fois que + *sub*; **~ he had left/it was done** une fois qu'il fut parti/que ce fut terminé; **at ~** tout de suite, immédiatement; (*simultaneously*) à la fois; **all at ~** *adv* tout d'un coup; **~ a week** une fois par semaine; **~ more** encore une fois; **~ and for all** une fois pour toutes; **~ upon a time there was ...** il y avait une fois ..., il était une fois ...

**oncoming** [ˈɒnkʌmɪŋ] *adj* (*traffic*) venant en sens inverse

 **KEYWORD**

**one** [wʌn] *num* un(e); **one hundred and fifty** cent cinquante; **one by one** un(e) à *or* par un(e); **one day** un jour ▷ *adj* **1** (*sole*) seul(e), unique; **the one book which** l'unique *or* le seul livre qui; **the one man who** le seul (homme) qui **2** (*same*) même; **they came in the one car** ils sont venus dans la même voiture ▷ *pron* **1**: **this one** celui-ci (celle-ci); **that one** celui-là (celle-là); **I've already got one/a red one** j'en ai déjà un(e)/un(e) rouge; **which one do you want?** lequel voulez-vous? **2**: **one another** l'un(e) l'autre; **to look at one another** se regarder **3** (*impersonal*) on; **one never knows** on ne sait jamais; **to cut one's finger** se couper le doigt; **one needs to eat** il faut manger

**one-off** [wʌnˈɒf] (*BRIT inf*) *n* exemplaire *m* unique

**oneself** [wʌnˈsɛlf] *pron* se; (*after prep, also emphatic*) soi-même; **to hurt ~** se faire mal; **to keep sth for ~** garder qch pour soi; **to talk to ~** se parler à soi-même; **by ~** tout seul

**one:** **one-shot** [wʌnˈʃɒt] (*US*) *n* = **one-off**; **one-sided** *adj* (*argument, decision*) unilatéral(e); **one-to-one** *adj* (*relationship*) univoque; **one-way** *adj* (*street, traffic*) à sens unique

**ongoing** [ˈɒngəʊɪŋ] *adj* en cours; (*relationship*) suivi(e)

**onion** [ˈʌnjən] *n* oignon *m*

**on-line** [ˈɒnlaɪn] *adj* (*Comput*) en ligne; (: *switched on*) connecté(e)

**onlooker** [ˈɒnlʊkəʳ] *n* spectateur(-trice)

**only** [ˈəʊnlɪ] *adv* seulement ▷ *adj* seul(e), unique ▷ *conj* seulement, mais; **an ~ child** un enfant unique; **not ~ ... but also** non seulement ... mais aussi; **I** **~ took one** j'en ai seulement pris un, je n'en ai pris qu'un

**on-screen** [ɒnˈskriːn] *adj* à l'écran

**onset** [ˈɒnsɛt] *n* début *m*; (*of winter, old age*) approche *f*

**onto** [ˈɒntu] *prep* = **on to**

**onward(s)** [ˈɒnwəd(z)] *adv* (*move*) en avant; **from that time ~** à partir de ce moment

**oops** [ʊps] *excl* houp!

**ooze** [uːz] *vi* suinter

**opaque** [əʊˈpeɪk] *adj* opaque

**open** [ˈəʊpn] *adj* ouvert(e); (*car*) découvert(e); (*road, view*) dégagé(e); (*meeting*) public(-ique); (*admiration*) manifeste ▷ *vt* ouvrir ▷ *vi* (*flower, eyes, door, debate*) s'ouvrir; (*shop, bank, museum*) ouvrir; (*book etc: commence*) commencer, débuter; **is it ~ to public?** est-ce ouvert au public?; **what time do you ~?** à quelle heure ouvrez-vous?; **in the ~ (air)** en plein air; **open up** *vt* ouvrir; (*blocked road*) dégager ▷ *vi* s'ouvrir; **open-air** *adj* en plein air; **opening** *n* ouverture *f*; (*opportunity*) occasion *f*; (*work*) débouché *m*; (*job*) poste vacant; **opening hours** *npl* heures *fpl* d'ouverture; **open learning** *n* enseignement universitaire à la carte, notamment par correspondance; (*distance learning*) télé-enseignement *m*; **openly** *adv* ouvertement; **open-minded** *adj* à l'esprit ouvert; **open-necked** *adj* à col ouvert; **open-plan** *adj* sans cloisons; **Open University** *n* (*BRIT*) cours universitaires par correspondance

● **OPEN UNIVERSITY**
●
● L'**Open University** a été fondée en
● 1969. L'enseignement comprend
● des cours (certaines plages horaires
● sont réservées à cet effet à la
● télévision et à la radio), des devoirs
● qui sont envoyés par l'étudiant à son
● directeur ou sa directrice d'études, et
● un séjour obligatoire en université
● d'été. Il faut préparer un certain

- nombre d'unités de valeur pendant
- une période de temps déterminée
- et obtenir la moyenne à un certain
- nombre d'entre elles pour recevoir le
- diplôme visé.

**opera** ['ɔpərə] n opéra m; **opera house** n opéra m; **opera singer** n chanteur(-euse) d'opéra

**operate** ['ɔpəreɪt] vt (machine) faire marcher, faire fonctionner ▷ vi fonctionner; **to ~ on sb (for)** (Med) opérer qn (de)

**operating room** n (US: Med) salle f d'opération

**operating theatre** n (BRIT: Med) salle f d'opération

**operation** [ɔpə'reɪʃən] n opération f; (of machine) fonctionnement m; **to have an ~ (for)** se faire opérer (de); **to be in ~** (machine) être en service; (system) être en vigueur; **operational** adj opérationnel(le); (ready for use) en état de marche

**operative** ['ɔpərətɪv] adj (measure) en vigueur ▷ n (in factory) ouvrier(-ière)

**operator** ['ɔpəreɪtəʳ] n (of machine) opérateur(-trice); (Tel) téléphoniste m/f

**opinion** [ə'pɪnjən] n opinion f, avis m; **in my ~** à mon avis; **opinion poll** n sondage m d'opinion

**opponent** [ə'pəunənt] n adversaire m/f

**opportunity** [ɔpə'tjuːnɪtɪ] n occasion f; **to take the ~ to do** or **of doing** profiter de l'occasion pour faire

**oppose** [ə'pəuz] vt s'opposer à; **to be ~d to sth** être opposé(e) à qch; **as ~d to** par opposition à

**opposite** ['ɔpəzɪt] adj opposé(e); (house etc) d'en face ▷ adv en face ▷ prep en face de ▷ n opposé m, contraire m; (of word) contraire

**opposition** [ɔpə'zɪʃən] n opposition f

**oppress** [ə'prɛs] vt opprimer

**opt** [ɔpt] vi: **to ~ for** opter pour; **to ~ to do** choisir de faire; **opt out** vi: **to ~ out of** choisir de ne pas participer à or de

ne pas faire

**optician** [ɔp'tɪʃən] n opticien(ne)

**optimism** ['ɔptɪmɪzəm] n optimisme m

**optimist** ['ɔptɪmɪst] n optimiste m/f; **optimistic** [ɔptɪ'mɪstɪk] adj optimiste

**optimum** ['ɔptɪməm] adj optimum

**option** ['ɔpʃən] n choix m, option f; (Scol) matière f à option; **optional** adj facultatif(-ive)

**or** [ɔːʳ] conj ou; (with negative): **he hasn't seen or heard anything** il n'a rien vu ni entendu; **or else** sinon; ou bien

**oral** ['ɔːrəl] adj oral(e) ▷ n oral m

**orange** ['ɔrɪndʒ] n (fruit) orange f ▷ adj orange inv; **orange juice** n jus m d'orange; **orange squash** n orangeade f

**orbit** ['ɔːbɪt] n orbite f ▷ vt graviter autour de

**orchard** ['ɔːtʃəd] n verger m

**orchestra** ['ɔːkɪstrə] n orchestre m; (US: seating) (fauteuils mpl d')orchestre

**orchid** ['ɔːkɪd] n orchidée f

**ordeal** [ɔː'diːl] n épreuve f

**order** ['ɔːdəʳ] n ordre m; (Comm) commande f ▷ vt ordonner; (Comm) commander; **in ~** en ordre; (of document) en règle; **out of ~** (not in correct order) en désordre; (machine) hors service; (telephone) en dérangement; **a machine in working ~** une machine en état de marche; **in ~ to do/that** pour faire/que + sub; **could I ~ now, please?** je peux commander, s'il vous plaît?; **to be on ~** être en commande; **to ~ sb to do** ordonner à qn de faire; **order form** n bon m de commande; **orderly** n (Mil) ordonnance f; (Med) garçon m de salle ▷ adj (room) en ordre; (mind) méthodique; (person) qui a de l'ordre

**ordinary** ['ɔːdnrɪ] adj ordinaire, normal(e); (pej) ordinaire, quelconque; **out of the ~** exceptionnel(le)

**ore** [ɔːʳ] n minerai m

**oregano** [ɔrɪ'gɑːnəu] n origan m

**organ** ['ɔːgən] n organe m; (Mus) orgue m, orgues fpl; **organic** [ɔː'gænɪk] adj

organique; (*crops etc*) biologique,
naturel(le); **organism** *n* organisme *m*
**organization** [ɔːɡənaɪˈzeɪʃən] *n*
organisation *f*
**organize** [ˈɔːɡənaɪz] *vt* organiser;
**organized** [ˈɔːɡənaɪzd] *adj* (*planned*)
organisé(e); (*efficient*) bien organisé;
**organizer** *n* organisateur(-trice)
**orgasm** [ˈɔːɡæzəm] *n* orgasme *m*
**orgy** [ˈɔːdʒɪ] *n* orgie *f*
**oriental** [ɔːrɪˈɛntl] *adj* oriental(e)
**orientation** [ɔːrɪɛnˈteɪʃən] *n* (*attitudes*)
tendance *f*; (*in job*) orientation *f*; (*of building*) orientation, exposition *f*
**origin** [ˈɔrɪdʒɪn] *n* origine *f*
**original** [əˈrɪdʒɪnl] *adj* original(e);
(*earliest*) originel(le) ▷ *n* original *m*;
**originally** *adv* (*at first*) à l'origine
**originate** [əˈrɪdʒɪneɪt] *vi*: **to ~ from**
être originaire de; (*suggestion*) provenir
de; **to ~ in** (*custom*) prendre naissance
dans, avoir son origine dans
**Orkney** [ˈɔːknɪ] *n* (*also*: **the ~s, the ~ Islands**) les Orcades *fpl*
**ornament** [ˈɔːnəmənt] *n* ornement *m*;
(*trinket*) bibelot *m*; **ornamental**
[ɔːnəˈmɛntl] *adj* décoratif(-ive);
(*garden*) d'agrément
**ornate** [ɔːˈneɪt] *adj* très orné(e)
**orphan** [ˈɔːfn] *n* orphelin(e)
**orthodox** [ˈɔːθədɔks] *adj* orthodoxe
**orthopaedic** (*us* **orthopedic**)
[ɔːθəˈpiːdɪk] *adj* orthopédique
**osteopath** [ˈɔstɪəpæθ] *n* ostéopathe
*m/f*
**ostrich** [ˈɔstrɪtʃ] *n* autruche *f*
**other** [ˈʌðəʳ] *adj* autre ▷ *pron*: **the ~ (one)** l'autre; **~s** (*other people*) d'autres
▷ *adv*: **~ than** autrement que; à part;
**the ~ day** l'autre jour; **otherwise** *adv*,
*conj* autrement
**Ottawa** [ˈɔtəwə] *n* Ottawa
**otter** [ˈɔtəʳ] *n* loutre *f*
**ouch** [autʃ] *excl* aïe!
**ought** (*pt* **~**) [ɔːt] *aux vb*: **I ~ to do it** je
devrais le faire, il faudrait que je le
fasse; **this ~ to have been corrected**
cela aurait dû être corrigé; **he ~ to win**

(*probability*) il devrait gagner
**ounce** [auns] *n* once *f* (*28.35g*; *16 in a pound*)
**our** [ˈauəʳ] *adj* notre, nos *pl*; *see also* **my**;
**ours** *pron* le (la) nôtre, les nôtres; *see
also* **mine¹**; **ourselves** *pron pl* (*reflexive,
after preposition*) nous; (*emphatic*) nous-mêmes; *see also* **oneself**
**oust** [aust] *vt* évincer
**out** [aut] *adv* dehors; (*published, not at
home etc*) sorti(e); (*light, fire*) éteint(e); **~
there** là-bas; **he's ~** (*absent*) il est sorti;
**to be ~ in one's calculations** s'être
trompé dans ses calculs; **to run/back**
*etc* **~** sortir en courant/en reculant
*etc*; **~ loud** *adv* à haute voix; **~ of** *prep*
(*outside*) en dehors de; (*because of: anger
etc*) par; (*from among*): **10 ~ of 10** 10 sur
10; (*without*): **~ of petrol** sans essence,
à court d'essence; **~ of order** (*machine*)
en panne; (*Tel: line*) en dérangement;
**outback** *n* (*in Australia*) intérieur *m*;
**outbound** *adj*: **outbound (from/for)**
en partance (de/pour); **outbreak**
*n* (*of violence*) éruption *f*, explosion
*f*; (*of disease*) de nombreux cas; **the
outbreak of war south of the border**
la guerre qui s'est déclarée au sud de
la frontière; **outburst** *n* explosion *f*,
accès *m*; **outcast** *n* exilé(e); (*socially*)
paria *m*; **outcome** *n* issue *f*, résultat *m*;
**outcry** *n* tollé (général); **outdated** *adj*
démodé(e); **outdoor** *adj* de *or* en plein
air; **outdoors** *adv* dehors; au grand air
**outer** [ˈautəʳ] *adj* extérieur(e); **outer
space** *n* espace *m* cosmique
**outfit** [ˈautfɪt] *n* (*clothes*) tenue *f*
**out**: **outgoing** *adj* (*president, tenant*)
sortant(e); (*character*) ouvert(e),
extraverti(e); **outgoings** *npl* (*BRIT:
expenses*) dépenses *fpl*; **outhouse** *n*
appentis *m*, remise *f*
**outing** [ˈautɪŋ] *n* sortie *f*; excursion *f*
**out**: **outlaw** *n* hors-la-loi *m inv* ▷ *vt*
(*person*) mettre hors la loi; (*practice*)
proscrire; **outlay** *n* dépenses *fpl*;
(*investment*) mise *f* de fonds; **outlet**
*n* (*for liquid etc*) issue *f*, sortie *f*; (*for

*emotion*) exutoire m; (*also:* **retail outlet**) point m de vente; (*us: Elec*) prise f de courant; **outline** n (*shape*) contour m; (*summary*) esquisse f, grandes lignes ▷ vt (*fig: theory, plan*) exposer à grands traits; **outlook** n perspective f; (*point of view*) attitude f; **outnumber** vt surpasser en nombre; **out-of-date** adj (*passport, ticket*) périmé(e); (*theory, idea*) dépassé(e); (*custom*) désuet(-ète); (*clothes*) démodé(e); **out-of-doors** adv = **outdoors**; **out-of-the-way** adj loin de tout; **out-of-town** adj (*shopping centre etc*) en périphérie; **outpatient** n malade m/f en consultation externe; **outpost** n avant-poste m; **output** n rendement m, production f; (*Comput*) sortie f ▷ vt (*Comput*) sortir

**outrage** ['autreɪdʒ] n (*anger*) indignation f; (*violent act*) atrocité f, acte m de violence; (*scandal*) scandale m ▷ vt outrager; **outrageous** [aut'reɪdʒəs] adj atroce; (*scandalous*) scandaleux(-euse)

**outright** adv [aut'raɪt] complètement; (*deny, refuse*) catégoriquement; (*ask*) carrément; (*kill*) sur le coup ▷ adj ['autraɪt] complet(-ète); catégorique

**outset** ['autset] n début m

**outside** [aut'saɪd] n extérieur m ▷ adj extérieur(e) ▷ adv (au) dehors, à l'extérieur ▷ prep hors de, à l'extérieur de; (*in front of*) devant; **at the ~** (*fig*) au plus or maximum; **outside lane** n (*Aut: in Britain*) voie f de droite; (*: in US, Europe*) voie de gauche; **outside line** n (*Tel*) ligne extérieure; **outsider** n (*stranger*) étranger(-ère)

**out**: **outsize** adj énorme; (*clothes*) grande taille inv; **outskirts** npl faubourgs mpl; **outspoken** adj très franc (franche); **outstanding** adj remarquable, exceptionnel(le); (*unfinished: work, business*) en suspens, en souffrance; (*debt*) impayé(e); (*problem*) non réglé(e)

**outward** ['autwəd] adj (*sign, appearances*) extérieur(e); (*journey*)

(d')aller; **outwards** adv (*esp BRIT*) = **outward**

**outweigh** [aut'weɪ] vt l'emporter sur

**oval** ['əuvl] adj, n ovale m

**ovary** ['əuvərɪ] n ovaire m

**oven** ['ʌvn] n four m; **oven glove** n gant m de cuisine; **ovenproof** adj allant au four; **oven-ready** adj prêt(e) à cuire

**over** ['əuvər] adv (par-)dessus ▷ adj (or adv) (*finished*) fini(e), terminé(e); (*too much*) en plus ▷ prep sur; par-dessus; (*above*) au-dessus de; (*on the other side of*) de l'autre côté de; (*more than*) plus de; (*during*) pendant; (*about, concerning*): **they fell out ~ money/her** ils se sont brouillés pour des questions d'argent/à cause d'elle; **~ here** ici; **~ there** là-bas; **all ~** (*everywhere*) partout; **~ and ~ (again)** à plusieurs reprises; **~ and above** en plus de; **to ask sb ~** inviter qn (à passer); **to fall ~** tomber; **to turn sth ~** retourner qch

**overall** ['əuvərɔ:l] adj (*length*) total(e); (*study, impression*) d'ensemble ▷ n (*BRIT*) blouse f ▷ adv [əuvər'ɔ:l] dans l'ensemble, en général; **overalls** npl (*boiler suit*) bleus mpl (de travail)

**overboard** ['əuvəbɔ:d] adv (*Naut*) par-dessus bord

**overcame** [əuvə'keɪm] pt of **overcome**

**overcast** ['əuvəka:st] adj couvert(e)

**overcharge** [əuvə'tʃɑ:dʒ] vt: **to ~ sb for sth** faire payer qch trop cher à qn

**overcoat** ['əuvəkəut] n pardessus m

**overcome** [əuvə'kʌm] vt (*irreg: like* **come**) (*defeat*) triompher de; (*difficulty*) surmonter ▷ adj (*emotionally*) bouleversé(e); **~ with grief** accablé(e) de douleur

**over**: **overcrowded** adj bondé(e); (*city, country*) surpeuplé(e); **overdo** vt (*irreg: like* **do**) exagérer; (*overcook*) trop cuire; **to overdo it**, **to overdo things** (*work too hard*) en faire trop, se surmener; **overdone** [əuvə'dʌn] adj (*vegetables, steak*) trop cuit(e); **overdose** n dose excessive; **overdraft** n découvert m;

**overdrawn** adj (account) à découvert; **overdue** adj en retard; (bill) impayé(e); (change) qui tarde; **overestimate** vt surestimer

**overflow** vi [əuvə'fləu] déborder ▷ n ['əuvəfləu] (also: ~ **pipe**) tuyau m d'écoulement, trop-plein m

**overgrown** [əuvə'grəun] adj (garden) envahi(e) par la végétation

**overhaul** vt [əuvə'hɔ:l] réviser ▷ n ['əuvəhɔ:l] révision f

**overhead** adv [əuvə'hɛd] au-dessus ▷ adj, n ['əuvəhɛd] ▷ adj aérien(ne); (lighting) vertical(e) ▷ n (US) = **overheads**; **overhead projector** n rétroprojecteur m; **overheads** npl (BRIT) frais généraux

**over**: **overhear** vt (irreg: like **hear**) entendre (par hasard); **overheat** vi (engine) chauffer; **overland** adj, adv par voie de terre; **overlap** vi se chevaucher; **overleaf** adv au verso; **overload** vt surcharger; **overlook** vt (have view of) donner sur; (miss) oublier, négliger; (forgive) fermer les yeux sur

**overnight** adv [əuvə'naɪt] (happen) durant la nuit; (fig) soudain ▷ adj ['əuvənaɪt] d'une (or de) nuit; soudain(e); **to stay ~ (with sb)** passer la nuit (chez qn); **overnight bag** n nécessaire m de voyage

**overpass** ['əuvəpɑːs] n (US: for cars) pont autoroutier; (: for pedestrians) passerelle f, pont m

**overpower** [əuvə'pauə<sup>r</sup>] vt vaincre; (fig) accabler; **overpowering** adj irrésistible; (heat, stench) suffocant(e)

**over**: **overreact** [əuvəri:'ækt] vi réagir de façon excessive; **overrule** vt (decision) annuler; (claim) rejeter; (person) rejeter l'avis de; **overrun** vt (irreg: like **run**) (Mil: country etc) occuper; (time limit etc) dépasser ▷ vi dépasser le temps imparti

**overseas** [əuvə'si:z] adv outre-mer; (abroad) à l'étranger ▷ adj (trade) extérieur(e); (visitor) étranger(-ère)

**oversee** [əuvə'si:] vt (irreg: like **see**) surveiller

**overshadow** [əuvə'ʃædəu] vt (fig) éclipser

**oversight** ['əuvəsaɪt] n omission f, oubli m

**oversleep** [əuvə'sli:p] vi (irreg: like **sleep**) se réveiller (trop) tard

**overspend** [əuvə'spɛnd] vi (irreg: like **spend**) dépenser de trop

**overt** [əu'və:t] adj non dissimulé(e)

**overtake** [əuvə'teɪk] vt (irreg: like **take**) dépasser; (BRIT: Aut) dépasser, doubler

**over**: **overthrow** vt (irreg: like **throw**) (government) renverser; **overtime** n heures fpl supplémentaires

**overtook** [əuvə'tuk] pt of **overtake**

**over**: **overturn** vt renverser; (decision, plan) annuler ▷ vi se retourner; **overweight** adj (person) trop gros(se); **overwhelm** vt (subj: emotion) accabler, submerger; (enemy, opponent) écraser; **overwhelming** adj (victory, defeat) écrasant(e); (desire) irrésistible

**ow** [au] excl aïe!

**owe** [əu] vt devoir; **to ~ sb sth, to ~ sth to sb** devoir qch à qn; **how much do I ~ you?** combien est-ce que je vous dois?; **owing to** prep à cause de, en raison de

**owl** [aul] n hibou m

**own** [əun] vt posséder ▷ adj propre; **a room of my ~** une chambre à moi, ma propre chambre; **to get one's ~ back** prendre sa revanche; **on one's ~** tout(e) seul(e); **own up** vi avouer; **owner** n propriétaire m/f; **ownership** n possession f

**ox** (pl **oxen**) [ɔks, 'ɔksn] n bœuf m

**Oxbridge** ['ɔksbrɪdʒ] n (BRIT) les universités d'Oxford et de Cambridge

**oxen** ['ɔksən] npl of **ox**

**oxygen** ['ɔksɪdʒən] n oxygène m

**oyster** ['ɔɪstə<sup>r</sup>] n huître f

**oz.** abbr = **ounce(s)**

**ozone** ['əuzəun] n ozone m; **ozone friendly** adj qui n'attaque pas or qui préserve la couche d'ozone; **ozone layer** n couche f d'ozone

# p

**p** abbr (BRIT) = **penny**; **pence**

**P.A.** n abbr = **personal assistant**; **public address system**

**p.a.** abbr = **per annum**

**pace** [peɪs] n pas m; (speed) allure f; vitesse f ▷ vi: **to ~ up and down** faire les cent pas; **to keep ~ with** aller à la même vitesse que; (events) se tenir au courant de; **pacemaker** n (Med) stimulateur m cardiaque; (Sport: also: **pacesetter**) meneur(-euse) de train

**Pacific** [pəˈsɪfɪk] n: **the ~ (Ocean)** le Pacifique, l'océan m Pacifique

**pacifier** [ˈpæsɪfaɪəʳ] n (us: dummy) tétine f

**pack** [pæk] n paquet m; (of hounds) meute f; (of thieves, wolves etc) bande f; (of cards) jeu m; (us: of cigarettes) paquet; (back pack) sac m à dos ▷ vt (goods) empaqueter, emballer; (in suitcase etc) emballer; (box) remplir; (cram) entasser ▷ vi: **to ~ (one's bags)** faire ses bagages; **pack in** (BRIT inf) ▷ vi (machine) tomber en panne ▷ vt (boyfriend) plaquer; **~ it in!** laisse tomber!; **pack off** vt: **to ~ sb off to** expédier qn à; **pack up** vi (BRIT inf: machine) tomber en panne; (: person) se tirer ▷ vt (belongings) ranger; (goods, presents) empaqueter, emballer

**package** [ˈpækɪdʒ] n paquet m; (also: ~ **deal**: agreement) marché global; (: purchase) forfait m; (Comput) progiciel m ▷ vt (goods) conditionner; **package holiday** n (BRIT) vacances organisées; **package tour** n voyage organisé

**packaging** [ˈpækɪdʒɪŋ] n (wrapping materials) emballage m

**packed** [pækt] adj (crowded) bondé(e); **packed lunch** (BRIT) n repas froid

**packet** [ˈpækɪt] n paquet m

**packing** [ˈpækɪŋ] n emballage m

**pact** [pækt] n pacte m, traité m

**pad** [pæd] n bloc(-notes m) m; (to prevent friction) tampon m ▷ vt rembourrer; **padded** adj (jacket) matelassé(e); (bra) rembourré(e)

**paddle** [ˈpædl] n (oar) pagaie f; (us: for table tennis) raquette f de ping-pong ▷ vi (with feet) barboter, faire trempette ▷ vt: **to ~ a canoe** etc pagayer; **paddling pool** n petit bassin

**paddock** [ˈpædək] n enclos m; (Racing) paddock m

**padlock** [ˈpædlɔk] n cadenas m

**paedophile** (us **pedophile**) [ˈpiːdəufaɪl] n pédophile m

**page** [peɪdʒ] n (of book) page f; (also: ~ **boy**) groom m, chasseur m; (at wedding) garçon m d'honneur ▷ vt (in hotel etc) (faire) appeler

**pager** [ˈpeɪdʒəʳ] n bip m (inf), Alphapage® m

**paid** [peɪd] pt, pp of **pay** ▷ adj (work, official) rémunéré(e); (holiday) payé(e); **to put ~ to** (BRIT) mettre fin à, mettre par terre

**pain** [peɪn] n douleur f; (inf: nuisance) plaie f; **to be in ~** souffrir, avoir mal; **to take ~s to do** se donner du mal pour faire; **painful** adj douloureux(-euse); (difficult) difficile, pénible; **painkiller**

*n* calmant *m*, analgésique *m*;
**painstaking** ['peɪnzteɪkɪŋ] *adj* (*person*) soigneux(-euse); (*work*) soigné(e)

**paint** [peɪnt] *n* peinture *f* ▷ *vt* peindre; **to ~ the door blue** peindre la porte en bleu; **paintbrush** *n* pinceau *m*; **painter** *n* peintre *m*; **painting** *n* peinture *f*; (*picture*) tableau *m*

**pair** [pɛəʳ] *n* (*of shoes, gloves etc*) paire *f*; (*of people*) couple *m*; **~ of scissors** (paire de) ciseaux *mpl*; **~ of trousers** pantalon *m*

**pajamas** [pəˈdʒɑːməz] *npl* (*US*) pyjama(s) *m(pl)*

**Pakistan** [pɑːkɪˈstɑːn] *n* Pakistan *m*; **Pakistani** *adj* pakistanais(e) ▷ *n* Pakistanais(e)

**pal** [pæl] *n* (*inf*) copain (copine)

**palace** ['pæləs] *n* palais *m*

**pale** [peɪl] *adj* pâle; **~ blue** *adj* bleu pâle *inv*

**Palestine** ['pælɪstaɪn] *n* Palestine *f*; **Palestinian** [pælɪsˈtɪnɪən] *adj* palestinien(ne) ▷ *n* Palestinien(ne)

**palm** [pɑːm] *n* (*Anat*) paume *f*; (*also:* **~ tree**) palmier *m* ▷ *vt*: **to ~ sth off on sb** (*inf*) refiler qch à qn

**pamper** ['pæmpəʳ] *vt* gâter, dorloter

**pamphlet** ['pæmflət] *n* brochure *f*

**pan** [pæn] *n* (*also:* **sauce~**) casserole *f*; (*also:* **frying ~**) poêle *f*

**pancake** ['pænkeɪk] *n* crêpe *f*

**panda** ['pændə] *n* panda *m*

**pane** [peɪn] *n* carreau *m* (de fenêtre), vitre *f*

**panel** ['pænl] *n* (*of wood, cloth etc*) panneau *m*; (*Radio, TV*) panel *m*, invités *mpl*; (*for interview, exams*) jury *m*

**panhandler** ['pænhændləʳ] *n* (*US inf*) mendiant(e)

**panic** ['pænɪk] *n* panique *f*, affolement *m* ▷ *vi* s'affoler, paniquer

**panorama** [pænəˈrɑːmə] *n* panorama *m*

**pansy** ['pænzɪ] *n* (*Bot*) pensée *f*

**pant** [pænt] *vi* haleter

**panther** ['pænθəʳ] *n* panthère *f*

**panties** ['pæntɪz] *npl* slip *m*, culotte *f*

**pantomime** ['pæntəmaɪm] *n* (*BRIT*) spectacle *m* de Noël; *voir encadré*

● **PANTOMIME**
●
● Une **pantomime** (à ne pas confondre
● avec le mot tel qu'on l'utilise en
● français), que l'on appelle également
● de façon familière "panto", est un
● genre de farce où le personnage
● principal est souvent un jeune
● garçon et où il y a toujours une
● "dame", c'est-à-dire une vieille
● femme jouée par un homme, et
● un méchant. La plupart du temps,
● l'histoire est basée sur un conte de
● fées comme Cendrillon ou Le Chat
● botté, et le public est encouragé
● à participer en prévenant le héros
● d'un danger imminent. Ce genre de
● spectacle, qui s'adresse surtout aux
● enfants, vise également un public
● d'adultes au travers des nombreuses
● plaisanteries faisant allusion à des
● faits d'actualité.

**pants** [pænts] *n* (*BRIT*: *woman's*) culotte *f*, slip *m*; (: *man's*) slip *m*, caleçon *m*; (*US*: *trousers*) pantalon *m*

**pantyhose** ['pæntɪhəuz] (*US*) *npl* collant *m*

**paper** ['peɪpəʳ] *n* papier *m*; (*also:* **wall~**) papier peint; (*also:* **news~**) journal *m*; (*academic essay*) article *m*; (*exam*) épreuve écrite ▷ *adj* en or de papier ▷ *vt* tapisser (de papier peint); **papers** *npl* (*also:* **identity ~s**) papiers *mpl* (d'identité); **paperback** *n* livre broché or non relié; (*small*) livre *m* de poche; **paper bag** *n* sac *m* en papier; **paper clip** *n* trombone *m*; **paper shop** *n* (*BRIT*) marchand *m* de journaux; **paperwork** *n* papiers *mpl*; (*pej*) paperasserie *f*

**paprika** ['pæprɪkə] *n* paprika *m*

**par** [pɑːʳ] *n* pair *m*; (*Golf*) normale *f* du parcours; **on a ~ with** à égalité avec, au même niveau que

**paracetamol** [pærə'si:təmɔl] (BRIT) n paracétamol m

**parachute** ['pærəʃu:t] n parachute m

**parade** [pə'reɪd] n défilé m ▷ vt (fig) faire étalage de ▷ vi défiler

**paradise** ['pærədaɪs] n paradis m

**paradox** ['pærədɔks] n paradoxe m

**paraffin** ['pærəfɪn] n (BRIT): ~ (oil) pétrole (lampant)

**paragraph** ['pærəɡrɑ:f] n paragraphe m

**parallel** ['pærəlɛl] adj: ~ (with or to) parallèle (à); (fig) analogue (à) ▷ n (line) parallèle f; (fig, Geo) parallèle m

**paralysed** ['pærəlaɪzd] adj paralysé(e)

**paralysis** [pə'rælɪsɪs, -si:z] (pl **paralyses**) [pə'rælɪsɪs, -si:z] n paralysie f

**paramedic** [pærə'mɛdɪk] n auxiliaire m/f médical(e)

**paranoid** ['pærənɔɪd] adj (Psych) paranoïaque; (neurotic) paranoïde

**parasite** ['pærəsaɪt] n parasite m

**parcel** ['pɑ:sl] n paquet m, colis m ▷ vt (also: ~ **up**) empaqueter

**pardon** ['pɑ:dn] n pardon m; (Law) grâce f ▷ vt pardonner à; (Law) gracier; ~! pardon!; ~ **me!** (after burping etc) excusez-moi!; **I beg your ~!** (I'm sorry) pardon!, je suis désolé!; **(I beg your) ~?**, (US) ~ **me?** (what did you say?) pardon?

**parent** ['pɛərənt] n (father) père m; (mother) mère f; **parents** npl parents mpl; **parental** [pə'rɛntl] adj parental(e), des parents

**Paris** ['pærɪs] n Paris

**parish** ['pærɪʃ] n paroisse f; (BRIT: civil) ≈ commune f

**Parisian** [pə'rɪzɪən] adj parisien(ne), de Paris ▷ n Parisien(ne)

**park** [pɑ:k] n parc m, jardin public ▷ vt garer ▷ vi se garer; **can I ~ here?** est-ce que je peux me garer ici?

**parking** ['pɑ:kɪŋ] n stationnement m; "**no ~**" "stationnement interdit"; **parking lot** n (US) parking m, parc m de stationnement; **parking meter** n parc(o)mètre m; **parking ticket** n P.-V. m

▌ Be careful not to translate **parking** by the French word **parking**.

**parkway** ['pɑ:kweɪ] n (US) route f express (en site vert ou aménagé)

**parliament** ['pɑ:ləmənt] n parlement m; **parliamentary** [pɑ:lə'mɛntərɪ] adj parlementaire

**Parmesan** [pɑ:mɪ'zæn] n (also: ~ **cheese**) Parmesan m

**parole** [pə'rəul] n: **on ~** en liberté conditionnelle

**parrot** ['pærət] n perroquet m

**parsley** ['pɑ:slɪ] n persil m

**parsnip** ['pɑ:snɪp] n panais m

**parson** ['pɑ:sn] n ecclésiastique m; (Church of England) pasteur m

**part** [pɑ:t] n partie f; (of machine) pièce f; (Theat etc) rôle m; (of serial) épisode m; (US: in hair) raie f ▷ adv = **partly** ▷ vt séparer ▷ vi (people) se séparer; (crowd) s'ouvrir; **to take ~ in** participer à, prendre part à; **to take sb's ~** prendre le parti de qn, prendre parti pour qn; **for my ~** en ce qui me concerne; **for the most ~** en grande partie; dans la plupart des cas; **in ~** en partie; **to take sth in good/bad ~** prendre qch du bon/mauvais côté; **part with** vt fus (person) se séparer de; (possessions) se défaire de

**partial** ['pɑ:ʃl] adj (incomplete) partiel(le); **to be ~ to** aimer, avoir un faible pour

**participant** [pɑ:'tɪsɪpənt] n (in competition, campaign) participant(e)

**participate** [pɑ:'tɪsɪpeɪt] vi: **to ~ (in)** participer (à), prendre part (à)

**particle** ['pɑ:tɪkl] n particule f; (of dust) grain m

**particular** [pə'tɪkjulə'] adj (specific) particulier(-ière); (special) particulier, spécial(e); (fussy) difficile, exigeant(e); (careful) méticuleux(-euse); **in ~** en particulier, surtout; **particularly** adv particulièrement; (in particular) en particulier; **particulars** npl détails mpl; (information) renseignements mpl

**parting** ['pɑ:tɪŋ] n séparation f; (BRIT:

*in hair)* raie f

**partition** [pɑːˈtɪʃən] n *(Pol)* partition f, division f; *(wall)* cloison f

**partly** [ˈpɑːtlɪ] adv en partie, partiellement

**partner** [ˈpɑːtnər] n *(Comm)* associé(e); *(Sport)* partenaire m/f; *(spouse)* conjoint(e); *(lover)* ami(e); *(at dance)* cavalier(-ière); **partnership** n association f

**part of speech** n *(Ling)* partie f du discours

**partridge** [ˈpɑːtrɪdʒ] n perdrix f

**part-time** [ˈpɑːtˈtaɪm] adj, adv à mi-temps, à temps partiel

**party** [ˈpɑːtɪ] n *(Pol)* parti m; *(celebration)* fête f; *(: formal)* réception f; *(: in evening)* soirée f; *(group)* groupe m; *(Law)* partie f

**pass** [pɑːs] vt *(time, object)* passer; *(place)* passer devant; *(friend)* croiser; *(exam)* être reçu(e) à, réussir; *(overtake)* dépasser; *(approve)* approuver, accepter ▷ vi passer; *(Scol)* être reçu(e) or admis(e), réussir ▷ n *(permit)* laissez-passer m inv; *(membership card)* carte f d'accès or d'abonnement; *(in mountains)* col m; *(Sport)* passe f; *(Scol: also:* ~ **mark**): **to get a ~** être reçu(e) (sans mention); **to ~ sb sth** passer qch à qn; **could you ~ the salt/oil, please?** pouvez-vous me passer le sel/l'huile, s'il vous plaît?; **to make a ~ at sb** *(inf)* faire des avances à qn; **pass away** vi mourir; **pass by** vi passer ▷ vt *(ignore)* négliger; **pass on** vt *(hand on)*: **to ~ on (to)** transmettre (à); **pass out** vi s'évanouir; **pass over** vt *(ignore)* passer sous silence; **pass up** vt *(opportunity)* laisser passer; **passable** adj *(road)* praticable; *(work)* acceptable

> Be careful not to translate **to pass an exam** by the French expression *passer un examen*.

**passage** [ˈpæsɪdʒ] n *(also: ~way)* couloir m; *(gen, in book)* passage m; *(by boat)* traversée f

**passenger** [ˈpæsɪndʒər] n passager(-ère)

**passer-by** [pɑːsəˈbaɪ] n passant(e)

**passing place** n *(Aut)* aire f de croisement

**passion** [ˈpæʃən] n passion f; **passionate** adj passionné(e); **passion fruit** n fruit m de la passion

**passive** [ˈpæsɪv] adj *(also Ling)* passif(-ive)

**passport** [ˈpɑːspɔːt] n passeport m; **passport control** n contrôle m des passeports; **passport office** n bureau m de délivrance des passeports

**password** [ˈpɑːswəːd] n mot m de passe

**past** [pɑːst] prep *(in front of)* devant; *(further than)* au delà de, plus loin que; après; *(later than)* après ▷ adv: **to run ~** passer en courant ▷ adj passé(e); *(president etc)* ancien(ne) ▷ n passé m; **he's ~ forty** il a dépassé la quarantaine, il a plus de or passé quarante ans; **ten/quarter ~ eight** huit heures dix/un or et quart; **for the ~ few/3 days** depuis quelques/3 jours; ces derniers/3 derniers jours

**pasta** [ˈpæstə] n pâtes fpl

**paste** [peɪst] n pâte f; *(Culin: meat)* pâté m (à tartiner); *(: tomato)* purée f, concentré m; *(glue)* colle f (de pâte) ▷ vt coller

**pastel** [ˈpæstl] adj pastel inv ▷ n *(Art: pencil)* (crayon m) pastel m; *(: drawing)* (dessin m au) pastel; *(colour)* ton m pastel inv

**pasteurized** [ˈpæstəraɪzd] adj pasteurisé(e)

**pastime** [ˈpɑːstaɪm] n passe-temps m inv, distraction f

**pastor** [ˈpɑːstər] n pasteur m

**past participle** [-ˈpɑːtɪsɪpl] n *(Ling)* participe passé

**pastry** [ˈpeɪstrɪ] n pâte f; *(cake)* pâtisserie f

**pasture** [ˈpɑːstʃər] n pâturage m

**pasty¹** n [ˈpæstɪ] petit pâté (en croûte)

**pasty²** [ˈpeɪstɪ] adj *(complexion)* terreux(-euse)

**pat** [pæt] vt donner une petite tape à; *(dog)* caresser

**patch** [pætʃ] n (of material) pièce f; (eye patch) cache m; (spot) tache f; (of land) parcelle f; (on tyre) rustine f ▷ vt (clothes) rapiécer; **a bad ~** (BRIT) une période difficile; **patchy** adj inégal(e); (incomplete) fragmentaire

**pâté** ['pæteɪ] n pâté m, terrine f

**patent** ['peɪtnt, US 'pætnt] n brevet m (d'invention) ▷ vt faire breveter ▷ adj patent(e), manifeste

**paternal** [pə'tɜːnl] adj paternel(le)

**paternity leave** [pə'tɜːnɪtɪ-] n congé m de paternité

**path** [pɑːθ] n chemin m, sentier m; (in garden) allée f; (of missile) trajectoire f

**pathetic** [pə'θɛtɪk] adj (pitiful) pitoyable; (very bad) lamentable, minable

**pathway** ['pɑːθweɪ] n chemin m, sentier m; (in garden) allée f

**patience** ['peɪʃns] n patience f; (BRIT: Cards) réussite f

**patient** ['peɪʃnt] n malade m/f; (of dentist etc) patient(e) ▷ adj patient(e)

**patio** ['pætɪəʊ] n patio m

**patriotic** [pætrɪ'ɒtɪk] adj patriotique; (person) patriote

**patrol** [pə'trəʊl] n patrouille f ▷ vt patrouiller dans; **patrol car** n voiture f de police

**patron** ['peɪtrən] n (in shop) client(e); (of charity) patron(ne); **~ of the arts** mécène m

**patronizing** ['pætrənaɪzɪŋ] adj condescendant(e)

**pattern** ['pætən] n (Sewing) patron m; (design) motif m; **patterned** adj à motifs

**pause** [pɔːz] n pause f, arrêt m ▷ vi faire une pause, s'arrêter

**pave** [peɪv] vt paver, daller; **to ~ the way for** ouvrir la voie à

**pavement** ['peɪvmənt] n (BRIT) trottoir m; (US) chaussée f

**pavilion** [pə'vɪlɪən] n pavillon m; (Sport) stand m

**paving** ['peɪvɪŋ] n (material) pavé m, dalle f

**paw** [pɔː] n patte f

**pawn** [pɔːn] n (Chess, also fig) pion m ▷ vt mettre en gage; **pawnbroker** n prêteur m sur gages

**pay** [peɪ] n salaire m; (of manual worker) paie f ▷ vb (pt, pp **paid**) ▷ vt payer ▷ vi payer; (be profitable) être rentable; **can I ~ by credit card?** est-ce que je peux payer par carte de crédit?; **to ~ attention (to)** prêter attention (à); **to ~ sb a visit** rendre visite à qn; **to ~ one's respects to sb** présenter ses respects à qn; **pay back** vt rembourser; **pay for** vt fus payer; **pay in** vt verser; **pay off** vt (debts) régler, acquitter; (person) rembourser ▷ vi (scheme, decision) se révéler payant(e); **pay out** vt (money) payer, sortir de sa poche; **pay up** vt (amount) payer; **payable** adj payable; **to make a cheque payable to sb** établir un chèque à l'ordre de qn; **pay day** n jour m de paie; **pay envelope** n (US) paie f; **payment** n paiement m; (of bill) règlement m; (of deposit, cheque) versement m; **monthly payment** mensualité f; **payout** n (from insurance) dédommagement m; (in competition) prix m; **pay packet** n (BRIT) paie f; **pay phone** n cabine f téléphonique, téléphone public; **pay raise** n (US) = **pay rise**; **pay rise** n (BRIT) augmentation f (de salaire); **payroll** n registre m du personnel; **pay slip** n (BRIT) bulletin m de paie, feuille f de paie; **pay television** n chaînes fpl payantes

**PC** n abbr = **personal computer**; (BRIT) = **police constable** ▷ adj abbr = **politically correct**

**p.c.** abbr = **per cent**

**PDA** n abbr (= personal digital assistant) agenda m électronique

**PE** n abbr (= physical education) EPS f

**pea** [piː] n (petit) pois

**peace** [piːs] n paix f; (calm) calme m, tranquillité f; **peaceful** adj paisible, calme

**peach** [piːtʃ] n pêche f

**peacock** ['pi:kɔk] n paon m
**peak** [pi:k] n (mountain) pic m, cime f; (of cap) visière f; (fig: highest level) maximum m; (: of career, fame) apogée n; **peak hours** npl heures fpl d'affluence or de pointe
**peanut** ['pi:nʌt] n arachide f, cacahuète f; **peanut butter** n beurre m de cacahuète
**pear** [pɛə<sup>r</sup>] n poire f
**pearl** [pə:l] n perle f
**peasant** ['pɛznt] n paysan(ne)
**peat** [pi:t] n tourbe f
**pebble** ['pɛbl] n galet m, caillou m
**peck** [pɛk] vt (also: ~ at) donner un coup de bec à; (food) picorer ▷ n coup m de bec; (kiss) bécot m; **peckish** adj (BRIT inf): **I feel peckish** je mangerais bien quelque chose, j'ai la dent
**peculiar** [pɪ'kju:lɪə<sup>r</sup>] adj (odd) étrange, bizarre, curieux(-euse); (particular) particulier(-ière); ~ **to** particulier à
**pedal** ['pɛdl] n pédale f ▷ vi pédaler
**pedalo** ['pɛdələu] n pédalo m
**pedestal** ['pɛdəstl] n piédestal m
**pedestrian** [pɪ'dɛstrɪən] n piéton m; **pedestrian crossing** n (BRIT) passage clouté; **pedestrianized** adj: **a pedestrianized street** une rue piétonne; **pedestrian precinct** (US **pedestrian zone**) n (BRIT) zone piétonne
**pedigree** ['pɛdɪgri:] n ascendance f; (of animal) pedigree m ▷ cpd (animal) de race
**pedophile** ['pi:dəufaɪl] (US) n = **paedophile**
**pee** [pi:] vi (inf) faire pipi, pisser
**peek** [pi:k] vi jeter un coup d'œil (furtif)
**peel** [pi:l] n pelure f, épluchure f; (of orange, lemon) écorce f ▷ vt peler, éplucher ▷ vi (paint etc) s'écailler; (wallpaper) se décoller; (skin) peler
**peep** [pi:p] n (BRIT: look) coup d'œil furtif; (sound) pépiement m ▷ vi (BRIT) jeter un coup d'œil (furtif)
**peer** [pɪə<sup>r</sup>] vi: **to ~ at** regarder attentivement, scruter ▷ n (noble) pair

m; (equal) pair, égal(e)
**peg** [pɛg] n (for coat etc) patère f; (BRIT: also: **clothes ~**) pince f à linge
**pelican** ['pɛlɪkən] n pélican m; **pelican crossing** n (BRIT Aut) feu m à commande manuelle
**pelt** [pɛlt] vt: **to ~ sb (with)** bombarder qn (de) ▷ vi (rain) tomber à seaux; (inf: run) courir à toutes jambes ▷ n peau f
**pelvis** ['pɛlvɪs] n bassin m
**pen** [pɛn] n (for writing) stylo m; (for sheep) parc m
**penalty** ['pɛnltɪ] n pénalité f; sanction f; (fine) amende f; (Sport) pénalisation f; (Football) penalty m; (Rugby) pénalité f
**pence** [pɛns] npl of **penny**
**pencil** ['pɛnsl] n crayon m; **pencil in** vt noter provisoirement; **pencil case** n trousse f (d'écolier); **pencil sharpener** n taille-crayon(s) m inv
**pendant** ['pɛndnt] n pendentif m
**pending** ['pɛndɪŋ] prep en attendant ▷ adj en suspens
**penetrate** ['pɛnɪtreɪt] vt pénétrer dans; (enemy territory) entrer en
**penfriend** ['pɛnfrɛnd] n (BRIT) correspondant(e)
**penguin** ['pɛŋgwɪn] n pingouin m
**penicillin** [pɛnɪ'sɪlɪn] n pénicilline f
**peninsula** [pə'nɪnsjulə] n péninsule f
**penis** ['pi:nɪs] n pénis m, verge f
**penitentiary** [pɛnɪ'tɛnʃərɪ] n (US) prison f
**penknife** ['pɛnnaɪf] n canif m
**penniless** ['pɛnɪlɪs] adj sans le sou
**penny** (pl **pennies** or **pence**) ['pɛnɪ, 'pɛnɪz, pɛns] n (BRIT) penny m; (US) cent m
**penpal** ['pɛnpæl] n correspondant(e)
**pension** ['pɛnʃən] n (from company) retraite f; **pensioner** n (BRIT) retraité(e)
**pentagon** ['pɛntəgən] n: **the P~** (US Pol) le Pentagone
**penthouse** ['pɛnthaus] n appartement m (de luxe) en attique
**penultimate** [pɪ'nʌltɪmət] adj pénultième, avant-dernier(-ière)
**people** ['pi:pl] npl gens mpl; personnes

*fpl*; (*inhabitants*) population *f*; (*Pol*)
peuple *m* ▷ *n* (*nation, race*) peuple *m*;
**several ~ came** plusieurs personnes
sont venues; **~ say that ...** on dit or les
gens disent que ...

**pepper** ['pɛpəʳ] *n* poivre *m*; (*vegetable*)
poivron *m* ▷ *vt* (*Culin*) poivrer;
**peppermint** *n* (*sweet*) pastille *f* de
menthe

**per** [pəːʳ] *prep* par; **~ hour** (*miles etc*) à
l'heure; (*fee*) (de) l'heure; **~ kilo** *etc* le kilo
*etc*; **~ day/person** par jour/personne; **~
annum** per an

**perceive** [pəˈsiːv] *vt* percevoir; (*notice*)
remarquer, s'apercevoir de

**per cent** *adv* pour cent

**percentage** [pəˈsɛntɪdʒ] *n*
pourcentage *m*

**perception** [pəˈsɛpʃən] *n* perception *f*;
(*insight*) sensibilité *f*

**perch** [pəːtʃ] *n* (*fish*) perche *f*; (*for bird*)
perchoir *m* ▷ *vi* (se) percher

**percussion** [pəˈkʌʃən] *n* percussion *f*

**perennial** [pəˈrɛnɪəl] *n* (*Bot*) (plante *f*)
vivace *f*, plante plurianuelle

**perfect** ['pəːfɪkt] *adj* parfait(e) ▷ *n*
(*also*: **~ tense**) parfait *m* ▷ *vt* [pəˈfɛkt]
(*technique, skill, work of art*) parfaire;
(*method, plan*) mettre au point;
**perfection** [pəˈfɛkʃən] *n* perfection *f*;
**perfectly** ['pəːfɪktlɪ] *adv* parfaitement

**perform** [pəˈfɔːm] *vt* (*carry out*)
exécuter; (*concert etc*) jouer, donner ▷ *vi*
(*actor, musician*) jouer; **performance**
*n* représentation *f*, spectacle *m*; (*of an
artist*) interprétation *f*; (*Sport: of car,
engine*) performance *f*; (*of company,
economy*) résultats *mpl*; **performer** *n*
artiste *m/f*

**perfume** ['pəːfjuːm] *n* parfum *m*

**perhaps** [pəˈhæps] *adv* peut-être

**perimeter** [pəˈrɪmɪtəʳ] *n* périmètre *m*

**period** ['pɪərɪəd] *n* période *f*; (*History*)
époque *f*; (*Scol*) cours *m*; (*full stop*)
point *m*; (*Med*) règles *fpl* ▷ *adj* (*costume,
furniture*) d'époque; **periodical**
[pɪərɪˈɔdɪkl] *n* périodique *m*;
**periodically** *adv* périodiquement

**perish** ['pɛrɪʃ] *vi* périr, mourir; (*decay*)
se détériorer

**perjury** ['pəːdʒərɪ] *n* (*Law: in court*) faux
témoignage; (*breach of oath*) parjure *m*

**perk** [pəːk] *n* (*inf*) avantage *m*, à-côté *m*

**perm** [pəːm] *n* (*for hair*) permanente *f*

**permanent** ['pəːmənənt] *adj*
permanent(e); **permanently** *adv*
de façon permanente; (*move abroad*)
définitivement; (*open, closed*)
en permanence; (*tired, unhappy*)
constamment

**permission** [pəˈmɪʃən] *n* permission *f*,
autorisation *f*

**permit** *n* ['pəːmɪt] permis *m*

**perplex** [pəˈplɛks] *vt* (*person*) rendre
perplexe

**persecute** ['pəːsɪkjuːt] *vt* persécuter

**persecution** [pəːsɪˈkjuːʃən] *n*
persécution *f*

**persevere** [pəːsɪˈvɪəʳ] *vi* persévérer

**Persian** ['pəːʃən] *adj* persan(e); **the ~
Gulf** le golfe Persique

**persist** [pəˈsɪst] *vi*: **to ~ (in doing)**
persister (à faire), s'obstiner (à faire);
**persistent** *adj* persistant(e), tenace

**person** ['pəːsn] *n* personne *f*;
**in ~** en personne; **personal** *adj*
personnel(le); **personal assistant** *n*
secrétaire personnel(le); **personal
computer** *n* ordinateur individuel,
PC *m*; **personality** [pəːsəˈnælɪtɪ]
*n* personnalité *f*; **personally** *adv*
personnellement; **to take sth
personally** se sentir visé(e) par
qch; **personal organizer** *n* agenda
(personnel) (*style Filofax®*); (*electronic*)
agenda électronique; **personal stereo**
*n* Walkman® *m*, baladeur *m*

**personnel** [pəːsəˈnɛl] *n* personnel *m*

**perspective** [pəˈspɛktɪv] *n*
perspective *f*

**perspiration** [pəːspɪˈreɪʃən] *n*
transpiration *f*

**persuade** [pəˈsweɪd] *vt*: **to ~ sb to do
sth** persuader qn de faire qch, amener
or décider qn à faire qch

**persuasion** [pəˈsweɪʒən] *n* persuasion

f; (*creed*) conviction f

**persuasive** [pə'sweɪsɪv] *adj*
persuasif(-ive)

**perverse** [pə'vəːs] *adj* pervers(e);
(*contrary*) entêté(e), contrariant(e)

**pervert** *n* ['pəːvəːt] perverti(e) ▷ *vt*
[pə'vəːt] pervertir; (*words*) déformer

**pessimism** ['pesɪmɪzəm] *n*
pessimisme *m*

**pessimist** ['pesɪmɪst] *n* pessimiste
*m/f*; **pessimistic** [pesɪ'mɪstɪk] *adj*
pessimiste

**pest** [pest] *n* animal *m* (*or* insecte *m*)
nuisible; (*fig*) fléau *m*

**pester** ['pestəʳ] *vt* importuner, harceler

**pesticide** ['pestɪsaɪd] *n* pesticide *m*

**pet** [pet] *n* animal familier ▷ *cpd*
(*favourite*) favori(e) ▷ *vt* (*stroke*)
caresser, câliner; **teacher's ~** chouchou
*m* du professeur; **~ hate** bête noire

**petal** ['petl] *n* pétale *m*

**petite** [pə'tiːt] *adj* menu(e)

**petition** [pə'tɪʃən] *n* pétition f

**petrified** ['petrɪfaɪd] *adj* (*fig*) mort(e)
de peur

**petrol** ['petrəl] *n* (*BRIT*) essence f; **I've
run out of ~** je suis en panne d'essence

⚠ Be careful not to translate **petrol** by
the French word **pétrole**.

**petroleum** [pə'trəulɪəm] *n* pétrole *m*

**petrol**: **petrol pump** *n* (*BRIT*: *in car,
at garage*) pompe f à essence; **petrol
station** *n* (*BRIT*) station-service f;
**petrol tank** *n* (*BRIT*) réservoir *m*
d'essence

**petticoat** ['petɪkəut] *n* jupon *m*

**petty** ['petɪ] *adj* (*mean*) mesquin(e);
(*unimportant*) insignifiant(e), sans
importance

**pew** [pjuː] *n* banc *m* (d'église)

**pewter** ['pjuːtəʳ] *n* étain *m*

**phantom** ['fæntəm] *n* fantôme *m*

**pharmacist** ['fɑːməsɪst] *n*
pharmacien(ne)

**pharmacy** ['fɑːməsɪ] *n* pharmacie f

**phase** [feɪz] *n* phase f, période f; **phase
in** *vt* introduire progressivement;
**phase out** *vt* supprimer

progressivement

**Ph.D.** *abbr* = **Doctor of Philosophy**

**pheasant** ['feznt] *n* faisan *m*

**phenomena** [fə'nɔmɪnə] *npl of*
**phenomenon**

**phenomenal** [fɪ'nɔmɪnl] *adj*
phénoménal(e)

**phenomenon** [fə'nɔmɪnən] (*pl* **phenomena**)
[fə'nɔmɪnən, -nə] *n* phénomène *m*

**Philippines** ['fɪlɪpiːnz] *npl* (*also*:
**Philippine Islands**): **the ~** les
Philippines *fpl*

**philosopher** [fɪ'lɔsəfəʳ] *n*
philosophe *m*

**philosophical** [fɪlə'sɔfɪkl] *adj*
philosophique

**philosophy** [fɪ'lɔsəfɪ] *n* philosophie f

**phlegm** [flem] *n* flegme *m*

**phobia** ['fəubjə] *n* phobie f

**phone** [fəun] *n* téléphone *m* ▷ *vt*
téléphoner à ▷ *vi* téléphoner; **to be
on the ~** avoir le téléphone; (*be calling*)
être au téléphone; (*phone back *vt, vi*
rappeler; **phone up** *vt* téléphoner à ▷ *vi*
téléphoner; **phone book** *n* annuaire *m*;
**phone box** (*US* **phone booth**) *n* cabine
f téléphonique; **phone call** *n* coup *m*
de fil *or* de téléphone; **phonecard** *n*
télécarte f; **phone number** *n* numéro
*m* de téléphone

**phonetics** [fə'netɪks] *n* phonétique f

**phoney** ['fəunɪ] *adj* faux (fausse),
factice; (*person*) pas franc (franche)

**photo** ['fəutəu] *n* photo f; **photo album**
*n* album *m* de photos; **photocopier** *n*
copieur *m*; **photocopy** *n* photocopie f
▷ *vt* photocopier

**photograph** ['fəutəgræf] *n*
photographie f ▷ *vt* photographier;
**photographer** [fə'tɔgrəfəʳ] *n*
photographe *m/f*; **photography**
[fə'tɔgrəfɪ] *n* photographie f

**phrase** [freɪz] *n* expression f; (*Ling*)
locution f ▷ *vt* exprimer; **phrase
book** *n* recueil *m* d'expressions (pour
touristes)

**physical** ['fɪzɪkl] *adj* physique;
**physical education** *n* éducation

f physique; **physically** adv
physiquement
**physician** [fɪˈzɪʃən] n médecin m
**physicist** [ˈfɪzɪsɪst] n physicien(ne)
**physics** [ˈfɪzɪks] n physique f
**physiotherapist** [fɪzɪəuˈθerəpɪst] n
kinésithérapeute m/f
**physiotherapy** [fɪzɪəuˈθerəpɪ] n
kinésithérapie f
**physique** [fɪˈziːk] n (appearance)
physique m; (health etc) constitution f
**pianist** [ˈpiːənɪst] n pianiste m/f
**piano** [pɪˈænəu] n piano m
**pick** [pɪk] n (tool: also: **~-axe**) pic m,
pioche f ⊳ vt choisir; (gather) cueillir;
(remove) prendre; (lock) forcer; **take
your ~** faites votre choix; **the ~ of** le
(la) meilleur(e) de; **to ~ one's nose** se
mettre les doigts dans le nez; **to ~
one's teeth** se curer les dents; **to ~
a quarrel with sb** chercher noise à
qn; **pick on** vt fus (person) harceler;
**pick out** vt choisir; (distinguish)
distinguer; **pick up** vi (improve)
remonter, s'améliorer ⊳ vt ramasser;
(collect) passer prendre; (Aut: give lift
to) prendre; (learn) apprendre; (Radio)
capter; **to ~ up speed** prendre de la
vitesse; **to ~ o.s. up** se relever
**pickle** [ˈpɪkl] n (also: **~s**: as condiment)
pickles mpl ⊳ vt conserver dans du
vinaigre or dans de la saumure; **in a ~**
(fig) dans le pétrin
**pickpocket** [ˈpɪkpɔkɪt] n pickpocket m
**pick-up** [ˈpɪkʌp] n (also: **~ truck**)
pick-up m inv
**picnic** [ˈpɪknɪk] n pique-nique m ⊳ vi
pique-niquer; **picnic area** n aire f de
pique-nique
**picture** [ˈpɪktʃə] n (also TV) image
f; (painting) peinture f, tableau m;
(photograph) photo(graphie) f;
(drawing) dessin m; (film) film m; (fig:
description) description f ⊳ vt (imagine)
se représenter; **pictures** npl: **the ~s**
(BRIT) le cinéma; **to take a ~ of sb/sth**
prendre qn/qch en photo; **would you
take a ~ of us, please?** pourriez-vous

nous prendre en photo, s'il vous plaît?;
**picture frame** n cadre m; **picture
messaging** n picture messaging m,
messagerie f d'images
**picturesque** [pɪktʃəˈresk] adj
pittoresque
**pie** [paɪ] n tourte f; (of fruit) tarte f; (of
meat) pâté m en croûte
**piece** [piːs] n morceau m; (item): **a ~ of
furniture/advice** un meuble/conseil
⊳ vt: **to ~ together** rassembler; **to take
to ~s** démonter
**pie chart** n graphique m à secteurs,
camembert m
**pier** [pɪə] n jetée f
**pierce** [pɪəs] vt percer, transpercer;
**pierced** adj (ears) percé(e)
**pig** [pɪg] n cochon m, porc m; (pej:
unkind person) mufle m; (: greedy person)
goinfre m
**pigeon** [ˈpɪdʒən] n pigeon m
**piggy bank** [ˈpɪgɪ-] n tirelire f
**pigsty** [ˈpɪgstaɪ] n porcherie f
**pigtail** [ˈpɪgteɪl] n natte f, tresse f
**pike** [paɪk] n (fish) brochet m
**pilchard** [ˈpɪltʃəd] n pilchard m (sorte
de sardine)
**pile** [paɪl] n (pillar, of books) pile f; (heap)
tas m; (of carpet) épaisseur f; **pile up** vi
(accumulate) s'entasser, s'accumuler
⊳ vt (put in heap) empiler, entasser;
(accumulate) accumuler; **piles** npl
hémorroïdes fpl; **pile-up** n (Aut)
télescopage m, collision f en série
**pilgrim** [ˈpɪlgrɪm] n pèlerin m

- **PILGRIM FATHERS**
-
- Les "Pères pèlerins" sont un
- groupe de puritains qui quittèrent
- l'Angleterre en 1620 pour fuir les
- persécutions religieuses. Ayant
- traversé l'Atlantique à bord du
- "Mayflower", ils fondèrent New
- Plymouth en Nouvelle-Angleterre,
- dans ce qui est aujourd'hui le
- Massachusetts. Ces Pères pèlerins
- sont considérés comme les

- fondateurs des États-Unis, et l'on
- commémore chaque année, le jour
- de "Thanksgiving", la réussite de leur
- première récolte.

**pilgrimage** ['pɪlgrɪmɪdʒ] n
pèlerinage m

**pill** [pɪl] n pilule f; **the ~** la pilule

**pillar** ['pɪləʳ] n pilier m

**pillow** ['pɪləu] n oreiller m; **pillowcase,
pillowslip** n taie f d'oreiller

**pilot** ['paɪlət] n pilote m ▷ cpd (scheme
etc) pilote, expérimental(e) ▷ vt piloter;
**pilot light** n veilleuse f

**pimple** ['pɪmpl] n bouton m

**PIN** n abbr (= personal identification
number) code m confidentiel

**pin** [pɪn] n épingle f; (Tech) cheville f ▷ vt
épingler; **~s and needles** fourmis fpl; **to
~ sth down** (fig) coincer qn; **to ~ sth on
sb** (fig) mettre qch sur le dos de qn

**pinafore** ['pɪnəfɔːʳ] n tablier m

**pinch** [pɪntʃ] n pincement m; (of salt
etc) pincée f ▷ vt pincer; (inf: steal)
piquer, chiper ▷ vi (shoe) serrer; **at a ~**
à la rigueur

**pine** [paɪn] n (also: **~ tree**) pin m ▷ vi: **to
~ for** aspirer à, désirer ardemment

**pineapple** ['paɪnæpl] n ananas m

**ping** [pɪŋ] n (noise) tintement m; **ping-
pong®** n ping-pong® m

**pink** [pɪŋk] adj rose ▷ n (colour) rose m

**pinpoint** ['pɪnpɔɪnt] vt indiquer (avec
précision)

**pint** [paɪnt] n pinte f (BRIT = 0.57 l; US =
0.47 l); (BRIT inf) = demi m, ≈ pot m

**pioneer** [paɪə'nɪəʳ] n pionnier m

**pious** ['paɪəs] adj pieux(-euse)

**pip** [pɪp] n (seed) pépin m; **pips** npl: **the
~s** (BRIT: time signal on radio) le top

**pipe** [paɪp] n tuyau m, conduite f; (for
smoking) pipe f ▷ vt amener par tuyau;
**pipeline** n (for gas) gazoduc m, pipeline
m; (for oil) oléoduc m; **piper** n (flautist)
joueur(-euse) de pipeau; (of
bagpipes) joueur(-euse) de cornemuse

**pirate** ['paɪərət] n pirate m ▷ vt (CD,
video, book) pirater

**Pisces** ['paɪsiːz] n les Poissons mpl

**piss** [pɪs] vi (inf!) pisser (!); **pissed** (inf!)
adj (BRIT: drunk) bourré(e); (US: angry)
furieux(-euse)

**pistol** ['pɪstl] n pistolet m

**piston** ['pɪstən] n piston m

**pit** [pɪt] n trou m, fosse f; (also: **coal ~**)
puits m de mine; (also: **orchestra ~**)
fosse d'orchestre; (US: fruit stone) noyau
m ▷ vt: **to ~ o.s.** or **one's wits against**
se mesurer à

**pitch** [pɪtʃ] n (BRIT Sport) terrain m; (Mus)
ton m; (fig: degree) degré m; (tar) poix
f ▷ vt (throw) lancer; (tent) dresser ▷ vi
(fall): **to ~ into/off** tomber dans/de;
**pitch-black** adj noir(e) comme poix

**pitfall** ['pɪtfɔːl] n piège m

**pith** [pɪθ] n (of orange etc) intérieur m
de l'écorce

**pitiful** ['pɪtɪful] adj (touching) pitoyable;
(contemptible) lamentable

**pity** ['pɪtɪ] n pitié f ▷ vt plaindre; **what a
~!** quel dommage!

**pizza** ['piːtsə] n pizza f

**placard** ['plækɑːd] n affiche f; (in march)
pancarte f

**place** [pleɪs] n endroit m, lieu m;
(proper position, rank, seat) place
f; (home): **at/to his ~** chez lui ▷ vt
(position) placer, mettre; (identify)
situer; reconnaître; **to take ~** avoir
lieu; **to change ~s with sb** changer
de place avec qn; **out of ~** (not suitable)
déplacé(e), inopportun(e); **in the first
~** d'abord, en premier; **place mat** n set
m de table; (in linen etc) napperon m;
**placement** n (during studies) stage m

**placid** ['plæsɪd] adj placide

**plague** [pleɪg] n (Med) peste f ▷ vt (fig)
tourmenter

**plaice** [pleɪs] n (pl inv) carrelet m

**plain** [pleɪn] adj (in one colour) uni(e);
(clear) clair(e), évident(e); (simple)
simple; (not handsome) quelconque,
ordinaire ▷ adv franchement,
carrément ▷ n plaine f; **plain
chocolate** n chocolat m à croquer;
**plainly** adv clairement; (frankly)

carrément, sans détours
**plaintiff** ['pleɪntɪf] n plaignant(e)
**plait** [plæt] n tresse f, natte f
**plan** [plæn] n plan m; (scheme) projet m
▷ vt (think in advance) projeter; (prepare)
organiser ▷ vi faire des projets; **to ~ to
do** projeter de faire
**plane** [pleɪn] n (Aviat) avion m; (also:
**~ tree**) platane m; (tool) rabot m; (Art,
Math etc) plan m; (fig) niveau m, plan
▷ vt (with tool) raboter
**planet** ['plænɪt] n planète f
**plank** [plæŋk] n planche f
**planning** ['plænɪŋ] n planification f;
**family ~** planning familial
**plant** [plɑːnt] n plante f; (machinery)
matériel m; (factory) usine f ▷ vt
planter; (bomb) déposer, poser;
(microphone, evidence) cacher
**plantation** [plæn'teɪʃən] n
plantation f
**plaque** [plæk] n plaque f
**plaster** ['plɑːstəʳ] n plâtre m; (also: **~
of Paris**) plâtre à mouler; (BRIT: also:
**sticking ~**) pansement adhésif ▷ vt
plâtrer; (cover): **to ~ with** couvrir de;
**plaster cast** n (Med) plâtre m; (model,
statue) moule m
**plastic** ['plæstɪk] n plastique m ▷ adj
(made of plastic) en plastique; **plastic
bag** n sac m en plastique; **plastic
surgery** n chirurgie f esthétique
**plate** [pleɪt] n (dish) assiette f; (sheet of
metal, on door; Phot) plaque f; (in book)
gravure f; (dental) dentier m
**plateau** (pl **~s** or **~x**) ['plætəu, -z] n
plateau m
**platform** ['plætfɔːm] n (at meeting)
tribune f; (stage) estrade f; (Rail) quai m;
(Pol) plateforme f
**platinum** ['plætɪnəm] n platine m
**platoon** [plə'tuːn] n peloton m
**platter** ['plætəʳ] n plat m
**plausible** ['plɔːzɪbl] adj plausible;
(person) convaincant(e)
**play** [pleɪ] n jeu m; (Theat) pièce f (de
théâtre) ▷ vt (game) jouer à; (team,
opponent) jouer contre; (instrument)

jouer de; (part, piece of music, note)
jouer; (CD etc) passer ▷ vi jouer; **to ~
safe** ne prendre aucun risque; **play
back** vt repasser, réécouter; **play up** vi
(cause trouble) faire des siennes; **player**
n joueur(-euse); (Mus) musicien(ne);
**playful** adj enjoué(e); **playground**
n cour f de récréation; (in park) aire
f de jeux; **playgroup** n garderie f;
**playing card** n carte f à jouer;
**playing field** n terrain m de sport;
**playschool** n = **playgroup**; **playtime**
n (Scol) récréation f; **playwright** n
dramaturge m
**plc** abbr (BRIT: = public limited company)
≈ SARL f
**plea** [pliː] n (request) appel m; (Law)
défense f
**plead** [pliːd] vt plaider; (give as excuse)
invoquer ▷ vi (Law) plaider; (beg):
**to ~ with sb (for sth)** implorer qn
(d'accorder qch); **to ~ guilty/not guilty**
plaider coupable/non coupable
**pleasant** ['plɛznt] adj agréable
**please** [pliːz] excl s'il te (or vous) plaît
▷ vt plaire à ▷ vi (think fit): **do as you ~**
faites comme il vous plaira; **~ yourself!**
(inf) (faites) comme vous voulez!;
**pleased** adj: **pleased (with)** content(e)
(de); **pleased to meet you** enchanté
(de faire votre connaissance)
**pleasure** ['plɛʒəʳ] n plaisir m; **"it's a ~"**
"je vous en prie"
**pleat** [pliːt] n pli m
**pledge** [plɛdʒ] n (promise) promesse f
▷ vt promettre
**plentiful** ['plɛntɪful] adj abondant(e),
copieux(-euse)
**plenty** ['plɛntɪ] n: **~ of** beaucoup de;
(sufficient) (bien) assez de
**pliers** ['plaɪəz] npl pinces fpl
**plight** [plaɪt] n situation f critique
**plod** [plɔd] vi avancer péniblement;
(fig) peiner
**plonk** [plɔŋk] (inf) n (BRIT: wine) pinard
m, piquette f ▷ vt: **to ~ sth down** poser
brusquement qch
**plot** [plɔt] n complot m, conspiration f;

*(of story, play)* intrigue f; *(of land)* lot m de terrain, lopin m ▷ vt *(mark out)* tracer point par point; *(Naut)* pointer; *(make graph of)* faire le graphique de; *(conspire)* comploter ▷ vi comploter

**plough** *(US* **plow)** [plau] n charrue f ▷ vt *(earth)* labourer; **to ~ money into** investir dans; **ploughman's lunch** n *(BRIT)* assiette froide avec du pain, du fromage et des pickles

**plow** [plau] *(US)* = **plough**

**ploy** [plɔɪ] n stratagème m

**pluck** [plʌk] vt *(fruit)* cueillir; *(musical instrument)* pincer; *(bird)* plumer; **to ~ one's eyebrows** s'épiler les sourcils; **to ~ up courage** prendre son courage à deux mains

**plug** [plʌg] n *(stopper)* bouchon m, bonde f; *(Elec)* prise f de courant; *(Aut: also:* **spark(ing) ~)** bougie f ▷ vt *(hole)* boucher; *(inf: advertise)* faire du battage pour, matraquer; **plug in** vt *(Elec)* brancher; **plughole** n *(BRIT)* trou m *(d'écoulement)*

**plum** [plʌm] n *(fruit)* prune f

**plumber** ['plʌmə'] n plombier m

**plumbing** ['plʌmɪŋ] n *(trade)* plomberie f; *(piping)* tuyauterie f

**plummet** ['plʌmɪt] vi *(person, object)* plonger; *(sales, prices)* dégringoler

**plump** [plʌmp] adj rondelet(te), dodu(e), bien en chair; **plump for** vt fus *(inf: choose)* se décider pour

**plunge** [plʌndʒ] n plongeon m; *(fig)* chute f ▷ vt plonger ▷ vi *(fall)* tomber, dégringoler; *(dive)* plonger; **to take the ~** se jeter à l'eau

**pluperfect** [plu:'pə:fɪkt] n *(Ling)* plus-que-parfait m

**plural** ['pluərl] adj pluriel(le) ▷ n pluriel m

**plus** [plʌs] n *(also:* **~ sign)** signe m plus; *(advantage)* atout m ▷ prep plus; **ten/twenty ~** plus de dix/vingt

**ply** [plaɪ] n *(of wool)* fil m ▷ vt *(a trade)* exercer ▷ vi *(ship)* faire la navette; **to ~ sb with drink** donner continuellement à boire à qn; **plywood** n contreplaqué m

**P.M.** n abbr *(BRIT)* = **prime minister**

**p.m.** adv abbr *(= post meridiem)* de l'après-midi

**PMS** n abbr *(= premenstrual syndrome)* syndrome prémenstruel

**PMT** n abbr *(= premenstrual tension)* syndrome prémenstruel

**pneumatic drill** [nju:'mætɪk-] n marteau-piqueur m

**pneumonia** [nju:'məunɪə] n pneumonie f

**poach** [pəutʃ] vt *(cook)* pocher; *(steal)* pêcher *(or* chasser*)* sans permis ▷ vi braconner; **poached** adj *(egg)* poché(e)

**P.O. Box** n abbr = **post office box**

**pocket** ['pɔkɪt] n poche f ▷ vt empocher; **to be (£5) out of ~** *(BRIT)* en être de sa poche (pour 5 livres); **pocketbook** n *(US: wallet)* portefeuille m; **pocket money** n argent m de poche

**pod** [pɔd] n cosse f

**podcast** n podcast m

**podiatrist** [pɔ'di:ətrɪst] n *(US)* pédicure m/f

**podium** ['pəudɪəm] n podium m

**poem** ['pəuɪm] n poème m

**poet** ['pəuɪt] n poète m; **poetic** [pəu'ɛtɪk] adj poétique; **poetry** n poésie f

**poignant** ['pɔɪnjənt] adj poignant(e)

**point** [pɔɪnt] n point m; *(tip)* pointe f; *(in time)* moment m; *(in space)* endroit m; *(subject, idea)* point, sujet m; *(purpose)* but m; *(also:* **decimal ~)**: **2 ~ 3 (2.3)** 2 virgule 3 (2,3); *(BRIT Elec: also:* **power ~)** prise f *(de courant)* ▷ vt *(show)* indiquer; *(gun etc)*: **to ~ sth at** braquer *or* diriger qch sur ▷ vi: **to ~ at** montrer du doigt; **points** npl *(Rail)* aiguillage m; **to make a ~ of doing sth** ne pas manquer de faire qch; **to get/miss the ~** comprendre/ne pas comprendre; **to come to the ~** en venir au fait; **there's no ~ (in doing)** cela ne sert à rien *(de faire)*, à quoi ça sert?; **to be on the ~ of doing sth** être sur le point de faire qch; **point out** vt (mention) faire remarquer, souligner; **point-blank** adv (fig) catégoriquement; (also: **at point-blank range**) à bout portant; **pointed** adj (shape) pointu(e); (remark) plein(e) de sous-entendus; **pointer** n (needle) aiguille f; (clue) indication f; (advice) tuyau m; **pointless** adj inutile, vain(e); **point of view** n point m de vue

**poison** ['pɔɪzn] n poison m ▷ vt empoisonner; **poisonous** adj (snake) venimeux(-euse); (substance, plant) vénéneux(-euse); (fumes) toxique

**poke** [pəuk] vt (jab with finger, stick etc) piquer; pousser du doigt; (put): **to ~ sth in(to)** fourrer or enfoncer qch dans; **poke about** vi fureter; **poke out** vi (stick out) sortir

**poker** ['pəukə<sup>r</sup>] n tisonnier m; (Cards) poker m

**Poland** ['pəulənd] n Pologne f

**polar** ['pəulə<sup>r</sup>] adj polaire; **polar bear** n ours blanc

**Pole** [pəul] n Polonais(e)

**pole** [pəul] n (of wood) mât m, perche f; (Elec) poteau m; (Geo) pôle m; **pole bean** n (us) haricot m (à rames); **pole vault** n saut m à la perche

**police** [pə'liːs] npl police f ▷ vt maintenir l'ordre dans; **police car** n voiture f de police; **police constable** n (BRIT) agent m de police; **police force** n police f, forces fpl de l'ordre; **policeman** (irreg) n agent m de police, policier m; **police officer** n agent m de police; **police station** n commissariat m de police; **policewoman** (irreg) n femme-agent f

**policy** ['pɔlɪsɪ] n politique f; (also: **insurance ~**) police f (d'assurance)

**polio** ['pəulɪəu] n polio f

**Polish** ['pəulɪʃ] adj polonais(e) ▷ n (Ling) polonais m

**polish** ['pɔlɪʃ] n (for shoes) cirage m; (for floor) cire f, encaustique f; (for nails) vernis m; (shine) éclat m, poli m; (fig: refinement) raffinement m ▷ vt (put polish on: shoes, wood) cirer; (make shiny) astiquer, faire briller; **polish off** vt (food) liquider; **polished** adj (fig) raffiné(e)

**polite** [pə'laɪt] adj poli(e); **politeness** n politesse f

**political** [pə'lɪtɪkl] adj politique; **politically** adv politiquement; **politically correct** politiquement correct(e)

**politician** [pɔlɪ'tɪʃən] n homme/ femme politique, politicien(ne)

**politics** ['pɔlɪtɪks] n politique f

**poll** [pəul] n scrutin m, vote m; (also: **opinion ~**) sondage m (d'opinion) ▷ vt (votes) obtenir

**pollen** ['pɔlən] n pollen m

**polling station** n (BRIT) bureau m de vote

**pollute** [pə'luːt] vt polluer

**pollution** [pə'luːʃən] n pollution f

**polo** ['pəuləu] n polo m; **polo-neck** adj à col roulé ▷ n (sweater) pull m à col roulé; **polo shirt** n polo m

**polyester** [pɔlɪ'ɛstə<sup>r</sup>] n polyester m

**polystyrene** [pɔlɪ'staɪriːn] n polystyrène m

**polythene** ['pɔlɪθiːn] n (BRIT) polyéthylène m; **polythene bag** n sac m en plastique

**pomegranate** ['pɔmɪgrænɪt] n grenade f

**pompous** ['pɔmpəs] adj pompeux(-euse)

**pond** [pɔnd] n étang m; (stagnant) mare f

**ponder** ['pɔndə<sup>r</sup>] vt considérer, peser

**pony** ['pəunɪ] n poney m; **ponytail** n queue f de cheval; **pony trekking** n (BRIT) randonnée f équestre or à cheval

**poodle** ['puːdl] n caniche m

**pool** [puːl] n (of rain) flaque f; (pond) mare f; (artificial) bassin m; (also: **swimming ~**) piscine f; (sth shared) fonds commun; (billiards) poule f ▷ vt mettre en commun; **pools** npl (football) ≈ loto sportif

**poor** [puə<sup>r</sup>] adj pauvre; (mediocre) médiocre, faible, mauvais(e) ▷ npl: **the ~** les pauvres mpl; **poorly** adv (badly)

mal, médiocrement ▷ *adj* souffrant(e),
malade

**pop** [pɔp] *n* (*noise*) bruit sec; (*Mus*)
musique *f* pop; (*inf: drink*) soda *m*; (*us
inf: father*) papa *m* ▷ *vt* (*put*) fourrer,
mettre (rapidement) ▷ *vi* éclater;
(*cork*) sauter; **pop in** *vi* entrer en
passant; **pop out** *vi* sortir; **popcorn** *n*
pop-corn *m*

**pope** [pəup] *n* pape *m*

**poplar** ['pɔplə<sup>r</sup>] *n* peuplier *m*

**popper** ['pɔpə<sup>r</sup>] *n* (*BRIT*) bouton-
pression *m*

**poppy** ['pɔpɪ] *n* (*wild*) coquelicot *m*;
(*cultivated*) pavot *m*

**Popsicle®** ['pɔpsɪkl] *n* (*us*) esquimau
*m* (*glace*)

**pop star** *n* pop star *f*

**popular** ['pɔpjulə<sup>r</sup>] *adj* populaire;
(*fashionable*) à la mode; **popularity**
[pɔpju'lærɪtɪ] *n* popularité *f*

**population** [pɔpju'leɪʃən] *n*
population *f*

**pop-up** *adj* (*Comput: menu, window*) pop
up *inv* ▷ *n* pop up *m inv*, fenêtre *f* pop up

**porcelain** ['pɔːslɪn] *n* porcelaine *f*

**porch** [pɔːtʃ] *n* porche *m*; (*us*) véranda *f*

**pore** [pɔː<sup>r</sup>] *n* pore *m* ▷ *vi*: **to ~ over**
s'absorber dans, être plongé(e) dans

**pork** [pɔːk] *n* porc *m*; **pork chop** *n* côte
*f* de porc; **pork pie** *n* pâté *m* de porc
en croûte

**porn** [pɔːn] *adj* (*inf*) porno ▷ *n* (*inf*)
porno *m*; **pornographic** [pɔːnə'græfɪk]
*adj* pornographique; **pornography**
[pɔː'nɔgrəfɪ] *n* pornographie *f*

**porridge** ['pɔrɪdʒ] *n* porridge *m*

**port** [pɔːt] *n* (*harbour*) port *m*; (*Naut:
left side*) bâbord *m*; (*wine*) porto *m*;
(*Comput*) port *m*, accès *m*; **~ of call**
(port d')escale *f*

**portable** ['pɔːtəbl] *adj* portatif(-ive)

**porter** ['pɔːtə<sup>r</sup>] *n* (*for luggage*) porteur *m*;
(*doorkeeper*) gardien *m*; portier *m*

**portfolio** [pɔːt'fəuliəu] *n* portefeuille
*m*; (*of artist*) portfolio *m*

**portion** ['pɔːʃən] *n* portion *f*, part *f*

**portrait** ['pɔːtreɪt] *n* portrait *m*

**portray** [pɔː'treɪ] *vt* faire le portrait
de; (*in writing*) dépeindre, représenter;
(*subj: actor*) jouer

**Portugal** ['pɔːtjugl] *n* Portugal *m*

**Portuguese** [pɔːtju'giːz] *adj*
portugais(e) ▷ *n* (*pl inv*) Portugais(e);
(*Ling*) portugais *m*

**pose** [pəuz] *n* pose *f* ▷ *vi* poser;
(*pretend*): **to ~ as** se faire passer pour
▷ *vt* poser; (*problem*) créer

**posh** [pɔʃ] *adj* (*inf*) chic *inv*

**position** [pə'zɪʃən] *n* position *f*; (*job,
situation*) situation *f* ▷ *vt* mettre en
place *or* en position

**positive** ['pɔzɪtɪv] *adj* positif(-ive);
(*certain*) sûr(e), certain(e); (*definite*)
formel(le), catégorique; **positively** *adv*
(*affirmatively, enthusiastically*) de façon
positive; (*inf: really*) carrément

**possess** [pə'zes] *vt* posséder;
**possession** [pə'zeʃən] *n* possession
*f*; **possessions** *npl* (*belongings*)
affaires *fpl*; **possessive** *adj*
possessif(-ive)

**possibility** [pɔsɪ'bɪlɪtɪ] *n* possibilité *f*;
(*event*) éventualité *f*

**possible** ['pɔsɪbl] *adj* possible; **as big
as ~** aussi gros que possible; **possibly**
*adv* (*perhaps*) peut-être; **I cannot
possibly come** il m'est impossible
de venir

**post** [pəust] *n* (*BRIT: mail*) poste *f*;
(: *letters, delivery*) courrier *m*; (*job,
situation*) poste *m*; (*pole*) poteau *m* ▷ *vt*
(*BRIT: send by post*) poster; (: *appoint*):
**to ~ to** affecter à; **where can I ~
these cards?** où est-ce que je peux
poster ces cartes postales?; **postage** *n*
tarifs *mpl* d'affranchissement; **postal**
*adj* postal(e); **postal order** *n*
mandat(-poste *m*) *m*; **postbox** *n* (*BRIT*)
boîte *f* aux lettres (*publique*); **postcard**
*n* carte postale; **postcode** *n* (*BRIT*)
code postal

**poster** ['pəustə<sup>r</sup>] *n* affiche *f*

**postgraduate** ['pəust'grædjuət] *n*
≈ étudiant(e) de troisième cycle

**postman** ['pəustmən] (*BRIT: irreg*)

facteur m

**postmark** ['pəʊstmɑːk] n cachet m
(de la poste)

**post-mortem** [pəʊst'mɔːtəm] n
autopsie f

**post office** n (building) poste f;
(organization): **the Post Office** les
postes fpl

**postpone** [pəs'pəʊn] vt remettre (à
plus tard), reculer

**posture** ['pɒstʃəʳ] n posture f; (fig)
attitude f

**postwoman** [pəʊst'wʊmən] (BRIT:
irreg) n factrice f

**pot** [pɒt] n (for cooking) marmite f,
casserole f; (teapot) théière f; (for coffee)
cafetière f; (for plants, jam) pot m; (inf:
marijuana) herbe f ▷ vt (plant) mettre en
pot; **to go to ~** (inf) aller à vau-l'eau

**potato** (pl **~es**) [pə'teɪtəʊ] n pomme
f de terre; **potato peeler** n épluche-
légumes m

**potent** ['pəʊtnt] adj puissant(e); (drink)
fort(e), très alcoolisé(e); (man) viril

**potential** [pə'tɛnʃl] adj potentiel(le)
▷ n potentiel m

**pothole** ['pɒthəʊl] n (in road) nid m
de poule; (BRIT: underground) gouffre
m, caverne f

**pot plant** n plante f d'appartement

**potter** ['pɒtəʳ] n potier m ▷ vi (BRIT): **to
~ around** or **about** bricoler; **pottery**
n poterie f

**potty** ['pɒtɪ] n (child's) pot m

**pouch** [paʊtʃ] n (Zool) poche f; (for
tobacco) blague f; (for money) bourse f

**poultry** ['pəʊltrɪ] n volaille f

**pounce** [paʊns] vi: **to ~ (on)** bondir
(sur), fondre (sur)

**pound** [paʊnd] n livre f (weight = 453g,
16 ounces; money = 100 pence); (for dogs,
cars) fourrière f ▷ vt (beat) bourrer de
coups, marteler; (crush) piler, pulvériser
▷ vi (heart) battre violemment, taper;
**pound sterling** n livre f sterling

**pour** [pɔːʳ] vt verser ▷ vi couler à flots;
(rain) pleuvoir à verse; **to ~ sb a drink**
verser or servir à boire à qn; **pour in**

vi (people) affluer, se précipiter; (news,
letters) arriver en masse; **pour out** vi
(people) sortir en masse ▷ vt vider; (fig)
déverser; (serve: a drink) verser; **pouring**
adj: **pouring rain** pluie torrentielle

**pout** [paʊt] vi faire la moue

**poverty** ['pɒvətɪ] n pauvreté f, misère f

**powder** ['paʊdəʳ] n poudre f ▷ vt
poudrer; **powdered milk** n lait m en
poudre

**power** ['paʊəʳ] n (strength, nation)
puissance f, force f; (ability, Pol: of party,
leader) pouvoir m; (of speech, thought)
faculté f; (Elec) courant m; **to be in ~**
être au pouvoir; **power cut** n (BRIT)
coupure f de courant; **power failure**
n panne f de courant; **powerful** adj
puissant(e); (performance etc) très
fort(e); **powerless** adj impuissant(e);
**power point** n (BRIT) prise f de courant;
**power station** n centrale f électrique

**p.p.** abbr (= per procurationem: by
proxy) p.p.

**PR** n abbr = **public relations**

**practical** ['præktɪkl] adj pratique;
**practical joke** n farce f; **practically**
adv (almost) pratiquement

**practice** ['præktɪs] n pratique f; (of
profession) exercice m; (at football etc)
entraînement m; (business) cabinet m
▷ vt, vi (US) = **practise; in ~** (in reality) en
pratique; **out of ~** rouillé(e)

**practise** (US **practice**) ['præktɪs]
vt (work at: piano, backhand etc)
s'exercer à, travailler; (train for: sport)
s'entraîner à; (a sport, religion, method)
pratiquer; (profession) exercer ▷ vi
s'exercer, travailler; (train) s'entraîner;
(lawyer, doctor) exercer; **practising**
(US **practicing**) adj (Christian etc)
pratiquant(e); (lawyer) en exercice

**practitioner** [præk'tɪʃənəʳ] n
praticien(ne)

**pragmatic** [præg'mætɪk] adj
pragmatique

**prairie** ['prɛərɪ] n savane f

**praise** [preɪz] n éloge(s) m(pl),
louange(s) f(pl) ▷ vt louer, faire

l'éloge de

**pram** [præm] n (BRIT) landau m, voiture f d'enfant

**prank** [præŋk] n farce f

**prawn** [prɔ:n] n crevette f (rose); **prawn cocktail** n cocktail m de crevettes

**pray** [preɪ] vi prier; **prayer** [prɛəʳ] n prière f

**preach** [pri:tʃ] vi prêcher; **preacher** n prédicateur m; (US: clergyman) pasteur m

**precarious** [prɪˈkɛərɪəs] adj précaire

**precaution** [prɪˈkɔːʃən] n précaution f

**precede** [prɪˈsiːd] vt, vi précéder; **precedent** [ˈprɛsɪdənt] n précédent m; **preceding** [prɪˈsiːdɪŋ] adj qui précède (or précédait)

**precinct** [ˈpriːsɪŋkt] n (US: district) circonscription f, arrondissement m; **pedestrian ~** (BRIT) zone piétonnière; **shopping ~** (BRIT) centre commercial

**precious** [ˈprɛʃəs] adj précieux(-euse)

**precise** [prɪˈsaɪs] adj précis(e); **precisely** adv précisément

**precision** [prɪˈsɪʒən] n précision f

**predator** [ˈprɛdətəʳ] n prédateur m, rapace m

**predecessor** [ˈpriːdɪsɛsəʳ] n prédécesseur m

**predicament** [prɪˈdɪkəmənt] n situation f difficile

**predict** [prɪˈdɪkt] vt prédire; **predictable** adj prévisible; **prediction** [prɪˈdɪkʃən] n prédiction f

**predominantly** [prɪˈdɔmɪnəntlɪ] adv en majeure partie; (especially) surtout

**preface** [ˈprɛfəs] n préface f

**prefect** [ˈpriːfɛkt] n (BRIT: in school) élève chargé de certaines fonctions de discipline

**prefer** [prɪˈfəːʳ] vt préférer; **preferable** [ˈprɛfrəbl] adj préférable; **preferably** [ˈprɛfrəblɪ] adv de préférence; **preference** [ˈprɛfrəns] n préférence f

**prefix** [ˈpriːfɪks] n préfixe m

**pregnancy** [ˈprɛgnənsɪ] n grossesse f

**pregnant** [ˈprɛgnənt] adj enceinte adj f; (animal) pleine

**prehistoric** [ˈpriːhɪsˈtɔrɪk] adj

préhistorique

**prejudice** [ˈprɛdʒudɪs] n préjugé m; **prejudiced** adj (person) plein(e) de préjugés; (in a matter) partial(e)

**preliminary** [prɪˈlɪmɪnərɪ] adj préliminaire

**prelude** [ˈprɛljuːd] n prélude m

**premature** [ˈprɛmətʃuəʳ] adj prématuré(e)

**premier** [ˈprɛmɪəʳ] adj premier(-ière), principal(e) ▷ n (Pol: Prime Minister) premier ministre; (Pol: President) chef m de l'État

**premiere** [ˈprɛmɪɛəʳ] n première f

**Premier League** n première division

**premises** [ˈprɛmɪsɪz] npl locaux mpl; **on the ~** sur les lieux; sur place

**premium** [ˈpriːmɪəm] n prime f; **to be at a ~** (fig: housing etc) être très demandé(e), être rarissime

**premonition** [prɛməˈnɪʃən] n prémonition f

**preoccupied** [priːˈɔkjupaɪd] adj préoccupé(e)

**prepaid** [priːˈpeɪd] adj payé(e) d'avance

**preparation** [prɛpəˈreɪʃən] n préparation f; **preparations** npl (for trip, war) préparatifs mpl

**preparatory school** n école primaire privée; (US) lycée privé

**prepare** [prɪˈpɛəʳ] vt préparer ▷ vi: **to ~ for** se préparer à

**prepared** [prɪˈpɛəd] adj: **~ for** préparé(e) à; **~ to** prêt(e) à

**preposition** [prɛpəˈzɪʃən] n préposition f

**prep school** n = **preparatory school**

**prerequisite** [priːˈrɛkwɪzɪt] n condition f préalable

**preschool** [ˈpriːˈskuːl] adj préscolaire; (child) d'âge préscolaire

**prescribe** [prɪˈskraɪb] vt prescrire

**prescription** [prɪˈskrɪpʃən] n (Med) ordonnance f; (: medicine) médicament m (obtenu sur ordonnance); **could you write me a ~?** pouvez-vous me faire une ordonnance?

**presence** [ˈprɛzns] n présence f; **in**

**sb's ~** en présence de qn; **~ of mind** présence d'esprit

**present** ['prɛznt] *adj* présent(e); *(current)* présent, actuel(le) ▷ *n* cadeau *m*; *(actuality)* présent *m* ▷ *vt* [prɪ'zɛnt] présenter; *(prize, medal)* remettre; *(give)*: **to ~ sb with sth** offrir qch à qn; **at ~** en ce moment; **to give sb a ~** offrir un cadeau à qn; **presentable** [prɪ'zɛntəbl] *adj* présentable; **presentation** [prɛzn'teɪʃən] *n* présentation *f*; *(ceremony)* remise *f* du cadeau *(or* de la médaille *etc)*; **present-day** *adj* contemporain(e), actuel(le); **presenter** [prɪ'zɛntə'] *n* (BRIT Radio, TV) présentateur(-trice); **presently** *adv* (soon) tout à l'heure, bientôt; *(with verb in past)* peu après; *(at present)* en ce moment; **present participle** [-'pɑ:tɪsɪpl] *n* participe *m* présent

**preservation** [prɛzə'veɪʃən] *n* préservation *f*, conservation *f*

**preservative** [prɪ'zə:vətɪv] *n* agent *m* de conservation

**preserve** [prɪ'zə:v] *vt* (keep safe) préserver, protéger; *(maintain)* conserver, garder; *(food)* mettre en conserve ▷ *n* (for game, fish) réserve *f*; *(often pl: jam)* confiture *f*

**preside** [prɪ'zaɪd] *vi* présider

**president** ['prɛzɪdənt] *n* président(e); **presidential** [prɛzɪ'dɛnʃl] *adj* présidentiel(le)

**press** [prɛs] *n* (tool, machine, newspapers) presse *f*; (for wine) pressoir *m* ▷ *vt* (push) appuyer sur; *(squeeze)* presser, serrer; *(clothes: iron)* repasser; *(insist)*: **to ~ sth on sb** presser qn d'accepter qch; *(urge, entreat)*: **to ~ sb to do** *or* **into doing sth** pousser qn à faire qch ▷ *vi* appuyer; **we are ~ed for time** le temps nous manque; **to ~ for sth** faire pression pour obtenir qch; **press conference** *n* conférence *f* de presse; **pressing** *adj* urgent(e), pressant(e); **press stud** *n* (BRIT) bouton-pression *m*; **press-up** *n* (BRIT) traction *f*

**pressure** ['prɛʃə'] *n* pression *f*; *(stress)* tension *f*; **to put ~ on sb (to do sth)** faire pression sur qn (pour qu'il fasse qch); **pressure cooker** *n* cocotte-minute *f*; **pressure group** *n* groupe *m* de pression

**prestige** [prɛs'ti:ʒ] *n* prestige *m*

**prestigious** [prɛs'tɪdʒəs] *adj* prestigieux(-euse)

**presumably** [prɪ'zju:məblɪ] *adv* vraisemblablement

**presume** [prɪ'zju:m] *vt* présumer, supposer

**pretence** (US **pretense**) [prɪ'tɛns] *n* (claim) prétention *f*; **under false ~s** sous des prétextes fallacieux

**pretend** [prɪ'tɛnd] *vt* (feign) feindre, simuler ▷ *vi* (feign) faire semblant

**pretense** [prɪ'tɛns] *n* (US) = **pretence**

**pretentious** [prɪ'tɛnʃəs] *adj* prétentieux(-euse)

**pretext** ['pri:tɛkst] *n* prétexte *m*

**pretty** ['prɪtɪ] *adj* joli(e) ▷ *adv* assez

**prevail** [prɪ'veɪl] *vi* (win) l'emporter, prévaloir; *(be usual)* avoir cours; **prevailing** *adj* (widespread) courant(e), répandu(e); *(wind)* dominant(e)

**prevalent** ['prɛvələnt] *adj* répandu(e), courant(e)

**prevent** [prɪ'vɛnt] *vt*: **to ~ (from doing)** empêcher (de faire); **prevention** [prɪ'vɛnʃən] *n* prévention *f*; **preventive** *adj* préventif(-ive)

**preview** ['pri:vju:] *n* (of film) avant-première *f*

**previous** ['pri:vɪəs] *adj* (last) précédent(e); *(earlier)* antérieur(e); **previously** *adv* précédemment, auparavant

**prey** [preɪ] *n* proie *f* ▷ *vi*: **to ~ on** s'attaquer à; **it was ~ing on his mind** ça le rongeait *or* minait

**price** [praɪs] *n* prix *m* ▷ *vt* (goods) fixer le prix de; **priceless** *adj* sans prix, inestimable; **price list** *n* tarif *m*

**prick** [prɪk] *n* (sting) piqûre *f* ▷ *vt* piquer; **to ~ up one's ears** dresser *or* tendre l'oreille

**prickly** ['prɪklɪ] *adj* piquant(e),

épineux(-euse); (fig: person) irritable

**pride** [praɪd] n fierté f; (pej) orgueil m ▷ vt: **to ~ o.s. on** se flatter de; s'enorgueillir de

**priest** [priːst] n prêtre m

**primarily** ['praɪmərɪlɪ] adv principalement, essentiellement

**primary** ['praɪmərɪ] adj primaire; (first in importance) premier(-ière), primordial(e) ▷ n (us: election) (élection f) primaire f; **primary school** n (BRIT) école f primaire

**prime** [praɪm] adj primordial(e), fondamental(e); (excellent) excellent(e) ▷ vt (fig) mettre au courant ▷ n: **in the ~ of life** dans la fleur de l'âge; **Prime Minister** n Premier ministre

**primitive** ['prɪmɪtɪv] adj primitif(-ive)

**primrose** ['prɪmrəuz] n primevère f

**prince** [prɪns] n prince m

**princess** [prɪn'sɛs] n princesse f

**principal** ['prɪnsɪpl] adj principal(e) ▷ n (head teacher) directeur m, principal m; **principally** adv principalement

**principle** ['prɪnsɪpl] n principe m; **in ~** en principe; **on ~** par principe

**print** [prɪnt] n (mark) empreinte f; (letters) caractères mpl; (fabric) imprimé m; (Art) gravure f, estampe f; (Phot) épreuve f ▷ vt imprimer; (publish) publier; (write in capitals) écrire en majuscules; **out of ~** épuisé(e); **print out** vt (Comput) imprimer; **printer** n (machine) imprimante f; (person) imprimeur m; **printout** n (Comput) sortie f imprimante

**prior** ['praɪə'] adj antérieur(e), précédent(e); (more important) prioritaire ▷ adv: **~ to doing** avant de faire

**priority** [praɪ'ɔrɪtɪ] n priorité f; **to have** or **take ~ over sth/sb** avoir la priorité sur qch/qn

**prison** ['prɪzn] n prison f ▷ cpd pénitentiaire; **prisoner** n prisonnier(-ière); **prisoner of war** n prisonnier(-ière) de guerre

**pristine** ['prɪstiːn] adj virginal(e)

**privacy** ['prɪvəsɪ] n intimité f, solitude f

**private** ['praɪvɪt] adj (not public) privé(e); (personal) personnel(le); (house, car, lesson) particulier(-ière); (quiet: place) tranquille ▷ n soldat m de deuxième classe; **"~"** (on envelope) "personnelle"; (on door) "privé"; **in ~** en privé; **privately** adv en privé; (within oneself) intérieurement; **private property** n propriété privée; **private school** n école privée

**privatize** ['praɪvɪtaɪz] vt privatiser

**privilege** ['prɪvɪlɪdʒ] n privilège m

**prize** [praɪz] n prix m ▷ adj (example, idiot) parfait(e); (bull, novel) primé(e) ▷ vt priser, faire grand cas de; **prizegiving** n distribution f des prix; **prizewinner** n gagnant(e)

**pro** [prəu] n (inf: Sport) professionnel(le) ▷ prep pro …; **pros** npl: **the ~s and cons** le pour et le contre

**probability** [prɔbə'bɪlɪtɪ] n probabilité f; **in all ~** très probablement

**probable** ['prɔbəbl] adj probable

**probably** ['prɔbəblɪ] adv probablement

**probation** [prə'beɪʃən] n: **on ~** (employee) à l'essai; (Law) en liberté surveillée

**probe** [prəub] n (Med, Space) sonde f; (enquiry) enquête f, investigation f ▷ vt sonder, explorer

**problem** ['prɔbləm] n problème m

**procedure** [prə'siːdʒə'] n (Admin, Law) procédure f; (method) marche f à suivre, façon f de procéder

**proceed** [prə'siːd] vi (go forward) avancer; (act) procéder; (continue): **to ~ (with)** continuer, poursuivre; **to ~ to do** se mettre à faire; **proceedings** npl (measures) mesures fpl; (Law: against sb) poursuites fpl; (meeting) réunion f, séance f; (records) compte rendu; actes mpl; **proceeds** ['prəusiːdz] npl produit m, recette f

**process** ['prəusɛs] n processus m; (method) procédé m ▷ vt traiter

**procession** [prə'sɛʃən] n défilé m,

cortège m; **funeral ~** (on foot) cortège funèbre; (in cars) convoi m mortuaire

**proclaim** [prə'kleɪm] vt déclarer, proclamer

**prod** [prɒd] vt pousser

**produce** n ['prɒdjuːs] (Agr) produits mpl ▷ vt [prə'djuːs] produire; (show) présenter; (cause) provoquer, causer; (Theat) monter, mettre en scène; (TV: programme) réaliser; (: play, film) mettre en scène; (Radio: programme) réaliser; (: play) mettre en ondes; **producer** n (Theat) metteur m en scène; (Agr, Comm, Cine) producteur m; (TV: of programme) réalisateur m; (: of play, film) metteur en scène; (Radio: of programme) réalisateur; (: of play) metteur en ondes

**product** ['prɒdʌkt] n produit m; **production** [prə'dʌkʃən] n production f; (Theat) mise f en scène; **productive** [prə'dʌktɪv] adj productif(-ive); **productivity** [prɒdʌk'tɪvɪtɪ] n productivité f

**Prof.** [prɒf] abbr (= professor) Prof

**profession** [prə'fɛʃən] n profession f; **professional** n professionnel(le) ▷ adj professionnel(le); (work) de professionnel

**professor** [prə'fɛsər] n professeur m (titulaire d'une chaire); (us: teacher) professeur m

**profile** ['prəʊfaɪl] n profil m

**profit** ['prɒfɪt] n (from trading) bénéfice m; (advantage) profit m ▷ vi: **to ~ (by or from)** profiter (de); **profitable** adj lucratif(-ive), rentable

**profound** [prə'faʊnd] adj profond(e)

**programme** (us **program**) ['prəʊɡræm] n (Comput: also BRIT: **program**) programme m; (Radio, TV) émission f ▷ vt programmer; **programmer** (us **programer**) n programmeur(-euse); **programming** (us **programing**) n programmation f

**progress** n ['prəʊɡrɛs] progrès m(pl) ▷ vi [prə'ɡrɛs] progresser, avancer; **in ~** en cours; **progressive** [prə'ɡrɛsɪv] adj progressif(-ive); (person) progressiste

**prohibit** [prə'hɪbɪt] vt interdire, défendre

**project** n ['prɒdʒɛkt] (plan) projet m, plan m; (venture) opération f, entreprise f; (Scol: research) étude f, dossier m ▷ vb [prə'dʒɛkt] ▷ vt projeter ▷ vi (stick out) faire saillie, s'avancer; **projection** [prə'dʒɛkʃən] n projection f; (overhang) saillie f; **projector** [prə'dʒɛktər] n projecteur m

**prolific** [prə'lɪfɪk] adj prolifique

**prolong** [prə'lɒŋ] vt prolonger

**prom** [prɒm] n abbr = **promenade** (us: ball) bal m d'étudiants; **the P~s** série de concerts de musique classique; voir encadré

● **PROM**
●
● En Grande-Bretagne, un **promenade**
● **concert** ou **prom** est un concert
● de musique classique, ainsi appelé
● car, à l'origine, le public restait
● debout et se promenait au lieu de
● rester assis. De nos jours, une partie
● du public reste debout, mais il y a
● également des places assises (plus
● chères). Les **Proms** les plus connus
● sont les Proms londoniens. La
● dernière séance (the "Last Night of
● the Proms") est un grand événement
● médiatique où se jouent des airs
● traditionnels et patriotiques. Aux
● États-Unis et au Canada, le **prom**
● ou **promenade** est un bal organisé
● par le lycée.

**promenade** [prɒmə'nɑːd] n (by sea) esplanade f, promenade f

**prominent** ['prɒmɪnənt] adj (standing out) proéminent(e); (important) important(e)

**promiscuous** [prə'mɪskjuəs] adj (sexually) de mœurs légères

**promise** ['prɒmɪs] n promesse f ▷ vt, vi promettre; **promising** adj prometteur(-euse)

**promote** [prə'məut] vt promouvoir; (new product) lancer; **promotion**

[prə'məʊʃən] n promotion f

**prompt** [prɒmpt] adj rapide ▷ n (Comput) message m (de guidage) ▷ vt (cause) entraîner, provoquer; (Theat) souffler (son rôle or ses répliques) à; **at 8 o'clock ~** à 8 heures précises; **to ~ sb to do** inciter or pousser qn à faire; **promptly** adv (quickly) rapidement, sans délai; (on time) ponctuellement

**prone** [prəʊn] adj (lying) couché(e) (face contre terre); (liable): **~ to** enclin(e) à

**prong** [prɒŋ] n (of fork) dent f

**pronoun** ['prəʊnaʊn] n pronom m

**pronounce** [prə'naʊns] vt prononcer; **how do you ~ it?** comment est-ce que ça se prononce?

**pronunciation** [prənʌnsɪ'eɪʃən] n prononciation f

**proof** [pru:f] n preuve f ▷ adj: **~ against** à l'épreuve de

**prop** [prɒp] n support m, étai m; (fig) soutien m ▷ vt (also: **~ up**) étayer, soutenir; **props** npl accessoires mpl

**propaganda** [prɒpə'gændə] n propagande f

**propeller** [prə'pɛlər] n hélice f

**proper** ['prɒpər] adj (suited, right) approprié(e), bon (bonne); (seemly) correct(e), convenable; (authentic) vrai(e), véritable; (referring to place): **the village ~** le village proprement dit; **properly** adv correctement, convenablement; **proper noun** n nom m propre

**property** ['prɒpətɪ] n (possessions) biens mpl; (house etc) propriété f; (land) terres fpl, domaine m

**prophecy** ['prɒfɪsɪ] n prophétie f

**prophet** ['prɒfɪt] n prophète m

**proportion** [prə'pɔːʃən] n proportion f; (share) part f, partie f; **proportions** npl (size) dimensions fpl; **proportional, proportionate** adj proportionnel(le)

**proposal** [prə'pəʊzl] n proposition f, offre f; (plan) projet m; (of marriage) demande f en mariage

**propose** [prə'pəʊz] vt proposer, suggérer ▷ vi faire sa demande en mariage; **to ~ to do** avoir l'intention de faire

**proposition** [prɒpə'zɪʃən] n proposition f

**proprietor** [prə'praɪətər] n propriétaire m/f

**prose** [prəʊz] n prose f; (Scol: translation) thème m

**prosecute** ['prɒsɪkjuːt] vt poursuivre; **prosecution** [prɒsɪ'kjuːʃən] n poursuites fpl judiciaires; (accusing side: in criminal case) accusation f; (: in civil case) la partie plaignante; **prosecutor** n (lawyer) procureur m; (also: **public prosecutor**) ministère public; (us: plaintiff) plaignant(e)

**prospect** n ['prɒspɛkt] perspective f; (hope) espoir m, chances fpl ▷ vt, vi [prə'spɛkt] prospecter; **prospects** npl (for work etc) possibilités fpl d'avenir, débouchés mpl; **prospective** [prə'spɛktɪv] adj (possible) éventuel(le); (future) futur(e)

**prospectus** [prə'spɛktəs] n prospectus m

**prosper** ['prɒspər] vi prospérer; **prosperity** [prɒ'spɛrɪtɪ] n prospérité f; **prosperous** adj prospère

**prostitute** ['prɒstɪtjuːt] n prostituée f; **male ~** prostitué m

**protect** [prə'tɛkt] vt protéger; **protection** [prə'tɛkʃən] n protection f; **protective** adj protecteur(-trice); (clothing) de protection

**protein** ['prəʊtiːn] n protéine f

**protest** n ['prəʊtɛst] protestation f ▷ vb [prə'tɛst] ▷ vi: **to ~ against/ about** protester contre/à propos de; **to ~ (that)** protester que

**Protestant** ['prɒtɪstənt] adj, n protestant(e)

**protester, protestor** [prə'tɛstər] n (in demonstration) manifestant(e)

**protractor** [prə'træktər] n (Geom) rapporteur m

**proud** [praʊd] adj fier(-ère); (pej) orgueilleux(-euse)

**prove** [pruːv] vt prouver, démontrer

▷ *vi*: **to ~ correct** *etc* s'avérer juste *etc*; **to ~ o.s.** montrer ce dont on est capable

**proverb** ['provɜːb] *n* proverbe *m*

**provide** [prə'vaɪd] *vt* fournir; **to ~ sb with sth** fournir qch à qn; **provide for** *vt fus* (*person*) subvenir aux besoins de; (*future event*) prévoir; **provided** *conj*: **provided (that)** à condition que + *sub*; **providing** [prə'vaɪdɪŋ] *conj* à condition que + *sub*

**province** ['provɪns] *n* province *f*; (*fig*) domaine *m*; **provincial** [prə'vɪnʃəl] *adj* provincial(e)

**provision** [prə'vɪʒən] *n* (*supplying*) fourniture *f*; approvisionnement *m*; (*stipulation*) disposition *f*; **provisions** *npl* (*food*) provisions *fpl*; **provisional** *adj* provisoire

**provocative** [prə'vɔkətɪv] *adj* provocateur(-trice), provocant(e)

**provoke** [prə'vəuk] *vt* provoquer

**prowl** [praul] *vi* (*also*: **~ about, ~ around**) rôder

**proximity** [prɔk'sɪmɪtɪ] *n* proximité *f*

**proxy** ['prɔksɪ] *n*: **by ~** par procuration

**prudent** ['pruːdnt] *adj* prudent(e)

**prune** [pruːn] *n* pruneau *m* ▷ *vt* élaguer

**pry** [praɪ] *vi*: **to ~ into** fourrer son nez dans

**PS** *n abbr* (= *postscript*) PS *m*

**pseudonym** ['sjuːdənɪm] *n* pseudonyme *m*

**PSHE** *n abbr* (BRIT: *Scol*: = *personal, social and health education*) cours d'éducation personnelle, sanitaire et sociale préparant à la vie adulte

**psychiatric** [saɪkɪ'ætrɪk] *adj* psychiatrique

**psychiatrist** [saɪ'kaɪətrɪst] *n* psychiatre *m/f*

**psychic** ['saɪkɪk] *adj* (*also*: **~al**) (méta)psychique; (*person*) doué(e) de télépathie ou d'un sixième sens

**psychoanalysis** (*pl* **-ses**) [saɪkəuə'nælɪsɪs, -siːz] *n* psychanalyse *f*

**psychological** [saɪkə'lɔdʒɪkl] *adj* psychologique

**psychologist** [saɪ'kɔlədʒɪst] *n* psychologue *m/f*

**psychology** [saɪ'kɔlədʒɪ] *n* psychologie *f*

**psychotherapy** [saɪkəu'θɛrəpɪ] *n* psychothérapie *f*

**pt** *abbr* = **pint(s)**; **point(s)**

**PTO** *abbr* (= *please turn over*) TSVP

**pub** [pʌb] *n abbr* (= *public house*) pub *m*

**puberty** ['pjuːbətɪ] *n* puberté *f*

**public** ['pʌblɪk] *adj* public(-ique) ▷ *n* public *m*; **in ~** en public; **to make ~** rendre public

**publication** [pʌblɪ'keɪʃən] *n* publication *f*

**public**: **public company** *n* société *f* anonyme; **public convenience** *n* (BRIT) toilettes *fpl*; **public holiday** *n* (BRIT) jour férié; **public house** *n* (BRIT) pub *m*

**publicity** [pʌb'lɪsɪtɪ] *n* publicité *f*

**publicize** ['pʌblɪsaɪz] *vt* (*make known*) faire connaître, rendre public; (*advertise*) faire de la publicité pour

**public**: **public limited company** *n* ≈ société *f* anonyme (SA) (*cotée en Bourse*); **publicly** *adv* publiquement, en public; **public opinion** *n* opinion publique; **public relations** *n* or *npl* relations publiques (RP); **public school** *n* (BRIT) école privée; (US) école publique; **public transport** (US **public transportation**) *n* transports *mpl* en commun

**publish** ['pʌblɪʃ] *vt* publier; **publisher** *n* éditeur *m*; **publishing** *n* (*industry*) édition *f*

**pub lunch** *n* repas *m* de bistrot

**pudding** ['pudɪŋ] *n* (BRIT: *dessert*) dessert *m*, entremets *m*; (*sweet dish*) pudding *m*, gâteau *m*

**puddle** ['pʌdl] *n* flaque *f* d'eau

**puff** [pʌf] *n* bouffée *f* ▷ *vt* (*also*: **~ out**: *sails, cheeks*) gonfler ▷ *vi* (*pant*) haleter; **puff pastry** (US **puff paste**) *n* pâte feuilletée

**pull** [pul] *n* (*tug*): **to give sth a ~** tirer sur qch ▷ *vt* tirer; (*trigger*) presser;

(strain: muscle, tendon) se claquer
▷ vi tirer; **to ~ to pieces** mettre en
morceaux; **to ~ one's punches** (also
fig) ménager son adversaire; **to ~ one's
weight** y mettre du sien (fig); **to ~ o.s.
together** se ressaisir; **to ~ sb's leg** (fig)
faire marcher qn; **pull apart** vt (break)
mettre en pièces, démantibuler; **pull
away** vi (vehicle: move off) partir; (draw
back) s'éloigner; **pull back** vt (lever etc)
tirer sur; (curtains) ouvrir ▷ vi (refrain)
s'abstenir; (Mil: withdraw) se retirer;
**pull down** vt baisser, abaisser; (house)
démolir; **pull in** vi (Aut) se ranger; (Rail)
entrer en gare; **pull off** vt enlever,
ôter; (deal etc) conclure; **pull out** vi
démarrer, partir; (Aut: come out of line)
déboîter ▷ vt (from bag, pocket) sortir;
(remove) arracher; **pull over** vi (Aut) se
ranger; **pull up** vi (stop) s'arrêter ▷ vt
remonter; (uproot) déraciner, arracher
**pulley** ['pʊlɪ] n poulie f
**pullover** ['pʊləʊvəʳ] n pull-over m,
tricot m
**pulp** [pʌlp] n (of fruit) pulpe f; (for paper)
pâte f à papier
**pulpit** ['pʊlpɪt] n chaire f
**pulse** [pʌls] n (of blood) pouls m; (of
heart) battement m; **pulses** npl (Culin)
légumineuses fpl
**puma** ['pjuːmə] n puma m
**pump** [pʌmp] n pompe f; (shoe)
escarpin m ▷ vt pomper; **pump up**
vt gonfler
**pumpkin** ['pʌmpkɪn] n potiron m,
citrouille f
**pun** [pʌn] n jeu m de mots, calembour m
**punch** [pʌntʃ] n (blow) coup m de poing;
(tool) poinçon m; (drink) punch m ▷ vt
(make a hole in) poinçonner, perforer;
(hit): **to ~ sb/sth** donner un coup de
poing à qn/sur qch; **punch-up** n (BRIT
inf) bagarre f
**punctual** ['pʌŋktjuəl] adj ponctuel(le)
**punctuation** [pʌŋktju'eɪʃən] n
ponctuation f
**puncture** ['pʌŋktʃəʳ] n (BRIT) crevaison
f ▷ vt crever

**punish** ['pʌnɪʃ] vt punir; **punishment** n
punition f, châtiment m
**punk** [pʌŋk] n (person: also: ~ **rocker**)
punk m/f; (music: also: ~ **rock**) le punk;
(us inf: hoodlum) voyou m
**pup** [pʌp] n chiot m
**pupil** ['pjuːpl] n élève m/f; (of eye)
pupille f
**puppet** ['pʌpɪt] n marionnette f,
pantin m
**puppy** ['pʌpɪ] n chiot m, petit chien
**purchase** ['pəːtʃɪs] n achat m ▷ vt
acheter
**pure** [pjʊəʳ] adj pur(e); **purely** adv
purement
**purify** ['pjʊərɪfaɪ] vt purifier, épurer
**purity** ['pjʊərɪtɪ] n pureté f
**purple** ['pəːpl] adj violet(te); (face)
cramoisi(e)
**purpose** ['pəːpəs] n intention f, but m;
**on ~** exprès
**purr** [pəːʳ] vi ronronner
**purse** [pəːs] n (BRIT: for money) porte-
monnaie m inv; (us: handbag) sac m (à
main) ▷ vt serrer, pincer
**pursue** [pə'sjuː] vt poursuivre
**pursuit** [pə'sjuːt] n poursuite f;
(occupation) occupation f, activité f
**pus** [pʌs] n pus m
**push** [pʊʃ] n poussée f ▷ vt pousser;
(button) appuyer sur; (fig: product)
mettre en avant, faire de la publicité
pour ▷ vi pousser; **to ~ for** (better
pay, conditions) réclamer; **push in**
vi s'introduire de force; **push off** vi
(inf) filer, ficher le camp; **push on** vi
(continue) continuer; **push over** vt
renverser; **push through** vi (in crowd)
se frayer un chemin; **pushchair** n
(BRIT) poussette f; **pusher** n (also: **drug
pusher**) revendeur(-euse) (de drogue),
ravitailleur(-euse) (en drogue); **push-
up** n (us) traction f
**pussy(-cat)** ['pusɪ-] n (inf) minet m
**put** (pt, pp ~) [put] vt mettre; (place)
poser, placer; (say) dire, exprimer; (a
question) poser; (case, view) exposer,
présenter; (estimate) estimer; **put**

**aside** *vt* mettre de côté; **put away**
*vt* (*store*) ranger; **put back** *vt* (*replace*)
remettre, replacer; (*postpone*) remettre;
**put by** *vt* (*money*) mettre de côté,
économiser; **put down** *vt* (*parcel etc*)
poser, déposer; (*in writing*) mettre
par écrit, inscrire; (*suppress: revolt
etc*) réprimer, écraser; (*attribute*)
attribuer; (*animal*) abattre; (*cat, dog*)
faire piquer; **put forward** *vt* (*ideas*)
avancer, proposer; **put in** *vt* (*complaint*)
soumettre; (*time, effort*) consacrer; **put
off** *vt* (*postpone*) remettre à plus tard,
ajourner; (*discourage*) dissuader; **put
on** *vt* (*clothes, lipstick, CD*) mettre; (*light
etc*) allumer; (*play etc*) monter; (*weight*)
prendre; (*assume: accent, manner*)
prendre; **put out** *vt* (*take outside*)
mettre dehors; (*one's hand*) tendre; (*light
etc*) éteindre; (*person: inconvenience*)
déranger, gêner; **put through** *vt* (*Tel:
caller*) mettre en communication;
(: *call*) passer; (*plan*) faire accepter;
**put together** *vt* mettre ensemble,
(*assemble: furniture*) monter, assembler;
(*meal*) préparer; **put up** *vt* (*raise*) lever,
relever, remonter; (*hang*) accrocher;
(*build*) construire, ériger; (*increase*)
augmenter; (*accommodate*) loger; **put
up with** *vt fus* supporter
**putt** [pʌt] *n* putt *m*; **putting green**
*n* green *m*
**puzzle** ['pʌzl] *n* énigme *f*, mystère *m*;
(*game*) jeu *m*, casse-tête *m*; (*jigsaw*)
puzzle *m*; (*also:* **crossword ~**) mots
croisés ▷ *vt* intriguer, rendre perplexe
▷ *vi:* **to ~ over** chercher à comprendre;
**puzzled** *adj* perplexe; **puzzling** *adj*
déconcertant(e), inexplicable
**pyjamas** [pɪˈdʒɑːməz] *npl* (*BRIT*)
pyjama *m*
**pylon** ['paɪlən] *n* pylône *m*
**pyramid** ['pɪrəmɪd] *n* pyramide *f*
**Pyrenees** [pɪrəˈniːz] *npl* Pyrénées *fpl*

# q

**quack** [kwæk] *n* (*of duck*) coin-coin *m
inv*; (*pej: doctor*) charlatan *m*
**quadruple** [kwɔˈdruːpl] *vt, vi*
quadrupler
**quail** [kweɪl] *n* (*Zool*) caille *f* ▷ *vi:* **to ~ at**
*or* **before** reculer devant
**quaint** [kweɪnt] *adj* bizarre; (*old-
fashioned*) désuet(-ète); (*picturesque*) au
charme vieillot, pittoresque
**quake** [kweɪk] *vi* trembler ▷ *n abbr*
= **earthquake**
**qualification** [kwɔlɪfɪˈkeɪʃən]
*n* (*often pl: degree etc*) diplôme *m*;
(*training*) qualification(s) *f(pl)*; (*ability*)
compétence(s) *f(pl)*; (*limitation*) réserve
*f*, restriction *f*
**qualified** ['kwɔlɪfaɪd] *adj* (*trained*)
qualifié(e); (*professionally*) diplômé(e);
(*fit, competent*) compétent(e),
qualifié(e); (*limited*) conditionnel(le)
**qualify** ['kwɔlɪfaɪ] *vt* qualifier; (*modify*)
atténuer, nuancer ▷ *vi:* **to ~ (as)**
obtenir son diplôme (de); **to ~ (for)**
remplir les conditions requises (pour);

(Sport) se qualifier (pour)
**quality** ['kwɒlɪtɪ] n qualité f
**qualm** [kwɑːm] n doute m; scrupule m
**quantify** ['kwɒntɪfaɪ] vt quantifier
**quantity** ['kwɒntɪtɪ] n quantité f
**quarantine** ['kwɒrntiːn] n
quarantaine f
**quarrel** ['kwɒrl] n querelle f, dispute f
▷ vi se disputer, se quereller
**quarry** ['kwɒrɪ] n (for stone) carrière f;
(animal) proie f, gibier m
**quart** [kwɔːt] n ≈ litre m
**quarter** ['kwɔːtər] n quart m; (of year)
trimestre m; (district) quartier m; (US,
CANADA: 25 cents) (pièce f de) vingt-cinq
cents ▷ vt partager en quartiers or
en quatre; (Mil) caserner, cantonner;
**quarters** npl logement m; (Mil)
quartiers mpl, cantonnement m; **a ~
of an hour** un quart d'heure; **quarter
final** n quart m de finale; **quarterly** adj
trimestriel(le) ▷ adv tous les trois mois
**quartet(te)** [kwɔː'tɛt] n quatuor m;
(jazz players) quartette m
**quartz** [kwɔːts] n quartz m
**quay** [kiː] n (also: **~side**) quai m
**queasy** ['kwiːzɪ] adj: **to feel ~** avoir
mal au cœur
**Quebec** [kwɪ'bɛk] n (city) Québec f;
(province) Québec m
**queen** [kwiːn] n (gen) reine f; (Cards
etc) dame f
**queer** [kwɪər] adj étrange,
curieux(-euse); (suspicious) louche ▷ n
(inf: highly offensive) homosexuel m
**quench** [kwɛntʃ] vt: **to ~ one's thirst**
se désaltérer
**query** ['kwɪərɪ] n question f ▷ vt
(disagree with, dispute) mettre en doute,
questionner
**quest** [kwɛst] n recherche f, quête f
**question** ['kwɛstʃən] n question f ▷ vt
(person) interroger; (plan, idea) mettre
en question or en doute; **beyond
~** sans aucun doute; **out of the ~**
hors de question; **questionable** adj
discutable; **question mark** n point
m d'interrogation; **questionnaire**

[kwɛstʃə'nɛər] n questionnaire m
**queue** [kjuː] (BRIT) n queue f, file f ▷ vi
(also: **~ up**) faire la queue
**quiche** [kiːʃ] n quiche f
**quick** [kwɪk] adj rapide; (mind) vif
(vive); (agile) agile, vif (vive) ▷ n: **cut
to the ~** (fig) touché(e) au vif; **be ~!**
dépêche-toi; **quickly** adv (fast) vite,
rapidement; (immediately) tout de suite
**quid** [kwɪd] n (pl inv: BRIT inf) livre f
**quiet** ['kwaɪət] adj tranquille,
calme; (voice) bas(se); (ceremony,
colour) discret(-ète) ▷ n tranquillité
f, calme m; (silence) silence m;
**quietly** adv tranquillement;
(silently) silencieusement; (discreetly)
discrètement
**quilt** [kwɪlt] n édredon m; (continental
quilt) couette f
**quirky** ['kwɜːkɪ] adj singulier(-ère)
**quit** [kwɪt] (pt, pp **~** or **~ted**) vt quitter
▷ vi (give up) abandonner, renoncer;
(resign) démissionner
**quite** [kwaɪt] adv (rather) assez, plutôt;
(entirely) complètement, tout à fait;
**~ a few of them** un assez grand
nombre d'entre eux; **that's not ~
right** ce n'est pas tout à fait juste; **~ (so)!**
exactement!
**quits** [kwɪts] adj: **~ (with)** quitte
(envers); **let's call it ~** restons-en là
**quiver** ['kwɪvər] vi trembler, frémir
**quiz** [kwɪz] n (on TV) jeu-concours m
(télévisé); (in magazine etc) test m de
connaissances ▷ vt interroger
**quota** ['kwəʊtə] n quota m
**quotation** [kwəʊ'teɪʃən] n citation f;
(estimate) devis m; **quotation marks**
npl guillemets mpl
**quote** [kwəʊt] n citation f; (estimate)
devis m ▷ vt (sentence, author) citer;
(price) donner, soumettre ▷ vi: **to
~ from** citer; **quotes** npl (inverted
commas) guillemets mpl

# r

**Rabat** [rəˈbɑːt] n Rabat
**rabbi** [ˈræbaɪ] n rabbin m
**rabbit** [ˈræbɪt] n lapin m
**rabies** [ˈreɪbiːz] n rage f
**RAC** n abbr (BRIT: = Royal Automobile
  Club) ≈ ACF m
**rac(c)oon** [rəˈkuːn] n raton m laveur
**race** [reɪs] n (species) race f; (competition,
  rush) course f ▷ vt (person) faire la
  course avec ▷ vi (compete) faire la
  course, courir; (pulse) battre très
  vite; **race car** n (US) = **racing car**;
  **racecourse** n champ m de courses;
  **racehorse** n cheval m de course;
  **racetrack** n piste f
**racial** [ˈreɪʃl] adj racial(e)
**racing** [ˈreɪsɪŋ] n courses fpl; **racing
  car** n (BRIT) voiture f de course; **racing
  driver** n (BRIT) pilote m de course
**racism** [ˈreɪsɪzəm] n racisme m; **racist**
  [ˈreɪsɪst] adj, n raciste m/f
**rack** [ræk] n (for guns, tools) râtelier m;
  (for clothes) portant m; (for bottles) casier
  m; (also: **luggage ~**) filet m à bagages;

(also: **roof ~**) galerie f; (also: **dish ~**)
  égouttoir m ▷ vt tourmenter; **to ~
  one's brains** se creuser la cervelle
**racket** [ˈrækɪt] n (for tennis) raquette f;
  (noise) tapage m, vacarme m; (swindle)
  escroquerie f
**racquet** [ˈrækɪt] n raquette f
**radar** [ˈreɪdɑːʳ] n radar m
**radiation** [reɪdɪˈeɪʃən] n rayonnement
  m; (radioactive) radiation f
**radiator** [ˈreɪdɪeɪtəʳ] n radiateur m
**radical** [ˈrædɪkl] adj radical(e)
**radio** [ˈreɪdɪəu] n radio f ▷ vt (person)
  appeler par radio; **on the ~** à la radio;
  **radioactive** adj radioactif(-ive); **radio
  station** n station f de radio
**radish** [ˈrædɪʃ] n radis m
**RAF** n abbr (BRIT) = **Royal Air Force**
**raffle** [ˈræfl] n tombola f
**raft** [rɑːft] n (craft: also: **life ~**) radeau m;
  (logs) train m de flottage
**rag** [ræg] n chiffon m; (pej: newspaper)
  feuille f, torchon m; (for charity)
  attractions organisées par les étudiants
  au profit d'œuvres de charité; **rags** npl
  haillons mpl
**rage** [reɪdʒ] n (fury) rage f, fureur f ▷ vi
  (person) être fou (folle) de rage; (storm)
  faire rage, être déchaîné(e); **it's all the
  ~** cela fait fureur
**ragged** [ˈrægɪd] adj (edge) inégal(e),
  qui accroche; (clothes) en loques;
  (appearance) déguenillé(e)
**raid** [reɪd] n (Mil) raid m; (criminal) hold-
  up m inv; (by police) descente f, rafle f
  ▷ vt faire un raid sur or un hold-up dans
  or une descente dans
**rail** [reɪl] n (on stair) rampe f; (on
  bridge, balcony) balustrade f; (of ship)
  bastingage m; (for train) rail m; **railcard**
  n (BRIT) carte f de chemin de fer;
  **railing(s)** n(pl) grille f; **railway** (US
  **railroad**) n chemin m de fer; (track)
  voie f ferrée; **railway line** n (BRIT) ligne
  f de chemin de fer; (track) voie ferrée;
  **railway station** n (BRIT) gare f
**rain** [reɪn] n pluie f ▷ vi pleuvoir; **in
  the ~** sous la pluie; **it's ~ing** il pleut;

**rainbow** n arc-en-ciel m; **raincoat** n imperméable m; **raindrop** n goutte f de pluie; **rainfall** n chute f de pluie; (measurement) hauteur f des précipitations; **rainforest** n forêt tropicale; **rainy** adj pluvieux(-euse)

**raise** [reɪz] n augmentation f ⊳ vt (lift) lever; hausser; (increase) augmenter; (morale) remonter; (standards) améliorer; (a protest, doubt) provoquer, causer; (a question) soulever; (cattle, family) élever; (crop) faire pousser; (army, funds) rassembler; (loan) obtenir; **to ~ one's voice** élever la voix

**raisin** ['reɪzn] n raisin sec

**rake** [reɪk] n (tool) râteau m; (person) débauché m ⊳ vt (garden) ratisser

**rally** ['rælɪ] n (Pol etc) meeting m, rassemblement m; (Aut) rallye m; (Tennis) échange m ⊳ vt rassembler, rallier; (support) gagner ⊳ vi (sick person) aller mieux; (Stock Exchange) reprendre

**RAM** [ræm] n abbr (Comput: = random access memory) mémoire vive

**ram** [ræm] n bélier m ⊳ vt (push) enfoncer; (crash into: vehicle) emboutir; (: lamppost etc) percuter

**Ramadan** [ræmə'dæn] n Ramadan m

**ramble** ['ræmbl] n randonnée f ⊳ vi (walk) se promener, faire une randonnée; (pej: also: **~ on**) discourir, pérorer; **rambler** n promeneur(-euse), randonneur(-euse); **rambling** adj (speech) décousu(e); (house) plein(e) de coins et de recoins; (Bot) grimpant(e)

**ramp** [ræmp] n (incline) rampe f; (Aut) dénivellation f; (in garage) pont m; **on/off ~** (us Aut) bretelle f d'accès

**rampage** [ræm'peɪdʒ] n: **to be on the ~** se déchaîner

**ran** [ræn] pt of **run**

**ranch** [rɑːntʃ] n ranch m

**random** ['rændəm] adj fait(e) or établi(e) au hasard; (Comput, Math) aléatoire ⊳ n: **at ~** au hasard

**rang** [ræŋ] pt of **ring**

**range** [reɪndʒ] n (of mountains) chaîne f; (of missile, voice) portée f; (of products) choix m, gamme f; (also: **shooting ~**) champ m de tir; (also: **kitchen ~**) fourneau m (de cuisine) ⊳ vt (place) mettre en rang, placer ⊳ vi: **to ~ over** couvrir; **to ~ from ... to** aller de ... à

**ranger** ['reɪndʒəʳ] n garde m forestier

**rank** [ræŋk] n rang m; (Mil) grade m; (BRIT: also: **taxi ~**) station f de taxis ⊳ vi: **to ~ among** compter or se classer parmi ⊳ adj (smell) nauséabond(e); **the ~ and file** (fig) la masse, la base

**ransom** ['rænsəm] n rançon f; **to hold sb to ~** (fig) exercer un chantage sur qn

**rant** [rænt] vi fulminer

**rap** [ræp] n (music) rap m ⊳ vt (door) frapper sur or à; (table etc) taper sur

**rape** [reɪp] n viol m; (Bot) colza m ⊳ vt violer

**rapid** ['ræpɪd] adj rapide; **rapidly** adv rapidement; **rapids** npl (Geo) rapides mpl

**rapist** ['reɪpɪst] n auteur m d'un viol

**rapport** [ræ'pɔːʳ] n entente f

**rare** [reəʳ] adj rare; (Culin: steak) saignant(e); **rarely** adv rarement

**rash** [ræʃ] adj imprudent(e), irréfléchi(e) ⊳ n (Med) rougeur f, éruption f; (of events) série f (noire)

**rasher** ['ræʃəʳ] n fine tranche (de lard)

**raspberry** ['rɑːzbərɪ] n framboise f

**rat** [ræt] n rat m

**rate** [reɪt] n (ratio) taux m, pourcentage m; (speed) vitesse f, rythme m; (price) tarif m ⊳ vt (price) évaluer, estimer; (people) classer; **rates** npl (BRIT: property tax) impôts locaux; **to ~ sb/sth as** considérer qn/qch comme

**rather** ['rɑːðəʳ] adv (somewhat) assez, plutôt; (to some extent) un peu; **it's ~ expensive** c'est assez cher; (too much) c'est un peu cher; **there's ~ a lot** il y en a beaucoup; **I would** or **I'd ~ go** j'aimerais mieux or je préférerais partir; **or ~** (more accurately) ou plutôt

**rating** ['reɪtɪŋ] n (assessment) évaluation f; (score) classement m; (Finance) cote f; **ratings** npl (Radio) indice(s) m(pl) d'écoute; (TV) Audimat®

**ratio** ['reɪʃɪəu] n proportion f; **in the ~ of 100 to 1** dans la proportion de 100 contre 1

**ration** ['ræʃən] n ration f ▷ vt rationner; **rations** npl (food) vivres mpl

**rational** ['ræʃənl] adj raisonnable, sensé(e); (solution, reasoning) logique; (Med: person) lucide

**rat race** n foire f d'empoigne

**rattle** ['rætl] n (of door, window) battement m; (of coins, chain) cliquetis m; (of train, engine) bruit m de ferraille; (for baby) hochet m ▷ vi cliqueter; (car, bus): **to ~ along** rouler en faisant un bruit de ferraille ▷ vt agiter (bruyamment); (inf: disconcert) décontenancer

**rave** [reɪv] vi (in anger) s'emporter; (with enthusiasm) s'extasier; (Med) délirer ▷ n (inf: party) rave f, soirée f techno

**raven** ['reɪvən] n grand corbeau

**ravine** [rə'viːn] n ravin m

**raw** [rɔː] adj (uncooked) cru(e); (not processed) brut(e); (sore) à vif, irrité(e); (inexperienced) inexpérimenté(e); **~ materials** matières premières

**ray** [reɪ] n rayon m; **~ of hope** lueur f d'espoir

**razor** ['reɪzər] n rasoir m; **razor blade** n lame f de rasoir

**Rd** abbr = **road**

**RE** n abbr (BRIT) = **religious education**

**re** [riː] prep concernant

**reach** [riːtʃ] n portée f, atteinte f; (of river etc) étendue f ▷ vt atteindre, arriver à; (conclusion, decision) parvenir à ▷ vi s'étendre; **out of/within ~** (object) hors de/à portée; **reach out** vt tendre ▷ vi: **to ~ out (for)** allonger le bras (pour prendre)

**react** [riː'ækt] vi réagir; **reaction** [riː'ækʃən] n réaction f; **reactor** [riː'æktər] n réacteur m

**read** (pt, pp **~**) [riːd, rɛd] vi lire ▷ vt lire; (understand) comprendre, interpréter; (study) étudier; (meter) relever; (subj: instrument etc) indiquer, marquer; **read out** vt lire à haute voix; **reader** n

lecteur(-trice)

**readily** ['rɛdɪlɪ] adv volontiers, avec empressement; (easily) facilement

**reading** ['riːdɪŋ] n lecture f; (understanding) interprétation f; (on instrument) indications fpl

**ready** ['rɛdɪ] adj prêt(e); (willing) prêt, disposé(e); (available) disponible ▷ n: **at the ~** (Mil) prêt à faire feu; **when will my photos be ~?** quand est-ce que mes photos seront prêtes?; **to get ~** (as vi) se préparer; (as vt) préparer; **ready-cooked** adj précuit(e); **ready-made** adj tout(e) faite(e)

**real** [rɪəl] adj (world, life) réel(le); (genuine) véritable; (proper) vrai(e) ▷ adv (US inf: very) vraiment; **real ale** n bière traditionnelle; **real estate** n biens fonciers or immobiliers; **realistic** [rɪə'lɪstɪk] adj réaliste; **reality** [riː'ælɪtɪ] n réalité f

**reality TV** n téléréalité f

**realization** [rɪəlaɪ'zeɪʃən] n (awareness) prise f de conscience; (fulfilment: also: of asset) réalisation f

**realize** ['rɪəlaɪz] vt (understand) se rendre compte de, prendre conscience de; (a project, Comm: asset) réaliser

**really** ['rɪəlɪ] adv vraiment; **~?** vraiment?, c'est vrai?

**realm** [rɛlm] n royaume m; (fig) domaine m

**realtor** ['rɪəltɔːr] n (US) agent immobilier

**reappear** [riːə'pɪər] vi réapparaître, reparaître

**rear** [rɪər] adj de derrière, arrière inv; (Aut: wheel etc) arrière ▷ n arrière m ▷ vt (cattle, family) élever ▷ vi (also: **~ up**: animal) se cabrer

**rearrange** [riːə'reɪndʒ] vt réarranger

**rear**: **rear-view mirror** n (Aut) rétroviseur m; **rear-wheel drive** n (Aut) traction f arrière

**reason** ['riːzn] n raison f ▷ vi: **to ~ with sb** raisonner qn, faire entendre raison à qn; **it stands to ~ that** il va sans dire que; **reasonable** adj raisonnable;

(*not bad*) acceptable; **reasonably** adv
(*behave*) raisonnablement; (*fairly*) assez;
**reasoning** n raisonnement m
**reassurance** [riːəˈʃuərəns] n (*factual*)
assurance f, garantie f; (*emotional*)
réconfort m
**reassure** [riːəˈʃuəʳ] vt rassurer
**rebate** [ˈriːbeɪt] n (*on tax etc*)
dégrèvement m
**rebel** n [ˈrɛbl] rebelle m/f ▷ vi [rɪˈbɛl]
se rebeller, se révolter; **rebellion**
[rɪˈbɛljən] n rébellion f, révolte f;
**rebellious** [rɪˈbɛljəs] adj rebelle
**rebuild** [riːˈbɪld] vt (*irreg: like* **build**)
reconstruire
**recall** vt [rɪˈkɔːl] rappeler; (*remember*)
se rappeler, se souvenir de ▷ n [ˈriːkɔl]
rappel m; (*ability to remember*) mémoire f
**rec'd** abbr of **received**
**receipt** [rɪˈsiːt] n (*document*) reçu m;
(*for parcel etc*) accusé m de réception;
(*act of receiving*) réception f; **receipts**
npl (*Comm*) recettes fpl; **can I have a
~, please?** je peux avoir un reçu, s'il
vous plaît?
**receive** [rɪˈsiːv] vt recevoir; (*guest*)
recevoir, accueillir; **receiver** n (*Tel*)
récepteur m, combiné m; (*Radio*)
récepteur; (*of stolen goods*) receleur
m; (*for bankruptcies*) administrateur m
judiciaire
**recent** [ˈriːsnt] adj récent(e); **recently**
adv récemment
**reception** [rɪˈsɛpʃən] n réception
f; (*welcome*) accueil m, réception;
**reception desk** n réception f;
**receptionist** n réceptionniste m/f
**recession** [rɪˈsɛʃən] n (*Econ*) récession f
**recharge** [riːˈtʃɑːdʒ] vt (*battery*)
recharger
**recipe** [ˈrɛsɪpɪ] n recette f
**recipient** [rɪˈsɪpɪənt] n (*of payment*)
bénéficiaire m/f; (*of letter*) destinataire
m/f
**recital** [rɪˈsaɪtl] n récital m
**recite** [rɪˈsaɪt] vt (*poem*) réciter
**reckless** [ˈrɛkləs] adj (*driver
etc*) imprudent(e); (*spender etc*)

**reckon** [ˈrɛkən] vt (*count*) calculer,
compter; (*consider*) considérer, estimer;
(*think*): **I ~ (that) ...** je pense (que) ...,
j'estime (que) ...
**reclaim** [rɪˈkleɪm] vt (*land: from sea*)
assécher; (*demand back*) réclamer (le
remboursement *or* la restitution de);
(*waste materials*) récupérer
**recline** [rɪˈklaɪn] vi être allongé(e) *or*
étendu(e)
**recognition** [rɛkəgˈnɪʃən] n
reconnaissance f; **transformed
beyond ~** méconnaissable
**recognize** [ˈrɛkəgnaɪz] vt: **to ~ (by/as)**
reconnaître (à/comme étant)
**recollection** [rɛkəˈlɛkʃən] n
souvenir m
**recommend** [rɛkəˈmɛnd] vt
recommander; **can you ~ a good
restaurant?** pouvez-vous me
conseiller un bon restaurant?;
**recommendation** [rɛkəmɛnˈdeɪʃən] n
recommandation f
**reconcile** [ˈrɛkənsaɪl] vt (*two people*)
réconcilier; (*two facts*) concilier,
accorder; **to ~ o.s. to** se résigner à
**reconsider** [riːkənˈsɪdəʳ] vt
reconsidérer
**reconstruct** [riːkənˈstrʌkt] vt
(*building*) reconstruire; (*crime, system*)
reconstituer
**record** n [ˈrɛkɔːd] rapport m, récit
m; (*of meeting etc*) procès-verbal m;
(*register*) registre m; (*file*) dossier m;
(*Comput*) article m; (*also*: **police ~**)
casier m judiciaire; (*Mus: disc*) disque
m; (*Sport*) record m ▷ adj record inv ▷ vt
[rɪˈkɔːd] (*set down*) noter; (*Mus: song
etc*) enregistrer; **public ~s** archives
fpl; **in ~ time** dans un temps record;
**recorded delivery** n (*BRIT Post*): **to
send sth recorded delivery** ≈ envoyer
qch en recommandé; **recorder** n
(*Mus*) flûte f à bec; **recording** n (*Mus*)
enregistrement m; **record player** n
tourne-disque m
**recount** [rɪˈkaʊnt] vt raconter

**recover** [rɪ'kʌvəʳ] vt récupérer ▷ vi
(*from illness*) se rétablir; (*from shock*) se
remettre; **recovery** n récupération
f; rétablissement m; (*Econ*)
redressement m

**recreate** [ri:krɪ'eɪt] vt recréer

**recreation** [rɛkrɪ'eɪʃən] n (*leisure*)
récréation f, détente f; **recreational
drug** n drogue récréative;
**recreational vehicle** n (*us*) camping-
car m

**recruit** [rɪ'kru:t] n recrue f
▷ vt recruter; **recruitment** n
recrutement m

**rectangle** ['rɛktæŋgl] n rectangle m;
**rectangular** [rɛk'tæŋgjuləʳ] adj
rectangulaire

**rectify** ['rɛktɪfaɪ] vt (*error*) rectifier,
corriger

**rector** ['rɛktəʳ] n (*Rel*) pasteur m

**recur** [rɪ'kə:ʳ] vi se reproduire; (*idea,
opportunity*) se retrouver; (*symptoms*)
réapparaître; **recurring** adj (*problem*)
périodique, fréquent(e); (*Math*)
périodique

**recyclable** [ri:'saɪkləbl] adj recyclable

**recycle** [ri:'saɪkl] vt, vi recycler

**recycling** [ri:'saɪklɪŋ] n recyclage m

**red** [rɛd] n rouge m; (*Pol: pej*) rouge m/f
▷ adj rouge; (*hair*) roux (rousse); **in the
~** (*account*) à découvert; (*business*) en
déficit; **Red Cross** n Croix-Rouge f;
**redcurrant** n groseille f (rouge)

**redeem** [rɪ'di:m] vt (*debt*) rembourser;
(*sth in pawn*) dégager; (*fig, also Rel*)
racheter

**red**: **red-haired** adj roux (rousse);
**redhead** n roux (rousse); **red-hot** adj
chauffé(e) au rouge, brûlant(e); **red
light** n: **to go through a red light** (*Aut*)
brûler un feu rouge; **red-light district**
n quartier mal famé

**red meat** n viande f rouge

**reduce** [rɪ'dju:s] vt réduire; (*lower*)
abaisser; **"~ speed now"** (*Aut*)
"ralentir"; **to ~ sb to tears** faire pleurer
qn; **reduced** adj réduit(e); **"greatly
reduced prices"** "gros rabais"; **at a**

**reduced price** (*goods*) au rabais; (*ticket
etc*) à prix réduit; **reduction** [rɪ'dʌkʃən]
n réduction f; (*of price*) baisse f;
(*discount*) rabais m; réduction; **is there
a reduction for children/students?** y
a-t-il une réduction pour les enfants/
les étudiants?

**redundancy** [rɪ'dʌndənsɪ] n (*BRIT*)
licenciement m, mise f au chômage

**redundant** [rɪ'dʌndnt] adj (*BRIT:
worker*) licencié(e), mis(e) au chômage;
(*detail, object*) superflu(e); **to be made
~** (*worker*) être licencié, être mis au
chômage

**reed** [ri:d] n (*Bot*) roseau m

**reef** [ri:f] n (*at sea*) récif m, écueil m

**reel** [ri:l] n bobine f; (*Fishing*) moulinet
m; (*Cine*) bande f; (*dance*) quadrille
écossais ▷ vi (*sway*) chanceler

**ref** [rɛf] n abbr (*inf: = referee*) arbitre m

**refectory** [rɪ'fɛktərɪ] n réfectoire m

**refer** [rɪ'fə:ʳ] vt: **to ~ sb to** (*inquirer,
patient*) adresser qn à; (*reader: to text*)
renvoyer qn à ▷ vi: **to ~** (*allude to*)
parler de, faire allusion à; (*consult*) se
reporter à; (*apply to*) s'appliquer à

**referee** [rɛfə'ri:] n arbitre m; (*BRIT:
for job application*) répondant(e) ▷ vt
arbitrer

**reference** ['rɛfrəns] n référence f,
renvoi m; (*mention*) allusion f, mention
f; (*for job application: letter*) références;
lettre f de recommandation; **with ~
to** en ce qui concerne; (*Comm: in letter*)
me référant à; **reference number** n
(*Comm*) numéro m de référence

**refill** vt [ri:'fɪl] remplir à nouveau; (*pen,
lighter etc*) recharger ▷ n ['ri:fɪl] (*for pen
etc*) recharge f

**refine** [rɪ'faɪn] vt (*sugar, oil*) raffiner;
(*taste*) affiner; (*idea, theory*) peaufiner;
**refined** adj (*person, taste*) raffiné(e);
**refinery** n raffinerie f

**reflect** [rɪ'flɛkt] vt (*light, image*)
réfléchir, refléter ▷ vi (*think*) réfléchir,
méditer; **it ~s badly on him** cela le
discrédite; **it ~s well on him** c'est tout
à son honneur; **reflection** [rɪ'flɛkʃən]

*n* réflexion *f*; (*image*) reflet *m*; **on reflection** réflexion faite

**reflex** ['ri:flɛks] *adj*, *n* réflexe (*m*)

**reform** [rɪ'fɔ:m] *n* réforme *f* ▷ *vt* réformer

**refrain** [rɪ'freɪn] *vi*: **to ~ from doing** s'abstenir de faire ▷ *n* refrain *m*

**refresh** [rɪ'frɛʃ] *vt* rafraîchir; (*subj: food, sleep etc*) redonner des forces à; **refreshing** *adj* (*drink*) rafraîchissant(e); (*sleep*) réparateur(-trice); **refreshments** *npl* rafraîchissements *mpl*

**refrigerator** [rɪ'frɪdʒəreɪtər] *n* réfrigérateur *m*, frigidaire *m*

**refuel** [ri:'fjuəl] *vi* se ravitailler en carburant

**refuge** ['rɛfju:dʒ] *n* refuge *m*; **to take ~ in** se réfugier dans; **refugee** [rɛfju'dʒi:] *n* réfugié(e)

**refund** *n* ['ri:fʌnd] remboursement *m* ▷ *vt* [rɪ'fʌnd] rembourser

**refurbish** [ri:'fə:bɪʃ] *vt* remettre à neuf

**refusal** [rɪ'fju:zəl] *n* refus *m*; **to have first ~ on sth** avoir droit de préemption sur qch

**refuse**[1] ['rɛfju:s] *n* ordures *fpl*, détritus *mpl*

**refuse**[2] [rɪ'fju:z] *vt*, *vi* refuser; **to ~ to do sth** refuser de faire qch

**regain** [rɪ'geɪn] *vt* (*lost ground*) regagner; (*strength*) retrouver

**regard** [rɪ'gɑ:d] *n* respect *m*, estime *f*, considération *f* ▷ *vt* considérer; **to give one's ~s to** faire ses amitiés à; **"with kindest ~s"** "bien amicalement"; **as ~s, with ~ to** en ce qui concerne; **regarding** *prep* en ce qui concerne; **regardless** *adv* quand même; **regardless of** sans se soucier de

**regenerate** [rɪ'dʒɛnəreɪt] *vt* régénérer ▷ *vi* se régénérer

**reggae** ['rɛgeɪ] *n* reggae *m*

**regiment** ['rɛdʒɪmənt] *n* régiment *m*

**region** ['ri:dʒən] *n* région *f*; **in the ~ of** (*fig*) aux alentours de; **regional** *adj* régional(e)

**register** ['rɛdʒɪstər] *n* registre *m*;

(*also*: **electoral ~**) liste électorale ▷ *vt* enregistrer, inscrire; (*birth*) déclarer; (*vehicle*) immatriculer; (*letter*) envoyer en recommandé; (*subj: instrument*) marquer ▷ *vi* s'inscrire; (*at hotel*) signer le registre; (*make impression*) être (bien) compris(e); **registered** *adj* (BRIT: *letter*) recommandé(e)

**registered trademark** *n* marque déposée

**registrar** ['rɛdʒɪstrɑ:ʳ] *n* officier *m* de l'état civil

**registration** [rɛdʒɪs'treɪʃən] *n* (*act*) enregistrement *m*; (*of student*) inscription *f*; (BRIT Aut: *also*: **~ number**) numéro d'immatriculation

**registry office** ['rɛdʒɪstrɪ-] *n* (BRIT) bureau *m* de l'état civil; **to get married in a ~** ≈ se marier à la mairie

**regret** [rɪ'grɛt] *n* regret *m* ▷ *vt* regretter; **regrettable** *adj* regrettable, fâcheux(-euse)

**regular** ['rɛgjulər] *adj* régulier(-ière); (*usual*) habituel(le), normal(e); (*soldier*) de métier; (Comm: *size*) ordinaire ▷ *n* (*client etc*) habitué(e); **regularly** *adv* régulièrement

**regulate** ['rɛgjuleɪt] *vt* régler; **regulation** [rɛgju'leɪʃən] *n* (*rule*) règlement *m*; (*adjustment*) réglage *m*

**rehabilitation** ['ri:əbɪlɪ'teɪʃən] *n* (*of offender*) réhabilitation *f*; (*of addict*) réadaptation *f*

**rehearsal** [rɪ'hə:səl] *n* répétition *f*

**rehearse** [rɪ'hə:s] *vt* répéter

**reign** [reɪn] *n* règne *m* ▷ *vi* régner

**reimburse** [ri:ɪm'bə:s] *vt* rembourser

**rein** [reɪn] *n* (*for horse*) rêne *f*

**reincarnation** [ri:ɪnkɑ:'neɪʃən] *n* réincarnation *f*

**reindeer** ['reɪndɪəʳ] *n* (*pl inv*) renne *m*

**reinforce** [ri:ɪn'fɔ:s] *vt* renforcer; **reinforcements** *npl* (Mil) renfort(s) *m(pl)*

**reinstate** [ri:ɪn'steɪt] *vt* rétablir, réintégrer

**reject** *n* ['ri:dʒɛkt] (Comm) article *m* de rebut ▷ *vt* [rɪ'dʒɛkt] refuser; (*idea*) rejeter; **rejection** [rɪ'dʒɛkʃən] n rejet m, refus m

**rejoice** [rɪ'dʒɔɪs] vi: **to ~ (at** or **over)** se réjouir (de)

**relate** [rɪ'leɪt] vt (tell) raconter; (connect) établir un rapport entre ▷ vi: **to ~ to** (connect) se rapporter à; **to ~ to sb** (interact) entretenir des rapports avec qn; **related** adj apparenté(e); **related to** (subject) lié(e) à; **relating to** prep concernant

**relation** [rɪ'leɪʃən] n (person) parent(e); (link) rapport m, lien m; **relations** npl (relatives) famille f; **relationship** n rapport m, lien m; (personal ties) relations fpl, rapports; (also: **family relationship**) lien de parenté; (affair) liaison f

**relative** ['rɛlətɪv] n parent(e) ▷ adj relatif(-ive); (respective) respectif(-ive); **relatively** adv relativement

**relax** [rɪ'læks] vi (muscle) se relâcher; (person: unwind) se détendre ▷ vt relâcher; (mind, person) détendre; **relaxation** [riːlæk'seɪʃən] n relâchement m; (of mind) détente f; (recreation) détente, délassement m; **relaxed** adj relâché(e); détendu(e); **relaxing** adj délassant(e)

**relay** ['riːleɪ] n (Sport) course f de relais ▷ vt (message) retransmettre, relayer

**release** [rɪ'liːs] n (from prison, obligation) libération f; (of gas etc) émission f; (of film etc) sortie f; (new recording) disque m ▷ vt (prisoner) libérer; (book, film) sortir; (report, news) rendre public, publier; (gas etc) émettre, dégager; (free: from wreckage etc) dégager; (Tech: catch, spring etc) déclencher; (let go: person, animal) relâcher; (: hand, object) lâcher; (: grip, brake) desserrer

**relegate** ['rɛləgeɪt] vt reléguer; (BRIT Sport): **to be ~d** descendre dans une division inférieure

**relent** [rɪ'lɛnt] vi se laisser fléchir; **relentless** adj implacable; (non-stop) continuel(le)

**relevant** ['rɛləvənt] adj (question) pertinent(e); (corresponding) approprié(e); (fact) significatif(-ive); (information) utile

**reliable** [rɪ'laɪəbl] adj (person, firm) sérieux(-euse), fiable; (method, machine) fiable; (news, information) sûr(e)

**relic** ['rɛlɪk] n (Rel) relique f; (of the past) vestige m

**relief** [rɪ'liːf] n (from pain, anxiety) soulagement m; (help, supplies) secours m(pl); (Art, Geo) relief m

**relieve** [rɪ'liːv] vt (pain, worry) soulager; (fear, worry) dissiper; (bring help) secourir; (take over from: gen) relayer; (: guard) relever; **to ~ sb of sth** débarrasser qn de qch; **to ~ o.s.** (euphemism) se soulager, faire ses besoins; **relieved** adj soulagé(e)

**religion** [rɪ'lɪdʒən] n religion f

**religious** [rɪ'lɪdʒəs] adj religieux(-euse); (book) de piété; **religious education** n instruction religieuse

**relish** ['rɛlɪʃ] n (Culin) condiment m; (enjoyment) délectation f ▷ vt (food etc) savourer; **to ~ doing** se délecter à faire

**relocate** [riːləʊ'keɪt] vt (business) transférer ▷ vi se transférer, s'installer or s'établir ailleurs

**reluctance** [rɪ'lʌktəns] n répugnance f

**reluctant** [rɪ'lʌktənt] adj peu disposé(e), qui hésite; **reluctantly** adv à contrecœur, sans enthousiasme

**rely on** [rɪ'laɪ-] vt fus (be dependent on) dépendre de; (trust) compter sur

**remain** [rɪ'meɪn] vi rester; **remainder** n reste m; (Comm) fin f de série; **remaining** adj qui reste; **remains** npl restes mpl

**remand** [rɪ'mɑːnd] n: **on ~** en détention préventive ▷ vt: **to be ~ed in custody** être placé(e) en détention préventive

**remark** [rɪ'mɑːk] n remarque f, observation f ▷ vt (faire) remarquer, dire; **remarkable** adj remarquable

**remarry** [riː'mærɪ] vi se remarier

**remedy** ['rɛmədɪ] n: **~ (for)** remède m

(contre *or* à) ▷ *vt* remédier à

**remember** [rɪˈmɛmbəʳ] *vt* se rappeler, se souvenir de; (*send greetings*): **~ me to him** saluez-le de ma part; **Remembrance Day** [rɪˈmɛmbrəns-] *n* (BRIT) ≈ (le jour de) l'Armistice *m*, ≈ le 11 novembre

● **REMEMBRANCE DAY**
●
● **Remembrance Day** ou
● **Remembrance Sunday** est le
● dimanche le plus proche du 11
● novembre, jour où la Première
● Guerre mondiale a officiellement
● pris fin. Il rend hommage aux
● victimes des deux guerres
● mondiales. À cette occasion, on
● observe deux minutes de silence
● à 11h, heure de la signature de
● l'armistice avec l'Allemagne en
● 1918; certaines membres de la
● famille royale et du gouvernement
● déposent des gerbes de coquelicots
● au cénotaphe de Whitehall, et des
● couronnes sont placées sur les
● monuments aux morts dans toute
● la Grande-Bretagne; par ailleurs,
● les gens portent des coquelicots
● artificiels fabriqués et vendus
● par des membres de la légion
● britannique blessés au combat, au
● profit des blessés de guerre et de
● leur famille.

**remind** [rɪˈmaɪnd] *vt*: **to ~ sb of sth** rappeler qch à qn; **to ~ sb to do** faire penser à qn à faire, rappeler à qn qu'il doit faire; **reminder** *n* (Comm: *letter*) rappel *m*, (*note etc*) pense-bête *m*; (*souvenir*) souvenir *m*

**reminiscent** [rɛmɪˈnɪsnt] *adj*: **~ of** qui rappelle, qui fait penser à

**remnant** [ˈrɛmnənt] *n* reste *m*, restant *m*; (*of cloth*) coupon *m*

**remorse** [rɪˈmɔːs] *n* remords *m*

**remote** [rɪˈməʊt] *adj* éloigné(e), lointain(e); (*person*) distant(e);

(*possibility*) vague; **remote control** *n* télécommande *f*; **remotely** *adv* au loin; (*slightly*) très vaguement

**removal** [rɪˈmuːvəl] *n* (*taking away*) enlèvement *m*; suppression *f*; (BRIT: *from house*) déménagement *m*; (*from office: dismissal*) renvoi *m*; (*of stain*) nettoyage *m*; (Med) ablation *f*; **removal man** (*irreg*) *n* (BRIT) déménageur *m*; **removal van** *n* (BRIT) camion *m* de déménagement

**remove** [rɪˈmuːv] *vt* enlever, retirer; (*employee*) renvoyer; (*stain*) faire partir; (*abuse*) supprimer; (*doubt*) chasser

**Renaissance** [rɪˈneɪsɑ̃s] *n*: **the ~** la Renaissance

**rename** [riːˈneɪm] *vt* rebaptiser

**render** [ˈrɛndəʳ] *vt* rendre

**rendezvous** [ˈrɒndɪvuː] *n* rendez-vous *m inv*

**renew** [rɪˈnjuː] *vt* renouveler; (*negotiations*) reprendre; (*acquaintance*) renouer

**renovate** [ˈrɛnəveɪt] *vt* rénover; (*work of art*) restaurer

**renowned** [rɪˈnaʊnd] *adj* renommé(e)

**rent** [rɛnt] *pt, pp of* **rend** ▷ *n* loyer *m* ▷ *vt* louer; **rental** *n* (*for television, car*) (*prix m de*) location *f*

**reorganize** [riːˈɔːɡənaɪz] *vt* réorganiser

**rep** [rɛp] *n abbr* (Comm) = **representative**

**repair** [rɪˈpɛəʳ] *n* réparation *f* ▷ *vt* réparer; **in good/bad ~** en bon/mauvais état; **where can I get this ~ed?** où est-ce que je peux faire réparer ceci?; **repair kit** *n* trousse *f* de réparations

**repay** [riːˈpeɪ] *vt* (*irreg: like* **pay**) (*money, creditor*) rembourser; (*sb's efforts*) récompenser; **repayment** *n* remboursement *m*

**repeat** [rɪˈpiːt] *n* (Radio, TV) reprise *f* ▷ *vt* répéter; (*promise, attack, also* Comm: *order*) renouveler; (Scol: *a class*) redoubler ▷ *vi* répéter; **can you ~ that, please?** pouvez-vous répéter,

s'il vous plaît?; **repeatedly** adv
souvent, à plusieurs reprises; **repeat
prescription** n (BRIT): **I'd like a repeat
prescription** je voudrais renouveler
mon ordonnance
**repellent** [rɪ'pɛlənt] adj repoussant(e)
▷ n: **insect ~** insectifuge m
**repercussions** [ri:pə'kʌʃənz] npl
répercussions fpl
**repetition** [rɛprɪ'tɪʃən] n répétition f
**repetitive** [rɪ'pɛtɪtɪv] adj (movement,
work) répétitif(-ive); (speech) plein(e)
de redites
**replace** [rɪ'pleɪs] vt (put back)
remettre, replacer; (take the place
of) remplacer; **replacement** n
(substitution) remplacement m; (person)
remplaçant(e)
**replay** ['ri:pleɪ] n (of match) match
rejoué; (of tape, film) répétition f
**replica** ['rɛplɪkə] n réplique f, copie
exacte
**reply** [rɪ'plaɪ] n réponse f ▷ vi répondre
**report** [rɪ'pɔ:t] n rapport m; (Press
etc) reportage m; (BRIT: also: **school
~**) bulletin m (scolaire); (of gun)
détonation f ▷ vt rapporter, faire un
compte rendu de; (Press etc) faire un
reportage sur; (notify: accident) signaler;
(: culprit) dénoncer ▷ vi (make a report)
faire un rapport; **I'd like to ~ a theft**
je voudrais signaler un vol; (present
o.s.): **to ~ (to sb)** se présenter (chez
qn); **report card** n (US, SCOTTISH)
bulletin m (scolaire); **reportedly** adv:
**she is reportedly living in Spain** elle
habiterait en Espagne; **he reportedly
told them to ...** il leur aurait dit de ...;
**reporter** n reporter m
**represent** [rɛprɪ'zɛnt] vt représenter;
(view, belief) présenter, expliquer;
(describe): **to ~ sth as** présenter or
décrire qch comme; **representation** f;
[rɛprɪzɛn'teɪʃən] n représentation f;
**representative** n représentant(e); (US
Pol) député m ▷ adj représentatif(-ive),
caractéristique
**repress** [rɪ'prɛs] vt réprimer;

**repression** [rɪ'prɛʃən] n répression f
**reprimand** ['rɛprɪmɑ:nd] n
réprimande f ▷ vt réprimander
**reproduce** [ri:prə'dju:s] vt reproduire
▷ vi se reproduire; **reproduction**
[ri:prə'dʌkʃən] n reproduction f
**reptile** ['rɛptaɪl] n reptile m
**republic** [rɪ'pʌblɪk] n république f;
**republican** adj, n républicain(e)
**reputable** ['rɛpjutəbl] adj de bonne
réputation; (occupation) honorable
**reputation** [rɛpju'teɪʃən] n
réputation f
**request** [rɪ'kwɛst] n demande f;
(formal) requête f ▷ vt: **to ~ (of or from
sb)** demander (à qn); **request stop** n
(BRIT: for bus) arrêt facultatif
**require** [rɪ'kwaɪə'] vt (need: subj: person)
avoir besoin de; (: thing, situation)
nécessiter, demander; (want) exiger;
(order): **to ~ sb to do sth/sth of sb**
exiger que qn fasse qch/qch de qn;
**requirement** n (need) exigence f;
besoin m; (condition) condition f
(requise)
**resat** [ri:'sæt] pt, pp of **resit**
**rescue** ['rɛskju:] n (from accident)
sauvetage m; (help) secours mpl ▷ vt
sauver
**research** [rɪ'sə:tʃ] n recherche(s) f(pl)
▷ vt faire des recherches sur
**resemblance** [rɪ'zɛmbləns] n
ressemblance f
**resemble** [rɪ'zɛmbl] vt ressembler à
**resent** [rɪ'zɛnt] vt être contrarié(e)
par; **resentful** adj irrité(e), plein(e)
de ressentiment; **resentment** n
ressentiment m
**reservation** [rɛzə'veɪʃən] n (booking)
réservation f; **to make a ~ (in an
hotel/a restaurant/on a plane)**
réserver or retenir une chambre/une
table/une place; **reservation desk** n
(US: in hotel) réception f
**reserve** [rɪ'zə:v] n réserve f; (Sport)
remplaçant(e) ▷ vt (seats etc) réserver,
retenir; **reserved** adj réservé(e)
**reservoir** ['rɛzəvwɑ:'] n réservoir m

**reshuffle** [ri:'ʃʌfl] n: **Cabinet ~** (Pol) remaniement ministériel

**residence** ['rezidəns] n résidence f; **residence permit** n (BRIT) permis m de séjour

**resident** ['rezidənt] n (of country) résident(e); (of area, house) habitant(e); (in hotel) pensionnaire ▷ adj résidant(e); **residential** [rezi'dɛnʃəl] adj de résidence; (area) résidentiel(le); (course) avec hébergement sur place

**residue** ['rezidju:] n reste m; (Chem, Physics) résidu m

**resign** [ri'zaɪn] vt (one's post) se démettre de ▷ vi démissionner; **to ~ o.s. to** (endure) se résigner à; **resignation** [rezig'neɪʃən] n (from post) démission f; (state of mind) résignation f

**resin** ['rezin] n résine f

**resist** [ri'zist] vt résister à; **resistance** n résistance f

**resit** (BRIT) vt [ri:'sit] (pt, pp **resat**) (exam) repasser ▷ n ['ri:sit] deuxième session f (d'un examen)

**resolution** [rezə'lu:ʃən] n résolution f

**resolve** [ri'zɔlv] n résolution f ▷ vt (decide): **to ~ to do** résoudre or décider de faire; (problem) résoudre

**resort** [ri'zɔ:t] n (seaside town) station f balnéaire; (for skiing) station de ski; (recourse) recours m ▷ vi: **to ~ to** avoir recours à; **in the last ~** en dernier ressort

**resource** [ri'sɔ:s] n ressource f; **resourceful** adj ingénieux(-euse), débrouillard(e)

**respect** [ris'pɛkt] n respect m ▷ vt respecter; **respectable** adj respectable; (quite good: result etc) honorable; **respectful** adj respectueux(-euse); **respective** adj respectif(-ive); **respectively** adv respectivement

**respite** ['rɛspaɪt] n répit m

**respond** [ris'pɔnd] vi répondre; (react) réagir; **response** [ris'pɔns] n réponse f; (reaction) réaction f

**responsibility** [rispɔnsɪ'bɪlɪtɪ] n

responsabilité f

**responsible** [ris'pɔnsibl] adj (liable): **~ (for)** responsable (de); (person) digne de confiance; (job) qui comporte des responsabilités; **responsibly** adv avec sérieux

**responsive** [ris'pɔnsiv] adj (student, audience) réceptif(-ive); (brakes, steering) sensible

**rest** [rɛst] n repos m; (stop) arrêt m, pause f; (Mus) silence m; (support) support m, appui m; (remainder) reste m, restant m ▷ vi se reposer; (be supported): **to ~ on** appuyer or reposer sur ▷ vt (lean): **to ~ sth on/against** appuyer qch sur/contre; **the ~ of them** les autres

**restaurant** ['rɛstərɔŋ] n restaurant m; **restaurant car** n (BRIT Rail) wagon-restaurant m

**restless** ['rɛstlis] adj agité(e)

**restoration** [rɛstə'reɪʃən] n (of building) restauration f; (of stolen goods) restitution f

**restore** [ri'stɔ:r] vt (building) restaurer; (sth stolen) restituer; (peace, health) rétablir; **to ~ to** (former state) ramener à

**restrain** [ris'treɪn] vt (feeling) contenir; (person): **to ~ (from doing)** retenir (de faire); **restraint** n (restriction) contrainte f; (moderation) retenue f; (of style) sobriété f

**restrict** [ris'trikt] vt restreindre, limiter; **restriction** [ris'trikʃən] n restriction f, limitation f

**rest room** n (US) toilettes fpl

**restructure** [ri:'strʌktʃər] vt restructurer

**result** [ri'zʌlt] n résultat m ▷ vi: **to ~ in** aboutir à, se terminer par; **as a ~ of** à la suite de

**resume** [ri'zju:m] vt (work, journey) reprendre ▷ vi (work etc) reprendre

**résumé** ['reɪzju:meɪ] n (summary) résumé m; (us: curriculum vitae) curriculum vitae m inv

**resuscitate** [ri'sʌsiteɪt] vt (Med) réanimer

**retail** ['riːteɪl] adj de or au détail ▷ adv
au détail; **retailer** n détaillant(e)
**retain** [rɪ'teɪn] vt (keep) garder,
conserver
**retaliation** [rɪtælɪ'eɪʃən] n représailles
fpl, vengeance f
**retarded** [rɪ'tɑːdɪd] adj retardé(e)
**retire** [rɪ'taɪəʳ] vi (give up work) prendre
sa retraite; (withdraw) se retirer, partir;
(go to bed) (aller) se coucher; **retired**
adj (person) retraité(e); **retirement**
n retraite f
**retort** [rɪ'tɔːt] vi riposter
**retreat** [rɪ'triːt] n retraite f ▷ vi battre
en retraite
**retrieve** [rɪ'triːv] vt (sth lost) récupérer;
(situation, honour) sauver; (error, loss)
réparer; (Comput) rechercher
**retrospect** ['rɛtrəspɛkt] n: **in ~**
rétrospectivement, après coup;
**retrospective** [rɛtrə'spɛktɪv] adj
rétrospectif(-ive), (law) rétroactif(-ive)
▷ n (Art) rétrospective f
**return** [rɪ'təːn] n (going or coming back)
retour m; (of sth stolen etc) restitution
f; (Finance: from land, shares) rapport
m ▷ cpd (journey) de retour; (BRIT:
ticket) aller et retour; (match) retour
▷ vi (person etc: come back) revenir;
(: go back) retourner ▷ vt rendre; (bring
back) rapporter; (send back) renvoyer;
(put back) remettre; (Pol: candidate)
élire; **returns** npl (Comm) recettes fpl;
(Finance) bénéfices mpl; **many happy
~s (of the day)!** bon anniversaire!; **by
~ (of post)** par retour (du courrier); **in
~ (for)** en échange (de); **a ~ (ticket) for ...**
un billet aller et retour pour ...; **return
ticket** n (esp BRIT) billet m aller-retour
**reunion** [riː'juːnɪən] n réunion f
**reunite** [riːjuː'naɪt] vt réunir
**revamp** [riː'væmp] vt (house) retaper;
(firm) réorganiser
**reveal** [rɪ'viːl] vt (make known) révéler;
(display) laisser voir; **revealing** adj
révélateur(-trice); (dress) au décolleté
généreux or suggestif
**revel** ['rɛvl] vi: **to ~ in sth/in doing** se

délecter de qch/à faire
**revelation** [rɛvə'leɪʃən] n révélation f
**revenge** [rɪ'vɛndʒ] n vengeance f; (in
game etc) revanche f ▷ vt venger; **to
take ~ (on)** se venger (sur)
**revenue** ['rɛvənjuː] n revenu m
**Reverend** ['rɛvərənd] adj (in titles):
**the ~ John Smith** (Anglican) le révérend
John Smith; (Catholic) l'abbé (John)
Smith; (Protestant) le pasteur (John)
Smith
**reversal** [rɪ'vəːsl] n (of opinion)
revirement m; (of order) renversement
m; (of direction) changement m
**reverse** [rɪ'vəːs] n contraire m, opposé
m; (back) dos m, envers m; (of paper)
verso m; (of coin) revers m; (Aut: also:
**~ gear**) marche f arrière ▷ adj (order,
direction) opposé(e), inverse ▷ vt (order,
position) changer, inverser; (direction,
policy) changer complètement de;
(decision) annuler; (roles) renverser
▷ vi (BRIT Aut) faire marche arrière;
**reverse-charge call** n (BRIT Tel)
communication f en PCV; **reversing
lights** npl (BRIT Aut) feux mpl de marche
arrière or de recul
**revert** [rɪ'vəːt] vi: **to ~ to** revenir à,
retourner à
**review** [rɪ'vjuː] n revue f; (of book, film)
critique f; (of situation, policy) examen
m, bilan m; (US: examination) examen
▷ vt passer en revue; faire la critique
de; examiner
**revise** [rɪ'vaɪz] vt réviser, modifier;
(manuscript) revoir, corriger ▷ vi (study)
réviser; **revision** [rɪ'vɪʒən] n révision f
**revival** [rɪ'vaɪvəl] n reprise f;
(recovery) rétablissement m; (of faith)
renouveau m
**revive** [rɪ'vaɪv] vt (person) ranimer;
(custom) rétablir; (economy) relancer;
(hope, courage) raviver, faire renaître;
(play, fashion) reprendre ▷ vi (person)
reprendre connaissance; (: from ill
health) se rétablir; (hope etc) renaître;
(activity) reprendre
**revolt** [rɪ'vəult] n révolte f ▷ vi se

révolter, se rebeller ▷ vt révolter,
dégoûter; **revolting** adj dégoûtant(e)
**revolution** [rɛvə'lu:ʃən] n révolution
f; (of wheel etc) tour m, révolution;
**revolutionary** adj, n révolutionnaire
(m/f)
**revolve** [rɪ'vɒlv] vi tourner
**revolver** [rɪ'vɒlvə*] n revolver m
**reward** [rɪ'wɔ:d] n récompense f ▷ vt:
**to ~ (for)** récompenser (de); **rewarding**
adj (fig) qui (en) vaut la peine,
gratifiant(e)
**rewind** [ri:'waind] vt (irreg: like **wind**)
(tape) réembobiner
**rewritable** [ri:'raitəbl] adj (CD, DVD)
réinscriptible
**rewrite** [ri:'rait] (pt **rewrote**, pp
**rewritten**) vt récrire
**rheumatism** ['ru:mətizəm] n
rhumatisme m
**Rhine** [rain] n: **the (River) ~** le Rhin
**rhinoceros** [rai'nɒsərəs] n
rhinocéros m
**Rhône** [rəun] n: **the (River) ~** le Rhône
**rhubarb** ['ru:bɑ:b] n rhubarbe f
**rhyme** [raim] n rime f; (verse) vers mpl
**rhythm** ['riðm] n rythme m
**rib** [rib] n (Anat) côte f
**ribbon** ['ribən] n ruban m; **in ~s** (torn)
en lambeaux
**rice** [rais] n riz m; **rice pudding** n riz
m au lait
**rich** [ritʃ] adj riche; (gift, clothes)
somptueux(-euse); **to be ~ in sth** être
riche en qch
**rid** [rid] (pt, pp **~**) vt: **to ~ sb of**
débarrasser qn de; **to get ~ of** se
débarrasser de
**riddle** ['ridl] n (puzzle) énigme f ▷ vt: **to
be ~d with** être criblé(e) de; (fig) être
en proie à
**ride** [raid] n promenade f, tour m;
(distance covered) trajet m ▷ vb (pt **rode**,
pp **ridden**) ▷ vi (as sport) monter (à
cheval), faire du cheval; (go somewhere:
on horse, bicycle) aller (à cheval or
bicyclette etc); (travel: on bicycle, motor
cycle, bus) rouler ▷ vt (a horse) monter;

(distance) parcourir, faire; **to ~ a horse/
bicycle** monter à cheval/à bicyclette;
**to take sb for a ~** (fig) faire marcher qn;
(cheat) rouler qn; **rider** n cavalier(-ière);
(in race) jockey m; (on bicycle) cycliste
m/f; (on motorcycle) motocycliste m/f
**ridge** [ridʒ] n (of hill) faîte m; (of roof,
mountain) arête f; (on object) strie f
**ridicule** ['ridikju:l] n ridicule m;
dérision f ▷ vt ridiculiser, tourner en
dérision; **ridiculous** [rɪ'dɪkjuləs] adj
ridicule
**riding** ['raidiŋ] n équitation f;
**riding school** n manège m, école f
d'équitation
**rife** [raif] adj répandu(e); **~ with**
abondant(e) en
**rifle** ['raifl] n fusil m (à canon rayé) ▷ vt
vider, dévaliser
**rift** [rift] n fente f, fissure f; (fig:
disagreement) désaccord m
**rig** [rig] n (also: **oil ~**: on land) derrick m;
(: at sea) plate-forme pétrolière ▷ vt
(election etc) truquer
**right** [rait] adj (true) juste, exact(e);
(correct) bon (bonne); (suitable)
approprié(e), convenable; (just) juste,
équitable; (morally good) bien inv; (not
left) droit(e) ▷ n (moral good) bien m;
(title, claim) droit m; (not left) droite
f ▷ adv (answer) correctement; (treat)
bien, comme il faut; (not on the left) à
droite ▷ vt redresser ▷ excl bon!; **do
you have the ~ time?** avez-vous l'heure
juste or exacte?; **to be ~** (person) avoir
raison; (answer) être juste or correct(e);
**by ~s** en toute justice; **on the ~** à
droite; **to be in the ~** avoir raison; **~ in
the middle** en plein milieu; **~ away**
immédiatement; **right angle** n (Math)
angle droit; **rightful** adj (heir) légitime;
**right-hand** adj: **the right-hand side**
la droite; **right-hand drive** n (BRIT)
conduite f à droite; (vehicle) véhicule
m avec la conduite à droite; **right-
handed** adj (person) droitier(-ière);
**rightly** adv bien, correctement; (with
reason) à juste titre; **right of way** n

(on path etc) droit m de passage; (Aut) priorité f; **right-wing** adj (Pol) de droite
**rigid** ['rɪdʒɪd] adj rigide; (principle, control) strict(e)
**rigorous** ['rɪgərəs] adj rigoureux(-euse)
**rim** [rɪm] n bord m; (of spectacles) monture f; (of wheel) jante f
**rind** [raɪnd] n (of bacon) couenne f; (of lemon etc) écorce f, zeste m; (of cheese) croûte f
**ring** [rɪŋ] n anneau m; (on finger) bague f; (also: **wedding ~**) alliance f; (of people, objects) cercle m; (of spies) réseau m; (of smoke etc) rond m; (arena) piste f, arène f; (for boxing) ring m; (sound of bell) sonnerie f ▷ vb (pt **rang**, pp **rung**) ▷ vi (telephone, bell) sonner; (person: by telephone) téléphoner; (ears) bourdonner; (also: **~ out**: voice, words) retentir ▷ vt (BRIT Tel: also: **~ up**) téléphoner à, appeler; **to ~ the bell** sonner; **to give sb a ~** (Tel) passer un coup de téléphone or de fil à qn; **ring back** vt, vi (BRIT Tel) rappeler; **ring off** vi (BRIT Tel) raccrocher; **ring up** (BRIT) ▷ vt (Tel) téléphoner à, appeler; **ringing tone** n (BRIT Tel) tonalité f d'appel; **ringleader** n (of gang) chef m, meneur m; **ring road** n (BRIT) rocade f; (motorway) périphérique m; **ringtone** n (on mobile) sonnerie f (de téléphone portable)
**rink** [rɪŋk] n (also: **ice ~**) patinoire f
**rinse** [rɪns] n rinçage m ▷ vt rincer
**riot** ['raɪət] n émeute f, bagarres fpl ▷ vi (demonstrators) manifester avec violence; (population) se soulever, se révolter; **to run ~** se déchaîner
**rip** [rɪp] n déchirure f ▷ vt déchirer ▷ vi se déchirer; **rip off** vt (inf: cheat) arnaquer; **rip up** vt déchirer
**ripe** [raɪp] adj (fruit) mûr(e); (cheese) fait(e)
**rip-off** ['rɪpɔf] n (inf): **it's a ~!** c'est du vol manifeste!, c'est de l'arnaque!
**ripple** ['rɪpl] n ride f, ondulation f; (of applause, laughter) cascade f ▷ vi se rider, onduler

**rise** [raɪz] n (slope) côte f, pente f; (hill) élévation f; (increase: in wages: BRIT) augmentation f; (: in prices, temperature) hausse f, augmentation; (fig: to power etc) ascension f ▷ vi (prices, numbers) augmenter, monter; (waters, river) monter; (sun, wind, person: from chair, bed) se lever; (also: **~ up**: tower, building) s'élever; (: rebel) se révolter; se rebeller; (in rank) s'élever; **to give ~ to** donner lieu à; **to ~ to the occasion** se montrer à la hauteur; **risen** ['rɪzn] pp of **rise**; **rising** adj (increasing: number, prices) en hausse; (tide) montant(e); (sun, moon) levant(e)
**risk** [rɪsk] n risque m ▷ vt risquer; **to take** or **run the ~ of doing** courir le risque de faire; **at ~** en danger; **at one's own ~** à ses risques et périls; **risky** adj risqué(e)
**rite** [raɪt] n rite m; **the last ~s** les derniers sacrements
**ritual** ['rɪtjuəl] adj rituel(le) ▷ n rituel m
**rival** ['raɪvl] n rival(e); (in business) concurrent(e) ▷ adj rival(e); qui fait concurrence ▷ vt (match) égaler; **rivalry** n rivalité f; (in business) concurrence f
**river** ['rɪvə'] n rivière f; (major: also fig) fleuve m ▷ cpd (port, traffic) fluvial(e); **up/down ~** en amont/aval; **riverbank** n rive f, berge f
**rivet** ['rɪvɪt] n rivet m ▷ vt (fig) river, fixer
**Riviera** [rɪvɪ'eərə] n: **the (French) ~** la Côte d'Azur
**road** [rəud] n route f; (in town) rue f; (fig) chemin, voie f ▷ cpd (accident) de la route; **major/minor ~** route principale or à priorité/voie secondaire; **which ~ do I take for ...?** quelle route dois-je prendre pour aller à...?; **roadblock** n barrage routier; **road map** n carte routière; **road rage** n comportement très agressif de certains usagers de la route; **road safety** n sécurité routière; **roadside** n bord m de la route, bas-

côté m; **roadsign** n panneau m de signalisation; **road tax** n (BRIT Aut) taxe f sur les automobiles; **roadworks** npl travaux mpl (de réfection des routes)

**roam** [rəum] vi errer, vagabonder

**roar** [rɔː] n rugissement m; (of crowd) hurlements mpl; (of vehicle, thunder, storm) grondement m ▷ vi rugir; hurler; gronder; **to ~ with laughter** rire à gorge déployée; **to do a ~ing trade** faire des affaires en or

**roast** [rəust] n rôti m ▷ vt (meat) (faire) rôtir; (coffee) griller, torréfier; **roast beef** n rôti m de bœuf, rosbif m

**rob** [rɔb] vt (person) voler; (bank) dévaliser; **to ~ sb of sth** voler or dérober qch à qn; (fig: deprive) priver qn de qch; **robber** n bandit m, voleur m; **robbery** n vol m

**robe** [rəub] n (for ceremony etc) robe f; (also: **bath~**) peignoir m; (us: rug) couverture f ▷ vt revêtir (d'une robe)

**robin** ['rɔbɪn] n rouge-gorge m

**robot** ['rəubɔt] n robot m

**robust** [rəu'bʌst] adj robuste; (material, appetite) solide

**rock** [rɔk] n (substance) roche f, roc m; (boulder) rocher m, roche; (us: small stone) caillou m; (BRIT: sweet) ≈ sucre m d'orge ▷ vt (swing gently: cradle) balancer; (: child) bercer; (shake) ébranler, secouer ▷ vi se balancer; être ébranlé(e) or secoué(e); **on the ~s** (drink) avec des glaçons; (marriage etc) en train de craquer; **rock and roll** n rock (and roll) m, rock'n'roll m; **rock climbing** n varappe f

**rocket** ['rɔkɪt] n fusée f; (Mil) fusée, roquette f; (Culin) roquette

**rocking chair** ['rɔkɪŋ-] n fauteuil m à bascule

**rocky** ['rɔkɪ] adj (hill) rocheux(-euse); (path) rocailleux(-euse)

**rod** [rɔd] n (metallic) tringle f; (Tech) tige f; (wooden) baguette f; (also: **fishing ~**) canne f à pêche

**rode** [rəud] pt of **ride**

**rodent** ['rəudnt] n rongeur m

**rogue** [rəug] n coquin(e)

**role** [rəul] n rôle m; **role-model** n modèle m à émuler

**roll** [rəul] n rouleau m; (of banknotes) liasse f; (also: **bread ~**) petit pain; (register) liste f; (sound: of drums etc) roulement m ▷ vt rouler; (also: **~ up**: string) enrouler; (also: **~ out**: pastry) étendre au rouleau, abaisser ▷ vi rouler; **roll over** vi se retourner; **roll up** vi (inf: arrive) arriver, s'amener ▷ vt (carpet, cloth, map) rouler; (sleeves) retrousser; **roller** n rouleau m; (wheel) roulette f; (for road) rouleau compresseur; (for hair) bigoudi m; **roller coaster** n montagnes fpl russes; **roller skates** npl patins mpl à roulettes; **roller-skating** n patin m à roulettes; **to go roller-skating** faire du patin à roulettes; **rolling pin** n rouleau m à pâtisserie

**ROM** [rɔm] n abbr (Comput: = read-only memory) mémoire morte, ROM f

**Roman** ['rəumən] adj romain(e) ▷ n Romain(e); **Roman Catholic** adj, n catholique (m/f)

**romance** [rə'mæns] n (love affair) idylle f; (charm) poésie f; (novel) roman m à l'eau de rose

**Romania** etc [rəu'meɪnɪə] = **Rumania** etc

**Roman numeral** n chiffre romain

**romantic** [rə'mæntɪk] adj romantique; (novel, attachment) sentimental(e)

**Rome** [rəum] n Rome

**roof** [ruːf] n toit m; (of tunnel, cave) plafond m ▷ vt couvrir (d'un toit); **the ~ of the mouth** la voûte du palais; **roof rack** n (Aut) galerie f

**rook** [ruk] n (bird) freux m; (Chess) tour f

**room** [ruːm] n (in house) pièce f; (also: **bed~**) chambre f (à coucher); (in school etc) salle f; (space) place f; **roommate** n camarade m/f de chambre; **room service** n service m des chambres (dans un hôtel); **roomy** adj spacieux(-euse);

(garment) ample

**rooster** ['ruːstəʳ] n coq m

**root** [ruːt] n (Bot, Math) racine f; (fig: of problem) origine f, fond m ▷ vi (plant) s'enraciner

**rope** [rəup] n corde f; (Naut) cordage m ▷ vt (tie up or together) attacher; (climbers: also: **~ together**) encorder; (area: also: **~ off**) interdire l'accès de; (: divide off) séparer; **to know the ~s** (fig) être au courant, connaître les ficelles

**rose** [rəuz] pt of **rise** ▷ n rose f; (also: **~bush**) rosier m

**rosé** ['rəuzeɪ] n rosé m

**rosemary** ['rəuzmərɪ] n romarin m

**rosy** ['rəuzɪ] adj rose; **a ~ future** un bel avenir

**rot** [rɒt] n (decay) pourriture f; (fig: pej: nonsense) idioties fpl, balivernes fpl ▷ vt, vi pourrir

**rota** ['rəutə] n liste f, tableau m de service

**rotate** [rəu'teɪt] vt (revolve) faire tourner; (change round: crops) alterner; (: jobs) faire à tour de rôle ▷ vi (revolve) tourner

**rotten** ['rɒtn] adj (decayed) pourri(e); (dishonest) corrompu(e); (inf: bad) mauvais(e), moche; **to feel ~** (ill) être mal fichu(e)

**rough** [rʌf] adj (cloth, skin) rêche, rugueux(-euse); (terrain) accidenté(e); (path) rocailleux(-euse); (voice) rauque, rude; (person, manner: coarse) rude, fruste; (: violent) brutal(e); (district, weather) mauvais(e); (sea) houleux(-euse); (plan) ébauché(e); (guess) approximatif(-ive) ▷ n (Golf) rough m ▷ vt: **to ~ it** vivre à la dure; **to sleep ~** (BRIT) coucher à la dure; **roughly** adv (handle) rudement, brutalement; (speak) avec brusquerie; (make) grossièrement; (approximately) à peu près, en gros

**roulette** [ruː'lɛt] n roulette f

**round** [raund] adj rond(e) ▷ n rond m, cercle m; (BRIT: of toast) tranche f; (duty: of policeman, milkman etc)

tournée f; (: of doctor) visites fpl; (game: of cards, in competition) partie f; (Boxing) round m; (of talks) série f ▷ vt (corner) tourner ▷ prep autour de ▷ adv: **right ~, all ~** tout autour; **~ of ammunition** cartouche f; **~ of applause** applaudissements mpl; **~ of drinks** tournée f; **~ of sandwiches** (BRIT) sandwich m; **the long way ~** (par) le chemin le plus long; **all (the) year ~** toute l'année; **it's just ~ the corner** (fig) c'est tout près; **to go ~ to sb's (house)** aller chez qn; **go ~ the back** passez par derrière; **enough to go ~** assez pour tout le monde; **she arrived ~ (about) noon** (BRIT) elle est arrivée vers midi; **~ the clock** 24 heures sur 24; **round off** vt (speech etc) terminer; **round up** vt rassembler; (criminals) effectuer une rafle de; (prices) arrondir (au chiffre supérieur); **roundabout** n (BRIT Aut) rond-point m (à sens giratoire); (at fair) manège m (de chevaux de bois) ▷ adj (route, means) détourné(e); **round trip** n (voyage m) aller et retour m; **roundup** n rassemblement m; (of criminals) rafle f

**rouse** [rauz] vt (wake up) réveiller; (stir up) susciter, provoquer; (interest) éveiller; (suspicions) susciter, éveiller

**route** [ruːt] n itinéraire m; (of bus) parcours m; (of trade, shipping) route f

**routine** [ruː'tiːn] adj (work) ordinaire, courant(e); (procedure) d'usage ▷ n (habits) habitudes fpl; (pej) train-train m; (Theat) numéro m

**row¹** [rəu] n (line) rangée f; (of people, seats, Knitting) rang m; (behind one another: of cars, people) file f ▷ vi (in boat) ramer; (as sport) faire de l'aviron ▷ vt (boat) faire aller à la rame or à l'aviron; **in a ~** (fig) d'affilée

**row²** [rau] n (noise) vacarme m; (dispute) dispute f, querelle f; (scolding) réprimande f, savon m ▷ vi (also: **to have a ~**) se disputer, se quereller

**rowboat** ['rəubəut] n (US) canot m (à rames)

**rowing** ['rəʊɪŋ] n canotage m; (as sport)
aviron m; **rowing boat** n (BRIT) canot
m (à rames)

**royal** ['rɔɪəl] adj royal(e); **royalty** n
(royal persons) (membres mpl de la)
famille royale; (payment: to author)
droits mpl d'auteur; (: to inventor)
royalties fpl

**rpm** abbr (= revolutions per minute) t/mn
(= tours/minute)

**R.S.V.P.** abbr (= répondez s'il vous plaît)
RSVP

**Rt. Hon.** abbr (BRIT: = Right Honourable)
titre donné aux députés de la Chambre des
communes

**rub** [rʌb] n: **to give sth a ~** donner un
coup de chiffon or de torchon à qch
▷ vt frotter; (person) frictionner; (hands)
se frotter; **to ~ sb up** (BRIT) or **to ~ sb**
(US) **the wrong way** prendre qn à
rebrousse-poil; **rub in** vt (ointment)
faire pénétrer; **rub off** vi partir; **rub
out** vt effacer

**rubber** ['rʌbə']ʳ n caoutchouc m; (BRIT:
eraser) gomme f (à effacer); **rubber
band** n élastique m; **rubber gloves** npl
gants mpl en caoutchouc

**rubbish** ['rʌbɪʃ] n (from household)
ordures fpl; (fig: pej) choses fpl sans
valeur; camelote f; (nonsense) bêtises
fpl, idioties fpl; **rubbish bin** n (BRIT)
boîte f à ordures, poubelle f; **rubbish
dump** n (BRIT: in town) décharge
publique, dépotoir m

**rubble** ['rʌbl] n décombres mpl; (smaller)
gravats mpl; (Constr) blocage m

**ruby** ['ruːbɪ] n rubis m

**rucksack** ['rʌksæk] n sac m à dos

**rudder** ['rʌdə']ʳ n gouvernail m

**rude** [ruːd] adj (impolite: person)
impoli(e); (: word, manners)
grossier(-ière); (shocking) indécent(e),
inconvenant(e)

**ruffle** ['rʌfl] vt (hair) ébouriffer; (clothes)
chiffonner; (fig: person): **to get ~d**
s'énerver

**rug** [rʌg] n petit tapis; (BRIT: blanket)
couverture f

**rugby** ['rʌgbɪ] n (also: **~ football**)
rugby m

**rugged** ['rʌgɪd] adj (landscape)
accidenté(e); (features, character) rude

**ruin** ['ruːɪn] n ruine f ▷ vt ruiner; (spoil:
clothes) abîmer; (: event) gâcher; **ruins**
npl (of building) ruine(s)

**rule** [ruːl] n règle f; (regulation)
règlement m; (government) autorité
f, gouvernement m ▷ vt (country)
gouverner; (person) dominer; (decide)
décider ▷ vi commander; (Law): **as
a ~** normalement, en règle générale;
**rule out** vt exclure; **ruler** n (sovereign)
souverain(e); (leader) chef m (d'État); (for
measuring) règle f; **ruling** adj (party) au
pouvoir; (class) dirigeant(e) ▷ n (Law)
décision f

**rum** [rʌm] n rhum m

**Rumania** [ruːˈmeɪnɪə] n Roumanie f;
**Rumanian** adj roumain(e) ▷ n
Roumain(e); (Ling) roumain m

**rumble** ['rʌmbl] n grondement m; (of
stomach, pipe) gargouillement m ▷ vi
gronder; (stomach, pipe) gargouiller

**rumour** (US **rumor**) ['ruːmə']ʳ n rumeur
f, bruit m (qui court) ▷ vt: **it is ~ed that**
le bruit court que

**rump steak** n romsteck m

**run** [rʌn] n (race) course f; (outing)
tour m or promenade f (en voiture);
(distance travelled) parcours m, trajet m;
(series) suite f, série f; (Theat) série de
représentations; (Ski) piste f; (Cricket,
Baseball) point m; (in tights, stockings)
maille filée, échelle f ▷ vb (pt **ran**, pp
**~**) ▷ vt (business) diriger; (competition,
course) organiser; (hotel, house) tenir;
(race) participer à; (Comput: program)
exécuter; (to pass: hand, finger): **to
~ sth over** promener or passer qch
sur; (water, bath) faire couler; (Press:
feature) publier ▷ vi courir; (pass: road
etc) passer; (work: machine, factory)
marcher; (bus, train) circuler; (continue:
play) se jouer, être à l'affiche; (: contract)
être valide or en vigueur; (flow: river,
bath, nose) couler; (colours, washing)

déteindre; (*in election*) être candidat, se présenter; **at a ~** au pas de course; **to go for a ~** aller courir or faire un peu de course à pied; (*in car*) faire un tour or une promenade (en voiture); **there was a ~ on** (*meat, tickets*) les gens se sont rués sur; **in the long ~** à la longue; **on the ~** en fuite; **I'll ~ you to the station** je vais vous emmener or conduire à la gare; **to ~ a risk** courir un risque; **run after** vt fus (*to catch up*) courir après; (*chase*) poursuivre; **run away** vi s'enfuir; **run down** vt (*Aut: knock over*) renverser; (BRIT: *reduce: production*) réduire progressivement; (: *factory/shop*) réduire progressivement la production/l'activité de; (*criticize*) critiquer, dénigrer; **to be ~ down** (*tired*) être fatigué(e) or à plat; **run into** vt fus (*meet: person*) rencontrer par hasard; (: *trouble*) se heurter à; (*collide with*) heurter; **run off** vi s'enfuir ▷ vt (*water*) laisser s'écouler; (*copies*) tirer; **run out** vi (*person*) sortir en courant; (*liquid*) couler; (*lease*) expirer; (*money*) être épuisé(e); **run out of** vt fus se trouver à court de; **run over** vt (*Aut*) écraser ▷ vt fus (*revise*) revoir, reprendre; **run through** vt fus (*recap*) reprendre, revoir; (*play*) répéter; **run up** vi: **to ~ up against** (*difficulties*) se heurter à; **runaway** adj (*horse*) emballé(e); (*truck*) fou (folle); (*person*) fugitif(-ive); (*child*) fugueur(-euse)

**rung** [rʌŋ] pp of **ring** ▷ n (*of ladder*) barreau m

**runner** ['rʌnəʳ] n (*in race: person*) coureur(-euse); (: *horse*) partant m; (*on sledge*) patin m; (*for drawer etc*) coulisseau m; **runner bean** n (BRIT) haricot m (à rames); **runner-up** n second(e)

**running** ['rʌnɪŋ] n (*in race etc*) course f; (*of business, organization*) direction f, gestion f ▷ adj (*water*) courant(e); (*commentary*) suivi(e); **6 days ~** 6 jours de suite; **to be in/out of the ~ for sth** être/ne pas être sur les rangs pour qch

**runny** ['rʌnɪ] adj qui coule

**run-up** ['rʌnʌp] n (BRIT): **~ to sth** période f précédant qch

**runway** ['rʌnweɪ] n (*Aviat*) piste f (d'envol or d'atterrissage)

**rupture** ['rʌptʃəʳ] n (*Med*) hernie f

**rural** ['rʊərl] adj rural(e)

**rush** [rʌʃ] n (*of crowd, Comm: sudden demand*) ruée f; (*hurry*) hâte f; (*of anger, joy*) accès m; (*current*) flot m; (*Bot*) jonc m ▷ vt (*hurry*) transporter or envoyer d'urgence ▷ vi se précipiter; **to ~ sth off** (*do quickly*) faire qch à la hâte; **rush hour** n heures fpl de pointe or d'affluence

**Russia** ['rʌʃə] n Russie f; **Russian** adj russe ▷ n Russe m/f; (*Ling*) russe m

**rust** [rʌst] n rouille f ▷ vi rouiller

**rusty** ['rʌstɪ] adj rouillé(e)

**ruthless** ['ruːθlɪs] adj sans pitié, impitoyable

**RV** n abbr (US) = **recreational vehicle**

**rye** [raɪ] n seigle m

# S

**Sabbath** ['sæbəθ] n (Jewish) sabbat m; (Christian) dimanche m

**sabotage** ['sæbətɑ:ʒ] n sabotage m ▷ vt saboter

**saccharin(e)** ['sækərɪn] n saccharine f

**sachet** ['sæʃeɪ] n sachet m

**sack** [sæk] n (bag) sac m ▷ vt (dismiss) renvoyer, mettre à la porte; (plunder) piller, mettre à sac; **to get the ~** être renvoyé(e) or mis(e) à la porte

**sacred** ['seɪkrɪd] adj sacré(e)

**sacrifice** ['sækrɪfaɪs] n sacrifice m ▷ vt sacrifier

**sad** [sæd] adj (unhappy) triste; (deplorable) triste, fâcheux(-euse); (inf: pathetic: thing) triste, lamentable; (: person) minable

**saddle** ['sædl] n selle f ▷ vt (horse) seller; **to be ~d with sth** (inf) avoir qch sur les bras

**sadistic** [sə'dɪstɪk] adj sadique

**sadly** ['sædlɪ] adv tristement; (unfortunately) malheureusement; (seriously) fort

**sadness** ['sædnɪs] n tristesse f

**s.a.e.** n abbr (BRIT: = stamped addressed envelope) enveloppe affranchie pour la réponse

**safari** [sə'fɑ:rɪ] n safari m

**safe** [seɪf] adj (out of danger) hors de danger, en sécurité; (not dangerous) sans danger; (cautious) prudent(e); (sure: bet etc) assuré(e) ▷ n coffre-fort m; **could you put this in the ~, please?** pourriez-vous mettre ceci dans le coffre-fort?; **~ and sound** sain(e) et sauf (sauve); **(just) to be on the ~ side** pour plus de sûreté, par précaution; **safely** adv (assume, say) sans risque d'erreur; (drive, arrive) sans accident; **safe sex** n rapports sexuels protégés

**safety** ['seɪftɪ] n sécurité f; **safety belt** n ceinture f de sécurité; **safety pin** n épingle f de sûreté or de nourrice

**saffron** ['sæfrən] n safran m

**sag** [sæg] vi s'affaisser, fléchir; (hem, breasts) pendre

**sage** [seɪdʒ] n (herb) sauge f; (person) sage m

**Sagittarius** [sædʒɪ'tɛərɪəs] n le Sagittaire

**Sahara** [sə'hɑ:rə] n: **the ~ (Desert)** le (désert du) Sahara m

**said** [sɛd] pt, pp of **say**

**sail** [seɪl] n (on boat) voile f; (trip): **to go for a ~** faire un tour en bateau ▷ vt (boat) manœuvrer, piloter ▷ vi (travel: ship) avancer, naviguer; (set off) partir, prendre la mer; (Sport) faire de la voile; **they ~ed into Le Havre** ils sont entrés dans le port du Havre; **sailboat** n (US) bateau m à voiles, voilier m; **sailing** n (Sport) voile f; **to go sailing** faire de la voile; **sailing boat** n bateau m à voiles, voilier m; **sailor** n marin m, matelot m

**saint** [seɪnt] n saint(e)

**sake** [seɪk] n: **for the ~ of** (out of concern for) pour (l'amour de), dans l'intérêt de; (out of consideration for) par égard pour

**salad** ['sæləd] n salade f; **salad cream** n (BRIT) (sorte f de) mayonnaise f; **salad dressing** n vinaigrette f

**salami** [sə'lɑːmɪ] n salami m
**salary** ['sælərɪ] n salaire m, traitement m
**sale** [seɪl] n vente f; (at reduced prices) soldes mpl; **sales** npl (total amount sold) chiffre m de ventes; **"for ~"** "à vendre"; **on ~** en vente; **sales assistant** (US **sales clerk**) n vendeur(-euse); **salesman** (irreg) n (in shop) vendeur m; **salesperson** (irreg) n (in shop) vendeur(-euse); **sales rep** n (Comm) représentant(e) m/f; **saleswoman** (irreg) n (in shop) vendeuse f
**saline** ['seɪlaɪn] adj salin(e)
**saliva** [sə'laɪvə] n salive f
**salmon** ['sæmən] n (pl inv) saumon m
**salon** ['sælɔn] n salon m
**saloon** [sə'luːn] n (US) bar m; (BRIT Aut) berline f; (ship's lounge) salon m
**salt** [sɔːlt] n sel m ▷ vt saler; **saltwater** adj (fish etc) (d')eau) de mer; **salty** adj salé(e)
**salute** [sə'luːt] n salut m; (of guns) salve f ▷ vt saluer
**salvage** ['sælvɪdʒ] n (saving) sauvetage m; (things saved) biens sauvés or récupérés ▷ vt sauver, récupérer
**Salvation Army** [sæl'veɪʃən-] n Armée f du Salut
**same** [seɪm] adj même ▷ pron: **the ~** le (la) même, les mêmes; **the ~ book as** le même livre que; **at the ~ time** en même temps; (yet) néanmoins; **all** or **just the ~** tout de même, quand même; **to do the ~** faire de même, en faire autant; **to do the ~ as sb** faire comme qn; **and the ~ to you!** et à vous de même!; (after insult) toi-même!
**sample** ['sɑːmpl] n échantillon m; (Med) prélèvement m ▷ vt (food, wine) goûter
**sanction** ['sæŋkʃən] n approbation f, sanction f ▷ vt cautionner, sanctionner; **sanctions** npl (Pol) sanctions
**sanctuary** ['sæŋktjuərɪ] n (holy place) sanctuaire m; (refuge) asile m; (for wildlife) réserve f

**sand** [sænd] n sable m ▷ vt (also: ~ **down**: wood etc) poncer
**sandal** ['sændl] n sandale f
**sand**: **sandbox** n (US: for children) tas m de sable; **sandcastle** n château m de sable; **sand dune** n dune f de sable; **sandpaper** n papier m de verre; **sandpit** n (BRIT: for children) tas m de sable; **sands** npl plage f (de sable); **sandstone** ['sændstəun] n grès m
**sandwich** ['sændwɪtʃ] n sandwich m ▷ vt (also: ~ **in**) intercaler; **~ed between** pris en sandwich entre; **cheese/ham ~** sandwich au fromage/jambon
**sandy** ['sændɪ] adj sablonneux(-euse); (colour) sable inv, blond roux inv
**sane** [seɪn] adj (person) sain(e) d'esprit; (outlook) sensé(e), sain(e)
**sang** [sæŋ] pt of **sing**
**sanitary towel** (US **sanitary napkin**) ['sænɪtərɪ-] n serviette f hygiénique
**sanity** ['sænɪtɪ] n santé mentale; (common sense) bon sens
**sank** [sæŋk] pt of **sink**
**Santa Claus** [sæntə'klɔːz] n le Père Noël
**sap** [sæp] n (of plants) sève f ▷ vt (strength) saper, miner
**sapphire** ['sæfaɪəʳ] n saphir m
**sarcasm** ['sɑːkæzm] n sarcasme m, raillerie f
**sarcastic** [sɑː'kæstɪk] adj sarcastique
**sardine** [sɑː'diːn] n sardine f
**SASE** n abbr (US: = self-addressed stamped envelope) enveloppe affranchie pour la réponse
**sat** [sæt] pt, pp of **sit**
**Sat.** abbr (= Saturday) sa
**satchel** ['sætʃl] n cartable m
**satellite** ['sætəlaɪt] n satellite m; **satellite dish** n antenne f parabolique; **satellite television** n télévision f par satellite
**satin** ['sætɪn] n satin m ▷ adj en or de satin, satiné(e)
**satire** ['sætaɪəʳ] n satire f
**satisfaction** [sætɪs'fækʃən] n satisfaction f

**satisfactory** [sætɪs'fæktərɪ] *adj* satisfaisant(e)

**satisfied** ['sætɪsfaɪd] *adj* satisfait(e); **to be ~ with sth** être satisfait de qch

**satisfy** ['sætɪsfaɪ] *vt* satisfaire, contenter; (*convince*) convaincre, persuader

**Saturday** ['sætədɪ] *n* samedi *m*

**sauce** [sɔːs] *n* sauce *f*; **saucepan** *n* casserole *f*

**saucer** ['sɔːsəʳ] *n* soucoupe *f*

**Saudi Arabia** ['saudɪ-] *n* Arabie *f* Saoudite

**sauna** ['sɔːnə] *n* sauna *m*

**sausage** ['sɔsɪdʒ] *n* saucisse *f*; (*salami etc*) saucisson *m*; **sausage roll** *n* friand *m*

**sautéed** ['səuteɪd] *adj* sauté(e)

**savage** ['sævɪdʒ] *adj* (*cruel, fierce*) brutal(e), féroce; (*primitive*) primitif(-ive), sauvage ▷ *n* sauvage *m/f* ▷ *vt* attaquer férocement

**save** [seɪv] *vt* (*person, belongings*) sauver; (*money*) mettre de côté, économiser; (*time*) (faire) gagner; (*keep*) garder; (*Comput*) sauvegarder; (*Sport: stop*) arrêter; (*avoid: trouble*) éviter ▷ *vi* (*also: ~ up*) mettre de l'argent de côté ▷ *n* (*Sport*) arrêt *m* (du ballon) ▷ *prep* sauf, à l'exception de

**savings** ['seɪvɪŋz] *npl* économies *fpl*; **savings account** *n* compte *m* d'épargne; **savings and loan association** (*us*) *n* ≈ société *f* de crédit immobilier

**savoury** (*us* **savory**) ['seɪvərɪ] *adj* savoureux(-euse); (*dish: not sweet*) salé(e)

**saw** [sɔː] *pt of* **see** ▷ *n* (*tool*) scie *f* ▷ *vt* (*pt* **~ed**, *pp* **~ed** *or* **~n**) scier; **sawdust** *n* sciure *f*

**sawn** [sɔːn] *pp of* **saw**

**saxophone** ['sæksəfəun] *n* saxophone *m*

**say** [seɪ] *n*: **to have one's ~** dire ce qu'on a à dire ▷ *vt* (*pt, pp* **said**) dire; **to have a ~** avoir voix au chapitre; **could you ~ that again?** pourriez-vous répéter ce que vous venez de dire?; **to ~ yes/no** dire oui/non; **my watch ~s 3 o'clock** ma montre indique 3 heures, il est 3 heures à ma montre; **that is to ~** c'est-à-dire, cela va sans dire, cela va de soi; **saying** *n* dicton *m*, proverbe *m*

**scab** [skæb] *n* croûte *f*; (*pej*) jaune *m*

**scaffolding** ['skæfəldɪŋ] *n* échafaudage *m*

**scald** [skɔːld] *n* brûlure *f* ▷ *vt* ébouillanter

**scale** [skeɪl] *n* (*of fish*) écaille *f*; (*Mus*) gamme *f*; (*of ruler, thermometer etc*) graduation *f*, échelle (graduée) (*of salaries, fees etc*) barème *m*; (*of map, also size, extent*) échelle *f* ▷ *vt* (*mountain*) escalader; **scales** *npl* balance *f*; (*larger*) bascule *f*; (*also*: **bathroom ~s**) pèse-personne *m inv*; **~ of charges** tableau *m* des tarifs; **on a large ~** sur une grande échelle, en grand

**scallion** ['skæljən] *n* (*us: salad onion*) ciboule *f*

**scallop** ['skɔləp] *n* coquille *f* Saint-Jacques; (*Sewing*) feston *m*

**scalp** [skælp] *n* cuir chevelu ▷ *vt* scalper

**scalpel** ['skælpl] *n* scalpel *m*

**scam** [skæm] *n* (*inf*) arnaque *f*

**scampi** ['skæmpɪ] *npl* langoustines (frites), scampi *mpl*

**scan** [skæn] *vt* (*examine*) scruter, examiner; (*glance at quickly*) parcourir; (*TV, Radar*) balayer ▷ *n* (*Med*) scanographie *f*

**scandal** ['skændl] *n* scandale *m*; (*gossip*) ragots *mpl*

**Scandinavia** [skændɪ'neɪvɪə] *n* Scandinavie *f*; **Scandinavian** *adj* scandinave ▷ *n* Scandinave *m/f*

**scanner** ['skænəʳ] *n* (*Radar, Med*) scanner *m*, scanographe *m*; (*Comput*) scanner, numériseur *m*

**scapegoat** ['skeɪpgəut] *n* bouc *m* émissaire

**scar** [skɑːʳ] *n* cicatrice *f* ▷ *vt* laisser une cicatrice *or* une marque à

**scarce** [skɛəs] *adj* rare, peu

abondant(e); **to make o.s. ~** (inf)
se sauver; **scarcely** adv à peine,
presque pas

**scare** [skɛəʳ] n peur f, panique f ▷ vt
effrayer, faire peur à; **to ~ sb stiff** faire
une peur bleue à qn; **bomb ~** alerte f à
la bombe; **scarecrow** n épouvantail m;
**scared** adj **to be scared** avoir peur

**scarf** (pl **scarves**) [skɑːf, skɑːvz] n (long)
écharpe f; (square) foulard m

**scarlet** ['skɑːlɪt] adj écarlate

**scarves** [skɑːvz] npl of **scarf**

**scary** ['skɛərɪ] adj (inf) effrayant(e);
(film) qui fait peur

**scatter** ['skætəʳ] vt éparpiller,
répandre; (crowd) disperser ▷ vi se
disperser

**scenario** [sɪ'nɑːrɪəu] n scénario m

**scene** [siːn] n (Theat, fig etc) scène f; (of
crime, accident) lieu(x) m(pl), endroit m;
(sight, view) spectacle m, vue f; **scenery**
n (Theat) décor(s) m(pl); (landscape)
paysage m; **scenic** adj offrant de beaux
paysages or panoramas

**scent** [sɛnt] n parfum m, odeur f; (fig:
track) piste f

**sceptical** (us **skeptical**) ['skɛptɪkl] adj
sceptique

**schedule** ['ʃɛdjuːl, us 'skɛdjuːl] n
programme m, plan m; (of trains) horaire
m; (of prices etc) barème m, tarif m ▷ vt
prévoir; **on ~** à l'heure (prévue); à la
date prévue; **to be ahead of/behind ~**
avoir de l'avance/du retard; **scheduled
flight** n vol régulier

**scheme** [skiːm] n plan m, projet
m; (plot) complot m, combine f;
(arrangement) arrangement m,
classification f; (pension scheme
etc) régime m ▷ vt, vi comploter,
manigancer

**schizophrenic** [skɪtsə'frɛnɪk] adj
schizophrène

**scholar** ['skɔləʳ] n érudit(e); (pupil)
boursier(-ère); **scholarship** n
érudition f; (grant) bourse f (d'études)

**school** [skuːl] n (gen) école f; (secondary
school) collège m, lycée m; (in university)

faculté f; (us: university) université
f ▷ cpd scolaire; **schoolbook** n livre
m scolaire or de classe; **schoolboy**
n écolier m; (at secondary school)
collégien m, lycéen m; **schoolchildren**
npl écoliers mpl; (at secondary school)
collégiens mpl, lycéens mpl; **schoolgirl**
n écolière f; (at secondary school)
collégienne f, lycéenne f; **schooling** n
instruction f, études fpl; **schoolteacher**
n (primary) instituteur(-trice);
(secondary) professeur m

**science** ['saɪəns] n science f; **science
fiction** n science-fiction f; **scientific**
[saɪən'tɪfɪk] adj scientifique; **scientist**
n scientifique m/f; (eminent) savant m

**sci-fi** ['saɪfaɪ] n abbr (inf: = science
fiction) SF f

**scissors** ['sɪzəz] npl ciseaux mpl; **a pair
of ~** une paire de ciseaux

**scold** [skəuld] vt gronder

**scone** [skɔn] n sorte de petit pain rond
au lait

**scoop** [skuːp] n pelle f (à main); (for ice
cream) boule f à glace; (Press) reportage
exclusif or à sensation

**scooter** ['skuːtəʳ] n (motor cycle) scooter
m; (toy) trottinette f

**scope** [skəup] n (capacity: of plan,
undertaking) portée f, envergure f; (: of
person) compétence f, capacités fpl;
(opportunity) possibilités fpl

**scorching** ['skɔːtʃɪŋ] adj torride,
brûlant(e)

**score** [skɔːʳ] n score m, décompte m
des points; (Mus) partition f ▷ vt (goal,
point) marquer; (success) remporter;
(cut: leather, wood, card) entailler, inciser
▷ vi marquer des points; (Football)
marquer un but; (keep score) compter
les points; **on that ~** sur ce chapitre,
à cet égard; **a ~ of** (twenty) vingt; **~s of**
(fig) des tas de; **to ~ 6 out of 10** obtenir
6 sur 10; **score out** vt rayer, barrer,
biffer; **scoreboard** n tableau m; **scorer**
n (Football) auteur m du but; buteur m;
(keeping score) marqueur m

**scorn** [skɔːn] n mépris m, dédain m

**Scorpio** ['skɔːpɪəu] n le Scorpion

**scorpion** ['skɔːpɪən] n scorpion m

**Scot** [skɔt] n Écossais(e)

**Scotch** [skɔtʃ] n whisky m, scotch m

**Scotch tape®** (US) n scotch® m, ruban adhésif

**Scotland** ['skɔtlənd] n Écosse f

**Scots** [skɔts] adj écossais(e); **Scotsman** (irreg) n Écossais m; **Scotswoman** (irreg) n Écossaise f; **Scottish** ['skɔtɪʃ] adj écossais(e); **Scottish Parliament** n Parlement écossais

**scout** [skaut] n (Mil) éclaireur m; (also: **boy ~**) scout m; **girl ~** (US) guide f

**scowl** [skaul] vi se renfrogner, avoir l'air maussade; **to ~ at** regarder de travers

**scramble** ['skræmbl] n (rush) bousculade f, ruée f ▷ vi grimper/descendre tant bien que mal; **to ~ for** se bousculer or se disputer pour (avoir); **to go scrambling** (Sport) faire du trial; **scrambled eggs** npl œufs brouillés

**scrap** [skræp] n bout m, morceau m; (fight) bagarre f; (also: **~ iron**) ferraille f ▷ vt jeter, mettre au rebut; (fig) abandonner, laisser tomber ▷ vi se bagarrer; **scraps** npl (waste) déchets mpl; **scrapbook** n album m

**scrape** [skreɪp] vt, vi gratter, racler ▷ n: **to get into a ~** s'attirer des ennuis; **scrape through** vi (exam etc) réussir de justesse

**scrap paper** n papier m brouillon

**scratch** [skrætʃ] n égratignure f, rayure f; (on paint) éraflure f; (from claw) coup m de griffe ▷ vt (rub) (se) gratter; (paint etc) érafler; (with claw, nail) griffer ▷ vi (se) gratter; **to start from ~** partir de zéro; **to be up to ~** être à la hauteur; **scratch card** n carte f à gratter

**scream** [skriːm] n cri perçant, hurlement m ▷ vi crier, hurler

**screen** [skriːn] n écran m; (in room) paravent m; (fig) écran, rideau m ▷ vt masquer, cacher; (from the wind etc) abriter, protéger; (film) projeter; (candidates etc) filtrer; **screening** n (of film) projection f; (Med) test m (or tests) de dépistage; **screenplay** n scénario m; **screen saver** n (Comput) économiseur m d'écran

**screw** [skruː] n vis f ▷ vt (also: **~ in**) visser; **screw up** vt (paper etc) froisser; **to ~ up one's eyes** se plisser les yeux; **screwdriver** n tournevis m

**scribble** ['skrɪbl] n gribouillage m ▷ vt gribouiller, griffonner

**script** [skrɪpt] n (Cine etc) scénario m, texte m; (writing) (écriture f) script m

**scroll** [skrəul] n rouleau m ▷ vt (Comput) faire défiler (sur l'écran)

**scrub** [skrʌb] n (land) broussailles fpl ▷ vt (floor) nettoyer à la brosse; (pan) récurer; (washing) frotter

**scruffy** ['skrʌfɪ] adj débraillé(e)

**scrum(mage)** ['skrʌm(ɪdʒ)] n mêlée f

**scrutiny** ['skruːtɪnɪ] n examen minutieux

**scuba diving** ['skuːbə-] n plongée sous-marine (autonome)

**sculptor** ['skʌlptər] n sculpteur m

**sculpture** ['skʌlptʃər] n sculpture f

**scum** [skʌm] n écume f, mousse f; (pej: people) rebut m, lie f

**scurry** ['skʌrɪ] vi filer à toute allure; **to ~ off** détaler, se sauver

**sea** [siː] n mer f ▷ cpd marin(e), de (la) mer, maritime; **by** or **beside the ~** (holiday, town) au bord de la mer; **by ~** par mer, en bateau; **out to ~** au large; (out) **at ~** en mer; **to be all at ~** (fig) nager complètement; **seafood** n fruits mpl de mer; **sea front** n bord m de mer; **seagull** n mouette f

**seal** [siːl] n (animal) phoque m; (stamp) sceau m, cachet m ▷ vt sceller; (envelope) coller; (: with seal) cacheter; **seal off** vt (forbid entry to) interdire l'accès à

**sea level** n niveau m de la mer

**seam** [siːm] n couture f; (of coal) veine f, filon m

**search** [səːtʃ] n (for person, thing, Comput) recherche(s) f(pl); (of drawer, pockets) fouille f; (Law: at sb's home) perquisition f ▷ vt fouiller; (examine)

examiner minutieusement; scruter
▷ *vi*: **to ~ for** chercher; **in ~ of** à la
recherche de; **search engine** *n*
(*Comput*) moteur *m* de recherche;
**search party** *n* expédition *f* de secours
**sea**: **seashore** *n* rivage *m*, plage *f*,
bord *m* de (la) mer; **seasick** *adj*: **to be
seasick** avoir le mal de mer; **seaside**
*n* bord *m* de mer; **seaside resort** *n*
station *f* balnéaire
**season** ['si:zn] *n* saison *f* ▷ *vt*
assaisonner, relever; **to be in/out of ~**
être/ne pas être de saison; **seasonal**
*adj* saisonnier(-ière); **seasoning** *n*
assaisonnement *m*; **season ticket** *n*
carte *f* d'abonnement
**seat** [si:t] *n* siège *m*; (*in bus, train*:
*place*) place *f*; (*buttocks*) postérieur *m*;
(*of trousers*) fond *m* ▷ *vt* faire asseoir,
placer; (*have room for*) avoir des places
assises pour, pouvoir accueillir; **I'd like
to book two ~s** je voudrais réserver
deux places; **to be ~ed** être assis; **seat
belt** *n* ceinture *f* de sécurité; **seating** *n*
sièges *fpl*, places assises
**sea**: **sea water** *n* eau *f* de mer; **seaweed**
*n* algues *fpl*
**sec.** *abbr* (= *second*) sec
**secluded** [sɪˈklu:dɪd] *adj* retiré(e),
à l'écart
**second** ['sɛkənd] *num* deuxième,
second(e) ▷ *adv* (*in race etc*) en seconde
position ▷ *n* (*unit of time*) seconde *f*;
(*Aut: also*: **~ gear**) seconde; (*Comm*:
*imperfect*) article *m* de second choix;
(*Brit Scol*) ≈ licence *f* avec mention ▷ *vt*
(*motion*) appuyer; **seconds** *npl* (*inf: food*)
rab *m* (*inf*); **secondary** *adj* secondaire;
**secondary school** *n* collège *m*; lycée *m*;
**second-class** *adj* de deuxième classe;
(*Rail*) de seconde (classe); (*Post*) au
tarif réduit; (*pej*) de qualité inférieure
▷ *adv* (*Rail*) en seconde; (*Post*) au tarif
réduit; **secondhand** *adj* d'occasion;
(*information*) de seconde main;
**secondly** *adv* deuxièmement; **second-
rate** *adj* de deuxième ordre, de qualité
inférieure; **second thoughts** *npl*: **to**

**have second thoughts** changer d'avis;
**on second thoughts** *or* **thought** (*us*)
à la réflexion
**secrecy** ['si:krəsɪ] *n* secret *m*
**secret** ['si:krɪt] *adj* secret(-ète)
▷ *n* secret *m*; **in ~** *adv* en secret,
secrètement, en cachette
**secretary** ['sɛkrətrɪ] *n* secrétaire *m/f*;
**S~ of State (for)** (*Brit Pol*) ministre
*m* (de)
**secretive** ['si:krətɪv] *adj* réservé(e);
(*pej*) cachottier(-ière), dissimulé(e)
**secret service** *n* services secrets
**sect** [sɛkt] *n* secte *f*
**section** ['sɛkʃən] *n* section *f*; (*Comm*)
rayon *m*; (*of document*) section, article
*m*, paragraphe *m*; (*cut*) coupe *f*
**sector** ['sɛktər] *n* secteur *m*
**secular** ['sɛkjulər] *adj* laïque
**secure** [sɪˈkjuər] *adj* (*free from anxiety*)
sans inquiétude, sécurisé(e); (*firmly
fixed*) solide, bien attaché(e) (*or*
fermé(e) *etc*); (*in safe place*) en lieu sûr,
en sûreté ▷ *vt* (*fix*) fixer, attacher; (*get*)
obtenir, se procurer
**security** [sɪˈkjuərɪtɪ] *n* sécurité *f*,
mesures *fpl* de sécurité; (*for loan*)
caution *f*, garantie *f*; **securities** *npl*
(*Stock Exchange*) valeurs *fpl*, titres *mpl*;
**security guard** *n* garde chargé
de la sécurité; (*transporting money*)
convoyeur *m* de fonds
**sedan** [səˈdæn] *n* (*us Aut*) berline *f*
**sedate** [sɪˈdeɪt] *adj* calme; posé(e) ▷ *vt*
donner des sédatifs à
**sedative** ['sɛdɪtɪv] *n* calmant *m*,
sédatif *m*
**seduce** [sɪˈdju:s] *vt* séduire; **seductive**
[sɪˈdʌktɪv] *adj* séduisant(e);
(*smile*) séducteur(-trice); (*fig: offer*)
alléchant(e)
**see** [si:] *vb* (*pt* **saw**, *pp* **~n**) ▷ *vt* (*gen*)
voir; (*accompany*): **to ~ sb to the
door** reconduire *or* raccompagner qn
jusqu'à la porte ▷ *vi* voir; **to ~ that**
(*ensure*) veiller à ce que + *sub*, faire en
sorte que + *sub*, s'assurer que; **~ you
soon/later/tomorrow!** à bientôt/plus

tard/demain!; **see off** vt accompagner
(à la gare or à l'aéroport etc); **see out**
vt (take to door) raccompagner à la
porte; **see through** vt mener à bonne
fin ▷ vt fus voir clair dans; **see to** vt fus
s'occuper de, se charger de

**seed** [si:d] n graine f; (fig) germe m;
(Tennis etc) tête f de série; **to go to
~** (plant) monter en graine; (fig) se
laisser aller

**seeing** ['si:ɪŋ] conj: **~ (that)** vu que,
étant donné que

**seek** (pt, pp sought) [si:k, sɔ:t] vt
chercher, rechercher

**seem** [si:m] vi sembler, paraître;
**there ~s to be ...** il semble qu'il y a ...,
on dirait qu'il y a ...; **seemingly** adv
apparemment

**seen** [si:n] pp of **see**

**seesaw** ['si:sɔ:] n (jeu m de) bascule f

**segment** ['sɛgmənt] n segment m; (of
orange) quartier m

**segregate** ['sɛgrɪgeɪt] vt séparer, isoler

**Seine** [seɪn] n: **the (River) ~** la Seine

**seize** [si:z] vt (grasp) saisir, attraper;
(take possession of) s'emparer de;
(opportunity) saisir

**seizure** ['si:ʒəʳ] n (Med) crise f, attaque
f; (of power) prise f

**seldom** ['sɛldəm] adv rarement

**select** [sɪ'lɛkt] adj choisi(e), d'élite;
(hotel, restaurant, club) chic inv, sélect
inv ▷ vt sélectionner, choisir; **selection**
n sélection f, choix m; **selective** adj
sélectif(-ive); (school) à recrutement
sélectif

**self** [sɛlf] n (pl **selves**): **the ~** le moi
inv ▷ prefix auto-; **self-assured** adj
sûr(e) de soi, plein(e) d'assurance;
**self-catering** adj (BRIT: flat) avec
cuisine, où l'on peut faire sa cuisine;
(: holiday) en appartement (or chalet etc)
loué; **self-centred** (US **self-centered**)
adj égocentrique; **self-confidence**
n confiance f en soi; **self-confident**
adj sûr(e) de soi, plein(e) d'assurance;
**self-conscious** adj timide, qui
manque d'assurance; **self-contained**

adj (BRIT: flat) avec entrée particulière,
indépendant(e); **self-control** n
maîtrise f de soi; **self-defence** (US
**self-defense**) n autodéfense f; (Law)
légitime défense f; **self-drive** adj (BRIT):
**self-drive car** voiture f de location;
**self-employed** adj qui travaille à
son compte; **self-esteem** n amour-
propre m; **self-indulgent** adj qui ne
se refuse rien; **self-interest** n intérêt
personnel; **selfish** adj égoïste; **self-
pity** n apitoiement m sur soi-même;
**self-raising** [sɛlf'reɪzɪŋ] (US **self-rising**
[sɛlf'raɪzɪŋ]) adj: **self-raising flour**
farine f pour gâteaux (avec levure
incorporée); **self-respect** n respect m de
soi, amour-propre m; **self-service** adj, n
libre-service (m), self-service (m)

**sell** (pt, pp sold) [sɛl, səuld] vt vendre
▷ vi se vendre; **to ~ at or for 10 euros** se
vendre 10 euros; **sell off** vt liquider; **sell
out** vi: **to ~ out (of sth)** (use up stock)
vendre tout son stock (de qch); **sell-by
date** n date f limite de vente; **seller** n
vendeur(-euse), marchand(e)

**Sellotape®** ['sɛləuteɪp] n (BRIT)
scotch® m

**selves** [sɛlvz] npl of **self**

**semester** [sɪ'mɛstəʳ] n (esp US)
semestre m

**semi...** ['sɛmɪ] prefix semi-, demi-; à
demi, à moitié; **semicircle** n demi-
cercle m; **semidetached (house)**
n (BRIT) maison jumelée or jumelle;
**semi-final** n demi-finale f

**seminar** ['sɛmɪnɑːʳ] n séminaire m

**semi-skimmed** ['sɛmɪ'skɪmd] adj
demi-écrémé(e)

**senate** ['sɛnɪt] n sénat m; (US): **the S~** le
Sénat; **senator** n sénateur m

**send** (pt, pp sent) [sɛnd, sɛnt] vt
envoyer; **send back** vt renvoyer; **send
for** vt fus (by post) se faire envoyer,
commander par correspondance; **send
in** vt (report, application, resignation)
remettre; **send off** vt (goods) envoyer,
expédier; (BRIT Sport: player) expulser
or renvoyer du terrain; **send on** vt

(BRIT: *letter*) faire suivre; (*luggage etc: in advance*) (faire) expédier à l'avance; **send out** vt (*invitation*) envoyer (par la poste); (*emit: light, heat, signal*) émettre; **send up** vt (*person, price*) faire monter; (BRIT: *parody*) mettre en boîte, parodier; **sender** n expéditeur(-trice); **send-off** n: **a good send-off** des adieux chaleureux

**senile** ['si:naɪl] adj sénile

**senior** ['si:nɪə'] adj (*high-ranking*) de haut niveau; (*of higher rank*): **to be ~ to sb** être le supérieur de qn; **senior citizen** n personne f du troisième âge; **senior high school** n (US) ≈ lycée m

**sensation** [sɛnˈseɪʃən] n sensation f; **sensational** adj qui fait sensation; (*marvellous*) sensationnel(le)

**sense** [sɛns] n sens m; (*feeling*) sentiment m; (*meaning*) sens, signification f; (*wisdom*) bon sens ▷ vt sentir, pressentir; **it makes ~** c'est logique; **senseless** adj insensé(e), stupide; (*unconscious*) sans connaissance; **sense of humour** (US **sense of humor**) n sens m de l'humour

**sensible** ['sɛnsɪbl] adj sensé(e), raisonnable; (*shoes etc*) pratique

▌ Be careful not to translate *sensible* by the French word *sensible*.

**sensitive** ['sɛnsɪtɪv] adj: **~ (to)** sensible (à)

**sensual** ['sɛnsjuəl] adj sensuel(le)

**sensuous** ['sɛnsjuəs] adj voluptueux(-euse), sensuel(le)

**sent** [sɛnt] pt, pp of **send**

**sentence** ['sɛntns] n (*Ling*) phrase f; (*Law: judgment*) condamnation f, sentence f; (: *punishment*) peine f ▷ vt: **to ~ sb to death/to 5 years** condamner qn à mort/à 5 ans

**sentiment** ['sɛntɪmənt] n sentiment m; (*opinion*) opinion f, avis m; **sentimental** [sɛntɪˈmɛntl] adj sentimental(e)

**Sep.** abbr (= *September*) septembre

**separate** adj ['sɛprɪt] séparé(e); (*organization*) indépendant(e); (*day,*

*occasion, issue*) différent(e) ▷ vb ['sɛpəreɪt] ▷ vt séparer; (*distinguish*) distinguer ▷ vi se séparer; **separately** adv séparément; **separates** npl (*clothes*) coordonnés mpl; **separation** [sɛpəˈreɪʃən] n séparation f

**September** [sɛpˈtɛmbə'] n septembre m

**septic** ['sɛptɪk] adj (*wound*) infecté(e); **septic tank** n fosse f septique

**sequel** ['si:kwl] n conséquence f; séquelles fpl; (*of story*) suite f

**sequence** ['si:kwəns] n ordre m, suite f; (*in film*) séquence f; (*dance*) numéro m

**sequin** ['si:kwɪn] n paillette f

**Serb** [sə:b] adj, n = **Serbian**

**Serbia** ['sə:bɪə] n Serbie f

**Serbian** ['sə:bɪən] adj serbe ▷ n Serbe m/f; (*Ling*) serbe m

**sergeant** ['sa:dʒənt] n sergent m; (*Police*) brigadier m

**serial** ['sɪərɪəl] n feuilleton m; **serial killer** n meurtrier m tuant en série; **serial number** n numéro m de série

**series** ['sɪərɪz] n série f; (*Publishing*) collection f

**serious** ['sɪərɪəs] adj sérieux(-euse); (*accident etc*) grave; **seriously** adv sérieusement; (*hurt*) gravement

**sermon** ['sə:mən] n sermon m

**servant** ['sə:vənt] n domestique m/f; (*fig*) serviteur (servante)

**serve** [sə:v] vt (*employer etc*) servir, être au service de; (*purpose*) servir à; (*customer, food, meal*) servir; (*subj: train*) desservir; (*apprenticeship*) faire, accomplir; (*prison term*) faire; purger ▷ vi (*Tennis*) servir; (*be useful*): **to ~ as/for/to do** servir de/à/à faire ▷ n (*Tennis*) service m; **it ~s him right** c'est bien fait pour lui; **server** n (*Comput*) serveur m

**service** ['sə:vɪs] n (*gen*) service m; (*Aut*) révision f; (*Rel*) office m ▷ vt (*car etc*) réviser; **services** npl (*Econ: tertiary sector*) (secteur m) tertiaire m, secteur des services; (BRIT: *on motorway*) station-service f; (*Mil*): **the**

**S~s** npl les forces armées; **to be of ~ to sb**, **do sb a ~** rendre service à qn; **~ included/not included** service compris/non compris; **service area** n (on motorway) aire f de services; **service charge** n (BRIT) service m; **serviceman** (irreg) n militaire m; **service station** n station-service f

**serviette** [sə:vi'ɛt] n (BRIT) serviette f (de table)

**session** ['sɛʃən] n (sitting) séance f; **to be in ~** siéger, être en session or en séance

**set** [sɛt] n série f, assortiment m; (of tools etc) jeu m; (Radio, TV) poste m; (Tennis) set m; (group of people) cercle m, milieu m; (Cine) plateau m; (Theat: stage) scène f; (: scenery) décor m; (Math) ensemble m; (Hairdressing) mise f en plis ▷ adj (fixed) fixe, déterminé(e); (ready) prêt(e) ▷ vb (pt, pp ~) ▷ vt (place) mettre, poser, placer; (fix, establish) fixer; (: record) établir; (assign: task, homework) donner; (exam) composer; (adjust) régler; (decide: rules etc) fixer, choisir ▷ vi (sun) se coucher; (jam, jelly, concrete) prendre; (bone) se ressouder; **to be ~ on doing** être résolu(e) à faire; **to ~ to music** mettre en musique; **to ~ on fire** mettre le feu à; **to ~ free** libérer; **to ~ sth going** déclencher qch; **to ~ sail** partir, prendre la mer; **set aside** vt mettre de côté; (time) garder; **set down** vt (subj: bus, train) déposer; **set in** vi (infection, bad weather) s'installer; (complications) survenir, surgir; **set off** vi se mettre en route, partir ▷ vt (bomb) faire exploser; (cause to start) déclencher; (show up well) mettre en valeur, faire valoir; **set out** vi: **to ~ out (from)** partir (de) ▷ vt (arrange) disposer; (state) présenter, exposer; **to ~ out to do** entreprendre de faire; avoir pour but or intention de faire; **set up** vt (organization) fonder, créer; **setback** n (hitch) revers m, contretemps m; **set menu** n menu m

**settee** [sɛ'ti:] n canapé m

**setting** ['sɛtɪŋ] n cadre m; (of jewel) monture f; (position: of controls) réglage m

**settle** ['sɛtl] vt (argument, matter, account) régler; (problem) résoudre; (Med: calm) calmer ▷ vi (bird, dust etc) se poser; **to ~ for sth** accepter qch, se contenter de qch; **to ~ on sth** opter or se décider pour qch; **settle down** vi (get comfortable) s'installer; (become calmer) se calmer; se ranger; (live quietly) se fixer; **settle in** vi s'installer; **settle up** vi: **to ~ up with sb** régler (ce que l'on doit à) qn; **settlement** n (payment) règlement m; (agreement) accord m; (village etc) village m, hameau m

**setup** ['sɛtʌp] n (arrangement) manière f dont les choses sont organisées; (situation) situation f, allure f des choses

**seven** ['sɛvn] num sept; **seventeen** num dix-sept; **seventeenth** [sevn'ti:nθ] num dix-septième; **seventh** num septième; **seventieth** ['sevntiiθ] num soixante-dixième; **seventy** num soixante-dix

**sever** ['sɛvər] vt couper, trancher; (relations) rompre

**several** ['sɛvərl] adj, pron plusieurs pl; **~ of us** plusieurs d'entre nous

**severe** [sɪ'vɪər] adj (stern) sévère, strict(e); (serious) grave, sérieux(-euse); (plain) sévère, austère

**sew** (pt ~ed, pp ~n) [səu, səud, səun] vt, vi coudre

**sewage** ['su:ɪdʒ] n vidange(s) f(pl)

**sewer** ['su:ər] n égout m

**sewing** ['səuɪŋ] n couture f; (item(s)) ouvrage m; **sewing machine** n machine f à coudre

**sewn** [səun] pp of **sew**

**sex** [sɛks] n sexe m; **to have ~ with** avoir des rapports (sexuels) avec; **sexism** ['sɛksɪzəm] n sexisme m; **sexist** adj sexiste; **sexual** ['sɛksjuəl] adj sexuel(le); **sexual intercourse** n rapports sexuels; **sexuality** [sɛksju'ælɪtɪ] n sexualité f; **sexy** adj sexy inv

**shabby** ['ʃæbɪ] adj miteux(-euse);

(*behaviour*) mesquin(e), méprisable

**shack** [ʃæk] n cabane f, hutte f

**shade** [ʃeɪd] n ombre f; (*for lamp*) abat-jour m inv; (*of colour*) nuance f, ton m; (*us: window shade*) store m; (*small quantity*): **a ~ of** un soupçon de ▷ vt abriter du soleil, ombrager; **shades** npl (*us: sunglasses*) lunettes fpl de soleil; **in the ~** à l'ombre; **a ~ smaller** un tout petit peu plus petit

**shadow** ['ʃædəʊ] n ombre f ▷ vt (*follow*) filer; **shadow cabinet** n (BRIT Pol) cabinet parallèle formé par le parti qui n'est pas au pouvoir

**shady** ['ʃeɪdɪ] adj ombragé(e); (*fig: dishonest*) louche, véreux(-euse)

**shaft** [ʃɑːft] n (*of arrow, spear*) hampe f; (Aut, Tech) arbre m; (*of mine*) puits m; (*of lift*) cage f; (*of light*) rayon m, trait m

**shake** [ʃeɪk] vb (pt **shook**, pp **~n**) ▷ vt secouer; (*bottle, cocktail*) agiter; (*house, confidence*) ébranler ▷ vi trembler; **to ~ one's head** (*in refusal etc*) dire or faire non de la tête; (*in dismay*) secouer la tête; **to ~ hands with sb** serrer la main à qn; **shake off** vt secouer; (*pursuer*) se débarrasser de; **shake up** vt secouer; **shaky** adj (*hand, voice*) tremblant(e); (*building*) branlant(e), peu solide

**shall** [ʃæl] aux vb: **I ~ go** j'irai; **~ I open the door?** j'ouvre la porte?; **I'll get the coffee, ~ I?** je vais chercher le café, d'accord?

**shallow** ['ʃæləʊ] adj peu profond(e); (*fig*) superficiel(le), qui manque de profondeur

**sham** [ʃæm] n frime f

**shambles** ['ʃæmblz] n confusion f, pagaïe f, fouillis m

**shame** [ʃeɪm] n honte f ▷ vt faire honte à; **it is a ~ (that/to do)** c'est dommage (que + sub/de faire); **what a ~!** quel dommage!; **shameful** adj honteux(-euse), scandaleux(-euse); **shameless** adj éhonté(e), effronté(e)

**shampoo** [ʃæm'puː] n shampooing m ▷ vt faire un shampooing à

**shandy** ['ʃændɪ] n bière panachée

**shan't** [ʃɑːnt] = **shall not**

**shape** [ʃeɪp] n forme f ▷ vt façonner, modeler; (*sb's ideas, character*) former; (*sb's life*) déterminer ▷ vi (*also*: **~ up**: *events*) prendre tournure; (: *person*) faire des progrès, s'en sortir; **to take ~** prendre forme or tournure

**share** [ʃɛəʳ] n part f; (Comm) action f ▷ vt partager; (*have in common*) avoir en commun; **to ~ out (among** or **between)** partager (entre); **shareholder** n (BRIT) actionnaire m/f

**shark** [ʃɑːk] n requin m

**sharp** [ʃɑːp] adj (*razor, knife*) tranchant(e), bien aiguisé(e); (*point, voice*) aigu(ë); (*nose, chin*) pointu(e); (*outline, increase*) net(te); (*cold, pain*) vif (vive); (*taste*) piquant(e), âcre; (Mus) dièse; (*person: quick-witted*) vif (vive), éveillé(e); (: *unscrupulous*) malhonnête ▷ n (Mus) dièse m ▷ adv: **at 2 o'clock ~** à 2 heures pile or tapantes; **sharpen** vt aiguiser; (*pencil*) tailler; (*fig*) aviver; **sharpener** n (*also*: **pencil sharpener**) taille-crayon(s) m inv; **sharply** adv (*turn, stop*) brusquement; (*stand out*) nettement; (*criticize, retort*) sèchement, vertement

**shatter** ['ʃætəʳ] vt briser; (*fig: upset*) bouleverser; (: *ruin*) briser, ruiner ▷ vi voler en éclats, se briser; **shattered** adj (*overwhelmed, grief-stricken*) bouleversé(e); (*inf: exhausted*) éreinté(e)

**shave** [ʃeɪv] vt raser ▷ vi se raser ▷ n: **to have a ~** se raser; **shaver** n (*also*: **electric shaver**) rasoir m électrique

**shaving cream** n crème f à raser

**shaving foam** n mousse f à raser

**shavings** ['ʃeɪvɪŋz] npl (*of wood etc*) copeaux mpl

**shawl** [ʃɔːl] n châle m

**she** [ʃiː] pron elle

**sheath** [ʃiːθ] n gaine f, fourreau m, étui m; (*contraceptive*) préservatif m

**shed** [ʃed] n remise f, resserre f ▷ vt (pt, pp **~**) (*leaves, fur etc*) perdre; (*tears*) verser, répandre; (*workers*) congédier

**she'd** [ʃiːd] = **she had**; **she would**

**sheep** [ʃiːp] n (pl inv) mouton m;
  **sheepdog** n chien m de berger;
  **sheepskin** n peau f de mouton

**sheer** [ʃɪəʳ] adj (utter) pur(e), pur et
  simple; (steep) à pic, abrupt(e); (almost
  transparent) extrêmement fin(e) ▷ adv à
  pic, abruptement

**sheet** [ʃiːt] n (on bed) drap m; (of paper)
  feuille f; (of glass, metal etc) feuille,
  plaque f

**sheik(h)** [ʃeɪk] n cheik m

**shelf** (pl **shelves**) [ʃelf, ʃelvz] n étagère
  f, rayon m

**shell** [ʃel] n (on beach) coquillage m; (of
  egg, nut etc) coquille f; (explosive) obus
  m; (of building) carcasse f ▷ vt (peas)
  écosser; (Mil) bombarder (d'obus)

**she'll** [ʃiːl] = **she will; she shall**

**shellfish** [ʃelfɪʃ] n (pl inv: crab etc)
  crustacé m; (: scallop etc) coquillage m
  ▷ npl (as food) fruits mpl de mer

**shelter** [ʃeltəʳ] n abri m, refuge m
  ▷ vt abriter, protéger; (give lodging to)
  donner asile à ▷ vi s'abriter, se mettre
  à l'abri; **sheltered** adj (life) retiré(e), à
  l'abri des soucis; (spot) abrité(e)

**shelves** [ʃelvz] npl of **shelf**

**shelving** [ʃelvɪŋ] n (shelves)
  rayonnage(s) m(pl)

**shepherd** [ʃepəd] n berger m ▷ vt
  (guide) guider, escorter; **shepherd's pie**
  n ≈ hachis m Parmentier

**sheriff** [ʃerɪf] (us) n shérif m

**sherry** [ʃerɪ] n xérès m, sherry m

**she's** [ʃiːz] = **she is; she has**

**Shetland** [ʃetlənd] n (also: **the ~s, the
  ~ Isles** or **Islands**) les îles fpl Shetland

**shield** [ʃiːld] n bouclier m; (protection)
  écran m de protection ▷ vt: **to ~ (from)**
  protéger (de or contre)

**shift** [ʃɪft] n (change) changement m;
  (work period) période f de travail; (of
  workers) équipe f, poste m ▷ vt déplacer,
  changer de place; (remove) enlever ▷ vi
  changer de place, bouger

**shin** [ʃɪn] n tibia m

**shine** [ʃaɪn] n éclat m, brillant m ▷ vb
  (pt, pp **shone**) ▷ vi briller ▷ vt (torch): **to**

**~ on** braquer sur; (polish: pt, pp **~d**) faire
  briller or reluire

**shingles** [ʃɪŋglz] n (Med) zona m

**shiny** [ʃaɪnɪ] adj brillant(e)

**ship** [ʃɪp] n bateau m; (large) navire
  m ▷ vt transporter (par mer); (send)
  expédier (par mer); **shipment** n
  cargaison f; **shipping** n (ships)
  navires mpl; (traffic) navigation f; (the
  industry) industrie navale; (transport)
  transport m; **shipwreck** n épave
  f; (event) naufrage m ▷ vt: **to be
  shipwrecked** faire naufrage; **shipyard**
  n chantier naval

**shirt** [ʃəːt] n chemise f; (woman's)
  chemisier m; **in ~ sleeves** en bras de
  chemise

**shit** [ʃɪt] excl (inf!) merde (!)

**shiver** [ʃɪvəʳ] n frisson m ▷ vi frissonner

**shock** [ʃɔk] n choc m; (Elec) secousse
  f, décharge f; (Med) commotion
  f, choc ▷ vt (scandalize) choquer,
  scandaliser; (upset) bouleverser;
  **shocking** adj (outrageous) choquant(e),
  scandaleux(-euse); (awful)
  épouvantable

**shoe** [ʃuː] n chaussure f, soulier m;
  (also: **horse~**) fer m à cheval ▷ vt (pt,
  pp **shod**) (horse) ferrer; **shoelace** n lacet
  m (de soulier); **shoe polish** n cirage m;
  **shoeshop** n magasin m de chaussures

**shone** [ʃɔn] pt, pp of **shine**

**shook** [ʃuk] pt of **shake**

**shoot** [ʃuːt] n (on branch, seedling)
  pousse f ▷ vb (pt, pp **shot**) ▷ vt (game:
  hunt) chasser; (: aim at) tirer; (: kill)
  abattre; (person) blesser/tuer d'un
  coup de fusil (or de revolver); (execute)
  fusiller; (arrow) tirer; (gun) tirer un
  coup de; (Cine) tourner ▷ vi (with gun,
  bow): **to ~ (at)** tirer (sur); (Football)
  shooter, tirer; **shoot down** vt (plane)
  abattre; **shoot up** vi (fig: prices etc)
  monter en flèche; **shooting** n (shots)
  coups mpl de feu; (attack) fusillade f;
  (murder) homicide m (à l'aide d'une arme
  à feu); (Hunting) chasse f

**shop** [ʃɔp] n magasin m; (workshop)

atelier *m* ▷ *vi* (*also*: **go ~ping**) faire ses courses *or* ses achats; **shop assistant** *n* (BRIT) vendeur(-euse); **shopkeeper** *n* marchand(e), commerçant(e); **shoplifting** *n* vol *m* à l'étalage; **shopping** *n* (*goods*) achats *mpl*, provisions *fpl*; **shopping bag** *n* sac *m* (à provisions); **shopping centre** (US **shopping center**) *n* centre commercial; **shopping mall** *n* centre commercial; **shopping trolley** *n* (BRIT) Caddie® *m*; **shop window** *n* vitrine *f*

**shore** [ʃɔːʳ] *n* (*of sea, lake*) rivage *m*, rive *f* ▷ *vt*: **to ~ (up)** étayer; **on ~** à terre

**short** [ʃɔːt] *adj* (*not long*) court(e); (*soon finished*) court, bref (brève); (*person, step*) petit(e); (*curt*) brusque, sec (sèche); (*insufficient*) insuffisant(e) ▷ *n* (*also*: **~ film**) court métrage; (*Elec*) court-circuit *m*; **to be ~ of sth** être à court de *or* manquer de qch; **in ~** bref; en bref; **~ of doing** à moins de faire; **everything ~ of** tout sauf; **it is ~ for** c'est l'abréviation *or* le diminutif de; **to cut ~** (*speech, visit*) abréger, écourter; **to fall ~ of** ne pas être à la hauteur de; **to run ~ of** arriver à court de, venir à manquer de; **to stop ~** s'arrêter net; **to stop ~ of** ne pas aller jusqu'à; **shortage** *n* manque *m*, pénurie *f*; **shortbread** *n* ≈ sablé *m*; **shortcoming** *n* défaut *m*; **short(crust) pastry** *n* (BRIT) pâte brisée; **shortcut** *n* raccourci *m*; **shorten** *vt* raccourcir; (*text, visit*) abréger; **shortfall** *n* déficit *m*; **shorthand** *n* (BRIT) sténo(graphie) *f*; **shortlist** *n* (BRIT: *for job*) liste *f* des candidats sélectionnés; **short-lived** *adj* de courte durée; **shortly** *adv* bientôt, sous peu; **shorts** *npl*: **(a pair of) shorts** un short; **short-sighted** *adj* (BRIT) myope; (*fig*) qui manque de clairvoyance; **short-sleeved** *adj* à manches courtes; **short story** *n* nouvelle *f*; **short-tempered** *adj* qui s'emporte facilement; **short-term** *adj* (*effect*) à court terme

**shot** [ʃɔt] *pt, pp* *of* **shoot** ▷ *n* coup *m*

(*de feu*); (*try*) coup, essai *m*; (*injection*) piqûre *f*; (*Phot*) photo *f*; **to be a good/ poor ~** (*person*) tirer bien/mal; **like a ~** comme une flèche; (*very readily*) sans hésiter; **shotgun** *n* fusil *m* de chasse

**should** [ʃud] *aux vb*: **I ~ go now** je devrais partir maintenant; **he ~ be there now** il devrait être arrivé maintenant; **I ~ go if I were you** si j'étais vous j'irais; **I ~ like to** j'aimerais bien, volontiers

**shoulder** [ˈʃəʊldəʳ] *n* épaule *f* ▷ *vt* (*fig*) endosser, se charger de; **shoulder blade** *n* omoplate *f*

**shouldn't** [ˈʃudnt] = **should not**

**shout** [ʃaut] *n* cri *m* ▷ *vt* crier ▷ *vi* crier, pousser des cris

**shove** [ʃʌv] *vt* pousser; (*inf: put*): **to ~ sth in** fourrer *or* ficher qch dans ▷ *n* poussée *f*

**shovel** [ˈʃʌvl] *n* pelle *f* ▷ *vt* pelleter, enlever (*or* enfourner) à la pelle

**show** [ʃəu] *n* (*of emotion*) manifestation *f*, démonstration *f*; (*semblance*) semblant *m*, apparence *f*; (*exhibition*) exposition *f*, salon *m*; (*Theat, TV*) spectacle *m*; (*Cine*) séance *f* ▷ *vb* (*pt* **~ed**, *pp* **~n**) ▷ *vt* montrer; (*film*) passer; (*courage etc*) faire preuve de, manifester; (*exhibit*) exposer ▷ *vi* se voir, être visible; **can you ~ me where it is, please?** pouvez-vous me montrer où c'est?; **to be on ~** être exposé(e); **it's just for ~** c'est juste pour l'effet; **show in** *vt* faire entrer; **show off** *vi* (*pej*) crâner ▷ *vt* (*display*) faire valoir; (*pej*) faire étalage de; **show out** *vt* reconduire à la porte; **show up** *vi* (*stand out*) ressortir; (*inf: turn up*) se montrer ▷ *vt* (*unmask*) démasquer, dénoncer; (*flaw*) faire ressortir; **show business** *n* le monde du spectacle

**shower** [ˈʃauəʳ] *n* (*for washing*) douche *f*; (*rain*) averse *f*; (*of stones etc*) pluie *f*, grêle *f*; (*US: party*) réunion organisée pour la remise de cadeaux ▷ *vi* prendre une douche, se doucher ▷ *vt*: **to ~ sb with** (*gifts etc*) combler qn de; **to have**

*or* **take a ~** prendre une douche, se doucher; **shower cap** *n* bonnet *m* de douche; **shower gel** *n* gel *m* douche

**showing** ['ʃəʊɪŋ] *n* (*of film*) projection *f*

**show jumping** [-dʒʌmpɪŋ] *n* concours *m* hippique

**shown** [ʃəʊn] *pp of* **show**

**show**: **show-off** *n* (*inf*: *person*) crâneur(-euse), m'as-tu-vu(e); **showroom** *n* magasin *m* or salle *f* d'exposition

**shrank** [ʃræŋk] *pt of* **shrink**

**shred** [ʃred] *n* (*gen pl*) lambeau *m*, petit morceau; (*fig*: *of truth, evidence*) parcelle *f* ▷ *vt* mettre en lambeaux, déchirer; (*documents*) détruire; (*Culin*: *grate*) râper; (: *lettuce etc*) couper en lanières

**shrewd** [ʃruːd] *adj* astucieux(-euse), perspicace; (*business person*) habile

**shriek** [ʃriːk] *n* cri perçant *or* aigu, hurlement *m* ▷ *vt*, *vi* hurler, crier

**shrimp** [ʃrɪmp] *n* crevette grise

**shrine** [ʃraɪn] *n* (*place*) lieu *m* de pèlerinage

**shrink** (*pt* **shrank**, *pp* **shrunk**) [ʃrɪŋk, ʃræŋk, ʃrʌŋk] *vi* rétrécir; (*fig*) diminuer; (*also*: **~ away**) reculer ▷ *vt* (*wool*) (faire) rétrécir ▷ *n* (*inf*: *pej*) psychanalyste *m/f*; **to ~ from (doing) sth** reculer devant (la pensée de faire) qch

**shrivel** ['ʃrɪvl] (*also*: **~ up**) *vt* ratatiner, flétrir ▷ *vi* se ratatiner, se flétrir

**shroud** [ʃraud] *n* linceul *m* ▷ *vt*: **~ed in mystery** enveloppé(e) de mystère

**Shrove Tuesday** ['ʃrəuv-] *n* (le) Mardi gras

**shrub** [ʃrʌb] *n* arbuste *m*

**shrug** [ʃrʌg] *n* haussement *m* d'épaules ▷ *vt*, *vi*: **to ~ (one's shoulders)** hausser les épaules; **shrug off** *vt* faire fi de

**shrunk** [ʃrʌŋk] *pp of* **shrink**

**shudder** ['ʃʌdər] *n* frisson *m*, frémissement *m* ▷ *vi* frissonner, frémir

**shuffle** ['ʃʌfl] *vt* (*cards*) battre; **to ~ (one's feet)** traîner les pieds

**shun** [ʃʌn] *vt* éviter, fuir

**shut** (*pt*, *pp* **~**) [ʃʌt] *vt* fermer ▷ *vi* (se) fermer; **shut down** *vt* fermer

définitivement ▷ *vi* fermer définitivement; **shut up** *vi* (*inf*: *keep quiet*) se taire ▷ *vt* (*close*) fermer; (*silence*) faire taire; **shutter** *n* volet *m*; (*Phot*) obturateur *m*

**shuttle** ['ʃʌtl] *n* navette *f*; (*also*: **~ service**) (*service m de*) navette *f*; **shuttlecock** *n* volant *m* (*de badminton*)

**shy** [ʃaɪ] *adj* timide

**siblings** ['sɪblɪŋz] *npl* (*formal*) frères et sœurs *mpl* (*de mêmes parents*)

**Sicily** ['sɪsɪlɪ] *n* Sicile *f*

**sick** [sɪk] *adj* (*ill*) malade; (*BRIT*: *vomiting*): **to be ~** vomir; (*humour*) noir(e), macabre; **to feel ~** avoir envie de vomir, avoir mal au cœur; **to be ~ of** (*fig*) en avoir assez de; **sickening** *adj* (*fig*) écœurant(e), révoltant(e), répugnant(e); **sick leave** *n* congé *m* de maladie; **sickly** *adj* maladif(-ive), souffreteux(-euse); (*causing nausea*) écœurant(e); **sickness** *n* maladie *f*; (*vomiting*) vomissement(s) *m(pl)*

**side** [saɪd] *n* côté *m*; (*of lake, road*) bord *m*; (*of mountain*) versant *m*; (*fig*: *aspect*) côté, aspect *m*; (*team*: *Sport*) équipe *f*; (*TV*: *channel*) chaîne *f* ▷ *adj* (*door, entrance*) latéral(e) ▷ *vi*: **to ~ with sb** prendre le parti de qn, se ranger du côté de qn; **by the ~ of** au bord de; **~ by ~** côte à côte; **to rock from ~ to ~** se balancer; **to take ~s (with)** prendre parti (pour); **sideboard** *n* buffet *m*; **sideboards** (*BRIT*), **sideburns** *npl* (*whiskers*) pattes *fpl*; **side effect** *n* effet *m* secondaire; **sidelight** *n* (*Aut*) veilleuse *f*; **sideline** *n* (*Sport*) (ligne *f* de) touche *f*; (*fig*) activité *f* secondaire; **side order** *n* garniture *f*; **side road** *n* petite route, route transversale; **side street** *n* rue transversale; **sidetrack** *vt* (*fig*) faire dévier de son sujet; **sidewalk** *n* (*US*) trottoir *m*; **sideways** *adv* de côté

**siege** [siːdʒ] *n* siège *m*

**sieve** [sɪv] *n* tamis *m*, passoire *f* ▷ *vt* tamiser, passer (au tamis)

**sift** [sɪft] *vt* passer au tamis *or* au crible; (*fig*) passer au crible

**sigh** [saɪ] n soupir m ▷ vi soupirer, pousser un soupir

**sight** [saɪt] n (faculty) vue f; (spectacle) spectacle m; (on gun) mire f ▷ vt apercevoir; **in ~** visible; (fig) en vue; **out of ~** hors de vue; **sightseeing** n tourisme m; **to go sightseeing** faire du tourisme

**sign** [saɪn] n (gen) signe m; (with hand etc) signe, geste m; (notice) panneau m, écriteau m; (also: **road ~**) panneau de signalisation ▷ vt signer; **where do I ~?** où dois-je signer?; **sign for** vt fus (item) signer le reçu pour; **sign in** vi signer le registre (en arrivant); **sign on** vi (BRIT: as unemployed) s'inscrire au chômage; (enrol) s'inscrire ▷ vt (employee) embaucher; **sign over** vt: **to ~ sth over to sb** céder qch par écrit à qn; **sign up** vi (Mil) s'engager; (for course) s'inscrire

**signal** ['sɪɡnl] n signal m ▷ vi (Aut) mettre son clignotant ▷ vt (person) faire signe à; (message) communiquer par signaux

**signature** ['sɪɡnətʃəʳ] n signature f

**significance** [sɪɡ'nɪfɪkəns] n signification f; importance f

**significant** [sɪɡ'nɪfɪkənt] adj significatif(-ive); (important) important(e), considérable

**signify** ['sɪɡnɪfaɪ] vt signifier

**sign language** n langage m par signes

**signpost** ['saɪnpəʊst] n poteau indicateur

**Sikh** [siːk] adj, n Sikh m/f

**silence** ['saɪləns] n silence m ▷ vt faire taire, réduire au silence

**silent** ['saɪlnt] adj silencieux(-euse); (film) muet(te); **to keep** or **remain ~** garder le silence, ne rien dire

**silhouette** [sɪluː'ɛt] n silhouette f

**silicon chip** ['sɪlɪkən-] n puce f électronique

**silk** [sɪlk] n soie f ▷ cpd de or en soie

**silly** ['sɪlɪ] adj stupide, sot(te), bête

**silver** ['sɪlvəʳ] n argent m; (money) monnaie f (en pièces d'argent); (also: **~ware**) argenterie f ▷ adj (made of

silver) d'argent, en argent; (in colour) argenté(e); **silver-plated** adj plaqué(e) argent

**similar** ['sɪmɪləʳ] adj: **~ (to)** semblable (à); **similarity** [sɪmɪ'lærɪtɪ] n ressemblance f, similarité f; **similarly** adv de la même façon, de même

**simmer** ['sɪməʳ] vi cuire à feu doux, mijoter

**simple** ['sɪmpl] adj simple; **simplicity** [sɪm'plɪsɪtɪ] n simplicité f; **simplify** ['sɪmplɪfaɪ] vt simplifier; **simply** adv simplement; (without fuss) avec simplicité; (absolutely) absolument

**simulate** ['sɪmjuleɪt] vt simuler, feindre

**simultaneous** [sɪməl'teɪnɪəs] adj simultané(e); **simultaneously** adv simultanément

**sin** [sɪn] n péché m ▷ vi pécher

**since** [sɪns] adv, prep depuis ▷ conj (time) depuis que; (because) puisque, étant donné que, comme; **~ then**, **ever ~** depuis ce moment-là

**sincere** [sɪn'sɪəʳ] adj sincère; **sincerely** adv sincèrement; **Yours sincerely** (at end of letter) veuillez agréer, Monsieur (or Madame) l'expression de mes sentiments distingués or les meilleurs

**sing** (pt **sang**, pp **sung**) [sɪŋ, sæŋ, sʌŋ] vt, vi chanter

**Singapore** [sɪŋɡə'pɔːʳ] n Singapour m

**singer** ['sɪŋəʳ] n chanteur(-euse)

**singing** ['sɪŋɪŋ] n (of person, bird) chant m

**single** ['sɪŋgl] adj seul(e), unique; (unmarried) célibataire; (not double) simple ▷ n (BRIT: also: **~ ticket**) aller m (simple); (record) 45 tours m; **singles** npl (Tennis) simple m; **every ~ day** chaque jour sans exception; **single out** vt choisir; (distinguish) distinguer; **single bed** n lit m d'une personne or à une place; **single file** n: **in single file** en file indienne; **single-handed** adv tout(e) seul(e), sans (aucune) aide; **single-minded** adj résolu(e), tenace; **single parent** n parent unique (or célibataire); **single-parent family** famille monoparentale; **single room** n chambre f à un lit or pour une personne

**singular** ['sɪŋgjuləʳ] adj singulier(-ière); (odd) singulier, étrange; (outstanding) remarquable; (Ling) (au) singulier, du singulier ▷ n (Ling) singulier m

**sinister** ['sɪnɪstəʳ] adj sinistre

**sink** [sɪŋk] n évier m; (washbasin) lavabo m ▷ vb (pt **sank**, pp **sunk**) ▷ vt (ship) (faire) couler, faire sombrer; (foundations) creuser ▷ vi couler, sombrer; (ground etc) s'affaisser; **to ~ into sth** (chair) s'enfoncer dans qch; **sink in** vi (explanation) rentrer (inf), être compris

**sinus** ['saɪnəs] n (Anat) sinus m inv

**sip** [sɪp] n petite gorgée ▷ vt boire à petites gorgées

**sir** [səʳ] n monsieur m; **S~ John Smith** sir John Smith; **yes ~** oui Monsieur

**siren** ['saɪərn] n sirène f

**sirloin** ['səːlɔɪn] n (also: ~ **steak**) aloyau m

**sister** ['sɪstəʳ] n sœur f; (nun) religieuse f, (bonne) sœur; (BRIT: nurse) infirmière f en chef; **sister-in-law** n belle-sœur f

**sit** (pt, pp **sat**) [sɪt, sæt] vi s'asseoir; (be sitting) être assis(e); (assembly) être en séance, siéger; (for painter) poser ▷ vt (exam) passer, se présenter à; **sit back** vi (in seat) bien s'installer, se carrer; **sit down** vi s'asseoir; **sit on** vt fus (jury, committee) faire partie de; **sit up** vi s'asseoir; (straight) se redresser; (not go to bed) rester debout, ne pas se coucher

**sitcom** ['sɪtkɔm] n abbr (TV: = situation comedy) sitcom f, comédie f de situation

**site** [saɪt] n emplacement m, site m; (also: **building ~**) chantier m ▷ vt placer

**sitting** ['sɪtɪŋ] n (of assembly etc) séance f; (in canteen) service m; **sitting room** n salon m

**situated** ['sɪtjueɪtɪd] adj situé(e)

**situation** [sɪtjuˈeɪʃən] n situation f; **"~s vacant/wanted"** (BRIT) "offres/demandes d'emploi"

**six** [sɪks] num six; **sixteen** num seize; **sixteenth** [sɪksˈtiːnθ] num seizième; **sixth** ['sɪksθ] num sixième; **sixth form** n (BRIT) ≈ classes fpl de première et de terminale; **sixth-form college** n lycée n'ayant que des classes de première et de terminale; **sixtieth** ['sɪkstɪɪθ] num soixantième; **sixty** num soixante

**size** [saɪz] n dimensions fpl; (of person) taille f; (of clothing) taille; (of shoes) pointure f; (of problem) ampleur f; (glue) colle f; **sizeable** adj assez grand(e); (amount, problem, majority) assez important(e)

**sizzle** ['sɪzl] vi grésiller

**skate** [skeɪt] n patin m; (fish: pl inv) raie f ▷ vi patiner; **skateboard** n skateboard m, planche f à roulettes; **skateboarding** n skateboard m; **skater** n patineur(-euse); **skating** n patinage m; **skating rink** n patinoire f

**skeleton** ['skɛlɪtn] n squelette m; (outline) schéma m

**skeptical** ['skɛptɪkl] (US) = **sceptical**

**sketch** [skɛtʃ] n (drawing) croquis m, esquisse f; (outline plan) aperçu m; (Theat) sketch m, saynète f ▷ vt esquisser, faire un croquis or une esquisse de; (plan etc) esquisser

**skewer** ['skjuːəʳ] n brochette f

**ski** [skiː] n ski m ▷ vi skier, faire du ski; **ski boot** n chaussure f de ski

**skid** [skɪd] n dérapage m ▷ vi déraper

**ski: skier** n skieur(-euse); **skiing** n ski m; **to go skiing** (aller) faire du ski

**skilful** (US **skillful**) ['skɪlful] adj habile, adroit(e)

**ski lift** n remonte-pente m inv

**skill** [skɪl] n (ability) habileté f, adresse f, talent m; (requiring training) compétences fpl; **skilled** adj habile, adroit(e); (worker) qualifié(e)

**skim** [skɪm] vt (soup) écumer; (glide over) raser, effleurer ▷ vi: **to ~ through** (fig) parcourir; **skimmed milk** (US **skim milk**) n lait écrémé

**skin** [skɪn] n peau f ▷ vt (fruit etc) éplucher; (animal) écorcher; **skinhead**

*n* skinhead *m*; **skinny** *adj* maigre, maigrichon(ne)

**skip** [skɪp] *n* petit bond *or* saut; (BRIT: *container*) benne *f* ▷ *vi* gambader, sautiller; (*with rope*) sauter à la corde ▷ *vt* (*pass over*) sauter

**ski**: **ski pass** *n* forfait-skieur(s) *m*; **ski pole** *n* bâton *m* de ski

**skipper** ['skɪpəʳ] *n* (*Naut, Sport*) capitaine *m*; (*in race*) skipper *m*

**skipping rope** ['skɪpɪŋ-] (US **skip rope**) *n* (BRIT) corde *f* à sauter

**skirt** [skəːt] *n* jupe *f* ▷ *vt* longer, contourner

**skirting board** ['skəːtɪŋ-] *n* (BRIT) plinthe *f*

**ski slope** *n* piste *f* de ski

**ski suit** *n* combinaison *f* de ski

**skull** [skʌl] *n* crâne *m*

**skunk** [skʌŋk] *n* mouffette *f*

**sky** [skaɪ] *n* ciel *m*; **skyscraper** *n* gratte-ciel *m inv*

**slab** [slæb] *n* (*of stone*) dalle *f*; (*of meat, cheese*) tranche épaisse

**slack** [slæk] *adj* (*loose*) lâche, desserré(e); (*slow*) stagnant(e); (*careless*) négligent(e), peu sérieux(-euse) *or* consciencieux(-euse); **slacks** *npl* pantalon *m*

**slain** [sleɪn] *pp of* **slay**

**slam** [slæm] *vt* (*door*) (faire) claquer; (*throw*) jeter violemment, flanquer; (*inf: criticize*) éreinter, démolir ▷ *vi* claquer

**slander** ['slɑːndəʳ] *n* calomnie *f*; (*Law*) diffamation *f*

**slang** [slæŋ] *n* argot *m*

**slant** [slɑːnt] *n* inclinaison *f*; (*fig*) angle *m*, point *m* de vue

**slap** [slæp] *n* claque *f*, gifle *f*; (*on the back*) tape *f* ▷ *vt* donner une claque *or* une gifle (*or* une tape) à; **to ~ on** (*paint*) appliquer rapidement ▷ *adv* (*directly*) tout droit, en plein

**slash** [slæʃ] *vt* entailler, taillader; (*fig: prices*) casser

**slate** [sleɪt] *n* ardoise *f* ▷ *vt* (*fig: criticize*) éreinter, démolir

**slaughter** ['slɔːtəʳ] *n* carnage *m*,

massacre *m*; (*of animals*) abattage *m* ▷ *vt* (*animal*) abattre; (*people*) massacrer; **slaughterhouse** *n* abattoir *m*

**Slav** [slɑːv] *adj* slave

**slave** [sleɪv] *n* esclave *m/f* ▷ *vi* (*also*: **~ away**) trimer, travailler comme un forçat; **slavery** *n* esclavage *m*

**slay** (*pt* **slew**, *pp* **slain**) [sleɪ, sluː, sleɪn] *vt* (*literary*) tuer

**sleazy** ['sliːzɪ] *adj* miteux(-euse), minable

**sled** [slɛd] (US) = **sledge**

**sledge** [slɛdʒ] *n* luge *f*

**sleek** [sliːk] *adj* (*hair, fur*) brillant(e), luisant(e); (*car, boat*) aux lignes pures *or* élégantes

**sleep** [sliːp] *n* sommeil *m* ▷ *vi* (*pt, pp* **slept**) dormir; **to go to ~** s'endormir; **sleep in** *vi* (*oversleep*) se réveiller trop tard; (*on purpose*) faire la grasse matinée; **sleep together** *vi* (*have sex*) coucher ensemble; **sleeper** *n* (*person*) dormeur(-euse); (BRIT Rail: *on track*) traverse *f*; (: *train*) train-couchettes *m*; (: *berth*) couchette *f*; **sleeping bag** *n* sac *m* de couchage; **sleeping car** *n* wagon-lits *m*, voiture-lits *f*; **sleeping pill** *n* somnifère *m*; **sleepover** *n* nuit *f* chez un copain *or* une copine; **we're having a sleepover at Jo's** nous allons passer la nuit chez Jo; **sleepwalk** *vi* marcher en dormant; **sleepy** *adj* (*fig*) endormi(e)

**sleet** [sliːt] *n* neige fondue

**sleeve** [sliːv] *n* manche *f*; (*of record*) pochette *f*; **sleeveless** *adj* (*garment*) sans manches

**sleigh** [sleɪ] *n* traîneau *m*

**slender** ['slɛndəʳ] *adj* svelte, mince; (*fig*) faible, ténu(e)

**slept** [slɛpt] *pt, pp of* **sleep**

**slew** [sluː] *pt of* **slay**

**slice** [slaɪs] *n* tranche *f*; (*round*) rondelle *f*; (*utensil*) spatule *f*; (*also*: **fish ~**) pelle *f* à poisson ▷ *vt* couper en tranches (*or* en rondelles)

**slick** [slɪk] *adj* (*skilful*) bien ficelé(e);

(*salesperson*) qui a du bagout ▷ *n* (*also*: **oil ~**) nappe *f* de pétrole, marée noire

**slide** [slaɪd] *n* (*in playground*) toboggan *m*; (*Phot*) diapositive *f*; (BRIT: *also*: **hair ~**) barrette *f*; (*in prices*) chute *f*, baisse *f* ▷ *vb* (*pt, pp* **slid**) ▷ *vt* (faire) glisser ▷ *vi* glisser; **sliding** *adj* (*door*) coulissant(e)

**slight** [slaɪt] *adj* (*slim*) mince, menu(e); (*frail*) frêle; (*trivial*) faible, insignifiant(e); (*small*) petit(e), léger(-ère) *before n* ▷ *n* offense *f*, affront *m* ▷ *vt* (*offend*) blesser, offenser; **not in the ~est** pas le moins du monde, pas du tout; **slightly** *adv* légèrement, un peu

**slim** [slɪm] *adj* mince ▷ *vi* maigrir; (*diet*) suivre un régime amaigrissant; **slimming** *n* amaigrissement *m* ▷ *adj* (*diet, pills*) amaigrissant(e), pour maigrir; (*food*) qui ne fait pas grossir

**slimy** ['slaɪmɪ] *adj* visqueux(-euse), gluant(e)

**sling** [slɪŋ] *n* (*Med*) écharpe *f*; (*for baby*) porte-bébé *m*; (*weapon*) fronde *f*, lance-pierre *m* ▷ *vt* (*pt, pp* **slung**) lancer, jeter

**slip** [slɪp] *n* faux pas *m*; (*mistake*) erreur *f*, bévue *f*; (*underskirt*) combinaison *f*; (*of paper*) petite feuille, fiche *f* ▷ *vt* (*slide*) glisser ▷ *vi* (*slide*) glisser; (*move smoothly*): **to ~ into/out of** se glisser or se faufiler dans/hors de; (*decline*) baisser; **to ~ sth on/off** enfiler/enlever qch; **to give sb the ~** fausser compagnie à qn; **a ~ of the tongue** un lapsus; **slip up** *vi* faire une erreur, gaffer

**slipped disc** [slɪpt-] *n* déplacement *m* de vertèbre

**slipper** ['slɪpəʳ] *n* pantoufle *f*

**slippery** ['slɪpərɪ] *adj* glissant(e)

**slip road** *n* (BRIT: *to motorway*) bretelle *f* d'accès

**slit** [slɪt] *n* fente *f*; (*cut*) incision *f* ▷ *vt* (*pt, pp* **~**) fendre; couper, inciser

**slog** [slɒg] *n* (BRIT: *effort*) gros effort; (: *work*) tâche fastidieuse ▷ *vi* travailler très dur

**slogan** ['sləʊgən] *n* slogan *m*

**slope** [sləʊp] *n* pente *f*, côte *f*; (*side of mountain*) versant *m*; (*slant*) inclinaison *f* ▷ *vi*: **to ~ down** être *or* descendre en pente; **to ~ up** monter; **sloping** *adj* en pente, incliné(e); (*handwriting*) penché(e)

**sloppy** ['slɒpɪ] *adj* (*work*) peu soigné(e), bâclé(e); (*appearance*) négligé(e), débraillé(e)

**slot** [slɒt] *n* fente *f* ▷ *vt*: **to ~ sth into** encastrer *or* insérer qch dans; **slot machine** *n* (BRIT: *vending machine*) distributeur *m* (automatique), machine *f* à sous; (*for gambling*) appareil *m* *or* machine à sous

**Slovakia** [sləʊ'vækɪə] *n* Slovaquie *f*

**Slovene** [sləʊ'viːn] *adj* slovène ▷ *n* Slovène *m/f*; (*Ling*) slovène *m*

**Slovenia** [sləʊ'viːnɪə] *n* Slovénie *f*; **Slovenian** *adj*, *n* = **Slovene**

**slow** [sləʊ] *adj* lent(e); (*watch*): **to be ~** retarder ▷ *adv* lentement ▷ *vt*, *vi* ralentir; **"~"** (*road sign*) "ralentir"; **slow down** *vi* ralentir; **slowly** *adv* lentement; **slow motion** *n*: **in slow motion** au ralenti

**slug** [slʌg] *n* limace *f*; (*bullet*) balle *f*; **sluggish** *adj* (*person*) mou (molle), lent(e); (*stream, engine, trading*) lent(e)

**slum** [slʌm] *n* (*house*) taudis *m*; **slums** *npl* (*area*) quartiers *mpl* pauvres

**slump** [slʌmp] *n* baisse soudaine, effondrement *m*; (*Econ*) crise *f* ▷ *vi* s'effondrer, s'affaisser

**slung** [slʌŋ] *pt, pp of* **sling**

**slur** [sləːʳ] *n* (*smear*): **~ (on)** atteinte *f* (à); insinuation *f* (contre) ▷ *vt* mal articuler

**slush** [slʌʃ] *n* neige fondue

**sly** [slaɪ] *adj* (*person*) rusé(e); (*smile, expression, remark*) sournois(e)

**smack** [smæk] *n* (*slap*) tape *f*; (*on face*) gifle *f* ▷ *vt* donner une tape à; (*on face*) gifler; (*on bottom*) donner la fessée à ▷ *vi*: **to ~ of** avoir des relents de, sentir

**small** [smɔːl] *adj* petit(e); **small ads** *npl* (BRIT) petites annonces; **small change** *n* petite *or* menue monnaie

**smart** [smɑːt] *adj* élégant(e), chic

*inv*; (*clever*) intelligent(e); (*quick*) vif
(vive), prompt(e) ▷ *vi* faire mal, brûler;
**smartcard** *n* carte *f* à puce

**smash** [smæʃ] *n* (*also*: **~-up**) collision
*f*, accident *m*; (*Mus*) succès foudroyant
▷ *vt* casser, briser, fracasser; (*opponent*)
écraser; (*Sport: record*) pulvériser ▷ *vi* se
briser, se fracasser; s'écraser; **smashing**
*adj* (*inf*) formidable

**smear** [smɪəʳ] *n* (*stain*) tache *f*; (*mark*)
trace *f*; (*Med*) frottis *m* ▷ *vt* enduire;
(*make dirty*) salir; **smear test** *n* (BRIT
*Med*) frottis *m*

**smell** [smɛl] *n* odeur *f*; (*sense*) odorat
*m* ▷ *vb* (*pt, pp* **smelt** *or* **~ed**) ▷ *vt* sentir
▷ *vi* (*pej*) sentir mauvais; **smelly** *adj* qui
sent mauvais, malodorant(e)

**smelt** [smɛlt] *pt, pp of* **smell**

**smile** [smaɪl] *n* sourire *m* ▷ *vi* sourire

**smirk** [smə:k] *n* petit sourire suffisant
*or* affecté

**smog** [smɔg] *n* brouillard mêlé de
fumée

**smoke** [sməuk] *n* fumée *f* ▷ *vt, vi*
fumer; **do you mind if I ~?** ça ne vous
dérange pas que je fume?; **smoke
alarm** *n* détecteur *m* de fumée;
**smoked** *adj* (*bacon, glass*) fumé(e);
**smoker** *n* (*person*) fumeur(-euse); (*Rail*)
wagon *m* fumeurs; **smoking** *n*: **"no
smoking"** (*sign*) "défense de fumer";
**smoky** *adj* enfumé(e); (*taste*) fumé(e)

**smooth** [smu:ð] *adj* lisse; (*sauce*)
onctueux(-euse); (*flavour, whisky*)
moelleux(-euse); (*movement*)
régulier(-ière), sans à-coups *or* heurts;
(*flight*) sans secousses; (*pej: person*)
doucereux(-euse), mielleux(-euse) ▷ *vt*
(*also*: **~ out**) lisser, défroisser; (*creases,
difficulties*) faire disparaître

**smother** ['smʌðəʳ] *vt* étouffer

**SMS** *n abbr* (= *short message service*)
SMS *m*; **SMS message** *n* message
*m* SMS

**smudge** [smʌdʒ] *n* tache *f*, bavure *f* ▷ *vt*
salir, maculer

**smug** [smʌg] *adj* suffisant(e),
content(e) de soi

**smuggle** ['smʌgl] *vt* passer en
contrebande *or* en fraude; **smuggling** *n*
contrebande *f*

**snack** [snæk] *n* casse-croûte *m inv*;
**snack bar** *n* snack(-bar) *m*

**snag** [snæg] *n* inconvénient *m*,
difficulté *f*

**snail** [sneɪl] *n* escargot *m*

**snake** [sneɪk] *n* serpent *m*

**snap** [snæp] *n* (*sound*) claquement
*m*, bruit sec; (*photograph*) photo *f*,
instantané *m* ▷ *adj* subit(e), fait(e) sans
réfléchir ▷ *vt* (*fingers*) faire claquer;
(*break*) casser net ▷ *vi* se casser net
avec un bruit sec; (*speak sharply*) parler
d'un ton brusque; **to ~ open/shut**
s'ouvrir/se refermer brusquement;
**snap at** *vt fus* (*subj: dog*) essayer de
mordre; **snap up** *vt* sauter sur, saisir;
**snapshot** *n* photo *f*, instantané *m*

**snarl** [snɑ:l] *vi* gronder

**snatch** [snætʃ] *n* (*small amount*) ▷ *vt*
saisir (*d'un geste vif*); (*steal*) voler; **to ~
some sleep** arriver à dormir un peu

**sneak** [sni:k] (*US: pt* **snuck**) *vi*: **to ~
in/out** entrer/sortir furtivement *or* à
la dérobée ▷ *n* (*inf: pej: informer*) faux
jeton; **to ~ up on sb** s'approcher de qn
sans faire de bruit; **sneakers** *npl* tennis
*mpl*, baskets *fpl*

**sneer** [snɪəʳ] *vi* ricaner; **to ~ at sb/sth**
se moquer de qn/qch avec mépris

**sneeze** [sni:z] *vi* éternuer

**sniff** [snɪf] *vi* renifler ▷ *vt* renifler,
flairer; (*glue, drug*) sniffer, respirer

**snigger** ['snɪgəʳ] *vi* ricaner

**snip** [snɪp] *n* (*cut*) entaille *f*; (BRIT: *inf:
bargain*) (bonne) occasion *or* affaire
▷ *vt* couper

**sniper** ['snaɪpəʳ] *n* (*marksman*) tireur
embusqué

**snob** [snɔb] *n* snob *m/f*

**snooker** ['snu:kəʳ] *n* sorte de jeu de
billard

**snoop** [snu:p] *vi*: **to ~ about** fureter

**snooze** [snu:z] *n* petit somme ▷ *vi*
faire un petit somme

**snore** [snɔːʳ] *vi* ronfler ▷ *n*

ronflement m

**snorkel** ['snɔːkl] n (of swimmer) tuba m

**snort** [snɔːt] n grognement m ▷ vi grogner; (horse) renâcler

**snow** [snəu] n neige f ▷ vi neiger; **snowball** n boule f de neige; **snowdrift** n congère f; **snowman** (irreg) n bonhomme m de neige; **snowplough** (US **snowplow**) n chasse-neige m inv; **snowstorm** n tempête f de neige

**snub** [snʌb] vt repousser, snober ▷ n rebuffade f

**snug** [snʌg] adj douillet(te), confortable; (person) bien au chaud

 **KEYWORD**

**so** [səu] adv **1** (thus, likewise) ainsi, de cette façon; **if so** si oui; **so do** or **have I** moi aussi; **it's 5 o'clock - so it is!** il est 5 heures - en effet! or c'est vrai!; **I hope/think so** je l'espère/le crois; **so far** jusqu'ici, jusqu'à maintenant; (in past) jusque-là

**2** (in comparisons etc: to such a degree) si, tellement; **so big (that)** si or tellement grand (que); **she's not so clever as her brother** elle n'est pas aussi intelligente que son frère

**3**: **so much** adj, adv tant (de); **I've got so much work** j'ai tant de travail; **I love you so much** je vous aime tant; **so many** tant (de)

**4** (phrases): **10 or so** à peu près or environ 10; **so long!** (inf: goodbye) au revoir!, à un de ces jours!; **so (what)?** (inf) (bon) et alors?, et après?

▷ conj **1** (expressing purpose): **so as to do** pour faire, afin de faire; **so (that)** pour que or afin que + sub

**2** (expressing result) donc, par conséquent; **so that** si bien que, de (telle) sorte que; **so that's the reason!** c'est donc (pour) ça!; **so you see, I could have gone** alors tu vois, j'aurais pu y aller

**soak** [səuk] vt faire or laisser tremper; (drench) tremper ▷ vi tremper; **soak up** vt absorber; **soaking** adj (also: **soaking wet**) trempé(e)

**so-and-so** ['səuənsəu] n (somebody) un(e) tel(le)

**soap** [səup] n savon m; **soap opera** n feuilleton télévisé (quotidienneté réaliste ou embellie); **soap powder** n lessive f, détergent m

**soar** [sɔːʳ] vi monter (en flèche), s'élancer; (building) s'élancer

**sob** [sɔb] n sanglot m ▷ vi sangloter

**sober** ['səubəʳ] adj qui n'est pas (or plus) ivre; (serious) sérieux(-euse), sensé(e); (colour, style) sobre, discret(-ète); **sober up** vi se dégriser

**so-called** ['səu'kɔːld] adj soi-disant inv

**soccer** ['sɔkəʳ] n football m

**sociable** ['səuʃəbl] adj sociable

**social** ['səuʃl] adj social(e); (sociable) sociable ▷ n (petite) fête; **socialism** n socialisme m; **socialist** adj, n socialiste (m/f); **socialize** vi: **to socialize with** (meet others) fréquenter; (get to know) lier connaissance or parler avec; **social life** n vie sociale; **socially** adv socialement, en société; **social security** n aide sociale; **social services** npl services sociaux; **social work** n assistance sociale; **social worker** n assistant(e) sociale(e)

**society** [sə'saɪətɪ] n société f; (club) société, association f; (also: **high ~**) (haute) société, grand monde

**sociology** [səusɪ'ɔlədʒɪ] n sociologie f

**sock** [sɔk] n chaussette f

**socket** ['sɔkɪt] n cavité f; (Elec: also: **wall ~**) prise f de courant

**soda** ['səudə] n (Chem) soude f; (also: **~ water**) eau f de Seltz; (US: also: **~ pop**) soda m

**sodium** ['səudɪəm] n sodium m

**sofa** ['səufə] n sofa m, canapé m; **sofa bed** n canapé-lit m

**soft** [sɔft] adj (not rough) doux (douce); (not hard) doux, mou (molle); (not loud) doux, léger(-ère); (kind) doux, gentil(le); **soft drink** n boisson non alcoolisée;

**soft drugs** npl drogues douces; **soften**
['sɔfn] vt (r)amollir; (fig) adoucir ▷ vi
se ramollir; (fig) s'adoucir; **softly** adv
doucement; (touch) légèrement; (kiss)
tendrement; **software** n (Comput)
logiciel m, software m

**soggy** ['sɔgɪ] adj (clothes) trempé(e);
(ground) détrempé(e)

**soil** [sɔɪl] n (earth) sol m, terre f ▷ vt salir;
(fig) souiller

**solar** ['səulər] adj solaire; **solar power**
n énergie f solaire; **solar system** n
système m solaire

**sold** [səuld] pt, pp of **sell**

**soldier** ['səuldʒər] n soldat m,
militaire m

**sold out** adj (Comm) épuisé(e)

**sole** [səul] n (of foot) plante f; (of shoe)
semelle f; (fish: pl inv) sole f ▷ adj
seul(e), unique; **solely** adv seulement,
uniquement

**solemn** ['sɔləm] adj solennel(le);
(person) sérieux(-euse), grave

**solicitor** [sə'lɪsɪtər] n (BRIT: for wills etc)
≈ notaire m; (: in court) ≈ avocat m

**solid** ['sɔlɪd] adj (not liquid) solide; (not
hollow: mass) compact(e); (: metal, rock,
wood) massif(-ive) ▷ n solide m

**solitary** ['sɔlɪtərɪ] adj solitaire

**solitude** ['sɔlɪtjuːd] n solitude f

**solo** ['səuləu] n solo m ▷ adv (fly) en
solitaire; **soloist** n soliste m/f

**soluble** ['sɔljubl] adj soluble

**solution** [sə'luːʃən] n solution f

**solve** [sɔlv] vt résoudre

**solvent** ['sɔlvənt] adj (Comm) solvable
▷ n (Chem) (dis)solvant m

**sombre** (us **somber**) ['sɔmbər] adj
sombre, morne

 **KEYWORD**

**some** [sʌm] adj 1 (a certain amount
or number of): **some tea/water/ice
cream** du thé/de l'eau/de la glace;
**some children/apples** des enfants/
pommes; **I've got some money but
not much** j'ai de l'argent mais pas
beaucoup

2 (certain: in contrasts): **some people
say that ...** il y a des gens qui disent
que ...; **some films were excellent,
but most were mediocre** certains
films étaient excellents, mais la plupart
étaient médiocres

3 (unspecified): **some woman was
asking for you** il y avait une dame qui
vous demandait; **he was asking for
some book (or other)** il demandait un
livre quelconque; **some day** un de ces
jours; **some day next week** un jour la
semaine prochaine

▷ pron 1 (a certain number) quelques-
un(e)s, certain(e)s; **I've got some**
(books etc) j'en ai (quelques-uns); **some
(of them) have been sold** certains ont
été vendus

2 (a certain amount) un peu; **I've got
some** (money, milk) j'en ai (un peu);
**would you like some?** est-ce que vous
en voulez?, en voulez-vous?; **could I
have some of that cheese?** pourrais-
je avoir un peu de ce fromage?; **I've
read some of the book** j'ai lu une
partie du livre

▷ adv: **some 10 people** quelque 10
personnes, 10 personnes environ;
**somebody** ['sʌmbədɪ] pron
= **someone**; **somehow** adv d'une
façon ou d'une autre; (for some
reason) pour une raison ou une
autre; **someone** pron quelqu'un;
**someplace** adv (us) = **somewhere**;
**something** pron quelque chose m;
**something interesting** quelque
chose d'intéressant; **something to do**
quelque chose à faire; **sometime** adv
(in future) un de ces jours, un jour ou
l'autre; (in past): **sometime last month**
au cours du mois dernier; **sometimes**
adv quelquefois, parfois; **somewhat**
adv quelque peu, un peu; **somewhere**
adv quelque part; **somewhere else**
ailleurs, autre part

**son** [sʌn] n fils m

**song** [sɒŋ] n chanson f; (of bird) chant m
**son-in-law** ['sʌnɪnlɔː] n gendre m,
beau-fils m
**soon** [suːn] adv bientôt; (early) tôt;
**~ afterwards** peu après; see also **as**;
**sooner** adv (time) plus tôt; (preference):
**I would sooner do that** j'aimerais
autant or je préférerais faire ça; **sooner
or later** tôt ou tard
**soothe** [suːð] vt calmer, apaiser
**sophisticated** [səˈfɪstɪkeɪtɪd] adj
raffiné(e), sophistiqué(e); (machinery)
hautement perfectionné(e), très
complexe
**sophomore** ['sɒfəmɔːʳ] n (us)
étudiant(e) de seconde année
**soprano** [səˈprɑːnəu] n (singer)
soprano m/f
**sorbet** ['sɔːbeɪ] n sorbet m
**sordid** ['sɔːdɪd] adj sordide
**sore** [sɔːʳ] adj (painful)
douloureux(-euse), sensible ▷ n plaie f
**sorrow** ['sɒrəu] n peine f, chagrin m
**sorry** ['sɒrɪ] adj désolé(e); (condition,
excuse, tale) triste, déplorable; **~!**
pardon!, excusez-moi!; **~?** pardon?; **to
feel ~ for sb** plaindre qn
**sort** [sɔːt] n genre m, espèce f, sorte f;
(make: of coffee, car etc) marque f ▷ vt
(also: **~ out**: select which to keep) trier;
(classify) classer; (tidy) ranger; **sort out**
vt (problem) résoudre, régler
**SOS** n SOS m
**so-so** ['səusəu] adv comme ci
comme ça
**sought** [sɔːt] pt, pp of **seek**
**soul** [səul] n âme f
**sound** [saund] adj (healthy) en bonne
santé, sain(e); (safe, not damaged)
solide, en bon état; (reliable, not
superficial) sérieux(-euse), solide;
(sensible) sensé(e) ▷ adv: **~ asleep**
profondément endormi(e) ▷ n (noise,
volume) son m; (louder) bruit m; (Geo)
détroit m, bras m de mer ▷ vt (alarm)
sonner ▷ vi sonner, retentir; (fig: seem)
sembler (être); **to ~ like** ressembler à;
**sound bite** n phrase toute faite (pour

être citée dans les médias); **soundtrack** n
(of film) bande f sonore
**soup** [suːp] n soupe f, potage m
**sour** ['sauəʳ] adj aigre; **it's ~ grapes**
c'est du dépit
**source** [sɔːs] n source f
**south** [sauθ] n sud m ▷ adj sud inv;
(wind) du sud ▷ adv au sud, vers le
sud; **South Africa** n Afrique f du Sud;
**South African** adj sud-africain(e)
▷ n Sud-Africain(e); **South America**
n Amérique f du Sud; **South
American** adj sud-américain(e) ▷ n
Sud-Américain(e); **southbound** adj
en direction du sud; (carriageway)
sud inv; **south-east** n sud-est m;
**southeastern** [sauθˈiːstən] adj du or
au sud-est; **southern** ['sʌðən] adj (du)
sud; méridional(e); **South Korea** n
Corée f du Sud; **South of France** n: **the
South of France** le Sud de la France,
le Midi; **South Pole** n Pôle m Sud;
**southward(s)** adv vers le sud; **south-
west** n sud-ouest m; **southwestern**
[sauθˈwestən] adj du or au sud-ouest
**souvenir** [suːvəˈnɪəʳ] n souvenir m
(objet)
**sovereign** ['sɒvrɪn] adj, n souverain(e)
**sow¹** [səu] (pt **~ed**, pp **~n**) vt semer
**sow²** n [sau] truie f
**soya** ['sɔɪə] (us **soy** [sɔɪ]) n: **~ bean**
graine f de soja; **~ sauce** sauce f au soja
**spa** [spɑː] n (town) station thermale;
(us: also: **health ~**) établissement m de
cure de rajeunissement
**space** [speɪs] n (gen) espace m; (room)
place f, espace; (length of time) laps m
de temps ▷ cpd spatial(e) ▷ vt (also:
**~ out**) espacer; **spacecraft** n engin
or vaisseau spatial; **spaceship** n
= **spacecraft**
**spacious** ['speɪʃəs] adj spacieux(-euse),
grand(e)
**spade** [speɪd] n (tool) bêche f, pelle
f; (child's) pelle; **spades** npl (Cards)
pique m
**spaghetti** [spəˈgetɪ] n spaghetti mpl
**Spain** [speɪn] n Espagne f

# spam | 532

**spam** [spæm] n (Comput) spam m
**span** [spæn] n (of bird, plane) envergure
f; (of arch) portée f; (in time) espace m de
temps, durée f ▷ vt enjamber, franchir;
(fig) couvrir, embrasser
**Spaniard** ['spænjəd] n Espagnol(e)
**Spanish** ['spænɪʃ] adj espagnol(e),
d'Espagne ▷ n (Ling) espagnol m; **the
Spanish** npl les Espagnols
**spank** [spæŋk] vt donner une fessée à
**spanner** ['spænə'] n (BRIT) clé f (de
mécanicien)
**spare** [spɛə'] adj de réserve, de
rechange; (surplus) de or en trop, de
reste ▷ n (part) pièce f de rechange,
pièce détachée ▷ vt (do without) se
passer de; (afford to give) donner,
accorder, passer; (not hurt) épargner;
**to ~** (surplus) en surplus, de trop; **spare
part** n pièce f de rechange, pièce
détachée; **spare room** n chambre f
d'ami; **spare time** n moments mpl de
loisir; **spare tyre** (US **spare tire**) n (Aut)
pneu m de rechange; **spare wheel** n
(Aut) roue f de secours
**spark** [spɑːk] n étincelle f; **spark(ing)
plug** n bougie f
**sparkle** ['spɑːkl] n scintillement m,
étincellement m, éclat m ▷ vi étinceler,
scintiller
**sparkling** ['spɑːklɪŋ] adj (wine)
mousseux(-euse), pétillant(e); (water)
pétillant(e), gazeux(-euse)
**sparrow** ['spærəʊ] n moineau m
**sparse** [spɑːs] adj clairsemé(e)
**spasm** ['spæzəm] n (Med) spasme m
**spat** [spæt] pt, pp of **spit**
**spate** [speɪt] n (fig): **~ of** avalanche f or
torrent m de
**spatula** ['spætjʊlə] n spatule f
**speak** (pt **spoke**, pp **spoken**) [spiːk,
spəʊk, 'spəʊkn] vt (language) parler;
(truth) dire ▷ vi parler; (make a speech)
prendre la parole; **to ~ to sb/of** or
**about sth** parler à qn/de qch; **I don't
~ French** je ne parle pas français; **do
you ~ English?** parlez-vous anglais?;
**can I ~ to ...?** est-ce que je peux parler

à ...?; **speaker** n (in public) orateur m;
(also: **loudspeaker**) haut-parleur m; (for
stereo etc) baffle m, enceinte f; (Pol): **the
Speaker** (BRIT) le président de la Chambre
des communes or des représentants; (US) le
président de la Chambre
**spear** [spɪə'] n lance f ▷ vt transpercer
**special** ['spɛʃl] adj spécial(e); **special
delivery** n (Post): **by special delivery**
en express; **special effects** npl
(Cine) effets spéciaux; **specialist** n
spécialiste m/f; **speciality** [spɛʃɪˈælɪtɪ]
n (BRIT) spécialité f; **specialize** vi:
**to specialize (in)** se spécialiser
(dans); **specially** adv spécialement,
particulièrement; **special needs** npl
(BRIT) difficultés fpl d'apprentissage
scolaire; **special offer** n (Comm)
réclame f; **special school** n (BRIT)
établissement m d'enseignement
spécialisé; **specialty** n (US) = **speciality**
**species** ['spiːʃiːz] n (pl inv) espèce f
**specific** [spəˈsɪfɪk] adj (not vague)
précis(e), explicite; (particular)
particulier(-ière); **specifically**
adv explicitement, précisément;
(intend, ask, design) expressément,
spécialement
**specify** ['spɛsɪfaɪ] vt spécifier, préciser
**specimen** ['spɛsɪmən] n spécimen
m, échantillon m; (Med: of blood)
prélèvement m; (: of urine) échantillon m
**speck** [spɛk] n petite tache, petit point m;
(particle) grain m
**spectacle** ['spɛktəkl] n spectacle m;
**spectacles** npl (BRIT) lunettes fpl;
**spectacular** [spɛkˈtækjʊlə'] adj
spectaculaire
**spectator** [spɛkˈteɪtə'] n
spectateur(-trice)
**spectrum** (pl **spectra**) ['spɛktrəm, -rə]
n spectre m; (fig) gamme f
**speculate** ['spɛkjuleɪt] vi spéculer; (try
to guess): **to ~ about** s'interroger sur
**sped** [spɛd] pt, pp of **speed**
**speech** [spiːtʃ] n (faculty) parole f; (talk)
discours m, allocution f; (manner of
speaking) façon f de parler, langage m;

*(enunciation)* élocution f; **speechless** adj muet(te)

**speed** [spi:d] n vitesse f; *(promptness)* rapidité f ▷ vi *(pt, pp* **sped**) *Aut: exceed speed limit)* faire un excès de vitesse; **at full** or **top ~** à toute vitesse or allure; **speed up** *(pt, pp* **~ed up**) vi aller plus vite, accélérer vt accélérer; **speedboat** n vedette f, hors-bord m inv; **speeding** n *(Aut)* excès m de vitesse; **speed limit** n limitation f de vitesse, vitesse maximale permise; **speedometer** [spɪˈdɔmɪtəʳ] n compteur m *(de vitesse)*; **speedy** adj rapide, prompt(e)

**spell** [spɛl] n *(also:* **magic ~**) sortilège m, charme m; *(period of time)* *(courte)* période ▷ vt *(pt, pp* **spelt** or **~ed**) *(in writing)* écrire, orthographier; *(aloud)* épeler; *(fig)* signifier; **to cast a ~ on sb** jeter un sort à qn; **he can't ~** il fait des fautes d'orthographe; **spell out** vt *(explain)*: **to ~ sth out for sb** expliquer qch clairement à qn; **spellchecker** [ˈspɛltʃɛkəʳ] n *(Comput)* correcteur m or vérificateur m orthographique; **spelling** n orthographe f

**spelt** [spɛlt] pt, pp of **spell**

**spend** *(pt, pp* **spent**) [spɛnd, spɛnt] vt *(money)* dépenser; *(time, life)* passer; *(devote)* consacrer; **spending** n: **government spending** les dépenses publiques

**spent** [spɛnt] pt, pp of **spend** ▷ adj *(cartridge, bullets)* vide

**sperm** [spəːm] n spermatozoïde m; *(semen)* sperme m

**sphere** [sfɪəʳ] n sphère f; *(fig)* sphère, domaine m

**spice** [spaɪs] n épice f ▷ vt épicer

**spicy** [ˈspaɪsɪ] adj épicé(e), relevé(e); *(fig)* piquant(e)

**spider** [ˈspaɪdəʳ] n araignée f

**spike** [spaɪk] n pointe f; *(Bot)* épi m

**spill** *(pt, pp* **spilt** or **~ed**) [spɪl, -t, -d] vt renverser; répandre ▷ vi se répandre; **spill over** vi déborder

**spin** [spɪn] n *(revolution of wheel)* tour m; *(Aviat)* *(chute f en)* vrille f; *(trip in car)* petit tour, balade f; *(on ball)* effet m ▷ vb *(pt, pp* **spun**) ▷ vt *(wool etc)* filer; *(wheel)* faire tourner ▷ vi *(turn)* tourner, tournoyer

**spinach** [ˈspɪnɪtʃ] n épinards mpl

**spinal** [ˈspaɪnl] adj vertébral(e), spinal(e)

**spinal cord** n moelle épinière

**spin doctor** n *(inf)* personne employée pour présenter un parti politique sous un jour favorable

**spin-dryer** [spɪnˈdraɪəʳ] n *(BRIT)* essoreuse f

**spine** [spaɪn] n colonne vertébrale; *(thorn)* épine f, piquant m

**spiral** [ˈspaɪərl] n spirale f ▷ vi *(fig: prices etc)* monter en flèche

**spire** [ˈspaɪəʳ] n flèche f, aiguille f

**spirit** [ˈspɪrɪt] n *(soul)* esprit m, âme f; *(ghost)* esprit, revenant m; *(mood)* esprit, état m d'esprit; *(courage)* courage m, énergie f; **spirits** npl *(drink)* spiritueux mpl, alcool m; **in good ~s** de bonne humeur

**spiritual** [ˈspɪrɪtjuəl] adj spirituel(le); *(religious)* religieux(-euse)

**spit** [spɪt] n *(for roasting)* broche f; *(spittle)* crachat m; *(saliva)* salive f ▷ vi *(pt, pp* **spat**) cracher; *(sound)* crépiter; *(rain)* crachiner

**spite** [spaɪt] n rancune f, dépit m ▷ vt contrarier, vexer; **in ~ of** en dépit de, malgré; **spiteful** adj malveillant(e), rancunier(-ière)

**splash** [splæʃ] n *(sound)* plouf m; *(of colour)* tache f ▷ vt éclabousser ▷ vi *(also:* **~ about**) barboter, patauger; **splash out** vi *(BRIT)* faire une folie

**splendid** [ˈsplɛndɪd] adj splendide, superbe, magnifique

**splinter** [ˈsplɪntəʳ] n *(wood)* écharde f; *(metal)* éclat m ▷ vi *(wood)* se fendre; *(glass)* se briser

**split** [splɪt] n fente f, déchirure f; *(fig: Pol)* scission f ▷ vb *(pt, pp* **~**) ▷ vt fendre, déchirer; *(party)* diviser; *(work, profits)* partager, répartir ▷ vi *(break)* se fendre, se briser; (*divide*) se diviser; **split up** vi (*couple*) se séparer, rompre; (*meeting*) se disperser

**spoil** (*pt, pp* **~ed** *or* **~t**) [spɔɪl, -d, -t] vt (*damage*) abîmer; (*mar*) gâcher; (*child*) gâter

**spoilt** [spɔɪlt] *pt, pp of* **spoil** ▷ adj (*child*) gâté(e); (*ballot paper*) nul(le)

**spoke** [spəuk] *pt of* **speak** ▷ n rayon m

**spoken** ['spəukn] *pp of* **speak**

**spokesman** ['spəuksmən] (*irreg*) n porte-parole m inv

**spokesperson** ['spəukspə:sn] n porte-parole m inv

**spokeswoman** ['spəukswumən] (*irreg*) n porte-parole m inv

**sponge** [spʌndʒ] n éponge f; (*Culin: also:* **~ cake**) ≈ biscuit m de Savoie ▷ vt éponger ▷ vi: **to ~ off** *or* **on** vivre aux crochets de; **sponge bag** n (*BRIT*) trousse f de toilette

**sponsor** ['spɔnsər] n (*Radio, TV, Sport*) sponsor m; (*for application*) parrain m, marraine f; (*for fund-raising event*) donateur(-trice) ▷ vt sponsoriser, parrainer, faire un don à; **sponsorship** n sponsoring m, parrainage m; dons mpl

**spontaneous** [spɔn'teɪnɪəs] adj spontané(e)

**spooky** ['spu:kɪ] adj (*inf*) qui donne la chair de poule

**spoon** [spu:n] n cuiller f; **spoonful** n cuillerée f

**sport** [spɔ:t] n sport m; (*person*) chic type m/chic fille f ▷ vt (*wear*) arborer; **sport jacket** n (*us*) = **sports jacket**; **sports car** n voiture f de sport; **sports centre** n (*BRIT*) centre sportif; **sports jacket** n (*BRIT*) veste f de sport; **sportsman** (*irreg*) n sportif m; **sports utility vehicle** n véhicule m de loisirs (*de type SUV*); **sportswear** n vêtements mpl de sport; **sportswoman** (*irreg*) n sportive f; **sporty** adj sportif(-ive)

**spot** [spɔt] n tache f; (*dot: on pattern*) pois m; (*pimple*) bouton m; (*place*) endroit m, coin m; (*small amount*): **a ~ of** un peu de ▷ vt (*notice*) apercevoir,

repérer; **on the ~** sur place, sur les lieux; (*immediately*) sur le champ; **spotless** adj immaculé(e); **spotlight** n projecteur m; (*Aut*) phare m auxiliaire

**spouse** [spauz] n époux (épouse)

**sprain** [spreɪn] n entorse f, foulure f ▷ vt: **to ~ one's ankle** se fouler *or* se tordre la cheville

**sprang** [spræŋ] *pt of* **spring**

**sprawl** [sprɔ:l] vi s'étaler

**spray** [spreɪ] n jet m (en fines gouttelettes); (*from sea*) embruns mpl; (*aerosol*) vaporisateur m, bombe f; (*for garden*) pulvérisateur m; (*of flowers*) petit bouquet ▷ vt vaporiser, pulvériser; (*crops*) traiter

**spread** [spred] n (*distribution*) répartition f; (*Culin*) pâte f à tartiner; (*inf: meal*) festin m ▷ vb (*pt, pp* **~**) ▷ vt (*paste, contents*) étendre, étaler; (*rumour, disease*) répandre, propager; (*wealth*) répartir ▷ vi s'étendre; se répandre; se propager; (*stain*) s'étaler; **spread out** vi (*people*) se disperser; **spreadsheet** n (*Comput*) tableur m

**spree** [spri:] n: **to go on a ~** faire la fête

**spring** [sprɪŋ] n (*season*) printemps m; (*leap*) bond m, saut m; (*coiled metal*) ressort m; (*of water*) source f ▷ vb (*pt* **sprang**, *pp* **sprung**) ▷ vi bondir, sauter; **spring up** vi (*problem*) se présenter, surgir; (*plant, buildings*) surgir de terre; **spring onion** n (*BRIT*) ciboule f, cive f

**sprinkle** ['sprɪŋkl] vt: **to ~ water** *etc* **on, ~ with water** *etc* asperger d'eau *etc*; **to ~ sugar** *etc* **on, ~ with sugar** *etc* saupoudrer de sucre *etc*

**sprint** [sprɪnt] n sprint m ▷ vi courir à toute vitesse; (*Sport*) sprinter

**sprung** [sprʌŋ] *pp of* **spring**

**spun** [spʌn] *pt, pp of* **spin**

**spur** [spə:r] n éperon m; (*fig*) aiguillon m ▷ vt (*also:* **~ on**) éperonner; aiguillonner; **on the ~ of the moment** sous l'impulsion du moment

**spurt** [spə:t] n jet m; (*of blood*) jaillissement m; (*of energy*) regain m, sursaut m ▷ vi jaillir, gicler

**spy** [spaɪ] n espion(ne) ▷ vi: **to ~ on** espionner, épier ▷ vt (see) apercevoir

**sq.** abbr = **square**

**squabble** ['skwɔbl] vi se chamailler

**squad** [skwɔd] n (Mil, Police) escouade f, groupe m; (Football) contingent m

**squadron** ['skwɔdrn] n (Mil) escadron m; (Aviat, Naut) escadrille f

**squander** ['skwɔndər] vt gaspiller, dilapider

**square** [skwɛər] n carré m; (in town) place f ▷ adj carré(e) ▷ vt (arrange) régler; arranger; (Math) élever au carré; (reconcile) concilier; **all ~** quitte; à égalité; **a ~ meal** un repas convenable; **2 metres ~** (de) 2 mètres sur 2; **1 ~ metre** 1 mètre carré; **square root** n racine carrée

**squash** [skwɔʃ] n (BRIT: drink): **lemon/ orange ~** citronnade f/orangeade f; (Sport) squash m; (US: vegetable) courge f ▷ vt écraser

**squat** [skwɔt] adj petit(e) et épais(se), ramassé(e) ▷ vi (also: ~ **down**) s'accroupir; **squatter** n squatter m

**squeak** [skwiːk] vi (hinge, wheel) grincer; (mouse) pousser un petit cri

**squeal** [skwiːl] vi pousser un or des cri(s) aigu(s) or perçant(s); (brakes) grincer

**squeeze** [skwiːz] n pression f ▷ vt presser; (hand, arm) serrer

**squid** [skwɪd] n calmar m

**squint** [skwɪnt] vi loucher

**squirm** [skwəːm] vi se tortiller

**squirrel** ['skwɪrəl] n écureuil m

**squirt** [skwəːt] vi jaillir, gicler ▷ vt faire gicler

**Sr** abbr = **senior**

**Sri Lanka** [srɪ'læŋkə] n Sri Lanka m

**St** abbr = **saint; street**

**stab** [stæb] n (with knife etc) coup m (de couteau etc); (of pain) lancée f; (inf: try): **to have a ~ at (doing) sth** s'essayer à (faire) qch ▷ vt poignarder

**stability** [stə'bɪlɪtɪ] n stabilité f

**stable** ['steɪbl] n écurie f ▷ adj stable

**stack** [stæk] n tas m, pile f ▷ vt empiler, entasser

**stadium** ['steɪdɪəm] n stade m

**staff** [stɑːf] n (work force) personnel m; (BRIT Scol: also: **teaching ~**) professeurs mpl, enseignants mpl, personnel enseignant ▷ vt pourvoir en personnel

**stag** [stæg] n cerf m

**stage** [steɪdʒ] n scène f; (platform) estrade f; (point) étape f, stade m; (profession): **the ~** le théâtre ▷ vt (play) monter, mettre en scène; (demonstration) organiser; **in ~s** par étapes, par degrés

> Be careful not to translate *stage* by the French word *stage*.

**stagger** ['stægər] vi chanceler, tituber ▷ vt (person: amaze) stupéfier; (hours, holidays) étaler, échelonner; **staggering** adj (amazing) stupéfiant(e), renversant(e)

**stagnant** ['stægnənt] adj stagnant(e)

**stag night, stag party** n enterrement m de vie de garçon

**stain** [steɪn] n tache f; (colouring) colorant m ▷ vt tacher; (wood) teindre; **stained glass** n (decorative) verre coloré; (in church) vitraux mpl; **stainless steel** n inox m, acier m inoxydable

**staircase** ['stɛəkeɪs] n = **stairway**

**stairs** [stɛəz] npl escalier m

**stairway** ['stɛəweɪ] n escalier m

**stake** [steɪk] n pieu m, poteau m; (Comm: interest) intérêts mpl; (Betting) enjeu m ▷ vt risquer, jouer; (also: ~ **out**: area) marquer, délimiter; **to be at ~** être en jeu

**stale** [steɪl] adj (bread) rassis(e); (food) pas frais (fraîche); (beer) éventé(e); (smell) de renfermé; (air) confiné(e)

**stalk** [stɔːk] n tige f ▷ vt traquer

**stall** [stɔːl] n (BRIT: in street, market etc) éventaire m, étal m; (in stable) stalle f ▷ vt (Aut) caler; (fig: delay) retarder ▷ vi (Aut) caler; (fig) essayer de gagner du temps; **stalls** npl (BRIT: in cinema, theatre) orchestre m

**stamina** ['stæmɪnə] n vigueur f, endurance f

**stammer** ['stæmə$^r$] n bégaiement m
▷ vi bégayer

**stamp** [stæmp] n timbre m; (also:
**rubber ~**) tampon m; (mark, also fig)
empreinte f; (on document) cachet
m ▷ vi (also: **~ one's foot**) taper du
pied ▷ vt (letter) timbrer; (with rubber
stamp) tamponner; **stamp out** vt (fire)
piétiner; (crime) éradiquer; (opposition)
éliminer; **stamped addressed
envelope** n (BRIT) enveloppe
affranchie pour la réponse

**stampede** [stæm'pi:d] n ruée f; (of
cattle) débandade f

**stance** [stæns] n position f

**stand** [stænd] n (position) position f;
(for taxis) station f (de taxis); (Comm)
étalage m, stand m; (Sport: also: **~s**)
tribune f; (also: **music ~**) pupitre m
▷ vb (pt, pp **stood**) ▷ vi être or se tenir
(debout); (rise) se lever, se mettre
debout; (be placed) se trouver; (remain:
offer etc) rester valable ▷ vt (place)
mettre, poser; (tolerate, withstand)
supporter; (treat, invite) offrir, payer;
**to make a ~** prendre position; **to ~
for parliament** (BRIT) se présenter
aux élections (comme candidat à la
députation); **I can't ~ him** je ne peux
pas le voir; **stand back** vi (move back)
reculer, s'écarter; **stand by** vi (be ready)
se tenir prêt(e) ▷ vt fus (opinion) s'en
tenir à; (person) ne pas abandonner,
soutenir; **stand down** vi (withdraw)
se retirer; **stand for** vt fus (signify)
représenter, signifier; (tolerate)
supporter, tolérer; **stand in for** vt fus
remplacer; **stand out** vi (be prominent)
ressortir; **stand up** vi (rise) se lever,
se mettre debout; **stand up for** vt fus
défendre; **stand up to** vt fus tenir tête
à, résister à

**standard** ['stændəd] n (norm) norme
f, étalon m; (level) niveau m (voulu);
(criterion) critère m; (flag) étendard m
▷ adj (size etc) ordinaire, normal(e);
(model, feature) standard inv; (practice)
courant(e); (text) de base; **standards**

npl (morals) morale f, principes mpl;
**standard of living** n niveau m de vie

**stand-by ticket** n (Aviat) billet m
stand-by

**standing** ['stændɪŋ] adj debout
inv; (permanent) permanent(e) ▷ n
réputation f, rang m, standing m; **of
many years' ~** qui dure or existe depuis
longtemps; **standing order** n (BRIT:
at bank) virement m automatique,
prélèvement m bancaire

**stand**: **standpoint** n point m de vue;
**standstill** n: **at a standstill** à l'arrêt,
(fig) au point mort; **to come to a
standstill** s'immobiliser, s'arrêter

**stank** [stæŋk] pt of **stink**

**staple** ['steɪpl] n (for papers) agrafe f
▷ adj (food, crop, industry etc) de base
principal(e) ▷ vt agrafer

**star** [stɑ:$^r$] n étoile f; (celebrity) vedette f
▷ vt (Cine) avoir pour vedette; **stars** npl:
**the ~s** (Astrology) l'horoscope m

**starboard** ['stɑ:bəd] n tribord m

**starch** [stɑ:tʃ] n amidon m; (in food)
fécule f

**stardom** ['stɑ:dəm] n célébrité f

**stare** [stɛə$^r$] n regard m fixe ▷ vi: **to ~ at**
regarder fixement

**stark** [stɑ:k] adj (bleak) désolé(e),
morne ▷ adv: **~ naked** complètement
nu(e)

**start** [stɑ:t] n commencement m,
début m; (of race) départ m; (sudden
movement) sursaut m; (advantage)
avance f, avantage m ▷ vt commencer;
(cause: fight) déclencher; (rumour)
donner naissance à; (fashion) lancer;
(found: business, newspaper) lancer, créer;
(engine) mettre en marche ▷ vi (begin)
commencer; (begin journey) partir, se
mettre en route; (jump) sursauter;
**when does the film ~?** à quelle heure
est-ce que le film commence?; **to ~
doing** or **to do sth** se mettre à faire qch;
**start off** vi commencer; (leave) partir;
**start out** vi (begin) commencer; (set
out) partir; **start up** vi commencer;
(car) démarrer ▷ vt (fight) déclencher;

(*business*) créer; (*car*) mettre en marche; **starter** n (*Aut*) démarreur m; (*Sport: official*) starter m; (BRIT *Culin*) entrée f; **starting point** n point m de départ

**startle** ['stɑːtl] vt faire sursauter; donner un choc à; **startling** adj surprenant(e), saisissant(e)

**starvation** [stɑːˈveɪʃən] n faim f, famine f

**starve** [stɑːv] vi mourir de faim ▷ vt laisser mourir de faim

**state** [steɪt] n état m; (*Pol*) État ▷ vt (*declare*) déclarer, affirmer; (*specify*) indiquer, spécifier; **States** npl: **the S~s** les États-Unis; **to be in a ~** être dans tous ses états; **stately home** n manoir m or château m (*ouvert au public*); **statement** n déclaration f; (*Law*) déposition f; **state school** n école publique; **statesman** (*irreg*) n homme m d'État

**static** ['stætɪk] n (*Radio*) parasites mpl; (*also*: **~ electricity**) électricité f statique ▷ adj statique

**station** ['steɪʃən] n gare f; (*also*: **police ~**) poste m or commissariat m (de police) ▷ vt placer, poster

**stationary** ['steɪʃnərɪ] adj à l'arrêt, immobile

**stationer's (shop)** n (BRIT) papeterie f

**stationery** ['steɪʃnərɪ] n papier m à lettres, petit matériel de bureau

**station wagon** n (US) break m

**statistic** [stəˈtɪstɪk] n statistique f; **statistics** n (*science*) statistique f

**statue** ['stætjuː] n statue f

**stature** ['stætʃəʳ] n stature f; (*fig*) envergure f

**status** ['steɪtəs] n position f, situation f; (*prestige*) prestige m; (*Admin, official position*) statut m; **status quo** [-ˈkwəu] n: **the status quo** le statu quo

**statutory** ['stætjutrɪ] adj statutaire, prévu(e) par un article de loi

**staunch** [stɔːntʃ] adj sûr(e), loyal(e)

**stay** [steɪ] n (*period of time*) séjour m ▷ vi rester; (*reside*) loger; (*spend some time*) séjourner; **to ~ put** ne pas bouger; **to ~ the night** passer la nuit; **stay away** vi (*from person, building*) ne pas s'approcher; (*from event*) ne pas venir; **stay behind** vi rester en arrière; **stay in** vi (*at home*) rester à la maison; **stay on** vi rester; **stay out** vi (*of house*) ne pas rentrer; (*strikers*) rester en grève; **stay up** vi (*at night*) ne pas se coucher

**steadily** ['stedɪlɪ] adv (*regularly*) progressivement; (*firmly*) fermement; (*walk*) d'un pas ferme; (*fixedly: look*) sans détourner les yeux

**steady** ['stedɪ] adj stable, solide, ferme; (*regular*) constant(e), régulier(-ière); (*person*) calme, pondéré(e) ▷ vt assurer, stabiliser; (*nerves*) calmer; **a ~ boyfriend** un petit ami

**steak** [steɪk] n (*meat*) bifteck m, steak m; (*fish, pork*) tranche f

**steal** (*pt* **stole**, *pp* **stolen**) [stiːl, stəul, 'stəuln] vt, vi voler; (*move*) se faufiler, se déplacer furtivement; **my wallet has been stolen** on m'a volé mon portefeuille

**steam** [stiːm] n vapeur f ▷ vt (*Culin*) cuire à la vapeur ▷ vi fumer; **steam up** vi (*window*) se couvrir de buée; **to get ~ed up about sth** (*fig: inf*) s'exciter à propos de qch; **steamy** adj humide; (*window*) embué(e); (*sexy*) torride

**steel** [stiːl] n acier m ▷ cpd d'acier

**steep** [stiːp] adj raide, escarpé(e); (*price*) très élevé(e), excessif(-ive) ▷ vt (faire) tremper

**steeple** ['stiːpl] n clocher m

**steer** [stɪəʳ] vt diriger; (*boat*) gouverner; (*lead: person*) guider, conduire ▷ vi tenir le gouvernail; **steering** n (*Aut*) conduite f; **steering wheel** n volant m

**stem** [stem] n (*of plant*) tige f; (*of glass*) pied m ▷ vt contenir, endiguer; (*attack, spread of disease*) juguler

**step** [step] n pas m; (*stair*) marche f; (*action*) mesure f, disposition f ▷ vi: **to ~ forward/back** faire un pas en avant/arrière, avancer/reculer; **steps** npl (BRIT) = **stepladder**; **to be in/out of**

**~ (with)** (fig) aller dans le sens (de)/être déphasé(e) (par rapport à); **step down** vi (fig) se retirer, se désister; **step in** vi (fig) intervenir; **step up** vt (production, sales) augmenter; (campaign, efforts) intensifier; **stepbrother** n demi-frère m; **stepchild** (pl **~ren**) n beau-fils m, belle-fille f; **stepdaughter** n belle-fille f; **stepfather** n beau-père m; **stepladder** n (BRIT) escabeau m; **stepmother** n belle-mère f; **stepsister** n demi-sœur f; **stepson** n beau-fils m

**stereo** ['stɛrɪəʊ] n (sound) stéréo f; (hi-fi) chaîne f stéréo ▷ adj (also: **~phonic**) stéréo(phonique)

**stereotype** ['stɛrɪətaɪp] n stéréotype m ▷ vt stéréotyper

**sterile** ['stɛraɪl] adj stérile; **sterilize** ['stɛrɪlaɪz] vt stériliser

**sterling** ['stə:lɪŋ] adj (silver) de bon aloi, fin(e) ▷ n (currency) livre f sterling inv

**stern** [stə:n] adj sévère ▷ n (Naut) arrière m, poupe f

**steroid** ['stɪərɔɪd] n stéroïde m

**stew** [stju:] n ragoût m ▷ vt, vi cuire à la casserole

**steward** ['stju:əd] n (Aviat, Naut, Rail) steward m; **stewardess** n hôtesse f

**stick** [stɪk] n bâton m; (for walking) canne f; (of chalk etc) morceau m ▷ vb (pt, pp **stuck**) ▷ vt (glue) coller; (thrust): **to ~ sth into** piquer ou planter ou enfoncer qch dans; (inf: put) mettre, fourrer; (: tolerate) supporter ▷ vi (adhere) tenir, coller; (remain) rester; (get jammed: door, lift) se bloquer; **stick out** vi dépasser, sortir; **stick up** vi dépasser, sortir; **stick up for** vt fus défendre; **sticker** n auto-collant m; **sticking plaster** n sparadrap m, pansement adhésif; **stick insect** n phasme m; **stick shift** n (US Aut) levier m de vitesses

**sticky** ['stɪkɪ] adj poisseux(-euse); (label) adhésif(-ive); (fig: situation) délicat(e)

**stiff** [stɪf] adj (gen) raide, rigide; (door, brush) dur(e); (difficult) difficile, ardu(e); (cold) froid(e), distant(e); (strong, high) fort(e), élevé(e) ▷ adv: **to be bored/scared/frozen ~** s'ennuyer à mourir/être mort(e) de peur/froid

**stifling** ['staɪflɪŋ] adj (heat) suffocant(e)

**stigma** ['stɪgmə] n stigmate m

**stiletto** [stɪ'lɛtəʊ] n (BRIT: also: **~ heel**) talon m aiguille

**still** [stɪl] adj immobile ▷ adv (up to this time) encore, toujours; (even) encore; (nonetheless) quand même, tout de même

**stimulate** ['stɪmjuleɪt] vt stimuler

**stimulus** (pl **stimuli**) ['stɪmjuləs, 'stɪmjulaɪ] n stimulant m; (Biol, Psych) stimulus m

**sting** [stɪŋ] n piqûre f; (organ) dard m ▷ vt, vi (pt, pp **stung**) piquer

**stink** [stɪŋk] n puanteur f ▷ vi (pt **stank**, pp **stunk**) puer, empester

**stir** [stə:ʳ] n agitation f, sensation f ▷ vt remuer ▷ vi remuer, bouger; **stir up** vt (trouble) fomenter, provoquer; **stir-fry** vt faire sauter ▷ n: **vegetable stir-fry** légumes sautés à la poêle

**stitch** [stɪtʃ] n (Sewing) point m; (Knitting) maille f; (Med) point de suture; (pain) point de côté ▷ vt coudre, piquer; (Med) suturer

**stock** [stɔk] n réserve f, provision f; (Comm) stock m; (Agr) cheptel m, bétail m; (Culin) bouillon m; (Finance) valeurs fpl, titres mpl; (descent, origin) souche f ▷ adj (fig: reply etc) classique ▷ vt (have in stock) avoir, vendre; **in ~** en stock, en magasin; **out of ~** épuisé(e); **to take ~** (fig) faire le point; **~s and shares** valeurs (mobilières), titres; **stockbroker** ['stɔkbrəʊkəʳ] n agent m de change; **stock cube** n (BRIT Culin) bouillon-cube m; **stock exchange** n Bourse f (des valeurs); **stockholder** ['stɔkhəʊldəʳ] n (US) actionnaire m/f

**stocking** ['stɔkɪŋ] n bas m

**stock market** n Bourse f, marché financier

**stole** [stəʊl] pt of **steal** ▷ n étole f

**stolen** ['stəʊln] pp of **steal**

**stomach** ['stʌmək] n estomac m; (abdomen) ventre m ▷ vt supporter, digérer; **stomachache** n mal m à l'estomac or au ventre

**stone** [stəun] n pierre f; (pebble) caillou m, galet m; (in fruit) noyau m; (Med) calcul m; (BRIT: weight) = 6.348 kg; 14 pounds ▷ cpd de or en pierre ▷ vt (person) lancer des pierres sur, lapider; (fruit) dénoyauter

**stood** [stud] pt, pp of **stand**

**stool** [stu:l] n tabouret m

**stoop** [stu:p] vi (also: **have a ~**) être voûté(e); (also: **~ down**: bend) se baisser, se courber

**stop** [stɔp] n arrêt m; (in punctuation) point m ▷ vt arrêter; (break off) interrompre; (also: **put a ~ to**) mettre fin à; (prevent) empêcher ▷ vi s'arrêter; (rain, noise etc) cesser, s'arrêter; **to ~ doing sth** cesser or arrêter de faire qch; **to ~ sb (from) doing sth** empêcher qn de faire qch; **~ it!** arrête!; **stop by** vi s'arrêter (au passage); **stop off** vi faire une courte halte; **stopover** n halte f; (Aviat) escale f; **stoppage** n (strike) arrêt m de travail; (obstruction) obstruction f

**storage** ['stɔːrɪdʒ] n emmagasinage m

**store** [stɔːʳ] n (stock) provision f, réserve f; (depot) entrepôt m; (BRIT: large shop) grand magasin; (US: shop) magasin m ▷ vt emmagasiner; (information) enregistrer; **stores** npl (food) provisions; **who knows what is in ~ for us?** qui sait ce que l'avenir nous réserve or ce qui nous attend?; **storekeeper** n (US) commerçant(e)

**storey** (US **story**) ['stɔːrɪ] n étage m

**storm** [stɔːm] n tempête f; (thunderstorm) orage m ▷ vi (fig) fulminer ▷ vt prendre d'assaut; **stormy** adj orageux(-euse)

**story** ['stɔːrɪ] n histoire f; (Press: article) article m; (US) = **storey**

**stout** [staut] adj (strong) solide; (fat) gros(se), corpulent(e) ▷ n bière brune

**stove** [stəuv] n (for cooking) fourneau m;

(: small) réchaud m; (for heating) poêle m

**straight** [streɪt] adj droit(e); (hair) raide; (frank) honnête, franc (franche); (simple) simple ▷ adv (tout) droit; (drink) sec, sans eau; **to put or get** en ordre, mettre de l'ordre dans; (fig) mettre au clair; **~ away, ~ off** (at once) tout de suite; **straighten** vt ajuster; (bed) arranger; **straighten out** vt (fig) débrouiller; **straighten up** vi (stand up) se redresser; **straightforward** adj simple; (frank) honnête, direct(e)

**strain** [streɪn] n (Tech) tension f; pression f; (physical) effort m; (mental) tension f (nerveuse); (Med) entorse f; (breed: of plants) variété f; (: of animals) race f ▷ vt (fig: resources etc) mettre à rude épreuve, grever; (hurt: back etc) se faire mal à; (vegetables) égoutter; **strains** npl (Mus) accords mpl, accents mpl; **strained** adj (muscle) froissé(e); (laugh etc) forcé(e), contraint(e); (relations) tendu(e); **strainer** n passoire f

**strait** [streɪt] n (Geo) détroit m; **straits** npl: **to be in dire ~s** (fig) avoir de sérieux ennuis

**strand** [strænd] n (of thread) fil m, brin m; (of rope) toron m; (of hair) mèche f ▷ vt (boat) échouer; **stranded** adj en rade, en plan

**strange** [streɪndʒ] adj (not known) inconnu(e); (odd) étrange, bizarre; **strangely** adv étrangement, bizarrement; see also **enough**; **stranger** n (unknown) inconnu(e); (from somewhere else) étranger(-ère)

**strangle** ['stræŋgl] vt étrangler

**strap** [stræp] n lanière f, courroie f, sangle f; (of slip, dress) bretelle f

**strategic** [strə'tiːdʒɪk] adj stratégique

**strategy** ['strætɪdʒɪ] n stratégie f

**straw** [strɔː] n paille f; **that's the last ~!** ça c'est le comble!

**strawberry** ['strɔːbərɪ] n fraise f

**stray** [streɪ] adj (animal) perdu(e), errant(e); (scattered) isolé(e) ▷ vi s'égarer; **~ bullet** balle perdue

**streak** [striːk] n bande f, filet m; (in hair) raie f ▷ vt zébrer, strier

**stream** [striːm] n (brook) ruisseau m; (current) courant m, flot m; (of people) défilé ininterrompu, flot f vt (Scol) répartir par niveau ▷ vi ruisseler; **to ~ in/out** entrer/sortir à flots

**street** [striːt] n rue f; **streetcar** n (US) tramway m; **street light** n réverbère m; **street map, street plan** n plan m des rues

**strength** [strɛŋθ] n force f; (of girder, knot etc) solidité f; **strengthen** vt renforcer; (muscle) fortifier; (building, Econ) consolider

**strenuous** ['strɛnjuəs] adj vigoureux(-euse), énergique; (tiring) ardu(e), fatigant(e)

**stress** [strɛs] n (force, pressure) pression f; (mental strain) tension (nerveuse), stress m; (accent) accent m; (emphasis) insistance f ▷ vt insister sur, souligner; (syllable) accentuer; **stressed** adj (tense) stressé(e); (syllable) accentué(e); **stressful** adj (job) stressant(e)

**stretch** [strɛtʃ] n (of sand etc) étendue f ▷ vi s'étirer; (extend): **to ~ to** or **as far as** s'étendre jusqu'à ▷ vt tendre, étirer; (fig) pousser (au maximum); **at a ~** d'affilée; **stretch out** vi s'étendre ▷ vt (arm etc) allonger, tendre; (to spread) étendre

**stretcher** ['strɛtʃər] n brancard m, civière f

**strict** [strɪkt] adj strict(e); **strictly** adv strictement

**stride** [straɪd] n grand pas, enjambée f ▷ vi (pt **strode**, pp **stridden**) marcher à grands pas

**strike** [straɪk] n grève f; (of oil etc) découverte f; (attack) raid m ▷ vb (pt, pp **struck**) ▷ vt frapper; (oil etc) trouver, découvrir; (make: agreement, deal) conclure ▷ vi faire grève; (attack) attaquer; (clock) sonner; **to go on** or **come out on ~** se mettre en grève, faire grève; **to ~ a match** frotter une allumette; **striker** n gréviste

m/f; (Sport) buteur m; **striking** adj frappant(e), saisissant(e); (attractive) éblouissant(e)

**string** [strɪŋ] n ficelle f, fil m; (row: of beads) rang m; (Mus) corde f ▷ vt (pt, pp **strung**); **to ~ out** échelonner; **to ~ together** enchaîner; **the strings** npl (Mus) les instruments mpl à cordes; **to pull ~s** (fig) faire jouer le piston

**strip** [strɪp] n bande f; (Sport) tenue f ▷ vt (undress) déshabiller; (paint) décaper; (fig) dégarnir, dépouiller; (also: ~ **down**: machine) démonter ▷ vi se déshabiller; **strip off** vt (paint etc) décaper ▷ vi (person) se déshabiller

**stripe** [straɪp] n raie f, rayure f; (Mil) galon m; **striped** adj rayé(e), à rayures

**stripper** ['strɪpər] n strip-teaseuse f

**strip-search** ['strɪpsəːtʃ] vt: **to ~ sb** fouiller qn (en le faisant se déshabiller)

**strive** (pt **strove**, pp ~**n**) [straɪv, strəuv, 'strɪvn] vi: **to ~ to do/for sth** s'efforcer de faire/d'obtenir qch

**strode** [strəud] pt of **stride**

**stroke** [strəuk] n coup m; (Med) attaque f; (Swimming: style) (sorte f de) nage f ▷ vt caresser; **at a ~** d'un (seul) coup

**stroll** [strəul] n petite promenade ▷ vi flâner, se promener nonchalamment; **stroller** n (US: for child) poussette f

**strong** [strɔŋ] adj (gen) fort(e); (healthy) vigoureux(-euse); (heart, nerves) solide; **they are 50 ~** ils sont au nombre de 50; **stronghold** n forteresse f, fort m; (fig) bastion m; **strongly** adv fortement, avec force; vigoureusement; solidement

**strove** [strəuv] pt of **strive**

**struck** [strʌk] pt, pp of **strike**

**structure** ['strʌktʃər] n structure f; (building) construction f

**struggle** ['strʌgl] n lutte f ▷ vi lutter, se battre

**strung** [strʌŋ] pt, pp of **string**

**stub** [stʌb] n (of cigarette) bout m, mégot m; (of ticket etc) talon m ▷ vt: **to ~ one's toe (on sth)** se heurter le doigt de pied (contre qch); **stub out** vt écraser

**stubble** ['stʌbl] n chaume m; (on chin) barbe f de plusieurs jours

**stubborn** ['stʌbən] adj têtu(e), obstiné(e), opiniâtre

**stuck** [stʌk] pt, pp of **stick** ▷ adj (jammed) bloqué(e), coincé(e)

**stud** [stʌd] n (on boots etc) clou m; (collar stud) bouton m de col; (earring) petite boucle d'oreille; (of horses: also: ~ **farm**) écurie f, haras m; (also: ~ **horse**) étalon m ▷ vt (fig): ~**ded with** parsemé(e) or criblé(e) de

**student** ['stju:dənt] n étudiant(e) ▷ adj (life) estudiantin(e), étudiant(e), d'étudiant; (residence, restaurant) universitaire; (loan, movement) étudiant; **student driver** n (us) (conducteur(-trice)) débutant(e); **students' union** (BRIT: association) ≈ union f des étudiants; (: building) ≈ foyer m des étudiants

**studio** ['stju:dɪəu] n studio m, atelier m; (TV etc) studio; **studio flat** (us **studio apartment**) n studio m

**study** ['stʌdɪ] n étude f; (room) bureau m ▷ vt étudier; (examine) examiner ▷ vi étudier, faire ses études

**stuff** [stʌf] n (gen) chose(s) f(pl), truc m; (belongings) affaires fpl, trucs; (substance) substance f ▷ vt rembourrer; (Culin) farcir; (inf: push) fourrer; **stuffing** n bourre f, rembourrage m; (Culin) farce f; **stuffy** adj (room) mal ventilé(e) or aéré(e); (ideas) vieux jeu inv

**stumble** ['stʌmbl] vi trébucher; **to ~ across** or **on** (fig) tomber sur

**stump** [stʌmp] n souche f; (of limb) moignon m ▷ vt: **to be ~ed** sécher, ne pas savoir que répondre

**stun** [stʌn] vt (blow) étourdir; (news) abasourdir, stupéfier

**stung** [stʌŋ] pt, pp of **sting**

**stunk** [stʌŋk] pp of **stink**

**stunned** [stʌnd] adj assommé(e); (fig) sidéré(e)

**stunning** ['stʌnɪŋ] adj (beautiful) étourdissant(e); (news etc) stupéfiant(e)

**stunt** [stʌnt] n (in film) cascade f, acrobatie f; (publicity) truc m publicitaire ▷ vt retarder, arrêter

**stupid** ['stju:pɪd] adj stupide, bête; **stupidity** [stju:'pɪdɪtɪ] n stupidité f, bêtise f

**sturdy** ['stə:dɪ] adj (person, plant) robuste, vigoureux(-euse); (object) solide

**stutter** ['stʌtər] n bégaiement m ▷ vi bégayer

**style** [staɪl] n style m; (distinction) allure f, cachet m, style; (design) modèle m; **stylish** adj élégant(e), chic inv; **stylist** n (hair stylist) coiffeur(-euse)

**sub...** [sʌb] prefix sub..., sous-; **subconscious** adj subconscient(e)

**subdued** [səb'dju:d] adj (light) tamisé(e); (person) qui a perdu de son entrain

**subject** n ['sʌbdʒɪkt] sujet m; (Scol) matière f ▷ vt [səb'dʒɛkt]: **to ~ to** soumettre à; **to be ~ to** (law) être soumis(e) à; **subjective** [səb'dʒɛktɪv] adj subjectif(-ive); **subject matter** n (content) contenu m

**subjunctive** [səb'dʒʌŋktɪv] n subjonctif m

**submarine** [sʌbmə'ri:n] n sous-marin m

**submission** [səb'mɪʃən] n soumission f

**submit** [səb'mɪt] vt soumettre ▷ vi se soumettre

**subordinate** [sə'bɔ:dɪnət] adj (junior) subalterne; (Grammar) subordonné(e) ▷ n subordonné(e)

**subscribe** [səb'skraɪb] vi cotiser; **to ~ to** (opinion, fund) souscrire à; (newspaper) s'abonner à; être abonné(e) à

**subscription** [səb'skrɪpʃən] n (to magazine etc) abonnement m

**subsequent** ['sʌbsɪkwənt] adj ultérieur(e), suivant(e); **subsequently** adv par la suite

**subside** [səb'saɪd] vi (land) s'affaisser;

(*flood*) baisser; (*wind, feelings*) tomber

**subsidiary** [səbˈsɪdɪərɪ] *adj*
subsidiaire; accessoire; (*BRIT Scol: subject*) complémentaire ▷ *n* filiale *f*

**subsidize** [ˈsʌbsɪdaɪz] *vt*
subventionner

**subsidy** [ˈsʌbsɪdɪ] *n* subvention *f*

**substance** [ˈsʌbstəns] *n* substance *f*

**substantial** [səbˈstænʃl] *adj*
substantiel(le); (*fig*) important(e)

**substitute** [ˈsʌbstɪtjuːt] *n* (*person*)
remplaçant(e); (*thing*) succédané *m*
▷ *vt*: **to ~ sth/sb for** substituer qch/qn
à, remplacer par qch/qn; **substitution**
*n* substitution *f*

**subtitles** [ˈsʌbtaɪtlz] *npl* (*Cine*) sous-
titres *mpl*

**subtle** [ˈsʌtl] *adj* subtil(e)

**subtract** [səbˈtrækt] *vt* soustraire,
retrancher

**suburb** [ˈsʌbəːb] *n* faubourg *m*; **the ~s**
banlieue; **suburban** [səˈbəːbən] *adj* de
banlieue, suburbain(e)

**subway** [ˈsʌbweɪ] *n* (*BRIT: underpass*)
passage souterrain; (*US: railway*)
métro *m*

**succeed** [səkˈsiːd] *vi* réussir ▷ *vt*
succéder à; **to ~ in doing** réussir à faire

**success** [səkˈsɛs] *n* succès *m*; réussite *f*;
**successful** *adj* (*business*) prospère,
qui réussit; (*attempt*) couronné(e) de
succès; **to be successful (in doing)**
réussir (à faire); **successfully** *adv*
avec succès

**succession** [səkˈsɛʃən] *n* succession *f*

**successive** [səkˈsɛsɪv] *adj*
successif(-ive)

**successor** [səkˈsɛsər] *n* successeur *m*

**succumb** [səˈkʌm] *vi* succomber

**such** [sʌtʃ] *adj* tel (telle); (*of that kind*):
**~ a book** un livre de ce genre *or* pareil,
un tel livre; (*so much*): **~ courage** un
tel courage ▷ *adv* tel (telle); **~ a long trip** un
si long voyage; **~ a lot of** tellement
*or* tant de; **~ as** (*like*) tel (telle) que,
comme; **as ~** *adv* en tant que tel (telle),
à proprement parler; **such-and-such**
*adj* tel ou tel (telle ou telle)

**suck** [sʌk] *vt* sucer; (*breast, bottle*) téter

**Sudan** [suˈdɑːn] *n* Soudan *m*

**sudden** [ˈsʌdn] *adj* soudain(e),
subit(e); **all of a ~** soudain, tout à coup;
**suddenly** *adv* brusquement, tout à
coup, soudain

**sue** [suː] *vt* poursuivre en justice,
intenter un procès à

**suede** [sweɪd] *n* daim *m*, cuir suédé

**suffer** [ˈsʌfər] *vt* souffrir, subir; (*bear*)
tolérer, supporter, subir ▷ *vi* souffrir;
**to ~ from** (*illness*) souffrir de, avoir;
**suffering** *n* souffrance(s) *f(pl)*

**suffice** [səˈfaɪs] *vi* suffire

**sufficient** [səˈfɪʃənt] *adj* suffisant(e)

**suffocate** [ˈsʌfəkeɪt] *vi* suffoquer;
étouffer

**sugar** [ˈʃuɡər] *n* sucre *m* ▷ *vt* sucrer

**suggest** [səˈdʒɛst] *vt* suggérer,
proposer; (*indicate*) sembler
indiquer; **suggestion** [səˈdʒɛstʃən] *n*
suggestion *f*

**suicide** [ˈsuɪsaɪd] *n* suicide *m*; **~
bombing** attentat *m* suicide; *see also*
**commit**; **suicide bomber** *n* kamikaze
*m/f*

**suit** [suːt] *n* (*man's*) costume *m*, complet
*m*; (*woman's*) tailleur *m*, ensemble *m*;
(*Cards*) couleur *f*; (*lawsuit*) procès *m*
▷ *vt* (*subj: clothes, hairstyle*) aller à; (*be
convenient for*) convenir à; (*adapt*): **to
~ sth to** adapter *or* approprier qch à;
**well ~ed** (*couple*) faits l'un pour l'autre,
très bien assortis; **suitable** *adj* qui
convient; approprié(e), adéquat(e);
**suitcase** *n* valise *f*

**suite** [swiːt] *n* (*of rooms, also Mus*) suite
*f*; (*furniture*): **bedroom/dining room ~**
(ensemble *m* de) chambre *f* à coucher/
salle *f* à manger; **a three-piece ~** un
salon (canapé et deux fauteuils)

**sulfur** [ˈsʌlfər] (*US*) *n* = **sulphur**

**sulk** [sʌlk] *vi* bouder

**sulphur** (*US* **sulfur**) [ˈsʌlfər] *n* soufre *m*

**sultana** [sʌlˈtɑːnə] *n* (*fruit*) raisin (sec)
de Smyrne

**sum** [sʌm] *n* somme *f*; (*Scol etc*) calcul *m*;
**sum up** *vt* résumer ▷ *vi* résumer

**summarize** ['sʌməraɪz] vt résumer

**summary** ['sʌmərɪ] n résumé m

**summer** ['sʌmə<sup>r</sup>] n été m ▷ cpd d'été, estival(e); **in (the) ~** en été, pendant l'été; **summer holidays** npl grandes vacances; **summertime** n (season) été m

**summit** ['sʌmɪt] n sommet m; (also: **~ conference**) (conférence f au) sommet m

**summon** ['sʌmən] vt appeler, convoquer; **to ~ a witness** citer or assigner un témoin

**Sun.** abbr (= Sunday) dim

**sun** [sʌn] n soleil m; **sunbathe** vi prendre un bain de soleil; **sunbed** n lit pliant; (with sun lamp) lit à ultra-violets; **sunblock** n écran m total; **sunburn** n coup m de soleil; **sunburned, sunburnt** adj bronzé(e), hâlé(e); (painfully) brûlé(e) par le soleil

**Sunday** ['sʌndɪ] n dimanche m

**sunflower** ['sʌnflauə<sup>r</sup>] n tournesol m

**sung** [sʌŋ] pp of **sing**

**sunglasses** ['sʌnglɑ:sɪz] npl lunettes fpl de soleil

**sunk** [sʌŋk] pp of **sink**

**sun:** **sunlight** n (lumière f du) soleil m; **sun lounger** n chaise longue; **sunny** adj ensoleillé(e); **it is sunny** il fait (du) soleil, il y a du soleil; **sunrise** n lever m du soleil; **sun roof** n (Aut) toit ouvrant; **sunscreen** n crème f solaire; **sunset** n coucher m du soleil; **sunshade** n (over table) parasol m; **sunshine** n (lumière f du) soleil m; **sunstroke** n insolation f, coup m de soleil; **suntan** n bronzage m; **suntan lotion** n lotion f or lait m solaire; **suntan oil** n huile f solaire

**super** ['su:pə<sup>r</sup>] adj (inf) formidable

**superb** [su:'pə:b] adj superbe, magnifique

**superficial** [su:pə'fɪʃəl] adj superficiel(le)

**superintendent** [su:pərɪn'tɛndənt] n directeur(-trice); (Police) ≈ commissaire m

**superior** [su:'pɪərɪə<sup>r</sup>] adj supérieur(e);

(smug) condescendant(e), méprisant(e) ▷ n supérieur(e)

**superlative** [su:'pə:lətɪv] n (Ling) superlatif m

**supermarket** ['su:pəmɑ:kɪt] n supermarché m

**supernatural** [su:pə'nætʃərəl] adj surnaturel(le) ▷ n: **the ~** le surnaturel

**superpower** ['su:pəpauə<sup>r</sup>] n (Pol) superpuissance f

**superstition** [su:pə'stɪʃən] n superstition f

**superstitious** [su:pə'stɪʃəs] adj superstitieux(-euse)

**superstore** ['su:pəstɔ:<sup>r</sup>] n (BRIT) hypermarché m, grande surface

**supervise** ['su:pəvaɪz] vt (children etc) surveiller; (organization, work) diriger; **supervision** [su:pə'vɪʒən] n surveillance f; (monitoring) contrôle m; (management) direction f; **supervisor** n surveillant(e); (in shop) chef m de rayon

**supper** ['sʌpə<sup>r</sup>] n dîner m; (late) souper m

**supple** ['sʌpl] adj souple

**supplement** n ['sʌplɪmənt] supplément m ▷ vt [sʌplɪ'mɛnt] ajouter à, compléter

**supplier** [sə'plaɪə<sup>r</sup>] n fournisseur m

**supply** [sə'plaɪ] vt (provide) fournir; (equip): **to ~ (with)** approvisionner or ravitailler (en); fournir (en) ▷ n provision f, réserve f; (supplying) approvisionnement m; **supplies** npl (food) vivres mpl; (Mil) subsistances fpl

**support** [sə'pɔ:t] n (moral, financial etc) soutien m, appui m; (Tech) support m, soutien ▷ vt soutenir, supporter; (financially) subvenir aux besoins de; (uphold) être pour, être partisan de, appuyer; (Sport: team) être pour; **supporter** n (Pol etc) partisan(e); (Sport) supporter m

**suppose** [sə'pəuz] vt, vi supposer; imaginer; **to be ~d to do/be** être censé(e) faire/être; **supposedly** [sə'pəuzɪdlɪ] adv soi-disant; **supposing** conj si, à supposer que + sub

**suppress** [sə'prɛs] vt (revolt, feeling)
réprimer; (information) faire disparaître;
(scandal, yawn) étouffer

**supreme** [su'priːm] adj suprême

**surcharge** ['səːtʃɑːdʒ] n surcharge f

**sure** [ʃuə'] adj (gen) sûr(e); (definite,
convinced) sûr, certain(e); **~!** (of course)
bien sûr!; **to make ~ of sth/that** s'assurer de
qch/que, vérifier qch/que; **surely** adv
sûrement; certainement

**surf** [səːf] n (waves) ressac m ▷ vt: **to
~ the Net** surfer sur Internet, surfer
sur le net

**surface** ['səːfɪs] n surface f ▷ vt (road)
poser un revêtement sur ▷ vi remonter
à la surface; (fig) faire surface; **by ~
mail** par voie de terre; (by sea) par voie
maritime

**surfboard** ['səːfbɔːd] n planche f
de surf

**surfer** ['səːfə'] n (in sea) surfeur(-euse);
**web** or **net ~** internaute m/f

**surfing** ['səːfɪŋ] n surf m

**surge** [səːdʒ] n (of emotion) vague f ▷ vi
déferler

**surgeon** ['səːdʒən] n chirurgien m

**surgery** ['səːdʒərɪ] n chirurgie f; (BRIT:
room) cabinet m (de consultation); (also:
**~ hours**) heures fpl de consultation

**surname** ['səːneɪm] n nom m de
famille

**surpass** [səː'pɑːs] vt surpasser,
dépasser

**surplus** ['səːpləs] n surplus m, excédent
m ▷ adj en surplus, de trop; (Comm)
excédentaire

**surprise** [sə'praɪz] n (gen) surprise
f; (astonishment) étonnement m ▷ vt
surprendre, étonner; **surprised** adj
(look, smile) surpris(e), étonné(e); **to
be surprised** être surpris; **surprising**
adj surprenant(e), étonnant(e);
**surprisingly** adv (easy, helpful)
étonnamment, étrangement;
**(somewhat) surprisingly, he agreed**
curieusement, il a accepté

**surrender** [sə'rɛndə'] n reddition f,

capitulation f ▷ vi se rendre, capituler

**surround** [sə'raund] vt entourer;
(Mil etc) encercler; **surrounding** adj
environnant(e); **surroundings** npl
environs mpl, alentours mpl

**surveillance** [səː'veɪləns] n
surveillance f

**survey** n ['səːveɪ] enquête f, étude f; (in
house buying etc) inspection f, (rapport
m d')expertise f; (of land) levé m ▷ vt
[səː'veɪ] (situation) passer en revue;
(examine carefully) inspecter; (building)
expertiser; (land) faire le levé de; (look
at) embrasser du regard; **surveyor** n (of
building) expert m; (of land) (arpenteur
m) géomètre m

**survival** [sə'vaɪvl] n survie f

**survive** [sə'vaɪv] vi survivre; (custom
etc) subsister ▷ vt (accident etc) survivre
à, réchapper de; (person) survivre à;
**survivor** n survivant(e)

**suspect** adj, n ['sʌspɛkt] suspect(e)
▷ vt [səs'pɛkt] soupçonner, suspecter

**suspend** [səs'pɛnd] vt suspendre;
**suspended sentence** n (Law)
condamnation f avec sursis;
**suspenders** npl (BRIT) jarretelles fpl;
(US) bretelles fpl

**suspense** [səs'pɛns] n attente f,
incertitude f; (in film etc) suspense m; **to
keep sb in ~** tenir qn en suspens, laisser
qn dans l'incertitude

**suspension** [səs'pɛnʃən] n (gen, Aut)
suspension f; (of driving licence) retrait m
provisoire; **suspension bridge** n pont
suspendu

**suspicion** [səs'pɪʃən] n
soupçon(s) m(pl); **suspicious** adj
(suspecting) soupçonneux(-euse),
méfiant(e); (causing suspicion)
suspect(e)

**sustain** [səs'teɪn] vt soutenir; (subj:
food) nourrir, donner des forces à;
(damage) subir; (injury) recevoir

**SUV** n abbr (esp US: = sports utility vehicle)
SUV m, véhicule m de loisirs

**swallow** ['swɔləu] n (bird) hirondelle f
▷ vt avaler; (fig: story) gober

**swam** [swæm] pt of **swim**

**swamp** [swɔmp] n marais m, marécage m ▷ vt submerger

**swan** [swɔn] n cygne m

**swap** [swɔp] n échange m, troc m ▷ vt: **to ~ (for)** échanger (contre), troquer (contre)

**swarm** [swɔːm] n essaim m ▷ vi (bees) essaimer; (people) grouiller; **to be ~ing with** grouiller de

**sway** [sweɪ] vi se balancer, osciller ▷ vt (influence) influencer

**swear** [swɛəʳ] (pt **swore**, pp **sworn**) vt, vi jurer; **swear in** vt assermenter; **swearword** n gros mot, juron m

**sweat** [swɛt] n sueur f, transpiration f ▷ vi suer

**sweater** ['swɛtəʳ] n tricot m, pull m

**sweatshirt** ['swɛtʃəːt] n sweat-shirt m

**sweaty** ['swɛtɪ] adj en sueur, moite or mouillé(e) de sueur

**Swede** [swiːd] n Suédois(e)

**swede** [swiːd] n (BRIT) rutabaga m

**Sweden** ['swiːdn] n Suède f; **Swedish** ['swiːdɪʃ] adj suédois(e) ▷ n (Ling) suédois m

**sweep** [swiːp] n (curve) grande courbe; (also: **chimney ~**) ramoneur m ▷ vb (pt, pp **swept**) ▷ vt balayer; (subj: current) emporter

**sweet** [swiːt] n (BRIT: pudding) dessert m; (candy) bonbon m ▷ adj doux (douce); (not savoury) sucré(e); (kind) gentil(le); (baby) mignon(ne); **sweetcorn** n maïs doux; **sweetener** ['swiːtnəʳ] n (Culin) édulcorant m; **sweetheart** n amoureux(-euse); **sweetshop** n (BRIT) confiserie f

**swell** [swɛl] n (of sea) houle f ▷ adj (us: inf: excellent) chouette ▷ vb (pt **~ed**, pp **swollen** or **~ed**) ▷ vt (increase) grossir, augmenter ▷ vi (increase) grossir, augmenter; (sound) s'enfler; (Med: also: **~ up**) enfler; **swelling** n (Med) enflure f; (: lump) grosseur f

**swept** [swɛpt] pt, pp of **sweep**

**swerve** [swəːv] vi (to avoid obstacle) faire une embardée or un écart; (off the road) dévier

**swift** [swɪft] n (bird) martinet m ▷ adj rapide, prompt(e)

**swim** [swɪm] n: **to go for a ~** aller nager or se baigner ▷ vb (pt **swam**, pp **swum**) ▷ vi nager; (Sport) faire de la natation; (fig: head, room) tourner ▷ vt traverser (à la nage); **to ~ a length** nager une longueur; **swimmer** n nageur(-euse); **swimming** n nage f, natation f; **swimming costume** n (BRIT) maillot m (de bain); **swimming pool** n piscine f; **swimming trunks** npl maillot m de bain; **swimsuit** n maillot m (de bain)

**swing** [swɪŋ] n (in playground) balançoire f; (movement) balancement m, oscillations fpl; (change in opinion etc) revirement m ▷ vb (pt, pp **swung**) ▷ vt balancer, faire osciller; (also: **~ round**) tourner, faire virer ▷ vi se balancer, osciller; (also: **~ round**) virer, tourner; **to be in full ~** battre son plein

**swipe card** [swaɪp-] n carte f magnétique

**swirl** [swəːl] vi tourbillonner, tournoyer

**Swiss** [swɪs] adj suisse ▷ n (pl inv) Suisse(-esse)

**switch** [swɪtʃ] n (for light, radio etc) bouton m; (change) changement m, revirement m ▷ vt (change) changer; **switch off** vt éteindre; (engine, machine) arrêter; **could you ~ off the light?** pouvez-vous éteindre la lumière?; **switch on** vt allumer; (engine, machine) mettre en marche; **switchboard** n (Tel) standard m

**Switzerland** ['swɪtsələnd] n Suisse f

**swivel** ['swɪvl] vi (also: **~ round**) pivoter, tourner

**swollen** ['swəulən] pp of **swell**

**swoop** [swuːp] n (by police etc) rafle f, descente f ▷ vi (bird: also: **~ down**) descendre en piqué, piquer

**swop** [swɔp] n, vt = **swap**

**sword** [sɔːd] n épée f; **swordfish** n espadon m

**swore** [swɔːʳ] pt of **swear**

**sworn** [swɔːn] pp of **swear** ▷ adj

(*statement, evidence*) donné(e) sous
serment; (*enemy*) juré(e)
**swum** [swʌm] *pp of* **swim**
**swung** [swʌŋ] *pt, pp of* **swing**
**syllable** ['sɪləbl] *n* syllabe *f*
**syllabus** ['sɪləbəs] *n* programme *m*
**symbol** ['sɪmbl] *n* symbole *m*;
 **symbolic(al)** [sɪm'bɒlɪk(l)] *adj*
 symbolique
**symmetrical** [sɪ'mɛtrɪkl] *adj*
 symétrique
**symmetry** ['sɪmɪtrɪ] *n* symétrie *f*
**sympathetic** [sɪmpə'θɛtɪk] *adj*
 (*showing pity*) compatissant(e);
 (*understanding*) bienveillant(e),
 compréhensif(-ive); **~ towards** bien
 disposé(e) envers

> Be careful not to translate
> *sympathetic* by the French word
> *sympathique*.

**sympathize** ['sɪmpəθaɪz] *vi*: **to ~
 with sb** plaindre qn; (*in grief*) s'associer
 à la douleur de qn; **to ~ with sth**
 comprendre qch
**sympathy** ['sɪmpəθɪ] *n* (*pity*)
 compassion *f*
**symphony** ['sɪmfənɪ] *n* symphonie *f*
**symptom** ['sɪmptəm] *n* symptôme
 *m*; indice *m*
**synagogue** ['sɪnəgɒg] *n* synagogue *f*
**syndicate** ['sɪndɪkɪt] *n* syndicat *m*,
 coopérative *f*; (*Press*) agence *f* de presse
**syndrome** ['sɪndrəum] *n* syndrome *m*
**synonym** ['sɪnənɪm] *n* synonyme *m*
**synthetic** [sɪn'θɛtɪk] *adj* synthétique
**Syria** ['sɪrɪə] *n* Syrie *f*
**syringe** [sɪ'rɪndʒ] *n* seringue *f*
**syrup** ['sɪrəp] *n* sirop *m*; (BRIT: *also*:
 **golden ~**) mélasse raffinée
**system** ['sɪstəm] *n* système *m*;
 (*Anat*) organisme *m*; **systematic**
 [sɪstə'mætɪk] *adj* systématique;
 méthodique; **systems analyst** *n*
 analyste-programmeur *m/f*

**ta** [tɑː] *excl* (BRIT *inf*) merci!
**tab** [tæb] *n* (*label*) étiquette *f*; (*on drinks
 can etc*) languette *f*; **to keep ~s on** (*fig*)
 surveiller
**table** ['teɪbl] *n* table *f* ▷ *vt* (BRIT: *motion
 etc*) présenter; **a ~ for 4, please** une
 table pour 4, s'il vous plaît; **to lay** *or*
 **set the ~** mettre le couvert *or* la table;
 **tablecloth** *n* nappe *f*; **table d'hôte**
 [tɑːbl'dəut] *adj* (*meal*) à prix fixe; **table
 lamp** *n* lampe décorative *or* de table;
 **tablemat** *n* (*for plate*) napperon *m*,
 set *m*; (*for hot dish*) dessous-de-plat *m*
 *inv*; **tablespoon** *n* cuiller *f* de service;
 (*also*: **tablespoonful**: *as measurement*)
 cuillerée *f* à soupe
**tablet** ['tæblɪt] *n* (*Med*) comprimé *m*; (*of
 stone*) plaque *f*
**table tennis** *n* ping-pong *m*, tennis
 *m* de table
**tabloid** ['tæblɔɪd] *n* (*newspaper*)
 quotidien *m* populaire
**taboo** [tə'buː] *adj, n* tabou (*m*)
**tack** [tæk] *n* (*nail*) petit clou; (*fig*)

direction f ▷ vt (nail) clouer; (sew) bâtir
▷ vi (Naut) tirer un or des bord(s); **to ~
sth on to (the end of) sth** (of letter,
book) rajouter qch à la fin de qch

**tackle** ['tækl] n matériel m,
équipement m; (for lifting) appareil m de
levage; (Football, Rugby) plaquage m ▷ vt
(difficulty, animal, burglar) s'attaquer
à; (person: challenge) s'expliquer avec;
(Football, Rugby) plaquer

**tacky** ['tækɪ] adj collant(e); (paint) pas
sec (sèche); (pej: poor-quality) minable;
(: showing bad taste) ringard(e)

**tact** [tækt] n tact m; **tactful** adj plein(e)
de tact

**tactics** ['tæktɪks] npl tactique f

**tactless** ['tæktlɪs] adj qui manque
de tact

**tadpole** ['tædpəʊl] n têtard m

**taffy** ['tæfɪ] n (US) (bonbon m au)
caramel m

**tag** [tæg] n étiquette f

**tail** [teɪl] n queue f; (of shirt) pan m ▷ vt
(follow) suivre, filer; **tails** npl (suit) habit
m; see also **head**

**tailor** ['teɪlə'] n tailleur m (artisan)

**Taiwan** ['taɪ'wɑːn] n Taïwan (no
article); **Taiwanese** [taɪwə'niːz] adj
taïwanais(e) ▷ n inv Taïwanais(e)

**take** [teɪk] vb (pt **took**, pp **~n**) ▷ vt
prendre; (gain: prize) remporter; (require:
effort, courage) demander; (tolerate)
accepter, supporter; (hold: passengers
etc) contenir; (accompany) emmener,
accompagner; (bring, carry) apporter,
emporter; (exam) passer, se présenter
à; **to ~ sth from** (drawer etc) prendre
qch dans; (person) prendre qch à; **I ~
it that** je suppose que; **to be ~n ill**
tomber malade; **it won't ~ long** ça ne
prendra pas longtemps; **I was quite
~n with her/it** elle/cela m'a beaucoup
plu; **take after** vt fus ressembler
à; **take apart** vt démonter; **take
away** vt (carry off) emporter; (remove)
enlever; (subtract) soustraire; **take
back** vt (return) rendre, rapporter;
(one's words) retirer; **take down** vt

(building) démolir; (letter etc) prendre,
écrire; **take in** vt (deceive) tromper,
rouler; (understand) comprendre,
saisir; (include) couvrir, inclure; (lodger)
prendre; (dress, waistband) reprendre;
**take off** vi (Aviat) décoller ▷ vt (remove)
enlever; **take on** vt (work) accepter,
se charger de; (employee) prendre,
embaucher; (opponent) accepter de
se battre contre; **take out** vt sortir;
(remove) enlever; (invite) sortir avec; **to
~ sth out of** (out of drawer etc) prendre
qch dans; **to ~ sb out to a restaurant**
emmener qn au restaurant; **take over**
vt (business) reprendre ▷ vi: **to ~ over
from sb** prendre la relève de qn; **take
up** vt (one's story) reprendre; (dress)
raccourcir; (occupy: time, space) prendre,
occuper; (engage in: hobby etc) se mettre
à; (accept: offer, challenge) accepter;
**takeaway** (BRIT) adj (food) à emporter
▷ n (shop, restaurant) ≈ magasin m qui
vend des plats à emporter; **taken** pp of
**take**; **is this seat taken?** la place est
prise?; **takeoff** n (Aviat) décollage m;
**takeout** adj, n (US) = **takeaway**;
**takeover** n (Comm) rachat m; **takings**
npl (Comm) recette f

**talc** [tælk] n (also: **~um powder**) talc m

**tale** [teɪl] n (story) conte m, histoire
f; (account) récit m; **to tell ~s** (fig)
rapporter

**talent** ['tælnt] n talent m, don m;
**talented** adj doué(e), plein(e) de talent

**talk** [tɔːk] n (a speech) causerie f, exposé
m; (conversation) discussion f; (interview)
entretien m; (gossip) racontars mpl (pej)
▷ vi parler; (chatter) bavarder; **talks**
npl (Pol etc) entretiens mpl; **to ~ about**
parler de; **to ~ sb out of/into doing**
persuader qn de ne pas faire/de faire;
**to ~ shop** parler métier or affaires; **talk
over** vt discuter (de); **talk show** n (TV,
Radio) émission-débat f

**tall** [tɔːl] adj (person) grand(e); (building,
tree) haut(e); **to be 6 feet ~** ≈ mesurer
1 mètre 80

**tambourine** [tæmbə'riːn] n

tambourin m

**tame** [teɪm] adj apprivoisé(e); (fig:
story, style) insipide

**tamper** ['tæmpə'] vi: **to ~ with** toucher
à (en cachette ou sans permission)

**tampon** ['tæmpən] n tampon m
hygiénique or périodique

**tan** [tæn] n (also: **sun~**) bronzage m
▷ vt, vi bronzer, brunir ▷ adj (colour)
marron clair inv

**tandem** ['tændəm] n tandem m

**tangerine** [tændʒə'riːn] n mandarine f

**tangle** ['tæŋgl] n enchevêtrement m;
**to get in(to) a ~** s'emmêler

**tank** [tæŋk] n réservoir m; (for fish)
aquarium m; (Mil) char m d'assaut,
tank m

**tanker** ['tæŋkə'] n (ship) pétrolier m,
tanker m; (truck) camion-citerne m

**tanned** [tænd] adj bronzé(e)

**tantrum** ['tæntrəm] n accès m de colère

**Tanzania** [tænzə'nɪə] n Tanzanie f

**tap** [tæp] n (on sink etc) robinet m;
(gentle blow) petite tape ▷ vt frapper or
taper légèrement; (resources) exploiter,
utiliser; (telephone) mettre sur écoute;
**on ~** (fig: resources) disponible; **tap
dancing** n claquettes fpl

**tape** [teɪp] n (for tying) ruban m; (also:
**magnetic ~**) bande f (magnétique);
(cassette) cassette f; (sticky) Scotch®
m ▷ vt (record) enregistrer (au
magnétoscope or sur cassette); (stick)
coller avec du Scotch®; **tape measure**
n mètre m à ruban; **tape recorder** n
magnétophone m

**tapestry** ['tæpɪstrɪ] n tapisserie f

**tar** [tɑː] n goudron m

**target** ['tɑːgɪt] n cible f; (fig: objective)
objectif m

**tariff** ['tærɪf] n (Comm) tarif m; (taxes)
tarif douanier

**tarmac** ['tɑːmæk] n (BRIT: on road)
macadam m; (Aviat) aire f d'envol

**tarpaulin** [tɑː'pɔːlɪn] n bâche
goudronnée

**tarragon** ['tærəgən] n estragon m

**tart** [tɑːt] n (Culin) tarte f; (BRIT inf: pej:
prostitute) poule f ▷ adj (flavour) âpre,
aigrelet(te)

**tartan** ['tɑːtn] n tartan m ▷ adj
écossais(e)

**tartar(e) sauce** n sauce f tartare

**task** [tɑːsk] n tâche f; **to take to ~**
prendre à partie

**taste** [teɪst] n goût m; (fig: glimpse,
idea) idée f, aperçu m ▷ vt goûter ▷ vi:
**to ~ of** (fish etc) avoir le or un goût de;
**you can ~ the garlic (in it)** on sent
bien l'ail; **to have a ~ of sth** goûter (à)
qch; **can I have a ~?** je peux goûter?;
**to be in good/bad** or **poor ~** être de
bon/mauvais goût; **tasteful** adj de
bon goût; **tasteless** adj (food) insipide;
(remark) de mauvais goût; **tasty** adj
savoureux(-euse), délicieux(-euse)

**tatters** ['tætəz] npl: **in ~** (also: **tattered**)
en lambeaux

**tattoo** [tə'tuː] n tatouage m; (spectacle)
parade f militaire ▷ vt tatouer

**taught** [tɔːt] pt, pp of **teach**

**taunt** [tɔːnt] n raillerie f ▷ vt railler

**Taurus** ['tɔːrəs] n le Taureau

**taut** [tɔːt] adj tendu(e)

**tax** [tæks] n (on goods etc) taxe f; (on
income) impôts mpl, contributions fpl
▷ vt taxer; imposer; (fig: patience etc)
mettre à l'épreuve; **tax disc** n (BRIT Aut)
vignette f (automobile); **tax-free** adj
exempt(e) d'impôts

**taxi** ['tæksɪ] n taxi m ▷ vi (Aviat) rouler
(lentement) au sol; **can you call me
a ~, please?** pouvez-vous m'appeler
un taxi, s'il vous plaît?; **taxi driver** n
chauffeur m de taxi; **taxi rank** (BRIT),
**taxi stand** n station f de taxis

**tax payer** [-peɪə'] n contribuable m/f

**tax return** n déclaration f d'impôts or
de revenus

**TB** n abbr = **tuberculosis**

**tea** [tiː] n thé m; (BRIT: snack: for children)
goûter m; **high ~** (BRIT) collation
combinant goûter et dîner; **tea bag** n
sachet m de thé; **tea break** n (BRIT)
pause-thé f

**teach** (pt, pp **taught**) [tiːtʃ, tɔːt] vt: **to**

~ sb sth, to ~ sth to sb apprendre qch
à qn; (in school etc) enseigner qch à qn
▷ vi enseigner; **teacher** n (in secondary
school) professeur m; (in primary
school) instituteur(-trice); **teaching** n
enseignement m

**tea**: **tea cloth** n (BRIT) torchon m;
**teacup** n tasse f à thé

**tea leaves** npl feuilles fpl de thé

**team** [ti:m] n équipe f; (of animals)
attelage m; **team up** vi: to ~ up (with)
faire équipe (avec)

**teapot** ['ti:pɔt] n théière f

**tear**[1] ['tɪə[r]] n larme f; **in ~s** en larmes

**tear**[2] n [tɛə[r]] déchirure f ▷ vb (pt **tore**,
pp **torn**) ▷ vt déchirer ▷ vi se déchirer;
**tear apart** vt (also fig) déchirer; **tear
down** vt (building, statue) démolir;
(poster, flag) arracher; **tear off** vt (sheet
of paper etc) arracher; (one's clothes)
enlever à toute vitesse; **tear up** vt
(sheet of paper etc) déchirer, mettre en
morceaux or pièces

**tearful** ['tɪəful] adj larmoyant(e)

**tear gas** ['tɪə-] n gaz m lacrymogène

**tearoom** ['ti:ru:m] n salon m de thé

**tease** [ti:z] vt taquiner; (unkindly)
tourmenter

**tea**: **teaspoon** n petite cuiller; (also:
**teaspoonful**: as measurement)
≈ cuillerée f à café; **teatime** n l'heure f
du thé; **tea towel** n (BRIT) torchon m
(à vaisselle)

**technical** ['tɛknɪkl] adj technique

**technician** [tɛk'nɪʃən] n
technicien(ne)

**technique** [tɛk'ni:k] n technique f

**technology** [tɛk'nɔlədʒɪ] n
technologie f

**teddy (bear)** ['tɛdɪ-] n ours m (en
peluche)

**tedious** ['ti:dɪəs] adj fastidieux(-euse)

**tee** [ti:] n (Golf) tee m

**teen** [ti:n] adj =**teenage** ▷ n (US)
=**teenager**

**teenage** ['ti:neɪdʒ] adj (fashions etc)
pour jeunes, pour adolescents; (child)
qui est adolescent(e); **teenager** n

adolescent(e)

**teens** [ti:nz] npl: to be in one's ~ être
adolescent(e)

**teeth** [ti:θ] npl of **tooth**

**teetotal** ['ti:'təutl] adj (person) qui ne
boit jamais d'alcool

**telecommunications**
['tɛlɪkəmju:nɪ'keɪʃənz] n
télécommunications fpl

**telegram** ['tɛlɪgræm] n télégramme m

**telegraph pole** ['tɛlɪgrɑ:f-] n poteau
m télégraphique

**telephone** ['tɛlɪfəun] n téléphone m
▷ vt (person) téléphoner à; (message)
téléphoner; to be on the ~ (be speaking)
être au téléphone; **telephone book**
n =**telephone directory**; **telephone
booth** (BRIT), **telephone box** n cabine
f téléphonique; **telephone call** n appel
m téléphonique; **telephone directory**
n annuaire m (du téléphone);
**telephone number** n numéro m de
téléphone

**telesales** ['tɛlɪseɪlz] npl télévente f

**telescope** ['tɛlɪskəup] n télescope m

**televise** ['tɛlɪvaɪz] vt téléviser

**television** ['tɛlɪvɪʒən] n télévision
f; **on ~** à la télévision; **television
programme** n émission f de télévision

**tell** (pt, pp **told**) [tɛl, təuld] vt dire;
(relate: story) raconter; (distinguish):
to ~ sth from distinguer qch de ▷ vi
(talk): to ~ of parler de; (have effect)
se faire sentir, se voir; to ~ sb to do
dire à qn de faire; to ~ the time (know
how to) savoir lire l'heure; **tell off** vt
réprimander, gronder; **teller** n (in bank)
caissier(-ière)

**telly** ['tɛlɪ] n abbr (BRIT inf: = television)
télé f

**temp** [tɛmp] n (BRIT = temporary worker)
intérimaire m/f ▷ vi travailler comme
intérimaire

**temper** ['tɛmpə[r]] n (nature) caractère
m; (mood) humeur f; (fit of anger) colère f
▷ vt (moderate) tempérer, adoucir; **to be
in a ~** être en colère; **to lose one's ~** se
mettre en colère

**temperament** ['tɛmprəmənt]
n (nature) tempérament m;
**temperamental** [tɛmprə'mɛntl] adj
capricieux(-euse)

**temperature** ['tɛmprətʃəʳ] n
température f; **to have** or **run a ~** avoir
de la fièvre

**temple** ['tɛmpl] n (building) temple m;
(Anat) tempe f

**temporary** ['tɛmpərərɪ] adj
temporaire, provisoire; (job, worker)
temporaire

**tempt** [tɛmpt] vt tenter; **to ~ sb into
doing** induire qn à faire; **temptation** n
tentation f; **tempting** adj tentant(e);
(food) appétissant(e)

**ten** [tɛn] num dix

**tenant** ['tɛnənt] n locataire m/f

**tend** [tɛnd] vt s'occuper de ▷ vi: **to ~ to
do** avoir tendance à faire; **tendency**
['tɛndənsɪ] n tendance f

**tender** ['tɛndəʳ] adj tendre; (delicate)
délicat(e); (sore) sensible ▷ n (Comm:
offer) soumission f; (money): **legal ~**
cours légal ▷ vt offrir

**tendon** ['tɛndən] n tendon m

**tenner** ['tɛnəʳ] n (BRIT inf) billet m de
dix livres

**tennis** ['tɛnɪs] n tennis m; **tennis ball**
n balle f de tennis; **tennis court** n
(court m de) tennis m; **tennis match**
n match m de tennis; **tennis player** n
joueur(-euse) de tennis; **tennis racket**
n raquette f de tennis

**tenor** ['tɛnəʳ] n (Mus) ténor m

**tenpin bowling** ['tɛnpɪn-] n (BRIT)
bowling m (à 10 quilles)

**tense** [tɛns] adj tendu(e) ▷ n (Ling)
temps m

**tension** ['tɛnʃən] n tension f

**tent** [tɛnt] n tente f

**tentative** ['tɛntətɪv] adj timide,
hésitant(e); (conclusion) provisoire

**tenth** [tɛnθ] num dixième

**tent**: **tent peg** n piquet m de tente; **tent
pole** n montant m de tente

**tepid** ['tɛpɪd] adj tiède

**term** [təːm] n terme m; (Scol) trimestre

m ▷ vt appeler; **terms** npl (conditions)
conditions fpl; (Comm) tarif m; **in the
short/long ~** à court/long terme; **to
come to ~s with** (problem) faire face à;
**to be on good ~s with** bien s'entendre
avec, être en bons termes avec

**terminal** ['təːmɪnl] adj (disease) dans sa
phase terminale; (patient) incurable ▷ n
(Elec) borne f; (for oil, ore etc, also Comput)
terminal m; (also: **air ~**) aérogare f;
(BRIT: also: **coach ~**) gare routière

**terminate** ['təːmɪneɪt] vt mettre fin à;
(pregnancy) interrompre

**termini** ['təːmɪnaɪ] npl of **terminus**

**terminology** [təːmɪ'nɔlədʒɪ] n
terminologie f

**terminus** (pl **termini**) ['təːmɪnəs,
'təːmɪnaɪ] n terminus m inv

**terrace** ['tɛrəs] n terrasse f; (BRIT: row of
houses) rangée f de maisons (attenantes
les unes aux autres); **the ~s** (BRIT Sport)
les gradins mpl; **terraced** adj (garden)
en terrasses; (in a row: house, cottage etc)
attenant(e) aux maisons voisines

**terrain** [tɛ'reɪn] n terrain m (sol)

**terrestrial** [tɪ'rɛstrɪəl] adj terrestre

**terrible** ['tɛrɪbl] adj terrible, atroce;
(weather, work) affreux(-euse),
épouvantable; **terribly** adv
terriblement; (very badly) affreusement
mal

**terrier** ['tɛrɪəʳ] n terrier m (chien)

**terrific** [tə'rɪfɪk] adj (very
great) fantastique, incroyable,
terrible; (wonderful) formidable,
sensationnel(le)

**terrified** ['tɛrɪfaɪd] adj terrifié(e); **to be
~ of sth** avoir très peur de qch

**terrify** ['tɛrɪfaɪ] vt terrifier; **terrifying**
adj terrifiant(e)

**territorial** [tɛrɪ'tɔːrɪəl] adj
territorial(e)

**territory** ['tɛrɪtərɪ] n territoire m

**terror** ['tɛrəʳ] n terreur f; **terrorism** n
terrorisme m; **terrorist** n terroriste
m/f; **terrorist attack** n attentat m
terroriste

**test** [tɛst] n (trial, check) essai m; (: of

*courage etc*) épreuve *f*; (*Med*) examen *m*;
(*Chem*) analyse *f*; (*Scol*) interrogation *f*
de contrôle; (*also:* **driving ~**) (examen
du) permis *m* de conduire ▷ *vt* essayer;
mettre à l'épreuve; examiner; analyser;
faire subir une interrogation (de
contrôle) à

**testicle** ['tɛstɪkl] *n* testicule *m*

**testify** ['tɛstɪfaɪ] *vi* (*Law*) témoigner,
déposer; **to ~ to sth** (*Law*) attester qch

**testimony** ['tɛstɪmənɪ] *n* (*Law*)
témoignage *m*, déposition *f*

**test**: **test match** *n* (*Cricket, Rugby*)
match international; **test tube** *n*
éprouvette *f*

**tetanus** ['tɛtənəs] *n* tétanos *m*

**text** [tɛkst] *n* texte *m*; (*on mobile phone*)
texto *m*, SMS *m inv* ▷ *vt* (*inf*) envoyer un
texto *or* SMS à; **textbook** *n* manuel *m*

**textile** ['tɛkstaɪl] *n* textile *m*

**text message** *n* texto *m*, SMS *m inv*

**text messaging** [-'mɛsɪdʒɪŋ] *n*
messagerie textuelle

**texture** ['tɛkstʃəʳ] *n* texture *f*; (*of skin,
paper etc*) grain *m*

**Thai** [taɪ] *adj* thaïlandais(e) ▷ *n*
Thaïlandais(e)

**Thailand** ['taɪlænd] *n* Thaïlande *f*

**Thames** [tɛmz] *n*: **the (River) ~** la
Tamise

**than** [ðæn, ðən] *conj* que; (*with
numerals*): **more ~ 10/once** plus de
10/d'une fois; **I have more/less ~
you** j'en ai plus/moins que toi; **she
has more apples ~ pears** elle a plus
de pommes que de poires; **it is better
to phone ~ to write** il vaut mieux
téléphoner (plutôt) qu'écrire; **she is
older ~ you think** elle est plus âgée
que tu le crois

**thank** [θæŋk] *vt* remercier, dire merci
à; **thanks** *npl* remerciements *mpl*
▷ *excl* merci!; **~ you (very much)**
merci (beaucoup); **~ God** Dieu merci!;
**~s to** *prep* grâce à; **thankfully**
*adv* (*fortunately*) heureusement;
**Thanksgiving (Day)** *n* jour *m* d'action
de grâce; *voir encadré*

 **KEYWORD**

**that** [ðæt] *adj* (*demonstrative: pl* **those**)
ce, cet + *vowel or* h *mute*, cette *f*; **that
man/woman/book** cet homme/cette
femme/ce livre; (*not this*) cet homme-
là/cette femme-là/ce livre-là; **that one**
celui-là (celle-là)

▷ *pron* **1** (*demonstrative: pl* **those**) ce;
(*not this one*) cela, ça; (*that one*) celui
(celle); **who's that?** qui est-ce?; **what's
that?** qu'est-ce que c'est?; **is that
you?** c'est toi?; **I prefer this to that** je
préfère ceci à cela *or* ça; **that's what he
said** c'est *or* voilà ce qu'il a dit; **will you
eat all that?** est-ce que tu vas manger
tout ça?; **that is (to say)** c'est-à-dire,
à savoir

**2** (*relative: subject*) qui; (: *object*) que;
(: *after prep*) lequel (laquelle), lesquels
(lesquelles) *pl*; **the book that I read** le
livre que j'ai lu; **the books that are in
the library** les livres qui sont dans la
bibliothèque; **all that I have** tout ce
que j'ai; **the box that I put it in** la boîte
dans laquelle je l'ai mis; **the people
that I spoke to** les gens auxquels *or* à
qui j'ai parlé

**3** (*relative: of time*) où; **the day that he
came** le jour où il est venu

▷ *conj* que; **he thought that I was ill** il
pensait que j'étais malade

▷ *adv* (*demonstrative*): **I don't like it that much** ça ne me plaît pas tant que ça; **I didn't know it was that bad** je ne savais pas que c'était si *or* aussi mauvais; **it's about that high** c'est à peu près de cette hauteur

**thatched** [θætʃt] *adj* (*roof*) de chaume; **~ cottage** chaumière *f*

**thaw** [θɔː] *n* dégel *m* ▷ *vi* (*ice*) fondre; (*food*) dégeler ▷ *vt* (*food*) (faire) dégeler

 **KEYWORD**

**the** [ðiː, ðə] *def art* **1** (*gen*) le, la *f*, l' + *vowel or h mute*, les *pl* (*NB: à + le(s) =* **au(x)**; *de + le =* **du**; *de + les =* **des**): **the boy/girl/ink** le garçon/la fille/l'encre; **the children** les enfants; **the history of the world** l'histoire du monde; **give it to the postman** donne-le au facteur; **to play the piano/flute** jouer du piano/de la flûte
**2** (+ *adj to form n*) le, la *f*, l' + *vowel or h mute*, les *pl*; **the rich and the poor** les riches et les pauvres; **to attempt the impossible** tenter l'impossible
**3** (*in titles*): **Elizabeth the First** Elisabeth première; **Peter the Great** Pierre le Grand
**4** (*in comparisons*): **the more he works, the more he earns** plus il travaille, plus il gagne de l'argent

**theatre** (*us* **theater**) ['θɪətər] *n* théâtre *m*; (*Med: also:* **operating ~**) salle *f* d'opération

**theft** [θεft] *n* vol *m* (*larcin*)

**their** [ðεər] *adj* leur, leurs *pl*; *see also* **my**; **theirs** *pron* le (la) leur, les leurs; *see also* **mine**¹

**them** [ðεm, ðəm] *pron* (*direct*) les; (*indirect*) leur; (*stressed, after prep*) eux (elles); **give me a few of ~** donnez m'en quelques uns (*or* quelques unes); *see also* **me**

**theme** [θiːm] *n* thème *m*; **theme park** *n* parc *m* à thème

**themselves** [ðəm'sεlvz] *pl pron* (*reflexive*) se; (*emphatic, after prep*) eux-mêmes (elles-mêmes); **between ~** entre eux (elles); *see also* **oneself**

**then** [ðεn] *adv* (*at that time*) alors, à ce moment-là; (*next*) puis, ensuite; (*and also*) et puis ▷ *conj* (*therefore*) alors, dans ce cas ▷ *adj*: **the ~ president** le président d'alors *or* de l'époque; **by ~** (*past*) à ce moment-là; (*future*) d'ici là; **from ~ on** dès lors; **until ~** jusqu'à ce moment-là, jusque-là

**theology** [θɪ'ɔlədʒɪ] *n* théologie *f*

**theory** ['θɪərɪ] *n* théorie *f*

**therapist** ['θεrəpɪst] *n* thérapeute *m/f*

**therapy** ['θεrəpɪ] *n* thérapie *f*

 **KEYWORD**

**there** [ðεər] *adv* **1**: **there is**, **there are** il y a; **there are 3 of them** (*people, things*) il y en a 3; **there is no-one here/no bread left** il n'y a personne/il n'y a plus de pain; **there has been an accident** il y a eu un accident
**2** (*referring to place*) là, là-bas; **it's there** c'est là(-bas); **in/on/up/down there** là-dedans/là-dessus/là-haut/en bas; **he went there on Friday** il y est allé vendredi; **I want that book there** je veux ce livre-là; **there he is!** le voilà!
**3**: **there, there** (*esp to child*) allons, allons!

**there**: **thereabouts** *adv* (*place*) par là, près de là; (*amount*) environ, à peu près; **thereafter** *adv* par la suite; **thereby** *adv* ainsi; **therefore** *adv* donc, par conséquent

**there's** ['ðεəz] = **there is**; **there has**

**thermal** ['θə:ml] *adj* thermique; **~ underwear** sous-vêtements *mpl* en Thermolactyl®

**thermometer** [θə'mɔmɪtər] *n* thermomètre *m*

**thermostat** ['θə:məustæt] *n* thermostat *m*

**these** [ðiːz] *pl pron* ceux-ci (celles-ci) ▷ *pl adj* ces; (*not those*): **~ books** ces

livres-ci
**thesis** (pl **theses**) ['θi:sɪs, 'θi:si:z] n
thèse f
**they** [ðeɪ] pl pron ils (elles); (stressed)
eux (elles); **~ say that ...** (it is said
that) on dit que ...; **they'd = they had**;
**they would**; **they'll = they shall**;
**they will**; **they're = they are**; **they've
= they have**
**thick** [θɪk] adj épais(se); (stupid) bête,
borné(e) ▷ n: **in the ~ of** au beau milieu
de, en plein cœur de; **it's 20 cm =** ça a
20 cm d'épaisseur; **thicken** vi s'épaissir
▷ vt (sauce etc) épaissir; **thickness** n
épaisseur f
**thief** (pl **thieves**) [θi:f, θi:vz] n
voleur(-euse)
**thigh** [θaɪ] n cuisse f
**thin** [θɪn] adj mince; (skinny) maigre;
(soup) peu épais(se); (hair, crowd)
clairsemé(e) ▷ vt (also: **~ down**: sauce,
paint) délayer
**thing** [θɪŋ] n chose f; (object) objet
m; (contraption) truc m; **things** npl
(belongings) affaires fpl; **the ~ is ...** c'est
que ...; **the best ~ would be to** le mieux
serait de; **how are ~s?** comment ça va?;
**to have a ~ about** (be obsessed by) être
obsédé(e) par; (hate) détester; **poor ~!**
le (or la) pauvre!
**think** (pt, pp **thought**) [θɪŋk, θɔ:t] vi
penser, réfléchir ▷ vt penser, croire;
(imagine) s'imaginer; **what did you ~
of them?** qu'avez-vous pensé d'eux?;
**to ~ about sth/sb** penser à qch/qn;
**I'll ~ about it** je vais y réfléchir; **to ~ of
doing** avoir l'idée de faire; **I ~ so/not** je
crois or pense que oui/non; **to ~ well
of** avoir une haute opinion de; **think
over** vt bien réfléchir à; **think up** vt
inventer, trouver
**third** [θə:d] num troisième ▷ n (fraction)
tiers m; (Aut) troisième (vitesse) f; (BRIT
Scol: degree) ≈ licence f avec mention
passable; **thirdly** adv troisièmement;
**third party insurance** n (BRIT)
assurance f au tiers; **Third World** n: **the
Third World** le Tiers-Monde

**thirst** [θə:st] n soif f; **thirsty** adj qui a
soif, assoiffé(e); (work) qui donne soif;
**to be thirsty** avoir soif
**thirteen** [θə:'ti:n] num treize;
**thirteenth** [-'ti:nθ] num treizième
**thirtieth** ['θə:tɪɪθ] num trentième
**thirty** ['θə:tɪ] num trente

 **KEYWORD**

**this** [ðɪs] adj (demonstrative: pl **these**)
ce, cet + vowel or h mute, cette f; **this
man/woman/book** cet homme/cette
femme/ce livre; (not that) cet homme-
ci/cette femme-ci/ce livre-ci; **this one**
celui-ci (celle-ci)
▷ pron (demonstrative: pl **these**) ce;
(not that one) celui-ci (celle-ci), ceci;
**who's this?** qui est-ce?; **what's this?**
qu'est-ce que c'est?; **I prefer this
to that** je préfère ceci à cela; **this is
where I live** c'est ici que j'habite; **this
is what he said** voici ce qu'il a dit; **this
is Mr Brown** (in introductions) je vous
présente Mr Brown; (in photo) c'est Mr
Brown; (on telephone) ici Mr Brown
▷ adv (demonstrative): **it was about this
big** c'était à peu près de cette grandeur
or grand comme ça; **I didn't know
it was this bad** je ne savais pas que
c'était si or aussi mauvais

**thistle** ['θɪsl] n chardon m
**thorn** [θɔ:n] n épine f
**thorough** ['θʌrə] adj (search)
minutieux(-euse); (knowledge,
research) approfondi(e); (work,
person) consciencieux(-euse);
(cleaning) à fond; **thoroughly** adv
(search) minutieusement; (study)
en profondeur; (clean) à fond; (very)
tout à fait
**those** [ðəuz] pl pron ceux-là (celles-là)
▷ pl adj ces; (not these): **~ books** ces
livres-là
**though** [ðəu] conj bien que + sub,
quoique + sub ▷ adv pourtant
**thought** [θɔ:t] pt, pp of **think** ▷ n

pensée f; (idea) idée f; (opinion) avis m; **thoughtful** adj (deep in thought) pensif(-ive); (serious) réfléchi(e); (considerate) prévenant(e); **thoughtless** adj qui manque de considération

**thousand** ['θaʊzənd] num mille; **one ~** mille; **two ~** deux mille; **~s of** des milliers de; **thousandth** num millième

**thrash** [θræʃ] vt rouer de coups; (as punishment) donner une correction à; (inf: defeat) battre à plate(s) couture(s)

**thread** [θrɛd] n fil m; (of screw) pas m, filetage m ▷ vt (needle) enfiler

**threat** [θrɛt] n menace f; **threaten** vi (storm) menacer ▷ vt: **to threaten sb with sth/to do** menacer qn de qch/de faire; **threatening** adj menaçant(e)

**three** [θriː] num trois; **three-dimensional** adj à trois dimensions; **three-piece suite** n salon m (canapé et deux fauteuils); **three-quarters** npl trois-quarts mpl; **three-quarters full** aux trois-quarts plein

**threshold** ['θrɛʃhəʊld] n seuil m

**threw** [θruː] pt of **throw**

**thrill** [θrɪl] n (excitement) émotion f, sensation forte; (shudder) frisson m ▷ vt (audience) électriser; **thrilled** adj: **thrilled (with)** ravi(e) de; **thriller** n film m (or roman m or pièce f) à suspense; **thrilling** adj (book, play etc) saisissant(e); (news, discovery) excitant(e)

**thriving** ['θraɪvɪŋ] adj (business, community) prospère

**throat** [θrəʊt] n gorge f; **to have a sore ~** avoir mal à la gorge

**throb** [θrɔb] vi (heart) palpiter; (engine) vibrer; **my head is ~bing** j'ai des élancements dans la tête

**throne** [θrəʊn] n trône m

**through** [θruː] prep à travers; (time) pendant, durant; (by means of) par, par l'intermédiaire de; (owing to) à cause de ▷ adj (ticket, train, passage) direct(e) ▷ adv à travers; **(from) Monday ~ Friday** (us) de lundi à vendredi; **to put sb ~ to sb** (Tel) passer qn à qn; **to be**

**~** (BRIT: Tel) avoir la communication; (esp us: have finished) avoir fini; **"no ~ traffic"** (us) "passage interdit"; **"no ~ road"** (BRIT) "impasse"; **throughout** prep (place) partout dans; (time) durant tout(e) le (la) ▷ adv partout

**throw** [θrəʊ] n jet m; (Sport) lancer m ▷ vt (pt **threw**, pp **~n**) lancer, jeter; (Sport) lancer; (rider) désarçonner; (fig) décontenancer; **to ~ a party** donner une réception; **throw away** vt jeter; (money) gaspiller; **throw in** vt (Sport: ball) remettre en jeu; (include) ajouter; **throw off** vt se débarrasser de; **throw out** vt jeter; (reject) rejeter; (person) mettre à la porte; **throw up** vi vomir

**thru** [θruː] (us) = **through**

**thrush** [θrʌʃ] n (Zool) grive f

**thrust** [θrʌst] vt (pt, pp **~**) pousser brusquement; (push in) enfoncer

**thud** [θʌd] n bruit sourd

**thug** [θʌɡ] n voyou m

**thumb** [θʌm] n (Anat) pouce m ▷ vt: **to ~ a lift** faire de l'auto-stop, arrêter une voiture; **thumbtack** n (us) punaise f (clou)

**thump** [θʌmp] n grand coup; (sound) bruit sourd ▷ vt cogner sur ▷ vi cogner, frapper

**thunder** ['θʌndər] n tonnerre m ▷ vi tonner; (train etc): **to ~ past** passer dans un grondement or un bruit de tonnerre; **thunderstorm** n orage m

**Thur(s)** abbr (= Thursday) jeu

**Thursday** ['θəːzdɪ] n jeudi m

**thus** [ðʌs] adv ainsi

**thwart** [θwɔːt] vt contrecarrer

**thyme** [taɪm] n thym m

**Tibet** [tɪ'bɛt] n Tibet m

**tick** [tɪk] n (sound: of clock) tic-tac m; (mark) coche f; (Zool) tique f; (BRIT inf): **in a ~** dans un instant ▷ vi faire tic-tac ▷ vt (item on list) cocher; **tick off** vt (item on list) cocher; (person) réprimander, attraper

**ticket** ['tɪkɪt] n billet m; (for bus, tube) ticket m; (in shop: on goods) étiquette f; (for library) carte f; (also: **parking ~**)

contravention f, p.-v. m; **ticket barrier**
n (BRIT: Rail) portillon m automatique;
**ticket collector** n contrôleur(-euse);
**ticket inspector** n contrôleur(-euse);
**ticket machine** n billetterie f
automatique; **ticket office** n guichet
m, bureau m de vente des billets

**tickle** ['tɪkl] vi chatouiller ▷ vt
chatouiller; **ticklish** adj (person)
chatouilleux(-euse); (problem)
épineux(-euse)

**tide** [taɪd] n marée f; (fig: of events)
cours m

**tidy** ['taɪdɪ] adj (room) bien rangé(e);
(dress, work) net (nette), soigné(e);
(person) ordonné(e), qui a de l'ordre ▷ vt
(also: ~ up) ranger

**tie** [taɪ] n (string etc) cordon m; (BRIT:
also: **neck~**) cravate f; (fig: link) lien m;
(Sport: draw) égalité f de points; match
nul ▷ vt (parcel) attacher; (ribbon)
nouer ▷ vi (Sport) faire match nul; finir
à égalité de points; **to ~ sth in a bow**
faire un nœud à or avec qch; **to ~ a knot
in sth** faire un nœud à qch; **tie down**
vt (fig): **to ~ sb down to** contraindre
qn à accepter; **to feel ~d down** (by
relationship) se sentir coincé(e); **tie up**
vt (parcel) ficeler; (dog, boat) attacher;
(prisoner) ligoter; (arrangements)
conclure; **to be ~d up** (busy) être pris(e)
or occupé(e).

**tier** [tɪəʳ] n gradin m; (of cake) étage m

**tiger** ['taɪgəʳ] n tigre m

**tight** [taɪt] adj (rope) tendu(e), raide;
(clothes) étroit(e), très juste; (budget,
programme, bend) serré(e); (control)
strict(e), sévère; (inf: drunk) ivre, rond(e)
▷ adv (squeeze) très fort; (shut) à bloc,
hermétiquement; **hold ~!** accrochez-
vous bien!; **tighten** vt (rope) tendre;
(screw) resserrer; (control) renforcer
▷ vi se tendre; se resserrer; **tightly** adv
(grasp) bien, très fort; **tights** npl (BRIT)
collant m

**tile** [taɪl] n (on roof) tuile f; (on wall or
floor) carreau m

**till** [tɪl] n caisse (enregistreuse) ▷ prep,

conj = **until**

**tilt** [tɪlt] vt pencher, incliner ▷ vi
pencher, être incliné(e)

**timber** ['tɪmbəʳ] n (material) bois m de
construction

**time** [taɪm] n temps m; (epoch: often
pl) époque f, temps; (by clock) heure
f; (moment) moment m; (occasion, also
Math) fois f; (Mus) mesure f ▷ vt (race)
chronométrer; (programme) minuter;
(visit) fixer; (remark etc) choisir le
moment de; **a long ~** un long moment,
longtemps; **four at a ~** quatre à la
fois; **for the ~ being** pour le moment;
**from ~ to ~** de temps en temps; **at ~s**
parfois; **in ~** (soon enough) à temps;
(after some time) avec le temps, à la
longue; (Mus) en mesure; **in a week's
~** dans une semaine; **in no ~** en un rien
de temps; **any ~** n'importe quand;
**on ~** à l'heure; **5 ~s 5** 5 fois 5; **what ~
is it?** quelle heure est-il?; **what ~ is
the museum/shop open?** à quelle
heure ouvre le musée/magasin?; **to
have a good ~** bien s'amuser; **time
limit** n limite f de temps, délai m;
**timely** adj opportun(e); **timer** n (in
kitchen) compte-minutes m inv; (Tech)
minuteur m; **time-share** n maison
f/appartement m en multipropriété;
**timetable** n (Rail) (indicateur m)
horaire m; (Scol) emploi m du temps;
**time zone** n fuseau m horaire

**timid** ['tɪmɪd] adj timide; (easily scared)
peureux(-euse)

**timing** ['taɪmɪŋ] n (Sport)
chronométrage m; **the ~ of his
resignation** le moment choisi pour sa
démission

**tin** [tɪn] n étain m; (also: ~ **plate**)
fer-blanc m; (BRIT: can) boîte f (de
conserve); (: for baking) moule m (à
gâteau); (for storage) boîte f; **tinfoil** n
papier m d'étain or d'aluminium

**tingle** ['tɪŋgl] vi picoter; (person) avoir
des picotements

**tinker** ['tɪŋkəʳ]; **tinker with** vt fus
bricoler, rafistoler

**tinned** [tɪnd] *adj* (BRIT: *food*) en boîte, en conserve

**tin opener** [-ˈəupnəʳ] *n* (BRIT) ouvre-boîte(s) *m*

**tinsel** [ˈtɪnsl] *n* guirlandes *fpl* de Noël (*argentées*)

**tint** [tɪnt] *n* teinte *f*; (*for hair*) shampooing colorant; **tinted** *adj* (*hair*) teint(e); (*spectacles, glass*) teinté(e)

**tiny** [ˈtaɪnɪ] *adj* minuscule

**tip** [tɪp] *n* (*end*) bout *m*; (*gratuity*) pourboire *m*; (BRIT: *for rubbish*) décharge *f*; (*advice*) tuyau *m* ▷ *vt* (*waiter*) donner un pourboire à; (*tilt*) incliner; (*overturn: also:* **~ over**) renverser; (*empty: also:* **~ out**) déverser; **how much should I ~?** combien de pourboire est-ce qu'il faut laisser?; **tip off** *vt* prévenir, avertir

**tiptoe** [ˈtɪptəu] *n*: **on ~** sur la pointe des pieds

**tire** [ˈtaɪəʳ] *n* (US) = **tyre** ▷ *vt* fatiguer ▷ *vi* se fatiguer; **tired** *adj* fatigué(e); **to be tired of** en avoir assez de, être las (lasse) de; **tire pressure** (US) = **tyre pressure**; **tiring** *adj* fatigant(e)

**tissue** [ˈtɪʃuː] *n* tissu *m*; (*paper handkerchief*) mouchoir *m* en papier, kleenex® *m*; **tissue paper** *n* papier *m* de soie

**tit** [tɪt] *n* (*bird*) mésange *f*; **to give ~ for tat** rendre coup pour coup

**title** [ˈtaɪtl] *n* titre *m*

**T-junction** [ˈtiːˈdʒʌŋkʃən] *n* croisement *m* en T

**TM** *n abbr* = **trademark**

 **KEYWORD**

**to** [tuː, tə] *prep* **1** (*direction*) à; (*towards*) vers; envers; **to go to France/Portugal/London/school** aller en France/au Portugal/à Londres/à l'école; **to go to Claude's/the doctor's** aller chez Claude/le docteur; **the road to Edinburgh** la route d'Édimbourg **2** (*as far as*) (jusqu')à; **to count to 10** compter jusqu'à 10; **from 40 to 50**

people de 40 à 50 personnes **3** (*with expressions of time*): **a quarter to 5** 5 heures moins le quart; **it's twenty to 3** il est 3 heures moins vingt **4** (*for, of*) de; **the key to the front door** la clé de la porte d'entrée; **a letter to his wife** une lettre (adressée) à sa femme **5** (*expressing indirect object*) à; **to give sth to sb** donner qch à qn; **to talk to sb** parler à qn; **to be a danger to sb** être dangereux(-euse) pour qn **6** (*in relation to*) à; **3 goals to 2** 3 (buts) à 2; **30 miles to the gallon** ≈ 9,4 litres aux cent (km) **7** (*purpose, result*): **to come to sb's aid** venir au secours de qn, porter secours à qn; **to sentence sb to death** condamner qn à mort; **to my surprise** à ma grande surprise ▷ *with vb* **1** (*simple infinitive*): **to go/eat** aller/manger **2** (*following another vb*): **to want/try/start to do** vouloir/essayer de/commencer à faire **3** (*with vb omitted*): **I don't want to** je ne veux pas **4** (*purpose, result*) pour; **I did it to help you** je l'ai fait pour vous aider **5** (*equivalent to relative clause*): **I have things to do** j'ai des choses à faire; **the main thing is to try** l'important est d'essayer **6** (*after adjective etc*): **ready to go** prêt(e) à partir; **too old/young to …** trop vieux/jeune pour … ▷ *adv*: **push/pull the door to** tirez/poussez la porte

**toad** [təud] *n* crapaud *m*; **toadstool** *n* champignon (vénéneux)

**toast** [təust] *n* (Culin) pain grillé, toast *m*; (*drink, speech*) toast ▷ *vt* (Culin) faire griller; (*drink to*) porter un toast à; **toaster** *n* grille-pain *m inv*

**tobacco** [təˈbækəu] *n* tabac *m*

**toboggan** [təˈbɔgən] *n* toboggan *m*; (*child's*) luge *f*

**today** [tə'deɪ] *adv*, *n* (*also fig*)
aujourd'hui (*m*)

**toddler** ['tɒdləʳ] *n* enfant *m/f* qui
commence à marcher, bambin *m*

**toe** [təʊ] *n* doigt *m* de pied, orteil *m*;
(*of shoe*) bout *m* ▷ *vt*: **to ~ the line** (*fig*)
obéir, se conformer; **toenail** *n* ongle
*m* de l'orteil

**toffee** ['tɒfɪ] *n* caramel *m*

**together** [tə'gɛðəʳ] *adv* ensemble;
(*at same time*) en même temps; **~ with**
*prep* avec

**toilet** ['tɔɪlət] *n* (*BRIT: lavatory*) toilettes
*fpl*, cabinets *mpl*; **to go to the ~** aller
aux toilettes; **where's the ~?** où sont
les toilettes?; **toilet bag** *n* (*BRIT*)
nécessaire *m* de toilette; **toilet paper**
*n* papier *m* hygiénique; **toiletries** *npl*
articles *mpl* de toilette; **toilet roll** *n*
rouleau *m* de papier hygiénique

**token** ['təʊkən] *n* (*sign*) marque *f*,
témoignage *m*; (*metal disc*) jeton *m* ▷ *adj*
(*fee, strike*) symbolique; **book/record ~**
(*BRIT*) chèque-livre/-disque *m*

**Tokyo** ['təʊkjəʊ] *n* Tokyo

**told** [təʊld] *pt*, *pp* *of* **tell**

**tolerant** ['tɒlərnt] *adj*: **~ (of)**
tolérant(e) (à l'égard de)

**tolerate** ['tɒləreɪt] *vt* supporter

**toll** [təʊl] *n* (*tax, charge*) péage *m* ▷ *vi*
(*bell*) sonner; **the accident ~ on the
roads** le nombre de victimes de la
route; **toll call** *n* (*us Tel*) appel *m* (à)
longue distance; **toll-free** *adj* (*us*)
gratuit(e) ▷ *adv* gratuitement

**tomato** [tə'mɑːtəʊ] (*pl* **~es**) *n* tomate *f*;
**tomato sauce** *n* sauce *f* tomate

**tomb** [tuːm] *n* tombe *f*; **tombstone** *n*
pierre tombale

**tomorrow** [tə'mɒrəʊ] *adv*, *n* (*also fig*)
demain (*m*); **the day after ~** après-
demain; **a week ~** demain en huit; **~
morning** demain matin

**ton** [tʌn] *n* tonne *f* (*BRIT*: = 1016 kg; *us*
= 907 kg; *metric* = 1000 kg); **~s of** (*inf*)
des tas de

**tone** [təʊn] *n* ton *m*; (*of radio*, *BRIT Tel*)
tonalité *f* ▷ *vi* (*also*: **~ in**) s'harmoniser;

**tone down** *vt* (*colour, criticism*) adoucir

**tongs** [tɒŋz] *npl* pinces *fpl*; (*for coal*)
pincettes *fpl*; (*for hair*) fer *m* à friser

**tongue** [tʌŋ] *n* langue *f*; **~ in cheek** *adv*
ironiquement

**tonic** ['tɒnɪk] *n* (*Med*) tonique *m*; (*also*: **~
water**) Schweppes® *m*

**tonight** [tə'naɪt] *adv*, *n* cette nuit; (*this
evening*) ce soir

**tonne** [tʌn] *n* (*BRIT: metric ton*) tonne *f*

**tonsil** ['tɒnsl] *n* amygdale *f*; **tonsillitis**
[tɒnsɪ'laɪtɪs] *n*: **to have tonsillitis**
avoir une angine *or* une amygdalite

**too** [tuː] *adv* (*excessively*) trop; (*also*)
aussi; **~ much** (*as adv*) trop; (*as adj*) trop
de; **~ many** *adj* trop de

**took** [tuk] *pt* *of* **take**

**tool** [tuːl] *n* outil *m*; **tool box** *n* boîte *f* à
outils; **tool kit** *n* trousse *f* à outils

**tooth** (*pl* **teeth**) [tuːθ, tiːθ] *n* (*Anat, Tech*)
dent *f*; **to brush one's teeth** se laver les
dents; **toothache** *n* mal *m* de dents;
**to have toothache** avoir mal aux
dents; **toothbrush** *n* brosse *f* à dents;
**toothpaste** *n* (*pâte f*) dentifrice *m*;
**toothpick** *n* cure-dent *m*

**top** [tɒp] *n* (*of mountain, head*) sommet
*m*; (*of page, ladder*) haut *m*; (*of box,
cupboard, table*) dessus *m*; (*lid: of box,
jar*) couvercle *m*; (: *of bottle*) bouchon *m*;
(*toy*) toupie *f*; (*Dress: blouse etc*) haut;
(: *of pyjamas*) veste *f* ▷ *adj* du haut; (*in
rank*) premier(-ière); (*best*) meilleur(e)
▷ *vt* (*exceed*) dépasser; (*be first in*) être
en tête de; **from ~ to bottom** de fond
en comble; **on ~ of** sur; (*in addition to*)
en plus de; **over the ~** (*inf: behaviour
etc*) qui dépasse les limites; **top up**
(*us top off*) *vt* (*bottle*) remplir; (*salary*)
compléter; **to ~ up one's mobile
(phone)** recharger son compte; **top
floor** *n* dernier étage; **top hat** *n* haut-
de-forme *m*

**topic** ['tɒpɪk] *n* sujet *m*, thème *m*;
**topical** *adj* d'actualité

**topless** ['tɒplɪs] *adj* (*bather etc*) aux
seins nus

**topping** ['tɒpɪŋ] *n* (*Culin*) couche de

*crème, fromage etc qui recouvre un plat*

**topple** ['tɔpl] *vt* renverser, faire tomber
▷ *vi* basculer; tomber

**top-up** ['tɔpʌp] *n* (*for mobile phone*)
recharge *f*, minutes *fpl*; **top-up card** *n*
(*for mobile phone*) recharge *f*

**torch** [tɔːtʃ] *n* torche *f*; (BRIT: *electric*)
lampe *f* de poche

**tore** [tɔːʳ] *pt of* **tear²**

**torment** *n* ['tɔːmɛnt] tourment *m*
▷ *vt* [tɔː'mɛnt] tourmenter; (*fig: annoy*)
agacer

**torn** [tɔːn] *pp of* **tear²**

**tornado** [tɔː'neɪdəu] (*pl* **-es**) *n*
tornade *f*

**torpedo** [tɔː'piːdəu] (*pl* **-es**) *n* torpille *f*

**torrent** ['tɔrnt] *n* torrent *m*; **torrential**
[tɔ'rɛnʃl] *adj* torrentiel(le)

**tortoise** ['tɔːtəs] *n* tortue *f*

**torture** ['tɔːtʃəʳ] *n* torture *f* ▷ *vt*
torturer

**Tory** ['tɔːrɪ] *adj, n* (BRIT *Pol*) tory *m/f*,
conservateur(-trice)

**toss** [tɔs] *vt* lancer, jeter; (BRIT: *pancake*)
faire sauter; (*head*) rejeter en arrière
▷ *vi*: **to ~ up for sth** (BRIT) jouer qch à
pile ou face; **to ~ a coin** jouer à pile ou
face; **to ~ and turn** (*in bed*) se tourner
et se retourner

**total** ['təutl] *adj* total(e) ▷ *n* total *m* ▷ *vt*
(*add up*) faire le total de, additionner;
(*amount to*) s'élever à

**totalitarian** [təutælɪ'tɛərɪən] *adj*
totalitaire

**totally** ['təutəlɪ] *adv* totalement

**touch** [tʌtʃ] *n* contact *m*, toucher *m*;
(*sense, skill: of pianist etc*) toucher ▷ *vt*
(*gen*) toucher; (*tamper with*) toucher à;
**a ~ of** (*fig*) un petit peu de; une touche
de; **to get in ~ with** prendre contact
avec; **to lose ~** (*friends*) se perdre de
vue; **touch down** *vi* (*Aviat*) atterrir;
(*on sea*) amerrir; **touchdown** *n* (*Aviat*)
atterrissage *m*; (*on sea*) amerrissage
*m*; (US *Football*) essai *m*; **touched**
*adj* (*moved*) touché(e); **touching**
*adj* touchant(e), attendrissant(e);
**touchline** *n* (*Sport*) (ligne *f* de) touche

*f*; **touch-sensitive** *adj* (*keypad*) à
effleurement; (*screen*) tactile

**tough** [tʌf] *adj* dur(e); (*resistant*)
résistant(e), solide; (*meat*) dur, coriace;
(*firm*) inflexible; (*task, problem, situation*)
difficile

**tour** ['tuəʳ] *n* voyage *m*; (*also:* **package**
**~**) voyage organisé; (*of town, museum*)
tour *m*, visite *f*; (*by band*) tournée *f* ▷ *vt*
visiter; **tour guide** *n* (*person*) guide *m/f*

**tourism** ['tuərɪzm] *n* tourisme *m*

**tourist** ['tuərɪst] *n* touriste *m/f* ▷ *cpd*
touristique; **tourist office** *n* syndicat
*m* d'initiative

**tournament** ['tuənəmənt] *n*
tournoi *m*

**tour operator** *n* (BRIT) organisateur *m*
de voyages, tour-opérateur *m*

**tow** [təu] *vt* remorquer; (*caravan,*
*trailer*) tracter; **"on ~"**, (US) **"in ~"** (*Aut*)
"véhicule en remorque"; **tow away** *vt*
(*subj: police*) emmener à la fourrière;
(: *breakdown service*) remorquer

**toward(s)** [tə'wɔːd(z)] *prep* vers;
(*of attitude*) envers, à l'égard de; (*of*
*purpose*) pour

**towel** ['tauəl] *n* serviette *f* (de toilette);
**towelling** *n* (*fabric*) tissu-éponge *m*

**tower** ['tauəʳ] *n* tour *f*; **tower block** *n*
(BRIT) tour *f* (d'habitation)

**town** [taun] *n* ville *f*; **to go to ~** aller
en ville; (*fig*) y mettre le paquet; **town**
**centre** *n* (BRIT) centre *m* de la ville,
centre-ville *m*; **town hall** *n* ≈ mairie *f*

**tow truck** *n* (US) dépanneuse *f*

**toxic** ['tɔksɪk] *adj* toxique

**toy** [tɔɪ] *n* jouet *m*; **toy with** *vt fus*
jouer avec; (*idea*) caresser; **toyshop** *n*
magasin *m* de jouets

**trace** [treɪs] *n* trace *f* ▷ *vt* (*draw*) tracer,
dessiner; (*follow*) suivre la trace de;
(*locate*) retrouver

**tracing paper** ['treɪsɪŋ-] *n* papier-
calque *m*

**track** [træk] *n* (*mark*) trace *f*; (*path:*
*gen*) chemin *m*, piste *f*; (: *of bullet etc*)
trajectoire *f*; (: *of suspect, animal*) piste *f*;
(*Rail*) voie ferrée, rails *mpl*; (*on tape,*

*Comput, Sport*) piste; (*on CD*) piste *f*; (*on record*) plage *f* ▷ *vt* suivre la trace *or* la piste de; **to keep ~ of** suivre; **track down** *vt* (*prey*) trouver et capturer; (*sth lost*) finir par retrouver; **tracksuit** *n* survêtement *m*

**tractor** ['træktə'] *n* tracteur *m*

**trade** [treɪd] *n* commerce *m*; (*skill, job*) métier *m* ▷ *vi* faire du commerce ▷ *vt* (*exchange*): **to ~ sth (for sth)** échanger qch (contre qch); **to ~ with/in** faire du commerce avec/le commerce de; **trade in** *vt* (*old car etc*) faire reprendre; **trademark** *n* marque *f* de fabrique; **trader** *n* commerçant(e), négociant(e); **tradesman** (*irreg*) *n* (*shopkeeper*) commerçant *m*; **trade union** *n* syndicat *m*

**trading** ['treɪdɪŋ] *n* affaires *fpl*, commerce *m*

**tradition** [trə'dɪʃən] *n* tradition *f*; **traditional** *adj* traditionnel(le)

**traffic** ['træfɪk] *n* trafic *m*; (*cars*) circulation *f* ▷ *vi*: **to ~ in** (*pej: liquor, drugs*) faire le trafic de; **traffic circle** *n* (*us*) rond-point *m*; **traffic island** *n* refuge *m* (pour piétons); **traffic jam** *n* embouteillage *m*; **traffic lights** *npl* feux *mpl* (de signalisation); **traffic warden** *n* contractuel(le)

**tragedy** ['trædʒədɪ] *n* tragédie *f*

**tragic** ['trædʒɪk] *adj* tragique

**trail** [treɪl] *n* (*tracks*) trace *f*, piste *f*; (*path*) chemin *m*, piste; (*of smoke etc*) traînée *f* ▷ *vt* (*drag*) traîner, tirer; (*follow*) suivre ▷ *vi* traîner; (*in game, contest*) être en retard; **trailer** *n* (*Aut*) remorque *f*; (*us*) caravane *f*; (*Cine*) bande-annonce *f*

**train** [treɪn] *n* train *m*; (*in underground*) rame *f*; (*of dress*) traîne *f*; (*Brit: series*): **~ of events** série *f* d'événements ▷ *vt* (*apprentice, doctor etc*) former; (*Sport*) entraîner; (*dog*) dresser; (*memory*) exercer; (*point: gun etc*): **to ~ sth on** braquer qch sur ▷ *vi* recevoir sa formation; (*Sport*) s'entraîner; **one's ~ of thought** le fil de sa pensée; **what**

**time does the ~ from Paris get in?** à quelle heure arrive le train de Paris?; **is this the ~ for ...?** c'est bien le train pour...?; **trainee** [treɪ'ni:] *n* stagiaire *m/f*; (*in trade*) apprenti(e); **trainer** *n* (*Sport*) entraîneur(-euse); (*of dogs etc*) dresseur(-euse); **trainers** *npl* (*shoes*) chaussures *fpl* de sport; **training** *n* formation *f*; (*Sport*) entraînement *m*; (*of dog etc*) dressage *m*; **in training** (*Sport*) à l'entraînement; (*fit*) en forme; **training course** *n* cours *m* de formation professionnelle; **training shoes** *npl* chaussures *fpl* de sport

**trait** [treɪt] *n* trait *m* (de caractère)

**traitor** ['treɪtə'] *n* traître *m*

**tram** [træm] *n* (*Brit: also*: **~car**) tram(way) *m*

**tramp** [træmp] *n* (*person*) vagabond(e), clochard(e); (*inf: pej: woman*): **to be a ~** être coureuse

**trample** ['træmpl] *vt*: **to ~ (underfoot)** piétiner

**trampoline** ['træmpəli:n] *n* trampoline *m*

**tranquil** ['træŋkwɪl] *adj* tranquille; **tranquillizer** (*us* **tranquilizer**) *n* (*Med*) tranquillisant *m*

**transaction** [træn'zækʃən] *n* transaction *f*

**transatlantic** ['trænzət'læntɪk] *adj* transatlantique

**transcript** ['trænskrɪpt] *n* transcription *f* (*texte*)

**transfer** *n* ['trænsfə'] (*gen, also Sport*) transfert *m*; (*Pol: of power*) passation *f*; (*of money*) virement *m*; (*picture, design*) décalcomanie *f*; (*: stick-on*) autocollant *m* ▷ *vt* [træns'fə:'] transférer; passer; virer; **to ~ the charges** (*Brit Tel*) téléphoner en P.C.V.

**transform** [træns'fɔ:m] *vt* transformer; **transformation** *n* transformation *f*

**transfusion** [træns'fju:ʒən] *n* transfusion *f*

**transit** ['trænzɪt] *n*: **in ~** en transit

**transition** [træn'zɪʃən] *n* transition *f*

**transitive** ['trænzɪtɪv] *adj* (*Ling*)
transitif(-ive)

**translate** [trænz'leɪt] *vt*: **to ~ (from/into)** traduire (du/en); **can you ~ this for me?** pouvez-vous me traduire ceci?; **translation** [trænz'leɪʃən] *n* traduction *f*; (*Scol: as opposed to prose*) version *f*; **translator** *n* traducteur(-trice)

**transmission** [trænz'mɪʃən] *n* transmission *f*

**transmit** [trænz'mɪt] *vt* transmettre; (*Radio, TV*) émettre; **transmitter** *n* émetteur *m*

**transparent** [træns'pærnt] *adj* transparent(e)

**transplant** n ['trænsplɑːnt] (*Med*) transplantation *f*

**transport** n ['trænspɔːt] transport *m* ⊳ *vt* [træns'pɔːt] transporter; **transportation** [trænspɔː'teɪʃən] *n* (moyen *m* de) transport *m*

**transvestite** [trænz'vɛstaɪt] *n* travesti(e)

**trap** [træp] *n* (*snare, trick*) piège *m*; (*carriage*) cabriolet *m* ⊳ *vt* prendre au piège; (*confine*) coincer

**trash** [træʃ] *n* (*pej: goods*) camelote *f*; (: *nonsense*) sottises *fpl*; (*us: rubbish*) ordures *fpl*; **trash can** *n* (*us*) poubelle *f*

**trauma** ['trɔːmə] *n* traumatisme *m*; **traumatic** [trɔː'mætɪk] *adj* traumatisant(e)

**travel** ['trævl] *n* voyage(s) *m(pl)* ⊳ *vi* voyager; (*news, sound*) se propager ⊳ *vt* (*distance*) parcourir; **travel agency** *n* agence *f* de voyages; **travel agent** *n* agent *m* de voyages; **travel insurance** *n* assurance-voyage *f*; **traveller** (*us* **traveler**) *n* voyageur(-euse); **traveller's cheque** (*us* **traveler's check**) *n* chèque *m* de voyage; **travelling** (*us* **traveling**) *n* voyage(s) *m(pl)*; **travel-sick** *adj*: **to get travel-sick** avoir le mal de la route (*or* de mer *or* de l'air); **travel sickness** *n* mal *m* de la route (*or* de mer *or* de l'air)

**tray** [treɪ] *n* (*for carrying*) plateau *m*; (*on desk*) corbeille *f*

**treacherous** ['trɛtʃərəs] *adj* traître(sse); (*ground, tide*) dont il faut se méfier

**treacle** ['triːkl] *n* mélasse *f*

**tread** [trɛd] *n* (*step*) pas *m*; (*sound*) bruit *m* de pas; (*of tyre*) chape *f*, bande *f* de roulement ⊳ *vi* (*pt* **trod**, *pp* **trodden**) marcher; **tread on** *vt fus* marcher sur

**treasure** ['trɛʒəʳ] *n* trésor *m* ⊳ *vt* (*value*) tenir beaucoup à; **treasurer** *n* trésorier(-ière)

**treasury** ['trɛʒərɪ] *n*: **the T~**, (*us*) **the T~ Department** ≈ le ministère des Finances

**treat** [triːt] *n* petit cadeau, petite surprise ⊳ *vt* traiter; **to ~ sb to sth** offrir qch à qn; **treatment** *n* traitement *m*

**treaty** ['triːtɪ] *n* traité *m*

**treble** ['trɛbl] *adj* triple ⊳ *vt, vi* tripler

**tree** [triː] *n* arbre *m*

**trek** [trɛk] *n* (*long walk*) randonnée *f*; (*tiring walk*) longue marche, trotte *f*

**tremble** ['trɛmbl] *vi* trembler

**tremendous** [trɪ'mɛndəs] *adj* (*enormous*) énorme; (*excellent*) formidable, fantastique

**trench** [trɛntʃ] *n* tranchée *f*

**trend** [trɛnd] *n* (*tendency*) tendance *f*; (*of events*) cours *m*; (*fashion*) mode *f*; **trendy** *adj* (*idea, person*) dans le vent; (*clothes*) dernier cri *inv*

**trespass** ['trɛspəs] *vi*: **to ~ on** s'introduire sans permission dans; **"no ~ing"** "propriété privée", "défense d'entrer"

**trial** ['traɪəl] *n* (*Law*) procès *m*, jugement *m*; (*test: of machine etc*) essai *m*; **trials** *npl* (*unpleasant experiences*) épreuves *fpl*; **trial period** *n* période *f* d'essai

**triangle** ['traɪæŋgl] *n* (*Math, Mus*) triangle *m*

**triangular** [traɪ'æŋgjuləʳ] *adj* triangulaire

**tribe** [traɪb] *n* tribu *f*

**tribunal** [traɪ'bjuːnl] *n* tribunal *m*

**tribute** ['trɪbjuːt] *n* tribut *m*, hommage

*m*; **to pay ~ to** rendre hommage à

**trick** [trɪk] *n* (*magic*) tour *m*; (*joke, prank*) tour, farce *f*; (*skill, knack*) astuce *f*; (*Cards*) levée *f* ▷ *vt* attraper, rouler; **to play a ~ on sb** jouer un tour à qn; **that should do the ~** (*fam*) ça devrait faire l'affaire

**trickle** ['trɪkl] *n* (*of water etc*) filet *m* ▷ *vi* couler en un filet *or* goutte à goutte

**tricky** ['trɪkɪ] *adj* difficile, délicat(e)

**tricycle** ['traɪsɪkl] *n* tricycle *m*

**trifle** ['traɪfl] *n* bagatelle *f*; (*Culin*) ≈ diplomate *m* ▷ *adv*: **a ~ long** un peu long

**trigger** ['trɪgə'] *n* (*of gun*) gâchette *f*

**trim** [trɪm] *adj* (*house, garden*) bien tenu(e); (*figure*) svelte ▷ *n* (*haircut etc*) légère coupe; (*on car*) garnitures *fpl* ▷ *vt* (*cut*) couper légèrement; (*decorate*): **to ~ (with)** décorer (de); (*Naut: a sail*) gréer

**trio** ['triːəu] *n* trio *m*

**trip** [trɪp] *n* voyage *m*; (*excursion*) excursion *f*; (*stumble*) faux pas ▷ *vi* faire un faux pas, trébucher; **trip up** *vi* trébucher ▷ *vt* faire un croc-en-jambe à

**triple** ['trɪpl] *adj* triple

**triplets** ['trɪplɪts] *npl* triplés(-ées)

**tripod** ['traɪpɔd] *n* trépied *m*

**triumph** ['traɪʌmf] *n* triomphe *m* ▷ *vi*: **to ~ (over)** triompher (de); **triumphant** [traɪˈʌmfənt] *adj* triomphant(e)

**trivial** ['trɪvɪəl] *adj* insignifiant(e); (*commonplace*) banal(e)

**trod** [trɔd] *pt of* **tread**

**trodden** ['trɔdn] *pp of* **tread**

**trolley** ['trɔlɪ] *n* chariot *m*

**trombone** [trɔmˈbəun] *n* trombone *m*

**troop** [truːp] *n* bande *f*, groupe *m*; **troops** *npl* (*Mil*) troupes *fpl*; (: *men*) hommes *mpl*, soldats *mpl*

**trophy** ['trəufɪ] *n* trophée *m*

**tropical** ['trɔpɪkl] *adj* tropical(e)

**trot** [trɔt] *n* trot *m* ▷ *vi* trotter; **on the ~** (*BRIT: fig*) d'affilée

**trouble** ['trʌbl] *n* difficulté(s) *f(pl)*, problème(s) *m(pl)*; (*worry*) ennuis *mpl*, soucis *mpl*; (*bother, effort*) peine *f*; (*Pol*)

conflit(s) *m(pl)*, troubles *mpl*; (*Med*): **stomach etc ~** troubles gastriques *etc* ▷ *vt* (*disturb*) déranger, gêner; (*worry*) inquiéter ▷ *vi*: **to ~ to do** prendre la peine de faire; **troubles** *npl* (*Pol etc*) troubles; (*personal*) ennuis, soucis; **to be in ~** avoir des ennuis; (*ship, climber etc*) être en difficulté; **to have ~ doing sth** avoir du mal à faire qch; **it's no ~!** je vous en prie!; **the ~ is ...** le problème, c'est que ...; **what's the ~?** qu'est-ce qui ne va pas?; **troubled** *adj* (*person*) inquiet(-ète); (*times, life*) agité(e); **troublemaker** *n* élément perturbateur, fauteur *m* de troubles; **troublesome** *adj* (*child*) fatigant(e), difficile; (*cough*) gênant(e)

**trough** [trɔf] *n* (*also*: **drinking ~**) abreuvoir *m*; (*also*: **feeding ~**) auge *f*; (*depression*) creux *m*

**trousers** ['trauzəz] *npl* pantalon *m*; **short ~** (*BRIT*) culottes courtes

**trout** [traut] *n* (*pl inv*) truite *f*

**trowel** ['trauəl] *n* truelle *f*; (*garden tool*) déplantoir *m*

**truant** ['truənt] *n*: **to play ~** (*BRIT*) faire l'école buissonnière

**truce** [truːs] *n* trêve *f*

**truck** [trʌk] *n* camion *m*; (*Rail*) wagon *m* à plate-forme; **truck driver** *n* camionneur *m*

**true** [truː] *adj* vrai(e); (*accurate*) exact(e); (*genuine*) vrai, véritable; (*faithful*) fidèle; **to come ~** se réaliser

**truly** ['truːlɪ] *adv* vraiment, réellement; (*truthfully*) sans mentir; **yours ~** (*in letter*) je vous prie d'agréer, Monsieur (*or* Madame *etc*), l'expression de mes sentiments respectueux

**trumpet** ['trʌmpɪt] *n* trompette *f*

**trunk** [trʌŋk] *n* (*of tree, person*) tronc *m*; (*of elephant*) trompe *f*; (*case*) malle *f*; (*us Aut*) coffre *m*; **trunks** *npl* (*also*: **swimming ~s**) maillot *m or* slip *m* de bain

**trust** [trʌst] *n* confiance *f*; (*responsibility*): **to place sth in sb's ~** confier la responsabilité de qch à qn; (*Law*) fidéicommis *m* ▷ *vt* (*rely on*) avoir confiance en; (*entrust*): **to ~ sth to sb** confier qch à qn; (*hope*): **to ~ (that)** espérer (que); **to take sth on ~** accepter qch les yeux fermés; **trusted** *adj* en qui l'on a confiance; **trustworthy** *adj* digne de confiance

**truth** [tru:θ, (*pl*) tru:ðz] *n* vérité *f*; **truthful** *adj* (*person*) qui dit la vérité; (*answer*) sincère

**try** [traɪ] *n* essai *m*, tentative *f*; (*Rugby*) essai *f* ▷ *vt* (*attempt*) essayer, tenter; (*test: sth new: also*: **~ out**) essayer, tester; (*Law: person*) juger; (*strain*) éprouver ▷ *vi* essayer; **to ~ to do** essayer de faire; (*seek*) chercher à faire; **try on** *vt* (*clothes*) essayer; **trying** *adj* pénible

**T-shirt** ['ti:ʃə:t] *n* tee-shirt *m*

**tub** [tʌb] *n* cuve *f*; (*for washing clothes*) baquet *m*; (*bath*) baignoire *f*

**tube** [tju:b] *n* tube *m*; (*BRIT: underground*) métro *m*; (*for tyre*) chambre *f* à air

**tuberculosis** [tjubə:kju'ləusɪs] *n* tuberculose *f*

**tube station** *n* (*BRIT*) station *f* de métro

**tuck** [tʌk] *vt* (*put*) mettre; **tuck away** *vt* cacher, ranger; (*money*) mettre de côté; (*building*): **to be ~ed away** être caché(e); **tuck in** *vt* rentrer; (*child*) border ▷ *vi* (*eat*) manger de bon appétit; attaquer le repas; **tuck shop** *n* (*BRIT Scol*) boutique *f* à provisions

**Tue(s)** *abbr* (= *Tuesday*) ma

**Tuesday** ['tju:zdɪ] *n* mardi *m*

**tug** [tʌg] *n* (*ship*) remorqueur *m* ▷ *vt* tirer (sur)

**tuition** [tju:'ɪʃən] *n* (*BRIT: lessons*) leçons *fpl*; (: *private*) cours particuliers; (*US: fees*) frais *mpl* de scolarité

**tulip** ['tju:lɪp] *n* tulipe *f*

**tumble** ['tʌmbl] *n* (*fall*) chute *f*, culbute *f* ▷ *vi* tomber, dégringoler; **to ~ to sth** (*inf*) réaliser qch; **tumble dryer** *n* (*BRIT*) séchoir *m* (à linge) à air chaud

**tumbler** ['tʌmblə'] *n* verre (droit), gobelet *m*

**tummy** ['tʌmɪ] *n* (*inf*) ventre *m*

**tumour** (*US* **tumor**) ['tju:mə'] *n* tumeur *f*

**tuna** ['tju:nə] *n* (*pl inv: also*: **~ fish**) thon *m*

**tune** [tju:n] *n* (*melody*) air *m* ▷ *vt* (*Mus*) accorder; (*Radio, TV, Aut*) régler, mettre au point; **to be in/out of ~** (*instrument*) être accordé/désaccordé; (*singer*) chanter juste/faux; **tune in** *vi* (*Radio, TV*): **to ~ in (to)** se mettre à l'écoute (de); **tune up** *vi* (*musician*) accorder son instrument

**tunic** ['tju:nɪk] *n* tunique *f*

**Tunis** ['tju:nɪs] *n* Tunis

**Tunisia** [tju:'nɪzɪə] *n* Tunisie *f*

**Tunisian** [tju:'nɪzɪən] *adj* tunisien(ne) ▷ *n* Tunisien(ne)

**tunnel** ['tʌnl] *n* tunnel *m*; (*in mine*) galerie *f* ▷ *vi* creuser un tunnel (*or* une galerie)

**turbulence** ['tə:bjuləns] *n* (*Aviat*) turbulence *f*

**turf** [tə:f] *n* gazon *m*; (*clod*) motte *f* (de gazon) ▷ *vt* gazonner

**Turk** [tə:k] *n* Turc (Turque)

**Turkey** ['tə:kɪ] *n* Turquie *f*

**turkey** ['tə:kɪ] *n* dindon *m*, dinde *f*

**Turkish** ['tə:kɪʃ] *adj* turc (turque) ▷ *n* (*Ling*) turc *m*

**turmoil** ['tə:mɔɪl] *n* trouble *m*, bouleversement *m*

**turn** [tə:n] *n* tour *m*; (*in road*) tournant *m*; (*tendency: of mind, events*) tournure *f*; (*performance*) numéro *m*; (*Med*) crise *f*, attaque *f* ▷ *vt* tourner; (*collar, steak*) retourner; (*change*): **to ~ sth into** changer qch en; (*age*) atteindre ▷ *vi* (*object, wind, milk*) tourner; (*person: look back*) se (re)tourner; (*reverse direction*) faire demi-tour; (*become*) devenir; **to ~ into** se changer en, se transformer en; **a good ~** un service; **it gave me quite a ~** ça m'a fait un coup; **"no left ~"** (*Aut*) "défense de tourner à gauche"; **~ left/right at the next junction** tournez à gauche/droite au prochain carrefour; **it's your ~** c'est (à) votre tour; **in ~** à son tour;

à tour de rôle; **to take ~s** se relayer;
**turn around** vi (person) se retourner
▷ vt (object) tourner; **turn away** vi se
détourner, tourner la tête ▷ vt (reject:
person) renvoyer; (: business) refuser;
**turn back** vi revenir, faire demi-tour;
**turn down** vt (refuse) rejeter, refuser;
(reduce) baisser; (fold) rabattre; **turn
in** vi (inf: go to bed) aller se coucher
▷ vt (fold) rentrer; **turn off** vi (from
road) tourner ▷ vt (light, radio etc)
éteindre; (tap) fermer; (engine) arrêter;
**I can't ~ the heating off** je n'arrive
pas à éteindre le chauffage; **turn on**
vt (light, radio etc) allumer; (tap) ouvrir;
(engine) mettre en marche; **I can't ~ the
heating on** je n'arrive pas à allumer
le chauffage; **turn out** vt (light, gas)
éteindre; (produce) produire ▷ vi (voters,
troops) se présenter; **to ~ out to be ...**
s'avérer ..., se révéler ...; **turn over**
vi (person) se retourner ▷ vt (object)
retourner; (page) tourner; **turn round**
vi faire demi-tour; (rotate) tourner;
**turn to** vt fus: **to ~ to sb** s'adresser à
qn; **turn up** vi (person) arriver,
se pointer (inf); (lost object) être
retrouvé(e) ▷ vt (collar) remonter;
(radio, heater) mettre plus fort;
**turning** n (in road) tournant m;
**turning point** n (fig) tournant m,
moment décisif
**turnip** ['tə:nɪp] n navet m
**turn**: **turnout** n (of voters) taux m de
participation; **turnover** n (Comm:
amount of money) chiffre m d'affaires;
(: of goods) roulement m; (of staff)
renouvellement m, changement m;
**turnstile** n tourniquet m (d'entrée);
**turn-up** n (BRIT: on trousers) revers m
**turquoise** ['tə:kwɔɪz] n (stone)
turquoise f ▷ adj turquoise inv
**turtle** ['tə:tl] n tortue marine;
**turtleneck (sweater)** n pullover m à
col montant
**tusk** [tʌsk] n défense f (d'éléphant)
**tutor** ['tju:tə<sup>r</sup>] n (BRIT Scol: in college)
directeur(-trice) d'études; (private

teacher) précepteur(-trice); **tutorial**
[tju:'tɔ:rɪəl] n (Scol) (séance f de)
travaux mpl pratiques
**tuxedo** [tʌk'si:dəu] n (US) smoking m
**TV** [ti:'vi:] n abbr (= television) télé f, TV f
**tweed** [twi:d] n tweed m
**tweezers** ['twi:zəz] npl pince f à épiler
**twelfth** [twelfθ] num douzième
**twelve** [twelv] num douze; **at ~
(o'clock)** à midi; (midnight) à minuit
**twentieth** ['twentɪɪθ] num vingtième
**twenty** ['twentɪ] num vingt
**twice** [twaɪs] adv deux fois; **~ as much**
deux fois plus
**twig** [twɪg] n brindille f ▷ vt, vi (inf)
piger
**twilight** ['twaɪlaɪt] n crépuscule m
**twin** [twɪn] adj, n jumeau(-elle) ▷ vt
jumeler; **twin(-bedded) room** n
chambre f à deux lits; **twin beds** npl lits
mpl jumeaux
**twinkle** ['twɪŋkl] vi scintiller; (eyes)
pétiller
**twist** [twɪst] n torsion f, tour m; (in
wire, flex) tortillon m; (bend: in road)
tournant m; (in story) coup m de théâtre
▷ vt tordre; (weave) entortiller; (roll
around) enrouler; (fig) déformer ▷ vi
(road, river) serpenter; **to ~ one's
ankle/wrist** (Med) se tordre la
cheville/le poignet
**twit** [twɪt] n (inf) crétin(e)
**twitch** [twɪtʃ] n (pull) coup sec, saccade
f; (nervous) tic m ▷ vi se convulser;
avoir un tic
**two** [tu:] num deux; **to put ~ and ~
together** (fig) faire le rapprochement
**type** [taɪp] n (category) genre m, espèce
f; (model) modèle m; (example) type m;
(Typ) type, caractère m ▷ vt (letter etc)
taper (à la machine); **typewriter** n
machine f à écrire
**typhoid** ['taɪfɔɪd] n typhoïde f
**typhoon** [taɪ'fu:n] n typhon m
**typical** ['tɪpɪkl] adj typique,
caractéristique; **typically** adv (as usual)
comme d'habitude; (characteristically)
typiquement

**typing** ['taɪpɪŋ] n dactylo(graphie) f
**typist** ['taɪpɪst] n dactylo m/f
**tyre** (US **tire**) ['taɪəʳ] n pneu m; **I've got a
flat ~** j'ai un pneu crevé; **tyre pressure**
n (BRIT) pression f (de gonflage)

**UFO** ['juːfəu] n abbr (= unidentified flying
object) ovni m
**Uganda** [juːˈgændə] n Ouganda m
**ugly** ['ʌglɪ] adj laid(e), vilain(e); (fig)
répugnant(e)
**UHT** adj abbr = **ultra-heat treated**; **~
milk** lait m UHT or longue conservation
**UK** n abbr = **United Kingdom**
**ulcer** ['ʌlsəʳ] n ulcère m; **mouth ~**
aphte f
**ultimate** ['ʌltɪmət] adj ultime, final(e);
(authority) suprême; **ultimately** adv (at
last) en fin de compte; (fundamentally)
finalement; (eventually) par la suite
**ultimatum** (pl **~s** or **ultimata**)
[ʌltɪˈmeɪtəm, -tə] n ultimatum m
**ultrasound** ['ʌltrəsaund] n (Med)
ultrason m
**ultraviolet** ['ʌltrəˈvaɪəlɪt] adj
ultraviolet(te)
**umbrella** [ʌmˈbrɛlə] n parapluie m; (for
sun) parasol m
**umpire** ['ʌmpaɪəʳ] n arbitre m; (Tennis)
juge m de chaise

**UN** *n abbr* = **United Nations**

**unable** [ʌnˈeɪbl] *adj*: **to be ~ to** ne (pas) pouvoir, être dans l'impossibilité de; (*not capable*) être incapable de

**unacceptable** [ʌnəkˈsɛptəbl] *adj* (*behaviour*) inadmissible; (*price, proposal*) inacceptable

**unanimous** [juːˈnænɪməs] *adj* unanime

**unarmed** [ʌnˈɑːmd] *adj* (*person*) non armé(e); (*combat*) sans armes

**unattended** [ʌnəˈtɛndɪd] *adj* (*car, child, luggage*) sans surveillance

**unattractive** [ʌnəˈtræktɪv] *adj* peu attrayant(e); (*character*) peu sympathique

**unavailable** [ʌnəˈveɪləbl] *adj* (*article, room, book*) (qui n'est) pas disponible; (*person*) (qui n'est) pas libre

**unavoidable** [ʌnəˈvɔɪdəbl] *adj* inévitable

**unaware** [ʌnəˈwɛəʳ] *adj*: **to be ~ of** ignorer, ne pas savoir, être inconscient(e) de; **unawares** *adv* à l'improviste, au dépourvu

**unbearable** [ʌnˈbɛərəbl] *adj* insupportable

**unbeatable** [ʌnˈbiːtəbl] *adj* imbattable

**unbelievable** [ʌnbɪˈliːvəbl] *adj* incroyable

**unborn** [ʌnˈbɔːn] *adj* à naître

**unbutton** [ʌnˈbʌtn] *vt* déboutonner

**uncalled-for** [ʌnˈkɔːldfɔːʳ] *adj* déplacé(e), injustifié(e)

**uncanny** [ʌnˈkænɪ] *adj* étrange, troublant(e)

**uncertain** [ʌnˈsəːtn] *adj* incertain(e); (*hesitant*) hésitant(e); **uncertainty** *n* incertitude *f*, doutes *mpl*

**unchanged** [ʌnˈtʃeɪndʒd] *adj* inchangé(e)

**uncle** [ˈʌŋkl] *n* oncle *m*

**unclear** [ʌnˈklɪəʳ] *adj* (qui n'est) pas clair(e) *or* évident(e); **I'm still ~ about what I'm supposed to do** je ne sais pas encore exactement ce que je dois faire

**uncomfortable** [ʌnˈkʌmfətəbl] *adj* inconfortable, peu confortable; (*uneasy*) mal à l'aise, gêné(e); (*situation*) désagréable

**uncommon** [ʌnˈkɔmən] *adj* rare, singulier(-ière), peu commun(e)

**unconditional** [ʌnkənˈdɪʃənl] *adj* sans conditions

**unconscious** [ʌnˈkɔnʃəs] *adj* sans connaissance, évanoui(e); (*unaware*): **~ (of)** inconscient(e) (de) ▷ *n*: **the ~** l'inconscient *m*

**uncontrollable** [ʌnkənˈtrəuləbl] *adj* (*child, dog*) indiscipliné(e); (*temper, laughter*) irrépressible

**unconventional** [ʌnkənˈvɛnʃənl] *adj* peu conventionnel(le)

**uncover** [ʌnˈkʌvəʳ] *vt* découvrir

**undecided** [ʌndɪˈsaɪdɪd] *adj* indécis(e), irrésolu(e)

**undeniable** [ʌndɪˈnaɪəbl] *adj* indéniable, incontestable

**under** [ˈʌndəʳ] *prep* sous; (*less than*) (de) moins de; *au-dessous de*; (*according to*) selon, en vertu de ▷ *adv* au-dessous; en dessous; **~ there** là-dessous; **~ the circumstances** étant donné les circonstances; **~ repair** en (cours de) réparation; **undercover** *adj* secret(-ète), clandestin(e); **underdone** *adj* (*Culin*) saignant(e); (: *pej*) pas assez cuit(e); **underestimate** *vt* sous-estimer, mésestimer; **undergo** *vt* (*irreg: like* **go**) subir; (*treatment*) suivre; **undergraduate** *n* étudiant(e) (qui prépare la licence); **underground** *adj* souterrain(e); (*fig*) clandestin(e) ▷ *n* (BRIT: *railway*) métro *m*; (*Pol*) clandestinité *f*; **undergrowth** *n* broussailles *fpl*, sous-bois *m*; **underline** *vt* souligner; **undermine** *vt* saper, miner; **underneath** [ʌndəˈniːθ] *adv* (en) dessous ▷ *prep* sous, au-dessous de; **underpants** *npl* caleçon *m*, slip *m*; **underpass** *n* (BRIT: *for pedestrians*) passage souterrain; (: *for cars*) passage inférieur;

**underprivileged** adj défavorisé(e);
**underscore** vt souligner; **undershirt**
n (US) tricot m de corps; **underskirt** n
(BRIT) jupon m

**understand** [ʌndə'stænd] vt, vi (irreg:
like **stand**) comprendre; **I don't ~** je
ne comprends pas; **understandable**
adj compréhensible; **understanding**
adj compréhensif(-ive) ▷ n
compréhension f; (agreement) accord m

**understatement** ['ʌndəsteɪtmənt]
n: **that's an ~** c'est (bien) peu dire, le
terme est faible

**understood** [ʌndə'stud] pt, pp of
**understand** ▷ adj entendu(e); (implied)
sous-entendu(e)

**undertake** [ʌndə'teɪk] vt (irreg: like
**take**) (job, task) entreprendre; (duty)
se charger de; **to ~ to do sth** s'engager
à faire qch

**undertaker** ['ʌndəteɪkə'] n (BRIT)
entrepreneur m des pompes funèbres,
croque-mort m

**undertaking** ['ʌndəteɪkɪŋ] n
entreprise f; (promise) promesse f

**under**: **underwater** adv sous l'eau
▷ adj sous-marin(e); **underway**
adj: **to be underway** (meeting,
investigation) être en cours; **underwear**
n sous-vêtements mpl; (women's
only) dessous mpl; **underwent** pt of
**undergo**; **underworld** n (of crime)
milieu m, pègre f

**undesirable** [ʌndɪ'zaɪərəbl] adj peu
souhaitable; (person, effect) indésirable

**undisputed** ['ʌndɪs'pjuːtɪd] adj
incontesté(e)

**undo** [ʌn'duː] vt (irreg: like **do**) défaire;
**undone** [ʌn'dʌn] pp of **undo** ▷ adj: **to
come ~** se défaire

**undoubtedly** [ʌn'dautɪdlɪ] adv sans
aucun doute

**undress** [ʌn'drɛs] vi se déshabiller

**unearth** [ʌn'ə:θ] vt déterrer; (fig)
dénicher

**uneasy** [ʌn'iːzɪ] adj mal à l'aise,
gêné(e); (worried) inquiet(-ète); (feeling)
désagréable; (peace, truce) fragile

**unemployed** [ʌnɪm'plɔɪd] adj sans
travail, au chômage ▷ n: **the ~** les
chômeurs mpl

**unemployment** [ʌnɪm'plɔɪmənt] n
chômage m; **unemployment benefit**
(US **unemployment compensation**) n
allocation f de chômage

**unequal** [ʌn'iːkwəl] adj inégal(e)

**uneven** [ʌn'iːvn] adj inégal(e); (quality,
work) irrégulier(-ière)

**unexpected** [ʌnɪk'spɛktɪd]
adj inattendu(e), imprévu(e);
**unexpectedly** adv (succeed) contre
toute attente; (arrive) à l'improviste

**unfair** [ʌn'fɛə'] adj: **~ (to)** injuste
(envers)

**unfaithful** [ʌn'feɪθful] adj infidèle

**unfamiliar** [ʌnfə'mɪlɪə'] adj étrange,
inconnu(e); **to be ~ with sth** mal
connaître qch

**unfashionable** [ʌn'fæʃnəbl] adj
(clothes) démodé(e); (place) peu chic inv

**unfasten** [ʌn'fɑːsn] vt défaire; (belt,
necklace) détacher; (open) ouvrir

**unfavourable** (US **unfavorable**)
[ʌn'feɪvrəbl] adj défavorable

**unfinished** [ʌn'fɪnɪʃt] adj inachevé(e)

**unfit** [ʌn'fɪt] adj (physically: ill) en
mauvaise santé; (: out of condition)
pas en forme; (incompetent): **~ (for)**
impropre (à); (work, service) inapte (à)

**unfold** [ʌn'fəuld] vt déplier ▷ vi se
dérouler

**unforgettable** [ʌnfə'gɛtəbl] adj
inoubliable

**unfortunate** [ʌn'fɔːtʃnət] adj
malheureux(-euse); (event, remark)
malencontreux(-euse); **unfortunately**
adv malheureusement

**unfriendly** [ʌn'frɛndlɪ] adj peu
aimable, froid(e)

**unfurnished** [ʌn'fə:nɪʃt] adj non
meublé(e)

**unhappiness** [ʌn'hæpɪnɪs] n tristesse
f, peine f

**unhappy** [ʌn'hæpɪ] adj triste,
malheureux(-euse); (unfortunate:
remark etc) malheureux(-euse); (not

*pleased*): ~ **with** mécontent(e) de, peu
satisfait(e) de

**unhealthy** [ʌn'hɛlθɪ] *adj* (*gen*)
malsain(e); (*person*) maladif(-ive)

**unheard-of** [ʌn'hə:dɔv] *adj* inouï(e),
sans précédent

**unhelpful** [ʌn'hɛlpful] *adj* (*person*) peu
serviable; (*advice*) peu utile

**unhurt** [ʌn'hə:t] *adj* indemne, sain(e)
et sauf (sauve)

**unidentified** [ʌnaɪ'dɛntɪfaɪd] *adj* non
identifié(e); *see also* **UFO**

**uniform** ['ju:nɪfɔ:m] *n* uniforme *m*
▷ *adj* uniforme

**unify** ['ju:nɪfaɪ] *vt* unifier

**unimportant** [ʌnɪm'pɔ:tənt] *adj* sans
importance

**uninhabited** [ʌnɪn'hæbɪtɪd] *adj*
inhabité(e)

**unintentional** [ʌnɪn'tɛnʃənəl] *adj*
involontaire

**union** ['ju:njən] *n* union *f*; (*also*: **trade**
~) syndicat *m* ▷ *cpd* du syndicat,
syndical(e); **Union Jack** *n* drapeau du
*Royaume-Uni*

**unique** [ju:'ni:k] *adj* unique

**unisex** ['ju:nɪsɛks] *adj* unisexe

**unit** ['ju:nɪt] *n* unité *f*; (*section: of
furniture etc*) élément *m*, bloc *m*; (*team,
squad*) groupe *m*, service *m*; **kitchen ~**
élément de cuisine

**unite** [ju:'naɪt] *vt* unir ▷ *vi* s'unir;
**united** *adj* uni(e); (*country, party*)
unifié(e); (*efforts*) conjugué(e); **United
Kingdom** *n* Royaume-Uni *m* (R.U.);
**United Nations (Organization)** *n*
(Organisation *f* des) Nations unies
(ONU); **United States (of America)** *n*
États-Unis *mpl*

**unity** ['ju:nɪtɪ] *n* unité *f*

**universal** [ju:nɪ'və:sl] *adj* universel(le)

**universe** ['ju:nɪvə:s] *n* univers *m*

**university** [ju:nɪ'və:sɪtɪ] *n* université
*f* ▷ *cpd* (*student, professor*) d'université;
(*education, year, degree*) universitaire

**unjust** [ʌn'dʒʌst] *adj* injuste

**unkind** [ʌn'kaɪnd] *adj* peu gentil(le),
méchant(e)

**unknown** [ʌn'nəun] *adj* inconnu(e)

**unlawful** [ʌn'lɔ:ful] *adj* illégal(e)

**unleaded** [ʌn'lɛdɪd] *n* (*also*: ~ **petrol**)
essence *f* sans plomb

**unleash** [ʌn'li:ʃ] *vt* (*fig*) déchaîner,
déclencher

**unless** [ʌn'lɛs] *conj*: ~ **he leaves** à
moins qu'il (ne) parte; ~ **otherwise
stated** sauf indication contraire

**unlike** [ʌn'laɪk] *adj* dissemblable,
différent(e) ▷ *prep* à la différence de,
contrairement à

**unlikely** [ʌn'laɪklɪ] *adj* (*result,
event*) improbable; (*explanation*)
invraisemblable

**unlimited** [ʌn'lɪmɪtɪd] *adj* illimité(e)

**unlisted** ['ʌn'lɪstɪd] *adj* (*US Tel*) sur la
liste rouge

**unload** [ʌn'ləud] *vt* décharger

**unlock** [ʌn'lɔk] *vt* ouvrir

**unlucky** [ʌn'lʌkɪ] *adj* (*person*)
malchanceux(-euse); (*object, number*)
qui porte malheur; **to be ~** (*person*) ne
pas avoir de chance

**unmarried** [ʌn'mærɪd] *adj* célibataire

**unmistak(e)able** [ʌnmɪs'teɪkəbl] *adj*
indubitable; qu'on ne peut ne pas
reconnaître

**unnatural** [ʌn'nætʃrəl] *adj* non
naturel(le); (*perversion*) contre nature

**unnecessary** [ʌn'nɛsəsərɪ] *adj* inutile,
superflu(e)

**UNO** ['ju:nəu] *n abbr* = **United Nations
Organization**

**unofficial** [ʌnə'fɪʃl] *adj* (*news*)
officieux(-euse), non officiel(le); (*strike*)
≈ sauvage

**unpack** [ʌn'pæk] *vi* défaire sa valise
▷ *vt* (*suitcase*) défaire; (*belongings*)
déballer

**unpaid** [ʌn'peɪd] *adj* (*bill*) impayé(e);
(*holiday*) non-payé(e), sans salaire;
(*work*) non rétribué(e)

**unpleasant** [ʌn'plɛznt] *adj*
déplaisant(e), désagréable

**unplug** [ʌn'plʌg] *vt* débrancher

**unpopular** [ʌn'pɔpjuləʳ] *adj*
impopulaire

**unprecedented** [ʌn'presɪdɛntɪd] *adj*
sans précédent

**unpredictable** [ʌnprɪ'dɪktəbl] *adj*
imprévisible

**unprotected** ['ʌnprə'tɛktɪd] *adj* (*sex*)
non protégé(e)

**unqualified** [ʌn'kwɔlɪfaɪd] *adj*
(*teacher*) non diplômé(e), sans titres;
(*success*) sans réserve, total(e); (*disaster*)
total(e)

**unravel** [ʌn'rævl] *vt* démêler

**unreal** [ʌn'rɪəl] *adj* irréel(le);
(*extraordinary*) incroyable

**unrealistic** ['ʌnrɪə'lɪstɪk] *adj* (*idea*)
irréaliste; (*estimate*) peu réaliste

**unreasonable** [ʌn'riːznəbl] *adj* qui
n'est pas raisonnable

**unrelated** [ʌnrɪ'leɪtɪd] *adj* sans
rapport; (*people*) sans lien de parenté

**unreliable** [ʌnrɪ'laɪəbl] *adj* sur qui
(*or* quoi) on ne peut pas compter,
peu fiable

**unrest** [ʌn'rɛst] *n* agitation *f*,
troubles *mpl*

**unroll** [ʌn'rəul] *vt* dérouler

**unruly** [ʌn'ruːlɪ] *adj* indiscipliné(e)

**unsafe** [ʌn'seɪf] *adj* (*in danger*) en
danger; (*journey, car*) dangereux(-euse)

**unsatisfactory** ['ʌnsætɪs'fæktərɪ] *adj*
peu satisfaisant(e)

**unscrew** [ʌn'skruː] *vt* dévisser

**unsettled** [ʌn'sɛtld] *adj* (*restless*)
perturbé(e); (*unpredictable*) instable;
incertain(e); (*not finalized*) non résolu(e)

**unsettling** [ʌn'sɛtlɪŋ] *adj* qui a un effet
perturbateur

**unsightly** [ʌn'saɪtlɪ] *adj*
disgracieux(-euse), laid(e)

**unskilled** [ʌn'skɪld] *adj*: ~ **worker**
manœuvre *m*

**unspoiled** ['ʌn'spɔɪld], **unspoilt**
['ʌn'spɔɪlt] *adj* (*place*) non dégradé(e)

**unstable** [ʌn'steɪbl] *adj* instable

**unsteady** [ʌn'stɛdɪ] *adj* mal assuré(e),
chancelant(e), instable

**unsuccessful** [ʌnsək'sɛsful] *adj*
(*attempt*) infructueux(-euse); (*writer,
proposal*) qui n'a pas de succès; **to be**

~ (*in attempting sth*) ne pas réussir; ne
pas avoir de succès; (*application*) ne pas
être retenu(e)

**unsuitable** [ʌn'suːtəbl] *adj* qui ne
convient pas, peu approprié(e); (*time*)
inopportun(e)

**unsure** [ʌn'ʃuər] *adj* pas sûr(e); **to be ~
of o.s.** ne pas être sûr de soi, manquer
de confiance en soi

**untidy** [ʌn'taɪdɪ] *adj* (*room*) en
désordre; (*appearance, person*)
débraillé(e); (*person: in character*) sans
ordre, désordonné; (*work*) peu
soigné(e)

**untie** [ʌn'taɪ] *vt* (*knot, parcel*) défaire;
(*prisoner, dog*) détacher

**until** [ən'tɪl] *prep* jusqu'à; (*after negative*)
avant ▷ *conj* jusqu'à ce que + *sub*; (*in
past, after negative*) avant que + *sub*; ~ **he
comes** jusqu'à ce qu'il vienne, jusqu'à
son arrivée; ~ **now** jusqu'à présent,
jusqu'ici; ~ **then** jusque-là

**untrue** [ʌn'truː] *adj* (*statement*) faux
(fausse)

**unused¹** [ʌn'juːzd] *adj* (*new*) neuf
(neuve)

**unused²** [ʌn'juːst] *adj*: **to be ~ to sth/
to doing sth** ne pas avoir l'habitude de
qch/de faire qch

**unusual** [ʌn'juːʒuəl] *adj* insolite,
exceptionnel(le), rare; **unusually** *adv*
exceptionnellement, particulièrement

**unveil** [ʌn'veɪl] *vt* dévoiler

**unwanted** [ʌn'wɔntɪd] *adj* (*child,
pregnancy*) non désiré(e); (*clothes etc*)
à donner

**unwell** [ʌn'wɛl] *adj* souffrant(e); **to feel**
~ ne pas se sentir bien

**unwilling** [ʌn'wɪlɪŋ] *adj*: **to be ~ to do**
ne pas vouloir faire

**unwind** [ʌn'waɪnd] *vb* (*irreg: like* **wind**)
▷ *vt* dérouler ▷ *vi* (*relax*) se détendre

**unwise** [ʌn'waɪz] *adj* imprudent(e),
peu judicieux(-euse)

**unwittingly** [ʌn'wɪtɪŋlɪ] *adv*
involontairement

**unwrap** [ʌn'ræp] *vt* défaire; ouvrir

**unzip** [ʌn'zɪp] *vt* ouvrir (la fermeture

éclair de); (*Comput*) dézipper

 **KEYWORD**

**up** [ʌp] *prep*: **he went up the stairs/the hill** il a monté l'escalier/la colline; **the cat was up a tree** le chat était dans un arbre; **they live further up the street** ils habitent plus haut dans la rue; **go up that road and turn left** remontez la rue et tournez à gauche
▷ *adv* **1** en haut; en l'air; (*upwards, higher*): **up in the sky/the mountains** (là-haut) dans le ciel/les montagnes; **put it a bit higher up** mettez-le un peu plus haut; **to stand up** (*get up*) se lever, se mettre debout; (*be standing*) être debout; **up there** là-haut; **up above** au-dessus
**2**: **to be up** (*out of bed*) être levé(e); (*prices*) avoir augmenté *or* monté; (*finished*): **when the year was up** à la fin de l'année
**3**: **up to** (*as far as*) jusqu'à; **up to now** jusqu'à présent
**4**: **to be up to** (*depending on*): **it's up to you** c'est à vous de décider; (*equal to*): **he's not up to it** (*job, task etc*) il n'en est pas capable; (*inf: be doing*): **what is he up to?** qu'est-ce qu'il peut bien faire?
▷ *n*: **ups and downs** hauts et bas *mpl*

**up-and-coming** [ʌpənd'kʌmɪŋ] *adj* plein(e) d'avenir *or* de promesses
**upbringing** ['ʌpbrɪŋɪŋ] *n* éducation *f*
**update** [ʌp'deɪt] *vt* mettre à jour
**upfront** [ʌp'frʌnt] *adj* (*open*) franc (franche) ▷ *adv* (*pay*) d'avance; **to be ~ about sth** ne rien cacher de qch
**upgrade** [ʌp'greɪd] *vt* (*person*) promouvoir; (*job*) revaloriser; (*property, equipment*) moderniser
**upheaval** [ʌp'hiːvl] *n* bouleversement *m*; (*in room*) branle-bas *m*; (*event*) crise *f*
**uphill** [ʌp'hɪl] *adj* qui monte; (*fig: task*) difficile, pénible ▷ *adv* (*face, look*) en amont, vers l'amont; **to go ~** monter
**upholstery** [ʌp'həulstərɪ] *n*

rembourrage *m*; (*cover*) tissu *m* d'ameublement; (*of car*) garniture *f*
**upmarket** [ʌp'maːkɪt] *adj* (*product*) haut de gamme *inv*; (*area*) chic *inv*
**upon** [ə'pɔn] *prep* sur
**upper** ['ʌpə'] *adj* supérieur(e); du dessus ▷ *n* (*of shoe*) empeigne *f*; **upper-class** *adj* de la haute société, aristocratique; (*district*) élégant(e), huppé(e); (*accent, attitude*) caractéristique des classes supérieures
**upright** ['ʌpraɪt] *adj* droit(e); (*fig*) droit, honnête
**uprising** ['ʌpraɪzɪŋ] *n* soulèvement *m*, insurrection *f*
**uproar** ['ʌprɔːʳ] *n* tumulte *m*, vacarme *m*; (*protests*) protestations *fpl*
**upset** *n* ['ʌpset] dérangement *m*
▷ *vt* (*irreg: like* **set** [ʌp'set]) (*glass etc*) renverser; (*plan*) déranger; (*person: offend*) contrarier; (*: grieve*) faire de la peine à; bouleverser ▷ *adj* [ʌp'set] contrarié(e); peiné(e); **to have a stomach ~** (BRIT) avoir une indigestion
**upside down** ['ʌpsaɪd-] *adv* à l'envers; **to turn sth ~** (*fig: place*) mettre sens dessus dessous
**upstairs** [ʌp'stɛəz] *adv* en haut ▷ *adj* (*room*) du dessus, d'en haut ▷ *n*: **the ~** l'étage *m*
**up-to-date** ['ʌptə'deɪt] *adj* moderne; (*information*) très récent(e)
**uptown** ['ʌptaun] (*US*) *adv* (*live*) dans les quartiers chics; (*go*) vers les quartiers chics ▷ *adj* des quartiers chics
**upward** ['ʌpwəd] *adj* ascendant(e); vers le haut; **upward(s)** *adv* vers le haut; (*more than*): **upward(s) of** plus de
**uranium** [juə'reɪnɪəm] *n* uranium *m*
**Uranus** [juə'reɪnəs] *n* Uranus *f*
**urban** ['əːbən] *adj* urbain(e)
**urge** [əːdʒ] *n* besoin (impératif), envie (pressante) ▷ *vt* (*person*): **to ~ sb to do** exhorter qn à faire, pousser qn à faire, recommander vivement à qn de faire
**urgency** ['əːdʒənsɪ] *n* urgence *f*; (*of tone*) insistance *f*

**urgent** ['ə:dʒənt] *adj* urgent(e); *(plea, tone)* pressant(e)

**urinal** ['juərɪnl] *n* (BRIT: *place*) urinoir *m*

**urinate** ['juərɪneɪt] *vi* uriner

**urine** ['juərɪn] *n* urine *f*

**URL** *abbr* (= *uniform resource locator*) URL *f*

**US** *n abbr* = **United States**

**us** [ʌs] *pron* nous; *see also* **me**

**USA** *n abbr* = **United States of America**

**use** *n* [ju:s] emploi *m*, utilisation *f*; *(usefulness)* utilité *f* ▷ *vt* [ju:z] se servir de, utiliser, employer; **in ~** en usage; **out of ~** hors d'usage; **to be of ~** servir, être utile; **it's no ~** ça ne sert à rien; **to have the ~ of** avoir l'usage de; **she ~d to do it** elle le faisait (autrefois), elle avait coutume de le faire; **to be ~d to** avoir l'habitude de, être habitué(e) à; **use up** *vt* finir, épuiser; *(food)* consommer; **used** [ju:zd] *adj* *(car)* d'occasion; **useful** *adj* utile; **useless** *adj* inutile; *(inf: person)* nul(le); **user** *n* utilisateur(-trice), usager *m*; **user-friendly** *adj* convivial(e), facile d'emploi

**usual** ['ju:ʒuəl] *adj* habituel(le); **as ~** comme d'habitude; **usually** *adv* d'habitude, d'ordinaire

**utensil** [ju:'tɛnsl] *n* ustensile *m*; **kitchen ~s** batterie *f* de cuisine

**utility** [ju:'tɪlɪtɪ] *n* utilité *f*; *(also:* **public ~)** service public

**utilize** ['ju:tɪlaɪz] *vt* utiliser; *(make good use of)* exploiter

**utmost** ['ʌtməust] *adj* extrême, le (la) plus grand(e) ▷ *n*: **to do one's ~** faire tout son possible

**utter** ['ʌtə'] *adj* total(e), complet(-ète) ▷ *vt* prononcer, proférer; *(sounds)* émettre; **utterly** *adv* complètement, totalement

**U-turn** ['ju:'tə:n] *n* demi-tour *m*; *(fig)* volte-face *f inv*

**v.** *abbr* = **verse** (= *vide*) v.; (= *versus*) c.; (= *volt*) V

**vacancy** ['veɪkənsɪ] *n* (BRIT: *job*) poste vacant; *(room)* chambre *f* disponible; **"no vacancies"** "complet"

**vacant** ['veɪkənt] *adj* *(post)* vacant(e); *(seat etc)* libre, disponible; *(expression)* distrait(e)

**vacate** [və'keɪt] *vt* quitter

**vacation** [və'keɪʃən] *n* *(esp US)* vacances *fpl*; **on ~** en vacances; **vacationer** (*US* **vacationist**) *n* vacancier(-ière)

**vaccination** [væksɪ'neɪʃən] *n* vaccination *f*

**vaccine** ['væksi:n] *n* vaccin *m*

**vacuum** ['vækjum] *n* vide *m*; **vacuum cleaner** *n* aspirateur *m*

**vagina** [və'dʒaɪnə] *n* vagin *m*

**vague** [veɪg] *adj* vague, imprécis(e); *(blurred: photo, memory)* flou(e)

**vain** [veɪn] *adj* *(useless)* vain(e); *(conceited)* vaniteux(-euse); **in ~** en vain

**Valentine's Day** ['væləntaɪnz-] *n*

Saint-Valentin f

**valid** ['vælɪd] adj (document) valide, valable; (excuse) valable

**valley** ['vælɪ] n vallée f

**valuable** ['væljuəbl] adj (jewel) de grande valeur; (time, help) précieux(-euse); **valuables** npl objets mpl de valeur

**value** ['vælju:] n valeur f ▷ vt (fix price) évaluer, expertiser; (appreciate) apprécier; **values** npl (principles) valeurs fpl

**valve** [vælv] n (in machine) soupape f; (on tyre) valve f; (Med) valve, valvule f

**vampire** ['væmpaɪəʳ] n vampire m

**van** [væn] n (Aut) camionnette f

**vandal** ['vændl] n vandale m/f; **vandalism** n vandalisme m; **vandalize** vt saccager

**vanilla** [və'nɪlə] n vanille f

**vanish** ['vænɪʃ] vi disparaître

**vanity** ['vænɪtɪ] n vanité f

**vapour** (us **vapor**) ['veɪpəʳ] n vapeur f; (on window) buée f

**variable** ['vɛərɪəbl] adj variable; (mood) changeant(e)

**variant** ['vɛərɪənt] n variante f

**variation** [vɛərɪ'eɪʃən] n variation f; (in opinion) changement m

**varied** ['vɛərɪd] adj varié(e), divers(e)

**variety** [və'raɪətɪ] n variété f; (quantity) nombre m, quantité f

**various** ['vɛərɪəs] adj divers(e), différent(e); (several) divers, plusieurs

**varnish** ['vɑ:nɪʃ] n vernis m ▷ vt vernir

**vary** ['vɛərɪ] vt, vi varier, changer

**vase** [vɑ:z] n vase m

**Vaseline®** ['væsɪli:n] n vaseline f

**vast** [vɑ:st] adj vaste, immense; (amount, success) énorme

**VAT** [væt] n abbr (BRIT: = value added tax) TVA f

**vault** [vɔ:lt] n (of roof) voûte f; (tomb) caveau m; (in bank) salle f des coffres; chambre forte ▷ vt (also: ~ over) sauter (d'un bond)

**VCR** n abbr = **video cassette recorder**

**VDU** n abbr = **visual display unit**

**veal** [vi:l] n veau m

**veer** [vɪəʳ] vi tourner; (car, ship) virer

**vegan** ['vi:gən] n végétalien(ne)

**vegetable** ['vɛdʒtəbl] n légume m ▷ adj végétal(e)

**vegetarian** [vɛdʒɪ'tɛərɪən] adj, n végétarien(ne); **do you have any ~ dishes?** avez-vous des plats végétariens?

**vegetation** [vɛdʒɪ'teɪʃən] n végétation f

**vehicle** ['vi:ɪkl] n véhicule m

**veil** [veɪl] n voile m

**vein** [veɪn] n veine f; (on leaf) nervure f

**Velcro®** ['vɛlkrəu] n velcro® m

**velvet** ['vɛlvɪt] n velours m

**vending machine** ['vɛndɪŋ-] n distributeur m automatique

**vendor** ['vɛndəʳ] n vendeur(-euse); **street ~** marchand ambulant

**Venetian blind** [vɪ'ni:ʃən-] n store vénitien

**vengeance** ['vɛndʒəns] n vengeance f; **with a ~** (fig) vraiment, pour de bon

**venison** ['vɛnɪsn] n venaison f

**venom** ['vɛnəm] n venin m

**vent** [vɛnt] n conduit m d'aération; (in dress, jacket) fente f ▷ vt (fig: one's feelings) donner libre cours à

**ventilation** [vɛntɪ'leɪʃən] n ventilation f, aération f

**venture** ['vɛntʃəʳ] n entreprise f ▷ vt risquer, hasarder ▷ vi s'aventurer, se risquer; **a business ~** une entreprise commerciale

**venue** ['vɛnju:] n lieu m

**Venus** ['vi:nəs] n (planet) Vénus f

**verb** [və:b] n verbe m; **verbal** adj verbal(e)

**verdict** ['və:dɪkt] n verdict m

**verge** [və:dʒ] n bord m; **"soft ~s"** (BRIT) "accotements non stabilisés"; **on the ~ of doing** sur le point de faire

**verify** ['vɛrɪfaɪ] vt vérifier

**versatile** ['və:sətaɪl] adj polyvalent(e)

**verse** [və:s] n vers mpl; (stanza) strophe f; (in Bible) verset m

**version** ['və:ʃən] n version f

**versus** ['vəːsəs] *prep* contre
**vertical** ['vəːtɪkl] *adj* vertical(e)
**very** ['vɛrɪ] *adv* très ▷ *adj*: **the ~ book which** le livre même que; **the ~ last** le tout dernier; **at the ~ least** au moins; **~ much** beaucoup
**vessel** ['vɛsl] *n* (Anat, Naut) vaisseau *m*; (container) récipient *m*; *see also* **blood**
**vest** [vɛst] *n* (BRIT: underwear) tricot *m* de corps; (US: waistcoat) gilet *m*
**vet** [vɛt] *n abbr* (BRIT: = veterinary surgeon) vétérinaire *m/f*; (US: = veteran) ancien(ne) combattant(e) ▷ *vt* examiner minutieusement
**veteran** ['vɛtərn] *n* vétéran *m*; (also: **war ~**) ancien combattant
**veterinary surgeon** ['vɛtrɪnərɪ-] (BRIT) (US **veterinarian** [vɛtrɪ'nɛərɪən]) *n* vétérinaire *m/f*
**veto** ['viːtəu] *n* (pl **~es**) veto *m* ▷ *vt* opposer son veto à
**via** ['vaɪə] *prep* par, via
**viable** ['vaɪəbl] *adj* viable
**vibrate** [vaɪ'breɪt] *vi*: **to ~ (with)** vibrer (de)
**vibration** [vaɪ'breɪʃən] *n* vibration *f*
**vicar** ['vɪkə[r]] *n* pasteur *m* (de l'Église anglicane)
**vice** [vaɪs] *n* (evil) vice *m*; (Tech) étau *m*; **vice-chairman** *n* vice-président(e)
**vice versa** ['vaɪsɪ'vəːsə] *adv* vice versa
**vicinity** [vɪ'sɪnɪtɪ] *n* environs *mpl*, alentours *mpl*
**vicious** ['vɪʃəs] *adj* (remark) cruel(le), méchant(e); (blow) brutal(e); (dog) méchant(e), dangereux(-euse); **a ~ circle** un cercle vicieux
**victim** ['vɪktɪm] *n* victime *f*
**victor** ['vɪktə[r]] *n* vainqueur *m*
**Victorian** [vɪk'tɔːrɪən] *adj* victorien(ne)
**victorious** [vɪk'tɔːrɪəs] *adj* victorieux(-euse)
**victory** ['vɪktərɪ] *n* victoire *f*
**video** ['vɪdɪəu] *n* (video film) vidéo *f*; (also: **~ cassette**) vidéocassette *f*; (also: **~ cassette recorder**) magnétoscope *m* ▷ *vt* (with recorder) enregistrer;

(with camera) filmer; **video camera** *n* caméra *f* vidéo *inv*; **video (cassette) recorder** *n* magnétoscope *m*; **video game** *n* jeu *m* vidéo *inv*; **video shop** *n* vidéoclub *m*; **video tape** *n* bande *f* vidéo *inv*; (cassette) vidéocassette *f*
**vie** [vaɪ] *vi*: **to ~ with** lutter avec, rivaliser avec
**Vienna** [vɪ'ɛnə] *n* Vienne
**Vietnam, Viet Nam** ['vjɛt'næm] *n* Viêt-nam *or* Vietnam *m*; **Vietnamese** [vjɛtnə'miːz] *adj* vietnamien(ne) ▷ *n* (pl inv) Vietnamien(ne)
**view** [vjuː] *n* vue *f*; (opinion) avis *m*, vue ▷ *vt* voir, regarder; (situation) considérer; (house) visiter; **on ~** (in museum etc) exposé(e); **in full ~ of sb** sous les yeux de qn; **in my ~** à mon avis; **in ~ of the fact that** étant donné que; **viewer** *n* (TV) téléspectateur(-trice); **viewpoint** *n* point *m* de vue
**vigilant** ['vɪdʒɪlənt] *adj* vigilant(e)
**vigorous** ['vɪgərəs] *adj* vigoureux(-euse)
**vile** [vaɪl] *adj* (action) vil(e); (smell, food) abominable; (temper) massacrant(e)
**villa** ['vɪlə] *n* villa *f*
**village** ['vɪlɪdʒ] *n* village *m*; **villager** *n* villageois(e)
**villain** ['vɪlən] *n* (scoundrel) scélérat *m*; (BRIT: criminal) bandit *m*; (in novel etc) traître *m*
**vinaigrette** [vɪneɪ'grɛt] *n* vinaigrette *f*
**vine** [vaɪn] *n* vigne *f*
**vinegar** ['vɪnɪgə[r]] *n* vinaigre *m*
**vineyard** ['vɪnjɑːd] *n* vignoble *m*
**vintage** ['vɪntɪdʒ] *n* (year) année *f*, millésime *m* ▷ *cpd* (car) d'époque; (wine) de grand cru
**vinyl** ['vaɪnl] *n* vinyle *m*
**viola** [vɪ'əulə] *n* alto *m*
**violate** ['vaɪəleɪt] *vt* violer
**violation** [vaɪə'leɪʃən] *n* violation *f*; **in ~ of** (rule, law) en infraction à, en violation de
**violence** ['vaɪələns] *n* violence *f*
**violent** ['vaɪələnt] *adj* violent(e)
**violet** ['vaɪələt] *adj* (colour) violet(te)

▷ n (plant) violette f
**violin** ['vaɪə'lɪn] n violon m
**VIP** n abbr (= very important person) VIP m
**virgin** ['və:dʒɪn] n vierge f
**Virgo** ['və:gəu] n la Vierge
**virtual** ['və:tjuəl] adj (Comput, Physics) virtuel(le); (in effect): **it's a ~ impossibility** c'est quasiment impossible; **virtually** adv (almost) pratiquement; **virtual reality** n (Comput) réalité virtuelle
**virtue** ['və:tju:] n vertu f; (advantage) mérite m, avantage m; **by ~ of** en vertu or raison de
**virus** ['vaɪərəs] n (Med, Comput) virus m
**visa** ['vi:zə] n visa m
**vise** [vaɪs] n (US Tech) = **vice**
**visibility** [vɪzɪ'bɪlɪtɪ] n visibilité f
**visible** ['vɪzəbl] adj visible
**vision** ['vɪʒən] n (sight) vue f, vision f; (foresight, in dream) vision f
**visit** ['vɪzɪt] n visite f; (stay) séjour m ▷ vt (person: US: also: **~ with**) rendre visite à; (place) visiter; **visiting hours** npl heures fpl de visite; **visitor** n visiteur(-euse); (to one's house) invité(e); **visitor centre** (US **visitor center**) n hall m or centre m d'accueil
**visual** ['vɪzjuəl] adj visuel(le); **visualize** vt se représenter
**vital** ['vaɪtl] adj vital(e); **of ~ importance (to sb/sth)** d'une importance capitale (pour qn/qch)
**vitality** [vaɪ'tælɪtɪ] n vitalité f
**vitamin** ['vɪtəmɪn] n vitamine f
**vivid** ['vɪvɪd] adj (account) frappant(e), vivant(e); (light, imagination) vif (vive)
**V-neck** ['vi:nɛk] n décolleté m en V
**vocabulary** [vəu'kæbjulərɪ] n vocabulaire m
**vocal** ['vəukl] adj vocal(e); (articulate) qui n'hésite pas à s'exprimer, qui sait faire entendre ses opinions
**vocational** [vəu'keɪʃənl] adj professionnel(le)
**vodka** ['vɔdkə] n vodka f
**vogue** [vəug] n: **to be in ~** être en vogue or à la mode

**voice** [vɔɪs] n voix f ▷ vt (opinion) exprimer, formuler; **voice mail** n (system) messagerie f vocale; (device) boîte f vocale
**void** [vɔɪd] n vide m ▷ adj (invalid) nul(le); (empty): **~ of** vide de, dépourvu(e) de
**volatile** ['vɔlətaɪl] adj volatil(e); (fig: person) versatile; (: situation) explosif(-ive)
**volcano** (pl **~es**) [vɔl'keɪnəu] n volcan m
**volleyball** ['vɔlɪbɔ:l] n volley(-ball) m
**volt** [vəult] n volt m; **voltage** n tension f, voltage m
**volume** ['vɔlju:m] n volume m; (of tank) capacité f
**voluntarily** ['vɔləntrɪlɪ] adv volontairement
**voluntary** ['vɔləntərɪ] adj volontaire; (unpaid) bénévole
**volunteer** [vɔlən'tɪər] n volontaire m/f ▷ vt (information) donner spontanément ▷ vi (Mil) s'engager comme volontaire; **to ~ to do** se proposer pour faire
**vomit** ['vɔmɪt] n vomissure f ▷ vt, vi vomir
**vote** [vəut] n vote m, suffrage m; (votes cast) voix f, vote; (franchise) droit m de vote ▷ vt (chairman) élire; (propose): **to ~ that** proposer que + sub ▷ vi voter; **~ of thanks** discours m de remerciement; **voter** n électeur(-trice); **voting** n scrutin m, vote m
**voucher** ['vautʃər] n (for meal, petrol, gift) bon m
**vow** [vau] n vœu m, serment m ▷ vi jurer
**vowel** ['vauəl] n voyelle f
**voyage** ['vɔɪɪdʒ] n voyage m par mer, traversée f
**vulgar** ['vʌlgər] adj vulgaire
**vulnerable** ['vʌlnərəbl] adj vulnérable
**vulture** ['vʌltʃər] n vautour m

**W**

**waddle** ['wɔdl] *vi* se dandiner
**wade** [weɪd] *vi*: **to ~ through** marcher dans, patauger dans; *(fig: book)* venir à bout de
**wafer** ['weɪfər] *n (Culin)* gaufrette *f*
**waffle** ['wɔfl] *n (Culin)* gaufre *f* ⊳ *vi* parler pour ne rien dire; faire du remplissage
**wag** [wæg] *vt* agiter, remuer ⊳ *vi* remuer
**wage** [weɪdʒ] *n (also:* **~s***)* salaire *m*, paye *f* ⊳ *vt*: **to ~ war** faire la guerre
**wag(g)on** ['wægən] *n (horse-drawn)* chariot *m*; *(BRIT Rail)* wagon *m* (de marchandises)
**wail** [weɪl] *n* gémissement *m*; *(of siren)* hurlement *m* ⊳ *vi* gémir; *(siren)* hurler
**waist** [weɪst] *n* taille *f*, ceinture *f*; **waistcoat** *n (BRIT)* gilet *m*
**wait** [weɪt] *n* attente *f* ⊳ *vi* attendre; **to ~ for sb/sth** attendre qn/qch; **to keep sb ~ing** faire attendre qn; **~ for me, please** attendez-moi, s'il vous plaît; **I can't ~ to ...** *(fig)* je meurs

d'envie de ...; **to lie in ~ for** guetter; **wait on** *vt fus* servir; **waiter** *n* garçon *m* (de café), serveur *m*; **waiting list** *n* liste *f* d'attente; **waiting room** *n* salle *f* d'attente; **waitress** ['weɪtrɪs] *n* serveuse *f*
**waive** [weɪv] *vt* renoncer à, abandonner
**wake** [weɪk] *vb* (*pt* **woke** *or* **~d**, *pp* **woken** *or* **~d**) ⊳ *vt (also:* **~ up***)* réveiller ⊳ *vi (also:* **~ up***)* se réveiller ⊳ *n (for dead person)* veillée *f* mortuaire; *(Naut)* sillage *m*
**Wales** [weɪlz] *n* pays *m* de Galles; **the Prince of ~** le prince de Galles
**walk** [wɔːk] *n* promenade *f*; *(short)* petit tour; *(gait)* démarche *f*; *(path)* chemin *m*; *(in park etc)* allée *f* ⊳ *vi* marcher; *(for pleasure, exercise)* se promener ⊳ *vt (distance)* faire à pied; *(dog)* promener; **10 minutes' ~ from** à 10 minutes de marche de; **to go for a ~** se promener; faire un tour; **from all ~s of life** de toutes conditions sociales; **walk out** *vi (go out)* sortir; *(as protest)* partir (en signe de protestation); *(strike)* se mettre en grève; **to ~ out on sb** quitter qn; **walker** *n (person)* marcheur(-euse); **walkie-talkie** ['wɔːkɪ'tɔːkɪ] *n* talkie-walkie *m*; **walking** *n* marche *f* à pied; **walking shoes** *npl* chaussures *fpl* de marche; **walking stick** *n* canne *f*; **Walkman®** *n* Walkman® *m*; **walkway** *n* promenade *f*, cheminement piéton
**wall** [wɔːl] *n* mur *m*; *(of tunnel, cave)* paroi *f*
**wallet** ['wɔlɪt] *n* portefeuille *m*; **I can't find my ~** je ne retrouve plus mon portefeuille
**wallpaper** ['wɔːlpeɪpər] *n* papier peint ⊳ *vt* tapisser
**walnut** ['wɔːlnʌt] *n* noix *f*; *(tree, wood)* noyer *m*
**walrus** (*pl* **~** *or* **~es**) ['wɔːlrəs] *n* morse *m*
**waltz** [wɔːlts] *n* valse *f* ⊳ *vi* valser
**wand** [wɔnd] *n (also:* **magic ~***)* baguette *f* (magique)
**wander** ['wɔndər] *vi (person)* errer, aller

sans but; (*thoughts*) vagabonder ▷ *vt* errer dans

**want** [wɔnt] *vt* vouloir; (*need*) avoir besoin de ▷ *n*: **for ~ of** par manque de, faute de; **to ~ to do** vouloir faire; **to ~ sb to do** vouloir que qn fasse; **wanted** *adj* (*criminal*) recherché(e) par la police; **"cook wanted"** on recherche un cuisinier

**war** [wɔːʳ] *n* guerre *f*; **to make ~ (on)** faire la guerre (à)

**ward** [wɔːd] *n* (*in hospital*) salle *f*; (*Pol*) section électorale; (*Law: child: also:* **~ of court**) pupille *m/f*

**warden** ['wɔːdn] *n* (*BRIT: of institution*) directeur(-trice); (*of park, game reserve*) gardien(ne); (*BRIT: also:* **traffic ~**) contractuel(le)

**wardrobe** ['wɔːdrəub] *n* (*cupboard*) armoire *f*; (*clothes*) garde-robe *f*

**warehouse** ['wɛəhaus] *n* entrepôt *m*

**warfare** ['wɔːfɛəʳ] *n* guerre *f*

**warhead** ['wɔːhɛd] *n* (*Mil*) ogive *f*

**warm** [wɔːm] *adj* chaud(e); (*person, thanks, welcome, applause*) chaleureux(-euse); **it's ~** il fait chaud; **I'm ~** j'ai chaud; **warm up** *vi* (*person, room*) se réchauffer; (*athlete, discussion*) s'échauffer ▷ *vt* (*food*) (faire) réchauffer; (*water*) (faire) chauffer; (*engine*) faire chauffer; **warmly** *adv* (*dress*) chaudement; (*thank, welcome*) chaleureusement; **warmth** *n* chaleur *f*

**warn** [wɔːn] *vt* avertir, prévenir; **to ~ sb (not) to do** conseiller à qn de (ne pas) faire; **warning** *n* avertissement *m*; (*notice*) avis *m*; **warning light** *n* avertisseur lumineux

**warrant** ['wɔrnt] *n* (*guarantee*) garantie *f*; (*Law: to arrest*) mandat *m* d'arrêt; (*: to search*) mandat de perquisition ▷ *vt* (*justify, merit*) justifier

**warranty** ['wɔrənti] *n* garantie *f*

**warrior** ['wɔriəʳ] *n* guerrier(-ière)

**Warsaw** ['wɔːsɔː] *n* Varsovie

**warship** ['wɔːʃip] *n* navire *m* de guerre

**wart** [wɔːt] *n* verrue *f*

**wartime** ['wɔːtaim] *n*: **in ~** en temps de guerre

**wary** ['wɛəri] *adj* prudent(e)

**was** [wɔz] *pt of* **be**

**wash** [wɔʃ] *vt* laver ▷ *vi* se laver; (*sea*): **to ~ over/against sth** inonder/baigner qch ▷ *n* (*clothes*) lessive *f*; (*washing programme*) lavage *m*; (*of ship*) sillage *m*; **to have a ~** se laver, faire sa toilette; **wash up** *vi* (*BRIT*) faire la vaisselle; (*US: have a wash*) se débarbouiller; **washbasin** *n* lavabo *m*; **wash cloth** *n* (*US*) gant *m* de toilette; **washer** *n* (*Tech*) rondelle *f*, joint *m*; **washing** *n* (*BRIT: linen etc: dirty*) linge *m*; (*: clean*) lessive *f*; **washing line** *n* (*BRIT*) corde *f* à linge; **washing machine** *n* machine *f* à laver; **washing powder** *n* (*BRIT*) lessive *f* (en poudre)

**Washington** ['wɔʃiŋtən] *n* Washington *m*

**wash**: **washing-up** *n* (*BRIT*) vaisselle *f*; **washing-up liquid** *n* (*BRIT*) produit *m* pour la vaisselle; **washroom** *n* (*US*) toilettes *fpl*

**wasn't** ['wɔznt] = **was not**

**wasp** [wɔsp] *n* guêpe *f*

**waste** [weist] *n* gaspillage *m*; (*of time*) perte *f*; (*rubbish*) déchets *mpl*; (*also:* **household ~**) ordures *fpl* ▷ *adj* (*land, ground: in city*) à l'abandon; (*leftover*): **~ material** déchets ▷ *vt* gaspiller; (*time, opportunity*) perdre; **waste ground** *n* (*BRIT*) terrain *m* vague; **wastepaper basket** *n* corbeille *f* à papier

**watch** [wɔtʃ] *n* montre *f*; (*act of watching*) surveillance *f*; (*guard: Mil*) sentinelle *f*; (*: Naut*) homme *m* de quart; (*Naut: spell of duty*) quart *m* ▷ *vt* (*look at*) observer; (*: match, programme*) regarder; (*spy on, guard*) surveiller; (*be careful of*) faire attention à ▷ *vi* regarder; (*keep guard*) monter la garde; **to keep ~** faire le guet; **watch out** *vi* faire attention; **watchdog** *n* chien *m* de garde; (*fig*) gardien(ne); **watch strap** *n* bracelet *m* de montre

**water** ['wɔːtəʳ] *n* eau *f* ▷ *vt* (*plant, garden*) arroser ▷ *vi* (*eyes*) larmoyer; **in**

**British ~s** dans les eaux territoriales Britanniques; **to make sb's mouth ~** mettre l'eau à la bouche de qn; **water down** vt (milk etc) couper avec de l'eau; (fig: story) édulcorer; **watercolour** (US **watercolor**) n aquarelle f; **watercress** n cresson m (de fontaine); **waterfall** n chute f d'eau; **watering can** n arrosoir m; **watermelon** n pastèque f; **waterproof** adj imperméable; **water-skiing** n ski m nautique

**watt** [wɔt] n watt m

**wave** [weɪv] n vague f; (of hand) geste m, signe m; (Radio) onde f; (in hair) ondulation f; (fig: of enthusiasm, strikes etc) vague f ▷ vi faire signe de la main; (flag) flotter au vent; (grass) ondoyer ▷ vt (handkerchief) agiter; (stick) brandir; **wavelength** n longueur f d'ondes

**waver** ['weɪvər] vi vaciller; (voice) trembler; (person) hésiter

**wavy** ['weɪvɪ] adj (hair, surface) ondulé(e); (line) onduleux(-euse)

**wax** [wæks] n cire f; (for skis) fart m ▷ vt cirer; (car) lustrer; (skis) farter ▷ vi (moon) croître

**way** [weɪ] n chemin m, voie f; (distance) distance f; (direction) chemin, direction f; (manner) façon f, manière f; (habit) habitude f, façon f; **which ~? — this ~/that ~** par où or de quel côté? — par ici/par là; **to lose one's ~** perdre son chemin; **on the ~ (to)** en route (pour); **to be on one's ~** être en route; **to be in the ~** bloquer le passage; (fig) gêner; **it's a long ~ a-** c'est loin d'ici; **to go out of one's ~ to do** (fig) se donner beaucoup de mal pour faire; **to be under ~** (work, project) être en cours; **in a ~** dans un sens; **by the ~** à propos; **"~ in"** (BRIT) "entrée"; **"~ out"** (BRIT) "sortie"; **the ~ back** le chemin du retour; **"give ~"** (BRIT Aut) "cédez la priorité"; **no ~!** (inf) pas question!

**W.C.** n abbr (BRIT: = water closet) w.-c. mpl, waters mpl

**we** [wiː] pl pron nous

**weak** [wiːk] adj faible; (health) fragile; (beam etc) peu solide; (tea, coffee) léger(-ère); **weaken** vi faiblir ▷ vt affaiblir; **weakness** n faiblesse f; (fault) point m faible

**wealth** [wɛlθ] n (money, resources) richesse(s) f(pl); (of details) profusion f; **wealthy** adj riche

**weapon** ['wɛpən] n arme f; **~s of mass destruction** armes fpl de destruction massive

**wear** [wɛər] n (use) usage m; (deterioration through use) usure f ▷ vb (pt **wore**, pp **worn**) ▷ vt (clothes) porter; (put on) mettre; (damage: through use) user ▷ vi (last) faire de l'usage; (rub etc through) s'user; **sports/baby~** vêtements mpl de sport/pour bébés; **evening ~** tenue f de soirée; **wear off** vi disparaître; **wear out** vt user; (person, strength) épuiser

**weary** ['wɪərɪ] adj (tired) épuisé(e); (dispirited) las (lasse); abattu(e) ▷ vi: **to ~ of** se lasser de

**weasel** ['wiːzl] n (Zool) belette f

**weather** ['wɛðər] n temps m ▷ vt (storm: lit, fig) essuyer; (crisis) survivre à; **under the ~** (fig: ill) mal fichu(e); **weather forecast** n prévisions fpl météorologiques, météo f

**weave** (pt **wove**, pp **woven**) [wiːv, wəuv, 'wəuvn] vt (cloth) tisser; (basket) tresser

**web** [wɛb] n (of spider) toile f; (on duck's foot) palmure f; (fig) tissu m; (Comput): **the (World-Wide) W~** le Web; **web page** n (Comput) page f Web; **website** n (Comput) site m web

**wed** [wɛd] (pt, pp **~ded**) vt épouser ▷ vi se marier

**Wed** abbr (= Wednesday) me

**we'd** [wiːd] = **we had**; **we would**

**wedding** ['wɛdɪŋ] n mariage m; **wedding anniversary** n anniversaire m de mariage; **silver/golden wedding anniversary** noces fpl d'argent/d'or; **wedding day** n jour m du mariage; **wedding dress** n robe f de mariée;

**wedding ring** n alliance f

**wedge** [wɛdʒ] n (of wood etc) coin m; (under door etc) cale f; (of cake) part f ▷ vt (fix) caler; (push) enfoncer, coincer

**Wednesday** ['wɛnzdɪ] n mercredi m

**wee** [wi:] adj (SCOTTISH) petit(e); tout(e) petit(e)

**weed** [wi:d] n mauvaise herbe ▷ vt désherber; **weedkiller** n désherbant m

**week** [wi:k] n semaine f; **a ~ today/on Tuesday** aujourd'hui/mardi en huit; **weekday** n jour m de semaine; (Comm) jour ouvrable; **weekend** n week-end m; **weekly** adv une fois par semaine, chaque semaine ▷ adj, n hebdomadaire (m)

**weep** [wi:p] (pt, pp **wept**) vi (person) pleurer

**weigh** [weɪ] vt, vi peser; **to ~ anchor** lever l'ancre; **weigh up** vt examiner

**weight** [weɪt] n poids m; **to put on/ lose ~** grossir/maigrir; **weightlifting** n haltérophilie f

**weir** [wɪə^r] n barrage m

**weird** [wɪəd] adj bizarre; (eerie) surnaturel(le)

**welcome** ['wɛlkəm] adj bienvenu(e) ▷ n accueil m ▷ vt accueillir; (also: **bid ~**) souhaiter la bienvenue à; (be glad of) se réjouir de; **you're ~!** (after thanks) de rien, il n'y a pas de quoi

**weld** [wɛld] vt souder

**welfare** ['wɛlfɛə^r] n (wellbeing) bien-être m; (social aid) assistance sociale; **welfare state** n État-providence m

**well** [wɛl] n puits m ▷ adv bien ▷ adj: **to be ~** aller bien ▷ excl eh bien!; (relief also) bon!; (resignation) enfin!; **~ done!** bravo!; **get ~ soon!** remets-toi vite!; **to do ~** bien réussir; (business) prospérer; **as ~** (in addition) aussi, également; **as ~ as** aussi bien que or de; en plus de

**we'll** [wi:l] = **we will; we shall**

**well**: **well-behaved** adj sage, obéissant(e); **well-built** adj (person) bien bâti(e); **well-dressed** adj bien habillé(e), bien vêtu(e)

**well-groomed** [-'gru:md] adj très soigné(e)

**wellies** ['wɛlɪz] (inf) npl (BRIT) = **wellingtons**

**wellingtons** ['wɛlɪŋtənz] npl (also: **wellington boots**) bottes fpl en caoutchouc

**well**: **well-known** adj (person) bien connu(e); **well-off** adj aisé(e), assez riche; **well-paid** [wɛl'peɪd] adj bien payé(e)

**Welsh** [wɛlʃ] adj gallois(e) ▷ n (Ling) gallois m; **the Welsh** npl (people) les Gallois; **Welshman** (irreg) n Gallois m; **Welshwoman** (irreg) n Galloise f

**went** [wɛnt] pt of **go**

**wept** [wɛpt] pt, pp of **weep**

**were** [wə:^r] pt of **be**

**we're** [wɪə^r] = **we are**

**weren't** [wə:nt] = **were not**

**west** [wɛst] n ouest m ▷ adj (wind) d'ouest; (side) ouest inv ▷ adv à or vers l'ouest; **the W~** l'Occident m, l'Ouest; **westbound** ['wɛstbaund] adj en direction de l'ouest; (carriageway) ouest inv; **western** adj occidental(e), de or à l'ouest ▷ n (Cine) western m; **West Indian** adj antillais(e) ▷ n Antillais(e)

**West Indies** [-'ɪndɪz] npl Antilles fpl

**wet** [wɛt] adj mouillé(e); (damp) humide; (soaked: also: **~ through**) trempé(e); (rainy) pluvieux(-euse); **to get ~** se mouiller; **"~ paint"** "attention peinture fraîche"; **wetsuit** n combinaison f de plongée

**we've** [wi:v] = **we have**

**whack** [wæk] vt donner un grand coup à

**whale** [weɪl] n (Zool) baleine f

**wharf** (pl **wharves**) [wɔ:f, wɔ:vz] n quai m

 **KEYWORD**

**what** [wɔt] adj **1** (in questions) quel(le); **what size is he?** quelle taille fait-il?; **what colour is it?** de quelle couleur est-ce?; **what books do you need?**

quels livres vous faut-il?
**2** (*in exclamations*): **what a mess!** quel
désordre!; **what a fool I am!** que je
suis bête!
▷ *pron* **1** (*interrogative*) que; de/à/en
*etc* quoi; **what are you doing?** que
faites-vous?, qu'est-ce que vous faites?;
**what is happening?** qu'est-ce qui se
passe?, que se passe-t-il?; **what are
you talking about?** de quoi parlez-
vous?; **what are you thinking about?**
à quoi pensez-vous?; **what is it called?**
comment est-ce que ça s'appelle?;
**what about me?** et moi?; **what about
doing ...?** et si on faisait ...?
**2** (*relative: subject*) ce qui; (*: direct object*)
ce que; (*: indirect object*) ce à quoi, ce
dont; **I saw what you did/was on the
table** j'ai vu ce que vous avez fait/ce
qui était sur la table; **tell me what
you remember** dites-moi ce dont
vous vous souvenez; **what I want is
a cup of tea** ce que je veux, c'est une
tasse de thé
▷ *excl* (*disbelieving*) quoi!, comment!

**whatever** [wɔt'ɛvəʳ] *adj*: **take ~ book
you prefer** prenez le livre que vous
préférez, peu importe lequel; **~ book
you take** quel que soit le livre que
vous preniez ▷ *pron*: **do ~ is
necessary** faites (tout) ce qui est
nécessaire; **~ happens** quoi qu'il
arrive; **no reason ~ or whatsoever**
pas la moindre raison; **nothing ~ or
whatsoever** rien du tout
**whatsoever** [wɔtsəu'ɛvəʳ] *adj see*
**whatever**
**wheat** [wi:t] *n* blé *m*, froment *m*
**wheel** [wi:l] *n* roue *f*; (*Aut: also*:
**steering ~**) volant *m*; (*Naut*)
gouvernail *m* ▷ *vt* (*pram etc*) pousser,
rouler ▷ *vi* (*birds*) tournoyer; (*also*:
**~ round**: *person*) se retourner, faire
volte-face; **wheelbarrow** *n* brouette *f*;
**wheelchair** *n* fauteuil roulant;
**wheel clamp** *n* (*Aut*) sabot *m* (de
Denver)

**wheeze** [wi:z] *vi* respirer bruyamment

 **KEYWORD**

**when** [wɛn] *adv* quand; **when did he
go?** quand est-ce qu'il est parti?
▷ *conj* **1** (*at, during, after the time that*)
quand, lorsque; **she was reading
when I came in** elle lisait quand *or*
lorsque je suis entré
**2** (*on, at which*): **on the day when I met
him** le jour où je l'ai rencontré
**3** (*whereas*) alors que; **I thought I was
wrong when in fact I was right** j'ai
cru que j'avais tort alors qu'en fait
j'avais raison

**whenever** [wɛn'ɛvəʳ] *adv* quand donc
▷ *conj* quand; (*every time that*) chaque
fois que
**where** [wɛəʳ] *adv, conj* où; **this is ~**
c'est là que; **whereabouts** *adv* où
donc ▷ *n*: **nobody knows his
whereabouts** personne ne sait où
il se trouve; **whereas** *conj* alors que;
**whereby** *adv* (*formal*) par lequel (*or*
laquelle *etc*); **wherever** *adv* où donc
▷ *conj* où que + *sub*; **sit wherever
you like** asseyez-vous (là) où vous
voulez
**whether** ['wɛðəʳ] *conj* si; **I don't know
~ to accept or not** je ne sais pas si je
dois accepter ou non; **it's doubtful ~** il
est peu probable que + *sub*; **~ you go or
not** que vous y alliez ou non

 **KEYWORD**

**which** [wɪtʃ] *adj* **1** (*interrogative: direct,
indirect*) quel(le); **which picture do
you want?** quel tableau voulez-vous?;
**which one?** lequel (laquelle)?
**2**: **in which case** auquel cas; **we got
there at 8pm, by which time the
cinema was full** quand nous
sommes arrivés à 20h, le cinéma
était complet
▷ *pron* **1** (*interrogative*) lequel (laquelle),

lesquels (lesquelles) pl; **I don't mind
which** peu importe lequel; **which
(of these) are yours?** lesquels sont à
vous?; **tell me which you want**
dites-moi lesquels or ceux que vous
voulez
**2** (relative: subject) qui; (: object) que;
sur/vers etc lequel (laquelle) (NB: à +
lequel = **auquel**; de + lequel = **duquel**;
**the apple which you ate/which is
on the table** la pomme que vous avez
mangée/qui est sur la table; **the
chair on which you are sitting** la
chaise sur laquelle vous êtes assis;
**the book of which you spoke** le livre
dont vous avez parlé; **he said he
knew, which is true/I was afraid
of** il a dit qu'il le savait, ce qui est
vrai/ce que je craignais; **after which**
après quoi

**whichever** [wɪtʃ'ɛvəʳ] adj: **take ~ book
you prefer** prenez le livre que vous
préférez, peu importe lequel; **~ book
you take** quel que soit le livre que
vous preniez
**while** [waɪl] n moment m ▷ conj
pendant que; (as long as) tant que; (as,
whereas) alors que; (though) bien que
+ sub, quoique + sub; **for a ~** pendant
quelque temps; **in a ~** dans un
moment
**whilst** [waɪlst] conj = **while**
**whim** [wɪm] n caprice m
**whine** [waɪn] n gémissement m; (of
engine, siren) plainte stridente ▷
vi gémir, geindre, pleurnicher; (dog,
engine, siren) gémir
**whip** [wɪp] n fouet m; (for riding)
cravache f; (Pol: person) chef m de file
(assurant la discipline dans son groupe
parlementaire) ▷ vt fouetter; (snatch)
enlever (or sortir) brusquement;
**whipped cream** n crème fouettée
**whirl** [wə:l] vi tourbillonner; (dancers)
tournoyer ▷ vt faire tourbillonner;
faire tournoyer
**whisk** [wɪsk] n (Culin) fouet m ▷ vt

(eggs) fouetter, battre; **to ~ sb away** or
**off** emmener qn rapidement
**whiskers** ['wɪskəz] npl (of animal)
moustaches fpl; (of man) favoris mpl
**whisky** (IRISH, US **whiskey**) ['wɪskɪ] n
whisky m
**whisper** ['wɪspəʳ] n chuchotement m
▷ vt, vi chuchoter
**whistle** ['wɪsl] n (sound) sifflement m;
(object) sifflet m ▷ vi siffler ▷ vt siffler,
siffloter
**white** [waɪt] adj blanc (blanche); (with
fear) blême ▷ n blanc m; (person) blanc
(blanche); **White House** n (US): **the
White House** la Maison-Blanche;
**whitewash** n (paint) lait m de chaux
▷ vt blanchir à la chaux; (fig) blanchir
**whiting** ['waɪtɪŋ] n (pl inv: fish)
merlan m
**Whitsun** ['wɪtsn] n la Pentecôte
**whittle** ['wɪtl] vt: **to ~ away, to ~ down**
(costs) réduire, rogner
**whizz** [wɪz] vi aller (or passer) à toute
vitesse
**who** [hu:] pron qui
**whoever** [hu:'ɛvəʳ] pron: **~ finds it**
celui (celle) qui le trouve (, qui que ce
soit), quiconque le trouve; **ask ~ you
like** demandez à qui vous voulez; **~ he
marries** qui que ce soit or quelle que
soit la personne qu'il épouse; **~ told
you that?** qui a bien pu vous dire ça?,
qui donc vous a dit ça?
**whole** [həul] adj (complete)
entier(-ière), tout(e); (not broken)
intact(e), entier(-ière) ▷ n (all):
**the ~ of** la totalité de, tout(e) le (la);
(entire unit) tout m; **the ~ of the town**
la ville tout entière; **on the ~, as a ~**
dans l'ensemble; **wholefood(s)** n(pl)
aliments complets; **wholeheartedly**
[həul'hɑ:tɪdlɪ] adv sans réserve;
**to agree wholeheartedly** être
entièrement d'accord; **wholemeal**
adj (BRIT: flour, bread) complet(-ète);
**wholesale** n (vente f en) gros m
▷ adj (price) de gros; (destruction)
systématique; **wholewheat**

*adj* = **wholemeal**; **wholly** *adv*
entièrement, tout à fait

 **KEYWORD**

**whom** [huːm] *pron* **1** (*interrogative*) qui;
**whom did you see?** qui avez-vous vu?;
**to whom did you give it?** à qui l'avez-
vous donné?
**2** (*relative*) que; à/de *etc* qui; **the
man whom I saw/to whom I spoke**
l'homme que j'ai vu/à qui j'ai parlé

**whore** [hɔːʳ] *n* (*inf: pej*) putain *f*

 **KEYWORD**

**whose** [huːz] *adj* **1** (*possessive:
interrogative*): **whose book is this?**,
**whose is this book?** à qui est ce livre?;
**whose pencil have you taken?** à qui
est le crayon que vous avez pris?, c'est
le crayon de qui que vous avez pris?;
**whose daughter are you?** de qui
êtes-vous la fille?
**2** (*possessive: relative*): **the man whose
son you rescued** l'homme dont *or*
de qui vous avez sauvé le fils; **the girl
whose sister you were speaking to**
la fille à la sœur de qui *or* de laquelle
vous parliez; **the woman whose car
was stolen** la femme dont la voiture
a été volée
▷ *pron* à qui; **whose is this?** à qui est
ceci?; **I know whose it is** je sais à
qui c'est

 **KEYWORD**

**why** [waɪ] *adv* pourquoi; **why not?**
pourquoi pas?
▷ *conj*: **I wonder why he said that** je
me demande pourquoi il a dit ça; **that's
not why I'm here** ce n'est pas pour ça
que je suis là; **the reason why** la raison
pour laquelle
▷ *excl* eh bien!, tiens!; **why, it's**

**you!** tiens, c'est vous!; **why, that's
impossible!** voyons, c'est impossible!

**wicked** ['wɪkɪd] *adj* méchant(e);
(*mischievous: grin, look*) espiègle,
malicieux(-euse); (*crime*) pervers(e);
(*inf: very good*) génial(e) (*inf*)
**wicket** ['wɪkɪt] *n* (Cricket: *stumps*)
guichet *m*; (: *grass area*) espace compris
entre les deux guichets
**wide** [waɪd] *adj* large; (*area, knowledge*)
vaste, très étendu(e); (*choice*) grand(e)
▷ *adv*: **to open ~** ouvrir tout grand;
**to shoot ~** tirer à côté; **it is 3 metres
~** cela fait 3 mètres de large; **widely**
*adv* (*different*) radicalement; (*spaced*)
sur une grande étendue; (*believed*)
généralement; (*travel*) beaucoup;
**widen** *vt* élargir ▷ *vi* s'élargir;
**wide open** grand(e) ouvert(e);
**widespread** *adj* (*belief etc*) très
répandu(e)
**widow** ['wɪdəu] *n* veuve *f*; **widower**
*n* veuf *m*
**width** [wɪdθ] *n* largeur *f*
**wield** [wiːld] *vt* (*sword*) manier; (*power*)
exercer
**wife** (*pl* **wives**) [waɪf, waɪvz] *n* femme
*f*, épouse *f*
**wig** [wɪg] *n* perruque *f*
**wild** [waɪld] *adj* sauvage; (*sea*)
déchaîné(e); (*idea, life*) fou (folle);
(*behaviour*) déchaîné(e), extravagant(e);
(*inf: angry*) hors de soi, furieux(-euse)
▷ *n*: **the ~** la nature; **wilderness**
['wɪldənɪs] *n* désert *m*, région *f*
sauvage; **wildlife** *n* faune *f* (et flore
*f*); **wildly** *adv* (*behave*) de manière
déchaînée; (*applaud*) frénétiquement;
(*hit, guess*) au hasard; (*happy*) follement

 **KEYWORD**

**will** [wɪl] *aux vb* **1** (*forming future tense*):
**I will finish it tomorrow** je le finirai
demain; **I will have finished it by
tomorrow** je l'aurai fini d'ici demain;
**will you do it? - yes I will/no I won't** le

ferez-vous? - oui/non

**2** (*in conjectures, predictions*): **he will** or **he'll be there by now** il doit être arrivé à l'heure qu'il est; **that will be the postman** ça doit être le facteur

**3** (*in commands, requests, offers*): **will you be quiet!** voulez-vous bien vous taire!; **will you help me?** est-ce que vous pouvez m'aider?; **will you have a cup of tea?** voulez-vous une tasse de thé?; **I won't put up with it!** je ne le tolérerai pas!
▷ *vt* (*pt, pp* **willed**): **to will sb to do** souhaiter ardemment que qn fasse; **he willed himself to go on** par un suprême effort de volonté, il continua
▷ *n* volonté *f*; (*document*) testament *m*; **against one's will** à contre-cœur

**willing** ['wɪlɪŋ] *adj* de bonne volonté, serviable; **he's ~ to do it** il est disposé à le faire, il veut bien le faire; **willingly** *adv* volontiers

**willow** ['wɪləu] *n* saule *m*

**willpower** ['wɪl'pauə'] *n* volonté *f*

**wilt** [wɪlt] *vi* dépérir

**win** [wɪn] *n* (*in sports etc*) victoire *f* ▷ *vb* (*pt, pp* **won**) ▷ *vt* (*battle, money*) gagner; (*prize, contract*) remporter; (*popularity*) acquérir ▷ *vi* gagner; **win over** *vt* convaincre

**wince** [wɪns] *vi* tressaillir

**wind¹** [wɪnd] *n* (*also Med*) vent *m*; (*breath*) souffle *m* ▷ *vt* (*take breath away*) couper le souffle à; **the ~(s)** (*Mus*) les instruments *mpl* à vent

**wind²** (*pt, pp* **wound**) [waɪnd, waund] *vt* enrouler; (*wrap*) envelopper; (*clock, toy*) remonter ▷ *vi* (*road, river*) serpenter; **wind down** *vt* (*car window*) baisser; (*fig: production, business*) réduire progressivement; **wind up** *vt* (*clock*) remonter; (*debate*) terminer, clôturer

**windfall** ['wɪndfɔ:l] *n* coup *m* de chance

**winding** ['waɪndɪŋ] *adj* (*road*) sinueux(-euse); (*staircase*) tournant(e)

**windmill** ['wɪndmɪl] *n* moulin *m* à vent

**window** ['wɪndəu] *n* fenêtre *f*; (*in car, train: also:* **~pane**) vitre *f*; (*in shop etc*) vitrine *f*; **window box** *n* jardinière *f*; **window cleaner** *n* (*person*) laveur(-euse) de vitres; **window pane** *n* vitre *f*, carreau *m*; **window seat** *n* (*in vehicle*) place *f* côté fenêtre; **windowsill** *n* (*inside*) appui *m* de la fenêtre; (*outside*) rebord *m* de la fenêtre

**windscreen** ['wɪndskri:n] *n* pare-brise *m inv*; **windscreen wiper** *n* essuie-glace *m inv*

**windshield** ['wɪndʃi:ld] (*us*) *n* = **windscreen**

**windsurfing** ['wɪndsə:fɪŋ] *n* planche *f* à voile

**windy** ['wɪndɪ] *adj* (*day*) de vent, venteux(-euse); (*place, weather*) venteux; **it's ~** il y a du vent

**wine** [waɪn] *n* vin *m*; **wine bar** *n* bar *m* à vin; **wine glass** *n* verre *m* à vin; **wine list** *n* carte *f* des vins; **wine tasting** *n* dégustation *f* (de vins)

**wing** [wɪŋ] *n* aile *f*; **wings** *npl* (*Theat*) coulisses *fpl*; **wing mirror** *n* (*BRIT*) rétroviseur latéral

**wink** [wɪŋk] *n* clin *m* d'œil ▷ *vi* faire un clin d'œil; (*blink*) cligner des yeux

**winner** ['wɪnə'] *n* gagnant(e)

**winning** ['wɪnɪŋ] *adj* (*team*) gagnant(e); (*goal*) décisif(-ive); (*charming*) charmeur(-euse)

**winter** ['wɪntə'] *n* hiver *m* ▷ *vi* hiverner; **in ~** en hiver; **winter sports** *npl* sports *mpl* d'hiver; **wintertime** *n* hiver *m*

**wipe** [waɪp] *n*: **to give sth a ~** donner un coup de torchon/de chiffon/d'éponge à qch ▷ *vt* essuyer; (*erase: tape*) effacer; **to ~ one's nose** se moucher; **wipe out** *vt* (*debt*) éteindre, amortir; (*memory*) effacer; (*destroy*) anéantir; **wipe up** *vt* essuyer

**wire** ['waɪə'] *n* fil *m* (de fer); (*Elec*) fil électrique; (*Tel*) télégramme *m* ▷ *vt* (*house*) faire l'installation électrique de; (*also:* **~ up**) brancher; (*person: send telegram to*) télégraphier à

**wiring** ['waɪərɪŋ] n (Elec) installation f électrique

**wisdom** ['wɪzdəm] n sagesse f; (of action) prudence f; **wisdom tooth** n dent f de sagesse

**wise** [waɪz] adj sage, prudent(e); (remark) judicieux(-euse)

**wish** [wɪʃ] n (desire) désir m; (specific desire) souhait m, vœu m ▷ vt souhaiter, désirer, vouloir; **best ~es** (on birthday etc) meilleurs vœux; **with best ~es** (in letter) bien amicalement; **to ~ sb goodbye** dire au revoir à qn; **he ~ed me well** il m'a souhaité bonne chance; **to ~ to do/sb to do** désirer or vouloir faire/que qn fasse; **to ~ for** souhaiter

**wistful** ['wɪstful] adj mélancolique

**wit** [wɪt] n (also: **~s**: intelligence) intelligence f, esprit m; (presence of mind) présence f d'esprit; (wittiness) esprit; (person) homme/femme d'esprit

**witch** [wɪtʃ] n sorcière f

 **KEYWORD**

**with** [wɪð, wɪθ] prep **1** (in the company of) avec; (at the home of) chez; **we stayed with friends** nous avons logé chez des amis; **I'll be with you in a minute** je suis à vous dans un instant

**2** (descriptive): **a room with a view** une chambre avec vue; **the man with the grey hat/blue eyes** l'homme au chapeau gris/aux yeux bleus

**3** (indicating manner, means, cause): **with tears in her eyes** les larmes aux yeux; **to walk with a stick** marcher avec une canne; **red with anger** rouge de colère; **to shake with fear** trembler de peur; **to fill sth with water** remplir qch d'eau

**4** (in phrases): **I'm with you** (I understand) je vous suis; **to be with it** (inf: up-to-date) être dans le vent

**withdraw** [wɪθ'drɔ:] vt (irreg: like **draw**) retirer ▷ vi se retirer; **withdrawal** n retrait m; (Med) état m de manque;

**withdrawn** pp of **withdraw** ▷ adj (person) renfermé(e)

**withdrew** [wɪθ'druː] pt of **withdraw**

**wither** ['wɪðəʳ] vi se faner

**withhold** [wɪθ'həuld] vt (irreg: like **hold**) (money) retenir; (decision) remettre; (permission): **to ~ (from)** (permission) refuser (à); (information): **to ~ (from)** cacher (à)

**within** [wɪð'ɪn] prep à l'intérieur de ▷ adv à l'intérieur; **~ his reach** à sa portée; **~ sight of** en vue de; **~ a mile of** à moins d'un mille de; **~ the week** avant la fin de la semaine

**without** [wɪð'aut] prep sans; **~ a coat** sans manteau; **~ speaking** sans parler; **to go** or **do ~ sth** se passer de qch

**withstand** [wɪθ'stænd] vt (irreg: like **stand**) résister à

**witness** ['wɪtnɪs] n (person) témoin m ▷ vt (event) être témoin de; (document) attester l'authenticité de; **to bear ~ to sth** témoigner de qch

**witty** ['wɪtɪ] adj spirituel(le), plein(e) d'esprit

**wives** [waɪvz] npl of **wife**

**wizard** ['wɪzəd] n magicien m

**wk** abbr = **week**

**wobble** ['wɔbl] vi trembler; (chair) branler

**woe** [wəu] n malheur m

**woke** [wəuk] pt of **wake**

**woken** ['wəukn] pp of **wake**

**wolf** (pl **wolves**) [wulf, wulvz] n loup m

**woman** (pl **women**) ['wumən, 'wɪmɪn] n femme f ▷ cpd: **~ doctor** femme f médecin; **~ teacher** professeur m femme

**womb** [wuːm] n (Anat) utérus m

**women** ['wɪmɪn] npl of **woman**

**won** [wʌn] pt, pp of **win**

**wonder** ['wʌndəʳ] n merveille f, miracle m; (feeling) émerveillement m ▷ vi: **to ~ whether/why** se demander si/pourquoi; **to ~ at** (surprise) s'étonner de; (admiration) s'émerveiller de; **to ~ about** songer à; **it's no ~ that** il n'est pas étonnant que + sub; **wonderful** adj merveilleux(-euse)

**won't** [wəunt] = **will not**

**wood** [wud] n (timber, forest) bois m;
**wooden** adj en bois; (fig: actor) raide;
(: performance) qui manque de naturel;
**woodwind** n: **the woodwind** (Mus) les
bois mpl; **woodwork** n menuiserie f

**wool** [wul] n laine f; **to pull the ~ over
sb's eyes** (fig) en faire accroire à qn;
**woollen** (US **woolen**) adj de or en laine;
**woolly** (US **wooly**) adj laineux(-euse);
(fig: ideas) confus(e)

**word** [wə:d] n mot m; (spoken) mot,
parole f; (promise) parole; (news)
nouvelles fpl ▷ vt rédiger, formuler; **in
other ~s** en d'autres termes; **to have
a ~ with sb** toucher un mot à qn; **to
break/keep one's ~** manquer à sa
parole/tenir (sa) parole; **wording** n
termes mpl, langage m; (of document)
libellé m; **word processing** n
traitement m de texte; **word processor**
n machine f de traitement de texte

**wore** [wɔːʳ] pt of **wear**

**work** [wə:k] n travail m; (Art, Literature)
œuvre f ▷ vi travailler; (mechanism)
marcher, fonctionner; (plan etc)
marcher; (medicine) agir ▷ vt (clay,
wood etc) travailler; (mine etc) exploiter;
(machine) faire marcher or fonctionner;
(miracles etc) faire; **works** n (BRIT:
factory) usine f; **how does this ~?**
comment est-ce que ça marche?; **the
TV isn't ~ing** la télévision est en
panne or ne marche pas; **to be out of
~** être au chômage or sans emploi; **to
~ loose** se défaire, se desserrer; **work
out** vi (plans etc) marcher; (Sport)
s'entraîner ▷ vt (problem) résoudre;
(plan) élaborer; **it ~s out at £100** ça fait
100 livres; **worker** n travailleur(-euse),
ouvrier(-ière); **work experience** n
stage m; **workforce** n main-d'œuvre f;
**working class** n classe ouvrière ▷ adj:
**working-class** ouvrier(-ière), de la
classe ouvrière; **working week** n
semaine f de travail; **workman** (irreg)
n ouvrier m; **work of art** n œuvre

f d'art; **workout** n (Sport) séance
f d'entraînement; **work permit** n
permis m de travail; **workplace** n lieu
m de travail; **worksheet** n (Scol) feuille
f d'exercices; **workshop** n atelier m;
**work station** n poste m de travail;
**work surface** n plan m de travail;
**worktop** n plan m de travail

**world** [wə:ld] n monde m ▷ cpd
(champion) du monde; (power, war)
mondial(e); **to think the ~ of sb** (fig)
ne jurer que par qn; **World Cup** n:
**the World Cup** (Football) la Coupe du
monde; **world-wide** adj universel(le);
**World-Wide Web** n: **the World-Wide
Web** le Web

**worm** [wə:m] n (also: **earth~**) ver m

**worn** [wɔːn] pp of **wear** ▷ adj usé(e);
**worn-out** adj (object) complètement
usé(e); (person) épuisé(e)

**worried** ['wʌrɪd] adj inquiet(-ète); **to
be ~ about sth** être inquiet au sujet
de qch

**worry** ['wʌrɪ] n souci m ▷ vt inquiéter
▷ vi s'inquiéter, se faire du souci;
**worrying** adj inquiétant(e)

**worse** [wə:s] adj pire, plus mauvais(e)
▷ adv plus mal ▷ n pire m; **to get
~** (condition, situation) empirer,
se dégrader; **a change for the ~**
une détérioration; **worsen** vt, vi
empirer; **worse off** adj moins à l'aise
financièrement; (fig): **you'll be worse
off this way** ça ira moins bien de
cette façon

**worship** ['wə:ʃɪp] n culte m ▷ vt (God)
rendre un culte à; (person) adorer

**worst** [wə:st] adj le (la) pire, le (la) plus
mauvais(e) ▷ adv le plus mal ▷ n pire
m; **at ~** au pis aller

**worth** [wə:θ] n valeur f ▷ adj: **to be ~**
valoir; **it's ~ it** cela en vaut la peine,
ça vaut la peine; **it is ~ one's while
(to do)** ça vaut le coup (inf) (de faire);
**worthless** adj qui ne vaut rien;
**worthwhile** adj (activity) qui en vaut la
peine; (cause) louable

**worthy** ['wə:ðɪ] adj (person) digne;

(*motive*) louable; **~ of** digne de

**would** [wud] *aux vb* **1** (*conditional tense*):
**if you asked him he would do it** si
vous le lui demandiez, il le ferait; **if
you had asked him he would have
done it** si vous le lui aviez demandé, il
l'aurait fait
**2** (*in offers, invitations, requests*): **would
you like a biscuit?** voulez-vous un
biscuit?; **would you close the door
please?** voulez-vous fermer la porte,
s'il vous plaît?
**3** (*in indirect speech*): **I said I would do it**
j'ai dit que je le ferais
**4** (*emphatic*): **it WOULD have to
snow today!** naturellement il neige
aujourd'hui! *or* il fallait qu'il neige
aujourd'hui!
**5** (*insistence*): **she wouldn't do it** elle
n'a pas voulu *or* elle a refusé de le faire
**6** (*conjecture*): **it would have been
midnight** il devait être minuit; **it
would seem so** on dirait bien
**7** (*indicating habit*): **he would go there
on Mondays** il y allait le lundi

**wouldn't** ['wudnt] = **would not**
**wound¹** [wu:nd] *n* blessure *f* ▷ *vt*
blesser
**wound²** [waund] *pt*, *pp of* **wind**
**wove** [wəuv] *pt of* **weave**
**woven** ['wəuvn] *pp of* **weave**
**wrap** [ræp] *vt* (*also*: **~ up**) envelopper;
(*parcel*) emballer; (*wind*) enrouler;
**wrapper** *n* (*on chocolate etc*) papier *m*;
(BRIT: *of book*) couverture *f*; **wrapping**
*n* (*of sweet, chocolate*) papier *m*; (*of
parcel*) emballage *m*; **wrapping paper**
*n* papier *m* d'emballage; (*for gift*) papier
cadeau
**wreath** [ri:θ, *pl* ri:ðz] *n* couronne *f*
**wreck** [rɛk] *n* (*sea disaster*) naufrage
*m*; (*ship*) épave *f*; (*vehicle*) véhicule
accidenté *m*; (*pej*: *person*) loque
(humaine) *f* ▷ *vt* démolir; (*fig*) briser,

ruiner; **wreckage** *n* débris *mpl*; (*of
building*) décombres *mpl*; (*of ship*)
naufrage *m*
**wren** [rɛn] *n* (*Zool*) troglodyte *m*
**wrench** [rɛntʃ] *n* (*Tech*) clé *f* (à
écrous); (*tug*) violent mouvement de
torsion; (*fig*) déchirement *m* ▷ *vt* tirer
violemment sur, tordre; **to ~ sth from**
arracher qch (violemment) à *or* de
**wrestle** ['rɛsl] *vi*: **to ~ (with sb)** lutter
(avec qn); **wrestler** *n* lutteur(-euse);
**wrestling** *n* lutte *f*; (*also*: **all-in
wrestling**: BRIT) catch *m*
**wretched** ['rɛtʃɪd] *adj* misérable
**wriggle** ['rɪgl] *vi* (*also*: **~ about**) se
tortiller
**wring** (*pt*, *pp* **wrung**) [rɪŋ, rʌŋ] *vt*
tordre; (*wet clothes*) essorer; (*fig*): **to ~
sth out of** arracher qch à
**wrinkle** ['rɪŋkl] *n* (*on skin*) ride *f*; (*on
paper etc*) pli *m* ▷ *vt* rider, plisser ▷ *vi*
se plisser
**wrist** [rɪst] *n* poignet *m*
**write** (*pt* **wrote**, *pp* **written**) [raɪt, rəut,
'rɪtn] *vt*, *vi* écrire; (*prescription*) rédiger;
**write down** *vt* noter; (*put in writing*)
mettre par écrit; **write off** *vt* (*debt*)
passer aux profits et pertes; (*project*)
mettre une croix sur; (*smash up*: *car etc*)
démolir complètement; **write out**
*vt* écrire; (*copy*) recopier; **write-off**
*n* perte totale; **the car is a write-off** la
voiture est bonne pour la casse; **writer**
*n* auteur *m*, écrivain *m*
**writing** ['raɪtɪŋ] *n* écriture *f*; (*of author*)
œuvres *fpl*; **in ~** par écrit; **writing paper**
*n* papier *m* à lettres
**written** ['rɪtn] *pp of* **write**
**wrong** [rɒŋ] *adj* (*incorrect*) faux
(fausse); (*incorrectly chosen*: *number,
road etc*) mauvais(e); (*not suitable*) qui
ne convient pas; (*wicked*) mal; (*unfair*)
injuste ▷ *adv* mal ▷ *n* tort *m* ▷ *vt* faire
du tort à, léser; **you are ~ to do it** tu as
tort de le faire; **you are ~ about that,
you've got it ~** tu te trompes; **what's
~?** qu'est-ce qui ne va pas?; **what's
with the car?** qu'est-ce qu'elle a, la

voiture?; **to go ~** (*person*) se tromper; (*plan*) mal tourner; (*machine*) se détraquer; **I took a ~ turning** je me suis trompé de route; **wrongly** *adv* à tort; (*answer, do, count*) mal, incorrectement; **wrong number** *n* (*Tel*): **you have the wrong number** vous vous êtes trompé de numéro

**wrote** [rəut] *pt of* **write**
**wrung** [rʌŋ] *pt, pp of* **wring**
**WWW** *n abbr* = **World-Wide Web**; **the ~** le Web

**XL** *abbr* (= *extra large*) XL
**Xmas** ['ɛksməs] *n abbr* = **Christmas**
**X-ray** ['ɛksreɪ] *n* (*ray*) rayon *m* X; (*photograph*) radio(graphie) *f* ▷ *vt* radiographier
**xylophone** ['zaɪləfəun] *n* xylophone *m*

**yacht** [jɔt] *n* voilier *m*; (*motor, luxury yacht*) yacht *m*; **yachting** *n* yachting *m*, navigation *f* de plaisance

**yard** [jɑːd] *n* (*of house etc*) cour *f*; (*us: garden*) jardin *m*; (*measure*) yard *m* (= 914 *mm*; 3 *feet*); **yard sale** *n* (*us*) brocante *f* (dans son propre jardin)

**yarn** [jɑːn] *n* fil *m*; (*tale*) longue histoire

**yawn** [jɔːn] *n* bâillement *m* ▷ *vi* bâiller

**yd.** *abbr* = **yard(s)**

**yeah** [jɛə] *adv* (*inf*) ouais

**year** [jɪə<sup>r</sup>] *n* an *m*, année *f*; (*Scol etc*) année; **to be 8 ~s old** avoir 8 ans; **an eight-~-old child** un enfant de huit ans; **yearly** *adj* annuel(le) ▷ *adv* annuellement; **twice yearly** deux fois par an

**yearn** [jəːn] *vi*: **to ~ for sth/to do** aspirer à qch/à faire

**yeast** [jiːst] *n* levure *f*

**yell** [jɛl] *n* hurlement *m*, cri *m* ▷ *vi* hurler

**yellow** [ˈjɛləu] *adj, n* jaune (*m*); **Yellow Pages®** *npl* (*Tel*) pages *fpl* jaunes

**yes** [jɛs] *adv* oui; (*answering negative question*) si ▷ *n* oui *m*; **to say ~ (to)** dire oui (à)

**yesterday** [ˈjɛstədɪ] *adv, n* hier (*m*); **~ morning/evening** hier matin/soir; **all day ~** toute la journée d'hier

**yet** [jɛt] *adv* encore; (*in questions*) déjà ▷ *conj* pourtant, néanmoins; **it is not finished ~** ce n'est pas encore fini *or* toujours pas fini; **have you eaten ~?** vous avez déjà mangé?; **the best ~** le meilleur jusqu'ici *or* jusque-là; **as ~** jusqu'ici, encore

**yew** [juː] *n* if *m*

**Yiddish** [ˈjɪdɪʃ] *n* yiddish *m*

**yield** [jiːld] *n* production *f*, rendement *m*; (*Finance*) rapport *m* ▷ *vt* produire, rendre, rapporter; (*surrender*) céder ▷ *vi* céder; (*us Aut*) céder la priorité

**yob(bo)** [ˈjɔb(əu)] *n* (*BRIT inf*) loubar(d) *m*

**yoga** [ˈjəugə] *n* yoga *m*

**yog(h)ourt** *n* = **yog(h)urt**

**yog(h)urt** [ˈjɔgət] *n* yaourt *m*

**yolk** [jəuk] *n* jaune *m* (d'œuf)

 **KEYWORD**

**you** [juː] *pron* **1** (*subject*) tu; (*polite form*) vous; (*plural*) vous; **you are very kind** vous êtes très gentil; **you French enjoy your food** vous autres Français, vous aimez bien manger; **you and I will go** toi et moi *or* vous et moi, nous irons; **there you are!** vous voilà!
**2** (*object: direct, indirect*) te, t' + *vowel*; vous; **I know you** je te *or* vous connais; **I gave it to you** je te l'ai donné, je vous l'ai donné
**3** (*stressed*) toi; vous; **I told YOU to do it** c'est à toi *or* vous que j'ai dit de le faire
**4** (*after prep, in comparisons*) toi; vous; **it's for you** c'est pour toi *or* vous; **she's younger than you** elle est plus jeune que toi *or* vous
**5** (*impersonal: one*) on; **fresh air does you good** l'air frais fait du bien; **you**

**never know** on ne sait jamais; **you can't do that!** ça ne se fait pas!

**you'd** [ju:d] = **you had**; **you would**

**you'll** [ju:l] = **you will**; **you shall**

**young** [jʌŋ] adj jeune ▷ npl (of animal) petits mpl; (people): **the ~** les jeunes, la jeunesse; **my ~er brother** mon frère cadet; **youngster** n jeune m/f; (child) enfant m/f

**your** [jɔːʳ] adj ton (ta), tes pl; (polite form, pl) votre, vos pl; see also **my**

**you're** [juəʳ] = **you are**

**yours** [jɔːz] pron le (la) tien(ne), les tiens (tiennes); (polite form, pl) le (la) vôtre, les vôtres; **is it ~?** c'est à toi (or à vous)?; **a friend of ~** un(e) de tes (or de vos) amis; see also **faithfully**; **mine¹**; **sincerely**

**yourself** [jɔː'sɛlf] pron (reflexive) te; (: polite form) vous; (after prep) toi; vous; (emphatic) toi-même; vous-même; see also **oneself**; **yourselves** pl pron vous; (emphatic) vous-mêmes; see also **oneself**

**youth** [ju:θ] n jeunesse f; (young man) (pl ~s) jeune homme m; **youth club** n centre m de jeunes; **youthful** adj jeune; (enthusiasm etc) juvénile; **youth hostel** n auberge f de jeunesse

**you've** [ju:v] = **you have**

**Yugoslav** ['ju:gəʊslɑ:v] adj yougoslave ▷ n Yougoslave m/f

**Yugoslavia** [ju:gəʊ'slɑ:viə] n (Hist) Yougoslavie f

**zeal** [zi:l] n (revolutionary etc) ferveur f; (keenness) ardeur f, zèle m

**zebra** ['zi:brə] n zèbre m; **zebra crossing** n (BRIT) passage clouté or pour piétons

**zero** ['zɪərəʊ] n zéro m

**zest** [zɛst] n entrain m, élan m; (of lemon etc) zeste m

**zigzag** ['zɪgzæg] n zigzag m ▷ vi zigzaguer, faire des zigzags

**Zimbabwe** [zɪm'bɑ:bwɪ] n Zimbabwe m

**zinc** [zɪŋk] n zinc m

**zip** [zɪp] n (also: **~ fastener**) fermeture f éclair® or à glissière ▷ vt (file) zipper; (also: **~ up**) fermer (avec une fermeture éclair®); **zip code** n (US) code postal; **zip file** n (Comput) fichier m zip inv; **zipper** n (US) = **zip**

**zit** [zɪt] (inf) n bouton m

**zodiac** ['zəʊdɪæk] n zodiaque m

**zone** [zəʊn] n zone f

**zoo** [zu:] n zoo m

**zoology** [zu:'ɔlədʒɪ] n zoologie f

Z

**zoom** [zuːm] *vi*: **to ~ past** passer en
  trombe; **zoom lens** *n* zoom *m*
**zucchini** [zuːˈkiːnɪ] *n(pl)* (*us*)
  courgette(s) *f(pl)*